Children

SIXTH EDITION

JOHN W. SANTROCK

UNIVERSITY OF TEXAS AT DALLAS

Boston   Burr Ridge, IL   Dubuque, IA   Madison, WI   New York   San Francisco   St. Louis
Bangkok   Bogotá   Caracas   Lisbon   London   Madrid
Mexico City   Milan   New Delhi   Seoul   Singapore   Sydney   Taipei   Toronto

McGraw-Hill Higher Education

A Division of The McGraw-Hill Companies

CHILDREN, SIXTH EDITION

This book is printed on recycled, acid-free paper containing 10% postconsumer waste.

1 2 3 4 5 6 7 8 9 0 QPD/QPD 0 9 8 7 6 5 4 3 2 1 0

ISBN 0–697–36447–X

Editorial director: *Jane E. Vaicunas*
Executive editor: *Mickey Cox*
Senior developmental editor: *Sharon Geary*
Senior marketing manager: *James Rozsa*
Senior project manager: *Marilyn Rothenberger*
Senior production supervisor: *Mary E. Haas*
Coordinator of freelance design: *Michelle D. Whitaker*
Photo research coordinator: *John C. Leland*
Supplement coordinator: *Brenda A. Ernzen*
Compositor: *GTS Graphics, Inc.*
Typeface: *10.5/12 Goudy*
Printer: *Quebecor Printing Book Group/Dubuque, IA*

Freelance cover/interior designer: *Diane Beasley*
Cover image: *©SuperStock, Inc.*
Photo research: *Meyers Photo-Art*

The credits section for this book begins on page C-1 and is considered an extension of the copyright page.

Library of Congress Cataloging-in-Publication Data

Santrock, John, W.
    Children/John W. Santrock.—6th ed.
       p. cm.
    Includes bibliographical references and index.
    ISBN 0–697–36447–X
    1. Child development. 2. Adolescence. I. Title.
HQ67.9.S268   2000
305.23—dc21   99–22738
                                             CIP

To My Family:

MARY JO, TRACY, AND JENNIFER

Brief Contents

Contents

Section 1

The Nature of Children's Development   3

Chapter 1

Introduction   4

Chapter 2

The Science of Child Development   28

Section II

Beginnings   61

Chapter 3

Biological Beginnings   62

Chapter 7

Cognitive Development in Infancy   170

Chapter 8

Socioemotional Development in Infancy   196

Section IV

Early Childhood   229

Chapter 9

Physical Development in Early Childhood   230

Chapter 10

Cognitive Development in Early Childhood   252

Chapter 11

Socioemotional Development in Early Childhood   286

Section V

Middle and Late Childhood   329

Chapter 12

Physical Development in Middle and Late Childhood   330

Chapter 13

Cognitive Development in Middle and Late Childhood   356

Chapter 14

Socioemotional Development in Middle and Late Childhood   398

Section VI

Adolescence   437

Chapter 15

Physical Development in Adolescence   438

Chapter 16

Cognitive Development in Adolescence   468

Chapter 17

Socioemotional Development in Adolescence   498

Guide to Important Coverage

Through the Eyes of Children

Caring for Children

Adventures for the Mind

Improving Developmental Skills

Summary Tables

Preface

NEW OR REVISED?

When a textbook reaches its sixth edition, it typically generates two reactions from instructors. The first is that it must be successful to have lasted this long. Second, because of its age, most instructors believe they already are sufficiently aware of the book's content and approach, either because they have used a previous edition or because they have given the book more than a cursory look.

We acknowledge the accuracy of the first impression—more than 120,000 students have used previous editions. However, to those instructors who would apply the second criticism to the sixth edition, we optimistically challenge them to put it to the test. Why? With the most extensive input from instructors, research experts, and students any edition of the book has ever received, the inclusion of many new topics, the deletion of others, a new illustration program, new learning and study aids, a new design, and line-by-line revision of existing material, WE ARE CONFIDENT THAT THIS EDITION MORE CLOSELY RESEMBLES A NEW, RATHER THAN A REVISED, EDITION. THE CLOSER YOU LOOK, THE MORE CONFIDENT WE ARE THAT YOU WILL BE PLEASANTLY SURPRISED BY THE CHANGES.

WHAT DID WE LEARN?

What do most instructors and students really want from a chronological child development text? In partnership (the author and the publisher) and in preparation for this revision, we were determined to obtain a concrete answer to this question. To accomplish this, THE PUBLISHER SOLICITED AND RECEIVED MORE FEEDBACK, THROUGH HIGHLY DETAILED REVIEWS, FROM INSTRUCTORS THAN FOR ANY PREVIOUS EDITION OF THE BOOK.

What did we learn? Instructors who teach the chronological child development course told us to do the following, and we did:

1. Increase the coverage of physical development
2. Increase the coverage of emotional development
3. Reorganize the socioemotional development and social contexts discussions within chapters
4. Reorganize material across chapters
5. Delete the chapter-ending section on improving the lives of children and incorporate this in the chapter when appropriate
6. Increase the educational applications
7. Update and revise specific content
8. Improve the pedagogical system
9. Improve the design and illustration program

Increased Coverage of Physical Development

The consensus of the reviewers who teach the chronological child development course was that *Children* needed a stronger focus on physical development in many places. Based on their recommendations, the discussion of physical development was significantly upgraded in the following places with new or revised material:

- CHAPTER 3 "Biological Beginnings"
  - Sperm-sorting strategy for determining a child's sex
  - Expanded coverage of high-tech assisted reproduction strategies
  - The Human Genome Project
  - Hernstein and Murray's controversial book, *The Bell Curve*, and evaluation of it
  - Judith Harris' controversial new book, *The Nurture Assumption*, and evaluation of it
  - Updated and improved discussion of conclusions about heredity and environment
- CHAPTER 4 "Prenatal Development"
  - New section on caffeine effects on the fetus
  - New section on paternal factors during pregnancy that influence prenatal development and the development of the child
- CHAPTER 5 "Birth"
  - New opener, "The Story of Tanner Roberts: A Fantastic Voyage"
  - New section that describes what the experience of the transition to birth is like for the fetus and newborn
  - Extensively revised, more contemporary section on childbirth strategies
  - Expanded discussion of the father's needs/contributions in the postpartum period
  - Updated discussion of bonding
- CHAPTER 6 "Physical Development in Infancy"
  - Much expanded coverage of the brain's role
  - Updated, more extensive discussion of SIDS
- CHAPTER 9 "Physical Development in Early Childhood"
  - Extensively revised and updated discussion of illness and health
- CHAPTER 12 "Physical Development in Middle and Late Childhood"
  - New section on tooth development and dental care
  - Expanded discussion of nutrition, with special attention to the problem of obesity
  - New section on cancer in children
  - New section on cardiovascular disease in children
  - New section on asthma
  - New section on accidents and injuries

– Completely overhauled and updated discussion of children with disabilities
– New section on sensory disorders
– New section on physical disorders
– New section on speech disorders

• CHAPTER 15 "Physical Development in Adolescence"
  – Expanded coverage of pubertal changes, including more extensive discussion of hormonal changes and sexual development
  – New section on menarche and the menstrual cycle
  – New section on body image
  – New section on adolescent health, with the second half of the chapter centered on this
  – Updated, contemporary information about substance abuse
  – New section on cigarette smoking and programs to decrease it
  – New section on cognitive and sociocultural factors in adolescent health

Increased Coverage of Emotional Development

The consensus of our panel of reviewers who teach the chronological course was that *Children* also should have more extensive coverage of emotional development. To that end, we made the following changes:

• CHAPTER 8 "Socioemotional Development in Infancy"
  – New coverage of stranger anxiety
  – New description of social referencing
  – Revised discussion of temperament, with a stronger tie to emotional development
  – New material on Type D babies
  – Expanded exploration of cultural variations in attachment
  – New section on caregiving styles and attachment styles

• CHAPTER 11 "Socioemotional Development in Early Childhood"
  – New section on the developmental timetable of young children's emotional language and understanding
  – Strategies teachers can use to help children understand emotion

• CHAPTER 14 "Socioemotional Development in Middle and Late Childhood"
  – New section on developmental changes in emotion; includes discussion of emotional intelligence
  – New section on coping with stress
  – New section on coping with death

• CHAPTER 17 "Socioemotional Development in Adolescence"
  – New story introduction on why youth kill
  – Expanded, updated coverage of depression and suicide

Reorganization of Socioemotional Development and Social Contexts Discussions Within Chapters

In the 5th edition, when socioemotional development and the social contexts of development were discussed, the social contexts material always preceded the socioemotional development information. The consensus of the instructors who served as reviewers for this new edition of the book was that this should be reversed, and it was. Thus, in the 6th edition of *Children*, the basic, core information about socioemotional development comes before the description of social contexts of development in the chapters on infancy, early childhood, middle and late childhood, and adolescence. For example, in Chapter 11, "Socioemotional Development in Early Childhood," the self, emotional development, moral development, and gender are explored before families, peer relations, play, and television.

Reorganization of Material Across Chapters

In several locations, instructors who teach the chronological child development course told us they wanted some material moved to other chapters. Based on their recommendations, the following topics were placed in different chapters:

• Autism, which was described in Chapter 8, "Socioemotional Development in Infancy," in the 5th edition, is now examined in Chapter 12, "Physical Development in Middle and Late Childhood."
• Juvenile delinquency, depression, suicide, interrelation of problems, and intervention/prevention of problems, which were described in Chapter 15, "Physical Development in Adolescence," are now explored in Chapter 17, "Socioemotional Development in Adolescence."

Deletion of Chapter Endpiece on Improving the Lives of Children and Incorporation of the Material in the Main Text or Caring for Children Boxes Where Appropriate

The 5th edition of *Children* included an extensive chapter endpiece, "Improving the Lives of Children." The consensus of the reviewers who teach the chronological course on child development was that some of this material was too tangential to the chapter but that, where appropriate, some of the material should be included in the main part of the chapter. Thus, in the 6th edition, this applied material is included in the main body of the text or in a boxed insert (introduced in the text and integrated with it) called "Caring for Children."

Increased Educational Applications

Reviewers who teach the chronological child development course told us they would like to see an expansion of the material on educational applications. Following are examples of new educational applications that were woven into the text:

- CHAPTER 8 "Socioemotional Development in Infancy"
  - Discussion of recent research on the quality of child care
- CHAPTER 10 "Cognitive Development in Early Childhood"
  - New discussion of teaching strategies based on Vygotsky's theory
  - Frequency of programs using developmentally appropriate practices
  - "Developmental Skills" insert on nourishing the young child's cognitive development
- CHAPTER 11 "Socioemotional Development in Early Childhood"
  - How teachers can help children better understand their emotions
  - Strategies for enriching the quality of children's play
  - "Developmental Skills" insert on guiding young children's socioemotional development
- CHAPTER 12 "Physical Development in Middle and Late Childhood"
  - Strategies for helping children cope with stress
  - Revised, expanded, and updated coverage of children with disabilities
  - Contemporary treatment of issues involved in the education of children with disabilities, including recommendations for improving the outcomes of inclusions
- CHAPTER 13 "Cognitive Development in Middle and Late Childhood"
  - Revised and updated material on educational applications of Piaget's theory
  - Strategies for improving children's memory and study skills
  - Critical thinking and schooling
  - The Jasper Project and Fostering a Community of Learners programs
  - Educational applications of Sternberg's theory of intelligence
  - Educational applications of Gardner's theory of intelligence
  - Completely overhauled discussion of reading, with extensive discussion of educational issues
  - "Caring for Children" box: a teacher's passion for literacy
  - Extensively revised, updated, and expanded discussion of bilingual education, including recommendations for working with linguistically and culturally diverse children
  - Goal setting, planning, and self-regulation
  - Classroom recommendations for technology
  - Cooperative learning
- CHAPTER 14 "Socioemotional Development in Middle and Late Childhood"
  - Strategies for making friends at school
  - Strategies for improving relations between ethnically diverse students
  - Strategies for increasing children's prosocial behavior
  - The Global Lab and other technology connections with students around the world
  - Strategies for reducing and eliminating gender bias in education
- CHAPTER 15 "Physical Development in Adolescence"
  - "Caring for Children" box: Life Science and Life Skills Education
- CHAPTER 16 "Cognitive Development in Adolescence"
  - New section on self-regulatory learning and educational applications
  - A successful program for increasing the academic skills of African American students
  - Revised, updated discussion of moral education
  - New section on service learning

Extensive Updating and Revision of Content

We already have noted the extensive expansion of physical and emotional development material. Many other aspects of the text also were updated and revised significantly, in many cases based on the recommendations of the reviewers who teach the chronological child development course and a panel of expert content reviewers, that included Urie Bronfenbrenner, Cornell University; Diana Baumrind, University of California–Berkeley; Peter C. Scales, PhD, The Search Institute; Tiffany M. Field, Touch Research Institute, University of Miami Medical School; Algea Harrison, Oakland University; Allan Wigfield, University of Maryland; James E. Marcia, Simon Fraser University; David Sadker, Phyllis Lerner, American University; Sandra Graham, UCLA; Florence L. Denmark, University of Pennsylvania.

Following is a brief overview of just a few of the many content additions to *Children*, 6th edition, in addition to those already mentioned on physical and emotional development:

Ch. 1: – New historical section on the modern study of child development

Ch. 2: – New section on Vygotsky's theory of child development

Ch. 7: – Revised and updated discussion of the information-processing perspective in infancy
– New section on early environmental influences (focused on nutrition and poverty) on infant cognitive development

Ch. 10: – Considerably expanded coverage of Vygotsky
– New section on evaluating and comparing Piaget and Vygotsky

Ch. 11: – Extensively revised, updated, and expanded coverage of the effects of divorce on children

Ch. 13: – New discussion of Piaget's ideas on seriation and transitivity
– Extensive discussion of Gardner's views and addition of his eighth type of intelligence

- Extensively updated and expanded discussion of reading
- Improved coverage of bilingualism

Ch. 14: – Extensively revised and updated discussion of stepfamilies
- Extensively revised and updated coverage of socioeconomic status and schools, including Jonathan Kozol's descriptions
- Updated coverage of ethnicity and schools
- Revised description of ethnicity, culture, and achievement
- Strategies teachers and parents can use to increase children's prosocial behavior

Ch. 15: – Extensively revised, updated discussion of adolescent sexuality

Ch. 16: – New section on information processing in adolescence
- New discussion of memory changes in adolescence
- New coverage of critical thinking in adolescence
- New material on decision making in adolescence
- New section on self-regulatory learning in adolescence
- New section on service learning

Ch. 17: – Extensively revised, updated, and expanded discussion of attachment issues in adolescence
- Extensively revised, updated, and expanded discussion of dating and romantic relationships in adolescence

Improved, Instructor- and Student-Driven Pedagogical System

Students not only should be challenged to study hard and think more deeply and productively about child development but also should be provided with an extensive pedagogical framework to help them learn. The learning and study aids that follow, some of which are unique to this text and many of which are new to this edition, have been class tested with students and endorsed by them. As a consequence, we are more confident than ever before that your students will find this edition of *Children* to be very student friendly.

The New Look and Design

Children, 6th ed., has a very different look and design. The new look is more colorful and attractive, with more student-relevant features. The new design is one column and more open.

This new design allows quotations, key term definitions, web icons, and other features to be placed in the margins, rather than interrupting the text. The new look and design were carried out at the recommendations of students and instructors.

BEGINNING OF CHAPTER

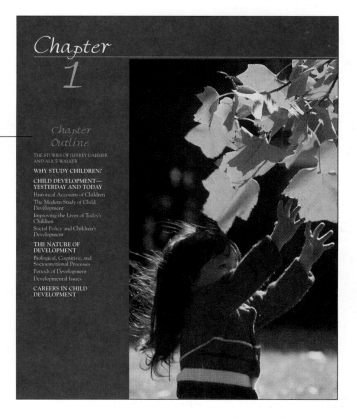

Chapter Outline

The chapter outline shows the organization of topics by heading levels.

"The Story of . . ."

Each chapter opens with a high-interest story that is linked to the chapter's content. Most of the chapter-opening stories are NEW in this edition.

Preview

The preview gives a brief look at what the chapter is about, including a series of questions that will be explored. (NEW)

Chapter
1

Chapter Outline

THE STORIES OF JEFFREY DAHMER AND ALICE WALKER

WHY STUDY CHILDREN?

CHILD DEVELOPMENT—YESTERDAY AND TODAY
Historical Accounts of Children
The Modern Study of Child Development
Improving the Lives of Today's Children
Social Policy and Children's Development

THE NATURE OF DEVELOPMENT
Biological, Cognitive, and Socioemotional Processes
Periods of Development
Developmental Issues

CAREERS IN CHILD DEVELOPMENT

Birth

There was a star danced, and under that I was born.
William Shakespeare
English Playwright, 17th Century

The Story of Tanner Roberts' Birth: A Fantastic Voyage

Tanner Roberts was born in a suite at St. Joseph's Medical Center in Burbank, California (Warrick, 1992). Let's examine what took place in the hours leading up to his birth. It is day 266 of his mother, Cindy's, pregnancy. She is in the frozen-food aisle of a convenience store and feels a sharp pain, starting in the small of her back and reaching around her middle, which causes her to gasp. For weeks, painless Braxton Hicks spasms (named for the gynecologist who discovered them) have been flexing her uterine muscles. But these practice contractions were not nearly as intense and painful as the one she just experienced. After six hours of irregular spasms, her uterus settles into a more predictable rhythm.

At 3 A.M., Cindy and her husband, Tom, are wide awake. They time Cindy's contractions with a stopwatch. The contractions are now only six minutes apart. It's time to call the hospital. At the hospital, Cindy goes to a labor-delivery suite. The nurse puts a webbed belt and fetal monitor around Cindy's middle to measure the labor. The monitor picks up the fetal heart rate. With each contraction of the uterine wall, Tanner's heartbeat jumps from its resting state of about 140 beats to 160–170 beats per minute. When the cervix is dilated to more than 4 centimeters, or almost half open, Cindy is given her first medication. As Demerol begins to drip in her veins, she becomes more relaxed. Tanner's heart rate dips to 130 and then 120.

Contractions are now coming every 3 to 4 minutes, each one lasting about 25 seconds. The Demerol does not completely obliterate Cindy's pain. She hugs her husband as the nurse urges her to "relax those muscles. Breathe deep. Relax. You are almost done."

Each contraction briefly cuts off Tanner's source of oxygen. However, the minutes of rest between each contraction resupply the oxygen and Cindy's deep breathing helps rush fresh blood to the fetal heart and brain.

At 8 A.M., Cindy's obstetrician arrives and determines that her cervix is almost completely dilated. Using a tool made for the purpose, he reaches into the birth canal and tears the membranes of the amnio sac, and about half a liter of clear fluid flows out. Contractions are now coming every two minutes, and each one is lasting a full minute.

By 9 A.M., the labor suite has been transformed into a delivery room. Tanner's body is compressed by his mother's contractions and pushes. As he nears his entrance into the world, the compressions help press the fluid from his lungs in preparation for his first breath.

Squeezed tightly in the birth canal, the top of Tanner's head emerges. His face is puffy and scrunched. Although fiercely squinting because of the sudden light, Tanner's eyes are open. Tiny bubbles of clear mucous are on his lips. Before any more of his body emerges, the obstetrician cradles Tanner's head and suctions his nose and mouth. Tanner takes his first breath, a large gasp followed by whimpering, and then a loud cry.

PREVIEW

The birth of a baby creates changes in a family. It is an event with long-lasting consequences. Although there are many ways to have a baby, the goal should always be to ensure the health of the mother and the baby. These are among the questions we will explore in this chapter:

• What are the stages of birth like?
• What is the birth experience like for the fetus and newborn?
• What is the current thinking about medicating mothers during the process of childbirth?
• What are some natural and prepared childbirth strategies?
• What determines whether a cesarean delivery will be carried out?
• What roles can fathers and siblings play in childbirth?
• What is the right stimulation for preterm infants?
• How is the newborn's health and responsiveness assessed?
• What is the nature of the postpartum period?

119

WITHIN CHAPTER

Single-Column Design (NEW)

The previous edition of *Children* had a dense, two-column format. Instructors and students told us to change this to a more open, one-column design. They said this makes the text material easier to read and allows the wider margins to be used for many pedagogical features, such as key term definitions and Internet sites.

"Through the Eyes of Children" (NEW)

This feature, appearing one or more times in each chapter, provides a glimpse of the real worlds of children in their own words.

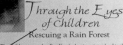

Web Icons (NEW)

Web icons appear a number of times in each chapter next to content that signals students to go to the Santrock, *Children*, 6th ed., web site, where they will find connecting links that provide additional information. The word(s) under the Internet icon is (are) repeated on the Santrock web site under that chapter for each access.

"Adventures for the Mind"

These critical thinking inserts appear periodically in each chapter to challenge students to stretch their minds.

"Caring for Children" (NEW)

This new box, appearing one or more times in each chapter, focuses on applications that involve providing a more caring world for children.

---

46   Santrock • Children

Caring for Children
An Important Mesosystem Connection—Family and School

In Bronfenbrenner's ecological theory, the mesosystem is the connection between microsystems or social contexts. An important mesosystem connection is between families and schools. Researchers have consistently found that many successful students receive long-term support from parents or other adults at home, as well as strong support from teachers and others at school. Involving parents in learning activities with their children at home is one kind of parental involvement that many educators believe is an important aspect of the child's learning. Family researcher and educator Ira Gordon (1978) concluded that parents of students in the early grades can play six key roles: volunteer, paid employee, teacher at home, audience, decision maker, and adult learner. These roles likely influence not only parents' behavior and their children's schoolwork but also the quality of schools and communities.

Today, after many decades of limited success, schools are beginning to put more thought into their communication with parents, recognizing that the initial contacts can make or break relationships and that first contacts affect later communication (Epstein, 1992). Recognizing the importance of parental involvement in education, a number of programs are being developed to enhance communication between schools and families.

Three types of school/family programs are face-to-face, technological, and written communication (D'Angelo & Adler, 1991). In Lima, Ohio, the main goal is for each school to establish a personal relationship with every parent. At an initial parent/teacher conference, parents are given a packet that is designed to increase their likelihood of engaging in learning activities with their children at home. Conferences, regular phone calls, and home visits establish an atmosphere of mutual understanding that makes other kinds of communication (progress reports, report cards, activity calendars, and discussions about problems that arise during the year) more welcome and successful.

Many programs are discovering new ways to use electronic communication to establish contact with a wider range of parents. In McAllen, Texas, the school district has developed a community partnership with local radio stations, and it sponsors "Discusiones Escolares," a weekly program in Spanish that encourages parents to become more involved in their children's education. Family and school relationships, parent involvement at school, the prevention of school dropouts, the creation of a learning atmosphere at home, and communication with adolescents are some of the topics the radio programs have addressed. Parents and others in the community may check out copies of the script or a cassette tape of each program from the parent coordinators at their schools.

In a joint effort of the New York City School System and the Children's Aid Society, since 1992 Salome Urena Middle Academies have invited community organizations to provide school-based programs for 1,200 students and their families (Carnegie Council on Adolescent Development, 1995). The school's family resource center, which is open from 8:30 A.M. to 8:30 P.M., is a valuable source of information and support for the community. Staffed by parents, social workers, and other volunteers, the center houses adult education, drug abuse prevention, and other activities. Since many of the families who send adolescents to the school are of Dominican origin, the school offers English-as-a-second-language classes for parents—400 parents are currently enrolled. Hanshaw Middle School in California's Stanislaus County includes a resource center for students' families. Parents can take classes in such areas as parenting or computers, and they can study for their high school equivalency degrees. Latino parents can get help in communicating with the school's teachers and administrators. The center also features a case management team and referral service that is available to students and their families.

In sum, extra care in developing and maintaining channels of communication between schools and families is an important aspect of children's development (Rosenthal & Sawyers, 1996).

development, there are many more "local" theories, or mini-models, that guide research in specific areas (Kuhn, 1998; Parke & Buriel, 1998). For example, in chapter 6 you will read about the recently developed dynamic systems theory (Thelen & Smith, 1998), which offers an explanation of infant perceptual-motor development, the new functionalist approach to understanding infants' emotional development in chapter 7, as well as the old and new approaches to parent-adolescent relationships in chapter 17.

"Improving Developmental Skills" (NEW)

Appearing one or more times in each chapter, this insert summarizes strategies that can be used to improve children's physical, cognitive, and socioemotional skills.

---

42   Santrock • Children

Improving Developmental Skills
Nurturing Children's Self-Efficacy

In Bandura's (1997) most recent book, he outlined the most important aspects of developing self-efficacy in children and adolescents:

- *Young children's requirement for extensive monitoring by competent adults.* Very young children lack knowledge of their own capabilities and the hazards of their world. Adult monitoring gets children through this early formative time until they become aware of what they can do and what situations require in the way of skills.
- *Recognizing that actions produce outcomes.* Infants need a stimulating environment that encourages them to sense that they can make things happen and to regard themselves as the doers.
- *Parental sources of self-efficacy.* Parental enabling activities increase infants' and children's exploratory and cognitive competence. Overprotective parents constrain children's mastery capabilities. By contrast, secure parents are more likely to encourage children's exploratory efforts and to give them an opportunity to experience a feeling of mastery.
- *The school's role.* As children master cognitive skills, they develop a growing sense of intellectual self-efficacy. A basic goal of education is to equip children with the self-control that enables them to master themselves. This self-regulation includes learning how to develop plans, be organized, become motivated, and use resources. Schools play an important role not only in children's intellectual self-efficacy but also in their health self-efficacy. The effectiveness of health education programs hinges on their ability to impart a sense of self-efficacy to manage one's health habits effectively.
- *The transition to adolescence.* As children move into adolescence, they have to assume increasing responsibility for their behavior. The way in which adolescents develop and exercise their self-efficacy can be critical in setting the courses that their life paths take. Being around competent parents, peers, and teachers who model self-efficacy increases adolescents' self-efficacy.

influence the environment, the environment can change the person's cognition, and so on.

Bandura believes that an important person factor in learning is **self-efficacy**, *the expectation that one can master a situation and produce positive outcomes.* A large number of studies reveal that, when children have high self-efficacy, they are more likely to do well in school and be more competent in a number of areas of life than when they have low self-efficacy (Bandura, 1997, 1998). The insert, Improving Developmental Skills, reveals how adults can improve children's self-efficacy.

Like the behavioral approach of Skinner, social learning theorists such as Bandura emphasize the importance of empirical research in studying children's development. This research focuses on the processes that explain children's development—the social and cognitive factors that influence what children are like.

Ethological Theories

Sensitivity to different kinds of experience varies over the life span. The presence or absence of certain experiences at particular times in the life span influences individuals well beyond the time the experiences first occur. Ethologists believe that most psychologists underestimate the importance of these special time frames in early development and the powerful roles that evolution and biological foundations play in development (Hinde, 1992).

Ethology emerged as an important view because of the work of European zoologists, especially Konrad Lorenz (1903–1989). **Ethology** stresses that behavior is strongly influenced by biology, is tied to evolution, and is characterized by critical or sensitive periods.

Working mostly with greylag geese, Lorenz (1965) studied a behavior pattern that was considered to be programmed within the bird's genes. A newly hatched gosling seemed to be born with the instinct to follow its mother. Observations showed that the gosling was capable of such behavior as soon as it hatched. Lorenz proved that it was incorrect to assume that such behavior was programmed in the animal. In a remarkable set of experiments, Lorenz separated the eggs laid by one goose into two groups. One group he returned to the goose to be hatched by her; the other group was hatched in an incubator. The goslings in the first group performed as predicted; they followed their mother as soon as they hatched. However, those in the second group, which saw Lorenz when they first hatched, followed him everywhere, as though he were their mother. Lorenz marked the goslings and then placed both groups under a box. Mother goose and "mother" Lorenz stood aside as the box was lifted. Each group of goslings went directly to its "mother." Based on such observations, Lorenz developed the ethological concept of **imprinting**, *rapid, innate learning within a limited critical period of time that involves attachment to the first moving object seen.* (See figure 2.7.)

The ethological view of Lorenz and the European zoologists forced American developmental psychologists to recognize the importance of the biological basis of

self-efficacy
Bandura's personal concept, which refers to the expectation that one can master a situation and produce positive outcomes.

ethology
A theory that stresses that behavior is strongly influenced by biology, is tied to evolution, and is characterized by critical or sensitive periods.

Key Terms

These are boldfaced in the text, and their definition follows in italics. They also appear in the margin near where they are presented, along with their definition. (NEW)

Summary Tables

Several times in each chapter, we review what has been discussed so far in that chapter by displaying the information in summary tables. This learning device helps students get a handle on material several times a chapter, so they don't have to wait until the end of a chapter and have too much information to digest.

Quotations

These appear at the beginning of the chapter and occasionally in the margins to stimulate further thought about a topic.

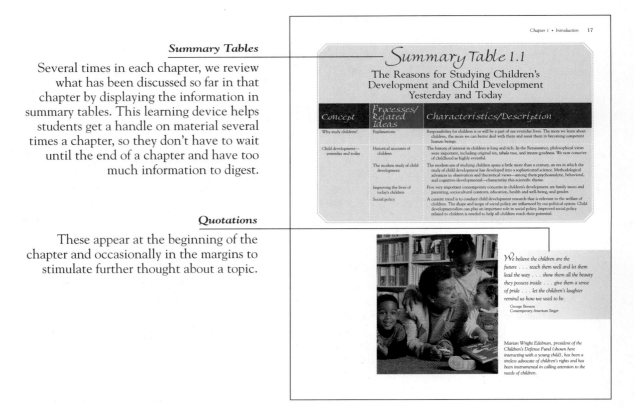

END OF CHAPTER

Chapter Review

This consists of two parts: (1) an overall cognitive map of the entire chapter and (2) a brief summary of the chapter.

Children Checklist (NEW)

This provides students with an opportunity to check their knowledge and understanding of the chapter's contents.

Cognitive Maps

A cognitive map completes each chapter and provides you with a visual organization of the chapter's main topics.

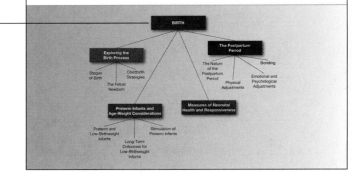

Key Terms

They are listed and page-referenced. Key terms also are defined and page-referenced in a comprehensive Glossary at the end of the book.

Children Resources

Students are provided information about both academic and practical resources in this feature. The resources include books, phone numbers, agencies, research journals, and organizations.

Taking It to the Net (NEW)

This presents students with questions to explore on the Internet that are related to the chapter. By going to the Santrock web site under Taking It to the Net, students will be able to connect to other web sites, where they can find information that will help them think more deeply about the questions posed.

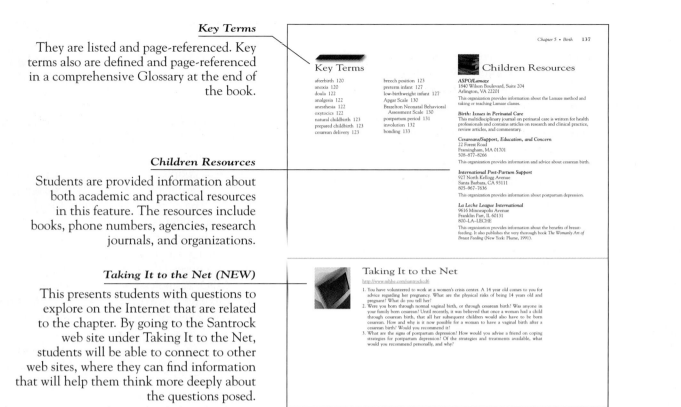

Chapter 5 • Birth 137

Key Terms

afterbirth 120
anoxia 120
doula 122
analgesia 122
anesthesia 122
oxytocics 122
natural childbirth 123
prepared childbirth 123
cesarean delivery 123

breech position 123
preterm infant 127
low-birthweight infant 127
Apgar Scale 130
Brazelton Neonatal Behavioral
   Assessment Scale 130
postpartum period 131
involution 132
bonding 133

Children Resources

ASPO/Lamaze
1840 Wilson Boulevard, Suite 204
Arlington, VA 22201
This organization provides information about the Lamaze method and taking or teaching Lamaze classes.

Birth: Issues in Perinatal Care
This multidisciplinary journal on perinatal care is written for health professionals and contains articles on research and clinical practice, review articles, and commentary.

Cesareans/Support, Education, and Concern
22 Forest Road
Framingham, MA 01701
508–877–8266
This organization provides information and advice about cesarean birth.

International Post-Partum Support
927 North Kellogg Avenue
Santa Barbara, CA 93111
805–967–7636
This organization provides information about postpartum depression.

La Leche League International
9616 Minneapolis Avenue
Franklin Part, IL 60131
800–LA–LECHE
This organization provides information about the benefits of breast-feeding. It also publishes the very thorough book *The Womanly Art of Breast Feeding* (New York: Plume, 1991).

Taking It to the Net

http://www.mhhe.com/santrockcd6

1. You have volunteered to work at a women's crisis center. A 14 year old comes to you for advice regarding her pregnancy. What are the physical risks of being 14 years old and pregnant? What do you tell her?
2. Were you born through normal vaginal birth, or through cesarean birth? Was anyone in your family born cesarean? Until recently, it was believed that once a woman had a child through cesarean birth, that all her subsequent children would also have to be born cesarean. How and why is it now possible for a woman to have a vaginal birth after a cesarean birth? Would you recommend it?
3. What are the signs of postpartum depression? How would you advise a friend on coping strategies for postpartum depression? Of the strategies and treatments available, what would you recommend personally, and why?

ANCILLARIES

The supplements listed here may accompany **Santrock, Children,** *sixth edition. Please contact your local McGraw-Hill representative for details concerning policies, prices, and availability as some restrictions may apply.*

For the Instructor:

Instructor's Manual
by Richard Marchesani (Elmira College)

This extensively revised and expanded manual provides the necessary tools for both the seasoned professor as well as professors new to the child development course. The new edition of the Instructor's Manual contains for each chapter, a chapter outline, a brief chapter overview, and a concise list of targeted learning objectives. Complete lecture suggestions are provided with further resource information included for each major chapter concept. Classroom activities provide hands-on suggestions for applying course material to students' every day lives in the form of classroom exercises and handouts. Discussion questions offer an alternative way for instructors to apply the text material in their lectures and incorporate interesting and controversial topics for students. The McGraw-Hill Child Developmental Psychology Image Database has been correlated to each chapter of the Instructor's Manual for easy lecture planning. A list of topical videos with brief content descriptions and running time information is included for each chapter as additional resources. Lastly, each chapter contains web site resources that direct instructors to the McGraw-Hill Developmental web site where hot links to related sites are available.

Test Bank
by Ruth Doyle (Casper College)

The Test Bank was extensively revised and expanded to include over 2,000 questions specifically related to the main text. Questions include a wide range of multiple-choice, case study, and critical thinking essay questions from which instructors can create their test material. Each item is designated as factual, conceptual, or applied as defined by Benjamin Bloom's Taxonomy of Educational Objectives (1956).

Computerized Test Bank
by Ruth Doyle (Casper College)

This computerized test bank contains all of the questions in the print version and is available in both Macintosh and Windows platforms.

The McGraw-Hill Child Developmental Psychology Image Database Overhead Transparencies and CD-ROM

This set of 174 full-color images was developed using the best selection of our child development art and tables and is available in both a print overhead transparency set as well as in a CD-ROM format with a fully functioning editing feature. Instructors can add their own lecture notes to the CD-ROM as well as organize the images to correspond to their particular classroom needs.

Videocases in Human Development

This set of videos features spontaneous, unrehearsed interviews on topics in child development. Each videotape features excerpts from real people as they talk about personal issues that have particular significance to them. Videocases in Human Development are the perfect supplement for the professor who wants to expose students to the real-life issues that face people at every developmental stage of life. Video One: Prenatal Issues; Video Two: Childhood Issues; Video Three: Adolescent Issues. Topics covered include alternative parenting, biracial adoption, ADD, homelessness, homosexual teens, substance abuse, and sexuality. An Instructor's Manual is included and provides an overview of each tape along with follow-up discussion questions.

PowerPoint™ Slide Presentation

This set of PowerPoint slides follows the chapter organization of *Children*, sixth edition and includes related text images for a more effective lecture presentation.

Web Site

You will find that the Santrock *Children*, sixth edition, web site has extensive links to helpful information about children. http://www.mhhe.com/ santrockcd.6

The AIDS Booklet

The fourth edition by Frank D. Cox of Santa Barbara City College is a brief but comprehensive introduction to acquired immune deficiency syndrome, which is caused by HIV (human immunodeficiency virus) and related viruses.

Annual Editions—Child Growth and Development 1999/2000

Published by Dushkin/McGraw-Hill, this is a collection of 32 articles on topics related to the latest research and thinking in child development. These editions are updated annually and contain helpful features including a topic guide, an annotated table of contents, and unit overviews, a topical index. Instructor's guide containing testing materials is also available.

Taking Sides

A debate-style reader designed to introduce students to controversial viewpoints on the field's most crucial issues. Each issue is carefully framed for the student, and the pro and con essays represent the arguments of leading scholars and commentators in their fields. Instructor's guide containing testing materials is available.

Student Study Guide
by Anita Rosenfield (Chaffey Community College)

The revised Study Guide has benefited from the author's experience in teaching courses in Student Success Strategies as well as her efforts to get student feedback on what makes an effective study guide. The Study Guide provides a complete introduction for students in the How to Use this Study Guide and Overall Course Objectives. Features include, for each chapter, learning objectives from the Instructor's Manual and a guided review for students with highlighted key terms. A self-test section provides an interactive workbook for students to complete the fill-in-the-blank format which corresponds to the main text chapters and sections. In addition, new to this edition of the Student Study Guide are research project ideas for students as well as in-text flash cards for more effective student learning. Internet resources and a sample midterm and final exam are also included in this useful study guide.

The Critical Thinker

Richard Mayer and Fiona Goodchild of the University of California, Santa Barbara, use excerpts from introductory psychology textbooks to show students how to think critically about psychology.

Guide to Life-Span Development for Future Educators
Guide to Life-Span Development for Future Nurses

These course supplements help students apply the concepts of human development to education. The supplements contain information, exercises, and sample tests designed to help students prepare for certification and understand human development from a professional perspective.

ACKNOWLEDGMENTS

A project of this magnitude requires the efforts of many people. I owe a special gratitude to Mickey Cox, Executive Editor, for providing outstanding guidance and support. Sharon Geary, Sr. Developmental Editor, showed a special enthusiasm and competence in monitoring this extensive revision of the book. The numerous members of the production team also did an excellent job in editing and redesigning the book—the particular members of the bookteam are listed at the beginning of the book. Thanks also go to Richard Marchesani, Elmira College; Ruth Doyle, Casper College; and Anita Rosenfield, Chaffey Community College for creating an excellent, significantly improved set of ancillaries.

I also owe special thanks to the reviewers who teach the chronological child development course. As indicated at the beginning of the preface, the substantial revision that was undertaken for this edition of the book was based on their detailed recommendations. I sincerely appreciate the time and effort that the following professors gave in this regard:

Carole Burke-Braxton
Austin Community College

Nancy Coghill
University of Southwest Louisiana

Sheridan DeWolf
Grossmont Community College

Linda Lavine
State University of New York–Cortland

Mary Ann McLaughlin
Clarion University of Pennsylvania

Joe Price
San Diego State University

Clyde Shepherd
Keene State College

Carol S. Soule
Appalachian State University

Carla Graham Wells
Odessa College

Alida Westman
Eastern Michigan University

Sarah Young
Longwood College

Earlier in the preface, the expert content consultants for this edition of the book were recognized. They deserve a great deal of thanks, as do the expert consultants for the 4th and 5th editions of *Children:*

Diana Baumrind
University of California–Berkeley

Phyllis Bronstein
University of Vermont

Rosalind Charlesworth
Weber State University

Jennifer Cousins
University of Houston

Florence Denmark
Pace University

Greta Fein
University of Maryland

Tiffany Field
University of Miami (FL)

Sandra Graham
UCLA

Algea Harrison
Oakland University

Michelle Paludi
Michelle Paludi & Affiliates

The following individuals also provided helpful recommendations on previous editions of the book:

Harry H. Avis
Sierra College

Patricia J. Bence
Tompkins Cortland Community College

Michael Bergmire
Jefferson College

Ruth Brinkman
St. Louis Community College, Florissant Valley

Dan W. Brunworth
Kishwaukee College

Dixie R. Crase
Memphis State University

JoAnn Farver
Oklahoma State University

Janet Fuller
Mansfield University

Thomas Gerry
Columbia Greene Community College

Barbara H. Harkness
San Bernardino Valley College

Susan Heidrich
University of Wisconsin

Alice S. Hoenig
Syracuse University

Sally Hoppstetter
Palo Alto College

Diane Carlson Jones
Texas A&M University

Ellen Junn
Indiana University

Claire B. Kopp
UCLA

Gloria Lopez
Sacramento City College

Mary Ann McLaughlin
Clarion University

Chloe Merrill
Weber State College

Karla Miley
Black Hawk College

Sandy Osborne
Montana State University

Richard Riggle
Coe College

James A. Rysberg
California State University, Chico

Marcia Rysztak
Lansing Community College

Diane Scott-Jones
University of Illinois

Ross A. Thompson
University of Nebraska, Lincoln

Dorothy A. Wedge
Fairmont State College

William H. Zachry
University of Tennessee, Martin

John A. Addleman
Messiah College

Lori A. Beasley
University of Central Oklahoma

Kathleen Crowley-Long
The College of Saint Rose

Swen H. Digranes
Northeastern State University

Ruth H. Doyle, N.C.C., L.P.C.
Casper College

Timothy P. Eicher
Dixie Community College

Robert J. Ivy
George Mason University

Deborah N. Margolis
Boston College

Richard L. Wagner
Mount Senario College

Marilyn E. Willis
Indiana University of Pennsylvania

Urie Bronfenbrenner Urie Bronfenbrenner is the Jacob Gould Schurman Professor of Human Development at Cornell University. He is the principal architect of the ecological theory of human development and also is one of the founders of Project Head Start. Urie Bronfenbrenner is widely recognized as one of the world's leading developmental psychologists. He has made major contributions to conceptualizing contextual influences on development, family processes, early childhood education, cultural influences, poverty, and many other domains. His pioneering work has significantly shaped the field of developmental psychology, and his influence continues today with such theoretical writings as his co-authored chapter "The Ecology of Developmental Processes" in *The Handbook of Child Psychology* (Vol. 1) (1998). Bronfenbrenner's work has received recognition from scientific societies and universities in the United States and in many countries around the world.

Dr. Diana Baumrind is a research scientist at the Institute of Human Development at the University of California in Berkeley (UCB). She received her Doctor of Philosophy in clinical, developmental, and social psychology at UCB, where for the last 30 years she has conducted her well-known longitudinal study, *The Family Socialization and Developmental Competence Project*. Dr. Baumrind is the leading authority on how contrasting patterns of parental authority affect the development of character and competence in children and adolescents. As a consequence of the author's seminal longitudinal research on the contrasting impact on children's character and competence of authoritative, authoritarian, permissive, and unengaged parenting styles, it is generally acknowledged that the authoritative pattern, which balances parental responsiveness (warmth, reciprocity, clear communication, and attachment) with demandingness (firm control, monitoring, maturity demands), most successfully promotes the welfare and social-emotional adjustment of middle-class children. In addition to her seminal work on child rearing, Dr. Baumrind is known for her work on ethics, and more recently on social policy applications of scholarly work on the family.

Dr. Tiffany M. Field is director of the Touch Research Institute and the Touch Research Institute Nursery School of the University of Miami School of Medicine, and Professor in the Department of Psychology, Pediatrics, and Psychiatry. She is a recipient of the American Psychological Association Distinguished Young Scientist Award and has had a research scientist award from NIMH for her research career. She is the author of *Infancy, Touch, and Advances in Touch Research*; the editor of a series of volumes entitled *High-Risk Infants* and *Stress and Coping*; and the author of over 200 journal papers. The mission of the Touch Research Institute is to conduct multidisciplinary and multiuniversity studies on touch as a basic sense, touch as communication, and the use of touch therapies in wellness and medical programs. Among the promising findings is that touch therapy enhances growth in premature infants, reduces stress (cortisol and norepinephrine levels) in child psychiatric patients, enhances alertness (decreases alpha waves, and increases math accuracy) in adults, and increases natural killer-cell activity in HIV men.

Peter C. Scales is a developmental psychologist who is widely recognized as one of the nation's foremost authorities on adolescent development, family life and sexuality education, middle schools, and healthy communities. He is Senior Fellow with Search Institute in Minneapolis, where he conducts research on the role that youth developmental assets play in risk reduction and promoting adolescent health. Among his positions, Dr. Scales has served as director of national initiatives for the Center for Early Adolescence at the University of North Carolina—Chapel Hill, chair of the Alaska Governor's Commission on Children and Youth and executive director of the Anchorage Center for Families, national director of education for Planned Parenthood Federation of America, and senior social scientist for Mathtech, where he was part of the team in the late 1970s that conducted the most extensive studies to date on sexuality education in America. Dr. Scales has authored more than 200 professional and popular articles, books, and other publications, appeared in the print and electronic media all over the country, including *The New York Times, USA Today,* and "Good Morning America," and has given more than 250 keynote speeches to groups ranging from the National Governor's Association to the National Council on Family Relations and the American School Health Association. His awards include the 1988 U.S. Administration for Children, Youth, and Families Commissioner Award for outstanding child abuse prevention, and the American Camping Association's 1998 Hedley S. Dimock award for outstanding contributions to youth development. He has appeared in numerous *Who's Who* volumes, including *Who's Who in the World.* He has three books coming out in 1999: *Developmental assets: A synthesis of the scientific research on adolescent development; A fragile foundation: developmental assets among American youth;* and *Building assets in school communities.*

Dr. Algea Harrison is a leading expert in the area of ethnic minority children and families and Professor of Psychology at Oakland University, Rochester, Michigan. She received her PhD from the University of Michigan and has been a visiting professor and scholar at the University of Zimbabwe; the Free University of Amsterdam; and Nanjing University, Peoples Republic of China. Dr. Harrison's research interests center on perceptions and behaviors of adolescents and working women that emerge from cultural contexts of development. The conceptual framework for her work is to illustrate the interaction between ethnicity and environment and its impact on social cognition, which subsequently has implications for developmental outcomes. She has been collaborating with international colleagues in a series of cross-cultural studies of adolescents' perceptions of support from their social networks. Dr. Harrison has published in leading journals and authored numerous book chapters.

Dr. Allan Wigfield is Professor of Human Development at the University of Maryland, College Park. He received his PhD from the University of Illinois.

His research focuses on the development and socialization of children's motivation and self-concepts. He also is interested in gender difference in motivation and self-concept. He holds several honors and awards, including the 1992 American Educational Research Association Human Development Research Award, for his work on how the transition to junior high school influences adolescents' motivation. Dr. Wigfield has published numerous journal articles and book chapters on his research, and has co-edited one book and four special issues of journals.

He serves on the editorial board of 8 leading journals in developmental and educational psychology.

Dr. James E. Marcia is a Professor of Psychology (Clinical/Developmental) at Simon Fraser University. He received his PhD in clinical psychology from Ohio State University and has directed the psychological training clinics at the State University of New York at Binghamton and at Simon Fraser University. He was both an intern and a visiting associate professor in psychiatry at Massachusetts Mental Health Center. His clinical interests are in psychotherapy and community mental health. His research interests are in construct validation of psychosocial developmental theory, with an initial emphasis on ego identity and a more recent focus on the adult stages of generativity and integrity. He co-authored the book *Ego Identity: A Handbook for Psychosocial Development* (1993). James Marcia developed the concept of identity status and is recognized as one of the world's leading experts on adolescent development.

David Sadker (Ed.D) is a professor at The American University (Washington, DC) and has been involved in training programs to combat sexism and sexual harassment in over 40 states and overseas. He has directed more than a dozen federal equity grants, authored five books and more than 75 articles in journals such as *Phi Delta Kappan, Harvard Educational Review,* and Psychology Today. His research and writing document sex bias from the classroom to the boardroom. He has published and trained in areas ranging from bias in professional communications to sexual harassment, from effective strategies in management to effective strategies in the classroom.

Together with his late wife Myra, David Sadker's work has been reported in hundreds of newspapers and magazines including *USA Today, USA Weekend, Parade Magazine, Business Week, The Washington Post, The London Times, The New York Times, Time* and *Newsweek.* They appeared on local and national television and radio shows such as "The Today Show," "Good Morning America," "The Oprah Winfrey Show," "Phil Donahue's The Human Animal," National Public Radio's "All Things Considered" and twice on "Dateline: NBC" with Jane Pauley. Dr. Sadker received the American Educational Research Association's award for the best review of research published in the United States in 1991, their professional service award in 1995, and the Eleanor Roosevelt Award from The American Association of University Women in 1995. The Sadker's book, *Failing at Fairness: How Our Schools Cheat Girls* was published by Touchstone Press in 1995.

Dr. Sandra Graham is a Professor in the Department of Education at the University of California–Los Angeles. She is also the Chair of the Interdepartmental Master's Program in African American Studies and the Associate Director of the Center for African American Studies at UCLA. She received her PhD from UCLA and holds degrees in history from Columbia University and Barnard College.

Among her research interests are cognitive approaches to motivation, the development of attributional processes, motivation in African Americans, and peer-directed aggression. She has received grants from the National Science Foundation and the Haynes Foundation to continue her research on childhood aggression and interventions to increase social skills and academic motivation in incarcerated adolescents. Professor Graham serves on the boards of many academic journals and professional associations, and is the author of many articles and book chapters. She is also the editor, with V. S. Folkes, of *Attribution Theory: Applications to Achievement, Mental Health, and Interpersonal Conflict* (Lawrence Erlbaum, 1990).

Dr. Florence L. Denmark is an internationally recognized scholar, administrator, leader, researcher, and policy maker. She received her PhD in social psychology from the University of Pennsylvania and has since made many contributions in that area, particularly to the psychology of women. However, her broad interests and distinguished accomplishments in psychology attest to her status as an eminent generalist in an age of specialization.

Denmark's impact on the field of psychology is widespread. She has authored more than 75 articles and 15 books, presented over 100 talks and invited addresses, and appeared on numerous radio and television shows. Denmark has also served as a leader in psychology in many capacities, including having been president of the American Psychological Association and president of the Council of International Psychologists. Her research and teaching achievements have earned her fellowship status in several APA distinctions. She is also the recipient of numerous other prestigious distinctions, including the APA's Distinguished Contributions to Psychology in the Public Interest/Senior Career Award as well as APA Division 35's (Psychology of Women) Carolyn Wood Sherif Award, and most recently, she received the APA's Distinguished Contributions to International Psychology Award.

Denmark has been the Thomas Hunter Professor of Psychology at Hunter College of the City University of New York. At present she is the Robert Scott Pace Distinguished Professor of Psychology at Pace University, where she is Chair of the Department of Psychology.

Phyllis Lerner (M.A.) is Director of interweave, (Bethesda, MD) an organization specializing in educational equity and effectiveness training. Interweave programs, typically designed for teachers and administrators from pre-school through graduate school, have also been adapted for community groups, including parents, social service personnel, and business leaders.

Ms. Lerner's background includes over two decades of teaching experience at the elementary, secondary, and university levels, as well as a special service consultant for the California State Department of Education's Title IX Office. Recently, she assisted in the development of and appeared in a Master of Arts in Teaching video series produced and disseminated by Lee Canter Educational Productions. Additionally, she worked to produce, direct, and present a gender equity inservice series for The Educational Channel, Baltimore County Public Schools and a similar program with Public Broadcasting in Springfield, Massachusetts.

As a national Trainer of Trainers in programs such as TESA and GESA, and as a leader in issues ranging from effectiveness in teaching to equity in athletics, Ms. Lerner has appeared on a variety of local and national public radio and television shows, and has been an invited speaker at hundreds of conferences.

Children

Prologue

If
I Had My Child to Raise Over Again

If I had my child to raise all over again,

I'd finger paint more, and point the finger less.

I'd do less correcting, and more connecting.

I'd take my eyes off my watch, and watch with my eyes.

I would care to know less, and know to care more.

I'd take more hikes and fly more kites.

I'd stop playing serious, and seriously play.

I would run through more fields, and gaze at more stars.

I'd do more hugging, and less tugging.

I would be firm less often, and affirm much more.

I'd build self-esteem first, and the house later.

I'd teach less about the love of power,

And more about the power of love.

DIANE LOOMANS

The Nature of Children's Development

In every child who is born, under no matter what circumstances, and of no matter what parents, the potentiality of the human race is born again.

—James Agee,
American Writer, 20th Century

Examining the shape of childhood allows us to understand it better. Every childhood is distinct, the first chapter of a new biography in the world. This book is about children's development—its universal features, its individual variations, its nature. *Children* is about the rhythm and meaning of children's lives, about turning mystery into understanding, and about weaving together a portrait of who each of us was, is, and will be. In Section I you will read two chapters: "Introduction" (chapter 1) and "The Science of Child Development" (chapter 2).

Chapter
1

Introduction

We reach back-ward to our parents and forward to our children and through their children to a future we will never see, but about which we need to care.

Carl Jung
Swiss Psychoanalyst, 20th Century

PREVIEW

By examining the shape of childhood, we can understand it better. This book is a window into the nature of children's development—your own and that of every other child of the human species.

Among the questions we will explore in this first chapter are

- How have children been treated at different points in history?
- What can we do to improve the lives of today's children?
- What are problems with America's social policy regarding children?
- What is development?
- What are some important issues involved in studying and thinking about how children develop?
- What are some career options in working with children?

The Stories of Jeffrey Dahmer and Alice Walker

Jeffrey Dahmer had a troubled childhood. His parents constantly bickered before they divorced, his mother had emotional problems and doted on his younger brother, and he felt that his father neglected him. When he was 8 years old, Jeffrey was sexually abused by an older boy. But most individuals who suffer through such childhood pains never go on to commit Dahmer's grisly crimes.

In 1991, a man in handcuffs dashed out of Dahmer's bizarrely cluttered apartment in a tough Milwaukee neighborhood, called the police, and stammered that Dahmer had tried to kill him. At least 17 other victims did not get away.

Alice Walker was born in 1944. She was the eighth child of Georgia sharecroppers who earned $300 a year. When Walker was 8, her brother accidentally shot her in the left eye with a BB gun. By the time her parents got her to the hospital a week later (they had no car), she was blind in that eye and it had developed a disfiguring layer of scar tissue.

Despite the counts against her, Alice Walker went on to become an essayist, a poet, and an award-winning novelist. She won the Pulitzer Prize for her book *The Color Purple*. Like her characters, especially the women, Alice Walker overcame pain and anger to celebrate the human spirit. Walker writes about people who "make it, who come out of nothing. People who triumph."

What leads one child to grow up and commit brutal acts of violence and another to turn poverty and trauma into a rich literary harvest? How can we explain how one child picks up the pieces of a life shattered

What are some possible causes of the brutal acts of violence that Jeffrey Dahmer committed?

Alice Walker won the Pulitzer Prize for her book The Color Purple. *Like the characters in her book (especially the women), Walker overcame pain and anger to triumph and celebrate the human spirit.*

Children are on a different plane. They belong to a generation and way of feeling properly their own.

George Santayana
Spanish-Born American Philosopher, 20th Century

Children's Issues

*Ah! What would the world be to us
If the children were no more?
We should dread the desert behind us
Worse than the dark before.*

Henry Wadsworth Longfellow
American Poet, 19th Century

History of Childhood

original sin view
Advocated during the Middle Ages, the belief that children were born into the world as evil beings and were basically bad.

by tragedy, while another becomes unhinged by life's stress? Why is it that some children are whirlwinds—full of energy, successful in school, and able to get along well with their peers—while others hang out on the sidelines, mere spectators of life? If you ever have wondered about what makes children develop into who they are, you have asked yourself the central questions we will explore in this book.

WHY STUDY CHILDREN?

Why study children? Perhaps you are or will be a parent or teacher. Responsibility for children is or will be a part of your everyday life. The more you learn about children, the better you can deal with them. Perhaps you hope to gain some insight into your own history—as an infant, as a child, and as an adolescent. Perhaps you just stumbled onto this course, thinking that it sounded interesting and that the topic of child development would raise some provocative and intriguing issues about how human beings grow and develop. Whatever your reasons, you will discover that the study of child development *is* provocative, *is* intriguing, and *is* filled with information about who we are and how we grew to be this way.

As you might imagine, understanding children's development, and our own personal journey through childhood, is a rich and complicated undertaking. You will discover that various experts approach the study of children in many different ways and ask many different questions. Amid this richness and complexity we seek a simple answer: to understand how children change as they grow up and the forces that contribute to this change.

CHILD DEVELOPMENT—YESTERDAY AND TODAY

Everywhere an individual turns in contemporary society, the development and well-being of children capture public attention, the interest of scientists, and the concern of policymakers. Historically, though, interest in the development of children has been uneven.

Historical Accounts of Children

Childhood has become such a distinct period that it is hard to imagine that it was not always thought of in that way. However, in medieval times, laws generally did not distinguish between child and adult offenses. After analyzing samples of art along with available publications, historian Philippe Ariès (1962) concluded that European societies did not accord any special status to children prior to 1600. In paintings, children were often dressed in smaller versions of adultlike clothing (see figure 1.1).

Were children actually treated as miniature adults with no special status in medieval Europe? Ariès' interpretation has been criticized. He primarily sampled aristocratic, idealized subjects, which led to the overdrawn conclusion that children were treated as miniature adults and not accorded any special status. In medieval times, children did often work, and their emotional bond with parents may not have been as strong as it is for many children today. However, in medieval times, childhood probably was recognized as a distinct phase of life more than Ariès believed. Also, we know that in ancient Egypt, Greece, and Rome rich conceptions of children's development were held.

Through history, philosophers have speculated at length about the nature of children and how they should be reared. Three such philosophical views are original sin, tabula rasa, and innate goodness. In the original sin view, *especially advocated during the Middle Ages, children were perceived as basically bad, being born into the world as evil beings.* The goal of child rearing was to provide salvation, to remove sin from the child's life. Toward the end of the seventeenth century, the tabula rasa view *was proposed by English philosopher John Locke. He argued that children are not innately bad but, instead, are like a "blank tablet," a tabula rasa.* Locke believed that childhood experiences are important in determining adult characteristics. He advised parents to spend time with their children and to help them become contributing members of society. In the eighteenth century, the innate goodness view *was presented by Swiss-born philosopher Jean-Jacques Rousseau, who stressed that children are inherently good.* Because children are basically good, said Rousseau, they should be permitted to grow naturally, with little parental monitoring or constraint.

In the past century and a half, our view of children has changed dramatically. We now conceive of childhood as a highly eventful and unique period of life that lays an important foundation for the adult years and is highly differentiated from them. In most approaches to childhood, distinct periods are identified, in which children master special skills and confront new life tasks. Childhood is no longer seen as an inconvenient "waiting" period during which adults must suffer the incompetencies of the young. We now value childhood as a special time of growth and change, and we invest great resources in caring for and educating our children. We protect them from the excesses of the adult work world through tough child labor laws; we treat their crimes against society under a special system of juvenile justice; and we have governmental provisions for helping children when ordinary family support systems fail or when families seriously interfere with children's well-being.

The Modern Study of Child Development

The modern era of studying children has a history that spans only a little more than a century (Cairns, 1983, 1998). This era began with some important developments in the late 1800s and extends through today. Why is this past century so special? During the past century, the study of child development has evolved into a sophisticated science. A number of major theories, along with elegant techniques and methods of study, help organize our thinking about children's development (Dixon & Lerner, 1999). New knowledge about children—based on direct observation and testing—is accumulating at a breathtaking pace.

During the last quarter of the nineteenth century, a major shift took place—from a strictly philosophical perspective on human psychology to a perspective that includes direct observation and experimentation. Most of the influential early psychologists were trained either in the natural sciences (such as biology or medicine) or in philosophy. In the field of child development, this was true of such influential thinkers as Charles Darwin, G. Stanley Hall, James Mark Baldwin, and Sigmund Freud. The natural scientists, even then, underscored the importance of conducting experiments and collecting reliable observations of what they studied. This approach had advanced the state of knowledge in physics, chemistry, and biology; however, these scientists were not at all sure that people, much less children or infants, could be profitably studied in this way. Their hesitation was due, in part, to a lack of examples to follow in studying children. In addition, philosophers of the time debated, on both intellectual and ethical grounds, whether the methods of science were appropriate for studying people.

The deadlock was broken when some daring and entrepreneurial thinkers began to study infants, children, and adolescents, trying new methods of study. For example, near the turn of the century, French psychologist Alfred Binet invented many tasks to study attention and memory. He used them to study his own daughters,

Figure 1.1
Historical Perception of Children

This artistic impression shows how children were viewed as miniature adults earlier in history. Artists' renditions of children as miniature adults may have been too stereotypical.

tabula rasa view
The idea, proposed by John Locke, that children are like a "blank tablet." *Parents*

innate goodness view
The idea, presented by Swiss-born philosopher Jean-Jacques Rousseau, that children are inherently good.

Figure 1.2
Gesell's Photographic Dome
Cameras rode on metal tracks at the top of the dome and were moved
as needed to record the child's activities. Others could observe from
outside the dome without being seen by the child.

other normal children, children with mental retardation, extremely gifted children,
and adults. Eventually, he collaborated in the development of the first modern test
of intelligence, which is named after him (the Binet). At about the same time, G.
Stanley Hall pioneered the use of questionnaires with large groups of children and
popularized the findings of earlier psychologists, whom he encouraged to do like-
wise. In one investigation, Hall tested 400 children in the Boston schools to find
out how much they "knew" about themselves and the world, asking them such questions as "Where are your ribs?"

Later, during the 1920s, a large number of child development research centers
were created (White, 1995), and their professional staffs began to observe and chart
a myriad of behaviors in infants and children. The centers at the Universities of
Minnesota, Iowa, California at Berkeley, Columbia, and Toronto became famous for
their investigations of children's play, friendship patterns, fears, aggression and conflict, and sociability. This work became closely associated with the so-called child
study movement, and a new organization, the Society for Research in Child Development, was formed at about the same time.

Another ardent observer of children was Arnold Gesell. With his photographic
dome, Gesell (1928) could systematically observe children's behavior without interrupting them (see figure 1.2). The direct study of children, in which investigators
directly observe children's behavior, conduct experiments, and obtain information
about children by questioning their parents and teachers, had an auspicious start in
the work of these child study experts. The flow of information about children, based
on direct study, has not slowed since that time.

Improving the Lives of Today's Children

Consider some of the newspaper articles you might read every day on important
dimensions of children's lives—such as their health and well-being, families and

*Children are the legacy we leave for the
time we will not live to see.*

—Aristotle
Greek Philosopher, 4th Century B.C.

parenting, education, culture and ethnicity, and gender. What the experts are discovering in each of these areas has direct and significant consequences for understanding children and for improving their lives (Zigler & Finn-Stevenson, 1999). An important theme of this book is to provide up-to-date coverage of the roles that health and well-being, families and parenting, education, culture and ethnicity, and gender play in improving children's lives.

Health and Well-Being Although we have become a nation obsessed with health and well-being, the health and well-being of our nation's children and children in many countries around the world raise serious concerns. The AIDS epidemic, starving children in Somalia, the poor quality of health care that many American families receive compared with that of their counterparts in other industrialized nations, inadequate nutrition and exercise, many teenagers succumbing to lives of alcohol and drug abuse, the ways in which children can most effectively cope with major life events such as the death of a parent or their parents' divorce, countless hassles and stressors, and the tragedy of poverty that invades too many children's lives are included on the virtually unending list of issues and dilemmas that affect children's health and well-being.

Asian physicians around 2600 B.C. and Greek physicians around 500 B.C. recognized that good habits are essential for good health. They did not blame the gods for illness and think that magic would cure it. They realized that people have some control over their health and well-being. A physician's role was as guide, assisting patients in restoring a natural and emotional balance.

As we enter the twenty-first century, once again we recognize the power of lifestyles and psychological states in promoting health and well-being. We are returning to the ancient view that the ultimate responsibility for our health and well-being, both ours and our children's, rests in our hands. Parents, teachers, nurses, physicians, and other adults serve as important models of health and well-being for children. They also can communicate effective strategies for health and well-being to children and monitor how effectively children are following these strategies (Weissberg & Greenberg, 1998).

Recognizing that adolescents are not getting adequate advice about health and well-being, the editors of the *Journal of the American Medical Association* devoted an entire issue (March, 1993) to encouraging doctors and nurses, who are used to curing with a stethoscope and prescription pad, to ask more personal questions of teenagers, to establish a doctor/teenager relationship instead of merely a doctor/parent relationship, and to explain that everything that goes on in the office is confidential, except when the teenagers are a danger to themselves or others.

Families and Parenting We hear a great deal from experts and popular writers about pressures on contemporary families (Cowan, Powell, & Cowan, 1998). To read about supports for families, see the box on Caring for Children. The number of families in which both parents work is increasing; at the same time, the number of one-parent families has risen over the past two decades as a result of a climbing divorce rate (Hetherington, 1999). With more children being raised by single parents or by parents who are both working, the time parents have to spend

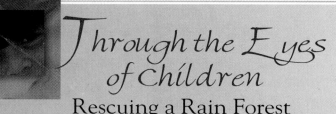

Through the Eyes of Children
Rescuing a Rain Forest

The children in teacher Ena Kern's class in a tiny school in the Swedish countryside learned that, with the destruction of rain forests in the Southern Hemisphere, many small animals were dying. A boy in her class made a simple suggestion, "Why don't we save the rain forest by buying it?"

The children began raising money. They organized country fairs. They wrote songs about the rain forests and performed them in public:

> *Oh, you beautiful rain forest*
> *Why do you have to die?*
> *All species need you*
> *We must prevent it!*
> *You cannot be cut down!*
> *We all need you.*

Soon schoolchildren across Sweden heard about the project, and thousands of them took up the effort—and the song. Even the king of Sweden went to the school and backed the project. The money was sent to an area in Costa Rica called Monte Verde, where a project had been established to raise money to save Costa Rica's rain forests. Ena Kern said that, if you have a problem, ask children for a solution and try it. They can change the world (Goleman, Kaufman, & Ray, 1993).

Prevention Programs

Caring for Children
Building a Pyramid of Services for Parents and Children

Children's health and well-being are enhanced when their parents have reasonable jobs, housing, and health care. And many families, especially those in low-income circumstances, need access to family services and support that will help them cope with challenges and stress that invade their lives. MaryLee Allen, Patricia Brown, and Belva Finlay (1992) proposed that communities need to offer a pyramid of services that range from provisions for all families to families whose children cannot be protected or treated at home (see figure 1.A). In between are families needing some extra support, families needing special assistance, and families in crisis.

There are essentially two types of programs that help families do a better job of nurturing and protecting their children. The first consists of programs that are variously called *family support programs*, *family resource programs*, or *parent education programs*. These programs offer low-intensity preventive services designed to strengthen family functioning early to avert crises. The second, more-intensive type of program, *family preservation services*, is intended to help families already in crisis change their behavior to remove the immediate risk to the children and, if possible, avert the need to remove the children from the home.

Figure 1.A
A Pyramid of Services to Improve Family Health and Well-Being

When communities are able to offer a pyramid of assistance that matches the pyramid of family needs, problems are likely to be solved or alleviated at earlier stages, when they are easier and less costly to address. As family needs grow in intensity, so do services to meet those needs.

Families whose children cannot be protected or treated at home

Families in crisis

Families needing special assistance

Families needing some extra support

All families

- Residential treatment centers
- Therapeutic group homes
- Foster family homes

- Intensive family preservation services
- Child protective services

- Comprehensive substance abuse treatment
- Respite (temporary) child care
- Family-based services
- Special health and education services

- Home visiting programs
- Family support centers
- Parent education programs

- Adequate income, housing, health care, child care, educational, and recreational services

with their children is being squeezed and the quality of child care is of concern to many (Harvey, 1999). Are working parents better using the decreased time with their children? Do day-care arrangements provide high-quality alternatives for parents? How troubled should we be about the increasing number of latchkey children—those at home alone after school, waiting for their parents to return from work? Answers to these questions can be formed by several different kinds of information obtained by experts in child development. This information comes from studies of the way working parents use the time with their children and the nature of their parenting approaches and behaviors, studies of the way various day-care arrangements influence children's social and intellectual growth in relation to home-care arrangements, and examination of the consequences of a child being without adult supervision for hours every day after school (Lamb, 1998; Lamb & others, 1999).

Twentieth-century Irish playwright George Bernard Shaw once commented that, although parenting is a very important profession, no test of fitness for it is ever imposed. If a test were imposed, some parents would turn out to be more fit than others. Parents want their children to grow into socially mature individuals, but they often are not sure about what to do to help their children reach this goal (Stenhouse, 1996). One reason for parents' frustration is that they often get conflicting messages about how to deal with their children. One "expert" might urge them to be more permissive with their children. Another might tell them to place stricter controls on them or they will grow up to be spoiled brats.

Most of you taking this course will be a parent someday; some of you already are. Each of you should take seriously the importance of rearing your children, because they are the future of our society. Good parenting takes considerable time. If you plan to become a parent, commit yourself day after day, week after week, month after month, and year after year to providing your children with a warm, supportive, safe, and stimulating environment that will make them feel secure and allow them to reach their full potential as human beings.

Understanding the nature of children's development can help you become a better parent. Many parents learn parenting practices and how to care for their children from their parents—some practices they accept but some they discard. Unfortunately, when parenting practices and child care strategies are passed from one generation to the next, both desirable and undesirable ones are usually perpetuated. This book and your instructor's lectures in this course can help you become much more knowledgeable about children's development and sort through which practices in your own upbringing you should continue with your own children and which you should abandon. To further evaluate your development as a child, see Adventures for the Mind.

Education   Like parenting, education is an extremely important dimension of children's lives (Parkay & Stanford, 1999; Santrock, in press). When we think of education, we usually associate it with schools. However, education also occurs in contexts other than schools. Children learn from their parents, from their siblings, from their peers, from books, from watching television, and from computers.

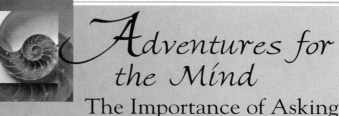

Adventures for the Mind
The Importance of Asking Questions—Exploring Your Own Development as a Child

Our question asking reflects our active curiosity. Children—especially young children—are remarkable for their ability to ask questions. When my granddaughter Jordan was 3½ years old, "Why?" was one of her favorite questions, and she used the word *why* relentlessly. As strong as question asking is early in our life, many of us ask far fewer questions as adults.

Asking questions can help us engage in critical thinking about children's development, including our own development as a child. As you go through this course, ask yourself questions about how you experienced a particular aspect of development. For example, consider your experiences in your family as you were growing up. Questions you can pose to yourself include the following: "How did my parents bring me up?" "How did the way they reared me influence what I'm like today?" "How did my relationship with my brothers or sisters affect my development?" Consider also questions about your experiences with peers and at school: "Did I have many close friends while I was growing up?" "How much time did I spend with my peers and friends at various points in childhood and adolescence compared with the time I spent with my parents?" "What were the schools I attended like?" "How good were my teachers?" "How did the schools and teachers affect my achievement orientation today?"

Be curious. Ask questions. Ask your friends and classmates about their experiences as they were growing up and compare them with yours. As you do this, though, keep in mind that, as we reconstruct our past, we may distort it, and it can reflect our biases.

If a community values its children, it must cherish their parents.

John Bowlby
Contemporary British Psychiatrist

Education Resources

Children learn to love when they are loved

You may look back on your own education and think of ways it could have been a lot better. Some, or even most, of your school years may have been spent in classrooms in which learning was not enjoyable but boring, stressful, and rigid. Some of your teachers may have not adequately considered your unique needs and skills. On the other hand, you may remember some classrooms and teachers that made learning exciting, something you looked forward to each morning you got up. You liked the teacher and the subject, and you learned.

There is widespread agreement that something needs to be done to improve the education our nation's children are receiving (Eccles & Roeser, 1999; Holtzmann, 1992). What can we do to make the education of children more effective? What can we do to make schools more productive and enjoyable contexts for children's development? Should we make the school days longer or shorter? the school year longer or shorter? or keep it the same and focus more on changing the curriculum itself? Should we emphasize less memorization and give more attention to the development of children's ability to process information more efficiently? Have schools become too soft and watered down? Should they make more demands on and have higher expectations of children? Should schools focus only on developing the child's knowledge and cognitive skills, or should they pay more attention to the whole child and consider the child's socioemotional and physical development as well? Should more tax dollars be spent on schools, and should teachers be paid more to educate our nation's children? Should schools be dramatically changed so that they serve as a locus for a wide range of services, such as primary health care, child care, preschool education, parent education, recreation, and family counseling, as well as traditional educational activities, such as learning in the classroom?

Diversity

Culture and Ethnicity   The tapestry of American culture has changed dramatically in recent years. Nowhere is the change more noticeable than in the increasing ethnic diversity of America's citizens. Ethnic minority groups—African American, Latino, Native American (American Indian), and Asian American, for example—made up 20 percent of all children and adolescents under the age of 17 in 1989. As we begin the twenty-first century, one-third of all school-aged children fall into this category. This changing demographic tapestry promises not only the richness that diversity produces but also difficult challenges in extending the American dream to individuals of all ethnic groups (McLoyd, 1999). Historically, ethnic minorities have found themselves at the bottom of the economic and social order. They have been disproportionately represented among the poor and the inadequately educated (Edelman, 1997). Half of all African American children and one-third of all Latino children live in poverty. School dropout rates for minority youth reach the alarming rate of 60 percent in some urban areas. These population trends and our nation's inability to prepare ethnic minority individuals for full participation in American life have produced an imperative for the social institutions that serve ethnic minorities (Halonen & Santrock, 1999). Schools, social services, health and mental health agencies, juvenile probation services, and other programs need to become more sensitive to ethnic issues and to provide improved services to ethnic minority and low-income individuals. (Hollins & Oliver, 1999; Hones & Cha, 1999).

Shown here are two Korean-born children on the day they became U.S. citizens. Asian American children are the fastest-growing group of ethnic minority children.

An especially important idea in considering ethnic minority groups is that, not only is there ethnic diversity within a culture such as the United States, but there is also considerable diversity within each ethnic group. Not all African American children come from low-income families. Not all Latino children are members of the Catholic church. Not all Asian American children are geniuses. Not all Native American children drop out of school. It is easy to make the mistake of stereotyping the members of an ethnic minority group as all being the same. Keep in mind, as we describe children from ethnic groups, that each group is heterogeneous.

Sociocultural contexts of development include three important concepts: contexts, culture, and ethnicity. These concepts are central to our discussion of children's development in this book, so we need to define them clearly. **Context** *refers to the setting in which development occurs, a setting that is influenced by historical, economic, social, and cultural factors.* To sense how important context is in understanding children's development, consider a researcher who wants to discover whether children today are more racially tolerant than children were a decade ago. Without reference to the historical, economic, social, and cultural aspects of race relations, students' racial tolerance cannot be fully understood. Every child's development occurs against a cultural backdrop of contexts (Greenfield & Suzuki, 1998; McLoyd, 1998). These contexts, or settings, include homes, schools, peer groups, churches, cities, neighborhoods, communities, university laboratories, the United States, China, Mexico, Japan, Egypt, and many others—each with meaningful historical, economic, social, and cultural legacies (Cole, 1999; Kagitcibasi, 1996).

Two sociocultural contexts that many child development researchers believe merit special attention are culture and ethnicity. **Culture** *refers to the behavior patterns, beliefs, and all other products of a particular group of people that are passed on from generation to generation.* The products result from the interaction between groups of people and their environment over many years. A cultural group can be as large as the United States or as small as an African hunter-gatherer group. Whatever its size, the group's culture influences the identity, learning, and social behavior of its members (Bornstein, 1999; Goodnow, 1995). For example, the United States is an achievement-oriented culture with a strong work ethic, but comparisons of American and Japanese children revealed that the Japanese are better at math, spend more time working on math in school, and spend more time doing homework than do Americans (Stevenson, 1995).

Cross-cultural studies—*comparisons of one culture with one or more other cultures—provide information about the degree to which children's development is similar, or universal, across cultures and to what degree it is culture-specific.* A special concern in comparing the United States with other cultures is our nation's unsatisfactory record in caring for its children. To further evaluate children's development in different cultural contexts, see Adventures for the Mind.

Ethnicity *(the word* ethnic *comes from the Greek word for "nation") is based on cultural heritage, nationality characteristics, race, religion, and language.* Ethnicity is central to the development of an **ethnic identity,** *which is a sense of membership in an ethnic group, based upon shared language, religion, customs, values, history, and race.* You are a member of one or more ethnic groups. Your ethnic identity reflects your deliberate decision to identify with an ancestor or ancestral group. If you are of Native American and African slave ancestry, you might choose to align yourself with the traditions and history of Native Americans, although an outsider might believe that your identity is African American.

Gender

Another important theme of this book is gender. Gender is receiving increased attention in studying children and in making their lives competent (Beal, 1994; Paludi, 1998). **Gender** *is the sociocultural dimension of being female or male.* Sex refers to the biological dimension of being female or male. Few aspects

Adventures for the Mind

Imagining What Your Development as a Child Would Have Been Like in Other Cultural Contexts

Imagine what your development as a child would have been like in a culture that offered few choices compared with that of the Western world—Communist China during the Cultural Revolution. Young people could not choose their jobs or their mates in rural China. They also were not given the choice of migrating to the city. Imagine also another cultural context, this one in the United States. Some areas of inner cities can be effective contexts for raising children, others not as effective. What would your life as a child have been like if you had grown up in an area of an inner city where most services had moved out, schools were inferior, poverty was extreme, and crime was common? Unfortunately, some of you did grow up in these circumstances.

context
The settings, influenced by historical, economic, social, and cultural factors, in which development occurs.

culture
The behavior patterns, beliefs, and all other products of a group that are passed on from generation to generation.

cross-cultural studies
Comparisons of one culture with one or more other cultures. These provide information about the degree to which children's development is similar, or universal, across cultures and about the degree to which it is culture-specific.

ethnicity
A characteristic based on cultural heritage, nationality characteristics, race, religion, and language.

ethnic identity
A sense of membership in an ethnic group based upon shared language, religion, customs, values, history, and race.

gender
The sociocultural dimension of being male or female.

Children Now

Children and Advocacy

Children and Poverty

17,051	women get pregnant.
2,773	of them are teenagers.
1,106	teenagers have abortions.
372	teenagers miscarry.
1,295	teenagers give birth.
689	babies are born to women who have had inadequate prenatal care.
719	babies are born at low birthweight.
129	babies are born at very low birthweight.
67	babies die before 1 month of life.
105	babies die before their first birthday.
27	children die from poverty.
10	children die from guns.
30	children are wounded by guns.
6	teenagers commit suicide.
135,000	children bring a gun to school.
7,742	teens become sexually active.
623	teenagers get syphilis or gonorrhea.
211	children are arrested for drug abuse.
437	children are arrested for drinking or drunken driving.
1,512	teenagers drop out of school.
1,849	children are abused or neglected.
3,288	children run away from home.
1,629	children are in adult jails.
2,556	children are born out of wedlock.
2,989	see their parents divorced.
34,285	people lose jobs.

Figure 1.3
One Day in the Lives of Children in the United States

of children's development are more central to their identity and to their social relationships than their gender or sex. Society's gender attitudes are changing, but how much? Is there a limit to how much society can determine what is appropriate behavior for females and males? These are among the provocative questions about gender we will explore in *Children*.

Earlier we indicated that diversity characterizes every ethnic group. Females and males are also very diverse. For example, some females excel at math; others do not. Some females have highly connected friendships, while others are lonely; the same is true for males. Diversity and individual differences exist in every ethnic, cultural, and gender group. Failure to recognize this strong diversity and individual variation results in the stereotyping of ethnic, cultural, and gender groups.

Social Policy and Children's Development

Social policy is *a national government's course of action designed to influence the welfare of its citizens.* A current trend is to conduct child development research that produces knowledge that will lead to wise and effective decision making in the area of social policy (Erwin, 1996; Sigel, 1998; Wilcox, 1999). When more than 20 percent of all children and more than half of all ethnic minority children are being raised in poverty, when between 40 and 50 percent of all children born in a particular era can expect to spend at least five years in a single-parent home, when children and young adolescents are giving birth, when the use and abuse of drugs are widespread, and when the specter and spread of AIDS is present, our nation needs a revised social policy related to children (Horowitz & O'Brien, 1989). Figure 1.3 vividly portrays one day in the lives of children in the United States.

The shape and scope of social policy related to children are heavily influenced by our political system, which is based on negotiation and compromise. The values held by individual lawmakers, the nation's economic strengths and weaknesses, and partisan politics all influence the policy agenda and whether the welfare of children will be improved. Periods of comprehensive social policy are often the outgrowth of concern over broad social issues. Child labor laws were established in the early twentieth century to protect children and jobs for adults as well; federal day-care funding during World War II was justified by the need for women laborers in factories; and Head Start and other War on Poverty programs in the 1960s were implemented to decrease intergenerational poverty (Zigler & Styfco, 1994).

Among the groups that have worked to improve the lives of children are UNICEF in New York and the Children's Defense Fund in Washington, DC. At a United Nations convention, a number of children's rights were declared (Limber & Wilcox, 1996). A sampling of these rights is presented in Figure 1.4. Marian Wright Edelman, president of the Children's Defense Fund, has been a tireless advocate of children's rights. Especially troubling to Edelman (1997) are the indicators that place the United States at or near the bottom of industrialized nations

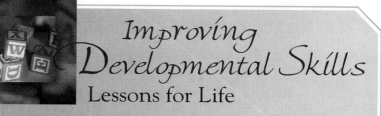

Improving Developmental Skills
Lessons for Life

Marian Wright Edelman (1992, 1997) is one of America's foremost crusaders in the quest for improving the lives of children. Following are some of the main strategies she believes we need to adopt, for improving not only children's lives but our own as well.

- **Don't feel as if you are entitled to anything that you don't sweat and struggle for.** Take the initiative to create opportunities. Don't wait around for people to give you favors. A door never has to stay closed. Push on it until it opens.
- **Take risks and don't worry about being criticized.** We all make mistakes. It is only through making mistakes that we learn how to do things right. It's not important how many times we fall down. What matters is how many times we get up. We need more courageous shepherds and fewer uncourageous sheep.
- **Never stop learning or you will get left behind.** College is a great investment but don't think you can park your mind there and everything you need to know will somehow be magically poured into it. Be an active learner. Be curious and ask questions. Explore new horizons.
- **Standing up for children is the most important mission in the world.** If Rosa Parks can sit down for civil rights, you can stand up for children. Parenting and nurturing the next generation of children are our society's most important functions and we need to take them more seriously than we have in the past. We hear a lot from politicians these days about "family values" but, when we examine our nation's policies for families, they don't reflect the politicians' promises.

social policy
A national government's course of action designed to influence the welfare of its citizens.

If our American way of life fails the child, it fails us all.

Pearl Buck
American Author, 20th Century

Social Policy

Children's Rights

Abuse and neglect	The need to protect children from all forms of maltreatment by parents and others: in cases of abuse and neglect, the government is obligated to undertake preventive and treatment programs
Best interests of the child	The need for the best interests of children to prevail in all legal and administrative decisions, taking into account children's opinions
Child labor	The need to protect children from economic exploitation and from engaging in work that is a threat to their health, education, and development
Children of ethnic minorities	The right of children from ethnic minority backgrounds to enjoy their own culture and to practice their own religion and language
Children without families	The right to receive special protection and assistance from the government when deprived of family support and to be provided with alternative care
Drug abuse	The need of children to be protected from illegal drugs, including their production or distribution
Education	The right to education: the government should be obligated to provide free and compulsory education and to ensure that school discipline reflects children's human dignity
Aims of education	Education that develops a child's personality and talents and fosters respect for human rights and for children's and others' cultural and national value
Sexual exploitation	The right of children to be protected from sexual exploitation and abuse, including prostitution and pornography
Freedom from discrimination	The need to protect children without exception from any form of discrimination
Handicapped children	The right of handicapped children to special care and training designed to help them achieve self-reliance and a full, active life in society
Health and health services	The right to the highest standard of health and access to medical services: the government should be obligated to ensure preventive health care, health care for expectant mothers, health education, and the reduction of infant and child mortality
Leisure and recreation	The right to leisure, play, and participation in cultural and artistic activities
Standard of living	The right to an adequate standard of living: the government should have a responsibility to assist parents who cannot meet this responsibility

$\mathcal{F}$*igure 1.4*
A Partial Listing of the Declaration of Children's Rights Presented to the United Nations

UNICEF

in the treatment of children. The insert, Improving Developmental Skills, profiles Edelman's ideas.

An overview of the main ideas we have discussed so far is presented in summary table 1.1. Next we explore some important developmental issues in the study of children.

Summary Table 1.1
The Reasons for Studying Children's Development and Child Development Yesterday and Today

Concept	Processes/ Related Ideas	Characteristics/Description
Why study children?	Explanations	Responsibility for children is or will be a part of our everyday lives. The more we learn about children, the more we can better deal with them and assist them in becoming competent human beings.
Child development— yesterday and today	Historical accounts of children	The history of interest in children is long and rich. In the Renaissance, philosophical views were important, including original sin, *tabula rasa*, and innate goodness. We now conceive of childhood as highly eventful.
	The modern study of child development	The modern era of studying children spans a little more than a century, an era in which the study of child development has developed into a sophisticated science. Methodological advances in observation and theoretical views—among them psychoanalytic, behavioral, and cognitive-developmental—characterize this scientific theme.
	Improving the lives of today's children	Five very important contemporary concerns in children's development are family issues and parenting, sociocultural contexts, education, health and well-being, and gender.
	Social policy	A current trend is to conduct child development research that is relevant to the welfare of children. The shape and scope of social policy are influenced by our political system. Child developmentalists can play an important role in social policy. Improved social policy related to children is needed to help all children reach their potential.

We believe the children are the future . . . teach them well and let them lead the way . . . show them all the beauty they possess inside . . . give them a sense of pride . . . let the children's laughter remind us how we used to be.

George Benson
Contemporary American Singer

Marian Wright Edelman, president of the Children's Defense Fund (shown here interacting with a young child), has been a tireless advocate of children's rights and has been instrumental in calling attention to the needs of children.

Figure 1.5
Biological, Cognitive, and Socioemotional Processes

Changes in development are the result of biological, cognitive, and socioemotional processes. These processes are interwoven as the child develops.

development
The pattern of change that begins at conception and continues through the life cycle.

biological processes
Changes in an individual's physical nature.

cognitive processes
Changes in an individual's thought, intelligence, and language.

socioemotional processes
Changes in an individual's relationships with other people, emotions, and personality.

THE NATURE OF DEVELOPMENT

Each of us develops in certain ways like all other individuals, like some other individuals, and like no other individuals. Most of the time, our attention is directed to a person's uniqueness, but psychologists who study development are drawn to our shared as well as our unique characteristics. As humans, each of us has traveled some common paths. Each of us—Leonardo da Vinci, Joan of Arc, George Washington, Martin Luther King, Jr., and you—walked at about the age of 1, engaged in fantasy play as a young child, and became more independent as a youth.

What do psychologists mean when they speak of an individual's development? **Development** *is the pattern of change that begins at conception and continues through the life span.* Most development involves growth, although it also includes decay (as in death and dying). The pattern of movement is complex because it is the product of several processes—biological, cognitive, and socioemotional.

Biological, Cognitive, and Socioemotional Processes

Biological processes *involve changes in an individual's physical nature.* Genes inherited from parents, the development of the brain, height and weight gains, motor skills, and the hormonal changes of puberty all reflect the role of biological processes in development.

Cognitive processes *involve changes in an individual's thought, intelligence, and language.* The tasks of watching a colorful mobile swinging above a crib, putting together a two-word sentence, memorizing a poem, solving a math problem, and imagining what it would be like to be a movie star all reflect the role of cognitive processes in children's development.

Socioemotional processes *involve changes in an individual's relationships with other people, changes in emotions, and changes in personality.* An infant's smile in response to her mother's touch, a young boy's aggressive attack on a playmate, a girl's development of assertiveness, and an adolescent's joy at the senior prom all reflect the role of socioemotional processes in children's development.

Remember as you read about biological, cognitive, and socioemotional processes that they are intricately interwoven. You will read about how socioemotional processes shape cognitive processes, how cognitive processes promote or restrict socioemotional processes, and how biological processes influence cognitive processes. Although it is helpful to study the various processes involved in children's development in separate sections of the book, keep in mind that you are studying the development of an integrated human child who has only one interdependent mind and body (see figure 1.5).

Periods of Development

For the purposes of organization and understanding, development is commonly described in terms of periods. The most widely used classification of developmental periods involves the following sequence: the prenatal period, infancy, early childhood, middle and late childhood, and adolescence. Approximate age ranges are placed on the periods to provide a general idea of when a period first appears and when it ends.

The **prenatal period** *is the time from conception to birth.* It is a time of tremendous growth—from a single cell to an organism, complete with a brain and behavioral capabilities, produced in approximately a nine-month period.

Infancy *is the developmental period that extends from birth to 18 to 24 months.* Infancy is a time of extreme dependence on adults. Many psychological activities are just beginning—language, symbolic thought, sensorimotor coordination, and social learning, for example.

Early childhood *is the developmental period that extends from the end of infancy to about 5 to 6 years; sometimes the period is called the preschool years.* During this time, young children learn to become more self-sufficient and to care for themselves, they develop school readiness skills (following instructions, identifying letters), and they spend many hours in play and with peers. First grade typically marks the end of this period.

Middle and late childhood *is the developmental period that extends from about 6 to 11 years of age, approximately corresponding to the elementary school years; sometimes the period is called the elementary school years.* Children master the fundamental skills of reading, writing, and arithmetic, and they are formally exposed to the larger world and its culture. Achievement becomes a more central theme of the child's world, and self-control increases.

Adolescence *is the developmental period of transition from childhood to early adulthood, entered approximately at 10 to 12 years of age and ending at 18 to 22 years of age.* Adolescence begins with rapid physical changes—dramatic gains in height and weight; changes in body contour; and the development of sexual characteristics such as enlargement of the breasts, development of pubic and facial hair, and deepening of the voice. At this point in development, the pursuit of independence and an identity are prominent. Thought is more logical, abstract, and idealistic. More and more time is spent outside of the family during this period.

Today, developmentalists do not believe that change ends with adolescence (Baltes, Lindenberger, & Staudinger, 1998; Santrock, 1999). They describe development as a lifelong process. However, the purpose of this text is to describe the changes in development that take place from conception through adolescence.

The periods of development from conception through adolescence are shown in figure 1.6, along with the processes of development—biological, cognitive, and socioemotional. The interplay of biological, cognitive, and socioemotional processes produces the periods of development.

Developmental Issues

Major issues raised in the study of children's development include the following: Is children's development due more to maturation (nature, heredity) or more to experience (nurture, environment)? Is development more continuous and smooth or more discontinuous and stagelike? Is development due more to early experience or more to later experience?

Maturation and Experience (Nature and Nurture) We can think of development as produced not only by the interplay of biological, cognitive, and socioemotional processes but also by the interplay of maturation and experience. **Maturation** *is the orderly sequence of changes dictated by the genetic blueprint we each have.* Just as a sunflower grows in an orderly way—unless flattened by an unfriendly environment—so does a human being grow in an orderly way, according to the maturational view. The range of environments can be vast, but the maturational approach argues that the genetic blueprint produces commonalities in our growth and development. We walk before we talk, speak one word before two words, grow rapidly in infancy and less so in early childhood, experience a rush of sexual hormones in puberty after a lull in childhood, reach the peak of our physical strength in late adolescence and early adulthood and then decline, and so on. The maturationists acknowledge that extreme environments—those that are psychologically

prenatal period
The time from conception to birth.

infancy
The developmental period that extends from birth to 18 to 24 months.

early childhood
The developmental period that extends from the end of infancy to about 5 to 6 years, sometimes called the preschool years.

middle and late childhood
The developmental period that extends from about 6 to 11 years of age, approximately corresponding to and sometimes called the elementary school years.

adolescence
The developmental period of transition from childhood to early adulthood, entered at approximately 10 to 12 years of age and ending at 18 to 22 years of age.

maturation
The orderly sequence of changes dictated by a genetic blueprint.

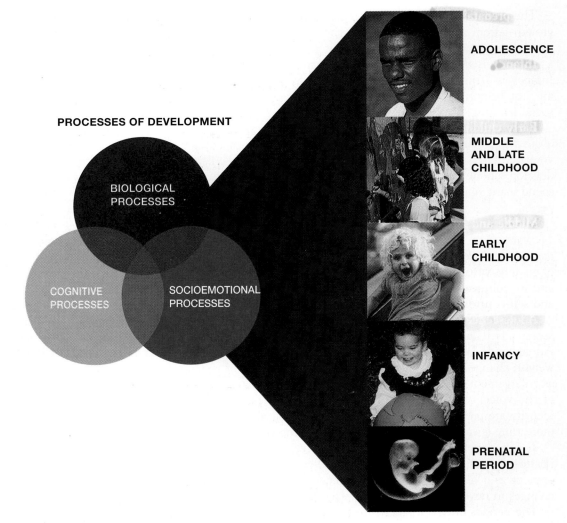

PROCESSES OF DEVELOPMENT

BIOLOGICAL PROCESSES

COGNITIVE PROCESSES

SOCIOEMOTIONAL PROCESSES

ADOLESCENCE

MIDDLE AND LATE CHILDHOOD

EARLY CHILDHOOD

INFANCY

PRENATAL PERIOD

Figure 1.6
Processes and Periods of Development

Development moves through the prenatal, infancy, early childhood, middle and late childhood, and adolescence periods. These periods of development are the result of biological, cognitive, and socioemotional processes. Development is the creation of increasingly complex forms.

barren or hostile—can depress development, but they believe that basic growth tendencies are genetically wired into human beings.

By contrast, other psychologists emphasize the importance of experiences in child development. Experiences run the gamut from individuals' biological environment (nutrition, medical care, drugs, and physical accidents) to their social environment (family, peers, schools, community, media, and culture).

The debate about whether development is primarily influenced by maturation or by experience has been a part of psychology since its beginning. This debate is often referred to as the **nature-nurture controversy.** Nature *refers to an organism's biological inheritance,* nurture *to environmental experiences. The "nature" proponents claim biological inheritance is the most important influence on development, the "nurture" proponents that environmental experiences are the most important.*

Continuity and Discontinuity   Think about your development for a moment. Did you gradually grow to become the person you are, in the slow cumulative way a seedling grows into a giant oak? Or did you experience sudden, distinct

nature-nurture controversy
Nature refers to an organism's biological inheritance, *nurture* to environmental influences. The "nature" proponents claim that biological inheritance is the most important influence on development; the "nurture" proponents claim that environmental experiences are the most important.

changes in your growth, the way a caterpillar changes into a butterfly? (See figure 1.7.) For the most part, developmentalists who emphasize experience have described development as a gradual, continuous process; those who emphasize maturation have described development as a series of distinct stages.

Some developmentalists emphasize the **continuity of development,** *the view that development involves gradual, cumulative change from conception to death.* A child's first word, while seemingly an abrupt, discontinuous event, is actually the result of months of growth and practice. Puberty, while also seemingly an abrupt, discontinuous occurrence, is actually a gradual process occurring over several years.

Other developmentalists focus on the **discontinuity of development,** *the view that development involves distinct stages in the life span.* This view sees each of us as passing through a sequence of stages in which change is qualitative rather than quantitative. As an oak moves from seedling to giant tree, it becomes *more* oak—its development is continuous. As a caterpillar changes into a butterfly, it does not become more caterpillar but, instead, becomes a *different kind* of organism—its development is discontinuous. For example, at a certain point a child moves from not being able to think abstractly about the world to being able to do so. This is a qualitative, discontinuous change in development, not a quantitative, continuous change.

Early and Later Experience   Another important developmental topic is the **early-later experience issue,** *which focuses on the degree to which early experiences (especially in infancy) or later experiences are the key determinants of the child's development.* That is, if infants experience negative, stressful circumstances in their lives, can those experiences be overcome by later, more-positive experiences? Or are the early experiences so critical—possibly because they are the infant's first, prototypical experiences—that they cannot be overridden by a later, more-enriched environment?

The early-later experience issue has a long history and continues to be hotly debated among developmentalists. Some believe that, unless infants experience warm, nurturant caregiving in the first year or so of life, their development will never be optimal (Bowlby, 1989; Sroufe, Egeland, & Carlson, 1999; Waters & others, 1995). Plato was sure that infants who are rocked frequently become better athletes. Nineteenth-century New England ministers told parents in Sunday sermons that the way they handled their infants would determine their children's future character. The emphasis on the importance of early experience rests on the belief that each life is an unbroken trail on which a psychological quality can be traced back to its origin (Kagan, 1984, 1992, 1998).

The early-experience doctrine contrasts with the later-experience view, which states that, rather than statuelike permanence after change in infancy, development continues to be like the ebb and flow of an ocean. The later-experience advocates argue that children are malleable throughout development and that later sensitive caregiving is just as important as earlier sensitive caregiving. A number of life-span developmentalists, who focus on the entire life span rather than only on child development, stress that too little attention has been given to later experiences in development (Baltes, 1987). They accept that early experiences are important contributors to development, but no more important than later experiences. Jerome Kagan (1992, 1998) points out that even children who show the qualities of an inhibited temperament, which is linked to heredity, have the capacity to change their behavior. In his research, almost one-third of a group of children who had an inhibited temperament at 2 years of age were not unusually shy or fearful when they were 4 years of age (Kagan & Snidman, 1991).

People in Western cultures, especially those steeped in the Freudian belief that the key experiences in development are children's relationships with their parents in the first five years of life, have tended to support the idea that early experiences are more important than later experiences (Chan, 1963; Lamb & Sternberg, 1992). By contrast, the majority of people in the world do not share this belief. For example, people in many Asian countries believe that experiences occurring after

*F*igure 1.7
Continuity and Discontinuity in Development

Is human development more like that of a seedling gradually growing into a giant oak or more like that of a caterpillar suddenly becoming a butterfly?

continuity of development
The view that development involves gradual, cumulative change from conception to death.

discontinuity of development
The view that development involves distinct stages in the life span.

early-later experience issue
The issue of the degree to which early experiences (especially infancy) or later experiences are the key determinants of the child's development.

What is the nature of the early and later experience issue in development?

about 6 to 7 years of age are more important aspects of development than are earlier experiences. This stance stems from the long-standing belief in Eastern cultures that children's reasoning skills begin to develop in important ways in the middle childhood years.

Evaluating the Developmental Issues   As we consider further these three salient developmental issues—nature and nurture, continuity and discontinuity, and early and later experiences—it is important to realize that most developmentalists recognize that it is unwise to take an extreme position on these issues. Development is not all nature or all nurture, not all continuity or all discontinuity, and not all early or later experiences. Nature and nurture, continuity and discontinuity, and early and later experiences all characterize our development through the human life cycle. For example, in considering the nature-nurture issue, the key to development is the *interaction* of nature and nurture rather than either factor alone (Plomin, 1993). Thus, an individual's cognitive development is the result of heredity-environment interaction, not heredity or environment alone. Much more about the role of heredity-environment interaction appears in chapter 3.

Nonetheless, although most developmentalists do not take extreme positions on these three important issues, this consensus has not meant the absence of spirited debate about how strongly development is influenced by each of these factors. Are girls less likely to do well in math because of their "feminine" nature or because of society's masculine bias? If, as children, adolescents experienced a world of poverty, neglect by parents, and poor schooling, can enriched experiences in adolescence remove the "deficits" they encountered earlier in their development? The answers developmentalists give to such questions depend on their stance on the issue of nature and nurture, continuity and discontinuity, and early and later experience. The answers to these questions also influence public policy decisions about children and how each of us lives through the human life span.

CAREERS IN CHILD DEVELOPMENT

Careers

A career in child development is one of the most rewarding vocational opportunities you can pursue. By choosing a career in child development, you will be able to help children who might not reach their potential as productive contributors to society develop into physically, cognitively, and socially mature individuals. Adults who work professionally with children invariably feel a sense of pride in their ability to contribute in meaningful ways to the next generation of human beings.

If you decide to pursue a career related to children's development, a number of options are available to you. College and university professors teach courses in child development, education, family development, and nursing; counselors, clinical psychologists, pediatricians, psychiatrists, school psychologists, pediatric nurses, psychiatric nurses, and social workers see children with problems and disturbances or illnesses; teachers instruct children in kindergartens, elementary schools, and secondary schools. In pursuing a career related to child development, you can expand your opportunities (and income) considerably by obtaining a graduate degree, although an advanced degree is not absolutely necessary.

Most college professors in child development and its related areas of psychology, education, family and consumer sciences, nursing, and social work have a master's degree and/or doctorate degree that required two to five years of academic work beyond their undergraduate degree. Becoming a child clinical psychologist or coun-

Summary Table 1.2
The Nature of Development and Careers in Child Development

Concept	Processes/ Related Ideas	Characteristics/Description
The nature of development	What is development?	Development is the pattern of movement or change that occurs throughout the life span.
	Biological, cognitive, and socioemotional processes	Development is influenced by an interplay of biological, cognitive, and socioemotional processes.
	Periods of development	Development is commonly divided into the following periods from conception through adolescence: the prenatal period, infancy, early childhood, middle and late childhood, and adolescence.
	Developmental issues	The debate over whether development is due primarily to maturation or to experience is another version of the nature-nurture controversy. Some developmentalists describe development as continuous (gradual, cumulative change), others as discontinuous (abrupt sequence of stages). The early-later experience issue focuses on whether early experiences (especially in infancy) are more important in development than are later experiences. Most developmentalists recognize that extreme positions on the nature-nurture, continuity-discontinuity, and early-later experience issues are unwise. Despite this consensus, spirited debate still occurs on these issues.
Careers in child development	Their nature	A wide range of opportunities are available to individuals who want to pursue a career related to child development. These opportunities include jobs in college and university teaching, child clinical psychology and counseling, school teaching and school psychology, nursing, pediatrics, psychiatry, and social work.

seling psychologist requires five to six years of graduate work to obtain the necessary Ph.D.; this includes both clinical and research training. School and career counselors pursue a master's or doctoral degree in counseling, often in graduate programs in education departments; these degrees require two to six years to complete. Becoming a pediatrician or psychiatrist requires four years of medical school, plus an internship and a residency in pediatrics or psychiatry, respectively; this career path takes seven to nine years beyond a bachelor's degree. School psychologists obtain either a master's degree (approximately two years) or a D.Ed. degree (approximately four to five years) in school psychology. School psychologists counsel children and parents when children have problems in school, often giving psychological tests to assess children's personality and intelligence. Social work positions may be obtained with an undergraduate degree in social work or related fields, but opportunities are expanded with an M.S.W. (master's of social work) or Ph.D., which require two and four to five years, respectively. Pediatric and psychiatric nursing positions can also be attained with an undergraduate R.N. degree; M.A. and Ph.D. degrees in nursing, which require two and four to five years of graduate training, respectively, are also available. To read further about jobs and careers that involve working with children, turn to figure 1.8. This list is not exhaustive but, rather, is meant to give you an idea of the many opportunities to pursue a rewarding career in child development and its related fields. Also keep in mind that majoring in child development or a related field can provide sound preparation for adult life.

At this point, we have discussed a number of ideas about the nature of development and careers in child development. An overview of these ideas is presented in summary table 1.2.

Nonacademic Careers in Psychology

Jobs/careers	Degree	Education required
Child clinical psychologist or counseling psychologist	Ph.D.	5–7 years postundergraduate
Child life specialist	Undergraduate degree	4 years of undergraduate study
Child psychiatrist	M.D.	7–9 years postundergraduate
Child welfare worker	Undergraduate degree (minimum)	4 years minimum
College/university professor in child development, education, family development, nursing, social work	Ph.D. or master's degree	5–6 years for Ph.D. (or D.Ed.) postundergraduate; 2 years for master's degree postundergraduate
Day care supervisor	Varies by state	Varies by state
Early childhood educator	Undergraduate degree (minimum)	4 years (minimum)
Elementary or secondary school teacher	Undergraduate degree (minimum)	4 years
Exceptional children teacher (special education teacher)	Undergraduate degree (minimum)	4 years or more (some states require a master's degree or passing a standardized exam to obtain a license to work with exceptional children)
Guidance counselor	Undergraduate degree (minimum); many have master's degree	4 years undergraduate; 2 years graduate
Pediatrician	M.D.	7–9 years medical school
Pediatric nurse	R.N.	2–5 years
Preschool/kindergarten teacher	Usually graduate degree	4 years
Psychiatric nurse	R.N.	2–5 years
School psychologist	Master's degree or Ph.D.	5–6 years of graduate work for Ph.D. or D.Ed.; 2 years for master's degree

Figure 1.8 Jobs and Careers in Child Development and Related Fields

Nature of training	Description of work
Includes both clinical and research training; involves a 1-year internship in a psychiatric hospital or mental health facility.	Child clinical psychologists or counseling psychologists diagnose children's problems and disorders, administer psychological tests, and conduct psychotherapy sessions. Some work at colleges and universities, where they do any combination of teaching, therapy, and research.
Many child life specialists have been trained in child development or education but undergo additional training in child life programs that includes parent education, developmental assessment, and supervised work with children and parents.	Child life specialists are employed by hospitals and work with children and their families before and after the children are admitted to the hospital. They often develop and monitor developmentally appropriate activities for child patients. They also help children adapt to their medical experiences and their stay at the hospital. Child life specialists coordinate their efforts with physicians and nurses.
Four years of medical school, plus an internship and residency in child psychiatry are required.	The role of the child psychiatrist is similar to that of the child clinical psychologist, but the psychiatrist can conduct biomedical therapy (for example, using drugs to treat clients); the child clinical or counseling psychologist cannot.
Coursework and training in social work or human services	Child welfare workers are employed by the Child Protective Services Unit of each state to protect children's rights. They especially monitor cases of child maltreatment and abuse and make decisions about what needs to be done to help protect the abused child from further harm and to help the child cope with prior abuse.
Take graduate courses, learn how to conduct research, attend and present papers at professional meetings	College and university professors teach courses in child development, family development, education, or nursing; conduct research; present papers at professional meetings; write and publish articles and books; and train undergraduate and graduate students for careers in these fields.
The Department of Public Welfare in many states publishes a booklet with the requirements for a day-care supervisor.	Day-care supervisors direct day-care or preschool programs, being responsible for the operation of the center. They often make decisions about the nature of the center's curriculum, may teach in the center themselves, work with and consult with parents, and conduct workshops for the staff or parents.
Coursework in early childhood education and practice in day-care or early childhood centers with supervised training	Early childhood educators usually teach in community colleges that award associate or bachelor's degrees in early childhood education with specialization in day care. They train individuals for careers in the field of day care.
Wide range of courses, with a major or concentration in education	Elementary and secondary teachers teach one or more subjects; prepare the curriculum; give tests, assign grades, and monitor students' progress; interact with parents and school administrators; attend lectures and workshops involving curriculum planning or help on special issues; and direct extracurricular programs.
Coursework in education, with a concentration in special education	Exceptional children teachers (also called special education teachers) work with children who are educationally handicapped (those who are mentally retarded, have a physical handicap, have a learning disability, or have a behavioral disorder) or who are gifted. They develop special curricula for the exceptional children and help them adapt to their exceptional circumstances. Special education teachers work with other school personnel and with parents to improve the adjustment of exceptional children.
Coursework in education and counseling in a school of education; counselor training experience	The majority of guidance counselors work with secondary school students, assisting them in educational and career planning. They often give students aptitude tests and evaluate their interests, as well as their abilities. Guidance counselors also see students who are having school-related problems, including emotional problems, referring them to other professionals, such as school psychologists or clinical psychologists, when necessary.
Four years of medical school, plus an internship and residency in pediatrics	Pediatricians monitor infants' and children's health and treat their diseases. They advise parents about infant and child development and the appropriate ways to deal with children.
Courses in biological sciences, nursing care, and pediatrics (often in a school of nursing); supervised clinical experiences in medical settings	Pediatric nurses promote health in infants and children, working to prevent disease or injury, assisting children with handicaps or health problems so they can achieve optimal health, and treating children with health deviations. Some pediatric nurses specialize in certain areas (for example, the neonatal intensive care unit clinician cares exclusively for newborns; the new-parent educator helps the parents of newborns develop better parenting skills). Pediatric nurses work in a variety of medical settings.
Coursework in education with a specialization in early childhood education; state certification usually required	Preschool teachers direct the activities of prekindergarten children, many of whom are 4-year-olds. They develop an appropriate curriculum for the age of the children that promotes their physical, cognitive, and social development in a positive atmosphere. The number of days per week and hours per day varies from one program to another. Kindergarten teachers work with young children who are between the age of preschool programs and the first year of elementary school; they primarily develop appropriate activities and curricula for 5-year-old children.
Courses in biological sciences, nursing care, and mental health in a school of nursing; supervised clinical training in child psychiatric settings	Psychiatric nurses promote the mental health of individuals; some specialize in helping children with mental health problems and work closely with child psychiatrists to improve these children's adjustment.
Includes coursework and supervised training in school settings, usually in a department of educational psychology	School psychologists evaluate and treat a wide range of normal and exceptional children who have school-related problems; work in a school system and see children from a number of schools; administer tests, interview and observe children, and consult with teachers, parents, and school administrators; and design programs to reduce the child's problem behavior.

Chapter Review

Children should have a special place in any society, for they are the society's future. An important concern is that too many children today will not reach their full potential because of inadequate rearing conditions. Far too many children live in poverty, have parents who do not adequately care for them, and go to schools where learning conditions are far from optimal.

In this chapter, you were introduced to the field of child development. You learned about the nature of child development through history, the modern study of child development, ways to improve children's lives, and social policy issues. You studied the nature of development by exploring biological, cognitive, and socioemotional processes; periods of development; and developmental issues. You also read about a number of careers in child development.

To obtain a more detailed review of the chapter, go back and again study the two summary tables on pages 17 and 23. In the next chapter, we will turn our attention to the field of child development as a science. You will learn about the importance of the scientific method, theories, and methods in studying children.

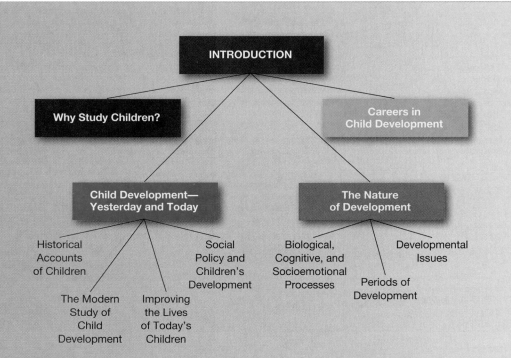

Children Checklist

Introduction

How much have you learned since the beginning of the chapter? Use the following statements to help you review your knowledge and understanding of the chapter material. First, read the statement and mentally or briefly demonstrate on paper that you can discuss the relevant information.

_____ I can describe historical accounts of children.

_____ I know about the developments in the modern study of child development.

_____ I am aware of the areas in which children's lives need to be improved.

_____ I understand the nature of social policy and children's development.

_____ I can discuss the processes involved in development.

_____ I can describe the periods of development.

_____ I know what some main developmental issues involve.

_____ I am aware of the many careers in child development.

For any items that you did not check, go back and locate the relevant material in the chapter. Review the material until you feel you can check off the item. You may want to use this checklist later in preparing for an exam.

Children Resources

Children's Defense Fund
25 E Street
Washington, DC 20001
800–424–9602

The Children's Defense Fund exists to provide a strong and effective voice for children and adolescents who cannot vote, lobby, or speak for themselves. The Children's Defense Fund is especially interested in the needs of poor, minority, and handicapped children and adolescents. The fund provides information, technical assistance, and support to a network of state and local child and youth advocates. The Children's Defense Fund publishes a number of excellent books and pamphlets related to children's needs.

Key Terms

original sin view 6
tabula rasa view 7
innate goodness view 7
context 13
culture 13
cross-cultural studies 13
ethnicity 13
ethnic identity 13
gender 13
social policy 15
development 18
biological processes 18
cognitive processes 18

socioemotional processes 18
prenatal period 19
infancy 19
early childhood 19
middle and late childhood 19
adolescence 19
maturation 19
nature-nurture controversy 20
continuity of development 21
discontinuity of development 21
early-later experience issue 21

Taking It to the Net

http://www.mhhe.com/santrockcd6

1. Bobbi loves mashed banana baby food, but not sweet potato baby food. LaRonda likes dolls, but not trucks. Chip is affectionate, while Suzi is shy. What are your likes and dislikes? Are these differences the result of heredity, or development?

2. Social policy is often motivated by changes in economics. One such change is the new trend by advertisers to target school-aged children, while they are in school. Consider the following statement, "Johnson Paper, the official notebook paper of Smith County Elementary Schools." Should children in school be allowed to become a new advertising market?

3. Delores is a single mother who cares greatly about her child. She also attends college and works 40 hours a week. Delores is worried that the hours she is at school and work, away from her child, may affect her child's development. What alternatives are there for working mothers and which alternative do you believe is the best alternative? And why?

Chapter

2

Chapter Outline

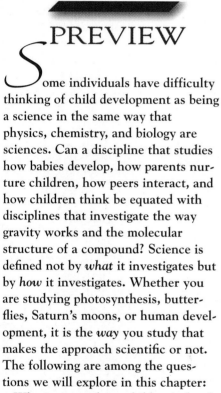

There is nothing quite so practical as a good theory.

Kurt Lewin
American Social Psychologist, 20th Century

PREVIEW

Some individuals have difficulty thinking of child development as being a science in the same way that physics, chemistry, and biology are sciences. Can a discipline that studies how babies develop, how parents nurture children, how peers interact, and how children think be equated with disciplines that investigate the way gravity works and the molecular structure of a compound? Science is defined not by *what* it investigates but by *how* it investigates. Whether you are studying photosynthesis, butterflies, Saturn's moons, or human development, it is the *way* you study that makes the approach scientific or not. The following are among the questions we will explore in this chapter:

• Why is research on children's development important? What information does it give us beyond personal experience and experts' findings?

• What steps are involved in using the scientific method to conduct research?

• What are the main theories of child development?

• What research methods do scientists use when they study children's development?

• What are some of the challenges that are involved in conducting research on children's development?

The Stories of Erik Erikson and Jean Piaget

Imagine that you have developed a major theory of child development. What would influence someone such as you to construct this theory? A person interested in developing such a theory usually goes through a long university training program that culminates in a doctoral degree. As part of the training, the future theorist is exposed to many ideas about a particular area of child development, such as biological, cognitive, or socioemotional development. Another factor that could explain why someone develops a particular theory is that person's life experiences. Two important developmental theorists, whose views will be described later in the chapter, are Erik Erikson and Jean Piaget. Let's examine a portion of their lives as they were growing up to discover how their experiences might have contributed to the theories they developed.

Erik Homberger Erikson (1902–1994) was born near Frankfurt, Germany, to Danish parents. Before Erik was born, his parents separated, and his mother left Denmark to live in Germany. At age 3, Erik became ill, and his mother took him to see a pediatrician named Homberger. Young Erik's mother fell in love with the pediatrician, married him, and named Erik after his new stepfather.

Erik attended primary school from the ages of 6 to 10 and then the gymnasium (high school) from 11 to 18. He studied art and a number of languages rather than science courses, such as biology and chemistry. Erik did not like the atmosphere of formal schooling, and this was reflected in his grades. Rather than go to college at age 18, the adolescent Erikson wandered around Europe, keeping a diary about his experiences. After a year of travel through Europe, he returned to Germany and enrolled in art school, became dissatisfied, and enrolled in another. Later he traveled to Florence, Italy. Psychiatrist Robert Coles described Erikson at this time:

> To the Italians he was . . . the young, tall, thin Nordic expatriate with long, blond hair. He wore a corduroy suit and was seen by his family and friends as not odd or "sick" but as a wandering artist who was trying to come to grips with himself, a not unnatural or unusual struggle. (Coles, 1970, p. 15)

The second major theorist whose life we will examine is Jean Piaget. Piaget (1896–1980) was born in Neuchâtel, Switzerland. Jean's father was an intellectual who taught young Jean to think systematically. Jean's mother was also very bright. His father had an air of detachment from his mother, whom Piaget described as prone to frequent outbursts of neurotic behavior.

In his autobiography, Piaget detailed why he chose to study cognitive development rather than social or abnormal development:

> I started to forego playing for serious work very early. Indeed, I have always detested any departure from reality, an attitude which I relate to . . . my mother's poor health. It was this disturbing factor which at the beginning of my studies in psychology made me keenly interested in psychoanalytic and pathological psychology. Though this interest helped me to achieve independence and widen my cultural

background, I have never since felt any desire to involve myself deeper in that particular direction, always much preferring the study of normalcy and of the workings of the intellect to that of the tricks of the unconscious. (Piaget, 1952a, p. 238)

These excerpts from Erikson's and Piaget's lives illustrate how personal experiences might influence the direction in which a particular theorist goes. Erikson's own wanderings and search for self contributed to his theory of identity development, and Piaget's intellectual experiences with his parents and schooling contributed to his emphasis on cognitive development.

WHY RESEARCH ON CHILD DEVELOPMENT IS IMPORTANT

It sometimes is said that experience is the most important teacher. We get a great deal of knowledge from personal experience. We generalize from what we observe and frequently turn memorable encounters into lifetime "truths." But how valid are these conclusions? Sometimes we err in making these personal observations or misinterpret what we see and hear. Chances are, you can think of many situations in which you thought other people read you the wrong the way, just as they may have felt that you misread them. When we base information only on personal experiences, we also aren't always completely objective, because sometimes we make judgments that protect our ego and self-esteem (McMillan, 1996).

We get information not only from personal experiences but also from authorities and experts. You may hear experts spell out a "best way" to parent children or educate them, but the authorities and experts don't always agree, do they? You may hear one expert proclaim that one strategy for interacting with children is the best and, the next week, see that another expert touts another strategy as the best. How can you tell which one to believe? One way to clarify the situation is to carefully examine research that has been conducted on the topic.

THE SCIENTIFIC RESEARCH APPROACH

Researchers take a skeptical, scientific attitude toward knowledge. When they hear someone claim that a particular method is effective in helping children cope with stress, they want to know if the claim is based on *good* research. The science part of child development seeks to sort fact from fancy by using particular strategies for obtaining information.

Scientific research *is objective, systematic, and testable*. It reduces the likelihood that information will be based on personal beliefs, opinions, and feelings. Scientific research is based on the **scientific method,** *an approach that can be used to discover accurate information. It includes these steps: conceptualize the problem, collect data, draw conclusions, and revise research conclusions and theory.*

The first step, *conceptualizing a problem*, involves identifying the problem, it may include theory, and it consists of developing one or more hypotheses. For example, a team of researchers decides that it wants to study ways to improve the achievement of children from impoverished backgrounds. The researchers have *identified a problem*, which, at a general level, may not seem like a difficult task. However, as part of the first step, they also must go beyond a general description of the problem by isolating, analyzing, narrowing, and focusing more specifically on what aspect of it they hope to study. Perhaps the researchers decide to discover if mentoring that involves sustained support, guidance, and concrete assistance to children from

Science refines everyday thinking.

Albert Einstein
German-born American Physicist, 20th Century

Truth is arrived at by the painstaking elimination of the untrue.

Arthur Conan Doyle
English Physician and Novelist, 20th Century

scientific research
Research that is objective, systematic, and testable.

scientific method
An approach that can be used to discover accurate information. It includes these steps: conceptualize the problem, collect data, draw conclusions, and revise research conclusions and theory.

Generating Research Ideas

Researchers use the scientific method to obtain accurate information about children's behavior and development. Data collection is part of the scientific method, demonstrated here by a researcher conducting a study of infant development.

impoverished backgrounds can improve their academic performance. At this point, even more narrowing and focusing needs to take place. What specific strategies do the researchers want the mentors to use? How often will the mentors see the children? How long will the mentoring program last? What aspects of the children's achievement do the researchers want to assess?

As researchers formulate a problem to study, they often draw on *theories and develop hypotheses.* A **theory** *is an interrelated, coherent set of ideas that helps to explain and to make predictions.* A theory contains **hypotheses,** *which are specific assumptions and predictions that can be tested to determine their accuracy.* For example, a theory on mentoring might attempt to explain and predict why sustained support, guidance, and concrete experience make a difference in the lives of children from impoverished backgrounds. The theory might focus on children's opportunities to model the behavior and strategies of mentors, or it might focus on the effects of individual attention, which might be missing in the children's lives.

The next step is to *collect information (data).* In the study of mentoring, the researchers might decide to conduct the mentoring program for six months. Their data might consist of classroom observations, teachers' ratings, and achievement tests given to the mentored children before the mentoring began and at the end of six months of mentoring.

Once data have been collected, child development researchers use *statistical procedures* to understand the meaning of quantitative data. Then they try to draw *conclusions.* In the study of mentoring, statistics would help determine whether or not their own observations are due to chance. After data have been analyzed, researchers compare their findings with those others have found about the same topic.

The final step in the scientific method is *revising research conclusions and theory.* A number of theories have been generated to describe and explain children's development. Over time, some theories have been discarded, others revised. Shortly in this chapter and throughout the text you will read about a number of theories of child development. Figure 2.1 illustrates the steps in the scientific method applied to the study of mentoring we have been discussing.

theory

An interrelated, coherent set of ideas that helps to explain and to make predictions.

hypotheses

Specific assumptions and predictions that can be tested to determine their accuracy.

Figure 2.1
The Scientific Method Applied to a Study of Mentoring

Step 1: Conceptualize the problem

A researcher identifies this problem: Many children from impoverished backgrounds have lower achievement than children from higher socioeconomic backgrounds. The researcher develops the hypothesis that mentoring will improve the achievement of the children from impoverished backgrounds.

Step 2: Collect information (data)

The researcher conducts the mentoring program for six months and collects data before the program begins and after its conclusion, using classroom observations, teachers' ratings, and achievement test scores.

Step 3: Draw conclusions

The researcher statistically analyzes the data and finds that the children's achievement improved over the six months of the study. The researcher concludes that mentoring is likely an important reason for the increase in the children's achievement.

Step 4: Revise research conclusions and theory

This research on mentoring, along with other research that obtains similar results, increases the likelihood that mentoring will be considered as an important component of theorizing about how to improve the achievement of children from low-income backgrounds.

THE FAR SIDE   By GARY LARSON

"So, Mr. Fenton . . . Let's begin with your mother."

THEORIES OF CHILD DEVELOPMENT

We will briefly explore five major theoretical perspectives on child development: psychoanalytic, cognitive, behavioral/social learning, ethological, and ecological. You will read more in-depth portrayals of these theories at different points in later chapters in the book.

The diversity of theories makes understanding children's development a challenging undertaking. Just when you think one theory correctly explains children's development, another theory crops up and makes you rethink your earlier conclusion. To keep from getting frustrated, remember that children's development is a complex, multifaceted topic, and no single theory has been able to account for all its aspects. Each theory has contributed an important piece to the child development puzzle. Although the theories sometimes disagree about certain aspects of children's development, much of their information is *complementary* rather than contradictory. Together the various theories let us see the total landscape of children's development in all its richness.

Psychoanalytic Theories

Psychoanalytic theorists describe development as primarily unconscious—that is, beyond awareness—and as heavily colored by emotion. Psychoanalytic theorists believe that behavior is merely a surface characteristic and that, to truly understand development, we have to analyze the symbolic meanings of behavior and the deep inner workings of the mind. Psychoanalytic theorists also stress that early experiences with parents extensively shape our development. These characteristics are highlighted in the main psychoanalytic theory, that of Sigmund Freud.

Freud's Theory   Freud (1856–1939) developed his ideas about psychoanalytic theory from work with mental patients. He was a medical doctor who specialized in neurology. He spent most of his years in Vienna, though he moved to London near the end of his career because of the Nazis' anti-Semitism.

Freud (1917) believed that personality has three structures: the id, the ego, and the superego. The **id** *is the Freudian structure of personality that consists of instincts, which are an individual's reservoir of psychic energy.* In Freud's view, the id is totally unconscious; it has no contact with reality. As children experience the demands and constraints of reality, a new structure of personality emerges—the **ego,** *the Freudian structure of personality that deals with the demands of reality.* The ego is called the executive branch of personality because it uses reasoning to make decisions. The id and the ego have no morality. They do not take into account whether something is right or wrong. The **superego** *is the Freudian structure of personality that is the moral branch of personality.* The superego takes into account whether something is right or wrong. Think of the superego as what we often refer to as our "conscience." You probably are beginning to sense that both the id and the superego make life rough for the ego. Your ego might say, "I will have sex only occasionally and be sure to take the proper precautions because I don't want the intrusion of a child in the development of my career." However, your id is saying, "I want to be satisfied; sex is pleasurable." Your superego is at work, too: "I feel guilty about having sex."

Remember that Freud considered personality to be like an iceberg; most of personality exists below our level of awareness, just as the massive part of an iceberg is beneath the surface of the water. Figure 2.2 illustrates this analogy.

How does the ego resolve the conflict among its demands for reality, the wishes of the id, and constraints of the superego? Through **defense mechanisms,** *the psychoanalytic term for unconscious methods the ego uses to distort reality, thereby protecting it from anxiety.* In Freud's view, the conflicting demands of the personality structures produce anxiety. For example, when the ego blocks the pleasurable pursuits of the id, inner anxiety is felt. This diffuse, distressed state develops when the ego senses that the id is going to cause harm to the individual. The anxiety alerts the ego to resolve the conflict by means of defense mechanisms.

Repression *is the most powerful and pervasive defense mechanism, according to Freud; it works to push unacceptable id impulses out of awareness and back into the unconscious mind.* Repression is the foundation from which all other defense mechanisms work; the goal of every defense mechanism is to repress, or push threatening impulses out of awareness. Freud said that our early childhood experiences, many of which he believed are sexually laden, are too threatening and stressful for us to deal with consciously. We reduce the anxiety of this conflict through the defense mechanism of repression.

As Freud listened to, probed, and analyzed his patients, he became convinced that their problems were the result of experiences early in life. Freud believed that we go through five stages of psychosexual development and that, at each stage of development, we experience pleasure in one part of the body more than in others. **Erogenous zones** *are, in Freud's theory, the parts of the body that have especially strong pleasure-giving qualities at each stage of development.*

Freud thought that the adult personality is determined by the way conflicts between the early sources of pleasure—the mouth, the anus, and then the genitals—and the demands of reality are resolved. When these conflicts are not resolved, the individual may become fixated at a particular stage of development. For example, a parent might wean a child too early, be too strict in toilet training, punish the child for masturbation, or smother the child with warmth.

The **oral stage** *is the first Freudian stage of development, occurring during the first 18 months of life, in which the infant's pleasure centers around the mouth.* Chewing,

Sigmund Freud, the pioneering architect of psychoanalytic theory.

Freud's Theory

id
The Freudian structure of personality that consists of instincts, which are an individual's reserve of psychic energy.

ego
The Freudian structure of personality that deals with the demands of reality.

superego
The Freudian structure of personality that is the moral branch of personality.

defense mechanisms
The psychoanalytic term for unconscious methods used by the ego to distort reality in order to protect itself from anxiety.

repression
The most powerful and pervasive defense mechanism; it pushes unacceptable id impulses out of awareness and back into the unconscious mind.

erogenous zones
Freud's concept of the parts of the body that have especially strong pleasure-giving qualities at each stage of development.

oral stage
The first Freudian stage of development, occurring during the first 18 months of life; the infant's pleasure centers around the mouth.

Figure 2.2
Conscious and Unconscious Processes: The Iceberg Analogy

This rather odd-looking diagram illustrates Freud's theory that most of the important personality processes occur below the level of conscious awareness. In examining people's conscious thoughts and their behaviors, we can see some reflections of the ego and the superego. Whereas the ego and superego are partly conscious and partly unconscious, the primitive id is the unconscious, totally submerged part of the iceberg.

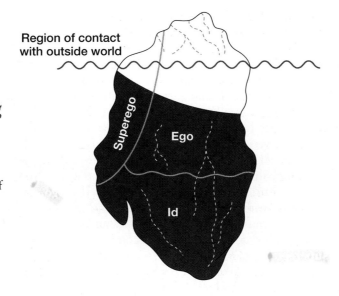

Region of contact with outside world

Superego

Ego

Id

anal stage

The second Freudian stage of development, occurring between 1½ and 3 years of age; the child's greatest pleasure involves the anus or the eliminative functions associated with it.

phallic stage

The third Freudian stage of development, occurring between the ages of 3 and 6; its name comes from the Latin word *phallus,* which means "penis."

Oedipus complex

In Freudian theory, the young child's development of an intense desire to replace the same-sex parent and to enjoy the affections of the opposite-sex parent.

latency stage

The fourth Freudian stage, occurring between approximately 6 years of age and puberty; the child represses all interest in sexuality and develops social and intellectual skills.

genital stage

The fifth and final Freudian stage of development, which occurs from puberty on; a sexual reawakening in which the source of sexual pleasure becomes someone outside of the family.

sucking, and biting are the chief sources of pleasure. These actions reduce tension in the infant.

The **anal stage** *is the second Freudian stage of development, occurring between 1½ and 3 years of age, in which the child's greatest pleasure involves the anus or the eliminative functions associated with it.* In Freud's view, the exercise of anal muscles reduces tension.

The **phallic stage** *is the third Freudian stage of development, which occurs between the ages of 3 and 6; its name comes from the Latin word* phallus, *which means "penis."* During the phallic stage, pleasure focuses on the genitals as the child discovers that self-manipulation is enjoyable.

In Freud's view, the phallic stage has a special importance in personality development because it is during this period that the Oedipus complex appears. This name comes from Greek mythology, in which Oedipus, the son of the King of Thebes, unwittingly kills his father and marries his mother. The **Oedipus complex,** *according to Freudian theory, is the young child's development of an intense desire to replace the same-sex parent and enjoy the affections of the opposite-sex parent.*

How is the Oedipus complex resolved? At about 5 to 6 years of age, children recognize that their same-sex parent might punish them for their incestuous wishes. To reduce this conflict, the child identifies with the same-sex parent, striving to be like him or her. If the conflict is not resolved, though, the individual may become fixated at the phallic stage.

The **latency stage** *is the fourth Freudian stage of development, which occurs between approximately 6 years of age and puberty; the child represses all interest in sexuality and develops social and intellectual skills.* This activity channels much of the child's energy into emotionally safe areas and helps the child forget the highly stressful conflicts of the phallic stage.

The **genital stage** *is the fifth and final Freudian stage of development, occurring from puberty on. The genital stage is a time of sexual reawakening; the source of sexual pleasure now becomes someone outside of the family.* Freud believed that unresolved conflicts with parents reemerge during adolescence. When resolved, the individual is capable of developing a mature love relationship and functioning independently as an adult.

Freud's theory has undergone significant revisions by a number of psychoanalytic theorists. Many contemporary psychoanalytic theorists place less emphasis on sexual instincts and more emphasis on cultural experiences as determinants of an individual's development. Unconscious thought remains a central theme, but most contemporary psychoanalysts believe that conscious thought makes up more of the iceberg than Freud envisioned. Next, we will explore the ideas of an important revisionist of Freud's ideas—Erik Erikson.

Erikson's Theory   Erik Erikson (1902–1994) recognized Freud's contributions but believed that Freud misjudged some important dimensions of human development. For one, Erikson (1950, 1968) said we develop in *psychosocial stages,* in contrast to Freud's psychosexual stages. For another, Erikson emphasized developmental change throughout the human life span, whereas Freud argued that our basic personality is shaped in the first five years of life. In Erikson's theory, eight stages of development unfold as we go through the life span (see figure 2.3). Each stage consists of a unique developmental task that confronts individuals with a crisis that must be faced. According to Erikson, this crisis is not a catastrophe but a turning point of increased vulnerability and enhanced potential. The more an individual resolves the crises successfully, the healthier development will be.

Trust versus mistrust *is Erikson's first psychosocial stage, which is experienced in the first year of life. A sense of trust requires a feeling of physical comfort and a minimal amount of fear and apprehension about the future. Trust in infancy sets the stage for a lifelong expectation that the world will be a good and pleasant place to live.*

Autonomy versus shame and doubt *is Erikson's second stage of development, occurring in late infancy and toddlerhood (1–3 years). After gaining trust in their caregivers, infants begin to discover that their behavior is their own. They*

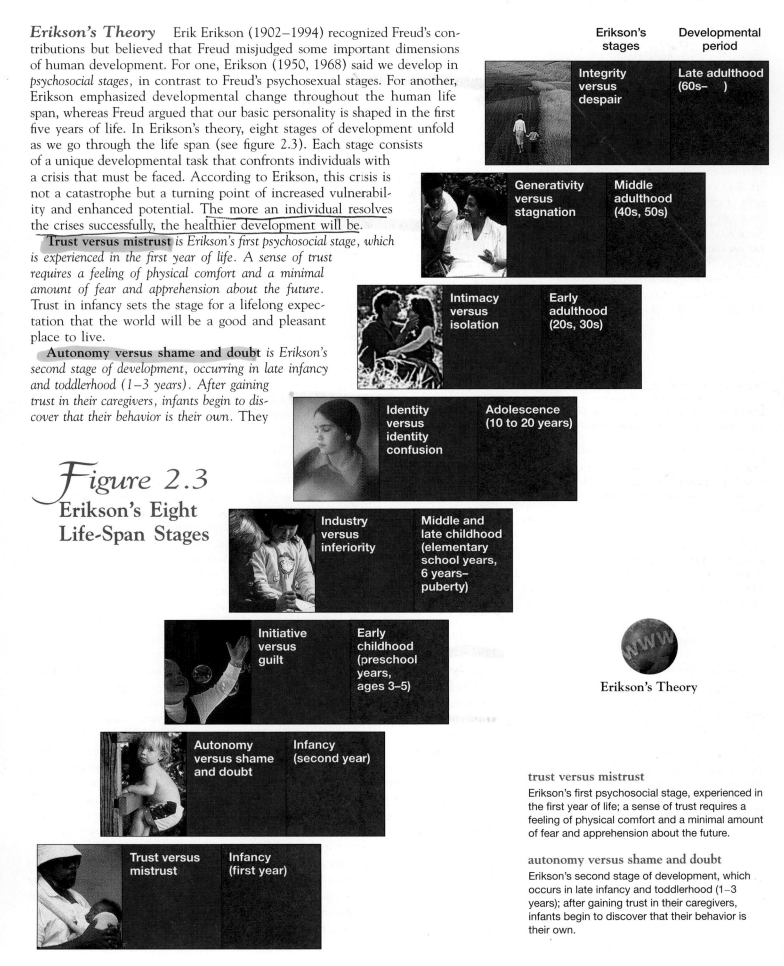

***F*igure 2.3**
**Erikson's Eight
Life-Span Stages**

Erikson's Theory

trust versus mistrust
Erikson's first psychosocial stage, experienced in the first year of life; a sense of trust requires a feeling of physical comfort and a minimal amount of fear and apprehension about the future.

autonomy versus shame and doubt
Erikson's second stage of development, which occurs in late infancy and toddlerhood (1–3 years); after gaining trust in their caregivers, infants begin to discover that their behavior is their own.

Erik Erikson with his wife, Joan, an artist. Erikson generated one of the most important developmental theories of the twentieth century.

initiative versus guilt
Erikson's third stage of development, which occurs during the preschool years; as preschool children encounter a widening social world, they are challenged more than they were as infants.

industry versus inferiority
Erikson's fourth stage of development, which occurs approximately in the elementary school years; children's initiative brings them into contact with a wealth of new experiences, and they direct their energy toward mastering knowledge and intellectual skills.

identity versus identity confusion
Erikson's fifth stage of development, which occurs during the adolescent years; adolescents are faced with finding out who they are, what they are all about, and where they are going in life.

intimacy versus isolation
Erikson's sixth stage of development, which occurs during the early adulthood years; young adults face the developmental task of forming intimate relationships with others.

generativity versus stagnation
Erikson's seventh stage of development, which occurs during middle adulthood; a chief concern is to assist the younger generation in developing and leading useful lives.

integrity versus despair
Erikson's eighth and final stage of development, which occurs during late adulthood; in the later years of life, we look back and evaluate what we have done with our lives.

start to assert their sense of independence, or autonomy. They realize their *will*. If infants are restrained too much or punished too harshly, they are likely to develop a sense of shame and doubt.

Initiative versus guilt *is Erikson's third stage of development, occurring during the preschool years. As preschool children encounter a widening social world, they are challenged more than when they were infants.* Active, purposeful behavior is needed to cope with these challenges. Children are asked to assume responsibility for their bodies, their behavior, their toys, and their pets. Developing a sense of responsibility increases initiative. Uncomfortable guilt feelings may arise, though, if the child is irresponsible and is made to feel too anxious. Erikson has a positive outlook on this stage. He believes that most guilt is quickly compensated for by a sense of accomplishment.

Industry versus inferiority *is Erikson's fourth developmental stage, occurring approximately in the elementary school years. Children's initiative brings them in contact with a wealth of new experiences. As they move into middle and late childhood, they direct their energy toward mastering knowledge and intellectual skills.* At no other time is the child more enthusiastic about learning than at the end of early childhood's period of expansive imagination. The danger in the elementary school years is the development of a sense of inferiority—of feeling incompetent and unproductive. Erikson believes that teachers have a special responsibility for children's development of industry. Teachers should "mildly but firmly coerce children into the adventure of finding out that one can learn to accomplish things which one would never have thought of by oneself" (Erikson, 1968, p. 127).

Identity versus identity confusion *is Erikson's fifth developmental stage, which individuals experience during the adolescent years. At this time, individuals are faced with finding out who they are, what they are all about, and where they are going in life.* Adolescents are confronted with many new roles and adult statuses—vocational and romantic, for example. Parents need to allow adolescents to explore many different roles and different paths within a particular role. If the adolescent explores such roles in a healthy manner and arrives at a positive path to follow in life, then a positive identity will be achieved. If an identity is pushed on the adolescent by parents, if the adolescent does not adequately explore many roles, and if a positive future path is not defined, then identity confusion reigns.

Intimacy versus isolation *is Erikson's sixth developmental stage, which individuals experience during the early adulthood years. At this time, individuals face the developmental task of forming intimate relationships with others.* Erikson describes intimacy as finding oneself yet losing oneself in another. If the young adult forms healthy friendships and an intimate relationship with another individual, intimacy will be achieved; if not, isolation will result.

Generativity versus stagnation *is Erikson's seventh developmental stage, which individuals experience during middle adulthood. A chief concern is to assist the younger generation in developing and leading useful lives*—this is what Erikson means by *generativity*. The feeling of having done nothing to help the next generation is *stagnation*.

Integrity versus despair *is Erikson's eighth and final developmental stage, which individuals experience during late adulthood. In the later years of life, we look back and evaluate what we have done with our lives.* Through many different routes, the older person may have developed a positive outlook in most or all of the previous stages of development. If so, the retrospective glances will reveal a picture of a life well spent, and the person will feel a sense of satisfaction—integrity will be achieved. If the older adult resolved many of the earlier stages negatively, the retrospective glances likely will yield doubt or gloom—the despair Erikson talks about.

Erikson does not believe that the proper solution to a stage crisis is always completely positive. Some exposure or commitment to the negative end of the person's bipolar conflict is sometimes inevitable—you cannot trust all people under all circumstances and survive, for example. Nonetheless, in the healthy solution to a stage crisis, the positive resolution dominates.

Cognitive Theories

Whereas psychoanalytic theories stress the importance of children's unconscious thoughts, cognitive theories emphasize their conscious thoughts. Two important cognitive theories are Piaget's cognitive development theory and information processing.

Piaget's theory will be covered in greater detail later in this book, when we discuss cognitive development in infancy, early childhood, middle and late childhood, and adolescence. Here we briefly present the main ideas of his theory.

Piaget's Cognitive Developmental Theory

The famous Swiss psychologist, Jean Piaget (1896–1980), stressed that children actively construct their own cognitive worlds; information is not just poured into their minds from the environment. Piaget believed that children adapt their thinking to include new ideas.

Two processes underlie our construction of the world: organization and adaptation. To make sense of our world, we organize our experiences. For example, we separate important ideas from less important ideas. We connect one idea to another. But not only do we organize our observations and experiences, we also *adapt* our thinking to include new ideas because additional information furthers understanding. Piaget (1954) believed that we adapt in two ways: assimilation and accommodation.

Assimilation *occurs when individuals incorporate new information into their existing knowledge.* **Accommodation** *occurs when individuals adjust to new information.* Consider a circumstance in which a 9-year-old girl is given a hammer and nails to hang a picture on the wall. She has never used a hammer, but from observation and vicarious experience she realizes that a hammer is an object to be held, that it is swung by the handle to hit the nail, and that it is usually swung a number of times. Recognizing each of these things, she fits her behavior into this information she already has (assimilation). However, the hammer is heavy, so she holds it near the top. She swings too hard and the nail bends, so she adjusts the pressure of her strikes. These adjustments reveal her ability to alter slightly her conception of the world (accommodation).

Piaget thought that assimilation and accommodation operate even in the very young infant's life. Newborns reflexively suck everything that touches their lips (assimilation), but, after several months of experience, they construct their understanding of the world differently. Some objects, such as fingers and the mother's breast, can be sucked, but others, such as fuzzy blankets, should not be sucked (accommodation).

Piaget also believed that we go through four stages in understanding the world (see figure 2.4). Each of the stages is age-related and consists of distinct ways of thinking. Remember, it is the *different* way of understanding the world that makes one stage more advanced than another; knowing *more* information does not make the child's thinking more advanced, in the Piagetian view. This is what Piaget meant when he said the child's cognition is *qualitatively* different in one stage compared to another. What are Piaget's four stages of cognitive development like?

The **sensorimotor stage,** *which lasts from birth to about 2 years of age, is the first Piagetian stage. In this stage, infants construct an understanding of the world by coordinating sensory experiences (such as seeing and hearing) with physical, motoric actions—hence the term* sensorimotor. At the beginning of this stage, newborns have little more than reflexive patterns with which to work. At the end of the stage, 2-year-

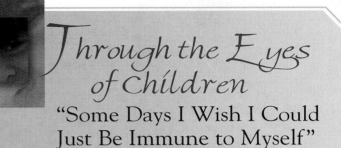

Through the Eyes of Children

"Some Days I Wish I Could Just Be Immune to Myself"

Following are some of 16-year-old Sandra's thoughts about herself:

The other day I started thinking about who I am. Then I started thinking about why I was thinking about who I am. Kind of confusing, huh?

My dad wants me to be a doctor and my mom wants me to be a lawyer, but I don't know what I want to be. I'll get it figured out at some point. I do know I don't want to be a waitress or a secretary.

I don't completely understand myself, but I don't think most other people do either. Sometimes I'm one way, then another. I'll be cheery and then moody. I'll be angry and then sensitive. I'm friendly to a lot of people, but I can be shy. Sometimes I get pretty stressed out with all the things I have to do. I'm so complicated that some days I wish I could just be immune to myself!

Piaget's Theory

assimilation
Individuals' incorporation of new information into their existing knowledge.

accommodation
Individuals' adjustment to new information.

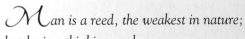

Man is a reed, the weakest in nature; but he is a thinking reed.

Blaise Pascal
French Philosopher and Mathematician, 17th Century

sensorimotor stage
The first of Piaget's stages, which lasts from birth to about 2 years of age; infants construct an understanding of the world by coordinating sensory experiences (such as seeing and hearing) with motoric actions.

Jean Piaget, the famous Swiss developmental psychologist, changed the way we think about the development of children's minds. For Piaget, a child's mental development is a continuous creation of increasingly complex forms.

Formal operational stage

The adolescent reasons in more abstract, idealistic, and logical ways.

11 years of age through adulthood

Concrete operational stage

The child can now reason logically about concrete events and classify objects into different sets.

7–11 years of age

Preoperational stage

The child begins to represent the world with words and images. These words and images reflect increased symbolic thinking and go beyond the connection of sensory information and physical action.

2–7 years of age

Sensorimotor stage

The infant constructs an understanding of the world by coordinating sensory experiences with physical actions. An infant progresses from reflexive, instinctual action at birth to the beginning of symbolic thought toward the end of the stage.

Birth to 2 years of age

Figure 2.4
Piaget's Four Stages of Cognitive Development

preoperational stage
The second Piagetian developmental stage, which lasts from about 2 to 7 years of age; children begin to represent the world with words, images, and drawings.

concrete operational stage
Piaget's third stage, which lasts from approximately 7 to 11 years of age; children can perform operations, and logical reasoning replaces intuitive thought as long as the reasoning can be applied to specific, concrete examples.

formal operational stage
Piaget's fourth and final stage, which occurs between the ages of 11 and 15; individuals move beyond concrete experiences and think in more abstract and logical ways.

olds have complex sensorimotor patterns and are beginning to operate with primitive symbols.

The **preoperational stage,** *which lasts from approximately 2 to 7 years of age, is the second Piagetian stage. In this stage, children begin to represent the world with words, images, and drawings.* Symbolic thought goes beyond simple connections of sensory information and physical action. However, although preschool children can symbolically represent the world, according to Piaget, they still lack the ability to perform *operations,* the Piagetian term for internalized mental actions that allow children to do mentally what they previously did physically.

The **concrete operational stage,** *which lasts from approximately 7 to 11 years of age, is the third Piagetian stage. In this stage, children can perform operations, and logical reasoning replaces intuitive thought as long as reasoning can be applied to specific or concrete examples.* For instance, concrete operational thinkers cannot imagine the steps necessary to complete an algebraic equation, which is too abstract for thinking at this stage of development.

The **formal operational stage,** *which appears between the ages of 11 and 15, is the fourth and final Piagetian stage. In this stage, individuals move beyond concrete experiences and think in abstract and more logical terms.* As part of thinking more abstractly, adolescents develop images of ideal circumstances. They might think about what an ideal parent is like and compare their parents to this ideal standard. They begin to entertain possibilities for the future and are fascinated with what they can be. In solving problems, formal operational thinkers are more systematic, developing hypotheses about why something is happening the way it is, then testing these hypotheses in a deductive fashion.

Vygotsky's Sociocultural Cognitive Theory Like Piaget, Russian Lev Vygotsky (1896–1934) also believed that children actively construct their knowledge. Vygotsky was born in Russia in the same year as Piaget, but he died much earlier, at the age of 37. Both Piaget's and Vygotsky's ideas remained virtually unknown to American scholars for many years, not being introduced to American audiences through English translations until the 1960s. In the past several decades, American psychologists and educators have shown increased interest in Vygotsky's (1962) views.

Three claims capture the heart of Vygotsky's view (Tappan, 1998): (1) the child's cognitive skills can be understood only when they are developmentally analyzed and interpreted, (2) cognitive skills are mediated by words, language, and forms of discourse, which serve as psychological tools for facilitating and transforming mental activity, and (3) cognitive skills have their origins in social relations and are embedded in a sociocultural backdrop.

For Vygotsky, taking a developmental approach means that, in order to understand any aspect of the child's cognitive functioning, one must examine its origins and transformations from earlier to later forms. Thus, a particular mental act, such as using private speech (speech-to-self), cannot be viewed accurately in isolation but should be evaluated as a step in a gradual developmental process.

Vygotsky's second claim, that to understand cognitive functioning it is necessary to examine the tools that mediate and shape it, led him to believe that language is the most important of these tools. Vygotsky argued that, in early childhood, language begins to be used as a tool that helps the child plan activities and solve problems.

Vygotsky's third claim was that cognitive skills originate in social relations and culture. Vygotsky portrayed the child's development as inseparable from social and cultural activities. He believed that the development of memory, attention, and reasoning involves learning to use the inventions of society, such as language, mathematical systems, and memory strategies. In one culture, this may consist of learning to count with the help of a computer. In another, it may consist of counting on one's fingers or using beads.

Vygotsky's theory has stimulated considerable interest in the view that knowledge is *situated* and *collaborative* (Greeno, Collins, & Resnick, 1996; Rogoff, 1998). That is, knowledge is distributed among people and environments, which include objects, artifacts, tools, books, and the communities in which people live. This suggests that knowing can best be advanced through interaction with others in cooperative activities.

Within these basic claims, Vygotsky articulated unique and influential ideas about the relation between learning and development. In chapter 10, "Cognitive Development in Early Childhood," we will further explore Vygotsky's contributions to our understanding of children's development.

Information Processing **Information processing** *involves the ways in which individuals process information about their world—how information enters the mind, how it is stored and transformed, and how it is retrieved to perform such complex activities as problem solving and reasoning.* A simple model of information processing is shown in figure 2.5.

There is considerable interest today in Lev Vygotsky's sociocultural cognitive theory of child development. What were Vygotsky's three basic claims about children's development?

Vygotsky's Theory

information processing
How individuals process information about their world; how information enters the mind, how it is stored and transformed, and how it is retrieved to perform such complex activities as problem solving and reasoning.

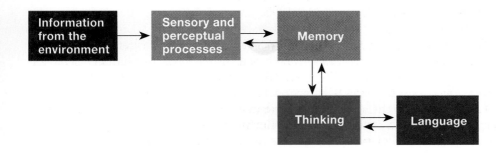

*F*igure 2.5
A Model of Information Processing

B. F. Skinner was a tinkerer who liked to make new gadgets. The younger of his two daughters, Deborah, was raised in Skinner's enclosed Air-Crib, which he invented because he wanted to control her environment completely. The Air-Crib was soundproofed and temperature-controlled. Some critics accused Skinner of monstrous experimentation with his children; however, the early controlled environment has not had any noticeable harmful effects. Debbie, shown here as a child with her parents, is currently a successful artist, is married, and lives in London.

Cognition begins when children detect information from the world through their sensory and perceptual processes. Then children store, transform, and retrieve the information through the processes of memory. Notice in our model that information can flow back and forth between memory and perceptual processes. For example, children are good at remembering the faces they see, yet their memory of a person's face may differ from the way the person actually looks. Keep in mind that our information-processing model is a simple one, designed to illustrate the main cognitive processes and their interrelations. We could have drawn other arrows—between memory and language, between thinking and sensory and perceptual processes, and between language and sensory and perceptual processes, for example. Also, it is important to know that the boxes in figure 2.5 do not represent sharp, distinct stages in processing information. There is continuity, flow, and overlap between the cognitive processes.

Behavioral and Social Learning Theories

Behaviorism and Social Learning Theory

Behaviorists believe we should examine only what can be directly observed and measured. At approximately the same time that Freud was interpreting his patients' unconscious minds through early childhood experiences, behaviorists such as Ivan Pavlov and John B. Watson were conducting detailed observations of behavior in controlled laboratory circumstances. Out of the behavioral tradition grew the belief that development is observable behavior, learned through experience with the environment. The two versions of the behavioral approach that are prominent today are the view of B. F. Skinner (1904–1990) and social learning theory.

behaviorism
The scientific study of observable behavioral responses and their environmental determinants.

Skinner's Behaviorism   **Behaviorism** *emphasizes the scientific study of observable behavioral responses and their environmental determinants.* In Skinner's behaviorism, the mind, conscious or unconscious, is not needed to explain behavior and development. Development is behavior. For example, observations of Sam reveal that his behavior is shy, achievement-oriented, and caring. Why is Sam's behavior this way? For Skinner, rewards and punishments in Sam's environment have shaped him into a shy, achievement-oriented, and caring person. Because of interactions with family members, friends, teachers, and others, Sam has *learned* to behave in this fashion.

Because behaviorists believe that development is learned and often changes according to environmental experiences, it follows that rearranging experiences can change development. For behaviorists, shy behavior can be transformed into outgoing behavior; aggressive behavior can be shaped into docile behavior; lethargic, boring behavior can be turned into enthusiastic, interesting behavior.

Social Learning Theory   Some psychologists believe that the behaviorists basically are right when they say development is learned and is influenced strongly by environmental experiences. However, they believe that Skinner went too far in declaring that cognition is unimportant in understanding development. **Social learning theory** *is the view of psychologists who emphasize behavior, environment, and cognition as the key factors in development.*

American psychologists Albert Bandura (1997, 1998) and Walter Mischel (1973, 1994) are the main architects of social learning theory's contemporary version, which Mischel (1973) labeled *cognitive* social learning theory. Both Bandura and Mischel believe that cognitive processes are important mediators of environment-behavior connections. Bandura's early research program focused heavily on observational learning, learning that occurs through observing what others do. Observational learning is also referred to as imitation or modeling. What is *cognitive* about observational learning in Bandura's view? Bandura (1925–) believes that people cognitively represent the behavior of others and then sometimes adopt this behavior themselves. For example, a young boy might observe his father's aggressive outbursts and hostile interchanges with people; when observed with his peers, the young boy's style of interaction is highly aggressive, showing the same characteristics as his father's behavior. A girl might adopt the dominant and sarcastic style of her teacher. When observed interacting with her younger brother, she says, "You are so slow. How can you do this work so slowly?" Social learning theorists believe that children acquire a wide range of such behaviors, thoughts, and feelings through observing others' behavior. These observations form an important part of children's development.

Bandura's (1986, 1997) most recent model of learning and development involves behavior, the person, and the environment. As shown in figure 2.6, behavior, personal (and cognitive), and environmental factors operate interactively. Behavior can influence personal factors and vice versa. The person's cognitive activities can

Albert Bandura has been one of the leading architects of the contemporary version of social learning theory— cognitive social learning theory.

Albert Bandura

social learning theory
A theory that emphasizes a combination of behavior, environment, and cognition as the key factors in development.

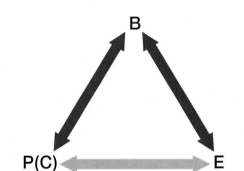

Figure 2.6
Bandura's Model of the Reciprocal Influence of Behavior, Personal and Cognitive Factors, and Environment

P(C) stands for personal and cognitive factors, *B* for behavior, and *E* for environment. The arrows reflect how relations between these factors are reciprocal rather than unidirectional. Examples of personal factors include intelligence, skills, and self-control.

Drawing by Opie; ©1978 The New Yorker Magazine, Inc.

Improving Developmental Skills
Nurturing Children's Self-Efficacy

In Bandura's (1997) most recent book, he outlined the most important aspects of developing self-efficacy in children and adolescents:

- *Young children's requirement for extensive monitoring by competent adults.* Very young children lack knowledge of their own capabilities and the hazards of their world. Adult monitoring gets children through this early formative time until they become aware of what they can do and what situations require in the way of skills.

- *Recognizing that actions produce outcomes.* Infants need a stimulating environment that encourages them to sense that they can make things happen and to regard themselves as the doers.

- *Parental sources of self-efficacy.* Parental enabling activities increase infants' and children's exploratory and cognitive competence. Overprotective parents constrain children's mastery capabilities. By contrast, secure parents are more likely to encourage children's exploratory efforts and to give them an opportunity to experience a feeling of mastery.

- *The school's role.* As children master cognitive skills, they develop a growing sense of intellectual self-efficacy. A basic goal of education is to equip children with the self-control that enables them to educate themselves. This self-regulation includes learning how to develop plans, be organized, become motivated, and use resources. Schools play an important role not only in children's intellectual self-efficacy but also in their health self-efficacy. The effectiveness of health education programs hinges on their ability to impart a sense of self-efficacy to manage one's health habits effectively.

- *The transition to adolescence.* As children move into adolescence, they have to assume increasing responsibility for their behavior. The way in which adolescents develop and exercise their self-efficacy can be critical in setting the courses that their life paths take. Being around competent parents, peers, and teachers who model self-efficacy increases adolescents' self-efficacy.

self-efficacy
Bandura's personal concept, which refers to the expectation that one can master a situation and produce positive outcomes.

ethology
A theory that stresses that behavior is strongly influenced by biology, is tied to evolution, and is characterized by critical or sensitive periods.

influence the environment, the environment can change the person's cognition, and so on.

Bandura believes that an important person factor in learning is **self-efficacy,** *the expectation that one can master a situation and produce positive outcomes.* A large number of studies reveal that, when children have high self-efficacy, they are more likely to do well in school and be more competent in a number of areas of life than when they have low self-efficacy (Bandura, 1997, 1998). The insert, Improving Developmental Skills, reveals how adults can improve children's self-efficacy.

Like the behavioral approach of Skinner, social learning theorists such as Bandura emphasize the importance of empirical research in studying children's development. This research focuses on the processes that explain children's development—the social and cognitive factors that influence what children are like.

Ethological Theories

Sensitivity to different kinds of experience varies over the life span. The presence or absence of certain experiences at particular times in the life span influences individuals well beyond the time the experiences first occur. Ethologists believe that most psychologists underestimate the importance of these special time frames in early development and the powerful roles that evolution and biological foundations play in development (Hinde, 1992).

Ethology emerged as an important view because of the work of European zoologists, especially Konrad Lorenz (1903–1989). **Ethology** *stresses that behavior is strongly influenced by biology, is tied to evolution, and is characterized by critical or sensitive periods.*

Working mostly with greylag geese, Lorenz (1965) studied a behavior pattern that was considered to be programmed within the bird's genes. A newly hatched gosling seemed to be born with the instinct to follow its mother. Observations showed that the gosling was capable of such behavior as soon as it hatched. Lorenz proved that it was incorrect to assume that such behavior was programmed in the animal. In a remarkable set of experiments, Lorenz separated the eggs laid by one goose into two groups. One group he returned to the goose to be hatched by her; the other group was hatched in an incubator. The goslings in the first group performed as predicted; they followed their mother as soon as they hatched. However, those in the second group, which saw Lorenz when they first hatched, followed him everywhere, as though he were their mother. Lorenz marked the goslings and then placed both groups under a box. Mother goose and "mother" Lorenz stood aside as the box was lifted. Each group of goslings went directly to its "mother." Based on such observations, Lorenz developed the ethological concept of **imprinting,** *rapid, innate learning within a limited critical period of time that involves attachment to the first moving object seen.* (See figure 2.7.)

The ethological view of Lorenz and the European zoologists forced American developmental psychologists to recognize the importance of the biological basis of

Ethology

imprinting

In ethological theories, rapid, innate learning, within a limited critical period of time, that involves attachment to the first moving object seen.

critical period

A fixed time period very early in development during which certain behaviors optimally emerge.

ecological theory

Bronfenbrenner's sociocultural view of development, which consists of five environmental systems ranging from the fine-grained inputs of direct interactions with social agents to the broad-based inputs of culture. The five systems in Bronfenbrenner's ecological theory are the microsystem, mesosystem, exosystem, macrosystem, and chronosystem.

microsystem

The setting, or context, in which an individual lives, including the person's family, peers, school, and neighborhood.

F*igure 2.7*
Imprinting

Konrad Lorenz, a pioneering student of animal behavior, is followed through the water by three imprinted greylag geese. Lorenz described imprinting as rapid, innate learning within a critical period that involves attachment to the first moving object seen. For goslings, the critical period is the first 36 hours after birth.

behavior. However, the research and theorizing of ethology still seemed to lack some ingredients that would elevate it to the ranks of the other theories discussed so far in this chapter. In particular, there was little or nothing in the classical ethological view about the nature of social relationships across the human life span, something that any major theory of development must explain. Also, its concept of **critical period,** *a fixed time period very early in development during which certain behaviors optimally emerge,* seemed to be overdrawn. Classical ethological theory was weak in stimulating studies with humans. Recent expansion of the ethological view has improved its status as a viable developmental perspective.

Like behaviorists, ethologists are careful observers of behavior. Unlike behaviorists, ethologists believe that laboratories are not good settings for observing behavior; rather, they meticulously observe behavior in its natural surroundings, in homes, playgrounds, neighborhoods, schools, hospitals, and so on.

Ecological Theory

Ethological theories place a strong emphasis on the biological foundations of children's development. In contrast to ethological theories, Urie Bronfenbrenner (1917–) has proposed a strong environmental view of children's development that is receiving increased attention. **Ecological theory** *is Bronfenbrenner's sociocultural view of development, which consists of five environmental systems ranging from the fine-grained inputs of direct interactions with social agents to the broad-based inputs of culture. The five systems in Bronfenbrenner's ecological theory are the microsystem, mesosystem, exosystem, macrosystem, and chronosystem.* We will consider each in turn. Bronfenbrenner's (1979, 1986, 1995; Bronfenbrenner & Morris, 1998) ecological model is shown in figure 2.8.

The **microsystem,** *in Bronfenbrenner's ecological theory, is the setting in which an individual lives. This context includes the person's family, peers, school, and neighborhood.* It is in the microsystem that most of the direct interactions with social agents take place—with parents, peers, and teachers, for example. The individual is not viewed as a passive recipient of experiences in these settings, but as someone who helps construct the settings. Bronfenbrenner points out that most of the research on environmental influences has focused on microsystems.

When imprinting studies go awry . . .

Figure 2.8
Bronfenbrenner's Ecological Theory of Development

Bronfenbrenner's ecological theory consists of five environmental systems: microsystem, mesosystem, exosystem, macrosystem, and chronosystem.

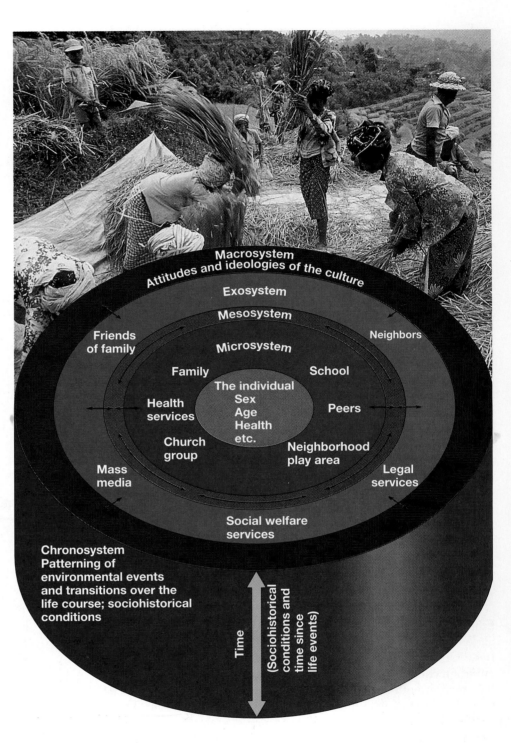

mesosystem

Relationships between microsystems or connections between contexts, such as the connection between family experience and the school experience.

Bronfenbrenner's Theory

The **mesosystem,** *in Bronfenbrenner's ecological theory, involves relationships between microsystems, or connections between contexts.* Examples are the relation of family experiences to school experiences, school experiences to church experiences, and family experiences to peer experiences. For instance, a boy whose parents have rejected him may have difficulty developing positive relations with teachers. Developmentalists increasingly believe it is important to observe behavior in multiple settings—such as in family, peer, and school contexts—to obtain a more complete picture of an individual's development (Booth & Dunn, 1996). The important mesosystem connection between families and schools is explored in the Caring for Children box.

The **exosystem,** *in Bronfenbrenner's ecological theory, is involved when experiences in a social setting in which an individual does not have an active role influence what that person experiences in an immediate context.* For example, work experiences may affect a woman's relationship with her husband and their child. The woman may receive a promotion that requires more travel, which might increase marital conflict and change patterns of parent-child interaction. Another example of an exosystem is a city government, which is responsible for the quality of parks, recreation centers, and library facilities for children and adolescents.

The **macrosystem,** *in Bronfenbrenner's ecological theory, involves the culture in which individuals live.* Remember from chapter 1 that *culture* refers to the behavior patterns, beliefs, and all other products of a group of people that are passed on from generation to generation. Remember also that *cross-cultural studies*—comparisons of one culture with one or more other cultures—provide information about the universality of children's development.

The **chronosystem,** *in Bronfenbrenner's ecological theory, involves the patterning of environmental events and transitions over the life course and sociohistorical circumstances.* For example, in studying the effects of divorce on children, researchers have found that the negative effects often peak in the first year after the divorce and that the effects are more negative for sons than for daughters (Hetherington, 1995; Hetherington, Cox, & Cox, 1982). By 2 years after the divorce, family interaction is less chaotic and more stable. With regard to sociocultural circumstances, girls today are much more likely to be encouraged to pursue a career than they were 20 to 30 years ago. In ways such as these, the chronosystem has a powerful impact on children's lives.

Bronfenbrenner (1995; Bronfenbrenner & Morris, 1998) recently added biological influences to his theory and now describes it as a bioecological theory. Nonetheless, ecological, environmental contexts still predominate in Bronfenbrenner's theory.

An Eclectic Theoretical Orientation

An **eclectic theoretical orientation** *does not follow any one theoretical approach but, rather, selects and uses from each theory whatever is considered the best in it.* No single theory described in this chapter is indomitable or capable of explaining entirely the rich complexity of child development. Each of the theories has made important contributions to our understanding of children's development, but none provides a complete description and explanation. Psychoanalytic theory best explains the unconscious mind. Erikson's theory best describes the changes that occur in adult development. Piaget's theory is the most complete description of children's cognitive development. The behavioral and social learning and ecological theories have been the most adept at examining the environmental determinants of development. The ethological theories have made us aware of biology's role and the importance of sensitive periods in development. It is important to recognize that, although theories are helpful guides, relying on a single theory to explain children's development is probably a mistake.

An attempt was made in this chapter to present five theoretical perspectives objectively. The same eclectic orientation will be maintained throughout the book. In this way, you can view the study of children's development as it actually exists—with different theorists making different assumptions, stressing different empirical problems, and using different strategies to discover information.

These theoretical perspectives, along with research issues that were discussed in chapter 1 and methods that will be described shortly, provide a sense of development's scientific nature. Figure 2.9 compares the main theoretical perspectives in terms of how they view important developmental issues and the methods used to study children.

In addition to the grand theories discussed in this chapter, which serve as general frameworks for thinking about and interpreting many aspects of children's

Urie Bronfenbrenner developed ecological theory, a perspective that is receiving increased attention. His theory emphasizes the importance of both micro and macro dimensions of the environment in which children live.

exosystem
The level at which experiences in another social setting—in which the individual does not have an active role—influence what the individual experiences in an immediate context.

macrosystem
The culture in which individuals live.

chronosystem
The patterning of environmental events and transitions over the life course and their sociohistorical contexts.

eclectic theoretical orientation
An approach not following any one theoretical approach but, rather, selecting from each theory whatever is considered the best in it.

Bronfenbrenner and a Multicultural Framework

Caring for Children

An Important Mesosystem Connection—Family and School

In Bronfenbrenner's ecological theory, the mesosystem is the connections between microsystems or social contexts. An important mesosystem connection is between families and schools. Researchers have consistently found that many successful students receive long-term support from parents or other adults at home, as well as strong support from teachers and others at school. Involving parents in learning activities with their children at home is one kind of parental involvement that many educators believe is an important aspect of the child's learning. Family researcher and educator Ira Gordon (1978) concluded that parents of students in the early grades can play six key roles: volunteer, paid employee, teacher at home, audience, decision maker, and adult learner. These roles likely influence not only parents' behavior and their children's schoolwork but also the quality of schools and communities.

Today, after many decades of limited success, schools are beginning to put more thought into their communication with parents, recognizing that the initial contacts can make or break relationships and that first contacts affect later communication (Epstein, 1992). Recognizing the importance of parental involvement in education, a number of programs are being developed to enhance communication between schools and families.

Three types of school/family programs are face-to-face, technological, and written communication (D'Angelo & Adler, 1991). In Lima, Ohio, the main goal is for each school to establish a personal relationship with every parent. At an initial parent/teacher conference, parents are given a packet that is designed to increase their likelihood of engaging in learning activities with their children at home. Conferences, regular phone calls, and home visits establish an atmosphere of mutual understanding that makes other kinds of communication (progress reports, report cards, activity calendars, and discussions about problems that arise during the year) more welcome and successful.

Many programs are discovering new ways to use electronic communication to establish contact with a wider range of parents. In McAllen, Texas, the school district has developed a community partnership with local radio stations, and it sponsors "Discusiones Escolares," a weekly program in Spanish that encourages parents to become more involved in their children's education. Family and school relationships, parent involvement at school, the prevention of school dropouts, the creation of a learning atmosphere at home, and communication with adolescents are some of the topics the radio programs have addressed. Parents and others in the community may check out copies of the script or a cassette tape of each program from the parent coordinators at their schools.

In a joint effort of the New York City School System and the Children's Aid Society, since 1992 Salome Urena Middle Academies have invited community organizations to provide school-based programs for 1,200 students and their families (Carnegie Council on Adolescent Development, 1995). The school's family resource center, which is open from 8:30 A.M. to 8:30 P.M., is a valuable source of information and support for the community. Staffed by parents, social workers, and other volunteers, the center houses adult education, drug abuse prevention, and other activities. Since many of the families who send adolescents to the school are of Dominican origin, the school offers English-as-a-second-language classes for parents—400 parents are currently enrolled.

Hanshaw Middle School in California's Stanislaus County includes a resource center for students' families. Parents can take classes in such areas as parenting or computers, and they can study for their high school equivalency degrees. Latino parents can get help in communicating with the school's teachers and administrators. The center also features a case management team and referral service that is available to students and their families.

In sum, extra care in developing and maintaining channels of communication between schools and families is an important aspect of children's development (Rosenthal & Sawyers, 1996).

development, there are many more "local" theories, or mini-models, that guide research in specific areas (Kuhn, 1998; Parke & Buriel, 1998). For example, in chapter 6 you will read about the recently developed dynamic systems theory (Thelen & Smith, 1998), which offers an explanation of infant perceptual-motor development, the new functionalist approach to understanding infants' emotional development in chapter 7, as well as the old and new approaches to parent-adolescent relationships in chapter 17.

Theory	Issues and methods			
	Continuity/discontinuity, early versus later experiences	*Biological and environmental factors*	*Importance of cognition*	*Research methods*
Psychoanalytic	Discontinuity between stages—continuity between early experiences and later development; early experiences very important; later changes in development emphasized in Erikson's theory	Freud's biological determination interacting with early family experiences; Erikson's more balanced biological-cultural interaction perspective	Emphasized, but in the form of unconscious thought	Clinical interviews, unstructured personality tests, psychohistorical analyses of lives
Cognitive	Discontinuity between stages—continuity between early experiences and later development in Piaget's theory; has not been important to information-processing psychologists	Piaget's emphasis on interaction and adaptation; environment provides the setting for cognitive structures to develop; information-processing view has not addressed this issue extensively but mainly emphasizes biological-environmental interaction	The primary determinant of behavior	Interviews and observations
Behavioral and social learning	Continuity (no stages); experience at all points of development important	Environment viewed as the cause of behavior in both views	Strongly deemphasized in the behavioral approach but an important mediator in social learning	Observation, especially laboratory observation
Ethological	Discontinuity but no stages; critical or sensitive periods emphasized; early experiences very important	Strong biological view	Not emphasized	Observation in natural settings
Ecological	Little attention to continuity/discontinuity; change emphasized more than stability	Strong environmental view	Not emphasized	Varied methods; especially stresses importance of collecting data in different social contexts

Figure 2.9
A Comparison of Theories and the Issues and Methods in Child Development

Summary Table 2.1
Research, Science, and Theories in Child Development

Concept	Processes/ Related Ideas	Characteristics/Description
Why research on child development is important	Its nature	Personal experiences and information from experts can sometimes help us understand children's development. However, the information we obtain from scientific research is extremely important.
The scientific research approach	Its nature	Scientific research is objective, systematic, and testable, reducing the probability that the information will be based on personal beliefs, opinions, or feelings. Scientific research is based on the scientific method, which includes these steps: (1) conceptualize the problem, (2) collect data, (3) draw conclusions, and (4) revise theory. A theory is a coherent set of ideas that helps to explain and to make predictions. A theory contains hypotheses.
Theories of child development	Psychoanalytic theories	Two important psychoanalytic theories are Freud's and Erikson's. Freud said personality is made up of three structures—id, ego, and superego—and that most of children's thoughts are unconscious. The conflicting demands of children's personality structures produce anxiety. Defense mechanisms, especially repression, protect the child's ego and reduce anxiety. Freud was convinced that problems develop because of early childhood experiences. He said individuals go through five psychosexual stages—oral, anal, phallic, latency, and genital. During the phallic stage, the Oedipus complex is a major source of conflict. Erikson developed a theory that emphasizes eight psychosocial stages of development: trust vs. mistrust, autonomy vs. shame and doubt, initiative vs. guilt, industry vs. inferiority, identity vs. identity confusion, intimacy vs. isolation, generativity vs. stagnation, and integrity vs. despair.
	Cognitive theories	Three important cognitive theories are Piaget's cognitive developmental theory, Vygotsky's sociocultural cognitive theory, and information processing. Piaget said that children are motivated to understand their world and use the processes of organization and adaptation (assimilation, accommodation) to do so. Piaget said children go through four cognitive stages: sensorimotor, preoperational, concrete operational, and formal operational. Vygotsky made three basic claims about children's development: (1) cognitive skills need to be interpreted developmentally, (2) cognitive skills are mediated by language, and (3) cognitive skills have their origins in social relations and culture. Information-processing theory is concerned with how individuals process information about their world. It includes how information gets into the child's mind, how it is stored and transformed, and how it is retrieved to allow the child to think and solve problems.
	Behavioral and social learning theories	Behaviorism emphasizes that cognition is not important in understanding children's behavior. Development is observed behavior, which is determined by rewards and punishments in the environment, according to B. F. Skinner, a famous behaviorist. Social learning theory, developed by Albert Bandura and others, states that the environment is an important determinant of behavior, but so are cognitive processes. Bandura's most recent model involves reciprocal interactions between person (cognition), behavior, and environment. Self-efficacy is currently the personal factor Bandura believes is especially important in children's development.
	Ethological theories	Konrad Lorenz was one of the important developers of ethological theories. Ethology emphasizes the biological and evolutionary basis of development. Imprinting and critical periods are key concepts.
	Ecological theory	In Bronfenbrenner's ecological theory, five environmental systems are important: microsystem, mesosystem, exosystem, macrosystem, and chronosystem.
	Eclectic theoretical orientation	No single theory can explain the rich, awesome complexity of children's development. Each of the theories has made a different contribution, and it probably is a wise strategy to adopt an eclectic theoretical perspective as we attempt to understand children's development. Many "local" theories, or mini-models, also guide research in specific areas of human development. Together, the grand theories and micro approaches give us a more complete portrait of how the journey of child development unfolds.

The "micro" theories focus on a specific aspect or time frame of development, seeking precise explanations of that particular dimension. As you read the remaining chapters of this book, you will come across many of these more focused views. Together, the grand theories and the micro approaches give us a more complete view of how the fascinating journey of children's development unfolds.

At this point, we have discussed a number of ideas about research, science, and theories in child development. An overview of these ideas is presented in summary table 2.1. Next, we will explore the methods child developmentalists use to study children, beginning with the measures they use.

RESEARCH METHODS

Remember that, in addition to theories, the scientific study of child development also involves research. We will begin our research inquiry with an overview of the measures child developmentalists use to obtain information about children.

When researchers want to find out, for example, if cocaine taken by pregnant women will affect the fetus, if academic preschool programs place too much stress on young children, and if watching a lot of MTV detracts from adolescents' learning in school, they can choose from many methods. We will discuss these methods separately, but recognize that often more than one is used in a single study.

Research is formalized curiosity. It is poking and searching with a purpose.

Zora Hurston
American Anthropologist and Author, 20th Century

Observation

Sherlock Holmes chided his assistant, Watson, "You see but you do not observe." We look at things all the time; however, casually watching two children interacting is not the same as the type of observation used in scientific studies. Scientific observation is highly systematic. It requires knowing what you are looking for, conducting observations in an unbiased manner, accurately recording and categorizing what you see, and effectively communicating your observations.

A common way to record observations is to write them down, often using shorthand or symbols. In addition, tape recorders, video cameras, special coding sheets, one-way mirrors, and computers increasingly are being used to make observations more efficient.

Observations can be made in either laboratories or naturalistic settings (Hartmann & George, 1999). A **laboratory** *is a controlled setting from which many of the complex factors of the real world have been removed.* Some researchers conduct studies in laboratories at the colleges or universities where they teach. Although laboratories often help researchers gain more control over the behavior of the participants, laboratory studies have been criticized as being artificial. In **naturalistic observation,** *behavior is observed outside of a laboratory, in the so-called real world.* Researchers conduct naturalistic observations of adolescents in classrooms, at home, at youth centers, at museums, in neighborhoods, and in other settings.

laboratory
A controlled setting from which many of the complex factors of the real world have been removed.

naturalistic observation
Observation that takes place in the real world instead of in a laboratory.

Interviews and Questionnaires

Sometimes the quickest and best way to get information about children is to ask them or adults who know them for it. Researchers use interviews and questionnaires (surveys) to find out about children's experiences, beliefs, and feelings. Most interviews take place face-to-face, although they can be done over the phone or via the Internet. Questionnaires are usually given to individuals in printed form, and they are asked to fill them out. This can be done in person, by mail, or via the Internet.

Good interviews and surveys involve concrete, specific, and unambiguous questions and a means of checking the authenticity of the respondents' replies. However, interviews and surveys are not without problems. One crucial limitation is that many individuals give socially desirable answers, responding in a way they think is

In this research study, an experimenter is communicating with a mother and child while the mother-child interaction is being videotaped. Later, the researchers will code the interaction of the mother and child using a number of precise, well-defined categories.

standardized tests
Commercially prepared tests that assess performance in different domains.

case study
An in-depth look at an individual.

correlational research
Research whose goal is to describe the strength of the relation between two or more events or characteristics.

Correlational Research

experimental research
Research involving experiments that permit the determination of cause. A carefully regulated procedure in which one or more of the factors believed to influence the behavior being studied are manipulated and all other factors are held constant.

most socially acceptable and desirable, rather than how they truly think or feel. For example, when asked whether they cheat on tests in school, some adolescents may say that they don't, even though they do, because it is socially undesirable to cheat. Skilled interviewing techniques and questions that increase forthright responses are critical in obtaining accurate information.

Standardized Tests

Standardized tests *are commercially prepared tests that assess children's performance in different domains. A standardized test often allows a child's performance to be compared with those of other children at the same age, in many cases on a national level.* Standardized tests can be given to children to assess their intelligence, achievement, personality, career interests, and other skills (Embretson & Hershberger, 1999). These tests may be given for a variety of purposes, including outcome measures in research studies, information that helps psychologists make decisions about individual children, or comparisons of students' performance across schools, states, and countries. In chapter 13, "Cognitive Development in Middle and Late Childhood," we will further explore standardized tests of intelligence.

Case Studies

A **case study** *is an in-depth look at an individual.* It often is used when unique aspects of a person's life cannot be duplicated, for either practical or ethical reasons. A case study provides information about an individual's fears, hopes, fantasies, traumatic experiences, upbringing, family relationships, health, and anything else that helps a psychologist understand that person's development. Some vivid case studies appear at different points in this text, among them one about a modern-day wild child named Genie, who lived in near isolation during her childhood.

Although case studies provide dramatic, in-depth portrayals of people's lives, we need to exercise caution when generalizing from this information. The subject of a case study is unique, with a genetic makeup and experiences no one else shares. In addition, case studies involve judgments of unknown reliability, in that usually no check is made to see if other psychologists agree with the observations.

Correlational Research

In **correlational research,** *the goal is to describe the strength of the relation between two or more events or characteristics.* Correlational research is useful because, the more strongly two events are correlated (related or associated), the more effectively we can predict one from the other. For example, if researchers find that low-involved, permissive parenting is correlated with a child's lack of self-control, it suggests that low-involved, permissive parenting might be one source of the lack of self-control.

A caution is in order, however. *Correlation does not equal causation.* The correlational finding just mentioned does not mean that permissive parenting necessarily causes low self-control in children. It could mean that, but it also could mean that a child's lack of self-control caused the parents to simply throw up their arms in despair and give up trying to control the child. It also could mean that other factors, such as heredity or poverty, caused the correlation between permissive parenting and low self-control in children. Figure 2.10 illustrates these possible interpretations of correlational data.

Experimental Research

Experimental research *allows researchers to determine the causes of behavior. They accomplish this task by performing an experiment, a carefully regulated procedure in which*

Observed correlation   **Possible explanations for this correlation**

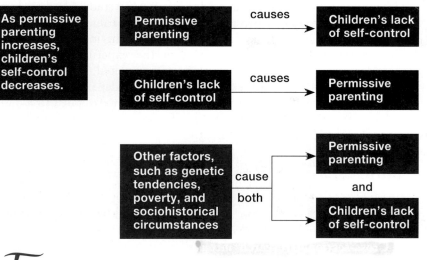

Figure 2.10
Possible Explanations for Correlational Data

An observed correlation between two events cannot be used to conclude that one event caused the other. Some possibilities are that the second event caused the first event or that a third, unknown event caused the correlation between the first two events.

one or more of the factors believed to influence the behavior being studied are manipulated and all other factors are held constant. If the behavior under study changes when a factor is manipulated, we say the manipulated factor causes the behavior to change. "Cause" is the event being manipulated. "Effect" is the behavior that changes because of the manipulation. Experimental research is the only truly reliable method of establishing cause and effect. Because correlational research does not involve the manipulation of factors, it is not a dependable way to isolate cause.

Experimental Research

Experiments involve at least one independent variable and one dependent variable. The **independent variable** *is the manipulated, influential, experimental factor.* The label "independent" indicates that this variable can be changed independently of any other factors. For example, suppose we want to design an experiment to study the effects of peer tutoring on children's achievement. In this example, the amount and type of peer tutoring could be independent variables. The **dependent variable** *is the factor that is measured in an experiment. It can change as the independent variable is manipulated.* The label "dependent" is used because this variable depends on what happens to the participants in an experiment as the independent variable is manipulated. In the peer tutoring study, achievement is the dependent variable. This might be assessed in a number of ways. Let's say in this study it is measured by scores on a nationally standardized achievement test.

In experiments, the independent variable consists of differing experiences that are given to one or more experimental groups and one or more control groups. An **experimental group** *is a group whose experience is manipulated.* A **control group** *is a group that is treated in every way like the experimental group except for the manipulated factor.* The control group serves as the baseline against which the effects of the manipulated condition can be compared. In the peer tutoring study, we need to have one group of adolescents that gets peer tutoring (experimental group) and one that doesn't (control group).

Another important principle of experimental research is **random assignment,** *which involves assigning participants to experimental and control groups by chance.* This practice reduces the likelihood that the experiment's results will be due to any preexisting differences between the groups. In our study of peer tutoring, random assignment greatly

independent variable
The manipulated, influential, experimental factor in an experiment.

dependent variable
The factor that is measured as the result of an experiment.

experimental group
A group whose experience is manipulated in an experiment.

control group
A comparison group in an experiment that is treated in every way like the experimental group except for the manipulated factor.

random assignment
In experimental research, the assignment of participants to experimental and control groups by chance.

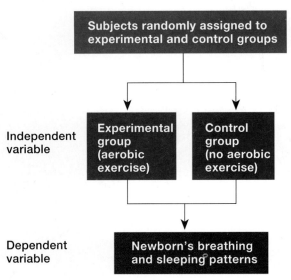

reduces the probability that the two groups will differ on such factors as age, family background, initial achievement, intelligence, personality, and health.

To summarize the peer tutoring–achievement study, children are randomly assigned to one of two groups: one (the experimental group) is given peer tutoring; the other (control group) is not. The independent variables consist of the differing experiences that the experimental and control groups receive. After the peer tutoring is completed, the adolescents are given a nationally standardized achievement test (dependent variable). Figure 2.11 illustrates the experimental research method applied to a different problem: the effects of aerobic exercise by pregnant women on their newborns' breathing and sleeping patterns.

Time Span of Research

Another research decision involves the time span of the research. There are several options—we can study individuals all at one time or we can study the same individuals over time.

Cross-sectional research *involves studying people all at one time.* For example, a researcher might be interested in studying the self-esteem of 8-, 12-, and 16-year-olds. In a cross-sectional study, the participants' self-esteem would be assessed at one time. The cross-sectional study's main advantage is that the researcher does not have to wait for the children to grow older. However, this approach provides no information about the stability of the children's and adolescents' self-esteem or how it might change over time.

Longitudinal research *involves studying the same individuals over a period of time, usually several years or more.* In a longitudinal study of self-esteem, the researcher might examine the self-esteem of a group of 8-year-old children, then assess their self-esteem again when they are 12, and then again when they are 16. One of the great values of longitudinal research is that we can evaluate how individual children and adolescents change as they get older. However, because longitudinal research is time consuming and costly, most research is cross-sectional.

$\diamond$ RESEARCH JOURNALS

Regardless of whether you pursue a career in child development, education, psychology, nursing, or a related field, you can benefit by learning about the journal process. Possibly as a student you will be required to look up original research in journals as part of writing a term paper. As a parent, teacher, or nurse you might want to consult journals to obtain information that will help you understand and work more effectively with children. And, as an inquiring person, you might want to look up information in journals after you have heard or read something that piqued your curiosity.

A *journal* publishes scholarly and academic information, usually in a specific domain, such as physics, math, sociology, or, in the case of our interest, adolescence. Scholars in these fields publish most of their research in journals, which are the core information source in virtually every academic discipline.

Journal articles are usually written for other professionals in the field of the journal's focus—such as geology, anthropology, or adolescence. Because the articles are written for other professionals, they often contain technical language and specialized terms related to a specific discipline that are difficult for nonprofessionals to understand. You have probably already had one or more courses in psychology, and you will be learning a great deal more about the specialized field of child development in this course, which should improve your ability to understand journal articles in this field.

An increasing number of journals publish information about children's development. Among the leading journals of child development are *Child Development*,

$\mathcal{F}$*igure 2.11*
Principles of the Experimental Strategy

The effects of aerobic exercise by pregnant women on their newborns' breathing and sleeping patterns.

cross-sectional research
Research that studies people all at one time.

longitudinal research
Research that studies the same people over a period of time, usually several years or more.

Child Development

Developmental Psychology, Infant Behavior and Development, Pediatric Nursing, Pediatrics, Early Childhood Research Quarterly, and *Journal of Research on Adolescence.* Also, a number of journals that do not focus solely on development include articles on children's development, such as *Journal of Educational Psychology, Sex Roles, Journal of Cross-Cultural Psychology, Journal of Marriage and the Family,* and *Journal of Consulting and Clinical Psychology.*

In psychology and the field of child development, most journal articles are reports of original research. Many journals also include review articles that present an overview of different studies on a particular topic, such as a review of day care, a review of the transition to elementary school, and a review of adolescent depression.

Many journals are highly selective about what they publish. Every journal has a board of experts that evaluates articles submitted for publication. One or more of the experts carefully examine the submitted paper and accept or reject it on such factors as its contribution to the field, its theoretical relevance, its methodological excellence, and its clarity of writing. Some of the most prestigious journals reject as many as 80 to 90 percent of the articles that are submitted because they fail to meet the journal's standards.

Where do you find journals, such as those previously listed? Your college or university library likely has one or more of the journals listed. Some public libraries also carry journals.

An *abstract* is a brief summary that appears at the beginning of a journal article. The abstract lets readers quickly determine whether the article is relevant to their interests and if they want to read the entire article. The *introduction,* as its title suggests, introduces the problem or issue that is being studied. It includes a concise review of research relevant to the topic, theoretical ties, and one or more hypotheses to be tested. The *method* section consists of a clear description of the subjects evaluated in the study, the measures used, and the procedures followed. The method section should be sufficiently clear and detailed so that, by reading it, another researcher could repeat, or replicate, the study. The *results* section reports the analysis of the data collected. In most cases, the results section includes statistical analyses that are difficult for nonprofessionals to understand. The *discussion* section describes the author's conclusions, inferences, and interpretation of the findings. Statements are usually made about whether the hypotheses presented in the introduction were supported, the limitations of the study, and suggestions for future research. The last part of a journal article is called *references,* which includes every citation in the article. The references section is often a good source for finding other articles relevant to the topic you are interested in.

Developmental Psychology

RESEARCH CHALLENGES

Research on children's development poses a number of challenges. Some of the challenges involve the pursuit of knowledge itself. Others involve the effects of research on participants. Still others relate to a better understanding of the information derived from research studies.

Ethics

Researchers exercise considerable caution to ensure the well-being of children participating in a study. Most colleges have review boards that evaluate whether the research is ethical.

The code of ethics adopted by the American Psychological Association (APA) instructs researchers to protect participants from mental and physical harm. The best interests of the participants always must be kept foremost in the researcher's mind (Kimmel, 1996). All participants, if they are old enough (typically 7 years or older), must give their informed consent to participate. If they are not old enough,

Ethics

their parents' or guardians' consent must be obtained. Informed consent means that the participants (and/or their parents/legal guardians) have been told what their participation will entail and any risks that might be involved. For example, if researchers want to study the effects of conflict in divorced families on children's self-esteem, the participants should be informed that in some instances discussion of a family's experiences might improve family relationships, but in other cases might raise unwanted family stress. After informed consent is given, participants retain the right to withdraw at any time.

Gender

Traditionally, science has been presented as nonbiased and value-free. However, many experts on gender believe that psychological research often has entailed gender bias (Anselmi, 1998; Doyle & Paludi, 1998). They argue that for too long the female experience was subsumed under the male experience. For example, conclusions have been drawn routinely about females based on research conducted only with males.

Following are three broad questions that female scholars have raised regarding gender bias in psychological research (Tetreault, 1997):

- How might gender be a bias that influences the choice of theory, questions, hypotheses, participants, and research design?
- How might research on topics of primary interest to females, such as relationships, feelings, and empathy, challenge existing theory and research?
- How has research that heretofore has exaggerated gender differences between females and males influenced the way parents, teachers, and others think about and interact with female and male adolescents? For example, gender differences in mathematics often have been exaggerated and fueled by societal bias.

Culture and Ethnicity

More children from ethnic minority backgrounds need to be included in research (Graham, 1992). Historically, ethnic minority children essentially have been ignored in research or simply have been viewed as variations from the norm, or average. Their developmental and educational problems have been viewed as "confounds," or "noise" in data. Researchers have deliberately excluded these children from the samples they have selected to study (Ryan-Finn, Cauce, & Grove, 1995). Because ethnic minority children have been excluded from research for so long, there likely is more variation in children's real lives than research studies have indicated (Stevenson, 1995, 1998, in press).

Researchers also have tended to practice what is called "ethnic gloss" when they select and describe ethnic minority samples (Trimble, 1989). *Ethnic gloss is using an ethnic label, such as African American or Latino, in a superficial way that makes an ethnic group look more homogeneous than it really is.* For example, a researcher might describe a sample as "20 Latinos and 20 Anglo Americans," when a more precise description of the Latino group would need to state, "The 20 Latino participants were Mexican Americans from low-income neighborhoods in the southwestern area of Los Angeles. Twelve were from homes in which Spanish is the dominant language spoken, 8 from homes in which English is the main spoken language. Ten were born in the United States, 10 in Mexico. Ten described themselves as Mexican American, 5 as Mexican, 3 as American, 2 as Chicano, and 1 as Latino." Ethnic gloss can cause researchers to obtain samples of ethnic groups that either are not representative or conceal the group's diversity, which can lead to overgeneralization and stereotyping.

Also, historically, when researchers have studied ethnic minority children, they have focused on the children's problems. It is important to study the problems, such

ethnic gloss

The use of an ethnic label, such as Latino, Asian American, or Native American, in a superficial way that makes an ethnic group seem more homogeneous than it really is.

as poverty, that ethnic minority adolescents face, but it also is important to examine their strengths as well, such as their pride, self-esteem, improvised problem-solving skills, and extended family support systems. Fortunately, now, in the context of a more pluralistic view of our society, researchers are increasingly studying the positive dimensions of ethnic minority children (Swanson, 1997).

Being a Wise Consumer of Information About Children's Development

We live in a society that generates a vast amount of information about children in various media ranging from research journals to newspaper and television accounts. The information varies greatly in quality. How can you evaluate this information?

Be Cautious of What Is Reported in the Popular Media
Television, radio, newspapers, and magazines frequently report research on child development. Many researchers regularly supply the media with information about children. In some cases, this research has been published in professional journals or presented at national meetings and then is picked up by the popular media. And most colleges have a media relations department, which contacts the press about current faculty research.

However, not all research on adolescents that appears in the media comes from professionals with excellent credentials and reputations. Journalists, television reporters, and other media personnel generally are not scientifically trained. It is not an easy task for them to sort through the avalanche of material they receive and to make sound decisions about which information to report.

Unfortunately, the media tend to focus on sensational, dramatic findings. They want you to stay tuned or buy their publication. When the information they gather from research journals is not sensational, they may embellish it and sensationalize it, going beyond what the researcher intended.

Another problem with research reported in the media is a lack of time or space to go into important details about a study. They often have only a few lines or a few minutes to summarize as best they can what may be complex findings. Too often this means that what is reported is overgeneralized and stereotyped.

Know How to Avoid Assuming Individual Needs on the Basis of Group Research
Nomothetic research *is research conducted at the level of the group.* Most research on children is nomothetic research. Individual variations in how children behave is not a common focus. For example, if researchers are interested in the effects of divorce on children's self-esteem, they might conduct a study with 50 children from divorced families and 50 children from intact, never divorced families. They might find that the children from divorced families, as a group, had lower self-esteem than did the children from intact families. That is a nomothetic finding that applies to children from divorced families as a group, and that is what is commonly reported in the media and in research journals. In this study, it likely was the case that some of the children from divorced families had higher school achievement than did the children from intact families—not as many, but some. Indeed, it is entirely possible that, of the 100 children in the study, the 2 or 3 children who had the highest school achievement were from divorced families, but that was never reported.

Nomothetic research provides valuable information about the characteristics of a group of children, revealing strengths and weaknesses of the group. However, in many instances, parents, teachers, and others want to know about how to help one particular child cope and learn more effectively. **Idiographic needs** *are needs of an individual, not the group.* Unfortunately, while nomothetic research can point up problems for certain groups of children, it does not always hold for an individual child.

nomothetic research
Research conducted at the level of the group.

idiographic needs
The needs of the individual, not the group.

Adventures for the Mind
Reading and Analyzing Reports About Children's Development

Information about children's development appears in research journals and in magazines and newspapers. Choose one of the topics covered in this book and course—such as day care, adolescent problems, or parenting. Find an article in a research journal (for example, *Child Development* or *Developmental Psychology*) and an article in a newspaper or magazine on the same topic. How did the research article on the topic differ from the newspaper or magazine article? What did you learn from this comparison?

Recognize How Easy It Is to Overgeneralize About a Small or Clinical Sample There often isn't space or time in media presentations to go into detail about the nature of the sample of the children on which a study was based. In many cases, samples are too small to let us generalize to a larger population. For example, if a study of children from divorced families is based on only 10 to 20 children, what is found in the study cannot be generalized to all children from divorced families. Perhaps the sample was drawn from families who have substantial economic resources, are Anglo American, live in a small southern town, and are undergoing therapy. From this study, we clearly would be making unwarranted generalizations if we thought the findings also characterize children from low- to moderate-income families, are from other ethnic backgrounds, live in a different geographic region, and are not undergoing therapy.

Be Aware That a Single Study Usually Is Not the Defining Word The media may identify an interesting research study and claim that it is something phenomenal with far-reaching implications. As a competent consumer of information, be aware that it is extremely rare for a single study to have earth-shattering, conclusive answers that apply to all children. In fact, where there are large numbers of studies that focus on a particular issue, it is not unusual to find conflicting results from one study to the next. Reliable answers about children's development usually emerge only after many researchers have conducted similar studies and have drawn similar conclusions. In our example of divorce, if one study reports that a counseling program for children from divorced families improved their self-esteem, we cannot conclude that the counseling program will work as effectively with all children from divorced families until many more studies have been conducted.

Remember That Causal Conclusions Cannot Be Made from Correlational Studies Drawing causal conclusions from correlational studies is one of the most common mistakes made by the media. In nonexperimental studies (remember that, in an experiment, participants are randomly assigned to treatments or experiences), two variables or factors may be related to each other. However, causal interpretations cannot be made when two or more factors simply are correlated; we cannot say that one causes the other. In the case of divorce, the headline might read "Divorce causes children to have low self-esteem." We read the story and find out that the information is based on the results of a research study. Since we obviously cannot, for ethical and practical reasons, randomly assign children to families that either will become divorced or will remain intact, this headline is based on a correlational study, and the causal statements are unproved. It may well be, for example, that another factor, such as family conflict or economic problems, is typically responsible for both children's poor school performance and parents' divorce.

Always Consider the Source of the Information and Evaluate Its Credibility Studies are not automatically accepted by the research community. As discussed earlier in the chapter, researchers usually have to submit their findings to a research journal, where it is reviewed by their colleagues, who decide whether or not to publish the paper. While the quality of research in journals is far from uniform, in most cases the quality of the research has undergone far more scrutiny and careful consideration than has research or other information that has not gone through the journal process. Within the media, we can distinguish between what is

Summary Table 2.2
Research Methods, Research Journals, and Research Challenges

Concept	Processes/ Related Ideas	Characteristics/Description
Research methods	Observation	Observations need to be conducted systematically. Observations can be made in a laboratory or in naturalistic settings.
	Interviews and questionnaires	Most interviews take place face-to-face, and most questionnaires (surveys) are given to individuals in printed form to be filled out. Social desirability and lying can be problematic in interviews and questionnaires.
	Standardized tests	They are commercially prepared tests that assess students' performance in different domains.
	Case studies	They represent an in-depth look at an individual. Generalizing from a case study to other individuals often is not warranted.
	Correlational research	The goal is to describe the strength of the relation between two or more events or characteristics. An important research principle is that correlation does not equal causation. When a correlation occurs between two events, the first could cause the second, the second could cause the first, or a third, unknown factor could cause the correlation between the first two events.
	Experimental research	This allows the determination of behavior's causes. Conducting an experiment involves examining the influence of at least one independent variable (the manipulated, influential, experimental factor) on one or more dependent variables (the measured factors). Experiments involve the random assignment of participants to one or more experimental groups (the groups whose experience is being manipulated) and one or more control groups (comparison groups treated in every way like the experimental group except for the manipulated factor).
	Time span of research	Cross-sectional research involves studying people all at one time. Longitudinal research consists of studying the same people over time.
Research journals	Their nature	A journal publishes scholarly and academic information. An increasing number of journals publish information about children's development. Most journal articles are reports of original research. Most research journal articles follow this format: abstract, introduction, method, results, discussion, and references.
Research challenges	Ethics	Researchers recognize that a number of ethical concerns have to be met when conducting studies. The best interests of the participants always have to be kept in mind.
	Gender	Every effort should be made to make research equitable for both females and males. In the past, research too often has been biased against females.
	Culture and ethnicity	We need to include more children from ethnic minority backgrounds in educational psychology research. A special concern is ethnic gloss.
	Being a wise consumer of information about children's development	Be cautious about what is reported in the media, avoid assuming individual needs on the basis of group research, recognize how easy it is to overgeneralize about a small or clinical sample, be aware that a single study usually is not the defining word, remember that causal conclusions cannot be drawn from correlational studies, and always consider the source of the information and evaluate its credibility.

presented in respected newspapers and magazines, such as the *New York Times* and *Newsweek,* and what appears in much less respected tabloids, such as the *National Enquirer.* To consider comparisons of information in research journals and magazines/newspapers, see Adventures for the Mind.

At this point, we have discussed many ideas about research methods, research journals, and research challenges. A review of these ideas is presented in summary table 2.2

Chapter Review

A discipline that studies pubertal change, parent-adolescent relationships, and peer interaction can be a science just as much as a science that investigates the way gravity works and a compound's molecular structure. That is, science is determined not by *what* it investigates but *how* it investigates.

We began this chapter by exploring the roles of research and science in child development and then turned our attention to these theories of adolescent development: psychoanalytic, cognitive, behavioral and social, ethological, ecological, contextual, and an eclectic theoretical orientation. Our coverage of research methods focused on observation, interviews and questionnaires, standardized tests, case studies, correlational research, experimental research, and the time span of research. We also studied the nature of research journals and examined research challenges that involve ethics, gender, culture and ethnicity, and wise consumerism of information about child development.

For a more detailed review of this chapter, again study the two summary tables on pages 48 and 57. This concludes Section One of the book. In Section Two, we will explore the beginnings of children's development, beginning with chapter 3, "Biological Beginnings."

✓ Children Checklist

The Science of Child Development

How much have you learned since the beginning of the chapter? Use the following statements to help you review your knowledge and understanding of the chapter material. First, read the statement and mentally or briefly demonstrate on paper that you can discuss the relevant information.

_*1*_ I can describe why research on children's development is important.
_*2*_ I know what the scientific method is and what steps are involved in it.
_____ I am aware of what psychoanalytic theories are like.
_____ I understand the nature of cognitive theories.
_____ I can discuss the behavioral and social learning theories.
_____ I can describe the ethological theories of development.
_____ I know about the ecological theory of development.
_____ I am aware of what an eclectic theoretical orientation is.
_____ I can discuss these research methods: observation, interviews and questionnaires, standardized tests, case studies, correlational research, experimental research, and the time span of research.
_____ I can describe the nature of research journals.
_____ I can evaluate research challenges involving ethics, gender, culture and ethnicity, and wise consumerism of information about children's development.

For any items that you did not check, go back and locate the relevant material in the chapter. Review the material until you feel that you can check off the item. You also may want to use this checklist later in preparing for an exam.

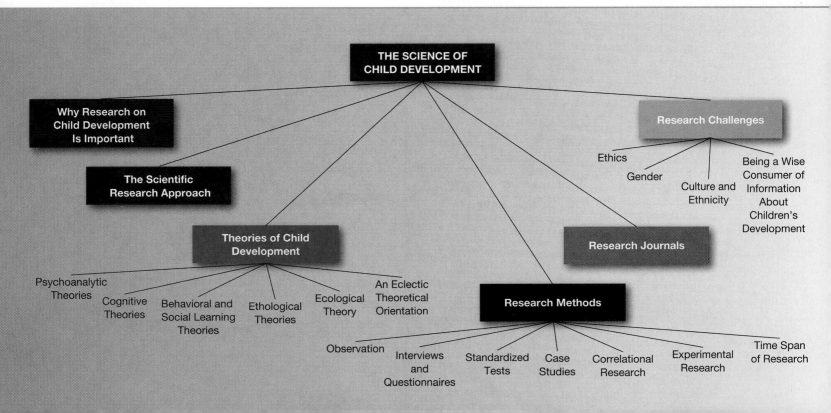

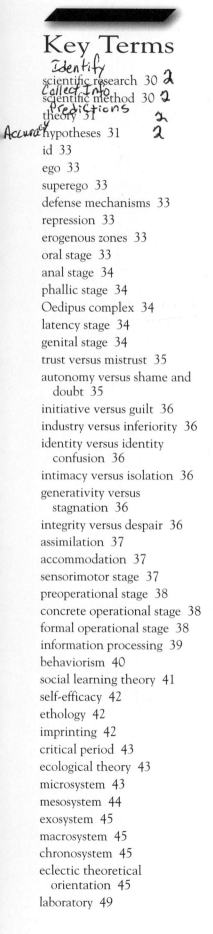

Key Terms

Identify
scientific research 30 2
Collect Info
scientific method 30 2
theory 31 *Predictions* 2
Accuracy hypotheses 31 2
id 33
ego 33
superego 33
defense mechanisms 33
repression 33
erogenous zones 33
oral stage 33
anal stage 34
phallic stage 34
Oedipus complex 34
latency stage 34
genital stage 34
trust versus mistrust 35
autonomy versus shame and
    doubt 35
initiative versus guilt 36
industry versus inferiority 36
identity versus identity
    confusion 36
intimacy versus isolation 36
generativity versus
    stagnation 36
integrity versus despair 36
assimilation 37
accommodation 37
sensorimotor stage 37
preoperational stage 38
concrete operational stage 38
formal operational stage 38
information processing 39
behaviorism 40
social learning theory 41
self-efficacy 42
ethology 42
imprinting 42
critical period 43
ecological theory 43
microsystem 43
mesosystem 44
exosystem 45
macrosystem 45
chronosystem 45
eclectic theoretical
    orientation 45
laboratory 49

naturalistic observation 49
standardized tests 50
case study 50
correlational research 50
experimental research 50
independent variable 51
dependent variable 51
experimental group 51
control group 51
random assignment 51
cross-sectional research 52
longitudinal research 52
ethnic gloss 54
nomothetic research 55
idiographic needs 55

Children Resources

Identity: Youth and Crisis
(1968) by Erik H. Erikson.
New York: W. W. Norton.

Erik Erikson was one of the leading theorists in the field of life-span development. In *Identity: Youth and Crisis*, he outlines his eight stages of life-span development and provides numerous examples from his clinical practice to illustrate the stages. Special attention is given to the fifth stage in Erikson's theory, identity versus identity confusion. Especially worthwhile are Erikson's commentaries about identity development in different cultures.

Observational Strategies of Child Study
(1990) by D. M. Irwin and M. M. Bushnell.
Fort Worth, TX: Harcourt Brace.

Being a good observer can benefit you a great deal in helping children reach their full potential. Observational skills can be learned. This practical book gives you a rich set of observational strategies that will assist you in becoming a more sensitive observer of children's behavior.

Taking It to the Net

http://www.mhhe.com/santrockcd6

1. Recall your pre-school experiences. Did your pre-school experiences mold you into the person you are today? Can the teaching methods used in pre-school affect a child's cognitive and socioemotional health a decade later?
2. Are scientists the only professionals qualified to conduct research in child development? Is there a role in child development research for teachers, nurses, or parents? For you?
3. As children grow, their brains get larger. As children grow, their knowledge base gets bigger. Does that mean that the larger your brain, the more you know? Correlational research provides the answer.

Section II

Beginnings

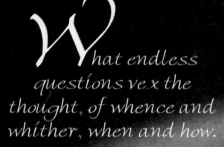

What endless questions vex the thought, of whence and whither, when and how.

Sir Richard Burton
British Explorer, 19th Century

The rhythm and meaning of life involve beginnings. Questions are raised about how, from so simple a beginning, endless forms develop, grow, and mature. What was this organism, what is this organism, and what will this organism be? In Section II, you will read three chapters: "Biological Beginnings" (chapter 3), "Prenatal Development" (chapter 4), and "Birth" (chapter 5).

Chapter

3

There are one hundred and ninety-three living species of monkeys and apes. One hundred and ninety-two of them are covered with hair. The exception is the naked ape, self-named Homo sapiens.

Desmond Morris
British Zoologist, 20th Century

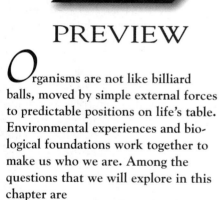

PREVIEW

*O*rganisms are not like billiard balls, moved by simple external forces to predictable positions on life's table. Environmental experiences and biological foundations work together to make us who we are. Among the questions that we will explore in this chapter are

- What are some fertility problems and possible solutions?
- What are some abnormalities in genes that can be passed on to offspring?
- How extensively does heredity influence children's development?
- How do scientists study hereditary influences on children?
- Is it ethical to breed for intelligence?
- What can we conclude about heredity-environment interaction and children's development?

The Story of the Jim and Jim Twins

Jim Springer and Jim Lewis are identical twins. They were separated at 4 weeks of age and did not see each other again until they were 39 years old. Both worked as part-time deputy sheriffs, vacationed in Florida, drive Chevrolets, had dogs named Toy, and married and divorced women named Betty. One twin named his son James Allan, and the other named his son James Alan. Both liked math but not spelling, enjoyed carpentry and mechanical drawing, chewed their fingernails down to the nubs, had almost identical drinking and smoking habits, had hemorrhoids, put on 10 pounds at about the same point in development, first suffered headaches at the age of 18, and had similar sleep patterns.

Jim Lewis (left) and Jim Springer (right).

But Jim and Jim have some differences. One wears his hair over his forehead, the other slicks it back and has sideburns. One expresses himself best orally; the other is more proficient in writing. But, for the most part, their profiles are remarkably similar.

Another pair, Daphne and Barbara, are called the "giggle sisters" because, after being reunited, they were always making each other laugh. A thorough search of their adoptive families' histories revealed no gigglers. And the identical sisters handled stress by ignoring it, avoided conflict and controversy whenever possible, and showed no interest in politics.

Two other female identical twin sisters were separated at 6 weeks and reunited in their fifties. Both had nightmares, which they describe in hauntingly similar ways: both dreamed of doorknobs and fishhooks in their mouths as they smothered to death! The nightmares began during early adolescence and stopped in the past 10 to 12 years. Both women were bed wetters until about 12 or 13 years of age, and they report educational and marital histories that were remarkably similar.

 # Love of beauty

Evolution and Behavior

natural selection
The evolutionary process that favors individuals of a species that are best adapted to survive and reproduce.

adaptive behavior
Behavior that promotes an organism's survival in the natural habitat.

These sets of twins are part of the Minnesota Study of Twins Reared Apart, directed by Thomas Bouchard and his colleagues. They bring identical twins (identical genetically because they come from the same fertilized egg) and fraternal twins (dissimilar genetically because they come from different fertilized eggs) from all over the world to Minneapolis to investigate their lives. The twins are given a number of personality tests, and detailed medical histories are obtained, including information about diet and smoking, exercise habits, chest X-rays, heart stress tests, and EEGs (brain-wave tests). The twins are interviewed and asked more than 15,000 questions about their family and childhood environment, personal interests, vocational orientation, values, and aesthetic judgments. They also are given ability and intelligence tests (Bouchard & others, 1990).

Critics of the Minnesota identical twins study point out that some of the separated twins were together several months prior to their adoption, that some of the twins had been reunited prior to their testing (in some cases, a number of years earlier), that adoption agencies often place twins in similar homes, and that even strangers who spend several hours together and start comparing their lives are likely to come up with some coincidental similarities (Adler, 1991). Still, even in the face of such criticism, the Minnesota study of identical twins indicates how scientists have recently shown an increased interest in the genetic basis of human development and that we need further research on genetic and environmental factors (Bouchard, 1995).

THE EVOLUTIONARY PERSPECTIVE

In evolutionary time, humans are relative newcomers to Earth, yet we have established ourselves as the most successful and dominant species. If we consider evolutionary time as a calendar year, humans arrived here in the last moments of December (Sagan, 1977). As our earliest ancestors left the forest to feed on the savannahs, and finally to form hunting societies on the open plains, their minds and behaviors changed. How did this evolution come about?

Natural Selection and Adaptive Behavior

Natural selection *is the evolutionary process that favors individuals of a species that are best adapted to survive and reproduce.* To understand natural selection, let's return to the middle of the nineteenth century, when Charles Darwin was traveling around the world, observing many different species of animals in their natural surroundings. Darwin, who published his observations and thoughts in *On the Origin of Species,* (1859), observed that most organisms reproduce at rates that would cause enormous increases in the population of most species and yet populations remain nearly constant. He reasoned that an intense, constant struggle for food, water, and resources must occur among the many young born each generation, because many of the young do not survive. Those that do survive pass on their genes to the next generation. Darwin believed that those who do survive to reproduce are probably superior in a number of ways to those who do not. In other words, the survivors are better adapted to their world than are the nonsurvivors (Enger & others, 1996). Over the course of many generations, organisms with the characteristics needed for survival would comprise a larger percentage of the population. Over many, many generations, this could produce a gradual modification of the whole population. If environmental conditions change, however, other characteristics might become favored by natural selection, moving the process in a different direction (Zubay, 1996).

A concept that is important for understanding the role of evolution in behavior is adaptive behavior (Crawford & Krebs, 1998; Knight, 1999). In evolutionary conceptions of psychology, **adaptive behavior** *is behavior that promotes an organism's* *survival in the natural habitat.* Adaptive behavior involves the organism's modification of its behavior to include its likelihood of survival. All organisms must adapt to particular places, climates, food sources, and ways of life. Natural selection designs adaptation to perform a certain function. An example of adaptation is an eagle's claws, designed by natural selection to facilitate predation. In the human realm, attachment is a system designed by natural selection to ensure an infant's closeness to the caregiver for feeding and protection from danger.

More than a million species have been classified, from bacteria to blue whales, with many varieties of beetles in between. The work of natural selection produced the disappearing acts of moths and the quills of porcupines, and the effects of evolution produced the technological advances, intelligence, and longer parental care of human beings (see figure 3.1).

Generally, evolution proceeds at a very slow pace. The lines that led to the emergence of human beings and the great apes diverged about 14 million years ago! Modern humans, *Homo sapiens,* came into existence only about 50,000 years ago. And the beginning of civilization as we know it began about 10,000 years ago. No sweeping evolutionary changes in humans have occurred since then—for example, our brain is not 10 times bigger than it was, we do not have a third eye in the back of our head, and we haven't learned to fly.

Although no dramatic evolutionary changes have occurred since *Homo sapiens* appeared on the fossil record 50,000 years ago, there have been sweeping cultural changes. Biological evolution shaped human beings into a culture-making species.

Race and Ethnicity

In keeping with one of the main themes of this text—exploration of sociocultural issues—let's examine the biological concept of race and see how it has taken on elaborate, often unfortunate, social meanings. **Race** *originated as a biological concept. It refers to a system for classifying plants and animals into subcategories according to specific physical and structural characteristics. Race* is one of the most misused and misunderstood words in the English language. Loosely, it has come to mean everything from religion to skin color.

The three main classifications of the human race are Mongoloid, or Asian; Caucasoid, or European; and Negroid, or African. Skin color, head shape, facial features, stature, and the color and texture of body hair are the physical characteristics most widely used to determine race.

These racial classifications presumably were created to define and clarify the differences among groups of people; however, they have not been very useful. Today many people define races as groups that are socially constructed on the basis of physical differences because race is a social construction and no longer a biological fact (Van den Berghe, 1978). For example, some groups, such as Native Americans, Australians, and Polynesians, do not fit into any of the three main racial categories. Also, obvious differences *within* groups are not adequately accounted for. Arabs, Hindus, and Europeans, for instance, are physically different, yet they are all called Caucasians. Although there are some physical characteristics that distinguish "racial" groups, there are, in fact, more similarities than differences among such groups.

Too often we are socialized to accept as facts many myths and stereotypes about people whose skin color, facial features, and hair texture differ from ours. For example, some people still believe that Asians are inscrutable, Jews are acquisitive, and Latinos are lazy. What people believe about race has profound social consequences. Until recently, for instance, African Americans were denied access to schools, hospitals, churches, and other social institutions attended by Whites.

*F*igure 3.1
The Better an Animal Is Adapted, the More Successful It Is

Humans, more than any other mammal, adapt to and control most types of environments. Because of longer parental care, humans learn more complex behavior patterns, which contribute to adaptation.

race

The term for a system for classifying plants and animals into subcategories according to specific physical and structural characteristics.

inpenetrable to Investigation

Fond of Acquiring

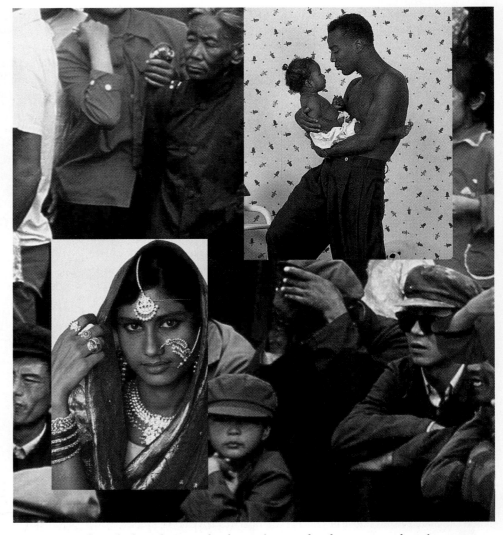

Race originated as a biological concept but has unfortunately taken on a number of negative social meanings as a sociocultural concept.

Although scientists are supposed to be a fair-minded lot, some also have used racial distinctions to further their own biases. Some even claim that one racial group has a biological inheritance that gives it an adaptive advantage over other racial groups. Nineteenth-century biologist Louis Agassiz, for example, asserted that God had created Blacks and Whites as separate species. Also, in Nazi Germany, where science and death made their grisliest alliance, Jews, homosexuals, and other "undesirables" were ascribed whatever characteristics were necessary to reinforce the conclusion that "survival of the fittest" demanded their elimination.

Unfortunately, racism cloaked in science still finds champions. Psychologist Philipe Rushton (1988) argues that evolution accounts for racial differences in sexual practices, fertility, intelligence, and criminality. Using these traits, he ranks Asians as superior, followed by Caucasians and people of African descent. Asians, Rushton claims, are the most intelligent, most sexually restrained, most altruistic, and least criminal of the races. Rushton ascribes a similar order to social classes: those who are impoverished resemble African Americans; those who earn high incomes resemble Asians and Whites. Rushton's theory, according to his critics, is full of "familiar vulgar stereotypes" (Weizmann & others, 1990). His notions are stitched together with frequent misinterpretations and overgeneralizations about racial differences and evolutionary history, and the data are tailored to fit his bias. Regrettably, even flimsy theories such as Rushton's provide whole cloth for anyone intent on justifying racism.

Exploring Racism

Remember that, although race is primarily a *biological* concept, ethnicity is primarily a *sociocultural* concept. In chapter 1, you read that cultural heritage, national characteristics, religion, language, *and* race constitute *ethnicity*. Race is just one component. However, the term *race* is often mistakenly used to refer to ethnicity. Jews, for example, are thought of as a race. Most are Caucasian, but they are too diverse to group into one racial subcategory. They also share too many anatomical features with other Caucasians to separate them as a distinct race (Thompson & Hughes, 1958). If we think of ethnicity predominantly in terms of social and cultural heritage, then Jews constitute an ethnic group.

Although we distinguish between race and ethnicity in this book, society usually does not. *Race* is used in a much broader way than many sociocultural psychologists recommend (Brislin, 1993). Social psychologist James Jones (1993) points out that thinking in racial terms has become embedded in cultures as an important factor in human interactions. For example, people often consider what race they will associate with when they decide on such things as where to live, who will make a suitable spouse, where to go to school, and what kind of job they want. Similarly, people often use race to judge whether or not another person is intelligent, competent, responsible, or socially acceptable. Children tend to adopt their parents' attitudes about race as they grow up, often perpetuating stereotypes and prejudice.

HEREDITY AND REPRODUCTION

Every species must have a mechanism for transmitting characteristics from one generation to the next. This mechanism is explained by the principles of genetics. Each of us carries a genetic code that we inherited from our parents. This code is located within every cell in our bodies. Our genetic codes are alike in one important way—they all contain the human genetic code. Because of the human genetic code, a fertilized human egg cannot grow into an egret, eagle, or elephant.

What Are Genes?

Each of us began life as a single cell weighing about one twenty-millionth of an ounce! This tiny piece of matter housed our entire genetic code—information about who we would become. These instructions orchestrated growth from that single cell to a person made of trillions of cells, each containing a perfect replica of the original genetic code (Miller & Harley, 1996).

The nucleus of each human cell contains 46 **chromosomes**, *which are threadlike structures that come in 23 pairs, one member of each pair coming from each parent. Chromosomes contain the remarkable genetic substance deoxyribonucleic acid, or DNA.* **DNA** *is a complex molecule that contains genetic information.* DNA's "double helix" shape looks like a spiral staircase (see figure 3.2). **Genes,** *the units of hereditary information, are short segments composed of DNA. Genes act as a blueprint for cells to reproduce themselves and manufacture the proteins that maintain life.* Chromosomes, DNA, and genes can be mysterious. To help you turn mystery into understanding, see figure 3.3.

Reproduction

Gametes *are human reproduction cells, which are created in the testes of males and the ovaries of females.* **Meiosis** *is the process of cell doubling and separation of chromosomes, with one member of each chromosomal pair going into each gamete, or daughter cell.* Thus, each human gamete has 23 unpaired chromosomes. The process of

Human Genome Project

chromosomes

Threadlike structures that come in 23 pairs, one member of each pair coming from each parent. Chromosomes contain the genetic substance DNA.

DNA

A complex molecule that contains genetic information.

genes

Units of hereditary information composed of DNA. Genes act as a blueprint for cells to reproduce themselves and manufacture the proteins that maintain life.

gametes

Human reproduction cells created in the testes of males and the ovaries of females.

meiosis

The process of cell doubling and separation of chromosomes in which each pair of chromosomes in a cell separates, with one member of each pair going into each gamete.

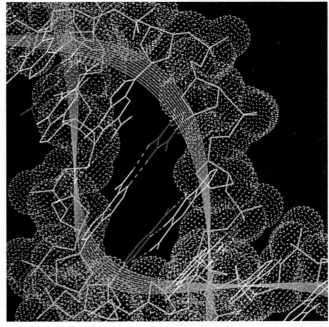

Figure 3.2
The Remarkable Substance Known as DNA

Genes are composed of DNA.

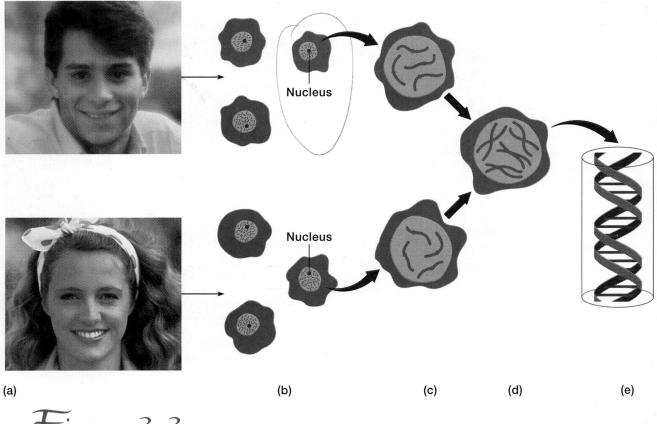

(a) (b) (c) (d) (e)

ℱigure 3.3
Facts About Chromosomes, DNA, and Genes

(*a*) The body contains billions of cells, which are organized into tissue and organs. (*b*) Each cell contains a central structure, the nucleus, which controls reproduction. (*c*) Chromosomes reside in the nucleus of each cell. The male's sperm and the female's egg are specialized reproductive cells that contain chromosomes. (*d*) At conception, the offspring receives matching chromosomes from the mother's egg and the father's sperm. (*e*) The chromosomes contain DNA, a chemical substance. Genes are short segments of the DNA molecule. They are the units of heredity information that act as a blueprint for cells to reproduce themselves and manufacture the proteins that sustain life.

reproduction

The process that, in humans, begins when a female gamete (ovum) is fertilized by a male gamete (sperm).

zygote

A single cell formed through fertilization.

Reproductive Health Issues

human **reproduction** *begins when a female gamete (ovum) is fertilized by a male gamete (sperm)* (see figure 3.4). A **zygote** *is a single cell formed through fertilization.* In the zygote, two sets of unpaired chromosomes combine to form one set of paired chromosomes—one member of each pair from the mother and the other member from the father. In this manner, each parent contributes 50 percent of the offspring's heredity.

An ovum is about 90,000 times as large as a sperm. Thousands of sperm must combine to break down the ovum's membrane barrier to allow a single sperm to penetrate the membrane barrier. Ordinarily, females have two X chromosomes, and males have one X and one Y chromosome. Because the Y chromosome is smaller and lighter than the X chromosome, Y-bearing sperm can be separated from X-bearing sperm in a centrifuge. This raises the possibility that the offspring's sex can be controlled. Not only are the Y-bearing sperm lighter, but they are more likely than the X-bearing sperm to coat the ovum. This results in the conception of 120 to 150 males for every 100 females. However, males are more likely to die (spontaneously abort) at every stage of prenatal development, so only about 106 males are born for every 100 females.

Considerable interest has recently been generated by the findings reported by the Genetics and IVF Institute in Fairfax, Virginia (Fugger & others, 1998). The clinic reported a 93 percent success rate with the births of 13 girls from 14 pregnancies in which the goal was to have a girl (the clinic also says that it achieved a similar

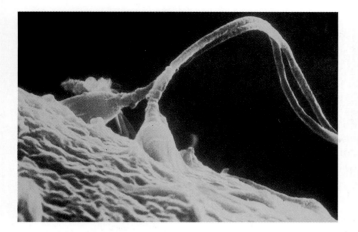

Figure 3.4
Union of Sperm and Egg

Figure 3.5
In Vitro Fertilization
Egg meets sperm in a laboratory dish.

success rate when the goal was to have a boy). How did they achieve this? They capitalized on the fact that sperm with a Y chromosome have about 2.8 percent less genetic material than sperm with an X chromosome. Based on this difference in the genetic material in X and Y chromosomes, the clinic sorted sperm and then artificially inseminated women with the sperm that had more genetic material in those cases in which parents wanted a girl. The first woman inseminated in this manner at the clinic wanted a daughter because the woman carried a gene for a rare disease that strikes boys almost exclusively.

Criticism of the clinic's strategy of sperm sorting for selecting the sex of an offspring has been extensive. Critics argue that the method should not be used for the family balancing of sex and that it interferes with nature's way of choosing sex with no medical benefit (Rosenwalks, 1998; Stillman, 1998). However, they acknowledge that it is appropriate to use when medical reasons are involved, as when there is a risk for a sex-linked disease, such as hemophilia. Critics also say the sample of 14 offspring is too small to determine whether the success rate will hold up over time. Since 1992, prior to the appearance of the new sex-sorting technique, researchers have been able to remove a cell from an eight-cell pre-embryo created through in-vitro fertilization (IVF) and determine its sex. Thus, for example, if parents are carriers of a genetic disease that affects boys, they can select a female pre-embryo for implantation. There is a cost differential in the sperm-sorting and IVF procedures: about $2,500 for sperm sorting and $10,000 for IVF.

Reproduction's fascinating moments have been made even more intriguing in recent years. In the United States, more than 2 million couples seek help for infertility every year. Of those, about 40,000 try high-tech assisted reproduction. The five most common techniques are

Infertility Resources

- *In vitro fertilization (IVF)*. An egg and a sperm are combined in a laboratory dish. If the egg is fertilized, the resulting embryo is transferred into the woman's uterus (see figure 3.5). The success rate is just under 20 percent.
- *Gamete intrafallopian transfer (GIFT)*. A doctor inserts eggs and sperm directly into a woman's fallopian tube. The success rate is almost 30 percent.
- *Intrauterine insemination (IUI)*. Frozen sperm—that of the husband or an unknown donor—is placed directly into the uterus, bypassing the cervix and upper vagina. The success rate is 10 percent.
- *Zygote intrafallopian transfer (ZIFT)*. This involves a two-step procedure. First, eggs are fertilized in the laboratory. Then, any resulting zygotes are

Drawing by Ziegler; ©1985 The New Yorker Magazine, Inc.

Females	
Problem	*Solution*
Damaged fallopian tubes	Surgery, in vitro fertilization
Abnormal ovulation	Hormone therapy, antibiotics, in vitro fertilization
Pelvic Inflammatory Disease (PID)	Antibiotics, surgery, change in birth control methods
Endometriosis*	Antibiotics, hormone therapy, surgery, artificial insemination
Damaged ovaries	Surgery, antibiotics, hormone therapy
Hostile cervical mucus	Antibiotics, artificial insemination, hormone therapy
Fibroid tumor	Surgery, antibiotics

Males	
Problem	*Solution*
Low sperm count	Antibiotics, hormone therapy, artificial insemination, lowered testicular temperature
Dilated veins around testicle	Surgery, lowered testicular temperature, antibiotics
Damaged sperm ducts	Surgery, antibiotics
Hormone deficiency	Hormone therapy
Sperm antibodies	Antibiotics, in vitro fertilization

*Endometriosis occurs when the uterine lining grows outside of the uterus and causes bleeding, blocking, or scarring that can interfere with conception or pregnancy.

Figure 3.6
Fertility Problems and Solutions

transferred to a fallopian tube. The success rate is approximately 25 percent.

- *Intracytoplasmic sperm injection (ICSI).* A doctor uses a microscopic pipette to inject a single sperm from a man's ejaculate into an egg. The zygote is returned to the uterus. The success rate is approximately 25 percent.

Approximately 10 to 15 percent of couples in the United States experience infertility, which is defined as the inability to conceive a child after 12 months of regular intercourse without contraception. The cause of infertility can rest with the woman or the man. The woman may not be ovulating, she may be producing abnormal ova, her fallopian tubes may be blocked, or she may have a disease that prevents implantation of the ova. The man may produce too few sperm, the sperm may lack motility (the ability to move adequately), or he may have a blocked passageway. In one study, long-term use of cocaine by men was related to low sperm count, low motility, and a higher number of abnormally formed sperm (Bracken & others, 1990). Cocaine-related infertility appears to be reversible if users stop taking the drug for at least one year. In some cases of infertility, surgery may correct the problem; in others, hormonal-based drugs may improve the probability of having a child. However, in some instances, fertility drugs have caused superovulation, producing three or more babies at a time. A summary of some of infertility's causes and solutions is presented in figure 3.6.

The creation of families by means of the new reproductive technologies raises important questions about the psychological consequences for children. In one study, the family relationships and socioemotional development of children were investigated in four types of families—two created by the most widely used reproductive technologies (in vitro fertilization and donor insemination) and two control groups (families with a naturally conceived child and adoptive families)

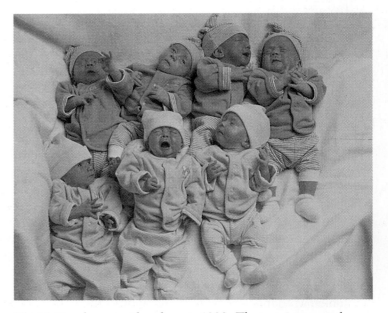

The McCaughey septuplets, born in 1998. The increasing use of fertility drugs is producing greater numbers of multiple births.

(Golombok & others, 1995). There were no differences between the four types of families on any of the measures of children's socioemotional development. The picture of families created by the new reproductive technologies was a positive one.

One consequence of fertility treatments is an increase in multiple births. Twenty-five to 30 percent of pregnancies achieved by fertility treatments—including in vitro fertilization—now result in multiple births. While parents may be thrilled at the prospect of having children, they also face serious risks. Any multiple birth increases the likelihood that the babies will have life-threatening and costly problems, such as extremely low birthweight.

With all of the possible complications of pregnancy, it is important to have some good pregnancy planning strategies. To read about several important ones, see the insert, Improving Developmental Skills.

Abnormalities in Genes and Chromosomes

What are some abnormalities that can occur in genes and chromosomes? What tests can be used to determine the presence of these abnormalities?

Types of Abnormalities Geneticists and developmentalists have identified a range of problems caused by major gene or chromosome defects. **Phenylketonuria (PKU)** *is a genetic disorder in which the individual cannot properly metabolize an amino acid. Phenylketonuria is now easily detected, but, if left untreated, mental retardation and hyperactivity result.* The disorder is treated by diet to prevent an excess accumulation of phenylalanine, an amino acid. Phenylketonuria involves a recessive gene and occurs about once in every 10,000 to 20,000 live births. Phenylketonuria accounts for about 1 percent of institutionalized mentally retarded individuals, and it occurs primarily in Whites.

Down syndrome *is a common genetically transmitted form of mental retardation, caused by the presence of an extra (47th) chromosome.* An individual with Down syndrome has a round face, a flattened skull, an extra fold of skin over the eyelids, a protruding tongue, short limbs, and retardation of motor and mental abilities. It is not known why the extra chromosome is present, but the health of the male sperm or female ovum may be involved. Women between the ages of 18 and 38 are less likely to give birth to a child with Down syndrome than are younger or older women. Down syndrome appears approximately once in every 700 live births. African American children are rarely born with Down syndrome. Some individuals have developed special programs to help children with Down syndrome. One such individual is Janet Marchese, adoptive mother of a baby with Down syndrome. She began putting the parents of children with Down syndrome together with couples who wanted to adopt them. Her adoption network has placed more than 1,500 children with Down syndrome and has a waiting list of couples who want to adopt.

Sickle-cell anemia, *which occurs most often in people of African descent, is a genetic disorder affecting the red blood cells.* A red blood cell is usually shaped like a disk, but in sickle-cell anemia a change in a recessive gene modifies its shape to a hook-shaped "sickle." These cells die quickly, causing anemia and early death of the individual because of their failure to carry oxygen to the body's cells. About 1 in 400

Improving Developmental Skills
Some Prepregnancy Strategies

- *Become knowledgeable about prepregnancy planning and health care providers.* The kinds of health care providers who are qualified to provide care for pregnant women include an obstetrician-gynecologist, a family practitioner, a nurse practitioner, and a certified nurse-midwife.
- *Meet with a health professional before conception.* A good strategy is for both potential parents to meet with a health professional prior to conception to assess their health and review personal and family histories. During this meeting, the health professional will discuss nutrition and other aspects of health that might affect the baby.
- *Find a health care provider who is competent.* The health care provider should
  —Take time to do a thorough family history
  —Not be patronizing
  —Be knowledgeable and stay current on prenatal testing
  —Be honest about risks, benefits, and side effects of any tests or treatments
  —Inspire trust

phenylketonuria (PKU)
A genetic disorder in which an individual cannot properly metabolize an amino acid. PKU is now easily detected but, if left untreated, results in mental retardation and hyperactivity.

Down syndrome
A common genetically transmitted form of mental retardation, caused by the presence of an extra (47th) chromosome.

Prenatal Testing and Down Syndrome

sickle-cell anemia
A genetic disorder that affects the red blood cells and occurs most often in people of African descent.

Figure 3.7
Sickle-Cell Anemia

During a physical examination for a college football tryout, Jerry Hubbard, 32, learned that he carried the gene for sickle-cell anemia. Daughter Sara is healthy but daughter Avery (in the print dress) has sickle-cell anemia. The couple says that they won't try to have any more children.

Klinefelter syndrome
A genetic disorder in which males have an extra X chromosome, making them XXY instead of XY.

Turner syndrome
A genetic disorder in which females are missing an X chromosome, making them XO instead of XX.

XYY syndrome
A genetic disorder in which males have an extra Y chromosome.

Genetic Disorders

Genetic Counseling

African American babies is affected. One in 10 African Americans is a carrier, as is 1 in 20 Latinos (see figure 3.7).

Other disorders are associated with sex-chromosome abnormalities. Remember that normal males have an X chromosome and a Y chromosome, and normal females have two X chromosomes. **Klinefelter syndrome** *is a genetic disorder in which males have an extra X chromosome, making them XXY instead of XY.* Males with this disorder have undeveloped testes, and they usually have enlarged breasts and become tall. Klinefelter syndrome occurs approximately once in every 800 live male births.

Turner syndrome *is a genetic disorder in which females are missing an X chromosome, making them XO instead of XX.* These females are short in stature and have a webbed neck. They may be mentally retarded and sexually underdeveloped. Turner syndrome occurs approximately once in every 3,000 live female births.

The **XYY syndrome** *is a genetic disorder in which the male has an extra Y chromosome. Early interest in this syndrome involved the belief that the Y chromosome found in males contributed to male aggression and violence.* It was then reasoned that if a male had an extra Y chromosome he would likely be extremely aggressive and possibly develop a violent personality. However, researchers subsequently found that XYY males are no more likely to commit crimes than are XY males (Witkin & others, 1976).

We have discussed six genetic disorders—phenylketonuria, Down syndrome, sickle-cell anemia, Klinefelter syndrome, Turner syndrome, and the XYY syndrome. A summary of these genetic disorders, as well as others, appears in figure 3.8.

Each year in the United States, 100,000 to 150,000 infants are born with a genetic disorder or malformation. These infants comprise about 3 to 5 percent of the 3 million births and account for at least 20 percent of infant deaths. Prospective parents increasingly are turning to genetic counseling for assistance, wanting to know their risk of having a child born with a genetic defect or malformation. To read further about genetic counseling, see the box Caring for Children.

The Human Genome Project (a *genome* is a complete set of genes), begun in the late 1970s, has as its goal the construction of the first detailed map of every human gene. Genetic engineers hope to use the knowledge derived from the project to reverse the course of many natural diseases (Olson, 1999; Sheffield, 1999). Recently, they isolated the genes for Huntington's disease, Lou Gehrig's disease, the so-called bubble-boy disease, and a common form of colon cancer, among others.

Name	Description	Treatment	Incidence	Prenatal detection	Carrier detection
Anencephaly	Neural-tube disorder that causes brain and skull malformations; most children die at birth.	Surgery	1 in 1,000	Ultrasound, amniocentesis	None
Cystic fibrosis	Glandular dysfunction that interferes with mucus production; breathing and digestion are hampered, resulting in a shortened life span.	Physical and oxygen therapy, synthetic enzymes, and antibiotics	1 in 2,000	Amniocentesis	Family history, DNA analysis
Down syndrome	Extra or altered 21st chromosome causes mild to severe retardation and physical abnormalities.	Surgery, early intervention, infant stimulation, and special learning programs	1 in 800 women, 1 in 350 women over 35	AFP, CVS, amniocentesis	Family history, chromosomal analysis
Hemophilia	Lack of the clotting factor causes excessive internal and external bleeding.	Blood transfusions and/or injections of the clotting factor	1 in 10,000 males	CVS, amniocentesis	Family history, DNA analysis
Klinefelter syndrome	An extra X chromosome causes physical abnormalities.	Hormone therapy	1 in 800 males	CVS, amniocentesis	None
Phenylketonuria (PKU)	Metabolic disorder that, left untreated, causes mental retardation.	Special diet	1 in 14,000	CVS, amniocentesis	Family history, blood test
Pyloric stenosis	Excess muscle in upper intestine causes severe vomiting and death if not treated.	Surgery	1 male in 200, 1 female in 1,000	None	None
Sickle-cell anemia	Blood disorder that limits the body's oxygen supply; it can cause joint swelling, sickle-cell crises, heart and kidney failure.	Penicillin, medication for pain, antibiotics, and blood transfusions	1 in 400 African American children (lower among other groups)	CVS, amniocentesis	Blood test
Spina bifida	Neural-tube disorder that causes brain and spine abnormalities.	Corrective surgery at birth, orthopedic devices, and physical/medical therapy	2 in 1,000	AFP, ultrasound, amniocentesis	None
Tay-Sachs disease	Deceleration of mental and physical development caused by an accumulation of lipids in the nervous system; few children live to age 5.	Medication and special diet	One in 30 American Jews is a carrier.	CVS, amniocentesis	Blood test
Thalassemia	Group of inherited blood disorders that causes anemic symptoms ranging from fatigue and weakness to liver failure.	Blood transfusions and antibiotics	1 in 400 children of Mediterranean descent	CVS, amniocentesis	Blood test
Turner syndrome	A missing or an altered X chromosome may cause sexual underdevelopment or physical abnormalities.	Hormone therapy	1 in 3,000 females	None	Blood test

Figure 3.8
Genetic Disorders and Conditions

Caring for Children
Genetic Counseling

In 1978, Richard Davidson was an athletic 37-year-old. A slip on an icy driveway landed him in the hospital for minor surgery for a broken foot. The day after the operation, he died. The cause of death was malignant hyperthermia (MH), a fatal allergylike reaction to certain anesthetics. The condition is hereditary and preventable—if the anesthesiologist is aware of the patient's susceptibility, alternative drugs can be used. Richard's death inspired his parents, Owen and Jean Davidson, to search their family tree for others with the MH trait. They mailed 300 letters to relatives, telling them of their son's death and warning about the hereditary risk. The gene, it turned out, came from Jean's side of the family. When her niece, Suellen Gallamore, informed the hospital where she was going to have infertility surgery about the MH in her bloodline, the doctors refused to treat her. In 1981, she co-founded the Malignant Hyperthermia Association to educate medical providers about MH, so that people at risk, like her sons, would not suffer as she had—or lose their lives, as her cousin had (Adato, 1995).

Consider also Bob and Mary Sims, who have been married for several years. They would like to start a family, but they are frightened. The newspapers and popular magazines are full of stories about infants who are born prematurely and don't survive, infants with debilitating physical defects, and babies found to have congenital mental retardation. The Simses feel that to have such a child would create a social, economic, and psychological strain on them and on society.

Accordingly, the Simses turn to a genetic counselor for help. Genetic counselors are usually physicians or biologists who are well versed in the field of medical genetics. They are familiar with the kinds of problems that can be inherited,

Suellen Gallamore with her sons, Scott and Greg Vincent. Among her immediate family, only Suellen has had the painful muscle biopsy for the MH gene. Scott, 24, and Greg, 26, assume that they carry the gene and protect against MH by alerting doctors about their family's medical history.

the odds of encountering them, and helpful measures for offsetting some of their effects. The Simses tell their counselor that there has been a history of mental retardation in Bob's family. Bob's younger sister was born with Down syndrome, a form of mental retardation. Mary's older brother has hemophilia, a condition in which bleeding is difficult to stop. They wonder what the chances are that a child of theirs might also be retarded or have hemophilia and what measures they can take to reduce their chances of having a mentally or physically defective child.

The counselor probes more deeply, because she understands that these facts in isolation do not give her a complete picture of the possibilities. She learns that no other relatives in Bob's family are retarded and that Bob's mother was in her late forties when his younger sister was born. She concludes that the retardation was probably due to the age of Bob's mother and not to a general tendency for members of his family to inherit retardation. It is well known that women over 40 have a much higher probability of giving birth to retarded children than are younger women. Apparently, in women over 40, the ova (egg cells) are not as healthy as in women under 40.

In Mary's case, the counselor determines that there is a small but clear possibility that Mary might be a carrier of hemophilia and might transmit that condition to a son. Otherwise, the counselor can find no evidence from the family history to indicate genetic problems.

The decision is then up to the Simses. In this case, the genetic problem will probably not occur, so the choice is fairly easy. But what should parents do if they face the strong probability of having a child with a major birth defect? Ultimately, the decision depends on the couple's ethical and religious beliefs (Wilfond, 1999).

Tests to Determine Abnormalities Scientists have developed a number of tests to determine whether a fetus is developing normally, among them amniocentesis, ultrasound sonography, the chorionic villus test, and the maternal blood test, each of which we will discuss in turn.

Amniocentesis *is a prenatal medical procedure in which a sample of amniotic fluid is withdrawn by syringe and tested to discover if the fetus is suffering from any chromosomal or metabolic disorders. Amniocentesis is performed between the 12th and 16th weeks of pregnancy.* The later amniocentesis is performed, the better its diagnostic potential. The earlier it is performed, the more useful it is in deciding whether a pregnancy should be terminated (see figure 3.9).

Ultrasound sonography *is a prenatal medical procedure in which high-frequency sound waves are directed into the pregnant woman's abdomen.* The echo from the sounds is transformed into a visual representation of the fetus's inner structures. This technique has been able to detect such disorders as microencephaly, a form of mental retardation involving an abnormally small brain. Ultrasound sonography is often used in conjunction with amniocentesis to determine the precise location of the fetus in the mother's abdomen (see figure 3.10).

As scientists have searched for more accurate, safer assessments of high-risk prenatal conditions, they have developed a new test. **Chorionic villi sampling** *is a prenatal medical procedure in which a small sample of the placenta is removed at some point between the 8th and 11th weeks of pregnancy.* Diagnosis takes approximately 10 days. Chorionic villi sampling allows a decision about abortion to be made near the end of the first trimester of pregnancy, a point when abortion is safer and less traumatic than after amniocentesis in the second trimester. These techniques provide valuable information about the presence of birth defects, but they also raise issues pertaining to whether an abortion should be obtained if birth defects are present.

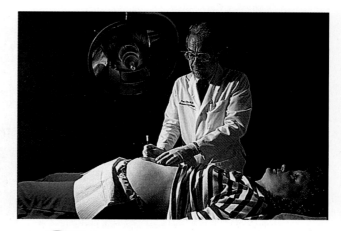

Figure 3.9

Amniocentesis Being Performed on a Pregnant Woman

amniocentesis
A prenatal medical procedure in which a sample of amniotic fluid is withdrawn by syringe and tested to discover if the fetus is suffering from any chromosomal or metabolic disorders. It is performed between the 12th and 16th weeks of pregnancy.

ultrasound sonography
A prenatal medical procedure in which high-frequency sound waves are directed into the pregnant woman's abdomen.

chorionic villi sampling
A prenatal medical procedure in which a small sample of the placenta is removed at a certain point in the pregnancy between the 8th and 11th weeks of pregnancy.

Amniocentesis
Obstetric Ultrasound
Chorionic Villi Sampling

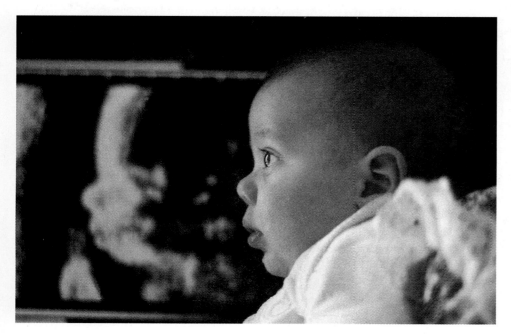

Figure 3.10
Ultrasound Sonography

A 6-month-old infant poses with the ultrasound sonography record taken four months into the baby's prenatal development.

Summary Table 3.1
The Evolutionary Perspective; Heredity and Reproduction

Concept	Processes/ Related Ideas	Characteristics/Description
The evolutionary perspective	Natural selection and adaptive behavior	Natural selection is the process that favors the individuals of a species that are best adapted to survive and reproduce. This concept was originally proposed by Charles Darwin. In evolutionary theory, adaptive behavior is behavior that promotes the organism's survival in a natural habitat. Although no dramatic evolutionary changes have occurred in humans since *Homo sapiens* first appeared in the fossil record 50,000 years ago, there have been sweeping cultural changes. Biological evolution shaped human beings into a culture-making species.
	Race and ethnicity	Race is a biological concept; ethnicity is a sociocultural concept. The concept of race has taken on a number of social meanings, some of which have resulted in discrimination and prejudice. Race continues to be a misunderstood and abused concept.
Heredity and reproduction	What are genes?	The nucleus of each human cell contains 46 chromosomes, which are composed of DNA. Genes are short segments of DNA and act as a blueprint for cells to reproduce and manufacture proteins that maintain life.
	Reproduction	Genes are transmitted from parents to offspring by gametes, or sex cells. Gametes are formed by the splitting of cells, a process called "meiosis." Reproduction takes place when a female gamete (ovum) is fertilized by a male gamete (sperm) to create a single-celled ovum. High-tech assisted reproduction has helped solve some infertility problems. Approximately 10 to 15 percent of couples in the United States experience infertility problems, some of which can be corrected through surgery or fertility drugs.
	Abnormalities in genes and chromosomes	A range of problems are caused by major gene or chromosome defects, among them PKU, Down syndrome, sickle-cell anemia, Klinefelter syndrome, Turner syndrome, and the XYY syndrome. Genetic counseling has increased in popularity as couples desire information about their risk of having a defective child. Amniocentesis, ultrasound sonography, chorionic villi sampling, and the maternal blood test are used to determine the presence of defects after pregnancy has begun.

maternal blood test
A prenatal diagnostic technique used to assess blood alphaprotein level, which is associated with neural-tube defects. This technique is also called the alpha-fetoprotein test (AFP).

The **maternal blood test** (*alpha-fetoprotein—AFP*) *is a prenatal diagnostic technique that is used to assess blood alphaprotein level, which is associated with neural-tube defects.* This test is administered to women 14 to 20 weeks into pregnancy only when they are at risk for bearing a child with defects in the formation of the brain and spinal cord.

So far in this chapter, we have discussed the evolutionary perspective; genes, chromosomes, and reproduction; and abnormalities in genes and chromosomes. An overview of these ideas is outlined in summary table 3.1.

GENETIC PRINCIPLES, METHODS, AND INFLUENCES

What are some basic genetic principles that affect children's development? What methods do behavior geneticists use to study heredity's influence? How does heredity influence such aspects of children's development as their intelligence? How do heredity and environment interact to produce children's development?

Genetic Principles

Genetic determination is a complex affair, and much is unknown about the way genes work (Collins, 1999; Tamarin, 1996). But a number of genetic principles have been discovered, among them those of dominant-recessive genes, sex-linked genes, polygenically inherited characteristics, reaction range, and canalization.

According to the **dominant-recessive genes principle,** *if one gene of a pair is dominant and one is recessive, the dominant gene exerts its effect, overriding the potential influence of the other, recessive gene. A recessive gene exerts its influence only if the two genes of a pair are both recessive.* If you inherit a recessive gene for a trait from each of your parents, you will show the trait. If you inherit a recessive gene from only one parent, you may never know you carry the gene. Brown eyes, farsightedness, and dimples rule over blue eyes, nearsightedness, and freckles in the world of dominant-recessive genes. Can two brown-eyed parents have a blue-eyed child? Yes, they can. Suppose that in each parent the gene pair that governs eye color includes a dominant gene for brown eyes and a recessive gene for blue eyes. Since dominant genes override recessive genes, the parents have brown eyes, but both are carriers of blueness and pass on their recessive genes for blue eyes. With no dominant gene to override them, the recessive genes can make the child's eyes blue. Figure 3.11 illustrates the dominant-recessive genes principle.

For thousands of years, people wondered what determined whether we become male or female. Aristotle believed that the father's arousal during intercourse determines the offspring's sex. The more excited the father is, the more likely it would be a son, he reasoned. Of course, he was wrong, but it was not until the 1920s that researchers confirmed the existence of human sex chromosomes, 2 of the 46

Lesser Biochemical Activity
↑
dominant-recessive genes principle
If one gene of a pair is dominant and one is recessive (goes back, or recedes), the dominant gene exerts its effect, overriding the potential influence of the recessive gene. A recessive gene exerts its influence only if both genes in a pair are recessive.

Heredity Resources

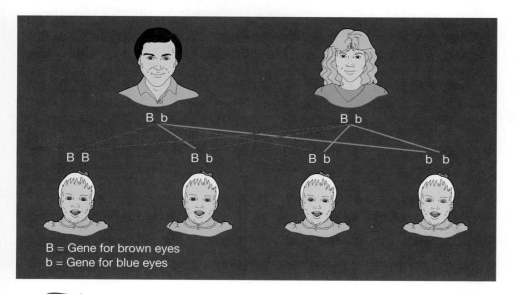

B = Gene for brown eyes
b = Gene for blue eyes

*F*igure 3.11
How Brown-Eyed Parents Can Have a Blue-Eyed Child

Although both parents have brown eyes, each parent can have a recessive gene for blue eyes. In this example, both parents have brown eyes, but each parent carries the recessive gene for blue eyes. Therefore, the odds of their child having blue eyes is one in four—the probability the child will receive a recessive gene (*b*) from each parent.

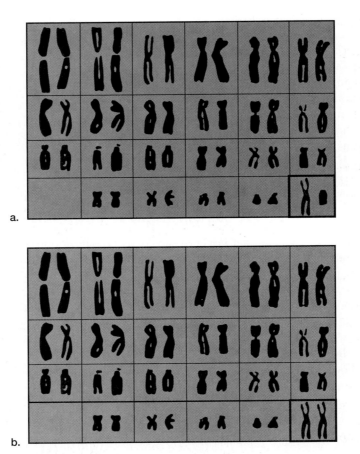

a.

b.

*F*igure 3.12
The Genetic Difference
Between Males and Females

Set (*a*) shows the chromosome structure of a male, and set (*b*) shows the chromosome structure of a female. The last pair of 23 pairs of chromosomes is in the bottom right box of each set. Notice that the Y chromosome of the male is smaller than that of the female. To obtain this kind of chromosomal picture, a cell is removed from a person's body, usually from the inside of the mouth. The chromosomes are stained by chemical treatment, magnified extensively, and then photographed.

That which comes of a cat will catch mice.

English Proverb

polygenic inheritance
The genetic principle that many genes can interact to produce a particular characteristic.

chromosomes human beings normally carry. As we saw earlier, ordinarily females have two X chromosomes, and males have an X and a Y. (Figure 3.12 shows the chromosomal makeup of a male and a female.)

Genetic transmission is usually more complex than the simple examples we have examined thus far (Hohner & Stevenson, 1999; Weaver & Hedrick, 1996). **Polygenic inheritance** *is the genetic principle that many genes can interact to produce a particular characteristic.* Few psychological characteristics are the result of single pairs. Most are determined by the interaction of many different genes. There are 50,000 or more genes, so you can imagine that possible combinations of these are staggering in number. Traits produced by this mixing of genes are said to be polygenically determined.

(handwritten annotations at top) * intro – Emotionally Stable, Calm — Autonomic ANS is not as Reactive
* Extra – Seeks Stimulation – Low brain Arousal

No one possesses all the characteristics that our genetic structure makes possible. A **genotype** *is the person's genetic heritage, the actual genetic material.* However, not all of this genetic material is apparent in our observed and measurable characteristics. A **phenotype** *is the way an individual's genotype is expressed in observed and measurable characteristics.* Phenotypes include physical traits (such as height, weight, eye color, and skin pigmentation) and psychological characteristics (such as intelligence, creativity, personality, and social tendencies).

For each genotype, a range of phenotypes can be expressed. Imagine that we could identify all of the genes that would make a person introverted or extraverted. Would measured introversion-extraversion be predictable from knowledge of the specific genes? The answer is no, because, even if our genetic model were adequate, introversion-extraversion is a characteristic shaped by experience throughout life. For example, parents may push an introverted child into social situations and encourage the child to become more gregarious. *sociable*

To understand how introverted a child is, think about a series of genetic codes that predispose the child to develop in a particular way, and imagine environments that are responsive or unresponsive to this development. For instance, the genotype of some persons may predispose them to be introverted in an environment that promotes a turning inward of personality, yet, in an environment that encourages social interaction and outgoingness, these individuals may become more extraverted. However, it would be unlikely for the individual with this introverted genotype to become a strong extravert. The **reaction range** *is the range of possible phenotypes for each genotype, suggesting the importance of an environment's restrictiveness or enrichment* (see figure 3.13).

Sandra Scarr (1984) explains reaction range this way: each of us has a range of potential. For example, an individual with "medium-tall" genes for height who grows up in a poor environment may be shorter than average; however, in an excellent nutritional environment, the individual may grow up taller than average. No matter how well fed the person is, though, someone with "short" genes will never be taller than average. Scarr believes that characteristics such as intelligence and introversion work the same way. That is, there is a range within which the environment can modify intelligence, but intelligence is not completely malleable. Reaction range gives us an estimate of how modifiable intelligence is. *Adaptable*

Although some traits have a wide reaction range, others are somewhat immune to extensive changes in the environment. These characteristics seem to stay on a particular developmental course, regardless of the environmental assaults on them (Waddington, 1957). **Canalization** *is the term chosen to describe the narrow path, or developmental course, that certain characteristics take. Apparently, preservative forces help protect, or buffer, a person from environmental extremes.* For example, American developmental psychologist Jerome Kagan (1984) points to his research on Guatemalan infants who had experienced extreme malnutrition as infants yet showed normal social and cognitive development later in childhood. And some abused children do not grow up to be abusers themselves.

Although the genetic influence of canalization exerts its power by keeping organisms on a particular developmental path, genes alone do not directly determine human behavior. Developmentalist Gilbert Gottlieb (1991) points out that genes are an integral part of the organism but that their activity (genetic expression) can be affected by the organism's environment. For example, hormones that circulate in the blood make their way into the cell, where they influence the cell's activity. The flow of hormones themselves can be affected by environmental events, such as light, day length, nutrition, and behavior.

Methods Used by Behavior Geneticists

Behavior genetics *is the study of the degree and nature of behavior's hereditary basis.* Behavior geneticists assume that behaviors are jointly determined by the interaction of heredity and environment (Dale & Dionne, 1999; Goldsmith,

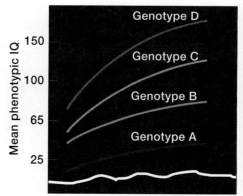

Figure 3.13
Responsiveness of Genotypes to Environmental Influences

Although each genotype responds favorably to improved environments, some are more responsive than others to environmental deprivation and enrichment.

genotype
A person's genetic heritage; the actual genetic material.

phenotype
The way an individual's genotype is expressed in observed and measurable characteristics.

reaction range *wide or narrow*
The range of possible phenotypes for each genotype, suggesting the importance of an environment's restrictiveness or enrichment.

canalization
The process by which characteristics take a narrow path or developmental course. Apparently, preservative forces help protect a person from environmental extremes.

(handwritten) Little or Lot of Genetic Inf. to be Channelled

Behavior Genetics

(handwritten) Short term memory – Canalization Phone #

behavior genetics
The study of the degree and nature of heredity basis.

Identical twins develop from a single fertilized egg that splits into two genetically identical organisms. Twin studies compare identical twins with fraternal twins. Fraternal twins develop from separate eggs, making them genetically no more similar than ordinary brothers and sisters.

twin study

A study in which the behavioral similarity of identical twins is compared with the behavioral similarity of fraternal twins.

identical twins

Twins who develop from a single fertilized egg that splits into two genetically identical replicas, each of which becomes a person.

fraternal twins

Twins who develop from separate eggs and separate sperm, making them genetically no more similar than ordinary siblings.

adoption study

A study in which investigators seek to discover whether, in behavior and psychological characteristics, adopted children are more like their adoptive parents, who provided a home environment, or more like their biological parents, who contributed their heredity. Another form of the adoption study is to compare adoptive and biological siblings.

Twin Research

1994). To study heredity's influence on behavior, behavior geneticists often use either twin studies or adoption studies.

In a **twin study,** *the behavioral similarity of identical twins is compared with the behavioral similarity of fraternal twins.* **Identical twins** *(called monozygotic twins) develop from a single fertilized egg that splits into two genetically identical replicas, each of which becomes a person.* **Fraternal twins** *(called dizygotic twins) develop from separate eggs and separate sperm, making them genetically no more similar than ordinary siblings.* Although fraternal twins share the same womb, they are no more alike genetically than are nontwin brothers and sisters, and they may be of different sexes. By comparing groups of identical and fraternal twins, behavior geneticists capitalize on the basic knowledge that identical twins are more similar genetically than are fraternal twins (Mitchell, 1999; Plomin & DeFries, 1998; Scarr, 1996). In one twin study, 7,000 pairs of Finnish identical and fraternal twins were compared on the personality traits of extraversion and neuroticism (psychological instability) (Rose & others, 1988). On both of these personality traits, the identical twins were much more similar than the fraternal twins were, suggesting the role of heredity in both traits. However, several issues crop up as a result of twin studies. Adults might stress the similarities of identical twins more than those of fraternal twins, and identical twins might perceive themselves as a "set" and play together more than fraternal twins do. If so, observed similarities in identical twins could be environmentally influenced.

In an **adoption study,** *investigators seek to discover whether, in behavior and psychological characteristics, adopted children are more like their adoptive parents, who provided a home environment, or more like their biological parents, who contributed their heredity. Another form of the adoption study is to compare adoptive and biological siblings.* In one investigation, the educational levels attained by the biological parents were better predictors of the adopted children's IQ scores than were the IQs of the children's adopted parents (Scarr & Weinberg, 1983). Because of the genetic relation between the adopted children and their biological parents, the implication is that heredity influences children's IQ scores.

Heredity's Influence on Development

What aspects of development are influenced by genetic factors? They all are. However, behavior geneticists are interested in more precise estimates of a characteristic's variation that can be accounted for by genetic factors (Ganger & others, 1999). Intelligence and temperament are among the most widely investigated aspects of heredity's influence on development.

Arthur Jensen (1969) sparked a lively and, at times, hostile debate when he presented his thesis that intelligence is primarily inherited. Jensen believes that environment and culture play only a minimal role in intelligence. He examined several studies of intelligence, some of which involved comparisons of identical and fraternal twins. Remember that identical twins have identical genetic endowments, so their IQs should be similar. Fraternal twins and ordinary siblings are less similar genetically, so their IQs should be less similar. Jensen found support for his argument in these studies. Studies with identical twins produced an average correlation of .82; studies with ordinary siblings produced an average correlation of .50. Note the difference of .32. To show that genetic factors are more important than environmental factors, Jensen compared identical twins reared together with those reared apart; the correlation for those reared together was .89 and for those reared apart was .78 (a difference of .11). Jensen argued that, if environmental influences are more important than genetic influences, then siblings reared apart, who experience different environments, should have IQs much further apart.

Many scholars have criticized Jensen's work. One criticism concerns the definition of intelligence itself. Jensen believes that IQ as measured by standardized

The Wizard of Ic *King Features Syndicate*

intelligence tests is a good indicator of intelligence. Critics argue that IQ tests tap only a narrow range of intelligence. Everyday problem solving, work, and social adaptability, say the critics, are important aspects of intelligence not measured by the traditional intelligence tests used in Jensen's sources. A second criticism is that most investigations of heredity and environment do not include environments that differ radically. Thus, it is not surprising that many genetic studies show environment to be a fairly weak influence on intelligence.

Intelligence is influenced by heredity, but most developmentalists have not found as strong a relationship as Jensen found in his work. Other experts estimate heredity's influence on intelligence to be in the 50 percent range (Plomin, DeFries, & McClearn, 1990).

The most recent controversy about heredity and intelligence focuses on the book *The Bell Curve: Intelligence and Class Structure in Modern Life* (1994) by Richard Hernstein and Charles Murray. The authors argue that America is rapidly evolving a huge underclass of intellectually deprived individuals whose cognitive abilities will never match the future needs of most employers. The authors believe that members of this underclass, a large percentage of whom are African American, might be doomed by their shortcomings to welfare dependency, poverty, crime, and lives devoid of any hope of ever reaching the American dream.

Hernstein and Murray believe that IQ can be quantitatively measured and that IQ test scores vary across ethnic groups. They point out that, in the United States, Asian Americans score several points higher than Whites, while African Americans score about 15 points lower than Whites. They also argue that these IQ differences are at least partly due to heredity and that government money spent on education programs such as Project Head Start is wasted, helping only the government's bloated bureaucracy.

Why do Hernstein and Murray call their book *The Bell Curve?* A bell curve is a normal distribution graph, which has the shape of a bell—bulging in the middle and thinning out at the edges (see figure 3.14). Normal distribution graphs are used to represent large numbers of people, who are sorted according to a shared characteristic, such as weight, exposure to asbestos, taste in clothes, or IQ.

Hernstein and Murray often refer to bell curves to make a point: that predictions about any individual based exclusively on the person's IQ are useless. Weak correlations between intelligence and job success have predictive value only when they are applied to large groups of people. Within such large groups, say Hernstein and Murray, the pervasive influence of IQ on human society becomes apparent.

Significant criticisms have been leveled at *The Bell Curve.* Experts on intelligence generally agree that African Americans score lower than Whites on IQ tests.

Genetics and Ethics

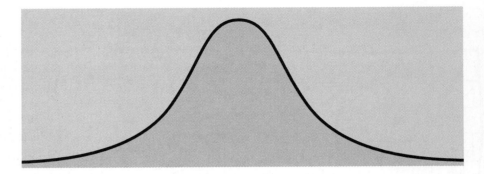

ℱigure 3.14
The Bell Curve

The term *bell curve* is used to describe a normal distribution graph, which looks like a bell—bulging in the middle and thinning out at the edges.

However, many of these experts raise serious questions about the ability of IQ tests to accurately measure a person's intelligence. Among the criticisms of IQ tests is that the tests are culturally biased against African Americans and Latinos. In 1971, the U.S. Supreme Court endorsed such criticisms and ruled that tests of general intelligence, in contrast to tests that solely measure fitness for a particular job, are discriminatory and cannot be administered as a condition of employment. Another criticism is that most investigations of heredity and environment do not include environments that differ radically. To read further about a controversial aspect of heredity, see the Adventures for the Mind insert.

Most experts today agree that the environment plays an important role in intelligence (Ceci & others, 1997). This means that improving children's environments can raise their intelligence. It also means that enriching children's environments can improve their school achievement and their acquisition of skills needed for employability. Craig Ramey and his associates (1988) found that high-quality early educational day care (through 5 years of age) significantly raised the tested intelligence of young children from impoverished backgrounds. Positive effects of this early intervention were still evident in the intelligence and achievement of these students when they were in middle school (Campbell & Ramey, 1994).

HEREDITY-ENVIRONMENT INTERACTION AND CHILDREN'S DEVELOPMENT

A common misconception is that behavior geneticists analyze only the effects of heredity on development. While they believe heredity plays an important role in children's development, they also carve up the environment's contribution to heredity-environment interaction (Rowe & Jacobson, 1999; Waldman & Rhee, 1999).

Genotype → Environment Concepts

Parents not only provide the genes for their child's biological blueprint for development; they also play important roles in determining the types of environments their children will encounter. Behavior geneticist Sandra Scarr (1993) believes that

---

passive genotype → environment correlation

This occurs when parents, who are genetically related to the child, provide a rearing environment for the child.

evocative genotype → environment correlation

This occurs when the child's genotype elicits certain types of physical and social environments.

active (niche-picking) genotype → environment correlation

This occurs when children seek out environments they find compatible and stimulating.

the environments parents select for their children depend to some degree on the parents' own genotypes. Behavior geneticists believe that the three ways heredity and environment interact are passively, evocatively, and actively. The arrow (→) in the heading for this section ("Genotype → Environment Concepts") expresses Scarr's emphasis that heredity drives the link between genotype and environment.

Passive genotype → environment correlation *occurs when parents who are genetically related to the child provide a rearing environment for the child.* For example, parents may have a genetic predisposition to be intelligent and to read skillfully. Because they read well and enjoy reading, they provide their child with books to read, with the likely outcome that their children will become skilled readers who enjoy reading.

Evocative genotype → environment correlation *occurs because a child's genotype elicits certain types of physical and social environments.* For example, active, smiling babies receive more social stimulation than do passive, quiet babies. Cooperative, attentive children evoke more pleasant and instructional responses from the adults around them than do uncooperative, distractible children.

Active (niche-picking) genotype → environment correlation *occurs when children seek out environments they find compatible and stimulating.* Niche-picking *refers to finding a niche, or setting, that is especially suited to the child's abilities.* Children select from their surrounding environment some aspects that they respond to, learn about, or ignore. Their active selections of certain environments are related to their particular genotype. Some children, because of their genotype, have the sensorimotor skills to perform well at sports. Others, because of their genotype, may have more ability in music. Children who are athletically inclined are more likely to actively seek out sports environments, in which they can perform well, while children who are musically inclined are more likely to spend time in musical environments, in which they can successfully perform their skills.

Scarr (1993) believes that the relative importance of the three genotype → environment correlations change as children develop from infancy through adolescence. In infancy, much of the environment that children experience is provided by adults. When those adults are genetically related to the child, the environment they provide is related to their own characteristics and genotypes. Although infants are active in structuring their experiences by actively attending to what is available to them, they cannot seek out and build their own environmental niches, as much as older children can. Therefore, passive genotype → environment correlations are more common in the lives of infants and young children than in the lives of older children, who can extend their experiences beyond the family's influences and create their environments to a greater degree.

Adventures for the Mind
The Nobel Prize Sperm Bank

In the 1980s, Dr. Robert Graham founded the Repository for Germinal Choice in Escondido, California, as a sperm bank for Nobel Prize winners and other bright individuals with the intent of producing geniuses. The sperm is available to women of "good stock" whose husbands are infertile, according to Graham.

Dr. Graham with the frozen sperm of a Nobel Prize–winning donor.

What are the odds that the sperm bank will yield that special combination of factors required to produce a creative genius? Twentieth-century Irish-born British playwright George Bernard Shaw once told a story about a beautiful woman who wrote him, saying that, with her body and his mind, they could produce marvelous offspring. Shaw responded by saying that, unfortunately, the offspring might get his body and her mind.

What do you think about the Nobel Prize sperm bank? Is it right to breed for intelligence? Does it raise visions of the German gene program of the 1930s and 1940s, in which the Nazis believed that certain traits are superior? They tried to breed children with such traits and killed people without them. Or does the sperm bank merely provide a social service for couples who cannot conceive a child, couples who want to maximize the probability that their offspring will have good genes?

Where do you stand on this controversial topic of breeding for intelligence? Do you think it is unethical? Can you see where it might bring hope for once childless couples?

Shared and Nonshared Environmental Experiences

Behavior geneticists also believe that another way the environment's role in heredity-environment interaction can be carved up is to consider the experiences of children that are in common with those of other children living in the same home, as well as experiences that are not shared (Finkel, Whitfield, & McGue, 1995; Perusse, 1999; Waldren & Turkheimer, 1999). Behavior geneticist Robert Plomin (1996) has found that common rearing, or shared environment, accounts for little of the variation in children's personality or interests. In other words, even though two children live under the same roof with the same parents, their personalities are often very different.

Shared environmental experiences *are children's common experiences, such as their parents' personalities and intellectual orientation, the family's social class, and the neighborhood in which they live.* By contrast, **nonshared environmental experiences** *are a child's unique experiences, both within the family and outside the family, that are not shared with another sibling. Thus, experiences occurring within the family can be part of the "nonshared environment."* Parents often interact differently with each sibling, and siblings interact differently with parents. Siblings often have different peer groups, different friends, and different teachers at school.

Conclusions About Heredity-Environment Interaction

The most recent controversy to hit the nature-nurture wars is Judith Harris' (1998) book *The Nurture Assumption: Why Children Turn Out the Way They Do; Parents Matter Less Than You Think and Peers Matter More.* Harris argues that there's nothing much parents can do to make a difference in their children's behavior, intelligence, or personality. Spank them, hug them, read to them, ignore them: Harris says it won't influence how they turn out. She argues that children's genes and peers are more important than parents in children's development. As with our earlier discussion of nature-nurture and intelligence, nature does matter. So does nurture. As respected child development expert T. Berry Brazelton (1998, p. C2) commented, "The Nurture Assumption is so disturbing it devalues what parents are trying to do. . . . Parents may say, 'If I don't matter, why should I bother?' That's terrifying and it's coming when children need a stronger home base."

In sum, both genes and environment are necessary for a person to even exist. Without genes, there is no person; without environment, there is no person (Scarr & Weinberg, 1980). Heredity and environment operate together—or cooperate—to produce a person's intelligence, temperament, height, weight, ability to pitch a baseball, reading skills, and so on (Gottlieb, Wahlsten, & Lickliter, 1998). If an attractive, popular, intelligent girl is elected president of her high school senior class, is her success due to heredity or to environment? Of course, the answer is both. Because the environment's influence depends on genetically endowed characteristics, the two factors *interact* (Mader, 1999).

The relative contributions of heredity and environment are not additive, as in such-and-such a percentage of nature and such-and-such a percentage of experience. That's the old view. Nor is it accurate to say that full genetic expression happens once, around conception or birth, after which we take our genetic legacy into the world to see how far it gets us. Genes produce proteins throughout the life span, in many different environments. Or they don't produce these proteins, depending on how harsh or nourishing those environments are. The interaction is so extensive that William Greenough (1997, 1999; Greenough & others, 1997) says that to ask which is more important, nature or nurture, is to ask which is more important to a rectangle, its length or its width.

shared environmental experiences
Children's common environmental experiences that are shared with their siblings, such as their parents' personalities and intellectual orientation, the family's social class, and the neighborhood in which they live.

nonshared environmental experiences
The child's unique experiences, both within the family and outside the family, that are not shared by another sibling. Thus, experiences occurring within the family can be part of the "nonshared environment."

Genes and Parenting

What is the theme of Judith Harris' (1998) controversial book, The Nurture Assumption? *What is the nature of the controversy?*

Summary Table 3.2
Genetic Principles, Methods, and Influences; Heredity-Environment Interaction

Concept	Processes/ Related Ideas	Characteristics/Description
Genetic principles, methods, and influences	Genetic principles	Genetic transmission is complex, but some principles have been worked out, among them dominant-recessive genes, sex-linked genes, polygenic inheritance, genotype-phenotype distinction, reaction range, and canalization.
	Methods used by behavior geneticists	Behavior genetics is the field concerned with the degree and nature of behavior's heredity basis. Among the most important methods used by behavior geneticists are twin studies and adoption studies.
	Heredity's influence on development	All aspects of development are influenced by heredity. Like Hernstein and Murray's, Jensen's argument that intelligence is due primarily to heredity sparked a lively and, at times, bitter debate. Intelligence is influenced by heredity, but not as strongly as Jensen and Hernstein and Murray envisioned. Most experts today agree that the environment plays an important role in intelligence.
Heredity-environment interaction	Genotype → environment concepts	Scarr believes that the environments parents select for their own children depend to some degree on the parents' genotypes. Three ways behavior geneticists believe heredity and environment are related in this manner are passively, evocatively, and actively. Passive genotype → environment correlation occurs when parents, who are genetically related to the child, provide a rearing environment for the child. Evocative genotype → environment correlation occurs because a child's genotype elicits certain types of physical and social environments. Active (niche-picking) genotype → environment correlation occurs when children seek out environments they find compatible and stimulating. Scarr believes the relative importance of these three forms of genotype/environment correlations change as children develop.
	Shared and nonshared environmental experiences	Shared environmental experiences are children's common experiences, such as their parents' personalities and intellectual orientation, the family's social class, and the neighborhood in which they live. *Nonshared environmental experiences* refers to the child's unique experiences, both within a family and outside the family, that are not shared by another sibling. Plomin argues that it is nonshared environmental experiences that primarily make up the environment's contribution to the reasons one sibling's personality is different from another's.
	Conclusions about heredity-environment interaction	Heredity and environment interact to produce human development. Without genes, there is no person; without environment, there is no person.

The emerging view is that many complex behaviors likely have some genetic loading that gives people a propensity for a particular developmental trajectory, but their actual development requires more: an environment. And that environment is complex, like the mixture of genes we inherit. Environmental influences range from the things we lump together under nurture (such as parenting, family dynamics, schooling, and neighborhood quality) to biological encounters (such as viruses, birth complications, and even biological events in cells).

An overview of the main ideas in our discussion of genetic principles and methods, heredity's influence on children's development, and the ways in which heredity and environment interact to produce development is presented in summary table 3.2. In the next chapter, we will continue to discuss biological beginnings, turning to the nature of prenatal development and birth.

Chapter Review

Biological beginnings raise questions of how we as a species came to be, how parents' genes are shuffled to produce a child, and how much experience can go against the grain of heredity.

In this chapter, we began by studying the Jim and Jim twins. We explored the evolutionary perspective, including natural selection and adaptive behavior, as well as the concepts of race and ethnicity. We studied these aspects of heredity and reproduction: what genes are, reproductive processes, and abnormalities in genes and chromosomes. We also read about genetic principles, methods, and influences. Our coverage of heredity-environment interaction focused on genotype → environment concepts, shared and nonshared environmental experiences, and conclusions about heredity-environment interaction. Remember that you can obtain a more detailed overview of the chapter by again studying the two summary tables on pages 76 and 85.

In the next chapter, we will continue our exploration of children's biological beginnings by discussing the dramatic unfolding of prenatal development.

✔ Children Checklist

Biological Beginnings

How much have you learned since the beginning of the chapter? Use the following statements to help you review your knowledge and understanding of the chapter material. First, read the statement and mentally or briefly demonstrate on paper that you can discuss the relevant information.

_____ I can describe natural selection and adaptive behavior.
_____ I know what the concepts of race and ethnicity mean.
_____ I understand the nature of genes and reproduction.
_____ I can discuss abnormalities in genes and chromosomes.
_____ I can describe some basic genetic principles, including dominant-recessive genes, polygenic inheritance, reaction range, and canalization.
_____ I know the methods used by behavior geneticists, such as twin studies and adoption studies.
_____ I am aware of heredity's influence on development and the controversy surrounding heredity's role in intelligence.
_____ I can discuss genotype → environment correlations.
_____ I know what shared and nonshared environmental experiences are.
_____ I can describe some conclusions about heredity-environment interaction.

For any items that you did not check, go back and locate the relevant material in the chapter. Review the material until you feel that you can check off the item. You also may want to use this checklist later in preparing for an exam.

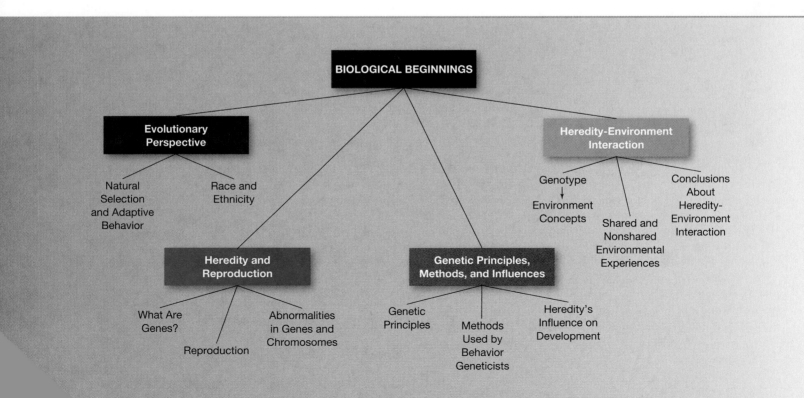

Key Terms

natural selection 64
adaptive behavior 64
race 65
chromosomes 67
DNA 67
genes 67
gametes 67
meiosis 67
reproduction 68
zygote 68
phenylketonuria (PKU) 71
Down syndrome 71
sickle-cell anemia 71
Klinefelter syndrome 72
Turner syndrome 72
XYY syndrome 72
amniocentesis 75
ultrasound sonography 75
chorionic villi sampling 75
maternal blood test 76
dominant-recessive genes
    principle 77

polygenic inheritance 78
genotype 79
phenotype 79
reaction range 79
canalization 79
behavior genetics 79
twin study 80
identical twins 80
fraternal twins 80
adoption study 80
passive genotype →
    environment correlation
    83
evocative genotype →
    environment correlation
    83
active (niche-picking)
    genotype → environment
    correlation 83
shared environmental
    experiences 84
nonshared environmental
    experiences 84

canalization
Reaction Range

Children Resources

American Fertility Society
2131 Magnolia Avenue
Birmingham, AL 35256
205–252–9764
This organization provides information about infertility and possible solutions to it.

How Healthy Is Your Family Tree?
(1995) by Carol Krause. New York: Simon & Schuster.
In this book, you will learn how to create a family medical tree. Once you put together a family medical tree, a specialist or genetic counselor can help you understand it.

National Organization for Rare Disorders (NORD)
Fairwood Professional Building
100 Route 37
New Fairfield, CT 06812
203–746–6518
This foundation supports awareness and education about rare birth defects and genetic disorders.

The Twins Foundation
P.O. Box 9487
Providence, RI 02940
401–274–6910
For information about twins and multiple births, contact this foundation.

Taking It to the Net

http://www.mhhe.com/santrockcd6

1. The evolutionary perspective of child development asks questions such as, "Are our brains the result of natural selection?" and "Is our behavior a form of adaptation to our environment?" According to evolutionary psychologists—yes. What is an evolutionary psychologist's perspective, and does it match your own perspective? Are your beliefs different from those of your fellow students?

2. Beth knows that her family has a history of colon cancer and that a genetic predisposition for some colon cancers may be passed on from generation to generation. Is it possible for Beth to be tested to see if she has inherited the possibility of developing colon cancer, and how would such a test work?

3. It has long been understood that genes control certain physical traits, such as eye color and height. Yet, can genes be responsible for our behavior? If you are funny, sad, or always on the go, are your genes responsible?

Chapter 4

Chapter Outline

The history of man for nine months preceding his birth would, probably, be far more interesting, and contain events of greater moment than all three score and ten years that follow it.

Samuel Taylor Coleridge
English Poet, Essayist, 19th Century

PREVIEW

This chapter chronicles the truly remarkable changes that take place from conception to birth. Imagine . . . at one time you were an organism floating around in a sea of fluid in your mother's womb. These are among the questions we will explore in this chapter:

- What changes take place during the course of prenatal development?
- What maternal diseases can a pregnant woman transmit to the fetus?
- What hazards do pregnant women pose for the fetus when they take various drugs?
- What paternal factors might harm the fetus?
- What constitutes good prenatal care?
- What are the best strategies parents can adopt when preparing for the baby's birth?

The Story of Bibinello

Although Jim and Sara did not plan to have a baby, they did not take precautions to prevent it, and it was not long before Sara was pregnant. Jim and Sara read the popular pregnancy book *What to Expect When You're Expecting* (Eisenberg, Murkoff, & Hathaway, 1991). They found a nurse-midwife they liked and invented a pet name—Bibinello—for the fetus. They signed up for birth preparation classes, and each Friday night for eight weeks they faithfully practiced simulated contractions. They drew up a birth plan that included their decisions about such matters as the type of care provider they wanted to use, the birth setting they wanted, and various aspects of labor and birth. They moved into a larger apartment so the baby could have its own room and spent weekends browsing through garage sales and second-hand stores to find good prices on baby furniture—a crib, a high chair, a stroller, a changing table, a crib mobile, a swing, a car seat.

Jim and Sara also spent a lot of time talking about Sara's pregnancy, what kind of parents they wanted to be, and what their child might be like. They also discussed what changes in their life the baby would make. One of their concerns was that Sara's maternity leave would last only six weeks. If she wanted to stay home longer, she would have to quit her job, something she and Jim were not sure they could afford. These are among the many questions that expectant couples face.

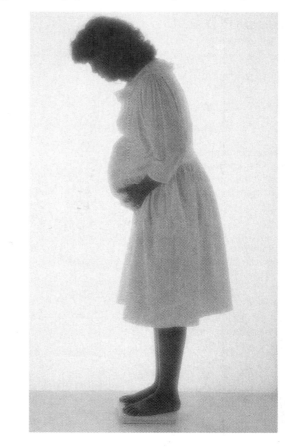

If I could have watched you grow
As a magical mother might.
If I could have seen through my magical
transparent belly,
There would have been such ripening
within . . .

Ann Sexton
American Poet, 20th Century

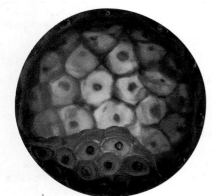

$\mathcal{F}$igure 4.1
The Blastocyst

The blastocyst produces a mass of cells when the fertilized egg repeatedly divides after conception. The blastocyst is the inner layer of cells that develops during the germinal period. These cells later develop into the embryo.

germinal period

The period of prenatal development that takes place in the first two weeks after conception. It includes the creation of the zygote, continued cell division, and the attachment of the zygote to the uterine wall.

blastocyst

The inner layer of cells that develops during the germinal period. These cells later develop into the embryo.

trophoblast

The outer layer of cells that develops in the germinal period. These cells provide nutrition and support for the embryo.

implantation

The attachment of the zygote to the uterine wall, which takes place about 10 days after conception.

THE COURSE OF PRENATAL DEVELOPMENT

Imagine how you came to be. Out of thousands of eggs and millions of sperm, one egg and one sperm united to produce you. Had the union of sperm and egg come a day or even an hour earlier or later, you might have been very different—maybe even of the opposite sex. Remember from chapter 3 that conception occurs when a single sperm cell from the male unites with an ovum (egg) in the female's fallopian tube in a process called fertilization. Remember also that the fertilized egg is called a zygote. By the time the zygote ends its three- to four-day journey through the fallopian tube and reaches the uterus, it has divided into approximately 12 to 16 cells.

The Germinal Period

The **germinal period** *is the period of prenatal development that takes place in the first 2 weeks after conception. It includes the creation of the zygote, continued cell division, and the attachment of the zygote to the uterine wall.* By approximately 1 week after conception, the zygote is composed of 100 to 150 cells. The differentiation of cells has already commenced, as inner and outer layers of the organism are formed. The **blastocyst** *is the inner layer of cells that develops during the germinal period. These cells later develop into the embryo* (see figure 4.1). The **trophoblast** *is the outer layer of cells that develops during the germinal period. It later provides nutrition and support for the embryo.* **Implantation,** *the attachment of the zygote to the uterine wall, takes place about 10 days after conception.* Figure 4.2 illustrates some of the most significant developments during the germinal period.

DENNIS THE MENACE

"My mom says I come from Heaven, my dad says he can't remember, an' Mr. Wilson is POSITIVE I came from Mars!"

DENNIS THE MENACE used by permission of Hank Ketcham and © by News American Syndicate.

The Embryonic Period

The **embryonic period** *is the period of prenatal development that occurs from two to eight weeks after conception. During the embryonic period, the rate of cell differentiation intensifies, support systems for the cells form, and organs appear.* As the zygote attaches to the uterine wall, its cells form two layers. At this time, the name of the mass of cells changes from *zygote* to *embryo*. The embryo's **endoderm** *is the inner layer of cells, which will develop into the digestive and respiratory systems.* The outer layer of cells is divided into two parts. The **ectoderm** *is the outermost layer, which will become the nervous system, sensory receptors (ears, nose, and eyes, for example), and skin parts (hair and nails, for example).* The **mesoderm** *is the middle layer, which will become the circulatory system, bones, muscles, excretory system, and reproductive system.* Every body part eventually develops from these three layers. The endoderm primarily produces internal body parts, the mesoderm primarily produces parts that surround the internal areas, and the ectoderm primarily produces surface parts.

As the embryo's three layers form, life-support systems for the embryo mature and develop rapidly. These life-support systems include the placenta, the umbilical cord, and the amnion. The **placenta** *is a life-support system that consists of a disk-shaped group of tissues in which small blood vessels from the mother and the offspring intertwine but do not join.* The **umbilical cord** *is a life-support system, containing two arteries and one vein, that connects the baby to the placenta.* Very small molecules—oxygen, water, salt, food from the mother's blood, as well as carbon dioxide and digestive wastes from the embryo's blood—pass back and forth between the mother and infant. Large molecules cannot pass through the placental wall; these include red blood cells and harmful substances, such as most bacteria, maternal wastes, and hormones. The mechanisms that govern the transfer of substances across the placental barrier are complex and are still not entirely understood (Rosenblith, 1992). Figure 4.3 provides an illustration of the placenta, the umbilical cord, and the nature of blood

embryonic period

The period of prenatal development that occurs two to eight weeks after conception. During the embryonic period, the rate of cell differentiation intensifies, support systems for the cells form, and organs appear.

endoderm

The inner layer of cells, which develops into digestive and respiratory systems.

ectoderm

The outermost layer of cells, which becomes the nervous system, sensory receptors (ears, nose, and eyes, for example), and skin parts (hair and nails, for example).

mesoderm

The middle layer of cells, which becomes the circulatory system, bones, muscles, excretory system, and reproductive system.

placenta

A life-support system that consists of a disk-shaped group of tissues in which small blood vessels from the mother and offspring intertwine.

umbilical cord

A life-support system, containing two arteries and one vein, that connects the baby to the placenta.

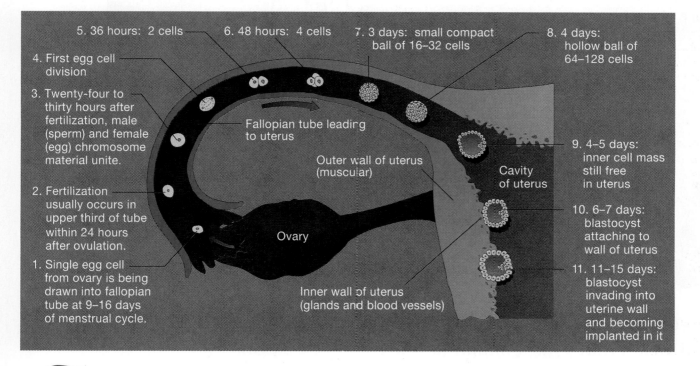

Figure 4.2
Significant Developments in the Germinal Period

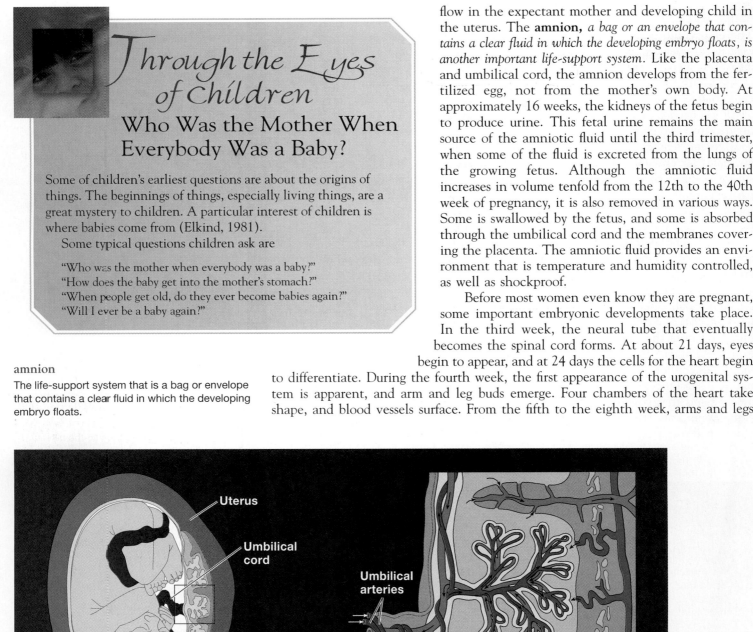

Through the Eyes of Children
Who Was the Mother When Everybody Was a Baby?

Some of children's earliest questions are about the origins of things. The beginnings of things, especially living things, are a great mystery to children. A particular interest of children is where babies come from (Elkind, 1981).

Some typical questions children ask are

"Who was the mother when everybody was a baby?"
"How does the baby get into the mother's stomach?"
"When people get old, do they ever become babies again?"
"Will I ever be a baby again?"

amnion
The life-support system that is a bag or envelope that contains a clear fluid in which the developing embryo floats.

flow in the expectant mother and developing child in the uterus. The **amnion,** *a bag or an envelope that contains a clear fluid in which the developing embryo floats,* is another important life-support system. Like the placenta and umbilical cord, the amnion develops from the fertilized egg, not from the mother's own body. At approximately 16 weeks, the kidneys of the fetus begin to produce urine. This fetal urine remains the main source of the amniotic fluid until the third trimester, when some of the fluid is excreted from the lungs of the growing fetus. Although the amniotic fluid increases in volume tenfold from the 12th to the 40th week of pregnancy, it is also removed in various ways. Some is swallowed by the fetus, and some is absorbed through the umbilical cord and the membranes covering the placenta. The amniotic fluid provides an environment that is temperature and humidity controlled, as well as shockproof.

Before most women even know they are pregnant, some important embryonic developments take place. In the third week, the neural tube that eventually becomes the spinal cord forms. At about 21 days, eyes begin to appear, and at 24 days the cells for the heart begin to differentiate. During the fourth week, the first appearance of the urogenital system is apparent, and arm and leg buds emerge. Four chambers of the heart take shape, and blood vessels surface. From the fifth to the eighth week, arms and legs

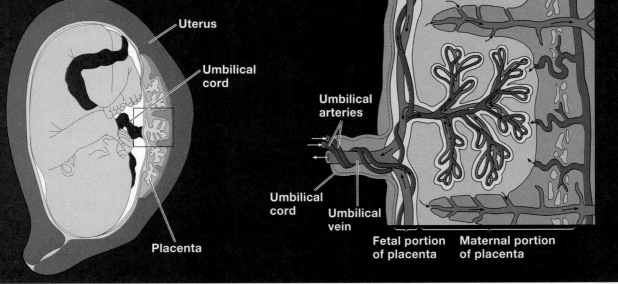

Figure 4.3
The Placenta and the Umbilical Cord

Maternal blood flows through the uterine arteries to the spaces housing the placenta, and it returns through the uterine veins to maternal circulation. Fetal blood flows through the umbilical arteries into the capillaries of the placenta and returns through the umbilical veins to the fetal circulation. The exchange of materials takes place across the layer separating the maternal and fetal blood supplies, so the bloods never come into contact. *Note:* The area bound by the square is enlarged in the right half of the illustration. Arrows indicate the direction of blood flow.

differentiate further; at this time, the face starts to form but still is not very recognizable. The intestinal tract develops and the facial structures fuse. At 8 weeks, the developing organism weighs about 1/30 ounce and is just over 1 inch long. **Organogenesis** *is the process of organ formation that takes place during the first two months of prenatal development.* When organs are being formed, they are especially vulnerable to environmental changes. Later in the chapter, we will describe the environmental hazards that are harmful during organogenesis.

organogenesis
Organ formation that takes place during the first two months of prenatal development.

The Fetal Period

The **fetal period** *is the prenatal period of development that begins two months after conception and lasts for seven months, on the average.* Growth and development continue their dramatic course during this time. Three months after conception, the fetus is about 3 inches long and weighs about 1 ounce. It has become active, moving its arms and legs, opening and closing its mouth, and moving its head. The face, forehead, eyelids, nose, and chin are distinguishable, as are the upper arms, lower arms, hands, and lower limbs. The genitals can be identified as male or female. By the end of the fourth month, the fetus has grown to 6 inches in length and weighs 4 to 7 ounces. At this time, a growth spurt occurs in the body's lower parts. Prenatal reflexes are stronger; arm and leg movements can be felt for the first time by the mother.

By the end of the fifth month, the fetus is about 12 inches long and weighs close to a pound. Structures of the skin have formed—toenails and fingernails, for example.

fetal period
The prenatal period of development that begins two months after conception and lasts for seven months, on the average.

The Visible Embryo

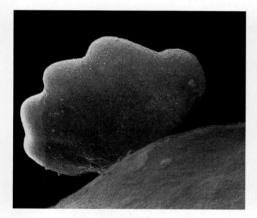

The hand of an embryo at 6 weeks

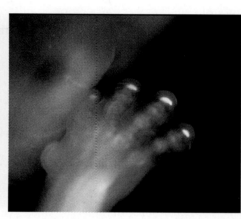

Fingers and thumb with pads seen at 8 weeks

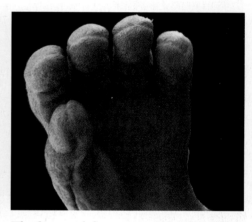

The finger pads have regressed by 13 weeks

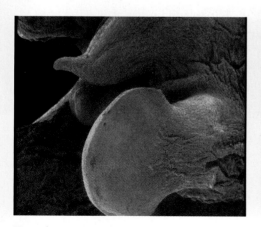

Toe ridges emerge after 7 weeks

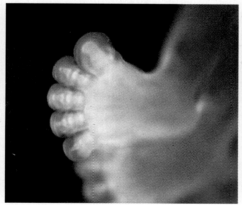

Toe pads and the emerging heel are visible by 9 weeks

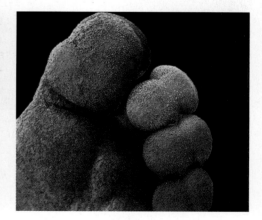

The toe pads have regressed by 13 weeks

The fingers and toes form rapidly during the first trimester. After 13 weeks of pregnancy, the hands and feet already look remarkably similar to those of a mature human, although they are still smaller than an adult's fingernail.

First trimester (first 3 months)		
Conception to 4 weeks	**8 weeks**	**12 weeks**
Fetal growth		
• Is less than ¹/₁₀ inch long • Beginning development of spinal cord, nervous system, gastrointestinal system, heart, and lungs • Amniotic sac envelops the preliminary tissues of entire body • Is called an "ovum"	• Is less than 1 inch long • Face is forming with rudimentary eyes, ears, mouth, and tooth buds • Arms and legs are moving • Brain is forming • Fetal heartbeat is detectable with ultrasound • Is called an "embryo"	• Is about 3 inches long and weighs about 1 ounce • Can move arms, legs, fingers, and toes • Fingerprints are present • Can smile, frown, suck, and swallow • Sex is distinguishable • Can urinate • Is called a "fetus"

Second trimester (middle 3 months)		
16 weeks	**20 weeks**	**24 weeks**
Fetal growth		
• Is about 5¹/₂ inches long and weighs about 4 ounces • Heartbeat is strong • Skin is thin, transparent • Downy hair (lanugo) covers body • Fingernails and toenails are forming • Has coordinated movements; is able to roll over in amniotic fluid	• Is 10 to 12 inches long and weighs ¹/₂ to 1 pound • Heartbeat is audible with ordinary stethoscope • Sucks thumb • Hiccups • Hair, eyelashes, eyebrows are present	• Is 11 to 14 inches long and weighs 1 to 1¹/₂ pounds • Skin is wrinkled and covered with protective coating (vernix caseoa) • Eyes are open • Meconium is collecting in bowel • Has strong grip

Third trimester (last 3¹/₂ months)		
28 weeks	**32 weeks**	**36 to 38 weeks**
Fetal growth		
• Is 14 to 17 inches long and weighs 2¹/₂ to 3 pounds • Is adding body fat • Is very active • Rudimentary breathing movements are present	• Is 16¹/₂ to 18 inches long and weighs 4 to 5 pounds • Has periods of sleep and wakefulness • Responds to sounds • May assume birth position • Bones of head are soft and flexible • Iron is being stored in liver	• Is 19 inches long and weighs 6 pounds • Skin is less wrinkled • Vernix caseosa is thick • Lanugo is mostly gone • Is less active • Is gaining immunities from mother

$\mathcal{F}$igure 4.4
The Three Trimesters of Prenatal Development

The Three Trimesters

The fetus is more active, showing a preference for a particular position in the womb. By the end of the sixth month, the fetus is about 14 inches long and already has gained another half pound to a pound. The eyes and eyelids are completely formed, and a fine layer of hair covers the head. A grasping reflex is present and irregular breathing movements occur. By the end of the seventh month, the fetus is about

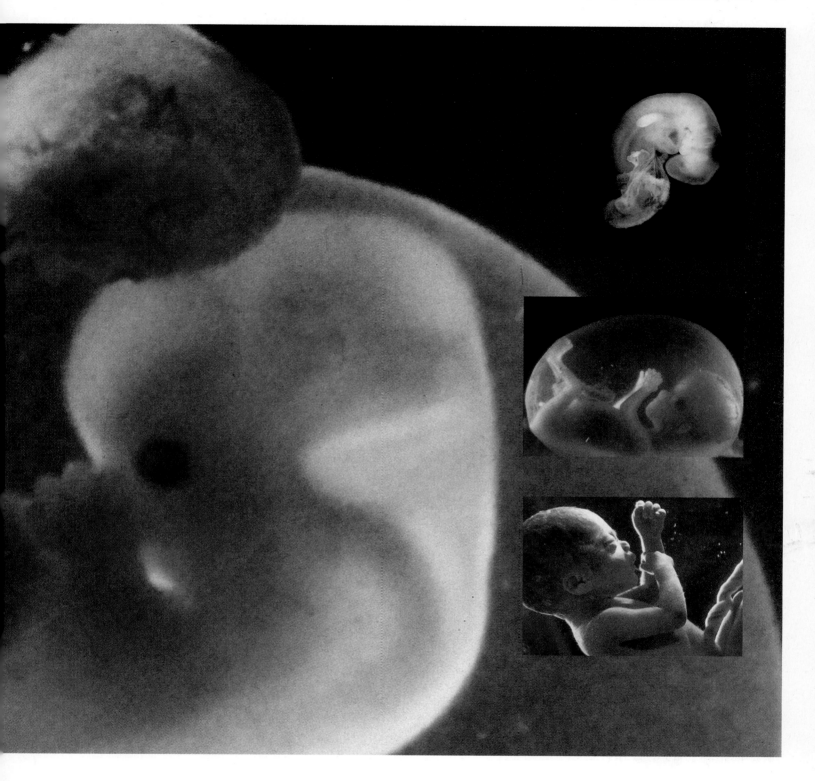

16 inches long and has gained another pound, now weighing about 3 pounds. During the eighth and ninth months, the fetus grows longer and gains substantial weight—about another 4 pounds. At birth, the average American baby weighs 7 pounds and is about 20 inches long. In these last two months, fatty tissues develop, and the functioning of various organ systems—heart and kidneys, for example—steps up.

We have described a number of developments in the germinal, embryonic, and fetal periods. An overview of some of the main developments we have discussed and some more specific changes in prenatal development are presented in figure 4.4.

Coping with Miscarriage

MISCARRIAGE AND ABORTION

A miscarriage, or spontaneous abortion, happens when pregnancy ends before the developing organism is mature enough to survive outside the womb. The embryo separates from the uterine wall and is expelled by the uterus. About 15 to 20 percent of all pregnancies end in a spontaneous abortion, most in the first two to three months. Many spontaneous abortions occur without the mother's knowledge, and many involve an embryo or a fetus that was not developing normally. Most spontaneous abortions are caused by chromosomal abnormalities.

Early in history, it was believed that a woman could be frightened into a miscarriage by loud thunder or a jolt in a carriage. Today, we recognize that this is highly unlikely. The developing organism is well protected. Abnormalities of the reproductive tract and viral or bacterial infections are more likely to cause spontaneous abortions. In some cases, severe traumas may be at fault.

Deliberate termination of pregnancy is a complex issue, medically, psychologically, socially, and legally. Carrying a baby to term can affect a woman's health, the woman's pregnancy may have resulted from rape or incest, the woman may not be married, or perhaps she is poor and wants to continue her education. Abortion is legal in the United States; in 1973, the U.S. Supreme Court ruled that any woman can obtain an abortion during the first six months of pregnancy, a decision that continues to generate ethical objections from antiabortion forces. The U.S. Supreme Court also has ruled that abortion in the first trimester is solely the decision of the mother and her doctor. Courts also have ruled that the baby's father and the parents of minor girls do not have any say during this time frame. In the second trimester, states can legislate the time and method of abortion for protection of the mother's health. In the third trimester, the fetus's right to live is a much stronger factor.

What are the psychological effects of having an abortion? In 1989, a research review panel appointed by the American Psychological Association examined more than 100 investigations of the psychological effects of abortion. The panel's conclusions follow. Unwanted pregnancies are stressful for most women. However, it is common for women to report feelings of relief as well as feelings of guilt after an abortion. These feelings are usually mild and tend to diminish rapidly over time without adversely affecting the woman's ability to function. Abortion is more stressful for women who have a history of serious emotional problems and who are not given support by family or friends. Only a small percentage of women fall into these high-risk categories. If an abortion is performed, it should not only involve competent medical care but care for the woman's psychological needs as well.

TERATOLOGY AND HAZARDS TO PRENATAL DEVELOPMENT

Some expectant mothers carefully tiptoe about in the belief that everything they do and feel has a direct effect on their unborn child. Others behave casually, assuming that their experiences will have little effect. The truth lies somewhere between these two extremes. Although living in a protected, comfortable environment, the fetus is not totally immune to the larger world surrounding the mother (McFarlane, Parker, & Soeken, 1996). The environment can affect the child in many well-documented ways. Thousands of babies born deformed or mentally retarded every year are the result of events that occurred in the mother's life, as early as one or two months before conception.

Exploring Health and Prenatal Development

Teratology

A **teratogen** *(the word comes from the Greek word* tera *meaning "monster") is any agent that causes a birth defect. The field of study that investigates the causes of birth defects is called teratology.* A specific teratogen (such as a drug) usually does not cause a specific birth defect (such as malformation of the legs). So many teratogens exist that practically every fetus is exposed to at least some teratogens. For this reason, it is difficult to determine which teratogen causes which birth defect. In addition, it may take a long time for the effects of a teratogen to show up. Only about half of all potential effects appear at birth.

Despite the many unknowns about teratogens, scientists have discovered the identity of some hazards to prenatal development and the particular point of fetal development at which they do their greatest damage. As figure 4.5 shows, sensitivity to teratogens begins about 3 weeks after conception. The probability of a structural defect is greatest early in the embryonic period, because this is when organs are being formed. After organogenesis is complete, teratogens are less likely to cause anatomical defects. Exposure later, during the fetal period, is more likely to stunt growth or to create problems in the way organs function. The precision of organogenesis is evident; teratologists point out that the vulnerability of the brain is greatest at 15 to 25 days after conception, the eyes at 24 to 40 days, the heart at 20 to 40 days, and the legs at 24 to 36 days.

teratogen

From the Greek word *tera,* meaning "monster," any agent that causes a birth defect. The field of study that investigates the causes of birth defects is called teratology.

Exploring Teratology

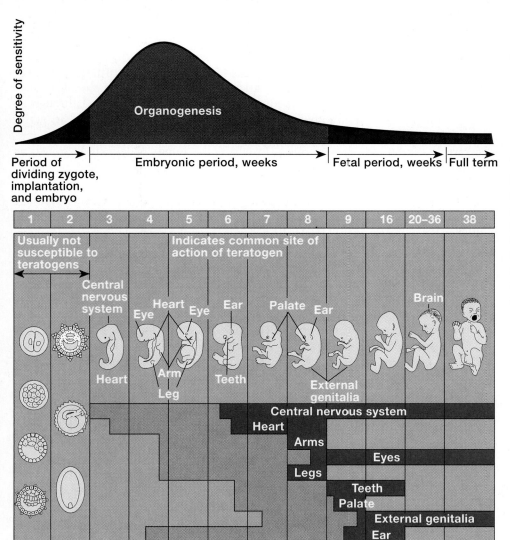

Figure 4.5
Teratogens and the Timing of Their Effects on Prenatal Development

The danger of structural defects caused by teratogens is greatest early in embryonic development. This is the period of organogenesis, and it lasts for several months. Damage caused by teratogens during this period is represented by the dark-colored bars. Later assaults by teratogens typically occur during the fetal period and, instead of structural damage, are more likely to stunt growth or cause problems of organ function.

Maternal Factors

Maternal characteristics that can affect prenatal development include maternal diseases and conditions and the mother's age, nutrition, emotional states, and stress.

Maternal Diseases and Conditions   Maternal diseases and infections can produce defects by crossing the placental barrier, or they can cause damage during the birth process itself. Rubella (German measles) is a maternal disease that can cause prenatal defects. A rubella outbreak in 1964–1965 resulted in 30,000 prenatal and neonatal (newborn) deaths, and more than 20,000 affected infants were born with malformations, including mental retardation, blindness, deafness, and heart problems. The greatest damage occurs when mothers contract rubella in the third and fourth weeks of pregnancy, although infection during the second month is also damaging. Elaborate preventive efforts ensure that rubella will never again have the disastrous effects it had in the mid-1960s. A vaccine that prevents German measles is now routinely administered to children, and women who plan to have children should have a blood test before they become pregnant to determine if they are immune to the disease.

Syphilis (a sexually transmitted disease) is more damaging later in prenatal development—four months or more after conception. Rather than affecting organogenesis, as rubella does, syphilis damages organs after they have formed. Damage includes eye lesions, which can cause blindness, and skin lesions. When syphilis is present at birth, other problems, involving the central nervous system and gastrointestinal tract, can develop. Most states require that pregnant women be given a blood test to detect the presence of syphilis.

Another infection that has received widespread attention recently is genital herpes. Newborns contract this virus when they are delivered through the birth canal of a mother with genital herpes. About one-third of babies delivered through an infected birth canal die; another one-fourth become brain damaged. If an active case of genital herpes is detected in a pregnant woman close to her delivery date, a cesarean section can be performed (in which the infant is delivered through an incision in the mother's abdomen) to keep the virus from infecting the newborn.

AIDS   The importance of women's health to the health of the offspring is nowhere better exemplified than when the mother has acquired immune deficiency syndrome (AIDS) (Bates & others, 1999). As the number of women with AIDS increases, more newborns are born exposed to and infected with AIDS (Cohen & others, 1996).

AIDS is currently the sixth leading cause of death for children 1–4 years of age in the United States. Between 15 and 30 percent of infants born to HIV-infected women become infected with the virus. This results in 1,500 to 2,000 children born with HIV annually in the United States. Treatment can help reduce the rate of HIV transmission from an infected woman to her baby to less than 10 percent.

A mother with AIDS can infect her offspring in three ways: (1) during gestation across the placenta; (2) during delivery through contact with maternal blood or fluids; and (3) postpartum through breast-feeding. Approximately one-third of infants born to infected mothers will ultimately become infected with HIV themselves (Caldwell & Rogers, 1991). Babies born to HIV-infected mothers can be (1) infected and symptomatic (show AIDS symptoms), (2) infected but asymptomatic (not show AIDS symptoms), or (3) not infected at all. An infant who is infected and asymptomatic may still develop HIV symptoms up until 15 months of age. One study documented a rare instance of the AIDS virus subsequently disappearing in an infant who was born infected with HIV (Bryon & others, 1995). This might have been an unusual transient or defective form of HIV.

Toxoplasmosis   Another disease that can be lethal for the fetus is **toxoplasmosis,** *which is caused by the parasite with which humans can become infected by eating raw meat or by not washing their hands after touching cats' feces or yard dirt.* Toxoplasmosis

Pregnancy and HIV

toxoplasmosis

A disease caused by a parasite with which humans can become infected by eating raw meat or by not washing their hands after touching cats' feces or yard dirt. It can be transmitted to the fetus and can cause eye defects, brain damage, or premature birth. A mild infection that causes coldlike symptoms in adults but can be a teratogen for the unborn baby.

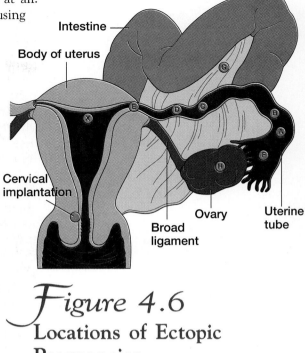

causes only a mild infection in adults, who get coldlike symptoms or none at all. However, toxoplasmosis can be transmitted from the mother to the fetus, causing possible eye defects, brain damage, or premature birth. To avoid getting toxoplasmosis, expectant mothers need to wash their hands after handling cats, litter boxes, and raw meat. In addition, pregnant women should make sure that all meats are thoroughly cooked before eating them and use gloves when working in the garden.

Ectopic Pregnancy   **Ectopic pregnancy** *is the presence of a developing embryo or fetus outside the normal location in the uterus.* Figure 4.6 illustrates the possible locations of ectopic pregnancies. More than 90 percent of ectopic pregnancies occur in the fallopian tubes. The incidence of ectopic pregnancy has more than tripled in recent years. Most of the increase is due to the increase in sexually transmitted tubal infections, such as genital chlamydia, and the tendency of women to delay childbearing until later in life, when the risk of ectopic pregnancy is greatest. Tubal ectopic pregnancies usually result in a rupture of the fallopian tube during the first eight weeks, resulting in the death of the embryo and hemorrhaging into the abdominal cavity. If a tubal pregnancy is detected prior to tubal rupture, it can be surgically terminated to avoid this dangerous event, which can be fatal to the mother because of the hemorrhaging.

The Mother's Age   When the mother's age is considered in terms of possible harmful effects on the fetus and infant, two time periods are of special interest: adolescence and the thirties and beyond. Approximately one of every five births is to an adolescent; in some urban areas, the figure reaches as high as one in every two births. Infants born to adolescents are often premature. The mortality rate of infants born to adolescent mothers is double that of infants born to mothers in their twenties. Although such figures probably reflect the mothers' immature reproductive system, they also may involve poor nutrition, lack of prenatal care, and low socioeconomic status. Prenatal care decreases the probability that a child born to an adolescent girl will have physical problems. However, adolescents are the least likely of women in all age groups to obtain prenatal assistance from clinics, pediatricians, and health services.

Increasingly, women seek to establish their careers before beginning a family, delaying childbearing until their thirties. Down syndrome, a form of mental retardation, is related to the mother's age. A baby with Down syndrome rarely is born to a mother under the age of 30, but the risk increases after the mother reaches 30. By age 40, the probability is slightly over 1 in 100, and, by age 50, it is almost 1 in 10. The risk also is higher before age 18.

Women also have more difficulty becoming pregnant after the age of 30. In one study, the clients of a French fertility clinic all had husbands who were sterile (Schwartz & Mayaux, 1982). To increase their chances of having a child, the women were artificially inseminated once a month for 1 year. Each woman had 12 chances to become pregnant. Seventy-five percent of the women in their twenties became pregnant, 62 percent of the women 31 to 35 years old became pregnant, and only 54 percent of the women over 35 years old became pregnant.

We still have much to learn about the role of the mother's age in pregnancy and childbirth. As women remain active, exercise regularly, and are careful about their nutrition, their reproductive systems may remain healthier at older ages than was thought possible in the past (Windridge, Certi & Berryman, 1999). Indeed, as we will see next, the mother's nutrition influences prenatal development.

Nutrition   A developing fetus depends completely on its mother for nutrition, which comes from the mother's blood. Nutritional status is not determined by any specific aspect of diet. Among the important factors are the total number of

*F*igure 4.6
Locations of Ectopic Pregnancies

The X marks the normal site of ectopic pregnancies. Abnormal sites are indicated by the other letters, in order of their frequency of occurrence.

ectopic pregnancy
The presence of a developing embryo or fetus outside the normal location in the uterus.

Ectopic Pregnancy

Later Age Pregnancy

Nutrition and Pregnancy

calories and appropriate levels of protein, vitamins, and minerals. The mother's nutrition even influences her ability to reproduce. In extreme instances of malnutrition, women stop menstruating, thus precluding conception. Children born to malnourished mothers are more likely to be malformed.

One study of Iowa mothers documents the important role of nutrition in prenatal development and birth (Jeans, Smith, & Stearns, 1955). The diets of 400 pregnant women were studied, and the status of their newborns was assessed. The mothers with the poorest diets had offspring who weighed the least, had the least vitality, were born prematurely, or died. In another study, diet supplements given to malnourished mothers during pregnancy improved the performance of their offspring during the first three years of life (Werner, 1979).

Emotional States and Stress   Tales abound about how a pregnant woman's emotional state affects the fetus. For centuries it was thought that frightening experiences—such as a severe thunderstorm or a family member's death—leave birthmarks on the child or affect the child in more serious ways. Today we believe that the mother's stress can be transmitted to the fetus, but we have gone beyond thinking that this transmission is magically produced (Parker & Barrett, 1992). We now know that, when a pregnant woman experiences intense fears, anxieties, and other emotions, physiological changes occur—among them, changes in respiration and glandular secretions. For example, producing adrenaline in response to fear restricts blood flow to the uterine area and may deprive the fetus of adequate oxygen.

The mother's emotional state during pregnancy can influence the birth process too. An emotionally distraught mother might have irregular contractions and a more difficult labor, which can cause irregularities in the baby's oxygen supply or can produce irregularities after birth. Babies born after extended labor also may adjust more slowly to their world and be more irritable.

Researchers have found that maternal anxiety during pregnancy is related to less than optimal outcomes (Stechler & Halton, 1982). In one study, maternal anxiety during pregnancy was associated with infants who were more hyperactive and irritable and who had more feeding and sleeping problems (Stanley, Soule, & Copens, 1979). Stresses during pregnancy that have been linked with maternal anxiety include marital discord, the death of a husband, and unwanted pregnancy (Field, 1990).

In one study, Tiffany Field and her colleagues (1985) attempted to reduce anxiety about pregnancy by giving video and verbal feedback during ultrasound assessments to assure the mother of the fetus's well-being. Compared with infants whose mothers did not receive such feedback, infants whose mothers got the intervention were less active in utero and had higher birthweights. As newborns, they were less irritable, and their performance on neonatal behavior assessments was superior. Thus, reassuring the mother of fetal well-being had positive outcomes for the infants in this study.

High Risk Situations

Fetal Alcohol Syndrome

Drugs   How do drugs affect prenatal development? Some pregnant women take drugs, smoke tobacco, and drink alcohol without thinking about the possible effects on the fetus. Occasionally, a rash of deformed babies are born, bringing to light the damage drugs can have on a developing fetus. This happened in 1961, when many pregnant women took a popular tranquilizer, thalidomide, to alleviate their morning sickness. In adults, the effects of thalidomide are mild; in embryos, however, they are devastating. Not all infants were affected in the same way. If the mother took thalidomide on day 26 (probably before she knew she was pregnant), an arm might not grow. If she took the drug 2 days later, the arm might not grow past the elbow. The thalidomide tragedy shocked the medical community and parents into the stark realization that the mother does not have to be a chronic drug user for the fetus to be harmed. Taking the wrong drug at the wrong time is enough to physically handicap the offspring for life.

Alcohol   Heavy drinking by pregnant women can also be devastating to offspring (Toth, Connor, & Streissguth, 1999). **Fetal alcohol syndrome (FAS)** *is a cluster of abnormalities that appears in the offspring of mothers who drink alcohol heavily during pregnancy.* The abnormalities include facial deformities and defective limbs, face, and heart. Most of these children are below average in intelligence, and some are mentally retarded (Olson & Burgess, 1996). Although many mothers of FAS infants are heavy drinkers, many mothers who are heavy drinkers do not have children with FAS or have one child with FAS and other children who do not have it. Figure 4.7 shows a child with fetal alcohol syndrome. Although no serious malformations such as those produced by FAS are found in infants born to mothers who are moderate drinkers, in one study, the infants whose mothers drank moderately (one to two drinks a day) during pregnancy were less attentive and alert, with the effects still present at 4 years of age (Streissguth & others, 1984). Also, in one recent study, adults with fetal alcohol syndrome had a high incidence of mental disorders, such as depression or anxiety (Famy, Streissguth, & Unis, 1998).

Expectant mothers are becoming more aware that alcohol and pregnancy do not mix. In one study of 1,712 pregnant women in 21 states, the prevalence of alcohol consumption by pregnant women declined from 32 percent in 1985 to 20 percent in 1988 (Serdula & others, 1991). The declines in drinking were greatest among the oldest and most educated pregnant women—19 percent of pregnant college graduates drank in 1988, a decline from the 41 percent rate in 1985. However, no decline in drinking was found among the least educated and youngest pregnant women. The proportion of drinkers among pregnant women with only a high school education stayed at 23 percent from 1985 to 1988.

Nicotine   Cigarette smoking by pregnant women can also adversely influence prenatal development, birth, and postnatal development (Johnson & others, 1993). Fetal and neonatal deaths are higher among smoking mothers. Also prevalent is a higher incidence of preterm births and lower birthweights (see figure 4.8). In one study, prenatal exposure to cigarette smoking was related to poorer language and cognitive development at 4 years of age (Fried & Watkinson, 1990). In another study, mothers who smoked during pregnancy had infants who were awake more on a consistent basis—an expected finding, since the active ingredient in cigarettes is

*F*igure 4.7
Fetal Alcohol Syndrome

Notice the wide-set eyes, flat bones, and thin upper lip.

fetal alcohol syndrome (FAS)
A cluster of abnormalities that appears in the offspring of mothers who drink alcohol heavily during pregnancy.

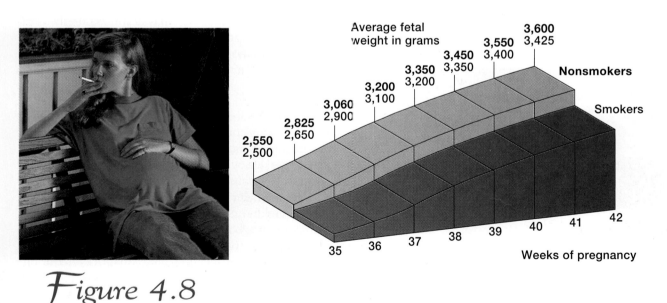

*F*igure 4.8
The Effects of Smoking by Expectant Mothers on Fetal Weight

Throughout prenatal development, the fetuses of expectant mothers who smoke weigh less than the fetuses of expectant mothers who do not smoke.

Adventures for the Mind

Intervention to Stop Pregnant Women from Smoking

Scientists have known about the negative consequences of smoking for more than three decades, but they have made little progress in developing effective interventions to help pregnant women quit smoking or to keep young women from becoming addicted to smoking. What needs to be done to get pregnant women to not smoke? Consider the role of health care providers and their training, the role of insurance companies, and specific programs targeted at pregnant women.

Smoking and Pregnancy

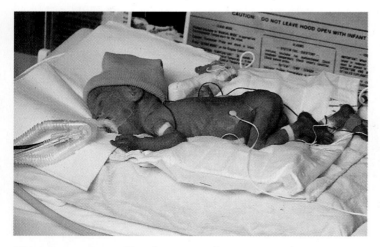

This baby was born addicted to cocaine because its mother was a cocaine addict. Researchers have found that the offspring of women who use cocaine during pregnancy often have hypertension and heart damage. Many of these infants face a childhood full of medical problems.

the stimulant nicotine (Landesman-Dwyer & Sackett, 1983). Respiratory problems and sudden infant death syndrome (also known as crib death) are also more common among the offspring of mothers who smoked during pregnancy (Schoendorf & Kiely, 1992). Intervention programs designed to get pregnant women to stop smoking can reduce some of smoking's negative effects on offspring, especially in raising birthweights (Chomitz, Cheung, & Lieberman, 1995). To further evaluate smoking by pregnant women, see Adventures for the Mind.

Caffeine   Might the caffeine that pregnant women take in by drinking coffee, tea, or cola, or by eating chocolate, possibly be transmitted to the fetus? In one study, no relation between caffeine consumption and infertility was found when caffeine intake was low to moderate (less than 3 cups of coffee per day) (Grodstein, Goldman, & Cramer, 1993). However, with heavier consumption, caffeine users were more than twice as likely to become pregnant than women who consumed less caffeine.

Once pregnancy has occurred, the effects of caffeine may depend on the level of consumption (Pinger & others, 1998). In one study, even low doses of caffeine (as little as one cup of coffee a day) were associated with miscarriage (Infante-Rivard & others, 1993). However, in another study drinking up to 3 cups of coffee a day did not increase the risk of miscarriage or have any adverse effects on the offspring (Mills & others, 1993). One review concluded that the small number of studies and the conflicting results of those studies make it impossible to reach a conclusion about the effects of caffeine use by pregnant women at this time (Astrid & Derby, 1994). Taking into account such results, the U.S. Food and Drug Administration recommends that pregnant women either abstain from caffeine or ingest it sparingly.

Marijuana   Marijuana use by pregnant women also has detrimental effects on a developing fetus. Marijuana use by pregnant women is associated with increased tremors and startles among newborns and poorer verbal and memory development at 4 years of age (Fried & Watkinson, 1990).

Cocaine   With the increased use of cocaine in the United States, there is growing concern about its effects on the embryos, fetuses, and infants of pregnant cocaine users (Hurt & others, 1999). Cocaine use during pregnancy has recently attracted considerable attention because of possible harm to the developing embryo and fetus (Eyler & others, 1998; Zelazo, Potter, & Valiante, 1995; Zeskind & others, 1999). The most consistent finding is that infants born to cocaine abusers have reduced birthweight and length (Chasnoff & others, 1992). There are increased frequencies of congenital abnormalities in the offspring of cocaine users during pregnancy, but other factors in the drug addict's lifestyle, such as malnutrition and other substance abuse, might be responsible for the congenital abnormalities (Eyler, Behnke, & Stewart, 1990). For example, cocaine users are more likely than nonusers to smoke cigarettes and marijuana, drink alcohol, and take amphetamines. Teasing apart these potential influences from the effects of cocaine use itself has not

Drug	Effects on fetus and offspring	Safe use of the drug
Alcohol	Small amounts increase risk of spontaneous abortion. Moderate amounts (one to two drinks a day) are associated with poor attention in infancy. Heavy drinking can lead to fetal alcohol syndrome. Some experts believe that even low to moderate amounts, especially in the first three months of pregnancy, increase the risk of FAS.	Avoid use.
Nicotine	Heavy smoking is associated with low-birthweight babies, which means the babies may have more health problems than other infants. Smoking may be especially harmful in the second half of pregnancy.	Avoid use.
Tranquilizers	Taken during the first three months of pregnancy, they may cause cleft palate or other congenital malformations.	Avoid use if you might become pregnant and during early pregnancy. Use only under a doctor's supervision.
Barbiturates	Mothers who take large doses may have babies who are addicted. Babies may have tremors, restlessness, and irritability.	Use only under a doctor's supervision.
Amphetamines	They may cause birth defects.	Use only under a doctor's supervision.
Cocaine	Cocaine may cause drug dependency and withdrawal symptoms at birth, as well as physical and mental problems, especially if the mother uses cocaine in the first three months of pregnancy. There is a higher risk of hypertension, heart problems, developmental retardation, and learning difficulties.	Avoid use.
Marijuana	It may cause a variety of birth defects and is associated with low birthweight and height.	Avoid use.

*F*igure 4.9
Drug Use During Pregnancy

yet been adequately accomplished (Lester, Freier, & LaGasse, 1995). Obtaining valid information about the frequency and type of drug use by mothers is also complicated, since many mothers fear prosecution or loss of custody because of their drug use.

Heroin   It is well documented that infants whose mothers are addicted to heroin show several behavioral difficulties (Hans, 1989). The young infants of these mothers are addicted and show withdrawal symptoms characteristic of opiate abstinence, such as tremors, irritability, abnormal crying, disturbed sleep, and impaired motor control. Behavioral problems are still often present at the first birthday, and attention deficits may appear later in the child's development. The most common treatment for heroin addicts, methadone, is associated with very severe withdrawal symptoms in newborns.

The effects of various other drugs on offspring and some guidelines for safe use of these drugs are presented in figure 4.9.

Paternal Factors

So far, we have been considering maternal factors during pregnancy that can influence prenatal development and the development of the child. Might there also be some paternal factors that can have this influence? Men's exposure to lead,

Reproductive Health Links

radiation, certain pesticides, and petrochemicals may cause abnormalities in sperm that lead to miscarriage or diseases, such as childhood cancer (Lindbohm, 1991; Taskinen, 1989). When fathers have a diet low in vitamin C, their offspring have a higher risk of birth defects and cancer (Fraga & others, 1991). Also, it has been speculated that, when fathers take cocaine, it may attach itself to sperm and cause birth defects, but the evidence for this is not yet strongly established. In some studies, chronic marijuana use has been shown to reduce testosterone levels and sperm counts, although the results have been inconsistent (Fields, 1998; Nahas, 1984).

The father's smoking during the mother's pregnancy also can cause problems for the offspring. In one investigation, the newborns of fathers who smoked during their wives' pregnancy were 4 ounces lighter at birth for each pack of cigarettes smoked per day than were the newborns whose fathers did not smoke during their wives' pregnancy (Rubin & others, 1986). In another study, in China, the longer the fathers smoked, the stronger the risk was for their children to develop cancer (Ji & others, 1997). In such studies, it is very difficult to tease apart prenatal and postnatal effects.

As is the case with older mothers, older fathers also may place their offspring at risk for certain birth defects. These include Down syndrome (about 5 percent of these children have older fathers), dwarfism, and Marfan's syndrome, which involves head and limb deformities.

Environmental Hazards

Radiation, chemicals, and other hazards in our modern industrial world can endanger the fetus. For instance, radiation can cause a gene mutation (an abrupt, permanent change in genetic material). Chromosomal abnormalities are higher among the offspring of fathers exposed to high levels of radiation in their occupations (Schrag & Dixon, 1985). Radiation from X rays also can affect the developing embryo and fetus, with the most dangerous time being the first several weeks after conception, when women do not yet know they are pregnant. It is important for women and their physicians to weigh the risk of an X ray when an actual or potential pregnancy is involved.

Environmental pollutants and toxic wastes are also sources of danger to unborn children. Researchers have found that various hazardous wastes and pesticides cause defects in animals exposed to high doses. Among the dangerous pollutants and wastes are carbon monoxide, mercury, and lead. Some children are exposed to lead because they live in houses in which lead-based paint flakes off the walls or near busy highways, where there are heavy automobile emissions from leaded gasoline. Researchers believe that early exposure to lead affects children's mental development. For example, in one study, 2-year-olds who prenatally had high levels of lead in their umbilical-cord blood performed poorly on a test of mental development (Bellinger & others, 1987).

Researchers also have found that manufacturing chemicals known as PCBs are harmful to prenatal development. In one study, the extent to which pregnant women ate PCB-polluted fish from Lake Michigan was examined, and subsequently their newborns were observed (Jacobson & others, 1984). The women who had eaten more PCB-polluted fish were more likely to have smaller, preterm infants who were more likely to react slowly to stimuli. And, in another study, prenatal exposure to PCBs was associated with problems in visual discrimination and short-term memory in 4-year-old children (Jacobson & others, 1992).

A current environmental concern involves women who spend long hours in front of computer monitors. The fear is that low-level electromagnetic radiation from the monitors might adversely affect their offspring, should these women become pregnant. In one study of 2,430 women telephone operators, half of the women worked at computer monitors (or video display terminals); half did not

(Schnorr & others, 1991). During the four years of the study, 730 of the women became pregnant, some more than once, for a total of 876 pregnancies. Over the four years, there was no significant difference in miscarriage rates between the two groups. The researchers concluded that working at a computer monitor does not increase miscarriage risk. Critics point out that there was no check for early fetal loss and that all of the women were younger than 34 years of age, so whether the findings hold for early fetal loss and older women awaits further research. In this study, miscarriages were higher among women who had more than 8 alcoholic drinks per month or smoked more than 20 cigarettes a day. Although computer monitors might not be related to miscarriage, they are associated with an increase in a variety of problems involving eye strain and the musculoskeletal system.

Yet another recent environmental concern for expectant mothers is prolonged exposure to heat in saunas or hot tubs that raises the mother's body temperature, creating a fever that endangers the fetus. The high temperature of a fever may interfere with cell division and may cause birth defects or even fetal death if the fever occurs repeatedly for prolonged periods of time. If the expectant mother wants to take a sauna or bathe in a hot tub, prenatal experts recommend that she take her oral temperature while she is exposed to the heat. When the expectant mother's body temperature rises a degree or more, she should get out and cool down. Ten minutes is a reasonable length of time for expectant mothers to spend in a sauna or hot tub, since the body temperature does not usually rise in this length of time. If the expectant mother feels uncomfortably hot in a sauna or hot tub, she should get out, even if she has been there only for a short time.

Fetal Surgery and Therapy

Unborn fetuses have become medicine's tiniest patients. Consider the following circumstance. At eight weeks into prenatal development, the diaphragm of the fetus had failed to close as it should have. The abdominal organs had grown up into the left lung's cavity, and the left lung had hardly developed at all. The abdomen had shrunk, and the heart had shifted to the center of the chest. This condition is called *diaphragmatic hernia*, which affects 1 in 2,200 babies. These fetuses have a 75 percent chance of dying before or soon after birth. To repair the hernia in the diaphragm, an incision is made through the mother's abdomen and uterus. Grasping the arm of the fetus, the surgeon gently rotates the tiny patient into position, then makes another incision under the fetus's rib cage. Next, the abdominal organs are moved out of the chest so the lungs will have room to grow. Then the diaphragm is rebuilt to keep the organs in their proper places. Wires connecting the fetus to a heart monitor make the surgical maneuvers especially difficult (see figure 4.10).

In addition to prenatal treatment of diaphragmatic hernia, surgeons have begun to prenatally treat such serious problems and diseases as hydrocephaly (a congenital malformation causing enlargement of the skull and compression of the brain), blocked bladder, and diseases now treated by bone marrow transplant—such as sickle-cell anemia, enzyme deficiencies, and various liver diseases. Also, drugs that might not pass through the placenta can be injected directly through the umbilical cord.

An important concern about fetal surgery is its risk. Before fetal surgery to correct a specific problem or disease is tried on the human fetus, it is tested on many animals. Still, any surgery involves considerable risk, especially in an organism as delicate and tiny as the human fetus. The advantages of prenatal surgery and therapy—such as rapid postoperative healing and the possible prevention of irreversible

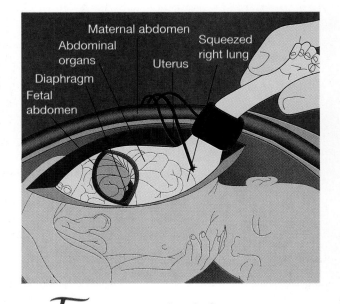

Figure 4.10
Fetal Surgery: The Repair of a Hernia in the Diaphragm of a Fetus

Summary Table 4.1

The Course of Prenatal Development, Miscarriage and Abortion, and Teratology and Hazards to Prenatal Development

Concept	Processes/ Related Ideas	Characteristics/Description
The course of prenatal development	The germinal period	This period is from conception to about 10 to 14 days later. A fertilized egg is called a zygote. The period ends when the zygote attaches to the uterine wall.
	The embryonic period	The embryonic period lasts from about 2 to 8 weeks after conception. The embryo differentiates into three layers, life-support systems develop, and organ systems form (organogenesis).
	The fetal period	The fetal period lasts from about 2 months after conception until 9 months, or when the infant is born. Growth and development continue their dramatic course, and organ systems mature to the point at which life can be sustained outside the womb.
Miscarriage and abortion	Their nature and ethical issues	A miscarriage, or spontaneous abortion, happens when pregnancy ends before the developing organism is mature enough to survive outside the womb. Estimates indicate that about 15 to 20 percent of all pregnancies end this way, many without the mother's knowledge. Induced abortion is a complex issue—medically, psychologically, ethically, and socially. An unwanted pregnancy is stressful for the woman, regardless of how it is resolved.
Teratology and hazards to prenatal development	Teratology	This field investigates the causes of congenital (birth) defects. Any agent that causes birth defects is called a teratogen.
	Maternal factors	Maternal diseases and infections can cause damage by crossing the placental barrier, or they can be destructive during the birth process. Among the maternal diseases and conditions believed to be involved in birth defects are rubella, syphilis, genital herpes, AIDS, toxoplasmosis, the mother's age, nutrition, and emotional state and stress. An ectopic pregnancy is the presence of a developing embryo or fetus outside the normal location in the uterus. Thalidomide was a tranquilizer given to pregnant women to alleviate their morning sickness. In the early 1960s, thousands of babies were malformed as a consequence of their mother having taken this drug. Alcohol, nicotine, caffeine, marijuana, cocaine, and heroin are some of the other drugs that may adversely affect prenatal and infant development.
	Paternal factors	Among the paternal factors that can adversely affect prenatal development is exposure to lead, radiation, certain pesticides, and petrochemicals. Vitamin C deficiencies, cocaine use, and smoking also may have harmful effects on the developing fetus. Older fathers, like older mothers, are linked with some birth defects.
	Environmental hazards	Among the environmental hazards that can endanger the fetus are radiation in jobs sites and X rays, environmental pollutants, toxic wastes, and prolonged exposure to heat in saunas and hot tubs.
	Fetal surgery and therapy	Recently developed medical treatment of the unborn fetus has focused on diaphragmatic hernia, hydrocephaly, sickle-cell anemia, and other diseases that have usually been treated by bone marrow transplants after birth. The advantages of prenatal surgery and therapy—such as rapid postoperative healing and the possible prevention of permanent damage—always have to be weighed against the surgical risks to the expectant mother and the fetus.

damage—always have to be weighed against the surgical risks to the expectant mother and the fetus.

At this point, we have discussed a number of ideas about the course of prenatal development, miscarriage and abortion, and teratology and hazards to prenatal development. An overview of these ideas is presented in summary table 4.1.

EXPECTANT PARENTS

For many people, becoming parents is one of the greatest life changes they will experience. Parenthood is permanent, and the physical and emotional nurturing of a child is both a time-intensive responsibility and a wonderful opportunity. So far, most of our discussion has focused on the embryo and the fetus, but it is also important to examine the effects of pregnancy on the expectant parents. An important first consideration is to confirm the pregnancy and then to calculate the due date. Then, as the pregnancy proceeds, a number of family issues emerge in the first, second, and third trimesters of pregnancy.

Exploring Pregnancy

Confirming the Pregnancy and Calculating the Due Date

Although pregnancy can be detected soon after conception, a woman might not suspect she is pregnant until she has missed a menstrual period. A pregnancy test checks the woman's urine or blood for human chorionic gonadotropin (HCG), a hormone produced during pregnancy. If a woman thinks she is pregnant, she should have her pregnancy confirmed early, so she can obtain prenatal care, avoid environmental hazards, and give special attention to nutritional needs. Figure 4.11 describes the early signs and symptoms of pregnancy.

Fetal life begins with the fertilization of the ovum, which occurs about 2 weeks after the woman's last menstrual period. However, the length of the pregnancy is calculated from the first day of the woman's last menstrual period and lasts an average of 280 days, or 40 weeks. When a doctor or midwife says that a woman is 8 weeks pregnant, it means that the fetus is 6 weeks old. The method of dating confuses many parents, who are certain they know just when conception occurred. When they are informed that the expectant mother is 8 weeks pregnant, they might know that the pregnancy is only just 6 weeks along, and they are correct. Birth is likely to occur anytime between 2 weeks before and after the so-called due date. Approximately two-thirds of all babies are born within 10 days of their due dates.

- Missed menstrual period
- Breast changes—a heavy and full feeling, tenderness, tingling in the nipple area, and a darkened areola
- Fullness or aching in the lower abdomen
- Fatigue and drowsiness, faintness
- Nausea, vomiting, or both
- Frequent urination
- Increased vaginal secretions
- Positive pregnancy test

$\mathcal{F}$*igure 4.11*
Early Signs and Symptoms of Pregnancy

The Three Trimesters and Preparation for the Baby's Birth

A common way of thinking about issues that arise during pregnancy is in terms of pregnancy's trimesters.

Interactive Pregnancy Calendar

The First Trimester   Earlier in this chapter, we learned that the first three calendar months of pregnancy (the first trimester) is a time when prenatal organ systems are being formed and begin to function. For the pregnant woman, the first trimester is a time of physical and emotional adjustment to her pregnant state.

The expectant mother may feel extraordinarily tired and require more sleep because of the new demands on her energy and because of the subsequent shift in her metabolic rate, especially in the second and third months of pregnancy. She also may experience nausea and vomiting during the early months of pregnancy. Although this is usually referred to as "morning sickness," it can occur at any time of day and is believed to be caused by human chorionic gonadotropin, produced by the developing placenta.

Although the female's breasts develop in puberty, the glandular tissue that produces milk does not completely develop until the woman becomes pregnant. As the levels of estrogen and other hormones change during pregnancy, the expectant mother's breasts change. They enlarge, veins are often more prominent, and a tingling sensation is often felt in the nipples. The expectant mother may also need to urinate more frequently as the enlarging uterus puts increased pressure on the bladder. In addition, her vagina and cervix become bluish in color, the cervix becomes softer, and vaginal secretions increase.

Emotional changes accompany physical changes in the early months of pregnancy. It is not unusual for the expectant mother to experience emotional ups and downs. The thought of motherhood may at times be pleasing and, at others, disturbing. She may cry easily. Such mood swings may be difficult to understand, for both the expectant mother and her partner.

Finding out that she is pregnant may not only bring about a mixture of emotions in the expectant mother but also in her partner: pride in the ability to produce a child; fear of losing independence; apprehension about changes in the marital relationship; doubts about one's ability to parent; and happiness about becoming parents. Sharing thoughts and feelings with each other can help expectant couples develop a closer relationship during the transition of parenthood.

A couple's sexual relationship may change during the first trimester. The expectant mother may experience an increased interest in spontaneous sexual activity because she no longer has to worry about trying to become pregnant or about avoiding pregnancy, or an expectant mother's sexual interest may decrease because of fatigue, nausea, breast changes, or fear of miscarriage. In a normal pregnancy, the expectant couple should discuss their feelings about sexual intercourse and do what is mutually desired.

Childbirth Classes

Might expectant parents benefit from a parent education class on pregnancy and prenatal development in the first trimester of pregnancy? It is important for expectant parents to become knowledgeable about the nature of pregnancy and prenatal development (Haertsch, Campbell, & Sanson-Fisher, 1999). To further evaluate the nature of prenatal care, see the box Caring for Children.

The Second Trimester   During the middle months of pregnancy, the expectant mother will probably feel better than she did earlier or than she will later. Nausea and fatigue usually lessen or disappear. As the baby's growth continues, the expectant mother's uterus expands into the abdominal cavity. By the end of the fifth month of pregnancy, the top of the uterus (called the fundus) reaches the navel. During monthly visits, the physician or caregiver measures the height of the fundus to ensure that the fetus is growing adequately and to estimate the length of the pregnancy. The expectant mother's breasts do not increase much in size during the

Caring for Children
Prenatal Care and Classes

Prenatal care varies enormously but usually involves a package of medical care services in a defined schedule of visits. In addition to medical care, prenatal care programs often include comprehensive educational, social, and nutritional services (Shiono & Behrman, 1995).

Prenatal care usually includes screening that can reveal manageable conditions and/or treatable diseases that could affect both the baby's life and the pregnant woman's. The education the mother receives about pregnancy, labor and delivery, and caring for the newborn can be extremely valuable, especially for first-time mothers. Prenatal care is also very important for women in poverty because it links them with other social services. The legacy of prenatal care continues after the birth because women who experience this type of care are more likely to get preventive care for their infants (Bates & others, 1994).

Women sometimes receive inadequate prenatal care for reasons related to the health care system, provider practices, and their own individual and social characteristics (Alexander & Korenbrot, 1995). In one national study, 71 percent of the low-income women experienced a problem in getting prenatal care (U.S. General Accounting Office, 1987). They cited finances, transportation, and child care as barriers. Motivating positive attitudes toward pregnancy is also important. Women who do not want to be pregnant, who have negative attitudes about being pregnant, or who unintentionally become pregnant are more likely to delay prenatal care or to miss appointments (Joseph, 1989).

Early prenatal classes may include couples in both early pregnancy and prepregnancy (Olds, London, &

Ladewig, 1988). The classes often focus on topics such as these:

- Changes in the development of the embryo and the fetus
- Self-care during pregnancy
- Fetal development concerns and environmental dangers for the fetus
- Sexuality during pregnancy
- Birth setting and types of care providers
- Nutrition, rest, and exercise
- Common discomforts of pregnancy and relief measures
- Psychological changes in both the expectant mother and her partner
- Information needed to get the pregnancy off to a good start

Early prenatal education classes focus on such topics as changes in the development of the fetus, while many later classes focus on preparation for the birth and care of the newborn.

Early classes also may include information about factors that place the expectant mother at risk for preterm labor and recognition of the possible signs and symptoms of preterm labor. Prenatal education classes also may include information on the advantages and disadvantages of breast- and bottle-feeding. Most expectant mothers (50 to 80 percent) make this infant feeding decision prior to the sixth month of pregnancy. Therefore, information about the issues involved in breast- versus bottle-feeding in an early prenatal education class is helpful.

So far, the prenatal education classes we have described focus on expectant couples in the first trimester of pregnancy. The later classes—those when the expectant mother is in the second or third trimester of pregnancy—focus on preparation for the birth, infant care and feeding, postpartum self-care, and birth choices. Much more about these topics appears in the next chapter.

second trimester, but colostrum (a yellowish fluid produced before breast milk) is usually present in the milk glands by the middle of pregnancy. This is the time for expectant mothers to begin preparing their breasts for breast-feeding if they have decided to breast-feed the baby.

Accompanying physical changes in the second trimester are psychological changes in response to advancing pregnancy and a changing body. Some expectant

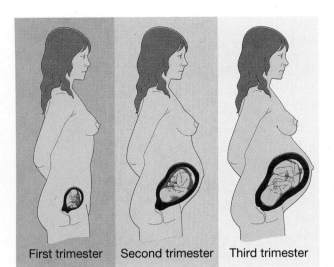

First trimester   Second trimester   Third trimester

*F*igure 4.12
The Changing Shape and Size of the Expectant Mother and the Fetus During the First, Second, and Third Trimesters of Pregnancy

mothers enjoy how they look; others consider themselves unattractive, inconvenienced, and restricted. If the expectant mother has not yet read books about child care in the first few years of life, this is a good time to purchase one or more of them. Later in this book, we will recommend some of the books as we discuss infants' physical, cognitive, and social development. This also is a good time to begin preparing the nursery for the baby's arrival.

During the second trimester, pregnancy becomes more of a reality for the expectant mother's partner. He can feel the baby move when he puts his hand on her abdomen or when she is in close contact with him. This contact with the baby increases his feelings of closeness and his interest in the pregnancy and the baby. He may or may not like the changing appearance of the expectant mother. In a normal pregnancy, the expectant couple can continue to have sexual intercourse without harming the fetus, which is believed to be adequately protected from penetrations and the strong contractions that sometimes accompany orgasm.

The Third Trimester   During the third trimester, the expectant mother's uterus expands to a level just below her breast bone (figure 4.12 shows the space taken up by the developing fetus in the first, second, and third trimesters of pregnancy). Crowding by the uterus, in addition to high levels of progesterone, may give the expectant mother heartburn and indigestion. She may also experience shortness of breath as her uterus presses upward on her diaphragm and ribs. Varicose veins in the legs, hemorrhoids, and swollen ankles sometimes appear because of the increased pressure within the abdomen, the decreased blood return from the lower limbs, and the effect of progesterone, which relaxes the walls of the blood vessels.

By the ninth month, the expectant mother often looks forward to the end of the pregnancy, relief from physical restrictions, and the long-awaited joy of having the baby. She may become more introspective and, at times, worry about labor, birth, and the baby. Through childbirth classes, the expectant couple can learn more about labor, birth, and how to cope with the stress of the latter part of pregnancy. In the next chapter, we will discuss different types of childbirth and childbirth classes.

In the third trimester of pregnancy, the expectant couple may feel protective of the developing baby. Adjustments in sexual activity continue as the expectant

In the third trimester of pregnancy, the expectant couple may feel protective of the developing baby. Lines of communication should be open between the expectant mother and her partner about their needs, feelings, and desires.

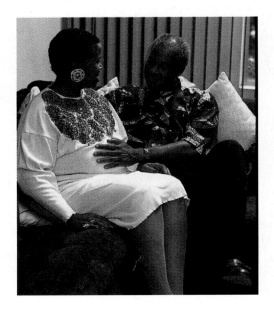

mother's abdomen enlarges. Lines of communication should be open between the expectant mother and her partner about their needs, feelings, and desires.

Preparation for the Baby's Birth   About two weeks before the baby's birth, the expectant mother's profile may change as the fetus descends into the pelvic cavity. The expectant mother may now feel less pressure on her diaphragm and thus find it easier to breathe and eat. However, because the head of the fetus can press on the expectant mother's bladder, she may need to urinate more frequently.

Toward the end of the pregnancy, noticeable contractions of the uterus (called Braxton Hicks contractions) increase in frequency. These contractions, which have occurred intermittently throughout pregnancy and which may or may not be felt by the expectant mother, help increase the efficiency of uterine circulation. Though usually not directly associated with labor, these contractions prepare the uterine muscles for labor. As the pregnancy comes to an end and the baby's head presses against the expectant mother's pelvis, her cervix becomes softer and thinner. This thinning is a sign of readiness for labor and birth.

Awkwardness and fatigue may add to the expectant mother's motivation for the pregnancy to end. She may feel as if she has been and will be pregnant forever. At the same time, the expectant mother may feel a "nesting urge" in the form of a spurt of energy that often results in preparations for the arrival of the new baby. She now visits her physician or midwife more often as these physical changes signal that her body is preparing for labor and birth.

The Expectant Mother's Nutrition, Weight Gain, and Exercise

Earlier we indicated that the mother's nutrition can have a strong influence on the development of the fetus. Here we will further discuss the mother's nutritional needs and optimal nutrition during pregnancy, as well as the role of exercise in the expectant mother's health.

*F*igure 4.13
Recommended Nutrient Increases for Expectant Mothers

Nutrition and Pregnancy

Exercise in Pregnancy

Nutrition and Weight Gain   The best assurance of an adequate caloric intake during pregnancy is a satisfactory weight gain over time. The optimal weight gain depends on the expectant mother's height, bone structure, and prepregnant nutritional state. However, maternal weight gains that average from 25 to 35 pounds are associated with the best reproductive outcomes. The pattern of weight gain is also important. The ideal pattern of weight gain during pregnancy is 2 to 4.4 pounds during the first trimester, followed by an average gain of 1 pound per week during the last two trimesters. In the second trimester, most of the weight gain is due to increased blood volume; the enlargement of breasts, uterus, and associated tissue and fluid; and the deposit of maternal fat. In the third trimester, weight gain mainly involves the fetus, placenta, and amniotic fluid. A 25-pound weight gain during pregnancy is generally distributed in the following way:

- 11 lb Fetus, placenta, and amniotic fluid
- 5 lb Maternal stores
- 4 lb Increased blood volume
- 3 lb Tissue fluid
- 2 lb Uterus and breasts

During the second and third trimesters, inadequate gains of less than 2.2 pounds per month or excessive gains of more than 6.6 pounds per month should be evaluated and the need for nutritional counseling considered. Inadequate weight gain has been associated with low-birthweight infants. Sudden sharp increases in weight of 3 to 5 pounds in a week may result from fluid retention and may require evaluation.

The recommended daily allowance (RDA) for all nutrients increases during pregnancy. The expectant mother should eat three meals a day, with nutritious snacks of fruits, cheese, milk, or other foods between meals if desired. More frequent, smaller meals also are recommended. Four to six glasses (8 ounces) of water and a total of 8 to 10 cups (8 ounces) of total fluid should be consumed daily. Water is an essential nutrient. The amount of the increase in nutrients depends on the nutrient. The need for protein, iron, vitamin D, calcium, phosphorous, and magnesium increases by 50 percent or more. Recommended increases for other nutrients range from 15 to 50 percent (see figure 4.13).

Exercise   How much and what type of exercise is best during pregnancy depend to some degree on the course of the pregnancy, the expectant mother's fitness, and her customary activity level. Normal participation in exercise can continue throughout an uncomplicated pregnancy. In general, the skilled sportswoman is no longer discouraged from participating in sports she participated in prior to her pregnancy. However, pregnancy is not the appropriate time to begin strenuous activity.

Because of the increased emphasis on physical fitness in our society, more women routinely jog as part of a physical fitness program prior to pregnancy. There are few concerns about continuing to jog during the early part of pregnancy, but in the latter part of pregnancy there is some concern about the jarring effect of jogging on breasts and abdomen. As pregnancy progresses, low-impact activities, such as swimming and bicycling, are safer and provide fitness as well as greater comfort, eliminating the bouncing associated with jogging.

Among the important information for the expectant mother to know about is the best nutrition for her and her developing fetus. The expectant mother should eat regularly, three meals a day, with nutritious snacks of fruits, cheese, milk, or other foods between meals if desired.

The following guidelines for exercise are recommended for expectant mothers (Olds, London, & Ladewig, 1988):

- Exercise for shorter time intervals. Exercising for 10 to 15 minutes, resting for a few minutes, and then exercising for another 10 to 15 minutes decreases potential problems associated with the shunting of blood to the musculoskeletal system and away from organs, such as the uterus.
- As pregnancy proceeds, expectant mothers should decrease the intensity of the exercise. The decreased intensity helps compensate for the expectant mother's decreased cardiac reserve, increased respiratory effort, and increased weight gain.
- Avoid prolonged overheating. Strenuous exercise, especially in a humid environment, can raise the body temperature and increase the risk of fetal problems. Remember also our earlier discussion about avoiding overheating in saunas and hot tubs.
- As pregnancy increases, the expectant mother should avoid high-risk activities, such as skydiving, mountain climbing, racquetball, and surfing. An expectant mother's changed center of gravity and softened joints may decrease her coordination and increase the risk of falls and injuries in such sports.
- Warm up and stretch to help prepare the joints for activity, and cool down with a period of mild activity to help restore circulation.
- After exercising, lie on the left side for 10 minutes to rest. This improves circulation from the extremities and promotes placental function.
- Wear supportive shoes and a supportive bra.
- Stop exercising and contact the physician or caregiver if dizziness, shortness of breath, tingling, numbness, vaginal bleeding, or abdominal pain occur.
- Reduce exercise in the last four weeks of pregnancy because there is some evidence that strenuous exercise near term increases the risk of low birthweight, stillbirth, and infant death.

Exercise during pregnancy helps prevent constipation, conditions the body, and is associated with a more positive mental state. However, it is important to remember to not overdo it. Pregnant women should always consult their physician before starting any exercise program.

At this point, we have discussed numerous ideas about prenatal development. An important agenda is to provide such information to expectant parents so that they can maximize positive prenatal outcomes. The insert, Improving Developmental Skills, profiles these strategies.

Culture and Prenatal Care

What is prenatal care in the United States like compared with that of other countries? What are some cultural beliefs about pregnancy?

Improving Developmental Skills
Maximizing Positive Prenatal Outcomes

What are some good strategies during pregnancy that are likely to maximize positive outcomes for prenatal development?

- *Eat nutritiously and monitor weight gain.* The recommended daily allowances for all nutrients increase during pregnancy. The pregnant woman should eat three balanced meals a day and nutritious snacks between meals if desired. Weight gains that average 25 to 35 pounds are associated with the best reproductive outcomes.
- *Engage in safe exercise.* How much and what type of exercise is best during pregnancy depends to some degree on the course of the pregnancy, the expectant mother's fitness, and her customary activity level. Normal participation in exercise can continue throughout an uncomplicated pregnancy. It is important to remember not to overdo exercise. Exercising for shorter intervals and decreasing the intensity of exercise as pregnancy proceeds are good strategies. Pregnant women should always consult a physician before starting an exercise program.
- *Don't drink alcohol or take other potentially harmful drugs.* An important strategy for pregnancy is to totally abstain from alcohol and other drugs, such as nicotine and cocaine. In this chapter, we described the harmful effects that these drugs can have on the developing fetus. Fathers also need to be aware of potentially harmful effects they can have on prenatal development.
- *Have a support system of family and friends.* The pregnant woman benefits from a support system of family members and friends. A positive relationship with a spouse helps keep stress levels down, as does a close relationship with one or more friends.
- *Reduce stress and stay calm.* Try to maintain an even, calm emotional state during pregnancy. High stress levels can harm the fetus. Pregnant women who are feeling a lot of anxiety can reduce their anxiety through a relaxation or stress management program.
- *Stay away from environmental hazards.* We saw in this chapter that some environmental hazards, such as pollutants and toxic wastes, can harm prenatal development. Be aware of these hazards and stay away from them.
- *Get excellent prenatal care.* The quality of prenatal care varies extensively. The education the mother receives about pregnancy, labor and delivery, and care of the newborn can be valuable, especially for first-time mothers.
- *Read a good book for expectant mothers.* An excellent one is *What to Expect When You Are Expecting*, which is profiled at the end of this chapter.

Prenatal Care

Health Care Providers

Prenatal Care in the United States and Around the World   As advanced a nation as the United States has become economically and technologically, it still has more low-birthweight infants than a number of other countries (Grant, 1996). Only 4 percent of the infants born in Sweden, Finland, the Netherlands, and Norway are low-birthweight, and only 5 percent of those born in New Zealand, Australia, France, and Japan are low-birthweight. In the United States, 7 percent of all infants are low-birthweight. In some developing countries, such as Bangladesh, where poverty is rampant and the health and nutrition of mothers are poor, the percentage of low-birthweight infants reaches as high as 50 percent of all infants.

In the United States, discrepancies occur between the prenatal development and birth of African American infants and White infants. African American infants are twice as likely to be born prematurely, have low birthweight, and have mothers who received late or no prenatal care. They are three times as likely to have their mothers die in childbirth. And they are five times as likely to be born to unmarried teenage mothers (Edelman, 1995).

In many of the countries with a lower percentage of low-birthweight infants than the United States, either free or very-low-cost prenatal and postnatal care is available to mothers. This care includes paid maternity leave from work that ranges from 9 to 40 weeks. In Norway and the Netherlands, prenatal care is coordinated with a general practitioner, an obstetrician, and a midwife.

Pregnant women in the United States do not receive the uniform prenatal care that women in many Scandinavian and Western European countries receive. The United States does not have a national policy of health care that assures high-quality assistance for pregnant women. The cost of giving birth is approximately $4,000 in the United States (more than $5,000 for a cesarean birth). More than 25 percent of all American women of prime childbearing age do not have insurance that will pay for hospital costs. More than one-fifth of all White mothers and one-third of all African American mothers do not receive prenatal care in the first trimester of their pregnancy. Five percent of White mothers and 10 percent of African American mothers receive no prenatal care at all (Wegman, 1986). Many infant-development researchers believe that the United States needs more comprehensive medical and educational services to improve the quality of prenatal care and to reduce the percentage of low-birthweight infants.

Cultural Beliefs About Pregnancy and Development   Specific actions in pregnancy are often determined by cultural beliefs. Certain behaviors are expected if a culture views pregnancy as a medical condition, whereas other behaviors are expected if pregnancy is viewed as a natural occurrence. Prenatal care may not be a priority for expectant mothers who view pregnancy as a natural occurrence. It is important for health care providers to become aware of the health practices of various cultural groups, including health beliefs about pregnancy and prenatal development. Cultural assessment is an important dimension of providing adequate health care for expectant mothers from various cultural groups. Cultural assessment includes identifying the main beliefs, values, and behaviors related to pregnancy and childbearing. Among the important cultural dimensions are ethnic background, degree of affiliation with the ethnic group, patterns of decision making, religious preference, language, communication style, and common etiquette practices.

Health care practices during pregnancy are influenced by numerous factors, including the prevalence of traditional home care remedies and folk beliefs, the importance of indigenous healers, and the influence of professional health care workers. Many Mexican American mothers are strongly influenced by their mothers and older women in their culture, often seeking and following their advice during pregnancy. In Mexican American culture, the indigenous healer is called a *curandero*. In some Native American tribes, the medicine woman or man fulfills the healing role. Herbalists are often found in Asian cultures, and faith healers, root doctors, and spiritualists are sometimes found in African American culture. When health care providers come into contact with expectant mothers, they need to assess

Summary Table 4.2
Expectant Parents

Concept	Processes/ Related Ideas	Characteristics/Description
Confirming the pregnancy and calculating the due date	Their nature	A pregnancy test checks the woman's urine or blood for human chorionic gonadotropin (HCG), a hormone produced during pregnancy. Fetal life begins with the fertilization of the ovum, which occurs about 2 weeks after the woman's last menstrual period. However, the length of the pregnancy is calculated from the first day of the woman's last menstrual period and lasts an average of 280 days, or 40 weeks.
The three trimesters and preparation for the baby's birth	The first trimester	The expectant mother may feel especially tired and require more sleep in the second and third months of pregnancy. She also may experience nausea and vomiting. The expectant mother's breasts enlarge, and she may need to urinate more often. Many expectant mothers experience emotional ups and downs about their pregnancy.
	The second trimester	During the middle months of pregnancy, the expectant mother often feels better than she did earlier or than she will later. Her uterus expands, and by the fifth month of pregnancy the top of her uterus reaches the navel. When colostrum appears in the milk glands, expectant mothers who plan to breast-feed should begin preparing their breasts for the breast-feeding. Psychological changes also occur in the second trimester.
	The third trimester	The expectant mother's uterus expands to a level just below her breast bone. At this time, she may experience indigestion and heartburn. She also may experience shortness of breath. Through childbirth classes, the expectant couple can learn more about labor, birth, and how to cope with the latter part of pregnancy.
	Preparation for the baby's birth	Two weeks prior to the baby's birth, the expectant mother's profile may change as the fetus descends into the pelvic cavity. She now feels less pressure on her diaphragm and may find it easier to breathe and eat. She often has to urinate more because of bladder pressure from the fetus's head. Toward the end of pregnancy, noticeable contractions of the uterus increase in frequency, which help increase the efficiency of uterine circulation and prepare the uterine muscles for labor. Her cervix becomes softer and thinner; the thinning is a sign of readiness for labor and birth.
The expectant mother's nutrition, weight gain, and exercise	Nutrition and weight gain	The best assurance of an adequate caloric intake during pregnancy is a satisfactory weight gain over time. Maternal weight gains that average 25 to 35 pounds are associated with the best reproductive outcomes. The pattern of the weight gain is also important.
	Exercise	How much and what type of exercise may be undertaken during pregnancy depend to some extent on the course of pregnancy, the expectant mother's fitness, and her customary activity level. Normal participation in exercise can continue throughout an uncomplicated pregnancy.
Culture and prenatal care	Prenatal care in the United States and around the world	Many countries, especially Scandinavian countries, have a lower percentage of low-birthweight infants than the United States. As many as one-third of African American mothers do not receive prenatal care in the first trimester of pregnancy.
	Cultural beliefs about pregnancy and prenatal development	Specific actions in pregnancy are often determined by cultural beliefs. Certain behaviors are expected if a culture views pregnancy as a medical condition or a natural occurrence. It is important for health care providers to become aware of the health practices of various cultural groups, including health beliefs about pregnancy and prenatal development.

whether such cultural practices pose a threat to the expectant mother and the fetus. If they pose no threat, there is no reason to try to change them. On the other hand, if certain cultural practices do pose a threat to the health of the expectant mother or the fetus, the health care provider should consider a culturally sensitive way to handle the problem. For example, some Philippinos will not take any medication during pregnancy.

At this point, we have discussed a number of ideas about expectant parents. An overview of these ideas is presented in summary table 4.2.

Chapter Review

When a species reproduces itself, life comes from life. Much of this chapter was about a state of becoming. Pregnancy is a state of becoming. An unborn baby is becoming a person capable of life outside the mother's body. And a woman and a man are becoming parents.

In this chapter, you read about the course of prenatal development, which includes the germinal, embryonic, and fetal periods. We also discussed the complexities of abortion. We studied teratology and hazards to prenatal development, focusing on such topics as maternal factors, paternal factors, environmental hazards, and fetal surgery and therapy. Our coverage of expectant parents examined confirmation of the pregnancy; calculation of the due date; the three trimesters of pregnancy; preparation for the baby's birth; the expectant mother's nutrition, weight gain, and exercise; and culture and prenatal care.

Remember that you can obtain a more detailed review of the chapter by again reading the two concept tables on pages 106 and 115. In the next chapter, we will turn our attention to the birth process itself.

✔ Children Checklist

Prenatal Development

How much have you learned since the beginning of the chapter? Use the following statements to help you review your knowledge and understanding of the chapter material. First, read the statement and mentally or briefly demonstrate on paper that you can discuss the relevant information.

_____ I can describe the course of prenatal development, including the germinal period, embryonic period, and fetal period.
_____ I understand the concepts of miscarriage and abortion.
_____ I know what teratology is.
_____ I can discuss how maternal factors, paternal factors, and environmental hazards influence prenatal development.
_____ I can describe some ideas about fetal surgery and therapy.
_____ I know the methods for confirming a pregnancy and calculating the due date.
_____ I can discuss the three trimesters and preparation for the baby's birth.
_____ I understand the importance of the expectant mother's nutrition, weight gain, and exercise.
_____ I am aware of cultural beliefs about pregnancy and prenatal care.

For any items that you did not check, go back and locate the relevant material in the chapter. Review the material until you feel you can check off the item. You may want to use this checklist later in preparing for an exam.

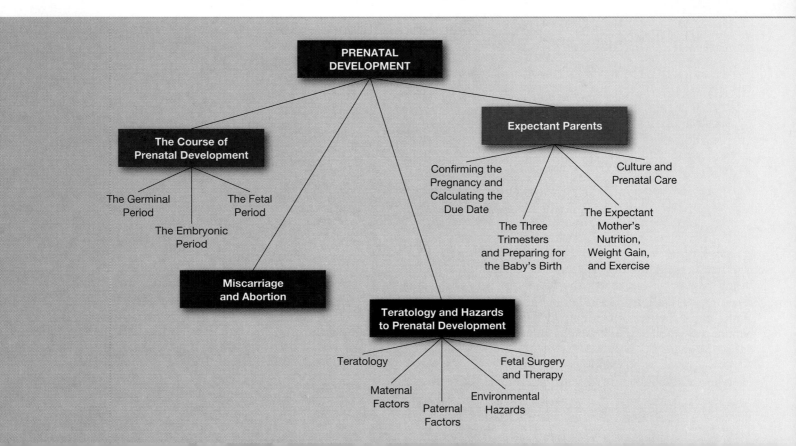

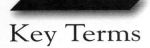

Key Terms

germinal period 90
blastocyst 90
trophoblast 90
implantation 90
embryonic period 91
endoderm 91
ectoderm 91
mesoderm 91
placenta 91

umbilical cord 91
amnion 92
organogenesis 93
fetal period 93
teratogen 97
toxoplasmosis 98
ectopic pregnancy 99
fetal alcohol syndrome
    (FAS) 101

Children Resources

National AIDS Information Clearinghouse
P.O. Box 6003
Rockville, MD 20850
301–217–0023

This clearinghouse provides accurate information and advice about AIDS and services for AIDS-infected mothers and infants.

National Center for Education in Maternal and Child Health
38th and R Streets NW
Washington, DC 20057
202–625–8400

This center answers questions about pregnancy and childbirth, high-risk infants, and maternal and child health programs. It also publishes a free guide, *Maternal and Child Health Publications*.

Prenatal Care Tips
Pregnant women can call this federal government toll-free number for prenatal care advice and referral to local health care providers 1–800–311–2229.

What to Expect When You're Expecting
(1989, 2nd ed.) by Arlene Eisenberg, Heidi Murkoff, and Sandee Hathaway. New York: Workman.

What to Expect When You're Expecting is a month-by-month, step-by-step guide to pregnancy and childbirth. The book tries to put expectant parents' normal fears into perspective by giving them comprehensive information and helping them enjoy this transition in their lives.

Taking It to the Net

http://www.mhhe.com/santrockcd6

1. Your best friend, Mary, found out yesterday that she is three weeks pregnant. She has been partying regularly the last three weeks and is concerned that her consumption of alcohol may have harmed her pregnancy. How can you help her find out what, if any, harm may have been done to the unborn child?

2. You and your partner are having a baby and the doctor has asked for permission to use the discarded placenta for research purposes. You have also been contacted by a local placental blood bank, which offers you money in exchange for the placenta. What decision do you make, and why?

3. Mothers with HIV often pass this virus on to the fetus, yet treatment can vastly reduce the number of babies born with HIV. Your best friend has just become pregnant. Should she be required to be tested for HIV? What if she is at a low-risk for having contracted HIV?

Birth

PREVIEW

The birth of a baby creates changes in a family. It is an event with long-lasting consequences. Although there are many ways to have a baby, the goal should always be to ensure the health of the mother and the baby. These are among the questions we will explore in this chapter:

- What are the stages of birth like?
- What is the birth experience like for the fetus and newborn?
- What is the current thinking about medicating mothers during the process of childbirth?
- What are some natural and prepared childbirth strategies?
- What determines whether a cesarean delivery will be carried out?
- What roles can fathers and siblings play in childbirth?
- What is the right stimulation for preterm infants?
- How is the newborn's health and responsiveness assessed?
- What is the nature of the postpartum period?

The Story of Tanner Roberts' Birth: A Fantastic Voyage

Tanner Roberts was born in a suite at St. Joseph's Medical Center in Burbank, California (Warrick, 1992). Let's examine what took place in the hours leading up to his birth. It is day 266 of his mother, Cindy's, pregnancy. She is in the frozen-food aisle of a convenience store and feels a sharp pain, starting in the small of her back and reaching around her middle, which causes her to gasp. For weeks, painless Braxton Hicks spasms (named for the gynecologist who discovered them) have been flexing her uterine muscles. But these practice contractions were not nearly as intense and painful as the one she just experienced. After six hours of irregular spasms, her uterus settles into a more predictable rhythm.

At 3 A.M., Cindy and her husband, Tom, are wide awake. They time Cindy's contractions with a stopwatch. The contractions are now only six minutes apart. It's time to call the hospital. At the hospital, Cindy goes to a labor-delivery suite. The nurse puts a webbed belt and fetal monitor around Cindy's middle to measure the labor. The monitor picks up the fetal heart rate. With each contraction of the uterine wall, Tanner's heartbeat jumps from its resting state of about 140 beats to 160–170 beats per minute. When the cervix is dilated to more than 4 centimeters, or almost half open, Cindy is given her first medication. As Demerol begins to drip in her veins, she becomes more relaxed. Tanner's heart rate dips to 130 and then 120.

Contractions are now coming every 3 to 4 minutes, each one lasting about 25 seconds. The Demerol does not completely obliterate Cindy's pain. She hugs her husband as the nurse urges her to "relax those muscles. Breathe deep. Relax. You are almost done."

Each contraction briefly cuts off Tanner's source of oxygen. However, the minutes of rest between each contraction resupply the oxygen and Cindy's deep breathing helps rush fresh blood to the fetal heart and brain.

At 8 A.M., Cindy's obstetrician arrives and determines that her cervix is almost completely dilated. Using a tool made for the purpose, he reaches into the birth canal and tears the membranes of the amnio sac, and about half a liter of clear fluid flows out. Contractions are now coming every two minutes, and each one is lasting a full minute.

By 9 A.M., the labor suite has been transformed into a delivery room. Tanner's body is compressed by his mother's contractions and pushes. As he nears his entrance into the world, the compressions help press the fluid from his lungs in preparation for his first breath.

Squeezed tightly in the birth canal, the top of Tanner's head emerges. His face is puffy and scrunched. Although fiercely squinting because of the sudden light, Tanner's eyes are open. Tiny bubbles of clear mucous are on his lips. Before any more of his body emerges, the obstetrician cradles Tanner's head and suctions his nose and mouth. Tanner takes his first breath, a large gasp followed by whimpering, and then a loud cry.

No single event can awaken within us a stranger totally unknown to us. To live is to be slowly born.

Antoine de Saint-Exupéry
French Novelist, 20th Century

**Birth Mailing Lists
and Newsgroups**

Preparing For Birth

afterbirth
The third stage of birth, when the placenta, umbilical cord, and other membranes are detached and expelled.

anoxia
The insufficient availability of oxygen to the fetus/newborn.

Tanner's trunk and head are luminescent pink. His limbs are still gray-blue from lack of oxygen. His fingers and toes are gray. His body is wet but only slightly bloody as the doctor lifts him onto his mother's abdomen.

The umbilical cord, still connecting Tanner with his mother, slows and stops pulsating. The obstetrician cuts it, severing Tanner's connection to his mother's womb. Now Tanner's blood flows not to his mother's blood for nourishment, but to his own lungs, intestines, and other organs

EXPLORING THE BIRTH PROCESS

As we saw in the opening story about Tanner Roberts, many changes take place during the birth of a baby. Let's further explore the birth process by examining the stages of birth, what the birth experience is like for the fetus and newborn, and a variety of childbirth strategies.

Stages of Birth

The birth process occurs in three stages. For a woman having her first child, the first stage lasts an average of 12 to 24 hours; it is the longest of the three stages. In the first stage, uterine contractions are 15 to 20 minutes apart at the beginning and last up to a minute. These contractions cause the woman's cervix to stretch and open. As the first stage progresses, the contractions come closer together, appearing every 2 to 5 minutes. Their intensity increases too. By the end of the first birth stage, contractions dilate the cervix to an opening of about 4 inches, so that the baby can move from the uterus to the birth canal.

The second birth stage begins when the baby's head starts to move through the cervix and the birth canal. It terminates when the baby completely emerges from the mother's body. This stage lasts approximately 1½ hours. With each contraction, the mother bears down hard to push the baby out of her body. By the time the baby's head is out of the mother's body, the contractions come almost every minute and last for about a minute.

Afterbirth *is the third stage, at which time the placenta, umbilical cord, and other membranes are detached and expelled.* This final stage is the shortest of the three birth stages, lasting only minutes (see figure 5.1).

The Fetus/Newborn

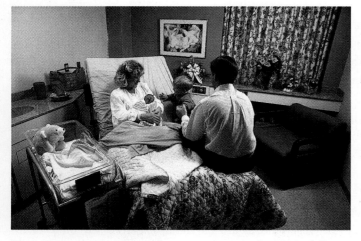

How is this scene in a hospital recovery room in the 1990s different from the childbirth scenes that were typical earlier in this century?

Being born involves considerable stress for the baby. (Albers, 1999). During each contraction, when the placenta and umbilical cord are compressed as the uterine muscles draw together, the supply of oxygen to the fetus is decreased. **Anoxia** *is the term used to describe the condition in which the fetus/newborn has an insufficient supply of oxygen.* Anoxia can cause brain damage. If the delivery takes too long, anoxia can develop.

The baby has considerable capacity to withstand the stress of birth. Large quantities of adrenaline and noradrenalin, hormones that are important in protecting the fetus in the event of oxygen deficiency, are secreted in stressful circumstances. These hormones increase the heart's pumping activity, speed up heart rate, channel blood flow to the brain, and raise blood-sugar level. Never again in life will such large amounts of these hormones be secreted. This circumstance underscores how stressful it is to be born but also how prepared and adapted the fetus is for birth (Von Beveren, 1998).

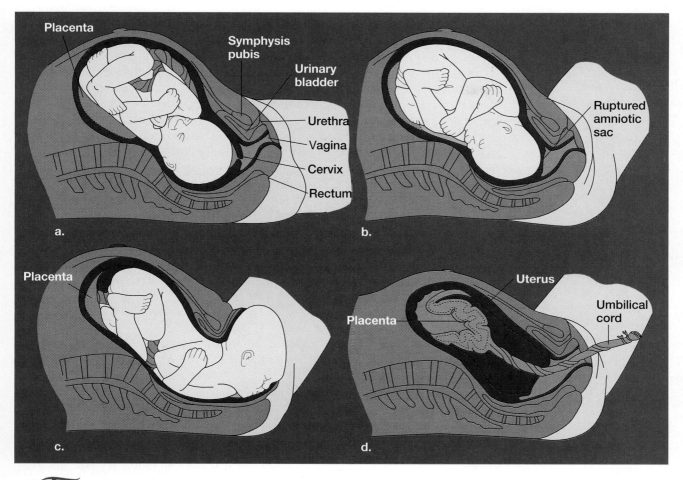

Figure 5.1
The Stages of Birth

(*a*) First stage: cervix is dilating; (*b*) late first stage (transition stage): cervix is fully dilated, and the amniotic sac has ruptured, releasing amniotic fluid; (*c*) second stage: birth of the infant; (*d*) third stage: delivery of the placenta (afterbirth).

As we saw in the case of Tanner Roberts at the beginning of the chapter, the umbilical cord is cut immediately after birth, and the baby is on its own. Now 25 million little air sacs in the lungs must be filled with air. Until now, these air sacs have held fluid, but this fluid is rapidly expelled in blood and lymph. The first breaths may be the hardest ones at any point in the life span. Until now, oxygen came from the mother via the umbilical cord, but now the baby has to be self-sufficient and breathe on its own. The newborn's bloodstream is redirected through the lungs and to all parts of the body.

At the time of birth, the baby is covered with what is called *vernix caseosa*, a protective skin grease. This vernix consists of fatty secretions and dead cells, thought to function in protecting the baby's skin against heat loss before and during birth. After the baby and mother have met and become acquainted with each other, the baby is taken to be cleaned, examined, weighed, and evaluated. Later in the chapter, we will discuss several measures that are used to examine the newborn's health and responsiveness.

Childbirth Strategies

Among the childbirth decisions that need to be made are what the setting will be and who the attendants will be, which childbirth technique will be used, and what the father's or sibling's role will be.

We must respect this instant of birth, this fragile moment. The baby is between two worlds, on a threshold, hesitating . . .

Frederick Leboyer
French Obstetrician, 20th Century

Newborn Care

Childbirth Strategies

**Childbirth Setting
and Attendants**

Midwifery

doula
A caregiver who provides continuous physical, emotional, and educational support to the mother before, during, and just after childbirth.

Doula

analgesia
Drugs used to alleviate pain, such as tranquilizers, barbiturates, and narcotics.

anesthesia
Drugs used in late first-stage labor and during expulsion of the baby to block sensation in an area of the body or to block consciousness.

oxytocics
Drugs that are synthetic hormones designed to stimulate contractions.

Labor Induction

Childbirth Setting and Attendants   In the United States, 99 percent of births take place in hospitals, and more over 90 percent are attended by physicians (Ventura & others, 1997). Many hospitals now have birthing centers, where fathers or birth coaches may be with the mother during labor and delivery. Some people believe this so-called alternative birthing center offers a good compromise between a technological, depersonalized hospital birth (which cannot offer the emotional experience of a home birth) and a birth at home (which cannot offer the medical backup of a hospital). A birthing room approximates a home setting as much as possible. The birthing room allows for a full range of birth experiences, from a totally unmedicated, natural birth to the most complex, medically intensive care. Some women with good medical histories and low risk for problem delivery choose a home delivery or a delivery in a freestanding birthing center, which is usually staffed by nurse-midwives.

Approximately 6 percent of women who deliver a baby in the United States are attended by a midwife (Ventura & others, 1997). Most midwives are nurses who have been specially trained in delivering babies (Webster & others, 1999).

In many countries around the world, babies are more likely to be delivered at home than they are in the United States. For example, in Holland, 35 percent of the babies are born at home, and more than 40 percent are delivered by midwives rather than doctors (Treffers & others, 1990).

In many countries, a doula attends a childbearing woman. *Doula* is a Greek word that means "a woman who helps." A **doula** *is a caregiver who provides continuous physical, emotional, and educational support for the mother before, during, and after childbirth.* Doulas remain with the mother throughout labor, assessing and responding to her needs. In one study, the mothers who received doula support reported less labor pain than the mothers who did not receive doula support (Klaus, Kennell, & Klaus, 1993). Doulas typically function as part of a "birthing team," serving as an adjunct to the midwife or the hospital obstetric staff (McGrath & others, 1999).

In the United States, most doulas work as independent providers hired by the expectant woman. Managed care organizations are increasingly offering doula support as a part of regular obstetric care. In many cultures, the practice of a knowledgeable woman helping a mother in labor is not officially labeled "doula" support but is simply an ingrained, centuries-old custom.

Methods of Delivery   Among the methods of delivery are medicated, natural and prepared, and cesarean.

Medicated   The American Academy of Pediatrics recommends the least possible medication during delivery (Hotchner, 1997). There are three basic kinds of drugs that are used for labor: analgesia, anesthesia, and oxytocics. **Analgesia** *is used to relieve pain.* Analgesics include tranquilizers, barbiturates, and narcotics (such as Demerol). **Anesthesia** *is used in late first-stage labor and during expulsion of the baby to block sensation in an area of the body or to block consciousness.* There is a trend toward not using general anesthesia in normal births because it can be transmitted through the placenta to the fetus. However, an epidural anesthesia does not cross the placenta. An *epidural block* is regional anesthesia that numbs the woman's body from the waist down. Even this drug, thought to be relatively safe, has come under recent criticism because it is associated with fever, extended labor, and increased risk for cesarean delivery (Lieberman & others, 1997). **Oxytocics** *are synthetic hormones that are used to stimulate contractions.* Pitocin is the most commonly used oxytocic.

Predicting how a particular drug will affect an individual pregnant woman and the fetus is difficult. While we have many commonalities as human beings, we also vary a great deal. Thus, a particular drug may have only a minimal effect on one fetus yet have a much stronger effect on another fetus. The drug's dosage also is a factor, with stronger doses of tranquilizers and narcotics given to decrease the mother's pain having a potentially more negative effect on the fetus than mild doses.

It is important for the mother to assess her level of pain and be an important voice in the decision of whether she should receive medication or not.

While the trend at one time was toward a natural childbirth without any medication, today the emphasis is on using some medication but keeping it to a minimum when possible. The emphasis today also is on broadly educating the pregnant woman so that she can be reassured and confident. Next, we will consider natural and prepared childbirth, which reflect this emphasis on education.

Natural and Prepared Childbirth   **Natural childbirth** *was developed in 1914 by an English obstetrician, Grantley Dick-Read. It attempts to reduce the mother's pain by decreasing her fear through education about childbirth and by teaching her to use breathing methods and relaxation techniques during delivery.* Dick-Read also believed that the doctor's relationship with the mother is an important dimension of reducing her perception of pain. He said the doctor should be present during her active labor prior to delivery and should provide reassurance.

Prepared childbirth *was developed by French obstetrician Ferdinand Lamaze. This childbirth strategy is similar to natural childbirth but includes a special breathing technique to control pushing in the final stages of labor and a more detailed anatomy and physiology course.* The Lamaze method has become very popular in the United States. The pregnant woman's husband or a friend usually serves as a coach, who attends childbirth classes with her and helps her with her breathing and relaxation during delivery.

Many other prepared childbirth techniques also have been developed (Samuels & Samuels, 1996). They usually include elements of Dick-Read's natural childbirth or Lamaze's method, plus one or more new components. For instance, the Bradley method places special emphasis on the father's role as a labor coach. Virtually all of the prepared childbirth methods emphasize some degree of education, relaxation and breathing exercises, and support. In recent years, new ways of teaching relaxation have been offered, including guided mental imagery, massage, and meditation. In sum, the current belief in prepared childbirth is that, when information and support are provided, women *know* how to give birth.

Cesarean Delivery   In a **cesarean delivery,** *the baby is removed from the mother's uterus through an incision made in her abdomen. This also is sometimes called a cesarean section.* A cesarean section is usually performed if the baby is in a **breech position,** *which causes the baby's buttocks to be the first part to emerge from the vagina.* Normally, the crown of the baby's head comes through the vagina first, but in 1 of every 25 babies, the head does not come through first. Breech babies' heads are still in the uterus while the rest of their bodies are out, which can cause respiratory problems.

Cesarean deliveries also are performed if the baby is lying crosswise in the uterus, if the baby's head is too large to pass through the mother's pelvis, if the baby develops complications, or if the mother is bleeding vaginally.

The benefits and risks of cesarean sections continue to be debated. Cesarean deliveries are safer than breech deliveries, but they involve a higher infection rate, longer hospital stay, and greater expense and stress that accompany any surgery.

Some critics believe that in the United States too many babies are delivered by cesarean section. More cesarean sections are performed in the United States than in any other country in the world. In the 1980s, births by cesarean section increased almost 50 percent in the United States, with almost one-fourth of babies delivered in this way. In the 1990s, the growing use of vaginal birth after a previous cesarean, greater public awareness, and peer pressure in the medical community led to some decline in cesarean sections.

Fathers and Childbirth   In the past several decades, fathers increasingly have participated in childbirth. Fathers-to-be are now more likely to go to at least one meeting with the obstetrician or caregiver during the pregnancy, attend childbirth

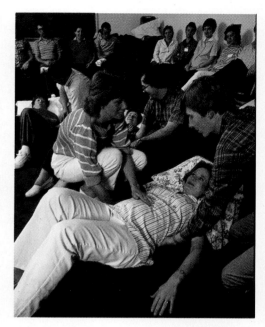

Many husbands, or coaches, take childbirth classes with their wives or friends as part of prepared or natural childbirth. This is a Lamaze training session. Lamaze training is available on a widespread basis in the United States and usually consists of six weekly classes.

natural childbirth
Developed in 1914 by Dick-Read, it attempts to reduce the mother's pain by decreasing her fear through education about childbirth and relaxation techniques during delivery.

prepared childbirth
Developed by French obstetrician Ferdinand Lamaze, this childbirth strategy is similar to natural childbirth but includes a special breathing technique to control pushing in the final stages of labor and a more detailed anatomy and physiology course.

cesarean delivery
The baby is removed from the mother's uterus through an incision made in her abdomen. This also is sometimes referred to as cesarean section.

breech position
The baby's position in the uterus that causes the buttocks to be the first part to emerge from the vagina.

Labor and Birth Resources
Lamaze
Cesarean Childbirth

Through the Eyes of Children

"That Baby Makes Silly Noises"

Four-year-old Robbie didn't know what his life was going to be like after his little brother was born. After they brought his new sibling, Terry, home from the hospital, Robbie watched as first his mother then his father cradled Terry and fussed over him. Robbie started to become more aloof. One day Robbie made a beeline for Terry and started to sock him. Fortunately, his mother was able to grab him before he hurt the baby. Several days later, he told his mom, "That baby makes silly noises."

His mother talked with Robbie about how important it is to be gentle with the baby and made a special effort to give Robbie more attention than she had been doing. Gradually, the parents let Robbie loose in Terry's presence, and no more baby assaults occurred.

It's hard for older siblings not to feel some jealousy when a new sibling arrives on the scene. By considering the older sibling's feelings and making sure the older sibling gets adequate attention, the sibling rivalry usually doesn't escalate into a problem.

Fathers and Childbirth

Siblings and Childbirth

preparation classes, learn about labor and birth, and be more involved in the care of the young infant. The change is consistent with our culture's movement toward less rigid concepts of "masculine" and "feminine."

For many expectant couples today, the father is trained to be the expectant mother's coach during labor, helping her learn relaxation methods and special breathing techniques for labor and birth. Most health professionals now believe that, just as with pregnancy, childbirth should be an intimate, shared moment between two people who are creating a new life together. Nonetheless, some men do not want to participate in prepared childbirth, and some women also still prefer that they not have a very active role. In such cases, other people can provide support for childbirth—mother, sister, friend, midwife, or physician, for example.

Husbands who are motivated to participate in childbirth have an important role at their wife's side. In the long stretches when there is no staff attendant present, a husband can provide companionship, support, and encouragement. In difficult moments of examination or medication, he can be comforting. Initially, he may feel embarrassed to use the breathing techniques he has learned in preparation classes, but he usually begins to feel more at home when he realizes he is performing a necessary function for his wife during each contraction.

Some individuals question whether the father is the best coach during labor. He may be nervous and feel uncomfortable in the hospital. Never having gone through labor himself, he might not understand the expectant mother's needs as well as another woman. There is no universal answer to this issue. Some laboring women want to depend on another woman, someone who has been through labor herself. Others want their husband to intimately share the childbirth experience. Many cultures exclude men from births, just as the American culture did until the past several decades. In some cultures, the woman's mother, or occasionally a daughter, serves as her assistant.

Siblings and Childbirth   If parents have a child and are expecting another, it is important for them to prepare the older child for the birth of a sibling. Sibling preparation includes providing the child with information about pregnancy, birth, and life with a newborn that is realistic and appropriate for the child's age.

Parents can prepare their older child for the approaching birth at any time during pregnancy. The expectant mother might announce the pregnancy early to explain her tiredness and vomiting. If the child is young and unable to understand waiting, parents may want to delay announcing the pregnancy until later, when the expectant mother's pregnancy becomes obvious and she begins to look "fat" to the child.

Parents may want to consider having the child present at the birth. Many family-centered hospitals, birth centers, and home births make this option available. Some parents wish to minimize or avoid separation from the older child, so they choose to give birth where sibling involvement is possible. These parents feel that, if there is no separation, the child will not develop separation anxiety and will not see the new baby as someone who took the mother away. Sibling involvement in the birth may enhance the attachment between the older child and the new baby. On the other hand, some children may not want to participate in the birthing process and should not be forced into it. Some preschool children may be overwhelmed by the whole process, and older children may feel embarrassed.

When parents have a child and are expecting another, they can provide the child with information about pregnancy, birth, and life with a newborn that is realistic and appropriate for the child's age. This information helps the child cope with the birth of a sibling. As part of the sibling preparation process, some parents choose to have the child present at the sibling's birth.

If the birth will be in a hospital with a typical stay of three to five days, parents need to consider the possibility that the child will feel separation anxiety by being separated from one or both parents. To ease the child's separation anxiety, the expectant mother should let the child know approximately when she will be going to the hospital, should tour the hospital with the child if possible, and, when labor begins, should tell the child where she is going. Before birth, the expectant mother can increase the father's role as a caregiver, if he is not already responsible for much of the child's daily care. Parents can ask about the regulations at the hospital or birth setting and, if possible, have the child visit the mother there. As sibling visitation has become recognized as a positive emotional experience for the entire family, hospitals are increasingly allowing children to visit their mothers after the birth of the baby. Some hospitals even allow siblings in the recovery room to see both the mother and the newborn.

In addition to being separated from the mother, the child now has to cope with another emotionally taxing experience: the permanent presence of a crying newborn who requires extensive care and attention from the mother. Life is never the same for the older child after the newborn arrives. Parents who once might have given extensive attention to the child now suddenly have less time available for the child—all because of the new sibling. It is not unusual for a child to ask a parent, "When are you going to take it back to the hospital?" Many children engage in regressive and attention-seeking behaviors after a new sibling arrives, such as sucking their thumb, directing anger at their parents or the baby (hitting, biting, or throwing things), wanting a bottle or the mother's breasts for themselves, or bedwetting. Such behaviors are natural and represent the child's way of coping with stress. Parents should not act as if they are disappointed because the child is behaving in such ways and should worry about such behaviors only if they persist after the child has had a reasonable amount of time to adjust to the new baby. To help the child cope with the arrival of a new baby, parents can (Simkin, Whalley, & Keppler, 1984)

- before and after the birth, read books to the child about living with a new baby.

Summary Table 5.1
Exploring the Birth Process

Concept	Processes/ Related Ideas	Characteristics/Description
Stages of birth	Their nature	Three stages of birth have been defined. The first lasts about 12 to 24 hours for a woman having her first child. The cervix dilates to about 4 centimeters. The second stage begins when the baby's head moves through the cervix and ends with the baby's complete emergence. The third stage is afterbirth.
The fetus/newborn	The transition to birth	Being born involves considerable stress for the baby, but the baby is well prepared and adapted to handle the stress. In some cases, though, anoxia occurs, in which there is an insufficient supply of oxygen to the fetus/newborn. Huge quantities of the stress-related hormones adrenaline and noradrenalin are secreted during the transition to birth.
Childbirth strategies	Childbirth setting and attendants	In the United States, 99 percent of births take place in hospitals, and more than 90 percent are attended by physicians. Many hospitals now have birthing centers. Some women with good medical histories and low risk for problem deliveries have babies at home. In many countries, such as Holland, much higher percentages of babies are born at home. Some births are attended by a midwife, and in many countries a doula attends.
	Methods of delivery	Among the methods of delivery are medicated, natural and prepared, and cesarean. The three basic kinds of drugs used in delivering a baby are analgesics (which relieve pain), anesthesia (which is used in late first-stage labor and during expulsion of the baby to block sensation in an area of the body or to block consciousness), and oxytocics (which stimulate contractions). Predicting how a particular drug will affect an individual pregnant woman and the fetus is difficult. Today the trend is toward using some medication during childbirth but keeping it at a minimum, if possible. Natural and prepared childbirth have become popular. The Lamaze method of childbirth has been especially used on a wide basis in the United States. Virtually all of the prepared childbirth methods emphasize some degree of education, relaxation or breathing exercises, and support. In a cesarean delivery, the baby is removed from the mother's uterus through an incision made in her abdomen. This sometimes is called a cesarean section. The benefits and risks of cesarean sections continue to be debated.
	Fathers and childbirth	In the past several decades, fathers increasingly have participated in childbirth. Fathers-to-be are more likely to go to at least one meeting with the obstetrician or caregiver during pregnancy, to attend childbirth preparation classes, to learn about labor and birth, and to be more involved in the care of the young infant. Husbands who are motivated to participate in childbirth have an important role at their wife's side. In some cultures, the father is excluded from childbirth, as was the case in the American culture until several decades ago.
	Siblings and childbirth	When parents have a child and are expecting another, it is important for them to prepare the older child for the birth of a sibling. Sibling preparation includes providing the child with information about the pregnancy, birth, and life with a newborn that is realistic and appropriate for the child's age.

- plan for time alone with the older child and do what he or she wants to do.
- use the time when the baby is asleep and the parent is rested to give special attention to the older child.
- give a gift to the older child in the hospital or at home.
- "tell" the baby about his or her special older brother or sister when the older sibling is listening.

At this point, we have discussed a number of ideas about the stages of birth, delivery complications, the use of drugs during childbirth, and childbirth strategies. An overview of these ideas is presented in summary table 5.1.

PRETERM INFANTS AND AGE-WEIGHT CONSIDERATIONS

How can we distinguish between a preterm infant and a low-birthweight infant? What are the developmental outcomes for low-birthweight infants? Do preterm infants have a different profile from that of full-term infants? What conclusions can we reach about preterm infants?

Preterm and Low-Birthweight Infants

preterm infant
An infant born prior to 38 weeks after conception.

low-birthweight infant
An infant born after a regular period of gestation (the length of time between conception and birth) of 38 to 42 weeks but who weighs less than 5½ pounds.

An infant is full-term when it has grown in the womb for a full 38 to 42 weeks between conception and delivery. A **preterm infant** *is one who is born prior to 38 weeks after conception.* A **low-birthweight infant** *is born after a regular gestation period (the length of time between conception and birth) of 38 to 42 weeks but weighs less than 5½ pounds.* Both preterm and low-birthweight infants are considered high-risk infants.

A short gestation period does not necessarily harm an infant. It is distinguished from retarded prenatal growth, in which the fetus has been damaged (Kopp, 1992). The neurological development of a short-gestation infant continues after birth on approximately the same timetable as if the infant still were in the womb. For example, consider an infant born after a gestation period of 30 weeks. At 38 weeks, approximately 2 months after birth, this infant shows the same level of brain development as a 38-week fetus who is yet to be born.

Some infants are born very early and have a precariously low birthweight. "Kilogram kids" weigh less than 2.3 pounds (which is 1 kilogram, or 1,000 grams) and are very premature. The task of saving such a baby is not easy. At the Stanford University Medical Center in Palo Alto, California, 98 percent of the preterm babies survive; however, 32 percent of those between 750 and 1,000 grams do not, and 76 percent of those below 750 grams do not. Approximately 250,000 preterm babies are born in the United States each year, and more than 15,000 of these weigh less than 1,000 grams.

Equal opportunity for life is an American ideal that is not fulfilled at birth (Paneth, 1995). African American babies are twice as likely as White babies to be born low-birthweight, to be born preterm, or to die at birth. Seventeen percent of all births are to African American families, yet 33 percent of all low-birthweight infants and 38 percent of all very-low-birthweight infants are born to African American families.

Long-Term Outcomes for Low-Birthweight Infants

Although most low-birthweight infants are normal and healthy, as a group they have more health and developmental problems than normal-birthweight infants (Chescheir & Hansen, 1999; Hack, Klein, & Taylor, 1995). The number and severity of these problems increase as birthweight decreases. (Barton, Hodgman, & Pavlova, 1999; Malloy, 1999). With the improved survival rates for infants who are born very early and very small come increases in severe brain damage. Cerebral palsy and other forms of brain injury are highly correlated with brain weight—the lower the brain weight, the greater the likelihood of brain injury. Approximately 7 percent of moderately low-birthweight infants (3 pounds 5 ounces to 5 pounds 8 ounces) have brain injuries. This figure increases to 20 percent for the smallest newborns (1 pound 2 ounces to 3 pounds 5 ounces). Low-birthweight infants are also more likely than normal-birthweight infants to have lung or liver diseases.

At school age, children who were born low in birthweight are more likely than

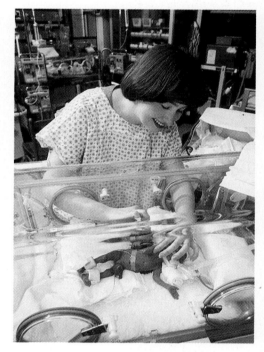

A "kilogram kid," weighing less than 2.3 pounds at birth. In the neonatal intensive care unit, banks of flashing lights, blinking numbers, and beeping alarms stand guard over kilogram kids, who are extremely preterm infants. They often lie on a water-bed that gently undulates; the water bed is in an incubator that is controlled for temperature and humidity by the baby's own body. Such vital signs as brain waves, heartbeat, blood gases, and respiratory rate are constantly monitored. All of this care can be very expensive. Though the cost can usually be kept within five figures, five or six months of neonatal intensive care can result in expenses of as much as a million dollars or more.

their normal-birthweight counterparts to have a learning disability, attention deficit disorder, or breathing problems, such as asthma (Taylor, Klein, & Hack, 1994). Children born very low in birthweight have more learning problems and lower levels of achievement in reading and math than moderately low-birthweight children. These problems are reflected in much higher percentages of low-birthweight children being enrolled in special education programs. Approximately 50 percent of all low-birthweight children are enrolled in special education programs.

Not all of these adverse consequences can be attributed solely to being born low in birthweight. Some of the less severe but more common developmental and physical delays occur because many low-birthweight children come from disadvantaged environments.

Some of the devastating effects of being born low in birthweight can be reversed (Blair & Ramey, 1996; Shino & Behrman, 1995). Intensive enrichment programs that provide medical and educational services for both the parents and the child have been shown to improve short-term developmental outcomes for low-birthweight children. Federal laws mandate that services for school-age disabled children (which include medical, educational, psychological, occupational, and physical care) be expanded to include family-based care for infants. At present, these services are aimed at children born with severe congenital disabilities. The availability of services for moderately low-birthweight children who do not have severe physical problems varies from state to state, but generally these services are not available.

**Low-Birthweight Infants
Exploring Low-Birthweight Issues
Social Factors in Low-Birthweight**

Stimulation of Preterm Infants

Just three decades ago, preterm infants were perceived to be too fragile to cope well with environmental stimulation, and the recommendation was to handle such infants as little as possible. The climate of opinion changed when the adverse effects of maternal deprivation (mothers' neglect of their infants) became known and was interpreted to include a lack of stimulation. A number of research studies followed that indicated a "more is better" approach in the stimulation of preterm infants. Today, however, experts on infant development argue that preterm infant care is far too complex to be described only in terms of amount of stimulation.

Following are some conclusions about the situation of preterm infants (Lester & Tronick, 1990):

1. Preterm infants' responses to stimulation vary with their conceptual age, illness, and individual makeup. The immature brain of the preterm infant may be more vulnerable to excessive, inappropriate, or mistimed stimulation. The very immature infant should probably be protected from stimulation that could destabilize its homeostatic condition.
2. As the healthy preterm infant becomes less fragile and approaches term, the issue of what is appropriate stimulation should be considered. Infants' behavioral cues can be used to determine appropriate interventions. An infant's signs of stress or avoidance behaviors indicate that stimulation should be terminated. Positive behaviors indicate that stimulation is appropriate.
3. Intervention with the preterm infant should be organized in the form of an individualized developmental plan. This plan should be constructed as a psychosocial intervention to include the parents and other immediate family members and to acknowledge the socioeconomic, cultural, and home environmental factors that will determine the social context in which the infant will be reared. The developmental plan should also include assessing the infant's behavior, working with the parents to help them understand the infant's medical and behavioral status, and helping the parents deal with their own feelings. To read further about stimulating preterm infants, see the box Caring for Children.

Touch Research Institute

Caring for Children

The Power of Touch and Massage in Development

There has been a recent surge of interest in the roles of touch and massage in improving the growth, health, and well-being of infants and children. This interest has been stimulated by the research of Tiffany Field (1998), director of the Touch Research Institute at the University of Miami School of Medicine. In one investigation, 40 preterm infants who had just been released from an intensive care unit and placed in a transitional nursery were studied (Field, Scafidi, & Schanberg, 1987). Twenty of the preterm babies were given special stimulation with massage and exercise for three 15-minute periods at the beginning of 3 consecutive hours every morning for 10 weekdays. For example, each infant was placed on its stomach and gently stroked. The massage began with the head and neck and moved downward to the feet. It also moved from the shoulders down to the hands. The infant was then rolled over. Each arm and leg was flexed and extended; then both legs were flexed and extended. Next, the massage was repeated.

The massaged and exercised preterm babies gained 47 percent more weight than their preterm counterparts who were not massaged and exercised, even though both groups had the same number of feedings per day and averaged the same intake of formula. The increased activity of the massaged, exercised infants would seem to work against weight gain. However, similar findings have been discovered with animals. The increased activity may increase gastrointestinal and metabolic efficiency. The massaged infants were more active and alert, and they performed better on developmental tests. Also,

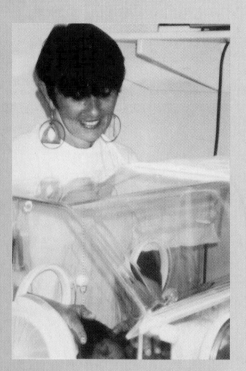

Shown here is Dr. Tiffany Field massaging a newborn infant. Dr. Field's research has clearly demonstrated the power of massage in improving the developmental outcome of at-risk infants. Under her direction, the Touch Research Institute in Miami, Florida, was recently developed to investigate the role of touch in a number of domains of health and well-being.

their hospital stays were about six days shorter than those of the nonmassaged, nonexercised group, which saved about $3,000 per preterm infant. Field has recently replicated these findings with preterm infants in another study.

In a more recent study, Field (1992) gave the same kind of massage (firm stroking with the palms of the hands) to preterm infants who were exposed to cocaine in utero. The infants also showed significant weight gain and improved scores on developmental tests. Currently, Field is using massage therapy with HIV-exposed preterm infants, with the hope that their immune system functioning will be improved. Others she has targeted include infants of depressed mothers, infants with colic, infants and children with sleep problems, and children who have diabetes, asthma, and juvenile arthritis.

In another study, Field and colleagues (1996) investigated 1- to 3-month-old infants born to depressed adolescent mothers. The infants were given 15 minutes of either massage or rocking for 2 days per week for a 6-week period. The infants who received massage therapy had lower stress, as well as improved emotionality, sociability, and soothability, when compared with the rocked infants.

Field (1992, 1995) also reports that touch benefits children and adolescents who have touch aversions, such as children who have been sexually abused, autistic children, and adolescents with eating disorders. Field also is studying the amount of touch a child normally receives during school activities. She hopes that positive forms of touch will return to school systems, where touching has been outlawed because of potential sexual abuse lawsuits.

MEASURES OF NEONATAL HEALTH AND RESPONSIVENESS

Apgar Scale

A widely used method to assess the health of newborns at one and five minutes after birth. The Apgar Scale evaluates infants' heart rate, respiratory effort, muscle tone, body color, and reflex irritability.

The **Apgar Scale** *is a method widely used to assess the health of newborns at one and five minutes after birth. The Apgar Scale evaluates infants' heart rate, respiratory effort, muscle tone, body color, and reflex irritability.* An obstetrician or a nurse does the evaluation and gives the newborn a score, or reading, of 0, 1, or 2 on each of these five health signs (see figure 5.2). A total score of 7 to 10 indicates that the newborn's condition is good. A score of 5 indicates there may be developmental difficulties. A score of 3 or below signals an emergency and indicates that the baby might not survive. The Apgar Scale is especially good at assessing the newborn's ability to respond to the stress of delivery, labor, and the new environment. (Butterfield, 1999). The Apgar Scale also identifies high-risk infants who need resuscitation.

Brazelton Neonatal Behavioral Assessment Scale

A test given several days after birth to assess newborns' neurological development, reflexes, and reactions to people.

To evaluate the newborn more thoroughly, the **Brazelton Neonatal Behavioral Assessment Scale** *is performed within 24–36 hours after birth to evaluate the newborn's*

$\mathcal{F}$igure 5.2
The Apgar Scale

	0	1	2
Heart rate	Absent	Slow—less than 100 beats per minute	Fast—100–140 beats per minute
Respiratory effort	No breathing for more than one minute	Irregular and slow	Good breathing with normal crying
Muscle tone	Limp and flaccid	Weak, inactive, but some flexion of extremities	Strong, active motion
Body color	Blue and pale	Body pink but extremities blue	Entire body pink
Reflex irritability	No response	Grimace	Coughing, sneezing, and crying

neurological development, reflexes, and reactions to people. When the Brazelton is given, the newborn is treated as an active participant, and the score attained is based on the newborn's best performance. Sixteen reflexes, such as sneezing, blinking, and rooting, are assessed, along with reactions to circumstances, such as the infant's reaction to a rattle. (We will have more to say about reflexes in the next chapter, when we discuss physical development in infancy.) The examiner rates the newborn on each of 27 categories (see figure 5.3). As an indication of how detailed the ratings are, consider item 15: "cuddliness." Nine categories are involved in assessing this item, with infant behavior scored on a continuum that ranges from the infant's being very resistant to being held to the infant's being extremely cuddly and clinging. The Brazelton scale not only is used as a sensitive index of neurological competence in the week after birth, but it also is used widely as a measure in many research studies on infant development. In scoring the Brazelton scale, Brazelton and his colleagues (Brazelton, Nugent, & Lester, 1987) categorize the 27 items into four categories—physiological, motoric, state, and interaction. They also classify the baby in global terms, such as "worrisome," "normal," or "superior," based on these categories.

A very low Brazelton score can indicate brain damage, or it can reflect stress to the brain that may heal in time. However, if an infant merely seems sluggish in responding to social circumstances, parents are encouraged to give the infant attention and become more sensitive to the infant's needs. Parents are shown how the newborn can respond to people and how to stimulate such responses. Researchers have found that the social interaction skills of both high-risk infants and healthy, responsive infants can be improved through such communication with parents (Worobey & Belsky, 1982).

1. Response decrement to repeated visual stimuli
2. Response decrement to rattle
3. Response decrement to bell

4. Response decrement to pinprick
5. Orienting response to inanimate visual stimuli
6. Orienting response to inanimate auditory stimuli

7. Orienting response to inanimate visual and auditory stimuli
8. Orienting response to animate visual stimuli—examiner's face
9. Orienting response to animate auditory stimuli—examiner's voice
10. Orienting response to animate visual and auditory stimuli
11. Quality and duration of alert periods
12. General muscle tone—in resting and in response to being handled, passive, and active

13. Motor activity
14. Traction responses as the infant is pulled to sit
15. Cuddliness—responses to being cuddled by examiner

16. Defensive movements—reactions to a cloth over the infant's face
17. Consolability with intervention by examiner
18. Peak of excitement and capacity to control self
19. Rapidity of buildup to crying state
20. Irritability during examination
21. General assessment of kind and degree of activity

22. Tremulousness
23. Amount of startling
24. Lability of skin color—measuring autonomic lability

25. Lability of states during entire examination
26. Self-quieting activity—attempts to console self and control state
27. Hand-to-mouth activity

*F*igure 5.3
The 27 Categories on the Brazelton Neonatal Behavioral Assessment Scale (NBAS)

THE POSTPARTUM PERIOD

Many health professionals believe that the best postpartum care is family centered, using the family's resources to support an early and smooth adjustment to the newborn by all family members. What is the postpartum period?

The Nature of the Postpartum Period

The **postpartum period** *is the period after childbirth or delivery. It is a time when the woman's body adjusts, both physically and psychologically, to the process of childbearing. It lasts for about six weeks or until the body has completed its adjustment and has returned to a near prepregnant state.* Some health professionals refer to the postpartum period as the "fourth trimester." While the time span of the postpartum period does not necessarily cover three months, the terminology of "fourth trimester" demonstrates the idea of continuity and the importance of the first several months after birth for the mother.

Postpartum Adjustment

postpartum period

The period after childbirth when the mother adjusts, both physically and psychologically, to the process of childbirth. This period lasts for about six weeks, or until her body has completed its adjustment and has returned to a near prepregnant state.

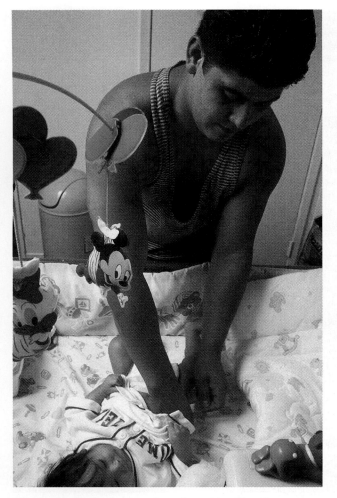

The postpartum period is a time of considerable adjustment and adaptation for both the mother and the father. Fathers can provide an important support system for mothers, especially in helping mothers care for young infants.

involution
The process by which the uterus returns to its prepregnant size.

Mothers, Fathers, and Newborns

The postpartum period is influenced by what preceded it. During pregnancy, the woman's body gradually adjusted to physical changes, but now it is forced to respond quickly. The method of delivery and circumstances surrounding the delivery affect the speed with which the woman's body readjusts during the postpartum period.

The postpartum period involves a great deal of adjustment and adaptation. The baby has to be cared for; the mother has to recover from childbirth; the mother has to learn how to take care of the baby; the mother needs to learn to feel good about herself as a mother; the father needs to learn how to take care of his recovering wife; the father needs to learn how to take care of the baby; and the father needs to learn how to feel good about himself as a father.

Physical Adjustments

The woman's body makes numerous physical adjustments in the first days and weeks after childbirth. She may have a great deal of energy or feel exhausted and let down. Most new mothers feel tired and need rest. Though these changes are normal, the fatigue can undermine the new mother's sense of well-being and confidence in her ability to cope with a new baby and a new family life.

Involution *is the process by which the uterus returns to its prepregnant size five or six weeks after birth.* Immediately following birth, the uterus weighs 2 to 3 pounds, and the fundus can be felt midway between the naval and the pubic bone. By the end of five or six weeks, the uterus weighs 2 to 3½ ounces and it has returned to its prepregnancy size. Nursing the baby helps contract the uterus at a rapid rate.

After delivery, a woman's body undergoes sudden and dramatic changes in hormone production. When the placenta is delivered, estrogen and progesterone levels drop steeply and remain low until the ovaries start producing hormones again. The woman will probably begin menstruating again in four to eight weeks if she is not breast-feeding. If she is breast-feeding, she might not menstruate for several months, though ovulation can occur during this time. The first several menstrual periods following delivery may be heavier than usual, but periods soon return to normal.

Some women and men want to resume sexual intercourse as soon as possible after the birth. Others feel constrained or afraid. A sore perineum (the area between the anus and vagina in the female), a demanding baby, lack of help, and extreme fatigue affect a woman's ability to relax and to enjoy making love. Physicians often recommend that women refrain from having sexual intercourse for approximately six weeks following the birth of the baby. However, it is probably safe to have sexual intercourse when the stitches heal, vaginal discharge stops, and the woman feels like it.

If the woman regularly engaged in conditioning exercises during pregnancy, exercise will help her recover her former body contour and strength during the postpartum period. With a caregiver's approval, the woman can begin some exercises as soon as one hour after delivery. In addition to recommending exercise in the postpartum period for women, health professionals also increasingly recommend that women practice the relaxation techniques they used during pregnancy and childbirth. Five minutes of slow breathing on a stressful day in the postpartum period can relax and refresh the new mother, as well as the new baby.

Emotional and Psychological Adjustments

Emotional fluctuations are common on the part of the mother in the postpartum period. These emotional fluctuations may be due to any of a number of factors: hormonal changes, fatigue, inexperience or lack of confidence with newborn babies, or the extensive time and demands involved in caring for a newborn. For some women, the emotional fluctuations decrease within several weeks after the delivery and are a minor aspect of their motherhood. For others, they are more long-lasting and may produce feelings of anxiety, depression, and difficulty in coping with stress. Mothers who have such feelings, even when they are getting adequate rest, may benefit from professional help in dealing with their problems. Following are some of the signs that may indicate a need for professional counseling about postpartum adaptation:

- Excessive worrying
- Depression
- Extreme changes in appetite
- Crying spells
- Inability to sleep

A special concern of many new mothers is whether they should stay home with the baby or go back to work. Some mothers want to return to work as soon as possible after the infant is born; others want to stay home with the infant for several months, then return to work; others want to stay home for a year before they return to work; and yet others did not work outside the home prior to the baby's arrival and do not plan to do so in the future.

Many women, because of a variety of pressures—societal, career, financial—do not have the option of staying at home after their babies are born (Eisenberg, Murkoff, & Hathaway, 1989). However, for women who have to make the choice, the process of decision making is often difficult and agonizing.

The father also undergoes considerable adjustment in the postpartum period, although in many cases he will be away at work all day, whereas the mother will be at home, at least in the first few weeks. One of the most common reactions of the husband is the feeling that the baby comes first and gets all of the attention. In some marriages, the man may have had that relationship with his wife and now feels that he has been replaced by the baby.

One strategy to help the man's postpartum reaction is for the parents to set aside some special time to be together with each other. The father's postpartum reaction also likely will be improved if he has taken childbirth classes with his wife and is an active participant in caring for the baby.

Important factors for both the mother and the father are the time and thought that go into being a competent parent of a young infant. It is important for both the mother and the father to become aware of the young infant's developmental needs—physical, psychological, and emotional. Both the mother and the father need to develop a sensitive, comfortable relationship with the baby. We will have more to say about the transition to parenting and the mother's and father's role in infant development in chapter 8. To think further about the postpartum period, see Adventures for the Mind.

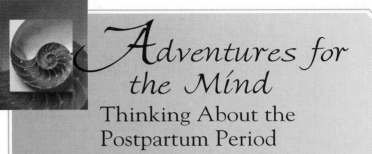

Adventures for the Mind

Thinking About the Postpartum Period

Get together with several other students in the class, making sure that the group includes at least one or more females and one or more males. After reading the material on the postpartum period, discuss your views on

- The most important adjustments the mother and father will have to make in their lives because of the newborn baby.
- Whether the mother should stay home with the baby or go back to work. If you think she should stay home, how long should she stay home with the baby before returning to work?
- The ways parents can help each other in adapting to the newborn baby in their lives.

Postpartum Resources

Bonding

A special component of the parent-infant relationship is **bonding,** *the occurrence of close contact, especially physical, between parents and newborn in the period shortly after birth.* Some physicians believe that this period shortly after birth is critical in development. During this time, the parents and child need to form an important emotional attachment that provides a foundation for optimal development in years to come (Kennell & McGrath, 1999). Special interest in bonding came about when some pediatricians argued that the circumstances surrounding delivery often separate

bonding
Close contact, especially physical, between parents and their newborn in the period shortly after birth.

Improving Developmental Skills
Some Good Birth Strategies

Following are some birth strategies that may benefit the baby and the mother:

- *Take a childbirth class.* These classes provide information about the childbirth experience.

- *Become knowledgeable about different childbirth techniques.* We described a number of different childbirth techniques in this chapter, including Lamaze and using doulas. Obtain more detailed information about such techniques by reading a good book, such as *Pregnancy and Childbirth* (1997) by Tracie Hotchner.

- *At-risk infants can benefit from positive intervention.* Massage can improve the developmental outcome of at-risk infants. Intensive enrichment programs that include medical, educational, psychological, occupational, and physical domains can benefit low-birthweight infants. Intervention with low-birthweight infants should involve an individualized plan.

- *Involve the family in the birth process.* If they are motivated to participate, the husband and siblings can benefit from being involved in the birth process. A mother, sister, or friend can also provide support.

- *Know about the adaptation required in the postpartum period.* The postpartum period involves considerable adaptation and adjustment by the mother. This adjustment is both physical and emotional. Exercise and relaxation techniques can benefit mothers in the postpartum period. So can an understanding, supportive husband.

mothers and their infants, preventing or making difficult the development of a bond. The pediatricians further argued that giving the mother drugs to make her delivery less painful may contribute to the lack of bonding. The drugs may make the mother drowsy, thus interfering with her ability to respond to and stimulate the newborn. Advocates of bonding also assert that preterm infants are isolated from their mothers to an even greater degree than are full-term infants, thereby increasing their difficulty in bonding.

Is there evidence that such close contact between mothers and newborns is critical for optimal development later in life? Although some research supports the bonding hypothesis (Klaus & Kennell, 1976), a body of research challenges the significance of the first few days of life as a critical period (Bakeman & Brown, 1980; Rode & others, 1981). Indeed, the extreme form of the bonding hypothesis—that the newborn must have close contact with the mother in the first few days of life to develop optimally—simply is not true.

Nonetheless, the weakness of the maternal-infant bonding research should not be used as an excuse to keep motivated mothers from interacting with their infants in the postpartum period. Such contact brings pleasure to many mothers. In some mother-infant pairs—including preterm infants, adolescent mothers, or mothers from disadvantaged circumstances—the practice of bonding may set in motion a climate for improved interaction after the mother and infant leave the hospital.

In recognition of the belief that bonding may have a positive effect on getting the parental-infant relationship off to a good start, many hospitals now offer a *rooming in* arrangement, in which the baby remains

A mother bonds with her infant moments after it is born. How critical is bonding for the development of social competence later in childhood?

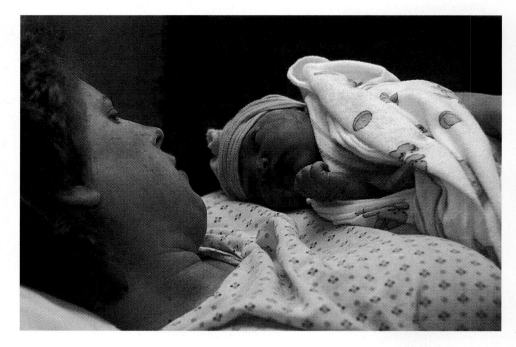

Summary Table 5.2

Preterm Infants and Age-Weight Considerations, Measures of Neonatal Health and Responsiveness, and the Postpartum Period

Concept	Processes/ Related Ideas	Characteristics/Description
Preterm infants and age-weight considerations	Preterm and low-birthweight infants	Preterm infants are those born after an abnormally short time period in the womb. Infants who are born after a regular gestation period of 38 to 42 weeks but who weigh less than 5½ pounds are called low-birthweight infants.
	Long-term outcomes for low-birthweight infants	Although most low-birthweight infants are normal and healthy, as a group they have more health and developmental problems than normal-birthweight infants. The number and severity of the problems increase as birthweight decreases.
	Stimulation	Preterm infant care is much too complex to be described only in terms of amount of stimulation. Preterm infants' responses vary according to their conceptual age, illness, and individual makeup. Infant behavioral cues can be used to indicate the appropriate stimulation. Intervention should be organized in the form of an individualized developmental plan.
Measures of neonatal health and responsiveness	Types	For many years, the Apgar Scale has been used to assess the newborn's health. A more recently developed test—the Brazelton Neonatal Behavioral Assessment Scale—is used for long-term neurological assessment. It assesses not only the newborn's neurological integrity but also its social responsiveness.
The postpartum period	Its nature	The postpartum period is the period after childbirth or delivery. It is a time when the woman's body adjusts, both physically and psychologically, to the process of childbearing. It lasts for about six weeks or until the body has completed its adjustment.
	Physical adjustments	These include fatigue, involution (the process by which the uterus returns to its prepregnant size five or six weeks after birth), hormonal changes that include a dramatic drop in estrogen and progesterone, consideration of when to resume sexual intercourse, and participation in exercises to recover former body contour and strength.
	Emotional and psychological adjustments	Emotional fluctuations on the part of the mother are common in the postpartum period. They may be due to hormonal changes, fatigue, inexperience or lack of confidence with newborn babies, or the extensive time and other demands involved in caring for a newborn. For some, the emotional fluctuations are minimal and disappear in several weeks; for others, they are more long-lasting. The father also goes through a postpartum adjustment. Another adjustment for both the mother and the father is the time and thought that go into being a competent parent of a young infant.
	Bonding	A special component of parent-infant relationships is bonding, which has not been found to be critical in the development of a competent infant or child but which may stimulate positive interaction between some mother-infant pairs. The new baby also changes the mother's and father's relationship with each other. A special concern of many new mothers is whether they should go back to work or stay home with the infant.

in the mother's room most of the time during its hospital stay. However, if parents choose not to use this rooming in arrangement, the weight of the research evidence suggests that it will not harm the infant emotionally (Lamb, 1994).

Throughout this chapter, we have discussed a number of positive birth strategies. The insert, Improving Developmental Skills, profiles some good birth strategies.

At this point, we have discussed a number of ideas about preterm infants and age-weight considerations, measures of neonatal health and responsiveness, and the postpartum period. An overview of these ideas is presented in summary table 5.2.

Chapter Review

The event of giving birth is a tremendous and unforgettable experience. Childbirth, with its personal drama and significance for the survival of the family, is an event that every society views as something special.

We began this chapter by describing Tanner Roberts' fantastic voyage of birth, then turned to a discussion of the stages of birth, what the birth transition is like for the fetus and newborn, and childbirth strategies. We explored the nature of preterm infants and age-weight considerations and examined measures of neonatal health and responsiveness. Our description of the postpartum period included information about physical adjustments, psychological and emotional adjustments, and bonding.

Don't forget that you can obtain a more detailed review of the chapter by again reading the two summary tables on pages 126 and 135. This concludes our discussion in Section Two, "Beginnings." In Section Three, we will turn our attention to the nature of infant development, beginning with chapter 6, "Physical Development in Infancy."

Children Checklist

Birth

How much have you learned since the beginning of the chapter? Use the following statements to help you review your knowledge and understanding of the chapter material. First, read the statement and mentally or briefly demonstrate on paper that you can discuss the relevant information.

_____ I can describe the stages of birth.
_____ I know what the current thinking is about medicating mothers during childbirth.
_____ I can discuss natural and prepared childbirth.
_____ I know about cesarean delivery.
_____ I can describe what roles father and siblings can play in childbirth.
_____ I can evaluate what the right stimulation is for preterm infants.
_____ I know how the newborn's health and responsiveness can be assessed.
_____ I can discuss the postpartum period.

For any items that you did not check, go back and locate the relevant material in the chapter. Review the material until you feel that you can check off the item. You may want to use this checklist later in preparing for an exam.

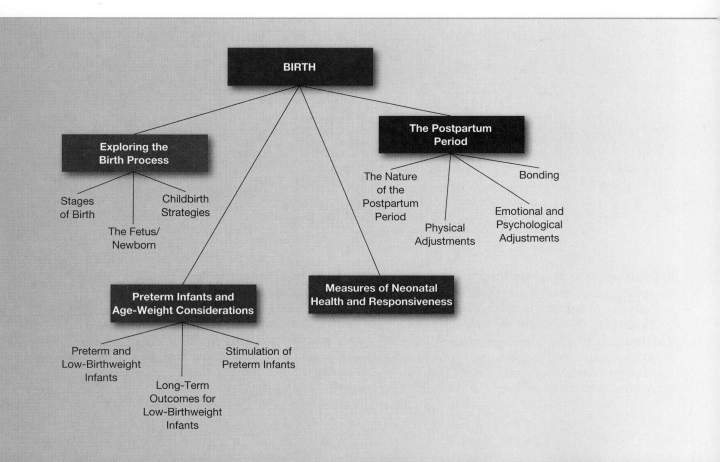

Key Terms

afterbirth 120
anoxia 120
doula 122
analgesia 122
anesthesia 122
oxytocics 122
natural childbirth 123
prepared childbirth 123
cesarean delivery 123

breech position 123
preterm infant 127
low-birthweight infant 127
Apgar Scale 130
Brazelton Neonatal Behavioral
    Assessment Scale 130
postpartum period 131
involution 132
bonding 133

Children Resources

ASPO/Lamaze
1840 Wilson Boulevard, Suite 204
Arlington, VA 22201

This organization provides information about the Lamaze method and taking or teaching Lamaze classes.

Birth: Issues in Perinatal Care
This multidisciplinary journal on perinatal care is written for health professionals and contains articles on research and clinical practice, review articles, and commentary.

Cesareans/Support, Education, and Concern
22 Forest Road
Framingham, MA 01701
508–877–8266

This organization provides information and advice about cesarean birth.

International Post-Partum Support
927 North Kellogg Avenue
Santa Barbara, CA 93111
805–967–7636

This organization provides information about postpartum depression.

La Leche League International
9616 Minneapolis Avenue
Franklin Part, IL 60131
800–LA–LECHE

This organization provides information about the benefits of breast-feeding. It also publishes the very thorough book *The Womanly Art of Breast Feeding* (New York: Plume, 1991).

Taking It to the Net

http://www.mhhe.com/santrockcd6

1. You have volunteered to work at a women's crisis center. A 14 year old comes to you for advice regarding her pregnancy. What are the physical risks of being 14 years old and pregnant? What do you tell her?
2. Were you born through normal vaginal birth, or through cesarean birth? Was anyone in your family born cesarean? Until recently, it was believed that once a woman had a child through cesarean birth, that all her subsequent children would also have to be born cesarean. How and why is it now possible for a woman to have a vaginal birth after a cesarean birth? Would you recommend it?
3. What are the signs of postpartum depression? How would you advise a friend on coping strategies for postpartum depression? Of the strategies and treatments available, what would you recommend personally, and why?

Section III

Infancy

*B*abies are such
a nice way to
start people.
Don Herold
American Writer, 20th Century

As newborns, we were not empty-headed organisms. We had some basic reflexes, among them crying, kicking, and coughing. We slept a lot and occasionally we smiled, although the meaning of our first smiles was not entirely clear. We ate and we grew. We crawled and then we walked, a journey of a thousand miles beginning with a single step. Sometimes we conformed; sometimes others conformed to us. Our development was a continuous creation of more complex forms. Our helpless kind demanded the meeting eyes of love. We juggled the necessity of curbing our will with becoming what we could will freely. Section III includes three chapters: "Physical Development in Infancy" (chapter 6), "Cognitive Development in Infancy" (chapter 7), and "Socioemotional Development in Infancy" (chapter 8).

Chapter

6

Chapter Outline

Physical Development in Infancy

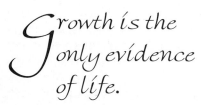

Growth is the only evidence of life.

John Henry, Cardinal Newman
English Churchman, 19th Century

PREVIEW

Among the first things developmentalists were able to demonstrate was that infants have highly developed perceptual motor systems. Until recently, even some nurses in maternity hospitals believed that newborns are blind at birth, and they told this to mothers. Most parents were also told that their newborns could not taste, smell, or feel pain. As you will discover later in this chapter, we now know that newborns can see (albeit fuzzily), taste, smell, and feel pain. These are among the questions that we will explore in this chapter:

- What is the nature of the brain's growth in infancy? How much can early experiences influence the brain's development?
- What is the best nutrition for infants? Is it best to breast-feed or bottle-feed infants?
- What are some good strategies for toilet training infants?
- What are some immunization schedules for infants? What is the best accident prevention for infants?
- How do infants' motor skills develop?
- How does infants' perceptual development unfold during infancy?
- What is the nature of perceptual-motor coupling and unification in infancy?

The Stories of Latonya and Ramona: Bottle- and Breast-Feeding in Africa

Latonya is a newborn baby in the African country of Ghana. The culture of the area in which she was born discourages breast-feeding. She has been kept apart from her mother and bottle-fed in her first days of infancy. Manufacturers of infant formula provide the hospital where she was born with free or subsidized milk powder. Her mother has been persuaded to bottle-feed rather than breast-feed her.

When her mother bottle-feeds Latonya, she overdilutes the milk formula with unclean water. Latonya's feeding bottles also have not been sterilized. Latonya starts getting sick, very sick. She dies before her first birthday.

By contrast, Ramona lives in the African country of Nigeria. Her mother is breast-feeding her. Ramona was born at a Nigerian hospital where a "baby-friendly" program had been initiated. In this program, babies are not separated from their mothers when they are born, and the mothers are encouraged to breast-feed them. The mothers are told of the perils that bottle-feeding can bring because of unsafe water and unsterilized bottles. They also are informed about the advantages of breast milk, which include its nutritious and hygienic qualities, its ability to immunize babies against common illnesses, and its role in reducing the mother's risk of breast and ovarian cancer. At 1 year of age, Ramona is very healthy.

For the past 10–15 years, the World Health Organization and UNICEF have been trying to reverse the trend toward bottle-feeding of infants, which emerged in many impoverished countries. They have instituted the "baby-friendly" program in many countries. They also have persuaded the International Association of Infant Formula Manufacturers to stop marketing their baby formulas to hospitals in countries where the governments support the baby-friendly initiatives. For the hospitals themselves, costs actually will be reduced as infant formula, feeding bottles, and separate nurseries become unnecessary. For example, a baby-friendly hospital in the Philippines, the Jose Fabella Memorial Hospital, already has reported saving 8 percent of its annual budget.

Hospitals play an important role in getting mothers to breast-feed their babies. For many years, maternity units were on the side of bottle-feeding babies and failed to give mothers adequate information about the benefits of breast-feeding. Fortunately, with the initiatives of the World Health Organization and UNICEF, that is beginning to change, but there still are many impoverished places in the world where the baby-friendly initiatives have not been implemented (Grant, 1993).

**International Society on
Infant Studies**

cephalocaudal pattern
The sequence in which the greatest growth occurs at the top—the head—with physical growth in size, weight, and feature differentiation gradually working from top to bottom.

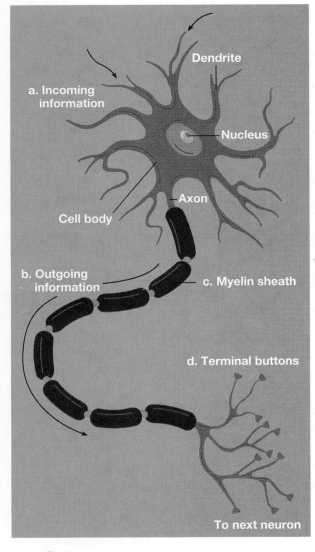

$\mathcal{F}$igure 6.1
The Neuron

(*a*) The dendrites of the cell body receive information from other neurons, muscles, or glands through the axon. (*b*) Axons transmit information away from the cell body. (*c*) A myelin sheath covers most axons and speeds information transmission. (*d*) As the axon ends, it branches out into terminal buttons.

PHYSICAL GROWTH AND DEVELOPMENT IN INFANCY

Infants' physical development in the first 2 years of life is extensive. At birth, neonates have a gigantic head (relative to the rest of the body), which flops around uncontrollably. They also possess reflexes that are dominated by evolutionary movements. In the span of 12 months, infants become capable of sitting anywhere, standing, stooping, climbing, and usually walking. During the second year, growth decelerates, but rapid increases in such activities as running and climbing take place. Let's now examine in greater detail the sequence of physical development in infancy.

Cephalocaudal and Proximodistal Patterns

The **cephalocaudal pattern** *is the sequence in which the greatest growth always occurs at the top—the head—with physical growth in size, weight, and feature differentiation gradually working its way down from top to bottom (for example, neck, shoulders, middle trunk, and so on).* This same pattern occurs in the head area, because the top parts of the head—the eyes and brain—grow faster than the lower parts, such as the jaw. An extraordinary proportion of the total body is occupied by the head during prenatal development and early infancy.

The **proximodistal pattern** *is the sequence in which growth starts at the center of the body and moves toward the extremities.* An example of this is the early maturation of muscular control of the trunk and arms, as compared with that of the hands and fingers.

Height and Weight

The average North American newborn is 20 inches long and weighs 7½ pounds. Ninety-five percent of full-term newborns are 18 to 22 inches long and weigh between 5½ and 10 pounds.

In the first several days of life, most newborns lose 5 to 7 percent of their body weight before they learn to adjust to neonatal feeding. Once infants adjust to sucking, swallowing, and digesting, they grow rapidly, gaining an average of 5 to 6 ounces per week during the first month. They have doubled their birthweight by the age of 4 months and have nearly tripled it by their first birthday. Infants grow about 1 inch per month during the first year, reaching approximately 1½ times their birth length by their first birthday.

Infants' rate of growth is considerably slower in the second year of life. By 2 years of age, infants weigh approximately 26 to 32 pounds, having gained a quarter to half a pound per month during the second year; now they have reached about one-fifth of their adult weight. At 2 years of age, the average infant is 32 to 35 inches in height, which is nearly one-half of their adult height.

The Brain

As an infant walks, talks, runs, shakes a rattle, smiles, and frowns, changes in its brain are occurring. Consider that the infant began life as a single cell and nine months later was born with a brain and nervous system that contained approximately 100 billion nerve cells, or neurons. A **neuron** *is a nerve cell that handles information processing at the cellular level* (see figure 6.1). Indeed, at birth the infant probably has all of the neurons it will ever have.

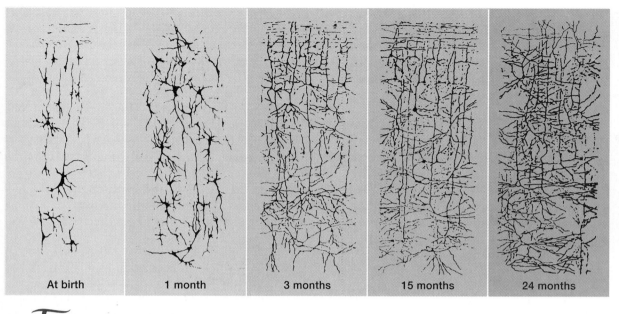

| At birth | 1 month | 3 months | 15 months | 24 months |

*F*igure 6.2
The Development of Dendritic Spreading

Note the increase in connectedness between neurons over the course of the first two years of life.

The Brain's Development   As the human embryo develops inside the womb, the central nervous system begins as a long, hollow tube on the embryo's back. About three weeks after conception, the brain forms into a large mass of neurons and loses its tubular appearance.

Scientists have identified three processes in the development of neurons: cell production, cell migration, and cell elaboration. Most neurons are produced between 10 and 26 weeks after conception. Amazingly, that means cells are generated at about 250,000 per minute in the human brain during this period. The second stage of neuron development involves cell migration, which occurs when cells move from the center of the brain, where neurons are produced, to their appropriate locations. Migration of neurons is completed 7 months after conception. The third stage of neuron development involves cell elaboration, which begins after cell migration. During cell migration, axons (the part of the neuron that carries information away from the cell to other neurons) and dendrites (the part of the neuron that collects information and routes it to the center of the cell) grow and form connections with other cells. Cell elaboration continues for years after birth and even has been documented in very old adults. As portrayed in figure 6.2, dendritic spreading in infancy is dramatic.

A myelin sheath, which is a layer of fat cells, encases most axons (review figure 6.1). Not only does the myelin sheath insulate nerve cells, but it also helps nerve impulses travel faster. Myelination, the process of encasing axons with fat cells, begins prenatally and continues after birth. Myelination for visual pathways occurs rapidly after birth, being completed in the first 6 months. Auditory myelination is not completed until 4–5 years of age. Some aspects of myelination continue even into adolescence.

At birth, the newborn's brain is about 25 percent of its adult weight. By the second birthday, the brain is about 75 percent of its adult weight. However, the brain's areas do not mature uniformly. Some areas, such as the primary motor areas, develop earlier than others, such as the primary sensory areas.

proximodistal pattern
The sequence in which growth starts at the center of the body and moves toward the extremities.

neuron
A nerve cell that handles information processing at the cellular level.

Neural Processes

Development of the Brain

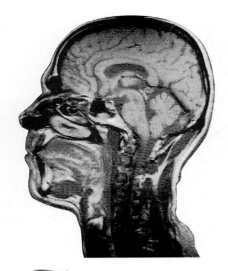

Figure 6.3
Cerebral Cortex

The cerebral cortex is located in the forebrain, the highest level of the brain. The cerebral cortex plays critical roles in important human functions, such as perception, thinking, and language.

cerebral cortex
Located in the forebrain, the structure that makes up about 80 percent of the brain's volume. It plays critical roles in perception, language, thinking, and many other important functions.

frontal lobe
In the cerebral cortex, the structure that is involved in voluntary movement and thinking.

occipital lobe
In the cerebral cortex, the structure that is involved in vision.

temporal lobe
In the cerebral cortex, the structure that is involved in hearing.

parietal lobe
In the cerebral cortex, the structure that is involved in bodily sensations, such as touch.

lateralization
Specialization in the brain's hemispheres. For example, speech and grammar are localized to the left hemisphere in most people.

The Brain's Lobes and Hemispheres   The forebrain is the highest level of the brain. It consists of a number of structures, including the **cerebral cortex,** *which makes up about 80 percent of the brain's volume and covers the lower portions of the brain like a cap. The cerebral cortex plays critical roles in many important human functions, such as perception, language, and thinking.* Figure 6.3 shows an image of the cerebral cortex.

The cerebral cortex is divided into four main areas called lobes: the **frontal lobe** *is involved in voluntary movement and thinking.* The **occipital lobe** *is involved in vision.* The **temporal lobe** *is involved in hearing.* The **parietal lobe** *is involved in processing information about body sensations, such as touch.* Figure 6.4 shows the locations of the four lobes in the brain.

The frontal lobes of the cerebral cortex are immature in the newborn. However, as neurons in the frontal lobes become myelinated and interconnected during the first year of life, infants develop an ability to regulate their physiological states (such as sleep) and gain more control over their reflexes. Cognitive skills that require deliberate thinking don't emerge until later (Bell & Fox, 1992). Indeed, the frontal lobes have the most prolonged development of any region in the human brain, with changes detectable at least into the adolescent years (Johnson, 1998).

The cerebral cortex is divided into two halves, or hemispheres (see figure 6.5). The term **lateralization** *is used to describe specialization in the brain's hemispheres.* There continues to be considerable interest in the degree to which each is involved in various aspects of thinking, feeling, and behavior.

The most extensive research on the brain's hemispheres involves language. At birth, the hemispheres already have started to specialize, with newborns showing greater electrical brain activity in the left hemisphere than the right hemisphere

Brandi Binder is evidence of the brain's hemispheric flexibility and resilience. Despite having had the right side of her cortex removed because of a severe case of epilepsy, Brandi engages in many activities often portrayed as only "right-brain" activities. She loves music, math, and art and is shown here working on one of her paintings.

when they are listening to speech sounds (Hahn, 1987). A common misconception is that virtually all language processing is carried out in the left hemisphere. Speech and grammar are localized to the left hemisphere in most people; however, the understanding of such aspects of language as appropriate language use in different contexts and the use of metaphor and humor involves the right hemisphere. Thus, language in general does not occur exclusively in the brain's left hemisphere (Johnson, 1998).

In the media and public, the left hemisphere has been described as the exclusive location of logical thinking and the right hemisphere the exclusive location of creative thinking. However, most neuroscientists point out that complex functions, such as reading, performing music, and creating art, involve both hemispheres. They believe labeling people as "left-brained" because they are logical thinkers and "right-brained" because they are creative thinkers does not correspond to the way the brain's hemispheres actually work. Such complex thinking in normal people is the outcome of communication between both sides of the brain.

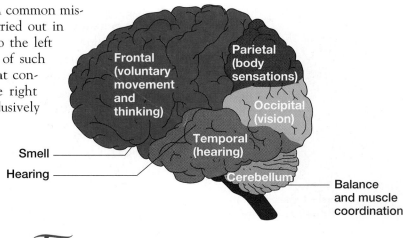

Figure 6.4
The Brain's Four Lobes

Shown here are the locations of the brain's four lobes: frontal, occipital, temporal, and parietal.

Early Experience and the Brain Until the middle of the twentieth century, scientists believed that the brain's development is determined by biological, hereditary factors. Researcher Mark Rosenzweig (1969) was curious about whether early experiences change the brain's development. He conducted a number of experiments with rats and other animals to investigate this possibility. Animals were randomly assigned to grow up in different environments. Animals in an enriched early environment lived in cages with stimulating features, such as wheels to rotate, steps to climb, levers to press, and toys to manipulate. In contrast, other animals had the early experience of growing up in standard cages or in barren, isolated conditions.

The results were stunning. The brains of the animals growing up in the enriched environment developed better than the brains of the animals reared in standard or isolated conditions. The brains of the "enriched" animals weighed more, had thicker layers, had more neuronal connections, and had higher levels of neurochemical activity.

Similar findings occurred when older animals were reared in vastly different environments, although the results were not as strong as for the younger animals. Such results give hope that enriching the lives of infants and young children who live in impoverished environments can produce positive changes in their development.

Scientists also now know that, starting shortly after birth, a baby's brain produces trillions more connections between neurons than it can possibly use. The brain eliminates connections that are seldom or never used. This pruning of brain connections continues at least until about 10 years of age.

The profusion of connections provides the growing brain with flexibility and resilience. Consider 13-year-old Brandi Binder, who developed such a severe case of epilepsy that surgeons at UCLA had to remove the right side of her cortex when she was 6. Binder lost virtually all the control she had established over muscles on the left side of her body, the side controlled by the right side of her brain, yet today, after years of therapy, ranging from leg lifts to math and music training, Binder is an A student. She loves music, math, and art—skills usually linked with the right side of the brain. Her recuperation is not 100 percent—for example, she never has regained the use of her left arm—however, her recovery is remarkable and shows that, if there is a way to compensate, the developing brain will find it.

Neuroscientists believe that what wires the brain—or rewires it, in the case of Brandi Binder—is repeated experience (Nash, 1997). Each time a baby tries to touch an attractive object or gazes intently at a face, tiny bursts of electricity shoot

Early Development of the Brain

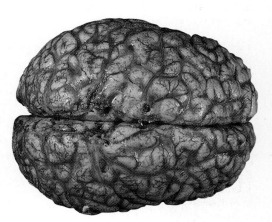

Figure 6.5
The Human Brain's Hemispheres

The two halves (hemispheres) of the human brain are clearly seen in this photograph.

through the brain, knitting together neurons into circuits. The results are some of the behavioral milestones we discuss in this and other chapters. For example, at about 2 months of age, the motor-control centers of the brain develop to the point at which infants can suddenly reach out and grab a nearby object. At about 4 months, the neural connections necessary for depth perception begin to take form. And, at about 12 months, the brain's speech centers are poised to produce one of infancy's magical moments: when the infant utters its first word.

Conclusions   In sum, neural connections are formed early in life (Johnson, 1999). The infant's brain literally is waiting for experiences to determine how connections are made. Before birth, it appears that genes mainly direct how the brain establishes basic wiring patterns. Neurons grow and travel to distinct places, waiting further instructions. After birth, environmental experiences are crucial to the brain's development (Greenough, 1999). The inflowing stream of sights, sounds, smells, touches, language, and eye contact helps the brain's connections take shape (Kuhl, 1997; Thelen, 1997).

Infant States

Not only do developmentalists chart infants' height and weight patterns, but they also examine the infants states, or states of consciousness, the levels of awareness that characterize individuals. One classification scheme describes eight infant states (Thoman & others, 1981):

1. *No* **REM (rapid eye movement) sleep,** *a recurring sleep stage during which vivid dreams commonly occur.* The infant's eyes are closed and still, and there is no motor activity other than occasional startle, rhythmic mouthing, or slight limb movement.
2. *Active sleep without REM.* The infant's eyes are closed and still; motor activity is present.
3. *REM sleep.* The infant's eyes are closed, although they may open briefly. Rapid eye movements can be detected through closed eyelids, and motor activity may or may not be present.
4. *Indeterminate sleep.* This category is reserved for all transitional states that cannot fit the above codes.
5. *Drowsy.* The infant's eyes may be opening and closing but have a dull, glazed appearance. Motor activity is minimal.
6. *Inactive alert.* The infant is relatively inactive, although there may be occasional limb movements. The eyes are wide open and bright and shiny.
7. *Active awake.* The infant's eyes are open, and there is motor activity.
8. *Crying.* The infant's eyes can be open or closed, and motor activity is present. Agitated vocalizations are also present.

Using classification schemes such as the one just described, researchers have identified many aspects of infant development. One such aspect is the sleeping-waking cycle (Henderson & France, 1999; Ingersoll & Thoman, 1999). When we were infants, sleep consumed more of our time than it does now. Newborns sleep 16 to 17 hours a day, although some sleep more and others less. The range is from a low of about 10 hours to a high of about 21 hours, although the longest period of sleep is not always between 11 P.M. and 7 A.M. Although total sleep remains somewhat consistent for young infants, their sleep during the day does not always follow a rhythmic pattern. An infant might change from sleeping several long bouts of 7 or 8 hours to three or four shorter sessions only several hours in duration. By about 1 month of age, most infants have begun to sleep longer at night, and, by about 4 months of age, they usually have moved closer to adultlike sleep patterns, spending their longest span of sleep at night and their longest span of waking during the day.

Researchers are intrigued by the various forms of infant sleep. They are especially interested in REM sleep. Most adults spend about one-fifth of their night in REM sleep, and REM sleep usually appears about 1 hour after non-REM sleep.

Early Experience and Brain Development

REM (rapid eye movement) sleep
A recurring sleep stage during which vivid dreams commonly occur.

*S*leep that knits up the ravelled sleave of care. . . .
Balm of hurt minds, nature's second course. Chief nourisher in life's feast.

William Shakespeare
English Playwright, 17th Century

However, about one-half of an infant's sleep is REM sleep, and infants often begin their sleep cycle with REM sleep rather than non-REM sleep. By the time infants reach 3 months of age, the percentage of time they spend in REM sleep falls to about 40 percent, and no longer does REM sleep begin their sleep cycle. The large amount of REM sleep may provide infants with added self-stimulation, since they spend less time awake than do older children. REM sleep also may promote the brain's development.

Of special concern is **sudden infant death syndrome (SIDS),** *a condition that occurs when an infant stops breathing, usually during the night, and suddenly dies without apparent cause.* SIDS is the leading cause of neonatal and infant death in the United States (Hunt, 1999; Lucey, 1999). Approximately 13 percent of all infant deaths are due to SIDS. It occurs in 1 to 2 of every 1,000 live births. It has not been determined whether the primary cause of death in SIDS is respiratory or cardiac failure (National Commission on Sleep Disorders Research, 1993).

Risk of SIDS is highest at 10–12 weeks of age. Unfortunately, at present there is no definitive way to predict the onset of the disorder. However, some infants are at particular risk (Maas, 1998):

* Low-birthweight infants are 5 to 10 times more likely to die of SIDS than are their normal-weight counterparts.
* Twins and triplets, even at normal birthweight, are twice as likely to die of SIDS; after one twin dies, the surviving twin also has an increased risk of dying from SIDS.
* Infants whose siblings have died of SIDS are two to four times as likely to die of it.
* Six percent of infants with sleep apnea, a temporary cessation of breathing in which the airway is completely blocked, usually 10 seconds or longer, die of SIDS.
* African American and Eskimo infants are four to six times as likely as all others to die of SIDS.
* SIDS is more common in lower socioeconomic groups.
* SIDS is more common in infants who are passively exposed to cigarette smoke (Klonoff-Cohen & others, 1995).

It is advisable that an infant be placed on its back, not on its side or stomach. This will make it less likely that its breathing will be obstructed.

Nutrition

Four-month-old Robert lives in Bloomington, Indiana, with his middle-class parents. He is well nourished and healthy. By contrast, 4-month-old Nikita lives in Ethiopia. Nikita and his parents live in impoverished conditions. Nikita is so poorly nourished that he has become emaciated and lies near death. The lives of Robert and Nikita reveal the vast diversity in nutritional status among today's children. Our coverage of infant nutrition begins with information about nutritional needs and eating behavior, then turns to the issue of breast- versus bottle-feeding, and concludes with an overview of malnutrition.

Nutritional Needs and Eating Behavior The importance of adequate energy and nutrient intake consumed in a loving and supportive environment during the infant years cannot be overstated (Yip, 1995). From birth to 1 year of age, human infants triple their weight and increase their length by 50 percent. Individual differences among infants in terms of their nutrient reserves, body composition, growth rates, and activity patterns make defining actual nutrient needs difficult. However, because parents need guidelines, nutritionists recommend that infants consume approximately 50 calories per day for each pound they weigh—more than twice an adult's requirement per pound.

SIDS

sudden infant death syndrome (SIDS)
A condition that occurs when an infant stops breathing, usually during the night, and suddenly dies without apparent cause.

Feeding Infants

Parents often want to know when to introduce new types of food. In the second half of the first year, human milk or formula continues to be the infant's primary nutritional source. The major change in feeding habits is the addition of solid foods to the infant's diet. The one generally accepted rule is to introduce infant cereal as the first food because of its high iron content. Because of its benefit as a source of iron, infant cereal should be continued until the infant is about 18 months of age. The addition of other foods is arbitrary. A common sequence is strained fruits, followed by vegetables and finally meats. At 6 months, foods such as cracker or zwieback can be offered as a type of finger and teething food.

Weaning—the process of giving up one method of feeding for another—usually refers to relinquishing the breast or bottle for a cup. In Western cultures, this is often regarded as an important task for infants, being psychologically significant because the infant has to give up a major source of oral pleasure. There is no one time for weaning that is best for every infant, but most infants show signs of being ready for weaning in the second half of the first year. Weaning should be gradual, by replacing one bottle- or breast-feeding at a time.

Some years ago, controversy surrounded the issue of whether a baby should be fed on demand or on a regular schedule. Famous behaviorist John Watson (1928) argued that scheduled feeding is superior because it increases the child's orderliness. An example of a recommended schedule for newborns is 4 ounces of formula every six hours. In recent years, demand feeding—in which the timing and amount of feeding are determined by the infant—has become more popular.

In the 1990s, we have become extremely nutrition-conscious. Does the same type of nutrition that makes us healthy adults also make young infants healthy? Some affluent, well-educated parents almost starve their babies by feeding them the low-fat, low-calorie diet they eat themselves. Diets designed for adult weight loss and prevention of heart disease may actually retard growth and development in babies. Fat is very important for babies. Nature's food—breast milk—is not low in fat or calories. No child under the age of 2 should be consuming skim milk.

In one investigation, seven cases were documented in which babies 7 to 22 months of age were unwittingly undernourished by their health-conscious parents (Lifshitz & others, 1987). In some instances, the parents had been fat themselves and were determined that their child was not going to be. The well-meaning parents substituted vegetables, skim milk, and other low-fat foods for what they called junk food. However, for infants, broccoli is not always a good substitute for a cookie. For growing infants, high-calorie, high-energy foods are part of a balanced diet.

Breast-Feeding

Breast- Versus Bottle-Feeding   Human milk, or an alternative formula, is the baby's source of nutrients and energy for the first four to six months. For years, developmentalists and nutritionists have debated whether breast-feeding an infant has substantial benefits over bottle-feeding. The growing consensus is that breast-feeding is better for the baby's health (Eiger, 1992; Bier & others, 1999). Breast-feeding provides milk that is clean and digestible and helps immunize the newborn from disease (Newman, 1995; Slusser & Powers, 1997). Breast-fed babies gain weight more rapidly than do bottle-fed babies. However, only about one-half of mothers nurse newborns, and even fewer continue to nurse their infants after several months. Mothers who work outside the home find it impossible to breast-feed their young infants for many months. Even though breast-feeding provides more ideal nutrition, some researchers argue that there is no long-term evidence of physiological or psychological harm to American infants when they are bottle-fed (Ferguson, Harwood, & Shannon, 1987). Despite these researchers' claims that no long-term negative consequences of bottle-feeding have been documented in American children, the American Academy of Pediatrics, the majority of physicians and nurses, and two leading publications for parents—the *Infant Care Manual* and *Parents* magazine—endorse breast-feeding as having physiological and psychological benefits (Young, 1990).

There is a consensus among experts that breast-feeding is the preferred practice, especially in developing countries where inadequate nutrition and poverty are common. In 1991, the Institute of Medicine, part of the National Academy of Sciences, issued a report that women should be encouraged to breast-feed their infants exclusively for the first four to six months of life. According to the report, the benefits of breast-feeding are protection against some gastrointestinal infections and food allergies for infants and possible reduction of osteoporosis and breast cancer for mothers. Nonetheless, while the majority of experts recommend breast-feeding, the issue of breast- versus bottle-feeding continues to be hotly debated. Many parents, especially working mothers, now follow a sequence of breast-feeding in the first several months and bottle-feeding thereafter. This strategy allows the mother's natural milk to provide nutritional benefits to the infant early in development and permits mothers to return to work after several months. Working mothers are also increasingly using "pumping," in which they use a pump to extract breast milk that can be stored for later feeding of the infant when the mother is not present.

Malnutrition in Infancy **Marasmus** *is a wasting away of body tissues in the infant's first year, caused by severe protein-calorie deficiency.* The infant becomes grossly underweight, and its muscles atrophy. The main cause of marasmus is early weaning from breast milk to inadequate nutrients, such as unsuitable and unsanitary cow's milk formula. Something that looks like milk but is not, usually a form of tapioca or rice, also might be used. In many of the world's developing countries, mothers used to breast-feed their infants for at least two years. To become more modern, they stopped breast-feeding much earlier and replaced it with bottle-feeding. Comparisons of breast-fed and bottle-fed infants in such countries as Afghanistan, Haiti, Ghana, and Chile document that the death rate of bottle-fed infants is up to five times greater than that of breast-fed infants (Grant, 1997).

Human milk, or an alternative formula, is a baby's source of nutrients for the first four to six months. The growing consensus is that breast-feeding is better for the baby's health, although controversy still swirls about the issue of breast- versus bottle-feeding.

marasmus
A wasting away of body tissues in the infant's first year, caused by severe deficiency of protein and calories.

Even if not fatal, severe and lengthy malnutrition is detrimental to physical, cognitive, and social development (Mortimer, 1992). In some cases, even moderate malnutrition can produce subtle difficulties in development. In one investigation, two groups of extremely malnourished 1-year-old South African infants were studied (Bayley, 1970). The children in one group were given adequate nourishment during the next six years; no intervention took place in the lives of the other group. After the seventh year, the poorly nourished group of children performed much worse on tests of intelligence than did the adequately nourished group. In yet another investigation, the diets of rural Guatemalan infants were associated with their social development at the time they entered elementary school (Barrett, Radke-Yarrow, & Klein, 1982). Children whose mothers had been given nutritious supplements during pregnancy and who themselves had been given more nutritious, high-calorie foods in their first two years of life were more active, more involved, more helpful with their peers, less anxious, and happier than their counterparts, who had not been given nutritional supplements. The undernourished Guatemalan infants were only mildly undernourished in infancy, suggesting how important it is for parents to be attentive to the nutritional needs of their infants.

Malnutrition in Infancy

In recent research on early supplementary feeding and children's cognitive development, Ernesto Pollitt and his colleagues (1993) conducted a longitudinal investigation over two decades in rural Guatemala. They found that early nutritional supplements in the form of protein and increased calories can have positive long-term effects on cognitive development. The researchers also found that the relation of nutrition to cognitive performance is moderated both by the time period during which the supplement is given and by the sociodemographic context. For example, the children in the lowest socioeconomic groups benefited more than did the children in higher socioeconomic groups. Although there still was a positive nutritional influence when supplementation began after 2 years of age, the effect on cognitive development was less powerful.

Toilet Training

Toilet Training

In the North American culture, being toilet trained is a physical and motor skill that is expected to be attained by 3 years of age (Charlesworth, 1987). By the age of 3, 84 percent of children are dry throughout the day, and 66 percent are dry throughout the night. The ability to control elimination depends on both muscular maturation and motivation. Children must be able to control their muscles to eliminate at the appropriate time, and they must want to eliminate in the toilet or potty, rather than in their pants.

In actuality, there are no data on the optimal time of toilet training, but developmentalists argue that, when it is initiated, it should be accomplished in a warm, relaxed, supportive manner. Many of today's parents begin toilet training of their infants at about 20 months to 2 years of age.

One argument being made today against late toilet training is that the "terrible twos" may be encountered. The 2-year-old's strong push for autonomy may lead to battles with parents trying to toilet train the 2-year-old. Late toilet training can become such a battleground that it extends to 4 to 5 years of age. Another argument against late toilet training is that many toddlers go to day care, and a child in diapers or training pants can be stigmatized by peers.

Immunization

Age	Immunization
2 months	Diphtheria Polio Influenza
4 months	Diphtheria Polio Influenza
6 months	Diphtheria Influenza
1 year	TB test
15 months	Measles Mumps Rubella Influenza
18 months	Diphtheria Polio
4–6 years	Diphtheria Polio
11–12 years	Measles Mumps Rubella
14–16 years	Tetanus-diphtheria

*F*igure 6.6
Recommended Immunization Schedule of Normal Infants and Children

Immunization

One of the most dramatic advances in infant health has been the decline of infectious diseases over the past four decades because of widespread immunization for preventable diseases. Though many presently available immunizations can be given to individuals of any age, the recommended schedule is to begin in infancy (Rodewald & others, 1999). The recommended age for various immunizations is shown in figure 6.6.

We have been discussing many aspects of the infant's physical development and health. It is very important for infants to get off to a healthy start in life. To read about one program that helps provide the support needed by high-risk families, see the box Caring for Children.

Accident Prevention

Accidents are a major cause of death in infancy, especially in the age range of 6 to 12 months. Infants need to be closely monitored as they gain increased locomotor and manipulative skills, along with a strong curiosity to explore the environment. Among the most common accidents in infancy are the aspiration of foreign objects, suffocation, falls, poisoning, burns, motor vehicle accidents, and bodily damage. Asphyxiation by foreign material in the respiratory tract is the leading cause of fatal injury in infants under 1 year of age. Toys need to be carefully inspected for potential danger. An active infant can grab a low-hanging mobile and rapidly chew off a piece. Balloons, whether partially inflated, uninflated, or popped, cause more infant deaths than any other kind of small object and should be kept away from infants and young children.

Caring for Children
A Healthy Start

The Hawaii Family Support/Healthy Start Program began in 1985 (Allen, Brown, & Finlay, 1992). It was designed by the Hawaii Family Stress Center in Honolulu, which already had been using home-visitor services to improve family functioning and reduce child abuse for more than a decade. Participation is voluntary. Families of newborns are screened for family risk factors, including unstable housing, histories of substance abuse, depression, parents' abuse as a child, late or no prenatal care, fewer than 12 years of schooling, poverty, and unemployment. Early identification workers screen and interview new mothers in the hospital. They also screen families referred by physicians, nurses, and others. Because the demand for services outstrips available resources, only families with a substantial number of risk factors can participate.

Each new participating family receives a weekly visit from a family support worker. Each of the program's eight home visitors works with approximately 25 families at a time. The worker helps the family cope with any immediate crises, such as un-

The Hawaii Family Support/Healthy Start Program provides overburdened families of newborns and young children many home-visitor services. This program has been very successful in reducing abuse and neglect in families.

employment or substance abuse. The family also is linked directly with a pediatrician to ensure that the children receive regular health care. Infants are screened for developmental delays and are immunized on schedule. Pediatricians have been educated about the program. They are notified when a child is enrolled in Healthy Start and when a family at risk stops participating.

The Family Support/Healthy Start Program recently hired a child development specialist to work with families of children with special needs. And, in some instances, the program's male family support worker also visits a father to talk specifically about his role in the family. The support workers encourage parents to participate in group activities held each week at the program center located in a neighborhood shopping center.

Over time, parents are encouraged to assume more responsibility for their family's health and well-being. Families can participate in Healthy Start until the child is 5 and enters public school.

Suffocation can cause infant deaths. Infants get caught under sheets or blankets, caregivers roll over and smother the infant when they sleep together, large plastic bags become wrapped around the infant's head, strings on toys become wrapped around the infant's neck, the infant strangles if its head gets caught between the crib slats and mattress or an object close to the crib, or the infant drowns when left unsupervised in a bathtub or near a source of water, such as a swimming pool, toilet, or bucket.

Falls are most common after 4 months of age, when the infant has learned to roll over, although they can occur at any age. The best advice is to never leave an infant unattended on a raised surface that has no guardrails. Changing tables, infant seats, high chairs, walkers, and swings are other locations of accidental falls.

Accidental poisoning is also one of the main causes of death in children under the age of 5. The highest incidence occurs in the 2-year-old age group, with the second highest incidence in the 1-year-old group. Once locomotion begins, danger from poisoning is present almost everywhere in the infant's environment. There are more than 500 toxic substances in the average home, and about one-third of all infant poisonings occur in the kitchen.

Injury Prevention

Burns are often not perceived to be a particular danger to infants, but several hazards exist, such as scalding from water that is too hot, excessive sunburn, and burns from electrical wires, sockets, and floor furnaces. One of the best burn safety devices is a smoke detector; parents are advised to have at least one in their homes.

Automobile accidents are the leading cause of accidental deaths in children over 1 year of age. The major danger for the infant is improper restraint within the motor vehicle. All infants, newborns included, should be secured in special car restraints, rather than being held or placed on the car seat.

Accidents can also cause bodily damage to infants in other ways. For example, sharp, jagged objects can cause skin wounds and long, pointed objects can be poked in the eye. Thus, a fork should not be given for self-feeding until the child has mastered the spoon, which usually happens by 18 months of age. Another often unrecognized danger to infants is attacks by young siblings and pets, especially dogs and cats.

MOTOR DEVELOPMENT

The study of motor development has seen a renaissance in the past decade. New insights are being made into the ways in which infants acquire motor skills. We will begin our exploration of motor development by examining reflexes and rhythmic movements, then turn our attention to gross and fine motor skills. To conclude, we will cover the fascinating field of developmental biodynamics, which is responsible for the awakened interest in the ways in which infants acquire motor skills.

Reflexes

The newborn is not an empty-headed organism. Among other things, it has some basic reflexes, which are genetically carried survival mechanisms. For example, the newborn has no fear of water, naturally holding its breath and contracting its throat to keep water out. Reflexes may serve as important building blocks for subsequent purposeful motor activity.

Reflexes govern the newborn's movements, which are automatic and beyond the newborn's control. They are built-in reactions to stimuli. In these reflexes, infants have adaptive responses to their environment before they have had the opportunity to learn. The **sucking reflex** *occurs when newborns automatically suck an object placed in their mouth. The sucking reflex enables newborns to get nourishment before they have associated a nipple with food.* The sucking reflex is an example of a reflex that is present at birth but later disappears. The **rooting reflex** *occurs when the infant's cheek is stroked or the side of the mouth is touched. In response, the infant turns its head toward the side that was touched in an apparent effort to find something to suck.* The sucking and rooting reflexes disappear when the infant is 3 to 4 months old. They are replaced by the infant's voluntary eating. The sucking and rooting reflexes have survival value for newborn mammals, who must find the mother's breast to obtain nourishment.

The **Moro reflex** *is a neonatal startle response that occurs in response to a sudden, intense noise or movement. When startled, the newborn arches its back, throws back its head, and flings out its arms and legs. Then the newborn rapidly closes its arms and legs to the center of its body.* The Moro reflex is a vestige from our primate ancestry, and it also has survival value. This reflex, which is normal in all newborns, also tends to disappear at 3 to 4 months of age. Steady pressure on any part of the infant's body calms the infant after it has been startled. Holding the infant's arm flexed at the shoulder will quiet the infant.

Some reflexes present in the newborn—coughing, blinking, and yawning, for example—persist throughout life. They are as important for the adult as they are for the infant. Other reflexes, though, disappear several months following birth, as the infant's brain functions mature, and voluntary control over many behaviors develops. The movements of some reflexes eventually become incorporated into

The experiences of the first three years of life are almost entirely lost to us, and when we attempt to enter into a small child's world, we come as foreigners who have forgotten the landscape and no longer speak the native tongue.

Selma Fraiberg
Developmentalist and Child Advocate, 20th Century

sucking reflex
A newborn's built-in reaction of automatically sucking an object placed in its mouth. The sucking reflex enables the infant to get nourishment before it has associated a nipple with food.

rooting reflex
The newborn's built-in reaction that occurs when the infant's cheek is stroked or the side of its mouth is touched. In response, the infant turns its head toward the side that was touched, in an apparent effort to find something to suck.

Moro reflex
A neonatal startle response that occurs in reaction to a sudden, intense noise or movement. When startled, the newborn arches its back, throws back its head, and flings out its arms and legs. Then the newborn rapidly closes its arms and legs to the center of its body.

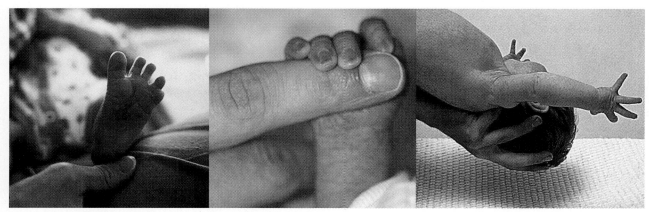

Babinski reflex	Grasping reflex	Moro reflex

Reflex	Stimulation	Infant's response	Developmental pattern
Blinking	Flash of light, puff of air	Closes both eyes	Permanent
Babinski	Sole of foot stroked	Fans out toes, twists foot in	Disappears after nine months to one year
Grasping	Palms touched	Grasps tightly	Weakens after three months, disappears after one year
Moro (startle)	Sudden stimulation, such as hearing loud noise or being dropped	Startles, arches back, throws head back, flings out arms and legs and then rapidly closes them to center of body	Disappears after three to four months
Rooting	Cheek stroked or side of mouth touched	Turns head, opens mouth, begins sucking	Disappears after three to four months
Stepping	Infant held above surface and feet lowered to touch surface	Moves feet as if to walk	Disappears after three to four months
Sucking	Object touching mouth	Sucks automatically	Disappears after three to four months
Swimming	Infant put face down in water	Makes coordinated swimming movements	Disappears after six to seven months
Tonic neck	Infant placed on back	Forms fists with both hands and usually turns head to the right (sometimes called the "fencer's pose" because the infant looks like it is assuming a fencer's position)	Disappears after two months

Figure 6.7
Infant Reflexes

more complex, voluntary actions. One important example is the **grasping reflex,** *which occurs when something touches the infant's palms. The infant responds by grasping tightly.* By the end of the third month, the grasping reflex diminishes, and the infant shows a more voluntary grasp, which is often produced by visual stimuli. For example, when an infant sees a mobile whirling above its crib, it may reach out and try to grasp it. As its motor development becomes smoother, the infant will grasp objects, carefully manipulate them, and explore their qualities.

An overview of the main reflexes we have discussed, along with others, is given in figure 6.7.

grasping reflex
A neonatal reflex that occurs when something touches the infant's palms. The infant responds by grasping tightly.

Sucking is an especially important reflex: it is the infant's route to nourishment. The sucking capabilities of newborns vary considerably. Some newborns are efficient at forceful sucking and obtaining milk; others are not as adept and get tired before they are full. Most newborns take several weeks to establish a sucking style that is coordinated with the way the mother is holding the infant, the way milk is coming out of the bottle or breast, and the infant's sucking speed and temperament.

A study by pediatrician T. Berry Brazelton (1956) involved observations of infants for more than a year to determine the incidence of their sucking when they were nursing and how their sucking changed as they grew older. Over 85 percent of the infants engaged in considerable sucking behavior unrelated to feeding. They sucked their fingers, their fists, and pacifiers. By the age of 1 year, most had stopped the sucking behavior.

Parents should not worry when infants suck their thumbs, fist, or even a pacifier. Many parents, though, do begin to worry when thumb sucking persists into the preschool and elementary school years. As much as 40 percent of children continue to suck their thumbs after they have started school (Kessen, Haith, & Salapatek, 1970). Most developmentalists do not attach a great deal of significance to this behavior and are not aware of parenting strategies that might contribute to it. Individual differences in children's biological makeup may be involved to some degree in the continuation of sucking behavior.

Gross and Fine Motor Skills

Gross motor skills *involve large muscle activities, such as moving one's arms and walking.* **Fine motor skills** *involve more finely tuned movements, such as finger dexterity.* Let's examine the changes in gross and fine motor skills in the first two years of life.

Gross Motor Skills   Ask any parents about their baby, and sooner or later you are likely to hear about one or more motor milestones, such as "Sallie just learned to crawl," "Jesse is finally sitting alone," or "Angela took her first step last week." It is no wonder that parents proudly announce such milestones. New motor skills are the most dramatic and observable changes in the infant's first year of life. These motor progressions transform babies from being unable to even lift their heads to being able to grab things off the grocery store shelf, to chase the cat, and to participate actively in the family's social life (Thelen, 1995).

At birth, infants have no appreciable coordination of the chest or arms, but in the first month they can lift their head from a prone position. At about 3 months, infants can hold their chest up and use their arms for support after being in a prone position. At 3 to 4 months, infants can roll over, and at 4 to 5 months they can support some weight with their legs. At about 6 months, infants can sit without support, and by 7 to 8 months they can crawl and stand without support. At approximately 8 months, infants can pull themselves up to a standing position, at 10 to 11 months they can walk using furniture for support (this is called cruising), and at 12 to 13 months they can walk without assistance. A summary of the developmental accomplishments in gross motor skills during the first year is shown in figure 6.8. The actual month at which the milestones occur varies by as much as 2 to 4 months, especially among older infants. What remains fairly uniform, however, is the sequence of accomplishments. An important implication of these infant motor accomplishments is the increasing degree of independence they bring. Older infants can explore their environment more extensively and initiate social interaction with caregivers and peers more readily than when they were younger.

In the second year of life, toddlers become more motorically skilled and mobile. They are no longer content with being in a playpen and want to move all over the place. Child development experts believe that motor activity during the second year is vital to the child's competent development and that few restrictions, except for safety purposes, should be placed on their motoric adventures (Fraiberg, 1959).

---

gross motor skills
Motor skills that involve large muscle activities, such as walking.

fine motor skills
Motor skills that involve more finely tuned movements, such as finger dexterity.

Developmental Milestones

A baby is an angel whose wings decrease as his legs increase.

French Proverb

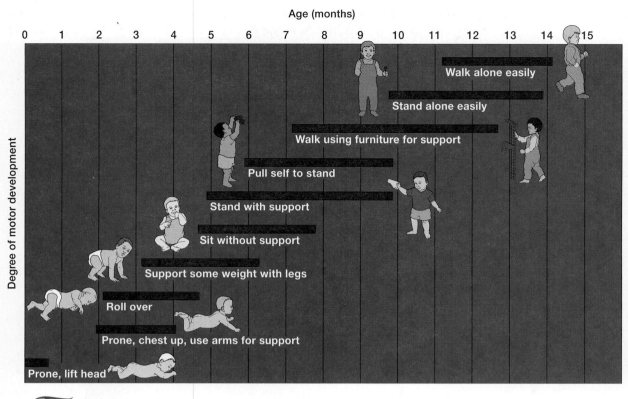

Figure 6.8
Milestones in Gross Motor Development

By 13 to 18 months, toddlers can pull a toy attached to a string, use their hands and legs to climb up a number of steps, and ride four-wheel wagons. By 18 to 24 months, toddlers can walk quickly or run stiffly for a short distance, balance on their feet in a squat position while playing with objects on the floor, walk backward without losing their balance, stand and kick a ball without falling, stand and throw a ball, and jump in place.

With the increased interest of today's adults in aerobic exercise and fitness, some parents have tried to give their infants a head start on becoming physically fit and physically talented. However, the American Academy of Pediatricians recently issued a statement that recommends against structured exercise classes for babies. Pediatricians are seeing more bone fractures and dislocations and more muscle strains in babies now than in the past. They point out that, when an adult is stretching and moving an infant's limbs, it is easy to go beyond the infant's physical limits without knowing it.

The physical fitness classes for infants range from passive fare—with adults putting infants through the paces—to programs called "aerobic" because they demand crawling, tumbling, and ball skills. However, exercise for infants is not aerobic. They cannot adequately stretch their bodies to achieve aerobic benefits.

Fine Motor Skills   Infants have hardly any control over fine motor skills at birth, although they have many components of what later become finely coordinated arm, hand, and finger movements (Rosenblith, 1992). The onset of reaching and grasping marks a significant achievement in infants' functional interactions with their surroundings. For many years it was believed that reaching for an object is visually guided—that is, the infant must continuously have sight of the hand and the target (White, Castle, & Held, 1964). However, in one study, Rachel Clifton and her colleagues (1993) demonstrated that infants do not have to see their own hands when

Birth to 6 months	
2 mo.	Holds rattle briefly
2 1/2 mo.	Glances from one object to another
3–4 mo.	Plays in simple way with rattle; inspects fingers; reaches for dangling ring; visually follows ball across table
4 mo.	Carries object to mouth
4–5 mo.	Recovers rattle from chest; holds two objects
5 mo.	Transfers object from hand to hand
5–6 mo.	Bangs in play; looks for object while sitting

6–12 months	
6 mo.	Secures cube on sight; follows adult's movements across room; immediately fixates on small objects and stretches out to grasp them; retains rattle
6 1/2 mo.	Manipulates and examines an object; reaches for, grabs, and retains rattle
7 mo.	Pulls string to obtain an object
7 1/2–8 1/2 mo.	Grasps with thumb and finger
8–9 mo.	Persists in reaching for toy out of reach on table; shows hand preference, bangs spoon; searches in correct place for toys dropped within reach of hands; may find toy hidden under cup
10 mo.	Hits cup with spoon; crude release of object
10 1/2–11 mo.	Picks up raisin with thumb and forefinger; pincer grasp; pushes car along
11–12 mo.	Puts three or more objects in a container

12–18 months	
	Places one 2-inch block on top of another 2-inch block (in imitation)
	Scribbles with a large crayon on large piece of paper
	Turns two to three pages in a large book with cardboard pages while sitting in an adult's lap
	Places three 1-inch cube blocks in a 6-inch diameter cup (in imitation)
	Holds a pencil and makes a mark on a sheet of paper
	Builds a four-block tower with 2-inch cube blocks (in imitation)

18–24 months	
	Draws an arc on piece of unlined paper with a pencil after being shown how
	Turns a doorknob that is within reach, using both hands
	Unscrews a lid put loosely on a small jar after being shown how
	Places large pegs in a pegboard
	Connects and takes apart a pop bead string of five beads
	Zips and unzips a large zipper after being shown how

Figure 6.9

The Development of Fine Motor Skills in Infancy

reaching for an object. They concluded that, because the infants could not see their hand or arm in the dark in the experiment, proprioceptive (muscle, tendon, joint sense) cues, not sight of the limb, guided the early reaching of the 4-month-old infants. The development of reaching and grasping becomes more refined during the first 2 years of life. Initially, infants show only crude shoulder and elbow movements, but later they show wrist movements, hand rotation, and coordination of the thumb and forefinger. The maturation of hand-eye coordination over the first 2 years of life is reflected in the improvement of fine motor skills. Figure 6.9 provides an overview of the development of fine motor skills in the first 2 years of life.

Developmental Biodynamics

Traditional views of motor development have chronicled the stagelike changes in posture and movement that characterize the first several years of life (Gesell, 1928; Shirley, 1933). In the past decade, advances in a number of domains have generated a new perspective on infant motor development. Rather than describing the ages at which various motor achievements are reached and explaining them as a result of brain and nervous-system maturation, the new perspective—**developmental biodynamics**—*seeks to explain how motor behaviors are assembled for perceiving and acting.* This perspective is an outgrowth of developments in the neurosciences, biomechanics, and the behavioral sciences (Lockman & Thelen, 1993). The research of Rachel Clifton and her colleagues (1993), which was described earlier, illustrates the developmental biodynamics view. They found that proprioceptive cues play an important role in early guided reaching. Their research shows *how* perception *and* action are linked in early manual skill development.

The developmental biodynamics view of infant motor development has especially been advanced by the theorizing and research of Esther Thelen (1995). Following are some of the main concepts in her developmental biodynamics perspective.

The new view of motor development emphasizes the importance of exploration and selection in finding solutions to new task demands. This means that infants need to assemble adaptive patterns by modifying their current movement patterns. The first step is to get the infant into the "ball park" of the task demands—a tentative crawl or several stumbling steps. Then, the infant has to "tune" these configurations to make them smoother and more effective. Such tuning is achieved through repeated cycles of action and perception of the consequences of that action in relation to the goal.

The developmental biodynamics view contrasts with the traditional maturational view by proposing that even the universal milestones, such as crawling, reaching, and walking, are learned through a process of adaptation. Infants modulate their movement patterns to fit a new task by exploring and selecting various possible configurations. The assumption is that the infant is motivated by the new challenge—a desire to get a new toy into one's mouth or to cross the room to join other family members. It is the new task, the challenge of the context, not prescribed genetic instructions that represents the driving force for change.

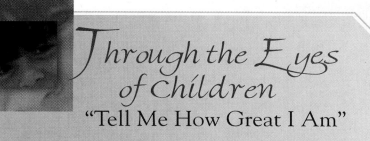

Through the Eyes of Children
"Tell Me How Great I Am"

T. Berry Brazelton, the well-known pediatrician, offers two blocks to an 8-month-old. Then he shows the baby how he wants her to put the two blocks together. Brazelton says that a baby who is hopeful about life will pick up one block, mouth it, rub it in her hair, then drop it over the side of the crib and watch whether you retrieve it for her. When you do, she completes the requested task by putting the two blocks together. Then she looks up at you with a bright-eyed look of expectancy that says, "Tell me how great I am" (Brazelton, 1992).

Brazelton says that babies like this little girl have gotten a good dose of approval and encouragement from their caregivers. Such babies expect to succeed in life's little challenges. By contrast, babies from homes that are bleak, chaotic, or neglectful go about the same task of putting the two blocks together in a way that signals they already expect to fail. Even when they bring the two blocks together, their demeanor often includes a drooped head that says, "I'm no good. See, I've failed." Brazelton believes that the two outlooks—one optimistic, the other pessimistic—begins to take shape in infancy (Goleman, 1995).

developmental biodynamics
The new perspective on motor development in infancy that seeks to explain how motor behaviors are assembled for perceiving and acting.

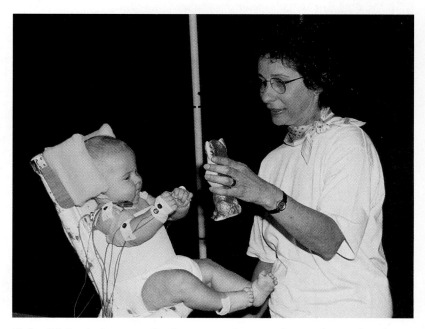

Esther Thelen is shown conducting an experiment to discover how infants learn to control their arms to reach and grasp for objects. A computer device is used to monitor the infants' arm movements and to track muscle patterns.

Improving Developmental Skills
Supporting the Infant's Physical and Motor Development

What are some good strategies for helping the infant develop in physically competent ways?

- *Be flexible about the infant's sleep patterns.* Don't try to put the infant on a rigid sleep schedule. By about 4 months of age, most infants have moved closer to adultlike sleep patterns.

- *Provide the infant with good nutrition.* Make sure the infant has adequate energy and nutrient intake. Provide this in a loving and supporting environment. Don't put an infant on a diet. Weaning should be gradual, not abrupt.

- *Breast-feed the infant, if possible.* Breast-feeding provides more ideal nutrition than bottle-feeding. If because of work demands the mother cannot breast-feed the infant, she should consider "pumping."

- *Toilet train the infant in a warm, relaxed, supportive manner.* Twenty months to 2 years of age is a recommended time to begin toilet training, so that it is accomplished before the "terrible twos." Like good strategies for the infant's sleep and nutrition, toilet training should not be done in a harsh, rigid way.

- *Give the infant extensive opportunities to explore safe environments.* Infants don't need exercise classes. What they should be provided are many opportunities to actively explore safe environments. Infants should not be constricted to small, confined environments for any length of time.

- *Don't push the infant's physical development or get up tight about physical norms.* In American culture, we tend to want our child to grow faster than other children. Remember that there is wide individual variation in normal physical development. Just because an infant is not at the top of a physical chart doesn't mean parents should start pushing the infant's physical skills. Infants develop at different paces. Respect and nurture the infant's individuality.

Consider the challenging task the infant faces when placed in a "Jolly Jumper" infant bouncer (see figure 6.10). The task for the infant is to first assemble the right movements to drive the spring and then to tune the spring to discover the "best bounce for the ounce." In one study involving the infant bouncer, infants began with only a few tentative bounces that varied considerably (Goldfield, Kay, & Warren, 1993). As weeks passed, they increased their bounces, but the variability of the bounces decreased. Studies such as those involving the infant bouncer are important because, rather than looking only for performance differences as a function of age, they emphasize discovering the processes involved in learning new motor skills.

At this point, we have discussed many ideas about physical and motor development. The insert, Improving Developmental Skills, profiles some positive strategies for supporting the infant's physical and motor development. Also, summary table 6.1 provides an overview of the ideas described so far in the chapter. A key theme in the developmental biodynamics view we just evaluated is that perception and action are coupled when new skills are learned. Let's now explore the nature of the infant's perceptual development.

Figure 6.10
Learning to Use an Infant Bouncer

Learning to use an infant bouncer is an excellent example of how the infant assembles the right movements over time to solve this challenging task.

Summary Table 6.1
Physical Growth, the Brain, and Motor Development

Concept	Processes/Related Ideas	Characteristics/Description
Physical growth and development in infancy	Cephalocaudal and proximodistal patterns	The cephalocaudal pattern is growth from the top down; the proximodistal pattern is growth from the center out.
	Height and weight	The average North American newborn is 20 inches long and weighs 7½ pounds. Infants grow about 1 inch per month during the first year and nearly triple their weight by their first birthday. Infants' rate of growth is slower in the second year.
	The brain	A neuron is a nerve cell that handles information processing at the cellular level. Three processes in the development of neurons are cell production, cell migration, and cell elaboration. Cell elaboration, as exemplified by dendritic spreading, continues for years after birth. Myelination insulates nerve cells and helps nerve impulses travel faster. At birth, the newborn's brain is about 25 percent of its adult weight; by the second birthday, it reaches 75 percent. The brains of animals growing up in enriched early environments develop better than those living in standard or isolated early environments. The forebrain is the highest level of the brain. One of its most important structures is the cerebral cortex, which has four lobes (frontal, occipital, temporal, and parietal), which are specialized for different functions, and two hemispheres (left, right). The frontal lobes are immature in newborns but show increasing maturity through the first several years and beyond. Lateralization is the term that describes the specialization of the brain's two hemispheres; it already has begun to occur in newborns. Speech and grammar are localized to the left hemisphere, but some aspects of language, such as context and humor, involve the right hemisphere. Neural connections are formed early in life. Before birth, genes mainly direct neurons to their locations. After birth, the inflowing stream of sights, sounds, smells, touches, language, and eye contact helps the brain's connections take shape.
	Infant states	Researchers have crafted different classification systems; one involves eight infant state categories, including deep sleep, drowsy, alert and focused, and inflexibly focused. Newborns usually sleep 16–17 hours a day. By 4 months, they approach adultlike sleeping patterns. REM sleep—during which dreaming occurs—occurs much more in early infancy than in childhood and adulthood. Sudden infant death syndrome (SIDS) is a condition that occurs when an infant stops breathing and suddenly dies without an apparent cause.
	Nutrition	Infants need to consume about 50 calories per day for each pound they weigh. A major change in the second year is the introduction of solid foods; in the first six months, human milk, or an alternative formula, is the baby's source of nutrition. The growing consensus is that breast-feeding is superior to bottle-feeding, but the increase in working mothers has meant fewer breast-fed babies. A current trend for working mothers is for them to breast-feed infants in the first several months to build up the infant's immune system, then bottle-feed after returning to work. Severe infant malnutrition is still prevalent in many parts of the world. Severe protein-calorie deficiency can cause marasmus. A special concern in impoverished countries is early weaning from breast milk. Even if not fatal, severe and lengthy malnutrition can impair physical, cognitive, and socioemotional development.
	Toilet training	Being toilet trained is expected to be attained by about 3 years of age in North America. There are no data on the optimal time for toilet training, but it should be initiated in a relaxed, supportive atmosphere. Some experts point out that late toilet training can lead to confrontations with the autonomy-seeking toddler.
	Immunization	Widespread immunization has led to a significant decline in infectious diseases.
	Accident prevention	Accidents are a major cause of death in infancy. The most common accidents in infancy include the aspiration of foreign objects, suffocation, falls, poisoning, burns, motor vehicle accidents, and bodily damage.
Motor development	Reflexes	The newborn is no longer viewed as a passive, empty-headed organism. Reflexes—automatic movements—govern the newborn's behavior. For infants, sucking is an important means of obtaining nutrition. Nonnutritive sucking is of interest to researchers, especially as a means of assessing attention and learning.
	Gross and fine motor skills	A number of gross motor and fine motor milestones occur in infancy.
	Developmental biodynamics	This approach seeks to explain how motor behaviors are assembled for perceiving and acting. It emphasizes the importance of exploration and selection in finding solutions to new task demands. A key theme is that perception and action are coupled when new skills are learned.

SENSORY AND PERCEPTUAL DEVELOPMENT

What are sensation and perception? Can a newborn see? If so, what can it perceive? What about the other senses—hearing, smell, taste, touch, and pain? What are they like in the newborn, and how do they develop in infancy? Can an infant put together information from two different modalities, such as sight and sound, in perceiving its world? These are among the intriguing questions we will now explore.

What Are Sensation and Perception?

How does a newborn know that her mother's skin is soft rather than rough? How does a 5-year-old know what color his hair is? How does an 8-year-old know that summer is warmer than winter? How does a 10-year-old know that a firecracker is louder than a cat's meow? Infants and children "know" these things because of their senses. All information comes to the infant through the senses. Without vision, hearing, touch, taste, smell, and other senses, the infant's brain would be isolated from the world; the infant would live in dark silence, a tasteless, colorless, feelingless void.

Sensation *occurs when information interacts with sensory receptors—the eyes, ears, tongue, nostrils, and skin*. The sensation of hearing occurs when waves of pulsating air are collected by the outer ear and transmitted through the bones of the inner ear to the auditory nerve. The sensation of vision occurs as rays of light contact the eyes and become focused on the retina.

Perception *is the interpretation of what is sensed*. The information about physical events that contacts the ears may be interpreted as musical sounds, for example. The physical energy transmitted to the retinas may be interpreted as a particular color, pattern, or shape.

Theories of Perceptual Development

Two main theoretical perspectives attempt to capture how the infant's perception develops: the constructivist view and the ecological view.

The Constructivist View
The **constructivist view,** *advocated by Piaget and information-processing psychologists, states that perception is a cognitive construction based on sensory input plus information retrieved from memory*. *In this view, perception is a representation of the world that builds up as the infant constructs an image of experiences*.

The constructivist view argues that perception is the process of internally representing information from the world. As information from the world is processed, it undergoes a series of internal manipulations. For example, information-processing psychologists ask the question, What is the purpose of vision (Marr, 1982)? Some of the answers to this question include to navigate through the environment without bumping into things, to be able to grasp things, and eventually to create a representation of visual objects that can be compared with representations in memory.

The Ecological View
Much of the research on perceptual development in infancy in the past several decades has been guided by the ecological view of Eleanor and James J. Gibson (Gibson, 1982, 1989; Gibson, 1966, 1979). They believe, unlike Piaget, that we can directly perceive information that exists in the world around us. We do not have to build up representations of the world in our mind; information about the world is available out there in the environment. Thus, the **ecological view** *states that perception has functional purposes of bringing the organism in contact with the environment and of increasing adaptation*. A key function of this perceptual adaptation is to detect perceptual invariants—those that remain stable—in a constantly changing world. A noticeable feature of the ecological view is that

Perceptual Development

sensation
The process that occurs when information interacts with the sensory receptors—the eyes, ears, tongue, nostrils, and skin.

perception
The interpretation of what is sensed.

constructivist view
Advocated by Piaget and the information-processing psychologists, this view states that perception is a cognitive construction based on sensory input plus information retrieved from memory. In this view, perception is a kind of representation of the world that builds up as the infant constructs an image of experiences.

ecological view
Advocated by the Gibsons, this view states that the purpose of perception is to detect perceptual invariants—those that remain stable—in a constantly changing world.

even complex things (such as a spatial layout) can be perceived directly without constructive activity.

The Gibsons believe that, if complex things can be perceived directly, perhaps they can be perceived even by young infants. Thus, the ecological view has inspired investigators to search for the competencies that young infants possess (Bower, 1989). Of course, ecological theorists do not deny that perception develops as infants and children develop. In fact, the ecological theorists stress that, as perceptual processes mature, a child becomes more efficient at discovering the invariant properties of objects available to the senses.

Visual Perception

Can newborns see? How does visual perception develop in infancy?

Visual Acuity and Color Psychologist William James (1890/1950) called the newborn's perceptual world a "blooming, buzzing" confusion. Was James right? A century later, we can safely say that he was wrong. The infant's perception of visual information is far more advanced than was previously thought.

Just how well can infants see? The newborn's vision is estimated to be 20/400 to 20/800 on the well-known Snellan chart, with which you are tested when you have your eyes examined (Haith, 1991). This is about 10 to 30 times lower than normal adult vision (20/20). By 6 months of age, though, vision is 20/100 or better, and, by about the first birthday, the infant's vision approximates that of an adult (Banks & Salapatek, 1983). Figure 6.11 shows a computer estimation of what a picture of a face looks like to a 1-month-old, and a 12-month-old and an adult from a distance of about 6 inches.

Can newborns see color? At birth, babies can distinguish between green and red (Adams, 1989). And adultlike functioning in all three types (red, blue, green) of color-sensitive receptors (cones) is present by 2 months of age.

Visual Preferences Robert Fantz (1963) is an important pioneer in the study of visual perception in infants. Fantz made an important discovery that advanced the ability of researchers to investigate infants' visual perception: infants look at different things for different lengths of time. Fantz placed infants in a "looking chamber," which had two visual displays on the ceiling above the infant's head. An experimenter viewed the infant's eyes by looking through a peephole. If the infant was fixating on one of the displays, the experimenter could see the display's reflection in the infant's eyes. This allowed the experimenter to determine how long the infant looked at each display. In figure 6.12 you can see Fantz's looking chamber and the results of his experiment. The infants preferred to look at patterns rather than at color or brightness. For example, they preferred to look at a face, a piece of printed matter, or a bull's-eye longer than at red, yellow, or white discs. In another experiment, Fantz found that younger infants—only 2 days old—look longer at patterned stimuli, such as faces and concentric circles, than at red, white, or yellow discs. Based on these results, it is likely that pattern perception has an innate basis, or at least is acquired after only minimal environmental experience. The newborn's visual world is not the blooming, buzzing confusion William James imagined.

Depth Perception How early can infants perceive depth? To investigate this question, infant perception researchers Eleanor Gibson and Richard Walk (1960) conducted a classic experiment. They constructed a miniature cliff with a drop-off covered by glass. The motivation for this experiment arose when Gibson was eating a picnic lunch on the edge of the Grand Canyon. She wondered whether an infant looking over the canyon's rim would perceive the dangerous drop-off and back up. In their laboratory, Gibson and Walk placed infants on the edge of a visual

Figure 6.11
Visual Acuity During the First Months of Life

The two photographs represent a computer estimation of what a picture of a face looks like to a 1-month-old and 12-month-old (approximating the vision of an adult).

Perceptual Development

Figure 6.12
Fantz's Experiment on Infants' Visual Perception

(a) Infants 2 to 3 months old preferred to look at some stimuli more than others. In Fantz's experiment, infants preferred to look at patterns rather than at color or brightness. For example, they looked longer at a face, a piece of printed matter, or a bull's-eye than at red, yellow, or white discs. (b) Fantz used a "looking chamber" to study infants' perception of stimuli.

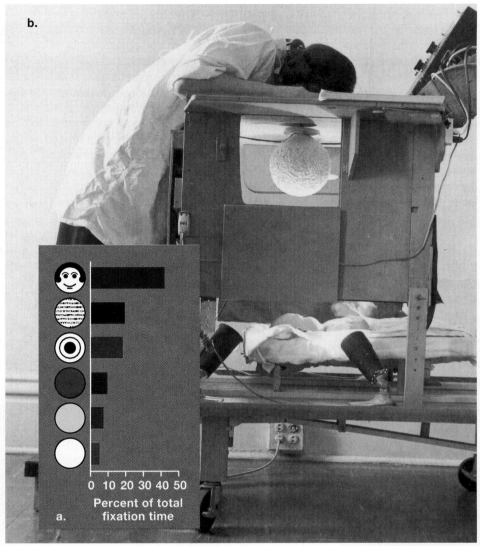

Figure 6.13
Examining Infants' Depth Perception on the Visual Cliff

Eleanor Gibson and Richard Walk (1960) found that most infants would not crawl out on the glass, which indicated that they had depth perception.

cliff and had their mothers coax them to crawl onto the glass (see figure 6.13). Most infants would not crawl out on the glass, choosing instead to remain on the shallow side, indicating that they could perceive depth. However, because the 6- to 14-month-old infants had extensive visual experience, this research did not answer the question of whether depth perception is innate.

Exactly how early in life does depth perception develop? Since younger infants do not crawl, this question is difficult to answer. Research with 2- to 4-month-old infants shows differences in heart rate when they are placed directly on the deep side of the visual cliff instead of on the shallow side (Campos, Langer, & Krowitz, 1970). However, an alternative interpretation is that young infants respond to differences in some visual characteristics of the deep and shallow cliffs, with no actual knowledge of depth.

Visual Expectations Infants not only see forms and figures at an early age but also develop expectations about future events in their world by the time they are 3 months of age. Marshall Haith and his colleagues (Canfield & Haith, 1991; Haith, Hazen, & Goodman, 1988) studied whether babies would form expectations about where an interesting picture would appear. The pictures were presented to the infants in either a regular alternating sequence—such as left, right, left, right—or an unpredictable sequence—such as right, right, left, right. When the sequence was predictable, the 3-month-old infants began to anticipate the location of the picture, looking at the side on which it was expected to appear. The young infants formed this visual expectation in less than one minute. However, younger infants did not develop expectations about where a picture would be presented.

Elizabeth Spelke (1988, 1991) also has demonstrated that young infants form visual expectations. She placed babies before a puppet stage and showed them a series of unexpected actions—for example, a ball seemed to roll through a solid barrier, another seemed to leap between two platforms, and a third appeared to hang in midair (Spelke, 1979) (see figure 6.14). Spelke measured the babies' looking times and recorded longer intervals for unexpected than expected actions. She concluded that, by 4 months of age, even though infants do not yet have the ability to talk about objects, move around objects, manipulate objects, or even see objects with high resolution, they can recognize where a moving object is when it has left their visual field and can infer where it should be when it comes into their sight again.

Other Senses

Considerable development also takes place in other sensory systems. We will explore development in hearing, touch and pain, smell, and taste.

Hearing   What is the nature of hearing in newborns? Can the fetus hear? What types of auditory stimulation should be used with infants at different points in the first year? We will examine each of these questions.

Immediately after birth, infants can hear, although their sensory thresholds are somewhat higher than those of adults (Trehub & others, 1991). That is, a stimulus must be louder to be heard by a newborn than by an adult. Also, in one study, as infants aged from 8 to 28 weeks, they became more proficient at localizing sounds (Morrongiello, Fenwick, & Chance, 1990). Not only can newborns hear, but the possibility has been raised that the fetus can hear as it nestles within its mother's womb. Let's examine this possibility further.

In the last few months of pregnancy, the fetus can hear sounds: the mother's voice, music, and so on (Kisilevsky, 1995). Given that the fetus can hear sounds, two psychologists wanted to find out if listening to Dr. Seuss' classic story *The Cat in the Hat*, while still in the mother's womb, would produce a preference for hearing the story after birth (DeCasper & Spence, 1986). Sixteen pregnant women read *The Cat in the Hat* to their fetuses twice a day over the last six weeks of their pregnancies. When the babies were born, their mothers read *The Cat in the Hat* or a story with a different rhyme and pace, *The King, the Mice, and the Cheese*. The infants sucked on a nipple in a different way when the mothers read *The Cat in the Hat*, suggesting that the infants recognized its pattern and tone (to which they had been exposed prenatally) (see figure 6.15).

Two important conclusions can be drawn from this investigation. First, it reveals how ingenious scientists have become at assessing the development not only of infants but of fetuses as well, in this case discovering a way to "interview" newborn babies who cannot yet talk. Second, it reveals the remarkable ability of an infant's brain to learn even before birth.

Babies are born into the world prepared to respond to the sounds of any human language. Even very young infants can discriminate subtle phonetic differences, such as those between the speech sounds of *ba* and *ga*. Young infants also will suck more on a nipple to hear a recording of their mother's voice than they will to hear the voice of an unfamiliar woman, and they will suck more to listen to their mother's native language than they will to listen to a foreign language (Mehler & others, 1988; Spence & DeCasper, 1987). And an interesting developmental change occurs during the first year: 6-month-old infants can discriminate phonetic sound contrasts from languages to which they have never been exposed, but they lose this discriminative

Figure 6.14
The Young Infant's Knowledge of the Perceptual World

A 4-month-old in Elizabeth Spelke's infant perception laboratory is tested to determine if it knows that an object in motion will not stop in midair. Spelke believes the young infant's knowledge about how the perceptual world works is innate.

Newborns' Senses

$\mathcal{F}$igure 6.15
Hearing in the Womb

(a) Pregnant mothers read *The Cat in the Hat* to their fetuses during the last few months of pregnancy. (b) When they were born, the babies preferred listening to a recording of their mothers reading *The Cat in the Hat*, as evidenced by their sucking on a nipple that produced this recording rather than another story, *The King, the Mice, and the Cheese*.

ability by their first birthday, demonstrating that experience with a specific language is necessary for maintaining this ability (Werker & LaDonde, 1988).

Touch and Pain   Do newborns respond to touch? What activities can adults engage in that involve tactile (touch) stimulation at various points in the infant's development? Can newborns feel pain?

Touch in the Newborn   Newborns respond to touch. A touch to the cheek produces a turning of the head, whereas a touch to the lips produces sucking movements. An important ability that develops in infancy is to connect information about vision with information about touch. One-year-olds clearly can do this, and it appears that 6-month-olds can, too (Acredolo & Hake, 1982). Whether still younger infants can coordinate vision and touch is yet to be determined. To further evaluate the nature of touch in infancy, see Adventures for the Mind.

Pain   If and when you have a son and need to consider whether he should be circumcised, the issue of an infant's pain perception probably will become important to you. Circumcision is usually performed on young boys about the third day after birth. Will your young son experience pain if he is circumcised when he is 3 days old? Increased crying and fussing occur during the circumcision procedure, suggesting that 3-day-old infants experience pain (Gunnar, Malone, & Fisch, 1987).

In the investigation by Megan Gunnar and her colleagues (1987), the healthy newborn's ability to cope with stress was evaluated. The newborn infant males cried intensely during the circumcision, indicating that it was stressful. The researchers pointed out that it is rather remarkable that the newborn infant does not suffer serious consequences from the surgery. Rather, the circumcised infant displays amazing resiliency and ability to cope. Within several minutes after the surgery, the infant can nurse and interact in a normal manner with his mother. And, if allowed to, the newly circumcised newborn drifts into a deep sleep, which seems to serve as a coping mechanism. In this experiment, the time spent in deep sleep was greater in the 60 to 240 minutes after the circumcision than before it.

For many years, doctors have performed operations on newborns without anesthesia. This medical practice was accepted because of the dangers of anesthesia and the supposition that newborns do not feel pain. Recently, as researchers have convincingly demonstrated that newborns can feel pain, the long-standing practice of operating on newborns without anesthesia is being challenged.

Smell   Newborns can differentiate odors. For example, by the expressions on their faces, they seem to indicate that they like the way vanilla and strawberry smell but do not like the way rotten eggs and fish smell (Steiner, 1979). In one investigation, young infants who were breast-fed showed a clear preference for smelling their mother's breast pad when they were 6 days old (MacFarlane, 1975) (see figure 6.16). However, when they were 2 days old, they did not show this preference (compared with a clean breast pad), indicating that they require several days of experience to recognize this odor.

Taste   Sensitivity to taste may be present before birth. When saccharin was added to the amniotic fluid of a near-term fetus, increased swallowing was observed (Windle, 1940). In one study, even at only 2 hours of age, babies made different facial expressions when they tasted sweet, sour, and bitter solutions (Rosenstein & Oster, 1988) (see figure 6.17). At about 4 months of age, infants begin to prefer salty tastes, which as newborns they had found to be aversive (Harris, Thomas, & Booth, 1990).

Intermodal Perception

Are young infants so competent that they can relate and integrate information through several senses? Imagine yourself playing basketball or tennis. You are experiencing

Adventures for the Mind
Devising Age-Appropriate Activities to Stimulate Infants' Different Sensory Modalities

Devise a list of age-appropriate activities for two of the sensory modalities we have just discussed—hearing and touch. For each modality, think about stimulation in the first six months and from six months to one year. Think about such auditory activities as listening to music boxes, musical mobiles, musical animals and dolls, and CDs, as well as about such tactile activities as touching stuffed animals and books with textures.

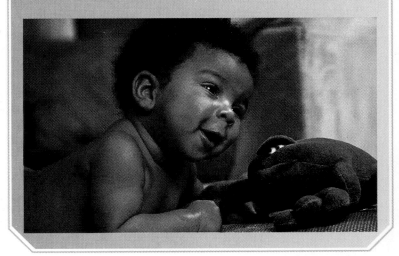

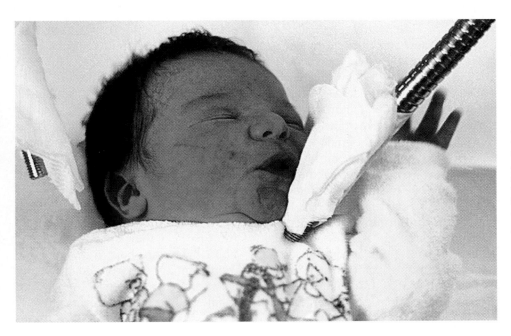

Figure 6.16
Newborns' Preference for the Smell of Their Mother's Breast Pad

In the experiment by MacFarlane (1975), 6-day-old infants preferred to smell their mother's breast pad over a clean one that had never been used, but 2-day-old infants did not show this preference, indicating that this odor preference requires several days of experience to develop.

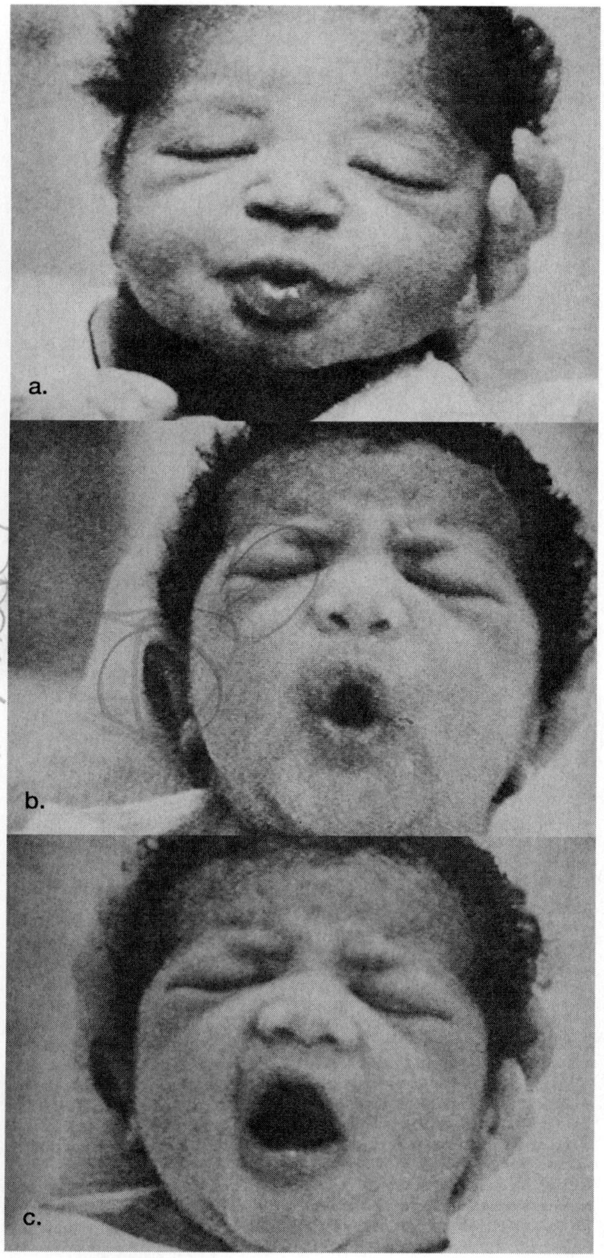

Figure 6.17
Newborns' Facial Responses to Basic Tastes

Facial expression elicited by (a) a sweet solution, (b) a sour solution, and (c) a bitter solution.

intermodal perception

The ability to relate and integrate information about two or more sensory modalities, such as vision and hearing.

many visual inputs: the ball coming and going, other players moving around, and so on. However, you are experiencing many auditory inputs as well: the sound of the ball bouncing or being hit, the grunts and groans, and so on. There is good correspondence between much of the visual and auditory information: when you see the ball bounce, you hear a bouncing sound; when a player stretches to hit a ball, you hear a groan.

We live in a world of objects and events that can be seen, heard, and felt. When mature observers simultaneously look and listen to an event, they experience a unitary episode. All of this is so commonplace that it scarcely seems worth mentioning, but consider the task of very young infants with little practice at perceiving. Can they put vision and sound together as precisely as adults do?

Intermodal perception *is the ability to relate and integrate information about two or more sensory modalities, such as vision and hearing.* The two main theories described earlier address the question of whether young infants develop intermodal perception. The ecological view argues that infants have intermodal perception capabilities very early in infancy. In this view, infants only have to attend to the appropriate sensory information; they do not have to build up an internal representation of the information through months of sensorimotor experiences. In contrast, the constructivist view advocated by Piaget states that perceptual abilities, such as vision, hearing, and touch, are not coordinated early in infancy; therefore, young infants do not have intermodal perception. According to Piaget, only through months of sensorimotor interaction with the world is intermodal perception possible. For example, infants can coordinate touch and vision only when they learn to look at objects as their hands grasp them.

To test intermodal perception, Elizabeth Spelke (1979) showed 4-month-old infants two films simultaneously. In each film, a puppet jumped up and down, but in one of the films the sound track matched the puppet's dancing movements; in the other film, it did not. By measuring the infants' gaze, Spelke found that the infants looked more at the puppet whose actions were synchronized with the sound track, suggesting that they recognized the visual-sound correspondence. Young infants can also coordinate visual-auditory information involving people. In one study, as early as at 3½ months old, infants looked more at their mother when they also heard her voice and longer at their father when they also heard his voice (Spelke & Owsley, 1979).

Might auditory-visual relations be coordinated even in newborns? Newborns do turn their eyes and their head toward the sound of a voice or rattle when the sound is maintained for several seconds (Clifton & others, 1981), but the newborn can localize a sound and look at an object only in a crude way (Bechtold, Bushnell, & Salapatek, 1979). Improved accuracy at auditory-visual coordination likely requires a sharpening through experience with visual and auditory stimuli. Nonetheless, although at a crude level, auditory-visual intermodal perception appears to be present at birth, likely having evolutionary value.

In sum, crude exploratory forms of intermodal perception exist in newborns. These exploratory forms of intermodal perception become sharpened with experience in the first year of life. In the first six months, infants have difficulty forming mental representations that connect sensory input from different modes, but in the second half of the first year they show an increased ability to make this connection mentally. Thus, babies are born into the world with some innate abilities to perceive relations among sensory modalities, but their intermodal abilities improve considerably through experience. As with all aspects of development, in perceptual development, nature and nurture interact and cooperate.

Summary Table 6.2
Sensory and Perceptual Development

Concept	Processes/Related Ideas	Characteristics/Description
What are sensation and perception?	Sensation	Sensation occurs when information interacts with sensory receptors—the eyes, ears, tongue, nostrils, and skin.
	Perception	Perception is the interpretation of what is sensed.
Theories of perceptual development	Constructivist view	Advocated by Piaget and information-processing psychologists, this view states that perception is a cognitive construction based on sensory input plus information retrieved from memory.
	Ecological view	Advocated by the Gibsons, this view states that perception has the functions of bringing organisms in contact with the environment and increasing adaptation. A key aspect of the ecological view involves perceptual invariants.
Visual perception	Visual acuity and color	William James was wrong—the newborn's visual world is not a blooming, buzzing confusion. Newborns can see and can distinguish greens and reds.
	Visual preferences	In Fantz's pioneering research, infants only 2 days old looked longer at patterned stimuli, such as faces, than at single-colored discs.
	Depth perception	A classic study by Gibson and Walk demonstrated through the use of the visual cliff that infants as young as 6 months have depth perception.
	Visual expectations	Spelke has demonstrated that infants develop expectations about future events in their world by the time they are 3 months old.
Other senses	Hearing	The fetus can hear several weeks before birth. Immediately after birth, newborns can hear, although their sensory threshold is higher than that of adults.
	Touch and pain	Newborns respond to touch and can feel pain. Research on circumcision shows that 3-day-old males experience pain and can adapt to stress.
Intermodal perception	Its nature	Intermodal perception is the ability to relate and integrate information about two or more sensory modalities, such as vision and hearing. The ecological view argues that young infants have intermodal perception; the constructivist view states that sensory modalities are not coordinated early in infancy. Spelke's research demonstrated that infants as young as 3 months of age can connect visual and auditory stimuli. Crude, exploratory forms of intermodal perception are present in newborns and become sharpened in the first year of life.
Perceptual-motor coupling and unification	Their nature	Thelen argues that perceptual and motor development are coupled and unified. She says that individuals perceive in order to move and move in order to perceive.

Perceptual-Motor Coupling and Unification

The main thrust of research in the Gibsonian tradition has been to discover how perception guides action. A less-well-studied but equally important issue is how action shapes perception. Motor activities may be crucial because they provide the means for exploring the world and learning about its properties. Only by moving one's eyes, head, hands, and arms and by traversing from one location to another can individuals fully experience their environment and learn effectively to adapt to it.

The distinction between perceiving and doing has been a time-honored tradition in psychology. However, Esther Thelen (1995) questions whether this distinction is real. She argues that individuals perceive in order to move and move in order to perceive. Thus, there is an increasing belief that perceptual and motor development do not develop in isolation from one other but, rather, are coupled (Bornstein & Arterberry, 1999). Babies are continually coordinating their movements with concurrent perceptual information to learn how to maintain balance, reach for objects in space, and locomote across various surfaces and terrains.

At this point, we have discussed many ideas about sensory and perceptual development. An overview of these ideas is presented in summary table 6.2.

Chapter Review

Once it was believed that newborns are virtually empty-headed organisms that experience the world as a blooming, buzzing confusion. Today, developmentalists believe that young infants have far more advanced capabilities. Infants assemble their motor and perceptual skills to adapt to their world.

Our coverage of physical growth and development focused on cephalocaudal and proximodistal patterns, height and weight, the brain, infant states, nutrition, toilet training, immunization, and accident prevention. We also studied a number of aspects of motor development, including reflexes, gross and fine motor skills, and developmental biodynamics. And we examined these aspects of sensory and perceptual development: what sensation and perception are, theories of perceptual development, visual perception, other senses, intermodal perception, and perceptual-motor coupling and unification.

Remember that you can obtain an overall summary of the chapter by again studying the two summary tables on pages 159 and 167. In the next chapter, we will study the infant's cognitive development.

✓ Children Checklist
Physical Development in Infancy

How much have you learned since the beginning of the chapter? Use the following statements to help you review your knowledge and understanding of the chapter material. First, read the statement and mentally or briefly demonstrate on paper that you can discuss the relevant information.

_____ I can describe the growth patterns in infancy.
_____ I understand the brain's growth in infancy.
_____ I know about the nature of infant states.
_____ I can discuss the role of nutrition in infancy.
_____ I can describe the issues involved in toilet training.
_____ I know about immunization and accident prevention.
_____ I can discuss infant motor development.
_____ I can describe what sensation and perception are, as well as theories of perceptual development.
_____ I am aware of the development of visual perception in infancy, including the aspects of visual acuity, color, visual preferences, depth perception, and visual expectations.
_____ I can discuss the development of the other senses, including hearing, touch and pain, smell, and taste.
_____ I know what intermodal perception is.
_____ I can describe perceptual-motor coupling and unification.

For any items that you did not check, go back and locate the relevant material in the chapter. Review the material until you feel you can check off the item. You may want to use this checklist later in preparing for an exam.

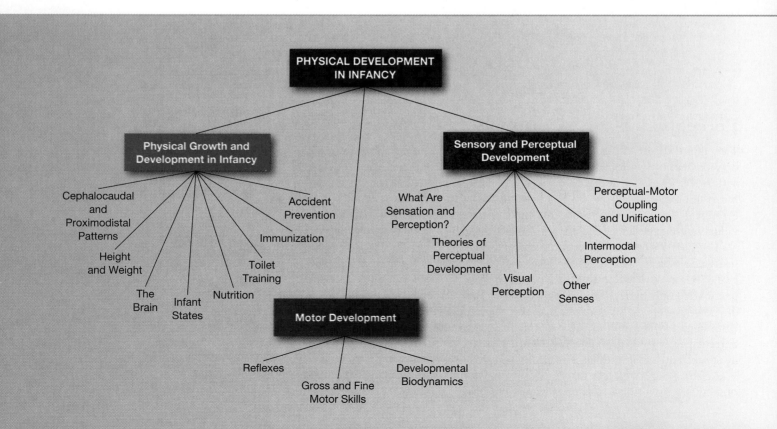

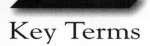

Key Terms

cephalocaudal pattern 142
proximodistal pattern 142
neuron 142
cerebral cortex 144
frontal lobe 144
occipital lobe 144
temporal lobe 144
parietal lobe 144
lateralization 144
REM (rapid eye movement)
  sleep 146
sudden infant death syndrome
  (SIDS) 147
marasmus 149 *wasting Away of muscle tissue Severe Malnu.*

sucking reflex 152
rooting reflex 152
Moro reflex 152 *Neonatal Startle Reflex*
grasping reflex 153
gross motor skills 154
fine motor skills 154 *Finger Flexibility*
developmental biodynamics
  157
sensation 160
perception 160 *what is Sensed*
constructivist view 160
ecological view 160
intermodal perception 166

Children Resources

Baby Steps
(1994) by Claire Kopp.
New York: W. H. Freeman.

Baby Steps is a guide to physical, cognitive, and socioemotional development in the first 2 years of life. The book is organized developmentally, with major sections divided into birth through 3 months, 4 through 7 months, 8 through 12 months, and the second year.

Infancy
(1990) by Tiffany Field.
Cambridge, MA: Harvard
University Press.

This is an outstanding book on infant development, written by one of the world's leading researchers on the topic. The book accurately captures the flavor of the young infant as an active learner and one far more competent than once was believed.

Solve Your Child's Sleep Problems
(1985) by Richard Ferber.
New York: Simon & Schuster.

Solve Your Child's Sleep Problems helps parents recognize when their infant or child has a sleep problem and tells them what to do about it.

Taking It to the Net

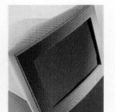

http://www.mhhe.com/santrockcd6

1. Your cousin confides in you that she is about to begin toilet training her first born son, and that she is concerned. What advice would you give her regarding how and when to toilet train her son?

2. You are working with a developmental psychologist who is interested in infant cognitive growth. She is in the initial stages of creating a series of experiments to test her ideas. She has asked you to identify three variables that would be important to research in this area. She would also like you to explain why you have selected these particular factors.

3. When a child sees an apple, do they see "the" apple, as it exists in "reality", or do they see only their perception of the apple? Do infants construct their own version of reality, or do they construct reality itself? You were once an infant, how do you know that what you call "real" is actually reality?

Chapter

7

I wish I could travel by the road that crosses the baby's mind where Reason makes kites of her laws and flies them...

Rabindranath Tagore
Bengali Poet, Essayist, 20th Century

PREVIEW

The current excitement and enthusiasm about infant cognition have been fueled by an interest in what an infant knows at birth and soon after, by continued fascination with innate and learned factors in the infant's cognitive development, and by controversies about whether infants construct their knowledge (as Piaget believed) or whether they know their world more directly. When you have completed this chapter you should have a good understanding of

- Piaget's theory of infant development
- The new look in infant cognitive development, which involves criticisms of Piaget's view
- The information-processing perspective
- Individual differences in intelligence
- What language is
- Biological influences on language
- Behavioral and environmental aspects of language
- How language develops

The Stories of Laurent, Lucienne, and Jacqueline

Jean Piaget, the famous Swiss psychologist, was a meticulous observer of his three children—Laurent, Lucienne, and Jacqueline. His books on cognitive development are filled with these observations. The following provide a glimpse of Piaget's observations of his children's cognitive development in infancy (Piaget, 1952).

- At 21 days of age, Laurent finds his thumb after three attempts; once he finds his thumb, prolonged sucking begins. But, when he is placed on his back, he doesn't know how to coordinate the movement of his arms with that of his mouth; his hands draw back, even when his lips seek them.
- During the third month, thumb sucking becomes less important to Laurent because of new visual and auditory interests. But, when he cries, his thumb goes to the rescue.
- Toward the end of Lucienne's fourth month, while she is lying in her crib, Piaget hangs a doll over her feet. Lucienne thrusts her feet at the doll and makes it move. Afterward, she looks at her motionless foot for a second, then kicks at the doll again. She has no visual control of her foot because her movements are the same whether she only looks at the doll or it is placed over her head. By contrast, she does have tactile control of her foot; when she tries to kick the doll and misses, she slows her foot movements to improve her aim.
- At 11 months, while seated, Jacqueline shakes a little bell. She then pauses abruptly so she can delicately place the bell in front of her right foot; then she kicks the bell hard. Unable to recapture the bell, she grasps a ball and places it in the same location where the bell was. She gives the ball a firm kick.
- At 1 year, 2 months, Jacqueline holds in her hands an object that is new to her: a round, flat box that she turns over and shakes; then she rubs it against her crib. She lets it go and tries to pick it up again. She succeeds only in touching it with her index finger, being unable to fully reach and grasp it. She keeps trying to grasp it and presses to the edge of her crib. She makes the box tilt up, but it nonetheless falls again. Jacqueline shows an interest in this result and studies the fallen box.
- At 1 year, 8 months, Jacqueline arrives at a closed door with a blade of grass in each hand. She stretches her right hand toward the doorknob but detects that she cannot turn it without letting go of the grass, so she puts the grass on the floor, opens the door, picks up the grass again, and then enters. But, when she wants to leave the room, things get complicated. She puts the grass on the floor and grasps the doorknob. Then she perceives that, by pulling the door toward her, she simultaneously chases away the grass that she had placed between the door and the threshold. She then picks up the grass and places it out of the door's range of movement.

For Piaget, these observations reflect important changes in the infant's cognitive development. Later in the chapter, you will learn that Piaget believed that infants go through six substages of development and that the behaviors you have just read about characterize those substages.

There was a child who went forth every day And the first object he looked upon, that object he became. And that object became part of him for the day, or a certain part of the day, or for many years, or stretching cycles of years.

Walt Whitman
American Poet, 19th Century

We are born capable of learning.

Jean-Jacques Rousseau
Swiss-Born French Philosopher, 18th Century

Piaget's Stages

scheme (or schema)
The basic unit (or units) for an organized pattern of sensorimotor functioning.

simple reflexes
Piaget's first sensorimotor substage, which corresponds to the first month after birth. In this substage, the basic means of coordinating sensation and action is through reflexive behaviors, such as rooting and sucking, which the infant has at birth.

PIAGET'S THEORY OF INFANT DEVELOPMENT

Poet Noah Perry once asked, "Who knows the thoughts of a child?" Piaget knew as much as anyone. Through careful, inquisitive interviews and observations of his own three children—Laurent, Lucienne, and Jacqueline—Piaget changed the way we think about children's conception of the world. Remember that we studied a general outline of Piaget's theory in chapter 2. You might want to review the basic features of his theory in chapter 2 at this time.

Piaget believed that the child passes through a series of stages of thought from infancy to adolescence. Passage through the stages results from biological pressures to *adapt* to the environment (through assimilation and accommodation) and to organize structures of thinking. The stages of thought are *qualitatively* different from one another. The way children reason at one stage is very different from the way they reason at another stage. This contrasts with the quantitative assessments of intelligence made through the use of standardized intelligence tests. In these tests, the focus is on what the child knows, or how many questions the child can answer correctly. According to Piaget, the mind's development is divided into four such quantitatively different stages: sensorimotor, preoperational, concrete operational, and formal operational. Here our concern is with the stage that characterizes infant thought—the sensorimotor stage.

The Stage of Sensorimotor Development

According to Piaget, the sensorimotor stage lasts from birth to about 2 years of age, corresponding to the period of infancy. During this time, mental development is characterized by considerable progression in the infant's ability to organize and coordinate sensations with physical movements and actions—hence the name sensorimotor (Piaget, 1952).

At the beginning of the sensorimotor stage, the infant has little more than reflexive patterns with which to work. By the end of the stage, the 2-year-old has complex sensorimotor patterns and is beginning to operate with a primitive system of symbols. Unlike other stages, the sensorimotor stage is subdivided into six substages, each of which involves qualitative changes in sensorimotor organization. The term **scheme (or schema)** *refers to the basic unit (or units) for an organized pattern of sensorimotor functioning.*

Within a substage, there may be different schemes—sucking, rooting, and blinking in substage 1, for example. In substage 1, the schemes are basically reflexive. From substage to substage, the schemes change in organization. This change is at the heart of Piaget's description of the stages. The six substages of sensorimotor development are (1) simple reflexes; (2) first habits and primary circular reactions; (3) secondary circular reactions; (4) coordination of secondary circular reactions; (5) tertiary circular reactions, novelty, and curiosity; and (6) internalization of schemes.

Simple reflexes *is Piaget's first sensorimotor substage, which corresponds to the first month after birth. In this substage, the basic means of coordinating sensation and action is through reflexive behaviors. These include rooting and sucking, which the infant has at birth.* In substage 1, the infant exercises these reflexes. More important, the infant develops an ability to produce behaviors that resemble reflexes in the absence of obvious reflexive stimuli. The newborn may suck when a bottle or nipple is only nearby, for example. When the baby was just born, the bottle or nipple would have produced the sucking pattern only when placed directly in its mouth or touched to the lips. Reflexlike actions in the absence of a triggering stimulus are evidence that the infant is initiating action and is actively structuring experiences in the first month of life.

First habits and primary circular reactions *is Piaget's second sensorimotor substage, which develops between 1 and 4 months of age. In this substage, the infant learns to coordinate sensation and types of schemes or structures—that is,* habits *and* primary circular reactions. A *habit* is a scheme based on a simple reflex, such as sucking, that has become completely separated from its eliciting stimulus. For example, an infant in substage 1 might suck when orally stimulated by a bottle or when visually shown the bottle. However, an infant in substage 2 might exercise the sucking scheme even when no bottle is present. A **primary circular reaction** *is a scheme based on the infant's attempt to reproduce an interesting or a pleasurable event that initially occurred by chance.* In a popular Piagetian example, a child accidentally sucks his fingers when they are placed near his mouth. Later, he searches for his fingers to suck them again, but the fingers do not cooperate in the search because the infant cannot coordinate visual and manual actions. Habits and circular reactions are stereotyped, in that the infant repeats them the same way each time. The infant's own body remains the center of attention. There is no outward pull by environmental events.

Secondary circular reactions *is Piaget's third sensorimotor substage, which develops between 4 and 8 months of age. In this substage, the infant becomes more object-oriented or focused on the world, moving beyond preoccupation with the self in sensorimotor interactions.* The chance shaking of a rattle, for example, may fascinate the infant. The infant will repeat this action for the sake of experiencing fascination. The infant imitates some simple actions of others, such as the baby talk or burbling of adults, and some physical gestures. However, these imitations are limited to actions the infant is already able to produce. Although directed toward objects in the world, the infant's schemes lack an intentional, goal-directed quality.

Coordination of secondary circular reactions *is Piaget's fourth sensorimotor substage, which develops between 8 and 12 months of age. In this substage, several significant changes take place that involve the coordination of schemes and intentionality.* Infants readily combine and recombine previously learned schemes in a *coordinated way.* They may look at an object and grasp it simultaneously, or they may visually inspect a toy, such as a rattle, and finger it simultaneously in obvious tactile exploration. Actions are even more outwardly directed than before. Related to this coordination is the second achievement—the presence of *intentionality,* the separation of means and goals in accomplishing simple feats. For example, infants might manipulate a stick (the means) to bring a desired toy within reach (the goal). They may knock over one block to reach and play with another one.

Tertiary circular reactions, novelty, and curiosity *is Piaget's fifth sensorimotor substage, which develops between 12 and 18 months of age. In this substage, infants become intrigued by the variety of properties that objects possess and by the many things they can make happen to objects.* A block can be made to fall, spin, hit another object, and slide across the ground. Tertiary circular reactions are schemes in which the infant purposely explores new possibilities with objects, continually changing what is done to them and exploring the results. Piaget says that this stage marks the developmental starting point for human curiosity and interest in novelty. Previous circular reactions have been devoted exclusively to reproducing former events, with the exception of imitation of novel acts, which occurs as early as substage 4. The tertiary circular act is the first to be concerned with novelty.

Internalization of schemes *is Piaget's sixth and final sensorimotor substage, which develops between 18 and 24 months of age. In this substage, the infant's mental functioning shifts from a purely sensorimotor plane to a symbolic plane, and the infant develops the ability to use primitive symbols.* For Piaget, a *symbol* is an internalized sensory image or word that represents an event. Primitive symbols permit the infant to think about concrete events without directly acting them out or perceiving them. Moreover, symbols allow the infant to manipulate and transform the represented events in simple ways. In a favorite Piagetian example, Piaget's young daughter saw a matchbox being opened and closed. Sometime later, she mimicked the event by opening and closing her mouth. This was an obvious expression of her image of the

first habits and primary circular reactions
Piaget's second sensorimotor substage, which develops between 1 and 4 months of age. In this substage, the infant learns to coordinate sensation and types of schemes or structures—that is, habits and primary circular reactions.

primary circular reaction
A scheme based on the infant's attempt to reproduce an interesting or a pleasurable event that initially occurred by chance.

secondary circular reactions
Piaget's third sensorimotor substage, which develops between 4 and 8 months of age. In this substage, the infant becomes more object-oriented, or focused on the world, moving beyond preoccupation with the self in sensorimotor interactions.

coordination of secondary circular reactions
Piaget's fourth sensorimotor substage, which develops between 8 and 12 months of age. In this substage, several significant changes take place involving the coordination of schemes and intentionality.

tertiary circular reactions, novelty, and curiosity
Piaget's fifth sensorimotor substage, which develops between 12 and 18 months of age. In this substage, infants become intrigued by the variety of properties that objects possess and by the multiplicity of things they can make happen to objects.

internalization of schemes
Piaget's sixth and final sensorimotor substage, which develops between 18 and 24 months of age. In this substage, the infant's mental functioning shifts from a purely sensorimotor plane to a symbolic plane, and the infant develops the ability to use primitive symbols.

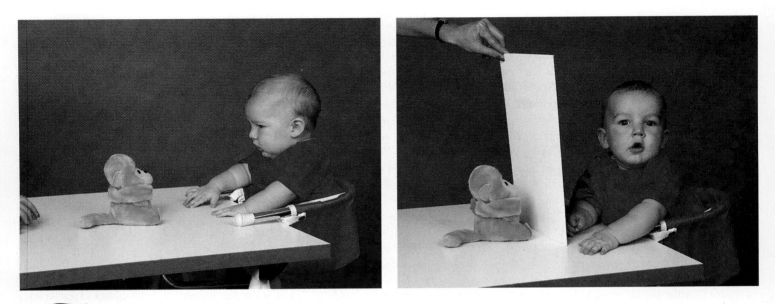

Figure 7.1
Object Permanence

Piaget thought that object permanence is one of infancy's landmark cognitive accomplishments. For this 5-month-old boy, "out-of-sight" is literally out of mind. The infant looks at the toy monkey *(left)*, but, when his view of the toy is blocked *(right)*, he does not search for it. Several months later, he will search for the hidden toy monkey, reflecting the presence of object permanence.

Sensorimotor Development

object permanence
The Piagetian term for one of an infant's most important accomplishments: understanding that objects and events continue to exist, even when they cannot directly be seen, heard, or touched.

event. In another example, a child opened a door slowly to avoid disturbing a piece of paper lying on the floor on the other side. Clearly, the child had an image of the unseen paper and what would happen to it if the door opened quickly. However, developmentalists have debated whether 2-year-olds really have such representations of action sequences at their command (Corrigan, 1981).

Object Permanence

Object permanence *is the Piagetian term for one of an infant's most important accomplishments: understanding that objects and events continue to exist, even when they cannot directly be seen, heard, or touched.* Imagine what thought would be like if you could not distinguish between yourself and your world. Your thought would be chaotic, disorganized, and unpredictable. This is what the mental life of a newborn is like, according to Piaget. There is no self-world differentiation and no sense of object permanence. By the end of the sensorimotor period, however, both are present.

The principal way that object permanence is studied is by watching an infant's reaction when an interesting object or event disappears (see figure 7.1). If infants show no reaction, it is assumed they believe the object no longer exists. By contrast, if infants are surprised at the disappearance and search for the object, it is assumed they believe it continues to exist.

At this point, we have discussed a number of characteristics of Piaget's stage of sensorimotor development. To help you remember the main characteristics of sensorimotor thought, turn to figure 7.2.

Evaluating Piaget's Sensorimotor Stage

Piaget opened up a whole new way of looking at infants by describing how their main task is to coordinate their sensory impressions with their motor activity. His view is a good summary of the general way that infants come to fathom the permanence of things in their world. However, the infant's cognitive world is not as neatly packaged as Piaget portrayed it, and some of Piaget's explanations for the cause of change are debated.

Piaget constructed his view of infancy mainly by observing the development of his own three children. Few laboratory techniques were available at the time. In the past several decades, sophisticated experimental techniques have been devised to study infants, and there have been a large number of research studies on infant development. Much of the new research suggests that Piaget's view of sensorimotor development needs to modified (Gounin-Decarie, 1996). The two research areas that have led researchers to a somewhat different understanding of infant development are (1) perceptual development and (2) conceptual development.

In chapter 6, we said that a number of theorists, such as Eleanor Gibson (1989), Elizabeth Spelke (1991; Spelke & Newport, 1998), and Tom Bower (1996), believe that infants' perceptual abilities are highly developed very early in development. For example, Spelke has demonstrated that infants as young as 4 months of age have intermodal perception—the ability to coordinate information from two or more sensory modalities, such as vision and hearing. Other research, by Renée Baillargeon (1995), documents that infants as young as 4 months expect objects to be substantial (in the sense that other objects cannot move through them) and permanent (in the sense that objects continue to exist when they are hidden). In sum, researchers believe that infants see objects as bounded, unitary, solid, and separate from their background, possibly at birth or shortly thereafter, but definitely by 3 to 4 months of age. Young infants still have much to learn about objects, but the world appears both stable and orderly to them and, thus, capable of being conceptualized. Infants are continually trying to structure and make sense of their world (Meltzoff & Gopnik, 1997).

It is more difficult to study what infants are thinking about than to study what they see. Still, researchers have devised ways to assess whether or not infants are thinking. One strategy is to look for symbolic activity, such as using a gesture to refer to something. Piaget (1952) used this strategy to document infants' motor recognition. For example, he observed his 6-month-old daughter make a gesture when she saw a familiar toy in a new location. She was used to kicking at the toy in her crib. When she saw it across the room, she made a brief kicking motion. However, Piaget did not consider this to be true symbolic activity because it was a motor movement, not a purely mental act. Nonetheless, Piaget suggested that his daughter was referring to, or classifying, the toy through her actions (Mandler, 1992). In a similar way, infants whose parents use sign language have been observed to start using conventional signs at about 6 to 7 months of age (Bonvillian, Orlansky, & Novack, 1983).

In summary, the recent research on infants' perceptual and conceptual development suggests that infants have more sophisticated perceptual abilities and can begin to think earlier than Piaget envisioned. These researchers believe that infants either are born with or acquire these abilities early in their development (Mandler, 1990, 1998).

It is clear from the new look at infant cognition that Piaget's view of sensorimotor development requires considerable revision (Lutz & Sternberg, 1999). Piaget's view is a general, unifying story of how biology and experience sculpt the infant's cognitive development: assimilation and accommodation always take the infant to higher ground through a series of substages. And, for Piaget, the motivation for change is general, an internal search for equilibrium. Many of today's researchers believe that Piaget wasn't specific enough about how infants learn about their world and that infants are far more competent than Piaget envisioned.

Ability to organize and coordinate sensations with physical movements

Is nonsymbolic through most of its duration

Consists of six substages of cognitive development

Object permanence develops

*F*igure 7.2
The Main Characteristics of Sensorimotor Thought, According to Piaget

Cognitive Milestones

Challenges to Piaget

However, according to infant development experts Marshall Haith and Janette Benson (1998), today it is difficult to tell such a unifying story of infant cognition. Many key questions are matters of debate. How much of the infant's cognitive development is innate? How much has strong biological foundations but requires considerable environmental input? How much is more perceptual than cognitive? How much emerges full-blown rather than gradually?

Like much of the modern world, the field of infant cognition is very specialized. There are many researchers working on different questions, with no general theory emerging that can connect all of the different findings (Nelson, 1999). Their theories are local theories, focused on specific research questions, rather than grand theories like Piaget's (Kuhn, 1998). If there are unifying themes, they are that investigators in infant development struggle with the big issues of nature and nurture, cognition and perception.

Some developmentalists, such as Haith (1993), believe that the following Piagetian ideas should not be discarded: that infants acquire knowledge about their world in a gradual rather than full-blown fashion and that each level of understanding builds on previous ones. They argue that the most accurate story of infant development is one of partial, graded accomplishments along the route to acquiring a concept.

Next, we will explore the information-processing perspective on infant development. It has contributed to the view which states that infants have more sophisticated cognitive abilities than Piaget envisioned.

THE INFORMATION-PROCESSING PERSPECTIVE

Piaget was interested in charting how children make sense of the world conceptually and how this ability changes developmentally. Information-processing psychologists often focus on more specific aspects of children's mental life. In chapter 2, "The Science of Child Development," we briefly discussed the information-processing perspective, which focuses on how individuals process information about their world—how information enters the mind, how it is stored and transformed in memory, and how it is retrieved to perform such complex activities as thinking and reasoning. Unlike Piaget, information-processing psychologists do not describe infancy as a stage or a series of substages. Rather, they emphasize the precise aspects of cognitive processes, such as attention, memory, and thinking (Carey, 1999; Case, 1999; Rose, 1995).

Piaget believed that the infant's ability to construct sensorimotor schemas, establish a coherent world of objects and events suitable to form the content of ideas, imitate, and form images that can stand for things is completed in the second half of the second year. However, many information-processing psychologists believe the young infant is more competent than Piaget believed. They think that attentional, symbolic, imitative, and conceptual capabilities are present earlier in infant development than Piaget envisioned (Meltzoff, 1992; Meltzoff & Moore, 1999).

Infant Cognition

Habituation and Dishabituation

If a stimulus—a sight or sound—is presented to infants several times in a row, they usually pay less attention to it each time. This suggests they are bored with it. This is the process of **habituation**—*repeated presentation of the same stimulus that causes reduced attention to the stimulus.* **Dishabituation** *is an infant's renewed interest in a stimulus.* Among the measures researchers use to study whether habituation is occurring are sucking behavior (sucking behavior stops when the young infant attends to a novel object), heart and respiration rates, and the length of time the infant looks at an object. Newborn infants can habituate to repetitive stimulation in virtually every stimulus modality—vision, hearing, touch, and so on (Rovee-Collier, 1987). However, habituation becomes more acute over the first three months of life. The extensive assessment of habituation in recent years has resulted in its use as a

habituation
Repeated presentation of the same stimulus, which causes reduced attention to the stimulus.

dishabituation
An infant's renewed interest in a stimulus.

Researchers use a variety of ingenious techniques to study infant development. In researcher Mark Johnson's laboratory at Carnegie Mellon University, babies have shown an ability to organize their world and to anticipate future events by learning and remembering sequences of colorful images on TV monitors.

measure of an infant's maturity and well-being. Infants who have brain damage or have suffered birth traumas, such as lack of oxygen, do not habituate well and may later have developmental and learning problems.

A knowledge of habituation and dishabituation can benefit parent-infant interaction. Infants respond to changes in stimulation. If stimulation is repeated often, the infant's response will decrease to the point that the infant no longer responds to the parent. In parent-infant interaction, it is important for parents to do novel things and to repeat them often until the infant stops responding. The wise parent senses when the infant shows an interest and that many repetitions of the stimulus may be necessary for the infant to process the information. The parent stops or changes behaviors when the infant redirects her attention (Rosenblith, 1992).

Memory

Memory *is a central feature of cognitive development, pertaining to all situations in which an individual retains information over time.* Sometimes information is retained for only a few seconds, and at other times it is retained for a lifetime. Memory is involved when we look up a telephone number and dial it, when we remember a telephone number and dial it, when we remember the name of our best friend from elementary school, when an infant remembers who her mother is, and when an older adult remembers to keep a doctor's appointment.

Popular child-rearing expert Penelope Leach (1990) tells parents that 6- to 8-month-old babies cannot hold in their mind a picture of their mother or father. And historically psychologists have believed that infants cannot store memories until they have the language skills required to form them and retrieve them. Recently, though, child development researchers have revealed that infants as young as 3 months of age show memory skills (Courage & Howe, 1999; Grunwald & others, 1993).

ℳan is the only animal that can be bored.

Erich Fromm
American Psychotherapist, 20th Century

Infant Memory Research

memory
A central feature of cognitive development, pertaining to all situations in which an individual retains information over time.

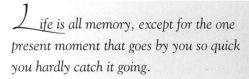

ℒife is all memory, except for the one present moment that goes by you so quick you hardly catch it going.

Tennessee Williams
American Playwright, 20th Century

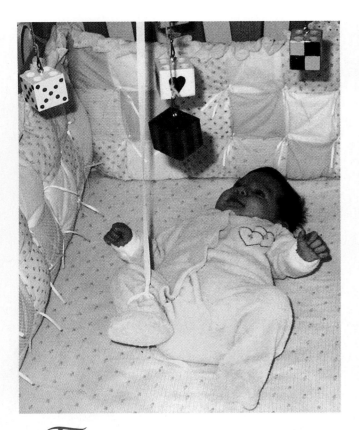

*F*igure 7.3
The Technique Used in Rovee-Collier's Investigation of Infant Memory

The mobile is connected to the infant's ankle by a ribbon and moves in direct proportion to the frequency and vigor of the infant's kicks. This infant is in a reinforcement period. During this period, the infant can see the mobile, but, because the ribbon is attached to a different stand, she cannot make the mobile move. Baseline activity is assessed during a nonreinforcement period prior to training, and all retention tests are also conducted during periods of nonreinforcement. As can be seen, this infant already has learned and is attempting to make the mobile move by kicking her leg with the ribbon attachments.

We are, in truth, more than half what we are by imitation.

Lord Chesterfield
English Statesman, 18th Century

In one study, infants were placed in large black boxes, where they lay looking up at TV screens, viewing a sequence of colorful objects that appeared repeatedly on the screens (Canfield & Haith, 1991). The babies' eye movements were monitored with an infrared camera linked to a computer. After viewing the sequence only five times, the babies could anticipate where the next object in the sequence would appear. With just a little more practice, they predicted a four-step sequence, and most could still remember it up to two weeks later.

Carolyn Rovee-Collier (1987) has found that infants can remember surprisingly intricate material. In a characteristic experiment, she places a baby in a crib underneath an elaborate mobile and ties one end of a ribbon to the baby's ankle and the other end to the mobile. Then she observes as the baby kicks and makes the mobile move. Weeks later, the baby is returned to the crib, but its foot is not tied to the mobile. The baby kicks, apparently trying to make the mobile move (see figure 7.3). However, if the mobile's makeup is changed even slightly, the baby doesn't kick. If the mobile is then restored to being exactly as it was when the baby's ankle was originally tied to it, the baby will begin kicking again. According to Rovee-Collier, even by 2½ months the baby's memory is incredibly detailed.

Nancy Myers and her colleagues (Myers, Clifton, & Clarkson, 1987) have found that 2-year-olds can remember experiences they had at 6 months of age. They placed 16 6-month-old babies in a dark room with objects that made different sounds. Using infrared cameras, they observed how and when the infants reached for objects. Two years later, the same children were brought back into the laboratory, along with a control group of 16 other 2½-year-old children (Perris, Myers, & Clifton, 1990). The experimental group revealed the same behavior they had shown at 6 months. They reached for the objects, displaying no fear, but fewer control group children reached for the objects and many of them cried. The experiment demonstrates that young children can remember experiences from up to 2 years earlier when put in the same context.

In summary, the capacity for memory appears much earlier in infancy than we used to believe. It also is more precise than earlier conclusions suggested.

Imitation

Can infants imitate someone else's emotional expressions? If an adult smiles, will the baby follow with a smile? If an adult protrudes her lower lip, wrinkles her forehead, and frowns, will the baby show a saddened look? If an adult opens his mouth, widens his eyes, and raises his eyebrows, will the baby follow suit? Can infants only a few days old do these things?

Infant development researcher Andrew Meltzoff (1992; Meltzoff, 1999; Meltzoff & Moore, 1999) has conducted numerous studies of infants' imitative abilities. He believes infants' imitative abilities are biologically based, because infants can imitate a facial expression within the first few days after birth. This occurs before they have had the opportunity to observe social agents in their environment protrude their tongues and engage in other behaviors. He also emphasizes that the infant's imitative abilities are not like what ethologists conceptualize as a hardwired, reflexive, innate releasing mechanism but, rather, involve flexibility, adaptability, and intermodal perception. In Meltzoff's observations of infants in the first 72 hours of life, the infants gradually displayed a full imitative response of an adult's facial expression, such as protruding the tongue or opening the mouth wide (see figure 7.4). Initially, the young infant may get its tongue only to the edge of its lips. However, after a number of attempts and observations of the adult behavior, the infant displays a more full-blown response.

Meltzoff has also studied **deferred imitation,** *which is imitation that occurs after a time delay of hours or days.* In one study, Meltzoff (1988) demonstrated that 9-month-old infants could imitate actions they had seen performed 24 hours earlier. Each action consisted of an unusual gesture—such as pushing a recessed button in a box (which produced a beeping sound). Piaget believed that deferred imitation does not occur until about 18 months of age; Meltzoff's research suggests that it occurs much earlier in infant development.

In sum, rather than assuming that infants' conceptual functioning—involving such important cognitive processes as memory and deferred imitation—can occur only as an outcome of a lengthy sensorimotor stage, information-processing psychologists believe that infants acquire them much earlier in infancy than Piaget believed. As we will see next, a third perspective on infant cognition also differs from Piaget's approach.

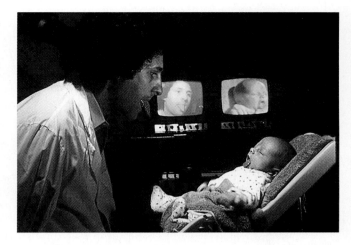

$\mathcal{F}$*igure 7.4*
Infant Imitation

Infant development researcher Andrew Meltzoff protrudes his tongue in an attempt to get the infant to imitate his behavior. Researchers have demonstrated that young infants can imitate adult behaviors far earlier than traditionally believed.

INDIVIDUAL DIFFERENCES IN INTELLIGENCE

So far, we have stressed general statements about how the cognitive development of infants progresses. We have emphasized what is typical of the largest number of infants or the average infant, but the results obtained for most infants do not apply to all infants. Individual differences in infant cognitive development have been studied primarily through the use of developmental scales, or infant intelligence tests.

It is advantageous to know whether an infant is advancing at a slow, a normal, or an advanced pace of development. In chapter 4, we discussed the Brazelton Neonatal Behavioral Assessment Scale, which is widely used to evaluate newborns. Developmentalists also want to know how development proceeds during the course of infancy. If an infant advances at an especially slow rate, then some form of enrichment may be necessary. If an infant develops at an advanced pace, parents may be advised to provide toys that stimulate cognitive growth in slightly older infants.

The infant testing movement grew out of the tradition of IQ testing of older children. However, the measures that assess infants are necessarily less verbal than IQ tests that assess the intelligence of older children. The infant developmental scales contain far more perceptual motor items. They also include measures of social interaction.

The most important early contributor to the developmental testing of infants was Arnold Gesell (1934). He developed a measure that was used as a clinical tool to help sort out potentially normal babies from abnormal ones. This was especially useful to adoption agencies, which had large numbers of babies awaiting placement. Gesell's examination was used widely for many years. It is still frequently used by pediatricians in their assessment of normal and abnormal infants. The current version of the Gesell test has four categories of behavior: motor, language, adaptive, and personal-social. The **developmental quotient (DQ)** *is an overall developmental score that combines subscores in motor, language, adaptive, and personal-social domains in the Gesell assessment of infants.* However, overall scores on tests like the Gesell do not correlate highly with IQ scores obtained later in childhood. This is not surprising, because the items on the developmental scales are considerably less verbal than the items on intelligence tests given to older children.

deferred imitation

Imitation that occurs after a time delay of hours or days.

developmental quotient (DQ)

An overall developmental score that combines subscores in motor, language, adaptive, and personal-social domains in the Gesell assessment of infants.

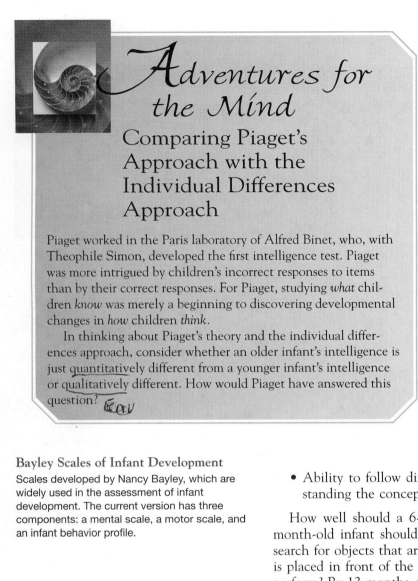

Adventures for the Mind
Comparing Piaget's Approach with the Individual Differences Approach

Piaget worked in the Paris laboratory of Alfred Binet, who, with Theophile Simon, developed the first intelligence test. Piaget was more intrigued by children's incorrect responses to items than by their correct responses. For Piaget, studying *what* children *know* was merely a beginning to discovering developmental changes in *how* children *think*.

In thinking about Piaget's theory and the individual differences approach, consider whether an older infant's intelligence is just *quantitatively* different from a younger infant's intelligence or *qualitatively* different. How would Piaget have answered this question?

Bayley Scales of Infant Development
Scales developed by Nancy Bayley, which are widely used in the assessment of infant development. The current version has three components: a mental scale, a motor scale, and an infant behavior profile.

Bayley Scales of Infant Development

The **Bayley Scales of Infant Development,** *developed by Nancy Bayley (1969), are widely used in the assessment of infant development. The current version has three components: a mental scale, a motor scale, and an infant behavior profile.* Unlike Gesell, whose scales were clinically motivated, Bayley wanted to develop scales that could assess infant behavior and predict later development. The early version of the Bayley scales covered only the first year of development. In the 1950s, the scales were extended to assess older infants. In 1993, the Bayley-II was published, with updated norms for diagnostic assessment at a younger age.

Because our discussion in this chapter centers on the infant's cognitive development, our primary interest is in Bayley's mental scale. It includes assessment of the following:

- Auditory and visual attention to stimuli
- Manipulation, such as combining objects or shaking a rattle
- Examiner interaction, such as babbling and imitation
- Relation with toys, such as banging spoons together
- Memory involved in object permanence, as when the infant finds a hidden toy
- Goal-directed behavior that involves persistence, such as putting pegs in a board
- Ability to follow directions and knowledge of objects' names, such as understanding the concept of "one"

How well should a 6-month-old perform on the Bayley mental scale? The 6-month-old infant should be able to vocalize pleasure and displeasure, persistently search for objects that are just out of immediate reach, and approach a mirror that is placed in front of the infant by the examiner. How well should a 12-month-old perform? By 12 months of age, the infant should be able to inhibit behavior when commanded to do so, imitate words the examiner says (such as *Mama*), and respond to simple requests (such as "Take a drink"). To further evaluate the individual differences approach, see Adventures for the Mind.

Tests of infant intelligence have been valuable in assessing the effects of malnutrition, drugs, maternal deprivation, and environmental stimulation on the development of infants. However, they have met with mixed results in predicting later intelligence. Global developmental quotient or IQ scores for infants have not been good predictors of childhood intelligence. However, specific aspects of infant intelligence are related to specific aspects of childhood intelligence. For example, in one study, infant language abilities as assessed by the Bayley test predicted language, reading, and spelling ability at 6 to 8 years of age (Siegel, 1989). Infant perceptual motor skills predicted visuospatial, arithmetic, and fine motor skills at 6 to 8 years of age. These results indicate that an item analysis of infant scales like Bayley's can provide information about the development of specific intellectual functions.

The explosion of interest in infant development has produced many new measures, especially using tasks that evaluate the way infants process information. Evidence is accumulating that measures of habituation and dishabituation predict intelligence in childhood (McCall & Carriger, 1993). Less cumulative attention by an infant in the habituation situation and greater amounts of attention in the dishabituation situation reflect more efficient information processing. Both types of attention—decrement and recovery—when measured in the first six months of infancy, are related to higher IQ scores on standardized intelligence tests given at various times between infancy and adolescence. In sum, more precise assessments of the infant's cognition with information-processing tasks involving attention have led to the conclusion that continuity between infant and childhood intelligence is greater than was previously believed.

It is important, however, not to go too far and think that the connections between early infant cognitive development and later childhood cognitive development are so strong that no discontinuity takes place. Rather than asking whether cognitive development is continuous *or* discontinuous, perhaps we should be examining the ways cognitive development is both continuous *and* discontinuous. Some important changes in cognitive development take place after infancy, changes that underscore the discontinuity of cognitive development. We will describe these changes in cognitive development in subsequent chapters, which focus on later periods of development.

An important agenda for caregivers is to engage in strategies that help the infant develop in cognitively competent ways. The insert, Improving Developmental Skills, profiles some of these strategies.

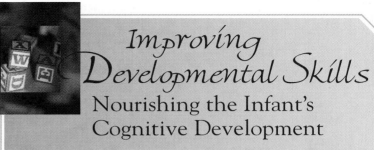

Improving Developmental Skills
Nourishing the Infant's Cognitive Development

What are some good strategies for helping the infant develop in cognitively competent ways?

- *Provide the infant with many play opportunities in a rich and varied environment.* Give the infant extensive opportunities to experience objects of different sizes, shapes, textures, and colors. Recognize that play with objects stimulates the infant's cognitive development.
- *Actively communicate with the infant.* Don't let the infant spend long bouts of waking hours in social isolation. Infants need caregivers who actively communicate with them. This active communication with adults is necessary for the infant's competent cognitive development.
- *Don't try to overaccelerate the infant's cognitive development.* Most experts believe infants' cognitive development benefits when they learn concepts naturally. The experts argue that restricting infants to a passive role and showing them flash cards to accelerate their cognitive development is not a good strategy.

EARLY ENVIRONMENTAL INFLUENCES ON INFANT COGNITIVE DEVELOPMENT

So far, we have discussed a number of approaches to infants' cognitive development, but an important aspect of this development remains to be examined. What are some early environmental experiences that might influence this cognitive development? Two areas in which researchers have investigated this question are nutrition and poverty.

Nutrition

When we think about how nutrition affects development, we usually think of physical development, such as skeletal growth, body shape, and susceptibility to disease. However, malnutrition also can restrict an infant's cognitive development.

In one study, two groups of extremely malnourished 1-year-old South African infants were examined (Bayley, 1970). The children in one group were given adequate nourishment during the next six years. No intervention took place in the lives of the other group of children. After the seventh year, the poorly nourished group of children performed worse on intelligence tests than did the adequately nourished group.

In another study, George Gutherie and his co-workers (1976) evaluated a group of severely underweight, malnourished infants in a rural area of the Philippines. They found that a combination of malnutrition, infection, and inadequate social stimulation from caregivers was associated with very low scores on the Bayley Scales of Infant Development.

In more recent research on nutrition and cognitive development, Ernesto Pollitt and his colleagues (1993) conducted a longitudinal study over two decades in rural Guatemala. They found that early nutritional supplements in the form of protein and increased calories can have positive long-term consequences for cognitive development. In the study, the link between nutrition and cognitive development was moderated by the time period in which the supplements were given and by the social context. For example, the children in the lowest socioeconomic groups benefited more than did the children in the higher socioeconomic groups. And, although there still was a positive nutritional influence when the supplements were given after 2 years of age, the effect was more powerful before the age of 2. In sum, good nutrition in infancy is important, not only for the child's physical development but also for the child's cognitive development.

Poverty

Children and Poverty

Researchers are increasingly interested in manipulating the early environment in children's lives when they are living in poverty, in hope that the changes will have a positive effect on their cognitive development (McLoyd, 1998, 1999). Two ways this can be carried out are (1) to change parents' adaptive and responsive functioning and (2) to provide competent educational day care.

In one study, called the Carolina Abecedarian Project, intensive intervention that began in infancy had positive results on children's intelligence (Campbell & Ramey, 1994; Ramey & Campell, 1984; Ramey & Ramey, 1998). The researchers identified more than 100 infants who were at risk for doing poorly in school because of their impoverished environment and low achievement of older siblings. As babies, they were randomly assigned to one of two groups: (1) a treatment group that was given educational day care or (2) a control group, which did not get the enriched day care. Both groups were given nutritional supplements and were provided with health care services. During the first three years of their lives, the children in the treatment group were given experiences designed to improve their motor, cognitive, language, and social skills. After 3 years of age, the treatment group also was given prereading instruction. Many efforts were made to involve the parents in their children's education in the treatment group. Through the age of 12, positive effects of the intervention were found on intelligence tests and in tests of achievement in reading and writing. The treatment group also was less likely than the control group to be placed in special education classes or to repeat a grade.

Early intervention programs for infants in poverty conditions vary. Some are center-based, like the Carolina program just described, others are home-based.

What are the characteristics of effective early intervention programs for infants in poverty conditions?

Some are brief interventions; others are long-term. Some are time-intensive (such as all-day educational day care), others less intensive (such as one-hour-a-day or once-a-week sessions). In general, researchers have found that early intervention programs for infants living in poverty have the most positive developmental outcomes when (1) the program is long-lasting, (2) the program is time-intensive, (3) the program provides direct educational benefits, often in educational contexts, and does not rely on parental training alone, and (4) the program is comprehensive and multidimensional, including educational, health, and counseling services for parents, in addition to working directly with infants. We will further explore intervention in the lives of children in poverty by discussing Project Head Start in chapter 10, "Cognitive Development in Early Childhood," and by examining many factors in poverty interventions in chapter 12, "Physical Development in Middle and Late Childhood."

At this point, we have studied many ideas about children's cognitive development. An overview of these ideas is presented in summary table 7.1. Next, we will explore another key dimension of infant development: language.

National Center for Children in Poverty

Zero to Three

LANGUAGE DEVELOPMENT

In France in 1799, a nude boy was observed running through the woods. The boy was captured when he was approximately 11 years old, and it was believed he had lived in the wild for at least 6 years. He was called the "Wild Boy of Aveyron" (Lane, 1976). When the boy was found, he made no effort to communicate; in fact, he never learned to communicate effectively. The Wild Boy of Aveyron raises an important issue in language: what are the biological, environmental, and cultural contributions to language? Later in the chapter, we will describe a modern-day wild child named Genie, who will shed some light on this issue. Indeed, the contributions of biology, environment, and culture figure prominently in our discussion of language.

What Is Language?

Every human culture has language. Human languages number in the thousands. They differ so much on the surface that many of us despair at learning more than one, yet all human languages have some common characteristics. A **language** *is a system of symbols used to communicate with others. In humans, language is characterized by infinite generativity and rule systems.* **Infinite generativity** *is an individual's ability to generate an infinite number of meaningful sentences using a finite set of words and rules. This makes language a highly creative enterprise.* Language's rule systems include phonology, morphology, syntax, semantics, and pragmatics, each of which we will discuss.

Language is made up of basic sounds, or *phonemes*. In the English language, there are approximately 36 phonemes. **Phonology** *is the study of a language's sound system.* Phonological rules specify that some sound sequences are permissible (for example, *sp, ba,* and *ar*) and others are not (for example, *zx* and *qp*). A good example of a phoneme in the English language is /k/, the sound represented by the letter *k* in the word *ski* and the letter *c* in the word *cat*. While the /k/ sound is slightly different in these two words, the variation is not distinguished, and the /k/ sound is described as a single phoneme. In some languages, such as Arabic, however, this kind of subtle variation represents separate phonemes. An increasing number of researchers believe that speech is an infant's gateway to language (Eimas, 1995; Morgan & Demuth, 1995).

What phonology does is provide a basis for constructing a large and expandable set of words—all that are or ever will be in that language—out of two or three dozen phonemes. We do not need 500,000. We need only two or three dozen.

Patricia Kuhl (1993) has conducted research which reveals that long before they actually begin to learn words, infants can sort through a number of spoken sounds

language
A system of symbols used to communicate with others. In humans, language is characterized by infinite generativity and rule systems.

infinite generativity
An individual's ability to generate an infinite number of meaningful sentences using a finite set of words and rules, which makes language a highly creative enterprise.

phonology
The study of a language's sound system.

Summary Table 7.1
Infant Cognitive Development

Concept	Processes/ Related Ideas	Characteristics/Description
Piaget's theory of infant development	Sensorimotor stage	This stage lasts from birth to about 2 years of age and involves progression in the infant's ability to organize and coordinate sensations with physical movements. The sensorimotor stage has six substages: simple reflexes; first habits and primary circular reactions; secondary circular reactions; coordination of secondary circular reactions; tertiary circular reactions, novelty, and curiosity; and internalization of schemes.
	Object permanence	*Object permanence* refers to the development of the ability to understand that objects and events continue to exist, even though the infant no longer is in contact with them. Piaget believed that this ability develops over the course of the six substages.
	Evaluating Piaget's sensorimotor stage	Piaget opened up a whole new way of looking at infant development in terms of coordinating sensory input with motor activities. However, in the past two decades, a large number of research studies have been conducted that suggest some revision of Piaget's view of sensorimotor development is needed. In perceptual development, researchers have found that a stable and differentiated perceptual world is established earlier than Piaget envisioned. In conceptual development, researchers have found that memory and other forms of symbolic activity occur by at least the second half of the first year of life, also much earlier than Piaget believed. Some developmentalists argue that it is hard to tell a unifying story about infant cognitive development, the way Piaget did many years ago. Debate flourishes about many issues, such as whether a concept is innate, as well as whether it emerges full-blown or more gradually.
The information-processing perspective and infant development	Its nature	Unlike Piaget, information-processing psychologists do not describe infancy as a stage or series of substages of sensorimotor development. Rather, they emphasize the importance of cognitive processes, such as attention, memory, and thinking. The information-processing psychologists believe that the young infant is more competent than Piaget envisioned, with attentional, symbolic, imitative, and conceptual abilities occurring much earlier in development than Piaget thought.
	Habituation and dishabituation	Habituation is the repeated presentation of the same stimulus, causing reduced attention to the stimulus. If a different stimulus is presented and the infant pays attention to it, dishabituation is occurring. Newborn infants can habituate, but habituation becomes more acute over the first three months of infancy.
	Memory	Memory is the retention of information over time. Memory develops much earlier in infancy than once was believed and is more specific than earlier conclusions suggested.
	Imitation	Infants can imitate the facial expressions of others in the first few days of life. Meltzoff demonstrated that deferred imitation occurs at about 9 months of age, much earlier than Piaget believed.
Individual differences in intelligence	History	Developmental scales for infants grew out of the tradition of IQ testing of older children. These scales are less verbal than IQ tests. Gesell was an early developer of an infant test. His scale is still widely used by pediatricians; it provides a developmental quotient (DQ).
	Bayley scales	The developmental scales most widely used today, developed by Nancy Bayley, consist of a motor scale, a mental scale, and an infant behavior profile.
	Conclusions about infant tests and continuity in mental development	Global infant intelligence measures are not good predictors of childhood intelligence. However, specific aspects of infant intelligence, such as information-processing tasks involving attention, have been better predictors of childhood intelligence, especially in a specific area. There is both continuity and discontinuity between infant cognitive development and cognitive development later in childhood.
Early environmental influences on infant cognitive development	Nutrition	Nutritional supplements given to malnourished infants have been found to improve infants' cognitive development.
	Poverty	Early intervention programs that target infants living in poverty are often more effective when they are (1) long-term, (2) time-intensive, (3) able to provide direct educational benefits, and (4) comprehensive and multidimensional.

in search of the ones that have meaning. Kuhl argues that from birth to about 4 months of age, infants are "universal linguists" who are capable of distinguishing all of the sounds that make up human speech. But, by about 6 months of age, they have started to specialize in the speech sounds of their native language. By 8 or 9 months of age, comprehension is more noticeable. For example, babies look at a ball when their mothers say "ball." Language experts say that it is impossible to determine how many words babies understand at this point in their development. However, research with slightly older children suggests that comprehension might outpace expression by a factor of 100 to 1. Researchers also have found that, although some babies are slow in beginning to talk, comprehension is often about equal between early and late talkers (Bates & Thal, 1991).

Morphology *is the study of what language users know about the units of meaning and the rules of combining morphemes.* A morpheme *is a meaningful string of phonemes (sounds) that has no smaller meaningful parts.* Every word in the English language is made up of one or more morphemes. Some words consist of a single morpheme (for example, *help*). Others are made up of more than one morpheme (for example, *helper*, which has two morphemes, *help* + *-er*, with the morpheme *-er* meaning "one who"—in this case, "one who helps"). However, not all morphemes are words (for example, *pre-*, *-tion*, and *-ing*). Just as the rules that govern phonemes ensure that certain sound sequences occur, the rules that govern morphemes ensure that certain strings of sounds occur in meaningful sequences. For example, we would not reorder *helper* as *erhelp*.

Syntax *involves the ways words are combined to form acceptable phrases and sentences.* For example, *He didn't stay, did he?* is a grammatical sentence, but *He didn't stay, didn't he?* is unacceptable and ambiguous. Similarly, if I say to you, "Bob slugged Tom" and "Bob was slugged by Tom," you know who did the slugging and who was slugged in each case because we share the same syntactic understanding of sentence structure. This concept of "who does what to whom" is called *grammatical relations*, and it is an important type of syntactic information.

The term **semantics** *refers to the meanings of words and sentences.* Every word has a set of semantic features. *Girl* and *woman*, for instance, both have some of the semantic features of the words *female* and *human*, but they also differ in meaning (for instance, regarding age). Words have semantic restrictions on how they can be used in sentences. The sentence *The bicycle talked the boy into buying a candy bar* is syntactically correct but semantically incorrect. The sentence violates our semantic knowledge that bicycles do not talk.

A final set of language rules involves **pragmatics**—*the use of appropriate conversation and the knowledge underlying the use of language in context.* The domain of pragmatics is broad, covering such circumstances as (1) taking turns in discussions instead of everyone talking at once; (2) using questions to convey commands ("Why is it so noisy in here?" "What is this, Grand Central Station?"); (3) using words such as *the* and *a* in a way that improves understanding ("I read *a* book last night. *The* plot was boring."); (4) using polite language in appropriate situations (for example, when talking to one's teacher); and (5) telling stories that are interesting, jokes that are funny, and lies that convince.

Do we learn this ability to generate rule systems for language and then use them to create an almost infinite number of words? Or is this remarkable ability the product of biology and evolution? (de Villiers & de Villiers, 1999)

Biological Influences

The strongest evidence for the biological basis of language is that children all over the world reach language milestones at about the same time developmentally and in about the same order. This occurs despite the vast variation in the language input they receive. For example, in some cultures, adults never talk to children under 1 year of age, yet these infants still acquire language. Also, there is no other convincing way to explain how *quickly* children learn language than through biological foundations.

"If you don't mind my asking, how much does a sentence diagrammer pull down a year?"

© Reprinted by permission of Bob Thaves.

morphology
The study of the rules for combining morphemes; morphemes are the smallest meaningful units of language.

syntax
The rules for combining words to form acceptable phrases and sentences.

semantics
The meaning of words and sentences.

pragmatics
The rules for appropriate conversation and the knowledge underlying the use of language in context.

The adjective is the banana peel of the parts of speech.

Clifton Fadiman
American Critic and Lecturer, 20th Century

Brain and Language Development

With these thoughts in mind, let's now explore these questions about biological influences on language: How strongly is language influenced by biological evolution? Are humans biologically wired to learn language? Is there a critical period for language acquisition?

Biological Evolution   A number of experts stress the biological foundations of language (Chomsky, 1957; Miller, 1981). They believe it is undeniable that biological evolution shaped humans into linguistic creatures (Scott, 1997). In terms of biological evolution, the brain, nervous system, and vocal system changed over hundreds of thousands of years. Prior to *Homo sapiens*, the physical equipment to produce language was not present. *Homo sapiens* went beyond the groans and shrieks of their predecessors with the development of abstract speech. Estimates vary as to how long ago humans acquired language—from about 20,000 to 70,000 years ago. In evolutionary time, then, language is a very recent acquisition.

language acquisition device (LAD)
A biological endowment that enables the child to detect certain language categories, such as phonology, syntax, and semantics.

Biological Prewiring   Linguist Noam Chomsky (1957) believes humans are biologically prewired to learn language at a certain time and in a certain way. He said that children are born into the world with a **language acquisition device (LAD),** *a biological endowment that enables the child to detect certain language categories, such as phonology, syntax, and semantics.* The LAD is a theoretical construct that flows from evidence about the biological basis of language.

Is there evidence for the existence of a LAD? Supporters of the LAD concept cite the uniformity of language milestones across languages and cultures, biological substrates for language, and evidence that children create language even in the absence of well-formed input. With regard to the last argument, most deaf children are the offspring of hearing parents. Some of these parents choose not to expose their deaf child to sign language, in order to motivate the child to learn speech while providing the child with a supportive social environment. Susan Goldin-Meadow (1979) has found that these children develop spontaneous gestures that are not based on their parents' gestures.

critical period
A period in which there is a learning readiness; beyond this period, learning is difficult or impossible.

**Critical Period Hypothesis
in Language**

Is There a Critical Period for Learning Language?   Have you ever encountered young children serving as unofficial "translators" for their non-English-speaking parents? Doctors and nurses sometimes encounter this when treating patients. Does this indicate that young children are able to easily learn language, while their parents have lost this ability? Such an explanation fits the view that there is a **critical period,** *a period in which there is a learning readiness. Beyond this period, learning is difficult or impossible.* The concept of a critical period applies nicely to certain varieties of songbirds. For example, baby white-crowned sparrows learn the song of their species quite well if they are exposed to it during a specific time as a chick. After this time, they can never develop a fully formed song pattern. But whether this notion can be extended to humans learning language is much less certain.

Almost all children learn one or more languages during their early years of development, so it is difficult to determine whether there is a critical period for language development (Obler, 1993). In the 1960s, Eric Lenneberg (1967) proposed a biological theory of language acquisition. He said that language is a maturational process and that there is a critical period between about 18 months of age and puberty, during which a first language must be acquired. Central to Lenneberg's thesis is the idea that language develops rapidly and with ease during the preschool years as a result of maturation. Lenneberg provided support for the critical-period concept from studies of several atypical populations. These included children with left-hemisphere brain damage, deaf children, and children with mental retardation (Tager-Flusberg, 1994). With regard to brain damage, Lenneberg believed that adults had already passed the critical period during which plasticity of brain function allows language skills to be relearned.

The stunted language development of a modern "wild child" supports the idea that there is a critical period for language acquisition (see figure 7.5). In 1970, a

California social worker made a routine visit to the home of a partially blind woman who had applied for public assistance. The social worker discovered that the woman and her husband had kept their 13-year-old daughter, Genie, locked away in almost total isolation during her childhood. Genie could not speak or stand erect. She had spent every day bound naked to a child's potty seat. She could move only her hands and feet. At night she was placed in a kind of straightjacket and caged in a crib with wire mesh sides and a cover. Whenever Genie made a noise, her father beat her. He never communicated with her in words but growled and barked at her instead (Rymer, 1992).

After she was rescued from her parents, Genie spent a number of years in extensive rehabilitation programs, such as speech and physical therapy (Curtiss, 1977). She eventually learned to walk, although with a jerky motion, and to use the toilet. Genie also learned to recognize many words and to speak in rudimentary sentences. At first, she spoke in one-word utterances. Later she was able to string together two-word combinations, such as "Big teeth," "Little marble," and "Two hand." Consistent with the language development of most children, three-word combinations (such as "Small two cup") followed. Unlike normal children, Genie has not learned to ask questions, and she does not understand grammar. She is not able to distinguish among pronouns or between passive and active verbs. Four years after she began stringing words together, Genie's speech still sounded like a garbled telegram. As an adult, she speaks in short, mangled sentences, such as "Father hit leg," "Big wood," and "Genie hurt."

Children like Genie, "Wild" Peter of Germany, and Kamala (the wolf-girl), who are abandoned, abused, and not exposed to language for many years, rarely speak normally. Such tragic evidence supports the critical-period hypothesis in language development. However, because these children also suffer severe emotional trauma and possible neurological deficits, the issue is still far from clear.

Let's go back to our "child translator" example. Why is it that children seem to do better than older people in learning language? Many researchers have proposed that the preschool years (until age 5) may be a critical period for language acquisition. Evidence for this notion comes from studies of brain development in young children, and from the amount of language learned by preschool children. However, other evidence suggests that we do not have a critical period for language learning. First of all, although much language learning takes place during the preschool years, learning continues well into the later school years and adulthood. Also, with respect to second-language learning, adults can do as well as or better than young children, provided they are motivated and spend equivalent amounts of learning time. In other words, young children's proficiency in language, while impressive, does not seem to involve a biologically salient critical period that older children and adults have passed.

Figure 7.5 "Wild Child" Genie

What were Genie's experiences like, and what implications do her experiences have for language acquisition?

Genie

Behavioral and Environmental Influences

Behaviorists view language as just another behavior, such as sitting, walking, and running. They argue that language represents chains of responses (Skinner, 1957) or imitation (Bandura, 1977). But many of the sentences we produce are novel; we have not heard them or spoken them before. For example, a child hears the sentence "The plate fell on the floor" and then says, "My mirror fell on the blanket," after dropping the mirror on the blanket. The behavioral mechanisms of reinforcement and imitation cannot completely explain this.

While spending long hours observing parents and their young children, child language researcher Roger Brown (1973) searched for evidence that parents reinforce their children for speaking in grammatical ways. He found that parents sometimes smile and praise their children for sentences they like. However, they also reinforce sentences that are ungrammatical. Brown concluded that no evidence exists to document that reinforcement is responsible for language's rule systems.

Another criticism of the behavioral view is that it fails to explain the extensive orderliness of language. The behavioral view predicts that vast individual differences should appear in children's speech development because of each child's unique learning history. But, as we have seen, a compelling fact about language is its structure and ever-present rule systems. All infants coo before they babble. All toddlers produce one-word utterances before two-word utterances. All state sentences in the active form before they state them in a passive form.

However, we do not learn language in a social vacuum. Most children are bathed in language from a very early age (Hart & Risley, 1995). We need this early exposure to language to acquire competent language skills (Snow, 1999). The Wild Boy of Aveyron did not learn to communicate effectively after being reared in social isolation for years. Genie's language is rudimentary, even after years of extensive training.

Today most language acquisition researchers believe that children from a wide variety of cultural contexts acquire their native language without explicit teaching. In some cases, they do so without apparent encouragement. Thus, there appear to be very few aids that are necessary for learning a language. However, the support and involvement of caregivers and teachers greatly facilitate a child's language learning (Dewey, 1999; Hoff-Ginsberg & Lerner, 1999). Of special concern are children who grow up in poverty-infested areas and are not exposed to guided participation in language.

John Locke (1993) argued that one reason social interactionist aspects have been underplayed in explaining language development is that linguists concentrate on language's complex structural properties, especially the acquisition of grammar. He believes they have given inadequate attention to the communicative aspects of language. Locke reminds us that language learning occurs in the very real context of physical and social maturation. Children are neither exclusively young biological linguists nor exclusively social beings. An interactionist view emphasizes the contributions of both biology and experience in language—that is, children are biologically prepared to learn language as they and their caregivers interact (MacWhinney, 1999; Nelson & Réger, 1995).

One intriguing role of the environment in the young child's acquisition of language is called **motherese**, *the kind of speech often used by mothers and other adults to talk to babies—in a higher pitch than normal and with simple words and sentences.* It is hard to talk in motherese when not in the presence of a baby. But, as soon as you start talking to a baby, you immediately shift into motherese. Much of this is automatic and something most parents are not aware they are doing. Motherese has the important functions of capturing the infant's attention and maintaining communication. When parents are asked why they use baby talk, they point out that it is designed to teach their baby to talk. Older peers also talk baby talk to infants, but observations of siblings indicate that the affectional features are dropped when sibling rivalry is sensed (Dunn & Kendrick, 1982).

Are there strategies other than motherese that adults use to enhance the child's acquisition of language? Four candidates are recasting, echoing, expanding, and labeling. **Recasting** *is rephrasing something the child has said in a different way, perhaps turning it into a question.* For example, if the child says, "The dog was barking," the adult can respond by asking, "When was the dog barking?" The effects of recasting fit with suggestions that "following in order to lead" helps a child learn language. That is, letting a child initially indicate an interest and then proceeding to elaborate that interest—commenting, demonstrating, and explaining—improve communication and help language acquisition. In contrast, an overly active, directive approach to communicating with the child may be harmful.

Echoing *is repeating what a child says, especially if it is an incomplete phrase or sentence.* **Expanding** *is restating, in a linguistically sophisticated form, what a child has said.* **Labeling** *is identifying the names of objects.* Young children are forever being asked to

motherese
The kind of speech often used by mothers and other adults to talk to babies—in a higher pitch than normal and with simple words and sentences.

recasting
Rephrasing a statement a child has said, perhaps turning it into a question.

echoing
Repeating what a child says, especially if it is an incomplete phrase or sentence.

expanding
Restating, in a linguistically sophisticated form, what a child has said.

labeling
Identifying the names of objects.

identify the names of objects. Roger Brown (1986) identified this as "the great word game" and claimed that much of the early vocabulary acquired by children is motivated by this adult pressure to identify the words associated with objects.

The strategies just described—recasting, echoing, expanding, and labeling—are used naturally and in meaningful conversations. Parents do not (and should not) use any deliberate method to teach their children to talk. Even for children who are slow in learning language, the experts agree that intervention should occur in natural ways, with the goal of being able to convey meaning.

It is important to recognize that children vary in their ability to acquire language and that this variation cannot be readily explained by differences in environmental input alone (Rice, 1996). For children who are slow in developing language skills, opportunities to talk and be talked with are important. Remember, though, that the encouragement of language development, not drill and practice, is the key (de Villiers, 1996; Snow, 1996). Language development is not a simple matter of imitation and reinforcement, a fact acknowledged even by most behaviorists today. To read further about ways that parents can facilitate children's language development, see Caring for Children.

Communicating with Babies

How Language Develops

In describing language, we have touched on language development many times. You just read about the motherese that parents use with their infants. Earlier we discussed the Wild Boy of Aveyron and Genie. Now let's examine in greater detail the developmental changes in language that take place in infancy.

In the first few months of life, infants show a startle response to sharp noises. Then, at 3 to 6 months, they begin to show an interest in sounds, they play with saliva, and they respond to voices. During the next 3 to 6 months, infants begin to babble, emitting such sounds as "goo-goo" and "ga-ga." The start of babbling is determined mainly by biological maturation, not reinforcement, hearing, or caregiver-infant interaction. Even deaf babies babble for a time (Lenneberg, Rebelsky, & Nichols, 1965). The purpose of the baby's earliest communication is to attract attention from parents and others in the environment. Infants engage the attention of others by making or breaking eye contact, by vocalizing sounds, and by performing manual actions, such as pointing. All of these behaviors involve the aspect of language we have called pragmatics.

At approximately 6 to 9 months, infants begin to understand their first words. **Receptive vocabulary** *refers to the words an individual understands.* Its growth increases dramatically in the second year, from an average of 12 words understood

Babbling
Language Milestones

receptive vocabulary
The words an individual understands.

Around the world, young children learn to speak in two-word utterances, in most cases, at about 18 to 24 months of age.

Caring for Children

How Parents Can Facilitate Children's Language Development

In *Growing Up with Language*, linguist Naomi Baron (1992) provides a number of ideas to help parents facilitate their child's language development. A summary of her ideas follows.

Infants

- *Be an active conversational partner.* Initiate conversation with the infant. If the infant is in a daylong child-care program, ensure that the baby gets adequate language stimulation from adults.
- *Talk as if the infant understands what you are saying.* Parents can generate self-fulfilling prophecies by addressing their young children as if they understand what is being said. The process may take four to five years, but children gradually rise to match the language model presented to them.
- *Use a language style with which you feel comfortable.* Don't worry about how you sound to other adults when you talk with your child. Your effect, not your content, is more important when talking with an infant. Use whatever type of baby talk with which you feel comfortable.

Toddlers

- *Continue to be an active conversational partner.* Engaging toddlers in conversation, even one-sided conversation, is the most important thing a parent can do to nourish a child linguistically.
- *Remember to listen.* Since toddlers' speech is often slow and laborious, parents are often tempted to supply words and thoughts for them. Be patient and let toddlers express themselves, no matter how painstaking the process is or how great a hurry you are in.
- *Use a language style with which you are comfortable, but consider ways of expanding your child's language abilities and horizons.* For example, using long sentences need not be problematic. Don't be afraid to use ungrammatical language to imitate the toddlers' novel forms (such as "No eat"). Use rhymes. Ask questions that encourage answers other than "Yes." Actively repeat, expand, and recast the child's utterances. Introduce new topics. And use humor in your conversation.

- *Adjust to your child's idiosyncrasies instead of working against them.* Many toddlers have difficulty pronouncing words and making themselves understood. Whenever possible, make toddlers feel they are being understood.
- *Avoid sexual stereotypes.* Don't let the toddler's sex unwittingly determine your amount or style of conversation. Many American mothers are more linguistically supportive of girls than of boys, and many fathers talk less with their children than mothers do. Active and cognitively enriching initiatives from both mothers and fathers benefit both boys and girls.
- *Resist making normative comparisons.* Be aware of the ages at which your child reaches specific milestones (first word, first 50 words, first grammatical combination). However, be careful not to measure this development rigidly against children of neighbors or friends. Such social comparisons can bring about unnecessary anxiety.

It is a good idea for parents to begin talking to their babies at the start. The best language teaching occurs when the talking is begun before the infant becomes capable of its first intelligible speech.

at the first birthday to an estimated 300 words or more understood at the second birthday. At approximately 9 to 12 months, infants first begin to understand instructions, such as "Wave bye-bye."

So far, we have not mentioned *spoken* vocabulary, which begins when the infant utters its first word. This is a milestone anticipated by every parent. This event usually occurs at about 10 to 15 months of age. Many parents view the onset of language development as coincident with this first word. However, as we have seen, some significant language milestones have already occurred. The infant's spoken vocabulary rapidly increases once the first word is spoken (Dapretto, 1999). It reaches an average of 200 to 275 words by the age of 2.

A child's first words include those that name important people (*dada*), familiar animals (*kitty*), vehicles (*car*), toys (*ball*), food (*milk*), body parts (*eye*), clothes (*hat*), household items (*clock*), and greeting terms (*bye*). These were the first words of babies 50 years ago. They are the first words of babies today. At times it is hard to tell what these one-word utterances mean. One possibility is that they stand for an entire sentence in the infant's mind. Because of the infant's limited cognitive or linguistic skills, possibly only one word comes out instead of the whole sentence. The **holophrase hypothesis** *states that a single word can be used to imply a complete sentence. Infants' first words characteristically are holophrastic.*

By the time children are 18 to 24 months of age, they usually utter two-word statements. During this two-word stage, they quickly grasp the importance of expressing concepts and of the role that language plays in communicating with others. To convey meaning with two-word utterances, the child relies heavily on gesture, tone, and context. The wealth of meaning children can communicate with a two-word utterance includes the following (Slobin, 1972):

- Identification: "See doggie."
- Location: "Book there."
- Repetition: "More milk."
- Nonexistence: "Allgone thing."
- Negation: "Not wolf."
- Possession: "My candy."
- Attribution: "Big car."
- Agent-action: "Mama walk."
- Action-direct object: "Hit you."
- Action-indirect object: "Give Papa."
- Action-instrument: "Cut knife."
- Question: "Where ball?"

These examples are from children whose first language is English, German, Russian, Finnish, Turkish, or Samoan. Although these two-word sentences omit many parts of speech, they are remarkably succinct in conveying many messages. In fact, in every language, a child's first combinations of words have this economical quality. **Telegraphic speech** *is the use of short and precise words to communicate. Young children's two- and three-word utterances characteristically are telegraphic.* When we send a telegram, we try to be short and precise, excluding any unnecessary words. As a result, articles, auxiliary verbs, and other connectives usually are omitted. Of course, telegraphic speech is not limited to two-word phrases. "Mommy give ice cream" and "Mommy give Tommy ice cream" also are examples of telegraphic speech. As children leave the two-word stage, they move rather quickly into three-, four-, and five-word combinations.

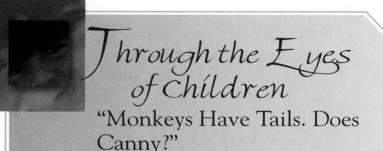

Through the Eyes of Children
"Monkeys Have Tails. Does Canny?"

At 17 months of age, Candy has just begun speaking her own name. She calls herself "Canny." She uses it to indicate ownership or a desire to be included. When her mother left for work in the car, she said, "Canny," and tried to climb into the car.

At 18 months of age, Candy's repetitious questions seek to determine similarities and differences between things. Candy asks over and over again to have objects identified. Then she tries to compare one with another. Candy says, "Monkeys have tails. So do bears. Does Canny? No. Does Mom? No," then around again, again, and again (Peterson, 1974).

holophrase hypothesis
The hypothesis that a single word can be used to imply a complete sentence; infants' first words characteristically are holophrastic.

Children pick up words as pigeons peas.

John Ray
English Naturalist, 17th Century

The Naming Explosion

telegraphic speech
The use of short and precise words to communicate; young children's two- and three-word utterances characteristically are telegraphic.

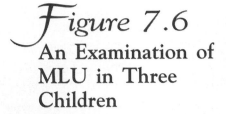

An Examination of MLU in Three Children

Shown here is the average length of utterances generated by three children who range in age from 1½ to just over 4 years.

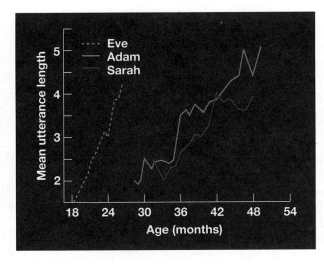

mean length of utterance (MLU)

An index of language development based on the number of morphemes per sentence a child produces in a sample of about 50 to 100 sentences; a good index of language maturity.

Roger Brown (1973) expanded this concept of classifying children's language development in terms of number of utterances. He proposed that the concept of **mean length of utterance (MLU),** *an index of language development based on the number of morphemes per sentence a child produces in a sample of about 50 to 100 sentences,* is a good index of language maturity. Brown identified five stages based on MLU:

Stage	MLU
1	1 + 2.0
2	2.5
3	3.0
4	3.5
5	4.0

The first stage begins when a child generates sentences with more than one morpheme, such as the examples of two-word utterances mentioned earlier. The 1 + designation suggests that the average number of morphemes in each utterance is greater than one but not yet two. This occurs because some of the child's utterances are still holophrases. This stage continues until the child averages two morphemes per utterance. Subsequent stages are marked by increments of 0.5 in mean length of utterance. Figure 7.6 shows Roger Brown's examination of MLU in three children.

Language Overview

As we have just seen, language unfolds sequentially (Elman, 1999). Language expert Lois Bloom (1998) concluded that three sequential frameworks help us better understand early language development:

- The emergence of words and a basic vocabulary, which begins toward the end of the first year and continues through the second year
- The transition from saying one word at a time to combining words and phrases into simple sentences, which begins to take place toward the end of the second year
- The transition from simple sentences expressing a single proposition to complex sentences, which begins between 2 and 3 years of age and continues into the elementary school years

We discussed the first two sequential frameworks in this chapter. We will discuss the third framework in chapters 10 and 13 on cognitive development in early childhood and in middle and late childhood, respectively.

Summary Table 7.2
Language Development

Concept	Processes/Related Ideas	Characteristics/Description
What is language?	Its nature	Language involves a system of symbols we use to communicate with each other. The system is characterized by infinite generativity and rule systems. The rule systems include phonology, morphology, syntax, semantics, and pragmatics.
Biological influences	Strongest evidence	Children all over the world acquire language milestones at about the same time developmentally and in about the same order, despite the vast variation in input they receive.
	Biological evolution	The fact that biological evolution shaped humans into linguistic creatures is undeniable.
	Biological prewiring	Chomsky argued that humans are biologically prewired to learn language and have a language acquisition device.
	Is there a critical period for learning language?	A critical period is a period when there is a learning readiness; beyond this period, learning is difficult or impossible. The stunted growth of "wild children," such as Genie, supports the notion that there is a critical period for language acquisition. However, the critical-period concept is still controversial.
Behavioral and environmental influences	The behavioral view	Language is just another behavior. Behaviorists believe language is learned primarily through reinforcement and imitation. These processes probably play a facilitative rather than a necessary role.
	Environmental influences	Most children are bathed in language early in their development. Among the ways adults teach language to infants are motherese, recasting, echoing, expanding, and labeling. Parents should talk to an infant extensively, especially about what the baby is attending to at the moment. Talk should be primarily live talk, not mechanical talk.
How language develops	Some developmental milestones	Among the milestones in infant language development are babbling (3 to 6 months), first words understood (6 to 9 months), the growth of receptive vocabulary (reaches 300 or more words at age 2), first instructions understood (9 months to 1 year), first word spoken (10 to 15 months), and the growth of spoken vocabulary (reaches 200 to 275 words at age 2). The holophrase hypothesis states that a single word is often used to imply a complete sentence; it characterizes infants' first words. At 18 to 24 months of age, infants often speak in two-word utterances. Telegraphic speech is the use of short and precise words to communicate—this characterizes toddlers' two-word utterances. Brown developed the concept of mean length of utterance (MLU). Five stages of MLU have been identified, providing a valuable indicator of language maturity.
Language overview	Its nature	Language unfolds sequentially. Three such important sequences are (1) the emergence of words and basic vocabulary (end of first year), (2) the transition from saying one word to combining words and phrases into simple sentences (end of second year), and (3) the transition from simple sentences that express a single proposition to complex sentences (2 to 3 years through the school years). At every point in development, linguistic interaction with others obeys certain principles. Also, not only is language development strongly influenced by the child's biological wiring, but the language environment the child is bathed in from an early age is more complex than was once envisioned.

We also have seen that, at every point in development, the child's linguistic interaction with others obeys certain principles. And, not only is language development strongly influenced by the child's biological wiring, but the language environment in which the child is bathed from an early age is far more complex than was envisioned in the past (Adamson, 1996).

At this point, we have discussed a number of ideas about language development. An overview of these ideas is presented in summary table 7.2. In the next chapter, we will continue our coverage of infant development by focusing on the infant's socioemotional development.

Chapter Review

Our knowledge of infant cognitive development has greatly expanded in the past two decades. We now know that infants have more sophisticated cognitive skills than we used to think.

We began this chapter with a glimpse at Piaget's observations of his own children. We studied Piaget's theory of infant development, focusing on the stage of sensorimotor development, object permanence, and evaluating Piaget's sensorimotor stage. We read about these aspects of the information-processing perspective: habituation and dishabituation, memory, and imitation. We also studied individual differences in intelligence in infancy, with special emphasis on the developmental testing of infants. We explored the early environmental influences of nutrition and poverty on infant cognitive development. Our coverage of language development focused on what language is, biological influences, behavioral and environmental influences, how language develops, and a language overview.

Don't forget that you can obtain an overall summary of the chapter by again reading the two summary tables on pages 184 and 193. In the next chapter, we will turn our attention to the study of socioemotional development in infancy.

✔ Children Checklist

Cognitive Development in Infancy

How much have you learned since the beginning of the chapter? Use the following statements to help you review your knowledge and understanding of the chapter material. First, read the statement and mentally or briefly demonstrate on paper that you can discuss the relevant information.

_____ I can describe Piaget's theory of infant development.
_____ I understand the new look at infant cognitive development and its criticisms of Piaget's view, as well as some remaining controversies in infant cognitive development.
_____ I know about the information-processing perspective, including habituation and dishabituation, memory, and imitation.
_____ I can discuss individual differences in intelligence.
_____ I can describe what language is.
_____ I can discuss biological influences on language.
_____ I can describe the behavioral and environmental dimensions of language.
_____ I know how language develops and can present a broad overview of basic aspects of language development in infancy.

For any items that you did not check, go back and locate the relevant material in the chapter. Review the material until you feel you can check off the item. You may want to use this checklist later in preparing for an exam.

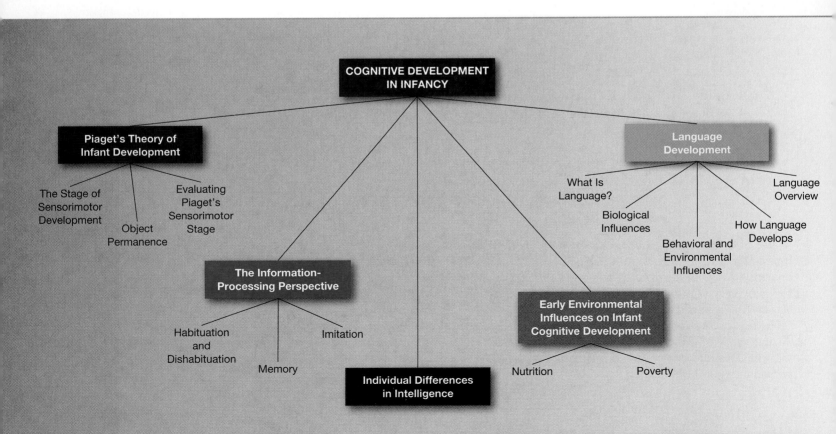

Key Terms

scheme (or schema) 172

simple reflexes 172

first habits and primary circular reactions 173

primary circular reaction 173

secondary circular reactions 173

coordination of secondary circular reactions 173

tertiary circular reactions, novelty, and curiosity 173

internalization of schemes 173

object permanence 174

habituation 176

dishabituation 176

memory 177

deferred imitation 179

developmental quotient (DQ) 179

Bayley Scales of Infant Development 180

language 183

infinite generativity 183

phonology 183

morphology 185

syntax 185

semantics 185

pragmatics 185

language acquisition device (LAD) 186

critical period 186

motherese 188

recasting 188

echoing 188

expanding 188

labeling 188

receptive vocabulary 189

holophrase hypothesis 191

telegraphic speech 191

mean length of utterance (MLU) 192

Children Resources

The First Three Years of Life
(1990, rev. ed.) by Burton White.
New York: Prentice-Hall.

The First Three Years of Life presents a broad-based approach to how parents can optimally rear their infants and young children. White strongly believes that most parents in America fail to provide an adequate intellectual and social foundation for their child's development, especially between the ages of 8 months and 3 years.

Growing Up With Language
(1992) by Naomi Baron.
Reading, MA: Addison-Wesley.

Baron focuses on three representative children and their families. She explores how children put their first words together, struggle to understand meaning, and use language as a creative tool. She shows parents how their own attitudes about language are extremely important in the child's language development.

Taking It to the Net

http://www.mhhe.com/santrockcd6

1. Individual differences in infant intelligence are often determined using a developmental assessment conducted by a developmental specialist. Under what circumstances would a child need to undergo a developmental assessment? What advice would you give to anxious parents before their child completes a developmental assessment? Should developmental assessments be required of all children? Why or why not?

2. At a recent party, a friend of yours who has an infant sister, states "Infants don't think, they only sense." Is your friend correct? What is the role of sense experience in thought and thinking?

3. It is generally known that language tends to develop rapidly between the ages of 2 and 5 years. This is often considered a "critical period," a time frame within which a child is more apt to learn a particular skill. Can you name 3 other skills and their critical periods? Are there more?

Chapter

8

Socioemotional Development in Infancy

PREVIEW

Because it cannot sustain itself, the human infant requires extensive care. Important topics in infant socioemotional development involve the kind of care needed and the best ways for the infant to begin the road to social maturity. Among the questions we will explore in this chapter are

- What emotions do infants show? When do they emerge?
- How can we classify the infant's temperament? What are some good parenting strategies that take into account the infant's temperament?
- When does the infant develop a sense of self?
- When does the infant push for independence? How can parents effectively handle this?
- How can we classify the way infants are attached to their caregivers? What parenting styles link up with different attachment categories?
- What is the transition to parenting like?
- What roles do mothers and fathers play in infants' development?
- What is the nature of child abuse?
- How does day care affect infants' development?

The Story of Tom's Fathering

Tom is a 1-year-old infant who is being reared by his father during the day. His mother works full-time at her job away from home, and his father is a writer who works at home; they prefer this arrangement over putting Tom in day care. Tom's father is doing a great job of caring for him. Tom's father keeps Tom nearby while he is writing and spends lots of time talking to him and playing with him. From their interactions, it is clear that they genuinely enjoy each other.

Tom's father is a far cry from the emotionally distant, conformist, traditional-gender-role fathers of the 1950s. He looks to the future and imagines the Little League games Tom will play in and the many other activities he can enjoy with Tom. Remembering how little time his own father spent with him, he is dedicated to making sure that Tom has an involved, nurturing experience with his father.

When Tom's mother comes home in the evening, she spends considerable time with him. Tom shows a positive attachment to both his mother and his father. His parents have cooperated and have successfully juggled their careers and work schedules to provide 1-year-old Tom with excellent child care.

Fathers are spending more time with their infants.

EMOTIONAL AND PERSONALITY DEVELOPMENT

Anyone who has been around infants for even a brief period of time can detect that they are emotional beings. Not only do we notice infants' expressions of emotions, but it doesn't take very long to sense that infants vary in their temperaments, with some being shy and others outgoing, some active and others much less so. Let's further explore these and other aspects of emotional and personality development in infants.

Emotional Development

Infants can express a number of emotions. We will explore what these are and how they develop, but first we need to define *emotion*.

Defining Emotion

Defining *emotion* is difficult because it is not easy to tell when a child or an adult is in an emotional state. Is a child in an emotional state when her heart beats fast, her palms sweat, and her stomach churns? Or is she in an emotional state when she smiles or grimaces? The body and face play important roles in understanding children's emotion. However, psychologists debate how important each is in determining whether a child is in an emotional state. For our purposes, we will define **emotion** as *feeling or affect that involves a mixture of physiological arousal (a fast heartbeat, for example) and overt behavior (a smile or grimace, for example).*

When we think about children's emotions, a few dramatic feelings, such as rage, fear, and glorious joy, usually spring to mind. But emotions can be subtle as well—the feeling a mother has when she holds her baby, the mild irritation of boredom, and the uneasiness of being in a new situation.

Psychologists classify emotions in many different ways, but one characteristic of almost all classifications is the designation of an emotion as positive or negative (Coy, 1999). **Positive affectivity (PA)** *refers to the range of positive emotions, from high energy, enthusiasm, and excitement to being calm, quiet, and withdrawn. Joy, happiness, and laughter involve positive affectivity.* **Negative affectivity (NA)** *refers to emotions that are negatively toned, such as anxiety, anger, guilt, and sadness.* PA and NA are independent dimensions in that a child can be high along both dimensions at the same time (for example, in a high-energy state and enthusiastic yet angry).

An important aspect of emotional development is emotional regulation (Posner, 1999; Saarni, Mumme, & Campos, 1998). During the first year of life, the infant gradually develops an ability to inhibit, or minimize, the intensity and duration of emotional reactions. At the same time, infants acquire a greater diversity of emotional responses. Examples of early emotional regulation are infants' soothing themselves by sucking or their withdrawing from excessive stimulation. Equally important is caregivers' assisting infants in learning how to regulate their emotions by attending to their distress and providing them with comfort.

Functionalism in Emotion

A number of developmentalists view the nature of emotion differently today than their predecessors did (Campos, 1994). The new view proposes that emotion is relational rather than intrapsychic, that there is a close link between emotion and the person's goals and effort, that emotional expressions can serve as social signals, and that the physiology of emotion involves much more than homeostasis and the person's interior. Emotion also incudes the ability to regulate and be regulated by social processes (Bruce, Olen, & Jensen, 1999).

The new approach is called "functionalism"—not because it focuses on evolutionary survival but because it links emotion with what the person is trying to do. In this view, the person and an environmental event constitute a whole. Emotion, thus, involves person-event transactions, in this perspective (see figure 8.1).

Blossoms are scattered by the wind
And the wind cares nothing, but
The blossoms of the heart
No wind can touch.

Youshida Kenko
Buddhist Monk, 14th Century

emotion
Feeling, or affect, that involves a mixture of physiological arousal and overt behavior. *'open to view'*

positive affectivity (PA)
The range of positive emotions from high energy, enthusiasm, and excitement to being calm, quiet, and withdrawn. Joy, happiness, and laughter involve positive affectivity.

negative affectivity (NA)
Emotions that are negatively toned, such as anger, anxiety, guilt, and sadness.

Exploring Emotion

$\mathcal{F}$*igure 8.1*
Functionalism in Emotion

Researcher Nathan Fox measured the brain waves of infants, such as this 4-month-old, who are stimulated with toys to elicit different emotional states. Fox demonstrated that very inhibited babies show a distinctive brain-wave pattern (as measured by the electroencephalogram [EEG] helmet in the photograph). Fox's research fits within the functionalist view of emotion, which argues that the physiology of emotion involves much more than homeostasis or an internal milieu. In functionalism, emotions are modes of adaptation to the environment.

More needs to be said about goals and emotion. Goals are related to emotion in a variety of ways. Regardless of what the goal is, an individual who overcomes an obstacle to attain a goal experiences happiness. By contrast, a person who must relinquish a goal as unattainable experiences sadness. And a person who faces difficult obstacles in pursuing a goal often experiences anger. The specific nature of the goal can affect the experience of a given emotion. For example, the avoidance of threat is linked with fear, the desire to atone is related to guilt, and the wish to avoid the scrutiny of others is associated with shame. Many of the functionalists focus their work on goal-related emotions (Hakim-Larson, 1995).

International Society for Research on Emotions

Affect in Parent-Child Relationships   Emotions are the first language with which parents and infants communicate before the infant acquires speech (Maccoby, 1992). Infants react to their parents' facial expressions and tone of voice. In return, parents "read" what the infant is trying to communicate, responding appropriately when their infants are either distressed or happy.

The initial aspects of infant attachment to parents are based on affectively toned interchanges, as when an infant cries and the caregiver sensitively responds. By the end of the first year, a mother's facial expression—either smiling or fearful—influences whether an infant will explore an unfamiliar environment. And, when children hear their parents quarreling, they often react with distressed facial expressions and inhibited play (Cummings, 1987). Exceptionally well-functioning families often

Emotional expression	Approximate time of emergence
Interest, neonatal smile (a sort of half smile that appears spontaneously for no apparent reason),* startled response,* distress,* disgust	Present at birth
Social smile	4 to 6 weeks
Anger, surprise, sadness	3 to 4 months
Fear	5 to 7 months
Shame/shyness	6 to 8 months
Contempt, guilt	2 years

* These expressions are precursors of the social smile and the emotions of surprise and sadness, which appear later. No evidence exists to suggest that they are related to inner feelings when they are observed in the first few weeks of life.

Figure 8.2
The Developmental Course of the Facial Expression of Emotions

Maximally Discriminative Facial Movement Coding System (MAX)
Izard's system of coding infants' facial expressions related to emotions. Using MAX, coders watch slow-motion and stop-action videotapes of infants' facial reactions to stimuli.

Infant Crying

basic cry
A rhythmic pattern usually consisting of a cry, a briefer silence, a shorter inspiratory whistle that is higher pitched than the main cry, and then a brief rest before the next cry.

anger cry
A cry similar to the basic cry, with more excess air forced through the vocal chords (associated with exasperation or rage).

pain cry
A sudden appearance of loud crying without preliminary moaning and a long initial cry followed by an extended period of breath holding.

include humor in their interactions, sometimes making each other laugh and developing light, pleasant mood states to defuse conflicts. And, when a positive mood has been induced in the child, the child is more likely to comply with a parent's directions.

Infant and adult affective communicative capacities make possible coordinated infant-adult interactions (Thompson, 1999). The face-to-face interactions of even 3-month-old infants and their adults are bidirectional (mutually regulated). That is, infants modify their affective displays and behaviors on the basis of their appreciation of their parents' affective displays and behaviors (Alexandrova, 1999). This coordination has led to characterizations of the mother-infant interaction as "reciprocal" or "synchronous." These terms are attempts to capture the quality of interaction when all is going well.

Developmental Timetable of Emotions   To determine whether infants are actually expressing a particular emotion, we need a system for measuring emotions. Carroll Izard (1982) developed such a system. The **Maximally Discriminative Facial Movement Coding System (MAX)** *is Izard's system of coding infants' facial expressions related to emotion. Using MAX, coders watch slow-motion and stop-action videotapes of infants' facial reactions to stimuli.* Among the stimulus conditions are giving an infant an ice cube, putting tape on the backs of the infant's hands, handing the infant a favorite toy and then taking it away, separating the infant from the mother and then reuniting them, having a stranger approach the infant, restraining the infant's head, placing a ticking clock next to the infant's ear, popping a balloon in front of the infant's face, and giving the infant camphor to sniff and lemon rind and orange juice to taste. To give just one example of how an emotion is coded, anger is indicated when the infant's brows are sharply lowered and drawn together, eyes are narrowed or squinted, and mouth is open in an angular, square shape. Based on Izard's classification system, interest, distress, and disgust are present at birth; a social smile appears at about 4 to 6 weeks; anger, surprise, and sadness emerge at about 3 to 4 months; fear is displayed at about 5 to 7 months; shame and shyness are displayed at about 6 to 8 months; and contempt and guilt don't appear until 2 years of age. A summary of the approximate timetable for the emergence of the facial expression of emotions is shown in figure 8.2.

Crying   Crying is the most important mechanism newborns have for communicating with their world (Gustafson, Green, & Kalinowski, 1993). This is true for the first cry, which tells the mother and doctor the baby's lungs have filled with air. Cries also may tell physicians and researchers something about the central nervous system.

Babies don't have just one type of cry. They have at least three (Wolff, 1969). The **basic cry** *is a rhythmic pattern that usually consists of a cry, followed by a briefer silence, then a shorter inspiratory whistle that is somewhat higher in pitch than the main cry, then another brief rest before the next cry.* Some infancy experts believe that hunger is one of the conditions that incite the basic cry. The **anger cry** *is a variation of the basic cry. However, in the anger cry, more excess air is forced through the vocal cords.* The **pain cry,** *which is stimulated by high-intensity stimuli, differs from other types of cries. A sudden appearance of loud crying without preliminary moaning and a long initial cry followed by an extended period of breath holding characterize the pain cry.*

Most parents, and adults in general, can determine whether an infant's cries signify anger or pain (Zeskind, Klein, & Marshall, 1992). Parents also can distinguish the cries of their own baby better than those of a strange baby. There is little consistent evidence to support the idea that mothers and females, but not fathers and males, are innately programmed to respond nurturantly to an infant's crying.

To soothe or not to soothe—should a crying baby be given attention and soothed, or does this spoil the infant? Many years ago, famous behaviorist John Watson (1928) argued that parents spend too much time responding to infant crying. As a consequence, he said, parents are actually rewarding infant crying and increasing its incidence. More recently, by contrast, infancy experts Mary Ainsworth (1979) and John Bowlby (1989) stress that you can't respond too much to infant crying in the first year of life. They believe that the caregiver's quick, comforting response to the infant's cries is an important ingredient in the development of secure attachment. In one of Ainsworth's studies, the mothers who responded quickly to their infants when they cried at 3 months of age had infants who cried less later in the first year of life (Bell & Ainsworth, 1972). On the other hand, behaviorist Jacob Gerwirtz (1977) found that a caregiver's quick, soothing response to crying increased subsequent crying.

Controversy, then, still swirls about the issue of whether parents should respond to an infant's cries (Lewis & Ramsay, 1999). However, developmentalists increasingly argue that an infant cannot be spoiled in the first year of life, which suggests that parents should soothe a crying infant rather than be unresponsive; in this manner, infants will likely develop a sense of trust and secure attachment to the caregiver in the first year of life.

Smiling   Smiling is another important communicative affective behavior of the infant. Two types of smiling can be distinguished in infants—one reflexive, the other social. A **reflexive smile** *does not occur in response to external stimuli. It appears during the first month after birth, usually during irregular patterns of sleep, not when the infant is in an alert state.* By contrast, a **social smile** *occurs in response to an external stimulus, which, early in development, typically is in response to a face.* Social smiling does not occur until 2 to 3 months of age (Emde, Gaensbauer, & Harmon, 1976), although some researchers believe that infants grin in response to voices as early as 3 weeks of age (Sroufe & Waters, 1976). The power of the infant's smiles was appropriately captured by British attachment theorist John Bowlby (1969): "Can we doubt that the more and better an infant smiles the better he is loved and cared for? It is fortunate for their survival that babies are so designed by nature that they beguile and enslave mothers."

reflexive smile

A smile that does not occur in response to external stimuli. It happens during the month after birth, usually during irregular patterns of sleep, not when the infant is in an alert state.

social smile

A smile in response to an external stimulus, which, early in development, typically is in response to a face.

Stranger Anxiety   The most frequent expression of an infant's fear involves **stranger anxiety,** *in which an infant shows a fear and wariness of strangers.* This tends to appear in the second half of the first year of life. There are individual variations in stranger anxiety, with not all infants showing distress when they encounter a stranger. Stranger anxiety usually emerges gradually, first appearing at about 6 months of age in the form of wary reactions. By age 9 months, the fear of strangers is often more intense and continues to escalate through the infant's first birthday (Emde, Gaensbauer, & Harmon, 1976).

A number of factors can influence whether an infant shows stranger anxiety, including the social context and the characteristics of the stranger. In terms of the social context, infants show less stranger anxiety when they are in familiar settings. For example, in one study, 10-month-olds showed little stranger anxiety when they met a stranger in their own home but much greater fear when they encountered a stranger in a research laboratory (Sroufe, Waters, & Matas, 1974). Also, infants show less stranger anxiety when they are sitting on their mothers' laps than when placed in an infant seat several feet away from their mothers (Bohlin & Hagekull, 1993). Thus, it appears that, when infants have a sense of security, they are less likely to show stranger anxiety.

Who the stranger is and how the stranger behaves also influence stranger anxiety in infants. Infants are less fearful of child strangers than adult strangers. They also are less fearful of friendly, outgoing, smiling strangers than of passive, unsmiling strangers (Bretherton, Stolberg, & Kreye, 1981).

stranger anxiety

An infant's fear and wariness of strangers; it tends to appear in the second half of the first year of life.

He who binds himself to joy
Does the winged life destroy;
But he who kisses the joy as it
Flies lives in eternity's sun rise.

William Blake
English Poet, 19th Century

What are some ways that developmentalists have classified infants' temperaments? Which classification makes the most sense to you, based on your observations of infants?

social referencing
"Reading" emotional cues in others to help determine how to act in a particular situation.

temperament
An individual's behavioral style and characteristic way of emotional response.

easy child
A child who is generally in a positive mood, who quickly establishes regular routines in infancy, and who adapts easily to new experiences.

difficult child
A child who tends to react negatively and cry frequently, who engages in irregular daily routines, and who is slow to accept new experiences.

slow-to-warm-up child
A child who has a low activity level, is somewhat negative, shows low adaptability, and displays a low intensity mood.

Infant Temperament

Social Referencing   Social referencing *involves "reading" emotional cues in others to help determine how to act in a particular situation.* The development of social referencing especially helps infants interpret ambiguous situations more accurately, as when they encounter a stranger and need to know whether to fear the person. In social referencing, infants often look to their mother for cues about how to react or behave in situations (Mumme, Fernald, & Herrera, 1996). Infants especially become better at social referencing in this manner during the second year of life. In their second year, infants show an increasing tendency to "check" with their mother before they act. That is, they check to see if she is happy, angry, or fearful. For example, in one study, 14- to 22-month-old infants were more likely to look at their mother's face as a source of information about how to react in a situation than were 6- to 9-month-old infants (Walden, 1991).

Temperament

Infants show different emotional responses. One infant may be cheerful and happy much of the time; another baby may cry a lot and more often display a negative mood. These behaviors reflect differences in their temperament (Halpern & Brand, 1999). Let's explore a definition of *temperament,* the ways in which it can be classified, and the implications of temperamental variations for parenting.

Defining and Classifying Temperament   **Temperament** *is an individual's behavioral style and characteristic way of emotional response.* Developmentalists are especially interested in the temperament of infants.

A widely debated issue is just what the key dimensions of temperament are. Psychiatrists Alexander Chess and Stella Thomas (Chess & Thomas, 1977; Thomas & Chess, 1991) believe there are three basic types, or clusters, of temperament—easy, difficult, and slow to warm up.

1. An **easy child** *is generally in a positive mood, quickly establishes regular routines in infancy, and adapts easily to new experiences.*
2. A **difficult child** *tends to react negatively and cry frequently, engages in irregular daily routines, and is slow to accept new experiences.*
3. A **slow-to-warm-up child** *has a low activity level, is somewhat negative, shows low adaptability, and displays a low intensity of mood.*

Various dimensions make up these three basic clusters of temperament. In their longitudinal investigation, Chess and Thomas found that 40 percent of the children they studied could be classified as easy, 10 percent as difficult, and 15 percent as slow to warm up. Researchers have found that these three basic clusters of temperament are moderately stable across the childhood years.

Children who have a difficult temperament or a temperament that reflects lack of control are at risk for problem behavior. In one study, a "difficult" temperament in adolescence was associated with higher levels of depression, drug use, and stressful life events, as well as lower levels of perceived family support (Tubman & Windle, 1995). In a longitudinal study, a temperament factor labeled "lack of control" (irritable, distractible) in early childhood (3 and 5 years of age) was related to externalized behavior problems (acting out, delinquent behavior) and less competent behavior in early adolescence (13 and 15 years of age) (Caspi & others, 1995). Across the same age span, a temperament factor labeled "approach" (friendliness, eagerness to explore new situations) was associated with fewer internalized problems (anxiety, depression) in boys. In an extension of this study, undercontrolled and inhibited 3-year-old children grew up to have more problem behaviors at 21 years of age than did well-adjusted, reserved, and confident children (Newman & Caspi, 1996).

New classifications of temperament continue to be forged (Lemery & others, 1999; Rothbart, 1999; Thompson, 1999). In a recent review of temperament, Mary Rothbart and John Bates (1998) concluded that, based on current research, the best framework for classifying temperament involves a revision of Chess and Thomas' categories of easy, difficult, and slow to warm up. The general classification of temperament now focuses more on (1) positive affect and approach (much like the personality trait of extraversion/introversion), (2) negative affectivity, and (3) effortful control (self-regulation).

A number of scholars conceive of temperament as a stable characteristic of newborns, which comes to be shaped and modified by the child's later experiences. This raises the question of heredity's role in temperament (Goldsmith, 1988). Twin and adoption studies have been conducted to answer this question (Plomin & others, 1994). The researchers have found a heritability index in the range of .50 to .60, suggesting a moderate influence of heredity on temperament. However, the strength of the association usually declines as infants become older (Goldsmith & Gottesman, 1981). This finding supports the belief that temperament becomes more mal- *Adaptable, Shaped* leable with experience. Alternatively, it may be that, as a child becomes older, behavior indicators of temperament are more difficult to spot.

Parenting and the Child's Temperament

Many parents don't become believers in temperament's importance until the birth of their second child. Many parents view the first child's behavior as being solely a result of how they socialized the child. However, management strategies that worked with the first child might not be as effective with the second child. Problems experienced with the first child (such as those involved in feeding, sleeping, and coping with strangers) might not exist with the second child, but new problems might arise. Such experiences strongly suggest that nature as well as nurture influence the child's development, that children differ from each other from very early in life, and that these differences have important implications for parent-child interaction (Kwak & others, 1999).

What are the implications of temperamental variations for parenting? Although answers to this question necessarily are speculative because of the incompleteness of the research literature, the following conclusions were reached by temperament experts Ann Sanson and Mary Rothbart (1995):

Complacent - Dom

- *Attention to and respect for individuality.* An important implication of taking children's individuality seriously is that it becomes difficult to generate prescriptions for "good parenting," other than possibly specifying that parents need to be sensitive and flexible. Parents need to be sensitive to the infant's signals and needs. A goal of parenting might be accomplished in one way with one child and in another way with another child, depending on the child's temperament.

    Some temperament characteristics pose more parenting challenges than others, at least in modern Western societies. Children's proneness to distress, as exhibited by frequent crying and irritability, can contribute to the emergence of avoidant or coercive parental responses. In one research study, though, extra support and training for mothers of distress-prone infants improved the quality of mother-infant interaction (van den Boom, 1989).

    Parents might react differently to a child's temperament, depending on whether the child is a girl or a boy and on the culture in which they live. For example, in one study, mothers were more responsive to the crying of irritable girls than to the crying of irritable boys (Crockenberg, 1986). Also, an active temperament might be valued in some cultures (such as the United States) but not in other cultures (such as China). Parents should respect each child's temperament, rather than try to fit all children into the same mold.

- *Structuring the child's environment.* Crowded, noisy environments can pose greater problems for some children (such as a "difficult child") than others

What are some good strategies for parents to adapt when responding to their infant's temperament?

(such as an "easygoing" child). We might also expect that a fearful, withdrawing child would benefit from slower entry into new contexts.

• *The "difficult child" and packaged parenting programs.* Some books and programs for parents focus specifically on temperament (Cameron, Hansen, & Rosen, 1989; Turecki & Tonner, 1989). These programs usually focus on children with "difficult" temperaments. Acknowledgment that some children are harder to parent is often helpful, and advice on how to handle particular difficult temperament characteristics can also be useful.

However, weighted against these potential advantages are several disadvantages. Whether a particular characteristic is difficult depends on its fit with the environment, whereas the notion of difficult temperament suggests that the problem rests solely with the child. To label a child "difficult" also has the danger of becoming a self-fulfilling prophecy. If a child is identified as "difficult," the labeling may maintain that categorization.

Children's temperament needs to be taken into account when considering caregiving behavior (Kochanska, 1999). Research does not yet allow for many highly specific recommendations, but, in general, caregivers should (1) be sensitive to the individual characteristics of the child, (2) be flexible in responding to these characteristics, and (3) avoid negative labeling of the child.

Personality Development

We have explored some important aspects of emotional development and temperament, which reveal individual variations in infants. Let's now examine the individual characteristics of the infant that often are thought of as central to personality development: trust and the development of self and independence.

Trust   According to Erik Erikson (1968), the first year of life is characterized by the trust-versus-mistrust stage of development. Following a life of regularity, warmth, and protection in the mother's womb, the infant faces a world that is less secure. Erikson believes that infants learn trust when they are cared for in a consistent, warm manner. If the infant is not well fed and kept warm on a consistent basis, a sense of mistrust is likely to develop.

Trust versus mistrust is not resolved once and for all in the first year of life. It arises again at each successive stage of development. There are both hope and danger in this. Children who enter school with a sense of mistrust may trust a particular teacher who has taken the time to make herself trustworthy. With this second chance, children overcome their early mistrust. By contrast, children who leave infancy with a sense of trust can still have their sense of mistrust activated at a later stage, perhaps if their parents are separated or divorced under conflicting circumstances.

An example is instructive (Elkind, 1970). A 4-year-old boy was being seen by a clinical psychologist at a court clinic. His adoptive parents, who had had him for six months, wanted to give him back to the agency. They said he was cold and unloving, stole things, and could not be trusted. He was indeed a cold and apathetic boy, but with good reason. One year after his illegitimate birth, he was taken away from his mother, who had a drinking problem, and was shuttled back and forth among several foster homes. At first, he tried to relate to people in the foster homes. The relationships never had an opportunity to develop because he was moved so frequently. In the end, he gave up trying to reach out to others, because the inevitable separations hurt too much. Like a burned child who dreads flame, this emotionally burned child shunned the pain of close relationships. He had trusted his mother, but now he trusted no one. Only years of devoted care and patience could undo the damage to this child's sense of trust.

The Developing Sense of Self and Independence   Individuals carry with them a sense of who they are and what makes them different from everyone else. They cling to this identity and begin to feel secure in the knowledge that this identity is becoming more stable. Real or imagined, this sense of self is a strong motivating force in life. When does the individual begin to sense a separate existence from others?

The Self   Infants are not "given" a self by their parents or the culture. Rather, they find and construct selves. Studying the self in infancy is difficult mainly because infants are unable to describe with language their experiences of themselves.

To determine whether infants can recognize themselves, psychologists have used mirrors. In the animal kingdom, only the great apes learn to recognize their reflection in a mirror, but human infants accomplish this feat by about 18 months of age. How does the mirror technique work? The mother puts a dot of rouge on her infant's nose. The observer watches to see how often the infant touches its nose. Next, the infant is placed in front of a mirror, and observers detect whether nose touching increases. In two independent investigations in the second half of the second year of life, infants recognized their own image and coordinated the image they saw with the actions of touching their own body (Amsterdam, 1968; Lewis & Brooks-Gunn, 1979).

Independence   Not only does the infant develop a sense of self in the second year of life, but independence also becomes a more central theme in the

Self Development in Infancy

Seeking Independence

Reprinted with special permission of North America Syndicate.

Erikson believed that autonomy versus shame and doubt is the key developmental theme of the toddler years.

I am what I can will freely.

Erik Erikson
*European-Born American Psychotherapist,
20th Century*

Are the Two's So Terrible?

infant's life. The theories of Margaret Mahler and Erik Erikson have important implications for both self-development and independence. Mahler (1979) believes that the child goes through a separation and then an individuation process. Separation involves the infant's movement away from the mother. Individuation involves the development of self.

Erikson (1968), like Mahler, believed that independence is an important issue in the second year of life. Erikson described the second stage of development as the stage of autonomy versus shame and doubt. Autonomy builds on the infant's developing mental and motor abilities. At this point in development, not only can infants walk, but they can also climb, open and close, drop, push and pull, and hold and let go. Infants feel pride in these new accomplishments and want to do everything themselves, whether it is flushing a toilet, pulling the wrapping off a package, or deciding what to eat. It is important for parents to recognize the motivation of toddlers to do what they are capable of doing at their own pace. Then they can learn to control their muscles and their impulses themselves. But, when caregivers are impatient and do for toddlers what they are capable of doing themselves, shame and doubt develop. Every parent has rushed a child from time to time. It is only when parents consistently overprotect toddlers or criticize accidents (wetting, soiling, spilling, or breaking, for example) that children develop an excessive sense of shame and doubt about their ability to control themselves and their world.

Erikson also believed that the stage of autonomy versus shame and doubt has important implications for the development of independence and identity during adolescence. The development of autonomy during the toddler years gives adolescents the courage to be independent individuals who can choose and guide their own future.

Too much autonomy, though, can be as harmful as too little. For instance, a 7-year-old boy who had a heart condition learned quickly how afraid his parents were of any signs of his having cardiac problems. It was not long before he ruled the household. The family could not go shopping or for a drive if the boy did not approve. On the rare occasions his parents defied him, he would get angry. His purple face and gagging frightened them into submission. This boy actually was scared of his power and eager to relinquish it. When the parents and the boy realized this, and recognized that a little shame and doubt were a healthy opponent of an inflated sense of autonomy, the family began to function more smoothly (Elkind, 1970).

Consider also Robert, age 22 months, who has just come home from watching his 5-year-old brother, William, take a swimming lesson. Their mother has gone in the kitchen to get dinner ready when she hears a scream. She hurries into the living room and sees Robert's teeth sunk into William's leg. The next day, Robert is playing with a new game and he can't get it right. He hurls it across the room and just misses his mother. That night his mother tells him it is time for bed. Robert's response is "No." Sometimes the world of 2-year-olds becomes very frustrating. Much of their frustration stems from their inability to control the adult world. Things are too big to manage, to push around, or to make happen. Toddlers want to be in the driver's seat of every car and to push every cart by themselves. Two-year-olds want to play the dominant role in almost every situation. When things don't go their way, toddlers can become openly defiant, even though they were placid as babies. Called the "terrible twos" by Arnold Gesell, this developmental time frame can try the patience of the most even-tempered parents. Nonetheless, calm, steady affection and firm patience can help disperse most of toddlerhood's tensions. Fortunately, the defiance is only temporary in most children's development.

Summary Table 8.1
Emotional and Personality Development

Concept	Processes/ Related Ideas	Characteristics/Description
Emotional development	What is emotion?	Emotion is feeling, or affect, that involves a mixture of physiological arousal and overt behavior. Emotions can be classified in terms of positive affectivity and negative affectivity. An important aspect of emotional development is self-regulation.
	Functionalism in emotion	The functionalist view emphasizes that emotion is relational rather than intrapsychic, that there is a close link between emotion and the person's goals and effort, that emotional expressions can serve as social signals, and that the physiology of emotion is much more than homeostasis and the person's interior—it also includes the ability to regulate and be regulated by social processes.
	Affect in parent-child relationships	Emotions are the first language with which parents and infants communicate before the infant acquires speech. Infant and adult affective communicative capacities make possible coordinated infant-adult interaction.
	Emotional development in infancy	Izard developed the Maximally Discriminative Facial Movement Coding System (MAX) for coding infants' expression of emotions. Based on this coding system, interest, distress, and disgust are present at birth; a social smile appears at about 4 to 6 weeks; anger, surprise, and sadness emerge at about 3 to 4 months; fear is displayed at about 5 to 7 months; shame and shyness emerge at about 6 to 8 months; and contempt and guilt appear at about 2 years of age.
	Crying	Crying is the most important mechanism newborns have for communicating with their world. Babies have at least three types of cries—basic cry, anger cry, and pain cry. Most parents, and adults in general, can tell whether an infant's cries signify anger or pain. Controversy still swirls about whether babies should be soothed when they cry. An increasing number of developmentalists support Ainsworth's and Bowlby's idea that infant crying should be responded to immediately in the first year of life.
	Smiling	Smiling is an important communicative affective behavior of the infant. Two types of smiling can be distinguished in infants: reflexive and social.
	Stranger anxiety	This involves an infant's fear and wariness of strangers, which tend to appear in the second half of the first year of life, intensifying toward the end of the first year. A number of factors influence stranger anxiety, including the social context and the characteristics of the stranger.
	Social referencing	This involves "reading" emotional cues in others to help determine how to act in a particular situation. Infants' use of social referencing increases considerably in the second year of life.
Temperament	Defining and classifying temperament	Temperament is an individual's behavioral style and characteristic way of emotional responding. Developmentalists are especially interested in the temperament of infants. Chess and Thomas classified infants as (1) easy, (2) difficult, or (3) slow to warm up. Recent classifications focus more on (1) positive affect and approach, (2) negative affectivity, and (3) effortful control.
	Parenting and the child's temperament	Although research evidence is sketchy at this point in time, some general recommendations are that caregivers should (1) be sensitive to the individual characteristics of the child, (2) be flexible in responding to these characteristics, and (3) avoid negative labeling of the child.
Personality development	Trust	Erikson argued that the first year is characterized by the crisis of trust versus mistrust; his ideas about trust have much in common with Ainsworth's concept of secure attachment.
	Developing a sense of self and independence	At some point in the second half of the second year of life, the infant develops a sense of self. Independence becomes a central theme in the second year of life. Mahler argues that the infant separates herself from her mother and then develops individuation. Erikson stressed that the second year of life is characterized by the stage of autonomy versus shame and doubt.

At this point, we have studied a number of ideas about the infant's emotional and personality development. An overview of these ideas is presented in summary table 8.1. Next, we will focus on another important aspect of infants' socioemotional development—their attachment to a caregiver.

Figure 8.3
Harlow's Classic "Contact Comfort" Study

Regardless of whether they were fed by a wire mother or by a cloth mother, the infant monkeys overwhelmingly preferred to be in contact with the cloth mother, demonstrating the importance of contact comfort in attachment.

attachment
A close emotional bond between an infant and a caregiver.

Harry Harlow

ATTACHMENT

A small curly-haired girl named Danielle, age 11 months, begins to whimper. After a few seconds, she begins to wail. The psychologist observing Danielle is conducting a research study on the nature of attachment between infants and their mothers. Subsequently, the mother reenters the room, and Danielle's crying ceases. Quickly, Danielle crawls over to where her mother is seated and reaches out to be held. The situation is one of the main ways that psychologists study the nature of attachment during infancy.

What Is Attachment?

In everyday language, attachment is a relationship between two individuals who feel strongly about each other and do a number of things to continue the relationship. Many pairs of people are attached: relatives, lovers, a teacher and student. In the language of developmental psychology, though, attachment is often restricted to a relationship between particular social figures and a particular phenomenon that is thought to reflect unique characteristics of the relationship. In this case, the developmental period is infancy, the social figures are the infant and one or more adult caregivers, and the phenomenon is a bond (Bowlby, 1969, 1989). To summarize, **attachment** *is a close emotional bond between the infant and the caregiver.*

There is no shortage of theories about infant attachment. Freud believed that infants become attached to the person or object that provides oral satisfaction. For most infants, this is the mother, since she is most likely to feed the infant.

Is feeding as important as Freud thought? A classic study by Harry Harlow and Robert Zimmerman (1959) reveals that the answer is no. These researchers evaluated whether feeding or contact comfort was more important to infant attachment. Infant monkeys were removed from their mothers at birth and reared for six months by surrogate (substitute) "mothers." As shown in figure 8.3, one of the mothers was made of wire, the other of cloth. Half of the infant monkeys were fed by the wire mother, half by the cloth mother. Periodically, the amount of time the infant monkeys spent with either the wire or the cloth monkey was computed. Regardless of whether they were fed by the wire or the cloth mother, the infant monkeys spent far more time with the cloth mother. This study clearly demonstrated that feeding is not the crucial element in the attachment process and that contact comfort is important.

Most toddlers develop a strong attachment to a favorite soft toy or blanket. Toddlers may carry the toy or blanket with them everywhere they go, just as Linus does in the "Peanuts" cartoon strip. Or they may run for the toy or blanket only in moments of crisis, such as after an argument or a fall. By the time they have outgrown the security object, all that may be left is a small fragment of the blanket, or a stuffed animal that is hardly recognizable, having had a couple of new faces and all its seams resewn half a dozen times. If parents try to replace the security object with something newer, the toddler will resist. There is nothing abnormal about a toddler carrying around a security blanket. Children know that the blanket or teddy bear is not their mother, yet they react affectively to these objects and derive comfort from them as if they were their mother. Eventually, they abandon the security object as they grow up and become more sure of themselves.

Might familiarity breed attachment? A famous study by ethologist Konrad Lorenz (1965) revealed that the answer is yes. Remember from our description of this study in chapter 2 that newborn goslings became attached to "father" Lorenz rather than to their mother because he was the first moving object they saw. The time period during which familiarity is important for goslings is the first 36 hours after birth; for human beings, it is more on the order of the first year of life. *imprinting*

Erik Erikson (1968) believed that the first year of life is the key time frame for the development of attachment. Recall his proposal—also discussed in chapter 2—that the first year of life represents the stage of trust versus mistrust. A sense of trust requires a feeling of physical comfort and a minimal amount of fear and apprehension about the future. Trust in infancy sets the stage for a lifelong expectation that the world will be a good and pleasant place to be. Erikson also believed that responsive, sensitive parenting contributes to an infant's sense of trust.

The ethological perspective of British psychiatrist John Bowlby (1969, 1989) also stresses the importance of attachment in the first year of life and the responsiveness of the caregiver. Bowlby believes that an infant and its mother instinctively form an attachment. He argues that the newborn is biologically equipped to elicit the mother's attachment behavior. The baby cries, clings, coos, and smiles. Later, the infant crawls, walks, and follows the mother. The infant's goal is to keep the mother nearby. Research on attachment supports Bowlby's view that, at about 6 to 7 months of age, the infant's attachment to the caregiver intensifies (Sroufe, 1985).

Attachment theorists argue that early experiences play an important role in a child's later social development. For example, Bowlby and Ainsworth argue that secure attachment to the caregiver in infancy is related to the development of social competence during the childhood years.

I am what I hope and give.

Erik Erikson
European-Born American Psychotherapist, 20th Century

Individual Differences

Although attachment to a caregiver intensifies midway through the first year, isn't it likely that some babies have a more positive attachment experience than others? Mary Ainsworth (1979) thinks so. She says that, in **secure attachment,** *infants use the caregiver, usually the mother, as a secure base from which to explore the environment. Ainsworth believes that secure attachment in the first year of life provides an important foundation for psychological development later in life.* The caregiver's sensitivity to the infant's signals increases secure attachment (DeWolff & van IJzendoorn, 1997). The securely attached infant moves freely away from the mother but processes her location through periodic glances. The securely attached infant responds positively to being picked up by others and, when put back down, freely moves away to play. An insecurely attached infant, by contrast, avoids the mother or is ambivalent toward her, fears strangers, and is upset by minor, everyday separations.

Ainsworth believes that insecurely attached infants can be classified as either anxious-avoidant or anxious-resistant, making four main attachment categories: secure (type B), avoidant (type A), ambivalent-resistant (type C), and disorganized (type D). **Type B babies** *use the caregiver as a secure base from which to explore the environment.* **Type A babies** *exhibit insecurity by avoiding the mother (for example, ignoring her, averting their gaze, and failing to seek proximity).* **Type C babies** *exhibit insecurity by resisting the mother (for example, clinging to her but at the same time fighting against the closeness, perhaps by kicking and pushing away).* **Type D babies** *are disorganized and disoriented. They may look dazed, show confusion, and be afraid.*

If early attachment to a caregiver is important, it should relate to a child's social behavior later in development. Research by Alan Sroufe (1985, 1996) documents this connection. In one study, infants who were securely attached to their mothers early in infancy were less frustrated and happier at 2 years of age than were insecurely attached counterparts (Matas, Arend, & Sroufe, 1978).

secure attachment

The infant uses a caregiver as a secure base from which to explore the environment. Ainsworth believes that secure attachment in the first year of life provides an important foundation for psychological development later in life.

type B babies

Infants who use a caregiver as a secure base from which to explore the environment.

vert

type A babies

Infants who exhibit insecurity by avoiding their mother (for example, ignoring her, averting their gaze, and failing to seek proximity).

ling + push

type C babies

Infants who exhibit insecurity by resisting the mother (for example, clinging to her but at the same time kicking and pushing away).

type D babies *disoriented disorganized*

Insecurely attached babies who are described as disorganized. They may be disoriented and afraid.

Forming a Secure Attachment

Through the Eyes of Children

Megan's and Diann's Smooth Dance

Two-year-old Megan goes to a high-quality infant care program. Diann has been Megan's teacher since Megan was a young infant. Their morning rituals are like two people engaged in a smooth dance, with Diann reaching out to Megan and Megan reciprocating.

In a clutched hand, Megan gives a flower to Diann. The two take turns touching the petals of the flower, exchanging many comments about the colors and the feel of the flower. They also exchange glances and smiles.

Later, Diann is sitting in the corner of the room. Megan stays with her for a little while, then moves away to play. After a few minutes, Megan looks back at Diann to make sure she is still there. Diann smiles, Megan smiles, and then Megan goes on with her play. In the afternoon, a tired Megan crawls into Diann's lap and puts her head on her teacher's shoulder.

Through Megan's eyes, her teacher is a secure attachment who is there when Megan needs her. Unfortunately, not all infant care is as good as what Megan is getting (Raikes, 1996).

A child forsaken, waking suddenly,
Whose gaze affeared on all things round
*   doth rove,*
And seeth only that it cannot see
The meeting eyes of love.

George Eliot
English Novelist, 19th Century

Strange Situation
An observational measure of infant attachment that requires the infant to move through a series of introductions, separations, and reunions with the caregiver and an adult stranger in a prescribed order.

Sroufe's more recent research involves following a group of 180 disadvantaged children—age 19—since before birth, examining the mother-infant attachment and social competence in children and youth (Ostoja & others, 1995; Sroufe, Egeland, & Carlson, 1999)). He found that, even though these children had unstable lives, those who had a secure mother-infant attachment were likely to be self-reliant in adolescence, have lower rates of problems, enjoy successful peer relations, and do well in school. Sroufe also has found that insecurely attached infants can become more securely attached if their mothers enter a more stable love relationship or alleviate their symptoms of depression.

Caregiving Styles and Attachment Classification

Attachment is defined as a close emotional bond between the infant and caregiver. Is the parent's caregiving style linked with this close emotional bond called attachment? Securely attached babies have caregivers who are sensitive to their signals and are consistently available to respond to their infants' needs (Gao, Elliot, & Waters, 1999). These caregivers often let their babies have an active part in determining the onset and pacing of interaction in the first year of life.

How do the caregivers of insecurely attached babies interact with them? Caregivers of avoidant babies tend to be unavailable or rejecting (Cassidy & Berlin, 1994). They often don't respond to their babies' signals and have little physical contact with them. When they do interact with their babies, they may behave in an angry and irritable way toward them. Caregivers of ambivalent-resistant babies tend to be inconsistently available to their babies (Cassidy & Berlin, 1994). That is, sometimes they respond to their babies' needs, and sometimes they don't. In general, they tend not to be very affectionate with their babies and show little synchrony when interacting with them. Caregivers of disorganized babies often neglect or physically abuse their babies (Main & Solomon, 1990). In some cases, these caregivers also have depression (Field, 1992; Levy, in press). Later in the chapter, we will have more to say about child abuse.

Measurement of Attachment

Much of the early research on attachment relied on caregivers' impressions rather than on direct observation of caregivers interacting with their infants. However, interview data might be flawed and unreliably related to what actually takes place when parents interact with their infant. In the past several decades, researchers have increasingly observed infants with their caregivers. The main setting that has been used to observe attachment in infancy is the Strange Situation developed by attachment researcher Mary Ainsworth (1967). The **Strange Situation** *is an observational measure of infant attachment that requires the infant to move through a series of introductions, separations, and reunions with the caregiver and an adult stranger in a prescribed order* (see figure 8.4).

Although the Strange Situation has been used in a large number of studies of infant attachment, some critics believe that the isolated, controlled events of the setting might not necessarily reflect what would happen if infants were observed with their caregiver in a natural environment. The issue of using controlled,

Episode	Persons present	Duration of episode	Description of setting
1	Caregiver, baby, and observer	30 seconds	Observer introduces caregiver and baby to experimental room, then leaves. (Room contains many appealing toys scattered about.)
2	Caregiver and baby	3 minutes	Caregiver is nonparticipant while baby explores; if necessary, play is stimulated after 2 minutes.
3	Stranger, caregiver, and baby	3 minutes	Stranger enters. First minute: stranger is silent. Second minute: stranger converses with caregiver. Third minute: stranger approaches baby. After 3 minutes caregiver leaves unobtrusively.
4	Stranger and baby	3 minutes or less	First separation episode. Stranger's behavior is geared to that of baby.
5	Caregiver and baby	3 minutes or more	First reunion episode. Caregiver greets and/or comforts baby, then tries to settle the baby again in play. Caregiver then leaves, saying "bye-bye."
6	Baby alone	3 minutes or less	Second separation episode.
7	Stranger and baby	3 minutes or less	Continuation of second separation. Stranger enters and gears behavior to that of baby.
8	Caregiver and baby	3 minutes	Second reunion episode. Caregiver enters, greets baby, then picks baby up. Meanwhile, stranger leaves unobtrusively.

Figure 8.4
The Ainsworth Strange Situation

Mary Ainsworth developed the Strange Situation to assess whether infants are securely or insecurely attached to their caregiver.

laboratory assessments versus naturalistic observations is widely debated in child development circles.

Attachment Research

Attachment, Temperament, and the Wider Social World

Not all research reveals the power of infant attachment to predict subsequent development (Fox, 1997). In one longitudinal study, attachment classification in infancy did not predict attachment classification at 18 years of age (Lewis, 1997). In this study, the best predictor of attachment classification at 18 was the occurrence of parent divorce in intervening years.

Thus, not all developmentalists believe that attachment in infancy is the only path to competence in life. Indeed, some developmentalists believe that too much emphasis is placed on the importance of the attachment bond in infancy. Jerome Kagan (1987), for example, believes that infants are highly resilient and adaptive; he argues that they are evolutionarily equipped to stay on a positive developmental course, even in the face of wide variations in parenting. Kagan and others stress that genetic and temperament characteristics play more important roles in a child's social competence than the attachment theorists, such as Bowlby, Ainsworth, and Sroufe, are willing to acknowledge (Chaudhuri & Williams, 1999; Young & Shahin-

In the Hausa culture, siblings and grandmothers provide a significant amount of care for infants.

far, 1995). For example, infants may have inherited a low tolerance for stress. This, rather than an insecure attachment bond, may be responsible for their inability to get along with peers.

Also, researchers have found cultural variations in attachment. German and Japanese babies often show different patterns of attachment than American babies. German babies are more likely than American babies to be categorized as avoidant, possibly because caregivers encourage them to be more independent (Grossmann & others, 1985). Japanese babies are more likely than American babies to be categorized as resistant-ambivalent. This may have more to do with the Ainsworth Strange Situation as a measure of attachment than with attachment insecurity itself. Japanese mothers rarely let anyone unfamiliar with their babies care for them. Thus, the Ainsworth Strange Situation may create considerably more stress for Japanese infants than for American infants, who are more accustomed to separation from their mothers (Takahashi, 1990). Even though there are cultural variations in attachment classification, the most frequent classification in every culture studied so far is secure attachment (van IJzendoorn & Kroonenberg, 1988).

Another criticism of attachment theory is that it ignores the diversity of socializing agents and contexts that exists in an infant's world. In some cultures, infants show attachments to many people. Among the Hausa (who live in Nigeria), both grandmothers and siblings provide a significant amount of care for infants (Harkness & Super, 1995). Infants in agricultural societies tend to form attachments to older siblings, who are assigned a major responsibility for younger siblings' care. The attachments formed by infants in group care in Israeli kibbutzim provide another challenge to the singular attachment thesis.

Researchers recognize the importance of competent, nurturant caregivers in an infant's development (Macoby, 1999). At issue, though, is whether or not secure attachment, especially to a single caregiver, is critical (Rosen & Burke, 1999).

SOCIAL CONTEXTS

Now that we have explored the infant's emotional and personality development and attachment, let's examine the social contexts in which these occur. We will begin by studying a number of aspects of the family and then turn to a social context in which infants increasingly spend time—day care.

The Family

Most of us began our lives in families and spent thousands of hours during our childhood interacting with our parents. Some of you are already parents; others of you may become parents. What is the transition to parenthood like?

The Transition to Parenthood   When people become parents through pregnancy, adoption, or stepparenting, they face disequilibrium and must adapt (Egeren, 1999; Klitzing, Simoni, & Burgin, 1999). Parents want to develop a strong attachment with their infant, but they still want to maintain strong attachments to their spouse and friends, and possibly continue their careers. Parents ask themselves how this new being will change their lives. A baby places new restrictions on partners; no longer will they be able to rush out to a movie on a moment's notice, and money may not be readily available for vacations and other luxuries. Dual-career parents ask, "Will it harm the baby to place her in day care? Will we be able to find responsible baby-sitters?"

AMBIVALENT - The coexistence of opposite & conflicting feelings of about the same person or object

The Transition To Parenting

In a longitudinal investigation of couples from late pregnancy until three and one-half years after the baby was born, Carolyn Cowan and her colleagues (1995) found that the couples enjoyed more positive marital relations before the baby was born than after. Still, almost one-third showed an increase in marital satisfaction. Some couples said that the baby had both brought them closer together *and* moved them further apart. They commented that being parents enhanced their sense of themselves and gave them a new, more stable identity as a couple. Babies opened men up to a concern with intimate relationships, and the demands of juggling work and family roles stimulated women to manage family tasks more efficiently and pay attention to their personal growth.

At some point during the early years of the child's life, parents face the difficult task of juggling their roles as parents and as self-actualizing adults. Until recently in our culture, nurturing our children and having a career were thought to be incompatible. Fortunately, we have come to recognize that the balance between caring and achieving, nurturing and working—although difficult to manage—can be accomplished (Hoffman & Youngblood, 1999).

Reciprocal Socialization   For many years, socialization between parents and children was viewed as a one-way process: children were considered to be the products of their parents' socialization techniques. Today, however, we view parent-child interaction as reciprocal (Hartup & Laursen, 1999; Schaffer, 1996). **Reciprocal socialization** *is socialization that is bidirectional. That is, children socialize parents just as parents socialize children.* For example, the interaction of mothers and their infants is symbolized as a dance or a dialogue in which successive actions of the partners are closely coordinated. This coordinated dance or dialogue can assume the form of mutual synchrony (each person's behavior depends on the partner's previous behavior) (Feldman, Greenbaum, & Yirmiya, 1999; Jaquay, Williams, & Bernieri, 1999). Or it can be reciprocal in a more precise sense. The actions of the partners can be matched, as when one partner imitates the other or when there is mutual smiling.

When reciprocal socialization has been studied in infancy, mutual gaze, or eye contact, plays an important role in early social interaction. In one investigation, the mother and infant engaged in a variety of behaviors while they looked at each other. By contrast, when they looked away from each other, the rate of such behaviors dropped considerably (Stern & others, 1977). In sum, the behaviors of mothers and infants involve substantial interconnection, mutual regulation, and synchronization.

Scaffolding *is parental behavior that supports children's efforts, allowing them to be more skillful than they would be if they were to rely only on their own abilities.* Caregivers provide a positive, reciprocal framework in which they and their children interact. Parents' efforts to time interactions in such a way that the infant experiences turn-taking with the parents illustrates an early parental scaffolding behavior. For example, in the game peek-a-boo, mothers initially cover their babies. Then they remove the covering, and finally they register "surprise" at the reappearance. As infants become more skilled at peek-a-boo, pat-a-cake, and so big, there are other caregiver games that exemplify scaffolding and turn-taking sequences. In one study, infants who had more extensive scaffolding experiences with their parents (especially in the form of turn-taking) were more likely to engage in turn-taking when they interacted with their peers (Vandell & Wilson, 1988). Scaffolding is not confined to parent-infant interaction but can be used by parents to support children's achievement-related efforts in school by adjusting and modifying the amount and type of support that best suits the child's level of development.

The Family as a System   As a social system, the family can be thought of as a constellation of subsystems defined in terms of generation, gender, and role (Davis, 1996). Divisions of labor among family members define particular subunits, and attachments define others. Each family member is a participant in several subsystems. Some are dyadic (involving two people), some polyadic (involving more

reciprocal socialization
Socialization that is bidirectional; children socialize parents, just as parents socialize children.

scaffolding
Parental behavior that supports children's efforts, allowing them to be more skillful than they would be if they relied only on their own abilities.

Family Resources

Figure 8.5

Interaction Between Children and Their Parents: Direct and Indirect Effects

Maternal Images and Portraits

Maternal Resources

than two people). The father and child represent one dyadic subsystem, the mother and father another. The mother-father-child represent one polyadic subsystem, the mother and two siblings another.

An organizational scheme that highlights the reciprocal influences of family members and family subsystems is shown in figure 8.5 (Belsky, 1981). As the arrows in the figure show, marital relations, parenting, and infant behavior and development can have both direct and indirect effects on each other. An example of a direct effect is the influence of the parents' behavior on the child. An example of an indirect effect is how the relationship between the spouses mediates the way a parent acts toward the child (McHale, Lauretti, & Kuerston-Hogan, 1999). For example, marital conflict might reduce the efficiency of parenting, in which case marital conflict would be an indirect effect on the child's behavior.

Mothers and Fathers as Caregivers The reality of motherhood is that, although fathers have increased their child-rearing responsibilities somewhat, the main responsibility for child rearing still falls on most mothers' shoulders (Paludi, 1998). Mothers do far more family work than fathers do—two to three times more. A few "exceptional" men do as much family work as their wives; in one study, the figure was 10 percent of the men (Berk, 1985).

The role of the mother brings with it benefits as well as limitations. Although motherhood is not enough to fill most women's entire lives, for most mothers, it is one of the most meaningful experiences in their lives.

Can fathers take care of infants as competently as mothers can? Observations of fathers and their infants suggest that fathers have the ability to act sensitively and responsively with their infants (McHale & others, 1995; Parke, 1995). The strongest evidence of the plasticity of male caregiving abilities is based on male primates, which are notoriously low in their interest in offspring. When forced to live with infants whose female caregivers are absent, the adult male competently rears the infants. Remember, however, that, although fathers can be active, nurturant, involved caregivers with their infants, many do not choose to follow this pattern.

Do fathers behave differently toward infants than mothers do? Maternal interactions usually center around child care activities—feeding, changing diapers, bathing. Paternal interactions are more likely to include play. Fathers engage in more rough-and-tumble play. They bounce infants, throw them up in the air, tickle them, and so on (Lamb, 1986; Lamb & others, 1999). Mothers do play with infants, but their play is less physical and arousing than that of fathers.

In stressful circumstances, do infants prefer their mother or father? In one study, 20 12-month-olds were observed interacting with their parents (Lamb, 1977). With both parents present, the infants preferred neither their mother nor their father. The same was true when the infants were alone with the mother or the father. However, the entrance of a stranger, combined with boredom and fatigue, produced a shift in the infants' social behavior toward the mother. In stressful circumstances, then, infants show a stronger attachment to the mother.

Might the nature of parent-infant interaction be different in families that adopt nontraditional gender roles? This question was investigated by Michael Lamb and his colleagues (1982). They studied Swedish families in which the fathers were the primary caregivers of their firstborn, 8-month-old infants. The mothers were working full-time. In all observations, the mothers were more likely to discipline, hold, soothe, kiss, and talk to the infants than were the fathers. These mothers and fathers dealt with their infants differently, along the lines of American fathers and mothers following traditional gender roles. Having fathers assume the primary caregiving role did not substantially alter the way they interacted with their infants. This may be for biological reasons or because of deeply ingrained socialization patterns in cultures.

One recent poll indicated that today's fathers feel they are better at parenting than their fathers were, in a number of ways (*Newsweek*, 1996):

- Fifty-five percent of today's fathers say being a parent is more important to them than it was to their fathers.
- Sixty-one percent of today's fathers say they understand their children better.
- Forty-nine percent rate themselves as better parents than their fathers were.
- Seventy percent say they spend more time with their children than their fathers spent with them.
- Fifty-two percent say they punish their children less severely.
- Eighty-six percent of the mothers who shared parenting said their mates did either a very good (52 percent) or a good (34 percent) parenting job.

Family responsibility was a major theme of the Million Man March in Washington, DC, in 1995. It also is the theme of the revival-style meetings of the Promise Keepers, an evangelical group that has been filling stadiums with men across the United States. Men today appear to be better fathers—when they are around. However, too many children growing up today see little of their fathers. In 1994, 16.3 million children in the United States were living with their mothers. Forty percent of these children had not seen their father in the past year.

Studies of different countries reveal that American fathers are about average in parental involvement, spending an average 45 minutes a day caring for children by themselves. The least involved fathers, Japanese, average only 3 minutes a day with their children. American mothers spend the most time in child care among women of any nation studied, more than 10 hours a day. Women are still doing twice as much child care as men, although 20 years ago they were doing three times as much (Levine, 1996). The consensus, then, is that, although men have improved their fathering, there is still room for improvement (Snarey, 1998).

Father-mother cooperation and mutual respect help the child develop positive attitudes toward both males and females (Biller, 1993). It is much easier for working parents to cope with changing family circumstances and day-care issues when the father and mother equitably share child-rearing responsibilities. Mothers feel less stress and have more positive attitudes toward their husbands when they are supportive partners.

Child Abuse   Unfortunately, parenting sometimes leads to the abuse of infants and children. Child abuse is an increasing problem in the United States. Estimates of its incidence vary, but some authorities say that as many as 500,000 children are physically abused every year. Laws in many states now require doctors and teachers to report suspected cases of child abuse, yet many cases go unreported, especially those of battered infants.

Child abuse is such a disturbing circumstance that many people have difficulty understanding or sympathizing with parents who abuse or neglect their children. Our response is often outrage and anger directed at the parent. This outrage focuses our attention on parents as bad, sick, monstrous, sadistic individuals who cause their children to suffer. Experts on child abuse believe that this view is too simple and deflects attention away from the social context of the abuse and parents' coping skills. It is especially important to recognize that child abuse is a diverse condition, that it is usually mild to moderate in severity, and that it is only partially caused by the individual personality characteristics of parents.

various form, different unlike

The Multifaceted Nature of Abuse   Whereas the public and many professionals use the term *child abuse* to refer to both abuse and neglect, developmentalists increasingly use the term *child maltreatment*. This term does not have quite the emotional impact of the term *abuse* and acknowledges that maltreatment includes

The Fatherhood Project

Online Resources For Fathers

National Clearinghouse on Child Abuse and Neglect

Child Abuse Prevention Network

International Aspects of Child Abuse

several different conditions. Among the different types of maltreatment are physical and sexual abuse; the fostering of delinquency; lack of supervision; medical, educational, and nutritional neglect; and drug or alcohol abuse. In one large survey, approximately 20 percent of the reported cases involved abuse alone, 46 percent neglect alone, 23 percent both abuse and neglect, and 11 percent sexual abuse (American Association for Protecting Children, 1986).

Severity of Abuse   The concern about child abuse began with the identification of "battered child syndrome," which continues to be associated with severe, brutal injury for several reasons. First, the media tend to underscore the most bizarre and vicious incidents. Second, much of the funding for child abuse prevention, identification, and treatment depends on the public's perception of the horror of child abuse and the medical profession's lobby for funds to investigate and treat abused children and their parents. The emphasis is often on the worst cases. These horrific cases do exist and are indeed terrible. However, they make up only a small minority of maltreated children. Less than 1 percent of maltreated children die. Another 11 percent suffer life-threatening, disabling injuries (American Association for Protecting Children, 1986). By contrast, almost 90 percent suffer temporary physical injuries. These milder injuries, though, are likely to be experienced repeatedly in the context of daily hostile family exchanges. Similarly, neglected children, who suffer no physical injuries, often experience extensive, long-term psychological harm.

The Cultural Context of Abuse   The extensive violence that takes place in the American culture is reflected in the occurrence of violence in the family. A regular diet of violence appears on television screens, and parents often resort to power assertion as a disciplinary technique. In China, where physical punishment is rarely used to discipline children, the incidence of child abuse is reported to be very low. In the United States, many abusing parents report that they do not have sufficient resources or help from others. This may be a realistic evaluation of the situation experienced by many low-income families, who do not have adequate preventive and supportive services.

Community support systems are especially important in alleviating stressful family situations, thereby helping prevent child abuse. An investigation of the support systems in 58 counties in New York State revealed a relation between the incidence of child abuse and the absence of support systems available to the family (Garbarino, 1976). Both family resources—relatives and friends, for example—and such formal community support systems as crisis centers and child abuse counseling were associated with a reduction in child abuse.

Family Influences   To understand abuse in the family, the interactions of all family members need to be considered, regardless of who actually performs the violent acts against the child (Margolin, 1994). For example, even though the father may be the one who physically abuses the child, contributions by the mother, the child, and siblings also should be evaluated. Many parents who abuse their children come from families in which physical punishment was used. These parents view physical punishment as a legitimate way of controlling the child's behavior. Physical punishment may be a part of this sanctioning. Children themselves may unwittingly contribute to child abuse. An unattractive child may receive more physical punishment than an attractive child. A child from an unwanted pregnancy may be especially vulnerable to abuse (Harter, Alexander, & Neimeyer, 1988). Husband-wife violence and financial problems may result in displaced aggression toward a defenseless child. Displaced aggression is commonly involved in child abuse. To further evaluate child abuse, see Adventures for the Mind.

Developmental Consequences of Abuse   Among the developmental consequences of child maltreatment are poor emotion regulation, attachment problems,

problems in peer relations, difficulty in adapting to school, and other psychological problems (Rogosch & others, 1995). Difficulties in initiating and modulating positive and negative affect have been observed in maltreated infants (Cicchetti, Ganiban, & Barnett, 1991). Maltreated infants also may show excessive negative affect or blunted positive affect.

Not only do maltreated infants show insecure patterns of attachment, but they also might show a form of attachment not often found in normal children. As we saw earlier in the chapter, maltreated children tend to display an attachment pattern referred to as *disorganized,* which involves high avoidance and high resistance (Main & Solomon, 1990). In one study, the disorganized attachment pattern was found in 80 percent of the maltreated infants observed (Carlson & others, 1989).

Maltreated children appear to be poorly equipped to develop successful peer relations, due to their aggressiveness, avoidance, and aberrant responses to both distress and positive approaches from peers (Mueller & Silverman, 1989). Two patterns of social behavior are common in maltreated children. Sometimes maltreated children show excessive physical and verbal aggression, while at other times maltreated children show a pattern of avoidance. These patterns have been described in terms of "fight or flight."

Maltreated children's difficulties in establishing effective relationships may show up in their interactions with teachers. Maltreated children might expect teachers to be unresponsive or unavailable, based on their relationships with their parents. For maltreated children, dealing with fears about abuse and searching for security in relationships with adults can take precedence over performing competently at academic tasks.

Being physically abused has been linked with children's anxiety, personality problems, depression, conduct disorder, and delinquency (Toth, Manley, & Cicchetti, 1992). Later, during the adult years, maltreated children show increased violence toward other adults, dating partners, and marital partners, as well as increased substance abuse, anxiety, and depression (Malinosky-Rummell & Hansen, 1993). In sum, maltreated children are at risk for developing a wide range of problems and disorders.

Thus far in our discussion of social contexts of infant development we have focused on the family, examining topics ranging from the transition to parenthood to child abuse. Next, we will explore the effects of another social context in which many American children spend many hours—day care.

Adventures for the Mind
Developing a Model of Intervention for Maltreating Families

What is the best way to help maltreated children? Intervention with maltreating families is difficult because of the multiple risk factors involved and the difficulty in getting such families to deal with the chaos in their lives. Poverty, intellectual and educational limitations, social isolation, and mental disorders are but a few of the factors that make it difficult to involve these families in effective treatment. With these limitations in mind, develop a model of intervention that you believe would benefit maltreated children and their families. Think about ways that therapists could assist families, about educational programs, and about recreational and activity possibilities.

Day Care

Each weekday at 8 A.M., Ellen Smith takes her 1-year-old daughter, Tanya, to the day-care center at Brookhaven College in Dallas. Then Mrs. Smith goes to work and returns in the afternoon to take Tanya home. After 3 years, Mrs. Smith reports that her daughter is adventuresome and interacts confidently with peers and adults. Mrs. Smith believes that day care has been a wonderful way to raise Tanya.

In Los Angeles, however, day care has been a series of horror stories for Barbara Jones. After 2 years of unpleasant experiences with sitters, day-care centers, and day-care homes, Mrs. Jones has quit her job as a successful real estate agent to stay home

Caring for Children

Child Care Policy Around the World

Sheila Kamerman (1989) surveyed the nature of child care policies around the world, with special attention given to European countries. Maternity and paternity policies for working parents include paid, job-protected leaves, which are sometimes supplemented by unpaid, job-protected leaves. Child care policy packages also often include full health insurance. An effective child care policy is designed to get an infant off to a competent start in life and to protect maternal health while maintaining income. More than a hundred countries around the world have such child care policies, including all of Europe, Canada, Israel, and many developing countries. Infants are assured of at least two to three months of maternal/paternal care, and in most European countries five to six months.

The maternity policy as now implemented in several countries involves a paid maternity leave that begins 2 to 6 weeks prior to expected childbirth and lasts from 8 to 20 or even 24 weeks after birth. This traditional maternal policy stems from an effort to protect the health of pregnant working women, new mothers, and their infants. Only since the 1960s has the maternity policy's link with employment become strong. A second child care policy emphasizes the importance of parenting and recognizes the potential of fathers as well as mothers to care for their infants. In Sweden, a par-

ent insurance benefit provides protection to the new mother before birth and for 6 to 12 weeks after birth but then allows the father to participate in the postchildbirth leave. Approximately one-fourth of Swedish fathers take at least part of the postchildbirth leave, in addition to the 2 weeks of paid leave all fathers are entitled to at the time of childbirth. In a typical pattern in Sweden, the working mother might take off 3 months, after which she and her husband might share child care between them, each working half-time for 6 months. In addition, Swedish parents have the option of taking an unpaid but fully protected job leave until their child is 18 months old and working a 6-hour day (without a reduction in pay) from the end of the parental leave until their child is 8 years old.

These policies are designed to let parents take maternity/paternity leave without losing employment or income. In sum, almost all the industrialized countries other than the United States have recognized the importance of developing maternity/paternity policies that allow working parents some time off after childbirth to recover physically, to adapt to parenting, and to improve the well-being of the infant.

and take care of her 2½-year-old daughter, Gretchen. "I didn't want to sacrifice my baby for my job," said Mrs. Jones, who was unable to find good substitute day-care homes. When she put Gretchen into a day-care center, she said that she felt her daughter was being treated like a piece of merchandise—dropped off and picked up.

Many parents worry whether day care will adversely affect their children. They fear that day care will reduce their infants' emotional attachment to them, retard the infants' cognitive development, fail to teach them how to control anger, and allow them to be unduly influenced by their peers. How extensive is day care? Are the worries of these parents justified?

In the 1990s, far more young children are in day care than at any other time in history; about 2 million children currently receive formal, licensed day care, and more than 5 million children attend kindergarten. Also, uncounted millions of children are cared for by unlicensed baby-sitters.

In Sweden, mothers or fathers are given paid maternity or paternity leave for up to 9 months. Sweden and many other European countries have well-developed child care policies. To learn about these policies, read Caring for Children. In Sweden, day care for infants under 1 year of age is usually not a major concern because one parent is on paid leave for child care.

Since the United States does not have a policy of paid leave for child care, day care in the United States has become a major national concern. The type of day care that young children receive varies extensively (Burchinal & others, 1996). Many day-care centers house large groups of children and have elaborate facilities. Some are commercial operations; others are non-profit centers run by churches, civic groups, and employers. Child care is frequently provided in private homes, at times by child care professionals, at others by mothers who want to earn extra money.

A special contemporary interest of researchers who study day care is the role of poverty (Huston, McLoyd, & Coll, 1994). In one study, day-care centers that served high-income children delivered better-quality care than did centers that served middle- and low-income children (Phillips & others, 1994). The indices of quality (such as teacher-child ratios) in subsidized centers for the poor were fairly good, but the quality of observed teacher-child interaction was lower than in high-income centers. To further evaluate the characteristics of competent care-givers, see Adventures for the Mind.

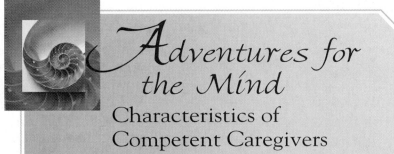

Adventures for the Mind
Characteristics of Competent Caregivers

Much of the health and well-being of infants is in the hands of caregivers. Whether the caregivers are parents or day-care personnel, these adults play significant roles in children's lives. What are the characteristics of competent caregivers? For one thing, competent caregivers enjoy caregiving. They reflect these positive feelings as they interact with infants and children. Try to come up with a list of five other characteristics of competent caregivers.

The provision of day care in most developing counties has improved, but this often has been in a form that denies access to the poorest children. In some locations in India, mobile day-care centers have provided intensive integrated child services to young children in slum settlements within large cities and rural villages.

Day Care Research

National Child Care Information Center

NICHD Study of Early Child Care

What constitutes quality child care? The following recommendations were made by the National Association for the Education of Young Children (1986). They are based on a consensus arrived at by experts in early childhood education and child development. It is especially important for parents to meet the adults who will care for their child. They are responsible for every aspect of the program's operation.

1. **The adult caregivers**

   • The adults should enjoy and understand how infants and young children grow.

   • There should be enough adults to work with a group and to care for the individual needs of children. The recommended ratios of adult caregivers for children of different ages are as follows (Kontos & Wilcox-Herzog, 1997):

Age of children	Adult:children ratio
0–1 Year	1:3
1–2 Years	1:5
2–3 Years	1:6
3–4 Years	1:8
4–5 Years	1:10

   • Caregivers should observe and record each child's progress and development.

2. **The program activities and equipment**

   • The environment should foster the growth and development of young children working and playing together.

   • A good center should provide appropriate and sufficient equipment and play materials and make them readily available.

   • Infants and children should be helped to increase their language skills and to expand their understanding of the world.

3. **The relation of staff to families and the community**

   • A good program should consider and support the needs of the entire family. Parents should be welcome to observe, discuss policies, make suggestions, and work in the activities of the center.

   • The staff in a good center should be aware of and contribute to community resources. The staff should share information about community recreational and learning opportunities with families.

4. **The design of the facility and the program to meet the varied demands of infants and young children, their families, and the staff**

   • The health of children, staff, and parents should be protected and promoted. The staff should be alert to the health of each child.

   • The facility should be safe for children and adults.

   • The environment should be spacious enough to accommodate a variety of activities and equipment. More specifically, there should be a minimum of 35 square feet of usable playroom floor space indoors per child and 75 square feet of play space outdoors per child.

Figure 8.6
What Is High-Quality Day Care?

The quality of care children experience in day care varies extensively. Some caregivers have no training, others have extensive training. Some day-care centers have a low caregiver-to-child ratio; others have a high caregiver-to-child ratio. Some experts have argued that the quality of day care most children receive in the United States is poor. Infancy researcher Jay Belsky (1989) not only believes that the quality of day care children experience is generally poor but also argues that this translates into negative developmental outcomes for children. Belsky concludes that extensive day-care experience during the first 12 months of life—as is typical in the United States—is associated with insecure attachment, as well as increased aggression, noncompliance, and possibly social withdrawal during the preschool and early elementary school years.

One study supports Belsky's beliefs (Vandell & Corasaniti, 1988). Extensive day care in the first year of life was associated with long-term negative outcomes. In contrast to children who began full-time day care later, children who began full-time day care (defined as more than 30 hours per week) as infants were rated by parents and teachers as being less compliant and as having poorer peer relations. In the first grade, they received lower grades and had poor work habits by comparison.

Belsky's conclusions about day care are controversial. Other respected researchers have arrived at a different conclusion; their review of the day-care research suggest no ill effects of day care (Scarr, Lande, & McCartney, 1989).

What constitutes a high-quality day-care program for infants? The demonstration program developed by Jerome Kagan and his colleagues (Kagan, Kearsley, & Zelazo, 1978) at Harvard University is exemplary. The day-care center included a pediatrician, a nonteaching director, and an infant-teacher ratio of 3 to 1. Teachers' aides assisted at the center. The teachers and aides were trained to smile frequently, to talk with the infants, and to provide them with a safe environment, which included many stimulating toys. No adverse effects of day care were observed in this project. More information about what to look for in a quality day-care center is presented in figure 8.6. Using such criteria, Carolee Howes (1988) discovered that children who entered low-quality child care as infants were least likely to be socially competent in early childhood (less compliant, less self-controlled, less task-oriented, more hostile, and having more problems in peer interaction). Unfortunately, children who come from families with few resources (psychological, social, and economic) are more likely to experience poor-quality day care than are children from more-advantaged backgrounds (Lamb, 1994).

Aware of the growing use of child care, the National Institute of Child Health and Human Development (NICHD) set out to develop a comprehensive, longitudinal study (a study that follows the same individuals over time, usually several years or more) that focuses on the child care experiences of children and their development (NICHD Early Child Care Research Network, 1997; Peth-Pierce, 1998). The study began in 1991, and data were collected on a diverse sample of almost 1,400 children and their families at 10 locations across the United States. Researchers are assessing children over seven years of their lives using multiple methods (trained observers, interviews, questionnaires, and testing) and measuring many facets of children's development, including physical health, cognitive development, and socioemotional development. Following are some of the results of this extensive study to date:

- The infants from low-income families were more likely to receive low-quality child care than were their higher-income counterparts. Quality of care was based on such characteristics as group size, child–adult ratio, physical environment, caregiver characteristics (such as formal education, specialized training, and

Quality day care includes having adult caregivers who enjoy being with infants and young children. The adult caregivers also should be knowledgeable about how infants and young children grow.

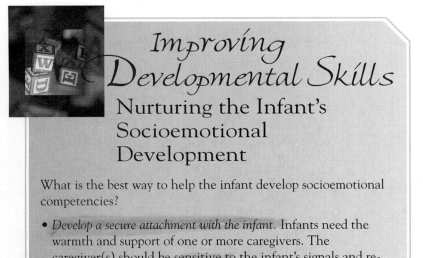

Improving Developmental Skills
Nurturing the Infant's Socioemotional Development

What is the best way to help the infant develop socioemotional competencies?

- *Develop a secure attachment with the infant.* Infants need the warmth and support of one or more caregivers. The caregiver(s) should be sensitive to the infant's signals and respond nurturantly.

- *Be sure that both the mother and the father nurture the infant.* Infants develop best when both the mother and the father provide warm, nurturant support. Fathers need to seriously evaluate their responsibility in rearing a competent infant.

- *Select competent day care.* If the infant will be placed in day care, spend time evaluating different options. Be sure the infant–caregiver ratio is low. Also assess whether the adults enjoy and are knowledgeable about interacting with infants. Determine if the facility is safe and provides stimulating activities.

- *Understand and respect the infant's temperament.* Be sensitive to the characteristics of each child. It may be necessary to provide extra support for distress-prone infants, for example. Avoid negative labeling of the infant.

- *Adapt to developmental changes in the infant.* An 18-month-old toddler is very different from a 6-month-old infant. Be knowledgeable about how infants develop and adapt to the changing infant. Let toddlers explore a wider, but safe environment.

- *Be physically and mentally healthy.* Infant's socioemotional development benefits when their caregivers are physically and mentally healthy. For example, a depressed parent may not sensitively respond to the infant's signals.

- *Read a good book on infant development.* Any of T. Berry Brazelton's books are a good start. One is *Touchpoints*. Two other good ones are *Infancy* by Tiffany Field and *Baby Steps* by Claire Kopp.

child care experience), and caregiver behavior (such as sensitivity to children).

- Child care in and of itself neither adversely affected nor promoted the security of infants' attachments to their mothers. Certain child care conditions, in combination with certain home environments, did increase the probability that infants would be insecurely attached to their mothers. The infants who received either poor quality of care or more than 10 hours per week of care or were in more than one setting in the first 15 months of life, were more likely to be insecurely attached, but only if their mothers were less sensitive in responding to them.

- Child care quality, especially sensitive and responsive attention from caregivers, was linked with fewer child problems. The higher the quality of child care over the first three years of life (more positive language stimulation and interaction between the child and the provider), the greater the child's language and cognitive abilities. No cognitive benefits were found for the children in the exclusive care of their mother.

At different points in this chapter, we have highlighted strategies for nurturing the infant's socioemotional development. The insert, Improving Developmental Skills, profiles some of the best ways to do this.

We have studied many ideas about attachment and social contexts. An overview of these ideas is presented in summary table 8.2.

We have all the knowledge necessary to provide absolutely first-rate child care in the United States. What is missing is the commitment and the will.

Edward Zigler
Contemporary American Developmental Psychologist

Summary Table 8.2
Attachment and Social Contexts

Concept	Processes/ Related Ideas	Characteristics/Description
Attachment	What is attachment?	Attachment is a close emotional bond between the infant and the caregiver. Feeding is not a critical element in attachment, although contact comfort, familiarity, and trust are. Bowlby's ethological theory stresses that the caregiver and the infant instinctively trigger attachment. Attachment to the caregiver intensifies at about 6–7 months.
	Individual differences	Ainsworth believes that secure attachment (type B babies) in the first year of life is optimal. In secure attachment, infants use the caregiver as a secure base from which to explore the environment. Three types of insecurely attached babies have been described: type A babies (avoidant), type C babies (ambivalent-resistant), and type D babies (disorganized).
	Caregiving styles and attachment classification	Caregivers of secure babies are sensitive to their signals and are consistently available to meet their needs. Caregivers of avoidant babies tend to be unavailable or rejecting. Caregivers of ambivalent-resistant babies tend to be inconsistently available to their babies and generally are not very affectionate. Caregivers of disorganized babies often neglect or physically abuse their babies.
	Measurement of attachment	The main way that attachment has been assessed is by using the Ainsworth Strange Situation, although it has been criticized for being too unnatural.
	Attachment, temperament, and the wider social world	Some critics argue that attachment theorists and researchers have not given adequate attention to genetics and temperament on the one hand and to the diversity of social agents and contexts on the other. Cultural variations in attachment have been found, but in all cultures studied to date secure attachment is the most common classification.
Social contexts	The family	The transition to parenting requires considerable adaptation and adjustment on the part of parents. Children socialize parents, just as parents socialize their children. Mutual regulation and scaffolding are important aspects of reciprocal socialization. The family is a system of interacting individuals; this system has different subsystems—some dyadic, others polyadic. Belsky's model describes direct and indirect effects. Although fathers have increased their child rearing, the main responsibility for child rearing still falls on most mothers' shoulders. Fathers can respond sensitively to infants. The mother's primary role when interacting with an infant involves caregiving; the father's, playful interaction. Father-mother cooperation and mutual respect help the child develop positive attitudes toward males and females.
		An understanding of child abuse requires information about cultural, familial, and community influences. Sexual abuse of children is now recognized as a more widespread problem than was believed in the past. Child maltreatment places the child at risk for a number of developmental problems.
	Day care	Day care has become a basic need of the American family; more children are in day care today than at any other time in history. The quality of day care is uneven. Belsky concluded that most day care is inadequate and that extensive day care in the first 12 months of an infant's life has negative developmental outcomes. Other experts disagree with Belsky. Day care remains a controversial topic. Quality day care can be achieved, and it seems to have few adverse effects on children.

Chapter Review

From birth, babies are wrapped in a socioemotional world with their caregivers. Babies and their caregivers communicate with each other through emotions, their senses, and their words. Through interaction with their caregivers, infants learn to adapt to their world.

We began this chapter by describing Tom's fathering experience and then we explored the following aspects of emotional and personality development: emotional development, temperament, and personality development. Our coverage of attachment focused on what it is, individual differences, caregiving styles and attachment classification, measurement of attachment, and attachment, temperament, and the wider social world. We also studied these two important social contexts in infancy: the family and day care.

Don't forget that you can obtain a more detailed review of the chapter by again studying the two summary tables on pages 207 and 223. This chapter concludes our coverage of infant development. Next, we will turn our attention to Section Four, "Early Childhood," beginning with chapter 9, "Physical Development in Early Childhood."

✔ Children Checklist

Socioemotional Development in Infancy

How much have you learned since the beginning of the chapter? Use the following statements to help you review your knowledge and understanding of the chapter material. First, read the statement and mentally or briefly demonstrate on paper that you can discuss the relevant information.

_____ I can discuss the nature of emotional development in infants.
_____ I know what temperament is and how it can be classified.
_____ I can describe personality development in infancy, including trust, the self, and independence.
_____ I am aware of what attachment is, individual differences in attachment, which parenting styles link up with different attachment classifications, and how attachment is assessed.
_____ I can evaluate attachment, temperament, and the wider social world.
_____ I can describe the transition to parenting, reciprocal socialization, and the family as a system.
_____ I can discuss mothers and fathers as caregivers, as well as child maltreatment.
_____ I can evaluate the effects of day care on infant development.

For any items that you did not check, go back and locate the relevant material in the chapter. Review the material until you feel you can check off the item. You may want to use this checklist later in preparing for an exam.

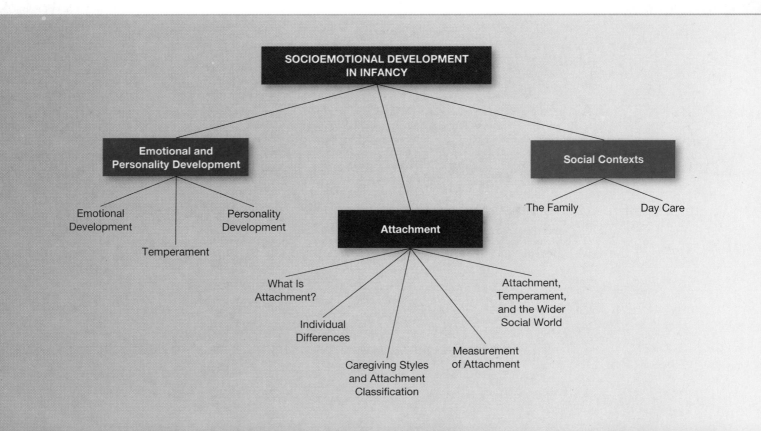

Key Terms

emotion 198
positive affectivity (PA) 198
negative affectivity (NA) 198
Maximally Discriminative
  Facial Movement Coding
  System (MAX) 200
basic cry 200
anger cry 200
pain cry 200
reflexive smile 201
social smile 201
stranger anxiety 201
social referencing 202
temperament 202

easy child 202
difficult child 202
slow-to-warm-up child 202
attachment 208
secure attachment 209
type B babies 209 *Best*
type A babies 209 *Aversive*
type C babies 209 *Cling+Push*
type D babies 209 *Disoriented*
Strange Situation 210
reciprocal socialization 213
scaffolding 213

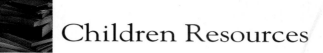

Children Resources

Daycare
(1993, rev. ed.) by Alison Clarke-Stewart.
Cambridge, MA: Harvard University Press.

This book draws on extensive research to survey the social, political, and economic contexts of day care. The author discusses options and consequences to help parents make informed choices.

Touchpoints
(1992) by T. Berry Brazelton.
Reading, MA: Addison-Wesley.

Covering the period from pregnancy to first grade, Brazelton focuses on the concerns and questions parents have about the child's feelings, behavior, and development.

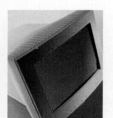

Taking It to the Net

http://www.mhhe.com/santrockcd6

1. You have an infant daughter who seems to lack a normal level of attachment to you and your spouse. What can be done to socialize the child into the family? Since infants naturally like to play, is there a way to use play to socialize your daughter into the family?
2. You are having a discussion with your sister concerning adoption. She is concerned about the emotional health of adopted children. What will the adoption agency be able to offer her in terms of information and support regarding this issue. What are some emotional issues encountered by adopted children?
3. You have been working at a day-care center for several weeks when you begin to notice that Lekisha does not like to be held and becomes upset when interacting with others. What are some strategies for developing social skills in infants? What strategies would you recommend, and why?

Infancy

Physical Development

Physical development in the first 2 years of life is extensive. Infants are born into the world equipped with a number of survival reflexes, such as coughing, blinking, yawning, and grasping. Cephalocaudal (top-down) and proximodistal (center-out) patterns characterize infant physical growth. Infants' rate of growth is much faster in the first year of life than in the second year. Both gross motor skills (such as walking) and fine motor skills (such as finger dexterity) make significant advances during infancy. As the infant ages from birth to 2 years, the interconnection of neurons increases dramatically. Newborns usually sleep 16 to 17 hours a day, but by 4 months they approach adultlike sleeping patterns. With regard to nutrition, infants need to consume about 50 calories per day for each pound they weigh. Breast- versus bottle-feeding continues to be a hotly debated issue. Many parents begin toilet training their toddlers at about 20 months to 2 years of age and conclude it by 3 years of age. The newborn's perception is much more advanced than we previously thought. Newborn vision is about 20/600, but by 6 months it has improved to at least 20/100. The visual cliff study demonstrated that depth perception is present by at least 6 months of age. Newborns, and even the fetus, can hear. Newborns also can feel pain, smell, and taste. Infants as young as 4 months of age have intermodal perception.

Cognitive Development

Piaget proposed that infant cognitive development involves the sensorimotor stage, or progression in the infant's ability to organize and coordinate sensations with physical movements. Piaget divided the sensorimotor stage into six substages, ranging from simple reflexes (birth to first month) to internalization of schemes (18–24 months). Piaget also found that object permanence is an important accomplishment in the first year. A number of contemporary developmentalists believe that Piaget underestimated some of the infant's competencies, especially competencies in developing a more stable and differentiated perceptual world and engaging in symbolic activity. The information-processing perspective emphasizes the infant's development of cognitive processes—such as attention and memory—rather than stages. Developmental scales that evaluate individual differences among infants have been developed. Milestones in infant language development include babbling (3–6 months), first words understood (6–9 months), the growth of receptive vocabulary (reaches 300 or more words by age 2), and the growth of spoken vocabulary (reaches 200–275 words by age 2). An infant's first words characteristically are holophrastic; at about 18–24 months, infants speak in two-word utterances. Mean length of utterance (MLU) has been used as an indicator of language maturity; five stages of MLU have been identified.

Socioemotional Development

Emotions are the first language with which parents and infants communicate before the infant acquires language. Various emotions emerge at different ages—for instance, a social smile at about 4–6 weeks, surprise at 3–4 months, and shame at 6–8 months. Stranger anxiety appears and intensifies in the second half of the first year of life, and social referencing increases in the second year. The infant's temperament involves a behavioral style and characteristic emotional response. Different classifications of temperament have been made, including easy, difficult, and slow to warm up. Erikson believed that the first year involves the stage of trust versus mistrust and the second year the stage of autonomy versus shame and doubt. Self-awareness emerges very early in infancy and develops over the first 3–4 months. Infants develop a rudimentary form of self-recognition at about 18 months of age. Attachment to the caregiver intensifies at about 6–7 months of age. Attachment has been classified as secure or insecure, with insecure babies described as avoidant, ambivalent-resistant, or disorganized. Different parenting styles link up with different attachment classifications. Secure attachment is described as the optimal course of development. Critics say that temperament and the wider social world need to be taken into account more in formulations of attachment. Two important social contexts for infant development are the family and day care. The transition to parenting requires adjustment and adaptation. Mutual regulation and scaffolding are two important aspects of reciprocal socialization in parent-infant interaction. Fathers have increased their interaction with infants, but in most families mothers still have the most responsibility for child rearing. Child maltreatment is a special concern. Day care has become a basic need of many American families. Day care itself does not harm infants, but low-quality day care can.

Early Childhood

You are troubled at seeing him spend his early years doing nothing. What! Is it nothing to be happy? Is it nothing to skip, to play, to run about all day long? Never in his life will he be so busy as now.

Jean-Jacques Rousseau
Swiss-Born French Philosopher,
18th Century

In early childhood, our greatest untold poem was being only 4 years old. We skipped and ran and played all the sun long, never in our lives so busy, busy being something we had not quite grasped yet. Who knew our thoughts, which we worked up into small mythologies all our own? Our thoughts and images and drawings took wings. The blossoms of our heart, no wind could touch. Our small world widened as we discovered new refuges and new people. When we said, "I," we meant something totally unique, not to be confused with any other. Section IV consists of three chapters: "Physical Development in Early Childhood" (chapter 9), "Cognitive Development in Early Childhood" (chapter 10), and "Socioemotional Development in Early Childhood" (chapter 11).

Chapter

9

Physical Development in Early Childhood

PREVIEW

As twentieth-century Welsh poet Dylan Thomas artfully observed, young children do "run all the sun long." And, as their physical development advances, children's small worlds widen. Among the questions we will explore in this chapter are

- How much do children grow in height and weight during early childhood?
- What changes in the brain and visual perception take place?
- How do young children's motor skills develop?
- What are some changes that occur in children's artistic drawings as they develop?
- What is the nature of young children's sleep? What sleep problems do some young children encounter?
- What are young children's energy needs and eating behavior like?
- What is the status of young children's illness and health in the United States and around the world?

The Story of Teresa Amabile and Her Creativity

Teresa Amabile remembers that, when she was in kindergarten, she rushed in every day, excited and enthusiastic about getting to the easel and playing with all those bright colors and big paint brushes. Children also had free access to a clay table with all kinds of art materials on it. Teresa remembers going home every day and telling her mother she wanted to draw, paint, and play with crayons.

Teresa's kindergarten experience, unfortunately, was the high point of her artistic interest. The next year, she entered a traditional elementary school and things began to change. Instead of Teresa's having free access to art materials every day, art became just another subject, something she had for an hour and a half every Friday afternoon.

Week after week, all through elementary school, it was the same art class. According to Teresa, her elementary school art classes were very restricted and demoralizing. She recalls being given small reprints of painting masterpieces, a different one each week. For example, one week in the second grade, children were presented with Leonardo da Vinci's *Adoration of the Magi.* This was meant for art appreciation, but that's not how the teacher used it. Instead, the children were told to take out their art materials and try to copy the masterpiece. For Teresa, and the other children, this was an exercise in frustration. She says that young elementary school children do not have the skill development even to make all those horses and angels fit on the page, let alone make them look like the masterpiece. Teresa easily could tell that she was not doing well at what the teacher asked her to do.

The children were not given any help in developing their skills. Also, the teacher graded the children on the art they produced, adding evaluation pressure to the situation. Teresa was aware at that time that her motivation for doing artwork was being completely destroyed. She no longer wanted to go home and paint at the end of the day.

Teresa Amabile eventually obtained her Ph.D. in psychology and became one of the leading researchers on creativity. Her hope is that more elementary schools will not crush children's enthusiasm for creativity, the way hers did. So many young children, like Teresa, are excited about exploring and creating, but, by the time they reach the third or fourth grade, many don't like school, let alone have any sense of pleasure in their own creativity (Goleman, Kaufman, & Ray, 1993).

**Preschool Growth
and Development**

BODY GROWTH AND CHANGE

Remember from chapter 6 that the infant's growth in the first year is rapid and follows cephalocaudal and proximodistal patterns. At some point around the first birthday, most infants begin to walk. During the infant's second year, the growth rate begins to slow down, but both gross and fine motor skills progress rapidly. The infant develops a sense of mastery through increased proficiency in walking and running. Improvement in fine motor skills—such as being able to turn the pages of a book, one at a time—also contributes to the infant's sense of mastery in the second year. The growth rate continues to slow down in early childhood. Otherwise, we would be a species of giants.

Height and Weight

The average child grows 2½ inches in height and gains between 5 and 7 pounds a year during early childhood. As the preschool child grows older, the percentage of increase in height and weight decreases with each additional year. Figure 9.1 shows the average height and weight of children as they age from 2 to 6 years. Girls are only slightly smaller and lighter than boys during these years, a difference that continues until puberty. During the preschool years, both boys and girls slim down as the trunks of their bodies lengthen. Although their heads are still somewhat large for their bodies, by the end of the preschool years most children have lost their top-heavy look. Body fat also shows a slow, steady decline during the preschool years. The chubby baby often looks much leaner by the end of early childhood. Girls have more fatty tissue than boys; boys have more muscle tissue.

Most preschool children are fascinated by bodies—especially their own, but also the bodies of family members and friends. Children have lots of questions about how their bodies work. Jonathan, age 4, says, "You know, I sometimes wonder about what is inside me. I bet it is all wet with blood and other stuff moving around. Outside of me it is all dry. You wouldn't know my inside by looking at the outside part." Jason, age 5, asks, "How does my brain work?" Jennifer, age 5, asks, "Why do we eat food? What happens to the food after we eat it?" Budding 4-year-old biologists such as Jonathan, Jason, and Jennifer are telling us they want to know more about the body's machinery. Two recommended books to help answer some of children's curious questions about their bodies are *The Body Book* by Claire Raynor and *Blood and Guts* by Linda Allison.

Growth patterns vary individually. Think back to your preschool years. This was probably the first time you noticed that some children were taller than you, some shorter; some were fatter, some thinner; some were stronger, some weaker. Much of the variation is due to heredity, but environmental experiences are involved to some extent. A review of the height and weight of children around the world concluded that the two most important contributors to height differences are ethnic origin and nutrition (Meredith, 1978). The urban, middle socioeconomic status, and firstborn children were taller than rural, lower socioeconomic status, and later-born children. The children whose mothers smoked during pregnancy were half an inch shorter than the children whose mothers did not smoke during pregnancy. In the United States, African American children are taller than White children.

Why are some children unusually short? The culprits are congenital factors (genetic or prenatal problems), a physical problem that develops in childhood, or an emotional difficulty. In many cases, children with congenital growth problems can be treated with hormones. Usually this treatment is directed at the pituitary, the body's master gland, located at the base of the brain. This gland secretes growth-related hormones. With regard to physical problems that develop during childhood, malnutrition and chronic infections can stunt growth. However, if the problems are properly treated, normal growth usually is attained. **Deprivation dwarfism** *is a type of growth retardation caused by emotional deprivation; children are deprived of affection, which causes stress and alters the release of hormones by the pituitary gland.* Some children who are not dwarfs may also show the effects of an impoverished

deprivation dwarfism
Growth retardation caused by emotional deprivation; children who are deprived of affection experience stress that affects the release of hormones by the pituitary gland.

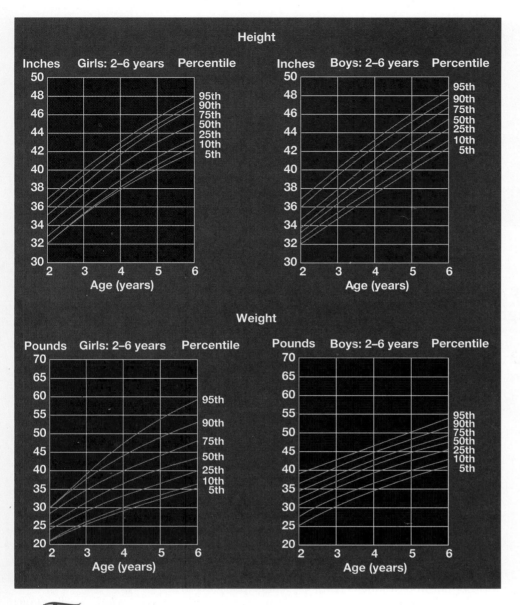

$\mathcal{F}$*igure 9.1*

Average Height and Weight of Girls and Boys from 2 to 6 Years of Age

emotional environment, although most parents of these children say they are small and weak because they have a poor body structure or constitution (Gardner, 1972).

The Brain

One of the most important physical developments during early childhood is the continuing development of the brain and nervous system. While the brain continues to grow in early childhood, it does not grow as rapidly as in infancy. By the time children have reached 3 years of age, the brain is three-quarters of its adult size. By age 5, the brain has reached about nine-tenths of its adult size.

The brain and the head grow more rapidly than any other part of the body. The top parts of the head, the eyes, and the brain grow faster than the lower portions, such as the jaw. Figure 9.2 reveals how the growth curve for the head and brain advances more rapidly than the growth curve for height and weight. At 5 years of

$\mathcal{S}$*wiftly the brain becomes an enchanted loom, where millions of flashing shuttles weave a dissolving pattern—always a meaningful pattern—though never an abiding one.*

Sir Charles Sherrington
English Neuroscientist, 20th Century

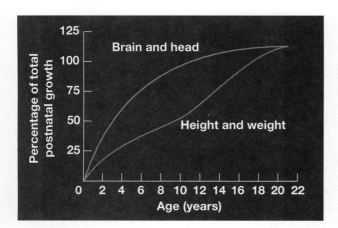

Figure 9.2
Growth Curves for the Head and Brain and for Height and Weight

The more rapid growth of the brain and head can easily be seen. Height and weight advance more gradually over the first two decades of life.

myelination
The process in which the nerve cells are covered and insulated with a layer of fat cells, which increases the speed at which information travels through the nervous system.

functional amblyopia
An eye defect that results from not using one eye enough to avoid the discomfort of double vision produced by imbalanced eye muscles; "lazy eye."

All the sun long I was running . . .
Dylan Thomas
Welsh Poet and Writer, 20th Century

age, when the brain has attained approximately 90 percent of its adult weight, the 5-year-old's total body weight is only about one-third of what it will be when the child reaches adulthood.

Some of the brain's increase in size is due to the increase in the number and size of nerve endings within and between areas of the brain. These nerve endings continue to grow at least until adolescence. Some of the brain's increase in size also is due to the increase in **myelination,** *in which nerve cells are covered and insulated with a layer of fat cells. This has the effect of increasing the speed of information traveling through the nervous system.* Some developmentalists believe myelination is important in the maturation of a number of children's abilities. For example, myelination in the areas of the brain related to hand-eye coordination is not complete until about 4 years of age. Myelination in the areas of the brain related to focusing attention is not complete until the end of the middle or late childhood.

The increasing maturation of the brain, combined with opportunities to experience a widening world, contribute to children's emerging cognitive abilities. Consider a child who is learning to read and is asked by a teacher to read aloud to the class. Input from the child's eyes is transmitted to the child's brain, then passed through many brain systems, which translate (process) the patterns of black and white into codes for letters, words, and associations. The output occurs in the form of messages to the child's lips and tongue. The child's own gift of speech is possible because brain systems are organized in ways that permit language processing.

Visual Perception

Visual maturity increases during the early childhood years. Only toward the end of early childhood are most children's eye muscles adequately developed to allow them to move their eyes efficiently across a series of letters. And preschool children are often farsighted, not being able to see up close as well as they can far away. By the time they enter the first grade, though, most children can focus their eyes and sustain their attention quite well.

Depth perception continues to mature during the preschool years. However, because of young children's lack of motor coordination, they may trip and spill drinks, fall from a jungle gym, or produce poor artwork.

Some children develop **functional amblyopia,** *or "lazy eye," which usually results from not using one eye enough to avoid the discomfort of double vision produced by imbalanced eye muscles.* Children with a lazy eye have no way of knowing that they are not seeing adequately, even though their vision is decreased because one eye is doing most of the work. Treatment may include patching the stronger eye for several months to encourage the use of the affected eye, wearing glasses, or doing eye exercises. Occasionally, surgery may be required on the muscles of the eye.

What signs suggest that a child might be having vision problems? These include rubbing the eyes, excessive blinking, squinting, appearing irritable when playing games that require good distance vision, shutting or covering one eye, and tilting the head or thrusting it forward when looking at something. A child who shows any of these behaviors should be examined by an ophthalmologist.

MOTOR DEVELOPMENT

Running as fast as you can, falling down, getting right back up and running just as fast as you can . . . building towers with blocks . . . scribbling, scribbling, and scribbling some more . . . cutting paper with scissors. During your preschool years, you probably developed the ability to perform all of these activities.

Gross and Fine Motor Skills

Considerable progress is made in both gross and fine motor skills during early childhood. First, let's explore changes in gross motor skills.

Developmental Milestones

Gross Motor Skills   The preschool child no longer has to make an effort simply to stay upright and to move around. As children move their legs with more confidence and carry themselves more purposefully, moving around in the environment becomes more automatic (Poest & others, 1990).

At 3 years of age, children enjoy simple movements, such as hopping, jumping, and running back and forth, just for the sheer delight of performing these activities. They take considerable pride in showing how they can run across a room and jump all of 6 inches. The run-and-jump will win no Olympic gold medals, but for the 3-year-old the activity is a source of considerable pride and accomplishment.

At 4 years of age, children are still enjoying the same kind of activities, but they have become more adventurous. They scramble over low jungle gyms as they display their athletic prowess. Although they have been able to climb stairs with one foot on each step for some time, they are just beginning to be able to come down the same way. They still often revert to marking time on each step.

At 5 years of age, children are even more adventuresome than when they were 4. It is not unusual for self-assured 5-year-olds to perform hair-raising stunts on practically any climbing object. Five-year-olds run hard and enjoy races with each other and their parents. A summary of development in gross motor skills during early childhood is shown in figure 9.3

You probably have arrived at one important conclusion about preschool children: they are very, very active. Indeed, 3-year-old children have the highest activity level of any age in the entire human life span. They fidget when they watch television. They fidget when they sit at the dinner table. Even when they sleep, they move around quite a bit. Because of their activity level and the development of large muscles, especially in the arms and legs, preschool children need daily exercise. To further evaluate gross motor skills in young children, see Adventures for the Mind.

It is important for preschool and kindergarten teachers to develop programs that encourage young children's gross motor skills. Catherine Poest and her colleagues (1990) provided some valuable suggestions for such programs. One set of

37–48 months	49–60 months	61–72 months
Throws ball underhanded (4′)	Bounces and catches ball	Throws ball (44′ boys; 25′ girls)
Pedals tricycle 10′	Runs 10′ and stops	Carries a 16-pound object
Catches large ball	Pushes/pulls a wagon/doll buggy	Kicks rolling ball
Completes forward somersault (aided)	Kicks 10″ ball toward target	Skips alternating feet
Jumps to floor from 12″	Carries 12-pound object	Roller skates
Hops three hops with both feet	Catches ball	Skips rope
Steps on footprint pattern	Bounces ball under control	Rolls ball to hit object
Catches bounced ball	Hops on one foot four hops	Rides two-wheel bike with training wheels

3-4 yr   4-5 yr   5+6 yr.

Figure 9.3
The Development of Gross Motor Skills in Early Childhood
The skills are listed in the approximate order of difficulty within each age period.

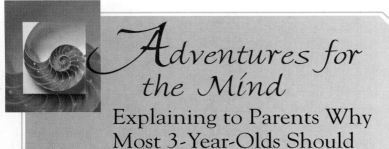

Adventures for the Mind

Explaining to Parents Why Most 3-Year-Olds Should Not Participate in Sports

Assume that you are the director of a preschool program and the parents ask you to develop a program to teach the children how to participate in sports. Think through how you would explain to the parents why most 3-year-olds are not ready for participation in sports programs. Include in your answer information about 3-year-olds' limited motor skills, as well as the importance of learning basic motor skills first.

their recommendations involves developing fundamental movement skills. Careful planning is needed to ensure that a variety of motor activities appropriate to the ages and individual skills of children are provided. Beam walking is one activity that can be used. The variety of balance beam pathways helps meet the individual motor needs of young children. Challenge children to walk the beams in different directions or walk while balancing bean bags on different body parts. Decrease the width of the beams, raise the height, or set up the beams on an incline.

Competent teachers of young children also plan daily fitness activities. Include a daily run or gallop to music on the bike path. Children love to run and get to do so too infrequently in early childhood education centers and at home. Several fast-paced fitness activities can be planned over the school year. Combine fitness with creative movement, music, and children's imaginations. Children enjoy moving like snakes, cats, bears, elephants, dinosaurs, frogs, kangaroos, seals, conductors and trains, police and police cars, pilots and airplanes, washing machines, and teeter-totters. Avoid recordings or activities that "program" children or that include group calisthenics and structured exercise routines that are not appropriate for young children.

The development of young children's gross motor skills also includes perceptual-motor activities. Teachers can ask children to copy their movements, such as putting hands on toes, hands on head, or hands on stomach. These activities help children learn body awareness and visual awareness. As the year progresses, teachers can gradually increase the difficulty of these exercises by touching body parts more difficult to name and locate (such as shoulders and elbows) (Weikart, 1987). Also provide children with many opportunities to move to a steady beat. They can tap and march to the tune of nursery rhymes, chants, songs, and parades, for example. Obstacle courses are enjoyable activities for children and help them understand such directions in space as "over," "under," "around," and "through," as well as help them practice moving through space without touching any of the obstacles.

In sum, designing and implementing a developmentally appropriate movement curriculum takes time and effort. Although time consuming, such a curriculum facilitates the development of children's gross motor skills. To read further about supporting young children's motor development, see Caring for Children.

Fine Motor Skills   At 3 years of age, children are still emerging from the infant ability to place and handle things. Although they have had the ability to pick up the tiniest objects between their thumb and forefinger for some time, they are still somewhat clumsy at it. Three-year-olds can build surprisingly high block towers, each block placed with intense concentration but often not in a completely straight line. When 3-year-olds play with a form board or a simple jigsaw puzzle, they are rather rough in placing the pieces. Even when they recognize the hole a piece fits into, they are not very precise in positioning the piece. They often try to force the piece in the hole or pat it vigorously.

By 4 years of age, children's fine motor coordination has improved substantially and become much more precise. Sometimes 4-year-old children have trouble building high towers with blocks because, in their desire to place each of the blocks perfectly, they may upset those already stacked. By age 5, children's fine motor coordination has improved further. Hand, arm, and body all move together under

Caring for Children
Supporting Young Children's Motor Development

Young children frequently engage in such activities as running, jumping, throwing, and catching. These activities form the basis of advanced, often sports-related skills. For children to progress to effective, coordinated, and controlled motor performance, interaction with and instruction from supportive adults can be beneficial.

How can early childhood educators support young children's motor development? When planning physical instruction for young children, it is important to keep in mind that their attention span is rather short, so instruction should be brief and to the point. Young children need to practice skills in order to learn them, so instruction should be followed with ample time for practice.

Fitness is an important dimension of people's lives, and it is beneficial to develop a positive attitude toward it early (Benelli & Yongue, 1995). Preschoolers need vigorous activities for short periods of time. They can be encouraged to rest or change to a quieter activity as needed. Movement,

even within the classroom, can improve a child's stamina. Such movement activities might be as basic as practicing locomotor skills or as complex as navigating an obstacle course. A number of locomotor skills (such as walking, running, jumping, sliding, skipping, and leaping) can be practiced forward and backward. And it is important to keep practice fun, allowing children to enjoy movement for the sheer pleasure of it.

There can be long-term negative effects for children who fail to develop basic motor skills. These children will not be as able to join in group games or participate in sports during their school years and in adulthood. However, the positive development of motor skills has other benefits besides participation in games and sports. Engaging in motor skills fulfills young children's needs and desires for movement, and exercise builds muscles, strengthens the heart, and enhances aerobic capacity.

better command of the eye. Mere towers no longer interest the 5-year-old, who now wants to build a house or a church, complete with steeple, though adults may still need to be told what each finished project is meant to be. A summary of the development of fine motor skills in early childhood is shown in figure 9.4.

How do developmentalists measure children's motor development? The **Denver Developmental Screening Test** *is a simple, inexpensive, fast method of diagnosing developmental delay in children from birth through 6 years of age. The test is individually administered and includes separate assessments of gross and fine motor skills, as well as language and personal-social ability.* Among the gross motor skills this test measures are the child's ability to sit, walk, long jump, pedal a tricycle, throw a ball overhand, catch a bounced ball, hop on one foot, and balance on one foot. Fine motor skills measured by the test include the child's ability to stack cubes, reach for objects, and draw a person (Frankenburg & others, 1992).

Denver Developmental Screening Test
A test used to diagnose developmental delay in children from birth to 6 years of age; includes separate assessments of gross and fine motor skills, language, and personal-social ability.

Young Children's Artistic Drawings

The development of fine motor skills in the preschool years allows children to become budding artists. There are dramatic changes in how children depict what they see. Art provides unique insights into children's perceptual worlds—what they are attending to, how space and distance are viewed, how they experience patterns and forms. Rhoda Kellogg is a creative teacher of preschool children who has observed and guided young children's artistic efforts for many decades. She has assembled an impressive array of tens of thousands of drawings produced by more than 2,000 preschool children. Adults who are unfamiliar with young children's art

"You moved."

Drawing by Lorenz; © 1987 The New Yorker Magazine, Inc.

placement stage
Kellogg's terms for 2- to 3-year-olds' drawings that are drawn in placement patterns.

shape stage
Kellogg's terms for 3-year-olds' drawings consisting of diagrams in different shapes.

design stage
Kellogg's terms for 3- to 4-year-olds' drawings that mix two basic shapes into more complex designs.

pictorial stage
Kellogg's terms for 4- to 5-year-olds' drawings depicting objects that adults can recognize.

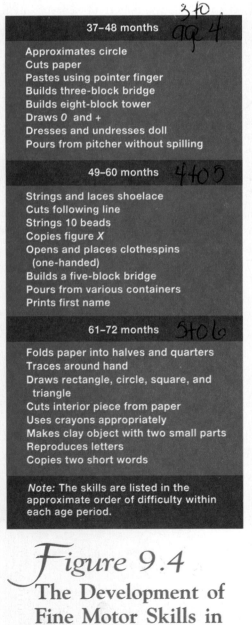

Figure 9.4
The Development of Fine Motor Skills in Early Childhood

often view the productions of this age group as meaningless scribbles. However, Kellogg (1970) documented that young children's artistic productions are orderly, meaningful, and structured.

By their second birthday, children can scribble. Scribbles represent the earliest form of drawing. Every form of graphic art, no matter how complex, contains the lines found in children's artwork, which Kellogg calls the 20 basic scribbles. These include vertical, horizontal, diagonal, circular, curving, waving or zigzag lines and dots. As young children progress from scribbling to picture making, they go through four distinguishable stages: placement, shape, design, and pictorial (see figure 9.5).

The **placement stage** *is Kellogg's term for 2- to 3-year-olds' drawings, drawn on a page in placement patterns.* One example of these patterns is the spaced border pattern shown in figure 9.5b. The **shape stage** *is Kellogg's term for 3-year-olds' drawings consisting of diagrams in different shapes* (figure 9.5c). Young children draw six basic shapes: circles, squares or rectangles, triangles, crosses, Xs, and forms. The **design stage** *is Kellogg's term for 3- to 4-year-olds' drawings in which young children mix two basic shapes into a more complex design* (figure 9.5d). This stage occurs rather quickly after the shape stage. The **pictorial stage** *is Kellogg's term for 4- to 5-year-olds' drawings that consist of objects that adults can recognize* (figure 9.5e). In the next chapter, we will look further at young children's art, paying special attention to the role of cognitive development in their art.

Young children often use the same formula for drawing different things. Though modified in small ways, one basic form can cover a range of objects. When children begin to draw animals, they portray them in the same way they portray humans: standing upright with a smiling face, legs, and arms (see figure 9.6). Pointed ears may be the only clue adults have as to the nature of the particular beast. As children become more aware of the nature of a cat, their drawings acquire more catlike features, and they show the cat on all four paws, tail in the air.

Not all children embrace art with equal enthusiasm, and the same child may want to draw one day but have no interest in it the next day. For most children, however, art is an important vehicle for conveying feelings and ideas that are not easily expressed in words (Schiller, 1995; Seefeldt, 1995). Drawing and constructing also provide children with a hands-on opportunity to use their problem-solving skills to develop creative ways to represent scale, space, and motion. Parents can provide a context for artistic exploration in their children by giving them a work space where they are not overly concerned about messiness or damage. They can make supplies available, have a bulletin board display space for the child's art, and support and encourage the child's art activity.

Handedness

For centuries, left-handers have suffered unfair discrimination in a world designed for right-handers. Even the devil himself has been portrayed as a left-hander. For many years, teachers forced all children to write with their right hand, even if they had a left-hand tendency. Fortunately, today most teachers let children write with the hand they favor.

Some children are still discouraged from using their left hand, even though many left-handed individuals have become very successful. Their ranks include Leonardo da Vinci, Benjamin Franklin, and Pablo Picasso. Each of these famous men was known for his imagination of spatial layouts, which may be stronger in left-handed individuals. Left-handed athletes also are often successful. Since there are fewer left-handed athletes, the opposition is not as accustomed to the style and approach of "lefties." Their tennis serve spins in the opposite direction, their curve ball in baseball swerves the opposite way, and their left foot in soccer is not the one children are used to defending against. Left-handed individuals also do well intellectually. In an analysis of the Scholastic Aptitude Test (SAT) scores of more than 100,000 students, 20 percent of the top-scoring group was left-handed, which is twice the rate of left-handedness found in the general population (Bower, 1985). Clearly, many left-handed people are competent in a wide variety of human activities, ranging from athletic skills to intellectual accomplishments.

When does hand preference develop? Adults usually notice a child's hand preference during early childhood, but researchers have found handedness tendencies in the infant years. Even newborns have some preference for one side of their body over the other. In one study, 65 percent of the infants turned their head to the right when they were lying on their stomach in the crib (Michel, 1981). Fifteen percent preferred to face toward the left. These preferences for the right or left were related to later handedness. At about 7 months of age, infants prefer grabbing with one hand or the other, and this is also related to later handedness (Ramsay, 1980). By 2 years of age, about 10 percent of children favor their left hand. Many preschool children, though, use both hands, with a clear hand preference not completely distinguished until later in development. Some children use one hand for writing and drawing, and the other hand for throwing a ball. My oldest daughter, Tracy, confuses the issue even further. She writes left-handed and plays tennis left-handed, but she plays golf right-handed. During early childhood, her handedness was still somewhat in doubt. My youngest daughter, Jennifer, was left-handed from early in infancy.

What is the origin of hand preference? Genetic inheritance and environmental experiences have been proposed as causes. In one study, a genetic interpretation was favored. The handedness of adopted children was not related to the handedness of their adoptive parents but was related to the handedness of their biological parents (Carter-Saltzman, 1980).

SLEEP AND SLEEP PROBLEMS

Most young children sleep through the night and have one daytime nap. Sometimes, though, it is difficult to get young children to go to sleep as they drag out their bedtime routine. Helping the child slow down before bedtime often contributes to less resistance in going to bed. Reading the child a story, playing quietly with the child in the bath, or letting the child sit on the caregiver's lap while listening to music are quieting activities.

Many young children want to take a soft, cuddly object, such as a favorite blanket, teddy bear, or other stuffed animal, to bed with them. **Transitional objects** *are those that children repeatedly use as bedtime companions. They usually are soft and cuddly, and most developmentalists view them as representing a transition from being a dependent person to being a more independent one.* Therefore, using transitional objects at bedtime is normal behavior for young children. In one study, children who relied on transitional objects at age 4 showed the same level of emotional adjustment at ages 11 and 16 as children who had not relied on transitional objects (Newson, Newson, & Mahalski, 1982).

Among the sleep problems that children may develop are nightmares, night terrors, sleepwalking, and sleeptalking (Gaylor, Anders, & Goodlin-Jones, 1999). **Nightmares** *are frightening dreams that awaken the sleeper, more often toward the morning than just after the child has gone to bed at night.* Caregivers should not

Figure 9.5
The Stages of Young Children's Artistic Drawings

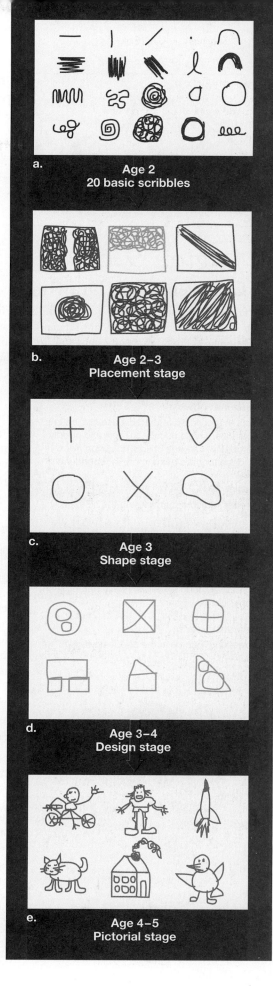

a. **Age 2**
20 basic scribbles

b. **Age 2–3**
Placement stage

c. **Age 3**
Shape stage

d. **Age 3–4**
Design stage

e. **Age 4–5**
Pictorial stage

Figure 9.6
Children's Cat Drawings

The first two cats are typical of a young child's early efforts at drawing animals. They are humanlike, standing upright. As children become more aware of the nature of cats, they draw them more catlike, standing on all four paws, as shown in the cat on the right.

transitional objects
Objects that children repeatedly use as bedtime companions. These usually are soft and cuddly and probably mark the child's transition from being dependent to being more independent.

nightmares
Frightening dreams that awaken the sleeper.

night terrors
Sudden arousal from sleep, characterized by intense fear and usually accompanied by physiological reactions, such as rapid heart rate and breathing, loud screams, heavy perspiration, and physical movement.

somnambulism
Sleepwalking; occurs in the deepest stage of sleep.

Handedness

Children and Sleep Disorders

worry about young children having occasional nightmares because almost every child has them. If children have nightmares persistently, it many indicate that they are feeling too much stress during their waking hours.

Night terrors *are characterized by a sudden arousal from sleep and an intense fear, usually accompanied by a number of physiological reactions, such as rapid heart rate and breathing, loud screams, heavy perspiration, and physical movement.* In most instances, the child has little or no memory of what happened during the night terror. Night terrors are less common than nightmares and occur more often in deep sleep than do nightmares. Many children who experience night terrors return to sleep rather quickly after the night terror. Caregivers tend to be especially worried when children have night terrors, although they are usually not a serious problem and are not believed to reflect any emotional problems in children.

Somnambulism *(sleepwalking) occurs during the deepest stage of sleep.* Approximately 15 percent of children sleepwalk at least once, and from 1 to 5 percent do it regularly. Most children outgrow the problem without professional intervention. Except for the danger of accidents while walking around asleep in the dark, there is nothing abnormal about sleepwalking. It is safe to awaken sleepwalking children, and it is a good idea to do so because they might harm themselves.

If children sleepwalk regularly, parents need to make the bedroom and house as safe from harm as possible. Sleeptalkers are soundly asleep as they speak, although occasionally they make fairly coherent statements for a brief period of time. Most of the time, though, you can't understand what children are saying during sleeptalking. There is nothing abnormal about sleeptalking, and there is no reason to try to stop it from occurring.

At this point, we have discussed a number of ideas about young children's body growth and change, motor development, and sleep. An overview of these ideas is presented in summary table 9.1.

NUTRITION

Four-year-old Bobby is on a steady diet of double cheeseburgers, french fries, and chocolate milkshakes. Between meals, he gobbles up candy bars and marshmallows. He hates green vegetables. Only a preschooler, Bobby already has developed poor nutritional habits. What are a preschool child's energy needs? What is a preschooler's eating behavior like?

Today, most teachers let children write with the hand they favor.

Summary Table 9.1
Body Growth and Change, Motor Development, and Sleep

Concept	Processes/ Related Ideas	Characteristics/Description
Body growth and change	Height and weight	The average child grows 2½ inches in height and gains between 5 and 7 pounds a year during early childhood. Growth patterns vary individually, though. Some children are unusually short because of congenital problems, a physical problem that develops in childhood, or emotional problems.
	The brain	The brain is a key aspect of growth. By age 5, the brain has reached nine-tenths of its adult size. Some of its increase in size is due to increases in the number and size of nerve endings, some to myelination. Increasing brain maturation contributes to improved cognitive abilities.
	Visual perception	Visual maturity increases in early childhood. Some children develop functional amblyopia, or "lazy eye."
Motor development	Gross motor skills	They increase dramatically during early childhood. Children become increasingly adventuresome as their gross motor skills improve. Young children's lives are extremely active, more active than at any other point in the life span. Rough-and-tumble play often occurs, especially in boys, and it can serve positive educational and developmental functions. It is important for preschool and kindergarten teachers to design and implement developmentally appropriate activities for young children's gross motor skills. Such activities include fundamental movement, daily fitness, and perceptual-motor opportunities.
	Fine motor skills	They also improve substantially during early childhood. The Denver Developmental Screening Test is one widely used measure of gross and fine motor skills.
	Young children's artistic drawings	The development of fine motor skills in the preschool years allows young children to become budding artists. Scribbling begins at 2 years of age and is followed by four stages of drawing, culminating in the pictorial stage at 4 to 5 years of age.
	Handedness	At one point, all children were taught to be right-handed. In today's world, the strategy is to allow children to use the hand they favor. Left-handed children are as competent in motor skills and intellect as right-handed children. Both genetic and environmental explanations of handedness have been given.
Sleep and sleep problems	Their nature	Most young children sleep through the night and have one daytime nap. Helping the child slow down before bedtime often contributes to less resistance in going to bed. Many young children want to take transitional objects to bed with them; these objects represent a transition from being dependent to being more independent. Among the problems in sleep that may develop are nightmares, night terrors, somnambulism (sleepwalking), and sleeptalking.

Energy Needs

Feeding and eating habits are important aspects of development during early childhood. What children eat affects their skeletal growth, body shape, and susceptibility to disease. Recognizing that nutrition is important for the child's growth and development, the federal government provides money for school lunch programs. An average preschool child requires 1,700 calories per day. Figure 9.7 shows the increasing energy needs of children as they move from infancy through the childhood years. Energy requirements for individual children are determined by the **basal metabolism rate (BMR),** *which is the minimum amount of energy a person uses in a resting state.* Energy needs of individual children of the same age, sex, and size vary. Reasons for these differences remain unexplained. Differences in physical activity,

Child Health Guide

basal metabolism rate (BMR)
The minimum amount of energy a person uses in a resting state.

Age	Weight (kg)	Height (cm)	Energy needs (calories)	Calorie ranges
1–3	13	90	1,300	900–1,800
4–6	20	112	1,700	1,300–2,300
7–10	28	132	2,400	1,650–3,300

Figure 9.7
Recommended Energy Intakes for Children Ages 1 Through 10

basal metabolism, and the efficiency with which children use energy are among the candidates for explanation.

Eating Behavior

Among the most important considerations for improving young children's eating behavior are knowing about basic daily routines, understanding the implications of fat and sugar intake, and recognizing a number of problems in eating behavior that may appear through the course of development.

Daily Eating Routines   What are the daily routines of eating for most 3-year-olds, 4-year-olds, and 5-year-olds (Allen & Marotz, 1989)?

3-year-olds

- Their appetite is fairly good, and they prefer small servings.
- They usually like only a few cooked vegetables but often eat about everything else.
- They feed themselves independently if they are hungry, using a spoon in a semiadult fashion; they may even spear with a fork.
- They dawdle over their food when they are not hungry.
- They can pour milk and juice and serve individual portions from a serving dish with prompts such as "fill it up to the line."
- They often begin to drink a lot of milk, so it is important to ensure that the 3-year-old does not fill up on milk to the exclusion of other needed foods.

4-year-olds

- Their appetite fluctuates from very good to fair.
- They may develop dislikes of certain foods and refuse to eat them to the point of tears if pushed.
- They use all eating utensils and become skilled at spreading jelly or peanut butter or at cutting soft foods, such as bread.
- Their eating and talking get in the way of each other; talking usually dominates eating.
- They like to help in the preparation of a meal, engaging in such activities as dumping premeasured ingredients, washing vegetables, and setting the table.

5-year-olds

- They usually eat well, but not at every meal.
- They like familiar foods.
- They become aware of other family members' food dislikes and declare that they, too, dislike these foods.
- They like to make their breakfast (pouring cereal, getting out milk and juice) and lunch (spreading peanut butter and jam on bread).

Spinach: Divide into little piles. Rearrange again into new piles. After five or six maneuvers, sit back and say you are full.

Delia Ephron
American Writer and Humorist, 20th Century

This would be a better world for children if parents had to eat the spinach.

Groucho Marx
American Comedian, 20th Century

Food	Calories	% of calories from fat
Burger King Whopper, fries, vanilla shake	1,250	43
Big Mac, fries, chocolate shake	1,100	41
McDonald's Quarter-Pounder with Cheese	418	52
Pizza Hut 10-inch pizza with sausage, mushrooms, pepperoni, and green pepper	1,035	35
Arby's roast beef sandwich, two potato patties, coleslaw, chocolate shake	1,200	30
Kentucky Fried Chicken dinner (three pieces chicken, mashed potatoes and gravy, coleslaw, roll)	830	50
Arthur Treacher's fish and chips (two pieces breaded and fried fish, french fries, cola drink)	900	43
Typical restaurant "diet plate" (hamburger patty, cottage cheese, etc.)	638	63

Figure 9.8
The Fat and Calorie Content of Selected Fast Foods

Source: From Virginia DeMoss, "Good, the Bad, and the Edible" in *Runner's World,* June 1980. © Virginia DeMoss. Reprinted by permission.

Fat and Sugar Consumption Caregivers' special concerns involve the appropriate amount of fat and sugar in young children's diets (Troiano & Flegal, 1998). While some health-conscious parents may be providing too little fat in their infants' and children's diets, other parents are raising their children on diets in which the percentage of fat is far too high. Our changing lifestyles, in which we often eat on the run and pick up fast-food meals, contribute to the increased fat levels in children's diets. Most fast-food meals are high in protein, especially meat and dairy products. But the average American child does not need to be concerned about getting enough protein. What must be of concern is the vast number of young children who are being weaned on fast foods that are not only high in protein but also high in fat. Eating habits become ingrained very early in life; unfortunately, it is during the preschool years that many people get their first taste of fast food (Poulton & Sexton, 1996). The American Heart Association recommends that the daily limit for calories from fat should be approximately 35 percent. Compare this percentage with the numbers in figure 9.8. Clearly, many fast-food meals contribute to excess fat intake by children.

Being overweight can be a serious problem in early childhood (Mei & others, 1998; Strauss & Knight, in press). Consider Ramón, a kindergartner who always begs to stay inside to help during recess. His teachers noticed that Ramón never joins the running games the small superheroes play as they propel themselves around the playground. Ramón is an overweight 4-year-old boy. Except for extreme cases of obesity, overweight preschool children are usually not encouraged to lose a great deal of weight but to slow their rate of weight gain so that they will grow into a more normal weight for their height by thinning out as they grow taller. Prevention of obesity in children includes helping children and parents see food as a way to satisfy hunger and nutritional needs, not as proof of love or as a reward for good behavior (Hill & Trowbridge, 1998). Snack foods should be low in fat, simple sugars, and salt, as well as high in fiber. Routine physical activity should be a daily occurrence. The child's life should be centered around activities, not meals (Kohl & Hobbs, 1998).

The concern is not only about excessive fat in children's diets but also about excessive sugar. Consider Robert, age 3, who loves chocolate. His mother lets him have three chocolate candy bars a day. He also drinks an average of four cans of caffeinated cola a day, and he eats sugar-coated cereal each morning at breakfast. The average American child consumes almost 2 pounds of sugar per week (Riddle

Exploring Childhood Obesity

Helping An Overweight Child

Eating Problems

**Harvard Center
for Children's Health**

& Prinz, 1984). How does sugar consumption influence the health and behavior of young children?

The association of sugar consumption with children's health problems—dental cavities and obesity, for example—has been widely documented (Rogers & Morris, 1986).

In sum, although there is individual variation in appropriate nutrition for children, their diets should be well-balanced and should include fats, carbohydrates, protein, vitamins, and minerals. An occasional candy bar does not hurt and can even benefit a growing body, but a steady diet of hamburgers, french fries, milkshakes, and candy bars should be avoided.

Sweets, Snacks, and "Fussy Eaters"   As we have seen, eating too many sweets contributes to eating problems during early childhood. When young children eat too many sweets—candy bars, cola, and sweetened cereals, for example—they can spoil their appetite and then not want to eat more nutritious foods when they are served at mealtime. Thus, caregivers need to be firm in limiting the amount of sweets young children eat.

Most preschool children need to eat more often than the adults in the family because preschool children use up so much energy. It is a long time from breakfast to lunch and from lunch to dinner for the active young child. Thus, a midmorning and midafternoon snack are recommended. A good strategy is to avoid giving sweets to young children during these snacktimes.

Many eating problems are carryovers from the toddler years. To avoid eating problems and "fussy eaters" in the preschool years, the following caregiver practices are recommended in the toddler and preschool years (Leach, 1991):

- Encourage the child's independence in eating.
- Let the child eat in any order or combination.
- Let the meal end when the child has had enough.
- Try to keep mealtimes enjoyable.
- Don't use food as a reward, punishment, bribe, or threat (that is, try to keep the child's eating completely separate from discipline).

Many young children get labeled as "fussy" or "difficult eaters" when they are only trying to exercise the same rights to personal taste and appetite adults take for granted. Allow for the child's developing tastes in food.

Malnutrition in Young Children from Low-Income Families   One of the most common nutritional problems in early childhood is iron deficiency anemia, which results in chronic fatigue. This is a problem that results from the failure to eat adequate amounts of quality meats and dark green vegetables. Young children from low-income families are most likely to develop iron deficiency anemia.

Poor nutrition is a special concern in the lives of young children from low-income families (Kleinman & others, 1998). In a review of hunger in the United States, it was estimated that 11 million preschool children are malnourished (Brown & Allen, 1988). Many of these children do not get essential amounts of iron, vitamins, or protein. Despite the proven effectiveness of the Special Supplemental Food Program for Women, Infants, and Children (WIC) in improving maternal and child health and in spite of the dramatic cost-effectiveness, only nine states and the District of Columbia supplement their federal WIC allotment to provide food and nutritional services to additional women, infants, and children (Children's Defense Fund, 1990). Only slightly more than half of all eligible women and children receive federal WIC funds.

ILLNESS AND HEALTH

Let's explore the nature of children's illness and health in the United States and around the world.

Young Children's Illness and Health in the United States

If a pediatrician stopped practicing 50 years ago and observed the illness and health of young children today, the sight might seem to be more science fiction than medical fact (Elias, 1998). The story of children's health in the past 50 years is a shift toward prevention and outpatient care.

In recent decades, vaccines have nearly eradicated disabling bacterial meningitis and have become available to prevent measles, rubella, mumps, and chicken pox. Figure 9.9 reveals the dramatic decline in deaths of children under the age of 5 that occurred from 1949 to 1996 for birth immaturity, birth defects, accidents, cancer, homicide, and heart disease. The disorders still most likely to be fatal during early childhood today are birth defects, cancer, and heart disease. Although the dangers of many diseases for children have been greatly diminished, it still is important for parents to keep young children on an immunization schedule.

A special concern about children's illness and health is exposure to parental smoking. Exposure to tobacco smoke increases children's risk for developing a number of medical problems, including pneumonia, bronchitis, middle ear infections, burns, and asthma. It also may lead to cancer in adulthood (AAP Committee on Environmental Health, 1997). As indicated in figure 9.10, more children under 5 years of age in the United States die from exposure to tobacco smoke (called passive smoking) than from car crashes and other injuries (Aligne & Stoddard, 1997). Because of such findings, most experts on children's health recommend that children be raised in a smoke-free environment.

Of special concern in the United States is the poor health status of many young children from low-income families. As we saw earlier in our discussion of nutrition and eating behavior, about 11 million preschool children in the United States are malnourished. Their malnutrition places their health at risk. Many have less

Cause	1949	1996
Birth immaturity/respiratory distress	1018.8	26.3
Birth defects (spina bifida, etc.)	443.9	36.8
Accidents	234.7	15.2
Cancer	45.7	2.7
Homicide	5.7	3.6
Heart disease	8.0	4.3

Figure 9.9
Deaths per 100,000 Children Under 5 Years of Age from 1949 to 1996

Preschoolers' Health

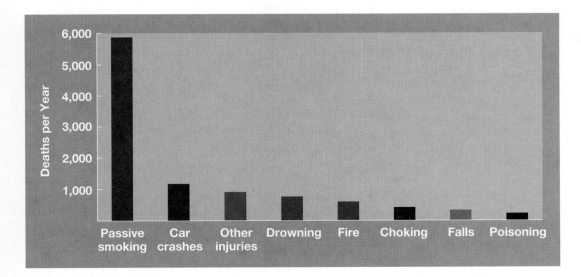

Figure 9.10
Number of Deaths per Year in Children Under the Age of 5 Due to Passive Smoking and Accidents

Ten percent of all children born in Bangladesh die before reaching the age of 5 from dehydration and malnutrition brought about by diarrhea.

resistance to diseases, including minor ones, such as colds, and major ones, such as influenza.

The State of Illness and Health in the World's Children

Of every three deaths in the world, one is a child under the age of 5. Every week, more than a quarter of a million young children die in developing countries in a quiet carnage of infection and undernutrition (Grant, 1996).

What are the main causes of death and child malnutrition in the world?

- *Diarrhea* is the leading cause of childhood death. However, approximately 70 percent of the more than 4 million children killed by diarrhea in 1990 could have been saved if all parents had available a low-cost breakthrough known as **oral rehydration therapy (ORT).** *This treatment encompasses a range of techniques designed to prevent dehydration during episodes of diarrhea by giving the child fluids by mouth.* When a child has diarrhea, dehydration can often be prevented by giving the child a large volume of water and other liquids.
- More than 3 million children were killed in 1990 by *measles, tetanus,* and *whooping cough.* Another 200,000 have been permanently disabled by polio. The efforts in the 1980s made immunization widely available, and the lives of many children have been saved by vaccination costing only about $5 a child. What is needed is improved communication to inform parents in developing countries and around the world of the importance of a course of vaccinations for their children.
- *Acute respiratory infections,* mainly *pneumonias,* killed 2 to 3 million children under the age of 5 in 1990. Most of these children could have been saved by 50 cents worth of antibiotics administered by a community health worker with a few months of training. Most of the children's parents could have sought out the low-cost help if they had known how to distinguish between a bad cough and a life-threatening lung infection.
- *Undernutrition* was a contributing cause in about one-third of the 14 million child deaths in the world in 1990. While not having enough to eat is still a fundamental problem in some of the world's poorest countries, the major cause of undernutrition in the world is not a shortage of food in the home. Rather, it is a lack of basic services and a shortage of information about preventing

Exploring the Health of the World's Children

oral rehydration therapy (ORT)
Treatment to prevent dehydration during episodes of diarrhea by giving fluids by mouth.

A simple child
That lightly draws its breath,
What should it know of death?

William Wordsworth
English Poet, 19th Century

infection and using food to promote growth. Making sure that parents know that they can protect their children's nutritional health by such means as birth spacing, care during pregnancy, breast-feeding, immunization, illness prevention, special feeding before and after illness, and regular checks of the child's weight gain can overcome many cases of malnutrition and poor growth in today's world.

- A contributing factor in at least one-fourth of today's child deaths is the *timing of births*. Births that are too numerous or too close, or mothers who are too young or too old, carry a much higher risk for both the mother and the child. Using this knowledge and today's low-cost ways of timing births is one of the most powerful and least expensive means of raising the child survival rate and improving children's health around the world.

- Also, more than half of all illnesses and deaths among children are associated with inadequate *hygiene*. In communities without a safe water supply and sanitation, it is very difficult to prevent the contamination of food and water. Some low-cost methods can prevent the spread of germs, and all families should be informed of these sanitation measures.

In summary, most child malnutrition, as well as most child deaths, can be prevented by parental actions that are almost universally affordable and are based on knowledge that is already available.

Nations with the highest mortality rate for children under age 5 include African nations, such as Angola, and Asian nations, such as Afghanistan. In Angola in 1991, for every 1,000 children born alive, 292 died before the age of 5; in Afghanistan, the figure was 257 per 1,000.

The countries with the lowest mortality rates for children under age 5 include Scandinavian countries, such as Sweden, where in 1991 only 5 of every 1,000 children under the age of 5 died. The U.S. mortality rate for children under the age of 5 is better than that of most countries, but, of the 129 countries for which figures were available in 1991, 22 countries had better rates than the United States. In 1991, the U.S. mortality rate for children under the age of 5 was 11 per 1,000.

Children's Health Around the World

Health, Illness, and Development

Although there has been great national interest in the psychological aspects of adult health, only recently has a developmental perspective on psychological aspects of children's health been proposed (Raman, 1999). The uniqueness of young children's health care needs is evident when we consider their motor, cognitive, and social development (Bolen, Bland, & Sacks, 1999; Maddux & others, 1986). For example, think about the infant's and preschool child's motor development—inadequate to ensure personal safety while riding in an automobile. Adults must take preventive measures to restrain infants and young children in car seats. Young children may lack the intellectual skills—including reading ability—to discriminate between safe and unsafe household substances. And they may lack the impulse control to keep from running out into a busy street while chasing after a ball or toy.

Children's Health Resources

Playgrounds for young children need to be designed with the child's safety in mind (Waltzman & others, in press). The initial steps in ensuring children's safety are to walk with children through the existing playground or the site where the playground is to be developed, talk with them about possible safety hazards, let them assist in identifying hazards, and indicate how they can use the playground safely. The outdoor play environment should enhance the child's motor, cognitive, and social development. The inadequate attention to the safety of children on playgrounds is evident in the following statistic: more than 305,000 preschool children were treated in emergency rooms with playground-related injuries from 1983 through 1987. One of the major problems is that playground

Child Safety Guide

Improving Developmental Skills
Supporting Young Children's Physical Development

What are some good strategies for supporting young children's physical development?

- *Give young children plenty of opportunities to be active and explore their world.* Young children are extremely active and should not be constrained for long periods of time. Competent teachers plan daily fitness activities for young children. Preschool-aged children are too young for organized sports.
- *Make sure that young children's motor activities are fun and appropriate for their age.* Young children should enjoy the motor activities they participate in. Also, don't try to push young children into activities that are more appropriate for older children. For example, don't try to train a 4-year-old to ride a bicycle or have a 5-year-old take tennis lessons.
- *Give young children ample opportunities to engage in art.* Don't constrain young children's drawing. Let them freely create their drawings.
- *Provide young children with good nutrition.* Know how many calories preschool children need to meet their energy needs, which are greater than in infancy. Too many young children are raised on fast foods. Monitor the amount of fat and sugar in young children's diet. Nutritious midmorning and midafternoon snacks are recommended in addition to breakfast, lunch, and dinner. Make sure that young children get adequate iron, vitamins, and protein.
- *Make sure that young children have regular medical checkups that include vision testing, immunizations, and dental care.* This is especially important for children living in impoverished conditions, who are less likely to get such checkups.
- *Be a positive health role model for young children.* When you have young children with you, control the speed of the vehicle you are driving. Don't smoke in their presence. Eat healthy foods. Just by being in your presence, young children will imitate many of your behaviors.
- *Make sure that where children play is safe.* Walk through the areas where children play and check for any potential hazards.

A Healthy Start

equipment—superstructures incorporating climbers, swings, slides, clatter bridges, and sliding poles—is not constructed over impact-absorbing surfaces, such as wood chips and sand. A 1-foot fall, headfirst into concrete or a 4-foot fall headfirst onto packed earth can be fatal. The wood chips and sand under equipment should be kept at a minimum of 8 inches deep.

Health-education programs for preschool children need to be cognitively simple. There are three simple but important goals for health-education programs for preschool children (Parcel & others, 1987): (1) be able to identify feelings of wellness and illness and be able to express them to adults; (2) be able to identify appropriate sources of assistance for health-related problems; and (3) be able to independently initiate the use of sources of assistance for health problems.

Caregivers play an important role in the health of young children (Gomel, Hanson, & Tinsley, 1999; Tinsley, Finley, & Ortiz, 1999). For example, by controlling the speed of the vehicles they drive, by decreasing or eliminating their drinking—especially before driving—and by not smoking around children, caregivers enhance children's health (Gergen & others, 1998). In one study, if the mother smoked, her children were twice as likely to have respiratory ailments (Etzel, 1988). The young children of single, unemployed, smoking mothers are also three times more likely to be injured. Smoking may serve as a marker to identify mothers less able to supervise young children. In sum, caregivers can actively affect young children's health and safety by training and monitoring children on recreational safety, self-protection skills, proper nutrition, and hygiene (Hoot & Robertson, 1994).

Illnesses, especially those that are not life threatening, provide an excellent opportunity for young children to expand their development (Deluca, 1999). The preschool period is a peak time for illnesses, such as respiratory infections (colds, flu) and gastrointestinal upsets (nausea, diarrhea). The illnesses usually are of short duration and are often handled outside the medical community through the family, day care, or school. Such minor illnesses can increase the young child's knowledge of health and illness and sense of empathy.

Young children may confuse terms such as *feel bad* with bad behavior and *feel good* with good behavior. Examples include the following:

- "I feel bad. I want aspirin."
- "I feel bad. My tummy hurts."
- "Bobby hurt me."
- "I bad girl. I wet my pants."
- "Me can do it. Me good girl."
- "I'm hurting your feeling, 'cause I was mean to you."
- "Stop, it doesn't feel good."

Summary Table 9.2
Nutrition, Illness, and Health

Concept	Processes/ Related Ideas	Characteristics/Description
Nutrition	Energy needs	They increase as children go through the childhood years. Energy requirements vary according to basal metabolism, rate of growth, and level of activity.
	Eating behavior	There are a number of daily routines in eating behaviors that 3-, 4-, and 5-year-old children follow. Many parents are raising children on diets that are too high in fat and sugar. Children's diets should include well-balanced proportions of fats, carbohydrates, protein, vitamins, and minerals. Eating too many sweets often contributes to eating problems in early childhood. Midmorning and midafternoon snacks are recommended for young children because children have high energy expenditures. Many eating problems are carryovers from the toddler years. Parents should try to keep the child's eating completely separate from discipline. A special concern is the poor nutrition of young children from low-income families. One problem these children may develop is iron deficiency anemia. Approximately 11 million preschool children are malnourished in the United States.
Illness and health	Young children's illness and health in the United States	In recent decades, vaccines have virtually eradicated many diseases that once were responsible for the deaths of many young children. The disorders still most likely to be fatal for young children are birth defects, cancer, and heart disease. A special concern about children's health and illness is exposure to parental smoking. Another special concern is the poor health status of many young children in low-income families. They often have less resistance to disease, including colds and influenza, than do their higher-socioeconomic status counterparts.
	The state of illness and health in the world's children	One death of every three in the world is the death of a child under age 5. Every week, more than a quarter of a millon children die in developing countries. The main causes of death and child malnutrition in the world are diarrhea, measles, tetanus, whooping cough, acute respiratory infections (mainly pneumonias), and undernutrition. Contributing factors include the timing of births and hygiene. Most child malnutrition and child deaths could be prevented by parental actions that are affordable and based on knowledge that is available today. The United States has a relatively low rate of child deaths, compared with that of other countries, although the Scandinavian countries have the best rates.
	Health, illness, and development	Children's health care needs are related to their motor, cognitive, and social development.

Young children often attribute their illness to what they view as a transgression, such as having eaten the wrong food or playing outdoors in the cold when told not to. In illness and wellness situations, adults can help children sort out distressed feelings resulting from emotional upsets from those resulting from physical illness. For example, a mother might say to her young daughter, "I know you feel bad because you are sick like your sister was last week, but you will be well soon, just as she is now." Or a mother might comment, "I know you feel bad because I'm going on a trip and I can't take you with me, but I'll be back in a few days" (Parmalee, 1986).

At various points in this chapter, we have described strategies that support young children's physical development. The insert, Improving Developmental Skills, provides a checklist for such strategies. Also, an overview of the ideas we have discussed about nutrition, health, and illness in early childhood is presented in summary table 9.2.

Children's Medical Library

Chapter Review

Although young children's physical growth and development are slower than in infancy, their lives are very active—the most active of any period in the human life span.

We began this chapter by evaluating young children's body growth and change, including height and weight, the brain, and visual perception. Then we studied motor development, focusing on gross motor skills, fine motor skills, young children's artistic drawings, and handedness. We also examined sleep and sleep problems. Our coverage of young children's nutrition involved energy needs and eating behavior, and our discussion of illness and health explored these topics in the United States and around the world, as well as health, illness, and development.

Don't forget that you can obtain an overall summary of the chapter by again reading the two summary tables on pages 241 and 249. In the next chapter, we will turn our attention to the young child's cognitive development.

✔ Children Checklist

Physical Development in Early Childhood

How much have you learned since the beginning of the chapter? Use the following statements to help you review your knowledge and understanding of the chapter material. First, read the statement and mentally or briefly demonstrate on paper that you can discuss the relevant information.

_____ I can describe body growth and change in early childhood, including height and weight, the brain, and visual perception.

_____ I know what changes take place in gross and fine motor skills.

_____ I know about young children's artistic drawings.

_____ I can discuss handedness.

_____ I can describe sleep and sleep problems.

_____ I can discuss the young child's energy needs.

_____ I can describe illness and health in young children in the United States.

_____ I know about illness and health in young children around the world.

_____ I can discuss the nature of health, illness, and development.

For any items that you did not check, go back and locate the relevant material in the chapter. Review the material until you feel you can check off the item. You may want to use this checklist later in preparing for an exam.

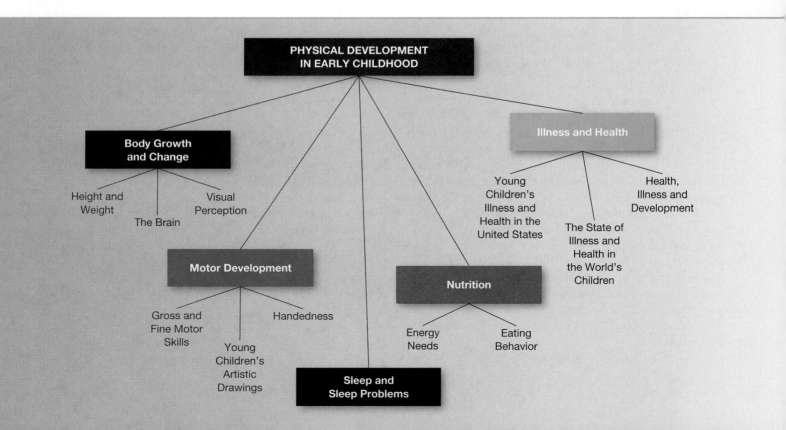

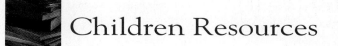

[handwritten: (Affection) Stress + pituitary Gland / Growth Retards from not releasing growth Hormone]

Key Terms

deprivation dwarfism 232

myelination 234

functional amblyopia 234 *[handwritten: Lazy Eye]*

Denver Developmental
   Screening Test 237

placement stage 238

shape stage 238

design stage 238

pictorial stage 238

transitional objects 240

nightmares 240 *[handwritten: } Non REM]*

night terrors 240

somnambulism 240 *[handwritten: Sleepwalk]*

basal metabolism rate (BMR)
   241

oral rehydration therapy
   (ORT) 246

Children Resources

Art for Kids' Sake

Child Welfare League of America
440 First Street NW, Suite 310
Washington, DC 20001

The best-known cartoonists in America have created an original collection of cartoon art to remind people of children's needs. Each cartoon conveys a theme, such as "Try a little tenderness." Cartoonists who volunteered their art include Gary Trudeau, Johnny Hart, Jim Davis, and Bill Keane.

Association for the Care of Children's Health

7910 Woodmont Avenue, Suite 300
Bethesda, MD 20814
301–654–6549

The primary focus of this health care organization is to ensure that all aspects of children's health care are family-centered, psychosocially sound, and developmentally supported.

Children's Aid International

P.O. Box 83220
San Diego, CA 92138
619–694–0095
800–942–2810

This multinational charitable organization provides nutritional, medical, and educational assistance to needy children in Southeast Asia, Africa, Latin America, Eastern Europe, and the United States.

Pediatric Report's Child Health Newsletter

This newsletter for parents, educators, and day-care and health professionals presents practical information needed by anyone who is caring for a child.

Taking It to the Net

http://www.mhhe.com/santrockcd6

1. Your younger brother sleepwalks on a regular basis but your mother tells you it is completely normal. Unfortunately, your brother often wanders into your room late at night, scaring you immensely and necessitating a solution to the problem. How would you find out how common sleepwalking is and what are some treatments, if any, to cure it?

2. Do you have a family member or friend who is left-handed? How do your left-handed friends differ from your right-handed friends? Are your left-handed friends more creative, more intelligent, or more easy-going than your right-handed friends? How might handedness affect thought processes? Can you name 5 famous lefties and the characteristics that may be attributed to their left-handedness?

3. There is a local group that is opposing the idea that elementary schools provide free or discounted breakfasts for qualified students. They see this program as a waste of money. Is there a relationship between nutrition, physical development, and cognitive development? What are your views on the issue of free or discounted breakfasts and how would you respond to an activist that is against free breakfasts?

Chapter 10

Learning is an ornament in prosperity, a refuge in adversity.

Aristotle
Greek Philosopher, 4th Century B.C.

PREVIEW

The cognitive world of the young child is creative, free, and fanciful. In the symbolic world of the young child's art, sometimes cars float on clouds, the sun is green, the sky is yellow, pelicans kiss seals, and people look like tadpoles. Young children's imaginations work overtime, and their mental grasp of the world improves. When you have completed this chapter, you should have a good understanding of

- Piaget's preoperational stage of development, including the symbolic function and intuitive thought substages
- Vygotsky's theory, including the zone of proximal development, language and thought, culture and society, and educational applications of his theory
- Information processing, including attention, memory, and task analysis
- The young child's theory of mind
- Changes in language development, including literacy
- Variations in early childhood education
- Developmentally appropriate and inappropriate practice
- Education for children who are disadvantaged
- The effects of early childhood education
- Whether preschool matters
- School readiness

The Story of Reggio Emilia's Children

The Reggio Emilia approach is an educational program for young children that was developed in the northern Italian city of Reggio Emilia. Children of single parents and children with disabilities have priority in admission; other children are admitted according to a scale of needs. Parents pay on a sliding scale based on income.

The children are encouraged to learn by investigating and exploring topics that interest them. A wide range of stimulating media and materials are available for children to use as they learn—music, movement, drawing, painting, sculpting, collages, puppets and disguises, and photography, for example.

In this program, children often explore topics in a group, which fosters a sense of community, respect for diversity, and a collaborative approach to problem solving. Two co-teachers are present to serve as guides for children. The Reggio Emilia teachers consider a project as an adventure, which can start from an adult's suggestion, from a child's idea, or from an event, such as a snowfall or something else unexpected. Every project is based on what the children say and do. The teachers allow children enough time to think and craft a project.

At the core of the Reggio Emilia approach is the image of children who are competent and have rights, especially the right to outstanding care and education (Bredekamp, 1993). Parent participation is considered essential, and cooperation is a major theme in the schools (Gandini, 1993). Many early childhood education experts believe the Reggio Emilia approach provides a supportive, stimulating context in which children are motivated to explore their world in a competent and confident manner (Firlik, 1996).

COGNITIVE DEVELOPMENTAL CHANGES

How do young children's minds change as they age through early childhood? Piaget had some thoughts about these changes, as did Lev Vygotsky. We will explore Piaget's ideas about the preoperational stage of development, Vygotsky's theory, the information-processing perspective, and the young child's theory of mind.

Piaget's Preoperational Stage of Development

What characterizes preoperational thought? What happens during the substages of symbolic function and intuitive thought?

Remember from chapter 7 that, during Piaget's sensorimotor stage of development, the infant progresses in the ability to organize and coordinate sensations and perceptions with physical movements and actions. What kinds of changes take place in the preoperational stage?

Since this stage of thought is called preoperational, it might seem that not much of importance occurs until full-fledged operational thought appears. Not so. The preoperational stage stretches from approximately 2 to 7 years of age. It is a time when stable concepts are formed, mental reasoning emerges, egocentrism begins strongly and then weakens, and magical beliefs are constructed. Preoperational thought is anything but a convenient waiting period for concrete operational thought. However, the label *preoperational* emphasizes that the child at this stage does not yet think in an operational way. What are operations? **Operations** *are internalized sets of actions that allow the child to do mentally what before she did physically.* Operations are highly organized and conform to certain rules and principles of logic. The operations appear in one form in concrete operational thought and in another form in formal operational thought. Thought in the preoperational stage is flawed and not well organized. Preoperational thought is the beginning of the ability to reconstruct at the level of thought what has been established in behavior. Preoperational thought also involves a transition from primitive to more sophisticated use of symbols. Preoperational thought can be divided into two substages: the symbolic function substage and the intuitive thought substage.

operations

In Piaget's theory, an internalized set of actions that allows a child to do mentally what she formerly did physically.

"*Mrs. Hammond! I'd know you anywhere from little Billy's portrait of you.*"

Drawing by Frascino; © 1988 The New Yorker Magazine, Inc.

Symbolic Function Substage   The **symbolic function substage** *is the first substage of preoperational thought, occurring roughly between the ages of 2 and 4. In this substage, the young child gains the ability to mentally represent an object that is not present.* The ability to engage in such symbolic thought is called symbolic function, and it vastly expands the child's mental world. Young children use scribbled designs to represent people, houses, cars, clouds, and so on. Other examples of symbolism in early childhood are language and the prevalence of pretend play. In sum, the ability to think symbolically and to represent the world mentally predominates in this early substage of preoperational thought. However, although young children make distinct progress during this substage, their thought still has several important limitations, two of which are egocentrism and animism.

Egocentrism *is a salient feature of preoperational thought. It is the inability to distinguish between one's own perspective and someone else's perspective.* The following telephone conversation between 4-year-old Mary, who is at home, and her father, who is at work, typifies Mary's egocentric thought:

Father:	Mary, is Mommy there?
Mary:	(Silently nods)
Father:	Mary, may I speak to Mommy?
Mary:	(Nods again silently)

Mary's response is egocentric in that she fails to consider her father's perspective before replying. A nonegocentric thinker would have responded verbally.

Piaget and Barbel Inhelder (1969) initially studied young children's egocentrism by devising the three mountains task (see figure 10.1). The child walks around the

Through the Eyes of Children
You're a Nice Book

Candy is 3 years old. She has just made up her first formal song. It goes like this:

> Book, book
> Tra la la
> Nice book
> You're a nice book
> Tra la la
> Book, book.

A week ago, she showed her father a picture of a yellow and green field with a long black mass across the top of the page. Before her father could offer an interpretation, Candy started explaining it to him. The yellow and green were a picnic, and the black mass was an umbrella to keep the picnickers from getting wet.

Parties and picnics interest her a lot. They frequently appear in her imaginary play, and her dolls all come to them. Some of the dolls have to be invited by telephone. Candy tells them that her name is Candy Clifford and that she lives on Stark Road at eleven nine two five. Then she describes the long drives by car or bicycle that her dolls must take to come to see her (Peterson, 1974).

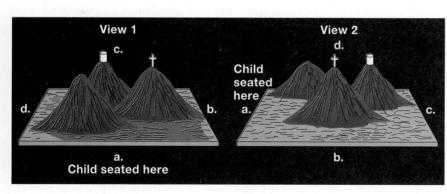

Symbolic Thinking

Figure 10.1
The Three Mountains Task

View 1 shows the child's perspective from where he or she is sitting. View 2 is an example of the photograph the child would be shown, mixed in with others from different perspectives. To correctly identify this view, the child has to take the perspective of a person sitting at spot (*b*). Invariably, a preschool child who thinks in a preoperational way cannot perform this task. When asked what a view of the mountains looks like from position (*b*), the child selects a photograph taken from location (*a*), the child's view at the time.

symbolic function substage
Piaget's first substage of preoperational thought, in which the child gains the ability to mentally represent an object that is not present (between 2 and 4 years of age).

egocentrism
The inability to distinguish between one's own perspective and someone else's (salient feature of the first substage of preoperational thought).

Figure 10.2
The Symbolic Drawings of Young Children

(*a*) A 3½-year-old's symbolic drawing. Halfway into this drawing, the 3½-year-old artist said it was "a pelican kissing a seal." (*b*) This 11-year-old's drawing is neater and more realistic but also less inventive.

animism
The belief that inanimate objects have "lifelike" qualities and are capable of action.

model of the mountains and becomes familiar with what the mountains look like from different perspectives, and they can see that there are different objects on the mountains. The child is then seated on one side of the table on which the mountains are placed. The experimenter moves a doll to different locations around the table, at each location asking the child to select, from a series of photos, the one photo that most accurately reflects the view the doll is seeing. Children in the preoperational stage often pick their view from where they are sitting, rather than the doll's view. Perspective-taking does not develop uniformly in preschool children, who frequently show perspective skills on some tasks but not others.

Animism, *another limitation within preoperational thought, is the belief that inanimate objects have "lifelike" qualities and are capable of action.* A young child might show animism by saying, "That tree pushed the leaf off, and it fell down," or "The sidewalk made me mad; it made me fall down." A young child who uses animism fails to distinguish the appropriate occasions for using human and nonhuman perspectives.

Possibly because young children are not very concerned about reality, their drawings are fanciful and inventive. Suns are blue, skies are yellow, and cars float on clouds in their symbolic, imaginative world. One 3½-year-old looked at a scribble he had just drawn and described it as a pelican kissing a seal (see figure 10.2a). The symbolism is simple but strong, like abstractions found in some modern art. As Picasso commented, "I used to draw like Raphael but it has taken me a lifetime to draw like young children." In the elementary school years, a child's drawings become more realistic, neat, and precise (see figure 10.2b). Suns are yellow, skies are blue, and cars travel on roads (Winner, 1986).

Intuitive Thought Substage   Tommy is 4 years old. Although he is starting to develop his own ideas about the world he lives in, his ideas are still simple, and he is not very good at thinking things out. He has difficulty understanding events he knows are taking place but which he cannot see. His fantasized thoughts bear little resemblance to reality. He cannot yet answer the question "What if . . . ?"

in any reliable way. For example, he has only a vague idea of what would happen if a car were to hit him. He also has difficulty negotiating traffic because he cannot do the mental calculations necessary to estimate whether an approaching car will hit him when he crosses the road.

The **intuitive thought substage** *is the second substage of preoperational thought, occurring between approximately 4 and 7 years of age. In this substage, children begin to use primitive reasoning and want to know the answers to all sorts of questions.* Piaget called this time period *intuitive* because, on the one hand, young children seem so sure about their knowledge and understanding, yet they are so unaware of how they know what they know. That is, they say they know something but know it without the use of rational thinking.

An example of young children's reasoning ability is the difficulty they have putting things into correct categories. Faced with a random collection of objects that can be grouped together on the basis of two or more properties, preoperational children are seldom capable of using these properties consistently to sort the objects into appropriate groupings. Look at the collection of objects in figure 10.3a. You would respond to the direction "Put the things together that you believe belong together" by sorting according to the characteristics of size and array. Your sorting might look something like that shown in figure 10.3b. In the social realm, the 4-year-old girl might be given the task of dividing her peers into groups according to whether they are friends and whether they are boys or girls. She would be unlikely to arrive at the following classification: friendly boys, friendly girls, unfriendly boys, unfriendly girls. Another example of classification shortcomings involves the preoperational child's understanding of religious concepts (Elkind, 1976). When asked "Can you be a Protestant and an American at the same time?" 6- and 7-year-olds usually say no. Nine-year-olds often say yes, understanding that objects can be cross-classified simultaneously.

Many of these examples show a characteristic of preoperational thought called **centration**— *the focusing, or centering, of attention on one characteristic to the exclusion of all others.* Centration

intuitive thought substage
Piaget's second substage of preoperational thought, in which children begin to use primitive reasoning and want to know the answers to all sorts of questions (between 4 and 7 years of age).

centration
The focusing of attention on one characteristic to the exclusion of all others.

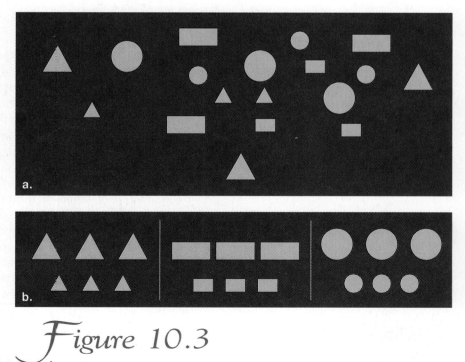

Figure 10.3
Arrays
(*a*) A random array of objects. (*b*) An ordered array of objects.

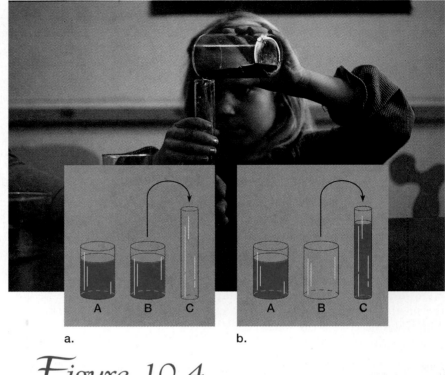

Figure 10.4
Piaget's Conservation Task

The beaker test is a well-known Piagetian test to determine whether a child can think operationally—that is, can mentally reverse actions and show conservation of the substance. *(a)* Two identical beakers are presented to the child. Then, the experimenter pours the liquid from B into C, which is taller and thinner than A or B. *(b)* The child is asked if these beakers (A and C) have the same amount of liquid. The preoperational child says no. When asked to point to the beaker that has more liquid, the preoperational child points to the tall, thin beaker.

conservation

The idea that an amount stays the same regardless of how its container changes.

is most clearly evidenced in young children's lack of **conservation**—*the idea that an amount stays the same regardless of how its container changes.* To adults, it is obvious that a certain amount of liquid stays the same, regardless of a container's shape. But this is not at all obvious to young children. Instead, they are struck by the height of the liquid in the container. In the conservation task—Piaget's most famous test— a child is presented with two identical beakers, each filled to the same level with liquid (see figure 10.4). The child is asked if these beakers have the same amount of liquid, and she usually says yes. Then the liquid from one beaker is poured into a third beaker, which is taller and thinner than the first two. The child is then asked if the amount of liquid in the tall, thin beaker is equal to that which remains in one of the original beakers. Children who are less than 7 or 8 years old usually say no and justify their answers in terms of the differing height or width of the beakers. Older children usually answer yes and justify their answers appropriately ("If you poured the milk back, the amount would still be the same").

In Piaget's theory, failing the conservation of liquid task is a sign that children are at the preoperational stage of cognitive development. Passing this test is a sign that they are at the concrete operational stage. In Piaget's view, the preoperational child fails to show conservation not only of liquid but also of number, matter, length, volume, and area (see figure 10.5).

The child's inability to mentally reverse actions is an important characteristic of preoperational thought. For example, in the conservation of matter shown in figure 10.5, preoperational children say that the longer shape has more clay because they

Type of conservation	Initial presentation	Manipulation	Preoperational child's answer
Number	Two identical rows of objects are shown to the child, who agrees they have the same number.	One row is lengthened and the child is asked whether one row now has more objects.	Yes, the longer row.
Matter	Two identical balls of clay are shown to the child. The child agrees that they are equal.	The experimenter changes the shape of one of the balls and asks the child whether they still contain equal amounts of clay.	No, the longer one has more.
Length	Two sticks are aligned in front of the child. The child agrees that they are the same length.	The experimenter moves one stick to the right, then asks the child if they are equal in length.	No, the one on the top is longer.
Volume	Two balls are placed in two identical glasses, with an equal amount of water. The child sees the balls displace equal amounts of water.	The experimenter changes the shape of one of the balls and asks the child if it still will displace the same amount of water.	No, the longer one on the right displaces more.
Area	Two identical sheets of cardboard have wooden blocks placed on them in identical positions. The child agrees that the same amount of space is left on each piece of cardboard.	The experimenter scatters the blocks on one piece of cardboard and then asks the child if one of the cardboard pieces has more space covered.	Yes, the one on the right has more space covered up.

*F*igure 10.5
Some Dimensions of Conservation: Number, Matter, Length, Volume, and Area

assume that "longer is more." Preoperational children cannot mentally reverse the clay-rolling process to see that the amount of clay is the same in both the shorter ball shape and the longer stick shape.

Some developmentalists do not believe Piaget was entirely correct in his estimate of when children's conservation skills emerge. For example, Rochel Gelman (1969) showed that, when the child's attention to relevant aspects of the conservation task is improved, the child is more likely to conserve. Gelman has also demonstrated

"I still don't have all the answers, but I'm beginning to ask the right questions."

Drawing by Lorenz; © 1989 The New Yorker Magazine, Inc.

that attentional training on one dimension, such as number, improves the preschool child's performance on another dimension, such as mass. Thus, Gelman believes that conservation appears earlier than Piaget thought and that attention is especially important in explaining conservation.

Yet another characteristic of preoperational children is that they ask a barrage of questions. Children's earliest questions appear around the age of 3, and by the age of 5 they have just about exhausted the adults around them with "why" questions. The child's questions yield clues about mental development and reflect intellectual curiosity. These questions signal the emergence of the child's interest in reasoning and figuring out why things are the way they are. Following are some samples of the questions children ask during the questioning period of 4 to 6 years of age (Elkind, 1976):

- "What makes you grow up?"
- "What makes you stop growing?"
- "Why does a lady have to be married to have a baby?"
- "Who was the mother when everybody was a baby?"
- "Why do leaves fall?"
- "Why does the sun shine?"

At this point we have discussed a number of characteristics of preoperational thought. To help you remember these characteristics, turn to figure 10.6.

Earlier, we mentioned that Gelman's research demonstrated that children may fail a Piagetian task because they do not attend to relevant dimensions of the task—length, shape, density, and so on. Gelman and other developmentalists also believe that many of the tasks used to assess cognitive development may not be sensitive to the child's cognitive abilities. Thus, any apparent limitations on cognitive development may be due to the tasks used to assess that

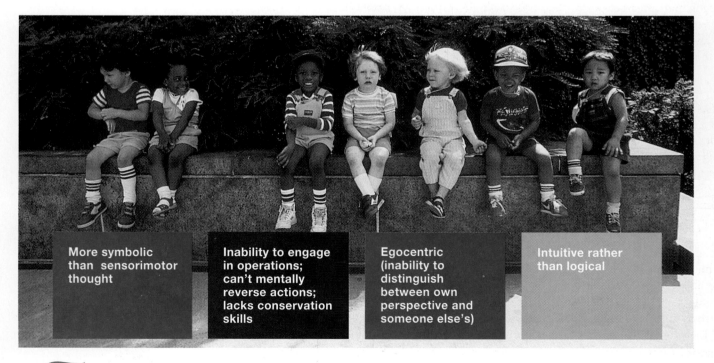

More symbolic than sensorimotor thought

Inability to engage in operations; can't mentally reverse actions; lacks conservation skills

Egocentric (inability to distinguish between own perspective and someone else's)

Intuitive rather than logical

Figure 10.6
Preoperational Thought's Characteristics

development. Gelman's research reflects the thinking of information-processing psychologists who place considerable importance on the tasks and procedures involved in assessing children's cognition.

Now that we have examined Piaget's ideas about how young children think, we will turn to the ideas of another important theorist, Lev Vygotsky.

Vygotsky's Theory of Development

In chapter 2, we described the basic principles of Vygotsky's theory (Tappan, 1998): (1) the child's cognitive skills can be understood only when they are developmentally analyzed and interpreted, (2) cognitive skills are mediated by words, language, and forms of discourse, which serve as psychological tools for facilitating and transforming mental activity, and (3) cognitive skills have their origins in social relations and are embedded in a sociocultural background. Here we expand on Vygotsky's theory of development, beginning with his unique ideas about the zone of proximal development.

The Zone of Proximal Development
The **zone of proximal development (ZPD)** *is Vygotsky's term for the range of tasks too difficult for children to master alone but which can be learned with the guidance and assistance of adults or more skilled children.* Thus, the lower limit of the ZPD is the level of problem solving reached by the child working independently. The upper limit is the level of additional responsibility the child can accept with the assistance of an able instructor (see figure 10.7). Vygotsky's emphasis on the ZPD underscores his belief in the importance of social influences, especially instruction, on children's cognitive development.

The ZPD captures the child's cognitive skills that are in the process of maturing and can be accomplished only with the assistance of a more skilled person (Panofsky, 1999). Vygotsky (1962) called these the "buds" or "flowers" of development, to distinguish them from the "fruits" of development, which the child already can accomplish independently.

Scaffolding
In chapter 7, we discussed the concept of scaffolding in socioemotional development. Here we describe its role in cognitive development. Closely linked to the idea of zone of proximal development is the concept of **scaffolding.** *Scaffolding means changing the level of support. Over the course of a teaching session, a more skilled person (teacher or more advanced peer of the child) adjusts the amount of guidance to fit the student's current performance level.* When the task the student is learning is new, the more skilled person may use direct instruction. As the student's competence increases, less guidance is given.

Dialogue is an important tool of scaffolding in the zone of proximal development (John-Steiner & Mahn, 1996; Tappan, 1998). Vygotsky viewed children as having rich but unsystematic, disorganized, and spontaneous concepts. These meet with the skilled helper's more systematic, logical, and rational concepts. As a result of the meeting and dialogue between the child and the skilled helper, the child's concepts become more systematic, logical, and rational.

Language and Thought
Vygotsky (1962) believed that young children use language not only for social communication but also to plan, guide, and monitor their behavior in a self-regulatory fashion. The use of language for self-regulation is called inner speech or private speech. For Piaget private speech is egocentric and immature, but for Vygotsky it is an important tool of thought during the early childhood years.

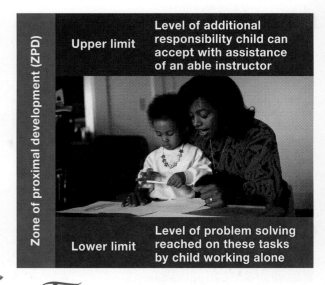

Upper limit — Level of additional responsibility child can accept with assistance of an able instructor

Lower limit — Level of problem solving reached on these tasks by child working alone

Zone of proximal development (ZPD)

Figure 10.7
Vygotsky's Zone of Proximal Development

Vygotsky's zone of proximal development has a lower limit and an upper limit. Tasks in the ZPD are too difficult for the child to perform alone. They require assistance from an adult or a skilled child. As children experience the verbal instruction or demonstration, they organize the information in their existing mental structures, so they can eventually perform the skill or task alone.

zone of proximal development (ZPD)
Vygotsky's term for tasks too difficult for children to master alone but that can be mastered with assistance. *w/significant instruction minimal performance Beyond childs Ability to do Alone*

scaffolding
In cognitive development, Vygotsky used this term to describe the changing support over the course of a teaching session, with the more skilled person adjusting guidance to fit the child's current performance level.

*better instruction
competence increases
guidance decreases as
performance improves*

Vygotsky on Language and Thought

Lev Vygotsky (1896–1934), shown here with his daughter, believed that children's cognitive development is advanced through social interaction with skilled individuals embedded in a sociocultural backdrop.

Vygotsky: Revolutionary Scientist

social constructivist approach
An approach that emphasizes the social contexts of learning and the fact that knowledge is mutually built and constructed; Vygotsky's theory is a social constructivist approach.

Vygotsky believed that language and thought initially develop independently of each other and then merge. He said that all mental functions have external, or social, origins. Children must use language to communicate with others before they can focus inward on their own thoughts. Children also must communicate externally and use language for a long period of time before the transition from external to internal speech takes place. This transition period occurs between the ages of 3 and 7 years of age and involves talking to oneself. After a while, the self-talk becomes second nature to children, and they can act without verbalizing. When this occurs, children have internalized their egocentric speech in the form of inner speech, which becomes their thoughts. Vygotsky believed that children who use a lot of private speech are more socially competent than those who don't. He argued that private speech represents an early transition in becoming more socially communicative.

Vygotsky's view challenged Piaget's ideas on language and thought. Vygotsky said that language, even in its earliest forms, is socially based. By contrast, Piaget emphasized young children's egocentric and nonsocial speech. For Vygotsky, when young children talk to themselves, they are using language to govern their behavior and guide themselves. Piaget believed that such self-talk reflects immaturity. However, researchers have found support for Vygotsky's view of the positive role of private speech in children's development (Winsler, Diaz, & Montero, 1997).

Evaluating and Comparing Vygotsky's and Piaget's Theories

Cognitively Ability to think

Vygotsky's theory came later than Piaget's theory, so it has not yet been evaluated as thoroughly. However, Vygotsky's theory already has been embraced by many teachers and has been successfully applied to education. His view of the importance of sociocultural influences on children's development fits with the current belief that it is important to evaluate the contextual factors in learning (Gojdamaschko, 1999). However, criticisms of his theory also have emerged. For example, some critics say he overemphasizes the role of language in thinking.

We already have mentioned several comparisons of Vygotsky's and Piaget's theories, such as Vygotsky's emphasis on the importance of inner speech in development and Piaget's view that such speech is immature. We also said earlier that both Vygotsky's and Piaget's theories are constructivist, emphasizing that children actively construct knowledge and understanding, rather than being passive receptacles.

Although both theories are constructivist, Vygotsky's is a **social constructivist approach,** *which emphasizes the social contexts of learning and the fact that knowledge is mutually built and constructed.* Piaget's theory does not have this social emphasis. The following analogies reflect the differing degree of social emphasis in the theories. For Piaget, the child is more like a little scientist; for Vygotsky, the child is more like a social child embedded in a sociocultural backdrop. Moving from Piaget to Vygotsky, the conceptual shift is from the individual to collaboration, social interaction, and sociocultural activity (Rogoff, 1998). For Piaget, children construct knowledge by transforming, organizing, and reorganizing previous knowledge. For Vygotsky, children construct knowledge through social interaction with others (Hogan & Tudge, 1999). The implication of Piaget's theory for teaching is that children need support to explore their world and discover knowledge. The main implication of Vygotsky's theory for teaching is that students need many opportunities to learn with the teacher and more skilled peers. In both Piaget's and Vygotsky's theories, teachers serve as facilitators and guides, rather than as directors and molders of learning. Figure 10.8 compares Vygotsky's and Piaget's theories.

Teaching Strategies Based on Vygotsky's Theory
Following are some ways that Vygotsky's theory can be incorporated in the classroom:

1. *Use the child's zone of proximal development in teaching.* Teaching should begin toward the zone's upper limit, where the child is able to reach the goal only

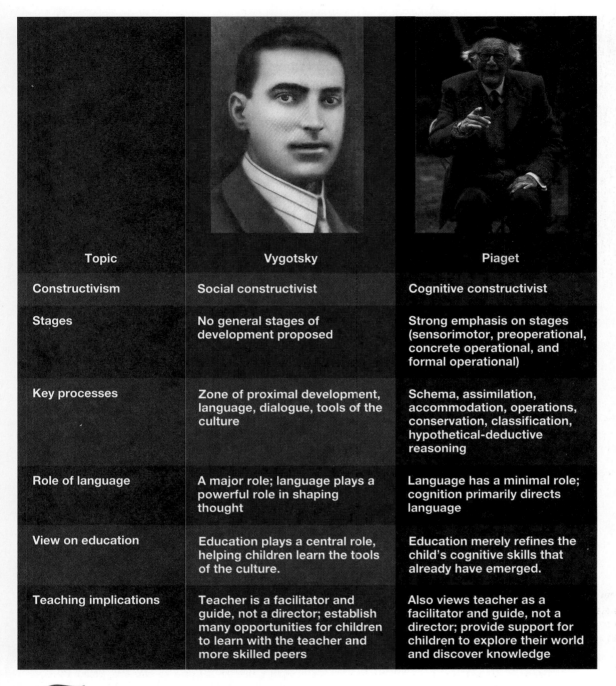

Topic	Vygotsky	Piaget
Constructivism	Social constructivist	Cognitive constructivist
Stages	No general stages of development proposed	Strong emphasis on stages (sensorimotor, preoperational, concrete operational, and formal operational)
Key processes	Zone of proximal development, language, dialogue, tools of the culture	Schema, assimilation, accommodation, operations, conservation, classification, hypothetical-deductive reasoning
Role of language	A major role; language plays a powerful role in shaping thought	Language has a minimal role; cognition primarily directs language
View on education	Education plays a central role, helping children learn the tools of the culture.	Education merely refines the child's cognitive skills that already have emerged.
Teaching implications	Teacher is a facilitator and guide, not a director; establish many opportunities for children to learn with the teacher and more skilled peers	Also views teacher as a facilitator and guide, not a director; provide support for children to explore their world and discover knowledge

*F*igure 10.8
Comparison of Vygotsky's and Piaget's Theories

through close collaboration with the instructor. With adequate continuing instruction and practice, the child organizes and masters the behavioral sequences required to perform the target skill. As the instruction continues, the performance transfers from the teacher to the child. The teacher gradually reduces the explanations, hints, and demonstrations until the student is able to perform the skill alone. Once the goal is achieved, it may become the foundation for the development of a new ZPD.

2. *Use scaffolding.* Look for opportunities to use scaffolding when children need help with self-initiated learning activities (Elicker, 1996). Also use scaffolding

Vygotsky Links

to help children move to a higher level of skill and knowledge. Offer just enough assistance. You might ask, "What can I do to help you?" Or simply observe the child's intentions and attempts, smoothly providing support when needed. When the child hesitates, offer encouragement. And encourage the child to practice the skill. You may watch and appreciate the child's practice or offer support when the child forgets what to do.

3. *Use more skilled peers as teachers.* Remember that it is not just adults that Vygotsky believed are important in helping children learn important skills. Children also benefit from the support and guidance of more skilled children.

4. *Monitor and encourage children's use of private speech.* Be aware of the developmental change from externally talking to oneself when solving a problem during the preschool years to privately talking to oneself in the early elementary school years. In the elementary school years, encourage children to internalize and self-regulate their talk to themselves.

5. *Assess the child's ZPD, not IQ.* Like Piaget, Vygotsky did not believe that formal, standardized tests are the best way to assess children's learning. Rather, Vygotsky argued that assessment should focus on determining the child's zone of proximal development. The skilled helper presents the child with tasks of varying difficulty to determine the best level at which to begin instruction. The ZPD is a measure of learning potential. IQ, also a measure of learning potential, emphasizes that intelligence is a property of the child. By contrast, ZPD emphasizes that learning is interpersonal. It is inappropriate to say that the child *has* a ZPD. Rather, a child *shares* a ZPD with a more skilled individual.

6. *Transform the classroom with Vygotskian ideas.* What does a Vygotskian classroom look like? The Kamehameha Elementary Education Program (KEEP) is based on Vygotsky's theory (Tharp, 1994). The zone of proximal development is the key element of instruction in this program. Children might read a story and then interpret its meaning. Many of the learning activities take place in small groups. All children spend at least 20 minutes each morning in an activity setting called "Center One." In this context, scaffolding is used to improve children's literary skills. The instructor asks questions, responds to students' queries, and builds on the ideas that students generate. Thousands of low-income children have attended KEEP public schools in Hawaii, on an Arizona Navajo Indian reservation, and in Los Angeles. Compared with a control group of non-KEEP children, the KEEP children participate more actively in classroom discussion, are more attentive in class, and have higher reading achievement (Tharp & Gallimore, 1988).

Piaget's cognitive development theory and Vygotsky's sociocultural cognitive theory have provided important insights about the way young children think and how this thinking changes developmentally. Next, we will explore a third major view on children's thinking—information processing.

Information Processing

Not only can we study the stages of cognitive development that young children go through, as Piaget did, but we can also study the different cognitive processes of young children's mental worlds. Two important aspects of preschool children's thoughts are attention and memory. What are the limitations and advances in attention and memory during the preschool years?

Attention   In chapter 7, we discussed attention in the context of habituation, which is something like being bored. In habituation, the infant becomes disinterested in a stimulus and no longer attends to it. Habituation involves a decrement in attention. Dishabituation is the recovery of attention. The importance of these aspects of attention in infancy for the preschool years was underscored by research showing that ~~both decrement and recovery of attention, when measured in the first six months of infancy, were associated with higher intelligence in the preschool years~~ (Bornstein & Sigman, 1986).

Although the infant's attention has important implications for cognitive development in the preschool years, the child's ability to pay attention changes significantly during the preschool years. The toddler wanders around, shifts attention from one activity to another, and seems to spend little time focused on any one object or event. By comparison, the preschool child might be observed watching television for a half hour. In one study, young children's attention to television in the natural setting of the home was videotaped (Anderson & others, 1985). Ninety-nine families comprising 460 individuals were observed for 4,672 hours. Visual attention to television dramatically increased during the preschool years.

One deficit in attention during the preschool years concerns those dimensions that ~~stand out,~~ or are *salient,* compared with those that are relevant to solving a problem or performing well on a task. For example, a problem might have a flashy, attractive clown that presents the directions for solving a problem. Preschool children are influenced strongly by the features of the task that stand out, such as the flashy, attractive clown. After the age of 6 or 7, children attend more efficiently to the dimensions of the task that are relevant, such as the directions for solving a problem. Developmentalists believe this change reflects a shift to cognitive control of attention, so that children act less impulsively and reflect more.

Memory   Memory is a central process in children's cognitive development; it involves the retention of information over time. Conscious memory comes into play as early as 7 months of age, although children and adults have little or no memory of events experienced before the age of 3. Among the interesting questions about memory in the preschool years are those involving short-term memory.

In **short-term memory,** *individuals retain information for up to 15 to 30 seconds, assuming there is no rehearsal.* Using rehearsal, we can keep information in short-term memory for a much longer period. One method of assessing short-term memory is the memory-span task. If you have taken an IQ test, you were probably exposed to one of these tasks. You simply hear a short list of stimuli—usually digits—presented at a rapid pace (one per second, for example). Then you are asked to repeat the digits. Research with the memory-span task suggests that short-term memory increases during early childhood. For example, in one investigation, memory span increased from about 2 digits in 2- to 3-year-old children to about 5 digits in 7-year-old children, yet, between 7 and 13 years of age, memory span increased only by 1½ digits (Dempster, 1981). Keep in mind, though, the individual differences in memory span, which is why IQ and various aptitude tests are used.

Why are there differences in memory span because of age? Rehearsal of information is important; older children rehearse the digits more than younger children. Speed and efficiency of processing information are important, too, especially the speed with which memory items can be identified. For example, in one study, children were tested on their speed at repeating words presented orally (Case, Kurland, & Goldberg, 1982). Speed of repetition was a powerful predictor of memory span. Indeed, when the speed of repetition was controlled, the 6-year-olds' memory spans were equal to those of young adults.

The speed-of-processing explanation highlights an important point in the information-processing perspective. That is, the speed with which a child processes information is an important aspect of the child's cognitive abilities.

Task Analysis   Another major emphasis of the information-processing perspective is on identifying the components of the task the child is performing. Information-processing psychologists are intrigued by the possibility that, if tasks are

short-term memory
The memory component in which individuals retain information for 15–30 seconds, assuming there is no rehearsal.

I come into the fields and spacious palaces of my memory, where are treasures of countless images of things in every manner.

St. Augustine
Roman Clergyman and Philosopher, 5th Century

made interesting and simple, children may display greater cognitive maturity than Piaget realized. This strategy was followed to determine if preschool children could reason about a *syllogism*—a type of reasoning problem consisting of two premises, or statements assumed to be true, plus a conclusion (Hawkins & others, 1984). To simplify problems, words such as *some* and *all* were made implicit rather than explicit. The problems focused on fantasy creatures alien to practical knowledge. Imagine how wide a child's eyes become when told stories about purple bangas who sneeze at people and merds who laugh and don't like mushrooms. The following are two syllogisms that were read to children:

> Every banga is purple.
> Purple animals always sneeze at people.
> Do bangas sneeze at people?

> Merds laugh when they're happy.
> Animals that laugh don't like mushrooms.
> Do merds like mushrooms?

By simplifying the problem and making its dimensions more understandable to young children, the researchers demonstrated that preschool children can reason about syllogisms.

The Young Child's Theory of Mind

Children are very curious about the nature of the human mind, and developmentalists have shown a flurry of interest in children's thoughts about what the human mind is like (Flavell, Green, & Flavell, 1995; Guajardo & Turley-Ames, 1999; Wellman, 1990).

Children's developing knowledge of the mind includes (Flavell, Miller, & Miller, 1993) the awareness that

- The mind exists
- The mind has connections to the physical world
- The mind can represent objects and events accurately or inaccurately
- The mind actively interprets reality and emotions

A child's first developmental acquisition is knowing that such a thing as a mind exists. By the age of 2 or 3, children refer to needs, emotions, and mental states— "I need my Mommy," "Tom feels bad," and "I forgot my doll." They also use intentional action or desire words, such as *wants to*. Cognitive terms such as *know*, *remember*, and *think* usually appear after perceptual and emotional terms but often are used by the age of 3. Later, children make finer distinctions between such mental phenomena as guessing versus knowing, believing versus fantasizing, and intending versus not on purpose.

At about 2 or 3 years of age, children develop the knowledge that people can be "cognitively connected" to objects and events in the external world. They understand that people can see them, hear them, like them, want them, fear them, and so on. By their awareness of the connections among stimuli, mental states, and behavior, young children possess a rudimentary mental theory of human action. On the input side, 2-year-olds sometimes hide objects, so that another person cannot see them, which involves manipulating stimuli to produce a certain perceptual state in another person. On the output side (mind to behavior), older 2-year-old children can predict action and emotional expression based on desires, as when comprehending that a child wants a cookie, tries to get one, and is happy if successful. However, 2-year-olds cannot predict actions based on beliefs. For instance, Ann wants to find her toy but can't find it in one location. Children predict she would be sad and look for it in another location, but they don't know that Ann's beliefs about possible locations influence where she will look.

In addition to inferring connections from stimuli to mental states, or from mental states to behavior or emotion, 3-year-olds can often infer mental states from behavior. When children use spontaneous language, they sometimes explain action by referring to mental causes. For example, a 3-year-old explains that he has paint on his hands because he thought his hands were paper. This gives new meaning to the term *finger painting!* In sum, children acquire knowledge about links between stimuli, mental states, and behavior fairly early in their development.

Young children also develop an understanding that the mind is separate from the physical world. They know that the mind is different from rocks, roller skates, and even the head. For example, a 3-year-old is told that one boy has a cookie and that another boy is thinking about a cookie. The 3-year-old knows which cookie can be seen by others, touched, eaten, shared, and saved for later. Three-year-olds also know that they can fantasize about things that don't exist, such as Martians, ghosts, and dragons.

Children also develop an understanding that the mind can represent objects and events accurately or inaccurately. Understanding of false beliefs usually appears in 4- or 5-year-old children, but not 3-year-olds. Consider the following story acted out for children with dolls. A boy places some chocolate in a blue cupboard and then goes out to play. While he is outside, his mother moves the chocolate to a green cupboard. When the boy returns and wants the chocolate, the subject is asked where the boy will look for it. Three-year-olds usually say, "The green cupboard," where the chocolate actually is, even though the boy had no way of knowing the chocolate had been moved. Thus, 3-year-olds do not understand that a person acts on the basis of what he or she believes to be true, rather than what they themselves know to be true. By contrast, 4- and 5-year-old children usually understand false beliefs.

Finally, children also develop an understanding that the mind actively mediates the interpretation of reality and the emotion experienced. The shift from viewing the mind as passive to viewing it as active appears in children's knowledge that prior experiences influence current mental states, which in turn affect emotions and social inferences. In the elementary school years, children change from viewing emotions as caused by external events without any mediation by internal states to viewing emotional reactions to an external event as influenced by a prior emotional state, experience, or expectations. For example, 6-year-old children do not understand that a child would be sad or scared when his friends suggest they ride bikes if that child previously was almost hit by a car while riding his bike.

In summary, young children are very curious about the human mind. By the age of 3, they turn some of their thoughts inward and understand that they and others have internal mental states. Beginning at about 3 years of age, children also show an understanding that the internal desires and beliefs of a person can be connected to that person's actions. Young children also know that they cannot physically touch thoughts, they believe that a person has to see an object to know it, and they grasp that their mental image of an object represents something that exists in the world.

At this point, we have discussed a number of ideas about cognitive developmental changes and early childhood. An overview of these ideas is presented in summary table 10.1.

LANGUAGE DEVELOPMENT

Young children's understanding sometimes gets way ahead of their speech. One 3-year-old, laughing with delight as an abrupt summer breeze stirred his hair and tickled his skin, commented, "It did winding me!" Adults would be understandably perplexed if a young child ventured, "Anything is not to break, only plates and glasses," when she meant, "Nothing is breaking except plates and glasses." Many of the oddities of young children's language sound like mistakes to adult listeners. However, from the children's point of view, they are not mistakes. They

Language Development

Summary Table 10.1
Cognitive Developmental Changes

Concept	Processes/ Related Ideas	Characteristics/Description
Piaget's stage of preoperational thought	Its nature	This is the beginning of the ability to reconstruct at the level of thought what has been established in behavior, and a transition from primitive to more sophisticated use of symbols. The child does not yet think in an operational way.
	Symbolic function substage	This substage occurs roughly between 2 and 4 years of age and is characterized by symbolic thought, egocentrism, and animism.
	Intuitive thought substage	This substage stretches from approximately 4 to 7 years of age. It is called intuitive because, on the one hand, children seem so sure about their knowledge, yet, on the other hand, they are so unaware of how they know what they know. The preoperational child lacks conservation and asks a barrage of questions.
Vygotsky's theory	Zone of proximal development	This is Vygotsky's term for the range of tasks too difficult for children to master alone but which can be learned with the guidance and assistance of adults and more skilled children.
	Scaffolding	This involves changing support over the course of a teaching session, with the more skilled person adjusting guidance to fit the student's current performance level. Dialogue is an important tool of scaffolding.
	Language and thought	Vygotsky believed that language plays a key role in guiding cognition. He said language and thought initially develop independently, but then children internalize their egocentric speech in the form of inner speech, which becomes their thoughts. This transition occurs from 3–7 years of age. This contrasts with Piaget's view that young children's speech is immature and egocentric.
	Evaluating and comparing Vygotsky's and Piaget's theories	Vygotsky's theory has increasingly been applied to education. Especially important are his ideas related to sociocultural influences on children's development and learning. Some critics say he overestimated the importance of language. Comparisons of Vygotsky's and Piaget's theories involve constructivism, metaphors for learning, stages, key processes, role of language, views on education, and teaching implications. Vygotsky's theory is social constructivist, Piaget's cognitive constructivist.
	Teaching strategies	These focus on using the child's zone of proximal development, using scaffolding and more skilled peers as teachers, monitoring and encouraging children's use of private speech, assessing the child's ZPD rather than IQ, and transforming the classroom with Vygotskian ideas.
Information processing	Attention	The child's attention dramatically improves during early childhood. One deficit in attention in early childhood is that the child attends to the salient rather than the relevant features of a task.
	Memory	Significant improvement in short-term memory occurs during early childhood. For example, memory span increases substantially in early childhood. Increased use of rehearsal and increased speed of processing are related to young children's memory improvement.
	Task analysis	Information-processing advocates believe a task's components should be analyzed. By making tasks more interesting and simple, some aspects of children's cognitive development have been shown to occur earlier than thought possible.
The young child's theory of mind	Its nature	Young children are very curious about the human mind. By about 3 years of age, they turn some of their thoughts inward and understand that they and others have internal mental states. Beginning at about 3, they also show an understanding that the internal beliefs and desires of another person can be connected to that person's actions. Young children also know that they cannot physically touch thoughts, they believe that a person has to see an object to know it, and they grasp that their mental image of an object represents something that exists in the world.

represent the way young children perceive and understand their world at that point in their development.

Stages and Rule Systems

What stages are involved in young children's language development? How do young children's rule systems for language change in early childhood?

Elaboration of Brown's Stages

In chapter 7, we briefly described Roger Brown's five stages of language development. Remember that Brown (1973) believes that mean length of utterance (MLU) is a good index of a child's language maturity. He identified five stages of a child's language development based on MLU.

In stage 1 (12 to 26 months of age), the MLU is 1.00 to 2.00. Vocabulary consists mainly of nouns and verbs, with several adjectives and adverbs. Word order is preserved. Typical sentences are "Mommy bye-bye" and "Big doggie."

In stage 2 (27 to 30 months), MLU is 2.00 to 2.50. Plurals are correctly formed, past tense is used, *be* is used, definite articles (*the*) and indefinite articles (*a, an*) are used, as are some prepositions. Typical sentences are "Dolly in bed," "Them pretty," and "Milk's all gone."

In stage 3 (31 to 34 months of age), MLU is 2.50 to 3.00. Yes-no questions appear, *wh-* questions (*who, what, where*) proliferate, negatives (*no, not, non*) are used, and so are imperatives (commands or requests). Typical sentences are "Daddy come home?" and "Susie no want milk."

In stage 4 (35 to 40 months), MLU is 3.00 to 3.75. One sentence is sometimes embedded in another. Typical sentences include "I think it's red" and "Know what I saw."

In stage 5 (41 to 46 months), MLU is 3.75 to 4.50. Simple sentences and propositional relations are coordinated. Typical sentences are "I went to Bob's and had ice cream" and "I like bunnies 'cause they're cute."

Rule Systems

Remember from our discussion of language development in chapter 7 that language consists of rule systems. These include morphology, syntax, semantics, and pragmatics. What kinds of changes take place in these rule systems during early childhood?

As children move beyond two-word utterances, they know morphology rules. Children begin using the plurals and possessive forms of nouns (such as *dogs* and *dog's*). They put appropriate endings on verbs (such as *-s* when the subject is third-person singular, *-ed* for the past tense, and *-ing* for the present progressive tense). They use prepositions (such as *in* and *on*), articles (such as *a* and *the*), and various forms of the verb *to be* (such as "I *was* going to the store"). Some of the best evidence for changes in children's use of morphological rules occurs in their overgeneralizations of the rules. Have you ever heard a preschool child say "foots" instead of "feet," or "goed" instead of "went"? If you do not remember having heard such oddities, talk to some parents who have young children, or to the young children themselves. You will hear some interesting errors in the use of morphological rule endings.

In a classic experiment, Jean Berko (1958) presented preschool children and first-grade children with cards such as the one shown in figure 10.9. Children were asked to look at the card while the experimenter read aloud the words on the card. Then the children were asked to supply the missing word. This might sound easy, but Berko was interested not just in the children's ability to recall the right word but also in their ability to say it "correctly" (with the ending that was dictated by morphological rules). "Wugs" would be the correct response for the card in figure 10.9.

This is a wug.

Now there is another one.
There are two of them.
There are two _____.

*F*igure 10.9
Stimuli in Berko's Study of Young Children's Understanding of Morphological Rules

In Jean Berko's (1958) study, young children were presented cards, such as this one with a "wug" on it. Then the children were asked to supply the missing word; in supplying the missing word, they had to say it correctly too. "Wugs" is the correct response here.

How do children's language abilities develop during early childhood?

Language Growth

Although the children's answers were not perfect, they were much better than chance. Moreover, the children demonstrated their knowledge of morphological rules, not only with the plural forms of nouns ("There are two wugs") but with possessive forms of nouns and the third-person singular and past-tense forms of verbs. What makes Berko's study impressive is that most of the words were fictional, created for the experiment. Thus, the children could not base their responses on remembering past instances of hearing the words. Instead, they were forced to rely on *rules*.

Similar evidence that children learn and actively apply rules occurs at the level of syntax. After advancing beyond two-word utterances, children speak word sequences that show a growing mastery of complex rules for how words should be ordered. Consider the case of *wh-* questions: "Where is Daddy going?" and "What is that boy doing?" for example. To ask these questions properly, the child has to know two important differences between *wh-* questions and simple affirmative statements (such as "Daddy is going to work" and "That boy is waiting on the school bus"). First, a *wh-* word must be added at the beginning of the sentence. Second, the auxiliary verb must be "inverted"—that is, exchanged with the subject of the sentence. Young children learn quite early where to put the *wh-* word. They take much longer to learn the auxiliary-inversion rule. Thus, it is common to hear preschool children asking such questions as "Where daddy is going?" and "What that boy is doing?"

As children move into the elementary school years, they become skilled at using syntactical rules to construct lengthy and complex sentences. Sentences such as "The man who fixed the house went home" and "I don't want you to use my bike" are impressive demonstrations of how the child can use syntax to combine ideas into a single sentence. How young children achieve the mastery of such complex rules and yet struggle with relatively simple arithmetic rules is a mystery we still must solve.

Regarding semantics, as children move beyond the 2-word stage, their knowledge of meanings also rapidly advances. The speaking vocabulary of a 6-year-old child ranges from 8,000 to 14,000 words. Assuming that word learning began when the child was 12 months old, this translates into a rate of 5 to 8 new word meanings a day between the ages of 1 and 6. After 5 years of word learning, the 6-year-old child does not slow down. According to some estimates, the average child of this age is moving along at the awe-inspiring rate of 22 words a day. How would you fare if you were given the task of learning 22 new words every day? It is truly miraculous how quickly children learn language.

Although there are many differences between a 2-year-old's language and a 6-year-old's language, none are more dramatic than those pertaining to pragmatics—rules of conversation (Ninio & Snow, 1996). A 6-year-old is simply a much better conversationalist than a 2-year-old. What are some of the improvements in pragmatics that are made in the preschool years? At about 3 years of age, children improve in their ability to talk about things that are not physically present. That is, they improve their command of the characteristic of language known as "displacement." One way displacement is revealed is in games of pretend. Although a 2-year-old might know the word *table*, he is unlikely to use this word to refer to an imaginary table that he pretends is standing in front of him. But a child over 3 probably has this ability, even if she does not always use it. There are large individual differences in preschoolers' talk about imaginary people and things.

Pragmatic Language

Literacy and Early Childhood Education

The concern about our nation's literacy—the ability to read and write—has led to a careful examination of preschool and kindergarten children's experiences, with the hope that a positive orientation toward reading and writing can be developed early in life (Mathes & Torgesen, 1999; Miller, 1999). Literacy begins in infancy. Reading and writing skills in young children should build on their existing understanding of oral and written language. Learning should occur in a supportive environment, one in which children can generate a positive perception of themselves and develop a positive attitude toward reading and writing (Golova & others, 1999; Stone, 1994).

Unfortunately, in the push to develop a nation of literate people by emphasizing the early development of reading and writing skills, some dangers have emerged (Early Childhood and Literacy Development Committee, 1986). Too many preschool children are being subjected to rigid, formal prereading programs with expectations and experiences that are too advanced for children of their levels of development. Too little attention is being given to the individual development of young children's learning styles and skills (Morrison, 1999). Too little attention is being placed on reading for pleasure, which may keep children from associating reading with enjoyment. The pressure to achieve high scores on standardized tests that often are inappropriate for preschool children has resulted in a curriculum that is too advanced and too intense. Such programs frequently restrict curiosity, critical thinking, and creative expression.

Literacy

What should a literacy program for preschool children be like? Instruction should be built on what children already know about oral language, reading, and writing. All young children should experience feelings of success and pride in their early reading and writing exercises (Fields & Spangler, 2000; Pianta, 1999). Teachers need to help them perceive themselves as people who can enjoy exploring oral and written language. Reading should be integrated into the broad communication process, which includes speaking, listening, and writing, as well as other communication systems, such as art, math, and music (Neuman & Roskos, 1993). Children's early writing attempts should be encouraged without concern for the proper formation of letters or correct conventional spelling. Children should be encouraged to take risks in reading and writing, and errors should be viewed as a natural part of the child's growth. Teachers and parents

Children's Writing
Supporting Young Children's Writing

Through the Eyes of Children

Learning About Bugs and Books

Dear State Committee:

We think Mrs. Hitchcock is the best teacher in the state because she was very nice to us on the very first day of school. She always has a smile on her face and she never frowns. She is kind and pretty. Mrs. Hitchcock teaches us good manners and how to help each other. We get to play with toys, learn about bugs, and have fun centers. She reads books to us and is a good storyteller.

At the end of the day, Mrs. Hitchcock gives us hugs and tells us goodbye when we go home. She loves us and we love her.

Mrs. Hitchcock's Happy Herd
(Letter dictated to Mrs.
Hitchcock's teacher assistant
by her kindergarten class at
Holley Navarre Primary School, FL)

Early Childhood Education
Reggio Emilia

child-centered kindergarten
Education that involves the whole child by considering both the child's physical, cognitive, and social development and the child's needs, interests, and learning styles.

should take time to regularly read to children from a wide variety of poetry, fiction, and nonfiction. Teachers and parents should present models for young children to emulate by using language appropriately, listening and responding to children's talk, and engaging in their own reading and writing. And children should be encouraged to be active participants in the learning process, rather than passive recipients of knowledge (Slavin, 1999). This can be accomplished by using activities that stimulate experimentation with talking, listening, writing, and reading.

EARLY CHILDHOOD EDUCATION

Our coverage of early childhood education focuses on variations in the education of young children, whether preschool is necessary, and school readiness.

Variations in Early Childhood Education

There are many variations in the way young children are educated. In the story that opened this chapter, you read about the Reggio Emilia program in northern Italy, a promising strategy that is receiving increased attention. First, we will explore the nature of the child-centered kindergarten, then turn our attention to Maria Montessori's approach. Next, we will examine the important concepts of developmentally appropriate and inappropriate education, followed by a discussion of what early childhood education's effects are.

The Child-Centered Kindergarten Kindergarten programs vary a great deal (Roopnarine & Johnson, 1999). Some approaches place more emphasis on young children's social development, others on their cognitive development. Some experts on early childhood education believe that the curriculum of too many of today's kindergarten and preschool programs place too much emphasis on achievement and success, putting pressure on young children too early in their development (Charlesworth, 1996; Elkind, 1988). Placing such heavy emphasis on success is not what kindergartens were originally intended to do. In the 1840s, Friedrich Froebel's concern for quality education for young children led to the founding of the kindergarten—literally, "a garden for children." The founder of the kindergarten understood that, like growing plants, children require careful nurturing. Unfortunately, too many of today's kindergartens have forgotten the importance of careful nurturing for our nation's young children.

In the **child-centered kindergarten,** *education involves the whole child and includes concern for the child's physical, cognitive, and social development.* Instruction is organized around the child's needs, interests, and learning styles. The process of learning, rather than what is learned, is emphasized (White & Coleman, 2000). Each child follows a unique developmental pattern, and young children learn best through firsthand experiences with people and materials. Play is extremely important in the child's total development. *Experimenting, exploring, discovering, trying out, restructuring, speaking,* and *listening* are all words that describe excellent kindergarten programs. Such programs are closely attuned to the developmental status of 4- and 5-year-old children. They are based on a state of being, not on a state of becoming.

The Montessori Approach Montessori schools are patterned after the educational philosophy of Maria Montessori, an Italian physician-turned-educator, who crafted a revolutionary approach to young children's education at the beginning of the twentieth century (Wentworth, 1999). Her work began in Rome with a group of children who were mentally retarded. She was successful in teaching them to read, write, and pass examinations designed for normal children. Some time later, she turned her attention to poor children from the slums of Rome and had similar success in teaching them. Her approach has since been adopted extensively in private nursery schools in the United States.

The **Montessori approach** *is a philosophy of education in which children are given considerable freedom and spontaneity in choosing activities. They are allowed to move from one activity to another as they desire.* The teacher acts as a facilitator rather than a director of learning. The teacher shows the child how to perform intellectual activities, demonstrates interesting ways to explore curriculum materials, and offers help when the child requests it.

Some developmentalists favor the Montessori approach, but others believe that it neglects children's social development (Chattin-McNichols, 1992). For example, while Montessori fosters independence and the development of cognitive skills, it deemphasizes verbal interaction between the teacher and child and peer interaction. Montessori's critics also argue that it restricts imaginative play.

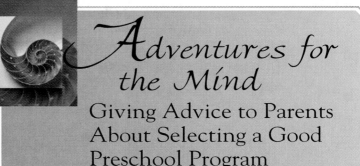

Adventures for the Mind

Giving Advice to Parents About Selecting a Good Preschool Program

Imagine that you are a preschool educational consultant. What kind of advice would you give parents about selecting a good preschool program? In developing your recommendations, consider what you would tell parents about the following:

• The relationship between the teacher-caregiver and the child
• Activities
• Teacher-caregiver development
• Staffing and group size
• The physical environment
• Health, safety, and nutrition
• The relationship between the parent and the teacher-caregiver

Montessori approach

An educational philosophy in which children are given considerable freedom and spontaneity in choosing activities and are allowed to move from one activity to another as they desire.

Facilitator –

High/Scope: Active Learning

Developmentally Appropriate and Inappropriate Practices in the Education of Young Children It is time for number games in a kindergarten class at the Greenbrook School in South Brunswick, New Jersey. With little prodding from the teacher, 23 5- and 6-year-old children fetch geometric puzzles, playing cards, and counting equipment from the shelves lining the room. At one round table, some young children fit together brightly colored shapes. One girl forms a hexagon out of triangles. Other children gather around her to count up how many parts were needed to make the whole. After about half an hour, the children prepare for story time. They put away their counting equipment and sit in a circle around one young girl. She holds up a giant book about a character named Mrs. Wishywashy, who insists on giving the farm animals a bath. The children recite the whimsical lines, clearly enjoying one of their favorite stories. The hallway outside the kindergarten is lined with drawings depicting the children's own interpretations of the book. After the first reading, volunteers act out various parts of the book. There is not one bored face in the room.

This is not reading, writing, and arithmetic the way most individuals remember it. A growing number of educators and psychologists believe that preschool and young elementary school children learn best through active, hands-on teaching methods such as games and dramatic play. They know that children develop at varying rates and that schools need to allow for these individual differences (Henninger, 1999; Jalongo & Isenberg, 2000). They also believe that schools should focus on improving children's social development, as well as their cognitive development. Educators refer to this type of schooling as **developmentally appropriate practice**, *which is based on knowledge of the typical development of children within an age span (age appropriateness) as well as the uniqueness of the child (individual appropriateness). Developmentally appropriate practice contrasts with developmentally inappropriate practice, which ignores the concrete, hands-on approach to learning. Direct teaching largely through*

developmentally appropriate practice

Education that focuses on the typical developmental patterns of children (age appropriateness) and the uniqueness of each child (individual appropriateness). Such practice contrasts with developmentally inappropriate practice, which ignores the concrete, hands-on approach to learning. Direct teaching largely through abstract paper-and-pencil activities presented to large groups of young children is believed to be developmentally inappropriate.

abstract paper-and-pencil activities presented to large groups of young children is believed to be developmentally inappropriate.

One of the most comprehensive documents addressing the issue of developmentally appropriate practice in early childhood programs is the position statement by the National Association for the Education of Young Children (NAEYC) (Bredekamp, 1987, 1997; National Association for the Education of Young Children, 1986). This document represents the expertise of many of the foremost experts in the field of early childhood education. By turning to figure 10.10, you can examine some of the NAEYC recommendations for developmentally appropriate practice. In one study, the children who attended developmentally appropriate kindergartens displayed more appropriate classroom behavior and had better conduct records and better work and study habits in the first grade than did the children who attended developmentally inappropriate kindergartens (Hart & others, 1993).

A special worry of early childhood educators is that the back-to-basics movement that has recently characterized educational reform is filtering down to kindergarten. Another worry is that many parents want their children to go to school earlier than kindergarten for the purpose of getting a "head start" in achievement. To further evaluate early childhood education, see Adventures for the Mind.

How common are programs that use developmentally appropriate practice? Unfortunately, as few as one-third to one-fifth of all early childhood programs follow this educational strategy. Even fewer elementary schools do. Child-initiated activities, divergent questioning, and small-group instruction are the exception rather than the rule (Dunn & Kontos, 1997).

Education for Children Who Are Disadvantaged For many years, children from low-income families did not receive any education before they entered the first grade. In the 1960s, an effort was made to try to break the cycle of poverty and poor education for young children in the United States through compensatory education. **Project Head Start** *is a compensatory education program designed to provide children from low-income families the opportunity to acquire the skills and experiences important for success in school.* Project Head Start began in the summer of 1965, funded by the Economic Opportunity Act, and it continues to serve disadvantaged children today.

Initially, Project Head Start consisted of many different types of preschool programs in different parts of the country. Little effort was made to find out whether some programs worked better than others, but it eventually became apparent that some programs did work better than others. **Project Follow Through** *was implemented in 1967 as an adjunct to Project Head Start. In Project Follow Through, different types of educational programs were devised to determine which programs were the most effective. In the Follow Through programs, the enriched programs were carried through the first few years of elementary school.*

Were some Follow Through programs more effective than others? Many of the variations were able to produce the desired effects in children. For example, children in academically oriented, direct-instruction approaches did better on achievement tests and were more persistent on tasks than were children in the other approaches. Children in affective education approaches were absent from school less often and showed more independence than children in other approaches. Thus, Project Follow Through was important in demonstrating that variation in early childhood education does have significant effects in a wide range of social and cognitive areas (Stallings, 1975).

The effects of early childhood compensatory education continue to be studied, and recent evaluations support the positive influence on both the cognitive and social worlds of disadvantaged young children (Bredekamp, 1996; Reynolds, 1999; Schweinhart, 1999). Of special interest are the long-term effects such intervention might produce. Model preschool programs lead to lower rates of placement

NAEYC

Project Head Start
Compensatory education designed to provide children from low-income families the opportunity to acquire the skills and experiences important for school success.

Project Follow Through
An adjunct to Project Head Start, in which the enrichment programs are carried through the first few years of elementary school.

Head Start Resources

in special education, dropping out of school, grade retention, delinquency, and use of welfare programs. Such programs might also lead to higher rates of high school graduation and employment. For every dollar invested in high-quality, model preschool programs, taxpayers receive about $1.50 in return by the time the participants reach the age of 20. The benefits include savings on public school education (such as special-education services), tax payments on additional earnings, reduced welfare payments, and savings in juvenile justice system costs. Predicted benefits over a lifetime are much greater to the taxpayer, a return of $5.73 on every dollar invested.

One long-term investigation of early childhood education was conducted by Irving Lazar, Richard Darlington, and their colleagues (1982). They pooled their resources into what they called a "consortium for longitudinal studies," developed to share information about the long-term effects of preschool programs, so that better designs and methods could be created. When the data from the eleven different early education studies were analyzed together, the children ranged in age from 9 to 19 years. The early education models varied substantially, but all were carefully planned and executed by experts in early childhood education. Outcome measures included indicators of school competence (such as special education and grade retention), abilities (as measured by standardized intelligence and achievement tests), attitudes and values, and impact on the family. The results indicated substantial benefits of competent preschool education with low-income children on all four dimensions investigated. In sum, ample evidence indicates that well-designed and well-implemented early childhood education programs with low-income children are successful.

Although educational intervention in impoverished children's lives is important, Head Start programs are not all created equal. One estimate is that 40 percent of the 1,400 Head Start programs are of questionable quality (Zigler & Styfco, 1994). More attention needs to be given to developing consistently high-quality Head Start programs (Bronfenbrenner, 1995; Parker & others, 1995). One high-quality early childhood education program (although not a Head Start program) is the Perry Preschool program in Ypsilanti, Michigan, designed by David Weikart (1982). The Perry Preschool program is a two-year preschool program that includes weekly home visits from program personnel. In a recent analysis of the long-term effects of the program, as young adults the Perry Preschool children have higher high school graduation rates, more are in the workforce, fewer need welfare, crime rates are lower among them, and there are fewer teen pregnancies than in a control group from the same background who did not get the enriched early childhood education experience (Weikart, 1993).

Too many young children go to substandard early childhood programs (Morrison, 2000). In a report by the Carnegie Corporation (1996), four out of five early childhood programs did not meet quality standards. Early childhood education should encourage adequate preparation for learning, varied learning activities, trusting relationships between adults and children, and increased parental involvement (Hildebrand, Phenice, & Hines, 2000).

The Effects of Early Childhood Education

Because kindergarten and preschool programs are so diverse, it is difficult to draw overall conclusions about their effects on children's development. Nonetheless, in one review of early

Adventures for the Mind
Observing Children in Preschool and Kindergarten

To learn about children, there is no substitute for interacting with them and observing them. Try to visit at least one preschool and one kindergarten. When I was trying to develop a meaningful idea for a master's thesis some years ago, my advisor suggested that I spend several weeks at different Head Start programs in Miami, Florida. The experience was invaluable and contributed significantly to my further pursuit of a career in the field of child development.

When you conduct your observations, consider whether the programs meet the criteria of developmentally appropriate education. Are the programs play- and child-centered or academics-centered?

Poverty and Learning

Early Childhood Care and Education Around the World

Component	Appropriate practice	Inappropriate practice
Curriculum goals	Experiences are provided in all developmental areas—physical, cognitive, social, and emotional.	Experiences are narrowly focused on cognitive development without recognition that all areas of the child's development are interrelated.
	Individual differences are expected, accepted, and used to design appropriate activities.	Children are evaluated only against group norms, and all are expected to perform the same tasks and achieve the same narrowly defined skills.
	Interactions and activities are designed to develop children's self-esteem and positive feelings toward learning.	Children's worth is measured by how well they conform to rigid expectations and perform on standardized tests.
Teaching strategies	Teachers prepare the environment for children to learn through active exploration and interaction with adults, other children, and materials.	Teachers use highly structured, teacher-directed lessons almost exclusively.
	Children select many of their own activities from among a variety the teacher prepares.	The teacher directs all activity deciding what children will do and when.
	Children are expected to be mentally and physically active.	Children are expected to sit down, be quiet, and listen or do paper-and-pencil tasks for long periods of time. A major portion of time is spent passively sitting, watching, and listening.
Guidance of socioemotional development	Teachers enhance children's self-control by using positive guidance techniques, such as modeling and encouraging expected behavior, redirecting children to a more acceptable activity, and setting clear limits.	Teachers spend considerable time enforcing rules, punishing unacceptable behavior, demeaning children who misbehave, making children sit and be quiet, and refereeing disagreements.
	Children are provided many opportunities to develop social skills, such as cooperating, helping, negotiating, and talking with the person involved to solve interpersonal problems.	Children work individually at desks and tables most of the time and listen to the teacher's directions to the total group.

Figure 10.10 NAEYC Recommendations for Developmentally

Component	Appropriate practice	Inappropriate practice
Language development, literacy, and cognitive development	Children are provided many opportunities to see how reading and writing are useful before they are instructed in letter names, sounds, and word identification. Basic skills develop when they are meaningful to children. An abundance of these activities is provided to develop language and literacy: listening to and reading stories and poems; taking field trips; dictating stories; participating in dramatic play; talking informally with other children and adults; and experimenting with writing.	Reading and writing instruction stresses isolated skill development, such as recognizing single letters, reading the alphabet, singing the alphabet song, coloring within predefined lines, and being instructed in correct formation of letters on a printed line.
	Children develop an understanding of concepts about themselves, others, and the world around them through observation, interaction with people and real objects, and the seeking of solutions to concrete problems. Learning about math, science, social studies, health, and other content areas is integrated through meaningful activities.	Instruction stresses isolated skill development through memorization. Children's cognitive development is seen as fragmented in content areas, such as math or science, and times are set aside for each of these.
Physical development	Children have daily opportunities to use large muscles, including running, jumping, and balancing. Outdoor activity is planned daily so children can freely express themselves.	Opportunity for large muscle activity is limited. Outdoor time is limited because it is viewed as interfering with instructional time, rather than as an integral part of the children's learning environment.
	Children have daily opportunities to develop small muscle skills through play activities, such as puzzles, painting, and cutting.	Small motor activity is limited to writing with pencils, coloring predrawn forms, and engaging in similar structured lessons.
Aesthetic development and motivation	Children have daily opportunities for aesthetic expression and appreciation through art and music. A variety of art media are available.	Art and music are given limited attention. Art consists of coloring predrawn forms or following adult-prescribed directions.
	Children's natural curiosity and desire to make sense of their world are used to motivate them to become involved in learning.	Children are required to participate in all activities to obtain the teacher's approval; to obtain extrinsic rewards, such as stickers or privileges; or to avoid punishment.

Appropriate and Inappropriate Education

Caring for Children

Parents and Schools as Partners in the Young Child's Education

Mothers and fathers play important roles in the development of young children's positive attitudes toward learning and education (Cowan, Heming, & Shuck, 1993). In one study, mothers and their preschool children were evaluated, and then the children's academic competence was assessed when they were in sixth grade (Hess & others, 1984). Maternal behavior in the preschool years was related to the children's academic competence in sixth grade. The best predictors of academic competence in sixth grade were the following maternal behaviors shown during the preschool years: effective communication with the child, a warm relationship with the child, positive expectations for achievement, use of rule-based rather than authority-based discipline, and not believing that success in school was based on luck.

The father's involvement with the child can also help build positive attitudes toward school and learning. Competent fathers of preschool children set aside regular time to be with the child, listen to the child and respond to questions, become involved in the child's play, and show an interest in the child's preschool and kindergarten activities. Fathers can help with the young child's schooling in the following ways:

- Supporting their children's efforts in school and their children's unique characteristics
- Helping children with their problems when the children seek advice
- Communicating regularly with teachers
- Participating in school functions

The relationship between the school and the parents of young children is an important aspect of preschool and kindergarten education (Stipek, Rosenblatt, & DiRocco, 1994). Schools and parents can cooperate to provide young children with the best possible preschool and kindergarten experience, as well as a positive orientation toward learning. In one study, the most important factor contributing to the success of the preschool program was the positive involvement of the parents in their young children's learning and education (Lally, Mangione, & Honig, 1987).

An important question that most parents of young children ask is, How can I evaluate whether or not a preschool program is a good one? Ellen Galinsky and Judy David (1988) provided some helpful guidelines for parents faced with choosing a preschool program; the guidelines centered around the relationship between the teacher-caregiver and the child, activities, teacher-caregiver development, staffing/group size, the physical environment, and the relationship between parents and the teacher-caregiver. Some of their suggestions for selecting a good preschool follow:

- Ask the teacher to describe another child she has cared for and see whether the description is warm and enthusiastic or judgmental and punitive.
- Ask the teacher "what if" questions, such as "What would you do if my child were fussy?" or "What would you do if my child refused to cooperate?"
- Listen to the tone of the room—is it pleasant and filled with happy, busy voices?
- Ask yourself if there are enough adults to have time to talk to and care for each child.
- Ask yourself if you would like to spend time there.
- Observe whether the space is childproof.
- Ask the teacher to describe other parents he has worked with—are the descriptions positive or negative?
- Ask for names of other parents with children in the program and call them as references—ask them what are the best and the worst aspects of the preschool.

Early Childhood Education Resources

childhood education's influence (Clarke-Stewart & Fein, 1983), it was concluded that children who attend preschool or kindergarten

- Interact more with peers, both positively and negatively
- Are less cooperative with and responsive to adults than home-reared children
- Are more socially competent and mature, in that they are more confident, extraverted, assertive, self-sufficient, independent, verbally expressive, knowledgeable about the social world, comfortable in social and stressful circumstances, and better adjusted when they go to school (exhibiting more task persistence, leadership, and goal direction, for example)

- Are less socially competent, in that they are less polite, less compliant to teacher demands, louder, and more aggressive and bossy, especially if the school or family supports such behavior

In sum, early childhood education generally has a positive effect on children's development, since the behaviors just mentioned—while at times negative—seem to be in the direction of developmental maturity, in that they increase as the child ages through the preschool years. To further evaluate children's development in early childhood, see Adventures for the Mind. And, to read about parents and schools as partners in the young child's education, see Caring for Children.

Nonsexist Early Childhood Education   Three important goals of nonsexist early childhood education are these: to free children from constraining stereotypes of gender roles, so that no aspect of their development will be closed off because of the children's sex; to promote equality for both sexes by facilitating each child's participation in activities necessary for optimal cognitive and socioemotional development; and to help children develop skills that will enable them to challenge sexist stereotypes and behaviors.

Young children's awareness of equitable gender roles can be expanded by having them participate in a number of activities, such as these (Derman-Sparks & the ABC Task Force, 1989):

- Read books about girls and boys that contradict gender stereotypes. Examples of such books are *William's Doll* (Zolotow, 1972), *Stephanie and the Coyote* (Crowder, 1969), and *Everybody Knows That* (Pearson, 1978).
- Get children to find and cut out magazine pictures of girls and boys, women and men, with a diversity of looks, dress, activities, and emotions.
- Create a display of photographs and pictures of women and men performing the same kind of tasks in the home and in the world of work. The display can be used to talk with children about the tasks that family members do and what kinds of tasks the children will do when they grow up.
- Be a nonsexist role model as a teacher, helping children learn new skills, and share tasks in a nonsexist manner.
- Invite members of children's families (including extended-family relatives) who have nontraditional jobs (such as a male flight attendant, nurse, or secretary; a female construction worker, engineer, or doctor) to come and talk with the class about their work.
- Support children's dramatic play that involves nontraditional gender roles.
- Tell stories about nonstereotyped dolls that support nontraditional behaviors and describe the conflicts they sometimes have when acting in ways that challenge stereotypical gender roles.

Does Preschool Matter?

According to child developmentalist David Elkind (1988), parents who are exceptionally competent and dedicated and who have both the time and the energy can provide the basic ingredients of early childhood education in their home. If parents have the competence and resources to provide young children with a variety of learning experiences and exposure to other children and adults (possibly through neighborhood play groups), along with opportunities for extensive play, then home schooling may sufficiently educate young children. However, if parents do not have the commitment, the time, the energy, and the resources to provide young children with an environment that approximates a good early childhood program, then it *does* matter whether a child attends preschool. In this case, the issue is not whether preschool is important but whether home schooling can closely duplicate what a competent preschool program can offer.

We should always keep in mind the unfortunate idea of early childhood education as an early start to ensure that the participants will finish early or on top

In most Japanese preschools, surprisingly little emphasis is put on academic instruction. In one study, 300 Japanese and 210 American preschool teachers, child development specialists, and parents were asked about various aspects of early childhood education (Tobin, Wu, & Davidson, 1989). Only 2 percent of the Japanese respondents listed "to give children a good start academically" as one of their top three reasons for a society to have preschools. In contrast, over half the American respondents chose this as one of their top three choices. To prepare children for successful careers in first grade and beyond, Japanese schools do not teach reading, writing, and mathematics but, rather, such skills as persistence, concentration, and the ability to function as a member of a group. The vast majority of young Japanese children are taught to read at home by their parents.

in an educational race. Elkind (1988) points out that perhaps the choice of the phrase *head start* for the education of disadvantaged children was a mistake. "Head Start program" does not imply a race. Not surprisingly, when middle socioeconomic status parents heard that low-income children were getting a "head start," they wanted a head start for their own young children. In some instances, starting children in formal academic training too early can produce more harm than good. In Denmark, where reading instruction follows a language experience approach and formal instruction is delayed until the age of 7, illiteracy is virtually nonexistent. By contrast, in France, where state-mandated formal instruction in reading begins at age 5, 30 percent of the children have reading problems. Education should not be stressful for young children. Early childhood education should not be solely an academic prep school.

Preschool is rapidly becoming a norm in early childhood education. Twenty-three states already have legislation pending to provide schooling for 4-year-old children, and there are already many private preschool programs. The increase in public preschools underscores the growing belief that early childhood education should be a legitimate component of public education. There are dangers, though. According to Elkind (1988), early childhood education is often not well understood at higher levels of education. The danger is that public preschool education for 4-year-old children will become little more than a downward extension of traditional elementary education. This is already occurring in preschool programs in which testing, workbooks, and group drills are imposed on 4- and 5-year-old children.

Elkind believes that early childhood education should become a part of public education, but on its own terms. Early childhood should have its own curriculum, its own methods of evaluation and classroom management, and its own teacher-training programs. Although there may be some overlap with the curriculum, evaluation, classroom management, and teacher training at the upper levels of schooling, they certainly should not be identical.

Researchers are already beginning to document some of the stress that increased academic pressure can bring to young children. In one study, Diane Burts and her colleagues (1989) compared the frequencies of stress-related behaviors observed in young children in classrooms with developmentally appropriate instructional practices with those of children in classrooms with developmentally inappropriate instructional practices. They found that the children in the developmentally inappropriate classrooms exhibited more stress-related behaviors than the children in the developmentally appropriate classrooms. In another study, children in a highly academically oriented early childhood education program were compared with children in a low academically oriented early childhood education program (Hirsch-Pasek & others, 1989). No benefits appeared for children in the highly academically oriented early childhood education program, but some possible harmful effects were noted. Higher test anxiety, less creativity, and a less positive attitude toward school characterized more of the children who attended the highly academic program than who attended the low academic program.

Improving Developmental Skills
Nourishing the Young Child's Cognitive Development

What are some good strategies for helping young children develop their cognitive competencies?

- *Provide opportunities for the young child's development of symbolic thought.* Give the child ample opportunities to scribble and draw. Provide the child opportunities to engage in make-believe play. Don't criticize the young child's art and play. Let the child's imagination flourish.
- *Encourage exploration.* Let the child select many of the activities he or she wants to explore. Don't have the child do rigid paper-and-pencil exercises that involve rote learning. The young child should not be spending lots of time passively sitting, watching, and listening.
- *Be an active language partner with the young child.* Encourage the young child to speak in entire sentences instead of using single words. Be a good listener. Ask the child lots of questions. Don't spend time correcting the child's grammar; simply model correct grammar yourself when you talk with the child. Don't correct the young child's writing. Spend time selecting age-appropriate books for the young child. Read books with the young child.
- *Become sensitive to the child's zone of proximal development.* Monitor the child's level of cognitive functioning. Know what tasks the child can competently perform alone and those that are too difficult, even with your help. Guide and assist the child in the proper performance of skills and use of tools in the child's zone of proximal development. Warmly support the young child's practice of these skills.
- *Evaluate the quality of the child's early childhood education program.* Make sure the early childhood program the child attends involves developmentally appropriate education. The program should be age-appropriate and individual-appropriate for the child. It should not be a high-intensity, academic-at-all-costs program. Don't pressure the child to achieve at this age.

School Readiness

Educational reform has prompted considerable concern about children's readiness to enter kindergarten and first grade. The issue gained national attention when the president and the nation's governors adopted school readiness as a national educational goal, vowing that by the year 2000 all children will start school ready to learn. The concept of school readiness is based on the assumption that all children need to possess a predetermined set of capabilities before they enter school. Thus, any discussions of school readiness should consider three important factors:

- The diversity and inequity of children's early life experiences
- The wide range of variation in young children's development and learning
- The degree to which school expectations for children entering kindergarten are reasonable, appropriate, and supportive of individual differences in children

The National Association for the Education of Young Children (1990) stresses that government officials and educators who promote universal school readiness should commit to the following:

- Addressing the inequities in early life experiences, so that all children have access to the opportunities that promote success in school
- Recognizing and supporting individual differences in children
- Establishing reasonable and appropriate expectations for children's capabilities on school entry

The National Association for the Education of Young Children believes that every child, except in the most severe instances of abuse, neglect, or disability, enters school ready to learn. However, not all children succeed in school. Inadequate health care and economic difficulties place many children at risk for academic failure before they enter school. Families who lack emotional resources and support also are not always capable of preparing their children to meet school expectations. Therefore, according to the NAEYC, it is important to provide families with access to the services and support necessary to prepare children to succeed in school. Such services include basic health care, economic support, basic nutrition, adequate housing, family support services, and high-quality early childhood education programs.

Expectations for young children's skills and abilities need to be based on knowledge of child development and the ways in which children learn. A basic principle of child development is that *there is tremendous normal variability both among children of the same chronological age and within an individual child.* Children's social skills, physical skills, cognitive skills, and emotional adjustment are equally important areas of development, and each contributes to how well children do in school. Within any group of children, one child may possess advanced language and cognitive skills but show poor social skills and emotional adjustment; another child may have advanced social skills, be well adjusted emotionally, and have good physical skills but have poor language skills. Readiness expectations should not be based on a narrow checklist focusing on only one or two dimensions of development. Such a narrow focus—considering only language or cognitive skills, for example—ignores the complexity and multidimensionality of children's development.

Wide variability also occurs in the rate of children's development. The precise time at which children will achieve a certain level of development or acquire specific skills is difficult to predict. Learning and development often do not occur in rigid, uniform ways. Thus, raising the legal entry age for school or holding a child out of school for a year may not be wise but could be a misdirected effort that only imposes a rigid schedule on the child's development, despite the child's normal differences from other children.

On a number of occasions in this chapter, we have talked about ways to nourish the young child's cognitive development. The insert, Improving Developmental Skills, profiles these strategies. At this point, we have discussed a number of ideas about language development and early childhood education. An overview of these ideas is presented in summary table 10.2

Summary Table 10.2

Language Development and Early Childhood Education

Concept	Processes/ Related Ideas	Characteristics/Description
Language development	Elaboration of Brown's stages	Roger Brown's five stages represent a helpful model for describing young children's language development. They involve mean length of utterance, age ranges, characteristics of language, and sentence variations.
	Rule systems	Rule systems involve changes in phonology, morphology, syntax, semantics, and pragmatics during the early childhood years.
	Literacy and early childhood	There has been increased interest in teaching young children reading and writing skills. Unfortunately, this has led to some dangers, with too many preschool children subjected to rigid, intense programs too advanced for their development. Young children need to develop positive feelings about their reading and writing skills through a supportive environment. Children should be active participants and be immersed in a wide range of interesting and enjoyable listening, talking, writing, and reading experiences.
Early childhood education	Variations	Child-centered kindergarten involves education of the whole child, with emphasis on individual variation, the process of learning, and the importance of play in development. The Montessori approach is another well-known early childhood education strategy. Developmentally appropriate practice is based on knowledge of the typical development of children within an age span (age appropriateness), as well as the uniqueness of the child (individual appropriateness). Developmentally appropriate practice contrasts with developmentally inappropriate practice, which ignores the concrete, hands-on approach to learning. Direct teaching largely through abstract paper-and-pencil activities presented to large groups of young children is believed to be developmentally inappropriate. The National Association for the Education of Young Children has been a strong proponent of developmentally appropriate practice and has developed extensive recommendations for its implementation. Compensatory education has tried to break through the poverty cycle with such programs as Head Start and Follow Through. Long-term studies reveal that model preschool programs have positive effects on development. The overall effects of early childhood education seem to be positive. However, outcome measures reveal areas in which social competence is more positive, others in which it is less positive. An important goal is to free children from constraining stereotypes of gender roles, so that no aspect of their development will be closed off because of their sex.
	Does preschool matter?	Parents can effectively educate their young children, just as schools can. However, many parents do not have the commitment, time, energy, and resources needed to provide young children with an environment that can compare with a competent early childhood education program. Too often, parents see education as a race, and preschool as a chance to get ahead in the race. However, education is not a race, and it should not be stressful for young children. Public preschools are appearing in many states. A concern is that they should not become merely simple versions of elementary school. Early childhood education has some issues that overlap with upper levels of schooling, but in many ways the agenda of early childhood is different.
	School readiness	Educational reform has prompted considerable concern about children's readiness to enter kindergarten and first grade. The National Association for the Education of Young Children believes that the proposed guidelines for school readiness often do not adequately take into account the diversity and inequity of children's early life experiences and the opportunities needed to succeed in school, they do not recognize and support individual differences in children, and they do not establish reasonable and appropriate expectations of children's capabilities on school entry.

Chapter Review

Young children make significant advances in cognitive development during early childhood. Their imagination soars and their mental grasp of the world improves.

We began this chapter by describing the excellent early childhood education program Reggio Emilia. Our coverage of cognitive developmental changes focused on Piaget's preoperational thought stage, Vygotsky's theory of development, information processing, and the young child's theory of mind. Then we turned our attention to changes in language development. We also studied numerous aspects of early childhood education, including variations in early childhood education, whether preschool matters, and school readiness.

Don't forget that you can obtain an overall summary of the chapter by again studying the two summary tables on pages 268 and 283. In the next chapter, we will continue our exploration of early childhood, focusing on socioemotional development.

✓ Children Checklist

Cognitive Development in Early Childhood

How much have you learned since the beginning of the chapter? Use the following statements to help you review your knowledge and understanding of the chapter material. First, read the statement and mentally or briefly demonstrate on paper that you can discuss the relevant information.

_____ I can describe Piaget's preoperational stage of development.
_____ I can discuss Vygotsky's theory.
_____ I can compare Piaget's and Vygotsky's theories.
_____ I know about young children's information processing.
_____ I am aware of the young child's theory of mind.
_____ I can describe changes in language development in early childhood, including ideas about literacy.
_____ I can discuss variations in early childhood education.
_____ I can describe developmentally appropriate and inappropriate education.
_____ I know about education for children who are disadvantaged.
_____ I can discuss the effects of early childhood education.
_____ I know about whether preschool matters.
_____ I can describe school readiness.

For any items that you did not check, go back and locate the relevant material in the chapter. Review the material until you feel you can check off the item. You may want to use this checklist later in preparing for an exam.

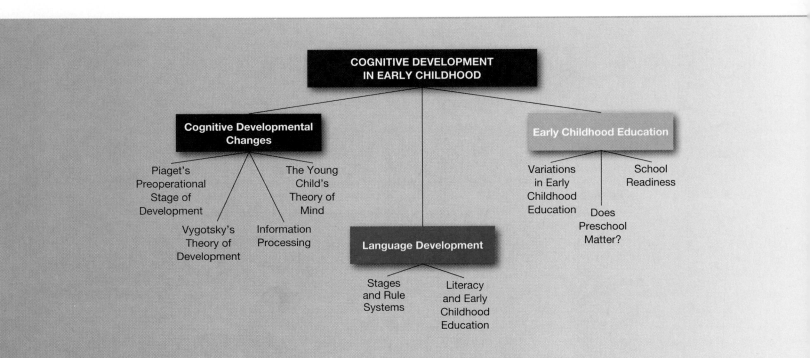

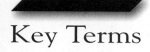

Key Terms

operations 254
symbolic function substage 255
egocentrism 255
animism 256
intuitive thought substage 257
centration 257
conservation 258
zone of proximal development (ZPD) 261
scaffolding 261

social constructivist approach 262
short-term memory 265
child-centered kindergarten 272
Montessori approach 273
developmentally appropriate practice 273
Project Head Start 274
Project Follow Through 274

Children Resources

National Association for the Education of Young Children (NAEYC)
1834 Connecticut Avenue NW
Washington, DC 20009
202–232–8777
800–424–2460

This large organization is an important advocacy group for young children and has developed guidelines for a number of dimensions of early childhood education. It publishes the excellent journal *Young Children*.

Raising Kids Who Want to Learn
Sesame Street
P.O. Box 40
Vernon, NH 07462

This 220-page book gives parents practical strategies for encouraging their children to learn without pushing them.

Reaching Potentials
Vols. 1 & 2
(1992, 1996)
edited by Sue Bredekamp and Teresa Rosegrant.
Washington, DC: National Association for the Education of Young Children.

Volume 1 addresses how to help young children reach their full potential—not only academically but also as healthy, sensitive, caring, and contributing members of society. Volume 2 focuses on recently developed national standards in various fields. Respected experts evaluate what early childhood educators need to know to develop meaningful, developmentally appropriate curriculum in such areas as science, math, health, visual arts, physical education, language, and literacy.

Taking It to the Net

http://www.mhhe.com/santrockcd6

1. Mr. Fosnelle recently read, and is interested in, an article that described the Reggio Emilia approach to education, but he is confused on how to begin using such a program. What would be your advice for how to begin to implement such an approach?
2. The theories of Piaget and Vygotsky are often discussed as the anithesis of each other. Yet you have been asked to explain the similarities between the developmental theories of Piaget and Vygotsky to a group of parents. What are the similarities? How might you address this issue?
3. You are talking to a woman that operates a local church's nursery. She says "I don't want to teach the five-year-olds, the kids at that age don't really know anything and really aren't ready to learn much." Is she correct? What is your response?

Chapter

11

Chapter Outline

Socioemotional Development in Early Childhood

PREVIEW

As they develop physically and cognitively, young children's socioemotional development also changes dramatically. Not only do young children need to adapt to changes in social contexts, but their caregivers must adapt to their many socioemotional changes. Among the questions that we will explore in this chapter are:

- What is the nature of the development of the young child's self?
- How do young children change emotionally?
- How does young children's moral development change?
- What influences a child's gender?
- Is there a best way to parent?
- How do siblings influence a child's development?
- What roles do peers play in the child's development?
- What is the function of play?
- How pervasive is television's influence on children's development?

The Story of Sara and Her Developing Sense of Morality and Values

Like many children, Sara Newland loves animals. When she was just 4 years old, she turned that love into social activism. During a trip to the zoo, she learned about the plight of an endangered species and became motivated to help. With her mother's assistance, Sara baked cakes and cookies and sold them on the sidewalk near her apartment building in New York City. She was elated when she raised $35, which she promptly mailed to the World Wildlife Fund. A few weeks later, her smiles turned into tears when the fund wrote Sara asking for more money. Sara was devastated because she thought she had taken care of the animal problem. Her mother told Sara that the endangered species problem and many others are so big that they require continual help from lots of people. That explanation apparently worked because Sara, now 9 years old, helps out at an inner-city child care center and regularly takes meals to homeless people in her neighborhood (Kantrowitz, 1991). Sara tells her friends not to be scared of homeless people. She says that some people wonder why she gives to them, then says, "If everyone gave food to them, they would all have decent meals."

Sensitive parents can make a difference in encouraging young children's sense of morality and values. Some experts on moral development believe that a capacity for goodness is present from the start, which reflects the "innate goodness" view of the child, which we discussed in chapter 1. But many developmentalists also believe that parents must nurture that goodness, just as they help their children become good readers, musicians, or athletes.

EMOTIONAL AND PERSONALITY DEVELOPMENT

In the story that opened the chapter, Sara displayed a positive sense of morality through her motivation to help an endangered species and the homeless. Let's further explore young children's moral development and other aspects of their emotional and personality development, beginning with the self.

The Self

We learned in chapter 7 that toward the end of the second year of life children develop a sense of self. During early childhood, some important developments in the self take place. Among these developments are facing the issue of initiative versus guilt and enhancing self-understanding.

Initiative Versus Guilt

According to Erikson (1968), the psychosocial stage that characterizes early childhood is *initiative versus guilt*. By now, children have become convinced that they are a person of their own; during early childhood, they must discover what kind of person they will become. They intensely identify with their parents, who most of the time appear to them to be powerful and beautiful, although often unreasonable, disagreeable, and sometimes even dangerous. During early childhood, children use their perceptual, motor, cognitive, and language skills to make things happen. They have a surplus of energy that permits them to forget failures quickly and to approach new areas that seem desirable—even if they seem dangerous—with undiminished zest and some increased sense of direction. On their own *initiative*, then, children at this stage exuberantly move out into a wider social world.

The great governor of initiative is *conscience*. Children now not only feel afraid of being found out, but they also begin to hear the inner voice of self-observation, self-guidance, and self-punishment (Bybee, 1999). Their initiative and enthusiasm may bring them not only rewards but also punishments. Widespread disappointment at this stage leads to an unleashing of guilt that lowers the child's self-esteem.

Whether children leave this stage with a sense of initiative that outweighs their sense of guilt depends in large part on how parents respond to their children's self-initiated activities. Children who are given the freedom and opportunity to initiate motor play, such as running, bike riding, sledding, skating, tussling, and wrestling, have their sense of initiative supported. Initiative is also supported when parents answer their children's questions and do not deride or inhibit fantasy or play activity. In contrast, if children are made to feel that their motor activity is bad, that their questions are a nuisance, and that their play is silly and stupid, then they often develop a sense of guilt over self-initiated activities that may persist through life's later stages (Elkind, 1970).

Self-Understanding

Self-understanding *is the child's cognitive representation of self, the substance and content of the child's self-conceptions.* For example, a 5-year-old girl understands that she is a girl, has blond hair, likes to ride her bicycle, has a friend, and is a swimmer. An 11-year-old boy understands that he is a student, a boy, a football player, a family member, a video-game lover, and a rock music fan. A child's self-understanding is based on the various roles and membership categories that define who children are. Though not the whole of personal identity, self-understanding provides its rational underpinnings (Damon & Hart, 1992).

The rudimentary beginning of self-understanding begins with self-recognition, which takes place by approximately 18 months of age. Since children can verbally communicate their ideas, research on self-understanding in childhood is not limited to visual self-recognition, as it was during infancy. Mainly by interviewing children, researchers have probed children's conceptions of many aspects of self-understanding. These include mind and body, self in relation to others, and pride and shame in self. In early childhood, children usually conceive of the self in physical terms. Most young children think the self is part of their body, usually their head. Young children

self-understanding
The child's cognitive representation of self, the substance and content of the child's self-conceptions.

usually confuse self, mind, and body. Because the self is a body part for them, they describe it along many material dimensions, such as size, shape, and color. Young children distinguish themselves from others through many different physical and material attributes. Says 4-year-old Sandra, "I'm different from Jennifer because I have brown hair and she has blond hair." Says 4-year-old Ralph, "I am different from Hank because I am taller, and I am different from my sister because I have a bicycle."

Researchers also believe that the *active dimension* is a central component of the self in early childhood (Keller, Ford, & Meacham, 1978). If we define the category *physical* broadly enough, we can include physical actions as well as body image and material possessions. For example, preschool children often describe themselves in terms of such activities as play. In sum, in early childhood, children frequently think of themselves in terms of a physical self or an active self.

Emotional Development

Children, like adults, experience many emotions during the course of a day. At times, children also try to make sense of other people's emotional reactions and feelings.

Developmental Timetable of Young Children's Emotion Language and Understanding

Among the most important changes in emotional development in early childhood are the increased use of emotion language and the understanding of emotion (Kuebli, 1994). Preschoolers become more adept at talking about their own and others' emotions. Between 2 and 3 years of age, children considerably increase the number of terms they use to describe emotion (Ridgeway, Waters, & Kuczaj, 1985). However, in the preschool years, children are learning more than just the "vocabulary" of emotion terms, they also are learning about the causes and consequences of feelings (Denham, 1999).

At 4–5 years of age, children show an increased ability to reflect on emotions. In this developmental time frame, they also begin to understand that the same event can elicit different feelings in different people. Moreover, they show a growing awareness about controlling and managing emotions to meet social standards (Bruce, Olen & Jensen, 1999). A summary of the characteristics of young children's emotion language and understanding is shown in figure 11.1.

Approximate age of child	Description
2–3 years	Increase emotion vocabulary most rapidly
	Correctly label simple emotions in self and others and talk about past, present, and future emotions
	Talk about the causes and consequences of some emotions and identify emotions associated with certain situations
	Use emotion language in pretend play
4–5 years	Show increased capacity to reflect verbally on emotions and to consider more complex relations between emotions and situations
	Understand that the same event may call forth different feelings in different people and that feelings sometimes persist long after the events that caused them
	Demonstrate growing awareness about controlling and managing emotions in accord with social standards

Figure 11.1
Some Characteristics of Young Children's Emotion Language and Understanding

Helping Children Understand Emotions Parents, teachers, and other adults can help children understand emotions. They can talk with children to help them cope with their feelings of distress, sadness, anger, or guilt. By being sensitive to children's emotional feelings and needs, adults can help children control their emotions and understand them. Learning to express some feelings and mask others are common, everyday lessons in children's lives. This has been called learning how to do "emotion work" (Hochschild, 1983).

Getting along with others often means handling emotions in a socially acceptable way. Children who get angry because they have to wait their turn or who laugh at a crying child who has fallen and skinned his knee can be encouraged to consider other children's feelings. Children who boast about winning something can be reminded how sad it feels to lose.

One way to help children understand their emotions is to get them to talk about their and others' emotions. Janet Kuebli (1994) described some strategies teachers can adopt to get children to do this:

- *Make sure the emotional climate of the classroom encourages emotional expression.* Caregivers need to make children feel comfortable in talking about their emotions and be motivated to help them understand what they are experiencing.
- *Structure the physical environment to help children learn about feelings.* Play centers vary in the opportunities they provide in experiencing and understanding emotion. Family-living and dramatic-play sections may encourage children to act out social interactions in which emotions are prominent. Teachers can observe children playing out emotion scripts and then introduce themes or ask

Children experience many emotions every day. An important aspect of child development is for children to understand and control their feelings. What are some strategies that adults can adopt to encourage children to talk about their emotions?

questions that stimulate children to explore the causes and consequences of emotions. Puppets and dolls also are good vehicles for emotion play.

- *The arts center is an excellent context for emotion conversation.* Teachers can encourage children to create pictures that tell about personal events in their lives. For example, children can be asked to draw about the time when they were upset with another child, afraid of something new, or happy they had done something good. Teachers can ask children about their drawings, giving them an opportunity to reflect on their emotions.
- *Stories and books with emotion themes can be used.* Teachers can select books for children that show other children being emotional and dealing with their feelings. Several examples include *The Grouchy Ladybug* (Carle, 1977), *I Feel Orange Today* (Godwin, 1993), *Even If I Did Something Awful* (Hazen, 1991), *I Was So Mad* and *That Bothered Kate* (Noll, 1991). Children and teachers can discuss the causes and consequences of story characters' emotions and then connect them with children's own experiences. Other media, such as TV, movies, plays, and children's magazines, provide similar options.
- *Deal with children's quarrels and disputes.* Fighting children learn more about anger if teachers do more than merely separate them. Teachers can ask each child to tell what happened and then to examine their personal contributions to the conflict. The children can be asked how the events made them feel and how they will respond differently the next time.

Moral Development

Increasingly, theorists and researchers are conceptualizing and studying moral development in terms of its emotional underpinnings. As we will see next, emotion (or feeling) is believed to be one of moral development's three main components.

What Is Moral Development?
Moral development concerns rules and conventions about what people should do in their interactions with other people. In studying these rules, developmentalists examine three domains. First, how do children *reason* or *think* about rules for ethical conduct? For example, consider cheating. The child can be presented with a story in which someone has a conflict about whether or not to cheat in a particular situation, such as taking a test in school. The child is asked to decide what is appropriate for the character to do and why. The focus is on the *reasoning* children use to justify their moral decisions.

moral development

Development regarding rules and conventions about what people should do in their interactions with other people.

Second, how do children actually *behave* in moral circumstances? In our example of cheating, the emphasis is on observing the child's cheating and the environmental circumstances that produced and maintained the cheating. Children might be shown some toys and then be asked to select the one they believe is the most attractive. The experimenter then tells the young children that that particular toy belongs to someone else and is not to be played with. Observations of different conditions under which the children deviate from the prohibition or resist temptation are then conducted.

Third, how do children *feel* about moral matters? In the example of cheating, do the children feel enough guilt to resist temptation? If children do cheat, do feelings of guilt after the transgression keep them from cheating the next time they face temptation? In the remainder of this section, we will focus on these three facets of moral development: thought, action, and feeling. Then we will evaluate the positive side of children's moral development: altruism.

Piaget's View of How Children's Moral Reasoning Develops
Interest in how the child thinks about moral issues was stimulated by Piaget (1932). He extensively observed and interviewed children from the age of 4 to 12. He watched them play marbles, seeking to learn how they used and thought about the game's rules. He also asked children questions about ethical rules—theft, lies,

Childhood innocence

heteronomous morality

The first stage of moral development, in Piaget's
theory, occurring from approximately 4 to 7 years
of age. Justice and rules are conceived of as
unchangeable properties of the world, removed
from the control of people.

autonomous morality

The second stage of moral development in
Piaget's theory, displayed by older children (about
10 years of age and older). The child becomes
aware that rules and laws are created by people
and that, in judging an action, one should
consider the actor's intentions as well as the
consequences.

imminent justice

The concept that, if a rule is broken, punishment
will be meted out immediately.

*W̶hat is moral is what you feel good after
and what is immoral is what you feel bad
after.*

Ernest Hemingway
American Author, 20th Century

punishment, and justice, for example. Piaget concluded that children think
in two distinctly different ways about morality, depending on their developmental maturity. **Heteronomous morality** *is the first stage of moral development, in Piaget's theory, occurring from approximately 4 to 7 years of age.
Justice and rules are conceived of as unchangeable properties of the world,
removed from the control of people.* **Autonomous morality** *is the second stage
of moral development, in Piaget's theory, displayed by older children (about 10
years of age and older). The child becomes aware that rules and laws are created by people and that, in judging an action, one should consider the actor's
intentions as well as the consequences.* Children 7 to 10 years of age are in a
transition between the two stages, showing some features of both.

Let's consider Piaget's two stages of moral development further. The
heteronomous thinker judges the rightness or goodness of behavior by
considering the consequences of the behavior, not the intentions of the
actor. For example, the heteronomous thinker says that breaking 12 cups
accidentally is worse than breaking 1 cup intentionally while trying to
steal a cookie. For the moral autonomist, the reverse is true. The actor's
intentions assume paramount importance. The heteronomous thinker
also believes that rules are unchangeable and are handed down by all-
powerful authorities. When Piaget suggested that new rules be introduced
into the game of marbles, the young children resisted. They insisted that
the rules had always been the same and could not be altered. By contrast,
older children—who were moral autonomists—accepted change and recognized that rules are merely convenient, socially agreed-upon conventions, subject to change by consensus.

The heteronomous thinker also believes in **imminent justice,** *the concept that, if a rule is broken, punishment will be meted out immediately.* The
young child believes that the violation is connected in some automatic way to the
punishment. Thus, young children often look around worriedly after committing a
transgression, expecting inevitable punishment. Older children, the moral autonomists, recognize that punishment is socially mediated and occurs only if a relevant
person witnesses the wrongdoing and that, even then, punishment is not inevitable.

Piaget argued that, as children develop, they become more sophisticated in thinking about social matters, especially about the possibilities and conditions of cooperation. Piaget believed that this social understanding comes about through the
mutual give-and-take of peer relations. In the peer group, where all members have
similar power and status, plans are negotiated and coordinated, and disagreements
are reasoned about and eventually settled. Parent-child relations, in which parents
have the power and the child does not, are less likely to advance moral reasoning,
because rules are often handed down in an authoritarian way.

Moral Behavior   The study of moral behavior has been influenced by social
learning theory. The processes of reinforcement, punishment, and imitation are used
to explain children's moral behavior. When children are rewarded for behavior that
is consistent with laws and social conventions, they are likely to repeat that behavior. When models who behave morally are provided, children are likely to adopt
their actions. And, when children are punished for immoral behavior, those behaviors are likely to be reduced or eliminated. However, because punishment may have
adverse side effects, it needs to be used judiciously and cautiously.

Another important point needs to be made about the social learning view of
moral development. Moral behavior is influenced extensively by the situation. What
children do in one situation is often only weakly related to what they do in other
situations. A child may cheat in math class but not in English class; a child may
steal a piece of candy when others are not present but not steal it when they are
present. More than half a century ago, morality's situational nature was observed in
a comprehensive study of thousands of children in many different situations—at

home, at school, and at church, for example. The totally honest child was virtually nonexistent; so was the child who cheated in all situations (Hartshorne & May, 1928–1930).

Social learning theorists also believe that the ability to resist temptation is closely tied to the development of self-control. Children must overcome their impulses toward something they want that is prohibited. To achieve this self-control, they must learn to be patient and to delay gratification. Today, social learning theorists believe that cognitive factors are important in the child's development of self-control. For example, in one study, children's cognitive transformations of desired objects helped them become more patient (Mischel & Patterson, 1976). Preschool children were asked to do a boring task. Close by was an exciting mechanical clown who tried to persuade the children to come play with him. The children who had been trained to say to themselves, "I'm not going to look at Mr. Clown when Mr. Clown says to look at him" controlled their behavior and continued working on the dull task much longer than those who did not instruct themselves.

Moral Feelings In chapter 2, we discussed Sigmund Freud's psychoanalytic theory. It describes the *superego* as one of the three main structures of personality—the id and ego being the other two. In Freud's classical psychoanalytic theory, the child's superego—the moral branch of personality—develops as the child resolves the Oedipus conflict and identifies with the same-sex parent in the early childhood years. Among the reasons children resolve the Oedipus conflict is the fear of losing their parents' love and of being punished for their unacceptable sexual wishes toward the opposite-sex parent. To reduce anxiety, avoid punishment, and maintain parental affection, children form a superego by identifying with the same-sex parent. Through their identification with the same-sex parent, children internalize the parents' standards of right and wrong that reflect societal prohibitions. And the child turns inward the hostility that was previously aimed externally at the same-sex parent. This inwardly directed hostility is now felt self-punitively as guilt, which is experienced unconsciously (beyond the child's awareness). In the psychoanalytic account of moral development, the self-punitiveness of guilt is responsible for keeping the child from committing transgressions. That is, children conform to societal standards to avoid guilt.

Positive feelings, such as empathy, contribute to the child's moral development. **Empathy** *is reacting to another's feelings with an emotional response that is similar to the other's feelings.* Although empathy is experienced as an emotional state, it often has a cognitive component. The cognitive component is the ability to discern another's inner psychological states, or what is called "perspective taking." Young infants have the capacity for some purely

Through the Eyes of Children
Amos Bear Gets Hurt

Amos is a large, squishy, plush bear that resides in a kindergarten class. Each weekend, he travels home with a different child, returning on Monday morning to relate his "adventures." He often is the first object children head to when they are tired, ill, or upset.

The teacher noticed that the children recently had been using Amos as a punching bag, so she arrived early the next day and bandaged Amos' arm with surgical gauze. When the children arrived, they wanted to know what was wrong with Amos. The teacher replied that he must have gotten hurt last night.

The children's response in caring for Amos was intense. One child wanted to fetch drugs, another to make coffee; still another went to search for money to pay Amos' doctor bills. Amos was given shots, rebandaged, and given medicine. Once they were sure that Amos had survived this ordeal, the children's consensus was that he needed a rest and some food. This led Amanda to remark, "Could we give him a diet cola? I think he is a vegetarian."

Throughout the ordeal, the children treated Amos in a caring, tender way. He was cradled in someone's arms most of the time, was not allowed to bump into anything, and was passed from one child to the next with great delicacy.

Amos' situation stimulated the children's empathy (Read, 1995). The Amos Bear situation took place at the Helen Turner School in Hayward, California, where Laurie Read taught until her death in 1992.

Amos bear and his caregivers.

Source: *Young Children,* 1995, p. 50, Laurie Reed National Association for the Education of Young Children, Washington, D.C.

empathy
Reacting to another's feelings with an emotional response that is similar to the other's feelings.

Gender Resources

gender
The social dimension of being female or male.

gender identity
The sense of being male or female, which most children acquire by the time they are 3 years old.

gender role
A set of expectations that prescribes how females or males should think, act, and feel.

estrogens
A main class of sex hormones; they influence the development of female physical characteristics.

androgens
A main class of sex hormones; they promote the development of male physical characteristics.

empathic responses, but for effective moral action children need to learn how to identify a wide range of emotional states in others. They also need to learn to anticipate what kinds of action will improve another person's emotional state.

We have seen that classical psychoanalytic theory emphasizes the power of unconscious guilt in moral development. However, other theorists, such as Martin Hoffman and William Damon, emphasize the role of empathy. Today, many child developmentalists believe that both positive feelings, such as empathy, sympathy, admiration, and self-esteem, as well as negative feelings, such as anger, outrage, shame, and guilt, contribute to the child's moral development (Eisenberg & others, in press; Roberts & Strayer, 1996). When strongly experienced, these emotions influence children to act in accord with standards of right and wrong. Emotions such as empathy, shame, guilt, and anxiety over other people's violation of standards are present early in development and undergo developmental change throughout childhood and beyond (Damon & Hart, 1992). These emotions provide a natural base for the child's acquisition of moral values, both orienting children toward moral events and motivating children to pay close attention to such events. But moral emotions do not operate in a vacuum to build the child's moral awareness, and they are not sufficient in themselves to generate moral responsiveness. They do not give the "substance" of moral regulation—the actual rules, values, and standards of behavior that children need to understand and act on. Moral emotions are inextricably interwoven with the cognitive and social aspects of children's development.

Gender

So far in this chapter, we have studied the self, emotional development, and moral development. Another important dimension of young children's socioemotional development is gender.

What Is Gender?   While *sex* refers to the biological dimension of being male or female, **gender** *refers to the social dimension of being male or female.* Two aspects of gender bear special mention—gender identity and gender role. **Gender identity** *is the sense of being male or female, which most children acquire by the time they are 3 years old.* **Gender role** *is a set of expectations that prescribe how females or males should think, act, and feel.*

Biological Influences   It was not until the 1920s that researchers confirmed the existence of human sex chromosomes, the genetic material that determines our sex. In chapter 3, you learned that humans normally have 46 chromosomes arranged in pairs. The 23rd pair may have two X chromosomes to produce a female, or it may have an X and a Y chromosome to produce a male.

Just as chromosomes are important in understanding biological influences, so are hormones. The two main classes of sex hormones are estrogens and androgens. **Estrogens,** *such as estradiol, influence the development of female physical sex characteristics.* **Androgens,** *such as testosterone, promote the development of male physical sex characteristics.* In the first few weeks of gestation, female and male embryos look alike. Male sex organs start to differ from female sex organs when XY chromosomes in the male embryo trigger the secretion of androgens. Low levels of androgens in the female embryo allow the normal development of female sex organs.

Some biological approaches to gender address the differences between the brains of females and those of males (Eisenberg, Martin, & Fabes, 1996). One approach focuses on the corpus callosum, the massive band of fibers that connects the brain's two hemispheres. Other approaches emphasize variations in the left and right hemispheres of the brains of males and females. At present, these are controversial views. What we do know is that the brains of females and males are far more similar than they are different. We also know that the brain has considerable plasticity and that experiences can modify its growth.

In gender development, however, biology is not completely destiny. When gender attitudes and behavior are at issue, children's socialization experiences matter a great deal.

Social Influences   In our culture, adults discriminate between the sexes shortly after the infant's birth. The "pink and blue" treatment may be applied to boys and girls before they leave the hospital. Soon afterward, differences in hairstyles, clothes, and toys become obvious. Adults and peers reward these differences throughout development. And boys and girls learn gender roles through imitation, or observational learning, by watching what other people say and do. In recent years, the idea that parents are the critical socializing agents in gender-role development has come under fire. Parents are only one of many sources through which the individual learns gender roles (Beal, 1994). Culture, schools, peers, the media, and other family members are others, yet it is important to guard against swinging too far in this direction because—especially in the early years of development—parents are important influences on gender development.

Identification and Social Learning Theories   Two prominent theories address the way children acquire masculine and feminine attitudes and behaviors from their parents. **Identification theory** *stems from Freud's view that the preschool child develops a sexual attraction to the opposite-sex parent. At 5 or 6 years of age the child renounces this attraction because of anxious feelings. Subsequently, the child identifies with the same-sex parent, unconsciously adopting the same-sex parent's characteristics.* However, today many child developmentalists do not believe gender development proceeds on the basis of identification, at least not in terms of Freud's emphasis on childhood sexual attraction. Children become gender-typed much earlier than 5 or 6 years of age, and they become masculine or feminine even when the same-sex parent is not present in the family.

The **social learning theory of gender** *emphasizes that children's gender development occurs through observation and imitation of gender behavior, and through the rewards and punishments children experience for gender-appropriate and inappropriate behavior.* Unlike identification theory, social learning theory argues that sexual attraction to parents is not involved in gender development. (A comparison of the identification and social learning views is presented in figure 11.2.) Parents often use rewards and punishments to teach their daughters to be feminine ("Karen, you are being a good girl when you play gently with your doll") and their sons to be masculine ("Keith, a boy as big as you is not supposed to cry"). Peers also extensively reward and punish gender behavior. And, by observing adults and peers at home, at school, in the neighborhood, and on television, children are widely exposed to a myriad of models who display masculine and feminine behavior. Critics of the social learning view argue that gender development is not as passively acquired as it indicates. Later, we will discuss the cognitive views of gender development, which stress that children actively construct their gender world.

Parental Influences   Parents, by action and by example, influence their children's gender development. Both mothers and fathers are psychologically important in children's gender development. Mothers are more consistently given responsibility for nurturance and physical care. Fathers are more likely to engage in playful interaction and to be given responsibility for ensuring that boys and girls conform

Theory	Processes	Outcome
Freud's identification theory	Sexual attraction to opposite-sex parent at 3–5 years of age; anxiety about sexual attraction and subsequent identification with same-sex parent at 5–6 years of age	Gender behavior similar to that of same-sex parent
Social learning theory	Rewards and punishments of gender-appropriate and -inappropriate behavior by adults and peers; observation and imitation of models' masculine and feminine behavior	Gender behavior

Figure 11.2

A Comparison of the Identification and Social Learning Views of Gender Development

Parents influence their children's development by action and example.

identification theory

A theory deriving from Freud's view that the preschool child develops a sexual attraction to the opposite-sex parent, by approximately 5 or 6 years of age renounces this attraction because of anxious feelings, and subsequently identifies with the same-sex parent, unconsciously adopting the same-sex parent's characteristics.

social learning theory of gender

A theory that emphasizes that children's gender development occurs through the observation and imitation of gender behavior and through the rewards and punishments children experience for gender-appropriate and inappropriate behavior.

Children need models rather than critics.

Joseph Joubert
French Essayist, 19th Century

As reflected in this tug-of-war battle between boys and girls, the playground in elementary school is like going to "gender school." Elementary school children show a clear preference for being with and liking same-sex peers. Eleanor Maccoby (inset) has studied children's gender development for many years. She believes peers play a powerful role in the development of gender behavior.

Fathers and Sons

to existing cultural norms. And, whether or not they have more influence on them, fathers are more involved in socializing their sons than their daughters. Fathers seem to play an especially important part in gender-role development. They are more likely than mothers to act differently toward sons and daughters. Thus, they contribute more to distinctions between the genders (Huston, 1983).

Many parents encourage boys and girls to engage in different types of play and activities (Fagot, Leinbach, & O'Boyle, 1992). Girls are more likely to be given dolls to play with during childhood. When old enough, they are more likely to be assigned baby-sitting duties. Girls are encouraged to be more nurturant and emotional than boys. Fathers are more likely to engage in aggressive play with their sons than with their daughters. As adolescents increase in age, parents permit boys more freedom than girls. They allow them to be away from home and stay out later without supervision. When parents place severe restrictions on their adolescent sons, it has a negative effect on the sons' development (Baumrind, 1989).

Peer Influences Parents provide the earliest discrimination of gender roles in development. Before long, though, peers join the societal process of responding to and modeling masculine and feminine behavior. Children who play in sex-appropriate activities tend to be rewarded for doing so by their peers. Those who play in cross-sexed activities tend to be criticized by their peers or left to play alone. Children show a clear preference for being with and liking same-sex peers (Maccoby, 1993). This tendency usually becomes stronger during the middle and late childhood years. After extensive observations of elementary school playgrounds, two researchers characterized the play settings as "gender school." They said that boys teach one another the required masculine behavior and enforce it strictly (Luria & Herzog, 1985). Girls also pass on the female culture and congregate mainly with one another. Individual "tomboy" girls can join boys' activities without losing their status in the girls' groups; however, the reverse is not true for boys, reflecting our society's greater sex-typing pressure for boys.

Peer demands for conformity to gender roles become especially intense during adolescence. Although there is greater social mixing of males and females during early adolescence, in both formal groups and in dating, peer pressure is strong for the adolescent boy to be the very best male possible and for the adolescent girl to be the very best female possible.

School and Teacher Influences In certain ways, both girls and boys might receive an education that is not fair (Sadker & Sadker, 1994)—for example,

- Girls' learning problems are not identified as often as boys' are.
- Boys are given the lion's share of attention in schools.
- Girls start school testing higher in every academic subject than boys yet graduate from high school scoring lower on the SAT exam.
- Boys are most often at the top of their classes, but they also are most often at the bottom as well—more likely to fail a class, miss promotion, or drop out of school.
- Pressure to achieve is more likely to be heaped on boys than on girls.

Media Influences As we have described, children encounter masculine and feminine roles in their everyday interactions with parents, peers, and teachers. The messages carried by the media about what is appropriate or inappropriate for males and for females are important influences on gender development as well.

A special concern is the way females are pictured on television. In the 1970s, it became apparent that television was portraying females as less competent than males. For example, about 70 percent of the prime-time characters were males, men were more likely to be shown in the work force, women were more likely to be shown as homemakers and in romantic roles, men were more likely to appear in higher-status jobs and in a greater diversity of occupations, and men were presented as more aggressive and constructive (Sternglanz & Serbin, 1974).

In the 1980s and 1990s, television networks became more sensitive to how males and females were portrayed on television shows. Consequently, many programs now focus on divorced families, cohabitation, and women in high-status roles. Even with the onset of this type of programming, researchers continue to find that television portrays males as more competent than females (Durkin, 1985). In one investigation, young adolescent girls indicated that television occupations are more extensively stereotyped than real-life occupations (Wroblewski & Huston, 1987).

Gender stereotyping also appears in the print media. In magazine advertising, females are shown more often in advertisements for beauty products, cleaning products, and home appliances. Males are shown more often in advertisements for cars, liquor, and travel. As with television programs, females are now being portrayed as more competent in advertisements than in the past, but advertisers have not yet given them equal status with males.

Cognitive Influences Developmentalists also recognize the important role that cognitive factors play in gender.

Cognitive Developmental Theory In the **cognitive developmental theory of gender,** *children's gender typing occurs after they have developed a concept of gender. Once they consistently conceive of themselves as male or female, children often organize their world on the basis of gender.* Initially proposed by Lawrence Kohlberg (1966), this theory argues that gender development proceeds in the following way. A child realizes, "I am a girl. I want to do girl things. Therefore, the opportunity to do girl things is rewarding." Kohlberg said that gender constancy develops at about 6–7 years of age in concert with the development of children's conservation and

Childhood decides.

Jean-Paul Sartre
French Existentialist Philosopher, 20th Century

cognitive developmental theory of gender
The theory that children's gender typing occurs after they have developed a concept of gender. Once they consistently conceive of themselves as male or female, children often organize their world on the basis of gender.

Theory	Processes	Outcome
Cognitive developmental theory	Development of gender constancy, especially around 6–7 years of age, when conservation skills develop; after children develop ability to consistently conceive of themselves as male or female, children often organize their world on the basis of gender, such as selecting same-sex models to imitate	Gender-typed behavior
Gender schema theory	Sociocultural emphasis on gender-based standards and stereotypes; children's attention and behavior are guided by an internal motivation to conform to these gender-based standards and stereotypes, allowing children to interpret the world through a network of gender-organized thoughts	Gender-typed behavior

Figure 11.3
A Comparison of Cognitive
Developmental and Gender Schema
Theories of Gender Development

categorization skills. After children consistently conceive of themselves as female or male, they begin to organize their world on the basis of gender, such as selecting same-sex models to imitate.

Gender Schema Theory   A **schema** *is a cognitive structure, a network of associations that organizes and guides an individual's perceptions.* A **gender schema** *organizes the world in terms of female and male.* **Gender schema theory** *states that an individual's attention and behavior are guided by an internal motivation to conform to gender-based sociocultural standards and stereotypes.* Gender schema theory suggests that "gender typing" occurs when individuals are ready to encode and organize information along the lines of what is considered appropriate cr typical for males and females in a society. Whereas Kohlberg's cognitive developmental theory argues that a particular cognitive prerequisite—gender constancy—is necessary for gender typing. **Gender constancy** refers to the understanding that sex remains the same even though activities, clothing, and hair style might change. Gender schema theory states that a general readiness to respond to and categorize information on the basis of culturally defined gender roles fuels children's gender-typing activities. A comparison of the cognitive developmental and gender schema theories is presented in figure 11.3.

Researchers have shown that the appearance of gender constancy in children is related to their level of cognitive development, especially the acquisition of conservation skills. This supports the cognitive developmental theory of gender (Serbin & Sprafkin, 1986). They also have shown that young children who are pregender-constant have more gender-role knowledge than the cognitive developmental theory of gender predicts (which supports gender schema theory) (Carter & Levy, 1988). Today, gender schema theorists acknowledge that gender constancy is one important aspect of gender-role development, but they stress that other cognitive factors—such as gender schema—are also important.

The Role of Language in Gender Development   Gender is present in the language children use and encounter. The language that children hear most of the time is sexist. That is, the English language contains sex bias, especially through the use of *he* and *man* to refer to everyone. For example, in one study, mothers and their 1- and 3-year-old children looked at popular children's books, such as *The Three Bears*, together (DeLoache, Cassidy, & Carpenter, 1987). The three bears were almost always referred to as boys; 95 percent of all the characters of indeterminate gender were referred to by the mothers as males.

At this point, we have studied a number of ideas about emotional and personality development in early childhood. An overview of these ideas is presented in summary table 11.1. In our discussion of emotional development, moral development, and gender, we explored ways that parents and peers contribute to these important aspects of development. Next, we will focus more closely on such social contexts of development in early childhood.

FAMILIES

In chapter 8, we learned that attachment is an important aspect of family relationships during infancy. Remember that some experts believe attachment to a caregiver during the first several years of life is the key ingredient in the child's socioemotional development. We also learned that other experts believe secure attachment has been overemphasized and that the child's temperament, other social agents and contexts, and the complexity of the child's social world are also important in determining the child's social competence and well-being. Some developmentalists also emphasize that the infant years have been overdramatized as determinants of life-span development. They argue that social experiences in

schema
A cognitive structure; a network of associations that organizes and guides an individual's perceptions.

gender schema
A schema that organizes the world in terms of female and male.

gender schema theory
The theory that an individual's attention and behavior are guided by an internal motivation to conform to gender-based sociocultural standards and stereotypes.

gender constancy
Refers to the understanding that sex remains the same even though activities, clothing, and hair style may change.

Summary Table 11.1
Emotional and Personality Development

Concept	Processes/ Related Ideas	Characteristics/Description
The self	Initiative vs. guilt	Erikson believed that early childhood is a period when development involves resolving the conflict of initiative versus guilt.
	Self-understanding	While a rudimentary form of self-understanding occurs at about 18 months in the form of self-recognition, in early childhood the physical and active self emerges.
Emotional development	Developmental timetable of young children's emotion language and understanding	Preschoolers become more adept at talking about their own and others' emotions. Two- and 3-year-olds considerably increase the number of terms they use to describe emotion and learn more about the causes and consequences of feelings. At 4–5 years of age, children show an increased ability to reflect on emotions and understand that a single event can elicit different emotions in different people. They also show a growing awareness about controlling and managing emotions to meet social standards.
	Helping children understand emotions	Strategies include making sure children have a positive climate in which to discuss their emotions, structuring the physical environment to help children learn about feelings, using art as a context for emotion conversation, selecting books for children with emotion themes, and effectively dealing with children's quarrels and disputes.
Moral development	What is it?	Moral development concerns rules and regulations about what people should do in their interactions with others. Developmentalists study how children think, behave, and feel about such rules and regulations.
	Piaget's view	Piaget distinguished between the heteronomous morality of younger children and the autonomous morality of older children.
	Moral behavior	Moral behavior is emphasized by social learning theorists. They believe there is considerable situational variability in moral behavior and that self-control is an important aspect of understanding children's moral behavior.
	Moral feelings	Freud's psychoanalytic theory emphasizes the importance of feelings with regard to the development of the superego, the moral branch of personality, which develops through the Oedipus conflict and identification with the same-sex parent. In Freud's view, children conform to societal standards to avoid guilt. Positive emotions, such as empathy, also are an important aspect of understanding moral feelings. In Damon's view, both positive and negative emotions contribute to children's moral development.
Gender	What is gender?	Gender is the social dimension of being male or female. Gender identity is acquired by 3 years of age for most children. A gender role is a set of expectations that prescribes how females or males should think, act, and feel.
	Biological influences	The 23rd pair of chromosomes may have two X chromosomes to produce a female, or one X and one Y chromosome to produce a male. The two main classes of sex hormones are estrogens, which are dominant in females, and androgens, which are dominant in males. Some biological approaches focus on differences between the brains of females and males. Biology is not completely destiny in gender development; children's socialization experiences matter a great deal.
	Social influences	Both identification theory and social learning theory emphasize the adoption of parents' gender characteristics. Peers are especially adept at rewarding gender-appropriate behavior. There is still concern about gender imbalance in education. Despite improvements, TV still portrays males as being more competent than females.
	Cognitive influences	Both cognitive developmental and gender schema theories emphasize the role of cognition in gender development. Gender is present in the language children use and encounter. Much of the language children hear is sexist.

the early childhood years and later deserve more attention than they have sometimes been given.

In this chapter, we will discuss early childhood experiences beyond attachment. We will explore the different types of parenting styles, sibling relationships, and the ways in which more children are now experiencing socialization in a greater variety of family structures than at any other point in history. Keep in mind, as we discuss these aspects of families, the importance of viewing the family as a system of interacting individuals who reciprocally socialize and mutually regulate each other.

Parenting

Two important dimensions of parenting are parenting styles and the adaptation of parenting to the child's developmental status.

Parenting Styles Parents want their children to grow into socially mature individuals, and they may feel frustrated in trying to discover the best way to accomplish this. Developmentalists have long searched for the ingredients of parenting that promote competent socioemotional development (Brooks, 1999). For example, in the 1930s, John Watson argued that parents are too affectionate with their children. In the 1950s, a distinction was made between physical and psychological discipline. Psychological discipline, especially reasoning, was emphasized as the best way to rear a child. In the 1970s and beyond, the dimensions of competent parenting have become more precise.

Especially widespread is the view of Diana Baumrind (1971). She believes parents should be neither punitive nor aloof. Rather, they should develop rules for their children and be affectionate with them. She emphasizes four types of parenting that are associated with different aspects of the child's socioemotional development: authoritarian, authoritative, neglectful, and indulgent. More recently, developmentalists have argued that permissive parenting comes in two different forms: neglectful and indulgent. What are these forms of parenting like?

Authoritarian parenting *is a restrictive, punitive style in which parents exhort the child to follow their directions and to respect work and effort. The authoritarian parent places firm limits and controls on the child and allows little verbal exchange. Authoritarian parenting is associated with children's social incompetence.* For example, an authoritarian parent might say, "You do it my way or else. There will be no discussion!"

Parenting

> *There's no vocabulary for love within a family, love that's lived in but not looked at, love within the light of which all else is seen, the love within which all other love finds speech. This love is silent.*
>
> T. S. Eliot
> *American-Born English Poet, 20th Century*

Control [handwritten]

authoritarian parenting warmth [handwritten]

A restrictive punitive style in which parents exhort the child to follow their directions and to respect work and effort. The authoritarian parent places firm limits and controls on the child and allows little verbal exchange. Authoritarian parenting is associated with children's social incompetence.

makes a difference w/warmth [handwritten]

Adventures for the Mind

Evaluating the Parenting Styles of Both Parents

In our discussion of parenting styles, authoritative parenting was associated with social competence in children. In some cases, though, a child's parents differ in their parenting styles. Consider all four styles of parenting—authoritarian, authoritative, neglectful, and indulgent—on the parts of the mother and the father. A best case is when both parents are authoritative. What might the effects on the child be if the father is authoritarian and the mother is indulgent, or the father is authoritarian and the mother is authoritative, and so on? Is it better for the child if both parents have the same parenting style, even if the styles both are authoritarian, both indulgent, or both neglectful, or is it better for the child to have at least one authoritative parent when the other parent is authoritarian, indulgent, or neglectful?

In thinking about parenting styles, consider also what style or styles your father and mother used in rearing you. Were they both authoritative; one authoritarian, the other indulgent; and so on? What effects do you think their parenting styles had on your development?

authoritative parenting

A parenting style in which parents encourage their children to be independent but still place limits and controls on their actions. Extensive verbal give-and-take is allowed, and parents are warm and nurturant toward the child. Authoritative parenting is associated with children's social competence.

neglectful parenting

A style of parenting in which the parent is very uninvolved in the child's life; it is associated with children's social incompetence, especially a lack of self-control.

indulgent parenting

A style of parenting in which parents are highly involved with their children but place few demands or controls on them. Indulgent parenting is associated with children's social incompetence, especially a lack of self-control.

Children of authoritarian parents are often anxious about social comparison, fail to initiate activity, and have poor communication skills. And, in one study, early harsh discipline was associated with child aggression (Weiss & others, 1992).

Authoritative parenting *encourages children to be independent but still places limits and controls on their actions. Extensive verbal give-and-take is allowed, and parents are warm and nurturant toward the child. Authoritative parenting is associated with children's social competence.* An authoritative parent might put his arm around the child in a comforting way and say, "You know you should not have done that. Let's talk about how you can handle the situation better next time." Children whose parents are authoritative are socially competent, self-reliant, and socially responsible.

Permissive parenting comes in two forms: neglectful and indulgent (Maccoby & Martin, 1983). **Neglectful parenting** *is a style in which the parent is very uninvolved in the child's life. It is associated with children's social incompetence, especially a lack of self-control.* This parent cannot answer the question "It is 10 P.M.—do you know where your child is?" Children whose parents are neglectful develop the sense that other aspects of the parents' lives are more important than they are. These children tend to be socially incompetent. Many have poor self-control and don't handle independence well.

Indulgent parenting *is a style of parenting in which parents are highly involved with their children but place few demands or controls on them. Indulgent parenting is associated with children's social incompetence, especially a lack of self-control.* Such parents let their children do what they want. The result is that the children never learn to control their own behavior and always expect to get their way. Some parents deliberately rear their children in this way because they believe the combination of warm involvement and few restraints will produce a creative, confident child. One boy I knew had parents who deliberately reared him in an indulgent manner. He moved his parents out of their bedroom suite and took it over for himself. He is now 18 years old and has not learned to control his behavior. When he can't get something he wants, he still throws temper tantrums. As you might expect, he is not popular with his peers. Children whose parents are indulgent rarely learn respect for others and have difficulty controlling their behavior.

The four classifications of parenting just discussed involve combinations of acceptance and responsiveness on the one hand and demand and control on the other. How these dimensions combine to produce authoritarian, authoritative, neglectful, and indulgent parenting is shown in figure 11.4. To further evaluate parenting styles, see Adventures for the Mind.

The Adaptation of Parenting to Developmental Changes in the Child
Parents also need to adapt their behavior to the child, based on the child's developmental maturity (Maccoby, 1999). Parents should not treat a 5-year-old the same as a 2-year-old. The 5-year-old and the 2-year-old have different needs and abilities. In the first year, parent-child interaction moves from a heavy focus on routine caretaking—feeding, changing diapers, bathing, and soothing—to later include more noncaretaking activities, such as play and visual-vocal exchanges. During the child's second and third years, parents often handle disciplinary mat-

	Accepting, responsive	Rejecting, unresponsive
Demanding, controlling	Authoritative	Authoritarian
Undemanding, uncontrolling	Indulgent	Neglectful

$\mathcal{F}$igure 11.4
Classification of Parenting Styles

The four types of parenting styles (authoritative, authoritarian, indulgent, and neglectful) involve the dimensions of acceptance and responsiveness on the one hand and demand and control on the other. For example, authoritative parenting involves being both accepting/responsive and demanding/controlling.

ters by physical manipulation: they carry the child away from a mischievous activity to the place they want the child to go. They put fragile and dangerous objects out of reach. They sometimes spank. But, as the child grows older, parents turn increasingly to reasoning, moral exhortation, and the giving or withholding of special privileges. As children move toward the elementary school years, parents show them less physical affection.

Sibling Relationships and Birth Order

Sandra describes to her mother what happened in a conflict with her sister:

> We had just come home from the ball game. I sat down on the sofa next to the light so I could read. Sally [the sister] said, "Get up. I was sitting there first. I just got up for a second to get a drink." I told her I was not going to get up and that I didn't see her name on the chair. I got mad and started pushing her. Her drink spilled all over her. Then she got really mad; she shoved me against the wall, hitting and clawing at me. I managed to grab a handful of hair.

$\mathcal{P}$arenting is a very important profession, but no test of fitness for it is ever imposed in the interest of children.

George Bernard Shaw
Irish Playwright, 20th Century

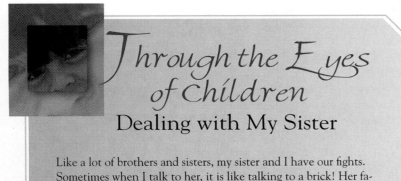

Through the Eyes of Children
Dealing with My Sister

Like a lot of brothers and sisters, my sister and I have our fights. Sometimes when I talk to her, it is like talking to a brick! Her favorite thing to do is to storm off and slam the door when she gets mad at me. After awhile, I cool off. When I calm down, I realize fighting with your sister is crazy. I go to my sister and apologize. It's a lot better to cool off and apologize than to keep on fighting and make things worse.

Cynthia, age 10

Big sisters are the crab grass in the lawn of life.

Charles Schulz
American Cartoonist, 20th Century

At this point, Sally comes into the room and begins to tell her side of the story. Sandra interrupts, "Mother, you always take her side."

Sibling Relationships   Any of you who have grown up with siblings probably have a rich memory of aggressive, hostile interchanges. But sibling relationships also have many pleasant, caring moments. Children's sibling relationships include helping, sharing, teaching, fighting, and playing. Children can act as emotional supports, rivals, and communication partners (Carlson, 1995). More than 80 percent of American children have one or more siblings (brothers or sisters). Because there are so many possible sibling combinations, it is difficult to generalize about sibling influences. Among the factors to consider are the number of siblings, the ages of siblings, birth order, age spacing, the sex of siblings, and whether sibling relationships are different from parent-child relationships.

Is sibling interaction different from parent-child interaction? There is some evidence that it is. Observations indicate that children interact more positively and in more varied ways with their parents than with their siblings (Baskett & Johnson, 1982). Children also follow their parents' dictates more than those of their siblings, and they behave more negatively and punitively with their siblings than with their parents.

In some instances, siblings may be stronger socializing influences on the child than parents are (Cicirelli, 1994). Someone close in age to the child—such as a sibling—may be able to understand the child's problems and communicate more effectively than parents can. In dealing with peers, coping with difficult teachers, and discussing such taboo subjects as sex, siblings may be more influential than parents in the socialization process.

Is sibling interaction the same around the world? In industrialized societies, such as the United States, the delegation of responsibility for younger siblings to older siblings tends to be carried out informally by parents. This is done primarily to give the parents freedom to pursue other activities. However, in nonindustrialized countries, such as Kenya, a much greater degree of importance is attached to the older sibling's role as a caregiver to younger siblings. In industrialized countries, the older sibling's caregiving role is often discretionary; in nonindustrialized countries, it is more obligatory (Cicirelli, 1994).

Birth Order   Birth order is a special interest of sibling researchers. When differences in birth order are found, they usually are explained by variations in interactions with parents and siblings associated with the unique experiences of being in a particular position in the family. This is especially true in the case of the firstborn child (Teti & others, 1993). The oldest child is the only one who does not have to share parental love and affection with other siblings—until another sibling comes along. An infant requires more attention than an older child; this means that the firstborn sibling now gets less attention than before the newborn arrived. Does this result in conflict between parents and the firstborn? In one research study, mothers became more negative, coercive, and restraining and played less with the firstborn following the birth of a second child (Dunn & Kendrick, 1982). Even though a new infant requires more attention from parents than does an older child, an especially intense relationship is often maintained between parents and firstborns throughout the life span. Parents have higher expectations for firstborn children than for later-born children. They put more pressure on them for achievement and responsibility. They also interfere more with their activities (Rothbart, 1971).

Birth order is also associated with variations in sibling relationships. The oldest sibling is expected to exercise self-control and show responsibility in interacting with younger siblings. When the oldest sibling is jealous or hostile, parents often protect the younger sibling. The oldest sibling is more dominant, competent, and powerful than the younger siblings. The oldest sibling is also expected to assist and teach younger siblings. Indeed, researchers have shown that older siblings are both more antagonistic—hitting, kicking, and biting—and more nurturant toward their younger siblings than vice versa (Abramovitch & others, 1986). There is also something unique about same-sex sibling relationships. Aggression and dominance occur more in same-sex relationships than in opposite-sex sibling relationships (Minnett, Vandell, & Santrock, 1983).

Given the differences in family dynamics involved in birth order, it is not surprising that firstborns and later-borns have different characteristics. Firstborn children are more adult-oriented, helpful, conforming, anxious, and self-controlled than their siblings. Parents give more attention to firstborns and this is related to firstborns' nurturant behavior (Stanhope & Corter, 1993). Parental demands and high standards established for firstborns result in these children's excelling in academic and professional endeavors. Firstborns are overrepresented in *Who's Who* and Rhodes scholars, for example. However, some of the same pressures placed on firstborns for high achievement may be the reason they also have more guilt, anxiety, and difficulty in coping with stressful situations, as well as higher admission to child guidance clinics.

What is the only child like? The popular conception is that the only child is a "spoiled brat," with such undesirable characteristics as dependency, lack of self-control, and self-centered behavior. But researchers present a more positive portrayal of the only child, who often is achievement-oriented and displays a desirable personality, especially in comparison with later-borns and children from large families (Falbo & Poston, 1993; Jiao, Ji, & Jing, 1996).

So far, our consideration of birth-order effects suggests that birth order might be a strong predictor of behavior. However, an increasing number of family researchers believe that birth order has been overdramatized and overemphasized. The critics argue that, when all of the factors that influence behavior are considered, birth order itself shows limited ability to predict behavior. Consider sibling relationships alone. They vary not only in birth order but also in number of siblings, age of siblings, age spacing of siblings, and sex of siblings.

Consider also the temperament of siblings. Researchers have found that siblings' temperamental traits ("easy" and "difficult," for example), as well as differential treatment of siblings by parents, influence how siblings get along (Stocker & Dunn, 1991). Siblings with "easy" temperaments who are treated in relatively equal ways by parents tend to get along with each other the best. By contrast, siblings with "difficult" temperaments, or whose parents have given one of them preferential treatment, get along the worst.

Beyond temperament and differential treatment of siblings by parents, think about some of the other important factors in children's lives that influence their behavior beyond birth order. They include heredity, models of competency or incompetency that parents present to children on a daily basis, peer influences, school influences, socioeconomic factors, sociohistorical factors, and cultural variations. When someone says firstborns are always like this but last-borns are always like that, you now know that the person is making overly simplistic statements that do not adequately take into account the complexity of influences on a child's behavior. Keep in mind, though, that, although birth order itself may not be a good predictor of children's behavior, sibling relationships and interaction are important dimensions of family processes.

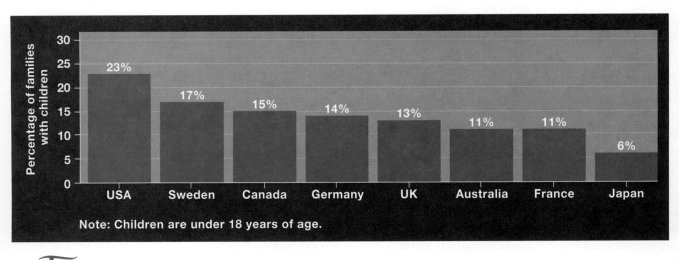

Figure 11.5
Single-Parent Families in Different Countries

The Changing Family in a Changing Society

Children are growing up in a greater variety of family structures than ever before. Many mothers spend the greatest part of their day away from their children, even their infants. More than one of every two mothers with a child under the age of 5 is in the labor force; more than two of every three with a child from 6 to 17 years of age is. And the increasing number of children growing up in single-parent families is staggering. As shown in figure 11.5, the United States has the highest percentage of single-parent families, compared with virtually all other countries. If current trends continue, by the year 2000 one in every four children also will have lived a portion of his or her life in a stepparent family.

Working Mothers

Because household operations have become more efficient and family size has decreased in America, it is not certain that children with mothers working outside the home actually receive less attention than children in the past whose mothers were not employed. Outside employment—at least for mothers with school-age children—may simply be filling time previously taken up by added household burdens and more children. It also cannot be assumed that, if the mother did not go to work, the child would benefit from the time freed up by streamlined household operations and smaller families. Mothering does not always have a positive effect on the child. The educated, nonworking mother may overinvest her energies in her children. This can foster an excess of worry and discourage the child's independence. In such situations, the mother may give more parenting than the child can profitably handle.

As Lois Hoffman (1989) commented, maternal employment is a part of modern life. It is not an aberrant aspect of it but a response to other social changes. It meets needs that cannot be met by the previous family ideal of a full-time mother and homemaker. Not only does it meet the parents' needs, but in many ways it may be a pattern better suited to socializing children for the adult roles they will occupy. This is especially true for daughters, but it is also true for sons. The broader range of emotions and skills that each parent presents is more consistent with this adult role. Just as his father shares the breadwinning role and the child-rearing role with his mother, so the son, too, may be more willing to share these roles. The rigid gender stereotyping perpetuated by the divisions of labor in the traditional family is not appropriate for the demands that will be made on children of either sex as adults.

Working Mothers

Family and the Workplace

The needs of the growing child require the mother to loosen her hold on the child. This task may be easier for the working woman, whose job is an additional source of identity and self-esteem. Overall, researchers have found no detrimental effects of maternal employment on children's development (Gottfried, Gottfried, & Bathurst, 1995; Richards & Duckett, 1994).

A common experience of working mothers (and working fathers) is feeling guilty about being away from their children. The guilt may be triggered by parents who miss their child, worry that their child is missing them, are concerned about the implications of working (such as whether the child is receiving good child care), and worry about the long-term effects of working (such as whether they are jeopardizing the child's future). To reduce guilt, the guilt needs to be acknowledged. Pediatrician T. Berry Brazelton (1983) believes that parents respond to guilt either by admitting it and working through it or by denying it and rationalizing it away. The latter tendency is not recommended. Working parents' guilt can also be reduced if they pay closer attention to how their children are doing.

Effects of Divorce on Children   These are the questions that we will explore that focus on the effects of divorce: Are children better adjusted in intact, never divorced families than in divorced families? Should parents stay together for the sake of their children? How much do parenting skills matter in divorced families? What factors are involved in the child's individual risk and vulnerability in a divorced family? What role does socioeconomic status play in the lives of children in divorced families?

Children's Adjustment in Divorced Families   Most researchers agree that children from divorced families show poorer adjustment than their counterparts in nondivorced families (Amato & Keith, 1991). Those that have experienced multiple divorces are at greater risk (Kurdek, Fine, & Sinclair, 1995). Children in divorced families are more likely than children in nondivorced families to have academic problems, to show externalized problems (such as acting out and delinquency) and internalized problems (such as anxiety and depression), to be less socially responsible, to have less competent intimate relationships, to drop out of school, to become sexually active at an early age, to take drugs, to associate with antisocial peers, and to have low self-esteem (Conger & Chao, 1996; McLanahan & Sandefur, 1994).

Although there is a consensus that children from divorced families show these adjustment problems to a greater extent than do children from nondivorced families, there is less agreement about the size of the effects (Hetherington, Bridges, & Insabella, 1998). Some researchers report that the divorce effects are modest and have become smaller as divorce has become more commonplace in society (Amato & Keith, 1991). However, others argue that approximately 20–25 percent of children in divorced families have these types of adjustment problems, in contrast to only 10 percent of children in nondivorced families, which is a notable two-fold increase (Hetherington & Jodl, 1994). Nonetheless, the majority of children in divorced families do not have these problems (Hetherington, 1999). The weight of the research evidence underscores that most children competently cope with their parents' divorce but that significantly more children from divorced families have adjustment problems (20–25 percent) than children from nondivorced families (10 percent).

Should Parents Stay Together for the Sake of Their Children?
Whether parents should stay in an unhappy or conflicted marriage for the sake of their children is one of the most commonly asked questions about divorce (Hetherington, 1999). If the stresses and disruptions in family relationships associated with an unhappy, conflictual marriage that erode the well-being of children are reduced by the move to a divorced, single-parent family, divorce may be

Children and Divorce
Divorce and Family Ties

advantageous. However, if the diminished resources and increased risks associated with divorce also are accompanied by inept parenting and sustained or increased conflict, not only between the divorced couple but also between the parents, children, and siblings, the best choice for the children would be for an unhappy marriage to be retained. These are "ifs," and it is difficult to determine how these will play out when parents either remain together in an acrimonious marriage or become divorced.

How Much Do Family Processes Matter in Divorced Families? Family processes matter a lot (Emery, 1999). When divorced parents' relationship with each other is harmonious and when they use authoritative parenting, the adjustment of children improves (Hetherington, Bridges, & Insabella, 1998). A number of researchers have shown that a disequilibrium, which includes diminished parenting skills, occurs in the year following the divorce but that, by two years after the divorce, restabilization has occurred and parenting skills have improved (Hetherington, 1989). About one-fourth to one-third of children in divorced families, compared with 10 percent in nondivorced families, become disengaged from their families, spending as little time as possible at home and in interaction with family members (Hetherington & Jodl, 1994). This disengagement is higher for boys than girls in divorced families. However, if there is a caring adult outside the home, such as a mentor, the disengagement may be a positive solution to a disrupted, conflicted family circumstance.

What Roles Do Noncustodial Parents Play in the Lives of Children in Divorced Families? Most nonresidential fathers have a friendly, companionate relationship with their children, rather than a traditional parental relationship (Munsch, Woodward, & Darling, 1995). They want their visits to be pleasant and entertaining, so they are reluctant to assume the role of a disciplinarian or teacher. They are less likely than nondivorced fathers to criticize, control, and monitor their child's behavior or to help them with such tasks as homework (Bray & Berger, 1993). The frequency of contact with noncustodial fathers and children's adjustment is usually found to be unrelated (Amato & Keith, 1991). The quality of the contact matters more. Under conditions of low conflict, when noncustodial fathers participate in a variety of activities with their offspring and engage in authoritative parenting, children, especially boys, benefit (Lindner-Gunnoe, 1993). We know less about noncustodial mothers than fathers, but these mothers are less adept than custodial mothers are at controlling and monitoring their child's behavior (Furstenberg & Nord, 1987). Noncustodial mothers' warmth, support, and monitoring can improve children's adjustment (Lindner-Gunnoe, 1993). To read about effective ways of communicating with children about divorce, see the Caring for Children box.

What Factors Are Involved in the Child's Individual Risk and Vulnerability in a Divorced Family? Among the factors involved in the child's risk and vulnerability are the child's adjustment prior to the divorce, as well as the child's personality and temperament, developmental status, gender, and custody situation. Children whose parents later divorce show poorer adjustment before the breakup (Amato & Booth, 1996). When antecedent levels of problem behaviors are controlled, differences in the adjustment of children in divorced and nondivorced families are reduced (Cherlin & others, 1991).

Personality and temperament also play a role in children's adjustment in divorced families. Children who are socially mature and responsible, who show few behavioral problems, and who have an easy temperament are better able to cope with their parents' divorce. Children with a difficult temperament often have problems in coping with their parents' divorce (Hetherington, 1995).

Focusing on the developmental status of the child involves taking into account

Divorce Resources

Caring for Children
Communicating with Children About Divorce

Ellen Galinsky and Judy David (1988) developed a number of guidelines for communicating with young children about divorce.

Explaining the Separation

As soon as the daily activities in the home make it obvious that one parent is leaving, tell the children. If possible, both parents should be present when the children are made aware of the separation to come. The reasons for the separation are very difficult for young children to understand. No matter what parents tell children, children can find reasons to argue against the separation. A child may say something like, "If you don't love each other anymore, you need to start trying harder." One set of parents told their 4-year-old, "We both love you. We will both always love you and take care of you, but we aren't going to live in the same house anymore. Daddy is moving to an apartment near the stores where we shop." It is extremely important for parents to tell the children who will take care of them and to describe the specific arrangements for seeing the other parent.

Explaining That the Separation Is Not the Child's Fault

Young children often believe their parents' separation or divorce is their own fault. Therefore, it is important to tell children that they are not the cause of the separation. Parents need to repeat this a number of times.

Explaining That It May Take Time to Feel Better

It is helpful to tell young children that it's normal to not feel good about what is happening, and that lots of other children feel this way when their parents become separated. It is also okay for divorced parents to share some of their emotions with children, by saying something like, "I'm having a hard time since the separation, just like you, but I know it's going to get better after a while." Such statements are best kept brief and should not criticize the other parent.

Keeping the Door Open for Further Discussion

Tell your children that, anytime they want to talk about the separation, to come to you. It is healthy for children to get out their pent-up emotions in discussions with their parents and to learn that the parents are willing to listen to their feelings and fears.

Providing as Much Continuity as Possible

The less children's worlds are disrupted by the separation, the easier their transition to a single-parent family will be. This means maintaining as much as possible the rules already in place. Children need parents who care enough to not only give them warmth and nurturance but also set reasonable limits. If the custodial parent has to move to a new home, it is important to preserve as much of what is familiar to the child as possible. In one family, the child helped arrange her new room exactly as it had been prior to the divorce. If children must leave friends behind, it is important for parents to help the children stay in touch by phone or by letter. Keeping the child busy and involved in the new setting can also keep their minds off the stressful thoughts about the separation.

Providing Support for Your Children and Yourself

After a divorce or separation, parents are as important to children as before the divorce or separation. Divorced parents need to provide children with as much support as possible. Parents function best when other people are available to give them support as adults and as parents. Divorced parents can find people who provide practical help and with whom they can talk about their problems. Too often, divorced parents criticize themselves and say they feel that they don't deserve help. One divorced parent commented, "I've made a mess of my life. I don't deserve anybody's help." However, seeking out others for support and feedback about problems can make the transition to a single-parent family more bearable.

---

the age of onset of the divorce and the time when the child's adjustment is assessed. In most studies, these factors are confounded with the length of time since the divorce occurred. Some researchers have found that preschool children whose parents divorce are at greater risk for long-term problems than are older children (Zill & others, 1993). The explanation for this focuses on their inability to realistically appraise the causes and consequences of divorce, their anxiety about the possibility of abandonment, their self-blame for the divorce, and their inability to use

What are some characteristics of families within different ethnic groups?

Father Custody

extrafamilial protective resources. However, adolescence may be a period in which problems in adjustment emerge or increase, even when divorce has occurred much earlier.

Earlier studies reported gender differences in response to divorce, with divorce being more negative for girls than boys in mother custody families. However, more recent studies have shown that gender differences are less pronounced and consistent than was previously believed. Some of the inconsistency may be due to the increase in father custody, joint custody, and increased involvement of noncustodial fathers, especially in their sons' lives. However, female adolescents in divorced families are more likely to drop out of high school and college than are their male counterparts. Male and female adolescents from divorced families are similarly affected in the likelihood of becoming teenage parents, but single parenthood more adversely affects girls.

In recent decades, an increasing number of children have lived in father custody and joint custody families (Maccoby, 1999; Stahl, 1999). What is their adjustment like, compared with that of children in mother custody families? Although there have been few thorough studies of the topic, there appear to be few advantages of joint custody over custody by one parent (Hetherington, Bridges, & Insabella, 1998). Some studies have shown that boys adjust better in father custody families, girls in mother custody families, while other studies have not. In one study, the adolescents in father custody families had higher rates of delinquency, believed to be due to less competent monitoring by the fathers (Maccoby & Mnookin, 1992).

What Role Does Socioeconomic Status Play in the Lives of Children in Divorced Families? Custodial mothers experience the loss of about one-fourth to one-half of their predivorce income, in comparison with a loss of only one-tenth by custodial fathers (Emery, 1994). This income loss for divorced mothers is accompanied by increased workloads, high rates of job instability, and residential moves to less desirable neighborhoods with inferior schools.

Cultural, Ethnic, and Socioeconomic Variations in Families
Cultures vary on a number of issues involving families, such as what the father's role in the family should be, the extent to which support systems are available to families, and the ways in which children should be disciplined. Although there are cross-cultural variations in parenting (Whiting & Edwards, 1988), in one study of parenting behavior in 186 cultures around the world, the most common pattern was a warm and controlling style, one that was neither permissive nor

restrictive (Rohner & Rohner, 1981). The investigators commented that the majority of cultures have discovered, over many centuries, a "truth" that only recently emerged in the Western world—namely, that children's healthy social development is most effectively promoted by love and at least some moderate parental control.

Families within different ethnic groups in the United States differ in their size, structure, composition, reliance on kinships networks, and levels of income and education (Parke & Buriel, 1998). Large and extended families are more common among minority groups than among the White majority. For example, 19 percent of Latino families have three or more children, compared with 14 percent of African American and 10 percent of White families. African American and Latino children interact more with grandparents, aunts, uncles, cousins, and more-distant relatives than do White children.

Single-parent families are more common among African Americans and Latinos than among White Americans. In comparison with two-parent households, single parents often have more limited resources of time, money, and energy. Ethnic minority parents also are less educated and more likely to live in low-income circumstances than their White counterparts. Still, many impoverished ethnic minority families manage to find ways to raise competent children.

Some aspects of home life can help protect ethnic minority children from injustice (Hill, 1999). The community and the family can filter out destructive racist messages, and parents can present alternative frames of reference to those presented by the majority. The extended family also can serve as an important buffer to stress (McAdou, 1999; Wakschlag, Chase-Lansdale, & Brooks-Gunn, 1996).

In America and most Western cultures, differences have been found in child rearing among different socioeconomic groups. Low-income parents often place a high value on external characteristics, such as obedience and neatness. By contrast, middle- and upper-income families frequently place a high value on internal characteristics, such as self-control and delay of gratification. Middle- and upper-income parents are more likely to explain something, praise, use reasoning to accompany their discipline, and ask their children questions. By contrast, low-income parents are more likely to use physical punishment and criticize their children (Hoff-Ginsburg & Tardif, 1995).

There also are socioeconomic differences in the way that parents think about education (Lareau, 1996). Middle- and upper-income parents more often think of education as something that should be mutually encouraged by parents and teachers. By contrast, low-income parents are more likely to view education as the teacher's job. Thus, increased school-family linkages especially can benefit students from low-income families.

Family Diversity

PEER RELATIONS, PLAY, AND TELEVISION

The family is an important social context for children's development. However, children's development also is strongly influenced by what goes on in other social contexts, such as peer relations, play, and television.

Peer Relations

As children grow older, peer relations consume an increasing amount of their time. What is the function of a child's peer group? Although children spend increasingly more time with peers as they become older, are there ways in which family and peer relations are coordinated?

peers
Children of about the same age or maturity level.

Peer Relations

Peer Group Functions

Peers *are children of about the same age or maturity level.* Same-age peer interaction fills a unique role in our culture. Age grading would occur even if schools were not age graded and children were left alone to determine the composition of their own societies. One of the most important functions of the peer group is to provide a source of information and comparison about the world outside the family. Children receive feedback about their abilities from their peer group. Children evaluate what they do in terms of whether it is better than, as good as, or worse than what other children do. It is hard to do this at home because siblings are usually older or younger.

Are peers necessary for development? When peer monkeys who have been reared together are separated, they become depressed and less advanced socially (Suomi, Harlow, & Domek, 1970). The human development literature contains a classic example of the importance of peers in social development. Anna Freud (Freud & Dann, 1951) studied six children from different families who banded together after their parents were killed in World War II. Intensive peer attachment was observed. The children formed a tightly knit group, dependent on one another and aloof with outsiders. Even though deprived of parental care, they neither became delinquent nor developed serious mental disorders.

Good peer relations may be necessary for normal socioemotional development (Ryan & Patrick, 1996). Social isolation, or the inability to "plug in" to a social network, is linked with many problems and disorders ranging from delinquency and problem drinking to depression (Kupersmidt & Coie, 1990). In one study, poor peer relations in childhood was associated with a tendency to drop out of school and delinquent behavior in adolescence (Roff, Sells, & Golden, 1972). In another study, harmonious peer relations in adolescence was related to positive mental health at midlife (Hightower, 1990).

The Distinct but Coordinated Worlds of Parent-Child and Peer Relations

What are some of the similarities and differences between peer and parent-child relationships? Children touch, smile, frown, and vocalize when they interact with parents and peers. However, rough-and-tumble play occurs mainly with other children, not with adults, and, in times of stress, children often move toward their parents rather than toward their peers.

Parent-child relationships can serve as emotional bases for exploring and enjoying peer relations (Posada, Lord, & Waters, 1995). Carollee Howes and her colleagues have conducted a number of research studies to demonstrate that relationships with teachers, as well as parents, can benefit children's socioemotional development and peer relations. In one study, children in child care settings who had secure attachment relationships with their teachers were more gregarious and less hostile toward their peers than were their counterparts with insecure attachments with their teachers (Howes, Hamilton, & Matheson, 1994). In another study, young children who were more sociable with parents *and* teachers also were more sociable with peers than were children who were less sociable with these adults (Howes & Clements, 1994). In yet another study, children's secure attachments with teachers compensated for insecure attachments with parents in terms of the children's social competence (Howes & others, 1988).

Peer researcher Daniel Olweus (1980) found that peer relations could be best predicted when knowledge of the relationship histories of both peers in a dyadic relationship are known (see Figure 11.6). Some boys were highly aggressive ("bullies"), and other boys were the recipients of aggression ("whipping boys") throughout their preschool years. The bullies and the whipping boys had distinctive relationship histories. The bullies' parents frequently rejected them, were authoritarian, and were permissive about their sons' aggression. Their families also were characterized by discord. By contrast, the whipping boys' parents were anxious and overprotective. They took special care to have their sons avoid aggression. The well-adjusted boys in the study were much less likely to be involved in aggressive peer interchanges than were the bullies and whipping boys. Their parents did not sanction aggression, and the parents' responsive involvement with their sons promoted the development of self-assertion rather than aggression or wimpish behavior.

Parents also may model or coach their children in the ways of relating to peers. In one study, parents recommended specific strategies to their children regarding peer relations (Rubin & Sloman, 1984). For example, parents told their children how to mediate disputes or how to become less shy with others. They also encouraged them to be tolerant and to resist peer pressure.

A key aspect of peer relations can be traced to basic lifestyle decisions by parents (Cooper & Ayers-Lopez, 1985). Parents' choices of neighborhoods, churches, schools, and their own friends influence the pool from which their children might select possible friends.

In sum, parent-child and peer worlds are coordinated and connected (Berndt, 1999; Maccoby, 1996). But they are also distinct. Earlier, we indicated that rough-and-tumble play occurs mainly with other children and not in parent-child interaction and that children often turn to parents, not peers, for support in times of stress. Peer relations also are more likely to consist of interaction on a much more equal basis than are parent-child relations. Because parents have greater knowledge and authority, children must often learn how to conform to rules and regulations laid down by parents. With peers, children learn to formulate and assert their own opinions, appreciate the perspective of peers, cooperatively negotiate solutions to disagreements, and evolve standards of conduct that are mutually acceptable.

Play

An extensive amount of peer interaction during childhood involves play. Although peer interaction can involve play, social play is but one type of play. **Play** *is a*

play
A pleasurable activity that is engaged in for its own sake.

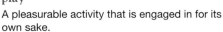

Figure 11.6
Peer Aggression: The Influence of the Relationship Histories of Each Peer

pleasurable activity that is engaged in for its own sake. Our coverage of play includes its functions, Parten's classic study of play, and types of play.

Play's Functions Play is essential to the young child's health. As today's children move into the twenty-first century and continue to experience pressure in their lives, play becomes even more crucial (VanHoorn & others, 1999). Play increases affiliation with peers, releases tension, advances cognitive development, increases exploration, and provides a safe haven in which to engage in potentially dangerous behavior. Play increases the probability that children will converse and interact with each other. During this interaction, children practice the roles they will assume later in life.

According to Freud and Erikson, play is an especially useful form of human adjustment, helping the child master anxieties and conflicts. Because tensions are relieved in play, the child can cope with life's problems. Play permits the child to work off excess physical energy and to release pent-up tensions. **Play therapy** *allows the child to work off frustrations. Through play therapy, the therapist can analyze the child's conflicts and ways of coping with them. Children may feel less threatened and be more likely to express their true feelings in the context of play.*

Piaget (1962) believed that play advances children's cognitive development. At the same time, he said that children's cognitive development *constrains* the way they play. Play permits children to practice their competencies and acquired skills in a relaxed, pleasurable way. Piaget thought that cognitive structures need to be exercised, and play provides the perfect setting for this exercise. For example, children who have just learned to add or multiply begin to play with numbers in different ways as they perfect these operations, laughing as they do so.

Vygotsky (1962), whose developmental theory was discussed in chapter 10, also believed that play is an excellent setting for cognitive development. He was

play therapy
Therapy that allows the child to work off frustrations and is a medium through which the therapist can analyze the child's conflicts and ways of coping with them. Children may feel less threatened and be more likely to express their true feelings in the context of play.

Mildred Parten classified play into six categories. Study this photograph and determine which of her categories are reflected in the behavior of the children.

especially interested in the symbolic and make-believe aspects of play, as when a child substitutes a stick for a horse and rides the stick as if it were a horse. For young children, the imaginary situation is real. Parents should encourage such imaginary play, because it advances the child's cognitive development, especially creative thought.

Daniel Berlyne (1960) described play as exciting and pleasurable in itself because it satisfies our exploratory drive. This drive involves curiosity and a desire for information about something new or unusual. Play is a means whereby children can safely explore and seek out new information—something they might not otherwise do. Play encourages this exploratory behavior by offering children the possibilities of novelty, complexity, uncertainty, surprise, and incongruity.

Parten's Classic Study of Play   Many years ago, Mildred Parten (1932) developed an elaborate classification of children's play. Based on observations of children in free play at nursery school, Parten arrived at these play categories:

1. **Unoccupied play** *occurs when the child is not engaging in play as it is commonly understood. The child may stand in one spot, look around the room, or perform random movements that do not seem to have a goal.* In most nursery schools, unoccupied play is less frequent than other forms of play.
2. **Solitary play** *occurs when the child plays alone and independently of others.* The child seems engrossed in the activity and does not care much about anything else that is happening. Two- and 3-year-olds engage more frequently in solitary play than older preschoolers do.
3. **Onlooker play** *occurs when the child watches other children play.* The child may talk with other children and ask questions but does not enter into their play behavior. The child's active interest in other children's play distinguishes onlooker play from unoccupied play.
4. **Parallel play** *occurs when the child plays separately from others, but with toys like those the others are using or in a manner that mimics their play.* The older children are, the less frequently they engage in this type of play. However even older preschool children engage in parallel play quite often.
5. **Associative play** *occurs when play involves social interaction with little or no organization.* In this type of play, children seem to be more interested in each other than in the tasks they are performing. Borrowing or lending toys and following or leading one another in line are examples of associative play.
6. **Cooperative play** *involves social interaction in a group with a sense of group identity and organized activity.* Children's formal games, competition aimed at winning, and groups formed by the teacher for doing things together are examples of cooperative play. Cooperative play is the prototype for the games of middle childhood. Little cooperative play is seen in the preschool years.

Types of Play   Parten's categories represent one way of thinking about the different types of play. However, today researchers and practitioners who are involved with children's play believe other types of play are important in children's development. Whereas Parten's categories emphasize the role of play in the child's social world, the contemporary perspective on play emphasizes both the cognitive and the social aspects of play. Among the most widely studied types of children's play today are sensorimotor and practice play, pretense/symbolic play, social play, constructive play, and games (Bergin, 1988). We will consider each of these types of play in turn.

Sensorimotor and Practice Play   **Sensorimotor play** *is behavior engaged in by infants to derive pleasure from exercising their existing sensorimotor schemas.* The development of sensorimotor play follows Piaget's description of sensorimotor thought,

And that park grew up with me; that small world widened as I learned its secret boundaries, as I discovered new refuges in the woods and jungles: hidden homes and lairs for the multitudes of imagination, for cowboys and Indians. . . . I used to dawdle on half holidays along the bent and devon-facing seashore, hoping for gold watches or the skull of a sheep or a message in a bottle to be washed up by the tide.

Dylan Thomas
Welsh Poet, 20th Century

unoccupied play
Play in which the child is not engaging in play as it is commonly understood and might stand in one spot, look around the room, or perform random movements that do not seem to have a goal.

solitary play
Play in which the child plays alone and independently of others.

onlooker play
Play in which the child watches other children play.

parallel play
Play in which the child plays separately from others, but with toys like those the others are using or in a manner that mimics their play.

associative play
Play that involves social interaction with little or no organization.

cooperative play
Play that involves social interaction in a group with a sense of group identity and organized activity.

sensorimotor play
Behavior engaged in by infants to derive pleasure from exercising their existing sensorimotor schemas.

Play

which we discussed in chapter 8. Infants initially engage in exploratory and playful visual and motor transactions in the second quarter of the first year of life. At 9 months of age, infants begin to select novel objects for exploration and play, especially those that are responsive, such as toys that make noise or bounce. At 12 months of age, infants enjoy making things work and exploring cause and effect. At this point in development, children like toys that perform when they act on them.

In the second year, infants begin to understand the social meaning of objects, and their play reflects this awareness. And 2-year-olds may distinguish between exploratory play that is interesting but not humorous and "playful" play, which has incongruous and humorous dimensions. For example, a 2-year-old might "drink" from a shoe or call a dog a "cow." When 2-year-olds find these deliberate incongruities funny, they are beginning to show evidence of symbolic play and the ability to play with ideas.

Practice play *involves the repetition of behavior when new skills are being learned or when physical or mental mastery and coordination of skills are required for games or sports. Sensorimotor play, which often involves practice play, is primarily confined to infancy, while practice play can be engaged in throughout life.* During the preschool years, children often engage in play that involves practicing various skills. Estimates indicate that practice play constitutes one-third of the preschool child's play activities but less than one-sixth of the elementary school child's play activities (Rubin, Fein, & Vandenberg, 1983). Practice play contributes to the development of the coordinated motor skills needed for later game playing. While practice play declines in the elementary school years, practice play activities such as running, jumping, sliding, twirling, and throwing balls or other objects are frequently observed on the playgrounds at elementary schools. These activities appear similar to the earlier practice play of the preschool years, but practice play in the elementary school years differs from earlier practice play because much of it is ends-rather than means-related. That is, elementary school children often engage in practice play for the purpose of improving the motor skills needed to compete in games or sports.

practice play
Play that involves repetition of behavior when new skills are being learned or when physical or mental mastery and coordination of skills are required for games or sports. Sensorimotor play, which often involves practice play, is primarily confined to infancy, while practice play can be engaged in throughout life.

pretense/symbolic play
Play in which the child transforms the physical environment into a symbol.

Pretense/Symbolic Play   **Pretense/symbolic play** *occurs when the child transforms the physical environment into a symbol.* Between 9 and 30 months of age, children increase their use of objects in symbolic play. They learn to transform objects—substituting them for other objects and acting toward them as if they were these other objects. For example, a preschool child treats a table as if it were a car and says, "I'm fixing the car," as he grabs a leg of the table.

Many experts on play consider the preschool years the "golden age" of symbolic/pretense play that is dramatic or sociodramatic in nature (Fein, 1986). This type of make-believe play often appears at about 18 months of age and reaches a peak at 4 to 5 years of age, then gradually declines. In the early elementary school years, children's interests often shift to games. In one observational study of nine children, at 4 years of age the children spent more than 12 minutes per hour in pretend play (Haight & Miller, 1993). In this study, a number of parents agreed with Piaget and Vygotsky that pretending helps develop children's imaginations.

social play
Play that involves social interactions with peers.

Social Play   **Social play** *is play that involves social interaction with peers.* Parten's categories, described earlier, are oriented toward social play. Social play with peers increases dramatically during the preschool years. In addition to general social play with peers and group pretense or sociodramatic play, another form of social play is rough-and-tumble play. The movement patterns of rough-and-tumble play are often similar to those of hostile behavior (running, chasing, wrestling, jumping, falling, hitting). However, in rough-and-tumble play these behaviors are accompanied by signals, such as laughter, exaggerated movement, and open rather than closed hands, that indicate that this is play.

In the sun that is young once only
Time let me play.

Dylan Thomas
Welsh Poet, 20th Century

Constructive Play   **Constructive play** *combines sensorimotor and practice repetitive activity with symbolic representation of ideas. Constructive play occurs when children engage in self-regulated creation or construction of a product or a problem solution.* Constructive play increases in the preschool years as symbolic play increases and sensorimotor play decreases. In the preschool years, some practice play is replaced by constructive play. For example, instead of moving their fingers around and around in finger paint (practice play), children are more likely to draw the outline of a house or a person in the paint (constructive play). Some researchers have found that constructive play is the most common type of play during the preschool years (Rubin, Maioni, & Hornung, 1976). Constructive play is also a frequent form of play in the elementary school years, both in and out of the classroom. Constructive play is one of the few playlike activities allowed in work-centered classrooms. For example, having children create a play about a social studies topic involves constructive play. Whether children consider such activities to be play usually depends on whether they get to choose whether to do it (it is play) or whether the teacher imposes it (it is not play), as well as whether it is enjoyable (it is play) or not (it is not play) (King, 1982).

Constructive play also can be used in the elementary school years to foster academic skill learning, thinking skills, and problem solving. Many educators plan classroom activities that include humor, encourage playing with ideas, and promote creativity (Bergin, 1988). Educators also often support the performance of plays, the writing of imaginative stories, the expression of artistic abilities, and the playful exploration of computers and other technological equipment. However, distinctions between work and play frequently become blurred in the elementary school classroom. Think of constructive play as a midway point between play and work.

Games   **Games** *are activities engaged in for pleasure. They include rules and often competition with one or more individuals.* Preschool children may begin to participate in social game play that involves simple rules of reciprocity and turn taking. However, games take on a much stronger role in the lives of elementary school children. In one study, the highest incidence of game playing occurred between 10 and 12 years of age (Eiferman, 1971). After age 12, games decline in popularity. They often are replaced by practice play, conversations, and organized sports (Bergin, 1988).

In the elementary years, games feature the meaningfulness of a challenge. This challenge is present if two or more children have the skills required to play and understand the rules of the game. Among the types of games children engage in are steady or constant games, such as tag, which are played consistently; recurrent or cyclical games, such as marbles and hopscotch, which seem to follow cycles of popularity and decline; sporadic games, which are rarely played; and one-time games, such as hula hoop contests, which rise to popularity once and then disappear.

In sum, play is a multidimensional, complex concept. It ranges from an infant's simple exercise of a newfound sensorimotor talent to a preschool child's riding a tricycle to an older child's participation in organized games. Children's play also can involve combinations of the play categories we have described. For example, social play can be sensorimotor (rough-and-tumble), symbolic, and constructive.

Strategies for Enriching the Quality of Children's Play   How can parents and teachers enrich the quality of children's play? Following are some helpful suggestions (Ward, 1996):

- *Time*. Provide children with long stretches of uninterrupted time to sustain sociodramatic and constructive play episodes. A rule of thumb is to allow for 30- to 50-minute blocks of time for free play at least several times a week.

constructive play

Play that combines sensorimotor/practice repetitive activity with symbolic representation of ideas. Constructive play occurs when children engage in self-regulated creation or construction of a product or a problem solution.

games

Activities engaged in for pleasure that include rules and often competition with one or more individuals.

- *Space.* Children need adequate space to play effectively. At least 25–30 square feet should be provided. Cramped space encourages aggression and decreases social play.
- *Experiences.* Children draw on past experiences when they play. Community field trips and classroom visits from individuals involved in various occupations and hobbies can stimulate rich episodes of pretend play. Relating fairy tales and folktales to children and reading stories to them can encourage fantasy play.
- *Play materials.* Home-living and theme-related props, dress-up clothes, dolls, trucks, and other vehicles promote social interaction and group dramatic play.

Adult involvement in the child's play should be minimally disruptive. It should be thought of as a way to support and extend play opportunities, not as a strategy forced on unwilling children. If children are playing unimaginatively, parents or teachers can sit next to them and silently begin to play. They can model a more interesting way of playing with the same materials.

Television

Television and Children

Few developments in society in the second half of the twentieth century had a greater impact on children than television (Comstock & Scharrar, 1999). Many children spend more time in front of the television set than they do with their parents. Although it is only one of the many mass media that affect children's behavior, television is the most influential. The persuasive capabilities of television are staggering. The 20,000 hours of television watched by the time the average American adolescent graduates from high school are greater than the number of hours spent in the classroom.

Television's Many Roles   Television can have a negative influence by taking children away from homework, making them passive learners, teaching them stereotypes, providing them with violent models of aggression, and presenting them with unrealistic views of the world. However, television can have a positive influence on children's development by presenting motivating educational programs, increasing their information about the world beyond their immediate environment, and providing models of prosocial behavior (Clifford, Gunter, & McAleer, 1995).

Television has been called many things, not all of them good. Depending on one's point of view, it may be a "window on the world," the "one-eyed monster," or the "boob tube." Television has been attacked as one of the reasons scores on national achievement tests in reading and mathematics are lower now than in the past. Television, it is claimed, attracts children away from books and schoolwork. In one study, children who read printed materials, such as books, watched television less than those who did not read (Huston, Seigle, & Bremer, 1983). Furthermore, critics argue, television trains children to become passive learners. Rarely, if ever, does television require active responses from the observer.

Television also is said to deceive. That is, it teaches children that problems are resolved easily and that everything always comes out right in the end. For example, TV detectives usually take only 30 to 60 minutes to sort through a complex array of clues to reveal the killer. And they *always* find the killer! Violence is a way of life on many shows, where it is all right for police to use violence and to break moral codes in their fight against evildoers. The lasting results of violence are rarely brought home to the viewer. A person who is injured suffers for only a few seconds. In real life, the person might need months or years to recover, or might not recover at all, yet one out of every two first-grade children says that the adults on television are like adults in real life.

A special concern is how ethnic minorities are portrayed on television (Greenberg & Brand, 1994). Ethnic minorities have historically been underrepresented and mis-

Television is a medium of entertainment which permits millions of people to listen to the same joke at the same time, and yet remain lonesome.

T. S. Eliot
American-Born English Poet, 20th Century

represented on television. Ethnic minority characters—whether African American, Latino, Asian American, or Native American—have traditionally been presented as less dignified and less positive than White characters. In one study, character portrayals of ethnic minorities were examined during heavy children's viewing hours (weekdays 4–6 P.M. and 7–11 P.M.) (Williams & Condry, 1989). The percentage of White characters far exceeded the actual percentage of Whites in the United States. The percentage of African American, Latino, and Asian American characters fell short of the population statistics. Latino characters were especially underrepresented. Only 0.6 percent of the characters were Latino, while the Latino population in the United States is 6.4 percent of the total U.S. population. Minorities tended to hold lower-status jobs and were more likely than Whites to be cast as criminals or victims.

There are some positive aspects to television's influence on children, however. For one, television presents children with a world that is different from the one in which they live. It exposes children to a wider variety of viewpoints and information than they might get from only their parents, teachers, and peers. And some television programs have educational and developmental benefits. One of television's major programming attempts to educate children is "Sesame Street." It is designed to teach children both cognitive and social skills. The program began in 1969 and is still going strong. "Sesame Street" demonstrates that education and entertainment can work well together (Green, 1995; Wright, 1995). Through "Sesame Street," children experience a world of learning that is both exciting and entertaining.

Amount of Television Watching by Children   Just how much television do young children watch? They watch a lot, and they seem to be watching more all the time. In the 1950s, 3-year-old children watched television for less than 1 hour a day; 5-year-olds watched just over 2 hours a day. But, in the 1970s, preschool children watched television for an average of 4 hours a day; elementary school children watched for as long as 6 hours a day (Friedrich & Stein, 1973). In the 1990s, children are averaging 11 to 28 hours of television per week, which is more than for any other activity except sleep.

As shown in figure 11.7, considerably more children in the United States than their counterparts in other developed countries watch television for long periods. For example, seven times as many 9-year-olds in the United States as their counterparts in Switzerland watch television more than 5 hours a day.

"Mrs. Horton, could you stop by school today?"
© Martha F. Campbell

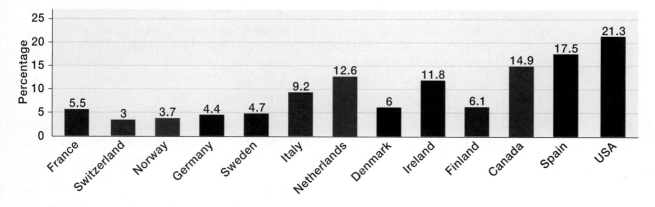

Figure 11.7
Percentage of 9-Year-Old Children Who Report Watching More Than Five Hours of Television per Weekday

Adventures for the Mind

Developing Parental Guidelines for Children's TV Viewing

Many parents do not carefully monitor their children's TV viewing and do not discuss the content of TV shows with them. Develop a series of guidelines that you would recommend to parents that you believe would help them make television a more positive influence in their children's lives. Consider such factors as the child's age, the child's activities other than TV, the parents' patterns of interaction with their children, and types of television shows.

Television and Violence

A special concern is the extent to which children are exposed to violence and aggression on television. Up to 80 percent of the prime-time shows include violent acts, including beatings, shootings, and stabbings. The frequency of violence increases on the Saturday morning cartoon shows, which average more than 25 violent acts per hour.

Effects of Television on Children's Aggression and Prosocial Behavior   What are the effects of television violence on children's aggression? Does television merely stimulate a child to go out and buy a *Star Wars* ray gun, or can it trigger an attack on a playmate? When children grow up, can television violence increase the likelihood they will violently attack someone?

In one longitudinal study, the amount of violence viewed on television at age 8 was significantly related to the seriousness of criminal acts performed as an adult (Huesmann, 1986). In another study, long-term exposure to television violence was significantly related to the likelihood of aggression in 1,565 12- to 17-year-old boys (Belson, 1978). Boys who watched the most aggression on television were the most likely to commit a violent crime, swear, be aggressive in sports, threaten violence toward another boy, write slogans on walls, or break windows. These studies are *correlational*, so we cannot conclude from them that television violence causes children to be more aggressive, only that watching television violence is *associated with* aggressive behavior. In one experiment, children were randomly assigned to one of two groups: one watched television shows taken directly from violent Saturday morning cartoon offerings on 11 different days; the second group watched television cartoon shows with all of the violence removed (Steur, Applefield, & Smith, 1971). The children were then observed during play at their preschool. The preschool children who saw the TV cartoon shows with violence kicked, choked, and pushed their playmates more than did the preschool children who watched nonviolent TV cartoon shows. Because the children were randomly assigned to the two conditions (TV cartoons with violence versus nonviolent TV cartoons), we can conclude that exposure to TV violence *caused* the increased aggression in the children in this investigation.

Some critics argue that the effects of television violence do not warrant the conclusion that TV violence causes aggression (Freedman, 1984). However, many experts argue that TV violence can induce aggressive or antisocial behavior in children (Strasburger, 1995). Of course, television is not the *only* cause of aggression. There is no *one* single cause of any social behavior. Aggression, like all other social behaviors, has a number of determinants.

Children need to be taught critical viewing skills to counter the adverse effects of television violence. In one study, elementary school children were randomly assigned to either an experimental or a control group (Huesmann & others, 1983). In the experimental group, children assisted in making a film to help children who had been fooled or harmed by television. The children also composed essays that focused on how television is not like real life and why it is bad to imitate TV violence or watch too much television. In the control group, the children received no training in critical viewing skills. The children who were trained in critical viewing skills developed more negative attitudes about TV violence and reduced their aggressive behavior.

Television also can teach children that it is better to behave in positive, prosocial ways than in negative, antisocial ways. Aimee Leifer (1973) demonstrated that

Developmental issues	What children see on TV	What children should see on TV
To establish a sense of *trust and safety*	The world is dangerous; enemies are everywhere; weapons are needed to feel safe.	A world where people can be trusted and help each other, where safety and predictability can be achieved, where fears can be overcome
To develop a sense of *autonomy with connectedness*	Autonomy is equated with fighting and weapons. Connectedness is equated with helplessness, weakness, and altruism.	A wide range of models of independence within meaningful relationships and of autonomous people helping each other
To develop a sense of *empowerment and efficacy*	Physical strength and violence equal power and efficacy. Bad guys always return, and a range of ways to have an impact is *not* shown.	Many examples of people having a positive effect on their world without violence
To establish *gender identity*	Exaggerated, rigid gender divisions—boys are strong, violent, and save the world; girls are helpless, victimized and irrelevant to world events	Complex characters with wide-ranging behaviors, interests, and skills; commonalities between the sexes overlapping in what both can do
To develop an *appreciation of diversity* among people	Racial and ethnic stereotyping. Dehumanized enemies. Diversity is dangerous. Violence against those who are different is justified.	Diverse peoples with varied talents, skills, and needs, who treat each other with respect, work out problems nonviolently, and enrich each others' lives
To construct the foundations of *morality and social responsibility*	One-dimensional characters who are all good or bad. Violence is the solution to interpersonal problems. Winning is the only acceptable outcome. Bad guys deserve to be hurt.	Complex characters who act responsibly and morally toward others—showing kindness and respect, working out moral problems, taking other people's points of view
To have opportunities for *meaningful play*	Program content is far removed from children's experience or level of understanding. Toys are linked to programs promoting imitative, not creative play.	Meaningful content to use in play, which resonates deeply with developmental needs; shows not linked to realistic toys so that children can create their own unique play

Figure 11.8
Television and Children's Development

television is associated with prosocial behavior in young children. She selected a number of episodes from the television show "Sesame Street" that reflected positive social interchanges. She was especially interested in situations that taught children how to use their social skills. For example, in one interchange, two men were fighting over the amount of space available to them. They gradually began to cooperate and to share the space. Children who watched these episodes copied these behaviors, and in later social situations they applied the prosocial lessons they had learned. To read about ways television could be improved to be more developmentally appropriate, see figure 11.8.

Children's Television Workshop

Improving Developmental Skills
Guiding Young Children's Socioemotional Development

How can young children's socioemotional skills be nourished? The following strategies can help.

- *Look for situations to help children with their emotions.* Parents, teachers, and other adults can help children understand and handle their emotions in socially acceptable ways.
- *Present positive moral models for the child and use emotional situations to promote moral development.* Children benefit when they are around people who engage in prosocial rather than antisocial behavior. Encourage children to show empathy and learn to deal with their emotions.
- *Be an authoritative parent.* Children's self-control and social competence benefit when both parents are authoritative. This means being neither punitive and overcontrolling nor permissive. Authoritative parents are nurturant, engage the child in verbal give-and-take, monitor the child, and use nonpunitive control.
- *Adapt to the child's developmental changes.* Parents should use less physical manipulation and more reasoning or withholding of special privileges in disciplining a 5-year-old, as opposed to disciplining a 2-year-old.
- *Communicate effectively with children in a divorced family.* Good strategies are to explain the separation and say it is not the child's fault, explain that it may take time to feel better, keep the door open for further discussion, provide as much continuity as possible, and provide a support system for the child.
- *Provide the child with opportunities for peer interaction.* Children learn a great deal from the mutual give-and-take of peer relations. Make sure the child gets considerable time to play with peers rather than watching TV or going to an academic early childhood program all day.
- *Provide the child with many opportunities for play.* Positive play experiences can play important roles in the young child's socioemotional development.
- *Monitor the child's TV viewing.* Keep exposure to TV violence to a minimum. Develop a set of guidelines for the child's TV viewing.

Television and Cognitive Development

Children bring various cognitive skills and abilities to their television viewing experience (Doubleday & Droege, 1993; Lorch, 1995; Rabin & Dorr, 1995). Compared with older children, preschoolers and young children attend to television more, comprehend less central content and more incidental content, and have difficulty making inferences about content. These youngest viewers have difficulty representing television content and often fill in their incomplete representations with stereotypes and familiar scripts derived from their limited general knowledge of television and the world. They usually are not aware that some content is intended to sell them toys and breakfast cereal, rather than to entertain and inform them. Older children have a better understanding in all of these areas, but they still process television information less effectively than adults do. Children's greater attention to television and their less complete and more distorted understanding of what they view suggest that they may miss some of the positive aspects of television and be more vulnerable to its negative aspects.

How does television influence children's creativity and verbal skills? Television is negatively related to children's creativity (Williams, 1986). Also, because television is primarily a visual modality, verbal skills—especially expressive language—are enhanced more by aural or print exposure (Beagles-Roos & Gat, 1983). Educational programming for young children can promote creativity and imagination, possibly because it has a slower pace, and auditory and visual modalities are better coordinated. Newer technologies, especially interactive television, hold promise for motivating children to learn and become more exploratory in solving problems (Singer, 1993). To further evaluate television and children's development, see Adventures for the Mind.

So far in the chapter, we have discussed numerous ways that young children's socioemotional development can be nourished. The insert, Improving Developmental Skills, profiles these recommendations. Also at this point, we have described many aspects of families, peers, play, and television. An overview of these ideas is presented in summary table 11.2.

Summary Table 11.2
Families, Peers, Play, and Television

Concept	Processes/ Related Ideas	Characteristics/Description
Families	Parenting	Authoritarian, authoritative, neglectful, and indulgent are four main parenting styles. Authoritative parenting is the style most often associated with children's social competence. Parents need to adapt their interaction strategies as the child grows older. Authoritative parenting is the most widely used style around the world.
	Sibling relationships and birth order	Siblings interact with each other in more negative and less varied ways than parents and children interact. Birth order is related in certain ways to child characteristics, but some critics argue that birth order is not a good predictor of behavior.
	The changing family	There is no indication that a mother's working full-time outside the home has negative long-term effects on children. Children in divorced families show more adjustment problems than their counterparts in nondivorced families, although the size of the effects are debated. Whether parents should stay together for the sake of children is difficult to determine, although conflict has negative effects on children. Children show better adjustment in divorced families when parents' relationship with each other is harmonious and authoritative parenting is used. Among other factors to be considered in children's adjustment in divorced families are adjustment prior to the divorce, personality and temperament, developmental status, gender, and custody. Income loss for divorced mothers may be linked with a number of stresses that may affect the child's adjustment. Cultures vary on a number of issues regarding families. African American and Latino children are more likely than White American children to live in single-parent families and larger families and to have extended family connections. Higher-income families are more likely to use discipline that encourages internalization; low-income families, discipline that focuses on external characteristics.
Peer relations, play, and television	Peer relations	Peers are powerful socialization agents. Peers are children who are of about the same age or maturity level. Peers provide a source of information and comparison about the world outside the family. Parent-child and peer relations represent distinct but coordinated worlds. Healthy family relations usually promote healthy peer relations.
	Play	Play's functions include affiliation with peers, tension release, advances in cognitive development, exploration, and provision of a safe haven. Parten developed the categories of unoccupied, solitary, onlooker, parallel, associative, and cooperative play. The contemporary perspective on play emphasizes both the cognitive and the social aspects of play. Among the most widely studied aspects of children's play today are sensorimotor play, practice play, pretense/symbolic play, social play, constructive play, and games. A number of strategies can be used to enrich children's play.
	Television	Television can have both negative influences (such as turning children into passive learners and presenting them with aggressive models) and positive influences (such as presenting motivating educational programs and providing models of prosocial behavior) on children's development. Children watch huge amounts of television. TV violence is not the only cause of children's aggression, but it can induce aggression. Prosocial behavior on TV is associated with increased positive behavior by children. Children's cognitive skills influence their TV-viewing experiences. Television viewing is negatively related to children's creativity and verbal skills.

Chapter Review

In early childhood, children's socioemotional worlds expand. Their emotion language increases, as does their understanding of emotion. They spend more time with peers and in play. Their small worlds widen as they discover new refuges and people, although parents continue to play important roles in their lives.

We began this chapter by considering the story of Sara and her developing sense of morality and values. Then we studied the following aspects of emotional and personality development: the self, emotional development, moral development, and gender. Our coverage of families focused on parenting, sibling relationships, and birth order, and the changing family in a changing society. We also examined peer relations, play, and television.

Don't forget that you can obtain a more detailed overview of the chapter by again studying the two summary tables on pages 300 and 323.

✓ Children Checklist

Socioemotional Development in Early Childhood

How much have you learned since the beginning of the chapter? Use the following statements to help you review your knowledge and understanding of the chapter material. First, read the statement and mentally or briefly demonstrate on paper that you can discuss the relevant information.

_____ I can evaluate the development of the self in young children.
_____ I know about emotional development in young children.
_____ I can describe young children's moral development.
_____ I can discuss gender development.
_____ I can describe parenting styles.
_____ I can discuss sibling relations and birth order.
_____ I am aware of the effects of divorce on children's development.
_____ I can describe cultural, ethnic, and socioeconomic variations in families.
_____ I can discuss peer relations.
_____ I can describe young children's play.
_____ I know how television affects children's development.

For any items that you did not check, go back and locate the relevant material in the chapter. Review the material until you feel you can check off the item. You may want to use this checklist later in preparing for an exam.

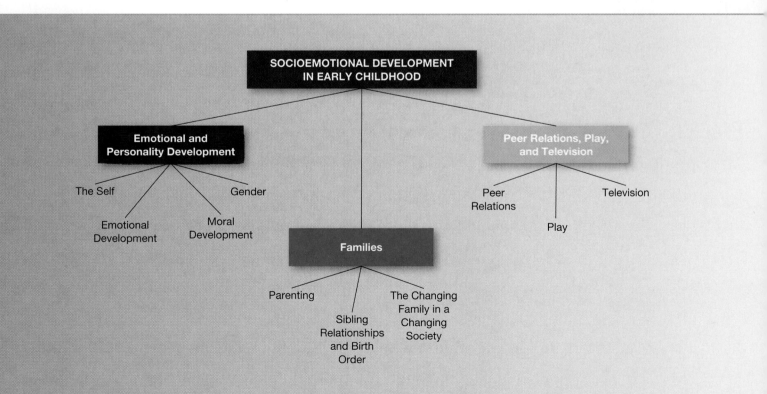

Key Terms

self-understanding 288
moral development 291
heteronomous morality 292
autonomous morality 292
imminent justice 292
empathy 293
gender 294
gender identity 294
gender role 294
estrogens 294
androgens 294
identification theory 295
social learning theory of
   gender 295
cognitive developmental
   theory of gender 297
schema 299
gender schema 299
gender schema theory 299
gender constancy 299

authoritarian parenting 301
authoritative parenting 302
neglectful parenting 302
indulgent parenting 302
peers 312
play 313
play therapy 314
unoccupied play 315
solitary play 315
onlooker play 315
parallel play 315
associative play 315
cooperative play 315
sensorimotor play 315
practice play 316
pretense/symbolic play 316
social play 316
constructive play 317
games 317

Children Resources

Alike and Different
(1992) edited by Bonnie Neugebauer. Washington, DC: National Association for the Education of Young Children.

This collection of practical essays addresses the many complex issues involved in educating young children from diverse ethnic backgrounds, as well as those with special needs. The essays cover many useful activities that promote an antibias atmosphere for early childhood education.

Children's Television Workshop
One Lincoln Plaza
New York, NY 10023
212–595–3456

This is a global educational institution that uses media, such as television, home video, and computer software, to facilitate learning among children at home, in the classroom, and in other community settings.

Growing Up with Divorce
(1990) by Neil Kalter. New York: Free Press.

Growing Up with Divorce is written for divorced parents and provides them with information to help their children avoid emotional problems. Kalter offers practical strategies for parents to help their children cope with the anxiety, anger, and confusion that can appear immediately after the separation or divorce, or that may develop after a number of years. Separate problems and concerns of children of different ages and sexes at each stage of divorce are portrayed.

The Preschool Years
(1988) by Ellen Galinsky and Judy David. New York: Times Books.

The Preschool Years describes normal child development in the 3- to 5-year-old age period and provides recommendations to parents for coping with specific problems in this period of development.

Taking It to the Net

http://www.mhhe.com/santrockcd6

1. Nikki is a happy child that loves to play with other children. Her mother often comments that she can make anyone a friend. Samantha, however, is generally abrasive with other children and has very few friends. What might you conclude regarding the value of healthy interpersonal peer relations?
2. Your neighbor is concerned about the impact of television on her 4-year-old. What are some activities she could engage in with her child to help the child understand the nature of television and to place television in an appropriate perspective?
3. Ms. Jones tells you that she is trying to raise her two boys and two girls to appreciate gender equity; however, she wonders how the emphasis on gender equity in the past 10–20 years has affected society. What are some of the social effects of the emphasis on gender equity? What would you tell Ms. Jones?

Early Childhood

Physical Development

The average child grows 2½ inches in height and gains 5 to 7 pounds a year during early childhood. Growth patterns vary individually, though. By age 5, the brain has reached nine-tenths of its adult size. Some of its size increase is due to the number and size of nerve endings, some to myelination. Gross motor skills increase dramatically during early childhood. Young children are more active than at any other period in the life span. Fine motor skills also increase substantially during early childhood. Energy needs increase as children go through the childhood years. One of every three deaths in the world is that of a child under 5. The most frequent cause of children's death is diarrhea. The United States has a relatively low mortality rate for children, although the Scandinavian countries have the lowest rates. The disorders most likely to be fatal for American children in early childhood are birth defects, cancer, and heart disease.

Cognitive Development

Piaget's stage of preoperational thought is the stage when children begin to be able to reconstruct at the level of thought what they have already learned to do in behavior, as well as a transition from a primitive to a more sophisticated use of symbols. The child does not yet think in an operational way. Preoperational thought consists of two substages: symbolic function (2–4 years of age) and intuitive thought (4–7 years of age). Vygotsky's theory emphasizes the zone of proximal development, the merging of language and thought from 3 to 7 years of age, and the sociocultural contexts of cognitive development. The child's attention improves dramatically during the early childhood years, as does short-term memory. Young children develop a curiosity about the nature of the human mind. Advances in language development also occur during early childhood. Child-centered kindergarten and developmentally appropriate education are important dimensions of early childhood education, as are quality Head Start programs. A current concern is that too many preschool and early childhood education programs place too much emphasis on academic achievement.

Socioemotional Development

Erikson believed that early childhood is characterized by the conflict of initiative versus conflict. In early childhood, the physical self becomes a part of the child's self-understanding. Preschoolers become more adept at talking about their own and others' emotions. Two- and 3-year-olds considerably increase the number of terms they use to describe emotion and learn about the causes and consequences of feelings. At 4–5 years of age, children show an increased ability to reflect on emotions and understand that a single event can elicit different feelings in different people. They also show a growing awareness about controlling and managing emotions to meet social standards. Piaget distinguished between the heteronomous morality of younger children and the autonomous morality of older children. In addition to moral thought, moral behavior and moral feelings are important dimensions of moral development. Gender identity is the sense of being female or male, which most children acquire by the age of 3. The identification, social learning, cognitive development, and gender schema theories have been proposed to explain children's gender development. Peers are especially adept at rewarding gender-appropriate behavior. Among the social contexts that are important in young children's lives are the family, peer relations, play, and television. Authoritative parenting is associated with children's social competence. Parents need to adapt their parenting strategies as their children become older, using less physical manipulation and more reasoning. In some cases, siblings are stronger socializing agents than parents. Children today live in many different types of families. More children today grow up in working-mother and divorced families. Cross-cultural, ethnic, and socioeconomic status differences in parenting exist. Peers are powerful social agents who provide a source of information and social comparison outside the family. Play also is an important context for development. Parten developed a number of categories of social play. Among the most important types of children's play are sensorimotor play, practice play, pretense/symbolic play, social play, constructive play, and games. Television is yet another powerful socializing influence on children, who watch huge amounts of TV. A special concern is the violence children see on television.

Middle and Late Childhood

Section V

> *Blessed be child-hood, which brings-something of heaven into the midst of our rough earthliness.*
>
> Henri Frédéric Amiel
> *Swiss Poet, Philosopher, 19th Century*

In middle and late childhood, children are on a different plane, belonging to a generation and feeling all their own. It is the wisdom of the human life span that at no time are children more ready to learn than during the period of expansive imagination at the end of early childhood. Children develop a sense of wanting to make things—and not just to make them, but to make them well and even perfectly. Their thirst is to know and to understand. They are remarkable for their intelligence and for their curiosity. Their parents continue to be important influences in their lives, but their growth also is shaped by successive choirs of friends. They don't think much about the future or about the past, but they enjoy the present moment. Section V consists of three chapters: "Physical Development in Middle and Late Childhood" (chapter 12), "Cognitive Development in Middle and Late Childhood" (chapter 13), and "Socioemotional Development in Middle and Late Childhood" (chapter 14).

Chapter 12

Physical Development in Middle and Late Childhood

PREVIEW

Considerable progress in children's physical development continues to be made in the middle and late childhood years. Children grow taller, heavier, and stronger. They become more adept at using their physical skills. Among the questions that we will explore in this chapter are

- What are the main changes in children's body growth in middle and late childhood?
- What motor development changes characterize school-age children? Does the motor development of girls differ from that of boys?
- What are some important nutritional recommendations for children? What roles do exercise and sports play in children's development?
- What are some health problems that children may encounter?
- How much do children understand health?
- What is the nature of children's disabilities and the educational issues that are involved?

The Story of Zhang Liyin

Standing on the balance beam at a sports school in Beijing, China, 6-year-old Zhang Liyin stretches her arms outward as she gets ready to perform a backflip. She wears the bright red gymnastic suit of the elite—a suit given to only the best 10 girls in her class of 6- to 8-year-olds (see figure 12.1). But her face wears a dreadful expression. She can't drum up enough confidence to do the flip. Maybe it is because she has had a rough week. A purple bruise decorates one leg, and a nasty gash disfigures the other. Her coach, a woman in her twenties, makes Zhang jump from the beam and escorts her to the high bar, where she is instructed to hang for three minutes. If Zhang falls, she must pick herself up and try again. But she does not fall, and she is escorted back to the beam, where her coach puts her through another tedious routine.

Zhang attends the sports school in the afternoon. The sports school is a privilege given to only 260,000 of China's 200 million students of elementary to college age. The Communist party has decided that sports is one avenue China can pursue to prove that China has arrived in the modern world. The sports schools designed to

Figure 12.1
The Training of Future Olympians in the Sports Schools of China

Six-year-old Zhang Liyin (*third from the left*) hopes someday to become an Olympic gymnastics champion. Attending the sports school is considered an outstanding privilege; only 260,000 of China's 200 million children are given this opportunity.

Child Health Guide

produce Olympic champions were the reason for China's success in the last three Olympics. These schools are the only road to Olympic stardom in China. There are precious few neighborhood playgrounds. And there is only one gymnasium for every 3.5 million people.

Many of the students who attend the sports schools in the afternoon live and study at the schools as well. Only a few attend a normal school and then go to a sports school in the afternoon. Because of her young age, Zhang stays at home during the mornings and goes to the sports school from noon until 6 P.M. A part-timer such as Zhang can stay enrolled until she no longer shows potential to move up to the next step. Any child who seems to lack potential is asked to leave.

Zhang was playing in a kindergarten class when a coach from a sports school spotted her. She was selected because of her broad shoulders, narrow hips, straight legs, symmetrical limbs, open-minded attitude, vivaciousness, and outgoing personality. If Zhang continues to show progress, she could be asked to move to full-time next year. At age 7, she would then go to school there and live in a dorm six days a week. If she becomes extremely competent at gymnastics, Zhang could be moved to Shishahai, where the elite gymnasts train and compete (Reilly, 1988).

BODY GROWTH AND PROPORTION

The period of middle and late childhood involves slow, consistent growth. This is a period of calm before the rapid growth spurt of adolescence. Among the important aspects of body growth and proportion in this developmental period are those involving skeletal and muscular systems, as well as tooth development and dental care.

Skeletal and Muscular Systems

During the elementary school years, children grow an average of 2 to 3 inches a year until, at the age of 11, the average girl is 4 feet, 10¾ inches tall, and the average boy is 4 feet, 9 inches tall. During the middle and late childhood years, children gain about 5 to 7 pounds a year. The weight increase is due mainly to increases in the size of the skeletal and muscular systems, as well as the size of some body organs. Muscle mass and strength gradually increase as "baby fat" decreases. The loose movements and knock knees of early childhood give way to improved muscle tone. The increase in muscular strength is due to heredity and to exercise. Children also double their strength capabilities during these years. Because of their greater number of muscle cells, boys are usually stronger than girls. A summary of the changes in height and weight in middle and late childhood appears in figure 12.2.

Proportional changes are among the most pronounced physical changes in middle and late childhood. Head circumference, waist circumference, and leg length decrease in relation to body height (Wong, 1997). A less noticeable physical change is that bones continue to ossify during middle and late childhood but yield to pressure and pull more than mature bones.

Tooth Development and Dental Care

Most of the teeth we have as adults begin to come in during middle and late childhood. Primary teeth start falling out at about 6 years of age and are replaced by the first permanent (secondary) teeth. Permanent teeth appear at the rate of approximately four per year for the next five years.

Because permanent teeth come in during middle and late childhood, it is important for children to have good dental hygiene during this period. Correct brushing techniques need to be taught and regular dental supervision carried out. Teeth

Height (inches)						
Age	Female percentiles			Male percentiles		
	25th	50th	75th	25th	50th	75th
6	43.75	45.00	46.50	44.25	45.75	47.00
7	46.00	47.50	49.00	46.25	48.00	49.25
8	48.00	49.75	51.50	48.50	50.00	51.50
9	50.25	53.00	53.75	50.50	52.00	53.50
10	52.50	54.50	56.25	52.50	54.25	55.75
11	55.00	57.00	58.75	54.50	55.75	57.25
Weight (pounds)						
6	39.25	43.00	47.25	42.00	45.50	49.50
7	43.50	48.50	53.25	46.25	50.25	55.00
8	49.00	54.75	61.50	51.00	55.75	61.50
9	55.75	62.75	71.50	56.00	62.00	69.25
10	63.25	71.75	82.75	62.00	69.25	78.50
11	71.75	81.25	94.25	69.00	77.75	89.00

Source: Data from R. E. Behman and V. C. Vaughan (eds.), *Nelson Textbook of Pediatrics*. W. B. Saunders, Philadelphia, PA, 1987.

Note: The percentile tells how the child compares with other children of the same age. The 50th percentile tells us that half of the children of a particular age are taller (heavier) or shorter (lighter). The 25th percentile tells us that 25 percent of the children of that age are shorter (lighter) and 75 percent are taller (heavier).

Figure 12.2
Changes in Height and Weight in Middle and Late Childhood

should be brushed after meals, after snacks, and before bedtime. Flossing following brushing is recommended, beginning at about 8–9 years of age.

In recent years, the use of fluoride in toothpaste, mouthwash, and water has greatly reduced the number of children who have cavities, with over half of all U.S. children 5–17 years of age being cavity-free. Periodontal disease, which involves inflammatory and degenerative conditions in the gums and tissues that support the teeth, often begins in childhood and accounts for a significant amount of tooth loss in adulthood. This disease is most often due to a buildup of plaque bacteria on the teeth. Conscientious brushing and flossing significantly reduce the risk of periodontal disease. Malocclusion occurs when the teeth of the upper and lower dental arches are not properly aligned. Orthodontic treatment for malocclusion, as well as uneven, crowded, or overlapping teeth, is usually most successful when begun toward the end of middle and late childhood or in early adolescence.

MOTOR DEVELOPMENT

During middle and late childhood, children's motor development becomes much smoother and more coordinated than it was in early childhood. For example, only one child in a thousand can hit a tennis ball over the net at the age of 3, yet by the age of 10 or 11 most children can learn to play the sport. Running, climbing, skipping rope, swimming, bicycle riding, and skating are just a few of the many physical skills elementary school children can master. And, when mastered, these physical skills are a source of great pleasure and accomplishment for children. In gross motor skills involving large muscle activity, boys usually outperform girls.

As children move through the elementary school years, they gain greater control over their bodies. Physical action is essential for them to refine their developing motor skills.

As children move through the elementary school years, they gain greater control over their bodies and can sit and attend for longer periods of time. However, elementary school children are far from having physical maturity, and they need to be active. Elementary school children become more fatigued by long periods of sitting than by running, jumping, or bicycling. Physical action is essential for these children to refine their developing skills, such as batting a ball, skipping rope, or balancing on a beam. An important principle of practice for elementary school children, therefore, is that they should be engaged in *active*, rather than passive, activities.

Increased myelinization of the central nervous system is reflected in the improvement of fine motor skills during middle and late childhood. Children's hands are used more adroitly as tools. Six-year-olds can hammer, paste, tie shoes, and fasten clothes. By 7 years of age, children's hands have become steadier. At this age, children prefer a pencil to a crayon for printing, and reversal of letters is less common. Printing becomes smaller. At 8 to 10 years of age, the hands can be used independently with more ease and precision. Fine motor coordination develops to the point at which children can write rather than print words. Letter size becomes smaller and more even. At 10 to 12 years of age, children begin to show manipulative skills similar to the abilities of adults. The complex, intricate, and rapid movements needed to produce fine-quality crafts or to play a difficult piece on a musical instrument can be mastered. Girls usually outperform boys in fine motor skills. A summary of changes in motor skills in middle and late childhood appears in figure 12.3.

CHILDREN'S HEALTH

Although we have become a health-conscious nation, many children as well as adults do not practice good health habits (Hayman, Mahon, & Turner, 1999). Too much junk food and too much couch-potato behavior describes all too many children. We begin our exploration of children's health with nutrition and exercise, then turn to a number of health problems that can emerge, and conclude with a discussion of children's understanding of health and illness.

Nutrition

In the middle and late childhood years, children's average body weight doubles. Children exert considerable energy as they engage in many different motor activities. To support their growth and active lives, children need to consume more food than they did in early childhood. From 1–3 years of age, infants and toddlers need to consume 1,300 calories per day on the average. At 4–6 years of age, young children need to take in 1,700 calories per day on the average. From 7–10 years of age, children need to consume 2,400 calories per day on the average; however, depending on the child's size, the range of recommended calories for 7- to 10-year-olds is 1,650 to 3,300 per day.

Within these calorie ranges, it is important to impress on children the value of a balanced diet to promote their growth. Children usually eat as their families eat, so the quality of their diet often depends largely on their family's pattern of eating. Most children acquire a taste for an increasing variety of food in middle and late childhood. However, with the increased availability of fast-food restaurants and media inducements, too many children fill up on food that has "empty calories" that

Age in years	Motor skills
6	Children can skip. Children can throw with proper weight shift and step. Girls can throw a small ball 19 feet, boys 34 feet. Girls and boys can vertically jump 7 inches. Girls can perform a standing long jump 33 inches, boys 36 inches. Children are more aware of their hands as tools. Children like to draw, paint, and color. Children can cut, paste paper toys, and sew crudely if needle is threaded. Children enjoy making simple figures in clay. Children can use a knife to spread butter or jam on bread.
7	Children balance on one foot without looking. Children can walk 2-inch-wide balance beams. Children can hop and jump accurately into small squares. Children can participate in jumping-jack exercise. Girls can throw a ball 25 feet, boys 45 feet. Girls can vertically jump 8 inches, boys 9 inches. Girls can perform standing long jump 41 inches, boys 43 inches. Children are able to maintain posture for a longer period of time. Children repeat physical performances to master them. Children brush and comb their hair, usually in an acceptable manner. Children use a table knife for cutting meat.
8	Children can engage in alternate rhythmic hopping in different patterns. Girls can throw a ball 34 feet, boys 59 feet. Girls can vertically jump 9 inches, boys 10 inches. Girls can perform standing long jump 50 inches, boys 55 inches. Grip strength increases. Children can use common tools, such as a hammer. Children can help with routine household tasks, such as dusting and sweeping.
9	Girls can throw a ball 41 feet, boys 71 feet. Girls can vertically jump 10 inches, boys 11 inches. Girls can perform standing long jump 53 inches, boys 57 inches. Perceptual-motor coordination becomes smoother.
10–11	Children can judge and intercept pathways of small balls thrown from distance. Girls can throw a small ball 49 feet, boys 94 feet at age 10; girls 58 feet and boys 106 feet at age 11. Girls can vertically jump 10 inches, boys 11 inches at age 10; girls 11 inches and boys 12 inches at age 11. Girls can perform standing long jump 57 inches, boys 61 inches at age 10; girls 62 inches and boys 66 inches at age 11. Children can make useful articles and do easy repair work. Children can cook and sew in small ways. Children can wash and dry their own hair.

*F*igure 12.3
Changes in Motor Skills During Middle and Late Childhood

do not promote effective growth. Many of these empty-calorie foods have a high content of sugar, starch, and excess fat.

Both parents and teachers can help children learn to eat better. In this vein, they can help children learn about the Food Guide Pyramid and what a healthy diet entails.

Children should begin their day by eating a healthy breakfast; according to nutritionists, breakfast should make up about one-fourth of the day's calories. A nutritious breakfast helps children have more energy and be more alert in the morning hours of school. In one study of low-income elementary-school-aged children, those who participated in a school breakfast program improved their standardized achievement test scores more and had fewer absences than the children who qualified for the program but did not participate (Meyers & others, 1989).

Exercise and Sports

How much exercise do children get? What are children's sports like?

Children and Exercise

The quality of life is determined by its activities.

Aristotle
Greek Philosopher, 4th Century B.C.

Exercise   Many of our patterns of health and illness are long-standing. Our experiences as children contribute to our health practices as adults. Did your parents seek medical help at your first sniffle, or did they wait until your temperature reached 104 degrees? Did they feed you heavy doses of red meat and sugar or a more rounded diet with vegetables and fruit? Did they involve you in sports or exercise programs, or did you lie around watching television all the time?

Are children getting enough exercise? The 1985 School Fitness Survey tested 18,857 children aged 6 to 17 on nine fitness tasks. Compared with a similar survey in 1975, there was virtually no improvement on the tasks. For example, 40 percent of the boys 6 to 12 years of age could not do more than one pull-up, and a full 25 percent could not do any. Fifty percent of the girls aged 6 to 17 and 30 percent of the boys aged 6 to 12 could not run a mile in less than 10 minutes. In the 50-yard dash, the adolescent girls in 1975 were faster than the adolescent girls in 1985.

Some experts suggest that television is at least partially to blame for the poor physical condition of our nation's children. In one study, children who watched little television were significantly more physically fit than their heavy-television-viewing counterparts (Tucker, 1987). The more children watch television, the more they are likely to be overweight. No one is quite sure whether this is because children spend their leisure time in front of the television set instead of chasing each other around the neighborhood or because they tend to eat a lot of junk food they see advertised on television.

Some of the blame also falls on the nation's schools, many of which fail to provide daily physical education classes. In the 1985 School Fitness Survey, 37 percent of the children in the first through fourth grades took gym classes only once or twice a week. The investigation also revealed that parents are poor role models when it comes to physical fitness. Less than 30 percent of the parents of the children in grades 1 through 4 exercised three days a week. Roughly half said they never get any vigorous exercise. In another study, observations of children's behavior in physical education classes at four elementary schools revealed how little vigorous exercise is done in these classes (Parcel & others, 1987). Children moved through space only 50 percent of the time they were in the class, and they moved continuously an average of only 2.2 minutes. In summary, not only do children's school weeks not include adequate physical education classes, but the majority of children do not exercise vigorously, even when they are in such classes. Furthermore, most children's parents are poor role models for vigorous physical exercise.

Does it make a difference if we push children to exercise more vigorously in elementary school? One study says yes (Tuckman & Hinkle, 1988). One hundred fifty-four elementary school children were randomly assigned either to three 30-minute running programs per week or to regular attendance in physical education classes. Although the results sometimes varied according to sex, for the most part, the cardiovascular health as well as the creativity of children in the running program were enhanced. For example, the boys in this program had less body fat, and the girls had more creative involvement in their classrooms.

In addition to the school, the family plays an important role in a child's exercise program. A wise strategy is for the family to take up activities involving vigorous physical exercise that parents and children can enjoy together. Running, swimming, cycling, and hiking are especially recommended. In encouraging children to exercise more, parents should not push them beyond their physical limits or expose them to competitive pressures that take the fun out of sports and exercise. For example, long-distance running may be too strenuous for young children and could result in bone injuries. Recently, there has been an increase in the number of children competing in strenuous athletic events, such as marathons and triathlons. Doctors are beginning to see some injuries in children that they previously saw only in adults. Some injuries, such as stress fractures and tendonitis, stem from the overuse of young, still-growing bodies. If left to their own devices, how many 8-year-old children would want to prepare for a marathon? It is recommended that parents downplay cutthroat striving and encourage healthy sports that children can enjoy, a topic we will discuss further in our examination of children's competitive sports.

Sports

In the story that opened the chapter, you read about 6-year-old Zhang Liyin, who attends a sports school that is designed to produce future Olympians. By American standards, Zhang's life sounds rigid and punitive. Even though sports has a lofty status in American society, children are not being trained with the intensity that characterizes Zhang Liyin's school. Sports have become an integral part of American culture. Thus, it is not surprising that more and more children become involved in sports every year. Both in public schools and in community agencies, children's sports programs that involve baseball, soccer, football, basketball, swimming, gymnastics, and other activities have grown to the extent that they have changed the shape of many children's lives.

Little league baseball, basketball, soccer, tennis, dance—as children's motor development becomes smoother and more coordinated, they are able to master these activities more competently in middle and late childhood than in early childhood.

Participation in sports can have both positive and negative consequences for children. Children's participation in sports can provide exercise, opportunities to learn how to compete, self-esteem, and a setting for developing peer relations and friendships. However, sports also can have negative outcomes for children: the pressure to achieve and win, physical injuries, a distraction from academic work, and unrealistic expectations for success as an athlete. Few people challenge the value of sports for children when conducted as part of a school physical education or intramural program. However, some critics question the appropriateness of highly competitive, win-oriented sports teams in schools and communities.

There is a special concern for children in high-pressure sports settings involving championship play with accompanying media publicity. Some clinicians and child developmentalists believe such activities not only put undue stress on the participants but also teach children the wrong values—namely, a win-at-all-costs philosophy. The possibility of exploiting children through highly organized, win-oriented sports programs is an ever present danger. Overly ambitious parents, coaches, and community boosters can unintentionally create a highly stressful atmosphere in children's sports. When parental, agency, or community prestige becomes the central focus of the child's participation in sports, the danger of exploitation is clearly present. Programs oriented toward such purposes often require long and arduous training sessions over many months and years, frequently leading to sports specialization at too early an age. In such circumstances, adults often transmit a distorted view of the role of the sport in the child's life, communicating to the child that the sport is the most important aspect of the child's existence. To read further about parents and children's sports, see Caring for Children.

We are underexercised as a nation. We look instead of play. We ride instead of walk. Our existence deprives us of the minimum of physical activity essential for healthy living.

John F. Kennedy
American President, 20th Century

Health Problems

For most children, middle and late childhood is a time of excellent health. Disease and death are less prevalent in this period than in other periods of childhood and

Diseases and Illnesses

Caring for Children

Parents and Children's Sports

Most sports psychologists believe it is important for parents to show an interest in their children's sports participation. Most children want their parents to watch them perform in sports. Many children whose parents do not come to watch them play in sporting events feel that their parents do not adequately support them. However, some children become extremely nervous when their parents watch them perform, or they get embarrassed when their parents cheer too loudly or make a fuss. If children request that their parents not watch them perform, parents should respect their children's wishes (Schreiber, 1990).

Parents should compliment their children for their sports performance. In the course of a game, there are dozens of circumstances when the child has done something positive—parents should stress a child's good performance, even if the child has limited abilities. Parents can tell their children how much the children hustled in the game and how enthusiastically they played. Even if the child strikes out in a baseball game, a parent can say, "That was a nice swing."

One of the hardest things for parents to do is to watch their children practicing or performing at a sport without helping them, to let their children make mistakes without interfering. Former Olympic swimmer Donna de Varona commented that the best way parents can help children in sports is to let them get to know themselves, and the only way they can do this is by having experiences in life. Naturally, parents want to provide their children with support and encouragement, but there is a point at which parental involvement becomes overinvolvement.

I (your author) have coached a number of young tennis players and have seen many parents who handled their roles as a nurturant, considerate parent well, but I have observed others who became overinvolved in their children's sport. Some parents were aware of their tendency to become overinvolved and backed off from pushing their children too intensely. However, some were not aware of their overintrusiveness and did not back off. The worst parent had a daughter who, at the age of 9, was already nationally ranked and showed great promise. Her father went to every lesson, every practice session, every tournament. Her tennis began to consume *his* life. At one tournament, he stormed onto the court during one of her matches and accused his daughter's 10-year-old opponent of cheating, embarrassing his daughter and himself. I called him the next day, told him I no longer could coach his daughter because of his behavior, and recommended that he seek counseling or not go to any more of her matches.

If parents do not become overinvolved, they can help their children build their physical skills and help them emotionally—discussing with them how to deal with a difficult coach, how to cope with a tough loss, and how to put in perspective a poorly played game. Parents need to carefully monitor their children as they participate in sports for signs of developing stress. If the problems appear to be beyond the intuitive skills of a volunteer coach or parent, a consultation with a counselor or clinician may be needed. Also, the parent needs to be sensitive to whether the sport in which the child is participating is the best one for the child and whether the child can handle its competitive pressures.

Some guidelines provided by the Women's Sports Foundation in its booklet *Parent's Guide to Girls' Sports* can benefit both parents and coaches of all children in sports:

The Dos

Make sports fun; the more children enjoy sports, the more they will want to play.

Remember that it is OK for children to make mistakes; it means they are trying.

Allow children to ask questions about the sport and discuss the sport in a calm, supportive manner.

Show respect for the child's sports participation.

Be positive and convince the child that he or she is making a good effort.

Be a positive role model for the child in sports.

The Don'ts

Yell or scream at the child

Condemn the child for poor play or continue to bring up failures long after they happen

Point out the child's errors in front of others

Expect the child to learn something immediately

Expect the child to become a pro

Ridicule or make fun of the child

Compare the child to siblings or to more talented children

Make sports all work and no fun

adolescence. However, some children do have health problems. Let's explore some of these, beginning with one of the most common problems—obesity.

Obesity   We will examine what constitutes obesity, what causes it, its consequences, and strategies for treating it.

When Is a Child Considered to Be Obese?

Defining when someone is obese is not a simple task. Weight for height is the most commonly used measure because it can be computed using a standard growth chart. If an individual is 20 percent over the expected weight for height, the individual is considered to be obese. In adults, body mass index (BMI) is currently in wide use, but for children this requires the development of age- and gender-based reference graphs. New BMI reference charts for children are in the process of being created (Klish, 1998). One problem in accurately measuring obesity is that variation in body fat in normal-weight individuals can range from 12 to 30 percent. When body mass index is used to define obesity in children, 22 percent of 6- to 19-year-olds are considered to be overweight; approximately one-half of these individuals, slightly more than 10 percent, are obese (Wolfe & others, 1994). This represents a 15 percent increase in obesity from just a decade earlier.

Girls are more likely than boys to be obese. Obesity is less common in African American than in White children during childhood, but during adolescence this reverses. Obesity at 6 years of age results in approximately a 25 percent probability that the child will be obese as an adult; obesity at age 12 results in approximately a 75 percent chance that the adolescent will be obese as an adult.

Consequences of Obesity in Children

We already have mentioned an important consequence of obesity in children: 25 percent of obese children become obese adults, and 75 percent of obese young adolescents become obese adults. Obesity also is a risk factor for many medical and psychological problems (Hill & Trowbridge, 1998). Obese children can develop pulmonary problems, such as sleep apnea (which we discussed in chapter 6, involving upper airway obstruction). Hip problems also are common in obese children. Obese children also are prone to have high blood pressure and elevated blood cholesterol levels. Low self-esteem and depression also are common outgrowths of obesity. Furthermore, obese children often are excluded from peer groups.

Treatment of Obesity

No evidence supports the use of surgical procedures in obese children. They should be used only when obesity is life-threatening (Klish, 1998). Diets only moderately deficient in calories are more successful over the long term than are those involving extreme deprivation of calories. Exercise is believed to be an extremely important component of a successful weight-loss program for overweight children. Exercise increases the child's lean body mass, which increases the child's resting metabolic rate. This results in more calories being burned in the resting state. Many experts on childhood obesity recommend a treatment that involves a combination of diet, exercise, and behavior modification. In a typical behavior modification program, children are taught to monitor their own behavior, keeping a food diary while attempting to lose weight. The diary should record not only the type and amount of food eaten but also when, with whom, and where it was eaten. That is, do children eat in front of the TV, by themselves, or because they are angry or depressed? A diary identifies behaviors that need to be changed.

What Causes Obesity?

Fat parents tend to have fat children, even if they are not living in the same household (Klish, 1998). Such characteristics as body type, height, body fat composition, and metabolism are inherited from parents. If both parents are obese, two-thirds of their children will become obese. If one parent is obese and the other is normal size, half of their children will become obese. If both

Overweight Children

parents are of normal size, less than 10 percent of their children will become obese (Whitaker & others, 1997).

In 1994, the first rodent gene for obesity, the ob gene, was identified. The product of the ob gene is the substance *leptin*, named for the Greek word for "thin." Leptin is circulated through the bloodstream to the hypothalamus in the brain, which plays important roles in eating behavior. Obese humans typically have high leptin levels (Considine, Sinha, & Heiman, 1996).

A child's insulin level is another important factor in eating behavior and obesity. Judy Rodin (1984) argues that what children eat influences their insulin levels. When children eat complex carbohydrates, such as cereals, bread, and pasta, insulin levels go up and fall of gradually. When children consume simple sugars, such as candy bars and soft drinks, insulin levels rise and then fall sharply—producing the sugar low with which many of us are all too familiar. Glucose levels in the blood are affected by these complex carbohydrates and simple sugars. Children are more likely to eat within the next several hours after eating simple sugars than after eating complex carbohydrates. And the food children eat at one meal influences what they will eat at the next meal. Thus, consuming doughnuts and candy bars, in addition to providing minimal nutritional value, sets up an ongoing sequence of what and how much children crave the next time they eat.

Thus, as can be seen in Rodin's analysis, the type of food children eat plays a role in obesity. Another factor that contributes to obesity is low activity level. A child's activity level is influenced by heredity but also by a child's motivation to engage in energetic activities and caregivers who model an active lifestyle or provide children with opportunities to be active.

Cancer in Children

Cancer   Cancer is the second leading cause of death (with injuries the leading cause) in children 5–14 years of age. Three percent of all children's deaths in this age period are due to cancer. In the 15–24 age group, cancer accounts for 13 percent of all deaths. Currently, 1 in every 330 children in the United States develops cancer before the age of 19. Morever, the incidence of cancer in children is increasing.

Child cancers have a different profile than adult cancers. Adult cancers attack mainly the lungs, colon, breast, prostrate, and pancreas. Child cancers are mainly those of the white blood cells (leukemia), brain, bone, lymph system, muscles, kidneys, and nervous system. All are characterized by an uncontrolled proliferation of abnormal cells.

As indicated in figure 12.4, the most common cancer in children is leukemia, a cancer of the tissues that make blood cells. In leukemia, the bone marrow makes an abundance of white blood cells that don't function properly. They invade the marrow and crowd out normal cells, making the child susceptible to bruising and infection. Lymphomas arise in the lymph system. Childhood lymphomas spread to the central nervous system and bone marrow. Treatments have been developed that can cure many children with lymphoma.

When cancer strikes children, it behaves differently than it does when it attacks adults. Children frequently have a more advanced stage of cancer when they are first diagnosed. When cancer is first diagnosed in adults, it has spread to distant parts of the body in only about 20 percent of the cases; however, that figure rises to 80 percent in children. Most adult cancers result from lifestyle factors, such as smoking, diet, occupation, and exposure to other cancer-causing agents. By contrast, little is known about the causes of childhood cancers (National Childhood Cancer Foundation, 1998).

Most adult cancer patients are treated in their local community by their family physician, consulting surgeon, or cancer specialist. Children with cancer are rarely treated by family physicians or pediatricians. They typically are treated by teams of physicians in children's hospitals, university medical centers, or cancer centers.

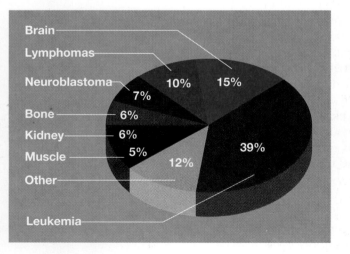

Figure 12.4
Types of Cancer in Children

Many children with cancer and other terminal illnesses may survive for a long period of time and experience problems associated with chronic illness or physical disability. Families initially may react with shock or denial when they find out that their child has cancer or any other type of terminal illness. Adjustment gradually follows and is usually characterized by an open admission that the illness exists. Most families move on to have realistic expectations for the child. A common pattern in parents of terminally ill children is chronic sorrow, in which acceptance of the child's illness is interspersed with periods of intense sorrow. Families with a terminally ill child benefit from the support of professionals and other families who have coped successfully with similar experiences.

Cardiovascular Disease   Cardiovascular disease is uncommon in children. Children with heart problems usually have one of the following, which usually can be corrected by surgery: holes in the heart, abnormal connections of heart vessels, abnormally narrow heart vessels, or abnormal heart valves. Unlike in adulthood, in which cardiovascular disease commonly arises from environmental experiences and behavior, such as smoking, most cases of cardiovascular disease in children are unrelated to environmental experiences and behavior.

Nonetheless, environmental experiences and behavior in the childhood years can sow the seeds for cardiovascular disease in adulthood. The precursors of cardiovascular disease often appear at a young age, with many elementary-school-aged children already possessing one or more of the risk factors, such as hypertension and obesity.

One large-scale investigation designed to improve children's cardiovascular health is the Bogalusa Heart Study, also called "Heart Smart." It involves an ongoing evaluation of 8,000 boys and girls in Bogalusa, Louisiana (Freedman & others, in press; Nicklas & others, 1995). The school is the focus of the Heart Smart intervention. Since 95 percent of children and adolescents aged 5 to 18 are in school, schools are an efficient context in which to educate individuals about health. Special attention is given to teachers, who serve as role models. Teachers who value the role of health in life and who engage in health-enhancing behavior present children and adolescents with positive models for health. Teacher in-service education is conducted by an interdisciplinary team of specialists, including physicians, psychologists, nutritionists, physical educators, and exercise physiologists. The school's staff is introduced to heart health education, the nature of cardiovascular disease, and risk factors for heart disease. Coping behavior, exercise behavior, and eating behavior are discussed with the staff, and a Heart Smart curriculum is explained. For example, the Heart Smart curriculum for grade 5 includes the content areas of cardiovascular health (such as risk factors associated with heart disease), behavior skills (for example, self-assessment and monitoring), eating behavior (for example, the effects of food on health), and exercise behavior (for example, the effects of exercise on the heart).

The physical education component of Heart Smart involves two to four class periods each week to incorporate a "Superkids-Superfit" exercise program. The physical education instructor teaches skills required by the school system plus aerobic activities aimed at cardiovascular conditioning, including jogging, racewalking, interval workouts, rope skipping, circuit training, aerobic dance, and games. Classes begin and end with 5 minutes of walking and stretching.

Through the Eyes of Children

Adam Rojo: An Optimistic 7-Year-Old Fights for His Life

Seven-year-old Adam Rojo has leukemia. He first found this out when he was 5, and he has been to the hospital often since then. Every month he has to go in for painful treatments for his bone marrow cancer. Sometimes he cries because of the pain. His weekly chemotherapy treatments make his hair fall out. Adam also has to wear a catheter, a long tube placed under his skin in his chest that allows medicine to be delivered to his body without needles being stuck in him all the time.

Adam says that his family treats him the same as when he was well and that it would be dumb for other people to treat him differently from other kids—he is the same person as before he got sick. He can't run or play as much as before, but he can read, sleep, do work, think, and do most of the things other people do. When people make fun of him because his hair fell out or he can't do sports, he tells them to take a hike.

Adam prays that he will live a long, happy life and that his brother and whole family will live long, happy lives. He says, "I would rather not have leukemia, but that's the way the cookie crumbles" (Krementz, 1989).

Heart Smart

Improving Developmental Skills

Nurturing and Supporting Children's Physical Development and Health

What are some good strategies for supporting children's physical development and health in the middle and late childhood years?

- *Elementary school children should participate mainly in active rather than passive activities.* This especially means reducing TV watching and increasing participation in such activities as swimming, skating, and bicycling.
- *Parents should monitor children's eating behavior.* Children need more calories now than when they were younger. However, a special concern is the increasing number of obese children. They need to have a medical checkup, to revise their diet, and to participate in a regular exercise program.
- *Elementary schools need to develop more and better physical education programs.* Only about one of every three elementary school children participates in a physical education program. Many of those who do aren't exercising much during the program.
- *Parents need to engage in physical activities that they can enjoy together with their children.* These activities include running, bicycling, hiking, and swimming.
- *Parents should try to make their children's experience in sports positive.* This means not stressing a win-at-all-costs philosophy.
- *Parents should help children avoid accidents and injuries.* Educate children about the hazards of risk taking and the improper use of equipment.

The school lunch program serves as an intervention site, where sodium, fat, and sugar levels are decreased. Children and adolescents are told reasons they should eat healthy foods, such as a tuna sandwich, and why they should not eat unhealthy foods, such as a hot dog with chili. The school lunch program includes a salad bar, where children and adolescents can serve themselves. The amount and type of snack foods sold on the school premises are monitored.

High-risk children—those with elevated blood pressure, cholesterol, and weight—are identified as part of Heart Smart. A multidisciplinary team of physicians, nutritionists, nurses, and behavioral counselors work with the high-risk boys and girls and their parents through group-oriented activities and individual-based family counseling. High-risk boys and girls and their parents receive diet, exercise, and relaxation prescriptions in an intensive 12-session program, followed by long-term monthly evaluations.

Extensive assessment is a part of this ongoing program. Short-term and long-term changes in children's knowledge about cardiovascular disease and changes in their behavior are assessed.

In one analysis in the Bogalusa Heart Study, more than half of the children exceeded the recommended intake of salt, fat, cholesterol, and sugar (Nicklas & others, 1995). Families with a history of heart disease have children with more risk factors than other families. Also, African American children have hormonal and renal factors that predispose them to develop hypertension.

Other school health programs that are being evaluated include the Minnesota Heart Health Program (Kelder & others, 1995) and the Southwest Cardiovascular Curriculum Project (Davis & others, 1995).

Medical Links

Asthma   Asthma involves an airway obstruction that consists of shortness of breath, wheezing, or tightness in the chest. The incidence of asthma has risen steadily in recent decades, possibly because of increased air pollution. Asthma is the most common chronic disease of childhood, is the primary reason for absences from school, and is responsible for a number of pediatric admissions to emergency rooms and hospitals (Wong, 1997).

The exact causes of asthma are not known, but it is believed that the disease results from hypersensitivity to environmental substances, which trigger an allergic reaction (Warman & others, 1999). Corticosteroids, which are generally inhaled, are the most effective anti-inflammatory drugs for treating asthma. Often, parents have kept asthmatic children from exercising because they fear the exercise will provoke an asthma attack. However, today it is believed that children with asthma should be encouraged to exercise, provided their asthma is under control, and participation should be evaluated on an individual basis. Some children with asthma lose their symptoms in adolescence; others do not. Why this differentiation occurs is not known.

Accidents and Injuries   The most common cause of severe injury and death in middle and late childhood is motor vehicle accidents, either as a pedestrian or as a passenger (Wong, 1997). The use of safety-belt restraints is important in reducing the severity of motor vehicle injuries (Bolen, Bland, & Sacks, 1999). The school-age child's motivation to ride a bicycle increases the risk of accidents. Other serious injuries involve skateboards, roller skates, and other sports equipment.

Most accidents occur in or near the child's home or school. The most effective prevention strategy is to educate the child about the hazards of risk taking and improper use of equipment. Appropriate safety helmets, protective eye and mouth shields, and protective padding are recommended for children who engage in active sports. Physically active school-aged children are more susceptible to fractures, strains, and sprains than are their less active counterparts (Furnival, Street, & Schunk, 1999). Also, boys are more likely than girls to experience these injuries.

Children's Understanding of Health and Illness

When elementary school children are asked about their health, they seem to understand that good health is something they have to work at on a regular basis. Early positive attitudes toward health and exercise are important in the child's ability to maintain a healthy lifestyle. But, while elementary school children and adolescents may recognize the contributions of nutrition and exercise to health, their behavior does not always follow suit.

Child Health

Adolescents seem to have an especially difficult time applying health information and knowledge to their own personal lives. For example, in one study, adolescents reported that they probably would never have a heart attack or a drinking problem but that other adolescents would (Weinstein, 1984). The adolescents also said that no relationship existed between their risk of heart attack and how much they exercised, smoked, or ate red meat or high-cholesterol foods, even though they correctly recognized that such factors as family history influence risk. Many adolescents appear to have unrealistic, overly optimistic beliefs about their immunity from health risks.

At various points so far, we have described ideas and strategies that can be used to improve children's developmental skills related to physical development and health. See the insert Improving Developmental Skills to read about these. We also have discussed many ideas about body growth, motor development, and children's health. An overview of these ideas is presented in summary table 12.1.

CHILDREN WITH DISABILITIES

Our discussion of children with health problems focused on some of the most common health problems in children, such as obesity, cancer, and accidents. In this section, we will turn our attention to children with disabilities and the issues involved in educating them.

Who Are Children with Disabilities?

Approximately 10 percent of all children in the United States receive special education or related services (Reschly, 1996). Figure 12.5 shows the approximate percentages of children with various disabilities who receive special education services (U.S. Department of Education, 1996). Within this group, a little more than half have a learning disability. Substantial percentages of children also have speech or language impairments (21 percent of those with disabilities), mental retardation (12 percent), and serious emotional disturbance (9 percent).

Exploring Disabilities

Educators now prefer to speak of "children with disabilities" rather than "handicapped children" to emphasize the person, not the disability (Culatta & Tompkins, 1999). The term "handicapping conditions" is still used to describe impediments to the learning and functioning of individuals with a disability that have been imposed by society. For example, when children who use a wheelchair do not have adequate access to a bathroom, transportation, and so on, this is referred to as a handicapping condition.

Summary Table 12.1
Body Growth and Proportion, Motor Development, and Children's Health

Concept	Processes/ Related Ideas	Characteristics/Description
Body growth and proportion	Skeletal and muscular systems	The period of middle and late childhood involves slow, consistent growth. During this period, children grow an average of 2 to 3 inches a year. Muscle mass and strength gradually increase. Among the most pronounced changes are decreases in head circumference, waist circumference, and leg length in relation to body height.
	Tooth development and dental care	Most of the teeth we have as adults begin to come in during middle and late childhood. First permanent teeth erupt at about 6 years of age and appear at the rate of approximately four teeth per year for the next 5 years. Good dental hygiene is important during this period.
Motor development	Its nature	During the middle and late childhood years, motor development becomes much smoother and more coordinated. Children gain greater control over their bodies and can sit and attend for longer periods of time. However, their lives should be activity-oriented and very active. Increased myelination of the central nervous system is reflected in improved motor skills. Improved fine motor skills appear in the form of handwriting development. Boys are usually better at gross motor skills, girls at fine motor skills.
Children's health	Nutrition	In the middle and late childhood years, children's weight doubles, and children exert considerable energy as they engage in motor activities. To support their growth, children need to consume more calories than when they were younger. Within recommended calorie ranges, it is important to impress on children the value of a balanced diet. A special concern is that too many children fill up on "empty calories," which are high in sugar, starch, and excess fat content. Beginning the day with a healthy breakfast promotes higher energy and better alertness in school.
	Exercise and sports	Every indication suggests that children in the United States are not getting enough exercise. Television viewing, parents being poor role models for exercise, and the lack of adequate physical education classes in schools are among the culprits. Children's participation in sports can have positive or negative consequences.
	Health problems	For most children, middle and late childhood is a time of excellent health. Disease and death are less prevalent in this period than in other periods of childhood and adolescence. However, some children do have health problems. An increasing problem is obesity. Slightly more than one-fifth of children are overweight, and 10 percent are obese. Heredity, insulin levels influenced by poor diet, and low activity level are implicated in obesity, which can have many negative physical and psychological consequences for children. Treatment of obesity focuses mainly on diet, exercise, and behavior modification. Cancer is the second leading cause of death in children (after accidents). Childhood cancers have a different profile from adult cancers—they usually already have spread to other parts of the body and they typically are of a different type. Leukemia is the most common childhood cancer. Cardiovascular disease is uncommon in children, but when it occurs it usually is not a product of experiences or behavior, which makes it different than when it occurs in adults. The precursors of adult cardiovascular disease often appear in the elementary school years, with many of these children already showing risk factors, such as hypertension or obesity. Heart Smart is one large-scale school-based study designed to lower risk for cardiovascular disease. Asthma is the most common chronic disease in childhood, but its exact cause is not known. The most common cause of severe injury and death in childhood is motor vehicle accidents, with most occurring at or near the child's home or school.
	Children's understanding of health and illness	Elementary school children seem to understand that health has to be worked at on a regular basis, but many of them do not adopt good health habits.

In the following sections, we will examine the following disabilities: sensory disorders, physical disorders, speech disorders, learning disabilities, attention deficit/hyperactivity disorder, and autism. In chapter 13, we will study mental retardation.

Sensory Disorders

Sensory disorders include visual and hearing impairments. Sometimes these impairments are described as part of a larger category called "communication disorders," along with speech and language disorders.

Visual Impairments   Some children may have mild vision problems that have not been corrected. If children squint a lot, hold books close to their face to read, frequently rub their eyes, complain that things appear blurred, or say that words move about the page, they need to be referred to appropriate professionals to have their vision checked (Boyles & Contadino, 1997). In many cases, they need only corrective lenses. However, a small portion of children (about 1 in 1,000) have more serious visual problems and are classified as visually impaired. This includes children who have low vision and children who are blind.

Children with **low vision** *have a visual acuity of between 20/70 and 20/200 (on the Snellen scale, in which 20/20 vision is normal) with corrective lenses*. Children with low vision can read with the aid of large-print books or a magnifying glass. Children who are **educationally blind** *cannot use their vision in learning and must use their hearing and touch to learn*. Approximately 1 in every 3,000 children is educationally blind. Almost one-half of these children were born blind, and another one-third lost their vision in the first year of life. Many children who are educationally blind have normal intelligence and function very well academically with appropriate supports and learning aids.

An important task when working with a child who is visually impaired is to determine the modality (such as touch or hearing) through which the child learns best. Preferential seating in the front of the class is also helpful.

Hearing Impairments   A hearing impairment can make learning difficult for children. Children who are born deaf or experience a significant hearing loss in the first several years of life usually do not develop normal speech and language. Some children in middle and late childhood have hearing impairments that have not yet been detected. If children turn one ear toward the speaker, frequently ask to have something repeated, don't follow directions, or frequently complain of earaches, colds, and allergies, their hearing needs to be evaluated by a specialist, such as an audiologist (Patterson & Wright, 1990).

Many children who are hearing impaired receive supplementary instruction beyond the regular classroom. Educational approaches to help children with hearing impairments learn fall into two categories: oral and manual. **Oral approaches** *include using lip reading, speech reading (relies on visual cues to teach reading), and whatever hearing the child has*. **Manual approaches** *involve sign language and finger spelling*. Sign language is a system of hand movements that symbolize words. Finger spelling consists of "spelling out" each word by placing the hand in different positions. A total communication approach that includes both oral and manual approaches is increasingly being used with children who are hearing impaired (Hallahan & Kaufmann, 1997; Heward, 1996).

Disability	Total	Percent of total
Specific learning disabilities	2,513,977	51.1
Speech or language impairments	1,023,665	20.8
Mental retardation	570,855	11.6
Serious emotional disturbance	428,168	8.7
Multiple disabilities	89,646	1.8
Hearing impairments	65,56	1.3
Orthopedic impairments	60,604	1.2
Other health impairments	106,5098	2.2
Visual impairments	24,877	0.5
Autism	22,780	0.5
Deaf-blindness	1,331	0.0
Traumatic brain injury	7,188	0.1
All disabilities	**4,915,168**	**100.0**

Note: The figures represent children with a disability who received special education services in the 1994–1995 school year. Children with multiple disabilities also have been counted under various single disabilities.

Figure 12.5
The Diversity of Children Who Have a Disability

Source: U.S. Department of Education, Office of Special Education Programs.

low vision
Visual acuity between 20/70 and 20/200.

educationally blind
Unable to use one's vision in learning. It implies a need to use hearing and touch to learn.

oral approaches
Educational approaches to help hearing-impaired children; they include lip reading, speech reading, and whatever hearing the child has.

Physical Disorders

Physical disorders that children may have include orthopedic impairments, such as cerebral palsy. Many children with physical disorders require special education, as well as related services. The related services may include transportation, physical therapy, school health services, and psychological services (Bowe, 2000).

Orthopedic impairments *involve restrictions in movement because of muscle, bone, or joint problems.* Depending on the severity of the restriction, some children may have only limited restriction, while others cannot move at all. Still other children cannot control the movement of their muscles. Orthopedic impairments can be caused by prenatal or perinatal problems, or they can be due to a disease or an accident during the childhood years. With the help of adaptive devices and medical technology, many children with an orthopedic impairment function well in the classroom (Boyles & Contadino, 1997).

Cerebral palsy *is a disorder that involves a lack of muscular coordination, shaking, or unclear speech.* The most common cause of cerebral palsy is lack of oxygen at birth. In the most common type of cerebral palsy, which is called *spastic,* children's muscles are stiff and difficult to move. The rigid muscles often pull the limbs into contorted positions. In a less common type, *ataxia,* children's muscles are rigid one moment and floppy the next moment, making movements clumsy and jerky.

Computers especially help children with cerebral palsy learn. If they have the coordination to use the keyboard, they can do their written work on the computer. A pen with a light can be added to a computer and used by the child as a pointer. Many children with cerebral palsy have unclear speech. For these children, speech and voice synthesizers, communication boards, talking notes, and page turners can improve their communication.

Speech Disorders

Speech disorders include articulation disorders, voice disorders, and fluency disorders. **Articulation disorders** *are problems in pronouncing sounds correctly.* A child's articulation at 6–7 years is still not always error-free, but it should be by age 8. A child with an articulation problem may find communication with peers and the teacher difficult or embarrassing. As a result, the child may avoid asking questions, participating in discussions, or communicating with peers. Articulation problems can usually be improved or resolved with speech therapy, though it may take months or years.

Voice disorders *are reflected in speech that is hoarse, harsh, too loud, too high-pitched, or too low-pitched. Children with cleft palate often have a voice disorder that makes their speech difficult to understand.* If a student speaks in a way that is consistently difficult to understand, the child should be referred to a speech therapist.

Fluency disorders *often involve what is commonly called "stuttering." Stuttering occurs when a child's speech has a spasmodic hesitation, prolongation, or repetition.* The anxiety many children feel because they stutter usually just makes their stuttering worse. Speech therapy is recommended.

Learning Disabilities

Paula doesn't like kindergarten and can't seem to remember the names of her teacher and classmates. Bobby's third-grade teacher complains that his spelling is awful. Eleven-year-old Tim says reading is really hard for him, and a lot of times the words don't make much sense. Each of these students has a learning disability.

The currently accepted description is "children with disabilities," rather than "handicapped children." Why the change in terminology?

manual approaches
Educational approaches to help hearing-impaired children; they include sign language and finger spelling.

orthopedic impairments
Restrictions in movement abilities due to muscle, bone, or joint problems.

cerebral palsy
A disorder that involves a lack of muscular coordination, shaking, or unclear speech.

articulation disorders
Problems in pronouncing sounds correctly.

voice disorders
Disorders reflected in speech that is hoarse, harsh, too loud, too high-pitched, or too low-pitched.

fluency disorders
Various disorders that involve what is commonly called "stuttering."

Speech Disorders

Learning Disabilities

Characteristics   Children with a **learning disability** *(1) are of normal intelligence or above, (2) have difficulties in at least one academic area and usually several, and (3) have a difficulty that is not attributable to any other diagnosed problem or disorder, such as mental retardation.* The global concept of learning disabilities includes problems in listening, concentrating, speaking, thinking.

About three times as many boys as girls are classified as having a learning disability (U.S. Department of Education, 1996). Among the explanations for this gender difference are a greater biological vulnerability of boys, as well as referral bias (boys are more likely to be referred by teachers for treatment because of their disruptive, hyperactive behavior).

By definition, children do not have a learning disability unless they have an academic problem. Among the most common academic areas in which children with a learning disability have problems are reading, written language, and math (Hallahan & Kaufmann, 1997).

About 5 percent of all school-age children in the United States receive special education or related services because of a learning disability. In the federal classification of children receiving special education and related services, attention deficit/hyperactivity disorder (ADHD) is included in the learning disabilities category. Because of the significant interest in ADHD today, we will discuss it by itself following learning disabilities.

In the past two decades, the percentage of children classified as having a learning disability has increased substantially—from less than 30 percent of all children receiving special education and related services in 1977–1978 to a little more than 50 percent today. Some experts say that the dramatic increase reflects poor diagnostic practices and overidentification. They believe that teachers sometimes are too quick to label children with the slightest learning problem as having a learning disability, instead of recognizing that the problem may rest in their ineffective teaching. Other experts say the increase in children being labeled with a "learning disability" is justified (Hallahan & Kaufmann, 1997).

The most common problem that characterizes children with a learning disability involves reading (Torgesen, 1999). Such children especially show problems with phonological skills (recall from chapter 7 "Cognitive Development in Infancy," that these involve being able to understand how sounds and letters match up to make words) (Lyon, 1999). **Dyslexia** *is a category that is reserved for individuals who have a severe impairment in their ability to read and spell.*

Children with a learning disability often have difficulties in handwriting, spelling, or composition. Their writing may be extremely slow, their writing products may be virtually illegible, and they may make numerous spelling errors because of their inability to match up sounds and letters.

Diagnosing whether a child has a learning disability is a difficult task. A learning disability often encompasses co-occurring conditions that can include problems in listening, concentrating, speaking, reading, writing, reasoning, math, or social interaction. Thus, individual children with a learning disability can have very different profiles. Learning disabilities often appear in association with such medical conditions as lead poisoning and fetal alcohol syndrome (American Psychiatric Association, 1994). And learning disabilities can occur with other disabilities, such as communication disorders and emotional/behavioral disorders (Polloway & others, 1997; Rock, Fessler, & Church, 1997; Schoenbrodt, Kumin, & Sloan, 1997). To further explore learning disabilities, see Adventures for the Mind.

Intervention Strategies   Many interventions have focused on improving the child's reading ability (Lyon & Moats, 1997). For example, in one study, instruction in phonological awareness at the kindergarten level had positive effects on reading development when the children reached the first grade (Blachman & others, 1994).

Unfortunately, not all children who have a learning disability that involves reading problems have the benefit of appropriate early intervention. Most children whose

learning disability
A disability that involves (1) having normal intelligence or above, (2) having difficulties in at least one academic area and usually several, and (3) having no other problem or disorder, such as mental retardation, that can be determined as causing the difficulty.

Learning Disabilities Association

dyslexia
A category of learning disabilities involving a severe impairment in the ability to read and spell.

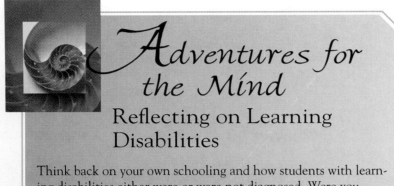

reading disability is not diagnosed until the third grade or later and who receive standard interventions fail to show noticeable improvement (Lyon, 1996). However, intensive instruction over a period of time by a competent teacher can remediate the deficient reading skills of many children. For example, in one study, 65 severely dyslexic children were given 65 hours of individual instruction in addition to group instruction in phonemic awareness and thinking skills (Alexander & others, 1991). The intensive intervention significantly improved the dyslexic children's reading skills.

Children with severe phonological deficits that lead to poor decoding and word recognition skills respond to intervention more slowly than do children with mild to moderate reading problems (Torgesen, 1995). Also, the success of even the best-designed reading intervention depends on the training and skills of the teacher.

Disability in basic reading skills has been the most common target of intervention studies because it is the most common form of learning disability, it is identifiable, and it represents the area of learning disabilities about which there is the most knowledge (Lyon, 1996). Interventions for other types of learning disabilities have been created but have not been extensively researched.

Improving outcomes for children with a learning disability is a challenging task and generally has required intensive intervention for even modest improvement in outcomes. However, no model program has proven to be effective for all children with learning disabilities (Terman & others, 1996).

Attention Deficit/Hyperactivity Disorder

Matthew has attention deficit/hyperactivity disorder, and the outward signs are fairly typical. He has trouble attending to the teacher's instructions and is easily distracted. He can't sit still for more than a few minutes at a time, and his handwriting is messy. His mother describes him as very fidgety.

attention deficit/hyperactivity disorder
A disability in which children consistently show one or more of the following characteristics: (1) inattention, (2) hyperactivity, and (3) impulsivity.

ADHD

Characteristics   **Attention deficit/hyperactivity disorder (ADHD)** *is a disability in which children consistently show one or more of the following characteristics over a period of time: (1) inattention, (2) hyperactivity, and (3) impulsivity.* Children who are inattentive have difficulty focusing on any one thing and may get bored with a task after only a few minutes. Children who are hyperactive show high levels of physical activity, almost always seeming to be in motion. Children who are impulsive have difficulty curbing their reactions and don't do a good job of thinking before they act. Depending on the characteristics that children with ADHD display, they can be diagnosed as (1) ADHD with predominantly inattention, (2) ADHD with predominantly hyperactivity/impulsivity, or (3) ADHD with both inattention and hyperactivity/impulsivity.

The U.S. Office of Education figures on children with a disability that were shown in figure 12.5 include children with ADHD in the category of children with specific learning disabilities, an overall category that comprises slightly more than one-half of all children who receive special education services. The number of children diagnosed and treated for ADHD has increased substantially, by some estimates doubling in the 1990s. The disorder occurs as much as four to nine times more in boys than in girls. There is controversy about the increased diagnosis of ADHD (Terman & others, 1996), however. Some experts attribute the increase mainly to heightened awareness of the disorder. Others are concerned that many children are

Many children with ADHD show impulsive behavior, such as this child who is jumping out of his seat and throwing a paper airplane at other children. How would you handle this situation if this were to happen in your classroom?

being diagnosed without undergoing extensive professional evaluation based on input from multiple sources.

Signs of ADHD may be present in the preschool years. Parents and preschool or kindergarten teachers may notice that the child has an extremely high activity level and a limited attention span. They may say the child is "always on the go," "can't sit still even for a second," or "never seems to listen." Many children with ADHD are difficult to discipline, have a low frustration tolerance, and have problems in peer relations. Other common characteristics of children with ADHD include general immaturity and clumsiness.

Although signs of ADHD are often present in the preschool years, their classification often doesn't take place until the elementary school years (Pueschel & others, 1995). The increased academic and social demands of formal schooling, as well as stricter standards for behavioral control, often illuminate the problems of the child with ADHD. Elementary school teachers typically report that this type of child has difficulty in working independently, completing seat work, and organizing work. Restlessness and distractibility also are often noted. These problems are more likely to be observed in repetitive or taxing tasks, or tasks the child perceives to be boring (such as completing worksheets or doing homework).

It used to be thought that ADHD decreased in adolescence, but now it is believed that this often is not the case. Estimates suggest that ADHD decreases in only about one-third of adolescents. Increasingly, it is being recognized that these problems may continue into adulthood.

Definitive causes of ADHD have not been found. For example, scientists have not been able to identify cause-related sites in the brain. However, a number of causes have been proposed, such as low levels of certain neurotransmitters (chemical messengers in the brain), prenatal and postnatal abnormalities, and environmental toxins, such as lead. Heredity also may play a role, as 30 to 50 percent of children with ADHD have a sibling or parent who has the disorder (Woodrich, 1994).

Students with ADHD have a failure rate in school that is two to three times that of other students (Reeve, 1994). About one-half of students with ADHD have repeated a grade by adolescence and more than one-third eventually drop out of school.

Many experts recommend a combination of academic, behavioral, and medical interventions to help students with ADHD learn and adapt more effectively (Appalachia Educational Laboratory, 1998). This intervention requires cooperation and effort on the part of the parents of students with ADHD, school personnel (teachers, administrators, special educators, and school psychologists), and health-care professionals.

It is estimated that about 85–90 percent of students with ADHD are taking stimulant medication such as Ritalin to control their behavior (Tousignant, 1995). A child should be given medication only after a complete assessment that includes a physical examination. Typically a small dose is administered as a trial to examine its effects. If the child adequately tolerates the small dose, the dosage may be increased.

The problem behaviors of students with ADHD can be temporarily controlled with prescriptive stimulants (Swanson & others, 1993). For many other children with ADHD, a combination of medication, behavior management, effective teaching, and parental monitoring improves their behavior. However, not all children with ADHD respond positively to prescription stimulants, and some critics believe that physicians are too quick in prescribing stimulants for children with milder forms of ADHD (Clay, 1997).

Autism

autism
A severe developmental disorder, has its onset in infancy. It includes deficiencies in social relationships, abnormalities in communication, and restricted, repetitive, and stereotyped patterns of behavior.

Autism

In giving rights to others that belong to them, we give rights to ourselves.

John F. Kennedy
U.S. President, 20th Century

Autism, *a severe developmental disorder, has its onset in infancy. It includes deficiencies in social relationships, abnormalities in communication, and restricted, repetitive, and stereotyped patterns of behavior.* Like other disorders, autism has a range of severity (Olley & Gutentag, 1999). Some children with autism never learn to speak, while others show communication and social irregularities. Some may display autistic behaviors many times a day, others more sporadically. Social deficiencies include a failure to make eye-to-eye contact when communicating and rarely seeking others for interaction or affection. Communication deficiencies include poor synchrony and lack of reciprocity in conversation, as well as stereotyped, repetitive use of language. Stereotyped patterns may include compulsive rituals and self-stimulatory actions, such as rocking, spinning, and finger flicking. Autistic individuals also may become distressed over small changes in the environment. The rearrangement of events or even furniture in the course of a day can cause children who are autistic to get extremely upset, reflecting their inflexibility in adapting to new routines.

What causes autism? The current consensus is that autism involves a brain dysfunction (Tsai, 1999). There is no evidence that family socialization causes autism (Rutter & Schopler, 1987). Mental retardation is present in some children with autism, while others show average or above-average intelligence.

Children with autism benefit from a well-structured classroom, individualized instruction, and small-group instruction (Pueschel & others, 1995). As with children who are mentally retarded, behavior modification sometimes has been effective in helping autistic children learn (Alberto & Troutman, 1995).

Educational Issues Involving Children with Disabilities

The legal requirement that schools serve all children with a disability is fairly recent. Beginning in the mid-1960s to mid-1970s, legislatures, the federal courts, and the United States Congress laid down special educational rights for children with disabilities. Prior to that time, most children with a disability were either refused enrollment or inadequately served by schools. In 1975, **Public Law 94-142,** *the Education for All Handicapped Children Act, required that all students with disabilities be given a free, appropriate public education and be provided the funding to help implement this education.*

In 1983, Public Law 94-142 was renamed the **Individuals with Disabilities Education Act (IDEA).** *The IDEA spells out broad mandates for services to all children with disabilities. These include evaluation and eligibility determination, appropriate education and the individualized education plan (IEP), and the least restrictive environment (LRE)* (Martin, Martin, & Terman, 1996).

Evaluation and Eligibility Determination Children who are thought to have a disability are evaluated to determine their eligibility for services under IDEA. Schools are prohibited from planning special education programs in advance and offering them on a space-available basis.

Children must be evaluated before a school can begin providing special services. Parents should be involved in the evaluation process. Reevaluation is required at least every three years (sometimes every year), when requested by parents, or when conditions suggest a reevaluation is needed. A parent who disagrees with the school's evaluation can obtain an independent evaluation, which the school is required to consider in providing special education services. If the evaluation finds that the child has a disability and requires special services, the school must provide them to the child.

The IDEA has many specific provisions that relate to the parents of a child with a disability. These include requirements that schools send notices to parents of proposed actions, of attendance at meetings regarding the child's placement or individualized education plan, and of the right to appeal school decisions to an impartial evaluator.

The Individuals with Disabilities Education Act (IDEA), including its 1997 amendments, requires that technology devices and services be provided to students with disabilities if they are necessary to ensure a free, appropriate education (Behrmann, 1994; Bryant & Seay, 1998; Lewis, 1998).

Two types of technology that can be used to improve the education of students with disabilities are instructional technology and assistance technology (Blackhurst, 1997). **Instructional technology** *includes various types of hardware and software, combined with innovative teaching methods, to accommodate students' needs in the classroom.* This technology includes videotapes, computer-assisted instruction, and complex hypermedia programs in which computers are used to control the display of audio and visual images stored on videodisc. The use of telecommunication systems, especially the Internet and its World

Public Law 94-142
The Education for All Handicapped Children Act, created in 1975, which requires that all children with disabilities be given a free, appropriate public education and which provides the funding to help with the costs of implementing this education.

Individuals with Disabilities Education Act (IDEA)
The IDEA spells out broad mandates for services to all children with disabilities (IDEA is a renaming of Public Law 94-142); these include evaluation and eligibility determination, appropriate education and the individualized education plan (IEP), and the least restrictive environment (LRE).

Education of Exceptional Children

Figure 12.6
Special Input Devices

Special input devices can help students with physical disabilities use computers more effectively.

Increasingly, children with disabilities are being taught in the regular classroom, as is this child with mild mental retardation.

instructional technology
Various types of hardware and software, combined with innovative teaching methods, to accommodate students' learning needs in the classroom.

assistive technology
Various services and devices to help children with disabilities function in their environment.

individualized education plan (IEP)
A written statement that spells out a program tailored to a child with a disability. The plan should be (1) related to the child's learning capacity, (2) specially constructed to meet the child's individual needs and not merely a copy of what is offered to other children, and (3) designed to provide educational benefits.

least restrictive environment (LRE)
The concept that a child with a disability must be educated in a setting that is as similar as possible to the one in which children who do not have a disability are educated.

inclusion
Educating a child with special education needs full-time in the regular classroom.

mainstreaming
Educating a child with special education needs partially in a special education classroom and partially in a regular classroom.

Inclusion

Wide Web, hold considerable promise for improving the education of students with or without a disability.

Assistive technology *consists of various services and devices to help students with disabilities function within their environment.* Examples include communication aids, alternative computer keyboards, and adaptive switches (see figure 12.6). To locate such services, educators can use computer databases, such as the Device Locator System (Academic Software, 1996).

Appropriate Education and the Individualized Education Plan (IEP)

The IDEA requires that students with disabilities have an **individualized education plan (IEP),** *a written statement that spells out a program specifically tailored for the student with a disability.* In general, the IEP should be (1) related to the child's learning capacity, (2) specially constructed to meet the child's individual needs and not merely a copy of what is offered to other children, and (3) designed to provide educational benefits.

Least Restrictive Environment (LRE)

Under the IDEA, a child with a disability must be educated in the **least restrictive environment (LRE).** *This means a setting that is as similar as possible to the one in which children who do not have a disability are educated.* This provision of the IDEA has given a legal basis to making an effort to educate children with a disability in the regular classroom (Crockett & Kaufmann, 1999). The term used to describe the education of children with a disability in the regular classroom used to be *mainstreaming.* However, that term has been replaced by the term **inclusion,** *which means educating a child with special education needs full-time in the general school program* (Idol, 1997). Today, **mainstreaming** *means educating a student with special education needs partially in a special education classroom and partially in a regular classroom* (Idol, 1997).

Not long ago, it was considered appropriate to educate children with disabilities outside the regular classroom. However, today, schools must make every effort to provide inclusion for children with disabilities (Heward, 2000; Siegel, 1997). These efforts can be very costly financially and very time consuming in terms of faculty effort.

The principle of least restrictive environment compels schools to examine possible modifications of the regular classroom before moving the child with a disability to a more restrictive placement. Also, regular classroom teachers often need specialized training to help some children with a disability, and state educational agencies are required to provide such training.

Many legal changes regarding children with disabilities have been extremely positive. Compared with several decades ago, far more children today are receiving competent, specialized services. For many children, inclusion in the regular classroom, with modifications or supplemental services, is appropriate (Kochhar, West, & Taymans, 2000; Turnbull & others, 1999). However, some experts believe that separate programs may be more effective and appropriate for children with disabilities (Martin, Martin, & Terman, 1996).

At various points in the chapter, we have described ideas and strategies that can be used to improve children's developmental skills. See the insert Improving Developmental Skills to read about these. We also discussed a number of ideas about children with disabilities. An overview of these ideas is presented in summary table 12.2.

Summary Table 12.2
Children with Disabilities

Concept	Processes/ Related Ideas	Characteristics/Description
Who are children with disabilities?	Their identity	An estimated 10 percent of U.S. children with a disability receive special education services. Slightly more than 50 percent of these students are classified as having a learning disability (in the federal government classification, this includes attention deficit/hyperactivity disorder (ADHD)). Substantial percentages also are represented by children who are mentally retarded, children with speech and language disorders, and children with a serious emotional disturbance. The term "students with disabilities" is now used, rather than "handicapped students."
Sensory disorders	Their nature	These include visual and hearing impairments. Sometimes they are described as part of a larger category called "communication disorders," along with speech and language disorders. Visual impairments include having low vision and being educationally blind. An important task is to determine in which modality (such as touch or hearing) the student who is visually impaired learns best.
Physical disorders	Their nature	These include orthopedic impairments, such as cerebral palsy.
Speech disorders	Their nature	They include a number of speech problems, such as articulation disorders, voice disorders, and fluency disorders. Articulation disorders are problems in pronouncing words correctly. Voice disorders are reflected in speech that is too hoarse, loud, high-pitched, or low-pitched. Children with cleft palate often have a voice disorder. Fluency disorders often involve what we commonly call "stuttering."
Learning disabilities	Characteristics	Children with a learning disability are of normal intelligence or above, have difficulties in at least one academic area and usually several, and have a difficulty that is not attributable to another diagnosed problem or disorder, such as mental retardation. The percentage of children diagnosed as "learning disabled" has increased dramatically in the past several decades. Diagnosing whether a child has a learning disability is difficult. About three times as many boys as girls have a learning disability. The most common problem that characterizes children with a learning disability involves reading. Dyslexia is a severe impairment in the ability to read and spell. Children with a learning disability often have difficulties in handwriting, spelling, or composition and increasingly are diagnosed with difficulties in math. Controversy surrounds the "learning disability" category, with some critics believing it is overdiagnosed, others arguing that it is not.
	Intervention strategies	Many interventions targeted for learning disabilities focus on reading ability and include such strategies as improving decoding skills. The success of even the best-designed interventions still depends on the training and skills of the teacher.
Attention deficit/ hyperactivity disorder	Characteristics	ADHD is a disability in which children consistently show problems in one or more of these areas: inattention, hyperactivity, and impulsivity. Individuals can be diagnosed as (1) ADHD with predominantly inattention, (2) ADHD with predominantly hyperactivity/impulsivity, or (3) ADHD with both of these categories present. Although signs of ADHD may be present in early childhood, diagnosis of ADHD often doesn't occur until the elementary school years.
	Intervention strategies	Many experts recommend a combination of academic, behavioral, and medical interventions to help students with ADHD learn and adapt more effectively.
Autism	Its nature	A severe disorder with an onset in infancy, autism includes deficiencies in social relationships, abnormalities in communication, and restricted, repetitive, and stereotyped patterns of behavior. The current consensus is that autism involves an organic brain dysfunction. There is no evidence that it is caused by family socialization. Children with autism benefit from a well-structured classroom, individualized instruction, and small-group instruction.
Educational issues involving children with disabilities	Historical background	Beginning in the mid-1960s to mid-1970s, the educational rights for children with disabilities were laid down. In 1975, Public Law 94-14, the Education for All Handicapped Children Act, required all children to be given a free, appropriate public education. In 1983, Public Law 94-142 was renamed the Individuals with Disabilities Education Act (IDEA), which spells out broad mandates for services to all children with disabilities.
	Evaluation and eligibility determination	Children who are thought to have a disability are evaluated to determine their eligibility for services. The IDEA has many provisions that relate to the parents of children with disabilities.
	Appropriate education and the individualized education plan (IEP)	An IEP consists of a written plan that spells out a program tailored to a child with a disability. The plan should (1) relate to the child's capacity, (2) be individualized and not a copy of a plan that is offered to other children, and (3) be designed to provide educational benefits.
	Least restrictive environment (LRE)	This concept, which is contained in the IDEA, states that children with disabilities must be educated in a setting that is as similar as possible to the one in which children without disabilities are educated. This provision of the IDEA has been given a legal basis to making an effort to educate children with disabilities in the regular classroom. The term *inclusion* means educating children with disabilities full-time in the regular classroom. The term *mainstreaming* means educating children with disabilities partially in the regular classroom and partially in a special education class. The trend is toward using inclusion more. Children's academic and social success is affected more by the quality of instruction than by where the child is placed.

Chapter Review

In middle and late childhood, most children lead active lives and are healthier than in any other child or adolescent period. Their physical skills become more rhythmic and smoothly coordinated than when they were younger. Nonetheless, some children develop health problems and have disabilities.

We began this chapter by reading about the training of future Olympians in the sports schools of China, then chronicled the body growth and proportion changes that occur during middle and late childhood. We also studied changes in school-age children's motor development. Our coverage of children's health focused on nutrition, exercise and sports, health problems, and children's understanding of health and illness. We examined the following aspects of children with disabilities: who are they, sensory disorders, physical disorders, speech disorders, learning disabilities, attention deficit/hyperactivity disorder, autism, and educational issues involving children with disabilities.

Don't forget that you can obtain a more detailed overview of the chapter by again studying the two summary tables on pages 344 and 353. In the next chapter, we will turn our attention to children's cognitive development in middle and late childhood.

Children Checklist

Physical Development in Middle and Late Childhood

How much have you learned since the beginning of the chapter? Use the following statements to help you review your knowledge and understanding of the chapter material. First, read the statement and mentally or briefly demonstrate on paper that you can discuss the relevant information.

_____ I can describe changes in body growth and proportion that occur in middle and late childhood.
_____ I can discuss motor development during the elementary school years.
_____ I know about nutritional requirements in school-age children.
_____ I can evaluate the roles of exercise and sports in children's development.
_____ I can discuss a number of health problems that can arise in children.
_____ I know about children's understanding of health and illness.
_____ I can describe who children with disabilities are.
_____ I can discuss children with disabilities.
_____ I can evaluate educational issues that involve children with disabilities.

For any items that you did not check, go back and locate the relevant material in the chapter. Review the material until you feel you can check off the item. You may want to use this checklist later in preparing for an exam.

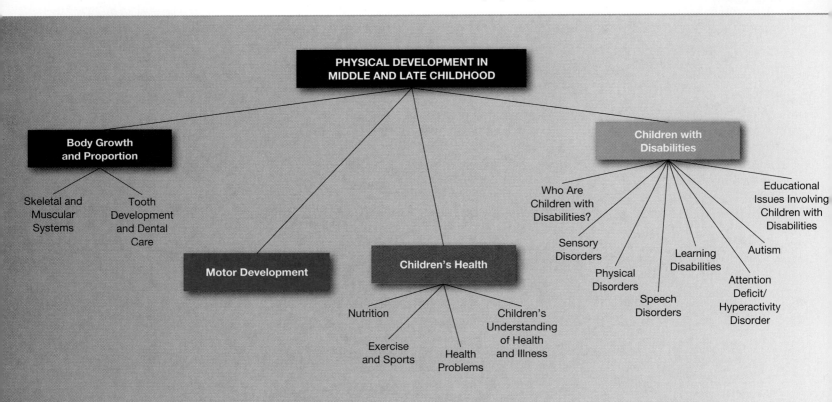

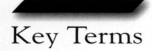

Key Terms

low vision 345
educationally blind 345
oral approaches 345
manual approaches 345
orthopedic impairments 346
cerebral palsy 346
articulation disorders 346
voice disorders 346
fluency disorders 346
learning disability 347
dyslexia 347
attention deficit/hyperactivity
   disorder (ADHD) 348

autism 350
Public Law 94-142 351
Individuals with Disabilities
   Education Act (IDEA) 351
instructional technology 351
assistive technology 352
individualized education plan
   (IEP) 352
least restrictive environment
   (LRE) 352
inclusion 352
mainstreaming 352

Children Resources

Children's Heartlink
5075 Arcadia Avenue
Minneapolis, MN 55436
612–928–4860

This organization provides treatment for needy children with heart disease and support for rheumatic fever prevention programs. It also supports the education of foreign medical professionals and provides technical advice and medical equipment and supplies.

Council for Exceptional Children
1920 Association Drive
Reston, VA 22091
703–620–3660

The CEC maintains an information center on the education of children and adolescents with disabilities and publishes materials on a wide variety of topics.

Learning Disabilities Association of America
4156 Library Road
Pittsburgh, PA 15234
412–341–1515

This organization provides education and support for parents of children with learning disabilities, interested professionals, and others. More than 500 chapters are in operation nationwide, offering information services, pamphlets, and book recommendations.

Taking It to the Net

http://www.mhhe.com/santrockcd6

1. You have agreed to coach a soccer team for children aged 7 and 8. What do you know about sports related injuries and how to reduce the risk of injury? What are the most common sport-related injuries for children, and how often do they occur?
2. You are tutoring a child with attention deficit/hyperactivity disorder. What are some appropriate instructional strategies for teaching this child with ADHD?
3. You have agreed to volunteer at a local school to work with students who have a disability. The teacher with whom you will be working tells you that parents often have a lot of questions regarding their child's education. Do you know what rights the child has? What rights the parents have?

Chapter

13

Cognitive Development in Middle and Late Childhood

PREVIEW

*I*n middle and late childhood, children spend more time in the achievement setting of school and are placed in circumstances that require them to display their intellectual skills under more pressure than they were in early childhood. Among the questions that we will explore in this chapter are

• What main changes did Piaget believe take place in the way children think during middle and late childhood?

• How does children's memory change during the elementary school years?

• What are some strategies for improving children's critical thinking skills?

• What are the key dimensions of intelligence?

• What controversies are involved in intelligence?

• How can children's creativity be enhanced?

• What are some language changes in middle and late childhood?

• Are some strategies for guiding children's achievement better than others?

The Story of Jessica Dubroff, Child Pilot

In 1996, Jessica Dubroff took off in cold rain and died when her single-engine Cessna nose-dived into a highway. Seven-year-old Jessica was only 4'2" tall and weighed just 55 lbs. What was she doing flying an airplane, especially in quest of being the youngest person ever to fly across the continent?

Jessica had been urged on by her parents, by a media drawn to a natural human-interest story, and by an ignoring Federal Aviation Administration. Jessica's feet did not even reach the rudder pedals. Was she granted too much freedom for a young child?

Jessica's parents gave their daughter independence from the beginning. She was delivered in a birthing tub without the benefit of a doctor or midwife. Her parents' philosophy was that real life is the best tutor, experience the best preparation for life. As a result, they kept Jessica, her brother (age 9), and her sister (age 3) at home without filing a home-schooling plan with local authorities. Jessica had no dolls, only tools. Instead of studying grammar, she did chores and sought what her mother called "mastery." Jessica had few if any boundaries. Parenting mainly consisted of cheerleading.

Jessica became interested in flying after her parents gave her an airplane ride for her sixth birthday, only 23 months before her fatal crash. Her father admitted the cross-country flight had been his idea but he had presented it to Jessica for her choice. The father became her press agent, courting TV, radio, and newspapers to publicize her flight.

After the crash, Jessica's mother said that, if she had it to do over again, she would have done nothing differently. She also commented that she did everything she could so Jessica could have freedom and choice. However, many developmentalists believe children should be given freedom and choice, but within the bounds of responsibility (Stengel, 1996).

While Jessica's story is a rare and tragic instance, the dangers of over-achieving, of growing up too soon, of intensely focusing on a single activity

Some critics argue that Jessica Dubroff was not allowed to be a child. Was she given too much freedom and choice? Did her parents act irresponsibly?

Children are remarkable for their intelligence and ardor, for their curiosity, their intolerance of shams, the clarity . . . of their vision.

Aldous Huxley
English Novelist, 20th Century

often show up in many different ways. The child actor grows up without an education, the tennis star mysteriously drops off the circuit to become a teenager, the figure skater takes part in a plot to club an opponent. Child athletes may ruin their bodies: ballerinas develop anorexia; teen football players take steroids. Are too many children's lives overscheduled, moving from one lesson to the next? Are they being robbed of the time to develop coping skills that they need to deal with life's realities?

While Jessica's story is tragic, remember that individual differences characterize children's development. Some children who are overachievers do quite well in life and have an intense desire to be successful. In such situations, it is not always all parental pressure but may involve the child's focused determination. Later in the chapter, we will further explore the nature of achievement, but first we will examine the cognitive changes that take place in middle and late childhood.

COGNITION

How does children's cognition—their mental processes, such as thinking, reasoning, and memory—change during middle and late childhood? To answer this question, we will explore three dimensions of cognition—Piaget's theory and concrete operational thought, information processing, and intelligence and creativity.

Piaget's Theory

According to Piaget (1967), the preschool child's thought is preoperational. Preoperational thought involves the formation of stable concepts, the emergence of mental reasoning, the prominence of egocentrism, and the construction of magical belief systems. Thought during the preschool years is still flawed and not well organized. Piaget believed that concrete operational thought does not appear until about the age of 7, but, as we learned in chapter 10, Piaget may have underestimated some of the cognitive skills of preschool children. For example, by carefully and cleverly designing experiments on understanding the concept of number, Rochel Gelman (1972) demonstrated that some preschool children show conservation, a concrete operational skill. In chapter 10, we explored concrete operational thought by describing the preschool child's flaws in thinking about such concrete operational skills as conservation and classification; here we will cover the characteristics of concrete operational thought again, this time emphasizing the competencies of elementary school children. We will also consider applications of Piaget's ideas to children's education and an evaluation of Piaget's theory.

Concrete Operational Thought Remember that, according to Piaget, concrete operational thought is made up of operations—mental actions that allow children to do mentally what they had done physically before. Concrete operations are also mental actions that are reversible. In the well-known test of reversibility of thought involving conservation of matter, the child is presented with two identical balls of clay. The experimenter rolls one ball into a long, thin shape; the other remains in its original ball shape. The child is then asked if there is more clay in the ball or in the long, thin piece of clay. By the time children reach the age of 7 or 8, most answer that the amount of clay is the same. To answer this problem correctly, children have to imagine that the clay ball is rolled out into a long, thin strip and then returned to its original round shape. This type of imagination involves a reversible mental action. Thus, a concrete operation is a reversible mental action on real, concrete objects. Concrete operations allow the child to coordinate several characteristics rather than focus on a single property of an object. In the clay example, the preoperational child is likely to focus on height *or* width. The concrete operational child coordinates information about both dimensions.

Many of the concrete operations Piaget identified focus on the way children reason about the properties of objects. One important skill that characterizes the concrete operational child is the ability to classify or divide things into different sets or subsets and to consider their interrelationships. An example of the concrete operational child's classification skills involves a family tree of four generations (see figure 13.1) (Furth & Wachs, 1975). This family tree suggests that the grandfather (A) has three children (B, C, and D), each of whom has two children (E through J), and that one of these children (J) has three children (K, L, and M). A child who comprehends the classification system can move up and down a level (vertically), across a level (horizontally), and up and down and across (obliquely) within the system. The concrete operational child understands that person J can at the same time be father, brother, and grandson, for example. A summary of concrete operational thought's characteristics is shown in figure 13.2.

Some Piagetian tasks require children to reason about relations between classes. One such task is **seriation,** *the concrete operation that involves ordering stimuli along a quantitative dimension (such as length).* To see if students can serialize, a teacher might haphazardly place eight sticks of different lengths on a table. The teacher then asks the students to order the sticks by length. Many young children end up with two or three small groups of "big" sticks or "little" sticks, rather than a correct ordering of all eight sticks. Another mistaken strategy they use is to evenly line up the tops of the sticks but ignore the bottoms. The concrete operational thinker simultaneously understands that each stick must be longer than the one that precedes it and shorter than the one that follows it.

Another aspect of reasoning about the relations between classes is **transitivity.** *This involves the ability to logically combine relations to understand certain conclusions.* In this case, consider three sticks (A, B, and C) of differing lengths. A is the longest, B is intermediate in length, and C is the shortest. Does the child understand that, if $A > B$ and $B > C$, then $A > C$? In Piaget's theory, concrete operational thinkers do; preoperational thinkers do not.

Piaget and Education   Piaget was not an educator and never pretended to be. However, he provided a sound conceptual framework from which to view learning and education. Earlier, we examined some specific suggestions for classroom activities based on Piaget's stages. Following are some more general principles in Piaget's theory that can be applied to teaching (Elkind, 1976; Heuwinkel, 1996):

1. *Take a constructivist approach.* In a constructivist vein, Piaget emphasized that children learn best when they are active and seek solutions for themselves. Piaget opposed teaching methods which imply that children are passive receptacles. The educational implication of Piaget's view is that, in all subjects, students learn best by making discoveries, reflecting on them, and discussing them, rather than blindly imitating the teacher or doing things by rote.
2. *Facilitate rather than direct learning.* Effective teachers design situations that allow students to learn by doing. These situations promote students' thinking and discovery. Teachers listen, watch, and question students to help them gain better understanding. Don't just examine *what* students think and the product of their learning. Rather, carefully observe them as they find out *how* they think. Ask relevant questions to stimulate their thinking and ask them to explain their answers.
3. *Consider the child's knowledge and level of thinking.* Students do not come to class with empty heads. They have many ideas about the physical and natural world. They have concepts of space, time, quantity, and causality. These ideas

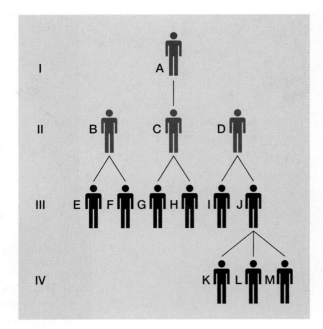

*F*igure 13.1
Classification: An Important Ability in Concrete Operational Thought

A family tree of four generations *(I to IV)*: The preoperational child has trouble classifying the members of the four generations; the concrete operational child can classify the members vertically, horizontally, and obliquely (up and down and across). For example, the concrete operational child understands that a family member can be a son, a brother, and a father, all at the same time.

seriation

The concrete operation that involves ordering stimuli along a quantitative dimension (such as length).

transitivity

In concrete operational thought, a mental concept that underlies the ability to logically combine relations to understand certain conclusions. It focuses on reasoning about the relations between classes.

Piaget and Education

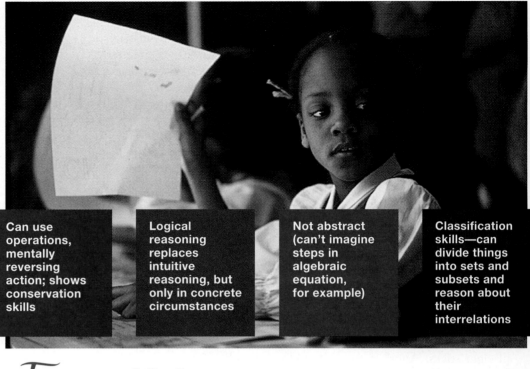

Can use operations, mentally reversing action; shows conservation skills

Logical reasoning replaces intuitive reasoning, but only in concrete circumstances

Not abstract (can't imagine steps in algebraic equation, for example)

Classification skills—can divide things into sets and subsets and reason about their interrelations

*F*igure 13.2
Characteristics of Concrete Operational Thought

differ from the ideas of adults. Teachers need to interpret what a student is saying and respond in a mode of discourse that is not too far from the student's level.

4. *Use ongoing assessment.* Individually constructed meanings cannot be measured by standardized tests. Math and language portfolios (which contain work in progress as well as finished products), individual conferences in which students discuss their thinking strategies, and students' written and verbal explanations of their reasoning can be used to evaluate progress.

5. *Promote the student's intellectual health.* When Piaget came to lecture in the United States, he was asked, "What can I do to get my child to a higher cognitive stage sooner?" He was asked this question so often here compared with other countries that he called it the American question. For Piaget, children's learning should occur naturally. Children should not be pushed and pressured into achieving too much too early in their development, before they are maturationally ready. Some parents spend long hours every day holding up large flash cards with words on them to improve their baby's vocabulary. In the Piagetian view, this is not the best way for infants to learn. It places too much emphasis on speeding up intellectual development, involves passive learning, and will not work.

6. *Turn the classroom into a setting of exploration and discovery.* What do actual classrooms look like when the teachers adopt Piaget's views? Several first- and second-grade math classrooms provide some good examples (Kamii, 1985, 1989). The teachers emphasize students' own exploration and discovery. The classrooms are less structured than what we think of as a typical classroom. Workbooks and predetermined assignments are not used. Rather, the teachers observe the students' interests and natural participation in activities to determine what the course of learning will be. For example, a math lesson might be constructed around counting the day's lunch money or dividing

supplies among students. Often, games are prominently used in the classroom to stimulate mathematical thinking. For example, a version of dominoes teaches children about even-numbered combinations. A variation on tic-tac-toe involves replacing Xs and Os with numbers. Teachers encourage peer interaction during the lessons and games because students' different viewpoints can contribute to advances in thinking.

Evaluating Piaget's Theory What were Piaget's main contributions? Has his theory withstood the test of time?

Contributions Piaget was a giant in the field of developmental psychology, the founder of the present field of children's cognitive development. Psychologists owe him a long list of masterful concepts of enduring power and fascination: assimilation, accommodation, object permanence, egocentrism, conservation, and others. Psychologists also owe him the current vision of children as active, constructive thinkers.

Piaget also was a genius when it came to observing children. His careful observations showed us inventive ways to discover how children act on and adapt to their world. Piaget showed us some important things to look for in cognitive development, such as the shift from preoperational to concrete operational thinking. He also showed us how children need to make their experiences fit their schemas (cognitive frameworks) yet simultaneously adapt their schemas to experience. Piaget also revealed how cognitive change is likely to occur if the context is structured to allow gradual movement to the next higher level and that a concept does not emerge suddenly, full-blown but, rather, through a series of partial accomplishments that lead to increasingly comprehensive understanding (Haith & Benson, 1998).

Piaget, shown here, was a genius at observing children. By carefully observing and interviewing children, he constructed a comprehensive theory of children's cognitive development.

Criticisms Piaget's theory has not gone unchallenged. Questions are raised about estimates of children's competence at different developmental levels; stages; the training of children to reason at higher levels; and culture and education.

- *Estimates of children's competence.* Some cognitive abilities emerge earlier than Piaget thought. For example, as previously noted, some aspects of object permanence emerge earlier than he believed. Even 2-year-olds are nonegocentric in some contexts. When they realize that another person will not see an object, they investigate whether the person is blindfolded or looking in a different direction. Conservation of number has been demonstrated as early as age 3, although Piaget did not think it emerged until 7. Young children are not as uniformly "pre" this and "pre" that (precausal, preoperational) as Piaget thought. Other cognitive abilities also can emerge later than Piaget thought. Many adolescents still think in concrete operational ways or are just beginning to master formal operations. Even many adults are not formal operational thinkers. In sum, recent theoretical revisions highlight more cognitive competencies of infants and young children and more cognitive shortcomings of adolescents and adults (Flavell, Miller, & Miller, 1993).
- *Stages.* Piaget conceived of stages as unitary structures of thought. Thus, his theory assumes developmental synchrony; that is, various aspects of a stage should emerge at the same time. However, some concrete operational concepts do not appear in synchrony. For example, children do not learn to conserve at the same time they learn to cross-classify. Thus, most contemporary developmentalists agree that children's cognitive development is not as stagelike as Piaget thought.

An outstanding teacher and education in the logic of science and mathematics are important cultural experiences that promote the development of operational thought. Schooling and education likely play more important roles in the development of operational thought than Piaget envisioned.

- *The training of children to reason at higher levels.* Some children who are at one cognitive stage (such as preoperational) can be trained to reason at a higher cognitive stage (such as concrete operational). This poses a problem for Piaget's theory. He argued that such training is only superficial and ineffective, unless the child is at a maturational transition point between the stages (Gelman & Williams, 1998).
- *Culture and education.* Culture and education exert stronger influences on children's development than Piaget believed (Gelman & Brenneman, 1994). The age at which children acquire conservation skills is related to the extent to which their culture provides relevant practice. An outstanding teacher and education in the logic of math and science can promote concrete and formal operational thought.

Still, some developmental psychologists believe we should now throw out Piaget altogether. These **neo-Piagetians** *argue that Piaget got some things right but that his theory needs considerable revision. In their revision of Piaget, more emphasis is given to how children process information through attention, memory, and strategy use* (Case, 1987, 1998). They especially believe that a more accurate vision of children's thinking requires more emphasis on strategies, the speed at which children process information, the particular cognitive task involved, and the division of cognitive problems into smaller, more precise steps.

Information Processing

Among the highlights of changes in information processing during middle and late childhood are improvements in memory, schemas, scripts, and scientific thinking. Remember also, from chapter 8, that the attention of most children improves dramatically during middle and late childhood and that at this time children attend more to the task-relevant features of a problem than to the salient features.

neo-Piagetians
Developmentalists who have elaborated on Piaget's theory, believing that children's cognitive development is more specific in many respects than Piaget thought.

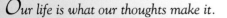

*O*ur life is what our thoughts make it.

Marcus Aurelius, *Meditations*
Roman Emperor, 2nd Century

Memory   In chapter 10, we concluded that short-term memory increases considerably during early childhood but after the age of 7 does not show as much increase. Is the same pattern found for **long-term memory,** *a relatively permanent and unlimited type of memory?* Long-term memory increases with age during middle and late childhood.

If we know anything at all about long-term memory, it is that long-term memory depends on the learning activities individuals engage in when learning and remembering information (Intons-Peterson, 1996; Pressley, 1996). **Control processes** *are cognitive processes that do not occur automatically but require work and effort. They are under the learner's conscious control and can be used to improve memory. They are also appropriately called strategies.*

In research conducted by Barbara Moely and her colleagues (1995), extensive variations in strategy instruction were found. Some teachers did try to help students with their memory and study strategies, but, overall, strategy instruction was low across a broad range of activities. Strategy instruction was most likely to occur in teaching math and problem solving. Following are some ways to help children improve their memory and study strategies:

- *Encourage them to pay close attention and minimize distraction.* Talk with children about how important it is to pay attention when they need to remember something. Give them exercises in which they get opportunities to give their undivided attention to something. Get children to generate their own words or pet phrases to say when they need to pay attention, such as "Focus" and "Zero in." Work with children to help them monitor and self-regulate how well they are paying attention and, when they catch their minds wandering, get them to say the word or pet phrase quietly but firmly to themselves.
- *Motivate children to remember material by understanding it, rather than rotely memorizing it.* Children will remember information better over the long term if they understand the information, rather than just rotely rehearsing and memorizing it. Rehearsal works well for encoding information into short-term memory, but, when children need to retrieve the information from long-term memory, it is much less efficient. Thus, for most information, encourage children to understand it, give it meaning, elaborate on it, and personalize it. Give children concepts and ideas to remember and then ask them how they can relate the concepts and ideas to their personal experiences. Give them practice on elaborating a concept, so they will process the information more deeply.
- *Help children organize what they put into their memory.* Children will remember information better if they organize it hierarchically. Give them some practice on arranging and reworking material that requires some structuring.
- *Give children some mnemonic strategies.* **Mnemonics** *refers to the use of specific memory aids for remembering information.* Mnemonic strategies can involve imagery and words. Following are some types of mnemonics:
  —Method of loci. In the **method of loci,** *children develop images of items to be remembered and store them in familiar locations.* Rooms of a house or stores on a street are common locations used in this memory strategy. For example, if children need to remember a list of concepts, they can mentally place them in the rooms of their house, such as entry foyer, living room, dining room, and kitchen. Then when they need to retrieve the information they can imagine the house, mentally go through the rooms, and retrieve the concepts.
  —Rhymes. Examples of using rhymes to remember something are the spelling rule "*i* before *e* except after *c*," the month rule of "Thirty days hath September, April, June, and November," and the turning bolts rule "Right is tight; left is loose." Singing the alphabet song is another example of using rhyming to remember something.
  —Acronyms. This refers to creating a word from the first letters of items to be remembered. For example, HOMES can be used as a cue for remembering the Great Lakes of Huron, Ontario, Michigan, Erie, and Superior.

long-term memory
A relatively permanent type of memory that holds huge amounts of information for a long period of time.

control processes
Cognitive processes that do not occur automatically but require work and effort. These processes are under the learner's conscious control and can be used to improve memory. They are also appropriately called strategies.

Memory Links
Strategies
Learning Technologies

mnemonics
Memory aids.

method of loci
A mnemonic technique in which individuals develop images of items to be remembered and store them in familiar locations.

keyword method
A mnemonic technique in which individuals use vivid imagery and attach the imagery to important words.

—Keyword method. Yet another mnemonic strategy that involves imagery is the **keyword method,** *in which vivid imagery is attached to important words.* This method has been used to practical advantage in teaching students how to rapidly master new information, such as foreign vocabulary words, the states and capitals of the United States, and the names of presidents of the United States. For example, in teaching students that Annapolis is the capital of Maryland, you could ask students to connect vivid images of Annapolis and Maryland, such as two apples getting married (Levin, 1980).

—Some educators argue against teaching students to use mnemonics to remember something because it involves rote memorization. Clearly, as we said earlier, remembering for understanding is preferred over rote memorization. However, if students need to learn lists of concepts, mnemonic devices can do the trick. Think of mnemonic devices as a way for students to learn some specific facts that they may need to reason about and solve problems that involve understanding.

- *Encourage children to spread out and consolidate their learning.* Talk with children about the importance of regularly reviewing what they learn. You can be a good model of this yourself, but also encourage children to do this on their own as well. When individuals have to prepare for a test, they will benefit from distributing their learning over a longer period rather than cramming for the test at the last minute. Cramming tends to produce short-term memory that is processed in a shallow rather than deep manner. A final, concentrated tune-up before the test instead of being faced with having to learn everything at the last minute is desirable.

- *Get children to ask themselves questions.* When children ask themselves questions about what they have read or an activity in class, they expand the number of associations they make with the information they need to retrieve. At least as early as the middle of elementary school, the self-questioning strategy can help children remember. For example, as children read, they can be encouraged to stop periodically and ask themselves such questions as "What is the meaning of what I just read?" "Why is this important?" and "What is an example of the concept I just read?" By reminding children periodically to generate questions about their experiences, teachers can help them remember the experiences.

- *Help children learn how to take good notes.* Taking good notes from either a lecture or a text benefits memory (Kiewra, 1989). When children are left to take notes without being given any strategies, they tend to take notes that are brief and disorganized. When they write something down, often it is verbatim. Encourage children not to write down everything someone says when they take notes. It is impossible to do this, anyway, and it can prevent them from getting the big picture of what someone is saying. Give children some practice in taking notes and then evaluate how good a job they have done. Secondary school students who are about to go to college will especially benefit from developing good note-taking skills. Some good note-taking strategies include

  —Summarizing. One note-taking strategy that you can help children practice is the summary method of listening for a few minutes and then writing down the main idea that a speaker is trying to get across in that time frame. Then the child listens for several more minutes and writes down another idea, and so on.

  —Outlining. Another note-taking strategy you can get children to practice is to outline what the speaker is saying, along the lines of how the chapters are organized in this book, with "A"-level heads as the main topics, "B"-level heads as subtopics under the "A" heads, and "C"-level heads under the "B" heads. Keep in mind that it is not enough to just tell children to "outline"; you will have to show them how.

  —Concept maps. Yet another strategy is to get children to practice drawing concept maps, much like the concept maps you have studied at the end of each chapter of this book. The concept maps are similar to outlines but visually portray information in a more spiderlike format. All three note-taking strategies—summarizing, outlining, and creating concept maps—described so far help children evaluate what are the most important ideas to remember. The last two strategies—outlining and making concept maps—also help children hierarchically arrange the material, which underscores an important theme of memory: it works best when it is organized.

• *Give children opportunities to practice the PQ4R method.* Various systems have been developed to help people remember information that they are studying. One of the earliest systems was called SQ3R, which stands for Survey, Question, Read, Recite, and Review. A more recently developed system is called **PQ4R,** *which stands for* **P***review,* **Q***uestion,* **R***ead,* **R***eflect,* **R***ecite, and* **R***eview.* Thus, the PQ4R system adds an additional step to the SQ3R system: reflect. Students from the later elementary school years on will benefit from practicing the PQ4R system (Adams, Carnine, & Gersten, 1982). The system benefits students by getting them to meaningfully organize information, ask questions about it, reflect on it, and review it. Following are more details about the steps in the PQ4R system:

PQ4R
A study strategy that stands for Preview, Question, Read, Reflect, Recite, and Review.

—*Preview.* Briefly survey the material to get a sense of the overall organization of ideas. Be sure to look at the headings to see the main topics and subtopics that will be covered. At the beginning of each chapter in this book, you scan an outline and read a section called Preview. Many books do not have these sections, so children need to learn to do this on their own.

—*Question.* Encourage children to ask themselves questions about the material as they read it. Earlier in our description of memory and study strategies, we highlighted the importance of self-generation of questions.

—*Read.* Now tell children to read the material. Encourage students to be *active* readers. This involves getting them to immerse themselves in what they are reading and striving to understand what the author is saying. This helps students avoid being *empty* readers, whose eyes just track the lines of text but whose minds fail to register anything important.

—*Reflect.* By occasionally stopping and reflecting on the material, students increase its meaningfulness. Encourage children to be *analytic* at this point in studying. After they have read something, challenge them to break open the ideas and scratch beneath the surface of the material. This is a good time to think about applications and interpretations of the information, as well as connecting it with other information already in long-term memory.

—*Recite.* This involves self-testing to see if students can remember the material and reconstruct it. At this point, encourage children to make up a series of questions about the material and then try to answer them.

—*Review.* Go over the material and evaluate what they know and don't know. Tell children at this point they should reread and study the material they don't remember or understand well. Several times each chapter in this book, you come across summary tables, in which the material you have read so far is reviewed. As with outlines, not all books have built-in reviews and summary tables. Give children practice on generating reviews or summary tables of what they have read and on going back to study the material they don't remember well.

In addition to these strategies, the characteristics of the child influence memory. Apart from the obvious variable of age, many characteristics of the child determine the effectiveness of memory. These characteristics include attitude, motivation, and health. However, the characteristic that has been examined the most thoroughly is the child's previously acquired knowledge. What the child knows has a tremendous effect on what the child remembers. In one investigation, 10-year-old chess experts remembered chessboard positions much better than did adults who did not play much chess (Chi, 1978). However, the children did not do as well as the adults

Children's Eyewitness Testimony

cognitive monitoring
The process of taking stock of what you are currently doing, what you will do next, and how effectively the mental activity is unfolding.

reciprocal teaching
An instructional procedure used by Brown and Palincsar to develop cognitive monitoring; it requires that students take turns leading a study group in the use of strategies for comprehending and remembering text content.

when both groups were asked to remember a group of random numbers; the children's expertise in chess gave them superior memories, but only in chess.

Children's memory is currently a topic of considerable interest in the nation's courtrooms. An emotional battle is being waged about the credibility of children's testimony (Brewer, 1996; Ceci, 1993). Listening to one side, it would seem that everything a child tells a therapist or social worker must be believed. For example, it is argued that it is hard for children to reveal the details of their victimization, so, when they do talk about it, we should believe them. On the other side, critics argue that, because children, especially young children, are vulnerable to erroneous suggestions and social demands, they should not be believed when they claim they have been molested.

What are we to believe? There are reliable age differences in suggestibility, with preschool children's reports being influenced more by the suggestibility of an interviewer's questioning and probing than are those of older children or adults. However, most children are neither as hypersuggestible or as coachable as some prodefense advocates have alleged, nor are they as resistant to suggestions about their own bodies as some proprosecution advocates have claimed. Children can be led to incorporate false suggestions into their memories of even intimate body touching, if the suggestions are made by powerful adult authority figures and are offered repeatedly over a long period of time. They also can be resistant to false suggestions and able to provide highly detailed and accurate reports of events that happened weeks or months ago. These findings underscore the need for considerable care in accepting claims by those who are eager to put a one-sided "spin" on the issue of children's memory accuracy and suggestibility.

Cognitive Monitoring   Cognitive monitoring *is the process of taking stock of what you are currently doing, what you will do next, and how effectively the mental activity is unfolding.* When children engage in an activity, such as reading, writing, or solving a math problem, they are repeatedly called on to take stock of what they are doing and what they plan to do next. For example, when children begin to solve a math problem—especially one that might take a while to finish—they must figure out what kind of problem they are working on and what would be a good approach in solving it. Once they undertake a problem solution, it is helpful to check whether the solution seems to be working or whether another approach would be better.

Instructional programs in reading comprehension, writing, and mathematics have been designed to foster the development of cognitive monitoring. Ann Brown and Annemarie Palincsar's (1989) program for reading comprehension is an excellent example of a cognitive monitoring instructional program. Students in the program acquire specific knowledge and learn strategies for monitoring their understanding. **Reciprocal teaching** *is an instructional procedure used by Brown and Palincsar to develop cognitive monitoring; it requires that students take turns in leading the group in the use of strategies for comprehending and remembering text content that the teacher models for the class.* The instruction involves a small group of students, often working with an adult leader, actively discussing a short text, with the goal of *summarizing* it, asking *questions* to promote understanding, offering *clarifying* statements for difficult or confusing words and ideas, and *predicting* what will come next. The procedure involves children in an active way, it teaches them some techniques to use for reflecting about their own understanding, and the group interaction is highly motivating and engaging.

Schemas and Scripts   In chapter 11, we described gender schema theory and defined a *schema* as a cognitive structure, a network of associations that organizes and guides an individual's perceptions. Schema is an important cognitive concept in memory and information processing. Schemas come from prior encounters with the environment and influence the way children encode, make inferences about, and retrieve information. Children have schemas for stories, scenes, spatial layouts (a bathroom or a park, for example), and common events (such as going to a restaurant, playing with toys, or practicing soccer).

Children frequently hear and tell stories. And, as they develop the ability to read, they are exposed to many kinds of stories in print. Simple stories have a structure and, after hearing enough stories, children develop a strong expectation about what kind of information will be contained in a story. This expectation is a *story schema*. For example, a story tells about what happens in a particular place and circumstance. This content is called the setting. A story also has at least one main character, the protagonist, who attempts to achieve a purposeful goal for a clear reason. The protagonist's actions are usually captured in one or more episodes of a story, which can be further broken down, depicting a fairly simple, one-episode story (see figure 13.3).

A **script** *is a schema for an event.* Children's first scripts appear very early in development, perhaps as early as the first year of life. Children clearly have scripts by the time they enter school. As they develop, their scripts become more sophisticated. For example, a 4-year-old's script for a restaurant might include information only about sitting down and eating food. By middle and late childhood, the child has added information to the restaurant script about the types of people who serve food, the process of paying the cashier, and so on.

Setting	1	Once there was a big gray fish named Albert.
	2	He lived in a pond near the edge of a forest.
Initiating event	3	One day Albert was swimming around the pond.
	4	Then he spotted a big juicy worm on top of the water.
Internal response	5	Albert knew how delicious worms tasted.
	6	He wanted to eat that one for his dinner.
Attempt	7	So he swam very close to the worm.
	8	Then he bit into him.
Consequence	9	Suddenly, Albert was pulled through the water into a boat.
	10	He had been caught by a fisherman.
Reaction	11	Albert felt sad.
	12	He wished he had been more careful.

Figure 13.3
"Albert, the Fish," a Representative Story

Critical Thinking

Currently, both psychologists and educators have considerable interest in critical thinking, although it is not an entirely new idea (Gardner, 1999; Runco, 1999). Famous educator John Dewey (1933) proposed a similar idea when he talked about the importance of getting students to think reflectively. Well-known psychologist Max Wertheimer (1945) talked about the importance of thinking productively, rather than blindly inducing a correct answer. **Critical thinking** *involves grasping the deeper meaning of ideas, keeping an open mind about different approaches and perspectives, and deciding for oneself what to believe or do.* In this book, the inserts called Adventures for the Mind, which appear in every chapter, challenge you to think critically about a topic or an issue related to the discussion. To think critically about developing a critical-thinking curriculum for first-graders, see Adventures for the Mind.

Critical Thinking and Schools

Jacqueline and Martin Brooks (1993) lament that so few schools really teach students to think critically and develop a deep understanding of concepts. For example, many high school students read *Hamlet* but don't think deeply about it, never transforming their prior notions of power, greed, and relationships. Deep understanding occurs when students are stimulated to rethink their prior ideas.

In Brooks and Brooks' view, schools spend too much time on getting students to give a single correct answer in an imitative way, rather than encouraging them to expand their thinking by coming up with new ideas and rethinking earlier conclusions. They believe that too often teachers ask students to recite, define, describe, state, and list, rather than to analyze, infer, connect, synthesize, criticize, create, evaluate, think, and rethink.

Brooks and Brooks point out that many successful students complete their assignments, do well on tests, and get good grades, yet they don't ever learn to think

script
A schema for events.

critical thinking
Thinking that involves grasping the deeper meaning of ideas, keeping an open mind about different approaches and perspectives, and deciding for oneself what to believe or do.

Critical Thinking Resources

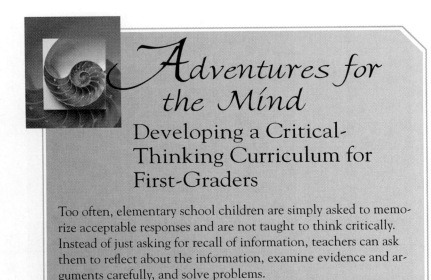

Adventures for the Mind

Developing a Critical-Thinking Curriculum for First-Graders

Too often, elementary school children are simply asked to memorize acceptable responses and are not taught to think critically. Instead of just asking for recall of information, teachers can ask them to reflect about the information, examine evidence and arguments carefully, and solve problems.

Imagine that you have been asked to develop a critical-thinking curriculum for first-graders. Review what was said in this chapter about the nature of critical thinking. Also consider how you have been challenged in the Adventures for the Mind inserts that have appeared in each chapter. What would be the curriculum's main themes?

critically and deeply. They believe our schools turn out students who think too superficially, staying on the surface of problems rather than stretching their minds and becoming deeply engaged in meaningful thinking.

Daniel Perkins and Sarah Tishman (1997) work with teachers to incorporate critical thinking into classrooms. Following are some of the critical-thinking skills they encourage teachers to help their students develop:

- *Open-mindedness*. This involves getting students to avoid narrow thinking and to explore options. For example, when teaching American literature, teachers might ask students to generate multiple critiques of Harriet Beecher Stowe's *Uncle Tom's Cabin*.
- *Intellectual curiosity*. This involves encouraging students to wonder, probe, question, and inquire. Getting students to recognize problems and inconsistencies also is wrapped up in intellectual curiosity. In history class, this might mean looking beyond culturally biased views of American history by reading British views on the American Revolution.
- *Planning and strategy*. Teachers work with students to help them develop plans, set goals, find direction and seek outcomes. In physical education, this might involve determining the best strategy to win a basketball or softball game.
- *Intellectual carefulness*. Teachers encourage students to check for inaccuracies, to be precise, and to be organized. For example, when students write a paper, they learn to structure the content and check the facts they include.

Jasper Project
Twelve videodisc adventures that focus on solving real-world math problems.

The Jasper Project

The Jasper Project   The **Jasper Project** *consists of 12 videodisc-based adventures that focus on solving real-world math problems.* The Jasper Project is the brainchild of the Cognition and Technology Group at Vanderbilt (1997). For students in grades 5 and up, *Jasper* helps students make connections with other disciplines, including science, history, and social studies. *Jasper*'s creators believe that too often math and other subjects are taught as isolated skills. They also think that students need to be exposed to real-world problems, rather than artificial problems that are unrelated to what happens in everyday life. *Jasper* also promotes collaborative problem solving among students. As students work together over several class periods, they have numerous opportunities to communicate about math, share their problem-solving strategies, and get feedback that helps them refine their thinking (see figure 13.4).

Jasper also encourages students to develop actual problem-solving projects. For example, in one school, after creating a business plan for the adventure *The Big Splash*, students were given the opportunity to gather relevant data to create a business plan to present to the principal. This resulted in the creation of a fun fair held for the entire school.

Jasper projects for other disciplines also have been developed. *Scientists in Action (SIA)* focuses on problem solving in science. One of the *SIA* stories is titled *Mystery of Stones River*, in which students explore issues related to water quality. They become familiar with ecosystems and the complex factors involved in developing healthy streams and rivers. The *Young Children's Literacy Series* is a multimedia language and literacy program for beginning readers. It is learner-centered and structured around video stories that anchor a series of activities that attempt to improve students' deep comprehension, composition, and oral communication.

"Blueprint for Success"

Christina and Marcus, two students from Trenton, visit an architectural firm on Career Day. While learning about the work of architects, Christina and Marcus hear about a vacant lot being donated in their neighborhood for a playground. This is exciting news because there is no place in their downtown neighborhood for children to play. Recently, several students have been hurt playing in the street. The challenge is for students to help Christina and Marcus design a playground and ballfield for the lot.

"The Big Splash"

Jasper's young friend Chris wants to help his school raise money to buy a new camera for the school TV station. His idea is to have a dunking booth in which teachers would be dunked when students hit a target. He must develop a business plan for the school principal in order to obtain a loan for his project. The overall problem centers on developing this business plan, including the use of a statistical survey to help him decide if this idea would be profitable.

$\mathcal{F}$igure 13.4
Problem-Solving Adventures in the *Jasper* Series

Transforming Schools into Communities of Thinking and Learning   Ann Brown (in press) has developed a program called "Fostering a Community of Learners (FCL)." It is being used in several schools and classrooms that serve inner-city students from 6 to 12 years of age. The program is successful in improving both children's literacy skills and their domain subject matter knowledge in such areas as biology.

Reflection and discussion are critical to the FCL classroom. Constructive commentary, questioning, querying, and criticism are the mode, rather than the exception. How are reflection and discussion encouraged? Three strategies are (1) using adults as role models, (2) having children teach children, and (3) implementing on-line computer consultation.

Schools for Thought

- *Adults as role models*. Visiting experts and classroom teachers introduce the big ideas and difficult principles at the beginning of a unit. The adults model thinking and self-reflection concerning how to go about finding a topic or how to reason with the information given. The adults continually ask students to justify opinions and then support them with evidence, to think of counterexamples to their rules, and so on. The adults also ask the group to summarize what is known and what still needs to be discovered. And the adults lead the class in setting new learning goals to guide the next stage of inquiry.

- *Children teaching children*. Children as well as adults enrich the classroom learning experience by contributing their particular expertise. Cross-age teaching occurs, in which older students teach younger students. This happens both face-to-face and via electronic mail (e-mail). Older students often serve as discussion leaders. Cross-age teaching provides students with invaluable opportunities to talk about learning, gives students responsibility and purpose, and fosters collaboration among peers.

- *On-line computer consultation*. Face-to-face communication is not the only way of building community and expertise. FCL classrooms benefit from using electronic mail. Experts provide coaching and advice, as well as commentary about what it means to learn and understand, through e-mail. On-line experts act as role models of thinking. They wonder, query, and make inferences based on incomplete knowledge (Brown & Campione, in press).

A culture of learning, negotiating, sharing, and producing work that is displayed to others is at the heart of FCL. The educational experience involves an interpretative

Figure 13.5
Defining Intelligence

Intelligence is an abstract concept that has been defined in various ways. The three most commonly agreed-on aspects of intelligence are the following: (*a*) verbal ability, (*b*) problem-solving skills, and (*c*) an ability to learn from and adapt to experiences of everyday life, as reflected in this child's adaptation to her inability to walk.

community that encourages active exchange and reciprocity. This approach has much in common with what Jerome Bruner (1996) has recommended for improving the culture of education.

Intelligence and Creativity

Twentieth-century English novelist Aldous Huxley said that children are remarkable for their curiosity and intelligence. What did Huxley mean when he used the word *intelligence?*

What Is Intelligence?   Intelligence is one of our most prized possessions, yet it is a concept that even the most intelligent people have not been able to agree on. Unlike such characteristics as height, weight, and age, intelligence cannot be directly measured. You can't peel back a student's scalp and observe the intelligence going on inside. You can evaluate students' intelligence only *indirectly,* by studying the intelligent acts they generate. For the most part, intelligence tests have been relied on to provide an estimate of a student's intelligence (Kail & Pelligrino, 1985).

Some experts describe intelligence as the possession of verbal ability and problem-solving skills. Others describe it as the ability to adapt to and learn from life's everyday experiences. Combining these ideas, we can arrive at a definition of **intelligence** *as verbal ability, problem-solving skills, and the ability to adapt to and learn from life's everyday experiences* (see figure 13.5).

intelligence
Verbal ability, problem-solving skills, and the ability to learn from and adapt to the experiences of everyday life.

Interest in intelligence has often focused on individual differences and assessment. **Individual differences** *are the stable, consistent ways in which people are different from each other.* We can talk about individual differences in personality or any other domain, but it is in the domain of intelligence that the most attention has been directed at individual differences. For example, an intelligence test purports to inform us about whether a student can reason better than others who have taken the test.

Robert J. Sternberg recalls being terrified of taking IQ tests as a child. He says that he literally froze when the time came to take such tests. Even as an adult, Sternberg stings with humiliation when he recalls being in the sixth grade and taking an IQ test with fifth-graders. Sternberg eventually overcame his anxieties about IQ tests. He not only began performing better on them but at age 13 he even devised his own IQ test and began using it to assess classmates—that is, until the school principal found out and scolded him. Sternberg became so fascinated by intelligence that he made its study one of his lifelong pursuits. Later in the chapter, we will discuss his theory of intelligence. To begin, though, let's go back in time and examine the first intelligence test.

The Binet Tests

In 1904, the French Ministry of Education asked psychologist Alfred Binet to devise a method of identifying children who were unable to learn in school. School officials wanted to reduce crowding by placing students who did not benefit from regular classroom teaching in special schools. Binet and his student Theophile Simon developed an intelligence test to meet this request. The test is called the 1905 Scale. It consisted of 30 questions on topics ranging from the ability to touch one's ear to the ability to draw designs from memory and define abstract concepts.

Binet developed the concept of **mental age (MA),** *an individual's level of mental development relative to others.* Not much later, in 1912, William Stern created the concept of **intelligence quotient (IQ),** *a person's mental age divided by chronological age (CA), multiplied by 100.* That is, IQ = MA/CA × 100. If mental age is the same as chronological age, then the person's IQ is 100. If mental age is above chronological age, then IQ is more than 100. If mental age is below chronological age, then IQ is less than 100. Scores noticeably above 100 are considered above average. Scores noticeably below 100 are labeled as below average. For example, a 6-year-old with a mental age of 8 would have an IQ of 133. A 6-year-old child with a mental age of 5 would have an IQ of 83.

The Binet test has been revised many times to incorporate advances in the understanding of intelligence and intelligence tests. These revisions are called the Stanford-Binet tests (Stanford University is where the revisions have been done). By administering the test to large numbers of people of different ages from different backgrounds, researchers have found that scores on the Stanford-Binet approximate a normal distribution (see figure 13.6). A **normal distribution** *is symmetrical, with a majority of the scores falling in the middle of the possible range of scores and few scores appearing toward the extremes of the range.*

The current Stanford-Binet is administered individually to people from the age of 2 through the adult years. It includes a variety of items, some of which require verbal responses, others nonverbal responses. For example, items that reflect a 6-year-old's performance on the test include the verbal ability to define at least six words, such as *orange* and *envelope,* as well as the nonverbal ability to trace a path through a maze. Items that reflect an average adult's intelligence include defining such words as *disproportionate* and *regard,* explaining a proverb, and comparing idleness and laziness.

The fourth edition of the Stanford-Binet was published in 1985. One important addition to this version was the analysis of the individual's responses in terms of four content areas: verbal reasoning, quantitative reasoning, abstract/visual reasoning, and short-term memory. A general composite score is still obtained to reflect overall intelligence. The Stanford-Binet continues to be one of the most widely used tests to assess a student's intelligence.

individual differences

The stable, consistent ways that people are different from each other.

As many people, as many minds; everyone his own way.

Terence
Roman Playwright, 2nd Century B.C.

mental age (MA)

Binet's measure of an individual's level of mental development, compared with that of others.

intelligence quotient (IQ)

A person's mental age divided by chronological age, multiplied by 100.

normal distribution

A distribution that is symmetrical, with most cases falling in the middle of the possible range of scores and a few scores appearing toward the extremes of the range.

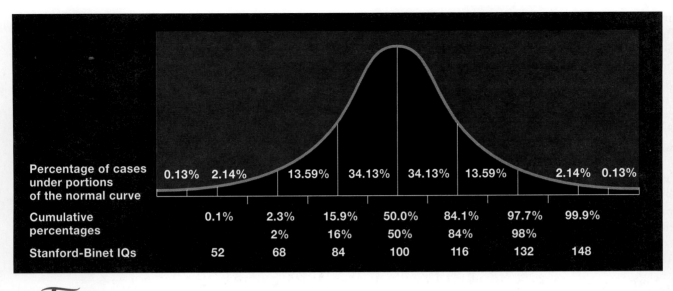

Percentage of cases under portions of the normal curve	0.13%	2.14%		13.59%	34.13%	34.13%	13.59%		2.14%	0.13%
Cumulative percentages		0.1%	2.3%	15.9%	50.0%	84.1%	97.7%	99.9%		
			2%	16%	50%	84%	98%			
Stanford-Binet IQs		52	68	84	100	116	132	148		

*F*igure 13.6
The Normal Curve and Stanford-Binet IQ Scores

The distribution of IQ scores approximates a normal curve. Most of the population falls in the middle range of scores. Notice that extremely high and extremely low scores are very rare. Slightly more than two-thirds of the scores fall between 84 and 116. Only about 1 in 50 individuals has an IQ of more than 132, and only about 1 in 50 individuals has an IQ of less than 68.

The Wechsler Scales   Another set of widely used tests to assess students' intelligence is called the Wechsler scales, developed by David Wechsler. They include the Wechsler Preschool and Primary Scale of Intelligence-Revised (WPPSI-R) to test children 4–6½ years of age; the Wechsler Intelligence Scale for Children-Revised (WISC-R) for children and adolescents 6–16 years of age; and the Wechsler Adult Intelligence Scale-Revised (WAIS-R).

Not only do the Wechsler scales provide an overall IQ, but they also yield verbal and performance IQs. Verbal IQ is based on six verbal subscales, performance IQ on five performance subscales. This allows the examiner to quickly see patterns of strengths and weaknesses in different areas of the student's intelligence. Several of the Wechsler subscales are shown in figure 13.7.

Types of Intelligence   Is it more appropriate to think of a child's intelligence as a general ability or as a number of specific abilities? Binet focused on a child's general intelligence. The IQ concept developed by William Stern was designed to capture this overall intellectual ability. Wechsler believed it was important to describe both a child's general intelligence and specific verbal and performance intelligences. This built on the ideas of Charles Spearman (1927), who said that people have both a general intelligence, which he called *g*, and specific types of intelligence, which he called *s*. As early as the 1930s, L. L. Thurstone (1938) said people have seven of these specific abilities, which he called primary abilities: verbal comprehension, number ability, word fluency, spatial visualization, associative memory, reasoning, and perceptual speed. More recently, the search for specific types of intelligence has heated up.

triarchic theory of intelligence
Sternberg's theory that intelligence consists of analytical, creative, and practical.

Sternberg's Triarchic Theory   Robert J. Sternberg (1986) developed the **triarchic theory of intelligence,** *which states that intelligence comes in three forms: analytical, creative, and practical.*

Analytical intelligence involves the ability to analyze, judge, evaluate, compare, and contrast. Creative intelligence consists of the ability to create, design, invent,

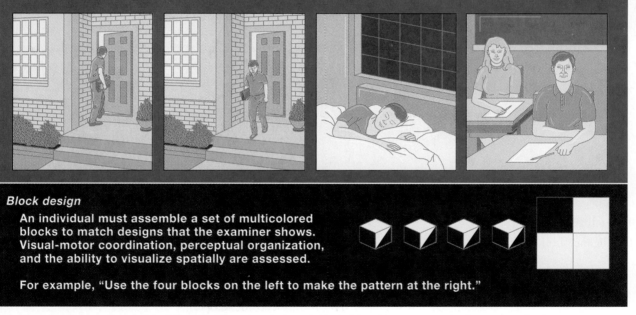

Verbal subscales

Similarities

An individual must think logically and abstractly to answer a number of questions about how things might be similar.

For example, "In what ways are boats and trains the same?"

Comprehension

This subtest is designed to measure an individual's judgment and common sense.

For example, "Why do individuals buy automobile insurance?"

Performance subscales

Picture arrangement

A series of pictures out of sequence is shown to an individual, who is asked to place them in their proper order to tell an appropriate story. This subtest evaluates how individuals integrate information to make it logical and meaningful.

For example, "The pictures below need to be placed in an appropriate order to tell a story."

Block design

An individual must assemble a set of multicolored blocks to match designs that the examiner shows. Visual-motor coordination, perceptual organization, and the ability to visualize spatially are assessed.

For example, "Use the four blocks on the left to make the pattern at the right."

Figure 13.7
Sample Subscales of the Wechsler Intelligence Scale for Children—Revised

Remember that the Wechsler includes 11 subscales, 6 verbal and 5 nonverbal. Four of the subscales are shown here.

originate, and imagine. Practical intelligence focuses on the ability to use, apply, implement, and put into practice. Some children are equally high in all three areas; others do well in only one or two of the areas. Consider three children:

- Ann, who scores high on traditional intelligence tests, such as the Stanford-Binet, and is a star analytical thinker (Analytical)

Sternberg's Theory

- Todd, who does not have the best test scores but has an insightful and creative mind (Creative)
- Art, who is street-smart and has learned to deal in practical ways with his world, although his scores on traditional intelligence tests are low (Practical)

Sternberg (1997) says that children with different triarchic patterns "look different" in school. Students with high analytic ability tend to be favored in conventional schooling. They often do well in direct instruction classes, in which the teacher lectures and gives students objective tests. They often are considered to be "smart" students, who get good grades, show up in high-level tracks, do well on traditional tests of intelligence and the SAT, and later get admitted to competitive colleges.

Children who are high in creative intelligence are often not in the top rung of their class. Sternberg says that many teachers have expectations about how assignments should be done, and creatively intelligent students may not conform to those expectations. Instead of giving conformist answers, they give unique answers, for which they might get reprimanded or marked down. No teacher wants to discourage creativity, but Sternberg believes that too often a teacher's desire to improve students' knowledge depresses creative thinking.

Like children high in creative intelligence, children who are practically intelligent often do not relate well to the demands of school. However, many of these children do well outside of the classroom's walls. They may have excellent social skills and good common sense. As adults, some become successful managers, entrepreneurs, or politicians, yet they have undistinguished school records.

Sternberg believes that few tasks are purely analytic, creative, or practical. Most tasks require a combination of these skills. For example, when children write a book report, they might (1) analyze the book's main themes, (2) generate new ideas about how the book might have been written better, and (3) think about how the book's themes can be applied to people's lives. He believes that what is important in teaching is to balance instruction related to the three types of intelligence. That is, students should be given opportunities to learn through analytical, creative, and practical thinking, in addition to the conventional strategy of having students memorize (Sternberg, 1999).

Gardner's Frames of Mind   Howard Gardner (1983, 1993) originally believed there are seven "frames of mind," or types of intelligence:

**Multiple Intelligences
Multiple Intelligence Links**

- Verbal skills
- Mathematical skills
- Ability to spatially analyze the world
- Movement skills
- Interpersonal skills
- Intrapersonal skills
- Musical skills

Gardner says that each of the seven types of intelligence can be destroyed by brain damage, that each involves unique cognitive skills, and that each shows up in an exaggerated way in both the gifted and idiots savants (individuals who are mentally retarded but have exceptional talent in a particular domain, such as drawing, music, or computing). Gardner recently added an eighth type of intelligence: skills related to natural history and the environment, such as observing, comparing, and categorizing, like those a naturalist uses.

The Key School in Indianapolis immerses students in activities that closely resemble Gardner's frames of mind (Goleman, Kaufman, & Ray, 1993). Each day, every student is exposed to materials that are designed to stimulate a range of human abilities, including art, music, computing, language skills, math skills, and physical games. In addition, attention is given to students' understanding of themselves and others.

Like other public schools, the Key School is open to any child in Indianapolis, but it is so popular that its students have to be chosen by lottery. The teachers are

Children in the Key School form "pods," in which they pursue activities of special interest to them. Every day, each child can choose from activities that draw on Gardner's eight frames of mind. The school has pods that range from gardening to architecture to gliding to dancing.

selected with an eye toward their special abilities in certain domains. For example, one teacher is competent at signing in the language of the deaf, a skill in both linguistic and kinesthetic domains.

The Key School's goal is to allow students to discover where they have natural curiosity and talent, then to let them explore those domains. Gardner says that, if teachers give students the opportunity to use their bodies, imaginations, and different senses, almost every student will find that he or she is good at something. Even students who are not outstanding in one area will find that they have relative strengths (Solomon, Powell, & Gardner, 1999).

Every nine weeks, the school emphasizes different themes, such as the Renaissance in sixteenth-century Italy and "Renaissance Now" in Indianapolis. Students develop projects related to the theme, but they are not graded. Instead, students present them to their classmates, explain them, and answer questions. Collaboration and teamwork are emphasized in the theme projects and in all areas of learning. Figure 13.8 further describes some strategies that are related to Gardner's eight types of intelligence.

Evaluating the Multiple Intelligence Approaches   Sternberg's and Gardner's approaches have much to offer. They have stimulated teachers to think more broadly about what makes up children's competencies. And they have motivated educators to develop programs that instruct students in multiple domains. These

Mathematical thinking
- Play games of logic with the child.
- Be on the lookout for appropriate situations for children to think about and construct numbers.
- Take children on field trips to computer labs, science museums, and electronics exhibits.
- Do math activities with the child, such as counting objects and experimenting with numbers.

Verbal skills
- Read to children and let them read to you.
- Discuss authors of books with children.
- Visit libraries and book stores with children.
- Have children keep a journal of significant events.
- Have children write stories and poems.
- Have children summarize and retell a story they have read.

Spatial skills
- Have a variety of arts and crafts materials that the child can use.
- Have children do mazes and create charts.
- Visit art museums and hands-on children's museums with the child.
- Have children draw the layout of their houses, neighborhoods, and other areas they know about.
- Go on walks with children. When they get back, ask them to visualize where they have been and then draw a map of their experiences.

Movement skills
- Provide children with opportunities for physical activity and encourage them to participate.
- Provide areas where children can play indoors and outdoors. If this is not possible, take them to a park.
- Take children to sporting events and the ballet.
- Encourage children to participate in dance activities.

Insightful skills for analyzing others
- Encourage children to work in groups.
- Help children develop communication skills.
- Provide group games for children to play.
- Encourage children to join clubs.

Insightful skills for self-understanding
- Encourage children to have hobbies and special interests.
- Listen to children's feelings and give them sensitive feedback.
- Encourage children to use their imagination.
- Have children keep a journal of their ideas.

Musical skills
- Provide children with a tape recorder or CD player they can use.
- Give children an opportunity to play a musical instrument.
- Take children to concerts.
- Encourage children to make up their own songs.

Naturalist skills
- Guide children in observing patterns in nature.
- Provide children with opportunities to classify objects in natural environments.
- Support children's exploration and comparison of natural and human-made systems.

*F*igure 13.8
Strategies for Helping Children Develop Gardner's Eight Frames of Mind

approaches also have contributed to the interest in assessing intelligence and class-room learning in innovative ways that go beyond conventional standardized and paper-and-pencil memory tasks. One way this assessment is carried out is by evaluating students' learning portfolios.

Some critics say that classifying musical skills as a main type of intelligence is off base. They ask whether there are possibly other skill domains that Gardner has left out. For example, there are outstanding chess players, prizefighters, writers, politicians, physicians, lawyers, ministers, and poets, yet we do not refer to chess intelligence, prizefighter intelligence, and so on. Other critics say that the research base to support the three intelligences of Sternberg and the eight intelligences of Gardner as the best ways to categorize intelligence has not yet been developed.

Controversies and Issues in Intelligence   The field of intelligence has its controversies. In one, inventor Robert Graham founded the Escondido Sperm Bank in California in an effort to produce geniuses. Graham collects the sperm of Nobel Prize–winners and offers it free of charge to intelligent women whose husbands are infertile. Critics say that breeding for intelligence is unethical. In reply, Graham says that the sperm bank provides a social service for couples who cannot conceive a child. And, in chapter 3, "Biological Beginnings," we discussed the controversial issue of how extensively intelligence is due to heredity or environment. We concluded that intelligence is due to an interaction of heredity and environment. Here, we will focus on several more issues, involving ethnicity and culture, as well as the use and misuse of intelligence tests.

Ethnicity and Culture   In the United States, children from African American and Latino families score below children from White families on standardized intelligence tests. Most comparisons have focused on African Americans and Whites. On the average, African American schoolchildren score 10 to 15 points lower than do White American schoolchildren (Neisser & others, 1996). Keep in mind that this figure of 10–15 points lower represents an average score. Many African American children score higher than many White children. Estimates are that 15–25 percent of all African American schoolchildren score higher than half of all White schoolchildren.

Are these differences based on heredity or environment? The consensus is environment (Brooks-Gunn, Klebanov, & Duncan, 1996). For example, in recent decades, as African Americans have experienced improved social, economic, and educational opportunities, the gap between White and African American children on conventional intelligence tests has narrowed (Jones, 1984). Between 1977 and 1996, as African Americans gained more educational opportunities, the gap between their SAT scores and those of their White counterparts shrank 23 percent (College Board, 1996). Also, when children from disadvantaged African American families are adopted by more advantaged middle-class families, their scores on intelligence tests become closer to the national average for middle-class children than to the national average for children from low-income families (Scarr & Weinberg, 1983).

Many of the early tests of intelligence were culturally biased, favoring urban children over rural children, children from middle-class families over children from low-income families, and White children over minority children (Miller-Jones, 1989). The standards for the early tests were almost exclusively based on White middle-class children. And some of the items were culturally biased. For example, one item on an early test asked what you should do if you find a 3-year-old in the street. The correct answer was "Call the police." However, children from impoverished inner-city families might not choose this answer if they have had bad experiences with the police. Children living in rural areas may not have police nearby. The contemporary versions of intelligence tests attempt to reduce such cultural bias.

Even if the content of test items is appropriate, another problem can characterize intelligence tests. Since many items are verbal, minority groups may encounter problems in understanding the language of the items. Consider Gregory Ochoa.

When he was in high school, he and his classmates were given an IQ test. Gregory looked at the test questions and didn't understand many of the words. Spanish was spoken at his home, and his English was not very good. Several weeks later, Gregory was placed in a "special" class. Many of the other students in the special class had names such as Ramirez and Gonzales. The special class was for students who were mentally retarded. Gregory lost interest in school and eventually dropped out. He joined the Navy, where he took high school courses and earned enough credits to attend college. He graduated from San Jose City College as an honor student, continued his education, and became a professor of social work at the University of Washington in Seattle.

culture-fair tests
Tests that are designed to be free of cultural bias.

Culture-fair tests *are tests of intelligence that attempt to be free of cultural bias.* Two types of culture-fair tests have been devised. The first includes items that are familiar to children from all socioeconomic and ethnic backgrounds, or items that at least are familiar to the children taking the test. For example, a child might be asked how a bird and a dog are different, on the assumption that all children have been exposed to birds and dogs. The second type of culture-fair test has all of the verbal items removed. Even though such tests are designed to be culture-fair, students with more education score higher on them than do their less-educated counterparts.

One test that takes children's socioeconomic backgrounds into account is called SOMPA, which stands for System of Multicultural Pluralistic Assessment. It can be given to children from 5–11 years of age. Instead of relying on a single test score, SOMPA is based on information about four areas of a student's life: (1) verbal and nonverbal intelligence in the conventional intelligence test mold, assessed by the WISC-R, (2) social and economic background of the family, obtained through a one-hour parent interview, (3) social adjustment to school, evaluated by an adaptive behavior inventory completed by parents, and (4) physical health, determined by a medical examination.

Cultural Bias and Testing

These attempts to produce culture-fair tests remind us that conventional intelligence tests probably are culturally biased, yet the effort to create a truly culture-fair test has not yielded a successful alternative. It also is important to consider that what is viewed as intelligent in one culture may not be thought of as intelligent in another (Lonner, 1990). In most Western cultures, children are considered intelligent if they are both smart (have considerable knowledge and can solve verbal problems) and fast (can process information quickly). By contrast, in the Buganda culture in Uganda, children who are wise, slow in thought, and say the socially correct thing are considered intelligent. And, in the widely dispersed Caroline Islands, one of the most important dimensions of intelligence is the ability to navigate by the stars.

The Use and Misuse of Intelligence Tests   Psychological tests are tools. Like all tools, their effectiveness depends on the knowledge, skill, and integrity of the user. A hammer can be used to build a beautiful kitchen cabinet, or it can be used as a weapon of assault. Like a hammer, psychological tests can be used for positive purposes, or they can be badly abused. Following are some cautions about IQ that can help you avoid the pitfalls of using information about a child's intelligence in negative ways.

- A special concern is that the scores on an IQ test easily can lead to stereotypes and expectations about students. Sweeping generalizations are too often made on the basis of an IQ score. Imagine that you are in the teacher's lounge the day after school has started in the fall. You mention a student—Johnny Jones—and another teacher remarks that she had Johnny in class last year. She comments that he was a real dunce and mentions he scored 83 on an IQ test. How hard is it to ignore this information as you go about teaching your class? Probably difficult. But it is important that you not develop the expectation that, because Johnny scored low on an IQ test, it is useless to spend much time teaching him. An IQ test should always be considered a measure of current performance. It is not a measure of fixed potential. Maturational changes and enriched environmental experiences can advance a student's intelligence.

- Another concern about IQ tests occurs when they are used as the main or sole characteristic of competence. A high IQ is not the ultimate human value. As we have seen in this chapter, it is important to consider not only students' intellectual competence in such areas as verbal skills but also their creative and practical skills.
- Especially be cautious in interpreting the meaningfulness of an overall IQ score. In evaluating a child's intelligence, it is wiser to think of intelligence as consisting of a number of domains. Keep in mind the different types of intelligence described by Sternberg and Gardner. Remember that, by considering the different domains of intelligence, you can find that every child has at least one or more strengths.

The Extremes of Intelligence   Intelligence tests have been used to discover indications of mental retardation or intellectual giftedness, the extremes of intelligence. At times, intelligence tests have been misused for this purpose. Keeping in mind the theme that an intelligence test should not be used as the sole indicator of mental retardation or giftedness, we will explore the nature of these intellectual extremes.

Mental Retardation   The most distinctive feature of mental retardation is inadequate intellectual functioning. Long before formal tests were developed to assess intelligence, the mentally retarded were identified by a lack of age-appropriate skills in learning and caring for themselves. Once intelligence tests were developed, numbers were assigned to indicate degree of mental retardation. It is not unusual to find two retarded people with the same low IQ, one of whom is married, employed, and involved in the community and the other requiring constant supervision in an institution. These differences in social competence led psychologists to include deficits in adaptive behavior in their definition of mental retardation. **Mental retardation** *is a condition of limited mental ability in which an individual has a low IQ, usually below 70 on a traditional intelligence test, and has difficulty adapting to everyday life.* About 5 million Americans fit this definition of mental retardation.

There are several classifications of mental retardation. About 89 percent of the mentally retarded fall into the mild category, with IQs of 55 to 70. About 6 percent are classified as moderately retarded, with IQs of 40 to 54; these people can attain a second-grade level of skills and may be able to support themselves as adults through some types of labor. About 3.5 percent of the mentally retarded are in the severe category, with IQs of 25 to 39; these individuals learn to talk and engage in very simple tasks but require extensive supervision. Less than 1 percent have IQs below 25; they fall into the profoundly mentally retarded classification and need constant supervision (Drew & Hardman, 2000).

Mental retardation can have an organic cause, or it can be social and cultural in origin. **Organic retardation** *is mental retardation caused by a genetic disorder or by brain damage;* organic *refers to the tissues or organs of the body, so there is some physical damage in organic retardation.* Down syndrome, one form of mental retardation, occurs when an extra chromosome is present in an individual's genetic makeup (see figure 13.9). It is not known why the extra chromosome is present, but it may involve the health or age of the female ovum or male sperm. Most people who suffer from organic retardation have IQs that range between 0 and 50.

Cultural-familial retardation *is a mental deficit in which no evidence of organic brain damage can be found; individuals' IQs range from 50 to 70.* Psychologists suspect that such mental deficits result from the normal variation that distributes people along the range of intelligence scores above 50, combined with growing up in a below-average

Figure 13.9
A Down Syndrome Child

What causes a child to develop Down syndrome? In what major classification of mental retardation does the condition fall?

mental retardation

A condition of limited mental ability in which an individual has a low IQ, usually below 70 on a traditional test of intelligence, and has difficulty adapting to everyday life.

Mental Retardation

organic retardation

Mental retardation that involves some physical damage and is caused by a genetic disorder or brain damage.

cultural-familial retardation

Retardation that is characterized by no evidence of organic brain damage, but the individual's IQ is between 50 and 70.

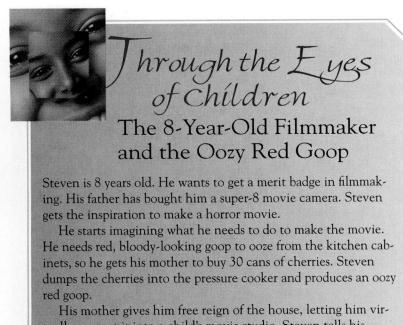

Through the Eyes of Children
The 8-Year-Old Filmmaker and the Oozy Red Goop

Steven is 8 years old. He wants to get a merit badge in filmmaking. His father has bought him a super-8 movie camera. Steven gets the inspiration to make a horror movie.

He starts imagining what he needs to do to make the movie. He needs red, bloody-looking goop to ooze from the kitchen cabinets, so he gets his mother to buy 30 cans of cherries. Steven dumps the cherries into the pressure cooker and produces an oozy red goop.

His mother gives him free reign of the house, letting him virtually convert it into a child's movie studio. Steven tells his mother he needs some costumes, which she obligingly makes.

The son's name: Steven Spielberg, whose mother supported his imagination and passion for filmmaking. Of course, Spielberg went on to become one of Hollywood's greatest producers with such films as *E.T.* and *Jurassic Park* (Goleman, Kaufman, & Ray, 1993).

gifted
Having above-average intelligence, usually an IQ of 120 or higher, and a superior talent for something.

Children Who Are Gifted
Gifted Education

intellectual environment. Children who are familially retarded can be detected in schools, where they often fail, need tangible rewards (candy rather than praise), and are highly sensitive to what others—both peers and adults—want from them (Feldman, 1996). However, as adults, the familially retarded are usually invisible, perhaps because adult settings don't tax their cognitive skills as sorely. It may also be that the familially retarded increase their intelligence as they move toward adulthood.

Giftedness   There have always been people whose abilities and accomplishments outshine others—the whiz kid in class, the star athlete, the natural musician. People who are **gifted** *have above-average intelligence (an IQ of 120 or higher) and/or superior talent for something.* When it comes to programs for the gifted, most school systems select children who have intellectual superiority and academic aptitude. Children who are talented in the visual and performing arts (arts, drama, dance), athletics, or other special aptitudes tend to be overlooked.

Until recently, giftedness and emotional distress were thought to go hand in hand. English novelist Virginia Woolf suffered from severe depression, for example, and eventually committed suicide. Sir Isaac Newton, Vincent van Gogh, Ann Sexton, Socrates, and Sylvia Plath all had emotional problems. However, these are the exception rather than the rule; in general, no relation between giftedness and mental disorder has been found. Recent studies support the conclusion that gifted people tend to be more mature and have fewer emotional problems than others (Feldman & Piirto, 1995). In one study, gifted children were more intrinsically motivated than were nongifted children.

Lewis Terman (1925) has followed the lives of approximately 1,500 children whose Stanford-Binet IQs averaged 150 into adulthood; the study will not be complete until the year 2010. Terman has found that this remarkable group is an accomplished lot. Of the 800 males, 78 have obtained doctorates (they include two past presidents of the American Psychological Association), 48 have earned M.D.s, and 85 have been granted law degrees. Most of these figures are 10 to 30 times greater than those found among the 800 men of the same age chosen randomly as a comparison group. These findings challenge the commonly held belief that the intellectually gifted are emotionally disordered or socially maladjusted.

The 672 gifted women studied by Terman (Terman & Oden, 1959) underscore the importance of relationships and intimacy in women's lives. Two thirds of these exceptional women graduated from college in the 1930s, and one fourth of them attended graduate school. Despite their impressive educational achievements, when asked to order their life's priorities, the gifted women placed families first, friendships second, and careers last. For these women, having a career often meant not having children. Of the 30 most successful women, 25 did not have any children. Such undivided commitments to the family are less true of women today. Many of the highly gifted women in Terman's study questioned their intelligence and concluded that their cognitive skills had waned in adulthood. Studies reveal that today gifted women have a stronger confidence in their cognitive skills and intellectual abilities than did the gifted women in Terman's study (Tomlinson-Keasey, 1990). Terman's gifted women represent a cohort who reached midlife prior to the women's movement and the current pervasiveness of the dual-career couple and the single-parent family (Tomlinson-Keasey, 1993).

In the most recent analysis of Terman's gifted children, two factors predicted longevity: personality and family stability (Friedman & others, 1995). With regard to personality, those who as children were conscientious and less impulsive lived significantly longer. With regard to family stability, those whose parents had divorced before the children reached age 21 faced a one-third greater mortality risk than did their counterparts whose parents had not divorced. Individuals who became divorced themselves also faced a shorter life. And not marriage itself but, rather, a stable marriage history was linked with increased longevity.

Ellen Winner (1996) has described three characteristics of gifted children, whether in the art, music, or academic domain:

1. *Precocity.* Gifted children are precocious. They begin to master an area earlier than their peers. Learning in their domain is more effortless than for ordinary children. In most instances, these gifted children are precocious because they have an inborn high ability in a particular domain or domains.
2. *Tendency to march to their own drummer.* Gifted children learn in a qualitatively different way than ordinary children. One way that they march to a different drummer is that they need minimal help, or scaffolding, from adults to learn. In many instances, they resist any kind of explicit instruction. They also make discoveries on their own and solve problems in unique ways.
3. *A passion to master.* Gifted children are driven to understand the domain in which they have high ability. They display an intense, obsessive interest and an ability to focus their motivation. They are not children who need to be pushed by their parents. They motivate themselves, says Winner.

Ten-year-old Alexandra Nechita is a gifted child in the domain of art. She is precocious, marches to the tune of a different drummer, and has a passion to master her domain.

Ten-year-old Alexandra Nechita has burst onto the child prodigy scene. She paints quickly and impulsively on large canvases, some as large as 5′ × 9′. It is not unusual for her to complete several of these large paintings in a week's time. Her paintings—in the modernist tradition—sell for up to $80,000 a piece. Alexandra used to color in coloring books for hours when she was only 2 years old. She had no interest in dolls or friends. Once she started school, as soon as she got home in the evening she painted. And she continues to paint—relentlessly and passionately. It is, she says, what she loves to do.

Creativity   **Creativity** *is the ability to think about something in novel and unusual ways and to come up with unique solutions to problems.* Thus, intelligence and creativity are not the same thing. This was recognized in Sternberg's account of intelligence earlier in this chapter and by J. P. Guilford (1967). Guilford distinguished between **convergent thinking,** *which produces one correct answer and is characteristic of the kind of thinking required on conventional intelligence tests,* and **divergent thinking,** *which produces many different answers to the same question and is more characteristic of creativity.* For example, a typical item on a conventional intelligence test is "How many quarters will you get in return for 60 dimes?" By contrast, the following question has many possible answers: "What image comes to mind when you hear the phrase 'Sitting alone in a dark room' or 'Can you think of some unique uses for a paper clip?'"

Are intelligence and creativity related? Although most creative children are quite intelligent, the reverse is not necessarily true. Many highly intelligent children (as measured by high scores on conventional intelligence tests) are not very creative. And, if Sternberg were to have his way, creative thinking would become part of a broader definition of intelligence.

An important goal is to help children become more creative (Ripple, 1999). What are the best strategies for accomplishing this goal?

creativity
The ability to think in novel and unusual ways and to come up with unique solutions to problems.

convergent thinking
Thinking that produces one correct answer and is characteristic of the kind of thinking tested by standardized intelligence tests.

divergent thinking
Thinking that produces many answers to the same question and is characteristic of creativity.

Never to be cast away are the gifts of the gods, magnificent.

Homer
Greek Poet, 9th Century B.C.

brainstorming
A technique in which individuals are encouraged to come up with ideas in a group, play off each other's ideas, and say practically whatever comes to mind.

**Teresa Amabile's Research
Csikszentmihalyi's Ideas**

- *Have children engage in brainstorming and come up with as many ideas as possible.* **Brainstorming** *is a technique in which children are encouraged to come up with creative ideas in a group, play off each other's ideas, and say practically whatever comes to mind* (Sternberg, 1995). Children are usually told to hold off from criticizing others' ideas at least until the end of the brainstorming session. Whether in a group or individually, a good creativity strategy is to come up with as many new ideas as possible. Famous twentieth-century Spanish artist Pablo Picasso produced more than 20,000 works of art. Not all of them were masterpieces. The more ideas children produce, the better their chance of creating something unique (Rickards, 1999). Creative children are not afraid of failing or getting something wrong. They may go down 20 dead-end streets before they come up with an innovative idea. They recognize that it's okay to win some and lose some. They are willing to take risks, just as Picasso was.

- *Provide children with environments that stimulate creativity.* Some settings nourish creativity; others depress it. People who encourage children's creativity often rely on their natural curiosity. They provide exercises and activities that stimulate children to find insightful solutions to problems, rather than asking a lot of questions that require rote answers. Adults also encourage creativity by taking children to locations where creativity is valued. Howard Gardner (1993) believes that science, discovery, and children's museums offer rich opportunities to stimulate childrens' creativity.

- *Don't overcontrol.* Teresa Amabile (1993) says that telling children exactly how to do things leaves them feeling that any originality is a mistake and any exploration is a waste of time. Letting children select their interests and supporting their inclinations are less likely to destroy their natural curiosity than dictating which activities they should engage in. Amabile also believes that, when adults constantly hover over children, the children feel they are being watched while they are working. When children are under constant surveillance, their creative risk-taking and adventurous spirit wane. Another strategy that can harm creativity is to have grandiose expectations for a child's performance and expect the child to do something perfectly, according to Amabile.

- *Encourage internal motivation.* The excessive use of prizes, such as gold stars, money, or toys, can stifle creativity by undermining the intrinsic pleasure children derive from creative activities. Creative children's motivation is the satisfaction generated by the work itself. Competition for prizes and formal evaluations often undermine intrinsic motivation and creativity (Amabile & Hennessey, 1992).

- *Foster flexible and playful thinking.* Creative thinkers are flexible and play with problems, which gives rise to a paradox. Although creativity takes effort, the effort goes more smoothly if students take it lightly. In a way, humor can grease the wheels of creativity (Goleman, Kaufman, & Ray, 1993). When children are joking around, they are more likely to consider unusual solutions to problems. Having fun helps disarm the inner censor that can condemn a child's ideas as off-base. As one clown named Wavy Gravy put it, "If you can't laugh about it, it just isn't funny anymore."

- *Introduce children to creative people.* You may not know a clown named Wavy Gravy whom you can ask to stimulate a child's creativity, but it is a good strategy to think about the identity of the most creative people in your community. Teachers can invite these people to their classrooms and ask them to describe what helps them become creative or to demonstrate their creative skills. A writer, poet, musician, scientist, and many others can bring their props and productions to the class, turning it into a theater for stimulating students' creativity. Poet Richard Lewis (1997) visits classrooms in New York City. He brings with him only the glassy spectrum that a shining marble holds. He lifts it above his head, so that every student can see its colored charms. He asks, "Who can see something playing inside?" Then he asks students to write about what they see. One student named Snigdha wrote that she sees the rainbow

Summary Table 13.1
Cognition in Middle and Late Childhood

Concept	Processes/ Related Ideas	Characteristics/Description
Piaget's theory	Concrete operational thought and education	Concrete operational thought involves operations, conservation, classification, seriation, and transitivity. Thought is not as abstract as later in development. Piaget's ideas have been applied extensively to education.
	Contributions and criticisms	We owe Piaget the field of cognitive development; he was a genius at observing children. Critics question his estimates of competence at different developmental levels, his stages concept, and other ideas. Neo-Piagetians believe that children's cognition is more specific than Piaget thought.
Information processing	Its nature	Long-term memory improves in middle and late childhood. Strategies are involved in this improvement. Schemas and scripts help children interpret their cognitive world. Cognitive monitoring can benefit school learning. There has been an increased interest in getting children to think more critically in recent years. The Jasper Project is an innovative program to help children learn mathematical skills. Ann Brown developed a program called "Fostering a Community of Learners." It uses adults as role models, children teaching children, and on-line consultation to encourage children's discussion and reflection.
Intelligence and creativity	What is intelligence?	Intelligence consists of verbal ability, problem-solving skills, and the ability to adapt to and learn from life's everyday experiences. Interest in intelligence often focuses on individual differences and assessment.
	The Binet and Wechsler tests	Binet and Simon developed the first intelligence test. Binet developed the concept of mental age, and Stern created the concept of IQ as = MA/CA × 100. The Stanford-Binet approximates a normal distribution. The Wechsler scales also are widely used to assess intelligence. They yield an overall IQ, as well as verbal and performance IQs.
	Types of intelligence	Spearman proposed that people have a general intelligence (g) and specific types of intelligence (s). Sternberg proposed the triarchic theory of intelligence, which states that intelligence comes in three forms: analytical, creative, and practical. Gardner believes there are 8 types of intelligence: verbal, math, spatial, movement, self insight, insight about others, musical skills, and skills related to natural history and the environment. The Key School involves educational applications of Gardner's multiple intelligences.
	Controversies and issues	These include ethnicity and culture (such as the extent to which ethnic differences in intelligence are due more to heredity or environment), cultural bias and culture-free tests, and the use and misuse of intelligence tests.
	Extremes of intelligence	Mental retardation involves low IQ and problems in adapting to everyday life. One way of classifying mental retardation is as organic or cultural-familial. A gifted child has above-average intelligence and/or superior talent for something. Terman's studies have contributed to our understanding of gifted children. Three characteristics of gifted children are precocity, individuality, and a passion to master.
	Creativity	Creativity is the ability to think about something in novel and unusual ways and to come up with unique solutions to problems. Guilford distinguished between convergent and divergent thinking. Encouraging children's creativity involves having children engage in brainstorming and coming up with as many ideas as possible, providing children with environments that stimulate creativity, not overcontrolling and criticizing, encouraging internal motivation, fostering flexible and playful thinking, and introducing children to creative people.

rising, the sun moving a lot, and the sun sleeping with the stars. She also wrote that she sees the rain dropping on the ground, stems breaking, apples falling from trees, and wind blowing the leaves.

At this point, we have discussed a number of ideas about cognition in middle and late childhood. An overview of these ideas is presented in summary table 13.1.

Harvard Project Zero

Children's reading is a complex process. What kinds of information-processing skills are involved?

LANGUAGE DEVELOPMENT

As children develop during middle and late childhood, changes in their vocabulary and grammar take place. Reading assumes a prominent role in their language world. An increasingly important consideration is bilingualism.

Vocabulary and Grammar

During middle and late childhood, a change occurs in the way children think about words. They become less tied to the actions and perceptual dimensions associated with words, and they become more analytical in their approach to words. For example, when asked to say the first thing that comes to mind when they hear a word, such as *dog*, preschool children often respond with a word related to the immediate context of a dog. A child might associate *dog* with a word that indicates its appearance (*black, big*) or to an action associated with it (*bark, sit*). Older children more frequently respond to *dog* by associating it with an appropriate category (*animal*) or to information that intelligently expands the context (*cat, veterinarian*). The increasing ability of elementary school children to analyze words helps them understand words that have no direct relation to their personal experiences. This allows children to add more abstract words to their vocabulary. For example, *precious stones* can be understood by understanding the common characteristics of *diamonds* and *emeralds*. Also, children's increasing analytic abilities allow them to distinguish between such similar words as *cousin* and *nephew* or *city, village,* and *suburb*.

Children make similar advances in grammar. The elementary school child's improvement in logical reasoning and analytical skills helps in the understanding of such constructions as the appropriate use of comparatives (*shorter, deeper*) and subjectives ("If you were president, . . ."). By the end of the elementary school years, children can usually apply many of the appropriate rules of grammar.

Reading

What are some approaches to teaching children how to read? Education and language experts continue to debate how children should be taught to read. The debate focuses on the whole-language approach versus the basic-skills-and-phonetics approach. The **whole-language approach** *stresses that reading instruction should parallel children's natural language learning. Reading materials should be whole and meaningful.* That is, in early reading instruction, children should be presented with materials in their complete form, such as stories and poems. In this way, say the whole-language advocates, children learn to understand language's communicative function.

In the whole-language approach, reading is integrated with other skills and subjects. Reading should be connected with listening and writing skills. Although there are variations in whole-language programs, most share the premise that reading should be integrated with other skills and subjects, such as science and social studies, and that it should focus on real-world, relevant material. Thus, a class might read newspapers, magazines, or books, then write about them and discuss them.

By contrast, the **basic-skills-and-phonetics approach** *emphasizes that reading instruction should teach phonetics and its basic rules for translating written symbols into sounds. Early reading instruction should involve simplified materials.* Only after they have learned phonological rules should children be given complex reading materials, such as books and poems.

Advocates of the basic-skills-and-phonetics approach often point to low reading achievement scores occurring as an outgrowth of the recent emphasis on holistic, literature-based instruction and the consequent lack of attention to basic skills and phonetics (Baumann & others, 1998). In California, a task force has recommended that children's reading skills be improved by pursuing a balanced approach, which

whole-language approach
An approach to reading instruction based on the idea that instruction should parallel children's natural language learning. Reading materials should be whole and meaningful.

basic-skills-and-phonetics approach
An approach to reading instruction that stresses phonetics and basic rules for translating symbols into sounds. Early reading instruction should involve simplified materials.

Reading Research

includes teaching phonemic awareness (sounds in words), phonics, and other decoding skills.

The term *balanced instruction* is now being used to describe combinations of reading approaches (Au, Carroll, & Scheu, in press; Freppon & Dahl, 1998; Pressley, in press; Tompkins, 1997; Weaver, in press). However, *balance* often means different things to different researchers and teachers. For some, *balanced* means a primary emphasis on phonics instruction with minimal whole-language emphasis; for others, the reverse.

Which approach is best? Researchers have not been able to document consistently that one approach is better than the other. There is very strong evidence that the decoding skills involved in recognizing sounds and words are important in becoming a good reader. A good strategy is to work with kindergarten and first-grade students on developing phonemic awareness, which involves recognizing that separate sounds make up words and that combining these sounds can make words. If students have not developed this phonemic awareness early in school, their literacy will still benefit if it is taught to them later in school (Pressley, 1996). Some critics believe that, because of the prominence of the whole-language approach, some teacher training programs have not adequately instructed future teachers in phonics and other structural rules of language.

There is also good evidence that students in the early years of school benefit from the whole-language approach of being immersed in a natural world of print (Graham & Harris, 1994). This approach helps them understand the purpose of learning to read and builds on their early home experiences with books and language.

Some experts believe that a combination of the two approaches should be followed (Freppon & Dahl, 1998; Spear-Swerling & Sternberg, 1994). In sum, there is every reason to believe that students learn to read best when they are exposed to both whole-language experiences and decoding skills. Indeed, a combination of whole-language and phonics approaches also recently was recommended by a national panel of experts after reviewing the research evidence on the effectiveness of reading approaches (Snow, 1998).

In a recent national survey of K–5 elementary school teachers' attitudes toward and experiences with different reading approaches, the following findings emerged (Baumann & others, 1998):

- A significant majority of teachers believed in using a balanced approach of combining skills with literature and language-rich activities (89%).
- A majority thought that phonics should be taught directly to help readers become skillful and fluent (63%).
- A majority believed that children need to be immersed in literature and literacy to achieve fluency (71%).
- When asked which reading skills were essential or important, the vast majority of K–2 teachers said "instruction in phonics" (99%), "meaning vocabulary" (99%), and "sight words" (96%).
- Teachers also used whole-language strategies. For example, K–2 teachers regularly read aloud (97%) and engaged children in oral language (83%) and journal writing (78%).

In sum, balance, eclecticism, and common sense characterize the reading and language arts instructional practices of many elementary school teachers. As educational psychologist David Berliner (1997) commented, teachers often are not extremist on the whole-language–phonics issue. They tend to be pragmatists, using what works. Caring for Children describes one teacher who successfully teaches reading.

Bilingualism

Octavio's parents moved to the United States one year before he was born. They do not speak English fluently and always have spoken to Octavio in Spanish. At age 6, Octavio has just entered the first grade in San Antonio. He speaks no English. What is the best way to teach Octavio?

Reading

Children's Literature

Caring for Children

A Teacher's Passion for Literacy

Betty Teuful teaches language arts to first-grade students in Plano, Texas. She was the school district's teacher of the year in 1998. Literacy is her passion. She is a strong advocate of literacy, not only in her school but throughout the nation. She envisions a literacy revival in which corps of volunteers become reading tutors in schools, community centers, and hospitals. Betty is working with nonprofit organizations to solicit publishers and businesses to contribute to a national "Read while you wait" campaign, which saturates clinics, restaurants, airports, and other public facilities with good literature.

She believes that, if children don't know how to read, if they don't understand language, and if they don't communicate with each other, it won't matter if they are computer literate. In her view, if teachers help children become competent at reading early in their schooling, their motivation to read should last a lifetime. In her words, "We ought to get them hooked on reading."

At Saigling Elementary School, Betty conducts literacy workshops for parents and places book baskets in locations where parents can read while they wait for conferences, meetings, and carpool groups. Using the musical talents of another Saigling teacher, Betty orchestrated the creation of Sing to Read, a program in which students observe patterns, rhymes, and rhythms in songs to help develop reading skills.

Every day after recess, first-grade classes gather to sing songs written on flip charts.

"My students know that every time we have a holiday, I'm going to buy a book and share it with the class," she says. They will say, "What did you find?" Then, they all sit down together to read.

Betty wants to guide children to develop self-worth, self-discipline, tolerance, a sense of humor, and an attitude toward life-long learning. One of the ways she encourages such traits is through the designation of "Joke Day" every Friday. Students get to write out jokes and leave them in a basket to be read during the day. They delight in trying to stump the teacher.

Betty says, "Anything that makes a teacher grow or stretch and think how he or she is instructing is good for children. The worst thing for a teacher is stagnation. I think you have to be willing to try out new ideas and explore new ways for children to learn."

The day after Betty received her Teacher of the Year award, Saigling first-graders honored her with a flower parade. They took many varieties of flowers to school—some from their gardens at home, others made with construction or tissue paper. When asked about their teacher, Ryan and Jordan chimed in, "She's nice and she's fair" (Fowler, 1998).

---

bilingual education

An educational approach whose aim is to teach academic subjects to immigrant children in their native languages (most often Spanish) while gradually adding English instruction.

Bilingual Education

As many as 10 million children in the United States come from homes in which English is not the primary language. Often, like Octavio, they live in a community in which English is the main form of communication. To be successful, they have to master the English language.

Bilingual education, *which has been the preferred strategy of schools for the past two decades, aims to teach academic subjects to immigrant children in their native languages (most often Spanish) while slowly and simultaneously adding English instruction.* Most bilingual programs are transitional programs developed to support students until they can understand English well enough to learn in the regular classroom. A typical program changes to English-only classes at the end of the second or third grade, although some programs continue instruction in the child's primary language until the sixth grade. In most programs, at least half of children's instruction is in English from the beginning (Garcia, 1992).

Proponents of bilingual education argue that teaching immigrants in their native language values their family and community culture, as well as increasing their self-esteem, thus making their academic success more likely. By contrast, critics stress that bilingual education harms immigrant children by failing to adequately instruct them in English, which will leave them unprepared for the workplace. In rebuttal, supporters of bilingual education say that it aims to teach English. Some states recently have passed laws declaring English to be their official language, creating conditions in which schools are not obligated to teach minority children in languages other than

English (Rothstein, 1998). In California, in 1998 voters repealed bilingual education altogether. Supporters of the appeal claimed that most Spanish-speaking voters opposed bilingual education, though polling after the election did not bear out this contention. Ironically, test scores that were released shortly after the election revealed that the scores of the children in bilingual programs in several large school districts were higher on average than the scores of the native English-speaking children.

Researchers have found that bilingualism does not interfere with performance in either language (Hakuta & Garcia, 1989; Oller, 1999). There is no evidence that children's use of their native language should be restricted because it might interfere with learning a second language.

Multilingual Multicultural Research

The United States is one of the few countries in the world in which most students graduate from high school knowing only their own language. For example, in Russia, schools have 10 grades, called forms, which roughly correspond to the 12 grades in American schools. Children begin school at age 7 in Russia. Russian students begin learning English in the third form. Because of the emphasis on teaching English in Russian schools, most Russian citizens under the age of 40 today are bilingual, able to speak at least some English in addition to their native language.

Is it better to learn a second language as a child or an adolescent? Adolescents make faster initial progress, but their eventual success in the second language is not as great as children's. For example, in one study, Chinese and Korean adults who had immigrated to the United States at different ages were given a test of grammatical knowledge (Johnson & Newport, 1989). Those who began learning English from 3 to 7 years of age scored as well as native speakers on the test, but as their age of arrival to the United States (and therefore of onset of learning) increased through later childhood and then adolescence, their test scores gradually declined. Children's ability to pronounce a second language with an accent also decreases with age, with an especially sharp decline occurring after the age of about 10 to 12 (Asher & Garcia, 1969). Adolescents can become competent in a second language, but this is a more difficult task than learning it as a child.

Following are some classroom recommendations for working effectively with linguistically and culturally diverse children (NAEYC, 1996):

- Recognize that all children are cognitively, linguistically, and emotionally connected to the language and culture of their home.
- Acknowledge that children can demonstrate their knowledge and capacity in many ways. Whatever language children speak, they should be able to demonstrate their capabilities and feel appreciated and valued.
- Understand that, without comprehensible input, second language learning can be difficult. It takes time to be linguistically competent in any language. Although verbal proficiency in a second language can be attained in two to three years, the skills needed to understand academic content through reading and writing may take four or more years. Children who do not become proficient in their second language after two to three years often are not proficient in their first language, either.
- Model appropriate use of English and provide the child with opportunities to use newly acquired vocabulary and language. The teacher also can learn a few words in the child's first language, thus demonstrating respect for the child's culture.
- Actively involve parents and families in the child's learning. Parents and families should be invited to engage in activities with their children. Encourage and assist parents in becoming knowledgeable about the value for children of knowing more than one language. Provide parents with strategies to support and maintain home-language learning.
- Recognize that children can and will acquire the use of English, even when their home language is used and respected. Bilingualism does not interfere with either language proficiency or cognitive development.
- To learn more about working with linguistic and culturally diverse children, collaborate with other teachers and educators.

ACHIEVEMENT

Yet another important dimension of cognitive development in middle and late childhood is children's achievement. We are a species motivated to do well at what we attempt, to gain mastery over the world in which we live, to explore unknown environments with enthusiasm and curiosity, and to achieve the heights of success. We live in an achievement-oriented world, with standards that tell children success is important. The standards suggest that success requires a competitive spirit, a desire to win, a motivation to do well, and the wherewithal to cope with adversity and to persist until an objective is reached. Some developmentalists, though, believe that we are becoming a nation of hurried, "wired" people who are raising our children to become the same way—uptight about success and failure and far too worried about what we accomplish in comparison with others. It was in the 1950s that an interest in achievement began to flourish. The interest initially focused on the need for achievement.

Need for Achievement

Think about yourself and your friends for a moment. Are you more achievement-oriented than they are, or are you less so? If we were to ask you and your friends to tell stories about achievement-related themes, could we accurately determine which of you is the most achievement-oriented?

Some individuals are highly motivated to succeed and expend a lot of effort, striving to excel. Other individuals are not as motivated to succeed and don't work as hard to achieve (Brophy, 1999). These two types of individuals vary in their **achievement motivation (need for achievement),** *the desire to accomplish something, to reach a standard of excellence, and to expend effort to excel.* David McClelland (1955) assessed achievement by showing individuals ambiguous pictures that were likely to stimulate achievement-related responses. The individuals were asked to tell a story about the picture, and their comments were scored according to how strongly they reflected achievement.

A host of studies have correlated achievement-related responses with different aspects of the individual's experiences and behavior. The findings are diverse, but they suggest that achievement-oriented individuals have a stronger hope for success than a fear of failure, are moderate rather than high or low in risk taking, and persist for appropriate lengths of time in solving difficult problems. Early research had indicated that independence training by parents promotes children's achievement, but more recent research reveals that parents, to increase achievement, need to set high standards for achievement, model achievement-oriented behavior, and reward their children for their achievements. And, in one study, the middle school students who had the highest grades were those whose parents, teachers, and schools were authoritative (Paulson, Marchant, & Rothlisberg, 1995).

Intrinsic and Extrinsic Motivation

Achievement motivation—whether in school, at work, or in sports—can be divided into two main types: **intrinsic motivation,** *the internal desire to be competent and to do something for its own sake,* and **extrinsic motivation,** *the influence of external rewards and punishments.* If you work hard in college because a personal standard of excellence is important to you, intrinsic motivation is involved. But, if you work hard in college because you know it will bring you a higher-paying job when you graduate, extrinsic motivation is at work.

An important consideration when motivating a child to do something is whether or not to offer an incentive. If a child is not doing competent work, is bored, or has a negative attitude, it may be worthwhile to consider incentives to improve motivation. However, there are times when external rewards can get in the way of motivation. In one investigation, children with a strong interest in art spent more

---

The trouble with being in the rat race is that even when you win you are still a rat.

Lily Tomlin
Contemporary American Actress

achievement motivation (need for achievement)
The desire to accomplish something, to reach a standard of excellence, and to expend effort to excel.

intrinsic motivation
The desire to be competent and to do something for its own sake.

extrinsic motivation
Motivation produced by external rewards and punishments.

time in a drawing activity when they expected no reward than did their counter-parts who knew they would be rewarded (Lepper, Greene, & Nisbett, 1973).

Intrinsic motivation implies that internal motivation should be promoted and external factors deemphasized. In this way, children learn to attribute to themselves the cause of their success and failure, and especially how much effort they expend. But, in reality, achievement is motivated by both internal and external factors; children are never divorced from their external environment. Some of the most achievement-oriented children are those who have a high personal standard for achievement and who are also highly competitive. In one study, low-achieving boys and girls who engaged in individual goal setting (intrinsic motivation) and were given comparative information about peers (extrinsic motivation) worked more math problems and got more of them correct than did their counterparts who experienced either condition alone (Schunk, 1983). Other research suggests that social comparison by itself is not a wise strategy (Nicholls, 1984). The argument is that social comparison puts the child in an ego-involved, threatening, self-focused state, rather than in a task-involved, effortful, strategy-focused state.

Another important consideration is the role of the child's home environment in promoting internal motivation (Gottfried, Fleming, & Gottfried, 1999). In one study, Adele Gottfried and Allen Gottfried (1989) found that greater variety of home experiences, parental encouragement of competence and curiosity, and home emphasis on academically related behaviors are related to children's internal motivation for achievement.

An extremely important aspect of internal causes of achievement is *effort*. Unlike many causes of success, effort is under the child's control and is amenable to change. Most children recognize the importance of effort in achievement. In one study, third- through sixth-grade students felt that effort was the most effective strategy for good school performance (Skinner, Wellborn, & Connell, 1990).

Mastery Orientation Versus Helpless and Performance Orientations

Closely related to an emphasis on intrinsic motivation, attributions of internal causes of behavior, and the importance of effort in achievement is a mastery orientation. Developmental psychologists Valanne Henderson and Carol Dweck (1990) have found that children show two distinct responses to difficult or challenging circumstances. Individuals with a **helpless orientation** *seem trapped by the experience of difficulty, and they attribute their difficulty to lack of ability.* They frequently say such things as "I'm not very good at this," even though they might earlier have demonstrated their ability through many successes. And, once they view their behavior as failure, they often feel anxious, and their performance worsens even further. Individuals with a **mastery orientation** *are task-oriented; instead of focusing on their ability, they are concerned about their learning strategies and the process of achievement rather than outcomes.* Mastery-oriented children often instruct themselves to pay attention, to think carefully, and to remember strategies that have worked for them in previous situations. They frequently report feeling challenged and excited by difficult tasks, rather than being threatened by them (Anderman, Maehr, & Midgley, 1996).

Another issue in motivation involves whether to adopt a mastery or a performance orientation. We have already described a mastery orientation. A **performance orientation** *involves being concerned with the achievement outcome; winning is what matters, and happiness is thought to result from winning.*

What sustains mastery-oriented individuals is the self-efficacy and satisfaction they feel from dealing effectively with the world in which they live. By contrast, what sustains performance-oriented individuals is winning. Although skills can be, and often are, involved in winning, performance-oriented individuals do not necessarily view themselves as having skills. Rather, they see themselves as using tactics, such as undermining others, to get what they want.

Does all of this mean that mastery-oriented individuals do not like to win and that performance-oriented individuals are not motivated to experience the self-efficacy

Intrinsic Motivation

The reward of a thing well done is to have done it.

Ralph Waldo Emerson
American Poet, Essayist, 19th Century

helpless orientation
An orientation in which one seems trapped by the experience of difficulty and attributes one's difficulty to a lack of ability.

mastery orientation
An orientation in which one is task-oriented and, instead of focusing on one's ability, is concerned with learning strategies.

performance orientation
An orientation in which one focuses on achievement outcomes; winning is what matters most, and happiness is thought to result from winning.

that comes from being able to take credit for one's accomplishments? No. A matter of emphasis or degree is involved, though. For mastery-oriented individuals, winning isn't everything; for performance-oriented individuals, skill development and self-efficacy take a back seat to winning.

Goal Setting, Planning, and Self-Regulation

Goal setting, planning, and self-regulation are important dimensions of achievement (Pintrich, 1999; Schunk, 2000). Goal setting and planning often work in concert. When individuals set goals, they need to plan how to reach those goals. Goals help people reach their dreams, increase their self-discipline, and maintain interest.

There has been little research on how children's goals develop (Eccles, Wigfield, & Schiefele, 1998). Performance goals likely are established in the elementary school years and become increasingly common in adolescence. However, there are vast individual variations in the extent to which children and adolescents, as well as adults, set goals and then develop plans to reach those goals. Especially in the secondary school years, youth should be encouraged to engage in goal-setting and planning activities.

Self-regulation involves the self-generation and self-monitoring of thoughts, feelings, and behaviors to reach a goal (Boekaerts, Pintrich, & Zeidner, 1999). These goals might be academic (such as improving reading comprehension, learning how to do multiplication, or asking relevant questions), or they might be socioemotional (such as controlling anger). Researchers have found that high-achieving students often engage in self-regulatory activities, such as setting specific learning goals, self-monitoring their learning, and systematically evaluating their progress toward a goal (Alderman, 1999; Schunk & Zimmerman, 1994). Parents and teachers who encourage children to become self-regulatory learners convey the message that children are responsible for their own behavior and that achievement requires active and dedicated effort (Zimmerman, Bonner, & Kovach, 1996).

In sum, we have seen that a number of psychological and motivational factors influence children's achievement. Especially important in the child's ability to adapt to new academic and social pressures are achievement motivation, internal attributions of causes of behavior, intrinsic motivation, a mastery orientation and goal setting, planning, and self-regulation. Next, we will explore the roles of ethnicity and culture in achievement.

Contextual Supports for Motivation

Ethnicity and Culture

What is the nature of achievement in ethnic minority children? How does culture influence children's achievement?

Ethnicity   The diversity that exists among ethnic minority children is evident in their achievement. For example, many Asian American students have a strong academic achievement orientation, but some do not.

In addition to recognizing the diversity that exists within every cultural group in terms of their achievement, it also is important to distinguish between difference and deficiency. Too often, the achievement of ethnic minority students—especially African Americans, Latinos, and Native Americans—have been interpreted as *deficits* by middle-socioeconomic-status White standards, when they simply are *culturally different and distinct* (Jones, 1994).

At the same time, many investigations overlook the socioeconomic status of ethnic minority students. In many instances, when ethnicity *and* socioeconomic status are investigated in a study, socioeconomic status predicts achievement better than ethnicity does. Students from middle- and upper-income families fare better than their counterparts from low-income backgrounds in a host of achievement situations—for example, expectations for success, achievement aspirations, and recognition of the importance of effort (Gibbs, 1989).

Sandra Graham (1986, 1990) has conducted a number of studies that reveal not only stronger socioeconomic-status than ethnic differences in achievement but also the importance of studying ethnic minority student motivation in the context of general motivational theory. Her inquiries fall within the framework of attribution theory and focus on the causes that African American students give for their achievement orientation, such as why they succeed or fail. She is struck by how consistently middle-income African American students do not fit the stereotype of being unmotivated. Like their White middle-income counterparts, they have high achievement expectations and understand that failure is usually due to a lack of effort, rather than bad luck.

A special challenge for many ethnic minority students, especially those living in poverty, is dealing with racial prejudice, conflict between the values of their group and those of the majority group, and a lack of high-achieving adults in their cultural group who can serve as positive role models.

It also is important to consider the nature of the schools that primarily serve ethnic minority students (Eccles, Wigfield, & Schiefele, 1998; Spencer, 1999). More than one third of all African American and almost one third of all Latino students attend schools in the 47 largest city school districts in the United States, compared with only 5 percent of all White and 22 percent of all Asian American students. Many of these ethnic minority students come from low-income families (more than one half are eligible for free or reduced-cost lunches). These inner-city schools are less likely than other schools to serve more advantaged populations or to offer high-quality academic support services, advanced courses, and courses that challenge students' active thinking skills. Even students who are motivated to learn and achieve may find it difficult to perform effectively in such contexts.

Culture   In the past decade, the poor performance of American children in math and science has become well publicized (Murray, 1996). For example, in one cross-national comparison of the math and science achievement of 9- to 13-year-old students, the United States finished 13th (out of 15) in science and 15th (out of 16) in math achievement (Educational Testing Service, 1992). In this study, Korean and Taiwanese students placed first and second, respectively.

Harold Stevenson's (1995; Stevenson & others, 1990) research explores reasons for the poor performance of American students. Stevenson and his colleagues have completed five cross-cultural comparisons of students in the United States, China, Taiwan, and Japan. In these studies, Asian students consistently outperform American students. And, the longer the students are in school, the wider the gap becomes between Asian and American students—the lowest difference is in the first grade, the highest in the eleventh grade (the highest grade studied).

To learn more about the reasons for these large cross-cultural differences, Stevenson and his colleagues spent thousands of hours observing in classrooms, as well as interviewing and surveying teachers, students, and parents. They found that the Asian teachers spent more of their time teaching math than did the American teachers. For example, more than one fourth of total classroom time in the first grade was spent on math instruction in Japan, compared with only one tenth of the time in the U.S. first-grade classrooms. Also, the Asian students were in school an average of 240 days a year, compared with 178 days in the United States.

In addition to the substantially greater time spent on math instruction in the Asian schools than the American schools, differences were found between the Asian and American parents. The American parents had much lower expectations for their children's education and achievement than did the Asian parents. Also, the American parents

Asian grade schools intersperse studying with frequent periods of activities. This approach helps children maintain their attention and likely makes learning more enjoyable. Shown here are Japanese fourth-graders making wearable masks.

were more likely to believe that their children's math achievement was due to innate ability; the Asian parents were more likely to say that their children's math achievement was the consequence of effort and training. The Asian students were more likely to do math homework than were the American students, and the Asian parents were far more likely to help their children with their math homework than were the American parents (Chen & Stevenson, 1989).

Critics of the cross-national comparisons argue that, in many comparisons, virtually all U.S. children are being compared with a "select" group of children from other countries, especially in the secondary school comparisons. Therefore, they conclude, it is no wonder that American students don't fare so well. That criticism holds for some international comparisons. However, even when the top 25 percent of students in different countries were recently compared, U.S. students move up some, but not a lot (Mullis & others, 1998).

CHILDREN AND COMPUTERS

At the middle of the twentieth century, commercial television had barely made its debut, and IBM had yet to bring its first computer to market. Now, as we move into the twenty-first century, both television *and* computers are important influences in children's lives (Calvert, 1999; Reeves, 1999). For some, the computer is a positive tool with the power to transform our schools and revolutionize children's learning. For others, the computer is a menacing force, more likely to undermine than to improve children's education and learning. Let's examine some of the possible positive and negative influences of computers in children's lives.

Positive Influences of Computers on Children

Among the potential positive influences of computers on children's development are its usefulness as a personal tutor, its function as a multipurpose tool, and its motivational and social effects (Lepper & Gurtner, 1989).

Computer-assisted instruction *uses the computer as a tutor to individualize instruction. The concept behind computer-assisted instruction is to use the computer to present information, give students practice, assess their level of understanding, and provide additional instruction if needed.* Computer-assisted instruction requires the active participation of the student and, in giving immediate feedback to students, is patient and nonjudgmental. Over the past two decades, more than 200 research studies involving computer-assisted instruction have been conducted. In general, the effects of computer-assisted instruction are positive. More precisely, the effects are more positive with programs involving tutorials rather than drill and practice, with younger rather than older students, and with students with lower than average ability or unselected populations.

The computer also serves as an important influence in children's lives through the role it can play in experiential learning (Linn & Hsi, 1999; Samaras, 1996). Some experts view the computer as an excellent medium for open-ended and exploratory learning (Fishman, 1999). The most widely studied activity has been the use of the Logo computing language, especially its simplified "turtle graphics" programming environment, as a way to improve children's planning and problem-solving abilities (Papert, 1980). The turtle graphics involve moving a small triangular cursor, called a "turtle," on the screen. However, the research on the effects of Logo are mixed. Although the early studies of Logo essentially found no benefits for children's learning, more recent studies have been supportive of Logo. In the successful recent studies, more favorable adult-child ratios are present, prepared support materials and explicit task requirements are included, younger children are studied, and a wider array of dependent variable measures are used (such as creativity, cognitive monitoring, and solution checking).

The computer can function in children's lives as a multipurpose tool in helping them achieve academic goals and become more creative (Bonk & King, 1999; Provenzo, Brett, & McClosky, 1999). The computer is especially helpful in improving children's

computer-assisted instruction
The teaching strategy that involves using computers as tutors to individualize instruction. Computers are used to present information, give students practice, assess student levels of understanding, and provide additional information when needed.

Webliography
Children's Software Review

writing and communication skills. Word-processing programs diminish the drudgery of writing, increasing the probability that children will edit and revise their work. Programs that assist students in outlining a paper may help students organize their thoughts before they write.

Several other themes appear in the discussion of the computer's positive influence on children's development. For one, computer adherents argue that the computer makes learning more intrinsically motivating. Computer enthusiasts also argue that the computer can make learning more fun. And lessons can often be embedded in instructional "games" or puzzles that encourage children's curiosity and sense of challenge. Some computer adherents also argue that expanded computer use in schools will increase students' cooperation and collaboration, as well as increase intellectual discussion among them. And, if the computer does increase student's interest, it may free teachers to spend more time working individually with students. Finally, computer adherents hope that the computer can increase the equality of educational opportunity. Since the computer allows students to work at their own pace, it may help students who do not normally succeed in schools. Because the computer is impartial, it should minimize the adverse influences of teacher prejudice and stereotyping.

The influence of computer use on children's learning, motivation, and social behavior continues to be a source of debate and controversy.

Negative Influences of Computers on Children

Among the potential negative influences of computers on children's development are those involving the regimentation and dehumanization of the classroom, unwarranted "shaping" of the curriculum, and generalization and limitations of computer-based teaching (Lepper & Gurtner, 1989), each of which we will discuss in turn.

Skeptics worry that, rather than increased individualization of instruction, computers will bring a much greater regimentation and homogenization of classroom learning experiences. Whereas some students may prefer to work autonomously and may learn most effectively when they are allowed to progress on their own, other students may rely on social interaction with guidance by the teacher for effective learning. And some computer skeptics worry that the computer will ultimately increase inequality, rather than equality, in educational outcomes. School funding in middle-class neighborhoods is usually better than in low-income areas, and the homes of children in middle-class neighborhoods are more likely to have computers than are those in low-income neighborhoods. Thus, an increasing emphasis on computer literacy may be inequitable for children from low-income backgrounds because they likely have had less opportunity to use computers. Some critics also worry about the dehumanization of the classroom. They argue that school is a social world as well as a cognitive, learning world. From this perspective, children plugged into a computer all day long have little opportunity to engage in social interaction.

A further concern is that computers may inadvertently and inappropriately shape the curriculum. Some subjects, such as mathematics and science, seem to be more easily and successfully adapted to computers than are such subjects as art and literature. Consequently, there is concern that the computer may eventually shape the curriculum in the direction of science and math because these areas are more easily computerized.

Yet another concern is the transfer of learning and motivation outside the computer domain. If the instructional effectiveness and motivational appeal of computer-based education depend on the use of impressive technical devices, such as color, animation, and sound effects, how effectively will student learning or motivation transfer to other contexts without these technical supports? Will children provided with the editorial assistance of the computer still learn the basic skills needed to progress to more complex forms of creative writing later in their careers? Will

Improving Developmental Skills
Strategies for Supporting Children's Cognitive Growth

What are the best strategies for helping elementary school children develop their cognitive skills?

- *Facilitate rather than direct children's learning.* Design situations that let children learn by doing and that actively promote their thinking and discovery. Listen, watch, and question children to help them attain a better understanding.
- *Provide opportunities for children to think critically.* Encourage children to think reflectively, rather than automatically accepting everything as correct. Ask children questions about similarities and differences in things. Ask them questions of clarification, such as "What is the main point?" and "Why?" Ask children to justify their opinion. Ask them "what if" questions.
- *Be a good cognitive role model.* Model thinking and self-reflection for the child to see and hear. When children are around people who think critically and reflectively, they incorporate these cognitive styles into their own thinking repertoire.
- *Encourage collaboration with other children.* Children learn not only from adults but from other children as well. Cross-age teaching, in which older children who are competent thinkers interact with younger children, can be especially helpful. Collaborative problem solving teaches children how to work cooperatively with others.
- *Stimulate children's creative thinking.* Encourage children to take risks in their thinking. Don't overcontrol by telling children precisely what to do; let their originality come through. Don't set up grandiose expectations; it can hurt creativity. Encourage the child to think freely and come up with as many different ways of doing something as possible.
- *Provide children with computer programs that promote thinking.* Encourage children to spend time practicing their thinking skills on a computer. A number of software programs are available that are designed to develop children's thinking skills. The programs can stimulate children to wonder and make inferences based on incomplete knowledge.

Children and Technology

children using computers in math gain the proficiency to deal with more complicated math in the future, or will their ability to solve complex conceptual problems in the absence of the computer have atrophied? Presently, we do not know the answers to these important questions, but they raise some vital concerns about the computer's role in children's development.

Classroom Recommendations for Technology

Following are some classroom recommendations on the use of technology (NAEYC, 1996):

- *Make appropriate judgments about whether the technology is age appropriate, individually appropriate, and culturally appropriate.* Take time to evaluate and choose the best software for effective learning.
- *Recognize that, when used appropriately, technology can enhance children's cognitive and social skills.* Computers are intrinsically interesting to children, and the sounds and graphics catch their attention. These computer characteristics can stimulate children's learning. Many children like to work with one or two partners on a computer. Their collaborative efforts can have social benefits (Clements & Nastasi, 1993).
- *Integrate appropriate technology into the regular learning environment and use it as one of many options to help children learn.* Locate computers in the classroom, rather than in a separate computer lab (Wright & Shade, 1994). Use computers to extend the curriculum.
- *Promote equitable access to technology for all children.* Consider girls' interests and interaction styles when selecting software for classroom use. Encourage children from low-income backgrounds to use computers. Learn about adaptive technology that is available for children with a disability.
- *Teachers, in collaboration with parents, should advocate for more appropriate technology applications to all children.* Teachers can provide information to parents on the benefits and use of appropriate software. They also can advocate for computer hardware that can be upgraded as new technology becomes available.
- *Recognize that the potentials of technology are far-reaching and ever changing.* It is important for educators to not become complacent and assume that their current knowledge or experience is adequate. As educators become competent users of technology, they can model appropriate use for children.

At various places in the chapter, we have discussed strategies that support children's cognitive growth. The insert, Improving Developmental Skills, profiles these strategies. At this point, we also have studied a number of ideas about language development, achievement, and computers. An overview of these ideas is presented in summary table 13.2.

Summary Table 13.2
Language Development, Achievement, and Computers

Concept	Processes/ Related Ideas	Characteristics/Description
Language development	Vocabulary and grammar	In middle and late childhood, children become more analytical and logical in their approach to words and grammar.
	Reading	Current debate focuses on the whole-language approach versus the basic-skills-and-phonics approach. The whole language-approach stresses that reading instruction should parallel children's natural language learning and give children whole-language materials, such as books and poems. The skills/phonics approach advocates instructing children in phonics and giving children simplified materials. Today, many experts recommend a balanced approach that combines the two approaches, although *balanced* often means different things to different people. There is good evidence that beginning readers benefit from an approach using both whole-language experiences and instruction in phonics and decoding.
	Bilingualism	Bilingual education aims to teach academic subjects to immigrant children in their native languages (most often in Spanish), while gradually adding English instruction. Proponents of bilingual education argue that it helps immigrants to value their family and culture, as well as increasing their self-esteem, thus making academic success more likely. Critics say it harms immigrant children by failing to adequately instruct them in English and leaving them unprepared for the workplace. However, researchers have found that bilingualism does not interfere with performance in either language. Success in learning a second language is greater in childhood than adolescence.
Achievement	Need for achievement	Achievement motivation (need for achievement) is the desire to accomplish something, to reach a standard of excellence, and to expend effort to excel. Researchers have found correlations between parenting practices and children's achievement motivation.
	Intrinsic and extrinsic motivation	An important dimension of achievement is whether the motivation is internal (intrinsic) or external (extrinsic). An extremely important dimension of internal causes of achievement is effort.
	Mastery orientation versus helpless and performance orientations	Children who have a mastery orientation are task-oriented and concerned with their learning strategies, rather than ability. They are interested in the process of achievement, rather than its outcomes. By contrast, children who have a helpless orientation seem trapped by the experience of difficulty and attribute their problems to lack of ability. The performance orientation involves being concerned with achievement outcomes, rather than achievement processes. To those with a performance orientation, winning is what matters, and happiness is thought to result from winning. Experts recommend a mastery rather than a helpless or performance orientation in achievement contexts.
	Goal setting, planning, and self-regulation	These are important dimensions of achievement. Self-regulation involves the self-generation and self-monitoring of thoughts, feelings, and behaviors to reach a goal. High-achieving students engage in self-regulatory activities.
	Ethnic and cross-cultural comparisons	Too often, research has characterized minority groups in terms of deficits. In addition to ethnic minority considerations, it also is important to determine whether socioeconomic status is a factor in achievement circumstances. It is always important to consider the diversity within an ethnic minority group. American children are more achievement-oriented than children in many other countries, but in recent years they have not fared well in achievement comparisons with children from Asian countries, such as China, Japan, and Korea.
Computers and children's development	Positive influences	Among the potential positive effects of computers on children's development are those involving the computer as a personal tutor (computer-assisted instruction), its use as a multipurpose tool, and the motivational and social aspects of its use.
	Negative influences	Among the potential negative effects of computers on children's development are regimentation and dehumanization of the classroom, unwarranted "shaping" of the curriculum, and limitations of computer-based teaching.
	Classroom recommendations for technology	These include making age-, individually, and culturally appropriate decisions; integrating technology into the classroom; promoting equitable access to technology; and other strategies.

Chapter Review

In middle and late childhood, competent children seek to know and understand. They enjoy learning and are remarkable for their curiosity.

We began this chapter by exploring cognition, including ideas about Piaget's theory, information processing, and intelligence and creativity. Our coverage of language development focused on vocabulary and grammar, reading, and bilingualism. We also studied achievement, including the need for achievement; intrinsic and extrinsic motivation; mastery versus helpless and performance orientations; goal setting, planning, and self-regulation; and ethnicity and culture. And we read about children and computers, their positive and negative influences, and some classroom recommendations for technology.

Don't forget that you can obtain a more detailed summary of the chapter by again studying the two summary tables on page 383 and 395. In the next chapter, we will continue our journey through middle and late childhood by exploring children's socioemotional development in this period.

Children Checklist

Cognitive Development in Middle and Late Childhood

How much have you learned since the beginning of the chapter? Use the following statements to help you review your knowledge and understanding of the chapter material. First, read the statement and mentally or briefly demonstrate on paper that you can discuss the relevant information.

_____ I can describe Piaget's stage of concrete operational thought.
_____ I can discuss changes in memory.
_____ I know about cognitive monitoring, schemas, and scripts.
_____ I am aware of the nature of critical thinking.
_____ I can describe what intelligence is, the Binet and Wechsler tests, Sternberg's triarchic theory, and Gardner's frames of mind.
_____ I can discuss controversies and issues in intelligence.
_____ I can describe the extremes of intelligence.
_____ I am aware of what is involved in children's creativity.
_____ I can discuss changes in vocabulary and grammar, reading, and bilingualism.
_____ I know about children's achievement.
_____ I can describe the role of computers in children's lives.

For any items that you did not check, go back and locate the relevant material in the chapter. Review the material until you feel you can check off the item. You may want to use this checklist later in preparing for an exam.

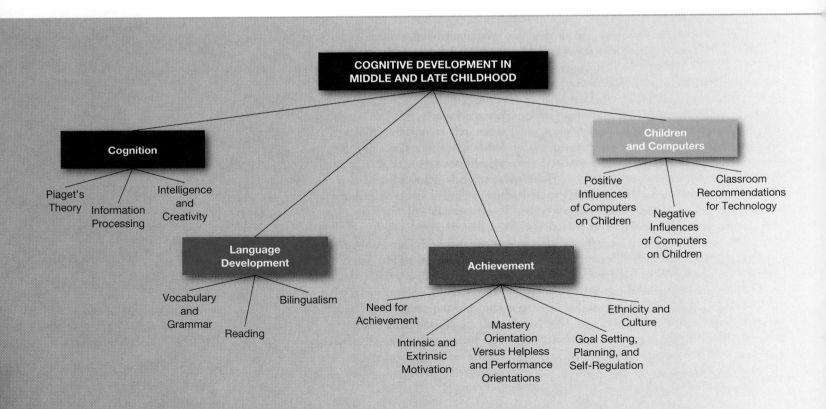

COGNITIVE DEVELOPMENT IN MIDDLE AND LATE CHILDHOOD

Cognition
- Piaget's Theory
- Information Processing
- Intelligence and Creativity

Language Development
- Vocabulary and Grammar
- Reading
- Bilingualism

Achievement
- Need for Achievement
- Intrinsic and Extrinsic Motivation
- Mastery Orientation Versus Helpless and Performance Orientations
- Goal Setting, Planning, and Self-Regulation
- Ethnicity and Culture

Children and Computers
- Positive Influences of Computers on Children
- Negative Influences of Computers on Children
- Classroom Recommendations for Technology

Key Terms

seriation 359
transitivity 359
neo-Piagetians 362
long-term memory 363
control processes 363
mnemonics 363
method of loci 363
keyword method 364
PQ4R 365
cognitive monitoring 366
reciprocal teaching 366
script 367
critical thinking 367
Jasper Project 368
intelligence 370
individual differences 371
mental age (MA) 371
intelligence quotient (IQ) 371
normal distribution 371
triarchic theory of intelligence 372
culture-fair tests 378

mental retardation 379
organic retardation 379
cultural-familial retardation 379
gifted 380
creativity 381
convergent thinking 381
divergent thinking 381
brainstorming 382
whole-language approach 384
basic-skills-and-phonetics approach 384
bilingual education 386
achievement motivation (need for achievement) 388
intrinsic motivation 388
extrinsic motivation 388
helpless orientation 389
mastery orientation 389
performance orientation 389
computer-assisted instruction 392

Children Resources

ERIC Clearinghouse on Elementary and Early Childhood Education
University of Illinois
College of Education
805 West Pennsylvania Avenue
Urbana, IL 61801
217–333–1386

ERIC provides wide-ranging references to many educational topics, including educational practices, parent-school relations, and community programs.

National Association for Gifted Children
1155 15th Street NW, #1002
Washington, DC 20005
202–785–4268

This is an association of academics, educators, and librarians. Its goal is to improve the education of gifted children. It publishes periodic reports on the education of gifted children and the journal *Gifted Children Quarterly*.

The New York Times Parents' Guide to the Best Books for Children
(1991) by Eden Lipson.
New York: Random House.

This revised and updated edition includes book recommendations for children of all ages. More than 1,700 titles are evaluated.

Taking It to the Net

http://www.mhhe.com/santrockcd6

1. Are you mathematically smart? Linguistically smart? Interpersonally smart? Take a multiple intelligences test and find out!
2. A friend asks you for a list of books that you believe he should read to his child. What children's books would you recommend, and why?
3. Most parents want to believe that their child is special, gifted, and above the norm. What does it mean to be "gifted?" How would you advise a parent that believed that his child was gifted? What characteristics would you tell him to look for and what would you tell him to expect from his child?

Chapter
14

Children are busy becoming something they have not quite grasped yet, something which keeps changing. . . .

Alastair Reid
American Poet, 20th Century

PREVIEW

The socioemotional worlds of children widen and become more complex in middle and late childhood. The following are among the questions that we will explore in this chapter:

- How does the child's self-understanding change?
- What is the nature of the child's self-esteem?
- What changes take place in the child's emotional development?
- What are some good strategies in helping children cope with stress?
- What changes occur in children's moral development?
- How extensive are gender differences in children?
- What are some new parenting issues in middle and late childhood?
- What are some important aspects of peer relations and friendship?
- What roles do socioeconomic status and ethnicity play in schools?

The Stories of Lafayette and Pharoah: The Tragedy of Poverty and Violence

Alex Kotlowitz (1991) followed the lives of two brothers, 10-year-old Lafayette and 7-year-old Pharoah, for two years. The boys lived in an impoverished housing project in Chicago. Their father had a drug habit and had trouble holding down a job.

Kotlowitz approached their mother, LaJoe, about the possibility of writing a book about Lafayette, Pharoah, and other children in the neighborhood. She liked the idea but hesitated. She then commented, "But you know, there are no children around here. They've seen too much to be children."

Over the two years, Lafayette and Pharoah struggled with school, resisted the lure of gangs, and mourned the deaths of friends. All the time they wondered why they were living in such a violent place and hoped they could get out.

Their older brother, 17-year-old Terrence, was a drug user. Lafayette told one of his friends, "You grow up 'round it. There are a lot of people in the projects who say they're not gonna do drugs, that they're not gonna drop out of school, that they won't be on the streets. But they're doing it now. Never say never. But I say never. My older brother didn't set a good example for me, but I'll set a good example for my younger brother."

A few days later, police arrested Terrence as a robbery suspect. They handcuffed him in the apartment in front of Lafayette and Pharoah. Pharoah told his mother, "I'm just too young to understand how life really is."

Several months later, shooting erupted in the housing complex, and their mother herded Lafayette and Pharoah into the hallway, where they crouched along the walls to avoid stray bullets. Lafayette said to his mother, "If we don't get away, someone's gonna end up dead. I feel it." Shortly thereafter, a 9-year-old friend of the boys was shot in the back of the head as he walked into his building just across the street. The bullet had been meant for someone else.

Poverty, stress, and violence were constants where Lafayette and Pharoah lived. There were so many shootings that many of them didn't even make the newspaper. Both boys wanted to move to a safe, quiet neighborhood, but their mother struggled just to make ends meet in the projects.

How might the stress of poverty and violence affect children's development? How might it affect the parent-child relationship? Although these kinds of circumstances are often harmful to children, might some children be resilient in the face of such stressors and have positive outcomes in life?

Some children triumph over life's adversities (Wilson & Gottman, 1996). Norman Garmezy (1985, 1993) has studied resilience amid disadvantage for many years. He concluded that three factors help children become resilient to stress and disadvantage: (1) good cognitive skills, especially attention, which helps children focus on tasks, such as school work; (2) a family—even if enveloped in poverty—characterized by warmth, cohesion, and a caring adult, such as a grandparent who takes responsibility in the absence of responsive parents or in the presence of intense marital conflict; and (3) external support, such as a teacher, a neighbor, a mentor, a caring agency, or a church. In one longitudinal study of resilient individuals from birth to 32 years of age in Kuaia, these three factors were present in their lives (Werner, 1989).

EMOTIONAL AND PERSONALITY DEVELOPMENT

In chapter 11, we discussed the development of the self, emotional development, moral development, and gender in early childhood. Here, we will focus on these important dimensions of children's development in middle and late childhood.

The Self

What is the nature of the child's self-understanding, self-esteem, and self-concept in the elementary school years? What aspect of the self did Erikson theorize to be an important developmental task in this period?

The Development of Self-Understanding

In middle and late childhood, self-understanding increasingly shifts from defining oneself through external characteristics to defining oneself through internal characteristics. Elementary school children are also more likely to define themselves in terms of social characteristics and social comparisons (Harter, 1999).

In middle and late childhood, children not only recognize differences between inner and outer states but also are more likely to include subjective inner states in their definition of self. For example, in one study, second-grade children were much more likely than younger children to name psychological characteristics (such as preferences or personality traits) in their self-definition and were less likely to name physical characteristics (such as eye color or possessions) (Aboud & Skerry, 1983). For example, 8-year-old Todd included in his self-description, "I am smart and I am popular." Ten-year-old Tina says about herself, "I am pretty good about not worrying most of the time. I used to lose my temper, but I'm better about that now. I also feel proud when I do well in school."

In addition to the increase of psychological characteristics in self-definition during the elementary school years, the *social aspects* of the self also increase at this point in development. In one investigation, elementary school children often included references to social groups in their self-descriptions (Livesly & Bromley, 1973). For example, some children referred to themselves as Girl Scouts, as Catholics, or as someone who has two close friends.

Children's self-understanding in the elementary school years also includes increasing reference to *social comparison*. At this point in development, children are more likely to distinguish themselves from others in comparative rather than in absolute terms. That is, elementary-school-age children are no longer as likely to think about what *I* do or do not do but are more likely to think about what *I* can do *in comparison with others*. This developmental shift provides an increased tendency to establish one's differences from others as an individual.

The Role of Perspective Taking in Self-Understanding

Many child developmentalists believe that perspective taking plays an important role in self-understanding. **Perspective taking** *is the ability to assume another person's perspective and understand his or her thoughts and feelings*. Robert Selman (1980) has proposed a developmental theory of perspective taking that has been given considerable attention. He believes perspective taking involves a series of five stages, ranging from 3

perspective taking
The ability to assume another person's perspective and understand his or her thoughts and feelings.

Stage	Perspective-taking stage	Ages	Description
0	Egocentric viewpoint	3–5	Child has a sense of differentiation of self and other but fails to distinguish between the social perspective (thoughts, feelings) of other and self. Child can label other's overt feelings but does not see the cause-and-effect relation of reasons to social actions.
1	Social-informational perspective taking	6–8	Child is aware that other has a social perspective based on other's own reasoning, which may or may not be similar to child's. However, child tends to focus on one perspective rather than coordinating viewpoints.
2	Self-reflective perspective taking	8–10	Child is conscious that each individual is aware of the other's perspective and that this awareness influences self's and other's view of each other. Putting self in other's place is a way of judging other's intentions, purposes, and actions. Child can form a coordinated chain of perspectives but cannot yet abstract from this process to the level of simultaneous mutuality.
3	Mutual perspective taking	10–12	Adolescent realizes that both self and other can view each other mutually and simultaneously as subjects. Adolescent can step outside the two-person dyad and view the interaction from a third-person perspective.
4	Social and conventional system perspective taking	12–15	Adolescent realizes mutual perspective taking does not always lead to complete understanding. Social conventions are seen as necessary because they are understood by all members of the group (the generalized other), regardless of their position, role, or experience.

Source: From R. L. Selman, "Social-Cognitive Understanding" in T. Lickona (ed.), *Moral Development and Behavior*, 1976. Reprinted by permission of Thomas Lickona.

Figure 14.1
Selman's Stages of Perspective Taking

years of age through adolescence (see figure 14.1). These stages begin with the egocentric viewpoint in early childhood and end with in-depth perspective taking in adolescence.

Self-Esteem and Self-Concept   High self-esteem and a positive self-concept are important characteristics of children's well-being (Harter, 1999).

What Are Self-Esteem and Self-Concept?   Self-esteem *refers to global evaluations of the self. Self-esteem is also referred to as self-worth or self-image.* For example, a child may perceive that she is not merely a person but a *good* person. Of course, not all children have an overall positive image of themselves. **Self-concept** *refers to domain-specific evaluations of the self.* Children can make self-evaluations in many domains of their lives—academic, athletic, appearance, and so on. In sum, *self-esteem* refers to global self-evaluations, *self-concept* to more domain-specific evaluations.

Investigators have not always made clear distinctions between self-esteem and self-concept, sometimes using the terms interchangeably or not precisely defining them. As you read the remaining discussion of self-esteem and self-concept, the

It is difficult to make people miserable when they feel worthy of themselves.

Abraham Lincoln
American President, 19th Century

self-esteem
The global evaluative dimension of the self. Self-esteem is also referred to as self-worth or self-image.

self-concept
Domain-specific evaluations of the self.

distinction between self-esteem as global self-evaluation and self-concept as domain-specific self-evaluation should help you keep the terms straight.

Measuring Self-Esteem and Self-Concept   Measuring self-esteem and self-concept hasn't always been easy. Recently, various measures have been developed to assess children and adolescents.

Susan Harter's (1985) Self-Perception Profile for Children is a revision of her original measure, the Perceived Competence Scale for Children (Harter, 1982). The **Self-Perception Profile for Children** *taps five specific domains of self-concept—scholastic competence, athletic competence, social acceptance, physical appearance, and behavioral conduct—plus general self-worth.* Harter's scale does an excellent job of separating children's self-evaluations in different skill domains, and, when general self-worth is assessed, questions focus on the overall self-evaluations rather than in specific skill domains.

The Self-Perception Profile for Children is designed to be used with third-grade through sixth-grade children. Harter also has developed a separate scale for adolescents, recognizing important developmental changes in self-perceptions. The Self-Perception Profile for Adolescents (Harter, 1989) taps eight domains—scholastic competence, athletic competence, social acceptance, physical appearance, behavioral conduct, close friendship, romantic appeal, and job competence—plus global self-worth. Thus, the adolescent version has three skill domains not present in the children's version—job competence, romantic appeal, and close friendship.

Parent-Child Relationships and Self-Esteem   In the most extensive investigation of parent-child relationships and self-esteem, the following parenting attributes were associated with boys' high self-esteem (Coopersmith, 1967):

- Expression of affection
- Concern about the child's problems
- Harmony in the home
- Participation in joint family activities
- Availability to give competent, organized help to the boys when they need it
- Setting clear and fair rules
- Abiding by these rules
- Allowing the children freedom within well-prescribed limits

Increasing Children's Self-Esteem   Four ways children's self-esteem can be improved are through (1) identification of the causes of low self-esteem and the domains of competence important to the self, (2) emotional support and social approval, (3) achievement, and (4) coping (see figure 14.2).

Identifying children's sources of self-esteem—that is, competence in domains important to the self—is critical to improving self-esteem. Susan Harter (1990) points out that the self-esteem enhancement programs of the 1960s, in which self-esteem itself was the target and individuals were encouraged to simply feel good about themselves, were ineffective. Rather, Harter believes that intervention must occur at the level of the *causes* of self-esteem if the individual's self-esteem is to improve significantly. Children have the highest self-esteem when they perform competently in domains that are important to them. Therefore, children should be encouraged to identify and value areas of competence.

Emotional support and social approval in the form of confirmation from others also powerfully influence children's self-esteem. Some children with low self-esteem come from conflicted families or conditions in which they experienced abuse or neglect—situations in which support was unavailable. In some cases, alternative sources of support can be implemented either informally through the encouragement of a teacher, a coach, or another significant adult or, more formally, through programs such as Big Brothers and Big Sisters. While peer approval becomes increasingly important during adolescence, both adult and peer support are important influences on the adolescent's self-esteem.

Self-Perception Profile for Children
A self-concept measure with five specific domains—scholastic competence, athletic competence, social acceptance, physical appearance, and behavioral conduct—plus general self-worth.

Identifying the causes of low self-esteem and which domains of competence are important to the self

Emotional support and social approval

Achievement

Coping

Figure 14.2
Four Key Aspects of Improving Self-Esteem

Achievement also can improve children's self-esteem (Bednar, Wells, & Peterson, 1995). For example, the straightforward teaching of real skills to children often results in increased achievement and, thus, in enhanced self-esteem. Children develop higher self-esteem because they know the important tasks to achieve goals, and they have experienced performing them or similar behaviors. The emphasis on the importance of achievement in improving self-esteem has much in common with Bandura's cognitive social learning concept of *self-efficacy*, which refers to individuals' beliefs that they can master a situation and produce positive outcomes.

Self-esteem also is often increased when children face a problem and try to cope with it, rather than avoid it. If coping rather than avoidance prevails, children often face problems realistically, honestly, and nondefensively. This produces favorable self-evaluative thoughts, which lead to the self-generated approval that raises self-esteem. The converse is true of low self-esteem. Unfavorable self-evaluations trigger denial, deception, and avoidance in an attempt to disavow that which has already been glimpsed as true. This process leads to self-generated disapproval as a form of feedback to the self about personal adequacy.

Industry Versus Inferiority   Erikson's fourth stage of the human life span, industry versus inferiority, appears during middle and late childhood. The term *industry* expresses a dominant theme of this period: children become interested in how things are made and how they work. It is the Robinson Crusoe age, in that the enthusiasm and minute detail Crusoe uses to describe his activities appeal to the child's budding sense of industry. When children are encouraged in their efforts to make, build, and work—whether building a model airplane, constructing a tree house, fixing a bicycle, solving an addition problem, or cooking—their sense of industry increases. However, parents who see their children's efforts at making things as "mischief" or "making a mess" encourage children's development of a sense of inferiority.

Children's social worlds beyond their families also contribute to a sense of industry. School becomes especially important in this regard. Consider children who are slightly below average in intelligence. They are too bright to be in special classes but not bright enough to be in gifted classes. They fail frequently in their academic efforts, developing a sense of inferiority. By contrast, consider children whose sense of industry is derogated at home. A series of sensitive and committed teachers may revitalize their sense of industry (Elkind, 1970).

Emotional Development

Emotional Intelligence

In chapter 11, we saw that preschoolers become more adept at talking about their own and others' emotions. They also show a growing awareness about controlling and managing emotions to meet social standards. Further developmental changes characterize emotion in middle and late childhood (Saarni, 1999).

Developmental Changes   Following are some important developmental changes in emotions during the elementary school years (Kuebli, 1994; Wintre & Vallance, 1994):

- An increased ability to understand such complex emotions as pride and shame (Kuebli, 1994). These emotions become more internalized and integrated with a sense of personal responsibility.
- Increased understanding that more than one emotion can be experienced in a particular situation
- An increased tendency to take into fuller account the events leading to emotional reactions
- Marked improvements in the ability to suppress or conceal negative emotional reactions
- The use of self-initiated strategies for redirecting feelings

Emotional Intelligence   The increased self-regulation of emotion that occurs during middle and late childhood is an important aspect of what Daniel Goleman (1995) calls "emotional intelligence." He believes that self-awareness of emotion is especially important because it enables individuals to exercise some self-control. The idea is not to completely suppress feelings but to become aware of them and then cope with them more effectively.

Using anxiety wisely is another aspect of emotional intelligence. Anxiety can serve a useful function, as long as it does not spin out of control. A little bit of worry can help children rehearse for problems and motivate the search for solving a problem. The downside of worry occurs when it becomes an end in itself and blocks thinking.

Perhaps the most visible aspects of emotional intelligence are the "people skills" of empathy, graciousness, and the ability to read a social situation. They help children and adults get along better with others and make the social world work more smoothly. Later in the chapter, we will explore some of these people skills in our discussion of appropriate and inappropriate strategies for making friends.

What are some examples of how schools are helping children with their emotional lives? One private school in San Francisco, the Nueva School, has a class in self science. The subject in self science is feelings—the child's own and those involved in relationships. Teachers speak to real issues, such as hurt over being left out, envy, and disagreements that could disrupt into a schoolyard battle. The list of the contents for self science matches up with many of Goleman's components of emotional intelligence. The topics in self science include:

- Having self-awareness (in the sense of recognizing feelings and building a vocabulary for them); seeing the links between thoughts, feelings, and reactions

- Knowing if thoughts or feelings are ruling a decision
- Seeing the consequences of alternative choices
- Applying these insights to decisions about such issues as drugs, smoking, and sex
- Recognizing strengths and weaknesses, and seeing oneself in a positive but realistic light
- Managing emotions; realizing what is behind a feeling (such as the hurt that triggers anger); learning ways to handle anxieties, anger, and sadness
- Taking responsibility for decisions and actions, as well as following through on commitments
- Understanding that empathy, understanding others' feelings, and respecting differences in how people feel about things are key dimensions of getting along in the social world
- Recognizing the importance of relationships and learning how to be a good listener and question asker; being assertive rather than passive or aggressive; learning how to cooperate, resolve conflicts, and negotiate

Names for these classes range from "social development" to "life skills" to "social and emotional learning." Their common goal is to raise every child's emotional competence as part of regular education, rather than focus on emotional skills as something to be taught only remedially to children who are faltering and are identified as "troubled."

Coping with Stress   An important aspect of children's emotional lives is learning how to cope effectively with stress. Also important is for caregivers to help children cope more effectively. Two effective strategies are to (1) remove at least one stressor from the child's life and (2) teach the child how to cope effectively.

Based on Michael Rutter's (1979) research on the multiple effects of stress, it makes sense that removing one stress or hassle can help children feel stronger and more competent. For example, consider Lisa, who had been coming to school hungry each morning. Her teacher arranged for Lisa to have hot breakfasts at school, which improved her concentration in school. This in turn helped Lisa suppress for a time her anxieties about her parents' impending divorce.

Children who have a number of coping techniques have the best chance of adapting and functioning competently in the face of stress. By learning new coping techniques, children might no longer feel as incompetent, and their self-confidence may improve. For example, Kim was relieved when a clinical psychologist helped her anticipate what it would be like to visit her seriously ill sister. She was frightened by the hospital and used withdrawal to cope. She said she did not want to see her sister, even though she missed her a great deal. Children tend to apply their coping strategies only in the situations in which stress develops. Adults can show children how to use these coping skills to their best advantage in many other situations as well. For example, Jennifer used altruism to cope when her mother was hospitalized for cancer. She coped with the separation by mothering her father, her little brother, and her classmates. Her classmates quickly became annoyed with her and began to tease her. Jennifer's teacher at school recognized the problem and helped Jennifer express her altruism by taking care of the class's pet animals and by being responsible for some daily cleanup chores. Her mothering of the children stopped, and so did the teasing. By following such guidelines, both professionals and laypeople can help children cope more effectively with stress.

Coping with Death   Children who have healthy and positive relationships with their parents before a parent dies cope with the death more effectively than children with unhappy prior relationships with the parent. The years of warmth and caring have probably taught the child effective ways of coping with such a traumatic event. Also, children who are given high-quality care by surviving family members during the mourning period, or who are effectively helped by caregivers in other contexts, experience less separation distress.

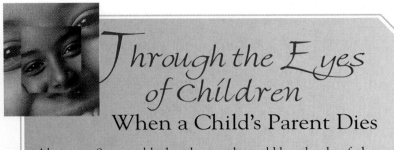

Through the Eyes of Children
When a Child's Parent Dies

Aletta was 9 years old when her mother told her that her father had died. She almost fell down, and her sister began screaming. Her hands still shake when she thinks about her father.

At school, the teacher told Aletta's class that her father had died. A lot of kids stopped playing with her when they heard her father had died. Aletta thinks they somehow might have been embarrassed or didn't know what to say.

Aletta says that if she knew anyone else whose father had died she would try to cheer them up. She would invite them over to her house a lot and play with them. Aletta says it would help if your friends would just play with you and treat you like a normal person.

Aletta still has dreams about her father—happy dreams. They make her feel good. The light on the garage shines in her window at night. Sometimes Aletta pretends that it is her father's spirit because the light shines only in her room. She says the light makes her happy (Krementz, 1983).

Sometimes the death of a sibling is even more difficult for children to understand and accept than the loss of a parent. Many children believe that only old people die, so the death of a child may stimulate children to think about their own immortality. The majority of children, though, seem to be able to cope with a sibling's death effectively if they are helped through a mourning period.

Knowing what children think about death can help adults understand their behavior in the period following the loss of a parent or sibling. When a 3-year-old boy creeps from his bed every night and runs down the street, searching for his mother who has just died, is he mourning for her? When a 6-year-old girl spends an entire afternoon drawing pictures of graveyards and coffins, is she grieving? When a 9-year-old boy can't wait to go back to school after the funeral so he can tell his classmates about how his sister died, is he denying grief? All of these are ways in which children cope with death. And all follow children's logic.

Children 3 to 5 years old think that dead people continue to live, but under changed circumstances. The missing person is simply missing, and young children expect the person to return at some point. When the person does not come back, they might feel hurt or angry at being abandoned. They might declare that they want to go to heaven to bring the dead person home. They might ask their caregivers where the dead person's house is, where the dead person eats, and why the dead person won't be cold if the person is buried without a coat and hat in winter.

Though children vary somewhat in the age at which they begin to understand death, the limitations of preoperational thought make it difficult for a child to comprehend death before the age of 7 or 8. Young children blame themselves for the death of someone they knew well, believing that the event may have happened because they disobeyed the person who died. Children under 6 rarely understand that death is universal, inevitable, and final. Instead, young children usually think that only people who want to die, or who are bad or careless, actually do die. At some point around the middle of the elementary school years, children begin to grasp the concept that death is the end of life and is not reversible. They come to realize that they, too, will die someday.

Moral Development

Remember from chapter 11 our description of Piaget's view of moral development. Piaget believed that younger children are characterized by heteronomous morality but that, by 10 years of age, they have moved into a higher stage called "autonomous" morality. According to Piaget, older children consider the intentions of the individual, believe that rules are subject to change, and are aware that punishment does not always follow a wrongdoing. A second major cognitive perspective on moral development was proposed by Lawrence Kohlberg.

Kohlberg's Theory of Moral Development   Kohlberg stressed that moral development is based primarily on moral reasoning and unfolds in stages (Kohlberg, 1958, 1976, 1986). Kohlberg arrived at his view after 20 years of using a unique interview with children. In the interview, children are presented with a series of stories in which characters face moral dilemmas. The following is the most popular Kohlberg dilemma:

Kohlberg's Theory

In Europe a woman was near death from a special kind of cancer. There was one drug that the doctors thought might save her. It was a form of radium that a druggist in the same town had recently discovered. The drug was expensive to make, but the druggist was charging ten times what the drug cost him to make. He paid $200 for the radium and charged $2,000 for a small dose of the drug. The sick woman's husband, Heinz, went to everyone he knew to borrow the money, but he could only get together $1,000 which is half of what it cost. He told the druggist that his wife was dying and asked him to sell it cheaper or let him pay later. But the druggist said, "No, I discovered the drug, and I am going to make money from it." So Heinz got desperate and broke into the man's store to steal the drug for his wife. (Kohlberg, 1969, p.379)

This story is one of 11 Kohlberg devised to investigate the nature of moral thought. After reading the story, the interviewee answers a series of questions about the moral dilemma. Should Heinz have stolen the drug? Was stealing it right or wrong? Why? Is it a husband's duty to steal the drug for his wife if he can get it no other way? Would a good husband steal? Did the druggist have the right to charge that much when there was no law setting a limit on the price? Why or why not?

Based on the reasons interviewees gave in response to this and other moral dilemmas, Kohlberg believed that three levels of moral development exist, each of which is characterized by two stages. A key concept in understanding moral development, especially Kohlberg's theory, is **internalization,** *the developmental change from behavior that is externally controlled to behavior that is internally controlled.*

Level One: Preconventional Reasoning

Preconventional reasoning *is the lowest level in Kohlberg's theory of moral development. At this level, the child shows no internalization of moral values—moral reasoning is controlled by external rewards and punishments.*

Stage 1. **Punishment and obedience orientation** *is the first stage in Kohlberg's theory of moral development. At this stage, moral thinking is based on punishment.* Children obey because adults tell them to obey.

Stage 2. **Individualism and purpose** *is the second stage in Kohlberg's theory of moral development. At this stage, moral thinking is based on rewards and self-interest.* Children obey when they want to obey and when it is in their best interest to obey. What is right is what feels good and what is rewarding.

Level Two: Conventional Reasoning

Conventional reasoning *is the second or intermediate level in Kohlberg's theory of moral development. At this level, the individual's internalization is intermediate. The person abides by certain standards (internal), but they are the standards of others (external), such as parents or the laws of society.*

Stage 3. **Interpersonal norms** *is the third stage in Kohlberg's theory of moral development. At this stage, the person values trust, caring, and loyalty to others as the basis of moral judgments.* Children often adopt their parents' moral standards at this stage, seeking to be thought of by their parents as a "good girl" or a "good boy."

Stage 4. **Social system morality** *is the fourth stage in Kohlberg's theory of moral development. At this stage, moral judgments are based on understanding the social order, law, justice, and duty.*

Level Three: Postconventional Reasoning

Postconventional reasoning *is the highest level in Kohlberg's theory of moral development. At this level, morality is completely internalized and not based on others' standards.* The person recognizes alternative moral courses, explores the options, and then decides on a personal moral code.

Stage 5. **Community rights versus individual rights** *is the fifth stage in Kohlberg's theory of moral development. At this stage, the person understands that values and laws are relative and that standards may vary from one person to another.* The person recognizes that laws are important for society but knows that laws can

internalization
The developmental change from behavior that is externally controlled to behavior that is internally controlled.

preconventional reasoning
The lowest level in Kohlberg's theory of moral development. At this level, the child shows no internalization of moral values—moral reasoning is controlled by external rewards and punishments.

punishment and obedience orientation
The first stage in Kohlberg's theory of moral development. At this stage, moral thinking is based on punishment.

individualism and purpose
The second stage in Kohlberg's theory of moral development. At this stage, moral thinking is based on rewards and self-interest.

conventional reasoning
The second, or intermediate, level in Kohlberg's theory of moral development. At this level, the individual's internalization is intermediate. The person abides by certain standards (internal), but they are the standards of others (external), such as parents or the laws of society.

interpersonal norms
The third stage in Kohlberg's theory of moral development. At this stage, the person values trust, caring, and loyalty to others as the basis of moral judgments.

social system morality
The fourth stage in Kohlberg's theory of moral development. At this stage, moral judgments are based on understanding the social order, law, justice, and duty.

postconventional reasoning
The highest level in Kohlberg's theory of moral development. At this level, morality is completely internalized and not based on others' standards.

community rights versus individual rights
The fifth stage in Kohlberg's theory of moral development. At this stage, the person understands that values and laws are relative and that standards may vary from one person to another.

Through the Eyes of Children

Life on the Make-Believe Planet of Pax

Elementary-school-aged children were asked to pretend that they had taken a long ride on a spaceship to a make-believe planet called Pax (Katz, 1987). The children were asked their opinions about various situations in which they found themselves.

All but two children believed that janitors should earn as much as teachers. The holdouts said teachers should make less because they stay in one room or because cleaning toilets is more disgusting and, therefore, deserves higher wages. All but one thought that not giving a job to a qualified applicant who has different characteristics (a striped rather than a dotted nose) is unfair.

In one situation, the mayor of a city on Pax was criticized by the press. Several children argued that the reporters should be jailed. One child said that if she were the mayor and was getting criticized, she would worry, make speeches, and say, "I didn't do anything wrong," not unlike what a lot of politicians do. Another child said that the mayor should not put the newspaper people out of work because that might make them print more bad things. The child recommended having them write comics instead.

universal ethical principles
The sixth and highest stage in Kohlberg's theory of moral development. At this stage, persons have developed a moral standard based on universal human rights.

be changed. The person believes that some values, such as liberty, are more important than the law.
Stage 6. **Universal ethical principles** *is the sixth and highest stage in Kohlberg's theory of moral development. At this stage, persons have developed a moral standard based on universal human rights.* When faced with a conflict between law and conscience, the person will follow conscience, even though the decision might involve personal risk.

Kohlberg believed that these levels and stages occur in a sequence and are age related: before age 9, most children reason about moral dilemmas in a preconventional way; by early adolescence, they reason in more conventional ways; and, by early adulthood, a small number of people reason in postconventional ways. In a 20-year longitudinal investigation, the uses of stages 1 and 2 decreased (Colby & others, 1983). Stage 4, which did not appear at all in the moral reasoning of the 10-year-olds, was reflected in 62 percent of the moral thinking of the 36-year-olds. Stage 5 did not appear until the age of 20 to 22 and never characterized more than 10 percent of the individuals. Thus, the moral stages appeared somewhat later than Kohlberg initially envisioned, and the higher stages, especially stage 6, were extremely elusive.

Kohlberg's Critics Kohlberg's provocative theory of moral development has not gone unchallenged (Lapsley, 1996; Rest, 1999). The criticisms involve the link between moral thought and moral behavior, inadequate consideration of culture's role and the family's role in moral development, and underestimation of the care perspective.

Moral Thought and Moral Behavior Kohlberg's theory has been criticized for placing too much emphasis on moral thought and not enough emphasis on moral behavior. Moral reasons can sometimes be a shelter for immoral behavior. Bank embezzlers and presidents endorse the loftiest of moral virtues when commenting about moral dilemmas, but their own behavior may be immoral. No one wants a nation of cheaters and thieves who can reason at the postconventional level. The cheaters and thieves may know what is right yet still do what is wrong.

Culture and Moral Development Yet another criticism of Kohlberg's view is that it is culturally biased (Banks, 1993; Miller, 1995). A review of research on moral development in 27 countries concluded that moral reasoning is more culture-specific than Kohlberg envisioned and that Kohlberg's scoring system does not recognize higher-level moral reasoning in certain cultural groups (Snarey, 1987). Examples of higher-level moral reasoning that would not be scored as such by Kohlberg's system are values related to communal equity and collective happiness in Israel, the unity and sacredness of all life forms in India, and the relation of the individual to the community in New Guinea. These examples of moral reasoning would not be scored at the highest level in Kohlberg's system because they do not emphasize the individual's rights and abstract principles of justice. One study assessed the moral development of 20 adolescent male Buddhist monks in Nepal (Huebner, Garrod, & Snarey, 1990). The issue of justice, a basic theme in Kohlberg's theory, was not of paramount importance in the monks' moral views, and their concerns about the prevention of suffering and the role of compassion are not captured by Kohlberg's theory. In sum, although Kohlberg's approach does capture much of the moral reasoning voiced in various cultures around the world, as we have just seen, there are some important moral concepts in particular cultures that his approach misses or misconstrues (Walker, 1996).

Family Processes and Moral Development   Kohlberg believed that family processes are essentially unimportant in children's moral development. He argued that parent-child relationships are usually power-oriented and provide children with little opportunity for mutual give and take or perspective taking. Rather, Kohlberg said that such opportunities are more likely to be provided by children's peer relations.

A number of developmentalists now believe that Kohlberg likely underestimated the contribution of family relationships to moral development. They emphasize that inductive discipline, which involves the use of reasoning and focuses children's attention on the consequences of their actions for others, positively influences moral development (Hoffman, 1970). They also stress that parents' moral values influence children's developing moral thoughts (Gibbs, 1993).

Gender and the Care Perspective   Carol Gilligan (1982, 1992, 1996) believes that Kohlberg's theory of moral development does not adequately reflect relationships and concern for others. The **justice perspective** *is a moral perspective that focuses on the rights of the individual; individuals stand alone and independently make moral decisions. Kohlberg's theory is a justice perspective.* By contrast, the **care perspective** *is a moral perspective that views people in terms of their connectedness with others and emphasizes interpersonal communication, relationships with others, and concern for others. Gilligan's theory is a care perspective.* According to Gilligan, Kohlberg greatly underplayed the care perspective in moral development. She believes that this may have happened because he was a male, because most of his research was with males rather than females, and because he used male responses as a model for his theory.

In extensive interviews with girls from 6 to 18 years of age, Gilligan and her colleagues found that girls consistently interpret moral dilemmas in terms of human relationships and base these interpretations on listening and watching other people (Gilligan, 1992, 1996). According to Gilligan, girls have the ability to sensitively pick up different rhythms in relationships and often are able to follow the pathways of feelings. Gilligan believes that girls reach a critical juncture in their development when they reach adolescence. Usually around 11 to 12 years of age, girls become aware that their intense interest in intimacy is not prized by the male-dominated culture, even though society values women as caring and altruistic. The dilemma is that girls are presented with a choice that makes them look either selfish or selfless. Gilligan believes that, as adolescent girls experience this dilemma, they increasingly silence their "distinctive voice." Researchers have found support for Gilligan's claim that females' and males' moral reasoning often centers around different concerns and issues (Galotti, Kozberg, & Farmer, 1990). However, one of Gilligan's initial claims—that traditional Kohlbergian measures of moral development are biased against females—has been extensively disputed. For example, most research studies using the Kohlberg stories and scoring system do not find sex differences (Walker,

Carol Gilligan is shown with some of the students she has interviewed about the importance of relationships in a female's development. According to Gilligan (center), the sense of relationship and connectedness is at the heart of female development.

justice perspective

A moral perspective that focuses on the rights of the individual; individuals stand alone and independently make moral decisions. Kohlberg's theory is a justice perspective.

care perspective

A moral perspective that views people in terms of their connectedness with others and emphasizes interpersonal communication, relationships with others, and concern for others. Gilligan's theory is a care perspective.

Gilligan's Care Perspective

1991). Thus, the strongest support for Gilligan's claims comes from studies that focus on items and scoring systems pertaining to close relationships, pathways of feelings, sensitive listening, and the rhythm of interpersonal behavior.

While females often articulate a care perspective and males a justice perspective, the gender difference is not absolute, and the two orientations are not mutually exclusive (Lyons, 1990). For example, in one study, 53 of the 80 females and males showed either a care or a justice perspective, but 27 subjects used both orientations, with neither predominating (Gilligan & Attanucci, 1988).

Contextual variations influence whether girls silence their "voice." In one study, Susan Harter and her colleagues (1996) found evidence for a refinement of Gilligan's position in that "feminine" girls reported lower levels of voice in public contexts (at school with teachers and classmates) but not in more private interpersonal relationships with close friends and parents. However, "androgynous" girls reported a strong voice in all contexts. Harter and her colleagues also found that adolescent girls who buy into societal messages that females should be seen and not heard are at most risk for problems in self development. The greatest self liabilities occurred for females who not only lacked a "voice" but who also emphasized the importance of appearance. In focusing on their outer selves, these girls face formidable challenges in meeting the punishing cultural standards of attractiveness.

Altruism   **Altruism** *is an unselfish interest in helping someone else.* Human acts of altruism are plentiful—the hardworking laborer who places $5 in a Salvation Army kettle; rock concerts to feed the hungry, help farmers, and fund AIDS research; and the child who takes in a wounded cat and cares for it. How do psychologists account for such acts of altruism?

Reciprocity and exchange are involved in altruism. Reciprocity is found throughout the human world. Not only is it the highest moral principle in Christianity, but it is also present in every widely practiced religion in the world—Judaism, Hinduism, Buddhism, and Islam. Reciprocity encourages children to do unto others as they would have others do unto them. Human sentiments are wrapped up in this reciprocity. Trust is probably the most important principle over the long run in altruism. Guilt surfaces if the child does not reciprocate, and anger may result if someone else does not reciprocate. Not all altruism is motivated by reciprocity and exchange, but self-other interactions and relationships help us understand altruism's nature. The circumstances most likely to involve altruism are empathic emotion for an individual in need or a close relationship between benefactor and recipient.

William Damon (1988) described a developmental sequence of children's altruism, especially of sharing. Most sharing during the first three years of life is done for nonempathic reasons, such as for the fun of the social play ritual or out of mere imitation. Then, at about 4 years of age, a combination of empathic awareness and adult encouragement produces a sense of obligation on the part of the child to share with others. This obligation forces the child to share, even though the child may not perceive this as the best way to have fun. Most 4-year-olds are not selfless saints, however. Children believe they have an obligation to share but do not necessarily think they should be as generous to others as they are to themselves. Neither do their actions always support their beliefs, especially when the object of contention is a coveted one. What is important developmentally is that the child has developed an internal belief that sharing is an obligatory part of a social relationship and that this involves a question of right and wrong. However, a preschool child's sense of reciprocity constitutes not a moral duty but, rather, a pragmatic means of getting one's way. Despite their shortcomings, these ideas about justice formed in early childhood set the stage for giant strides that children make in the years that follow.

By the start of the elementary school years, children genuinely begin to express more objective ideas about fairness. These notions about fairness have been used throughout history to distribute goods and to resolve conflicts. They involve the principles of equality, merit, and benevolence. *Equality* means that everyone is treated the same. *Merit* means giving extra rewards for hard work, a talented

altruism
An unselfish interest in helping someone else.

Every man takes care that his neighbor shall not cheat him. But a day comes when he begins to care that he does not cheat his neighbor. Then all goes well.

Ralph Waldo Emerson
American Poet, Essayist, 20th Century

performance, or other laudatory behavior. *Benevolence* means giving special consideration to individuals in a disadvantaged condition. Equality is the first of these principles used regularly by elementary school children. It is common to hear 6-year-old children use the word *fair* as synonymous with *equal* or *same*. By the mid to late elementary school years, children also believe that equity means special treatment for those who deserve it—the principles of merit and benevolence.

Missing from the factors that guide children's altruism is one that many adults might expect to be the most influential of all: the motivation to obey adult authority figures. Surprisingly, a number of studies have shown that adult authority has only a small influence on children's sharing. For example, when Nancy Eisenberg (1982) asked children to explain their own altruistic acts, they mainly gave empathic and pragmatic reasons for their spontaneous acts of sharing. Not one of the children referred to the demands of adult authority. Parental advice and prodding certainly foster standards of sharing, but the give-and-take of peer requests and arguments provides the most immediate stimulation of sharing. Parents may set examples that children carry into peer interaction and communication, but parents are not present during all of their children's peer exchanges. The day-to-day construction of fairness standards is done by children in collaboration and negotiation with each other. Over the course of many years and thousands of encounters, children's understanding of altruism deepens. With this conceptual elaboration, which involves such notions as equality, merit, benevolence, and compromise, come a greater consistency and generosity in children's sharing behavior (Damon & Hart, 1992).

What can parents and teachers do to promote children's altruism and prosocial behavior? Figure 14.3 provides a number of effective strategies.

Gender

In chapter 11, we discussed the biological, cognitive, and social influences on gender development. Gender is such a pervasive aspect of an individual's identity that we will further consider its role in children's development here. Among the gender-related topics we will examine are gender stereotypes, similarities, and differences; gender-role classification; and gender and ethnicity.

Gender Stereotypes   **Gender stereotypes** *are broad categories that reflect our impressions and beliefs about females and males.* All stereotypes, whether they are based on gender, ethnicity, or other groupings, refer to an image of what the typical member of a particular social category is like. The world is extremely complex. Every day we are confronted with thousands of different stimuli. The use of stereotypes is one way we simplify this complexity. If we simply assign a label (such as *soft*) to someone, we then have much less to consider when we think about the individual. However, once labels are assigned, they are remarkably difficult to abandon, even in the face of contradictory evidence.

How widespread is feminine and masculine stereotyping? According to a far-ranging study of college students in 30 countries, stereotyping of females and males is pervasive (Williams & Best, 1982). Males were widely believed to be dominant, independent, aggressive, achievement-oriented, and enduring, while females were widely believed to be nurturant, affiliative, less esteemed, and more helpful in times of distress.

In a subsequent study, women and men who lived in more highly developed countries perceived themselves as more similar than women and men who lived in less developed countries (Williams & Best, 1989). In the more highly developed countries, the women were more likely to attend college and be gainfully employed. Thus, as sexual equality increases, male and female stereotypes, as well as actual behavioral differences, may diminish. In this study, the women were more likely to perceive similarity between the sexes than the men were (Williams & Best, 1989). And the sexes were perceived more similarly in the Christian than in the Muslim societies.

Without civic morality communities perish; without personal morality their survival has no value.

Bertrand Russell
English Philosopher, 20th Century

gender stereotypes
Broad categories that reflect our impressions and beliefs about females and males.

Gender Stereotyping

What are little boys made of?
Frogs and snails
And puppy dogs' tails.

What are little girls made of?
Sugar and spice
And all that's nice

J. O. Halliwell
English Author, 19th Century

Alice Honig and Donna Wittmer (1994, 1996) provided the following recommendations for teachers and parents that focus on promoting children's prosocial behavior.

Value and emphasize consideration of other's needs.

This results in children's engaging in more helping activities. Nel Noddings (1992) explains the morality of caring as one of teaching children to feel for others, which leads to empathy and concern.

Model prosocial behaviors.

Children imitate what adults do. For example, an adult who comforts children in times of stress is likely to observe other children imitating her comforting behaviors with other peers. When parents or teachers yell at children, they likely will observe more incidences of children yelling at others.

Label and identify prosocial and antisocial behaviors.

Often go beyond just saying, "That's good" or "That's nice" to a child. Be specific in identifying prosocial behaviors. Say, "You are being very helpful" or "You gave him a tissue. That was very nice of you because he needed to wipe his nose."

Attribute positive social behaviors to each child.

Attributing positive intentions, such as "You shared because you like to help others," increases children's prosocial behavior.

Notice and positively encourage prosocial behaviors, but don't overuse external rewards.

Commenting on positive behaviors and attributing positive characteristics to children rather than using external rewards helps children internalize prosocial responses.

Facilitate perspective taking and understanding others' feelings.

Helping children notice and respond to others' feelings can increase their consideration of others (Mecca, 1996).

Use positive discipline strategies.

Reason with children when they do something wrong. If a child is too aggressive and harms another child, point out the consequences of the child's behavior for the victim. Avoid harsh, punitive behavior with the child. Redirect antisocial actions to more acceptable actions.

Actively lead discussions on prosocial interactions.

Set up discussion sessions and let children evaluate how goods and benefits are distributed justly among people with varying needs, temperaments, talents, and troubles.

Develop class and school projects that foster altruism.

Let children come up with examples of projects they can engage in that will help others. These projects might include cleaning up the schoolyard, writing as pen pals to children in troubled lands, collecting toys or food for individuals in need, and making friends with older adults during visits to a nursing home.

Use technology to promote prosocial behavior.

Videotape children who behave prosocially to increase sharing. In one study, third-grade children viewed videotapes of themselves and models in sharing situations (Devoe & Sherman, 1978). This strategy increased sharing immediately, and more sharing was still observed one week later.

Invite moral mentors to visit the class.

Recruit and involve moral mentors in the classroom. Invite people who have contributed altruistically to better the lives of others in the community. In one classroom, a teacher invited a high school swimming star who spends time helping children with a disability to talk with her class.

*F*igure 14.3
Strategies Teachers and Parents Can Use to Increase Children's Prosocial Behavior

Gender Similarities and Differences Let's now examine some of the differences between the sexes, keeping in mind that (a) the differences are averages—not all females versus all males; (b) even when differences are reported, there is considerable overlap between the sexes; and (c) the differences may be due primarily to biological factors, sociocultural factors, or both. First, we will examine physical differences, and then we will turn to cognitive and socioemotional differences.

Physical Similarities and Differences From conception on, females have a longer life expectancy than males, and females are less likely than males to develop physical or mental disorders. Estrogen strengthens the immune system, making females more resistant to infection, for example. Female hormones also signal the liver to produce more "good" cholesterol, which makes females' blood vessels more elastic than males'. Testosterone triggers the production of low-density lipoprotein, which clogs blood vessels. Males have twice the risk of coronary disease as females. Higher levels of stress hormones cause faster clotting in males, but also higher blood pressure than in females. Women have about twice the body fat of men, most concentrated around breasts and hips. In males, fat is more likely to go to the abdomen. On the average, males grow to be 10 percent taller than females. Male hormones promote the growth of long bones; female hormones stop such growth at puberty.

Similarity was the rule rather than the exception in a study of metabolic activity in the brains of females and males (Gur & others, 1995). The exceptions involved areas of the brain that involve emotional expression and physical expression, which are more active in females. However, there are many physical differences between females and males. Are there as many cognitive differences?

Cognitive Similarities and Differences In a classic review of gender differences, Eleanor Maccoby and Carol Jacklin (1974) concluded that males have better math and visuospatial skills (the kinds of skills an architect needs to design a building's angles and dimensions), while females have better verbal abilities. More recently, Maccoby (1987) revised her conclusion about several gender dimensions. She said that the accumulation of research evidence now suggests that verbal differences between females and males have virtually disappeared but that the math and visuospatial differences still exist. Another analysis found that males outperform females in spatial tasks (Voyer, Voyer, & Bryden, 1995).

Some experts in gender, such as Janet Shibley Hyde (1993), believe that the cognitive differences between females and males have been exaggerated. For example, Hyde points out that there is considerable overlap in the distributions of female and male scores on math and visuospatial tasks. Figure 14.4 shows that, although males outperform females on visuospatial tasks, female and male scores overlap substantially. Thus, while the *average* difference favors males, many females have higher scores on visuospatial tasks than most males do. The claim that "males outperform females in math" does not mean that all males outperform all females. Rather, it means that the average scores of males are higher than the average scores of females (Hyde & Plant, 1995).

Socioemotional Similarities and Differences Two areas of socioemotional development in which gender similarities and differences have been studied extensively are social relationships and aggression.

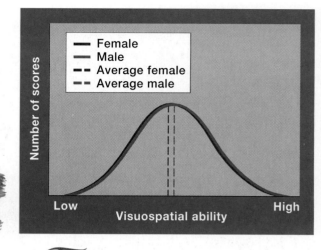

*F*igure 14.4
Visuospatial Ability of Males and Females

Notice that, although an average male's visuospatial ability is higher than an average female's, the overlap between the sexes is substantial. Not all males have better visuospatial ability than all females—the substantial overlap indicates that, although the average score of males is higher, many females outperform many males on such tasks.

*I*f you are going to generalize about women, you will find yourself up to here in exceptions.

Dolores Hitchens
American Mystery Writer, 20th Century

"So, according to the stereotype, you can put two and two together, but I can read the handwriting on the wall."

© 1986 Joel Pett, Phi Delta Kappan.

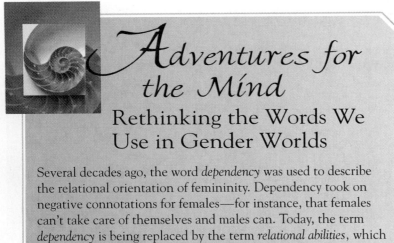

Adventures for the Mind
Rethinking the Words We Use in Gender Worlds

Several decades ago, the word *dependency* was used to describe the relational orientation of femininity. Dependency took on negative connotations for females—for instance, that females can't take care of themselves and males can. Today, the term *dependency* is being replaced by the term *relational abilities*, which has much more positive connotations. Rather than being thought of as dependent, women are now more often described as skilled in forming and maintaining relationships. Make up a list of words that you associate with masculinity and a list of words you associate with femininity. Do these words have any negative connotations for males or females? For the words that do have negative connotations, think about replacements for them that have more positive connotations.

rapport talk

The language of conversation and a way of establishing connections and negotiating relationships.

report talk

Talk that gives information, such as public speaking.

Gender and Communication

Gender differences occur in the communication aspect of social relationships, according to sociolinguist Deborah Tannen (1990). She distinguishes between rapport talk and report talk. **Rapport talk** *is the language of conversation and a way of establishing connections and negotiating relationships.* **Report talk** *is talk that gives information. Public speaking is an example of report talk.* Males hold center stage through report talk, with such verbal performances as storytelling, joking, and lecturing with information. By contrast, females enjoy private, rapport talk more and conversation that is relationship-oriented.

Tannen says that boys and girls grow up in different worlds of talk—parents, siblings, peers, teachers, and others talk to girls and boys differently. The play of boys and girls also is different. Boys tend to play in large groups that are hierarchically structured, and their groups usually have a leader, who tells the others what to do and how to do it. Boys' games have winners and losers and often are the subject of arguments. And boys often boast of their skill and argue about who is best at what. By contrast, girls are more likely to play in small groups or pairs, and the center of a girl's world is often a best friend. In girls' friendships and peer groups, intimacy is pervasive. Turn taking is more characteristic of girls' games than of boys' games. And, much of the time, girls simply like to sit and talk with each other, concerned more about being liked by others than about jockeying for status in any obvious way.

In sum, Tannen, like other gender experts, such as Carol Gilligan (1982, 1996), whose ideas you read about earlier in the chapter, believes that girls are more relationship-oriented than boys are and that this relationship orientation should be prized as a more important skill in our culture than it currently is. To further contemplate the socioemotional worlds of gender, see Adventures for the Mind.

One of the most consistent gender differences is that boys are more aggressive than girls. Another is that boys are more active than girls. The aggression differences is especially pronounced when children are provoked. Both biological and environmental factors have been proposed to account for gender differences in aggression. Biological factors include heredity and hormones. Environmental factors include cultural expectations, adult and peer models, and social agents who reward aggression in boys and punish aggression in girls.

An important skill is to be able to regulate and control your emotions and behavior. Males usually show less self-regulation than females (Eisenberg, Martin, & Fabes, 1996), and this low self-control can translate into behavioral problems. In one study, children's low self-regulation was linked with greater aggression, the teasing of others, overreaction to frustration, low cooperation, and inability to delay gratification (Block & Block, 1980).

Gender Controversy   Our coverage of gender similarities and differences reveals some areas in which gender differences are substantial and others in which they are small or nonexistent. Controversy swirls about such similarities and differences. Alice Eagly (1996) argues that the belief that gender differences are small or nonexistent is rooted in a feminist commitment to gender similarity and is seen as a route to political equality. Many feminists fear that gender differences will be interpreted as deficiencies on the part of females and will be seen as biologically based. They argue that such conclusions could revive traditional stereotypes that females are innately inferior to males (Unger & Crawford, 1992). Eagly responds to such criticisms by saying that a large body of research on gender now exists and reveals stronger gender differences than feminists acknowledge. This controversy is evidence that negotiating the science and politics of gender is not an easy task.

Gender-Role Classification   Not very long ago, it was accepted that boys should grow up to be masculine and girls to be feminine, that boys are made of "frogs and snails" and girls are made of "sugar and spice and all that is nice." Let's further explore such gender classifications of boys and girls as "masculine" and "feminine."

What Is Gender-Role Classification?   In the past, a well-adjusted boy was supposed to be independent, aggressive, and powerful. A well-adjusted girl was supposed to be dependent, nurturant, and uninterested in power. The masculine characteristics were considered to be healthy and good by society; the feminine characteristics were considered undesirable.

In the 1970s, as both females and males became dissatisfied with the burdens imposed by their stereotypic roles, alternatives to femininity and masculinity were proposed. Instead of describing masculinity and femininity as a continuum in which more of one means less of the other, it was proposed that individuals could have both masculine and feminine traits. This thinking led to the development of the concept of **androgyny,** *the presence of desirable masculine and feminine characteristics in the same person* (Bem, 1977; Spence & Helmreich, 1978). The androgynous boy might be assertive (masculine) and nurturant (feminine). The androgynous girl might be powerful (masculine) and sensitive to others' feelings (feminine).

Measures have been developed to assess androgyny. One of the most widely used measures is the Bem Sex-Role Inventory. To see whether your gender-role classification is masculine, feminine, or androgynous, see figure 14.5.

Gender experts, such as Sandra Bem, argue that androgynous individuals are more flexible, competent, and mentally healthy than their masculine or feminine counterparts. To some degree, though, deciding on which gender-role classification is best depends on the context involved. For example, in close relationships, feminine and androgynous orientations might be more desirable because of the expressive nature of close relationships. However, masculine and androgynous orientations might be more desirable in traditional academic and work settings because of the achievement demands in these contexts.

A special concern involves adolescent boys who adopt a strong masculine role. Researchers have found that high-masculinity adolescent boys often engage in problem behaviors, such as delinquency, drug abuse, and unprotected sexual intercourse (Pleck, 1995). Many of these boys, who present themselves as virile, macho, and aggressive, also do poorly in school. Too many adolescent males base their manhood on the caliber of gun they carry or the number of children they have fathered (Sullivan, 1991).

Androgyny and Education   Can and should androgyny be taught to students? In general, it is easier to teach androgyny to girls than to boys and easier to teach it before the middle school grades. For example, in one study, a gender curriculum was put in place for one year in the kindergarten, fifth, and ninth grades (Guttentag & Bray, 1976). It involved books, discussion materials, and classroom exercises with an androgynous bent. The program was most successful with the fifth-graders, least successful with the ninth-graders. The ninth-graders, especially the boys, showed a boomerang effect, in which they had more traditional gender-role attitudes after the year of androgynous instruction than before it.

Despite such mixed findings, the advocates of androgyny programs believe that traditional sex-typing is harmful for all students and especially has prevented many girls from experiencing equal opportunity. The detractors argue that androgynous educational programs are too value-laden and ignore the diversity of gender roles in our society.

androgyny
The presence of desirable masculine and feminine characteristics in the same individual.

Androgyny

The following items are from the Bem Sex-Role Inventory. To find out whether you score as androgynous, first rate yourself on each item, on a scale from 1 (never or almost never true) to 7 (always or almost always true).

1. self-reliant
2. yielding
3. helpful
4. defends own beliefs
5. cheerful
6. moody
7. independent
8. shy
9. conscientious
10. athletic
11. affectionate
12. theatrical
13. assertive
14. flatterable
15. happy
16. strong personality
17. loyal
18. unpredictable
19. forceful
20. feminine

21. reliable
22. analytical
23. sympathetic
24. jealous
25. has leadership abilities
26. sensitive to the needs of others
27. truthful
28. willing to take risks
29. understanding
30. secretive
31. makes decisions easily
32. compassionate
33. sincere
34. self-sufficient
35. eager to soothe hurt feelings
36. conceited
37. dominant
38. soft-spoken
39. likable
40. masculine

41. warm
42. solemn
43. willing to take a stand
44. tender
45. friendly
46. aggressive
47. gullible
48. inefficient
49. acts as a leader
50. childlike
51. adaptable
52. individualistic
53. does not use harsh language
54. unsystematic
55. competitive
56. loves children
57. tactful
58. ambitious
59. gentle
60. conventional

From Janet S. Hyde, *Half the Human Experience: The Psychology of Women*, 5th ed. Copyright © 1995 by D. C. Heath and Company, Lexington, MA. Used by permission of Houghton Mifflin Company.

Scoring

(a) Add up your ratings for items 1, 4, 7, 10, 13, 16, 19, 22, 25, 28, 31, 34, 37, 40, 43, 46, 49, 55, and 58. Divide the total by 20. That is your masculinity score.

(b) Add up your ratings for items 2, 5, 8, 11, 14, 17, 20, 23, 26, 29, 32, 35, 38, 41, 44, 47, 50, 53, 56, and 59. Divide the total by 20. That is your femininity score.

(c) If your masculinity score is above 4.9 (the approximate median for the masculinity scale), and your femininity score is above 4.9 (the approximate femininity median), then you would be classified as androgynous on Bem's scales.

*F*igure 14.5
The Bem Sex-Role Inventory: Are You Androgynous?

gender-role transcendence

The belief that, when an individual's competence is at issue, it should not be conceptualized on the basis of masculinity, femininity, or androgyny but, rather, on a personal basis.

To be meek, patient, tactful, modest, honorable, brave, is not to be either manly or womanly, it is to be humane.

Jane Harrison
English Writer, 20th Century

Gender-Role Transcendence Some critics of androgyny say enough is enough and that there is too much talk about gender. They believe that androgyny is less of a panacea than originally envisioned (Doyle & Paludi, 1998). An alternative is **gender-role transcendence,** *the view that when an individual's competence is at issue, it should be conceptualized on a personal basis, rather than on the basis of masculinity, femininity, or androgyny* (Pleck, 1983). That is, we should think about ourselves as people, not as masculine, feminine, or androgynous. Parents should rear their children to be competent boys and girls, not masculine, feminine, or androgynous, say the gender-role critics. They believe such gender-role classification leads to too much stereotyping.

Gender in Context The concept of gender-role classification involves a personality-traitlike categorization of a person. However, it may be helpful to think of personality in terms of person-situation interaction rather than personality traits alone. Thus, in our discussion of gender-role classification, we describe how different gender roles might be more appropriate, depending on the context, or setting, involved.

To see the importance of considering gender in context, let's examine helping behavior and emotion. The stereotype is that females are better than males at help-

In Egypt near the Aswan Dam, women are returning from the Nile River, where they have filled their water jugs. How might gender-role socialization for girls in Egypt compare with that in the United States?

ing. But it depends on the situation. Females are more likely than males to volunteer their time to help children with personal problems and to engage in caregiving behavior. However, in situations in which males feel a sense of competence and involve danger, males are more likely than females to help (Eagly & Crowley, 1986). For example, a male is more likely than a female to stop and help a person stranded by the roadside with a flat tire.

"She is emotional; he is not"—that is the master emotional stereotype. However, like differences in helping behavior, emotional differences in males and females depend on the particular emotion involved and the context in which it is displayed (Shields, 1991). Males are more likely to show anger toward strangers, especially male strangers, when they feel they have been challenged. Males also are more likely to turn their anger into aggressive action. Emotional differences between females and males often show up in contexts that highlight social roles and relationships. For example, females are more likely to discuss emotions in terms of relationships, and they are more likely to express fear and sadness.

The importance of considering gender in context is nowhere more apparent than when examining what is culturally prescribed behavior for females and males in different countries around the world. While there has been greater acceptance of androgyny and similarities in male and female behavior in the United States, in many countries gender roles have remained gender-specific. For example, in Egypt in the division of labor between Egyptian males and females is dramatic. Egyptian males are socialized and schooled to work in the public sphere, females in the private world of home and child rearing. The Islamic religion, which predominates in Egypt, dictates that the man's duty is to provide for his family and the woman's is to care for her family and household. Any deviations from this traditionally masculine and feminine behavior are severely disapproved of. China also has been a male-dominant culture. Although women have made some strides in China, the male role is still dominant. Androgynous behavior and gender equity are not what most males in China want to see happen.

At this point, we have studied a number of ideas about emotional and personality development in middle and late childhood. An overview of these ideas is presented in summary table 14.1. Next, we will explore how social contexts influence development in middle and late childhood, beginning with the family.

Gender and Culture

Summary Table 14.1
Emotional and Personality Development

Concept	Processes/ Related Ideas	Characteristics/Description
The self	Self-understanding and perspective taking	The internal self, the social self, and the socially comparative self become more prominent in middle and late childhood. Selman proposed a model of perspective taking with five stages.
	Self-esteem and self-concept	*Self-esteem* refers to global evaluations of the self; self-esteem is also referred to as self-worth or self-image. *Self-concept* refers to domain-specific self-evaluations. Harter has developed separate measures of self-evaluation for children and adolescents; these measures assess skill domain perceptions as well as general self-worth. Self-esteem and parenting, the increasing of self-esteem, and Erikson's stage of industry versus inferiority are other important dimensions of self in middle and late childhood.
Emotional development	Developmental changes	Among these are increased understanding of such complex emotions as pride and shame, increased understanding that more than one emotion can be experienced in a particular situation, increased tendency to take into account the events leading up to an emotional reaction, improved ability to suppress and conceal emotions, and the ability to use self-initiated strategies to redirect emotions.
	Emotional intelligence	This includes self-awareness, the understanding of one's own feelings, empathy for the feelings of others, and the regulation of emotion. Some educational programs seek to improve children's emotional skills.
	Coping with stress	Two good strategies for caregivers are (1) remove at least one stressor from the child's life and (2) help the child learn how to use effective coping strategies.
	Coping with death	Young children do not understand the nature of death, believing it is not final. At the middle of the elementary school years, they comprehend its final, irreversible nature.
Moral development	Kohlberg's theory	Kohlberg developed a provocative theory of moral reasoning with three levels—preconventional, conventional, and postconventional—and six stages (two at each level). Increased internalization characterizes movement to levels 2 and 3. Criticisms of Kohlberg's theory include the claims that Kohlberg overemphasizes cognition and underemphasizes behavior, underestimates culture's role as well as the family's role, and inadequately considers the care perspective. Gilligan advocates giving greater attention to the care perspective in moral development and believes that early adolescence is a critical juncture in female development.
	Altruism	Altruism is an unselfish interest in helping someone else. Damon described a developmental sequence of altruism.
Gender	Stereotypes, similarities, and differences	Gender stereotypes are widespread around the world. A number of physical differences exist between females and males. Some experts, such as Hyde, argue that cognitive differences between females and males have been exaggerated. In terms of socioemotional differences, males are more aggressive and active than females, while females emphasize their social ties. Currently, there is controversy about how similar or different females and males are in a number of areas.
	Gender-role classification	This focuses on how masculine, feminine, or androgynous an individual is. In the past, competent males were supposed to be masculine (powerful, for example); females were supposed to be feminine (nurturant, for example). In the 1970s there arose the concept of androgyny—that the most competent individuals have both positive masculine and feminine characteristics. Of special concern are adolescents who adopt a strong masculine role. Some programs have tried to teach androgyny to students but have had mixed results. Some experts believe that too much attention is given to gender in our society and that instead we should pursue gender-role transcendence.
	Gender in context	This view states that the best way to conceptualize gender is not as a traitlike category but as a person-situation concept in terms of gender in context. Areas such as emotion and helping illustrate the importance of the "gender in context" concept. Although androgyny and multiple gender roles are often available for American children to choose from, in many countries around the world, rigid, traditional gender roles are still in place. In these countries, such as China and Egypt, the male role is dominant.

FAMILIES

As children move into the middle and late childhood years, parents spend considerably less time with them. In one study, parents spent less than half as much time with their children aged 5 to 12 in caregiving, instruction, reading, talking, and playing as when the children were younger (Hill & Stafford, 1980). This drop in parent-child interaction may be even more extensive in families with little parental education. Although parents spend less time with their children in middle and late childhood than in early childhood, parents continue to be extremely important socializing agents in their children's lives. What are some of the most important parent-child issues in middle and late childhood?

Parent-Child Issues

Parent-child interactions during early childhood focus on such matters as modesty, bedtime regularities, control of temper, fighting with siblings and peers, eating behavior and manners, autonomy in dressing, and attention seeking. While some of these issues—fighting and reaction to discipline, for example—are carried forward into the elementary school years, many new issues have appeared by the age of 7 (Maccoby, 1984). These include whether children should be made to perform chores and, if so, whether they should be paid for them; how to help children learn to entertain themselves, rather than relying on parents for everything; and how to monitor children's lives outside the family in school and peer settings.

School-related matters are especially important for families during middle and late childhood. School-related difficulties are the number one reason that children in this age group are referred for clinical help. Children must learn to relate to adults outside the family on a regular basis—adults who interact with the child much differently than parents. During middle and late childhood, interactions with adults outside the family involve more formal control and achievement orientation.

School-Family Linkages

Discipline during middle and late childhood is often easier for parents than it was during early childhood; it may also be easier than during adolescence. In middle and late childhood, children's cognitive development has matured to the point where it is possible for parents to reason with them about resisting deviation and controlling their behavior. By adolescence, children's reasoning has become more sophisticated, and they may be less likely to accept parental discipline. Adolescents also push more strongly for independence, which contributes to parenting difficulties. Parents of elementary school children use less physical discipline than do parents of preschool children. By contrast, parents of elementary school children are more likely to use deprivation of privileges, appeals directed at the child's self-esteem, comments designed to increase the child's sense of guilt, and statements indicating to the child that he or she is responsible for his or her actions.

During middle and late childhood, some control is transferred from parent to child, although the process is gradual and involves *coregulation* rather than control by either the child or the parent alone. The major shift to autonomy does not occur until about the age of 12 or later. During middle and late childhood, parents continue to exercise general supervision and exert control, while children are allowed to engage in moment-to-moment self-regulation. This coregulation process is a transition period between the strong parental control of early childhood and the increased relinquishment of general supervision of adolescence.

During this coregulation, parents should:

- Monitor, guide, and support children at a distance
- Effectively use the times when they have direct contact with their children
- Strengthen in their children the ability to monitor their own behavior, to adopt appropriate standards of conduct, to avoid hazardous risks, and to sense when parental support and contact are appropriate

Life changes in parents also influence the nature of parent-child interaction in middle and late childhood; parents become more experienced in child rearing. As child-rearing demands are reduced in middle and late childhood, mothers are more likely to consider returning to a career or beginning a new career. Marital relationships change, as less time is spent in child rearing and more time is spent in career development, especially for mothers.

Societal Changes in Families

As we discussed in chapter 11, increasing numbers of children are growing up in divorced and working-mother families. But there are several other major shifts in the composition of family life that especially affect children in middle and late childhood. Parents are divorcing in greater numbers than ever before, but many of them remarry. It takes time for parents to marry, have children, get divorced, and then remarry. Consequently, there are far more elementary and secondary school children than infant or preschool children living in stepfamilies. In addition, an increasing number of elementary and secondary school children are latchkey children.

Stepfamilies
Stepfamily Resources
Stepfamily Support

Stepfamilies   The number of remarriages involving children has grown steadily in recent years, although the rate of remarriage actually has declined as the divorce rate has increased in the past several decades. Also, divorces occur at a 10 percent higher rate in remarriages than in first marriages (Cherlin & Furstenberg, 1994). As a result of their parents' successive marital transitions, about half of all children whose parents divorce will have a stepfather within four years of parental separation.

As in divorced families, children in stepfamilies have more adjustment problems than their counterparts in nondivorced families (Hetherington, Bridges, & Insabella, 1998). The adjustment problems of stepfamily children are much like those of children in divorced families—academic problems, externalizing and internalizing problems, lower self-esteem, early sexual activity, delinquency, and so on (Anderson & others, 1999). There is an increase in adjustment problems of children in newly remarried families (Hetherington & Clingempeel, 1992). Early adolescence seems to be an especially difficult time in which to have a remarriage occur, possibly because it exacerbates normal early adolescent concerns about autonomy, identity, and sexuality (Hetherington, 1993). Restabilization may take longer in stepfamilies, up to five years or more, than in divorced families, which often occurs in one to two years.

Boundary ambiguity, *the uncertainty in stepfamilies about who is in or out of the family and who is performing or responsible for certain tasks in the family system,* can present problems in stepfamilies. In the early stages of remarriage, stepfathers have been described as behaving like polite strangers, trying to win over their stepchildren by reducing negative behaviors and trying to control them less than do fathers in nondivorced families (Bray & Berger, 1993; Bray, Berger, & Boethel, 1999). In longer established stepfamilies, a distant, disengaged parenting style predominates for stepfathers, although conflict can remain high between stepfather and children. Stepmothers have a more difficult time integrating themselves into stepfamilies than do stepfathers. Children's relationships with custodial parents (biological father in stepmother families, biological mother in stepfather families) tend to be better than with stepparents (Santrock, Sitterle, & Warshak, 1988). Also, children in complex (or blended) stepfamilies (in which both parents bring offspring from previous marriages to live in the newly constituted stepfamily) show more adjustment problems than do children in simple stepfamilies (in which only one parent brings offspring into the stepfamily) (Hetherington, 1993; Santrock & Sitterle, 1987).

Latchkey Children   We concluded in chapter 11 that the mother's working outside the home does not necessarily have negative outcomes for her children. However, a certain subset of children from working-mother families deserves further scrutiny: latchkey children. These children typically do not see their parents from the time they leave for school in the morning until about 6 or 7 P.M. They are called "latchkey" children because they are given the key to their home, take the key to

boundary ambiguity
The uncertainty in stepfamilies about who is in or out of the family and who is performing or responsible for certain tasks in the family system.

Caring for Children
Parenting and Children in Stepfamilies

What are some problems frequently encountered by stepfamilies? What are some ways to build a strong, positive stepfamily? William Gladden (1991) recently provided the following guidelines, which address these questions.

Frequently Encountered Problems in Stepfamilies

- Adapting to multiple viewpoints, attitudes, and personalities
- Arranging to comply with the visitation and other custodial rights granted by a court to the absent natural parent—holidays and vacations can pose special problems, for example
- Conflicting ideas about how to discipline children and differing expectations about children
- Continuing battles over child custody issues
- Disagreements over expenses and how family finances are to be allocated
- Feelings of anger, hurt, mistrust, or guilt regarding the exspouse, which may be transferred to the new mate
- Interference by in-laws, especially grandparents, who have an interest in the children
- Reduced space, privacy, and personal time
- Refusal of the children to follow the rules or wishes of the stepparent
- Unwillingness of the children to accept the stepparent, with possible outright rejection of the stepparent
- Rivalry between children for attention and affection, especially when stepsiblings are involved
- Unresolved emotional problems of the children because of the disequilibrium they have experienced in their lives
- Unresolved personal problems of the parents, such as psychological or behavioral problems, that may accompany them into the newly created family

Strategies for Building a Strong, Positive Stepfamily

- Communicate about and come to an agreement on rules of conduct.
- Try to develop and maintain a cooperative relationship with the absent natural parent who still has legal rights to the children.
- Develop good communication between family members and learn to communicate clearly.
- Provide the children with age-appropriate responsibilities.
- Make a commitment to talk about and resolve disagreements based on mutual respect and kindness.
- Don't avoid dealing with the personal problems that create stress in the stepfamily; find positive ways to cope with them.
- Openly express affection.
- Plan for at least one mealtime per day that includes all the stepfamily members.
- Plan for family group entertainment and recreation.
- Respect the individual privacy rights of each member of the stepfamily.
- Support each stepfamily member's interests, hobbies, and goals.
- If family conflicts seem irreconcilable, or if the behavior of a child poses serious problems, it is usually wise to seek professional help. Most communities also have stepfamily support groups, whose members may share problems encountered by many stepfamilies. Such support groups can be especially beneficial for coping with stepfamily issues and problems.

school, and then use it to let themselves into the home while their parents are still at work. Latchkey children are largely unsupervised for two to four hours a day during each school week. During the summer months, they might be unsupervised for entire days, five days a week.

Thomas and Lynette Long (1983) interviewed more than 1,500 latchkey children. They concluded that a slight majority of these children had had negative latchkey experiences. Some latchkey children may grow up too fast, hurried by the responsibilities placed on them. How do latchkey children handle the lack of limits and structure during the latchkey hours? Without limits and parental supervision, latchkey children find their way into trouble more easily, possibly stealing, vandalizing, or abusing a sibling. The Longs point out that 90 percent of the juvenile delinquents in Montgomery County, Maryland, are latchkey children. Joan Lipsitz (1983), in testifying before the Select Committee on Children, Youth, and Families, called the lack of adult supervision of children in the after-school hours one of today's major problems. Lipsitz called it the "three-to-six o'clock problem" because it was during this time that the Center for Early Adolescence in North Carolina, when Lipsitz was director, experienced a peak of referrals for clinical help. And, in a 1987 national poll, teachers rated the latchkey children phenomenon the number one reason that children have problems in schools (Harris, 1987).

While latchkey children may be vulnerable to problems, the experiences of latchkey children vary enormously, as do the experiences of all children with working mothers (Belle, 1999). Parents need to give special attention to the ways in which their latchkey children's lives can be effectively monitored. Variations in latchkey experiences suggest that parental monitoring and authoritative parenting help the child cope more effectively with latchkey experiences, especially in resisting peer pressure (Galambos & Maggs, 1989; Steinberg, 1986). In one study, attending a formal after-school program that included academic, recreational, and remedial activities was associated with better academic achievement and social adjustment, in comparison with other types of after-school care (such as informal adult supervision or self-care) (Posner & Vandell, 1994). Practitioners and policymakers recommend that after-school programs have warm and supportive staff, a flexible and relaxed schedule, multiple activities, and opportunities for positive interactions with staff and peers (Pierce, Hamm, & Vandell, 1997; Vandell & Pierce, 1999).

PEER RELATIONS

During middle and late childhood, children spend an increasing amount of time in peer interaction. In one investigation, children interacted with peers 10 percent of their day at the age of 2, 20 percent at age 4, and more than 40 percent between the ages of 7 and 11 (Barker & Wright, 1951). The number of episodes with peers totaled 299 per typical school day.

What do children do when they are with their peers? In one study, sixth-graders were asked what they do when they are with their friends (Medrich & others, 1982). Team sports accounted for 45 percent of boys' activities but only 26 percent of girls'. General play, going places, and socializing were common listings for both sexes. Most peer interactions occur outside the home (although close to home), in private rather than public places, and between children of the same sex rather than between children of different sexes.

Peer Statuses

Children often think, "What can I do to get all of the kids at school to like me?" or "What's wrong with me? Something must be wrong, or I would be more popular." What makes a child popular with peers? **Popular children** *are frequently nominated as a best friend and are rarely disliked by their peers.* Researchers have found that popular children give out reinforcements, listen carefully, maintain open lines of communication with peers, are happy, act like themselves, show enthusiasm and concern for others, and are self-confident without being conceited (Hartup, 1983).

Developmentalists have distinguished among three types of children who have a different peer status than popular children: those who are neglected, those who are rejected, and those who are controversial (Ladd, 1999; Wentzal & Asher, 1995). **Neglected children** *are infrequently nominated as a best friend but are not disliked by their peers.* **Rejected children** *are infrequently nominated as someone's best friend and are actively disliked by their peers.* **Controversial children** *are frequently nominated both as someone's best friend and as being disliked.*

Rejected children often have more serious adjustment problems later in life than do neglected children (Dishion & Li, 1996; Kupersmidt & Patterson, 1993). For example, in one study, 112 fifth-grade boys were evaluated over a period of seven years until the end of high school (Kupersmidt & Coie, 1990). The key factor in predicting whether rejected children would engage in delinquent behavior or drop out of school later during adolescence was aggression toward peers in elementary school.

popular children
Children who are frequently nominated as a best friend and are rarely disliked by their peers.

neglected children
Children who are infrequently nominated as a best friend but are not disliked by their peers.

rejected children
Children who are infrequently nominated as a best friend and are actively disliked by their peers.

controversial children
Children who are frequently nominated both as someone's best friend and as being disliked.

Not all rejected children are aggressive. Although aggression and its related characteristics of impulsiveness and disruptiveness underlie rejection about half the time, approximately 10 to 20 percent of rejected children are shy.

An important question to ask is how neglected children and rejected children can be trained to interact more effectively with their peers. The goal of training programs with neglected children is often to help them attract attention from their peers in positive ways and to hold their attention by asking questions, by listening in a warm and friendly way, and by saying things about themselves that relate to the peers' interests. They also are taught to enter groups more effectively.

The goal of training programs with rejected children is often to help them listen to peers and "hear what they say" instead of trying to dominate peer interactions. Rejected children are trained to join peers without trying to change what is taking place in the peer group. Children may need to be motivated to use these strategies by being persuaded that they work effectively and are satisfying. In some programs, children are shown videotapes of appropriate peer interaction; then they are asked to comment on them and to draw lessons from what they have seen. In other training programs, popular children are taught to be more accepting of neglected or rejected peers.

Social Cognition

Children's social cognitions about their peers also become increasingly important for understanding peer relationships in middle and late childhood. Of special interest are the ways in which children process information about peer relations and their social knowledge (Crick & Dodge, 1994; Rubin & others, 1999).

Social Cognition

A boy accidentally trips and knocks a peer's soft drink out of his hand. The peer misinterprets the encounter as hostile, which leads him to retaliate aggressively against the boy. Through repeated encounters of this kind, other peers come to perceive the aggressive boy as habitually acting in inappropriate ways. Kenneth Dodge (1983) argues that children go through five steps in processing information about their social world. They decode social cues, interpret, search for a response, select an optimal response, and enact. Dodge has found that aggressive boys are more likely to perceive another child's actions as hostile when the child's intention is ambiguous. And, when aggressive boys search for cues to determine a peer's intention, they respond more rapidly, less efficiently, and less reflectively than do nonaggressive children. These are among the social cognitive factors believed to be involved in the nature of children's conflicts.

Lacking Clearness Double Meaning

Social knowledge is also involved in children's ability to get along with peers. An important part of children's social life involves knowing what goals to pursue in poorly defined or ambiguous situations. Social relationship goals, such as how to initiate and maintain a social bond, are also important. Children need to know what scripts to follow to get other children to be their friends. For example, as part of the script for getting friends, it helps to know that saying nice things, regardless of what the peer does or says, will make the peer like the child more.

From a social cognitive perspective, children who are maladjusted do not have adequate social cognitive skills to interact effectively with others. One investigation explored the possibility that children who are maladjusted do not have the social cognitive skills necessary for positive social interaction (Asarnow & Callan, 1985). Boys with and without peer adjustment difficulties were identified, and their social cognitive skills were assessed. Boys without peer adjustment problems generated more alternative solutions to problems, proposed more assertive and mature solutions, gave less intense aggressive solutions, showed more adaptive planning, and evaluated physically aggressive responses less positively than did boys with peer adjustment problems.

The world of peers is one of varying acquaintances; children interact with some children they barely know and with friends for hours every day. It is to the latter—friends—that we now turn.

*F*igure 14.6
Functions of Children's Friendships

Companionship | Stimulation | Physical support
Ego support | Social comparison | Intimacy/affection

Friendships

A man's growth is seen in the successive choirs of his friends.

Ralph Waldo Emerson
American Poet, Essayist, 19th Century

Friends

"My best friend is nice. She is honest and I can trust her. I can tell her my innermost secrets and know that nobody else will find out about them. I have other friends, but she is my best friend. We consider each other's feelings and don't want to hurt each other. We help each other out when we have problems. We make up funny names for people and laugh ourselves silly. We make lists of which boys we think are the ugliest, which are the biggest jerks, and so on. Some of these things we share with other friends, some we don't." This is a description of a friendship by a 10-year-old girl. It reflects the belief that children are interested in specific peers—not just any peers. They want to share concerns, interests, information, and secrets with them.

Why are children's friendships important? They serve six functions: companionship, stimulation, physical support, ego support, social comparison, and intimacy/affection (Gottman & Parker, 1987). Concerning companionship, friendship provides children with a familiar partner and playmate, someone who is willing to spend time with them and join in collaborative activities. Concerning stimulation, friendship provides children with interesting information, excitement, and amusement. Concerning physical support, friendship provides time, resources, and assistance. Concerning ego support, friendship provides the expectation of support, encouragement, and feedback, which helps children maintain an impression of themselves as competent, attractive, and worthwhile individuals. Concerning social comparison, friendship provides information about where the child stands vis-à-vis others and whether the child is doing OK. Concerning intimacy and affection, friendship provides children with a warm, close, trusting relationship with another individual in which self-disclosure takes place (Rose & Asher, 1999) (see figure 14.6).

In one study, the knowledge of both appropriate and inappropriate strategies for making friends was related positively to a child's prosocial behavior and peer acceptance but negatively to antisocial behavior (Wentzel & Erdley, 1993). The children's appropriate and inappropriate strategies are presented in figure 14.7.

Willard Hartup (1996; Hartup & Laursen, 1999; Hartup & Stevens, 1997) has studied peer relations and friendship for more than three decades. He recently concluded that friends can be cognitive and emotional resources from childhood through old age. Friends can foster self-esteem and a sense of well-being. Although having friends can be a developmental advantage, not all friendships are alike. People differ in the company they keep—that is, who their friends are. Developmental

Category	Examples
Strategies appropriate for making friends	
Initiate interaction.	Learn about friend: ask for his or her name, age, favorite activities. Prosocial overtures: introduce self, start conversation, invite him or her to do things.
Be nice.	Be nice, kind, considerate.
Prosocial behavior	Honesty and trustworthiness: tell the truth, keep promises. Be generous, sharing, cooperative.
Respect for self and others	Respect others, have good manners: be polite and courteous. Listen to what others say. Have a positive attitude and personality: be open to others, be friendly, be funny. Be yourself. Enhance your own reputation: be clean, dress neatly, be on best behavior.
Provide social support.	Be supportive: help, give advice, show you care. Engage in activities together: study or play, sit next to one another, be in same group. Enhance others: compliment them.
Strategies inappropriate for making friends	
Psychological aggression	Show disrespect, bad manners: be prejudiced and inconsiderate, use others, curse, be rude. Be exclusive, uncooperative: don't invite them to do things, ignore them, isolate them, don't share with or help them. Hurt their reputation or feelings: gossip, spread rumors, embarrass them, criticize them.
Negative self-presentation	Be self-centered: be snobby, conceited, and jealous; show off, care only about yourself. Be mean, have bad attitude or affect: be mean, cruel, hostile, a grouch, angry all the time. Hurt own reputation: be a slob, act stupidly, throw temper tantrums, start trouble, be a sissy.
Antisocial behavior	Physical aggression: fight, trip, spit, cause physical harm. Verbal aggression or control: yell at others, pick on them, make fun of them, call them names, be bossy. Dishonesty, disloyalty: tell lies, steal, cheat, tell secrets, break promises. Break school rules: skip school, drink alcohol, use drugs.

Figure 14.7
Appropriate and Inappropriate Strategies for Making Friends at School

advantages occur when children have friends who are socially skilled and supportive. However, it is not developmentally advantageous to have coercive and conflict-ridden friendships.

Two of friendship's most common characteristics are intimacy and similarity. **Intimacy in friendships** *is self-disclosure and the sharing of private thoughts.* Research reveals that intimate friendships may not appear until early adolescence (Berndt & Perry, 1990). Also, throughout childhood, friends are more similar than dissimilar in terms of age, sex, race, and many other factors. Friends often have similar attitudes toward school, similar educational aspirations, and closely aligned achievement orientations. Friends like the same music, the same kind of clothes, and the same kind of leisure activities.

intimacy in friendships
Self-disclosure and the sharing of private thoughts.

Hold a true friend with both hands.
Nigerian Proverb

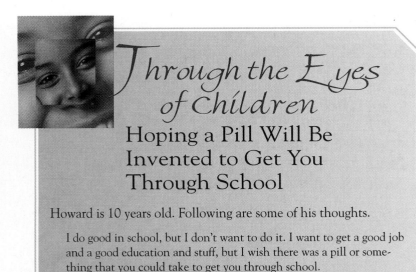

Through the Eyes of Children

Hoping a Pill Will Be Invented to Get You Through School

Howard is 10 years old. Following are some of his thoughts.

I do good in school, but I don't want to do it. I want to get a good job and a good education and stuff, but I wish there was a pill or something that you could take to get you through school.

I try to stay away from fights at school. I try to settle things just by talking, but if somebody pushes me too far I'll take them on.

I wish everybody would pay more attention to kids. Sometimes grown-ups pay attention, but not a lot. They are kind of wrapped up in their jobs and don't pay attention to us kids. I don't think kids would get into as much trouble if people spent more time with kids.

Elementary Education
Pathways to School Improvement

The world rests on the breath of the children in the schoolhouse.

The Talmud
Palestinian and Babylonian Source of Jewish Law and Schools, 4th Century

Knowledge which is acquired under compulsion obtains no hold on the mind.

Plato
Greek Philosopher, 4th Century B.C.

SCHOOLS

It is justifiable to be concerned about the impact of schools on children: by the time students graduate from high school, they have spent 10,000 hours in the classroom. Children spend many years in schools as members of a small society in which there are tasks to be accomplished, people to be socialized and socialized by, and rules that define and limit behavior, feelings, and attitudes.

The Transition to Elementary School

For most children, entering the first grade signals a change from being a "homechild" to being a "schoolchild"—a situation in which new roles and obligations are experienced. Children take up a new role (being a student), interact and develop relationships with new significant others, adopt new reference groups, and develop new standards by which to judge themselves. School provides children with a rich source of new ideas to shape their sense of self.

A special concern about children's early school experiences is emerging. Evidence is mounting that early schooling proceeds mainly on the basis of negative feedback. For example, children's self-esteem in the latter part of elementary school is lower than it is in the earlier part, and older children rate themselves as less smart, less good, and less hardworking than do younger ones (Blumenfeld & others, 1981).

In school as well as out of school, children's learning, like children's development, is *integrated* (NAEYC, 1988). One of the main pressures on elementary teachers has been the need to "cover the curriculum." Frequently, teachers have tried to do so by tightly scheduling discrete time segments for each subject. This approach ignores the fact that children often do not need to distinguish learning by subject area. For example, they advance their knowledge of reading and writing when they work on social studies projects; they learn mathematical concepts through music and physical education (Katz & Chard, 1989). A curriculum can be facilitated by providing learning areas in which children plan and select their activities. For example, the classroom may include a fully equipped publishing center, complete with materials for writing, illustrating, typing, and binding student-made books; a science area, with animals and plants for observation and books to study; and other similar areas. In this type of classroom, children learn reading as they discover information about science; they learn writing as they work together on interesting projects. Such classrooms also provide opportunities for spontaneous play, recognizing that elementary school children continue to learn in all areas through unstructured play, either alone or with other children.

Education experts Lilliam Katz and Sylvia Chard (1989) described two elementary school classrooms. In one, children spent an entire morning making identical pictures of traffic lights. The teacher made no attempt to get the children to relate the pictures to anything else the class was doing. In the other class, the children were investigating a school bus. They wrote to the district's school superintendent and asked if they could have a bus parked at their school for a few days. They studied the bus, discovered the functions of its parts, and discussed traffic rules. Then, in the classroom, they built their own bus out of cardboard. The children had fun, but they also practiced writing, problem solving, and even some arithmetic. When the class had their parents' night, the teacher was ready with reports on how each child was doing. However, all that the parents wanted to see was the bus because their children had been talking about it at home for weeks. Many contemporary education experts believe that this is the kind of education all children deserve. That is, they believe that children should be active, constructivist learners and taught through concrete, hands-on experience (Bonk & Cunningham, 1999).

Teachers

Teachers have a prominent influence in middle and late childhood. They symbolize authority and establish the classroom's climate, the conditions of interaction among students, and the nature of group functioning.

Almost everyone's life is affected in one way or another by teachers. You were influenced by teachers as you grew up; you may become a teacher yourself or work with teachers through counseling or psychological services; and you may one day have children whose education will be guided by many different teachers through the years. You can probably remember several of your teachers vividly: perhaps one never smiled, another required you to memorize everything in sight, and another always appeared happy and vibrant and encouraged verbal interaction. Psychologists and educators have tried to create a profile of a good teacher's personality traits, but the complexity of personality, education, learning, and individual differences makes the task difficult. Nonetheless, some teacher traits are associated with positive student outcomes more than others; enthusiasm, ability to plan, poise, adaptability, warmth, flexibility, and awareness of individual differences are a few (Gage, 1965).

Erik Erikson (1968) believes that good teachers should be able to produce a sense of industry, rather than inferiority, in their students. Good teachers are trusted and respected by the community and know how to alternate work and play, study and games, says Erikson. They know how to recognize special efforts and to encourage special abilities. They also know how to create a setting in which children feel good about themselves and how to handle those children to whom school is not important. In Erikson's (1968) own words, children should be "mildly but firmly coerced into the adventure of finding out that one can learn to accomplish things which one would never have thought of by oneself" (p. 127).

Teacher characteristics and styles are important, but they need to be considered in concert with what children bring to the school situation. Some children may benefit more from structure than others, and some teachers may be able to handle a flexible curriculum better than others. **Aptitude-treatment interaction (ATI)** *stresses the importance of children's aptitudes and characteristics and the treatments and experiences they are given in classrooms.* *Aptitude* refers to such characteristics as academic potential and personality characteristics on which students differ: *treatment* refers to educational techniques, such as structured versus flexible classrooms (Cronbach & Snow, 1977). Researchers have found that children's achievement level (aptitude) interacts with classroom structure (treatment) to produce the best learning (Peterson, 1977). For example, students who are highly achievement-oriented usually do well in a flexible classroom and enjoy it; low-achievement-oriented students usually fare worse and dislike the flexibility. The reverse often appears in structured classrooms.

Socioeconomic Status and Ethnicity in Schools

Children from low-income, ethnic minority backgrounds have more difficulties in school than do their middle-socioeconomic status, White counterparts. Why? Critics argue that schools have not done a good job of educating low-income, ethnic minority students to overcome the barriers to their achievement (Scott-Jones, 1995). Let's further explore the roles of socioeconomic status and ethnicity in schools.

The Education of Students from Low Socioeconomic Backgrounds

Many children in poverty face problems at home and at school that present barriers to their learning (Phillips & others, 1999; Wertheimer, 1999). At home, they may

I touch the future. I teach.

Christa McAuliffe
American Educator and Astronaut, 20th Century.

ERIC Clearinghouse on Teachers
Research on Teaching

aptitude-treatment interaction (ATI)
The interaction of children's aptitude and characteristics and the treatments and experiences they are given in classrooms.

Urban Education and
Children in Poverty

have parents who don't set high educational standards for them, who are incapable of reading to them, and who don't have enough money to pay for educational materials and experiences, such as books and trips to zoos and museums. They may experience malnutrition and live in areas where crime and violence are a way of life (Ceballo, 1999; DuRant, 1999).

Many of the schools that children from impoverished backgrounds attend have fewer resources than do the schools in higher-income neighborhoods (Shade, Kelly, & Oberg, 1997). Schools in low-income areas are more likely to have more students with lower achievement test scores, lower graduation rates, and smaller percentages of students going to college. And they are more likely to have young teachers with less experience than do schools in higher-income neighborhoods. In some instances, though, federal aid has provided a context for improved learning in schools located in low-income areas.

Schools in low-income areas also are more likely to encourage rote learning, while schools in higher-income areas are more likely to work with children to improve their thinking skills (Spring, 1998). Thus far too many schools in low-income neighborhoods provide students with environments that are not conducive to effective learning, and many of the schools' buildings and classrooms are old, crumbling, and poorly maintained.

Interview with Jonathan Kozol

Jonathan Kozol (1991) vividly described some of the problems that children of poverty face in their neighborhood and at school in *Savage Inequalities.* Following are some of his observations in one inner-city area. East St. Louis, Illinois, which is 98 percent African American, has no obstetric services, no regular trash collection, and few jobs. Nearly one third of the families live on less than $7,500 a year, and 75 percent of its population lives on welfare of some form. Blocks upon blocks of housing consist of dilapidated, skeletal buildings. Residents breathe the chemical pollution of nearby Monsanto Chemical Company. Raw sewage repeatedly backs up into homes. Lead from nearby smelters poisons the soil. Child malnutrition and fear of violence are common. The problems of the streets spill over into the schools, where sewage also backs up from time to time. Classrooms and hallways are old and unattractive, athletic facilities inadequate. Teachers run out of chalk and paper, the science labs are 30–50 years out of date, and the school's heating system has never worked correctly. A history teacher has 110 students but only 26 books.

Kozol says that anyone who visits places like East St. Louis, even for a brief time, comes away profoundly shaken. After all, these are innocent children who have done nothing wrong. Kozol's interest was in describing what life is like in the nation's inner-city neighborhoods and schools, which are predominantly African American and Latino. However, as indicated earlier, there are many non-Latino White children who live in poverty, although they often are in suburban or rural areas. Kozol argues that many inner-city schools are still segregated, are grossly underfunded, and do not provide adequate opportunities for children to learn effectively.

One recent trend in antipoverty programs is to conduct two-generational intervention (Huston, 1999; McLoyd, 1998, 1999). This involves providing both services for children (such as educational day care or preschool education) and services for parents (such as adult education, literacy training, and job skill training). Recent evaluations of the two-generational programs suggest that they have more positive effects on parents than they do on children (St. Pierre, Layzer, & Barnes, 1996). Also discouraging for children is that, when the two-generational programs show benefits, they are more likely to be in the form of health benefits than cognitive gains.

Ethnicity in Schools School segregation is still a factor in the education of children of color in the United States (Simons, Finlay, & Yang, 1991). Almost one third of all African American and Latino students attend schools in which 90 percent or more of the students are from minority groups.

The school experiences of students from different ethnic groups vary considerably (Hollins & Oliver, 1999). African American and Latino students are much less

Diversity and Education

likely than non-Latino White or Asian American students to be enrolled in academic, college preparatory programs and are much more likely to be enrolled in remedial and special education programs. Asian American students are far more likely than other ethnic minority groups to take advanced math and science courses in high school. African American students are twice as likely as Latinos, Native Americans, or Whites to be suspended from school. Ethnic minorities of color constitute the majority in 23 of the 25 largest school districts in the United States, a trend that is increasing (Banks, 1995). However, 90 percent of the teachers in America's schools are non-Latino White, and the percentage of minority teachers is projected to decrease even further in the coming years.

American anthropologist John Ogbu (1989) proposed the view that ethnic minority students are placed in a position of subordination and exploitation in the American educational system. He believes that students of color, especially African Americans and Latinos, have inferior educational opportunities, are exposed to teachers and school administrators who have low academic expectations for them, and encounter negative stereotypes of ethnic minority groups. In one study of middle schools in predominantly Latino areas of Miami, Latino and White teachers rated African American students as having more behavioral problems than African American teachers rated the same students as having (Zimmerman & others, 1995).

Like Ogbu, educational psychologist Margaret Beale Spencer (1990) says that a form of institutional racism permeates many American schools. That is, well-meaning teachers, acting out of misguided liberalism, fail to challenge children of color to achieve. Such teachers prematurely accept a low level of performance from these children, substituting warmth and affection for high standards of academic success.

Following are some strategies for improving relations between ethnically diverse students (Santrock, in press).

Multicultural Education

- *Turn the class into a jigsaw classroom.* When Eliot Aronson was a professor at the University of Texas at Austin, the school system contacted him for ideas on how to reduce the increasing racial tension in classrooms. Aronson (1986) developed the concept of "jigsaw classroom," in which students from different cultural backgrounds are placed in a cooperative group in which they have to construct different parts of a project to reach a common goal. Aronson used the term *jigsaw* because he saw the technique as much like a group of students cooperating to put different pieces together to complete a jigsaw puzzle. How might this work? Consider a class of students, some White, some African American, some Latino, and some Asian American. The lesson to be learned by the groups focuses on the life of Joseph Pulitzer. The class might be broken up into groups of six students each, with the groups being as equal as possible in terms of ethnic composition and achievement level. The lesson about Pulitzer's life is divided into six parts, with each part given to a member of each six-person group. The parts might be paragraphs from Pulitzer's biography, such as how the Pulitzer family came to the United States, Pulitzer's childhood, and his early work. All the students in each group are given an allotted time to study their parts. Then the groups meet, and each member tries to teach a part to the group. Learning depends on the students' interdependence and cooperation in reaching the same goal. Sometimes the jigsaw classroom strategy is referred to as creating a superordinate goal or common task for students. Team sports, drama productions, and music performances are examples of contexts in which students cooperatively participate to reach a superordinate goal.

James Comer (left) is shown with some of the inner-city African American children who attend a school that became a better learning environment because of Comer's intervention. Comer is convinced that a strong, familylike atmosphere is a key to improving the quality of inner-city schools.

Improving Developmental Skills

Strategies for Supporting Children's Socioemotional Development

What are some good strategies for nourishing children's socioemotional skills?

- *Improve children's self-esteem.* This can be accomplished by identifying the causes of the child's self-esteem, providing emotional support and social approval, helping the child achieve, and helping the child cope with stress.
- *Help children understand their emotions and cope with stress.* When children are experiencing considerable stress, try to remove at least one stressor from their lives. Also help the child learn effective coping strategies.
- *Nurture children's moral development.* Parents can improve their children's morality by being warm and supportive rather than punitive, using reasoning when disciplining, providing opportunities for children to learn about others' perspectives and feelings, involving children in family decision making, and modeling prosocial moral behavior. A number of other strategies for promoting children's prosocial behavior were discussed in the chapter.
- *Adapt to developmental changes in children.* Because parents typically spend less time with children in middle and late childhood, it is important to strengthen children's self-control. This is especially true in the case of latchkey children. As in early childhood, authoritative parenting should continue to be the choice, rather than authoritarian or permissive parenting.
- *Improve children's peer and friendship skills.* Peer and friendship relations become increasingly important to elementary school children. Adults can talk with children about the importance of being nice, engaging in prosocial behavior, and providing support in getting peers and friends to like them. Parents also can communicate to children that being aggressive, self-centered, and inconsiderate of others harms peer and friendship relations.
- *Create schools that support children's socioemotional development.* Not only do good teachers know how to challenge and stimulate children's cognitive development but they also know how to make children feel good about themselves. Too much of elementary school education involves negative feedback. We need more classrooms in which children are excited about learning. This learning should be designed to increase children's self-esteem, not wreck their emotional well-being. Parents need to encourage and support their children's educational accomplishments but not set unrealistic achievement expectations.

- *Encourage students to have positive personal contact with diverse other students.* Contact alone does not do the job of improving relationships with diverse others. For example, busing ethnic minority students to predominantly White schools, or vice versa, has not reduced prejudice or improved interethnic relations (Minuchin & Shapiro, 1983). What matters is what happens after children get to school. Especially beneficial in improving interethnic relations is sharing one's worries, successes, failures, coping strategies, interests, and other personal information with people of other ethnicities. When this happens, people are seen more as individuals than as a heterogeneous cultural group.
- *Encourage students to engage in perspective taking.* Exercises and activities that help students see others' perspectives can improve interethnic relations. This helps students "step into the shoes" of peers who are culturally different and feel what it is like to be treated in fair or unfair ways (Cushner, McClelland, & Safford, 1996).
- *Help students think critically and be emotionally intelligent when cultural issues are involved.* Students who think in narrow ways are prejudiced. Students who learn to think critically and deeply about interethnic relations are likely to decrease their prejudice. Becoming more emotionally intelligent includes understanding the causes of one's feelings, managing anger, listening to what others are saying, and being motivated to share and cooperate.
- *Reduce bias.* Teachers can reduce bias by displaying images of children from diverse ethnic and cultural groups, selecting play materials and classroom activities that encourage cultural understanding, helping students resist stereotyping, and working with parents (Derman-Sparks, 1989).
- *View the school and community as a team to help support teaching efforts.* James Comer (1988; Comer & others, 1996) believes that a community, team approach is the best way to educate children. Three important aspects of the Comer Project for Change are (1) a governance and management team that develops a comprehensive school plan, assessment strategy, and staff development plan; (2) a mental health or school support team; and (3) a parent's program. Comer believes that the entire school community should have a cooperative rather than an adversarial attitude. The Comer program is currently operating in more than 600 schools in 26 states.
- *Be a competent cultural mediator.* Teachers can play a powerful role as a cultural mediator by being sensitive to racist content in materials and classroom interactions, learning more about different ethnic groups, being sensitive to children's ethnic attitudes, viewing students of color positively, and thinking of positive ways to get parents of color more involved as partners with teachers in educating children (Banks, 1997; Cushner, 1999).

Summary Table 14.2
Families, Peer Relations, and Schools

Concept	Processes/ Related Ideas	Characteristics/Description
Families	Parent-child issues	Parents spend less time with children during middle and late childhood, including less time in caregiving, instruction, reading, talking, and playing. Nonetheless, parents still are powerful and important socializing agents during this period. New parent-child issues emerge, and discipline changes. Control is more coregulatory, children and parents label each other more, and parents mature just as children do.
	Societal changes in families	During middle and late childhood, two major changes in many children's lives are moving into a stepfamily and becoming a latchkey child. Like in divorced families, children living in stepfamilies have more adjustment problems than their counterparts in nondivorced families. Early adolescence is an especially difficult time for a remarriage to occur. Restabilization often takes longer in remarriages than in divorce. Boundary ambiguity is a common difficulty in stepfamilies. Children have better relationships with their biological parents than stepparents and show more problems in complex, blended families than simple stepfamilies. Latchkey children may become vulnerable when they are not monitored by adults in the after-school hours.
Peer relations	Peer statuses	Popular children are frequently nominated as a best friend and are rarely disliked by their peers. Neglected children are infrequently nominated as a best friend but are not disliked by their peers. Rejected children are infrequently nominated as a best friend and are actively disliked by peers. Controversial children are frequently nominated both as someone's best friend and as being disliked. Rejected children are at risk for a number of problems.
	Social cognition	Social information-processing skills and social knowledge are two important dimensions of social cognition in peer relations.
	Friends	Children's friendships serve six functions: companionship, stimulation, physical support, ego support, social comparison, and intimacy/affection. Intimacy and similarity are common characteristics of friendships.
Schools	The transition to elementary school	Children spend more than 10,000 hours in the classroom as members of a small society in which there are tasks to be accomplished, people to be socialized and socialized by, and rules that define and limit behavior. A special concern is that early schooling proceeds mainly on the basis of negative feedback to children.
	Teachers	Teachers have prominent influences in middle and late childhood. Aptitude-treatment interaction is an important consideration.
	Socioeconomic status and ethnicity	Children in poverty face problems at home and at school that present barriers to their learning. Schools in low-income neighborhoods often have fewer resources, have less experienced teachers, and are more likely to encourage rote learning rather than thinking skills. The school experiences of students from different ethnic groups vary considerably. It is important for teachers to have positive expectations for and challenge children of color to achieve. Among the strategies teachers can follow for improving relations among ethnically diverse students are to turn the classroom into a jigsaw classroom, to encourage positive personal contact among ethnically diverse students, to stimulate perspective taking, to reduce bias, to view the school and the community as a team, and to be a competent cultural mediator.

At various places in the chapter, we have discussed strategies that support children's socioemotional development. The insert, Improving Developmental Skills, profiles these strategies. We also have discussed many ideas about families, peers, and schools in middle and late childhood. An overview of these ideas is presented in summary table 14.2.

Chapter Review

Children's socioemotional development changes in many ways during middle and late childhood. Their socioemotional worlds widen and become more complex.

We began the chapter by exploring the poverty and violence in the lives of Lafayette and Pharoah, discussing factors that help children be resilient in the face of these stressful circumstances. Our coverage of emotional and personality development focused on the self, emotional development, moral development, and gender. We examined the following aspects of families: parent-child issues and societal changes in families. We also studied peer relations, including peer statuses, social cognition, and friends. In discussing schools, we evaluated the transition to school, teachers, and socioeconomic status and ethnicity in schools.

Remember that you can obtain a more detailed overview of the chapter by again studying the two summary tables on pages 418 and 431. This concludes our exploration of middle and late childhood. In Section VI, we will follow children's development through adolescence, beginning with chapter 15, "Physical Development in Adolescence."

Children Checklist

Socioemotional Development in Middle and Late Childhood

How much have you learned since the beginning of the chapter? Use the following statements to help you review your knowledge and understanding of the chapter material. First, read the statement and mentally or briefly demonstrate on paper that you can discuss the relevant information.

_____ I can discuss the development of the self in middle and late childhood.
_____ I know about emotional changes that take place in middle and late childhood.
_____ I can describe Kohlberg's theory of moral development.
_____ I can discuss altruism.
_____ I am aware of what is involved in gender development.
_____ I can describe parenting in this age period.
_____ I know about peer relations and friendship.
_____ I can describe schools in middle and late childhood.

For any items that you did not check, go back and locate the relevant material in the chapter. Review the material until you feel you can check off the item. You may want to use this checklist later in preparing for an exam.

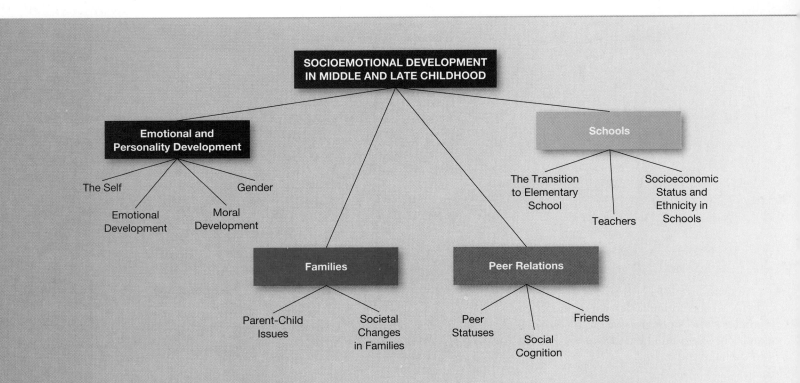

Key Terms

perspective taking 400

self-esteem 401

self-concept 401

Self-Perception Profile for
    Children 402

internalization 407

preconventional reasoning 407

punishment and obedience
    orientation 407

individualism and purpose
    407

conventional reasoning 407

interpersonal norms 407

social system morality 407

postconventional reasoning
    407

community rights versus
    individual rights 407

universal ethical principles 408

justice perspective 409

care perspective 409

altruism 410

gender stereotypes 411

rapport talk 414

report talk 414

androgyny 415

gender-role transcendence 416

boundary ambiguity 420

popular children 422

neglected children 422

rejected children 422

controversial children 422

intimacy in friendships 425

aptitude-treatment interaction
    (ATI) 427

Children Resources

Children: The Challenge
(1964) by Rudolph Dreikurs.
New York: Hawthorne Books.

Children: The Challenge tells parents how to discipline their children
more effectively. The author discusses a wide range of situations in
which discipline is called for. Although it was written over three
decades ago, this book is still one of the books on parental discipline
most widely recommended by mental health professionals.

Raising Black Children
(1992) by James P. Comer
and Alvin E. Poussaint.
New York: Plume.

This is an excellent book for African American parents. It includes wise
suggestions that are not in most child-rearing books (almost all others
are written for middle-class White parents and do not deal with special
problems faced by ethnic minority parents or parents from low-income
backgrounds).

Stepfamily Association of America
602 East Joppa Road
Baltimore, MD 21204
410–823–7570

This organization provides a support network for stepparents, remarried
parents, and their children. It has local chapters across the United
States and published materials on stepfamilies.

Taking It to the Net

http://www.mhhe.com/santrockcd6

1. Imagine you are a nurse at a local hospital. You have just had a conversation with a doctor
   and she asked you to complete several tasks immediately, even though you told her that
   you were very busy. What's the most beneficial emotion to exhibit? Anger? Defiance? Joy?
   Pity? Are you able to determine the difference between the emotion you have and the
   emotion you believe you should have? Is there an advantage to being emotionally
   intelligent? Are you emotionally intelligent?

2. Do you value yourself? How would you rate your own self worth? Low? High? Self-esteem,
   one's perception of self-worth, is an important aspect of one's self-concept. What is your
   self-esteem? Take a look and see!

3. Does the information age present a new twist on traditional morality issues? What special
   morality issues does cyberspace present? How are people coping with these issues? How
   would you cope with these issues?

Middle and Late Childhood

Physical Development

During the elementary school years, children grow an average of 2 to 3 inches a year. Muscle mass and strength gradually increase. Legs lengthen and trunks slim down. Growth is slow and consistent. Motor development becomes smoother and more coordinated. Boys are usually better at gross motor skills, girls at fine motor skills. Our nation's children are not getting enough exercise. A special concern is stress in children's lives—both life events and daily hassles can cause stress. Sociocultural factors, such as poverty, can place considerable stress on children. One of children's important buffers against stress is the long-term presence of a basic trusting relationship with at least one adult. A readily available support network is also important. Of special concern are children with a disability, including children with a learning disability or attention deficit/hyperactivity disorder.

Cognitive Development

According to Piaget, the cognitive development of children 7 to 11 years old is characterized by concrete operational thought. Concrete operations are mental actions that are reversible. We owe Piaget the present field of cognitive development. However, Piaget's theory, especially his stage concept, has not gone uncriticized. Neo-Piagetians believe that children's cognitive development is more specific than Piaget proposed. Children's long-term memory, scientific reasoning, and cognitive monitoring improve during middle and late childhood. It is important for children to engage in critical thinking. One issue in intelligence is whether it is a general ability or a number of specific abilities. Concerns include the cultural bias of intelligence tests and the misuse of the tests. The extremes of intelligence are mental retardation and giftedness. Children's creativity should be encouraged. In middle and late childhood, children become more analytical and logical in their approach to words and grammar. Reading is a more central aspect of language in the middle and late childhood years. No negative effects of bilingualism have been found. Contemporary ideas about achievement focus on the distinction between intrinsic and extrinsic motivation, a mastery versus helpless or performance orientations, and ethnic minority children's achievement.

Socioemotional Development

The internal self, the social self, and the socially comparative self become more prominent in self-understanding in middle and late childhood. Perspective taking increases in this period. Self-concept and self-esteem are important dimensions of the child's socioemotional development. Children show an increased understanding of such complex emotions as pride and shame, are more likely to suppress or conceal emotions, and use self-initiated strategies to redirect feelings. Emotional intelligence is increasingly believed to be an important aspect of social competence. Two good strategies for helping children cope with stress are to remove at least one stressor from their lives and to help them develop effective coping strategies. Kohlberg developed a provocative theory of moral reasoning, which involves three levels (preconventional, conventional, and postconventional) and six stages. Kohlberg's theory has been criticized, especially by Gilligan, who believes he underestimated the importance of the care perspective. Children's altruism changes developmentally. Gender is an important aspect of elementary school children's development, especially gender stereotypes, similarities and differences, gender-role classification, and gender in context. Parents spend less time with children in middle and late childhood, but parents are still very important socializing agents in this period. New parent-child issues emerge, and discipline changes. Control is more coregulatory. In middle and late childhood, two major changes in many children's lives are moving into a stepfamily and becoming a latchkey child. Children spend considerably more time with peers in this period. Distinctions in peer relations are made between popular children, rejected children, and neglected children. Friendships become more important in middle and late childhood. A special concern about early elementary education is that it proceeds mainly on the basis of negative feedback to children. Another special concern is the education of children from poverty backgrounds and the improvement of interethnic relations.

Adolescence

> *I*n no order of
> things is adolescence
> the simple time of life.
>
> **Jean Erskine Stewart**
> **American Writer, 20th Century**

Adolescents try on one face after another, seeking to find a face of their own. Their generation of young people is the fragile cable by which the best and the worst of their parents' generation is transmitted to the present. In the end, there are only two lasting bequests parents can leave youth—one being roots, the other wings. Section VI contains three chapters: "Physical Development in Adolescence" (chapter 15), "Cognitive Development in Adolescence" (chapter 16), and "Socioemotional Development in Adolescence" (chapter 17).

Chapter
15

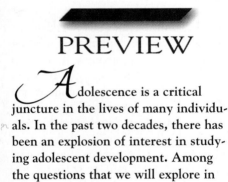

PREVIEW

Adolescence is a critical juncture in the lives of many individuals. In the past two decades, there has been an explosion of interest in studying adolescent development. Among the questions that we will explore in this chapter are

- Is adolescence primarily a biological stage, or is it a sociohistorical invention?
- What is the life of today's youth like?
- What causes puberty? What are some of puberty's main changes?
- How are adolescents affected by maturing early or late?
- What are the leading causes of death in adolescence?
- How sexually active are adolescents? How does the adolescent pregnancy rate in the United States compare with that in other countries?
- What are some eating disorders in adolescence?
- How do cognitive and sociocultural factors influence adolescent health?

Stories of the Mysteries and Curiosities of Adolescent Sexuality

I am 16 years old, and I really like this one girl. She wants to be a virgin until she marries. We went out last night, and she let me go pretty far, but not all the way. I know she really likes me, too, but she always stops me when things start getting hot and heavy. It is getting hard for me to handle. She doesn't know it, but I'm a virgin, too. I feel I am ready to have sex. I have to admit I think about having sex with other girls, too. Maybe I should be dating other girls.

Frank C.

I'm 14 years old. I have a lot of sexy thoughts. Sometimes, just before I drift off to sleep at night, I think about this hunk who is 16 years old and plays on the football team. He is so gorgeous, and I can feel him holding me in his arms and kissing and hugging me. When I'm walking down the hall between classes at school, I sometimes start daydreaming about guys I have met and wonder what it would be like to have sex with them. Last year I had this crush on the men's track coach. I'm on the girls' track team, so I saw him a lot during the year. He hardly knew I thought about him the way I did, although I tried to flirt with him several times.

Amy S.

Is it weird to be a 17-year-old guy and still be a virgin? Sometimes, I feel like the only 17-year-old male on the planet who has not had sex. I feel like I am missing out on something great, or at least that's what I hear. I'm pretty religious, and I sometimes feel guilty when I think about sex. The thought runs through my mind that maybe it is best to wait until I'm married or at least until I have a long-term relationship that matters a lot to me.

Tom B.

I'm 15 years old, and I had sex for the first time recently. I had all of these expectations about how great it was going to be. He didn't have much experience either. We were both pretty scared about the whole thing. It was all over in a hurry. My first thought was, "Is that all there is?" It was a very disappointing experience.

Claire T.

I've felt differently than most boys for a long time and I had my first crush on another boy when I was 13. I'm 16 years old now and I'm finally starting to come to grips with the fact that I am gay. I haven't told my parents yet. I don't know if they will be able to handle it. I'm still a little confused by all of this. I know I will have to "come out" at some point.

Jason R.

439

Adolescent Issues

storm-and-stress view
Hall's view that adolescence is a turbulent time, charged with conflict and mood swings.

inventionist view
The belief that adolescence is a sociohistorical creation. Especially important in the development of the inventionist view of adolescence were the sociohistorical circumstances at the beginning of the twentieth century, a time when legislation was enacted that ensured the dependency of youth and made their move into the economic sphere more manageable.

THE NATURE OF ADOLESCENCE

As in the development of children, genetic, biological, environmental, and social factors interact in adolescent development. Also, continuity and discontinuity characterize adolescent development. The genes inherited from parents still influence thought and behavior during adolescence, but inheritance now interacts with the social conditions of the adolescent's world—with family, peers, friendships, dating, and school experiences. An adolescent has experienced thousands of hours of interaction with parents, peers, and teachers in the past 10 to 13 years of development. Still new experiences and developmental tasks appear during adolescence. Relationships with parents take a different form, moments with peers become more intimate, and dating occurs for the first time, as do sexual exploration and possibly intercourse. The adolescent's thoughts are more abstract and idealistic. Biological changes trigger a heightened interest in body image. Adolescence, then, has both continuity and discontinuity with childhood.

The Biological and Sociohistorical Nature of Adolescence

Is adolescence a biologically based period, or is it a sociohistorical invention? Both views have been proposed. First, we will examine G. Stanley Hall's biological view, which emphasizes the storm and stress of adolescence; second, we will study the inventionist view of adolescence.

G. Stanley Hall's View   Historians label G. Stanley Hall (1844–1924) the father of the scientific study of adolescence. Hall's ideas were first published in 1904 in a two-volume set titled *Adolescence* (Hall, 1904). Hall was strongly influenced by Charles Darwin, the famous evolutionary theorist, and applied the scientific and biological dimensions of Darwin's view to the study of adolescent development. He believed that all development is controlled by genetically determined physiological factors and argued that environment plays a minimal role in development, especially during infancy and childhood. However, Hall did acknowledge that environment accounts for more change in development in adolescence than in earlier periods. Thus, at least with regard to adolescence, Hall believed—as we do today—that heredity interacts with environmental influences to determine an individual's development.

Hall said that adolescence is filled with storm and stress. The **storm-and-stress view** *is Hall's concept that adolescence is a turbulent time, charged with conflict and mood swings.* He borrowed the "storm and stress" label from the *Sturm und Drang* descriptions of such German writers as Goethe and Schiller, who wrote novels full of idealism, commitment to goals, passion, feeling, and revolution. Hall sensed a parallel between the themes of the German authors and the psychological development of adolescents. In Hall's view, adolescents' thoughts, feelings, and actions oscillate between conceit and humility, good and temptation, happiness and sadness. The adolescent may be nasty to a peer one moment, kind the next moment. At one time the adolescent may want to be alone but seconds later seek companionship.

The Inventionist View   While adolescence has a biological base, as G. Stanley Hall believed, adolescence also has a sociohistorical base. Indeed, sociohistorical conditions contributed to the emergence of the concept of adolescence. At a point not too long ago, the concept of "teenager" had not yet been invented. The **inventionist view** *states that adolescence is a sociohistorical creation. Especially important in the invention of the concept of adolescence were the sociohistorical circumstances at the beginning of the twentieth century, a time when legislation was enacted* *that ensured the dependency of youth and helped make their move into the economic sphere more manageable.* The sociohistorical circumstances included a decline in apprenticeship; increased mechanization during the Industrial Revolution, which also involved upgraded skills requirements of labor and specialized divisions of labor; the separation of home and work; the writings of G. Stanley Hall; urbanization; the appearance of youth groups, such as the YMCA and Boy Scouts; and age-segregated schools.

Schools, work, and economics are important dimensions of the inventionist view of adolescence (Lapsley, Enright, & Serlin, 1985). Some scholars of adolescence argue that the invention of the concept of adolescence was mainly a by-product of the motivation to create a system of compulsory public education. In this view, the function of secondary schools is to transmit intellectual skills to youth. However, other scholars of adolescence argue that the primary purpose of secondary schools is to deploy youth within the economic sphere and to serve as an important cog in the authority structure of the culture. In this view, the American society "inflicted" the status of adolescence on its youth through child-saving legislation. By developing laws for youth, the adult power structure placed youth in a submissive position that restricted their options, encouraged their dependency, and made their move into the world of work more manageable.

Today's Youth

Today's adolescents face demands and expectations, as well as risks and temptations, that appear to be more numerous and complex than those faced by adolescents only a generation ago. Nonetheless, contrary to the popular stereotype of adolescents as highly stressed and incompetent, the vast majority of adolescents successfully negotiate the path from childhood to adulthood. By some criteria, today's adolescents are doing better than their counterparts from a decade or two earlier. Today, more adolescents complete high school, especially African American adolescents. The majority of adolescents today have positive self-concept and positive relationships with others.

A cross-cultural study by Daniel Offer and his colleagues (1988) supported the contention that most adolescents have positive images of themselves and contradicted the stereotype that most adolescents have problems or are disturbed in some way. The self-images of adolescents around the world were sampled—in the United States, Australia, Bangladesh, Hungary, Israel, Italy, Japan, Taiwan, Turkey, and West Germany. A healthy self-image characterized at least 73 percent of the adolescents studied. They appeared to be moving toward adulthood with a healthy integration of previous experiences, self-confidence, and optimism about the future. Although there were some differences among the adolescents, they were happy most of the time, they enjoyed life, they perceived themselves as able to exercise self-control, they valued work and school, they expressed confidence about their sexual selves, they expressed positive feelings toward their families, and they felt they had the capability to cope with life's stresses: not exactly a storm-and-stress portrayal of adolescence.

According to adolescent researchers Shirley Feldman and Glenn Elliott (1990), public attitudes about adolescence emerge from a combination of personal experience and media portrayals, neither of which produce an objective picture of how normal adolescents develop. Some of the readiness to assume the worst about adolescents likely involves the short memories of adults. Many adults measure their current perceptions of adolescents by their memories of their own adolescence. Adults may portray today's adolescents as more troubled, less respectful, more self-centered, more assertive, and more adventurous than they were.

However, in matters of taste and manners, the young people of every generation have seemed radical, unnerving, and different from adults—different in how they look, in how they behave, in the music they enjoy, in their hairstyles, and

A few years ago it occurred to me that when I was a teenager, in the early depression years, there were no teenagers! The teenager has sneaked up on us in our own lifetime, and yet it seems he has always been with us. . . . The teenager had not yet been invented, though, and there did not yet exist a special class of beings, bounded in a certain way—not quite children and certainly not adults.

A. K. Cohen
American Writer, 20th Century

**Practical Resources and Research
Youth Information Directory**

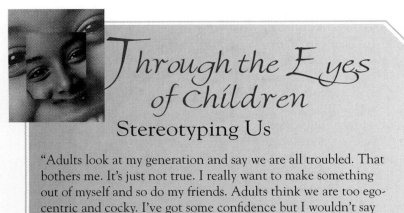

Through the Eyes of Children
Stereotyping Us

"Adults look at my generation and say we are all troubled. That bothers me. It's just not true. I really want to make something out of myself and so do my friends. Adults think we are too ego-centric and cocky. I've got some confidence but I wouldn't say I'm cocky. I've got some insecurities like everybody else."

—Germaine, Age 16,
New York City

Profile of America's Youth
American Youth Policy Forum

in the clothing they choose. It is an enormous error, though, to confuse adolescents' enthusiasm for trying on new identities and enjoying moderate amounts of outrageous behavior with hostility toward parental and societal standards. Acting out and boundary testing are time-honored ways in which adolescents move toward accepting, rather than rejecting, parental values.

Although the majority of adolescents experience the transition from childhood to adulthood more positively than is portrayed by many adults and the media, too many adolescents today are not provided with adequate opportunities and support to become competent adults. In many ways, today's adolescents are presented with a less stable environment than adolescents of a decade or two ago. High divorce rates, high adolescent pregnancy rates, and increased geographic mobility of families contribute to this lack of stability in adolescents' lives. Today's adolescents are exposed to a complex menu of lifestyle options through the media, and, although the adolescent drug rate is beginning to show signs of decline, the rate of adolescent drug use in the United States is higher than that of any other country in the industrialized Western world. Many of today's adolescents face these temptations, as well as sexual activity, at increasingly young ages.

Our discussion underscores an important point about adolescents: they do not make up a homogeneous group (Galambos & Tilton-Weaver, 1996). Most adolescents negotiate the lengthy path to adult maturity successfully, but too large a group does not. Ethnic, cultural, gender, socioeconomic, age, and lifestyle differences influence the actual life trajectory of every adolescent. Different portrayals of adolescence emerge, depending on the particular group of adolescents being described.

Now that we have considered some historical views of adolescents and have evaluated today's adolescents, let's turn our attention to the ways in which adolescents develop physically. We will begin with the dramatic changes of puberty.

PUBERTY

One father remarked that the problem with his teenage son was not that he grew, but that he did not know when to stop growing. As we will see, there is considerable variation in the timing of the adolescent growth spurt.

Puberty's Boundaries and Determinants

Puberty can be distinguished from adolescence. For most of us, puberty has ended long before adolescence is exited, although puberty is the most important marker of the beginning of adolescence. What is puberty? **Puberty** *is a period of rapid physical maturation involving hormonal and bodily changes that occur primarily during early adolescence.*

Imagine a toddler displaying all the features of puberty—a 3-year-old girl with fully developed breasts or a boy just slightly older with a deep voice. That is what we would see by the year 2250 if the age at which puberty arrives kept getting younger at its present pace. In Norway, **menarche**—*a girl's first menstruation*—occurs at just over 13 years of age, compared to 17 years of age in the 1840s. In the United States—where children mature up to a year earlier than children in European

puberty
A period of rapid skeletal and sexual maturation that occurs mainly in early adolescence.

menarche
First menstruation.

From *Penguin Dreams and Stranger Things* by *Berke Breathed. Copyright © 1985 by The Washington Post Company. By permission of Little, Brown and Company.*

countries—the average age of menarche has been declining an average of about 4 months per decade for the past century. Fortunately, however, we are unlikely to see pubescent toddlers, since what has happened in the past century is likely the result of a higher level of nutrition and health. The available information suggests that menarche began to occur earlier at about the time of the Industrial Revolution, a period associated with increased standards of living and advances in medical science (Petersen, 1979).

Genetic factors also are involved in puberty. Puberty is not simply an environmental accident. As indicated earlier, while nutrition, health, and other factors affect puberty's timing and variations in its makeup, the basic genetic program is wired into the nature of the species (Plomin, 1993).

Another key factor in puberty's occurrence is body mass, as was mentioned earlier. Menarche occurs at a relatively consistent weight in girls. A body weight approximating 106 ± 3 pounds can trigger menarche and the end of the pubertal growth spurt. For menarche to begin and continue, fat must make up 17 percent of the girl's body weight. Both teenage anorexics whose weight drops dramatically and female athletes in certain sports (such as gymnastics) may become amenorrheic (having an absence or suppression of menstrual discharge).

In summary, puberty's determinants include nutrition, health, heredity, and body mass. So far, our discussion of puberty has emphasized its dramatic changes. Keep in mind, though, that puberty is not a single, sudden event. We know when a young boy or girl is going through puberty, but pinpointing its beginning and its end is difficult. Except for menarche, which occurs rather late in puberty, no single marker heralds puberty. For boys, the first whisker or first wet dream is an event that could mark its appearance, but both may go unnoticed.

Hormonal Changes

Behind the first whisker in boys and the widening of hips in girls is a flood of **hormones,** *powerful chemical substances secreted by the endocrine glands and carried through the body by the bloodstream.* The endocrine system's role in puberty involves the interaction of the hypothalamus, the pituitary gland, and the gonads (sex glands). The **hypothalamus** *is a structure in the higher portion of the brain that monitors eating, drinking, and sex.* The **pituitary gland** *is an important endocrine gland that controls growth and regulates other glands.* The **gonads** *are the sex glands—the testes in males, the ovaries in females.* How does this hormonal system work? The pituitary sends a signal via

Biological Changes

hormones
Powerful chemical substances secreted by the endocrine glands and carried through the body by the bloodstream.

hypothalamus
A structure in the higher portion of the brain that monitors eating, drinking, and sex.

pituitary gland
An important endocrine gland that controls growth and regulates other glands.

gonads
The sex glands—the testes in males and the ovaries in females.

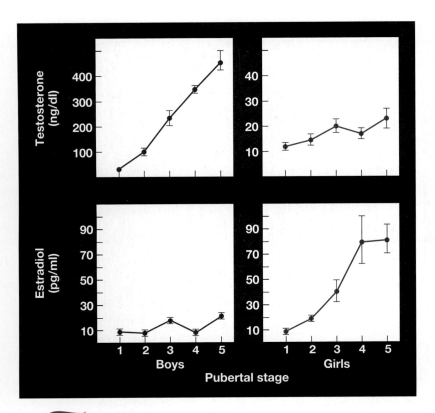

Figure 15.1
Hormone Levels by Sex and Pubertal Stage for Testosterone and Estradiol

The five stages range from the early beginning of puberty (stage 1) to the most advanced stage of puberty (stage 5).

androgens
The main class of male sex hormones.

estrogens
The main class of female sex hormones.

testosterone
A hormone associated in boys with the development of genitals, an increase in height, and a change in voice.

estradiol
A hormone associated in girls with breast, uterine, and skeletal development.

gonadotropins (hormones that stimulate the testes or ovaries) to the appropriate gland to manufacture the hormone. Then the pituitary gland, through interaction with the hypothalamus, detects when the optimal level of hormones is reached and responds by maintaining gonadotropin secretion.

Two primary classes of hormones are important in pubertal development—androgens and estrogens. **Androgens** *are the main class of male sex hormones.* **Estrogens** *are the main class of female hormones.* Researchers have examined which androgens and which estrogens show the strongest increases during puberty. **Testosterone** *is an androgen that plays an important role in male pubertal development.* Throughout puberty, increasing testosterone levels are associated with a number of physical changes in boys—the development of external genitals, an increase in height, and voice changes. **Estradiol** *is an estrogen that plays an important role in female pubertal development.* As the estradiol level rises, breast development, uterine development, and skeletal changes occur. In one study, testosterone levels increased eighteenfold in boys but only twofold in girls across the pubertal period; estradiol levels increased eightfold in girls but only twofold in boys during puberty (Nottleman & others, 1987) (see figure 15.1). Note that both testosterone and estradiol are present in the hormonal makeup of both boys and girls but that testosterone dominates in male pubertal development, estradiol in female pubertal development.

The same influx of hormones that puts hair on a male's chest and imparts curvature to a female's breast may contribute to psychological development in adolescence (Dorn & Lucas, 1995). In one study of 108 normal boys and girls ranging in age from 9 to 14, a higher concentration of testosterone was present in boys who rated themselves more socially competent (Nottelmann & others, 1987). In another study, of 60 normal boys and girls in the same age range, girls with higher estradiol levels expressed more anger and aggression (Inoff-Germain & others,1988). However, hormonal effects by themselves do not account for adolescent development. For example, in one study, social factors accounted for two to four times as much variance as did hormonal factors in young adolescent girls' depression and anger (Brooks-Gunn & Warren, 1989). Also, behavior and moods can affect hormones (Paikoff, Buchanan, & Brooks-Gunn, 1991). Stress, eating patterns, exercise, sexual activity, tension, and depression can activate or suppress various aspects of the hormonal system. In sum, the hormone-behavior link is complex.

One additional aspect of the pituitary gland's role in development still needs to be described. Not only does the pituitary gland release gonadotropins that stimulate the testes and ovaries, but through interaction with the hypothalamus the pituitary gland also secretes hormones that either directly lead to growth and skeletal maturation or produce such growth effects through interaction with the *thyroid gland*, located in the neck region.

An overview of the locations and functions of the major endocrine glands is shown in figure 15.2. Now that we have studied the endocrine system's important role in puberty, we will turn our attention to the external physical changes that characterize puberty.

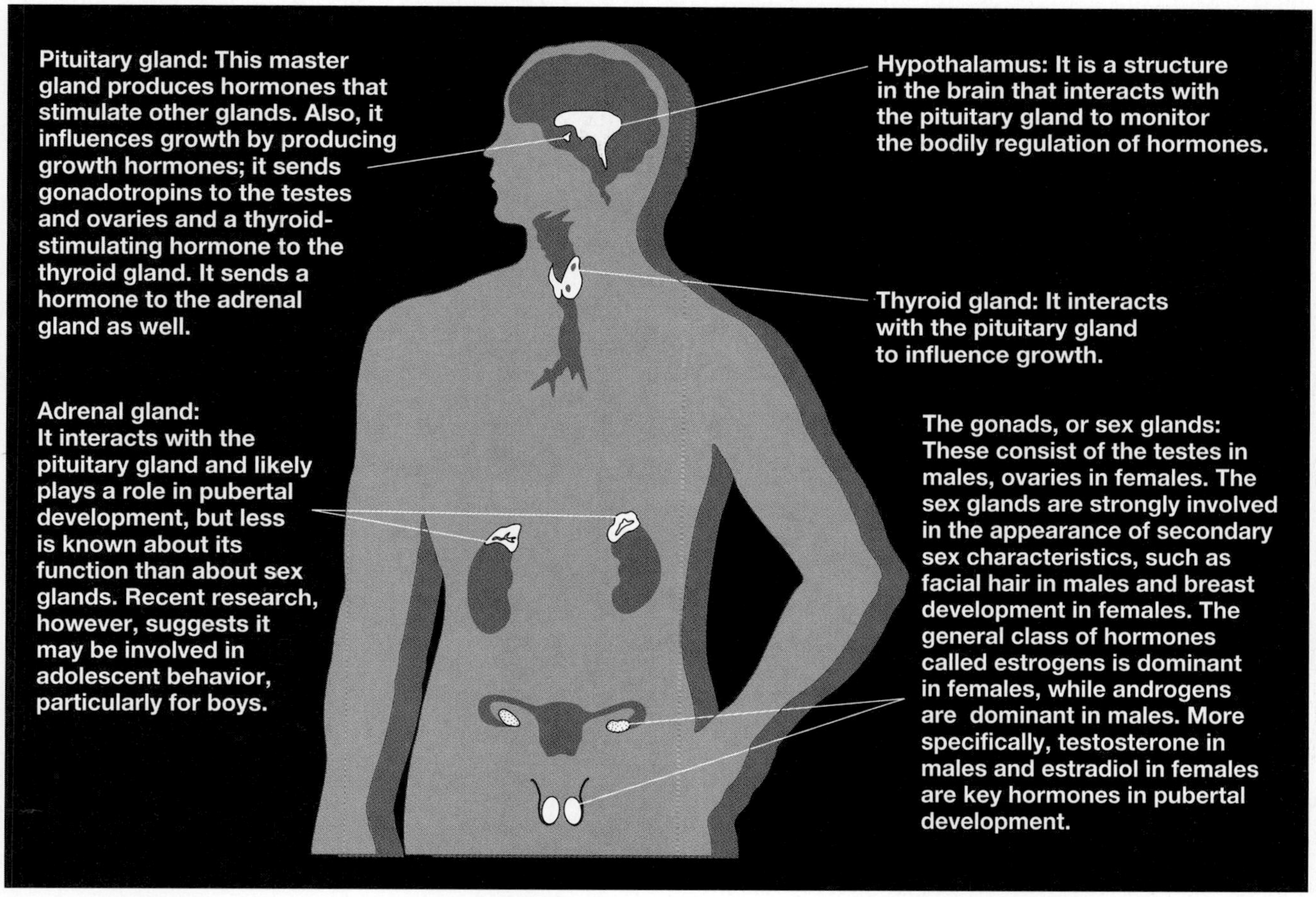

Pituitary gland: This master gland produces hormones that stimulate other glands. Also, it influences growth by producing growth hormones; it sends gonadotropins to the testes and ovaries and a thyroid-stimulating hormone to the thyroid gland. It sends a hormone to the adrenal gland as well.

Hypothalamus: It is a structure in the brain that interacts with the pituitary gland to monitor the bodily regulation of hormones.

Thyroid gland: It interacts with the pituitary gland to influence growth.

Adrenal gland: It interacts with the pituitary gland and likely plays a role in pubertal development, but less is known about its function than about sex glands. Recent research, however, suggests it may be involved in adolescent behavior, particularly for boys.

The gonads, or sex glands: These consist of the testes in males, ovaries in females. The sex glands are strongly involved in the appearance of secondary sex characteristics, such as facial hair in males and breast development in females. The general class of hormones called estrogens is dominant in females, while androgens are dominant in males. More specifically, testosterone in males and estradiol in females are key hormones in pubertal development.

Figure 15.2
The Major Endocrine Glands Involved in Pubertal Change

Height, Weight, and Sexual Maturation

Among the most noticeable physical changes during puberty are increases in height and weight, as well as sexual maturation.

Height and Weight   As indicated in figure 15.3, the growth spurt occurs approximately two years earlier for girls than for boys (Abbassi, 1998). The mean beginning of the growth spurt in girls is 9 years of age; for boys, it is 11 years of age. The peak rate of pubertal change occurs at 11.5 years for girls and 13.5 years for boys. During their growth spurt, girls increase in height about 3½ inches per year, boys about 4 inches.

Boys and girls who are shorter or taller than their peers before adolescence are likely to remain so during adolescence. In our society, there is a stigma attached to short boys. At the beginning of the adolescent period, girls tend to be as tall as or taller than boys of their age, but by the end of the middle school years most boys have caught up or, in many cases, have even surpassed girls in height. And, even though height in the elementary school years is a good predictor of height later in adolescence, there is still room for the individual's height to change in relation to the height of his or her peers. As much as 30 percent of the height of late adolescence is unexplained by height in the elementary school years.

The rate at which adolescents gain weight follows approximately the same developmental timetable as the rate at which they gain height. Marked weight gains

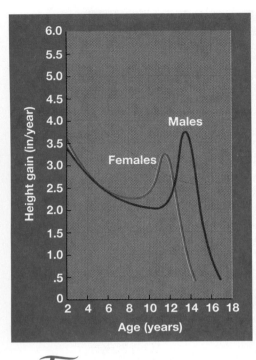

*F*igure 15.3
Pubertal Growth Spurt

On the average, the growth spurt that characterizes pubertal change occurs two years earlier for girls (10½) than for boys (12½).

coincide with the onset of puberty. During early adolescence, girls tend to outweigh boys, but, just as with height, by about age 14 boys begin to surpass girls.

Sexual Maturation   Think back to the onset of your puberty. Of the striking changes that were taking place in your body, what was the first change that occurred? Researchers have found that male pubertal characteristics develop in this order: increase in penis and testicle size, appearance of straight pubic hair, minor voice change, first ejaculation (which usually occurs through masturbation or a wet dream), appearance of kinky pubic hair, onset of maximum growth, growth of hair in armpits, more detectable voice changes, and growth of facial hair. Three of the most noticeable areas of sexual maturation in boys are penis elongation, testes development, and growth of facial hair. The normal range and average age of development for these sexual characteristics, along with height spurt, are shown in figure 15.4. Figure 15.5 shows the typical course of male sexual development during puberty.

What is the order of appearance of physical changes in females? First, either the breasts enlarge or pubic hair appears. Later, hair appears in the armpits. As these changes occur, the female grows in height, and her hips become wider than her shoulders. Her first menstruation comes rather late in the pubertal cycle. Initially, her menstrual cycles may be highly irregular. For the first several years, she might not ovulate every menstrual cycle. Some girls do not become fertile until 2 years after the period begins. No voice changes comparable to those in pubertal males occur in pubertal females. By the end of puberty, the female's breasts have become more fully rounded. Two of the most noticeable aspects of female pubertal change are pubic hair and breast development. Figure 15.4 shows the normal range and average development of these sexual characteristics and also provides information about menarche and height gain. Figure 15.5 shows the typical course of female sexual development during puberty.

It should be noted that less is known about the sequence of pubertal changes in females than is known about the sequence of such changes in males (Susman, 1995). Pubertal changes in females unfold in a less clear-cut way than they do in males.

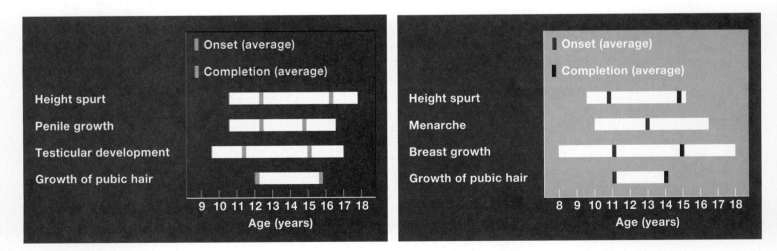

*F*igure 15.4
Normal Range and Average Development of Sexual Characteristics in Males and Females

MALE SEXUAL DEVELOPMENT

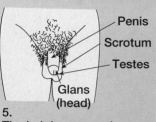

Penis
Scrotum
Testes
Glans (head)

1.
No pubic hair. The testes, scrotum, and penis are about the same size and shape as those of a child.

2.
A little soft, long, lightly colored hair, mostly at the base of the penis. This hair may be straight or a little curly. The testes and scrotum have enlarged, and the skin of the scrotum has changed. The scrotum, the sack holding the testes, has lowered a bit. The penis has grown only a little.

3.
The hair is darker coarser, and more curled. It has spread to thinly cover a somewhat larger area. The penis has grown mainly in length. The testes and scrotum have grown and dropped lower than in stage 2.

4.
The hair is now as dark, curly, and coarse as that of an adult male. However, the area that the hair covers is not as large as that of an adult male; it has not spread to the thighs. The penis has grown even larger and wider. The glans (the head of the penis) is bigger. The scrotum is darker and bigger because the testes have gotten bigger.

5.
The hair has spread to the thighs and is now like that of an adult male. The penis, scrotum, and testes are the size and shape of those of an adult male.

FEMALE SEXUAL DEVELOPMENT

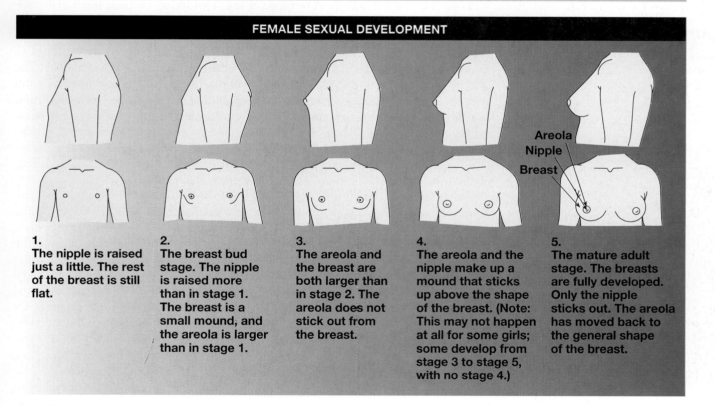

Areola
Nipple
Breast

1.
The nipple is raised just a little. The rest of the breast is still flat.

2.
The breast bud stage. The nipple is raised more than in stage 1. The breast is a small mound, and the areola is larger than in stage 1.

3.
The areola and the breast are both larger than in stage 2. The areola does not stick out from the breast.

4.
The areola and the nipple make up a mound that sticks up above the shape of the breast. (Note: This may not happen at all for some girls; some develop from stage 3 to stage 5, with no stage 4.)

5.
The mature adult stage. The breasts are fully developed. Only the nipple sticks out. The areola has moved back to the general shape of the breast.

Figure 15.5
The Five Pubertal Stages of Male and Female Sexual Development

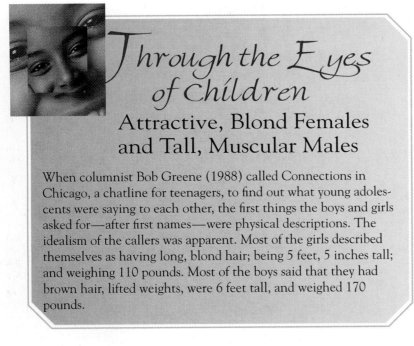

Through the Eyes of Children

Attractive, Blond Females and Tall, Muscular Males

When columnist Bob Greene (1988) called Connections in Chicago, a chatline for teenagers, to find out what young adolescents were saying to each other, the first things the boys and girls asked for—after first names—were physical descriptions. The idealism of the callers was apparent. Most of the girls described themselves as having long, blond hair; being 5 feet, 5 inches tall; and weighing 110 pounds. Most of the boys said that they had brown hair, lifted weights, were 6 feet tall, and weighed 170 pounds.

Individual Variation in Puberty The pubertal sequence may begin as early as 10 years of age or as late as 13½ for most boys. It may end as early as 13 years or as late as 17 years for most boys. The normal range is wide enough that, given two boys of the same chronological age, one might complete the pubertal sequence before the other one has begun it. For girls, the age range of the first menstrual period is even wider. Menarche is considered within a normal range if it appears between the ages of 9 and 15.

Menarche and the Menstrual Cycle

The onset of puberty and menarche has often been described as a "main event" in most historical accounts of adolescence (Erikson, 1968; Freud, 1958; Hall, 1904). Basically, these views suggest that pubertal changes and such events as menarche produce a different body that requires considerable change in self-conception, possibly resulting in an identity crisis. Only recently has there been empirical research directed at understanding the female adolescent's adaptation to menarche and the menstrual cycle (Brooks-Gunn, Graber, & Paikoff, 1994).

In one study of 639 girls, a wide range of reactions to menarche appeared (Brooks-Gunn & Ruble, 1982). However, most of the reactions were quite mild, as the girls described their first period as a little upsetting, a little surprising, or a little exciting and positive. In this study, 120 of the fifth- and sixth-grade girls were telephoned to obtain more personal, detailed information about their experience with menarche. The most frequent theme of the girls' responses was positive—namely, that menarche was an index of their maturity. Other positive reports indicated that the girls could now have children, were experiencing something that made them more like adult women, and now were more like their friends. The most frequent negative aspects of menarche reported by the girls were its hassle (having to carry supplies around) and its messiness. A minority of the girls also indicated that menarche involved physical discomfort, produced behavioral limitations, and created emotional changes.

In that study, questions also were asked about the extent to which the girls communicated with others about the appearance of menarche, the extent to which the girls were prepared for menarche, and how the experience was related to early/late maturation. Virtually all of the girls told their mothers immediately, but most of the girls did not tell anyone else about menarche, with only one in five informing a friend. However, after two or three periods had occurred, most of the girls had talked with girlfriends about menstruation. The girls not prepared for menarche indicated more negative feelings about menstruation than those who were more prepared for its onset. The girls who matured early had more negative reactions than the average- or late-maturing girls. In summary, menarche initially may be disruptive, especially for unprepared and early-maturing girls, but it typically does not reach the tumultuous, conflicting proportions described by some early theoreticians.

In discussing menarche, we have explored some of its psychological accompaniments. Let's now turn our attention to another psychological dimension of pubertal change: body image.

Body Image

One psychological aspect of physical change in puberty is certain: adolescents are preoccupied with their bodies and develop individual images of what their bodies are like. Perhaps you looked in the mirror on a daily and sometimes even hourly basis to see if you could detect anything different about your changing body. Preoccupation with one's body image is strong throughout adolescence, but it is especially acute during puberty, a time when adolescents are more dissatisfied with their bodies than in late adolescence (Wright, 1989).

There are gender differences in adolescents' perceptions of their bodies. In general, girls are less happy with their bodies and have more negative body images, compared with boys, throughout puberty (Brooks-Gunn & Paikoff, 1993; Henderson & Zivian, 1995). Also, as pubertal change proceeds, girls often become more dissatisfied with their bodies, probably because their body fat increases, while boys become more satisfied as they move through puberty, probably because their muscle mass increases (Gross, 1984).

Early and Late Maturation

Some of you entered puberty early, others late, and yet others on time. When adolescents mature earlier or later than their peers, might they perceive themselves differently? In the Berkeley Longitudinal Study some years ago, early-maturing boys perceived themselves more positively and had more successful peer relations than did their late-maturing counterparts (Jones, 1965). The findings for early-maturing girls were similar but not as strong as for boys. When the late-maturing boys were in their thirties, however, they had developed a

Adolescents show a strong preoccupation with their changing bodies and develop individual images of what their bodies are like. Adolescent boys, as well as adolescent girls, rate body build as one of the most important dimensions of physical attractiveness.

stronger sense of identity than the early-maturing boys had (Peskin, 1967). Possibly this occurred because the late-maturing boys had more time to explore life's options or because the early-maturing boys continued to focus on their advantageous physical status instead of on career development and achievement.

More recent research confirms, though, that at least during adolescence it is advantageous to be an early-maturing rather than a late-maturing boy (Simmons & Blyth, 1987). The more recent findings for girls suggest that early maturation is a mixed blessing: these girls experience more problems in school but also more independence and popularity with boys. The time that maturation is assessed also is a factor. In the sixth grade, early-maturing girls show greater satisfaction with their figures than do late-maturing girls, but by the tenth grade late-maturing girls are more satisfied. The reason for this is that, in late adolescence, early-maturing girls are shorter and stockier, whereas late-maturing girls are taller and thinner. Late-maturing girls in late adolescence have bodies that more closely approximate the current American ideal of feminine beauty—tall and thin.

In the past decade, an increasing number of researchers have found that early maturation increases girls' vulnerability to a number of problems (Brooks-Gunn & Paikoff, 1993). Early-maturing girls are more likely to smoke, drink, be depressed, have an eating disorder, request earlier independence from their parents, and have older friends; and their bodies are likely to elicit responses from males that lead to earlier dating and earlier sexual experiences. In one study, the early-maturing girls had lower educational and occupational attainment in adulthood (Stattin & Magnusson, 1990). Apparently as a result of their social and cognitive immaturity, combined with early physical development, early-maturing girls are easily lured into problem behaviors, not recognizing the possible long-term effects of these on their development (Petersen, 1993).

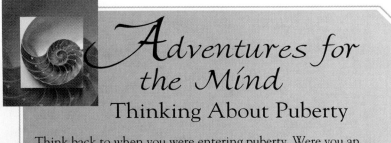

Some researchers now question whether the effects of puberty are as strong as once believed (Petersen, 1993). Puberty affects some adolescents more strongly than others and some behaviors more strongly than others. Body image, dating interest, and sexual behavior are affected by pubertal change. The recent questioning of puberty's effects suggests that, in terms of overall development and adjustment in the human life span, pubertal variations (such as early and late maturation) are less dramatic than is commonly thought. In thinking about puberty's effects, keep in mind that an adolescent's world involves cognitive and socioemotional changes, as well as physical changes. As with all periods of development, these processes work in concert to produce who we are in adolescence. To think further about early and late maturation, see Adventures for the Mind.

Pubertal Timing and Health Care

What can be done to identify off-time maturers who are at risk for health problems? Many adolescents whose development is extremely early or extremely late are likely to come to the attention of a physician—such as a boy who has not had a spurt in height by the age of 16 or a girl who has not menstruated by the age of 15. Girls and boys who are early or late maturers but are well within the normal range are less likely to be taken to a physician because of their maturational status. Nonetheless, these boys and girls may have fears and doubts about being normal that they do not raise unless a physician, a counselor, or another health care provider takes the initiative. A brief discussion outlining the sequence and timing of events and the large individual variations in them may be all that is required to reassure many adolescents who are maturing very early or very late.

Health care providers also may want to discuss the adolescent's off-time development with his or her parents. Information about the peer pressures of off-time development can be beneficial. Especially helpful to early-maturing girls is a discussion of peer pressures to date and to engage in adultlike behavior at an early age. The transition to middle school, junior high school, or high school may be more stressful for girls and boys who are in the midst of puberty than for those who are not (Brooks-Gunn & Reiter, 1990).

If pubertal development is extremely late, a physician may recommend hormonal treatment. In one study of extended pubertal delay in boys, hormonal treatment worked to increase the height, dating interest, and peer relations in several boys but resulted in little or no improvement in other boys (Lewis, Money, & Bobrow, 1977).

In sum, most early- and late-maturing individuals weather puberty's challenges and stresses competently. For those who do not, discussions with sensitive and knowledgeable health care providers and parents can improve the off-time maturing adolescent's coping abilities.

At this point, we have discussed a number of ideas about the nature of adolescence and pubertal development. An overview of these ideas is presented in summary table 15.1. Next, we will further examine the nature of adolescent health.

Adolescent Health

ADOLESCENT HEALTH

Many of the factors linked to poor health habits and early death in the adult years begin during adolescence. Some behaviors warrant considerable concern because of their potential for harm during adolescence, such as the use of drugs and the neu-

Summary Table 15.1
The Nature of Adolescence and Pubertal Development

Concept	Processes/ Related Ideas	Characteristics/Description
The nature of adolescence	The biological and sociohistorical natures of adolescence	G. Stanley Hall is the father of the scientific study of adolescence. His storm-and-stress view emphasizes the biological basis of adolescence. In contrast, the inventionist view states that adolescence is a sociohistorical creation; the concept of adolescence emerged at the beginning of the twentieth century, when the enactment of legislation ensured the dependency of youth and made their move into the economic sphere more manageable.
	Today's youth	Many stereotypes of adolescents are too negative. Most adolescents today successfully negotiate the path from childhood to adulthood. By some criteria, today's adolescents also are doing better than their counterparts from a decade or two earlier. However, too many of today's adolescents are not provided with adequate opportunities and support to become competent adults. In many ways, today's adolescents are presented with a less stable environment. It is important to view adolescents as a heterogeneous group because a different portrayal emerges, depending on the particular set of adolescents being described.
Puberty	Puberty's boundaries and determinants	Puberty is a rapid change to physical maturation involving hormonal and bodily changes that occur primarily during early adolescence. Puberty's determinants include nutrition, health, heredity, and body mass.
	Hormonal changes	The endocrine system's influence on puberty involves an interaction of the hypothalamus, the pituitary gland, and the gonads (sex glands). Testosterone, a member of the general class of hormones known as androgens, plays a key role in the pubertal development of males. Estradiol, a member of the general class of hormones known as estrogens, plays a key role in the pubertal development of females. Recent research has documented a link between hormonal levels and the adolescent's behavior. The pituitary gland also stimulates growth, either through the thyroid gland or, more directly, through growth hormones.
	Height, weight, and sexual maturation	The initial onset of pubertal growth occurs on the average at 9½ years for girls and 11½ years for boys, reaching a peak change at 11½ for girls and 13½ for boys. Girls grow an average of 3½ inches per year during pubertal change, boys 4 inches. Sexual maturation is a predominant feature of pubertal change and includes a number of changes in physical development, such as penile growth, testicular development, and pubic hair in boys and pubic hair and breast growth in girls. Individual variation in puberty is extensive, within a normal range that is wide enough that, given two boys of the same chronological age, one may complete the pubertal sequence before the other has begun it.
	Menarche and the menstrual cycle	Menarche is the girl's first period. Menarche and the menstrual cycle produce a wide range of reactions in girls. Those who are not prepared or who mature early tend to have more negative reactions.
	Body image	Adolescents show considerable interest in their body image. Young adolescents are more preoccupied and less satisfied with their body image than are late adolescents. Girls have more negative body images throughout puberty than boys do.
	Early and late maturation	Early maturation favors boys, at least during adolescence. As adults, though, late-maturing boys achieve more successful identities. Researchers are increasingly finding that early-maturing girls are vulnerable to many problems. Some researchers now question whether puberty's effects are as strong as once believed.
	Pubertal timing and health care	Most early- and late-maturing adolescents weather puberty's challenges competently. For those who do not, discussions with sensitive and knowledgeable health care providers and parents can improve the off-time maturing adolescent's coping abilities.

National Longitudinal Study of Adolescent Health

Youth and Mortality

If we listen to boys and girls at the very moment they seem most pimply, awkward and disagreeable, we can partly penetrate a mystery most of us once felt heavily within us, and have now forgotten. This mystery is the very process of creation of man and woman.

Colin Macinnes
Scottish Author, 20th Century

rological damage they can cause, as well as the potentially deadly combination of drugs and driving (Millstein, Petersen, & Nightingale, 1993).

We will begin our exploration of health and illness by examining the main causes of death in adolescence and then will turn to some areas in which health problems may arise, such as sexuality, substance use and abuse, and eating disorders.

Leading Causes of Death in Adolescence

Medical improvements have increased the life expectancy of today's adolescents, compared with that of their counterparts who lived earlier in the twentieth century. Still, life-threatening factors continue to exist in adolescents' lives.

The three leading causes of death in adolescence are accidents, suicide, and homicide (Takanishi, 1993). More than half of all deaths in adolescents ages 10 to 19 are due to accidents, and most of those involve motor vehicles, especially for older adolescents. Risky driving habits, such as speeding, tailgating, and driving under the influence of alcohol or other drugs, may be more important causes of these accidents than is lack of driving experience. In about 50 percent of the motor vehicle fatalities involving an adolescent, the driver has a blood alcohol level of 0.10 percent, twice the level needed to be "under the influence" in some states. A high rate of intoxication is also often present in adolescents who die as pedestrians or while using recreational vehicles.

Suicide accounts for 6 percent of the deaths in the 10-to-14 age group, a rate of 1.3 per 100,000 population; in the 15-to-19 age group, suicide accounts for 12 percent of deaths, or 9 per 100,000 population. Since the 1950s, the adolescent suicide rate has tripled. We will discuss suicide further in chapter 17, "Socioemotional Development in Adolescence."

Homicide is yet another leading cause of death in adolescence. Homicide is especially high among African American male adolescents; they are three times more likely to be killed by guns than by natural causes (Simons, Finlay, & Yang, 1991). We will discuss violence in youth further in chapter 17, "Socioemotional Development in Adolescence."

Next, we will turn out attention to some areas of adolescence in which health problems are common. To begin, we will explore adolescent sexuality.

Sexuality

During adolescence, the lives of males and females become wrapped in sexuality. Adolescence is a time of sexual exploration and experimentation, sexual fantasies and sexual realities, and the incorporation of sexuality into one's identity. At a time when sexual identity is an important developmental task of adolescence, the adolescent is confronted with conflicting sexual values and messages. Most adolescents eventually manage to develop a mature sexual identity, but most have periods of vulnerability and confusion along life's sexual journey.

Heterosexual Attitudes and Behavior
What is the current profile of the sexual activity of adolescents? Based on a national survey of adolescents, sexual intercourse is uncommon in early adolescence but becomes more common in the high school and college years (see figure 15.6) (Alan Guttmacher Institute, 1995, 1998). A summary of these findings includes

- Eight in 10 girls and 7 in 10 boys are virgins at age 15.
- The probability that adolescents will have sexual intercourse increases steadily with age, but one in five individuals has not yet had sexual intercourse by age 19.
- Initial sexual intercourse occurs in the mid- to late-adolescent years for most teenagers, about eight years before they marry; more than one-half of 17-year-olds have had sexual intercourse.

- Most adolescent females' first voluntary sexual partners are either younger, the same age, or no more than two years older; 27 percent are three to four years older; 12 percent are five or more years older.

Most studies find that adolescent males are more likely than adolescent females to report that they have had sexual intercourse and are sexually active (Hayes, 1987). Males also say that sexual intercourse is a more enjoyable experience for them. Males also report that they are sexually active at an earlier age than females do. And African American adolescents report that they are more sexually active than White or Latino adolescents (Hayes, 1987).

In some areas of the United States, the percentages of sexually active young adolescents may be even greater. In an inner-city area of Baltimore, 81 percent of the males at age 14 said that they already had engaged in sexual intercourse. Other surveys in inner-city, low-income areas also reveal a high incidence of early sexual intercourse (Clark, Zabin, & Hardy, 1984).

In sum, by the end of adolescence, most individuals have had sexual intercourse. Male, African American, and inner-city adolescents report being the most sexually active. While sexual intercourse can be a meaningful experience for older, mature adolescents, many adolescents are not emotionally prepared to handle sexual experiences, especially in early adolescence. In one study, the earlier in adolescence the boys and girls engaged in sexual intercourse, the more likely they were to show adjustment problems (Bingham & Crockett, 1996).

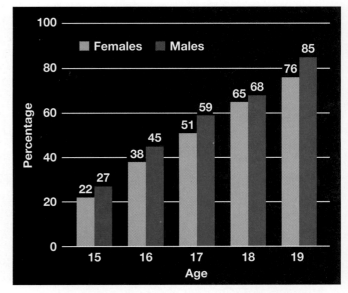

Source: Alan Guttmacher Institute (1995). 1995 National Survey of Family Growth and 1995 National Survey of Adolescent Males. New York: Alan Guttmacher Institute.

Figure 15.6
Percentage of Youth Who Say They Have Had Sexual Intercourse

Homosexual Attitudes and Behavior   Although the development of gay or lesbian identity has been widely studied in adults, few researchers have investigated the gay or lesbian identity (often referred to as the coming-out process) in adolescents. In one study of gay male adolescents, coming out was conceptualized in three stages: sensitization; awareness with confusion, denial, guilt, and shame; and acceptance (Newman & Muzzonigro, 1993). The majority of the gay adolescents said they felt different from other boys as children. The average age at having their first crush on another boy was 12.7 years, and the average age at realizing they were gay was 12.5 years. Most of the boys said they felt confused when they first became aware that they were gay. About half of the boys said they initially tried to deny their identity as a gay. The parents who had strong traditional family values (belief in the importance of religion, emphasis on marriage and having children) were less accepting of their gay sons than were the parents who had weaker traditional family values.

Both the early and more recent surveys indicate that about 4 percent of males and 3 percent of females are exclusively homosexual (Hunt, 1974; Kinsey, Pomeroy, & Martin, 1948). In a recent comprehensive survey of adolescent sexual orientation in almost 35,000 junior and senior high school students in Minnesota, 4.5 percent reported predominantly homosexual attractions (Remafedi & others, in press). Homosexual identities, attractions, and behaviors increased with age. More than 6 percent of the 18-year-olds said they had predominantly homosexual attractions. How many of these youth later become gay is not known, although it is widely accepted that many adolescents who engage in homosexual behavior in adolescence do not continue the practice into adulthood.

An individual's sexual orientation—heterosexual or homosexual—is most likely determined by a combination of genetic, hormonal, and environmental factors (Savin-Williams & Rodriguez, 1993). Most experts on homosexuality believe

Exploring Sexual Orientation

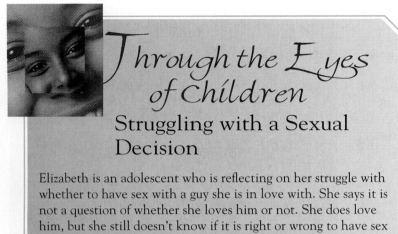

Through the Eyes of Children
Struggling with a Sexual Decision

Elizabeth is an adolescent who is reflecting on her struggle with whether to have sex with a guy she is in love with. She says it is not a question of whether she loves him or not. She does love him, but she still doesn't know if it is right or wrong to have sex with him. He wants her to have sex, but she knows her parents don't. Some of her friends say yes; others say no. Elizabeth is confused. After a few days of contemplation, in a moment of honesty, she admits that she is not his special love. This finally tilts the answer to not having sex with him. She realizes that, if the relationship falls through, she will look back and regret it if she does have sex. In the end, Elizabeth decides not to have sex with him.

Elizabeth's reflections reveal her struggle to understand what is right and what is wrong, whether to have sex or not. In her circumstance, the fact that in a moment of honesty she admitted that she was not his special love made a big difference in her decision (Bollerud, Christopherson, & Frank, 1990).

that no one factor alone causes homosexuality and that the relative weight of each factor may vary from one individual to the next. In truth, no one knows *exactly* what causes an individual to be homosexual; however, scientists have a clearer picture of what does *not* cause homosexuality. For example, children raised by gay or lesbian parents or couples are no more likely to be homosexual than are children raised by heterosexual parents. There also is no evidence that male homosexuality is caused by a dominant mother or a weak father or that female homosexuality is caused by girls choosing male role models. Among the biological factors believed to be involved in homosexuality are prenatal hormone conditions (Ellis & Ames, 1987). In the second to fifth months after conception, exposure to hormone levels characteristic of females is speculated to cause an individual (male or female) to become attracted to males. If this "prenatal critical period hypothesis" turns out to be correct, it would explain why researchers and clinicians have found it difficult to modify a homosexual orientation.

Adolescence may play an important role in the development of homosexuality (Gruskin, 1994). In one study, participation in homosexual behavior and sexual arousal by same-sex peers in adolescence was strongly related to an adult homosexual orientation (Bell, Weinberg, & Mammersmith, 1981). When interest in the same sex is intense and compelling, an adolescent often experiences severe conflict. American culture stigmatizes homosexuality; negative labels, such as *fag* and *queer*, are given to male homosexuals, and *lezzie* and *dyke* to female homosexuals. The sexual socialization of adolescent homosexuals becomes a process of learning to hide. Some gay males wait out their entire adolescence, hoping that heterosexual feelings will develop. Many female adolescent homosexuals have similar experiences. Many adult females who identify themselves as homosexuals had considered themselves predominantly heterosexual during adolescence.

Contraceptive Use   Adolescents are increasing their use of contraceptives. Adolescent girls' contraceptive use at first intercourse rose from 48 percent to 65 percent during the 1980s (Forrest & Singh, 1990). By 1995, use at first intercourse had reached 78 percent, with two thirds of that figure involving condom use. A sexually active adolescent who does not use contraception has a 90 percent chance of pregnancy within one year (Alan Guttmacher Institute, 1998). The method adolescent girls use most frequently is the pill (44 percent), followed by condoms (38 percent). About 10 percent rely on an injectable contraception, 4 percent on withdrawal, and 3 percent on an implant (Alan Guttmacher Institute, 1998). Approximately one third of adolescent girls who rely on condoms also take the pill or practice withdrawal.

Although adolescent contraceptive use is increasing, many sexually active adolescents still do not use contraceptives, or they use them inconsistently. Sexually active younger adolescents are less likely to take contraceptive precautions than older adolescents. Younger adolescents are more likely to use a condom or withdrawal, while older adolescents are more likely to use the pill or a diaphragm. In one study, more adolescent females than males reported changing their behavior in the direction of safer sex practices (Rimberg & Lewis, 1994).

The AIDS epidemic has led to an increased awareness of the importance of sex education in adolescence.

Sexually Transmitted Diseases

Tammy, age 15, has just finished listening to a lecture in her health class. We overhear her talking to one of her girlfriends as she walks down the school corridor: "That was a disgusting lecture. I can't believe all the diseases you can get by having sex. I think she was probably trying to scare us. She spent a lot of time talking about AIDS, which I've heard that normal people don't get. Right? I've heard that only homosexuals and drug addicts get AIDS, and I've also heard that gonorrhea and most other sexual diseases can be cured, so what's the big deal if you get something like that?" Tammy's view of sexually transmitted diseases (formerly called venereal disease, or VD) is common among adolescents. Teenagers tend to believe that sexually transmitted diseases always happen to someone else, can be easily cured without any harm done, and are too disgusting for a nice young person to even hear about, let alone get. This view is wrong. Adolescents who are having sex *do* run a risk of getting sexually transmitted diseases. Sexually transmitted diseases are fairly common among today's adolescents.

Sexually Transmitted Diseases

Chlamydia

Sexually transmitted diseases are primarily transmitted through sexual intercourse, although they can be transmitted orally. **Chlamydia** *is a sexually transmitted disease named for the bacteria that cause it.* Chlamydia affects as many as 10 percent of all college males and females. Males experience a burning sensation during urination and a mucoid discharge. Females experience painful urination or a vaginal discharge. These signs often mimic gonorrhea. However, when penicillin is prescribed for gonorrhealike symptoms, the problem does not go away, as it would if gonorrhea were the culprit. If left untreated, the disease can affect the entire reproductive tract. This can lead to problems left by scar tissue, which can prevent the female from becoming pregnant. Effective drugs are available to treat this common sexually transmitted disease.

chlamydia
A sexually transmitted disease named for the bacteria that cause it.

Herpes Simplex Virus II

An alarming increase in another sexually transmitted disease, herpes simplex virus II, has occurred in recent years. **Herpes simplex virus II** *is a sexually transmitted disease whose symptoms include irregular cycles of sores and blisters in the genital area.* Although this disease is more common among young

herpes simplex virus II
A sexually transmitted disease whose symptoms include irregular cycles of sores and blisters in the genital area.

adults (estimates range as high as 1 in 5 sexually active adults), as many as 1 in 35 adolescents have genital herpes. The herpes virus is potentially dangerous. If babies are exposed to the active virus during birth, they are vulnerable to brain damage or even death, and women with herpes are eight times more likely than unaffected women to develop cervical cancer. At present, herpes is incurable.

Syphilis   Sexual problems have plagued human beings throughout history. Hippocrates wrote about syphilis in 460 B.C. The first major recorded epidemic of syphilis appeared in Naples, Italy, 2 years after Columbus' first return. It is believed that millions of people died of the disease, which is sexually transmitted through intercourse, kissing, and intimate body contact. The cause of syphilis is a tiny bacterium that requires warm, moist surfaces to penetrate the body. It was not until 400 years after the Italian outbreak that penicillin, a successful treatment for syphilis, was discovered.

AIDS   Today, we harbor the same fear of sexually transmitted disease as in Columbus' time, but instead of syphilis it is AIDS, a major sexually related problem, that has generated considerable fear in today's world.

AIDS (acquired immune deficiency syndrome) *is caused by the human immunodeficiency virus (HIV), which destroys the body's immune system.* Many germs that usually would not harm a person with a healthy immune system can produce devastation and death in persons with AIDS.

In 1981, when AIDS was first recognized in the United States, there were fewer than 60 reported cases. Beginning in 1990, we began losing as many Americans each year to AIDS as died in the Vietnam War, almost 60,000 people. According to federal health officials, 1 to 1.5 million Americans are now asymptomatic carriers of AIDS—those who are infected with the virus and presumably capable of infecting others but who show no clinical symptoms of AIDS. In 1989, the first attempt to assess AIDS among college students was made. Testing of 16,861 students found 30 students infected with the virus (American College Health Association, 1989). If the 12.5 million students attending college were infected at the same rate, 25,000 students would have the AIDS virus.

The number of AIDS cases reported in the 13–19 age group each year has increased from one case in 1981 to almost 2,184 cases in 1995 (CDC National AIDS Clearinghouse, 1998). However, the average latency time from viral infection to time of illness is about five to seven years. Thus, most infected adolescents would not become ill until they are adults. Most individuals in their early twenties with an AIDS diagnosis likely were infected with HIV during adolescence—the early-twenties age group accounts for 17 percent of all AIDS cases in the United States.

There are some differences between AIDS in adolescents and AIDS in adults:

1. A higher percentage of adolescent AIDS cases are acquired by heterosexual transmission.
2. A higher percentage of adolescents are asymptomatic (they will become symptomatic in adulthood).
3. A higher percentage of African American and Latino cases occur in adolescence.
4. A special set of ethical and legal issues are involved in testing and informing partners and parents of adolescents.
5. There is less use and availability of contraceptives in adolescence.

In one study, condom use among adolescents who were at the greatest risk of contracting AIDS—for example, intravenous drug users—was significantly below average (Sonenstein, Pleck, & Ku, 1989). Only 21 percent of the adolescents who had used intravenous drugs or whose partners had used intravenous drugs used condoms. Among the adolescents who reported having sex with prostitutes, only

AIDS (acquired immune deficiency syndrome)
A syndrome caused by the human immunodeficiency virus (HIV), which destroys the body's immune system.

HIV/AIDS and Adolescents
STD Resources

The AIDS virus is not transmitted like colds or the flu, but by an exchange of infected blood, semen, or vaginal fluids. This usually occurs during sexual intercourse, in sharing drug needles, or to babies infected before or during birth.

You won't get AIDS from

- Everyday contact with individuals around you at school or the workplace, parties, child care centers, or stores.
- Swimming in a pool, even if someone in the pool has the AIDS virus.
- A mosquito bite or from bedbugs, lice, flies, or other insects.
- Saliva, sweat, tears, urine, or a bowel movement.
- A kiss.
- Clothes, telephones, or toilet seats.
- Using a glass or eating utensils that someone with the virus has used.
- Being on a bus, train, or crowded elevator with an individual who is infected with the virus or who has AIDS.

Blood donations and transfusions

- You will not come into contact with the AIDS virus by donating blood at a blood bank.
- The risk of getting AIDS from a blood transfusion has been greatly reduced. Donors are screened for risk factors, and donated blood is tested.

Risky behavior

- Having a number of sex partners
- Sharing drug needles and syringes
- Engaging in anal sex with or without a condom
- Performing vaginal or oral sex with someone who shoots drugs or engages in anal sex
- Engaging in sex with someone you don't know well or with someone who has several sexual partners
- Engaging in unprotected sex (without a condom) with an infected individual

Safe behavior

- Not having sex
- Sex with one mutually faithful, uninfected partner
- Sex with proper protection
- Not shooting drugs

Source: U.S. Government educational pamphlet: *America Responds to AIDS*, 1988.

Figure 15.7
Understanding AIDS: What's Risky, What's Not

17 percent said they used condoms. And, among the adolescents who reported having sex with five or more partners in the past year, only 37 percent reported using condoms. The adolescents who reported homosexual intercourse reported the highest condom use—66 percent.

Experts say that AIDS can be transmitted only by sexual contact, the sharing of needles, or blood transfusion (which in the past few years has been tightly monitored) (Kalichman, 1996). Although 90 percent of AIDS cases continue to occur among homosexual males and intravenous drug users, a disproportionate increase among females who are heterosexual partners of bisexual males or of intravenous drug users has been recently noted. This increase suggests that the risk of AIDS may be increasing among heterosexual individuals who have multiple sex partners (Jones, 1996). Figure 15.7 describes what's risky and what's not regarding AIDS.

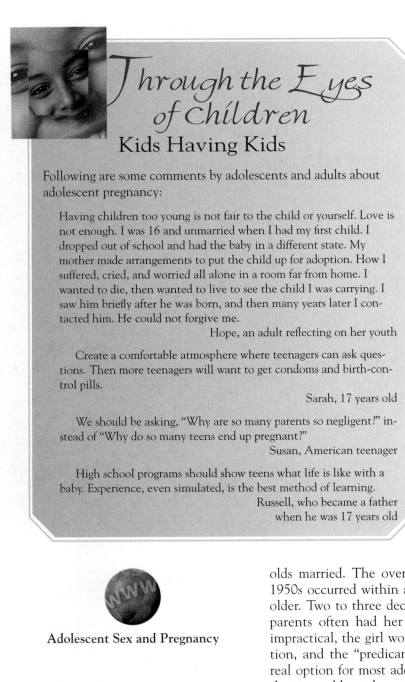

Through the Eyes of Children
Kids Having Kids

Following are some comments by adolescents and adults about adolescent pregnancy:

> Having children too young is not fair to the child or yourself. Love is not enough. I was 16 and unmarried when I had my first child. I dropped out of school and had the baby in a different state. My mother made arrangements to put the child up for adoption. How I suffered, cried, and worried all alone in a room far from home. I wanted to die, then wanted to live to see the child I was carrying. I saw him briefly after he was born, and then many years later I contacted him. He could not forgive me.
>
> Hope, an adult reflecting on her youth

> Create a comfortable atmosphere where teenagers can ask questions. Then more teenagers will want to get condoms and birth-control pills.
>
> Sarah, 17 years old

> We should be asking, "Why are so many parents so negligent?" instead of "Why do so many teens end up pregnant?"
>
> Susan, American teenager

> High school programs should show teens what life is like with a baby. Experience, even simulated, is the best method of learning.
>
> Russell, who became a father when he was 17 years old

Adolescent Sex and Pregnancy

Adolescent Pregnancy   Angela is 15 years old and pregnant. She reflects, "I'm three months pregnant. This could ruin my whole life. I've made all of these plans for the future and now they are down the drain. I don't have anybody to talk to about my problem. I can't talk to my parents. There is no way they can understand." Pregnant adolescents were once practically invisible and unmentionable, but yesterday's secret has become today's national dilemma.

They are from different backgrounds and from different places, but their circumstances have the same stressfulness. Each year, more than 500,000 American teenagers become pregnant, more than 70 percent of them unmarried (*Child Trends*, 1996). They represent a flaw in America's social fabric. Like Angela, far too many become pregnant in their early or middle adolescent years. More than 200,000 females in the United States have a child before their 18th birthday. As one 17-year-old Los Angeles mother of a 1-year-old son said, "We are children having children." The only bright spot in adolescent pregnancy statistics is that small declines in the teenage birthrate began to appear in 1992 and 1993; the rate had risen by one fourth between 1986 and 1991.

Despite the rise in the teenage birthrate that occurred in the late 1980s, the rate is lower now than it was in the 1950s and 1960s. What is different now, though, is the steady rise in the number of nonmarital teenage pregnancies. Dramatic changes have swept through the American culture in the past three decades, changes that involve sexual attitudes and social morals. Adolescents gave birth at a higher rate in 1950 than they do today, but that was a time of early marriage. Then, the vast majority of 15- to 19-year-olds married. The overwhelming majority of births to adolescent mothers in the 1950s occurred within a marriage and mainly involved females 17 years of age and older. Two to three decades ago, if an unwed adolescent girl became pregnant, her parents often had her swiftly married in a "shotgun" wedding. If marriage was impractical, the girl would discreetly disappear, the child would be put up for adoption, and the "predicament" would never be discussed again. Abortion was not a real option for most adolescent females until 1973, when the Supreme Court ruled that it could not be outlawed.

In today's world, if an adolescent girl does not choose to have an abortion (almost 40 percent do), she usually keeps the baby and raises it without the traditional involvement of marriage. With the stigma of illegitimacy less severe, adolescent girls are less likely to give up their babies for adoption. Fewer than 5 percent do, compared with approximately 35 percent in the early 1960s. But, while the stigma of illegitimacy has lessened, the lives of most pregnant adolescents is anything but rosy.

The adolescent pregnancy rate in the United States is much higher than in other industrialized countries (East & Felice, 1996). It is more than twice as high as the rates in England, France, and Canada; almost three times as high as the rate in Sweden; and seven times as high as the rate in the Netherlands (*Child Trends*, 1996; Jones & others, 1985; Kenney, 1987). Although American adolescents are no more sexually active than their counterparts in these other countries, they are many more times likely to become pregnant. Although the adolescent pregnancy rate in the

United States is still very high, the adolescent birthrate fell an estimated 3 percent in 1997, continuing a six-year trend (U.S. Department of Health and Human Services, 1998). Since 1990, the sharpest drop (20 percent) in the adolescent birth rate has occurred in 15- to 17-year-old African Americans. Fear of sexually transmitted diseases, especially AIDS, school/community health center health classes, and a greater hope for the future are the likely reasons for this decrease.

The consequences of our nation's high adolescent pregnancy rate are of great concern (Brooks-Gunn & Chase-Lansdale, 1995; Luster & others, 1995). Pregnancy in adolescence increases the health risks of both the child and the mother. Infants born to adolescent mothers are more likely to have low birthweights (a prominent cause of infant mortality), as well as neurological problems and childhood illnesses. Adolescent mothers often drop out of school, fail to gain employment, and become dependent on welfare. Although many adolescent mothers resume their education later in life, they generally do not catch up with women who postpone childbearing. In the National Longitudinal Survey of Work Experience of Youth, it was found that only half of the women 20 to 26 years old who first gave birth at age 17 had completed high school by their twenties. The percentage was even lower for those who gave birth at a younger age (Mott & Marsiglio, 1985). By contrast, among females who waited until age 20 to have a baby, more than 90 percent had obtained a high school education. Among the younger adolescent mothers, almost half had obtained a general equivalency diploma (GED), which does not often open up good employment opportunities. These educational deficits have negative consequences for the young women themselves and for their children. Adolescent parents are more likely than those who delay childbearing to have low-paying, low-status jobs or to be unemployed. The mean family income of White females who give birth before age 17 is approximately half that of families in which the mother delays birth until her mid- or late twenties.

What is the pattern of alcohol consumption among adolescents?

Substance Use and Abuse

The 1960s and 1970s were a time of marked increases in the use of illicit drugs. During the social and political unrest of those years, many youth turned to marijuana, stimulants, and hallucinogens. Increases in alcohol consumption by adolescents also were noted (Robinson & Greene, 1988). More precise data about drug use by adolescents have been collected in recent years. Each year since 1975, Lloyd Johnston, Patrick O'Malley, and Gerald Bachman (1997), working at the Institute of Social Research at the University of Michigan, have carefully monitored drug use by America's high school seniors in a wide range of public and private high schools. From time to time, they also sample the drug use of younger adolescents and adults.

Adolescent Substance Use

Drug use by American secondary school students rose again in 1996, continuing a trend that began in 1991 among eighth-grade students and in 1992 among tenth- and twelfth-grade students (Johnston, O'Malley, & Bachman, 1997). The proportion of eighth-graders taking any illicit drug in the past 12 months almost doubled from 1991 figures (from 11 percent to 21 percent). Since 1992, the proportion of adolescents using any illicit drugs in the prior 12 months increased by nearly two thirds among tenth-graders (from 20 to 33 percent) and by nearly half among twelfth-graders (from 27 to 39 percent).

In 1996, marijuana use, in particular, continued the strong resurgence that began in the early 1990s, with increased use at all three grade levels. Among eighth-graders, annual prevalence (the proportion reporting use in the 12 months prior to the survey) rose to three times its 1991 level, from 6 percent in 1991 to 18 percent in 1996. Among tenth-graders, annual prevalence nearly doubled from the low point in use in 1992 of 15 percent to 34 percent in 1996; among twelfth-graders, annual prevalence increased by more than half, from the low point of 22 percent in 1992 to 36 percent in 1996.

Although marijuana had the sharpest increase in use by adolescents, the use of a number of other illicit drugs, such as LSD, amphetamines, stimulants, and inhalants, also increased. Johnston, O'Malley, and Bachman (1995) concluded that drugs have recently been perceived as being less dangerous and that such a perception is usually accompanied by an increase in use.

A special concern is the increased use of drugs by young adolescents. Also, it is important to note that the United States has the highest rate of adolescent drug use of all the world's industrialized nations.

National Clearinghouse for Alcohol and Drug Information

Alcohol   Alcohol is the drug most widely used by adolescents in our society. For them, it has produced many enjoyable moments and many sad ones as well. Alcoholism is the third leading killer in the United States, with more than 13 million people classified as alcoholics, many of whom established their drinking habits during adolescence. Each year, approximately 25,000 people are killed and 1.5 million injured by drunk drivers. In 65 percent of the aggressive male acts against females, the offender is under the influence of alcohol (Goodman & others, 1986). In numerous instances of drunken driving and assaults on females, the offenders are adolescents.

How extensive is alcohol use by adolescents? Alcohol use by high school seniors has gradually declined. Monthly use declined from 72 percent in 1980 to 51 percent in 1996. The prevalence of drinking five or more drinks in a row in a two-week interval fell from 41 percent in 1980 to 31 percent in 1996. However, data from college students show little drop in alcohol use and an increase in heavy drinking. Heavy drinking at parties among college males is common and is becoming more common (Johnston, O'Malley, & Bachman, 1997).

Cigarette Smoking   Smoking begins primarily during childhood and adolescence. One study found that, once young adolescents begin to smoke cigarettes, the addictive properties of nicotine make it extremely difficult for them to stop (Melby & Vargas, 1996). Adolescent smoking peaked in the mid-1970s, then began to decline through 1980. However, in the 1990s, adolescent cigarette smoking increased (Johnston, O'Malley, & Bachman, 1997). Among both eighth- and tenth-graders, the proportion who reported smoking in the 30 days prior to the survey increased by one third since 1991. Nineteen percent of the eighth-graders and 28 percent of the tenth-graders reported such use. Since 1992, the smoking rate had risen by more than one fifth among high school seniors, with 34 percent saying they had smoked within the past 30 days. Peer disapproval of cigarette smoking had dropped over the past several years, and the percentage of adolescents who saw smoking as dangerous had been declining since 1993. Among eighth-graders, less than one half thought there was great risk to smoking a pack or more a day. Cigarettes were readily available to these underage youth. Of the eighth-graders, most of whom were 13 to 14 years of age, 76 percent said that they could get cigarettes fairly easily if they wanted them. Of the tenth-graders, more than 90 percent said they could buy cigarettes easily.

One comprehensive health approach that includes an attempt to curb cigarette smoking by adolescents was developed by clinical psychologist Cheryl Perry and her colleagues (1988). Three programs were developed based on peer group norms, healthy role models, and social skills training. Elected peer leaders were trained as instructors. In seventh grade, adolescents were offered "Keep It Clean," a six-session course emphasizing the negative effects of smoking. In eighth grade, students were involved in "Health Olympics," an approach that included exchanging greeting cards on smoking and health with peers in other countries. In ninth grade, students participated in "Shifting Gears," which included six sessions focused on social skills. In the social skills program, students critiqued media messages and created their own positive health videotapes. At the same time as the school intervention, a communitywide smoking cessation program, as well as a diet and health awareness campaign, was initiated. After five years, students who were involved in the smoking and health program were much less likely to smoke cigarettes, use marijuana, or drink alcohol than were their counterparts who were not involved in the program.

A Parent's Guide to Adolescent Drug Use

The Roles of Development, Parents, and Peers in Adolescent Drug Abuse Most adolescents become drug users at some point in their development, whether limited to alcohol, caffeine, and cigarettes or extended to marijuana, cocaine, and hard drugs. A special concern involves adolescents using drugs as a way of coping with stress, which can interfere with the development of competent coping skills and responsible decision making. Researchers have found that drug use in childhood or early adolescence has more detrimental long-term effects on the development of responsible, competent behavior than when drug use occurs in late adolescence (Newcomb & Bentler, 1983). When they use drugs to cope with stress, many young adolescents enter adult roles of marriage and work prematurely, without adequate socioemotional growth, and experience greater failure in adult roles.

How early are adolescents beginning drug use? National samples of eighth- and ninth-grade students were included for the first time in 1991 in the Institute for Social Research survey of drug use (Johnston, O'Malley, & Bachman, 1992). Early in the drug use increase in the United States (late 1960s, early 1970s), drug use was much higher among college students than among high school students, who in turn had much higher rates of drug use than middle or junior high school students. However, today the rates for college and high school students are similar, and the rates for young adolescents are not as different from those for older adolescents as might be anticipated.

Parents, peers, and social support play important roles in preventing adolescent drug abuse (Johnson & others, 1996; Pentz, 1994). Positive relationships with parents and others are important in reducing adolescents' drug use (Emshoff & others, 1996). In one study, social support (which consisted of good relationships with parents, siblings, adults, and peers) during adolescence substantially reduced drug abuse (Newcomb & Bentler, 1988). In another study, the adolescents were most likely to take drugs when both of their parents took drugs (such as tranquilizers, amphetamines, alcohol, or nicotine) and when their peers took drugs (Kandel, 1974).

Eating Disorders

A tall, slender, 16-year-old girl goes into the locker room of a fitness center, throws her towel across the bench, and looks squarely in the mirror. She yells, "You fat pig. You are nothing but a fat pig." America is a nation obsessed with food, spending extraordinary amounts of time thinking about, eating, and avoiding food. Eating disorders are complex, involving genetic inheritance, physiological factors, cognitive factors, and environmental experiences. In one study, girls who in early adolescence felt most negatively about their bodies were more likely to develop eating problems two years later (Attie & Brooks-Gunn, 1989). In one study, adolescent girls who had positive relationships with both parents tended to have healthier eating patterns (Swarr & Richards, 1996). In another study, the girls who were both

Anorexia nervosa has become an increasing problem for adolescent girls.

physically involved with their boyfriends and in pubertal transition were the most likely to be dieting or engaging in disordered eating patterns (Cauffman, 1994). The three most prominent eating disorders are obesity, anorexia nervosa, and bulimia. We discussed many aspects of obesity in chapter 12. Here, we will focus on anorexia nervosa and bulimia.

Fifteen-year-old Jane gradually eliminated foods from her diet to the point at which she subsisted by eating *only* applesauce and eggnog. She spent hours observing her body, wrapping her fingers around her waist to see if it was getting any thinner. She fantasized about becoming a beautiful fashion model who would wear designer bathing suits. Even when she reached 85 pounds, Jane still felt fat. She continued to lose weight, eventually emaciating herself. She was hospitalized and treated for **anorexia nervosa,** *an eating disorder that involves the relentless pursuit of thinness through starvation.* Eventually, anorexia nervosa can lead to death, as it did for popular gymnast Christy Henrich.

Most anorexics are White adolescent or young adult females from well-educated, middle- and upper-income families. They distort their body image, perceiving themselves as overweight even when they become skeletal. Numerous causes of anorexia nervosa have been proposed. One is the current fashion image of thinness, reflected in the saying "You can't be too rich or too thin." Many anorexics grow up in families with high achievement demands. Unable to meet these high expectations and control their grades, they turn to something they can control: their weight.

Bulimia *is an eating disorder in which the individual consistently follows a binge-and-purge eating pattern.* The bulimic goes on an eating binge and then purges by inducing vomiting or using a laxative. Sometimes the binges alternate with fasting, at other times with normal eating. Like anorexia nervosa, bulimia is primarily a female disorder.

Now that we have considered some health problems in adolescence, let's explore some of the cognitive and sociocultural factors that can be involved in those problems.

Cognitive and Sociocultural Factors in Adolescent Health

Adolescents often reach a level of health, strength, and energy they never will match during the remainder of their lives. They also have a sense of uniqueness and invulnerability that leads them to think that illness and disorder will not enter their lives. And they possess a time perspective that envisions the future as having few or no boundaries. Adolescents believe that they will recoup any lost health or modify any bad habits they might develop. Given this combination of physical and cognitive factors, is it any wonder that so many adolescents have poor health habits?

Health Beliefs, Knowledge, and Decision Making Adolescents' health beliefs include beliefs about vulnerability and behavior (Millstein, Petersen, & Nightingale, 1993). Adolescents, as well as adults, underestimate their vulnerability to harm (Kamler & others, 1987). While they usually recognize that such behaviors as substance abuse and unprotected sexual intercourse are potential health hazards, they often underestimate the potentially negative consequences of these behaviors.

Adolescents generally are poorly informed about health issues and have significant misperceptions about health (Centers for Disease Control, 1988). Younger adolescents have less factual knowledge about a variety of health topics, including sexually transmitted diseases and drug abuse, than older adolescents do.

Young adolescents are better at decision making than are children but are worse at decision making than are older adolescents. The decision-making skills of older adolescents and adults, however, are far from perfect. And the ability to make decisions does not guarantee that such decisions will be made in everyday life, where breadth of experience comes into play (Keating, 1990). For example, driver-training

anorexia nervosa
An eating disorder that involves the relentless pursuit of thinness through starvation.

Anorexia Nervosa

bulimia
An eating disorder in which the individual consistently follows a binge-purge eating pattern.

Adolescent Health Attitudes and Behavior

National Longitudinal Study of Adolescent Health

Caring for Children

Life Science and Life Skills Education

Early adolescence is a time when many health-compromising behaviors—drug abuse, unprotected sex, poor dietary habits, and lack of exercise, for example—either occur for the first time or intensify. As children move through puberty and often develop a feeling that they should be able to engage in adultlike behaviors, they essentially ask, "How should I use my body?" According to David Hamburg and his colleagues (1993), any responsible education must answer that basic question with a substantial life science curriculum that provides adolescents with accurate information about their own bodies, including what the consequences are for engaging in health-compromising behaviors.

Most adolescent health experts believe that a life science education program should be an important part of the curriculum in all middle schools (Hamburg, 1990; Kolbe, Collins, & Cortese, 1997). This education involves providing adolescents with a better understanding of adolescent development, including puberty (its biological and social ramifications), the reproductive system, sexual behavior, sexually transmitted diseases, nutrition, diet, and exercise. In addition, young adolescents should have readily accessible health services, nutritious food in the cafeteria, a smoke-free and physically safe environment, and appropriate physical fitness activities.

Many adolescent health experts also believe that life skills training should be part of the life science curriculum (Hamburg, 1990; Hamburg & others, 1993). Life skills training programs teach young adolescents how to make in-

formed, deliberate, and constructive decisions that will reduce their health-compromising behaviors. Life skills training programs also can improve the interpersonal skills of young adolescents, helping them relate better with others and solve interpersonal problems more effectively.

One new school-based model for enhancing the life opportunities of adolescents is the full-service school, which encompasses school-based primary health clinics, youth service programs, and other innovative services to improve access to health and social services. These programs have in common the use of school facilities for delivering services through partnerships with community agencies, a shared vision of youth development, and financial support from sources outside of school systems, especially states and foundations. Organizing a full-service school requires careful planning to involve school personnel, community agencies, parents, and students. Evaluation of the full-service school's effectiveness is still scattered, although some recent results are encouraging with regard to adolescents' health and mental health care, dropout rates, substance abuse, pregnancy prevention, and improved attendance (Dryfoos, 1995).

It is also important to remember that health promotion in adolescence should not be solely the responsibility of schools. Adolescent health can benefit from the cooperation and integration of a number of societal institutions: the family, schools, the health care system, the media, and community organizations (Hamburg & others, 1993).

courses improve adolescents' cognitive and motor skills to levels equal to, or sometimes superior to, those of adults. However, driver training has not been effective in reducing adolescents' high rate of traffic accidents (Potvin, Champagne, & Laberge-Nadeau, 1988). Thus, an important research agenda is to study the way adolescents make decisions in practical health situations (Crockett & Petersen, 1993). To read further about improving adolescents' health, see the Caring for Children box.

Sociocultural Factors in Adolescent Health Sociocultural factors influence health through their roles in setting cultural norms about health, through social relationships that provide emotional support, and through the encouragement of healthy or unhealthy behaviors.

In considering the health of ethnic minority group adolescents, it is important to recognize that there are large within-group differences in living conditions and lifestyles and that these differences are influenced by socioeconomic status, status as an immigrant, social skills, language skills, occupational opportunities, and social resources, such as the availability of meaningful social support networks. At present,

Improving Developmental Skills

Supporting and Guiding Adolescent Physical Development and Health

What are some good strategies for supporting and guiding adolescent physical development and health? They include

- *Develop more positive expectations for adolescents.* We negatively stereotype adolescents too much. These negative expectations have a way of becoming self-fulfilling prophecies and harming adult-adolescent communication. Don't view adolescence as a time of crisis and rebellion. View it as a time of evaluation, decision making, commitment, and the carving out of a place in the world.
- *Understand the many physical changes adolescents are going through.* The many physical changes adolescents go through can be very perplexing to them. They are not quite sure what they are going to change into, and this can create considerable uncertainty for them.
- *Be a good health role model for adolescents.* Adolescents benefit from being around adults who are good health models, individuals who exercise regularly, eat healthily, and don't take drugs.
- *Communicate more effectively with adolescents about sexuality.* Emphasize that young adolescents should abstain from sex. If adolescents are going to be sexually active, they need to take contraceptive precautions. Adolescents need to learn about sexuality and human reproduction before they become sexually active, no later than early adolescence. Adolescents should be encouraged to do community service in child care centers.

there is little research information about the role of ethnicity in adolescents' health beliefs and behavior. However, researchers do know what some of the important health issues are for various ethnic minority adolescents (Earls, 1993).

Poverty is related to poor health in adolescents. In the National Health Interview Study (1991), 7 percent of the adolescents living in poverty were in only fair or poor health, compared with 2 percent of adolescents in nonpoverty households. In another study, 9 percent of the 10- to 18-year-olds below the poverty line, compared with 6 percent of those above it, had a chronic condition that resulted in some loss of ability to conduct the normal activities of adolescence (Newacheck, 1989). What are some of the mechanisms that can produce poor health in adolescents who live in poverty conditions? They include income, family environment, schools and community groups, and psychological factors (Klerman, 1993). Having insufficient income to meet basic needs can make particular behaviors difficult—seeking medical care, for example. Low income often causes families to live in inner-city ghettos, where there are few role models who engage in health-enhancing behaviors. Many poor adolescents are less connected to sources that might advocate or model positive behaviors or urge the avoidance of negative ones. These sources include families, schools, and community organizations. Poor adolescents seem to be strongly influenced by peers who engage in health-compromising behaviors, possibly because of inadequate emotional support from the family. Adolescents may be likely to practice health-promoting behaviors if they believe they have the power to influence their future. Alienation or a sense of powerlessness or hopelessness is not likely to lead to health promotion. In a national study of eighth-graders, perception of personal control over one's life was highest among those from the highest social class status and lowest among those from the lowest social class status (Hafner & others, 1990). The poor adolescents were more likely than their more affluent counterparts to believe that goals can be reached through luck, rather than planning or effort.

Health Services

While adolescents have a greater number of acute health conditions than adults do, they use private physician services at a lower rate than any other age group does (Edelman, 1997). Adolescents often underutilize other health care systems as well (Millstein, 1988). Health services are especially unlikely to meet the health needs of younger adolescents, ethnic minority adolescents, and adolescents living in poverty. Among the chief barriers to better health services for adolescents are cost, poor organization, and unavailability of health services, as well as confidentiality of care. Also, few health care providers receive any special training for working with adolescents. Many say that they feel unprepared to provide

Health Risks and Adolescents

Summary Table 15.2
Adolescent Health

Concept	Processes/ Related Ideas	Characteristics/Description
Leading causes of death in adolescence	Their nature	The three leading causes of death in adolescence are accidents, suicide, and homicide.
Sexuality	Heterosexual attitudes and behavior	In the United States most adolescents are virgins at age 15, but most have had sexual intercourse by age 18.
	Homosexual attitudes and behavior	Rates of homosexuality have remained constant in the twentieth century. No definitive conclusions about the causes of homosexuality have been reached.
	Contraceptive use	Both male and female adolescents report increased contraceptive use in recent years but many adolescents, especially young adolescents, still have unprotected sex.
	Sexually transmitted diseases	Any adolescent who has sex runs the risk of getting a sexually transmitted disease, formerly called venereal disease, although many adolescents underestimate their own risk. Among the sexually transmitted diseases adolescents may get are chlamydia, herpes simplex virus II, syphilis, and AIDS.
	Adolescent pregnancy	More than 1 million American adolescents become pregnant each year. The U.S. adolescent pregnancy rate is the highest in the Western world. The consequences of adolescent pregnancy include health risks for the mother and the offspring.
Substance use and abuse	Their nature	The United States has the highest adolescent drug-use rate of any industrialized nation. In the mid-1980s, there was a slight downturn in use, but in the 1990s use began to increase again. Alcohol abuse by adolescents is a major problem. So is cigarette smoking. Development, parents, and schools play important roles in adolescent drug use.
Eating disorders	Their nature	Anorexia nervosa and bulimia increasingly have become problems for adolescent females. Societal, psychological, and physiological causes of these disorders have been proposed.
Cognitive and social factors in adolescent health	Cognitive factors	Cognitive factors in adolescents' health include concepts of health behavior, beliefs about health, health knowledge, and decision making.
	Sociocultural factors	These influence health through their roles in setting cultural norms about health, social relationships that provide support, and the encouragement of healthy or unhealthy behaviors.
Health services	Their nature	Adolescents use health services less than any other age group, even though they have a number of acute health conditions. There are many barriers to providing better services for adolescents, and these need to be examined.

such services as contraceptive counseling and an accurate evaluation of what constitutes abnormal behavior in adolescence (Irwin, 1993). Health care providers may transmit to their patients their discomfort in discussing such topics as sexuality, which may lead to adolescents' unwillingness to discuss sensitive issues with them.

At this point, we have studied many ideas about adolescent physical development and health. See Improving Developmental Skills for some positive strategies in these areas. To review the information we have discussed about adolescent health, see summary table 15.2.

Promoting Adolescent Health

Chapter Review

Adolescents flash from one end of the world to the other, both in body and in mind as they move through a seemingly endless preparation for life. In fragile moments, they may become acquainted with sex and other temptations that can compromise their health.

We began this chapter by exploring the following aspects of the nature of adolescence: the biological and sociohistorical determinants and what today's youth are like. Our coverage of puberty focused on its boundaries and determinants; hormonal changes; height, weight, and sexual maturation; menarche and the menstrual cycle; body image; early and late maturation; and pubertal change and health care. We examined the following dimensions of adolescent health: the leading causes of death in adolescence, sexuality, substance use and abuse, eating disorders, cognitive and sociocultural factors in adolescent health, and health services.

Don't forget that you can obtain a more detailed review of the chapter by again studying the two summary tables on pages 451 and 465. In the next chapter, we will continue our journey through adolescence by evaluating the nature of the cognitive changes that take place in this period.

Children Checklist

Physical Development in Adolescence

How much have you learned since the beginning of the chapter? Use the following statements to help you review your knowledge and understanding of the chapter material. First, read the statement and mentally or briefly demonstrate on paper that you can discuss the relevant information.

_____ I can describe the biological and sociohistorical natures of adolescence.
_____ I know what today's youth are like.
_____ I can discuss puberty's boundaries, determinants, and changes.
_____ I can evaluate the effects of early and late maturation.
_____ I am aware of the main causes of death in adolescence.
_____ I can discuss adolescent sexuality, including attitudes and behavior, sexually transmitted diseases, and adolescent pregnancy.
_____ I can describe substance use and abuse in adolescence.
_____ I am aware of what is involved in anorexia nervosa and bulimia.
_____ I can discuss cognitive and sociocultural factors in adolescent health.

For any items that you did not check, go back and locate the relevant material in the chapter. Review the material until you feel you can check off the item. You may want to use this checklist later in preparing for an exam.

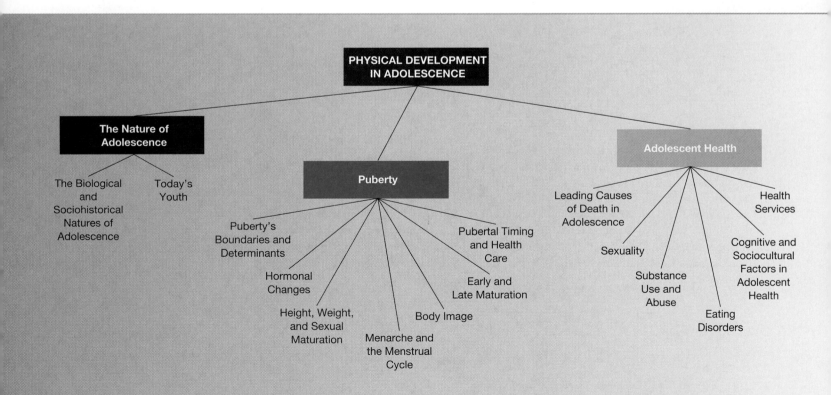

Key Terms

storm-and-stress view 440
inventionist view 440
puberty 442
menarche 442
hormones 443
hypothalamus 443
pituitary gland 443
gonads 443
androgens 444

estrogens 444
testosterone 444
estradiol 444
chlamydia 455
herpes simplex virus II 455
AIDS (acquired immune
   deficiency syndrome) 456
anorexia nervosa 462
bulimia 462

Children Resources

Search Institute
Thresher Square West
700 South Third Street, Suite 210
Minneapolis, MN 55415
612–376–8955

The Search Institute has available a large number of resources for improving the lives of adolescents. In 1995, the institute began distributing the excellent publications of the Center for Early Adolescence, University of North Carolina, which had just closed. The brochures and books available address school improvement, adolescent literacy, parent education, program planning, and adolescent health and include resource lists. A free quarterly newsletter is available.

The Society for Adolescent Medicine
10727 White Oak Avenue
Granada Hills, CA 91344

This organization is a valuable source of information about competent physicians who specialize in treating adolescents. It maintains a list of recommended adolescence specialists across the United States.

Taking It to the Net

http//www.mhhe.com/santrockcd6

1. You have been asked to give a brief talk on adolescence and substance abuse to a group of parents. Would you feel comfortable giving such a talk? What would you talk about? What are the major risk factors involved in adolescent substance abuse? What are some strategies that parents could use to reduce the risk of their adolescent using drugs?
2. You have noticed that your best friend talks about her appearance a lot. She's a bit underweight and she's lost 30 pounds in the last year. She's always asking you if she's too fat, if her breasts are too small, or if her cheeks are too round. Is she merely concerned about her appearance, or does she have a body image or eating disorder? How would you know? What should you do?
3. Mike and Sue are having an argument. Mike says "Wow, are you in a bad mood. PMS?" Sue explodes, "What?!" Do you think premenstrual syndrome (PMS) really exists, or is it a myth? Is it a physical or psychological disorder? What do you believe to be the social issues surrounding PMS?

Chapter 16

Chapter Outline

Cognitive Development in Adolescence

I remember my youth and that feeling that never came back to me anymore—the feeling that I could last forever, outlast the sea, the earth, and all men.

Joseph Conrad
Polish-Born English Novelist, 20th Century

PREVIEW

When people think of the changes that take place in adolescence, they often focus on pubertal changes or problems and disorders. However, there are some impressive cognitive changes that occur in adolescence as well. Among the questions that we will explore are

- What changes did Piaget believe characterize the way adolescents think?
- What is adolescent egocentrism?
- In what ways do adolescents process information differently than children do?
- What are adolescents' values like?
- What are some different ways that adolescents can be morally educated?
- What role does religion play in adolescents' lives?
- What is the nature of secondary education? What are effective middle schools like?
- What influences adolescents' career decisions?
- What role does work play in adolescent development?

The Story of Cleveland Wilkes

Cleveland Wilkes' family lives in Providence, Rhode Island. They never have had much money. He and his parents know what unemployment can do to a family. Nonetheless, Cleveland, who is 17 years old, is known as "the dresser" to his friends because of his penchant for flamboyant clothes, especially shoes. What little money Cleveland manages to scrape together is all channeled into maintaining a wardrobe. In Cleveland's own words,

Whole world floats by around here. There ain't nothing you can't see on these streets. See more in a month here than a lifetime where the rich folks live, all protected from the bad world. I ain't saying it's so great here. Only thing we don't have is the thing we need most of: jobs. Ain't no jobs for us here. Not a one, man, and I know, too, 'cause I been looking for three years, and I ain't all that old.

Country got no use for me, folks around here neither. Ain't nobody care too much what happens to us. Tell us, "Ain't you boys got nothing better to do than stand around all day? What you find to talk about all these hours? And ain't you supposed to be in school? Ain't you suppose to be doing this or doing that?"

If you want to know what the teenagers are doing on this side of town to pass the time of day, now you got it. We got so many folks out of work it's enough to blow your mind. I can hear my brain rotting it's been so long since I done anything. How they let this happen to a country like this, having all these kids walking around the streets, got their hands jammed in their pockets, got their head down? What do folks think these kids gonna do, when they go month after month, year after year without nothing that even smells like a job?

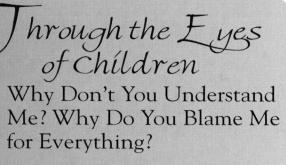

Through the Eyes of Children
Why Don't You Understand Me? Why Do You Blame Me for Everything?

Buba is 12 years old. Yesterday she wrote her parents a note. She began the note by thanking her parents for all of the wonderful things they had done for her. Then, very quickly, she nailed them right between the eyes with her criticism. She wanted to know why they never listen to her, why they don't understand her, why they blame her for everything, why they yell at her so much. Buba went on to say that she feels left out of the family and that she's not sure they (her parents) really love her (*Helping a Teenager Grow Up Gradually*, 1983).

This new criticalness of parents often happens rather abruptly, as it did in Buba's case. Buba's increasing idealistic thinking led her to compare her parents with what ideal parents are like. Like all parents, Buba's came up far short.

The thoughts of youth are long, long thoughts.

Henry Wadsworth Longfellow
American Poet, 19th Century

hypothetical-deductive reasoning
Piaget's formal operational concept that adolescents have the cognitive ability to develop hypotheses, or best guesses, about ways to solve problems, such as an algebraic equation.

ADOLESCENT COGNITION

Adolescents' developing power of thought opens up new cognitive and social horizons. Let's examine what their developing power of thought is like, beginning with Piaget's theory.

Piaget's Theory

What is the nature of Piaget's ideas about cognitive development in adolescence? To answer this question, we will study Piaget's stage of formal operational thought.

Most significantly, formal operational thought is more *abstract* than concrete operational thought. Adolescents are no longer limited to actual, concrete experiences as anchors for thought. They can conjure up make-believe situations, events that are purely hypothetical possibilities or strictly abstract propositions, and can try to reason logically about them.

The abstract quality of the adolescent's thought at the formal operational level is evident in the adolescent's verbal problem-solving ability. Whereas the concrete operational thinker needs to see the concrete elements A, B, and C to be able to make the logical inference that, if A = B and B = C, then A = C, the formal operational thinker can solve this problem merely through verbal presentation.

Another indication of the abstract quality of adolescents' thought is their increased tendency to think about thought itself. One adolescent commented, "I began thinking about why I was thinking what I was. Then I began thinking about why I was thinking about what I was thinking about what I was." If this sounds abstract, it is, and it characterizes the adolescent's enhanced focus on thought and its abstract qualities.

Accompanying the abstract nature of formal operational thought in adolescence is thought full of idealism and possibilities. While children frequently think in concrete ways, or in terms of what is real and limited, adolescents begin to engage in extended speculation about ideal characteristics—qualities they desire in themselves and in others. Such thoughts often lead adolescents to compare themselves with others in regard to such ideal standards. And, during adolescence, the thoughts of individuals are often fantasy flights into future possibilities. It is not unusual for the adolescent to become impatient with these newfound ideal standards and to become perplexed over which of many ideal standards to adopt. To read further about formal operational thought, see Adventures for the Mind.

At the same time that adolescents think more abstractly and idealistically, they also think more logically. Adolescents begin to think more as a scientist thinks, devising plans to solve problems and systematically testing solutions. This type of problem solving has an imposing name. **Hypothetical-deductive reasoning** *is Piaget's formal operational concept that adolescents have the cognitive ability to develop hypotheses, or best guesses, about ways to solve problems, such as an algebraic equation. Then they systematically deduce, or conclude, which is the best path to follow in solving the equation.* By contrast, children are more likely to solve problems in a trial-and-error fashion.

One example of hypothetical-deductive reasoning involves a modification of the familiar game Twenty Questions. Individuals are shown a set of 42 color pictures, displayed in a rectangular array (six rows of seven pictures each) and are asked to determine which picture the experimenter has in mind (that is, which is "correct"). The subjects are allowed to ask only questions to which the experimenter can answer yes or no. The object of the game is to select the correct picture by asking as few questions as possible. Adolescents who are deductive hypothesis testers formulate a plan and test a series of hypotheses, which considerably narrows the field of choices. The most effective plan is a "halving" strategy (*Q:* Is the picture in the right half of the array? *A:* No. *Q:* OK. Is it in the top half? And so on.). A correct halving strategy guarantees the answer in seven questions or less. By contrast, concrete operational thinkers may persist with questions that continue to test some of the same possibilities that previous questions could have eliminated. For example, they may ask whether the correct picture is in row 1 and are told that it is not. Later, they ask whether the picture is *x*, which is in row 1.

Thus, formal operational thinkers test their hypotheses with judiciously chosen questions and tests. By contrast, concrete operational thinkers often fail to understand the relation between a hypothesis and a well-chosen test of it, stubbornly clinging to ideas that already have been discounted.

Piaget believed that formal operational thought is the best description of how adolescents think. A summary of formal operational thought's characteristics is shown in figure 16.1. As we will see next, though, formal operational thought is not a homogeneous stage of development.

Some of Piaget's ideas on formal operational thought are being challenged (Overton & Byrnes, 1991). There is much more individual variation in formal operational thought than Piaget envisioned. Only about one in three young adolescents is a formal operational thinker. Many American adults never become formal operational thinkers, and neither do many adults in other cultures. Consider the following conversation between a researcher and an illiterate Kpelle farmer in the West African country of Liberia (Scribner, 1977):

Researcher: All Kpelle men are rice farmers. Mr. Smith is not a rice farmer. Is he a Kpelle man?

Kpelle farmer: I don't know the man. I have not laid eyes on the man myself.

Members of the Kpelle culture who had gone through formal schooling answered the researcher in a logical way. As with our discussion of concrete operational thought in chapter 10, we find that cultural experiences influence whether individuals reach a Piagetian stage of thought. Education in the logic of science and mathematics is an important cultural experience that promotes the development of formal operational thinking.

Also, for adolescents who become formal operational thinkers, assimilation (incorporating new information into existing knowledge) dominates the initial development of formal operational thought, and the world is perceived subjectively and idealistically. Later in adolescence, as intellectual balance is restored, these individuals accommodate (adjust to new information) to the cognitive upheaval that has occurred.

In addition to thinking more logically, abstractly, and idealistically, which characterize Piaget's formal operational thought stage, in what other ways does adolescent cognition change? One important way involves adolescent egocentrism.

Adventures for the Mind
Piaget, Children, Adolescents, and Political Conventions

Suppose an 8-year-old and a 16-year-old are watching a political convention on television. In view of where each child is likely to be in terms of Piaget's stages of cognitive development, how would their perceptions of the proceedings likely differ? What would the 8-year-old "see" and comprehend? What Piagetian changes would these differences reflect?

The error of youth is to believe that intelligence is a substitute for experience, while the error of age is to believe that experience is a substitute for intelligence.

Lyman Bryson
American Author, 20th Century

Abstract	Idealistic	Logical
Adolescents think more abstractly than children. Formal operational thinkers can solve abstract algebraic equations, for example.	Adolescents often think about what is possible. They think about ideal characteristics of themselves, others, and the world.	Adolescents begin to think more like scientists, devising plans to solve problems and systematically testing solutions. Piaget called this type of logical thinking hypothetical-deductive reasoning.

*F*igure 16.1
Characteristics of Formal Operational Thought

Adolescents begin to think more as scientists think, devising plans to solve problems and systematically testing solutions. Piaget gave this type of thinking the imposing name of hypothetical-deductive reasoning.

Adolescent Egocentrism

"Oh, my gosh! I can't believe it. Help! I can't stand it!" Tracy desperately yells. "What is wrong? What is the matter?" her mother asks. Tracy responds, "Everyone in here is looking at me." The mother queries, "Why?" Tracy says, "Look, this one hair just won't stay in place," as she rushes to the rest room of the restaurant. Five minutes later, she returns to the table in the restaurant after she has depleted an entire can of hair spray.

During a conversation between two 14-year-old girls, the one named Margaret says, "Are you kidding, I won't get pregnant." And, 13-year-old Adam describes himself, "No one understand me, particularly my parents. They have no idea of what I am feeling."

Adolescent egocentrism *is the heightened self-consciousness of adolescents, which is reflected in their belief that others are as interested in them as they themselves are, and in their sense of personal uniqueness.*

adolescent egocentrism

The heightened self-consciousness of adolescents that is reflected in their belief that others are as interested in them as they are in themselves, and in their sense of personal uniqueness.

David Elkind (1976) believes that adolescent egocentrism can be dissected into two types of social thinking—imaginary audience and personal fable. The **imaginary audience** *refers to the heightened self-consciousness of adolescents that is reflected in their belief that others are as interested in them as they themselves are. The imaginary audience involves attention-getting behavior—the attempt to be noticed, visible, and "on stage."* Tracy's comments and behavior, in the first paragraph of this section, reflect the imaginary audience. Another adolescent might think that others are as aware of a small spot on his trousers as he is, possibly knowing that he has masturbated. Another adolescent, an eighth-grade girl, walks into her classroom and thinks that all eyes are riveted on her complexion. Adolescents especially sense that they are "on stage" in early adolescence, believing they are the main actors and all others are the audience.

According to Elkind, the **personal fable** *is the part of adolescent egocentrism involving an adolescent's sense of uniqueness.* The comments of Margaret and Adam, mentioned earlier, reflect the personal fable. Adolescents' sense of personal uniqueness makes them feel that no one can understand how they really feel. For example, an adolescent girl thinks that her mother cannot possibly sense the hurt she feels because her boyfriend has broken up with her. As part of their effort to retain a sense of personal uniqueness, adolescents might craft a story about the self that is filled with fantasy, immersing themselves in a world that is far removed from reality. Personal fables frequently show up in adolescent diaries.

Developmentalists have increasingly studied adolescent egocentrism in recent years. The research interest focuses on what the components of egocentrism really are, the nature of self-other relationships, the reasons egocentric thought emerges in adolescence, and the role of egocentrism in adolescent problems. For example, David Elkind (1985) believes that adolescent egocentrism is brought about by formal operational thought. Others, however, argue that adolescent egocentrism is not entirely a cognitive phenomenon. Rather, they think the imaginary audience is due both to the ability to think hypothetically (formal operational thought) and to the ability to step outside oneself and anticipate the reactions of others in imaginative circumstances (perspective taking) (Lapsley, 1991).

Now that we have studied Piaget's stage of formal operational thought and some ideas about adolescent egocentrism, we will turn our attention to changes in information processing during adolescence. To begin, we will examine some changes in memory.

Many adolescent girls spend long hours in front of the mirror, depleting cans of hair spray, tubes of lipstick, and jars of cosmetics. How might this behavior be related to changes in adolescent cognitive and physical development?

imaginary audience
Adolescents' heightened self-consciousness, reflected in their belief that others are as interested in them as they themselves are; attention-getting behavior motivated by a desire to be noticed, visible, and "on stage."

personal fable
The part of adolescent egocentrism that involves an adolescent's sense of uniqueness.

Information Processing

The ability to process information improves during adolescence. Among the areas in which this improvement occurs are memory, decision making, critical thinking, and self-regulatory learning.

Memory How might short-term memory be used in problem solving? In a series of experiments, Robert Sternberg (1977) and his colleagues (Sternberg & Nigro, 1980; Sternberg & Rifkin, 1979) attempted to answer this question by giving third-grade, sixth-grade, ninth-grade, and college students analogies to solve. The main differences occurred between the younger (third- and sixth-grade) and older (ninth-grade and college) students. The older students were more likely to complete the information processing required to solve the analogy task. The children, by contrast, often stopped their processing of information before they had considered all of the necessary steps required to solve the problems. Sternberg believes that incomplete information processing occurred because the children's short-term memory was overloaded. Solving problems, such as analogies, requires individuals to make continued comparisons between newly encoded information and previously encoded information. Sternberg argues that adolescents probably have more storage space in short-term memory, which results in fewer errors on such problems as analogies.

In addition to more storage space, are there other reasons adolescents perform better on memory span tasks and in solving analogies? While many other factors may be involved, information-processing psychologists believe that changes in the speed and efficiency of information processing are important, especially the speed with which information can be identified.

Long-term memory increases substantially in the middle and late childhood years and likely continues to improve during adolescence, although this has not been well documented by researchers. If anything at all is known about long-term memory, it is that it depends on the learning activities engaged in when learning and remembering information (Pressley & Schneider, 1997; Siegler, 1996).

Memory changes represent one way that information processing develops in adolescence. Another set of information-processing changes involves the way adolescents make decisions.

Decision Making   Adolescence is a time of increased decision making—about the future, which friends to choose, whether to go to college, which person to date, whether to have sex, whether to buy a car, and so on (Byrnes, 1997; Galotti & Kozberg, 1996). How competent are adolescents at making decisions? In some reviews, older adolescents are described as more competent than younger adolescents, who, in turn, are more competent than children (Keating, 1990). Compared with children, young adolescents are more likely to generate options, to examine a situation from a variety of perspectives, to anticipate the consequences of decisions, and to consider the credibility of sources.

One study documents that older adolescents are better than younger adolescents at decision making (Lewis, 1981). Eighth-, tenth-, and twelfth-grade students were presented with dilemmas involving the choice of a medical procedure. The oldest students were most likely to spontaneously mention a variety of risks, to recommend consultation with an outside specialist, and to anticipate future consequences. For example, when asked a question about whether to have cosmetic surgery, a twelfth-grader said that different aspects of the situation need to be examined, along with its effects on the individual's future, especially relationships with other people. By contrast, an eighth-grader presented a more limited view, commenting on the surgery's effects on getting turned down for a date, the money involved, and being teased by peers.

In sum, older adolescents often make better decisions than do younger adolescents, who, in turn, make better decisions than children do. But the decision-making skills of older adolescents are far from perfect, as are those of adults. Indeed, some researchers have found that adolescents and adults do not differ in their decision-making skills (Quadrel, Fischoff, & Davis, 1993).

Adolescents need more opportunities to practice and discuss realistic decision making (Jones, Rasmussen, & Moffitt, 1997). Many real-world decisions occur in an atmosphere of stress that includes such factors as time constraints and emotional involvement. One strategy for improving adolescent decision making about real-world choices involving such matters as sex, drugs, and daredevil driving is for schools to provide more opportunities for adolescents to engage in role playing and group problem solving related to such circumstances.

Another strategy is for parents to involve their adolescents in appropriate decision-making activities. In one study of more than 900 young adolescents and a subsample of their parents, the adolescents were more likely to participate in family decision making when they perceived themselves to be in control of what happens to them and if they thought their input would have some bearing on the outcome of the decision-making process (Liprie, 1993).

Critical Thinking   Adolescence is an important transitional period in the development of critical thinking (Keating, 1990). Among the cognitive changes that allow improved critical thinking in adolescence are

- Increased speed, automaticity, and capacity of information processing, which free cognitive resources for other purposes
- More breadth of content knowledge in a variety of domains
- Increased ability to construct new combinations of knowledge
- A greater range and more spontaneous use of strategies or procedures for applying or obtaining knowledge, such as planning, consideration of alternatives, and cognitive monitoring

Critical Thinking

Although adolescence is an important period in the development of critical-thinking skills, if a solid basis of fundamental skills (such as literacy and math skills) is not developed during childhood, such critical-thinking skills are unlikely to mature in adolescence. For the subset of adolescents who lack such fundamental skills, potential gains in adolescent thinking are not likely.

We have seen that adolescents' ability to process information better than children involves improvements in memory, decision making, and critical thinking. Many adolescents also are better than children at monitoring and regulating their learning.

Self-Regulatory Learning   In chapter 14, we described *self-regulatory learning* as the self-generating and self-monitoring of thoughts to reach a goal. Here, we will further explore self-regulatory learning and apply it to learning in middle school. What are some characteristics of self-regulated learners? Self-regulatory learners (Winne, 1995, 1997)

Self-Regulatory Learning

- Set goals for extending their knowledge and sustaining their motivation
- Are aware of their emotional makeup and have strategies for managing their emotions
- Periodically monitor their progress toward a goal
- Fine-tune or revise their strategies, based on the progress they are making
- Evaluate obstacles that may arise and make the necessary adaptations

Teachers, tutors, mentors, counselors, and parents can help students become self-regulatory learners. Barry Zimmerman, Sebastian Bonner, and Robert Kovach (1996) developed a model for turning low self-regulatory students into students who engage in the following multistep strategies: (1) self-evaluation and monitoring, (2) goal setting and strategic planning, (3) implementation of a plan into action and monitoring of it, and (4) monitoring of outcomes and refining of strategies (see figure 16.2).

Zimmerman and his colleagues describe a seventh-grade student who is doing poorly in history and apply their self-regulatory model to her situation. In step 1, she self-evaluates her studying and test-preparation by keeping a detailed record of them. The teacher gives her some guidelines for keeping these records. After several weeks, the student turns in the records and traces her poor test performance to low comprehension of difficult reading material.

In step 2, the student sets a goal, in this case of improving reading comprehension, and plans how to achieve the goal. The teacher assists her in breaking the goal into

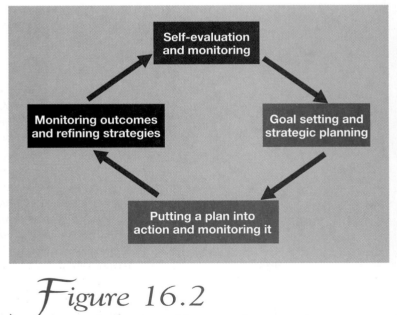

Figure 16.2
A Model of Self-Regulatory Learning

components, such as locating main ideas and setting specific goals for understanding a series of paragraphs in her textbook. The teacher also provides the student with strategies, such as focusing initially on the first sentence of each paragraph and then scanning the others as a means of identifying main ideas. Another support the teacher offers the student is adult or peer tutoring in reading comprehension.

In step 3, the student puts the plan into action and begins to monitor her progress. Initially, she may need help from the teacher or tutor in identifying the main ideas in the reading. This feedback can help her monitor her reading comprehension more effectively on her own.

In step 4, the student monitors her improvement in reading comprehension by evaluating whether it has had any impact on her learning outcomes. Most important, has her improvement in reading comprehension led to better performance on history tests?

The student's self-evaluations reveal that the strategy of finding main ideas has only partly improved her comprehension and only when the first sentence contained the paragraph's main idea. Thus, the teacher recommends further strategies.

Teachers who encourage students to be self-regulatory learners convey the message that students are responsible for their own behavior, for their education, and for their development into contributing citizens of society. Another message conveyed by self-regulatory learning is that learning is a personal experience that requires active and dedicated participation by the student (Zimmerman, Bonner, & Kovach, 1996).

Our coverage of adolescent cognitive development has taken us through Piaget's formal operational stage, adolescent egocentrism, and changes in the way adolescents process information. Next, we will turn our attention to some very different aspects of adolescents' thinking—how they think and make decisions about values and religion.

VALUES AND RELIGION

What are adolescents' values like today? What is the nature of moral education? How powerful is religion in adolescents' lives?

Values

Adolescents carry with them a set of values that influences their thoughts, feelings, and actions. What were your values when you were an adolescent? Are the values of today's adolescents changing?

Over the past two decades, adolescents have shown an increased concern for personal well-being and a decreased concern for the well-being of others, especially for the disadvantaged (Astin & others, 1994). As shown in figure 16.3, today's college freshmen are more strongly motivated to be well off financially and less motivated to develop a meaningful philosophy of life than were their counterparts of 20 or even 10 years ago. Student commitment to becoming very well-off financially as a "very important" reason for attending college reached a record high in the 1990s.

However, two values that increased during the 1960s continue to be important to many of today's youth: self-fulfillment and self-expression (Conger, 1988). As part of their motivation for self-fulfillment, many adolescents show great interest in their physical health and well-being. Greater self-fulfillment and self-expression can be laudable goals, but, if they become the only goals, self-destruction, loneliness, or alienation may result. Young people also need to develop a corresponding sense of commitment to others' welfare. Encouraging adolescents to have a strong commitment to others, in concert with an interest in self-fulfillment, is an important task for America at the close of the twentieth century.

Some signs indicate that today's students are shifting toward a stronger interest in the welfare of society (Yates, 1996). For example, between 1986 and 1994, there

Without civic morality communities perish; without personal morality their survival has no value.

Bertrand Russell
English Philosopher, 20th Century

Values

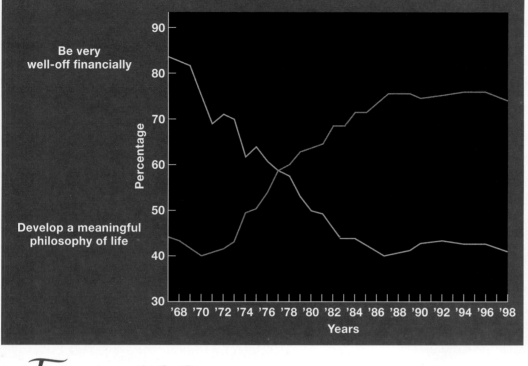

Figure 16.3
Changing Freshman Life Goals, 1968–1998

The percentages indicated are in response to the question of identifying a life goal as "essential" or "very important." There has been a significant reversal in freshman life goals in the past two decades, with a far greater percentage of today's college freshmen stating that a "very important" life goal is to be well off financially, and far fewer stating that developing a meaningful philosophy of life is a "very important" life goal.

was an increase in the percentage of freshmen who said that they were strongly interested in participating in community action programs (28 percent in 1994, 18 percent in 1986) and in helping promote racial understanding (40 percent in 1994, 27 percent in 1986). In one study, students' participation in community service stimulated them to reflect on society's political organization and moral order (Yates, 1995). More students are showing an active interest in the problems of the homeless, child abuse, hunger, and poverty (Conger, 1988). The percentage of students who believe that it is desirable to work for a social service organization rose from 11 percent in 1980 to 17 percent in 1989 (Johnston, Bachman, & O'Malley, 1990). Whether these small incremental increases in concern for the community and society will continue is difficult to predict.

Moral Education

Moral education is hotly debated in educational circles. We will study one of the earliest analyses of moral education, then turn to some contemporary views.

The Hidden Curriculum More than 60 years ago, educator John Dewey (1933) recognized that, even when schools do not have specific programs in moral education, they provide moral education through a "hidden curriculum." The **hidden curriculum** *is conveyed by the moral atmosphere that is a part of every school.* The moral atmosphere is created by school and classroom rules, the moral orientation of teachers and school administrators, and text materials. Teachers serve as models

Moral Development and Education

hidden curriculum
Dewey's concept that every school has a pervasive moral atmosphere, even if it doesn't have a program of moral education.

There are some signs that today's adolescents are shifting toward a stronger interest in the welfare of society, as evidenced by the volunteer work these adolescents are doing on Earth Day.

character education

A direct approach to moral education that involves teaching students a basic moral literacy to prevent them from engaging in immoral behavior and doing harm to themselves and others.

values clarification

An approach to moral education that emphasizes helping people clarify what their lives are for and what is worth working for. Students are encouraged to define their own values and to understand the values of others.

cognitive moral education

An approach to moral education based on the belief that students should develop such values as democracy and justice as their moral reasoning develops; Kohlberg's theory has been the basis of a number of cognitive moral education programs.

of ethical or unethical behavior. Classroom rules and peer relations at school transmit attitudes about cheating, lying, stealing, and consideration of others. And, through its rules and regulations, the school administration infuses the school with a value system.

Character Education   **Character education** *is a direct approach that involves teaching students a basic moral literacy to prevent them from engaging in immoral behavior and doing harm to themselves or others.* The argument is that such behaviors as lying, stealing, and cheating are wrong, and students should be taught this throughout their education. Every school should have an explicit moral code that is clearly communicated to students. Any violations of the code should be met with sanctions (Bennett, 1993). Instruction in specified moral concepts, such as cheating, can take the form of example and definition, class discussions and role playing, or rewarding students for proper behavior.

Some character education movements are the Character Education Partnership, the Character Education Network, the Aspen Declaration on Character Education, and the publicity campaign "Character Counts." Among the books that promote character education are William Bennett's (1993) *The Book of Virtues* and William Damon's (1995) *Greater Expectations*.

Values Clarification   **Values clarification** *means helping people clarify what their lives are for and what is worth working for.* In this approach, students are encouraged to define their own values and understand the values of others. Values clarification differs from character education in that students are not told what their values should be.

In the following values clarification exercise, students are asked to select from among 10 people the 6 who should be allowed to enter a safe shelter because a third world war has broken out (Johnson, 1990):

You work for a government agency in Washington and your group has to decide which six of the following ten people will be admitted to a small fallout shelter. Your group has only 20 minutes to make the decision. These are your choices:

- A 30-year-old male bookkeeper
- The bookkeeper's wife, who is 6 months pregnant
- A second-year African American male medical student who is a political activist
- A 42-year-old male who is a famous historian-author
- A Hollywood actress who is a singer and dancer
- A female biochemist
- A 54-year-old male Rabbi
- A male Olympic athlete who is good in all sports
- A female college student
- A policeman with a gun

In this type of values clarification exercise, there are no right or wrong answers. The clarification of values is left up to the individual student. Advocates of values clarification say it is value-free. However, critics argue that its controversial content offends community standards. They also say that, because of its relativistic nature, values clarification undermines accepted values and fails to stress right behavior.

Cognitive Moral Education   **Cognitive moral education** *is a concept based on the belief that students should learn to value such things as democracy and justice as their moral reasoning develops.* Kohlberg's theory, which we discussed in chapter 14, has been the basis for a number of cognitive moral education programs. In a typical program, high school students meet in a semester-long course to discuss a number of moral issues. The instructor acts as a facilitator, rather than as a director, of the class. The hope is that students will develop more advanced notions of such concepts as cooperation, trust, responsibility, and community. Toward the end of his career, Kohlberg (1986) recognized that the moral atmosphere of the school is more important than he initially envisioned. For example, in one study, a semester-long moral education class based on Kohlberg's theory was successful in advancing moral thinking in three democratic schools, but not in three authoritarian schools (Higgins, Power, & Kohlberg, 1983).

Shown here is an adolescent who has volunteered to work in the National Helpers Network. This program gives students an opportunity to participate in service learning. Among the services provided are helping with environmental concerns, improving neighborhoods, and tutoring. Students also participate in weekly seminars that encourage them to reflect on their active involvement in the community. For more information about the National Helpers Network, call 212–679–7461.

Service Learning   **Service learning** *is a form of education that promotes social responsibility and service to the community.* In service learning, students might engage in tutoring, help the elderly, work in a hospital, assist at a day-care center, or clean up a vacant lot to make a play area. An important goal of service learning is for students to become less self-centered and more motivated to help others (Waterman, 1997).

Service learning takes education out into the community (Levesque & Prosser, 1996). One eleventh-grade student worked as a reading tutor for students from low-income homes who had reading skills well below their grade levels. She commented that, until she did the tutoring, she didn't realize how many students had not experienced the same opportunities she had had when she was growing up. An especially rewarding moment was when one young girl told her, "I want to learn to read like you do so I can go to college when I grow up." Thus, service learning can benefit not only the students but also the recipients of their help.

Researchers have found that service learning benefits students in a number of ways:

- Their grades improve, they become more motivated, and they set more goals (Johnson & others, 1998; Serow, Ciechalski, & Daye, 1990).
- Their self-esteem improves (Hamburg, 1997).
- They become less alienated (Calabrese & Schumer, 1986).
- They increasingly reflect on society's political organization and moral order (Yates, 1995).

Required community service has increased in high schools. In one survey, 15 percent of the nation's largest school districts had such a requirement (National and Community Service Coalition, 1995). Even though required community service has increased in high schools, in another survey of 40,000 adolescents, two thirds said they had never done any volunteer work to help other people (Benson, 1993). The benefits of service learning, for both the volunteer and the recipient, suggest that more adolescents should be required to participate in such programs.

service learning
A form of education that promotes social responsibility and service to the community.

Service Learning

It is one of the beautiful compensations of life that no one can sincerely try to help another without helping himself.

Charles Warner
American Novelist, 19th Century

Religion

Many children and adolescents show an interest in religion, and religious institutions created by adults are designed to introduce certain beliefs and ensure that children will carry on a religious tradition. Societies have invented, for example, Sunday schools, parochial education, tribal transmission of religious traditions, and home schooling.

Does this indoctrination work? In many cases, it does (Paloutzian, 1996). In general, adults tend to adopt the religious teachings of their upbringing. For instance, if individuals are Catholics by the time they are 25 years of age, and were raised as Catholics, they likely will continue to be Catholics throughout their adult years. If a religious change or reawakening occurs, it is most likely to take place during adolescence (Argyle & Beit-Hallahmi, 1975).

Religion and Adolescents

Religious issues are important to adolescents (Paloutzian & Santrock, 1997). In one survey, 95 percent of 13- to 18-year-olds said they believe in God or a universal spirit (Gallup & Bezilla, 1992). Almost three fourths of the adolescents said they pray, and about one half indicated they had attended religious services in the past week. Almost one half said it is very important for a young person to learn religious faith.

Developmental Changes Adolescence might be an especially important juncture for religious development. Even if children have been indoctrinated into a religion by their parents, because of advances in their cognitive development they begin to question what their own religious beliefs truly are.

During adolescence, especially in late adolescence and the college years, identity development becomes a central focus (Erikson, 1968). Youth want to find answers to these kinds of questions: "Who am I?" "What am I all about as a person?" "What kind of life do I want to lead?" As part of their search for identity, adolescents begin to grapple in more sophisticated, logical ways with such questions as these: "Why am I on this planet?" "Is there really a God or higher spiritual being, or have I just been believing what my parents and the church imprinted in my mind?" "What really are my religious views?"

Piaget's (1962) cognitive developmental theory provides a theoretical backdrop for understanding religious development in children and adolescents. For example, in one study, children were asked about their understanding of certain religious pictures and Bible stories (Goldman, 1964). The children's responses fell into three stages closely related to Piaget's theory.

In the first stage (up until 7 or 8 years of age)—*preoperational intuitive religious thought*—children's religious thoughts were unsystematic and fragmented. Many of the children either did not fully understand the material in the stories or did not consider all of the evidence. For example, one child's response to the question "Why was Moses afraid to look at God?" (Exodus 3:6) was "Because God had a funny face!"

In the second stage (occurring from 7 or 8 to 13 or 14 years of age)—*concrete operational religious thought*—children focused on particular details of pictures and stories. For example, in response to the question about why Moses was afraid to look at God, one child said, "Because it was a ball of fire. He thought he might burn him." Said another child, "It was a bright light and to look at it might blind him."

In the third stage (age 14 through the remainder of adolescence)—*formal operational religious thought*—adolescents revealed a more abstract, hypothetical religious understanding. For example, one adolescent said Moses was afraid to look at God because "God is holy and the world is sinful." Another youth responded, "The awesomeness and almightiness of God would make Moses feel like a worm in comparison."

Other researchers have found similar developmental changes in children and adolescents. For example, in one study, at about 17 or 18 years of age adolescents increasingly commented about freedom, meaning, and hope—abstract concepts—when making religious judgments (Oser & Gmunder, 1991).

Religiousness and Sexuality in Adolescence One area of religion's influence on adolescent development involves sexual activity. Although variability and change in church teachings make it difficult to characterize religious doctrines simply, most churches discourage premarital sex. Thus, the degree of adolescents' participation in religious organizations may be more important than religious affiliation as a determinant of premarital sexual attitudes and behavior. Adolescents who attend religious services frequently may hear messages about abstaining from sex. The involvement of adolescents in religious organizations also enhances the probability that they will become friends with adolescents who have restrictive attitudes toward premarital sex. In one study, adolescents who attended church frequently and valued religion in their lives were less experienced sexually and had less permissive attitudes toward premarital sex than did their counterparts who attended church infrequently and said that religion did not play a strong role in their lives

(Thorton & Camburn, 1989). However, while religious involvement is associated with a lower incidence of sexual activity among adolescents, adolescents who are religiously involved and sexually active are less likely to use medical methods of contraception (especially the pill) than are their sexually active counterparts with low religious involvement.

Fowler's Developmental Theory   James Fowler (1981) proposed a theory of religious development that focuses on the motivation to discover meaning in life, either within or outside of organized religion. Fowler proposed six stages of religious development that are related to Erikson's, Piaget's, and Kohlberg's theories of development (Torney-Purta, 1993).

Stage 1. Intuitive-projective faith (early childhood). After infants learn to trust their caregiver (Erikson's formulation), they invent their own intuitive images of what good and evil are. As children move into Piaget's preoperational stage, their cognitive worlds open up a variety of new possibilities. Fantasy and reality are taken as being the same thing. Right and wrong are seen in terms of consequences to the self.

Stage 2. Mythical-literal faith (middle and late childhood). As children move into Piaget's concrete operational stage, they begin to reason in a more logical, but not abstract, way. They see the world as more orderly. Grade-school-age children interpret religious stories literally, and they perceive God as being much like a parent figure who rewards the good and punishes the bad. What is right is often perceived as fair exchange.

Stage 3. Synthetic-conventional faith (transition between childhood and adolescence, early adolescence). Adolescents start to develop formal operational thought (Piaget's highest stage) and begin to integrate what they have learned about religion into a coherent belief system. According to Fowler, although the synthetic-conventional faith stage is more abstract than the previous two stages, young adolescents still mainly conform to the religious beliefs of others (analogous to Kohlberg's conventional level of morality) and have not yet adequately analyzed alternative religious ideologies. Behavior that involves a question of right and wrong is seen in terms of the harm it does to a relationship or what others might say. Fowler believes that most adults become locked into this stage and never move on to higher stages of religious development.

Stage 4. Individuating-reflexive faith (transition between adolescence and adulthood, early adulthood). Fowler believes that at this stage, for the first time, individuals are capable of taking full responsibility for their religious beliefs. Often as a response to their leaving-home experience, young people begin to take responsibility for their lives. Young adults start to realize that they can choose the course of their life and that they must expend effort to follow a particular life course. Individuals come face-to-face with decisions about whether to consider themselves or the welfare of others first, and whether the religious doctrines they were taught when they were growing up are absolute or relative. Fowler believes that both formal operational thought and the intellectual challenges to an individual's values and religious ideologies that often take place in college are essential to developing individuating-reflexive faith.

Stage 5. Conjunctive faith (middle adulthood). Fowler believes that only a small number of adults ever move on to this stage, which involves being more open to paradox and opposing viewpoints. This openness stems from people's awareness of their finiteness and limitations. One woman Fowler (1981, p. 192) placed at this stage revealed the following complex religious understanding: "Whether you call it God or Jesus or Cosmic Flow or Reality or Love, it doesn't matter what you call it. It is there."

Stage 6. Universalizing faith (middle adulthood or late adulthood). Fowler says that the highest stage in religious development involves transcending specific belief systems to achieve a sense of oneness with all beings and a commitment to breaking down the barriers that are divisive to people on this planet. Conflictual events are no longer seen as paradoxes. Fowler argues that very, very few people ever achieve this elusive, highest stage of religious development. Three who he says have were Mahatma Gandhi, Martin Luther King, Jr., and Mother Teresa.

Summary Table 16.1
Adolescent Cognition, Values and Religion

Concept	Processes/ Related Ideas	Characteristics/Description
Adolescent cognition	Piaget's theory	Abstractness and idealism, as well as hypothetical-deductive reasoning, are highlighted in formal operational thought. Formal operational thought involves the ability to reason about what is possible and hypothetical, as opposed to what is real, and the ability to reflect on one's own thoughts. Formal operational thought occurs in two phases—an assimilation phase, in which reality is overwhelmed (early adolescence), and an accommodation phase, in which intellectual balance is restored through a consolidation of formal operational thought (middle years of adolescence). Individual variation is extensive, and Piaget did not give this adequate attention. Many young adolescents are not formal operational thinkers but, rather, are consolidating their concrete operational thought.
	Adolescent egocentrism	Elkind proposed that adolescents, especially young adolescents, develop an egocentrism that involves both the construction of an imaginary audience (the belief that others are as preoccupied with the adolescent as the adolescent is) and a personal fable (a sense of personal uniqueness). Elkind believes that egocentrism appears because of formal operational thought. Others argue that perspective taking also is involved.
	Information processing	Adolescents likely have a better memory than children because of increases in storage space, as well as speed and efficiency of information processing. Adolescence is a time of increased decision making. Older adolescents are more competent at decision making than younger adolescents, who are more competent at this than children. The ability to make competent decisions does not guarantee they will be made in life. Adolescence is an important transitional period in critical thinking because of such cognitive changes as increased speed, automaticity, and capacity of information processing; increased ability to construct new combinations of knowledge; and a greater range and more spontaneous use of strategies. Self-regulation consists of self-generating and self-monitoring thoughts, feelings, and behaviors to reach a goal. Self-regulation is an important aspect of learning in adolescence.
Values and religion	Values	Over the past two decades, adolescents have shown an increased concern for personal well-being and a decreased concern for the welfare of others. Recently, adolescents have shown a slight increase in concern for community and societal issues.
	Moral education	The hidden curriculum involves the belief that every school has a moral atmosphere. Character education is a direct education approach that advocates teaching students a basic moral literacy. Values clarification emphasizes helping students clarify what their lives are for and what is worth working for. Cognitive moral education states that students should develop such values as democracy and justice as their moral reasoning develops. Kohlberg's theory has been the basis of a number of cognitive moral education programs. Service learning involves educational experiences that promote social responsibility and service to the community. Researchers have found that service learning benefits students in a number of ways.
	Religion	Many children and adolescents show an interest in religion, and religious institutions are designed to introduce them to religious beliefs. Adolescence may be a special juncture in religious development for many individuals. Piaget's theory provides a cognitive background for understanding religious development. Linkages between religiousness and sexuality occur in adolescence. Fowler proposed a life-span theory of religious development.

As with other stage theories of development—such as Erikson's, Piaget's, and Kohlberg's—Fowler's theory does not adequately take into account individual variation in development. Not everyone goes through the stages as coherently as Fowler portrays them.

At this point, we have studied a number of ideas about cognition, values, and religion in adolescence. An overview of these ideas is presented in summary table 16.1.

SCHOOLS

What is the nature of schooling for adolescents? How many adolescents drop out of school?

Schools for Adolescents

The impressive changes in adolescents' cognition lead us to examine the nature of schools for adolescents. In chapter 14, we discussed different ideas about the effects of schools on children's development. Here, we will focus more exclusively on the nature of secondary schools. Among the questions we will try to answer are the following: What should be the function of secondary schools? What is the nature of the transition from elementary to middle or junior high school? What are effective schools for young adolescents?

The Controversy Surrounding Secondary Schools   During the twentieth century, schools have assumed a more prominent role in the lives of adolescents. From 1890 to 1920, virtually every state developed laws that excluded youth from work and required them to attend school. In this time frame, the number of high school graduates increased 600 percent (Tyack, 1976). By making secondary education compulsory, the adult power structure placed adolescents in a submissive position and made their move into the adult world of work more manageable. In the nineteenth century, high schools were mainly for the elite, with the main educational emphasis on classical liberal arts courses. In the 1920s, educators perceived that the secondary school curriculum needed to be changed. Schools for the masses, it was thought, should not just involve intellectual training but should also include training for work and citizenship. The curriculum of secondary schools became more comprehensive and grew to include general education, college preparatory, and vocational education courses. As the twentieth century unfolded, secondary schools continued to expand their orientation, adding courses in music, art, health, physical education, and other topics. By the middle of the twentieth century, schools had moved further toward preparing students for comprehensive roles in life. Today, secondary schools retain their comprehensive orientation, designed to train adolescents intellectually but in many other ways as well, such as vocationally and socially.

Although there has been a consistent trend of increased school attendance for more than 150 years, the distress over alienated and rebellious youth has led some educators and social scientists to question whether secondary schools actually benefit adolescents. During the early 1970s, these experts agreed that high schools contribute to adolescent alienation and interfere with the transition to adulthood (Martin, 1976). They said that adolescents should be given educational alternatives to the comprehensive high school, such as on-the-job community work, to increase their exposure to adult roles and to decrease their sense of isolation from adults. To some degree in response to these critics, a number of states lowered from 16 to 14 the age at which adolescents could leave school.

In the last decade of the twentieth century, the back-to-basics movement has gained momentum, with proponents arguing that the main function of schools should be rigorous training of intellectual skills through such subjects as English, math, and science. Advocates of the back-to-basics movement point to the excessive fluff in secondary school curricula, with students being allowed to select from many alternatives that will not give them a basic education in intellectual subjects. Some critics also point to the extensive time students spend in extracurricular activities. They argue that schools should be in the business of imparting knowledge to adolescents and not be so concerned about their social and emotional lives. Related to the proverbial dilemma of schools' functions is whether schools should include a vocational curriculum in addition to training in basic subjects, such as English, math, and science. Some critics of the fluff in secondary schools argue that the

Schools for Adolescents

In youth we learn, in age we understand.

Marie Ebner von Eschenbach
Austrian Author, 20th Century

National Center for Education Statistics
**United States Department
of Education**

school day should be longer and that the school year should be extended into the summer months. Such arguments are made by critics who believe that the main function of schools should be the training of intellectual skills. Little concern for adolescents' social and emotional development appears in these arguments.

Should the main—and perhaps only—major goal of schooling for adolescents be the development of an intellectually mature individual? Or should schools also focus on the adolescent's maturity in social and emotional development? Should schools be comprehensive, providing a multifaceted curriculum that includes many electives and alternative subjects? These are provocative questions that continue to be heatedly debated in educational and community circles.

The Transition to Middle or Junior High School   The emergence of junior high schools in the 1920s and 1930s was justified on the basis of the physical, cognitive, and social changes that characterize early adolescence, as well as the need for more schools for the growing student population. Old high schools became junior high schools, and new regional high schools were built. In most systems, the ninth grade remained a part of the high school in content, although physically separated from it in a 6-3-3 system. Gradually, the ninth grade was restored to the high school, as many school systems developed middle schools that include the seventh and eighth grades, or sixth, seventh, and eighth grades. The creation of middle schools was influenced by the earlier onset of puberty in recent decades.

One worry of educators and psychologists is that junior high and middle schools have simply become watered-down versions of high schools, mimicking their curricular and extracurricular schedules. The critics argue that unique curricular and extracurricular activities reflecting a wide range of individual differences in biological and psychological development in early adolescence should be incorporated into our junior high and middle schools. The critics also stress that many high schools foster passivity rather than autonomy and that schools should create a variety of pathways for students to achieve an identity.

The transition to middle school or junior high school from elementary schools interests developmentalists because, even though it is a normative experience for virtually all children, the transition can be stressful. Why? The transition takes place at a time when many changes—in the individual, in the family, and in school—are occurring simultaneously. These changes include puberty and related concerns about body image; the emergence of at least some aspects of formal operational thought, including accompanying changes in social cognition; increased responsibility and independence in association with decreased dependency on parents; change from a small, contained classroom structure to a larger, more impersonal school structure; change from one teacher to many teachers and from a small, homogeneous set of peers to a larger, more heterogeneous set of peers; and an increased focus on achievement and performance and their assessment. This list includes a number of negative, stressful features, but there can be positive aspects to the transition. Students are more likely to feel grown up, have more subjects from which to select, have more opportunities to spend time with peers and to locate compatible friends, and enjoy increased independence from direct parental monitoring, and they may be more challenged intellectually by academic work.

When students make the transition from elementary school to middle or junior high school, they experience the **top-dog phenomenon,** *the circumstance of moving from the top position (in elementary school, being the oldest, biggest, and most powerful students in the school) to the lowest position (in middle or junior high school, being the youngest, smallest, and least powerful students in the school).* Researchers who have charted the transition from elementary to middle or junior high school find that the first year of middle or junior high school can be difficult for many students (Hawkins & Berndt, 1985). For example, in one study of the transition from sixth grade in an elementary school to the seventh grade in a junior high school, adolescents' perceptions of the quality of their school life plunged in the seventh grade (Hirsch & Rapkin, 1987). In the seventh grade, the students were less satisfied with school,

Middle Schools
Educational Psychology Resources

top-dog phenomenon
The circumstance of moving from the top position in elementary school to the lowest position in middle or junior high school.

The transition from elementary to middle or junior high school occurs at the same time as a number of other developmental changes. Biological, cognitive, and socioemotional changes converge with this schooling transition to make it a time of considerable adaptation.

were less committed to school, and liked their teachers less. The drop in school satisfaction occurred regardless of how academically successful the students were.

Effective Schools for Young Adolescents
What makes a successful middle school? Joan Lipsitz (1984) and her colleagues searched the nation for the best middle schools. Extensive contacts and observations were made. Based on the recommendations of education experts and observations in schools in different parts of the United States, four middle schools were chosen for their outstanding ability to educate young adolescents. What were these middle schools like? The most striking feature was their willingness and ability to adapt all school practices to their students' individual differences in physical, cognitive, and social development. The schools took seriously the knowledge we have developed about young adolescents. This seriousness was reflected in the decisions about different aspects of school life. For example, one middle school fought to keep its schedule of minicourses on Friday, so that every student could be with friends and pursue personal interests. Two other middle schools expended considerable energy on a complex school organization, so that small groups of students worked with small groups of teachers who could vary the tone and pace of the school day, depending on the students' needs. Another middle school developed an advisory scheme, so that each student had daily contact with an adult who was willing to listen, explain, comfort, and prod the adolescent. Such school policies reflect thoughtfulness and personal concern about individuals who have compelling developmental needs.

Another aspect of the effective middle schools was that early in their existence—the first year in three of the schools and the second year in the fourth school—they emphasized the importance of creating an environment that was positive for adolescents' social and emotional development. This goal was established not only because such environments contribute to academic excellence but also because social and emotional development were valued as intrinsically important in adolescents' schooling.

Recognizing that the vast majority of middle schools do not approach the excellent schools described by Joan Lipsitz (1984), in 1989 the Carnegie Corporation issued an extremely negative evaluation of our nation's middle schools. In the report, "Turning Points: Preparing American Youth for the 21st Century," the

Middle School Resources

What does education often do? It makes a straight-cut ditch of a free, meandering brook.

Henry David Thoreau
American Poet, Essayist, 19th Century

**Secondary Schools and
Adolescent Issues**

Educating Young Adolescents

conclusion was put forth that most young adolescents attend massive, impersonal schools, learn from seemingly irrelevant curricula, trust few adults in school, and lack access to health care and counseling. The Carnegie Corporation (1989) report recommended the following:

- Develop smaller "communities" or "houses" to lessen the impersonal nature of large middle schools.
- Lower student-to-counselor ratios from several hundred-to-1 to 10-to-1.
- Involve parents and community leaders in schools.
- Develop curricula that produce students who are literate, understand the sciences, and have a sense of health, ethics, and citizenship.
- Have teachers team teach in more flexibly designed curriculum blocks that integrate several disciplines, instead of presenting students with disconnected, rigidly separated 50-minute segments.
- Boost students' health and fitness with more in-school programs and help students who need public health care to get it.

Many of these recommendations were echoed in a report from the National Governors' Association (*America in Transition,* 1989), which stated that the very structure of middle school education in America neglects the basic developmental needs of young adolescents. Many educators and psychologists strongly support these recommendations (Wigfield & Eccles, 1994, 1995). The Edna McConnell Clark Foundation's Program for Disadvantaged Youth is an example of a multiyear, multisite effort designed to implement many of the proposals for middle school improvement. The foundation has engaged the Center for Early Adolescence at the University of North Carolina to guide five urban school districts in their middle school reform (Scales, 1992). In sum, middle schools throughout the nation need a major redesign if they are to be effective in educating adolescents for becoming competent adults in the twenty-first century.

Through its Middle Grade School State Policy Initiative, the Carnegie Foundation of New York is implementing the "Turning Points" recommendations in nearly 100 schools and 15 states nationwide. A national evaluation of this initiative is currently underway. Data from the state of Illinois already show that, in 42 schools participating in at least one year of the study since 1991, enactment of the "Turning Points" recommendations was associated with significant improvements in students' reading, math, and language arts achievement. In 31 schools with several years of data, the same pattern of positive results was found within schools over time. That is, as schools continued to implement the "Turning Points" recommendations, students' achievement continued to improve (Carnegie Council on Adolescent Development, 1995). To think further about middle and junior high school education, see Adventures for the Mind.

One successful program for increasing the academic skills of African American adolescents was developed by Xavier College in New Orleans. Xavier's program is called SOAR (Stress on Analytical Reasoning). It is an intensive, 12-hour-a-day, 4-week summer program. SOAR treats problem solving as a step-by-step process. Students are given such word problems as "Cross out the letter after the letter in the word "pardon" which is in the same position in the word as it is in the alphabet." Rather than let students just guess at the answer, the teachers force the students to focus on such issues as the meaning of "the same position in the word."

In the SOAR program, the students are given verbal analogies (such as "Oven is to bake" as "Dishes are to dishwasher" or as "Carry is to automobile"). And they are required to identify the logical relation between words before being allowed to solve the problem. They are given jumbled sentences and are asked to rearrange them in logical order. In short, the students are encouraged to think a lot about thinking.

Recently, Eugene Williams, the director of Washington, DC's citywide program for public school students who hope to become National Merit Scholars, adopted many of Xavier College's methods for the Washington program. In the Washington program, students are divided into teams and are instructed to work through math problems out loud—as their partners criticize their thinking. Instead of just memorizing vocabulary lists, they are taught to create mental images of new words. The Washington program lasts for six weeks in the summer. The increased emphasis on developing thinking skills already has paid off. The number of merit scholars in Washington, DC, has increased. The program, which places a premium on analytic and abstract reasoning, requires students to be recommended by their principal and have the active support of their parents.

Maxine Bleich, president of the nonprofit Ventures in Education, is attempting to replicate SOAR's success in disadvantaged high schools—rural and urban—in many parts of the United States. It is important to note that these programs have focused on highly motivated students. It is not known if the methods will work with below average, unmotivated students.

High School Dropouts

For many decades, dropping out of high school has been viewed as a serious educational and societal problem. By leaving high school before graduating, many dropouts take with them educational deficiencies that severely curtail their economic and social well-being throughout their adult lives. We will study the scope of the problem, the causes of dropping out, and ways to reduce dropout rates. While dropping out of high school has negative consequences for youth, the picture is not entirely bleak. Over the past 40 years, the proportion of adolescents who have not finished high school has decreased considerably. In 1940, more than 60 percent of all individuals 25 to 29 years of age had not completed high school. By 1986, this proportion had dropped to less than 14 percent. From 1973 to 1983, the annual dropout rate nationwide fell by almost 20 percent, from 6.3 to 5.2 percent.

Despite the decline in overall high school dropout rates, a major concern is the higher dropout rate of minority-group and low-income students, especially in large cities (Cohen, 1994; Evans & others, 1995). The student dropout rates of most minority groups have been declining, but they remain substantially above those of White adolescents. The proportion of Latino youth who finish high school is not keeping pace with the gains by African Americans. High school completion rates for Latino youth dropped from 63 percent in 1985 to 56 percent in 1989; the completion rate was 52 percent in 1972. In contrast, the high school graduation rate for African American youth increased from 67 percent in 1972 to 76 percent in 1989. The comparable rates for White youth remained the same—82 percent in both 1972 and 1989.

Dropout rates are also high for Native Americans (fewer than 10 percent graduate from high school). In some inner-city areas, the dropout rate for ethnic minority students is especially high, reaching more than 50 percent in Chicago, for example.

Students drop out of schools for many reasons (Jacobs, Garnier, & Weisner, 1996; McDougall, Schonert-Reichel, & Hymel, 1996). In one study, almost 50 percent of the dropouts cited school-related reasons for leaving school, such as not liking school or being expelled or suspended (Rumberger, 1983). Twenty percent of the dropouts (but 40 percent of the Latino students) cited economic reasons for leaving school. One third of the female students dropped out for personal reasons, such as pregnancy or marriage.

Most research on dropouts has focused on high school students. One study focused on middle school dropouts (Rumberger, 1995). The observed differences in dropout rates among ethnic groups were related to differences in family background—especially socioeconomic status. Lack of parental academic support, low parental supervision, and low parental educational expectations for their adolescents were also related to dropping out of middle school.

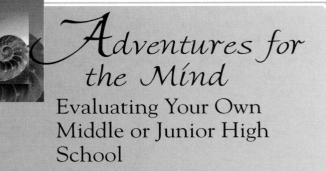

Adventures for the Mind

Evaluating Your Own Middle or Junior High School

What was your own middle or junior high school like? How did it measure up to Lipsitz's criteria for effective schools for young adolescents? Did the school characteristically take individual differences into account? Did the administrators and teachers adequately address the unique needs of young adolescents as separate from those of children and older adolescents? Was socioemotional development emphasized as much as cognitive development? Suppose you could redesign the middle school you attended in one or two significant ways to improve students' socioemotional development. What changes would you make?

Reducing the Dropout Rate

High School Education

To help reduce the dropout rate, community institutions, especially schools, need to break down the barriers between work and school. Many youth step off the education ladder long before reaching the level needed for a professional career, often with nowhere to step next, and are left to their own devices to search for work. These youth need more assistance than they are now receiving. Among the approaches worth considering are these (William T. Grant Foundation Commission, 1988):

• Monitored work experiences, such as those through cooperative education, apprenticeships, internships, preemployment training, and youth-operated enterprises
• Community and neighborhood services, including voluntary and youth-guided services
• Redirected vocational education, the principal thrust of which should not be preparation for specific jobs but acquisition of basic skills needed for a wide range of jobs
• Guarantees of continuing education, employment, or training, especially in conjunction with mentor programs
• Career information and counseling to expose youth to job opportunities and career options, as well as to successful role models
• School volunteer programs, not only for tutoring but also for access to adult friends and mentors

Career Planning

developmental career choice theory
Ginzberg's theory that children and adolescents go through three career choice stages—fantasy, tentative, and realistic.

CAREER DEVELOPMENT AND WORK

What is the nature of career development in adolescence? Does working part-time while going to school have a positive or negative affect on adolescent development?

Career Development

What theories have been developed to direct our understanding of adolescents' career choices? What roles do exploration, decision making, and planning play in career development? How do sociocultural factors affect career development?

Theories of Career Development   Three main theories describe the manner in which adolescents make choices about career development: Ginzberg's developmental theory, Super's self-concept theory, and Holland's personality-type theory.

Ginzberg's Developmental Theory   Developmental career choice theory *is Eli Ginzberg's theory that children and adolescents go through three career choice stages: fantasy, tentative, and realistic* (Ginzberg, 1972). When asked what they want to be when they grow up, young children might answer "a doctor," "a superhero," "a teacher," "a movie star," "a sports star," or any number of other occupations. In childhood, the future seems to hold almost unlimited opportunities. Ginzberg argues that, until about the age of 11, children are in the *fantasy stage* of career choice. From the ages of 11 to 17, adolescents are in the *tentative stage* of career development, a transition from the fantasy stage of childhood to the realistic decision making of young adulthood. Ginzberg believes that adolescents progress from evaluating their interests (11 to 12 years of age) to evaluating their capacities (13 to 14 years of age) to evaluating their values (15 to 16 years of age). Thinking shifts from less subjective to more realistic career choices at 17 to 18 years of age. Ginzberg calls the period from 17 to 18 years of age through the early twenties the *realistic stage* of career choice. During this time, the individual extensively explores available careers, then focuses on a particular career, and finally selects a specific job within the career (such as family practitioner or orthopedic surgeon, within the career of doctor).

Critics have attacked Ginzberg's theory on a number of grounds. For one, the initial data were collected from middle-class youth, who probably had more career options open to them. And, as with other developmental theories (such as Piaget's), the time frames are too rigid. Moreover, Ginzberg's theory does not take into account individual differences—some adolescents make mature decisions about careers (and stick with them) at much earlier ages than specified by Ginzberg. Not all children engage in career fantasies, either. In a revision of his theory, Ginzberg (1972) conceded that lower-class individuals do not have as many options available as middle-class individuals do. Ginzberg's general point—that at some point during late adolescence or early adulthood more realistic career choices are made—probably is correct.

Super's Self-Concept Theory   **Career self-concept theory** *is Donald Super's theory that individuals' self-concepts play central roles in their career choices. Super believes that it is during adolescence that individuals first construct a career self-concept* (Super, 1976). He emphasizes that career development consists of five phases. First, at about 14 to 18 years of age, adolescents develop ideas about work that mesh with their already existing global self-concept—this phase is called *crystallization*. Between 18 and 22 years of age, they narrow their career choices and initiate behavior that enables them to enter some type of career—this phase is called *specification*. Between 21 and 24 years of age, young adults complete their education or training and enter the world of work—this phase is called *implementation*. The decision on a specific, appropriate career is made between 25 and 35 years of age—this phase is called *stabilization*. Finally, after the age of 35, individuals seek to advance their careers and reach higher-status positions—this phase is called *consolidation*. The age ranges should be thought of as approximate rather than rigid. Super believes that career exploration in adolescence is a key ingredient of the adolescent's career self-concept. He constructed the Career Development Inventory to assist counselors in promoting adolescents' career exploration.

career self-concept theory
Super's theory that individuals' self-concepts play central roles in their career choices.

Holland's Personality-Type Theory   **Personality-type theory** *is John Holland's theory that an effort should be made to match an individual's career choice with his or her personality* (Holland, 1987). Once individuals find a career that fits with their personality, they are more likely to enjoy that career and stay in a job for a longer period of time than are individuals who work at jobs that are not suitable for their personality. Holland believes there are six basic personality types to be considered when matching the individual's psychological makeup with a career:

personality-type theory
Holland's theory that an effort should be made to match an individual's career choice with his or her personality.

- *Realistic.* These individuals show characteristically "masculine" traits. They are physically strong, deal in practical ways with problems, and have very little social know-how. They are best oriented toward practical careers, such as labor, farming, truck driving, and construction.
- *Intellectual.* These individuals are conceptually and theoretically oriented. They are thinkers, rather than doers. Often, they avoid interpersonal relations and are best suited to careers in math and science.
- *Social.* These individuals often show characteristically "feminine" traits, especially those associated with verbal skills and interpersonal relations. They are likely to be best equipped to enter "people" professions, such as teaching, social work, and counseling.
- *Conventional.* These youth show a distaste for unstructured activities. They are best suited for jobs as subordinates, such as bank tellers, secretaries, and file clerks.
- *Enterprising.* These individuals energize their verbal abilities toward leading others, dominating individuals, and selling people on issues or products. They are best counseled to enter such careers as sales, politics, and management.
- *Artistic.* These youth prefer to interact with their world through artistic expression, avoiding conventional and interpersonal situations in many instances, and should be oriented toward such careers as art and writing.

If all individuals were to fall conveniently into Holland's personality types, career counselors would have an easy job. But individuals are more varied and complex than Holland's theory suggests. Even Holland now admits that most individuals are not pure types. Still, the basic idea of matching individuals' abilities to particular

Exploring Career Development

careers is an important contribution to the career field (Brown, 1987). Holland's personality types are incorporated into the Strong-Campbell Vocational Interest Inventory, a widely used measure in career guidance.

Exploration, Decision Making, and Planning   Exploration, decision making, and planning play important roles in adolescents' career choices (Michelozzi, 1996; Wallace-Broscious, Serafica, & Osipow, 1994). In countries where equal employment opportunities have emerged—such as the United States, Canada, Great Britain, and France—the exploration of various career paths is critical in the adolescent's career development. Adolescents often approach career exploration and decision making with considerable ambiguity, uncertainty, and stress. Many of the career decisions they make involve floundering and unplanned changes. Many adolescents do not adequately explore careers on their own and receive little direction from school guidance counselors. On the average, high school students spend less than three hours per year with guidance counselors, and in some schools the average is even less (National Assessment of Educational Progress, 1976). In many schools, students not only do not know *what* information to seek about careers but also do not know *how* to seek it.

Among the important aspects of planning in career development is awareness of the educational requirements for a particular career. In one study, a sample of 6,029 high school seniors from 57 school districts in Texas was studied (Grotevant & Durrett, 1980). The students lacked knowledge about two aspects of careers: (1) accurate information about the educational requirements of careers they desired and (2) information about the vocational interests predominantly associated with their career choices.

Sociocultural Influences   Not every individual born into the world can grow up to become a nuclear physicist or a doctor—there is a genetic limitation that keeps some adolescents from performing at the high intellectual levels necessary to enter such careers. Similarly, there are genetic limitations that restrict some adolescents from becoming professional football players or professional golfers. But there usually are many careers available to each of us, careers that provide a reasonable match with our abilities. Our sociocultural experiences exert strong influences on our career choices from among the wide range available. Among the important sociocultural factors that influence career development are socioeconomic status, parents and peers, schools, and gender roles.

School-To-Work Transitions

Socioeconomic Status   The channels of upward mobility open to lower-socioeconomic status youth are largely educational. The school hierarchy from grade school through high school, as well as through college and graduate school, is programmed to orient individuals toward some type of career. Less than a hundred years ago, only eight years of education were believed to be necessary for vocational competence, and anything beyond that qualified the individual for advanced placement in higher-status occupations. By the middle of the twentieth century, the high school diploma had already lost ground as a ticket to career success. College rapidly became a prerequisite for entering a higher-status occupation. Employers reason that an individual with a college degree is a better risk than a high school graduate or a high school dropout.

Parents and Peers   Parents and peers also are strong influences on adolescents' career choices. David Elkind (1981) believes that today's parents are pressuring their adolescents to achieve too much too soon. In some cases, though, adolescents do not get challenged enough by their parents. Consider a 25-year-old woman who vividly describes the details of her adolescence that later prevented her from seeking a competent career. From early in adolescence, both of her parents encouraged her to finish high school, but at the same time they emphasized that she needed to get a job to help them pay the family's bills. She was never told that she could not go to college, but both parents encouraged her to find someone to marry who could support her financially. This very bright girl is now divorced and feels intellectually cheated by her parents, who socialized her in the direction of marriage and away from a college education.

From an early age, children see and hear about what jobs their parents have. In some cases, parents even take their children to work with them on jobs. When we (your author) were building our house, the bricklayer brought his two sons to help with the work. They were only 14 years old, yet were already engaging in apprenticeship work with their father.

Unfortunately, many parents want to live vicariously through their son's or daughter's career achievements. The mother who did not get into medical school and the father who did not make it as a professional athlete may pressure their youth to achieve a career status that is beyond the youth's talents.

Many factors influence the parent's role in the adolescent's career development. For one, mothers who work regularly outside the home and show effort and pride in their work probably have strong influences on their adolescents' career development. A reasonable conclusion is that, when both parents work and enjoy their work, adolescents learn work values from both parents. Peers also can influence the adolescent's career development. In one study, when adolescents had friends and parents with high career standards, they were more likely to seek higher career status jobs, even if they came from low-income families (Simpson, 1962).

These adolescents are at a job fair, seeking information about careers. Improving adolescents' awareness of career options and educational requirements is an important agenda for our nation.

School Influences   Schools, teachers, and counselors can exert a powerful influence on adolescents' career development. School is the primary setting where individuals first encounter the world of work. School provides an atmosphere for continuing self-development in relation to achievement and work. And school is the only institution in our society presently capable of providing the delivery systems necessary for career education—instruction, guidance, placement, and community connections.

A national survey revealed the nature of career information available to adolescents (Chapman & Katz, 1983). The single most common resource was the *Occupational Outlook Handbook (OOH)*, with 92 percent of the schools having one or more copies. The second major source was the *Dictionary of Occupational Titles (DOT)*, with 82 percent having this book available for students. Less than 30 percent had no established committee to review career information resources. When students talked to counselors, it was more often about high school courses than about career guidance.

School counseling has been criticized heavily, both inside and outside the educational establishment. Insiders complain about the large number of students per school counselor and the weight of noncounseling administrative duties. Outsiders complain that school counseling is ineffective, biased, and a waste of money. Short of a new profession, several options are possible (William T. Grant Foundation Commission, 1988). First, twice the number of counselors are needed to meet all students' needs. Second, there could be a redefinition of teachers' roles, accompanied by retraining and a reduction in teaching loads, so that classroom teachers could assume a stronger role in handling the counseling needs of adolescents. The professional counselor's role in this plan would be to train and assist teachers in their counseling and to provide direct counseling in situations the teacher could not handle. Third, the whole idea of school counselors would be abandoned, and counselors would be located elsewhere—in neighborhood social service centers or labor offices, for example. (Germany forbids teachers to give career counseling, reserving this task for officials in well-developed networks of labor offices.)

The College Board Commission on Precollege Guidance and Counseling (1986) recommends other alternatives. It believes that local school districts should develop broad-based planning that actively involves the home, school, and community. Advocating better-trained counselors, the commission supports stronger partnerships between home and school to increase two-way communication about student progress and better collaboration among schools, community agencies, colleges, businesses, and other community resources.

Gender Roles   Because many females have been socialized to adopt nurturing roles rather than career or achieving roles, traditionally they have not planned

Career Development Quarterly

The test for whether or not you can hold a job should not be the arrangement of your chromosomes.

Bella Abzug
American Congresswoman, 20th Century

The Working Adolescent

seriously for careers, have not explored career options extensively, and have restricted their career choices to careers that are gender-stereotyped (Jozefowicz, Barber, & Mollasis, 1994). The motivation for work is the same for both sexes. However, females and males make different choices because of their socialization experiences and the way that social forces structure the opportunities available to them. To read further about gender and science education, see the Caring for Children box.

As growing numbers of females pursue careers, they are faced with questions involving career and family. Should they delay marriage and childbearing and establish their career first? Or should they combine their career, marriage, and childbearing in their twenties? Some women in the past decade have embraced the domestic patterns of an earlier historical period. They have married, borne children, and committed themselves to full-time mothering. These "traditional" women have worked outside the home only intermittently, if at all, and have subordinated the work role to the family role.

Many other women, though, have veered from this time-honored path. They have postponed, and even forgotten, motherhood. They have developed committed, permanent ties to the workplace that resemble the pattern once reserved only for men. When they have had children, they have strived to combine a career and motherhood. While there have always been "career" women, today their numbers are growing at an unprecedented rate.

Work

One of the greatest changes in adolescents' lives in recent years has been the increased number of adolescents who work part-time and still attend school on a regular basis. Our discussion of adolescents and work includes information about the sociohistorical context of adolescent work, the advantages and disadvantages of part-time work, and adolescent unemployment.

The Sociohistorical Context of Adolescent Work   Over the past century, the percentage of youth who worked full-time as opposed to those who were in school has decreased dramatically. In the late 1800s, fewer than 1 of every 20 high-school-age adolescents was in school. Today, more than 9 of every 10 adolescents receive high school diplomas. In the nineteenth century, many adolescents learned a trade from their father or another adult member of the community.

Even though prolonged education has kept many contemporary youth from holding full-time jobs, it has not prevented them from working on a part-time basis while going to school. Most high school seniors have had some work experience. In a national survey of 17,000 high school seniors, three of four reported some job income during the average school week (Bachman, 1982). For 41 percent of the males and 30 percent of the females, this income exceeded $50 a week. The typical part-time job for high school seniors involves 16 to 20 hours of work per week, although 10 percent work 30 hours a week or more.

In 1940, only 1 of 25 tenth-grade males attended school and simultaneously worked part-time. In the 1970s, the number increased to more than 1 of every 4. And, in the 1980s, as just indicated, 3 of 4 combined school and part-time work. Adolescents also are working longer hours now than in the past. For example, the number of 14- to 15-year-olds who work more than 14 hours per week has increased substantially in the past three decades. A similar picture emerges for 16-year-olds. In 1960, 44 percent of 16-year-old males who attended school worked more than 14 hours a week, but, by the 1980s, the figure had increased to more than 60 percent.

What kinds of jobs are adolescents working at today? About 17 percent who work do so in restaurants, such as McDonald's and Burger King, waiting on customers and cleaning up. Other adolescents work in retail stores as cashiers or salespeople (about 20 percent), in offices as clerical assistants (about 10 percent), or as unskilled laborers (about 10 percent). In one study, boys reported higher self-esteem and well-being when they perceived that their jobs were providing skills that would be useful to them in the future (Mortimer & others, 1992).

Caring for Children

A Technology and Science Support Program for Ethnic Minority Girls

Special concerns are raised about the lack of modern technological equipment, such as computers and telecommunications equipment, in schools in low-income areas. Such concerns are magnified further for many ethnic minority girls who attend schools in impoverished neighborhoods because they often show less interest in technology than their male counterparts do.

In one recent effort to improve the interest of such girls in pursuing careers in the sciences and computer technology, the Young Women Scholars' Early Alert Initiative Program was created by Wayne State University, school districts in southeastern Michigan, and industry (Gipson, 1997). They surveyed elementary, middle, and high school teachers from 18 school districts. Almost 40 percent of the teachers had no computer equipment in their classrooms and even more lacked adequate computer training to fully utilize the computers they had.

Forty seventh-grade girls, primarily from low-income, ethnic minority families, were selected for the program. The girls were taken to Wayne State University on a number of occasions to participate in math, computer, and science workshops. The girls also were taken on field trips to the Medical School and the Information Technology Center, where they interacted with female scientists. These scientists described how they became interested in their specialty area, as well as their personal hardships, career paths, and current lives. Two field trips to industrial sites and three field trips to museums occurred during the five-month program. At each site, the girls met and spoke with scientists and museum staff. In addition, parents participated in some of the programs and assisted on at least one field trip.

Do male and female adolescents take the same types of jobs, and are they paid equally? Some jobs are held almost exclusively by male adolescents—busboy, gardener, manual laborer, and newspaper carrier—while other jobs are held almost exclusively by female adolescents—baby-sitter and maid. Male adolescents work longer hours and are paid more per hour than female adolescents (Helson, Elliot, & Leigh, 1989).

The Advantages and Disadvantages of Part-Time Work in Adolescence Does the increase in work have benefits for adolescents? In some cases, yes; in others, no. Ellen Greenberger and Laurence Steinberg (1981, 1986) examined the work experiences of students in four California high schools. Their findings disproved some common myths. For example, generally it is assumed that adolescents get extensive on-the-job training when they are hired for work. The reality is that they get little training at all. Also, it is assumed that youths—through work experiences—learn to get along better with adults. However, adolescents reported that they rarely felt close to the adults with whom they worked. However, the adolescents' work experiences did help them understand how the business world works, how to get and keep a job, and how to manage money. Working also helped adolescents learn to budget their time, take pride in their accomplishments, and evaluate their goals. But working adolescents often have to give up sports, social affairs with peers, and sometimes sleep. And they have to balance the demands of work, school, family, and peers.

Greenberger and Steinberg asked students about their grade point averages, school attendance, and satisfaction from school, as well as the number of hours spent studying and participating in extracurricular activities since they began working. They found that the working adolescents had lower grade point averages than nonworking adolescents. More than one of four students reported that their grades dropped when they began working; only one of nine said their grades improved. But it was not just working that affected adolescents' grades—more important, it was

Improving Developmental Skills

Strategies for Supporting Adolescents' Cognitive Development

What are some good strategies for nourishing adolescents' cognitive development?

- *Provide support for adolescents' information processing.* Provide opportunities and guide adolescents in making good decisions, especially in real-world settings; stimulate adolescents to think critically; and encourage them to engage in self-regulatory learning.
- *Give adolescents opportunities to discuss moral dilemmas.* Provide adolescents with group opportunities to discuss the importance of cooperation, trust, and caring.
- *Create better schools for adolescents.* Schools for adolescents need to

  —Emphasize socioemotional development as well as cognitive development
  —Take individual variation in adolescents seriously
  —Develop curricula that involve high expectations for success and the support to attain that success
  —Develop smaller communities
  —Involve parents and community leaders more
  —Break down the barriers between school and work to reduce the high school dropout rate

- *Provide adolescents with information about careers.* Adolescents do not get adequate information about careers. Career decision making needs to be given a higher priority in schools.
- *Don't let adolescents work too many hours while going to school.* Parents need to monitor how many hours adolescents work during the school year. A rule of thumb is that working more than 20 hours a week or more in the eleventh and twelfth grades lowers grades.

how long they worked. Tenth-graders who worked more than 14 hours a week suffered a drop in grades. Eleventh-graders worked up to 20 hours a week before their grades dropped. When adolescents spend more than 20 hours per week working, there is little time to study for tests and to complete homework assignments. In addition to the work affecting their grades, the working adolescents felt less involved in school, were absent more, and said they did not enjoy school as much as their nonworking counterparts did. The adolescents who worked also spent less time with their families—but just as much time with their peers—as their nonworking counterparts. The adolescents who worked long hours also were more frequent users of alcohol and marijuana.

More recent research confirms the link between part-time work during adolescence and problem behavior (Hansen, 1996). In one large-scale study, the role of part-time work in the adjustment of more than 70,000 high school seniors was investigated (Bachman & Schulenberg, 1993). Consistent with other research, part-time work in high school was associated with a number of problem behaviors: not getting enough sleep, not eating breakfast, not exercising, not having enough leisure time, and using drugs. For the most part, the results occurred even when students worked 1 to 5 hours per week, but they became more pronounced after 20 hours of work per week. And, in another study, taking on a job for more than 20 hours per week was associated with increasing disengagement from school, increased delinquency and drug use, increased autonomy from parents, and diminished self-reliance (Steinberg, Fegley, & Dornbusch, 1993). In sum, the overwhelming evidence is that working part-time while going to high school is associated with a number of problem behaviors, especially when the work consumes 20 or more hours of the adolescent's week.

Some states have responded to these findings by limiting the number of hours adolescents can work while they are attending secondary school. In 1986, in Pinellas County, Florida, a law placed a cap on the previously unregulated hours that adolescents can work while school is in session. The allowable limit is set at 30 hours, which—based on research evidence—is still too high.

School-to-Work Transitions

Adolescent Unemployment   In some cases, the media have exaggerated the degree of adolescent unemployment. For example, based on data collected by the U.S. Department of Labor, 9 of 10 adolescents are either in school, at a job, or both. Only 5 percent are out of school, without a job, and looking for full-time employment. Most unemployed adolescents are not unemployed for long. Only 10 percent are without a job for six months or longer. Most unemployed adolescents are school dropouts.

Certain segments of the adolescent population, however, are more likely than others to be unemployed. For example, a disproportionate percentage of unemployed adolescents are African American. The unemployment situation is especially acute for African American and Latino youth between the ages of 16 and 19. The job situation, however, has improved somewhat for African American adolescents: in

Summary Table 16.2
Schools, Careers, and Work in Adolescence

Concept	Processes/ Related Ideas	Characteristics/Description
Schools	The controversy surrounding secondary schools	In the 1980s, the back-to-basics movement gained momentum. The back-to-basics movement emphasizes rigorous academic training. Many experts on education and development believe that the back-to-basics movement does not adequately address individual variations among children and adolescents. They also believe that education should be more comprehensive, focusing on social as well as cognitive development.
	Transition to middle or junior high school	The emergence of junior highs in the 1920s and 1930s was justified on the basis of physical, cognitive, and social changes in early adolescence and the need for more schools in response to a growing student population. Middle schools have become more popular in recent years and coincide with puberty's earlier arrival. The transition to middle or junior high school coincides with many social, familial, and individual changes in the adolescent's life. The transition involves moving from the top-dog to the lowest position.
	Effective schools for young adolescents	Successful schools for young adolescents take individual differences in development seriously, show a deep concern for what is known about early adolescence, and emphasize social and emotional development as much as intellectual development. In 1989, the Carnegie Corporation recommended a major redesign of middle schools.
	High school dropouts	Dropping out has been a serious problem for decades. Many dropouts have educational deficiencies that curtail their economic and social well-being for much of their adult life. Some progress has been made in that dropout rates for most ethnic minority groups have declined in recent decades, although dropout rates for inner-city, low-income minorities and Latinos are still precariously high. Dropping out of school is associated with demographic, family-related, peer-related, school-related, economic, and individual factors. Reducing the dropout rate and improving the lives of noncollege youth could be accomplished by strengthening schools and bridging the gap between school and work.
Careers and work	Career development	Three theories are Ginzberg's developmental theory, Super's self-concept theory, and Holland's personality-type theory. Exploration of career options is a critical aspect of career development in countries where equal employment opportunities exist. Many youth flounder and make unplanned career choice changes. Students also need more knowledge about the education and ability requirements of various careers. Sociocultural influences involve social class, parents and peers, schools, and gender. The channels of opportunity for lower-class youth are largely educational. Many factors influence the parent's role in the adolescent's career development. School counseling has been criticized heavily, and recommendations have been made for its improvement. Parents play an important role in their sons' and daughters' career development. Because many females have been socialized to adopt nurturing rather than career or achieving roles, they have not adequately prepared for careers. As growing numbers of females pursue careers, they are faced with questions involving career and family. Parents often have different expectations, give different advice, and provide different opportunities in career development for their sons and daughters.
	Work	Adolescents are not as likely to hold full-time jobs today as their adolescent counterparts from the nineteenth century. There has been a tremendous increase in the number of adolescents who work part-time and go to school, which has both advantages and disadvantages. In some cases, adolescent unemployment has been exaggerated; however, for many minority-group adolescents, unemployment is a major problem.

1969, 44 percent of African American 16- to 19-year-olds were unemployed; today, that figure is approximately 32 percent.

At various places, we have discussed strategies for improving adolescents' cognitive development. The insert, Improving Developmental Skills, profiles those strategies. And, at this point, we have described a number of ideas about schools, careers, and work in adolescence. An overview of these ideas is presented in summary table 16.2.

Chapter Review

When we think of the changes that characterize adolescence, we often think of the high drama of puberty or the socioemotional changes of identity and independence. But some impressive cognitive changes also arrive with adolescence.

We began this chapter by exploring the cognitive world of adolescents, focusing on Piaget's stage of formal operational thought, adolescent egocentrism, and information processing. Our coverage then turned to values, moral education, and religion. We also studied schools for adolescents, examining the controversy surrounding secondary schools, the transition to middle or junior high school, health education, and high school dropouts. We read about career development, including theories of career development, exploration, planning, decision making, and sociocultural influences. We described the nature of work in adolescence by considering its sociohistorical contexts, the advantages/disadvantages of part-time work, and unemployment.

Remember that you can obtain an overall summary of the chapter by again reading the two summary tables on pages 482 and 495. In the next chapter, we will continue our study of adolescence by focusing on socioemotional development.

✓ Children Checklist

Cognitive Development in Adolescence

How much have you learned since the beginning of the chapter? Use the following statements to help you review your knowledge and understanding of the chapter material. First, read the statement and mentally or briefly demonstrate on paper that you can discuss the relevant information.

_____ I can describe Piaget's stage of formal operational thought.
_____ I can discuss adolescent egocentrism.
_____ I can describe some important information-processing changes in adolescence.
_____ I am aware of the nature of values in adolescence.
_____ I can discuss moral education.
_____ I can describe the role of religion in adolescents' lives.
_____ I know about the controversy surrounding secondary schools.
_____ I can discuss the transition to middle or junior high school.
_____ I know about effective schools for young adolescents.
_____ I can describe high school dropouts.
_____ I know about career development in adolescence.
_____ I am aware of the role of work in adolescents' lives.

For any items that you did not check, go back and locate the relevant material in the chapter. Review the material until you feel you can check off the item. You may want to use this checklist later in preparing for an exam.

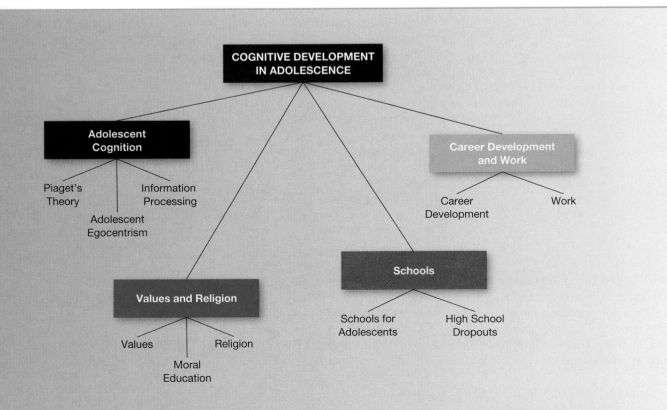

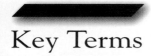

Key Terms

hypothetical-deductive reasoning 470

adolescent egocentrism 472

imaginary audience 473

personal fable 473

hidden curriculum 477

character education 478

values clarification 478

cognitive moral education 478

service learning 479

top-dog phenomenon 484

developmental career choice theory 488

career self-concept theory 489

personality-type theory 489

Children Resources

Successful Schools for Young Adolescents
(1984) by Joan Lipsitz. New Brunswick, NJ: Transaction Books.

This book is a classic resource for people involved in middle school education. The book establishes a set of criteria for evaluating middle school effectiveness. Emphasis is placed on understanding adolescent development, school effectiveness research, and public policy.

"Turning Points" (1989)
Carnegie Council on Adolescent Development
2400 N Street NW
Washington, DC 20037-1153
202–429–7979

This comprehensive report concludes that the education most of the nation's young adolescents are receiving is seriously inadequate. The report includes a number of recommendations for meeting the educational needs of young adolescents.

Taking It to the Net

http://www.mhhe.com/santrockcd6

1. Did you work while you were in high school? Do you believe that working, while an adolescent, is beneficial? Why, or why not? What might be the disadvantages of working during high school?

2. Do you believe that the morality of today's adolescents is lacking? Why or why not? If you had the ability to effect any change on society, for the purpose of increasing adolescent morality, what would that change be? How would you instill character in adolescents?

3. Your best friend has decided to drop out of high school. She says that a high school diploma doesn't mean anything anymore anyway. Is that true? Why or why not? What do you tell her?

Chapter
17

Chapter Outline

Socioemotional Development in Adolescence

In case you're worried about what's going to become of the younger generation, it's going to grow up and start worrying about the younger generation.

Roger Allen
Contemporary American Author

PREVIEW

The socioemotional worlds of adolescence are filled with many changes. Among the questions that we will explore in this chapter are

- What are some contemporary thoughts about identity development?
- What identity statuses can an adolescent have?
- What roles do families, culture, ethnicity, and gender play in identity development?
- How are autonomy and attachment involved in adolescent development?
- What is the nature of parent-adolescent conflict?
- How does the maturation of adolescents and their parents influence parent-adolescent interaction?
- What roles do peers, friendships, and cliques play in adolescent development?
- What characterizes dating and romantic relationships in adolescence?
- How similar or different are adolescents in various cultures?
- What role does ethnicity have in adolescent development?

The Stories of Kip Kinkel and Luke Woodham: Why Youth Kill

Slightly built 15-year-old Kip Kinkel has an innocent look and a shy smile. In May 1998, Kinkel strode into the cafeteria at Thurston High School in Springfield, Oregon, and opened fire on his fellow students, murdering two of them and injuring many others. Later that day, police went to Kip's home and found his parents lying dead on the floor, also victims of Kip's violence. A series of other school-related shootings also has recently occurred.

Is there any way that psychologists can predict whether a youth will turn violent? It's a complex task, but they have pieced together some clues (Cowley, 1998). The violent youth are overwhelmingly male, and many are driven by feelings of powerlessness. Violence seems to infuse these youth with a sense of power. Sixteen-year-old Luke Woodham was known as a chubby nerd at his school in Pearl, Mississippi. But, in the fall of 1997, he shed that image by stabbing his mother to death and shooting nine of his classmates, killing two of them. Woodham wrote in a letter, "I killed because people like me are mistreated every day. Murder is not weak and slow-witted. Murder is gutsy and daring."

In April, 1999 at Columbine High School in Littleton, Colorado, Eric Harris (18) and Dylan Kiebold (17), members of an outcast clique called "The Trenchcoat Mafia," killed 12 students and a teacher, planted bombs around the school, then committed suicide. Harris had a web page on which he had bragged of making four pipe bombs more than a year before the shootings but no one apparently took it seriously.

University of Virginia psychologist Dewey Cornell (1998) says that many youth give clear indications of their future violence but aren't taken seriously. Kip Kinkel had an obsession with guns and explosives, a history of abusing animals, and a nasty temper when crossed. When police examined his room, they found two pipe bombs, three larger bombs, and bomb-making recipes that Kip had downloaded from the Internet. Clearly, some signs were present in Kip's life to suggest some serious problems, but it is difficult to predict whether youth like Kip will actually act on their anger and sense of powerlessness to commit murder.

Kip Kinkel is accused of killing his parents and opening fire on his classmates in Springfield, Oregon. What causes youth to become so violent?

Identity Development

IDENTITY

By far the most comprehensive and provocative story of identity development has been told by Erik Erikson. As you may remember from chapter 2, identity versus identity confusion is the fifth stage in Erikson's eight stages of the life cycle, occurring at about the same time as adolescence. It is a time of being interested in finding out who one is, what one is all about, and where one is headed in life.

During adolescence, worldviews become important to the individual, who enters what Erikson (1968) calls a "psychological moratorium," a gap between the security of childhood and the autonomy of adulthood. Adolescents experiment with the numerous roles and identities they draw from the surrounding culture. Youth who successfully cope with these conflicting identities during adolescence emerge with a new sense of self that is both refreshing and acceptable (Moshman, 1999). Adolescents who do not successfully resolve this identity crisis are confused, suffering what Erikson calls "identity confusion." This confusion takes one of two courses: the individuals withdraw, isolating themselves from peers and family, or they lose their identity in the crowd.

Some Contemporary Thoughts About Identity

Contemporary views of identity development suggest several important considerations. First, identity development is a lengthy process; in many instances, it is a more gradual, less cataclysmic transition than Erikson's term *crisis* implies. Second, identity development is extraordinarily complex.

Identity formation neither begins nor ends with adolescence. It begins with the appearance of attachment, the development of a sense of self, and the emergence of independence in infancy, and it reaches its final phase with a life review and integration in old age. What is important about identity in adolescence, especially late adolescence, is that for the first time physical development, cognitive development, and social development advance to the point at which the individual can sort through and synthesize childhood identities and identifications to construct a viable pathway toward adult maturity. Resolution of the identity issue at adolescence does not mean that identity will be stable through the remainder of one's life. A person who develops a healthy identity is flexible, adaptive, and open to changes in society, in relationships, and in careers. This openness assures numerous reorganizations of identity features throughout the life of the person who has achieved identity.

Identity formation does not happen neatly, and it usually does not happen cataclysmically. At the bare minimum, it involves commitment to a vocational direction, an ideological stance, and a sexual orientation. Synthesizing the identity components can be a long, drawn-out process, with many negations and affirmations of various roles and faces (Marcia, 1996). Identities are developed in bits and pieces. Decisions are not made once and for all but have to be made again and again. And the decisions may seem trivial at the time: whom to date, whether or not to break up, whether or not to have intercourse, whether or not to take drugs, whether to go to college after high school or get a job, which major to choose, whether to study or whether to play, whether or not to be politically active, and so on. Over the years of adolescence, the decisions begin to form a core of what the individual is all about as a person—what is called "identity" (Arboleda, 1999).

Identity Statuses and Development

Canadian psychologist James Marcia (1980, 1994) analyzed Erikson's theory of identity development and concluded that four identity statuses, or modes of resolution, appear in the theory: identity diffusion, identity foreclosure, identity moratorium, and identity achievement. The extent of an adolescent's commitment and crisis is used to classify him or her, according to one of the four identity statuses. **Crisis** *is*

crisis
Marcia's term for a period of identity development during which the adolescent is choosing from among meaningful alternatives.

	Identity status			
Position on occupation and ideology	**Identity moratorium**	**Identity foreclosure**	**Identity diffusion**	**Identity achievement**
Crisis	Present	Absent	Absent	Present
Commitment	Absent	Present	Absent	Present

Figure 17.1
Marcia's Four Statuses of Identity

defined as a period of identity development during which the adolescent is choosing among meaningful alternatives. Most researchers now use the term *exploration* rather than *crisis*, although, in the spirit of Marcia's original formulation, we will use the term *crisis*. **Commitment** *is defined as the part of identity development in which adolescents show a personal investment in what they are going to do.*

Identity diffusion *is Marcia's term for adolescents who have not yet experienced a crisis (that is, they have not yet explored meaningful alternatives) or made any commitments.* Not only are they undecided about occupational and ideological choices, but they are also likely to show little interest in such matters. **Identity foreclosure** *is the term Marcia uses to describe adolescents who have made a commitment but have not experienced a crisis.* This occurs most often when parents hand down commitments to their adolescents, more often than not in an authoritarian manner. In these circumstances, adolescents have not had adequate opportunities to explore different approaches, ideologies, and vocations on their own. **Identity moratorium** *is the term Marcia uses to describe adolescents who are in the midst of a crisis, but their commitments are either absent or only vaguely defined.* **Identity achievement** *is Marcia's term for adolescents who have undergone a crisis and have made a commitment.* Marcia's four statuses of identity are summarized in figure 17.1.

Young adolescents are primarily in Marcia's identity diffusion, foreclosure, or moratorium status. At least three aspects of the young adolescent's development are important in identity formation: young adolescents must establish confidence in parental support, develop a sense of industry, and gain a self-reflective perspective on their future.

Some researchers believe the most important identity changes take place in the college years, rather than earlier in adolescence. For example, Alan Waterman

commitment
Marcia's term for the part of identity development in which adolescents show a personal investment in what they are going to do.

identity diffusion
Marcia's term for adolescents who have not yet experienced a crisis (explored meaningful alternatives) or made any commitments.

identity foreclosure
Marcia's term for adolescents who have made a commitment but have not experienced a crisis.

identity moratorium
Marcia's term for adolescents who are in the midst of a crisis, but their commitments are either absent or vaguely defined.

identity achievement
Marcia's term for adolescents who have undergone a crisis and have made a commitment.

Exploring Your Identity Development

Now that you have read about various aspects of identity development, this is a good time to explore your own identity development. How might you gain insight into your personal self or identity? One way is to list adjectives that describe yourself. You also could ask people who know you well, such as several family members and/or friends, to give you some feedback about how they honestly would describe you. How does their perception match your self-perception? Consider also your interests, attitudes, and hobbies. How did you develop your personal characteristics and interests? Try to trace their origins. Tracing the development of aspects of yourself can help you gain insight into your own identity formation.

_A_s long as one keeps searching, the answers come.

Joan Baez
American Folk Singer, 20th Century

individuality

According to Cooper and her colleagues, individuality consists of two dimensions: self-assertion (the ability to have and communicate a point of view) and separateness (the use of communication patterns to express how one is different from others).

connectedness

According to Cooper and her colleagues, connectedness consists of two dimensions: mutuality (sensitivity to and respect for others' views) and permeability (openness to others' views).

(1992) has found that, from the years preceding high school through the last few years of college, the number of individuals who are identity achieved increases, along with a decrease in those who are identity diffused. College upperclassmen are more likely than college freshmen or high school students to be identity achieved. Many young adolescents are identity diffused. These developmental changes are especially true in regard to vocational choice. For religious beliefs and political ideology, fewer college students have reached the identity achieved status, with a substantial number characterized by foreclosure and diffusion. Thus, the timing of identity may depend on the particular role involved, and many college students are still wrestling with ideological commitments.

Many identity status researchers believe that a common pattern of individuals who develop positive identities is to follow what are called "MAMA" cycles of _moratorium-achiever-moratorium-achiever_. These cycles may be repeated throughout life. Personal, family, and societal changes are inevitable, and, as they occur, the flexibility and skill required to explore new alternatives and develop new commitments are likely to facilitate an individual's coping skills.

Family Influences on Identity

Parents are important figures in the adolescent's development of identity. In studies that relate identity development to parenting styles, democratic parents, who encourage adolescents to participate in family decision making, foster identity achievement. Autocratic parents, who control the adolescent's behavior without giving the adolescent an opportunity to express opinions, encourage identity foreclosure. Permissive parents, who provide little guidance to adolescents and allow them to make their own decisions, promote identity diffusion (Enright & others, 1980).

In addition to doing studies on parenting styles, researchers have also examined the role of individuality and connectedness in the development of identity. The presence of a family atmosphere that promotes both individuality and connectedness is important in the adolescent's identity development (Cooper & Grotevant, 1989). **Individuality** _consists of two dimensions: self-assertion, the ability to have and communicate a point of view, and separateness, the use of communication patterns to express how one is different from others._ **Connectedness** _also consists of two dimensions: mutuality, sensitivity to, and respect for others' views, and permeability—openness to others' views._ In general, research findings reveal that identity formation is enhanced by family relationships that are both individuated, which encourages adolescents to develop their own point of view, and connected, which provides a secure base from which to explore the widening social worlds of adolescence. To further evaluate identity development, see Adventures for the Mind.

Culture, Ethnicity, and Gender

How do culture and ethnicity influence an adolescent's identity development? How does gender affect the nature of an adolescent's identity development?

Culture and Ethnicity   Erikson is especially sensitive to the role of culture in identity development. He points out that, throughout the world, ethnic minority groups have struggled to maintain their cultural identities while blending into the dominant culture (Erikson, 1968). Erikson says that this struggle for an inclusive identity, or an identity within the larger culture, has been the driving force in the founding of churches, empires, and revolutions throughout history.

For many ethnic minority individuals, adolescence is a special juncture in their development (Kurtz, Cantu, & Phinney, 1996; Spencer & Dornbusch, 1990). Although children are aware of some ethnic and cultural differences, most ethnic minority individuals consciously confront their ethnicity for the first time in adolescence. In contrast to children, adolescents have the ability to interpret ethnic and cultural information, to reflect on the past, and to speculate about the future. As they cognitively mature, ethnic minority adolescents become acutely aware of the evaluations of their ethnic group made by the majority White culture (Comer, 1988). As one researcher commented, the young African American child may learn that Black is beautiful but conclude as an adolescent that White is powerful (Semaj, 1985).

Ethnic minority youth's awareness of negative appraisals, conflicting values, and restricted occupational opportunities can influence life choices and plans for the future (Cross, Clark, & Fhagen-Smith, 1999; Spencer & Dornbusch, 1990; Swanson, Spencer, & Petersen, 1998). As one ethnic minority youth stated, "The future seems shut off, closed. Why dream? You can't reach your dreams. Why set goals? At least if you don't set any goals, you don't fail."

For many ethnic minority youth, a lack of successful ethnic minority role models with whom to identify is a special concern. The problem is especially acute for inner-city ethnic minority youth. Because of the lack of adult ethnic minority role models, some ethnic minority youth may conform to middle-class White values and identify with successful White role models. However, for many adolescents, their ethnicity and skin color limit their acceptance by the White culture. Thus, many ethnic minority adolescents have a difficult task: negotiating two value systems— that of their own ethnic group and that of the White society. Some adolescents reject the mainstream, foregoing the rewards controlled by White Americans; others adopt the values and standards of the majority White culture; yet others take the difficult path of biculturalism.

In one study, ethnic identity exploration was higher among ethnic minority than among White American college students (Phinney & Alipura, 1990). In this study, the ethnic minority college students who had thought about and resolved issues involving their ethnicity had higher self-esteem than their ethnic minority counterparts who had not. In another investigation, the ethnic identity development of Asian American, African American, Latino, and White American tenth-grade students in Los Angeles was studied (Phinney, 1989). The adolescents from each of the three ethnic minority groups faced a similar need to deal with their ethnic group identification in a predominantly White American culture. In some instances, the adolescents from the three ethnic minority groups perceived different issues to be important in their resolution of ethnic identity. For the Asian American adolescents, pressures to achieve academically and concerns about quotas that make it difficult to get into good colleges were salient issues. Many of the African American adolescent females discussed their realization that White American standards of beauty (especially hair and skin color) did not apply to them; the African American adolescent males were concerned with possible job discrimination and the need to distinguish themselves from a negative societal image of African American male adolescents. For the Latino adolescents, prejudice was a recurrent theme, as was the conflict of values between their Latino cultural heritage and the majority culture.

The contexts in which ethnic minority youth live influence their identity development. Many ethnic minority youth in the United States live in low-income urban settings, where support for developing a positive identity is absent. Many of these youth live in pockets of poverty; are exposed to drugs, gangs, and criminal activities; and interact with other youth and adults who have dropped out of school and/or are unemployed. In such settings, effective organizations and programs for youth can make important contributions to developing a positive identity (Cooper & others, 1996; Sheets, 1999; Taylor, 1999).

Researcher Margaret Beale Spencer, shown here talking with adolescents, believes that adolescence is often a critical juncture in the identity development of ethnic minority individuals. Most ethnic minority individuals consciously confront their ethnicity for the first time in adolescence.

Gender and Identity Development   In Erikson's (1968) classic presentation of identity development, the division of labor between the sexes was reflected in his assertion that males' aspirations were mainly oriented toward career and ideological commitments, while females' were centered around marriage and childbearing. In the 1960s and 1970s, researchers found support for Erikson's assertion about gender differences in identity. For example, vocational concerns were more central to the identity of males, and affiliative concerns were more important in the identity of females. However, in the past two decades, as females have developed stronger vocational interests, sex differences are turning into sex similarities.

Some investigators believe the order of stages proposed by Erikson is different for females and males. One view is that for males identity formation precedes the stage of intimacy, while for females intimacy precedes identity. These ideas are consistent with the belief that relationships and emotional bonds are more important concerns of females, while autonomy and achievement are more important concerns of males (Gilligan, 1990). In one study, the development of a clear sense of self by adolescent girls was related to their concerns about care and response in relationships (Rogers, 1987).

The task of identity exploration may be more complex for females than for males, in that females may try to establish identities in more domains than males. In today's world, the options for females have increased and thus may at times be confusing and conflicting, especially for females who hope to successfully integrate family and career roles (Archer, 1994).

FAMILIES

In chapter 14, we discussed how, during middle and late childhood, parents spend less time with their children than in early childhood. Discipline involves an increased use of reasoning and deprivation of privileges, and there is a gradual transfer of control from parents to children but still within the boundary of coregulation. One of the most important issues and questions that need to be raised about family relationships in adolescence is, What is the nature of autonomy and attachment?

Autonomy and Attachment

The adolescent's push for autonomy and responsibility puzzles and angers many parents. Parents see their teenager slipping from their grasp. They may have an urge to take stronger control as the adolescent seeks autonomy and responsibility. Heated emotional exchanges may ensue, with either side calling names, making threats, and doing whatever seems necessary to gain control. Parents may seem frustrated because they *expect* their teenager to heed their advice, to want to spend time with the family, and to grow up to do what is right. Most parents anticipate that their teenager will have some difficulty adjusting to the changes that adolescence brings, but few parents can imagine and predict just how strong an adolescent's desires will be to spend time with peers or how much adolescents will want to show that it is they—not their parents—who are responsible for their successes and failures.

The ability to attain autonomy and gain control over one's behavior in adolescence is acquired through appropriate adult reactions to the adolescent's desire for control (Keener & Boykin, 1996; Urberg & Wolowicz, 1996). At the onset of adolescence, the average individual does not have the knowledge to make appropriate or mature decisions in all areas of life. As the adolescent pushes for autonomy, the wise adult relinquishes control in those areas in which the adolescent can make reasonable decisions but continues to guide the adolescent to make reasonable decisions in areas in which the adolescent's knowledge is more limited. Gradually, adolescents acquire the ability to make mature decisions on their own.

In the past decade, developmentalists have begun to explore the role of secure attachment and related concepts, such as connectedness to parents, in adolescence (Allen, Hauser, & Borman-Spurrell, 1996; Cassidy & Shaver, 1999). They believe that secure attachment to parents in adolescence may facilitate the adolescent's social competence and well-being, as reflected in such characteristics as self-esteem, emotional adjustment, and physical health (Cooper, Shaver, & Collins, 1998; Juang & Nyuyen, 1997). In the research of Joseph Allen and his colleagues (Allen & Hauser, 1994; Allen & Kuperminc, 1995), securely attached adolescents had somewhat lower probabilities of engaging in problem behaviors.

Many studies that assess secure and insecure attachment in adolescence use the Adult Attachment Interview (AAI) (George, Main, & Kaplan, 1984). This measure examines an individual's memories of significant attachment relationships. Based on the responses to questions on the AAI, individuals are classified as *secure-autonomous* (which corresponds to secure attachment in infancy) or one of three following insecure categories.

Dismissing/avoidant attachment *is an insecure category in which individuals deemphasize the importance of attachment. This category is associated with consistent experiences of the rejection of attachment needs by caregivers.* One possible outcome of dismissing/avoidant attachment is that parents and adolescents may mutually distance themselves from each other, which lessens parents' influence. In one study, dismissing/avoidant attachment was related to violent and aggressive behavior on the part of the adolescent.

Preoccupied/ambivalent attachment *is an insecure category in which adolescents are hypertuned to attachment experiences. This is thought to occur mainly when parents are inconsistently available to the adolescent.* This may result in a high degree of attach-

dismissing/avoidant attachment
An insecure category in which individuals deemphasize the importance of attachment. This category is associated with consistent experiences of rejection of attachment needs by caregivers.

preoccupied/ambivalent attachment
An insecure category in which adolescents are hypertuned to attachment experiences. This is thought to mainly occur when parents are consistently unavailable to the adolescent.

unresolved/disorganized attachment
An insecure category in which the adolescent has an unusually high level of fear and being disoriented. This may result from traumatic experiences such as a parent's death or abuse by parents.

Parent-Adolescent Relationships
Parenting Today's Adolescents
Parent-Adolescent Conflict

When I was a boy of 14, my father was so ignorant I could hardly stand to have the man around. But when I got to be 21, I was astonished at how much he had learnt in 7 years.

Mark Twain
American Writer and Humorist, 20th Century

ment-seeking behavior, mixed with angry feelings. Conflict between parents and adolescents in this type of attachment may be too high for healthy development.

Unresolved/disorganized attachment *is an insecure category in which the adolescent has an unusually high level of fear and is disoriented. This may result from such traumatic experiences as a parent's death or abuse by parents.*

Secure attachment, or connectedness to parents, promotes competent peer relations and positive, close relationships outside of the family (Main, 1999). In one investigation in which attachment to parents and peers was assessed, adolescents who were securely attached to parents also were securely attached to peers; those who were insecurely attached to parents also were more likely to be insecurely attached to peers (Armsden & Greenberg, 1984). There are times when adolescents reject closeness, connection, and attachment to their parents as they assert their ability to make decisions and to develop an identity. But, for the most part, the worlds of parents and peers are coordinated and connected, not uncoordinated and disconnected.

Parent-Adolescent Conflict

While attachment to parents remains strong during adolescence, the connectedness is not always smooth. Early adolescence is a time when conflict with parents escalates beyond childhood levels. This increase may be due to a number of factors: the biological changes of puberty, cognitive changes involving increased idealism and logical reasoning, social changes focused on independence and identity, maturational changes in parents, and expectations that are violated by parents and adolescents. The adolescent compares her parents to an ideal standard and then criticizes their flaws. A 13-year-old girl tells her mother, "That is the tackiest-looking dress I have ever seen. Nobody would be caught dead wearing that." The adolescent demands logical explanations for comments and discipline. A 14-year-old boy tells his mother, "What do you mean I have to be home at 10 P.M. because it's the way we do things around here? Why do we do things around here that way? It doesn't make sense to me."

Many parents see their adolescent changing from a compliant child to someone who is noncompliant, oppositional, and resistant to parental standards. When this happens, parents tend to clamp down and put more pressure on the adolescent to conform to parental standards. Parents often expect their adolescents to become mature adults overnight, instead of understanding that the journey takes 10 to 15 years. Parents who recognize that this transition takes time handle their youth more competently and calmly than those who demand immediate conformity to adult standards. The opposite tactic—letting adolescents do as they please without supervision—is also unwise.

In one study, Reed Larson and Marsye Richards (1994) had mothers, fathers, and adolescents carry electronic pagers for a week and report their activities and emotions at random times. The result was a portrait of the hour-by-hour emotional realities lived by families with adolescents. Differences between the fast-paced daily realities lived by each family member created considerable potential for misunderstanding and conflict. Because each family member was often attending to different priorities, needs, and stressors, their realities were often out of sync. Even when they wanted to shared leisure activity, their interests were at odds. One father said that his wife liked to shop, his daughter liked to play video games, and he liked to stay home. Although the main theme of this work was the hazards of contemporary life, some of the families with adolescents were buoyant, and their lives were coordinated.

Conflict with parents increases in early adolescence, but it does not reach the tumultuous proportions G. Stanley Hall envisioned at the beginning of the twentieth century (Holmbeck, 1996; Holmbeck, Paikoff, & Brooks-Gunn, 1995). Rather, much of the conflict involves the everyday events of family life, such as keeping a bedroom clean, dressing neatly, getting home by a certain time, and not talking forever on the phone. The conflicts rarely involve major dilemmas, such as drugs and delinquency.

It is not unusual to hear parents of young adolescents ask, "Is it ever going to get better?" Things usually do get better as adolescents move from early to late adolescence. Conflict with parents often escalates during early adolescence, remains somewhat stable during the high school years, and then lessens as the adolescent reaches 17 to 20 years of age. Parent-adolescent relationships become more positive if adolescents go away to college than if they stay at home and go to college (Sullivan & Sullivan, 1980).

The everyday conflicts that characterize parent-adolescent relationships may actually serve a positive developmental function. These minor disputes and negotiations facilitate the adolescent's transition from being dependent on parents to becoming an autonomous individual. For example, in one study, adolescents who expressed disagreement with their parents explored identity development more actively than did adolescents who did not express disagreement with their parents (Cooper & others, 1982). As previously mentioned, one way for parents to cope with the adolescent's push for independence and identity is to recognize that adolescence is a 10- to 15-year transitional period in the journey to adulthood, rather than an overnight accomplishment. Recognizing that conflict and negotiation can serve a positive developmental function can tone down parental hostility too. Understanding parent-adolescent conflict, though, is not simple (Conger & Ge, 1999).

In sum, the old model of parent-adolescent relationships suggested that as adolescents mature they detach themselves from parents and move into a world of autonomy apart from parents. The old model also suggested that parent-adolescent conflict is intense and stressful throughout adolescence. The new model emphasizes that parents serve as important attachment figures and support systems as adolescents explore a wider, more complex social world. The new model also emphasizes that, in most families, parent-adolescent conflict is moderate rather than severe and that the everyday negotiations and minor disputes are normal and can serve the positive developmental function of helping the adolescent make the transition from childhood dependency to adult independence (see figure 17.2).

Still, a high degree of conflict characterizes some parent-adolescent relationships. One estimate of the proportion of parents and adolescents who engage in prolonged, intense, repeated, unhealthy conflict is about one in five families (Montemayor, 1982). While this figure represents a minority of adolescents, it indicates that 4 to 5 million American families encounter serious, highly stressful parent-adolescent conflict. And this prolonged, intense conflict is associated with a number of adolescent problems—movement out of the home, juvenile delinquency, school dropout, pregnancy and early marriage, membership in religious cults, and drug abuse (Brook & others, 1990).

The Maturation of Adolescents and Parents

Physical, cognitive, and socioemotional changes in the adolescent's development influence the nature of parent-adolescent relationships. Parental changes also influence the nature of these relationships. Among the changes in the adolescent are puberty; expanded logical reasoning and increased idealistic and egocentric thought; violated expectations; changes in schooling, peers, friendship, and dating; and movement toward independence. Conflict between parents and adolescents is the most stressful during the apex of pubertal growth (Silverberg & Steinberg, 1990).

Parental changes include those involving marital dissatisfaction, economic burdens, career reevaluation and time perspective, and health and bodily concerns. Marital dissatisfaction is greater when the offspring is an adolescent, rather than a child or an adult. A greater economic burden is placed on parents during the rearing of their adolescents. Parents may reevaluate their occupational achievement, deciding whether they have met their youthful aspirations for

Old model	
Autonomy detachment from parents; parent and peer worlds are isolated	Intense, stressful conflict throughout adolescence; parent-adolescent relationships are filled with storm and stress on virtually a daily basis

New model	
Attachment and autonomy; parents are important support systems and attachment figures; adolescent-parent and adolescent-peer worlds have some important connections	Moderate parent-adolescent conflict common and can serve a positive developmental function; conflict greater in early adolescence, especially during the apex of puberty

Figure 17.2
Old and New Models of Parent-Adolescent Relationships

It is not enough for parents to understand children. They must accord children the privilege of understanding them.

Milton Sapirstein
American Psychiatrist, 20th Century

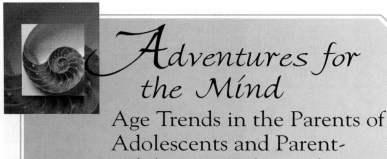

Adventures for the Mind
Age Trends in the Parents of Adolescents and Parent-Adolescent Relationships

In the future, many parents of adolescents will be older because many people are delaying marriage and childbearing. How do you think this will affect the nature of parent-adolescent relationships? Do you think the parents of adolescents who are in their fifties and sixties will be more strict or more permissive than parents who are in their late thirties and forties?

**Reengaging Families
with Adolescents**

Families as Asset Builders

Adolescent Peer Relationships

Peer Pressure

Youth Connections

success. Parents may look to the future and think about how much time they have remaining to accomplish what they want. Adolescents, however, look to the future with unbounded optimism, sensing that they have an unlimited amount of time to accomplish what they desire. Health concerns and an interest in bodily integrity and sexual attractiveness become prominent themes of adolescents' parents. Even when their bodies and sexual attractiveness are not deteriorating, many parents of adolescents perceive that they are. By contrast, adolescents are beginning to reach the peak of their physical attractiveness, strength, and health. While both adolescents and their parents show a heightened preoccupation with their bodies, adolescents' outcomes are probably more positive. To further evaluate parental age, see Adventures for the Mind.

We have seen that parents play very important roles in adolescent development. Although adolescents are moving toward independence, they still need to stay connected with their families. Competent adolescent development is most likely to happen when adolescents have parents who (Small, 1990)

- Show them warmth and mutual respect
- Demonstrate sustained interest in their lives
- Recognize and adapt to their cognitive and socioemotional development
- Communicate expectations for high standards of conduct and achievement
- Display authoritative, constructive ways of dealing with problems and conflict

At this point, we have studied many ideas about identity and about families in adolescence. An overview of these ideas is presented in summary table 17.1. Next, we will continue our exploration of the social contexts in which adolescents develop.

 PEERS

In chapter 14, we discussed how children spend more time with their peers in middle and late childhood than in early childhood. We also found that friendships become more important in middle and late childhood and that popularity with peers is a strong motivation for most children. Advances in cognitive development during middle and late childhood also allow children to take the perspective of their peers and friends more readily, and their social knowledge of how to make and keep friends increases.

Imagine you are back in junior or senior high school, especially during one of your good times. Peers, friends, cliques, dates, parties, and clubs probably come to mind. Adolescents spend huge chunks of time with peers, more than in middle and late childhood.

Peer Groups

How much pressure is there to conform to peers during adolescence? Consider the following statement made by an adolescent girl:

> Peer pressure is extremely influential in my life. I have never had very many friends, and I spend quite a bit of time alone. The friends I have are older. The closest friend I have had is a lot like me in that we are both sad and depressed a lot. I began to act even more

Summary Table 17.1
Identity and Families

Concept	Processes/ Related Ideas	Characteristics/Description
Identity	Erikson's theory	This is the most comprehensive and provocative view of identity development. Identity versus identity confusion is the fifth stage in Erikson's life-cycle theory. During adolescence, worldviews become important, and the adolescent enters a psychological moratorium, a gap between childhood security and adult autonomy.
	Some contemporary thoughts about identity	Identity development is extraordinarily complex. It is done in bits and pieces. For the first time in development, during adolescence, individuals are physically, cognitively, and socially mature enough to synthesize their lives and pursue a viable path toward adult maturity.
	Identity statuses and development	Marcia proposed that four statuses of identity exist, based on a combination of conflict and commitment: identity diffusion, identity foreclosure, identity moratorium, and identity achievement. Some experts believe that the main identity changes take place in late adolescence or youth, rather than in early adolescence. College upperclassmen are more likely to be identity achieved than are freshmen or high school students, although many college students are still wrestling with ideological commitments. Individuals often follow "moratorium-achievement-moratorium-achievement" cycles.
	Family influences	Parents are important figures in adolescents' identity development. Democratic parenting facilitates identity development in adolescence; autocratic and permissive parenting do not. Cooper and her colleagues have shown that both individuation and connectedness in family relations make important contributions to adolescent identity development.
	Culture, ethnicity, and gender	Erikson is especially sensitive to the role of culture in identity development, underscoring how throughout the world ethnic minority groups have struggled to maintain their cultural identities while blending into the majority culture. Adolescence is often a special juncture in the identity development of ethnic minority individuals because, for the first time, they consciously confront their ethnic identity. While Erikson's classical theory argued for sex differences in identity development, more recent studies have shown that, as females have developed stronger vocational interests, sex differences in identity are turning into similarities. However, others argue that relationships and emotional bonds are more central to the identity development of females than males and that female identity development today is more complex than male identity development.
Families	Autonomy and attachment	Many parents have a difficult time handling the adolescent's push for autonomy, even though this push is one of the hallmarks of adolescent development. Adolescents do not simply move into a world isolated from parents; attachment to parents increases the probability that the adolescent will be socially competent and will explore a widening social world in healthy ways. Increasingly, researchers are classifying attachment in adolescence as secure-autonomous and breaking down insecure attachment into these three categories (dismissing/avoidant, preoccupied/ambivalent, and unresolved/disorganized). The social worlds of parents and peers are coordinated and connected.
	Parent-adolescent conflict	Conflict with parents often increases in early adolescence. Such conflict is usually moderate. The increase in conflict probably serves the positive developmental function of promoting autonomy and identity. A small subset of adolescents experiences high parent-adolescent conflict that is related to various negative outcomes for adolescents.
	The maturation of adolescents and parents	Physical, cognitive, and socioemotional changes in the adolescent's development influence parent-adolescent relationships. Parental changes—marital dissatisfaction, economic burdens, career reevaluation and time perspective, and health and bodily concerns—also influence parent-adolescent relationships.

Each of you, individually, walkest with the tread of a fox, but collectively ye are geese.

Solon
Greek Poet, Statesman, 6th Century B.C.

crowd
The largest and least personal of adolescent groups.

cliques
Smaller groups that involve greater intimacy among members and have more cohesion than crowds.

Most adolescents conform to the mainstream standards of their peers. However, the rebellious, or anticonformist, adolescent reacts counter to the mainstream peer group's expectations, deliberately moving away from the actions or beliefs this group advocates.

depressed than before when I was with her. I would call her up and try to act even more depressed than I was because that is what I thought she liked. In that relationship, I felt pressure to be like her.

Conformity to peer pressure in adolescence can be positive or negative. Teenagers engage in all sorts of negative conformity behavior—use seedy language, steal, vandalize, and make fun of parents and teachers. However, a great deal of peer conformity is not negative and consists of the desire to be involved in the peer world, such as dressing like friends and wanting to spend large amounts of time with members of a clique. Such circumstances may involve prosocial activities as well, as when clubs raise money for worthy causes.

Young adolescents conform more to peer standards than children do. Investigators have found that, around the eighth and ninth grades, conformity to peers—especially to their antisocial standards—peaks (Leventhal, 1994). At this point, adolescents are most likely to go along with a peer to steal hubcaps off a car, draw graffiti on a wall, or steal cosmetics from a store counter.

Cliques and Crowds Most peer group relationships in adolescence can be categorized in one of three ways: the crowd, the clique, or individual friendships. The **crowd** *is the largest and least personal of adolescent groups.* Members of the crowd meet because of their mutual interest in activities, not because they are mutually attracted to each other. **Cliques** *are smaller, involve greater intimacy among members, and have more group cohesion than crowds.*

Allegiance to cliques, clubs, organizations, and teams exerts powerful control over the lives of many adolescents (Tapper, 1996). Group identity often overrides personal identity. The leader of a group may place a member in a position of considerable moral conflict by asking, in effect, "What's more important, our code or your parents'?" or "Are you looking out for yourself, or the members of the group?" Such labels as *brother* and *sister* sometimes are adopted and used in the members' conversations with each other. These labels symbolize the bond between the members and suggest the high status of group membership.

One of the most widely cited studies of adolescent cliques and crowds is that of James Coleman (1961). Students from 10 high schools were asked to identify the leading crowds in their schools. They also were asked to identify the students who were the most outstanding in athletics, popularity, and various school activities. Regardless of the school sampled, the leading crowds were composed of athletes and popular girls. Much less power in the leading crowd was attributed to bright students.

Think about your high school years. What were the cliques, and which one were you in? Although the names of cliques change, we could go to almost any high school in the United States and find three to six well-defined cliques or crowds. In one study, six peer group structures emerged: populars, unpopulars, jocks, brains, druggies, and average students (Brown & Mounts, 1989). The proportion of students in these cliques was much lower in multiethnic schools because of the additional existence of ethnically based crowds.

In one study, clique membership was associated with adolescent self-esteem (Brown & Lohr, 1987). The cliques included jocks (athletically oriented), populars (well-known students who led social activities), normals (middle-of-the-road students who made up the masses), druggies or toughs (known for illicit drug use or other delinquent activities), and nobodies (low in social skills or intellectual abilities). The self-esteem of the jocks and the populars was highest, whereas that of the nobodies was lowest. One group of adolescents not in a clique had self-esteem equivalent to that of the jocks and the populars; this group was the independents, who indicated that clique membership was not important to them. Keep in mind that these data are correlational; self-esteem could increase an adolescent's probability of becoming a clique member, just as clique membership could increase the adolescent's self-esteem.

Adolescent Groups Versus Children Groups

Children groups differ from adolescent groups in several important ways. The members of children groups often are friends or neighborhood acquaintances, and their groups usually are not as formalized as many adolescent groups. During the adolescent years, groups tend to include a broader array of members. In other words, adolescents other than friends or neighborhood acquaintances often are members of adolescent groups. Try to recall the student council, honor society, or football team at your junior high school. If you were a member of any of these organizations, you probably remember that they were made up of many people you had not met before and that it was a more heterogeneous group than your childhood peer groups. For example, peer groups in adolescence are more likely to have a mixture of individuals from different ethnic groups than are peer groups in childhood.

As ethnic minority children move into adolescence and enter schools with more heterogeneous school populations, they become more aware of their ethnic minority status. Ethnic minority adolescents may have difficulty joining peer groups and clubs in predominantly White schools. Similarly, White adolescents may have peer difficulties in predominately ethnic minority schools. However, schools are only one setting in which peer relations take place; they also occur in the neighborhood and in the community.

Ethnic minority adolescents often have two sets of peer relationships—one at school, the other in the community. Community peers are more likely to be from their own ethnic group in their immediate neighborhood. Sometimes, they go to the same church and participate in activities together, such as Black History Week, Chinese New Year's, or Cinco de Mayo Festival. Because ethnic group adolescents usually have two sets of peers and friends, when researchers ask about their peers and friends, questions should focus on both relationships at school and relationships in the neighborhood and community. Ethnic minority adolescents who are social isolates at school may be social stars in their segregated neighborhood. Also, because adolescents are more mobile than children, inquiries should be made about the scope of their social networks.

A well-known observational study by Dexter Dunphy (1963) supports the notion that opposite-sex participation in groups increases during adolescence. In late childhood, boys and girls participate in small, same-sex cliques. As they move into the early adolescent years, the same-sex cliques begin to interact with each other. Gradually, the leaders and high-status members form further cliques based on heterosexual relationships. Eventually, the newly created heterosexual cliques replace the same-sex cliques. The heterosexual cliques interact with each other in large crowd activities, too—at dances and athletic events, for example. In late adolescence, the crowd begins to dissolve, as couples develop more serious relationships and make long-range plans that may include engagement and marriage (see figure 17.3).

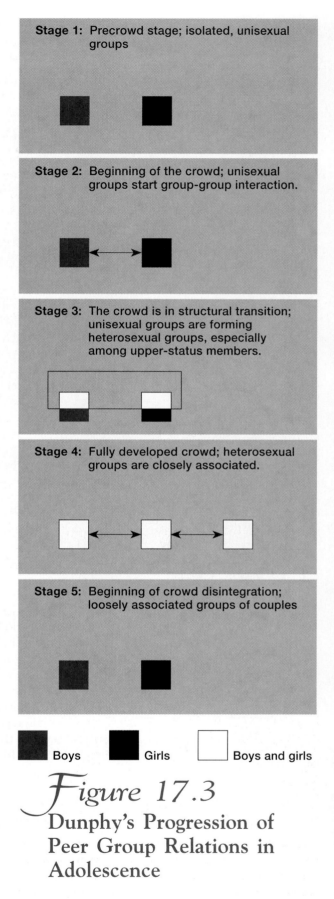

Stage 1: Precrowd stage; isolated, unisexual groups

Stage 2: Beginning of the crowd; unisexual groups start group-group interaction.

Stage 3: The crowd is in structural transition; unisexual groups are forming heterosexual groups, especially among upper-status members.

Stage 4: Fully developed crowd; heterosexual groups are closely associated.

Stage 5: Beginning of crowd disintegration; loosely associated groups of couples

Boys   Girls   Boys and girls

Figure 17.3
Dunphy's Progression of Peer Group Relations in Adolescence

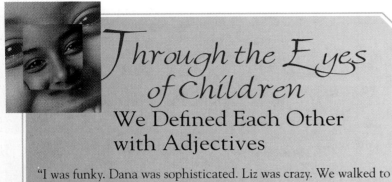

Through the Eyes of Children
We Defined Each Other with Adjectives

"I was funky. Dana was sophisticated. Liz was crazy. We walked to school together, went for bike rides, cut school, got stoned, talked on the phone, smoked cigarettes, slept over, discussed boys and sex, went to church together, and got angry at each other. We defined each other with adjectives and each other's presence. As high school friends, we simultaneously resisted and anticipated adulthood and womanhood.

What was possible when I was 15 and 16? We still had to tell our parents where we were going! We wanted to do excitedly forbidden activities like going out to dance clubs and drinking whiskey sours. Liz, Dana, and I wanted to do these forbidden things in order to feel: to have intense emotional and sensual experiences that removed us from the suburban sameness we shared with each other and everyone else we knew. We were tired of the repetitive experiences that our town, our siblings, our parents, and our school offered to us . . .

The friendship between Dana, Liz, and myself was born out of another emotional need: the need for trust. The three of us had reached a point in our lives when we realized how unstable relationships can be, and we all craved safety and acceptance. Friendships all around us were often uncertain. We wanted and needed to be able to like and trust each other (Garrod & others, 1992, pp. 199–200).

Friendships

Harry Stack Sullivan (1953) was the most influential theorist to discuss the importance of adolescent friendships. He argued that there is a dramatic increase in the psychological importance and intimacy of close friends during early adolescence. In contrast to other psychoanalytic theorists' narrow emphasis on the importance of parent-child relationships, Sullivan contended that friends also play important roles in shaping children's and adolescents' well-being and development. In terms of well-being, he argued that all people have a number of basic social needs, including the need for tenderness (secure attachment), playful companionship, social acceptance, intimacy, and sexual relations. Whether or not these needs are fulfilled largely determines our emotional well-being. For example, if the need for playful companionship goes unmet, then we become bored and depressed; if the need for social acceptance is not met, we suffer a lowered sense of self-worth. Developmentally, friends become increasingly depended on to satisfy these needs during adolescence; thus, the ups-and-downs of experiences with friends increasingly shape adolescents' state of well-being. In particular, Sullivan believed that the need for intimacy intensifies during early adolescence, motivating teenagers to seek out close friends. He felt that, if adolescents fail to forge such close friendships, they experience painful feelings of loneliness, coupled with a reduced sense of self-worth.

Research findings support many of Sullivan's ideas. For example, adolescents report disclosing intimate and personal information to their friends more often than do younger children (Buhrmester & Furman, 1987). Adolescents also say they depend more on friends than on parents to satisfy their needs for companionship, reassurance of worth, and intimacy (Furman & Buhrmester, 1992). In one study, daily interviews with 13- to 16-year-old adolescents over a 5-day period were conducted to find out how much time they spent engaged in meaningful interactions with friends and parents (Buhrmester & Carbery, 1992). Adolescents spent an average of 103 minutes per day in meaningful interactions with friends, compared with just 28 minutes per day with parents. In addition, the quality of friendship is more strongly linked to feelings of well-being during adolescence than during childhood. Teenagers with superficial friendships, or no close friendships at all, report feeling lonelier and more depressed, and they have a lower sense of self-esteem than do teenagers with intimate friendships (Yin, Buhrmester, & Hibbard, 1996). In another study, friendship in early adolescence was a significant predictor of self-worth in early adulthood (Bagwell, Newcomb, & Bukowski, 1994).

Although most adolescents develop friendships with individuals who are close to their own age, some adolescents become best friends with younger or older individuals. A common fear, especially among parents, is that adolescents who have older friends will be encouraged to engage in delinquent behavior or early sexual behavior. Researchers have found that adolescents who interact with older youths do engage in these behaviors more frequently, but it is not known whether the older youth guide younger adolescents toward deviant behavior or whether the younger adolescents were already prone to deviant behavior before they developed the friendship with the older youth (Billy, Rodgers, & Udry, 1984).

Youth Organizations

Youth organizations can have an important influence on the adolescent's development (Snider & Miller, 1993). More than 400 national youth organizations operate in the United States (Erickson, 1996). The organizations include career groups, such as Junior Achievement; groups aimed at building character, such as Girls Scouts and Boy Scouts; political groups, such as Young Republicans and Young Democrats; and ethnic groups, such as Indian Youth of America (Price & others, 1990). They serve approximately 30 million young people each year. The largest youth organization is 4-H, with nearly 5 million participants. The smallest are ASPIRA, a Latino youth organization that provides intensive educational enrichment programs for about 13,000 adolescents each year, and WAVE, a dropout-prevention program that serves about 8,000 adolescents each year.

Adolescents who join such groups are more likely to participate in community activities in adulthood; they have higher self-esteem, are better educated, and come from families with higher incomes than their counterparts who do not participate in youth groups (Erickson, 1982). Participation in youth groups can help adolescents practice the interpersonal and organizational skills that are important for success in adult roles.

To increase the participation of low-income and ethnic minority adolescents in youth groups, Girls Clubs and Boys Clubs are being established in locations where young adolescents are at high risk for dropping out of school, becoming delinquents, and developing substance-abuse problems. The locations are 15 housing projects in different American cities. The club programs are designed to provide individual, small-group, and drop-in supportive services that enhance educational and personal development. Preliminary results suggest that the Boys and Girls Clubs help reduce vandalism, drug abuse, and delinquency (Boys and Girls Clubs of America, 1989).

These adolescents are participating in Girls Club and Boys Club activities. This type of organization can have an important influence on adolescents' lives. Adolescents who participate in youth organizations on a regular basis participate more in community activities as adults and have higher self-esteem than their counterparts who do not.

Dating and Romantic Relationships

Dating takes on added importance during adolescence (Feiring, 1995). As comedian Dick Cavett (1974) remembers, the thought of an upcoming dance or sock hop was absolute agony: "I knew I'd never get a date. There seemed to be only this limited set of girls I could and should be seen with, and they were all taken by the jocks." Adolescents spend considerable time either dating or thinking about dating, which has gone far beyond its original courtship function to become a form of recreation, a source of status and achievement, and a setting for learning about close relationships. One function of dating, though, continues to be mate selection.

Dating and Romantic Relationships

Types of Dating and Developmental Changes   In their early romantic relationships, many adolescents are not motivated to fulfill attachment or even sexual needs. Rather, early romantic relationships serve as a context for adolescents to explore how attractive they are, how they should romantically interact with someone, and how all of this looks to the peer group (Brown, in press). Only after adolescents acquire some basic competencies in interacting with romantic partners does the fulfillment of attachment and sexual needs become central functions of these relationships (Furman & Wehner, in press).

In their early exploration of romantic relationships, today's adolescents often find comfort in numbers and begin hanging out together in heterosexual groups. Sometimes they just hang out at someone's house or get organized enough to get someone to drive them to a mall or a movie (Peterson, 1997). A special concern is early

He who would learn to fly one day must first learn to stand and walk and climb and dance: one cannot fly into flying.

Friedrich Nietzsche
German Philosopher, 19th Century

dating and "going with" someone, which is associated with adolescent pregnancy and problems at home and school (Downey & Bonica, 1997).

One new term on the adolescent dating scene is *hooking up*, which describes two individuals who casually see each other—usually only once or twice—and mainly just kiss and make out. *Seeing each other* also refers to a casual form of dating but it lasts longer than hooking up. When seeing each other, adolescents aren't tied down to one person. This allows an adolescent to see one person but still date others. *Going out* describes a dating relationship in which adolescents stop seeing other people and see each other exclusively. Going out can still involve a lot of group dates or it can involve more private dates.

Yet another form of dating recently has been added. *Cyberdating* is dating over the internet (Thomas, 1998). One 10-year-old girl posted this ad on the net:

> Hi! I'm looking for a Cyber Boyfriend! I'm 10. I have brown hair and brown eyes. I love swimming, playing basketball, and think kittens are adorable!!!

Cyberdating is especially becoming popular among middle school students. By the time they reach high school and are able to drive, dating usually has evolved into a more traditional real-life venture.

dating scripts
The cognitive models that adolescents and adults use to guide and evaluate dating interactions.

Dating Scripts   **Dating scripts** *are the cognitive models that guide individuals' dating interactions.* In one study, first dates were highly scripted along gender lines (Rose & Frieze, 1993). The males followed a proactive dating script, the females a reactive one. The male's script involved initiating the date (asking for and planning it), controlling the public domain (driving and opening doors), and initiating sexual interaction (making physical contact, making out, and kissing). The female's script focused on the private domain (concern about appearance, enjoying the date), participating in the structure of the date established by the male (being picked up, having doors opened), and responding to his sexual overtures. These gender differences give males more power in the initial stage of a dating relationship.

In another study, male and female adolescents brought different motivations to the dating experience (Feiring, 1996). The 15-year-old girls were more likely to describe romance in terms of interpersonal qualities, the boys in terms of physical attraction. The young adolescents frequently mentioned the affiliative qualities of companionship, intimacy, and support as positive aspects of romantic relationships, but not love and security. Also, the young adolescents described physical attraction more in terms of cute, pretty, or handsome than in sexual terms (such as being a good kisser). Possibly the failure to discuss sexual interests was due to the adolescents' discomfort in talking about such personal feelings with an unfamiliar adult.

Emotion and Romantic Relationships   The strong emotions of romantic relationships can thrust adolescents into a world in which things are turned upside down and ordinary reality recedes from view (Larson, Clore, & Wood, in press). One 14-year-old reports that he is so in love he can't think about anything else. A 15-year-old girl is enraged by the betrayal of her boyfriend. She is obsessed with ways to get back at him. The daily fluctuations in the emotions of romantic relationships can make the world seem almost surreal. Although the strong emotions of romance can have disruptive effects on adolescents, they also provide a source for possible mastery and growth. Learning to manage these strong emotions can give adolescents a sense of competence.

Romantic relationships often are involved in an adolescent's emotional experiences. In one study of ninth to twelfth graders, girls gave real and fantasized heterosexual relationships as the explanation for more than one third of their strong emotions and boys gave this reason for 25 percent of their strong emotions (Wilson-Shockley, 1995). Strong emotions were attached far less to school (13%), family (9%), and same-sex peer relations (8%). The majority of the emotions were reported as positive, but a substantial minority (42%), were reported as negative, including feelings of anxiety, anger, jealousy, and depression.

Relationships with Parents and Adolescent Romantic Relationships   Researchers recently have found that attachment history and early child care are precursors to forming positive couple relationships in adolescence (Sroufe, Egeland, & Carlson, 1999). For example, infants who had an anxious attachment with their caregiver in infancy were less likely to develop positive couple relationships in adolescence than their securely attached counterparts. It may be that having a history of secure attachment, in adolescence they may be better able to control their emotions and more comfortable in self-disclosure in adolescent romantic relationships.

Wyndol Furman and Elizabeth Wehner (in press) recently discussed how specific insecure attachment styles might link up with adolescents' romantic relationships. Adolescents with a secure attachment to parents are likely to approach romantic relationships expecting closeness, warmth, and intimacy. Thus, they are likely to feel comfortable in developing close, intimate romantic relationships. Adolescents with a dismissing/avoidant attachment to parents are likely to expect romantic partners to be unresponsive and unavailable. Thus, they may tend to behave in ways that distance themselves from romantic relationships. Adolescents with a preoccupied/ambivalent attachment to parents are likely to be disappointed and frustrated with intimacy and closeness in romantic relationships.

Sociocultural Contexts and Dating   The sociocultural context exerts a powerful influence on adolescent dating patterns. Values and religious beliefs of people in various cultures often dictate the age at which dating begins, how much freedom in dating is allowed, whether dates must be chaperoned by adults or parents, and the roles of males and females in dating. For example, Latino and Asian American cultures have more conservative standards regarding adolescent dating than does the Anglo-American culture. Dating may be a source of cultural conflict for many immigrants and their families who have come from cultures in which dating begins at a late age, little freedom in dating is allowed, dates are chaperoned, and adolescent girls' dating is especially restricted. Next, we will further explore the culture's role in adolescent socioemotional development.

CULTURE AND ADOLESCENT DEVELOPMENT

We live in an increasingly diverse world, one in which there is increasing contact between adolescents from different cultures and ethnic groups. How do adolescents vary cross-culturally? What rites of passage do adolescents experience? What is the nature of ethnic minority adolescents and their development?

Cross-Cultural Comparisons and Rites of Passage

Ideas about the nature of adolescents and orientation toward adolescents may vary from culture to culture and within the same culture over different time periods (Whiting, 1989). For example, some cultures (such as the Mangaian culture in the

---

Through the Eyes of Children
They Were Thinking about Having Sex with Girls from Budweiser Ads

"During 9th and 10th grade, I constantly fell in love with older boys I knew only slightly and shy boys my own age I knew well. I never went out on any dates with these boys; I just thought about them a lot. I knew some older guys from school government and committees. They were nice to me. Some flirted quite a bit with me. Bit I never went on dates with the older guys because they never asked me out. They usually had girlfriends who were Seniors. The shy boys my own age were not quite ready for dating. While I was thinking about true love and romantic walks through the park, they were thinking about videogames, rock music, and sex with girls from Budweiser ads. I never quite felt much like 'dating material.' I was tall and liked school and talked a lot in class. I wore weird clothes and wrote articles for the school newspaper and about local political candidates. Sometimes bizarre boys who wanted to be comic strip heroes or felt as stifled as I did by our relatively small town would confess their true love for me. These incidents never led to sexual relationships with these boys. I would tell them I knew how they felt, seeing that I had a few unfruitful crushes of my own. I never liked any of the boys who liked me" (Garrod & others, 1992, p. 203).

Source: Garrod, A., Smulyan, L., Powers, S.I., & Kilenny, R. (1992). *Adolescent portraits.* Boston: Allyn & Bacon.

Consider the flowers of a garden: though differing in kind, colour, form and shape, yet inasmuch as they are refreshed by the waters of one spring, revived by the breath of one wind, invigorated by the rays of one sun, this diversity increases their charm, and adds to their beauty. . . . How unpleasing to the eye if all the flowers and plants, the leaves and blossoms, the fruits, the branches and the trees of that garden were all of the same shape and colour! Diversity of hues, form and shape, enriches and adorns the garden. . . .

Àbud'l-Bahá
Persian Baha'i Religious Leader, 20th Century

South Sea islands) have more permissive attitudes toward adolescent sexuality than the American culture, and some cultures (the Ines Beag culture off the coast of Ireland, for example) have more conservative attitudes toward adolescent sexuality than the American culture. Over the course of the twentieth century, attitudes toward sexuality—especially for females—have become more permissive in the American culture.

Early in this century, overgeneralizations about the universal aspects of adolescents were made based on data and experience in a single culture—the middle-class culture of the United States. For example, it was believed that adolescents everywhere went through a period of "storm and stress," characterized by self-doubt and conflict. However, when Margaret Mead visited the island of Samoa, she found that the adolescents of the Samoan culture were not experiencing much stress.

cross-cultural studies

The comparison of a culture with one or more other cultures, which provides information about the degree to which development is similar (universal) across cultures or the degree to which it is culture-specific.

As we discovered in chapter 1, **cross-cultural studies** *involve the comparison of a culture with one or more other cultures, which provides information about the degree to which development is similar, or universal, across cultures, or the degree to which it is culture-specific*. The study of adolescence has emerged in the context of Western industrialized society, with the practical needs and social norms of this culture dominating thinking about adolescents. Consequently, the development of adolescents in Western cultures has evolved as the norm for all adolescents of the human species, regardless of economic and cultural circumstances. This narrow viewpoint can produce erroneous conclusions about the nature of adolescents. One variation in the experiences of adolescents in different cultures is whether the adolescents go through a rite of passage.

rite of passage

A ceremony or ritual that marks an individual's transition from one status to another. Most rites of passage focus on the transition to adult status.

Some societies have elaborate ceremonies that signal the adolescent's move to maturity and achievement of adult status. A **rite of passage** *is a ceremony or ritual that marks an individual's transition from one status to another. Most rites of passage focus on the transition to adult status*. In many primitive cultures, rites of passage are the avenue through which adolescents gain access to sacred adult practices, to knowledge, and to sexuality. These rites often involve dramatic practices intended to facilitate the adolescent's separation from the immediate family, especially the mother. The transformation is usually characterized by some form of ritual death and rebirth, or by means of contact with the spiritual world. Bonds are forged between the adolescent and the adult instructors through shared rituals, hazards, and secrets to allow the adolescent to enter the adult world. This kind of ritual provides a forceful and discontinuous entry into the adult world at a time when the adolescent is perceived to be ready for the change.

Africa has been the location of many rites of passage for adolescents, especially sub-Saharan Africa. Under the influence of Western culture, many of the rites are disappearing today, although some vestiges remain. In locations where formal education is not readily available, rites of passage are still prevalent.

Changing Contexts

Do we have such rites of passage for American adolescents? We certainly do not have universal formal ceremonies that mark the passage from adolescence to adulthood. Certain religious and social groups do have initiation ceremonies that indicate that an advance in maturity has been reached—the Jewish bar mitzvah, the Catholic confirmation, and social debuts, for example. School graduation ceremonies come the closest to being culturewide rites of passage in the United States. The high school graduation ceremony has become nearly universal for middle-class adolescents and increasing numbers of adolescents from low-income backgrounds. Nonetheless, high school graduation does not result in universal changes; many high school graduates continue to live with their parents, continue to be economically dependent on them, and continue to be undecided about career and lifestyle matters. Another rite of passage for increasing numbers of American adolescents is sexual intercourse (Halonen & Santrock, 1999). By the end of adolescence, more than 70 percent of American adolescents have had sexual intercourse.

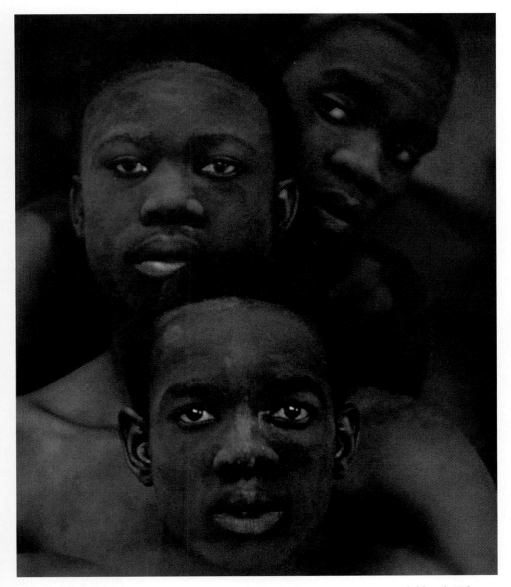

These Congolese Kota boys painted their faces as part of a rite of passage to adulthood. What kinds of rites of passage do American adolescents have?

Now that we have discussed the importance of a global perspective in understanding adolescence and the nature of rites of passage, we will turn our attention to the development of ethnic minority adolescents in the United States.

Ethnicity

First, we will examine the nature of ethnicity and socioeconomic status; second, we will examine the nature of differences and diversity; third, we will study the aspects of value conflicts, assimilation, and pluralism.

Ethnicity and Socioeconomic Status   Much of the research on ethnic minority adolescents has failed to tease apart the influences of ethnicity and socioeconomic status. Ethnicity and socioeconomic status can interact in ways that exaggerate the influence of ethnicity because ethnic minority individuals are overrepresented in the lower socioeconomic levels of American society. Consequently, researchers too often have given ethnic explanations of adolescent development that were largely due to socioeconomic status rather than ethnicity. For example, decades of research on group differences in self-esteem failed to consider the socioeconomic status of African American and White children and adolescents. When African American adolescents from low-income backgrounds are compared with White adolescents from middle-income backgrounds, the differences are often large but not informative because of the confounding of ethnicity and socioeconomic status (Scott-Jones, 1995).

Although some ethnic minority youth are from middle-income backgrounds, economic advantage does not entirely enable them to escape their ethnic minority status (Spencer & Dornbusch, 1990). Middle-income ethnic minority youth still encounter much of the prejudice, discrimination, and bias associated with being a member of an ethnic minority group. Often characterized as a "model minority" because of their strong achievement orientation and family cohesiveness, Japanese Americans still experience stress associated with ethnic minority status (Sue, 1990). Even though middle-income ethnic minority adolescents have more resources available to counter the destructive influences of prejudice and discrimination, they still cannot completely avoid the pervasive influence of negative stereotypes about ethnic minority groups.

Not all ethnic minority families are poor. However, poverty contributes to the stressful life experiences of many ethnic minority adolescents. Thus, many ethnic minority adolescents experience a double disadvantage: (1) prejudice, discrimination, and bias because of their ethnic minority status and (2) the stressful effects of poverty.

Differences and Diversity   There are legitimate differences between various ethnic minority groups, as well as between ethnic minority groups and the majority White group. Recognizing and respecting these differences are important aspects of getting along with others in a multicultural world. Historical, economic, and social experiences produce differences in ethnic groups (Coll, Meyer, & Brillion, 1995). Individuals living in a particular ethnic or cultural group adapt to the values, attitudes, and stresses of that culture. Their behavior, while possibly different from yours, is, nonetheless, often functional for them. It is important for adolescents to take the perspective of individuals from ethnic and cultural groups that are different from theirs and think, "If I were in their shoes, what kind of experiences might I have had?" "How would I feel if I were a member of their ethnic or cultural group?" "How would I think and behave if I had grown up in their world?" Such perspective taking often increases an adolescent's empathy and understanding of individuals from ethnic and cultural groups different from their own.

Another important dimension to continually keep in mind when studying ethnic minority adolescents is their diversity (Burton & Allison, 1995). Ethnic minority groups are not homogeneous; they have different social, historical, and economic backgrounds. For example, Mexican, Cuban, and Puerto Rican immigrants are all Latinos, but they migrated for different reasons, came from varying socioeconomic backgrounds in their native countries, and experience different rates and types of employment in the United States. The federal government now recognizes the existence of 511 *different* Native American tribes, each having a unique ancestral background with differing values and characteristics. Asian Americans include the Chinese, Japanese, Filipinos, Koreans, and Southeast Asians, each group having a distinct ancestry and language. As an indication of the diversity of Asian Americans, they not only show high educational attainments but also include a high proportion of individuals with no education whatsoever. For example, 90 percent of Korean American males graduate from high school, but only 71 percent of Vietnamese American males do.

Value Conflicts, Assimilation, and Pluralism   Stanley Sue (1990) believes that value conflicts are often involved when individuals respond to ethnic issues. These value conflicts have been a source of considerable controversy. According to Sue, without properly identifying the assumptions and effects of the conflicting values, it is difficult to resolve ethnic minority issues. Let's examine one of

Diversity and Pluralism

$\mathcal{W}$*e all know we are unique individuals, but we tend to see others as representatives of groups.*

Deborah Tannen
Contemporary American Sociolinguist

these value conflicts, assimilation versus pluralism, to see how it might influence an individual's response to an ethnic minority issue.

Assimilation *is the absorption of ethnic minority groups into the dominant group, which often means the loss of some or virtually all of the behavior and values of the ethnic minority group.* Individuals who adopt an assimilation stance usually advocate that ethnic minority groups become more American. By contrast, **pluralism** *is the coexistence of distinct ethnic and cultural groups in the same society. Individuals who adopt a pluralistic stance usually advocate that cultural differences be maintained and appreciated.*

Sue believes that one way to resolve value conflicts about sociocultural issues is to conceptualize or redefine them in innovative ways. For example, in the assimilation/pluralism conflict, rather than assume that assimilation is necessary for the development of functional skills, one strategy is to focus on the fluctuating criteria defining those skills considered to be functional; another is to consider the possibility that developing functional skills does not prevent the existence of pluralism. For instance, the classroom instructor might use multicultural examples when teaching social studies and still be able to discuss both culturally universal (etic) and culturally specific (emic) approaches to American and other cultures. To read about two programs that provide support for ethnic minority youth, see Caring for Children.

ADOLESCENT PROBLEMS

In chapter 15, we considered the adolescent problems involved in substance abuse and sexuality. Here, we will focus on the problems of juvenile delinquency, depression, and suicide. Then, we will explore the interrelation of problems and some strategies for prevention and intervention.

Juvenile Delinquency

Our coverage of juvenile delinquency focuses on its nature, its antecedents, and violence and youth.

The label **juvenile delinquent** *is applied to an adolescent who breaks the law or engages in behavior that is considered illegal.* Like other categories of disorders, juvenile delinquency is a broad concept; legal infractions range from littering to murder. Because the adolescent technically becomes a juvenile delinquent only after being judged guilty of a crime by a court of law, official records do not accurately reflect the number of illegal acts juvenile delinquents commit. Estimates of the number of juvenile delinquents in the United States are sketchy, but FBI statistics indicate that at least 2 percent of all youth are involved in juvenile court cases. The number of girls found guilty of juvenile delinquency has increased substantially in recent years. Delinquency rates among African Americans, other minority groups, and lower socioeconomic status youth are especially high in proportion to the overall population of these groups. However, such groups have less influence over the judicial decision-making process in the United States and, therefore, may be judged delinquent more readily than their White, middle-class counterparts.

What causes delinquency? Many causes have been proposed, including heredity, identity problems, community influences, and family experiences. Erik Erikson (1968), for example, believes that adolescents whose development has restricted them from acceptable social roles or has made them feel they cannot measure up to the demands placed on them may choose a negative identity. Adolescents with a negative identity may find support for their delinquent image among their peers, reinforcing the negative identity. For Erikson, delinquency is an attempt to establish an identity, although a negative one.

Although delinquency is less exclusively a lower-class phenomenon than it was in the past, some characteristics of the lower-class culture may promote delinquency. The norms of many lower-class peer groups and gangs are antisocial, or counterproductive, to the goals and norms of society at large. Getting into and staying out of trouble are

assimilation

The absorption of ethnic minority groups into the dominant group, which often involves the loss of some or virtually all of the behavior and values of the ethnic minority group.

pluralism

The coexistence of distinct ethnic and cultural groups in the same society. Individuals with a pluralistic stance usually advocate that cultural differences be maintained and appreciated.

I am here and you will know that I am the best and will hear me. The color of my skin or the kink of my hair or the spread of my mouth has nothing to do with what you are listening to.

Leontyne Price
American Opera Singer, 20th Century

juvenile delinquent

An adolescent who breaks the law or engages in behavior that is considered illegal.

Caring for Children
El Puente and Quantum

El Puente, which means "the bridge," was opened in New York City in 1983 because of community dissatisfaction with the health, education, and social services youth were receiving (Simons, Finlay, & Yang, 1991). El Puente emphasizes five areas of youth development: health, education, achievement, personal growth, and social growth.

El Puente is located in a former Roman Catholic church on the south side of Williamsburg in Brooklyn, a neighborhood made up primarily of low-income Latino families, many of which are far below the poverty line. Sixty-five percent of the residents receive some form of public assistance. The neighborhood has the highest school dropout rate for Latinos in New York City and the highest felony rate for adolescents in Brooklyn.

When the youth, ages 12 through 21, first enroll in El Puente, they meet with counselors and develop a four-month plan that includes the programs they are interested in joining. At the end of four months, the youth and staff develop a plan for continued participation. Twenty-six bilingual classes are offered in such subjects as the fine arts, theater, photography, and dance. In addition, a medical and fitness center, GED night school, and mental health and social services centers are a part of El Puente.

El Puente is funded through state, city, and private organizations and serves about 300 youth. The program has been replicated in Chelsea and Holyoke, Massachusetts, and two other sites in New York are being developed.

The Quantum Opportunities Program, funded by the Ford Foundation, was a four-year, year-around mentoring effort. The students were entering the ninth grade at a high school with high rates of poverty, were minorities, and came from families that received public assistance. Each day for four years, mentors provided sustained support, guidance, and concrete assistance to their students.

The Quantum program required students to participate in (1) academic-related activities outside school hours, including reading, writing, math, science, social studies, peer tutoring, and computer skills training; (2) community service projects, including tutoring elementary school students, cleaning up the neighborhood, and volunteering in hospitals, nursing homes, and libraries; and (3) cultural enrichment and personal development activities, including life skills training and college and job planning. In exchange for their commitment to the program, students were offered financial incentives that encouraged participation, completion, and long-range planning. A stipend of $1.33 was given to students for each hour they participated in these activities. For every 100 hours of education, service, or development activities, students received a bonus of $100. The average cost per participant was $10,600 for the 4 years, which is one half the cost of 1 year in prison.

An evaluation of the Quantum project compared the mentored students with a nonmentored control group. Sixty-three percent of the mentored students graduated from high school, but only 42 percent of the control group did; 42 percent of the mentored students are currently enrolled in college, but only 16 percent of the control group are. Further, the control-group students were twice as likely as the mentored students to receive food stamps or welfare, and they had more arrests. Such programs clearly have the potential to overcome the intergenerational transmission of poverty and its negative outcomes.

These adolescents participate in the programs of El Puente, located in a predominately low-income Latino neighborhood in Brooklyn, New York. The El Puente program stresses five areas of youth development: health, education, achievement, personal growth, and social growth.

Antecedent	Association with delinquency	Description
Identity	Negative identity	Erikson believes delinquency occurs because the adolescent fails to resolve a role identity.
Self-control	Low degree	Some children and adolescents fail to acquire the essential controls that others have acquired during the process of growing up.
Age	Early initiation	Early appearance of antisocial behavior is associated with serious offenses later in adolescence. However, not every child who acts out becomes a delinquent.
Sex	Males	Boys engage in more antisocial behavior than girls do, although girls are more likely to run away. Boys engage in more violent acts.
Expectations for education and school grades	Low expectations and low grades	Adolescents who become delinquents often have low educational expectations and low grades. Their verbal abilities are often weak.
Parental influences	Monitoring (low), support (low), discipline (ineffective)	Delinquents often come from families in which parents rarely monitor their adolescents, provide them with little support, and ineffectively discipline them.
Peer influences	Heavy influence, low resistance	Having delinquent peers greatly increases the risk of becoming delinquent.
Socioeconomic status	Low	Serious offenses are committed more frequently by lower-class males.
Neighborhood quality	Urban, high crime, high mobility	Communities often breed crime. Living in a high-crime area, which also is characterized by poverty and dense living conditions, increases the probability that a child will become a delinquent. These communities often have grossly inadequate schools.

Figure 17.4
The Antecedents of Juvenile Delinquency

prominent features of life for some adolescents in low-income neighborhoods. Adolescents from low-income backgrounds may sense that they can gain attention and status by performing antisocial actions. Being "tough" and "masculine" are high-status traits for lower-class boys, and these traits are often measured by the adolescent's success in performing and getting away with delinquent acts. A community with a high crime rate also lets the adolescent observe many models who engage in criminal activities. These communities may be characterized by poverty, unemployment, and feelings of alienation toward the middle class. Quality schooling, educational funding, and organized neighborhood activities may be lacking in these communities.

Family support systems are also associated with delinquency (Feldman & Weinberger, 1994). Parents of delinquents are less skilled in discouraging antisocial behavior and in encouraging skilled behavior than are parents of nondelinquents. Parental monitoring of adolescents is especially important in determining whether an adolescent becomes a delinquent (Patterson, DeBaryshe, & Ramsey, 1989). Family discord and inconsistent and inappropriate discipline are also associated with delinquency, as are relations. Having delinquent peers greatly increases the risk of becoming delinquent. A summary of the antecedents of delinquency is presented in figure 17.4

A recent, special concern in low-income areas is escalating gang violence.

Violence and Gangs

Prevention of Youth Violence

Of increasing concern is the high rate of violence displayed by adolescents. According to the U.S. Department of Education (1993), 16 percent of high school seniors reported that they had been threatened with a weapon at school; 7 percent said they had been injured with a weapon. One of every five high school students routinely carries a firearm, knife, or club. Many teachers say they have been verbally abused, physically threatened, or actually attacked by students. And homicide remains the leading cause of death among African Americans, regardless of gender or age.

Intervening with children before they develop ingrained antisocial behaviors is an important dimension of reducing violence in youth (Staub, 1996). Slogan campaigns and scare tactics do not work. In one successful intervention, Positive Adolescents Choices Training (PACT), African American 12- to 15-year-olds learn to manage their anger and resolve conflicts peacefully (Hammond, 1993). Through the use of culturally sensitive videotapes, students learn to give and receive feedback, control their anger, and negotiate and compromise. The videotapes show peer role models demonstrating these skills, along with adult role models who encourage the participants to practice the techniques. Students in the program have spent less time in juvenile court for violence-related offenses than have nonparticipants in a control group. The program students also have shown a drop in violence-related school suspensions and have improved their social and conflict-resolution skills.

The Safe Schools Act can help foster such programs as PACT. Under the bill, schools can receive grants up to $3 million a year over two years to develop their own violence prevention programs. The initiatives could include comprehensive school safety strategies, coordination with community programs and agencies, and improved security to keep weapons out of the schools. To ensure that programs focus on prevention more than on enforcement, the grants allow only 33 percent of the funds to be used for metal detectors and security guards.

As previously mentioned, interventions can reduce or prevent youth violence (Carnegie Council on Adolescent Development, 1995). Efforts at prevention should include developmentally appropriate schools, supportive families, and youth and community organizations. At a more specific level, one promising strategy for preventing youth violence is the teaching of conflict management as part of health education in elementary and middle schools. To build resources for such programs, the Carnegie Foundation is supporting a national network of violence prevention practitioners based at the United States Department of Education, linked with a national research center on youth violence at the University of Colorado.

Depression and Suicide

What is the nature of depression in adolescence? What causes an adolescent to commit suicide?

Depression   Depression is more likely to occur in adolescence than in childhood. Also, adolescent girls consistently have higher rates of depression than adolescent boys. Among the reasons for this sex difference are that

- Females tend to ruminate in their depressed mood and amplify it
- Females' self-images, especially their body images, are more negative than males'
- Females face more discrimination than males.

Certain family factors place adolescents at risk for developing depression. These include having a depressed parent, emotionally unavailable parents, parents who have high marital conflict, and parents with financial problems.

Poor peer relationships also are associated with adolescent depression. Not having a close relationship with a best friend, having less contact with friends, and experiencing peer rejection all increase depressive tendencies in adolescents.

The experience of difficult changes or challenges also is associated with depressive symptoms in adolescence (Compas & Grant, 1993), and parental divorce increases depressive symptoms in adolescents. Also, when adolescents go through puberty at the same time as they move from elementary school to middle or junior high school, they report being depressed more than do adolescents who go through puberty after the school transition.

Suicide   Suicide is a common problem in our society. Its rate has tripled in the past 30 years in the United States; each year, about 25,000 people take their own lives. Beginning with the 15-year-old age group, the suicide rate begins to rise rapidly.

Suicide is now the third leading cause of death in 15- to 24-year-olds (Shneidman, 1996). Males are about three times as likely to commit suicide as females are; this may be because of their choice of more active methods for attempting suicide—shooting, for example. By contrast, females are more likely to use passive methods, such as sleeping pills, which are less likely to produce death. Although males commit suicide more frequently, females attempt it more frequently.

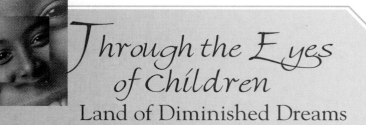

Through the Eyes of Children
Land of Diminished Dreams

The year is two-thousand fifty-four,
    The world is full of curses.
People walk the streets no more,
    No women carry purses.

The name of the game is survival now——
    Safety is far in the past.
Families are huge, with tons of kids
    In hopes that one will last.

Drugs are no longer looked down on,
    They are a way of life.
They help us escape the wrenching stress
    Of our fast world's endless strife . . .

I wake up now—it was only a dream,
    But the message was terribly clear.
We'd better think hard about the future
    Before our goals and our dreams disappear.

Jessica Inglis, 16

Depression is more likely to occur in adolescence than in childhood, and female adolescents are more likely than male adolescents to be depressed.

What to do

1. Ask direct, straightforward questions in a calm manner: "Are you thinking about hurting yourself?"

2. Assess the seriousness of the suicidal intent by asking questions about feelings, important relationships, who else the person has talked with, and the amount of thought given to the means to be used. If a gun, pills, a rope, or other means has been obtained and a precise plan developed, clearly the situation is dangerous. Stay with the person until help arrives.

3. Be a good listener and be very supportive without being falsely reassuring.

4. Try to persuade the person to obtain professional help and assist him or her in getting this help.

What not to do

1. Do not ignore the warning signs.

2. Do not refuse to talk about suicide if a person approaches you about it.

3. Do not react with humor, disapproval, or repulsion.

4. Do not give false reassurances by saying such things as "Everything is going to be OK." Also do not give out simple answers or platitudes, such as "You have everything to be thankful for."

5. Do not abandon the individual after the crisis has passed or after professional help has commenced.

Figure 17.5
What to Do and What Not to Do When You Suspect Someone Is Likely to Commit Suicide

Adolescent Depression

Suicide

Estimates indicate that, for every successful suicide in the general population, 6 to 10 attempts are made. For adolescents, the figure is as high as 50 attempts for every life taken. As many as two in every three college students has thought about suicide on at least one occasion; their methods range from overdosing on drugs to crashing into the White House in an airplane.

Why do adolescents attempt suicide? There is no simple answer to this important question. It is helpful to think of suicide in terms of proximal and distal factors. Proximal, or immediate, factors can trigger a suicide attempt. Highly stressful circumstances, such as the loss of a boyfriend or girlfriend, poor grades at school, or an unwanted pregnancy, can trigger a suicide attempt. Drugs have been involved more often in recent suicide attempts than in attempts in the past (Wagner, Cole, & Schwartzman, 1993).

Distal, or earlier, experiences often are involved in suicide attempts as well. A long-standing history of family instability and unhappiness may be present (Reinherz & others, 1994). Just as a lack of affection and emotional support, high control, and pressure for achievement by parents during childhood are related to adolescent depression, such combinations of family experiences are also likely to show up as distal factors in suicide attempts. The adolescent might also lack supportive friendships. In a study of suicide among gifted women, previous suicide attempts, anxiety, conspicuous instability in work and in relationships, depression, or alcoholism also was present in the women's lives (Tomlinson-Keasey, Warren, & Elliot, 1986). These factors are similar to those found to predict suicide among gifted men.

Just as genetic factors are associated with depression, they are also associated with suicide. The closer a person's genetic relationship to someone who has committed suicide, the more likely that person is to also commit suicide.

What is the psychological profile of the suicidal adolescent? Suicidal adolescents often have depressive symptoms (Gadpaille, 1996). Although not all depressed adolescents are suicidal, depression is the most frequently cited factor associated with adolescent suicide. A sense of hopelessness, low self-esteem, and high self-blame are also associated with adolescent suicide (Harter & Marold, 1992). Figure 17.5 provides valuable information about what to do and what not to do when you suspect someone is contemplating suicide.

Adventures for the Mind
Why Is a Course of Risk Taking in Adolescence Likely to Have More Serious Consequences Today Than in the Past?

The world is dangerous and unwelcoming for too many of America's teenagers, especially those from low-income families, neighborhoods, and schools. Many adolescents are resilient and cope with the challenges of adolescence without too many setbacks. Others struggle unsuccessfully to find jobs, are written off as losses by their schools, become pregnant before they are ready to become parents, or risk their health through drug abuse. Adolescents in virtually every era have been risk takers, testing limits and making shortsighted judgments. But why are the consequences of choosing a course of risk taking possibly more serious today than they have ever been?

The Interrelation of Problems and Successful Prevention/Intervention Programs

We have described some of the major adolescent problems in this chapter and the two preceding chapters: substance abuse; juvenile delinquency; school-related problems, such as dropping out of school; adolescent pregnancy and sexually transmitted diseases; depression; and suicide.

The most at-risk adolescents have more than one problem. Researchers are increasingly finding that problem behaviors in adolescence are interrelated (Tubman & Windle, 1995). For example, heavy substance abuse is related to early sexual activity, lower grades, dropping out of school, and delinquency. Early initiation of sexual activity is associated with the use of cigarettes and alcohol, the use of marijuana and other illicit drugs, lower grades, dropping out of school, and delinquency. Delinquency is related to early sexual activity, early pregnancy, substance abuse, and dropping out of school. As many as 10 percent of all adolescents in the United States have serious multiple-problem behaviors (for example, adolescents who have dropped out of school, are behind in their grade level, are users of heavy drugs, regularly use cigarettes and marijuana, and are sexually active but do not use contraception). Many, but not all, of these very high-risk youth "do it all." Another 15 percent of adolescents participate in many of these behaviors but with slightly lower frequency and less deleterious consequences. These high-risk youth often engage in two- or three-problem behaviors (Dryfoos, 1990). To further evaluate adolescent problems, see Adventures for the Mind.

In addition to understanding that many adolescents engage in multiple-problem behaviors, it also is important to develop programs that reduce adolescent problems.

Youth Risk Behavior
Treating Adolescent Problems

There is no easy path leading out of life, and few are the easy ones that lie within it.

Walter Savage Landor
English Poet, 10th Century

Improving Developmental Skills
Strategies for Supporting Adolescents' Socioemotional Development

What are some good strategies for helping adolescents improve their socioemotional competencies?

Let adolescents explore their identity. Adolescence is a time of identity exploration. Adults should encourage adolescents to try out different options as they seek to find what type of life they want to pursue.

• *Understand the importance of autonomy and attachment.* A common stereotype is that parents are less important in adolescent development than in child development. However, parents continue to play a crucial role in the adolescent's development. They need their parents as a resource and support system, especially in stressful times. Value the adolescent's motivation for independence. However, continue to monitor the adolescent's whereabouts, although less intrusively and directly than in childhood.

• *Keep parent-adolescent conflict from being turbulent, and use good communication skills with the adolescent.* Adolescents' socioemotional development benefits when conflict with parents is either low or moderate. Keep communication channels open with the adolescent. Be an active listener and show respect for the adolescent's advancing developmental status. As with childhood, authoritative parenting is the best choice in most situations. Communicate expectations for high standards of achievement and conduct.

• *Recognize the importance of peers, youth organizations, and mentors.* Respected peers need to be used more frequently in programs that promote health and education. Adolescents need greater access to youth organizations staffed by caring peers and adults. Mentors can play a strong role in supporting adolescents' socioemotional development.

• *Help adolescents better understand the nature of differences, diversity, and value conflicts.* Adolescents need to be encouraged to take the perspective of adolescents from diverse ethnic backgrounds.

• *Give adolescents individualized attention.* One of the reasons that adolescents develop problems is that they have not been given adequate attention.

• *Provide better communitywide collaboration for helping youth.* In successful programs, a number of different services and programs cooperate to help adolescents.

• *Prevent adolescent problems through early identification and intervention.* The seeds of many adolescent problems are already in place in childhood.

In a recent review of the programs that have been successful in preventing or reducing adolescent problems, adolescence researcher Joy Dryfoos (1990) described the common components of these successful programs:

1. *Intensive individualized attention.* In successful programs, high-risk children are attached to a responsible adult, who gives the child attention and deals with the child's specific needs. This theme occurs in a number of programs. In a successful substance-abuse program, a student assistance counselor is available full-time for individual counseling and referral for treatment.

2. *Communitywide multiagency collaborative approaches.* The basic philosophy of communitywide programs is that a number of different programs and services have to be in place. In one successful substance-abuse program, a communitywide health promotion campaign has been implemented that uses local media and community education, in concert with a substance-abuse curriculum in the schools.

3. *Early identification and intervention.* Reaching children and their families before children develop problems, or at the beginning of their problems, is a successful strategy. One preschool program serves as an excellent model for the prevention of delinquency, pregnancy, substance abuse, and dropping out of school. Operated by the High Schope Foundation in Ypsilanti, Michigan, the Perry Preschool has had a long-term positive impact on its students. This enrichment program, directed by David Weikart, serves disadvantaged African American children. They attend a high-quality two-year preschool program and receive weekly home visits from program personnel. Based on official police records, by age 19, individuals who had attended the Prerry Preschool program were less likely to have been arrested and reported fewer adult offenses than a control group. The Perry Preschool students also were less likely to drop out of school, and teachers rated their social behavior as more competent than that of a crowd group who had not receive the enriched preschool experience.

We have discussed a number of strategies for improving developmental skills at various points in the chapter. The insert Improving Developmental Skills highlights these strategies. At this point, we also have discussed many ideas about peers, culture, and adolescent problems. An overview of these ideas is presented in summary table 17.2.

Summary Table 17.2
Peers, Culture, and Adolescent Problems

Concept	Processes/ Related Ideas	Characteristics/Description
Peers	Peer groups	The pressure to conform to peers is strong during adolescence, especially during the eighth and ninth grades. There are usually three to six well-defined cliques in every secondary school. Membership in certain cliques—especially jocks and populars—is associated with increased self-esteem. Independents also show high self-esteem. Children groups are less formal, less heterogeneous, and less heterosexual than adolescent groups. Dunphy found that the development of adolescent groups moves through five stages.
	Friendships	Harry Stack Sullivan was the most influential theorist to discuss the importance of friendships. He argued that there is a dramatic increase in the psychological importance and intimacy of close friends in early adolescence.
	Youth organizations	Youth organizations can have an important influence on the adolescent's development. More than 400 national youth organizations currently exist.
	Dating and romantic relationships	Dating takes on added importance in adolescence, and it can have many functions. Younger adolescents often begin to hang out together in heterosexual groups. A special concern is early dating, which is linked with developmental problems. Male dating scripts are proactive, those of females reactive. Emotions are heavily involved in adolescent dating and romantic relationships. Researchers have found that adolescent romantic relationships are linked with relationships with parents. Culture can exert a powerful influence on adolescent dating.
Culture and rites of passage	Their nature	As in other periods of development, culture influences adolescents' development. Ceremonies mark an individual's transition from one status to another, especially into adulthood. In primitive cultures, rites of passage are often well defined. In contemporary America, rites of passage to adulthood are ill-defined.
	Ethnicity	Much of the research on ethnic minority adolescents has not teased apart the influences of ethnicity and social class. Because of this failure, too often researchers have given ethnic explanations that were largely due to socioeconomic factors. While not all ethnic minority families are poor, poverty contributes to the stress of many ethnic minority adolescents. There are legitimate differences between many ethnic groups, as well as between ethnic groups and the White majority. Recognizing these differences is an important aspect of getting along with others in a diverse, multicultural world. Too often, differences between ethnic groups and the White majority have been interpreted as deficits on the part of the ethnic minority group. Another important dimension of ethnic minority groups is their diversity. Ethnic minority groups are not homogeneous; they have different social, historical, and economic backgrounds. Failure to recognize diversity and individual variations results in the stereotyping of an ethnic minority group. Value conflicts are often involved when individuals respond to ethnic issues. One prominent value conflict involves assimilation versus pluralism.
Adolescent problems	Juvenile delinquency	A juvenile delinquent is an adolescent who breaks the law or engages in conduct that is considered illegal. Heredity, identity problems, community influences, and family experiences have been proposed as causes of delinquency. Parents' failure to discourage antisocial behavior and encourage skilled behavior, as well as parents' lack of monitoring of the adolescent's whereabouts, are related to delinquency. An increasing concern is the high rate of violence among youth.
	Depression and suicide	Adolescents have a higher rate of depression than children. Female adolescents are more likely to have mood and depressive disorders than male adolescents are. Adolescent suicide has tripled since the 1950s. Both proximal and distal factors are involved in suicide's causes.
	The interrelation of problems and successful prevention/intervention programs	Researchers are increasingly finding that problem behaviors in adolescence are interrelated. Dryfoos found a number of common components in programs designed to prevent or reduce adolescent problems: they provide individual attention to high-risk children, they develop communitywide intervention, and they include early identification and intervention.

Chapter Review

We began this chapter by evaluating why such adolescents as Kip Kinkel and Luke Woodham kill. They we described the following aspects of identity: some contemporary thoughts; identity statuses; family influences; and culture, ethnicity, and gender. Our coverage of families focused on autonomy and attachment, parent-adolescent conflict, and the maturation of adolescents and parents. We studied the following dimensions of peer relations: peer groups, friendships, youth organizations, and dating and romantic relationships. We also explored culture and adolescent development, including cross-cultural comparisons and rites of passage, as well as ethnicity. We examined adolescent programs by discussing juvenile delinquency, depression and suicide, and the interrelation of problems and successful prevention/intervention programs.

Don't forget that you can obtain a more detailed overview of the chapter by again reading the two summary tables on pages 509 and 527. This chapter on socioemotional development in adolescence is the last one in the book. However, a final part to the book—an epilogue—takes you on a journey through childhood.

✓ Children Checklist

Socioemotional Development in Adolescence

How much have you learned since the beginning of the chapter? Use the following statements to help you review your knowledge and understanding of the chapter material. First, read the statement and mentally or briefly demonstrate on paper that you can discuss the relevant information.

_____ I can describe some contemporary thoughts about identity.
_____ I am aware of the different identity statuses.
_____ I can evaluate the roles of families, culture, ethnicity, and gender in identity development.
_____ I can discuss autonomy and attachment in adolescence.
_____ I can evaluate the nature of parent-adolescent conflict.
_____ I know how the maturation of adolescents and parents can influence parent-adolescent interactions.
_____ I can describe peer groups and youth organizations.
_____ I can discuss dating and romantic relationships.
_____ I know about culture and adolescence.
_____ I can discuss ethnicity and adolescent development
_____ I can describe the nature of adolescent problems.

For any items that you did not check, go back and locate the relevant material in the chapter. Review the material until you feel you can check off the item. You may want to use this checklist later in preparing for an exam.

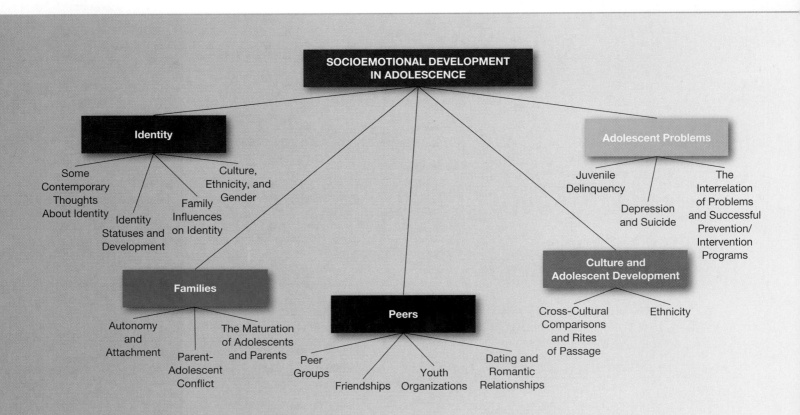

Key Terms

crisis 500
commitment 501
identity diffusion 501
identity foreclosure 501
identity moratorium 501
identity achievement 501
individuality 502
connectedness 502
dismissing/avoidant
   attachment 505
preoccupied/ambivalent
   attachment 505

unresolved/disorganized
   attachment 506
crowd 510
cliques 510
dating scripts 514
cross-cultural studies 516
rite of passage 516
assimilation 519
pluralism 519
juvenile delinquent 519

Children Resources

Great Transitions
(1995) by the Carnegie Council on Adolescent Development.
New York: Carnegie Corporation.

This report by the Carnegie Council on Adolescent Development
covers a wide range of topics. A number of discussions evaluate ways to
reduce adolescent risk and enhance their opportunities.

National Resource Center for Youth Services
University of Oklahoma College of Continuing Education
202 West 8th Street
Tulsa, OK 74119-1419
918–589–2986

This resource center has available a number of videotapes and
publications on adolescents. They also have an annual training
conference on working with America's youth that is sponsored by the
National Network for Youth.

You and Your Adolescent
(1997, 2nd ed.)
by Laurence Steinberg and Ann Levine. New York: HarperCollins.

You and Your Adolescent provides a broad, developmental overview of
adolescence, with parental advice mixed in along the way.

Taking It to the Net

http://www.mhhe.com/santrockcd6

1. You begin to notice that your 14-year-old is staying home more often than usual and even
   has been truant at school a few times. You also notice that he has become nervous,
   anxious, tense, and unsure of himself. Do you remember being anxious as an adolescent?
   What are some possible causes of this anxiety? How much anxiety is normal in
   adolescents?
2. Who were your role models growing up? Are you a role model for the adolescents in your
   life? Why or why not? What characteristics are necessary to be a role model?
3. Suicide is the third leading cause of death in adolescents, following accidents and
   homicide. Would you be able to recognize the symptoms of those who are vulnerable to
   suicide? What types of behavior would you look for, and why? What should you do if you
   suspect that someone you know is suicidal?

Adolescence

Physical Development

Puberty is a period of rapid skeletal and sexual maturation that occurs mainly in early adolescence. Testosterone plays an important role in male pubertal development, estradiol an important role in female pubertal development. The initial onset of pubertal growth occurs on the average at 9½ years for girls and 11½ for boys, reaching a peak change at 11½ for girls, 13½ for boys. Adolescents show a heightened interest in their body image. Early maturation favors boys during early adolescence, but, in terms of identity development in adulthood, later maturation is more favorable. Early-maturing girls are vulnerable to a number of problems. At issue is the extent to which puberty's effects have been exaggerated. The three leading causes of death in adolescence are accidents, suicide, and homicide. A majority of adolescents have had sexual intercourse by age 18, and sexual intercourse among adolescents is increasing. Both males and females report increased use of birth control in recent years. Sexually transmitted diseases and adolescent pregnancy are major problems in adolescence. So is substance abuse. Among the eating disorders that adolescents can experience are anorexia nervosa and bulimia. Cognitive and sociocultural factors influence adolescent health. Adolescents use health services less than any other age group, even though they may encounter a number of acute health conditions.

Cognitive Development

In Piaget's theory, formal operational thought emerges between 11 and 15 years of age. Formal operational thought is more abstract, idealistic, and logical than concrete operational thought. Piaget believed that adolescents become capable of hypothetical-deductive reasoning. Some of Piaget's ideas on formal operational thought are being challenged. Young adolescents are characterized by adolescent egocentrism, which includes an imaginary audience and a personal fable. Changes in information processing that characterize adolescence include improvements in memory, decision making, critical thinking, and self-regulatory learning. Values and spirituality are important to many adolescents. A number of strategies have been used in the moral education of adolescents. The function of schools for adolescents has been debated extensively. The transition to middle or junior high school often is stressful. A special concern is the number of adolescents who drop out of school, especially Latino adolescents. Career development becomes more important in adolescence, a time when many adolescents combine school with part-time work.

Socioemotional Development

Erikson proposed that adolescence is characterized by the stage of identity versus identity confusion. Marcia proposed four statuses of identity. Some experts believe that the most important changes in identity occur in late adolescence or youth, rather than early adolescence. Parents, culture, and gender influence identity development. Many parents have a difficult time handling the adolescent's push for autonomy, even though the push is one of the hallmarks of adolescent development. Adolescents do not simply move into a world isolated from their parents. Attachment to parents increases the probability that the adolescent will be socially competent and explore a widening social world in competent ways. Conflict with parents often increases in early adolescence, and this likely serves a positive developmental function, as long as it is not severe conflict. Both maturation of the adolescent and maturation of parents influence parent-adolescent interaction. The pressure for peer conformity increases in early adolescence. Friendships take on a more important role in adolescence than in childhood. Children's groups are less formal, less heterogeneous, and more same-sex than adolescent groups. Dating and romantic relationships become important aspects of the lives of many adolescents. In many primitive cultures, rites of passage mark a transition to adult status. In America, rites of passage are poorly defined. An increasing interest focuses on ethnic minority adolescents. Juvenile delinquency, depression, and suicide are problems that increase in adolescence. At-risk adolescents often have more than one problem. Two approaches that have widespread application in improving the lives of at-risk youth are (1) individual attention and (2) coordinated communitywide involvement.

531

Epilogue

The Journey of Childhood

I hope you can look back and say that you learned a lot about children—not only other children, but yourself as a child and how your childhood contributed to who you are today. The insightful words of philosopher Soren Kierkegaard capture the importance of looking back to understand ourselves: "Life is lived forward but understood backwards." I also hope that those of you who become the parents of children or who work with children in some capacity—whether as teacher, counselor, or community leader—feel that you have a better grasp of what children's development is all about.

Future generations depend on our ability to face our children. At some point in our adult lives, each one of us needs to examine the shape of our life and ask whether we have met the responsibility of competently and caringly carving out a better world for our children. Twenty-one centuries ago, Roman poet and philosopher Lucretius described one of adult life's richest meanings: grasping that the generations of living things pass in a short while and, like runners, pass on the torch of life. More than 20 centuries later, American writer James Agee captured yet another of life's richest meanings: in every child who is born, the potentiality of the human species is born again.

As we come to the end of this book, I leave you with the following montage of thoughts and images that conveys the beauty and complexity of children's development.

The rhythm and meaning of human development involve beginnings, when questions of whence and whither, when and how are asked. How, from so simple a beginning, do endless forms develop and grow and mature? What was this organism, what is it now, and what will it become? Birth's fragile moment arrives, when the newborn is on a threshold between two worlds.

As newborns, we were not empty-headed organisms. We cried, kicked, coughed, sucked, saw, heard, and tasted. We slept a lot and occasionally we smiled, although the meaning of our first smiles was not entirely clear. We crawled and then we walked, a journey of a thousand miles beginning with a single step. With each forward step we left some ghost of ourselves behind. Sometimes we conformed, sometimes others conformed to us. Our development was a continous creation of more-complex forms and our helpless kind demanded the "meeting eyes of love." We split the universe into two halves: "me" and "not me." And we juggled the need to curb our own will with becoming what we could will freely.

In early childhood, our greatest untold poem was being only 4 years old. We skipped, played, and ran all the day long, never in our lives so busy, busy becoming something we had not quite grasped yet. Who knew our thoughts, which we worked up into small mythologies all our own? While our thoughts and feelings took wings, the blossoms of our heart no wind could touch. Our small world widened as we discovered new refuges and new people. When we said "I," we meant something totally unique, not to be confused with any other.

In middle and late childhood, we were on a different plane, belonging to a generation and feeling properly our own. It is the wisdom of human development that at no other time are we more ready to learn than at the end of early childhood's period of expansive imagination. Our thirst was to know and to understand. Our parents continued to cradle our lives, but our growth was also being shaped by successive choirs of friends. We did not think much about the future or the past but enjoyed the present.

In no other order of things was adolescence the simple time of life for us. We clothed ourselves with rainbows and went brave as the zodiac, flashing from one end of the world to the other. We tried on one face after another , searching for a face of our own. We wanted our parents to understand us and hoped they would give us the privilege of understanding them. We wanted to fly but found that first we had to learn to stand and walk and climb and dance. In our most pimply and awkward moments, we became acquainted with sex. We played furiously at adult games but were confined to a society of our own peers. Our generation was the fragile cable by which the best and the worst of our parents' generation was transmitted to the present. In the end, there were but two lasting bequests our parents could leave us—one being roots, the other wings.

Glossary

A

accommodation Individuals' adjustment to new information. 37

achievement motivation (need for achievement) The desire to accomplish something, to reach a standard of excellence, and to expend effort to excel. 388

active (niche-picking) genotype → environment correlations The type of interactions that occur when children seek out environments they find compatible and stimulating. 82

adaptive behavior Behavior that promotes an organism's survival in the natural habitat. 64

adolescence The developmental period of transition from childhood to early adulthood, entered at approximately 10 to 12 years of age and ending at 18 to 22 years of age. 19

adolescent egocentrism The heightened self-consciousness of adolescents that is reflected in their belief that others are as interested in them as they are in themselves, and in their sense of personal uniqueness. 472

adoption study A study in which investigators seek to discover whether, in behavior and psychological characteristics, adopted children are more like their adoptive parents, who provided a home environment, or more like their biological parents, who contributed their heredity. Another form of the adoption study is to compare adoptive and biological siblings. 80

afterbirth The third stage of birth, when the placenta, umbilical cord, and other membranes are detached and expelled. 120

AIDS (acquired immune deficiency syndrome) A syndrome caused by the human immunodeficiency virus (HIV), which destroys the body's immune system. 456

altruism An unselfish interest in helping someone else. 410

amniocentesis A prenatal medical procedure in which a sample of amniotic fluid is withdrawn by syringe and tested to discover if the fetus is suffering from any chromosomal or metabolic disorders. It is performed between the 12th and 16th weeks of pregnancy. 75

amnion The life-support system that is a bag or envelope that contains a clear fluid in which the developing embryo floats. 92

anal stage The second Freudian stage of development, occurring between 1½ and 3 years of age; the child's greatest pleasure involves the anus or the eliminative functions associated with it. 34

analgesia Drugs used to alleviate pain, such as tranquilizers, barbiturates, and narcotics. 122

androgens The main class of male sex hormones. 294, 444

androgyny The presence of desirable masculine and feminine characteristics in the same individual. 415

anesthesia Drugs used in late first-stage labor and during expulsion of the baby to block sensation in an area of the body or to block consciousness. 122

anger cry A cry similar to the basic cry, with more excess air forced through the vocal chords (associated with exasperation or rage). 200

animism The belief that inanimate objects have "lifelike" qualities and are capable of action. 256

anorexia nervosa An eating disorder that involves the relentless pursuit of thinness through starvation. 462

anoxia The insufficient availability of oxygen to the fetus/newborn. 120

Apgar Scale A widely used method to assess the health of newborns at one and five minutes after birth. The Apgar Scale evaluates infants' heart rate, respiratory effort, muscle tone, body color, and reflex irritability. 130

aptitude-treatment interaction (ATI) The interaction of children's aptitude and characteristics and the treatments and experiences they are given in classrooms. 427

articulation disorders Problems in pronouncing sounds correctly. 346

assimilation Individuals' incorporation of new information into their existing knowledge. 37

assimilation The absorption of ethnic minority groups into the dominant group, which often involves the loss of some or virtually all of the behavior and values of the ethnic minority group. 519

assistive technology Various services and devices to help children with disabilities function in their environment. 352

associative play Play that involves social interaction with little or no organization. 315

attachment A close emotional bond between an infant and a caregiver. 208

attention deficit/hyperactivity disorder A disability in which children consistently show one or more of the following characteristics: (1) inattention, (2) hyperactivity, and (3) impulsivity. 348

authoritarian parenting A restrictive punitive style in which parents exhort the child to follow their directions and to respect work and effort. The authoritarian parent places firm limits and controls on the child and allows little verbal exchange. Authoritarian parenting is associated with children's social incompetence. 301

authoritative parenting A parenting style in which parents encourage their children to be independent but still place limits and controls on their actions. Extensive verbal give-and-take is allowed, and parents are warm and nurturant toward the child. Authoritative parenting is associated with children's social competence. 302

autism A severe developmental disorder, has its onset in infancy. It includes deficiencies in social relationships, abnormalities in communication and restricted, repetitive and stereotyped patterns of behavior. 350

autonomous morality The second stage of moral development in Piaget's theory, displayed by older children (about 10 years of age and older). The child becomes aware that rules and laws are created by people and that, in judging an action, one should consider the actor's intentions as well as the consequences. 292

autonomy versus shame and doubt Erikson's second stage of development, which occurs in late infancy and toddlerhood (1–3 years); after gaining trust in their caregivers, infants begin to discover that their behavior is their own. 35

B

basal metabolism rate (BMR) The minimum amount of energy a person uses in a resting state. 241

basic cry A rhythmic pattern usually consisting of a cry, a briefer silence, a shorter inspiratory whistle that is higher pitched than the main cry, and then a brief rest before the next cry. 200

basic-skills-and-phonetics approach An approach to reading instruction that stresses phonetics and basic rules for translating symbols into sounds. Early reading instruction should involve simplified materials. 384

Bayley Scales of Infant Development Scales developed by Nancy Bayley, which are widely used in the assessment of infant development. The current version has three components: a mental scale, a motor scale, and an infant behavior profile. 180

behavior genetics The study of the degree and nature of behavior's heredity basis. 79

behaviorism The scientific study of observable behavioral responses and their environmental determinants. 40

bilingual education An educational approach whose aim is to teach academic subjects to immigrant children in their native languages (most often Spanish) while gradually adding English instruction. 386

biological processes Changes in an individual's physical nature. 18

blastocyst The inner layer of cells that develops during the germinal period. These cells later develop into the embryo. 90

bonding Close contact, especially physical, between parents and their newborn in the period shortly after birth. 133

boundary ambiguity   The uncertainty in stepfamilies about who is in or out of the family and who is performing or responsible for certain tasks in the family system.   420

brainstorming   A technique in which individuals are encouraged to come up with ideas in a group, play off each other's ideas, and say practically whatever comes to mind.   382

Brazelton Neonatal Behavioral Assessment Scale   A test given several days after birth to assess newborns' neurological development, reflexes, and reactions to people.   130

breech position   The baby's position in the uterus that causes the buttocks to be the first part to emerge from the vagina.   123

bulimia   An eating disorder in which the individual consistently follows a binge-purge eating pattern.   462

C

canalization   The process by which characteristics take a narrow path or developmental course. Apparently, preservative forces help protect a person from environmental extremes.   79

care perspective   A moral perspective that views people in terms of their connectedness with others and emphasizes interpersonal communication, relationships with others, and concern for others. Gilligan's theory is a care perspective.   409

career self-concept theory   Super's theory that individuals' self-concepts play central roles in their career choices.   489

case study   An in-depth look at an individual.   50

centration   The focusing of attention on one characteristic to the exclusion of all others.   257

cephalocaudal pattern   The sequence in which the greatest growth occurs at the top—the head—with physical growth in size, weight, and feature differentiation gradually working from top to bottom.   142

cerebral cortex   Located in the forebrain, the structure that makes up about 80 percent of the brain's volume. It plays critical roles in perception, language, thinking, and many other important functions.   144

cerebral palsy   A disorder that involves a lack of muscular coordination, shaking, or unclear speech.   346

cesarean delivery   The baby is removed from the mother's uterus through an incision made in her abdomen. This also is sometimes referred to as cesarean section.   123

character education   A direct approach to moral education that involves teaching students a basic moral literacy to prevent them from engaging in immoral behavior and doing harm to themselves and others.   478

child-centered kindergarten   Education that involves the whole child by considering both the child's physical, cognitive, and social development and the child's needs, interests, and learning styles.   272

chlamydia   A sexually transmitted disease named for the bacteria that cause it.   455

chorionic villi test   A prenatal medical procedure in which a small sample of the placenta is removed at a certain point in the pregnancy between the 8th and 11th weeks of pregnancy.   75

chromosomes   Threadlike structures that come in 23 pairs, one member of each pair coming from each parent. Chromosomes contain the genetic substance DNA.   67

chronosystem   The patterning of environmental events and transitions over the life course and their sociohistorical contexts.   45

cliques   Smaller groups that involve greater intimacy among members and have more cohesion than crowds.   510

cognitive developmental theory of gender   The theory that children's gender typing occurs after they have developed a concept of gender. Once they consistently conceive of themselves as male or female, children often organize their world on the basis of gender.   297

cognitive monitoring   The process of taking stock of what you are currently doing, what you will do next, and how effectively the mental activity is unfolding.   366

cognitive moral education   An approach to moral education based on the belief that students should develop such values as democracy and justice as their moral reasoning develops; Kohlberg's theory has been the basis of a number of cognitive moral education programs.   478

cognitive processes   Changes in an individual's thought, intelligence, and language.   18

commitment   Marcia's term for the part of identity development in which adolescents show a personal investment in what they are going to do.   501

community rights versus individual rights   The fifth stage in Kohlberg's theory of moral development. At this stage, the person understands that values and laws are relative and that standards may vary from one person to another.   407

computer-assisted instruction   The teaching strategy that involves using computers as tutors to individualize instruction. Computers are used to present information, give students practice, assess student levels of understanding, and provide additional information when needed.   392

concrete operational stage   Piaget's third stage, which lasts from approximately 7 to 11 years of age; children can perform operations, and logical reasoning replaces intuitive thought as long as the reasoning can be applied to specific, concrete examples.   38

connectedness   According to Cooper and her colleagues, connectedness consists of two dimensions: mutuality (sensitivity to and respect for others' views) and permeability (openness to others' views).   502

conservation   The idea that an amount stays the same regardless of how its container changes.   258

constructive play   Play that combines sensorimotor/practice repetitive activity with symbolic representation of ideas. Constructive play occurs when children engage in self-regulated creation or construction of a product or a problem solution.   317

constructivist view   Advocated by Piaget and the information-processing psychologists, this view states that perception is a cognitive construction based on sensory input plus information retrieved from memory. In this view, perception is a kind of representation of the world that builds up as the infant constructs an image of experiences.   160

context   The settings, influenced by historical, economic, social, and cultural factors, in which development occurs.   13

continuity of development   The view that development involves gradual, cumulative change from conception to death.   21

control group   A comparison group in an experiment that is treated in every way like the experimental group except for the manipulated factor.   51

control processes   Cognitive processes that do not occur automatically but require work and effort. These processes are under the learner's conscious control and can be used to improve memory. They are also appropriately called strategies.   363

controversial children   Children who are frequently nominated both as someone's best friend and as being disliked.   422

conventional reasoning   The second, or intermediate, level in Kohlberg's theory of moral development. At this level, the individual's internalization is intermediate. The person abides by certain standards (internal), but they are the standards of others (external), such as parents or the laws of society.   407

convergent thinking   Thinking that produces one correct answer and is characteristic of the kind of thinking tested by standardized intelligence tests.   381

cooperative play   Play that involves social interaction in a group with a sense of group identity and organized activity.   315

coordination of secondary circular reactions   Piaget's fourth sensorimotor substage, which develops between 8 and 12 months of age. In this substage, several significant changes take place involving the coordination of schemes and intentionality.   173

correlational research   Research whose goal is to describe the strength of the relation between two or more events or characteristics.   50

creativity   The ability to think in novel and unusual ways and to come up with unique solutions to problems.   381

crisis   Marcia's term for a period of identity development during which the adolescent is choosing from among meaningful alternatives.   500

critical period   A fixed time period very early in development during which certain behaviors optimally emerge.   43, 186

critical thinking Thinking that involves grasping the deeper meaning of ideas, keeping an open mind about different approaches and perspectives, and deciding for oneself what to believe or do. 367

cross-cultural studies The comparison of a culture with one or more other cultures, which provides information about the degree to which development is similar (universal) across cultures or the degree to which it is culture-specific. 13, 516

cross-sectional research Research that studies people all at one time. 52

crowd The largest and least personal of adolescent groups. 510

cultural-familial retardation Retardation that is characterized by no evidence of organic brain damage, but the individual's IQ is between 50 and 70. 379

culture The behavior patterns, beliefs, and all other products of a group that are passed on from generation to generation. 13

culture-fair tests Tests that are designed to be free of cultural bias. 378

D

dating scripts The cognitive models that adolescents and adults use to guide and evaluate dating interactions. 514

defense mechanisms The psychoanalytic term for unconscious methods used by the ego to distort reality in order to protect itself from anxiety. 33

deferred imitation Imitation that occurs after a time delay of hours or days. 179

Denver Developmental Screening Test A test used to diagnose developmental delay in children from birth to 6 years of age; includes separate assessments of gross and fine motor skills, language, and personal-social ability. 237

dependent variable The factor that is measured as the result of an experiment. 51

deprivation dwarfism Growth retardation caused by emotional deprivation; children who are deprived of affection experience stress that affects the release of hormones by the pituitary gland. 232

design stage Kellogg's terms for 3- to 4-year-olds' drawings that mix two basic shapes into more complex designs. 238

development The pattern of change that begins at conception and continues through the life cycle. 18

developmental biodynamics The new perspective on motor development in infancy that seeks to explain how motor behaviors are assembled for perceiving and acting. 157

developmental career choice theory Ginzberg's theory that children and adolescents go through three career choice stages—fantasy, tentative, and realistic. 488

developmental quotient (DQ) An overall developmental score that combines subscores in motor, language, adaptive, and personal-social domains in the Gesell assessment of infants. 179

developmentally appropriate practice Education that focuses on the typical developmental patterns of children (age appropriateness) and the uniqueness of each child (individual appropriateness). Such practice contrasts with developmentally inappropriate practice, which ignores the concrete, hands-on approach to learning. Direct teaching largely through abstract paper-and-pencil activities presented to large groups of young children is believed to be developmentally inappropriate. 273

difficult child A child who tends to react negatively and cry frequently, who engages in irregular daily routines, and who is slow to accept new experiences. 202

discontinuity of development The view that development involves distinct stages in the life span. 21

dishabituation An infant's renewed interest in a stimulus. 176

dismissing/avoidant attachment An insecure category in which individuals deemphasize the importance of attachment. This category is associated with consistent experiences of rejection of attachment needs by caregivers. 505

divergent thinking Thinking that produces many answers to the same question and is characteristic of creativity. 381

DNA A complex molecule that contains genetic information. 67

dominant-recessive genes principle If one gene of a pair is dominant and one is recessive (goes back, or recedes), the dominant gene exerts its effect, overriding the potential influence of the recessive gene. A recessive gene exerts its influence only if both genes in a pair are recessive. 77

doula A caregiver who provides continuous physical, emotional, and educational support to the mother before, during, and just after childbirth. 122

Down syndrome A common genetically transmitted form of mental retardation, caused by the presence of an extra (47th) chromosome. 71

dyslexia A category of learning disabilities involving a severe impairment in the ability to read and spell. 347

E

early childhood The developmental period that extends from the end of infancy to about 5 to 6 years, sometimes called the preschool years. 19

early-later experience issue The issue of the degree to which early experiences (especially infancy) or later experiences are the key determinants of the child's development. 21

easy child A child who is generally in a positive mood, who quickly establishes regular routines in infancy, and who adapts easily to new experiences. 202

echoing Repeating what a child says, especially if it is an incomplete phrase or sentence. 188

eclectic theoretical orientation An approach not following any one theoretical approach but, rather, selecting from each theory whatever is considered the best in it. 45

ecological theory Bronfenbrenner's sociocultural view of development, which consists of five environmental systems ranging from the fine-grained inputs of direct interactions with social agents to the broad-based inputs of culture. The five systems in Bronfenbrenner's ecological theory are the microsystem, mesosystem, exosystem, macrosystem, and chronosystem. 43

ecological view Advocated by the Gibsons, this view states that the purpose of perception is to detect perceptual invariants—those that remain stable—in a constantly changing world. 160

ectoderm The outermost layer of cells, which becomes the nervous system, sensory receptors (ears, nose, and eyes, for example), and skin parts (hair and nails, for example). 91

ectopic pregnancy The presence of a developing embryo or fetus outside the normal location in the uterus. 99

educationally blind Unable to use one's vision in learning. It implies a need to use hearing and touch to learn. 345

ego The Freudian structure of personality that deals with the demands of reality. 33

egocentrism The inability to distinguish between one's own perspective and someone else's (salient feature of the first substage of preoperational thought). 255

embryonic period The period of prenatal development that occurs two to eight weeks after conception. During the embryonic period, the rate of cell differentiation intensifies, support systems for the cells form, and organs appear. 91

emotion Feeling, or affect, that involves a mixture of physiological arousal and overt behavior. 198

empathy Reacting to another's feelings with an emotional response that is similar to the other's feelings. 294

endoderm The inner layer of cells, which develops into digestive and respiratory systems. 91

erogenous zones Freud's concept of the parts of the body that have especially strong pleasure-giving qualities at each stage of development. 33

estradiol A hormone associated in girls with breast, uterine, and skeletal development. 444

estrogens The main class of female sex hormones. 294, 444

ethnic gloss The use of an ethnic label, such as Latino, Asian American, or Native American, in a superficial way that makes an ethnic group seem more homogeneous than it really is. 54

ethnic identity A sense of membership in an ethnic group based upon shared language, religion, customs, values, history, and race. 13

ethnicity A characteristic based on cultural heritage, nationality characteristics, race, religion, and language. 13

ethology A theory that stresses that behavior is strongly influenced by biology, is tied to evolution, and is characterized by critical or sensitive periods. 42

evocative genotype → environment correlations The type of interactions that occur when the child's genotype elicits certain types of physical and social environments. 82

exosystem The level at which experiences in another social setting—in which the individual does not have an active role—influence what the individual experiences in an immediate context. 45

expanding Restating, in a linguistically sophisticated form, what a child has said. 188

experimental group A group whose experience is manipulated in an experiment. 51

experimental research Research involving experiments that permit the determination of cause. A carefully regulated procedure in which one or more of the factors believed to influence the behavior being studied are manipulated and all other factors are held constant. 50

extrinsic motivation Motivation produced by external rewards and punishments. 388

F

fetal alcohol syndrome (FAS) A cluster of abnormalities that appears in the offspring of mothers who drink alcohol heavily during pregnancy. 101

fetal period The prenatal period of development that begins two months after conception and lasts for seven months, on the average. 93

fine motor skills Motor skills that involve more finely tuned movements, such as finger dexterity. 154

first habits and primary circular reactions Piaget's second sensorimotor substage, which develops between 1 and 4 months of age. In this substage, the infant learns to coordinate sensation and types of schemes or structures—that is, habits and primary circular reactions. 173

fluency disorders Various disorders that involve what is commonly called "stuttering." 346

formal operational stage Piaget's fourth and final stage, which occurs between the ages of 11 and 15; individuals move beyond concrete experiences and think in more abstract and logical ways. 38

fraternal twins Twins who develop from separate eggs and separate sperm, making them genetically no more similar than ordinary siblings. 80

frontal lobe In the cerebral cortex, the structure that is involved in voluntary movement and thinking. 144

functional amblyopia An eye defect that results from not using one eye enough to avoid the discomfort of double vision produced by imbalanced eye muscles; "lazy eye." 234

G

games Activities engaged in for pleasure that include rules and often competition with one or more individuals. 317

gametes Human reproduction cells created in the testes of males and the ovaries of females. 67

gender The sociocultural dimension of being male or female. 13, 294

gender constancy Refers to the understanding that sex remains the same even though activities, clothing, and hair style may change. 299

gender identity The sense of being male or female, which most children acquire by the time they are 3 years old. 294

gender role A set of expectations that prescribes how females or males should think, act, and feel. 294

gender-role transcendence The belief that, when an individual's competence is at issue, it should not be conceptualized on the basis of masculinity, femininity, or androgyny but, rather, on a personal basis. 416

gender schema A schema that organizes the world in terms of female and male. 299

gender schema theory The theory that an individual's attention and behavior are guided by an internal motivation to conform to gender-based sociocultural standards and stereotypes. 299

gender stereotypes Broad categories that reflect our impressions and beliefs about females and males. 411

generativity versus stagnation Erikson's seventh stage of development, which occurs during middle adulthood; a chief concern is to assist the younger generation in developing and leading useful lives. 36

genes Units of hereditary information composed of DNA. Genes act as a blueprint for cells to reproduce themselves and manufacture the proteins that maintain life. 67

genital stage The fifth and final Freudian stage of development, which occurs from puberty on; a sexual reawakening in which the source of sexual pleasure becomes someone outside of the family. 34

genotype A person's genetic heritage; the actual genetic material. 79

germinal period The period of prenatal development that takes place in the first two weeks after conception. It includes the creation of the zygote, continued cell division, and the attachment of the zygote to the uterine wall. 90

gifted Having above-average intelligence, usually an IQ of 120 or higher, and a superior talent for something. 380

gonads The sex glands—the testes in males and the ovaries in females. 443

grasping reflex A neonatal reflex that occurs when something touches the infants' palms. The infant responds by grasping tightly. 153

gross motor skills Motor skills that involve large muscle activities, such as walking. 154

H

habituation Repeated presentation of the same stimulus, which causes reduced attention to the stimulus. 176

helpless orientation An orientation in which one seems trapped by the experience of difficulty and attributes one's difficulty to a lack of ability. 389

herpes simplex virus II A sexually transmitted disease whose symptoms include irregular cycles of sores and blisters in the genital area. 455

heteronomous morality The first stage of moral development, in Piaget's theory, occurring from approximately 4 to 7 years of age. Justice and rules are conceived of as unchangeable properties of the world, removed from the control of people. 292

hidden curriculum Dewey's concept that every school has a pervasive moral atmosphere, even if it doesn't have a program of moral education. 477

holophrase hypothesis The hypothesis that a single word can be used to imply a complete sentence; infants' first words characteristically are holophrastic. 191

hormones Powerful chemical substances secreted by the endocrine glands and carried through the body by the bloodstream. 443

hypothalamus A structure in the higher portion of the brain that monitors eating, drinking, and sex. 443

hypotheses Specific assumptions and predictions that can be tested to determine their accuracy. 31

hypothetical-deductive reasoning Piaget's formal operational concept that adolescents have the cognitive ability to develop hypotheses, or best guesses, about ways to solve problems, such as an algebraic equation. 470

I

id The Freudian structure of personality that consists of instincts, which are an individual's reserve of psychic energy. 33

identical twins Twins who develop from a single fertilized egg that splits into two genetically identical replicas, each of which becomes a person. 80

identification theory A theory deriving from Freud's view that the preschool child develops a sexual attraction to the opposite-sex parent, by approximately 5 or 6 years of age renounces this attraction because of anxious feelings, and subsequently identifies with the same-sex parent, unconsciously adopting the same-sex parent's characteristics. 295

identity achievement Marcia's term for adolescents who have undergone a crisis and have made a commitment. 501

identity diffusion Marcia's term for adolescents who have not yet experienced a crisis (explored meaningful alternatives) or made any commitments. 501

identity foreclosure Marcia's term for adolescents who have made a commitment but have not experienced a crisis. 501

identity moratorium Marcia's term for adolescents who are in the midst of a crisis, but their commitments are either absent or vaguely defined. 501

identity versus identity confusion Erikson's fifth stage of development, which occurs during the adolescent years; adolescents are faced with finding out who they are, what they are all about, and where they are going in life. 36

idiographic needs The needs of the individual, not the group. 55

imaginary audience Adolescents' heightened self-consciousness, reflected in their belief that others are as interested in them as they themselves are; attention-getting behavior motivated by a desire to be noticed, visible, and "on stage." 473

imminent justice The concept that, if a rule is broken, punishment will be meted out immediately. 292

implantation The attachment of the zygote to the uterine wall, which takes place about 10 days after conception. 90

imprinting In ethological theories, rapid, innate learning, within a limited critical period of time, that involves attachment to the first moving object seen. 43

inclusion Educating a child with special education needs full-time in the regular classroom. 352

independent variable The manipulated, influential, experimental factor in an experiment. 51

individual differences The stable, consistent ways that people are different from each other. 371

individualism and purpose The second stage in Kohlberg's theory of moral development. At this stage, moral thinking is based on rewards and self-interest. 407

individuality According to Cooper and her colleagues, individuality consists of two dimensions: self-assertion (the ability to have and communicate a point of view) and separateness (the use of communication patterns to express how one is different from others). 502

individualized education plan (IEP) A written statement that spells out a program tailored to a child with a disability. The plan should be (1) related to the child's learning capacity, (2) specially constructed to meet the child's individual needs and not merely a copy of what is offered to other children, and (3) designed to provide educational benefits. 352

Individuals with Disabilities Education Act (IDEA) The IDEA spells out broad mandates for services to all children with disabilities (IDEA is a renaming of Public Law 98-142); these include evaluation and eligibility determination, appropriate education and the individualized education plan (IEP), and the least restrictive environment (LRE). 351

indulgent parenting A style of parenting in which parents are highly involved with their children but place few demands or controls on them. Indulgent parenting is associated with children's social incompetence, especially a lack of self-control. 302

industry versus inferiority Erikson's fourth stage of development, which occurs approximately in the elementary school years; children's initiative brings them into contact with a wealth of new experiences, and they direct their energy toward mastering knowledge and intellectual skills. 36

infancy The developmental period that extends from birth to 18 to 24 months. 19

infinite generativity An individual's ability to generate an infinite number of meaningful sentences using a finite set of words and rules, which makes language a highly creative enterprise. 183

information processing How individuals process information about their world; how information enters the mind, how it is stored and transformed, and how it is retrieved to perform such complex activities as problem solving and reasoning. 39

initiative versus guilt Erikson's third stage of development, which occurs during the preschool years; as preschool children encounter a widening social world, they are challenged more than they were as infants. 36

innate goodness view The idea, presented by Swiss-born philosopher Jean-Jacques Rousseau, that children are inherently good. 7

instructional technology Various types of hardware and software, combined with innovative teaching methods, to accommodate students' learning needs in the classroom. 352

integrity versus despair Erikson's eighth and final stage of development, which occurs during late adulthood; in the later years of life, we look back and evaluate what we have done with our lives. 36

intelligence Verbal ability, problem-solving skills, and the ability to learn from and adapt to the experiences of everyday life. 370

intelligence quotient (IQ) A person's mental age divided by chronological age, multiplied by 100. 371

intermodal perception The ability to relate and integrate information about two or more sensory modalities, such as vision and hearing. 166

internalization The developmental change from behavior that is externally controlled to behavior that is internally controlled. 407

internalization of schemes Piaget's sixth and final sensorimotor substage, which develops between 18 and 24 months of age. In this substage, the infant's mental functioning shifts from a purely sensorimotor plane to a symbolic plane, and the infant develops the ability to use primitive symbols. 173

interpersonal norms The third stage in Kohlberg's theory of moral development. At this stage, the person values trust, caring, and loyalty to others as the basis of moral judgments. 407

intimacy in friendships Self-disclosure and the sharing of private thoughts. 425

intimacy versus isolation Erikson's sixth stage of development, which occurs during the early adulthood years; young adults face the developmental task of forming intimate relationships with others. 36

intrinsic motivation The desire to be competent and to do something for its own sake. 388

intuitive thought substage Piaget's second substage of preoperational thought, in which children begin to use primitive reasoning and want to know the answers to all sorts of questions (between 4 and 7 years of age). 257

inventionist view The belief that adolescence is a sociohistorical creation. Especially important in the development of the inventionist view of adolescence were the sociohistorical circumstances at the beginning of the twentieth century, a time when legislation was enacted that ensured the dependency of youth and made their move into the economic sphere more manageable. 440

involution The process by which the uterus returns to its prepregnant size. 132

J

Jasper Project Twelve videodisc adventures that focus on solving real-world math problems. 368

justice perspective A moral perspective that focuses on the rights of the individual; individuals stand alone and independently make moral decisions. Kohlberg's theory is a justice perspective. 409

juvenile delinquent An adolescent who breaks the law or engages in behavior that is considered illegal. 519

K

keyword method A mnemonic technique in which individuals use vivid imagery and attach the imagery to important words. 364

Klinefelter syndrome A genetic disorder in which males have an extra X chromosome, making them XXY instead of XY. 72

L

labeling Identifying the names of objects. 188

laboratory A controlled setting from which many of the complex factors of the real world have been removed. 49

language A system of symbols used to communicate with others. In humans language is characterized by infinite generativity and rule systems. 183

language acquisition device (LAD) A biological endowment that enables the child to detect certain language categories, such as phonology, syntax, and semantics. 186

latency stage The fourth Freudian stage, occurring between approximately 6 years of age and puberty; the child represses all interest in sexuality and develops social and intellectual skills. 34

lateralization Specialization in the brain's hemispheres. For example, speech and grammar are localized to the left hemisphere in most people. 144

learning disability   A disability that involves (1) having normal intelligence or above, (2) having difficulties in at least one academic area and usually several, and (3) having no other problem or disorder, such as mental retardation, that can be determined as causing the difficulty. 347

least restrictive environment (LRE)   The concept that a child with a disability must be educated in a setting that is as similar as possible to the one in which children who do not have a disability are educated.   352

longitudinal research   Research that studies the same people over a period of time, usually several years or more.   52

long-term memory   A relatively permanent type of memory that holds huge amounts of information for a long period of time.   363

low vision   Visual acuity between 20/70 and 20/200.   345

low-birthweight infant   An infant born after a regular period of gestation (the length of time between conception and birth) of 38 to 42 weeks but who weighs less than 5½ pounds. 127

M

macrosystem   The culture in which individuals live.   45

mainstreaming   Educating a child with special education needs partially in a special education classroom and partially in a regular classroom. 352

manual approaches   Educational approaches to help hearing-impaired children; they include sign language and finger spelling.   346

marasmus   A wasting away of body tissues in the infant's first year, caused by severe deficiency of protein and calories.   149

mastery orientation   An orientation in which one is task-oriented and, instead of focusing on one's ability, is concerned with learning strategies.   389

maternal blood test   A prenatal diagnostic technique used to assess blood alphaprotein level, which is associated with neural-tube defects. This technique is also called the alpha-fetoprotein test (AFP).   76

maturation   The orderly sequence of changes dictated by a genetic blueprint.   19

Maximally Discriminative Facial Movement Coding System (MAX)   Izard's system of coding infants' facial expressions related to emotions. Using MAX, coders watch slow-motion and stop-action videotapes of infants' facial reactions to stimuli.   200

mean length of utterance (MLU)   An index of language development based on the number of morphemes per sentence a child produces in a sample of about 50 to 100 sentences; a good index of language maturity.   192

meiosis   The process of cell doubling and separation of chromosomes in which each pair of chromosomes in a cell separates, with one member of each pair going into each gamete. 67

memory   A central feature of cognitive development, pertaining to all situations in which an individual retains information over time.   177

menarche   First menstruation.   442

mental age (MA)   Binet's measure of an individual's level of mental development, compared with that of others.   371

mental retardation   A condition of limited mental ability in which an individual has a low IQ, usually below 70 on a traditional test of intelligence, and has difficulty adapting to everyday life.   379

mesoderm   The middle layer of cells, which becomes the circulatory system, bones, muscles, excretory system, and reproductive system.   91

mesosystem   Relationships between microsystems or connections between contexts, such as the connection between family experience and the school experience.   44

method of loci   A mnemonic technique in which individuals develop images of items to be remembered and store them in familiar locations.   363

microsystem   The setting, or context, in which an individual lives, including the person's family, peers, school, and neighborhood.   43

middle and late childhood   The developmental period that extends from about 6 to 11 years of age, approximately corresponding to and sometimes called the elementary school years.   19

mnemonics   Memory aids.   363

Montessori approach   An educational philosophy in which children are given considerable freedom and spontaneity in choosing activities and are allowed to move from one activity to another as they desire.   273

moral development   Development regarding rules and conventions about what people should do in their interactions with other people.   291

Moro reflex   A neonatal startle response that occurs in reaction to a sudden, intense noise or movement. When startled, the newborn arches its back, throws back its head, and flings out its arms and legs. Then the newborn rapidly closes its arms and legs to the center of its body.   152

morphology   The study of the rules for combining morphemes; morphemes are the smallest meaningful units of language.   185

motherese   The kind of speech often used by mothers and other adults to talk to babies—in a higher pitch than normal and with simple words and sentences.   188

myelination   The process in which the nerve cells are covered and insulated with a layer of fat cells, which increases the speed at which information travels through the nervous system. 234

N

natural childbirth   Developed in 1914 by Dick-Read, it attempts to reduce the mother's pain by decreasing her fear through education about childbirth and relaxation techniques during delivery.   123

natural selection   The evolutionary process that favors individuals of a species that are best adapted to survive and reproduce.   64

naturalistic observation   Observation that takes place in the real world instead of in a laboratory.   49

nature-nurture controversy   Nature refers to an organism's biological inheritance, *nurture* to environmental influences. The "nature" proponents claim biological inheritance is the most important influence on development; the "nurture" proponents claim that environmental experiences are the most important.   20

negative affectivity (NA)   Emotions that are negatively toned, such as anger, anxiety, guilt, and sadness.   198

neglected children   Children who are infrequently nominated as a best friend but are not disliked by their peers.   422

neglectful parenting   A style of parenting in which the parent is very uninvolved in the child's life; it is associated with children's social incompetence, especially a lack of self-control. 302

neo-Piagetians   Developmentalists who have elaborated on Piaget's theory, believing that children's cognitive development is more specific in many respects than Piaget thought. 362

neuron   A nerve cell that handles information processing at the cellular level.   143

night terrors   Sudden arousal from sleep, characterized by intense fear and usually accompanied by physiological reactions, such as rapid heart rate and breathing, loud screams, heavy perspiration, and physical movement.   240

nightmares   Frightening dreams that awaken the sleeper.   240

nomothetic research   Research conducted at the level of the group.   55

nonshared environmental experiences   The child's unique experiences, both within the family and outside the family, that are not shared by another sibling. Thus, experiences occurring within the family can be part of the "nonshared environment."   84

normal distribution   A distribution that is symmetrical, with most cases falling in the middle of the possible range of scores and a few scores appearing toward the extremes of the range. 371

O

object permanence   The Piagetian term for one of an infant's most important accomplishments: understanding that objects and events continue to exist, even when they cannot directly be seen, heard, or touched.   174

occipital lobe   In the cerebral cortex, the structure that is involved in vision.   144

Oedipus complex   In Freudian theory, the young child's development of an intense desire to replace the same-sex parent and to enjoy the affections of the opposite-sex parent.   34

onlooker play   Play in which the child watches other children play.   315

operations   In Piaget's theory, an internalized set of actions that allows a child to do mentally what she formerly did physically.   254

oral approaches Educational approaches to help hearing-impaired children; they include lip reading, speech reading, and whatever hearing the child has. 345

oral rehydration therapy (ORT) Treatment to prevent dehydration during episodes of diarrhea by giving fluids by mouth. 246

oral stage The first Freudian stage of development, occurring during the first 18 months of life; the infant's pleasure centers around the mouth. 33

organic retardation Mental retardation that involves some physical damage and is caused by a genetic disorder or brain damage. 379

organogenesis Organ formation that takes place during the first two months of prenatal development. 93

original sin view Advocated during the Middle Ages, the belief that children were born into the world as evil beings and were basically bad. 6

orthopedic impairments Restrictions in movement abilities due to muscle, bone, or joint problems. 346

oxytocics Drugs that are synthetic hormones designed to stimulate contractions. 122

P

pain cry A sudden appearance of loud crying without preliminary moaning and a long initial cry followed by an extended period of breath holding. 200

parallel play Play in which the child plays separately from others, but with toys like those the others are using or in a manner that mimics their play. 315

parietal lobe In the cerebral cortex, the structure that is involved in bodily sensations, such as touch. 144

passive genotype → environment correlations The type of interactions that occur when parents, who are genetically related to the child, provide a rearing environment for the child. 82

peers Children of about the same age or maturity level. 312

perception The interpretation of what is sensed. 160

performance orientation An orientation in which one focuses on achievement outcomes; winning is what matters most, and happiness is thought to result from winning. 389

personal fable The part of adolescent egocentrism that involves an adolescent's sense of uniqueness. 473

personality-type theory Holland's theory that an effort should be made to match an individual's career choice with his or her personality. 489

perspective taking The ability to assume another person's perspective and understand his or her thoughts and feelings. 400

phallic stage The third Freudian stage of development, occurring between the ages of 3 and 6; its name comes from the Latin word *phallus*, which means "penis." 34

phenotype The way an individual's genotype is expressed in observed and measurable characteristics. 79

phenylketonuria (PKU) A genetic disorder in which an individual cannot properly metabolize an amino acid. PKU is now easily detected but, if left untreated, results in mental retardation and hyperactivity. 71

phonology The study of a language's sound system. 183

pictorial stage Kellogg's terms for 4- to 5-year-olds' drawings depicting objects that adults can recognize. 238

pituitary gland An important endocrine gland that controls growth and regulates other glands. 443

placement stage Kellogg's terms for 2- to 3-year-olds' drawings that are drawn in placement patterns. 238

placenta A life-support system that consists of a disk-shaped group of tissues in which small blood vessels from the mother and offspring intertwine. 91

play A pleasurable activity that is engaged in for its own sake. 313

play therapy Therapy that allows the child to work off frustrations and is a medium through which the therapist can analyze the child's conflicts and ways of coping with them. Children may feel less threatened and be more likely to express their true feelings in the context of play. 314

pluralism The coexistence of distinct ethnic and cultural groups in the same society. Individuals with a pluralistic stance usually advocate that cultural differences be maintained and appreciated. 519

polygenic inheritance The genetic principle that many genes can interact to produce a particular characteristic. 78

popular children Children who are frequently nominated as a best friend and are rarely disliked by their peers. 422

positive affectivity (PA) The range of positive emotions from high energy, enthusiasm, and excitement to being calm, quiet, and withdrawn. Joy, happiness, and laughter involve positive affectivity. 198

postconventional reasoning The highest level in Kohlberg's theory of moral development. At this level, morality is completely internalized and not based on others' standards. 407

postpartum period The period after childbirth when the mother adjusts, both physically and psychologically, to the process of childbirth. This period lasts for about six weeks, or until her body has completed its adjustment and has returned to a near prepregnant state. 131

PQ4R A study strategy that stands for Preview, Question, Read, Reflect, Recite, and Review. 365

practice play Play that involves repetition of behavior when new skills are being learned or when physical or mental mastery and coordination of skills are required for games or sports. Sensorimotor play, which often involves practice play, is primarily confined to infancy, while practice play can be engaged in throughout life. 316

pragmatics The rules for appropriate conversation and the knowledge underlying the use of language in context. 185

preconventional reasoning The lowest level in Kohlberg's theory of moral development. At this level, the child shows no internalization of moral values—moral reasoning is controlled by external rewards and punishments. 407

prenatal period The time from conception to birth. 19

preoccupied/ambivalent attachment An insecure category in which adolescents are hypertuned to attachment experiences. This is thought to mainly occur when parents are consistently unavailable to the adolescent. 505

preoperational stage The second Piagetian developmental stage, which lasts from about 2 to 7 years of age; children begin to represent the world with words, images, and drawings. 38

prepared childbirth Developed by French obstetrician Ferdinand Lamaze, this childbirth strategy is similar to natural childbirth but includes a special breathing technique to control pushing in the final stages of labor and a more detailed anatomy and physiology course. 123

pretense/symbolic play Play in which the child transforms the physical environment into a symbol. 316

preterm infant An infant born prior to 38 weeks after conception. 127

primary circular reaction A scheme based on the infant's attempt to reproduce an interesting or a pleasurable event that initially occurred by chance. 173

Project Follow Through An adjunct to Project Head Start, in which the enrichment programs are carried through the first few years of elementary school. 274

Project Head Start Compensatory education designed to provide children from low-income families the opportunity to acquire the skills and experiences important for school success. 274

proximodistal pattern The sequence in which growth starts at the center of the body and moves toward the extremities. 143

puberty A period of rapid skeletal and sexual maturation that occurs mainly in early adolescence. 442

Public Law 94-142 The Education for All Handicapped Children Act, created in 1975, which requires that all children with disabilities be given a free, appropriate public education and which provides the funding to help with the costs of implementing this education. 351

punishment and obedience orientation The first stage in Kohlberg's theory of moral development. At this stage, moral thinking is based on punishment. 407

R

race The term for a system for classifying plants and animals into subcategories according to specific physical and structural characteristics. 65

random assignment   In experimental research, the assignment of participants to experimental and control groups by chance.   51

rapport talk   The language of conversation and a way of establishing connections and negotiating relationships.   414

reaction range   The range of possible phenotypes for each genotype, suggesting the importance of an environment's restrictiveness or enrichment.   79

recasting   Rephrasing a statement a child has said, perhaps turning it into a question.   188

receptive vocabulary   The words an individual understands.   189

reciprocal socialization   Socialization that is bidirectional; children socialize parents, just as parents socialize children.   213

reciprocal teaching   An instructional procedure used by Brown and Palincsar to develop cognitive monitoring; it requires that students take turns leading a study group in the use of strategies for comprehending and remembering text content.   366

reflexive smile   A smile that does not occur in response to external stimuli. It happens during the month after birth, usually during irregular patterns of sleep, not when the infant is in an alert state.   201

rejected children   Children who are infrequently nominated as a best friend and are actively disliked by their peers.   422

REM (rapid eye movement) sleep   A recurring sleep stage during which vivid dreams commonly occur.   146

report talk   Talk that gives information, such as public speaking.   414

repression   The most powerful and pervasive defense mechanism; it pushes unacceptable id impulses out of awareness and back into the unconscious mind.   33

reproduction   The process that, in humans, begins when a female gamete (ovum) is fertilized by a male gamete (sperm).   68

rite of passage   A ceremony or ritual that marks an individual's transition from one status to another. Most rites of passage focus on the transition to adult status.   516

rooting reflex   The newborn's built-in reaction that occurs when the infant's cheek is stroked or the side of its mouth is touched. In response, the infant turns its head toward the side that was touched, in an apparent effort to find something to suck.   152

S

scaffolding   Parental behavior that supports children's efforts, allowing them to be more skillful than they would be if they relied only on their own abilities.   213

scaffolding   In cognitive development, Vygotsky used this term to describe the changing support over the course of a teaching session, with the more skilled person adjusting guidance to fit the child's current performance level.   261

schema   A cognitive structure; a network of associations that organizes and guides an individual's perceptions.   299

scheme (or schema)   The basic unit (or units) for an organized pattern of sensorimotor functioning.   172

scientific method   An approach that can be used to discover accurate information. It includes these steps: conceptualize the problem, collect data, draw conclusions, and revise research conclusions and theory.   30

scientific research   Research that is objective, systematic, and testable.   30

script   A schema for events.   367

secondary circular reactions   Piaget's third sensorimotor substage, which develops between 4 and 8 months of age. In this substage, the infant becomes more object-oriented, or focused on the world, moving beyond preoccupation with the self in sensorimotor interactions.   173

secure attachment   The infant uses a caregiver as a secure base from which to explore the environment. Ainsworth believes that secure attachment in the first year of life provides an important foundation for psychological development later in life.   209

self-concept   Domain-specific evaluations of the self.   401

self-efficacy   Bandura's personal concept, which refers to the expectation that one can master a situation and produce positive outcomes.   42

self-esteem   The global evaluative dimension of the self. Self-esteem is also referred to as self-worth or self-image.   401

Self-Perception Profile for Children   A self-concept measure with five specific domains—scholastic competence, athletic competence, social acceptance, physical appearance, and behavioral conduct—plus general self-worth.   402

self-understanding   The child's cognitive representation of self, the substance and content of the child's self-conceptions.   288

semantics   The meaning of words and sentences.   185

sensation   The process that occurs when information interacts with the sensory receptors—the eyes, ears, tongue, nostrils, and skin.   160

sensorimotor play   Behavior engaged in by infants to derive pleasure from exercising their existing sensorimotor schemas.   315

sensorimotor stage   The first of Piaget's stages, which lasts from birth to about 2 years of age; infants construct an understanding of the world by coordinating sensory experiences (such as seeing and hearing) with motoric actions.   37

seriation   The concrete operation that involves ordering stimuli along a quantitative dimension (such as length).   359

service learning   A form of education that promotes social responsibility and service to the community.   479

shape stage   Kellogg's terms for 3-year-olds' drawings consisting of diagrams in different shapes.   238

shared environmental experiences   Children's common environmental experiences that are shared with their siblings, such as their parents' personalities and intellectual orientation, the family's social class, and the neighborhood in which they live.   84

short-term memory   The memory component in which individuals retain information for 15–30 seconds, assuming there is no rehearsal.   265

sickle-cell anemia   A genetic disorder that affects the red blood cells and occurs most often in people of African descent.   71

simple reflexes   Piaget's first sensorimotor substage, which corresponds to the first month after birth. In this substage, the basic means of coordinating sensation and action is through reflexive behaviors, such as rooting and sucking, which the infant has at birth.   172

slow-to-warm-up child   A child who has a low activity level, is somewhat negative, shows low adaptability, and displays a low intensity mood.   202

social constructivist approach   An approach that emphasizes the social contexts of learning and the fact that knowledge is mutually built and constructed; Vygotsky's theory is a social constructivist approach.   262

social learning theory   A theory that emphasizes a combination of behavior, environment, and cognition as the key factors in development.   41

social learning theory of gender   A theory that emphasizes that children's gender development occurs through the observation and imitation of gender behavior and through the rewards and punishments children experience for gender-appropriate and inappropriate behavior.   295

social play   Play that involves social interactions with peers.   316

social policy   A national government's course of action designed to influence the welfare of its citizens.   15

social referencing   "Reading" emotional cues in others to help determine how to act in a particular situation.   202

social smile   A smile in response to an external stimulus, which, early in development, typically is in response to a face.   201

social system morality   The fourth stage in Kohlberg's theory of moral development. At this stage, moral judgments are based on understanding the social order, law, justice, and duty.   407

socioemotional processes   Changes in an individual's relationships with other people, emotions, and personality.   18

solitary play   Play in which the child plays alone and independently of others.   315

somnambulism   Sleepwalking; occurs in the deepest stage of sleep.   240

standardized tests   Commercially prepared tests that assess performance in different domains.   50

storm-and-stress view   Hall's view that adolescence is a turbulent time, charged with conflict and mood swings.   440

Strange Situation   An observational measure of infant attachment that requires the infant to move through a series of introductions, separations, and reunions with the caregiver and an adult stranger in a prescribed order.   210

stranger anxiety   An infant's fear and wariness of strangers; it tends to appear in the second half of the first year of life.   201

sucking reflex   A newborn's built-in reaction of automatically sucking an object placed in its mouth. The sucking reflex enables the infant to get nourishment before it has associated a nipple with food.   152

sudden infant death syndrome (SIDS)   A condition that occurs when an infant stops breathing, usually during the night, and suddenly dies without apparent cause.   147

superego   The Freudian structure of personality that is the moral branch of personality.   33

symbolic function substage   Piaget's first substage of preoperational thought, in which the child gains the ability to mentally represent an object that is not present (between 2 and 4 years of age).   255

syntax   The rules for combining words to form acceptable phrases and sentences.   185

T

tabula rasa view   The idea, proposed by John Locke, that children are like a "blank tablet."   7

telegraphic speech   The use of short and precise words to communicate; young children's two- and three-word utterances characteristically are telegraphic.   191

temperament   An individual's behavioral style and characteristic way of emotional response.   202

temporal lobe   In the cerebral cortex, the structure that is involved in hearing.   144

teratogen   From the Greek word *tera*, meaning "monster," any agent that causes a birth defect. The field of study that investigates the causes of birth defects is called teratology.   97

tertiary circular reactions, novelty, and curiosity   Piaget's fifth sensorimotor substage, which develops between 12 and 18 months of age. In this substage, infants become intrigued by the variety of properties that objects possess and by the multiplicity of things they can make happen to objects.   173

testosterone   A hormone associated in boys with the development of genitals, an increase in height, and a change in voice.   444

theory   An interrelated, coherent set of ideas that helps to explain and to make predictions.   31

top-dog phenomenon   The circumstance of moving from the top position in elementary school to the lowest position in middle or junior high school.   484

toxoplasmosis   A disease caused by a parasite with which humans can become infected by eating raw meat or by not washing their hands after touching cats' feces or yard dirt. It can be transmitted to the fetus and can cause eye defects, brain damage, or premature birth. A mild infection that causes coldlike symptoms in adults but can be a teratogen for the unborn baby.   98

transitional objects   Objects that children repeatedly use as bedtime companions. These usually are soft and cuddly and probably mark the child's transition from being dependent to being more independent.   240

transitivity   In concrete operational thought, a mental concept that underlies the ability to logically combine relations to understand certain conclusions. It focuses on reasoning about the relations between classes.   359

triarchic theory   Sternberg's theory that intelligence consists of componential intelligence, experiential intelligence, and contextual intelligence.   372

trophoblast   The outer layer of cells that develops in the germinal period. These cells provide nutrition and support for the embryo.   90

trust versus mistrust   Erikson's first psychosocial stage, experienced in the first year of life; a sense of trust requires a feeling of physical comfort and a minimal amount of fear and apprehension about the future.   35

Turner syndrome   A genetic disorder in which females are missing an X chromosome, making them XO instead of XX.   72

twin study   A study in which the behavioral similarity of identical twins is compared with the behavioral similarity of fraternal twins.   80

type A babies   Infants who exhibit insecurity by avoiding their mother (for example, ignoring her, averting their gaze, and failing to seek proximity).   209

type B babies   Infants who use a caregiver as a secure base from which to explore the environment.   209

type C babies   Infants who exhibit insecurity by resisting the mother (for example, clinging to her but at the same time kicking and pushing away).   209

type D babies   Insecurely attached babies who are described as disorganized. They may be disoriented and afraid.   209

U

ultrasound sonography   A prenatal medical procedure in which high-frequency sound waves are directed into the pregnant woman's abdomen.   75

umbilical cord   A life-support system, containing two arteries and one vein, that connects the baby to the placenta.   91

universal ethical principles   The sixth and highest stage in Kohlberg's theory of moral development. At this stage, persons have developed a moral standard based on universal human rights.   408

unoccupied play   Play in which the child is not engaging in play as it is commonly understood and might stand in one spot, look around the room, or perform random movements that do not seem to have a goal.   315

unresolved/disorganized attachment   An insecure category in which the adolescent has an unusually high level of fear and being disoriented. This may result from traumatic experiences such as a parent's death or abuse by parents.   506

V

values clarification   An approach to moral education that emphasizes helping people clarify what their lives are for and what is worth working for. Students are encouraged to define their own values and to understand the values of others.   478

voice disorders   Disorders reflected in speech that is hoarse, harsh, too loud, too high-pitched, or too low-pitched.   346

W

whole-language approach   An approach to reading instruction based on the idea that instruction should parallel children's natural language learning. Reading materials should be whole and meaningful.   384

X

XYY syndrome   A genetic disorder in which males have an extra Y chromosome.   72

Z

zone of proximal development (ZPD)   Vygotsky's term for tasks too difficult for children to master alone but that can be mastered with assistance.   261

zygote   A single cell formed through fertilization.   68

A

Abbassi, V. (1998). Growth and normal puberty. *Pediatrics (Supplement)*, 102 (2) 507–511.

Aboud, F., & Skerry, S. (1983). Self and ethnic concepts in relation to ethnic constancy. *Canadian Journal of Behavioral Science*, 15, 3–34.

Abramovitch, R., Corter, C., Pepler, D.J., & Stanhope, L. (1986). Sibling and peer interaction: A final follow-up and comparison. *Child Development*, 47, 217–229.

Academic Software, Inc. (1996). *Adaptive device locator system (computer program)*. Lexington, KY: Author.

Acredolo, L.P., & Hake, J.L. (1982). Infant perception. In B.B. Wolman (Ed.), *Handbook of developmental psychology*. Englewood Cliffs, NJ: Prentice Hall.

Adams, A., Carnine, D., & Gersten, R. (1982). Instructional strategies for studying content area text in the intermediate grades. *Reading Research Quarterly*, 18, 27–53.

Adams, R.J. (1989). Newborns' discrimination among mid- and long-wavelength stimuli. *Journal of Experimental Child Psychology*, 47, 130–141.

Adamson, L.B. (1996). *Communication development in infancy*. Boulder, CO: Westview Press.

Adato, A. (1995, April). Living legacy? Is heredity destiny? *Life*, pp. 60–68.

Adler, T. (1991, January). Seeing double? Controversial twins study is widely reported, debated. *APA Monitor*, 22, 1, 8.

Ainsworth, M.D.S. (1967). Infancy in Uganda: Infant care and the growth of love. In B.M. Caldwell & H.N. Riccuiti (Eds.), *Review of child development research* (Vol. 3). Chicago: University of Chicago Press.

Ainsworth, M.D.S. (1979). Infant-mother attachment. *American Psychologist*, 34, 932–937.

Alan Guttmacher Institute (1993). *National survey of the American male's sexual habits*. Unpublished data. New York: Author.

Alan Guttmacher Institute (1995). *National survey of the American male's sexual habits*. New York: Alan Guttmacher Institute.

Alan Guttmacher Institute (1998). *Teen sex and pregnancy*. New York: Alan Guttmacher Institute.

Alberto, P., & Troutman, A. (1995). *Applied behavior analysis for teachers* (4th ed.). Upper Saddle River, NJ: Prentice-Hall.

Alderman, M.K. (1999). *Motivation for achievement*. Mahwah, NJ: Erlbaum.

Alexander, A., Anderson, H., Heilman, P.C., & Others. (1991). Phonological awareness training and remediation of analytic decoding deficits in a group of severe dyslexics. *Annals of Dyslexia*, 41, 193–206.

Alexander, G.R., & Korenbrot, C.C. (1995). The role of prenatal care in preventing low birth weight. *The Future of Children*, 5 (1), 103–120.

Alexandrova, E.O. (1999, April). *Emotional competence: Effects of indirect parental modeling in children*. Paper presented at the meeting of the Society for Research in Child Development, Albuquerque.

Aligne, C.A., & Stoddard, J.J. (1997). Tobacco and children: An economic evaluation of the medical effects of parental smoking. *Archives of Pediatric and Adolescent Medicine*, 151, 648–653.

Allen, J.P., & Hauser, S.T. (1994, February). *Adolescent-family interactions as predictors of qualities of parental, peer, and romantic relationships at age 25*. Paper presented at the meeting of the Society for Research on Adolescence, San Diego.

Allen, J.P., & Kuperminc, G.P. (1995, March). *Adolescent attachment, social competence, and problematic behavior*. Paper presented at the meeting of the Society for Research in Child Development, Indianapolis.

Allen, J.P., Hauser, S.T., & Borman-Spurrell, E. (1996). Attachment security and related sequalae of severe adolescent psychopathology: An eleven-year follow-up study. *Journal of Consulting and Clinical Psychology*, 64, 254–263.

Allen, K.E., & Marotz, L. (1989). *Developmental profiles: Birth-to-six*. Albany, NY: Delmar.

Allen, M., Brown, F., & Finlay, B. (1992). *Helping children by strengthening families*. Washington, DC: Children's Defense Fund.

Amabile, T. (1993). Commentary. In Goleman, D., Kaufman, P., & Ray, M. *The Creative Spirit*. New York: Plume.

Amabile, T.M., & Hennesey, B.A. (1992). The motivation for creativity in children. In A.K. Boggiano & T.S. Pittman (Eds.), *Achievement and motivation*. New York: Cambridge.

Amato, P.R., & Booth, A. (1996). A prospective study of divorce and parent–child relationships. *Journal of Marriage and the Family*, 58, 356–365.

Amato, P.R., & Keith, B. (1991). Parental divorce and the well-being of children: A meta-analysis. *Psychological Bulletin*, 110, 26–46.

America in Transition. (1989). Washington, DC: National Governors' Association Task Force on Children.

American Academy of Pediatrics (AAP) Committee on Environmental Health. (1997). Environmental tobacco smoke: A hazard to children. *Pediatrics*, 99, 639–642.

American Association for Protecting Children. (1986). *Highlights of official child neglect and abuse reporting: 1984*. Denver: American Humane Association.

American College Health Association. (1989, May). *Survey of AIDS on American college and university campuses*. Washington, DC: American College Health Association.

American Psychiatric Association. (1994). *Diagnostic and statistical manual of mental disorders* (4th ed.). Washington, DC: American Psychiatric Association.

Amsterdam, B.K. (1968). *Mirror behavior in children under two years of age*. Unpublished doctoral dissertation, University of North Carolina, Chapel Hill.

Anderman, E.M., Maehr, M.L., & Midgley, C. (1996). *Declining motivation after the transition to middle school: Schools can make a difference*. Unpublished manuscript, University of Kentucky, Lexington.

Anderson, D.R., Lorch, E.P., Field, D.E., Collins, P.A., & Nathan, J.G. (1985, April). *Television viewing at home: Age trends in visual attention and time with TV*. Paper presented at the biennial meeting of the Society for Research in Child Development, Toronto.

Anderson, E., Greene, S.M., Hetherington, E.M., & Clingempeel, W.G. (1999). The dynamics of parental remarriage. In E.M. Hetherington (Ed.), *Coping with divorce, single parenting, and remarriage*. Mahwah, NJ: Erlbaum.

Anselmi, D.L. (1998). *Questions of gender*. Burr Ridge, IL: McGraw-Hill.

Appalachia Educational Laboratory (1998). *ADHD–building academic success*. Charleston, WV: Appalachia Educational Laboratory.

Arboleda, T. (1999). *In the shadow of race*. Mahwah, NJ: Erlbaum.

Archer, S.L. (Ed.). (1994). *Intervention for adolescent identity development*. Newbury Park, CA: Sage.

Argyle, M., & Beit-Hallahmi, B. (1975). *The social psychology of religion*. London: Routledge & Kegan Paul.

Ariès, P. (1962). *Centuries of childhood* (R. Baldrick, Trans.). New York: Knopf.

Armsden, G., & Greenberg, M.T. (1984). *The inventory of parent and peer attachment: Individual differences and their relationship to psychological well-being in adolescence*. Unpublished manuscript. University of Washington.

Aronson, E. (1986, August). *Teaching students things they think they already know about: The case of prejudice and desegregation*. Paper presented at the meeting of the American Psychological Association, Washington, DC.

Asarnow, J.R., & Callan, J.W. (1985). Boys with peer adjustment problems: Social cognitive processes. *Journal of Consulting and Clinical Psychology*, 53, 80–87.

Asher, J., & Garcia, R. (1969). The optimal age to learn a foreign language. *Modern Language Journal*, 53, 334–341.

Astin, A.W., Korn, W.S., Sax, L.J., & Mahoney, K.M. (1994). *The American freshman: National norms for fall 1994*. Los Angeles: UCLA, Higher Education Research Institute.

Astrid, N., & Debry, G. (1994). Potential teratogenic and neurodevelopmental consequences of coffee and caffeine exposure: A review of human and animal data. *Neurotoxicology and Teratology*, 16, 531–543.

Attie, I., & Brooks-Gunn, J. (1989). Development of eating problems in adolescent girls: A longitudinal study. *Developmental Psychology*, 25, 70–79.

Au, K., Carroll, J., & Scheu, J. (in press). *Balanced literacy instruction: A teacher's resource book*. Norwood, MA: Christopher-Gordon.

B

Bachman, J.G. (1982, June 28). *The American high school student: A profile based on national survey data*. Paper presented at a conference entitled "The American High School Today and Tomorrow," Berkeley, CA.

Bachman, J.G., & Schulenberg, J. (1993). How part-time work intensity relates to drug use, problem behavior, time use, and satisfaction among high school seniors: Are these consequences or just correlates? *Developmental Psychology*, 29, 220–235.

Bagwell, C.L., Newcomb, A.F., & Bukowski, W.M. (1994, February). *Early adolescent friendship as a predictor of adult adjustment: A twelve-year follow-up investigation*. Paper presented at the biennial meeting of the Society for Research on Adolescence, San Diego.

Bakeman, R., & Brown, J.V. (1980). Early interaction: Consequences for social and mental development at three years. *Child Development*, 51, 437–447.

Baltes, P.B. (1987). Theoretical propositions of life-span developmental psychology: On the dynamics between growth and decline. *Developmental Psychology*, 23, 611–626.

Baltes, P.B., Lindenberger, U., & Staudinger, U.M. (1998). Life-span theory in developmental psychology. In W. Damon (ed.), *Handbook of child psychology* (5th ed., Vol. 1). New York: Wiley.

Bandura, A. (1977). *Social learning theory*. Englewood Cliffs, NJ: Prentice-Hall.

Bandura, A. (1986). *Social foundations of thought and action: A social cognitive theory*. Englewood Cliffs, NJ: Prentice Hall.

Bandura, A. (1997). *Self-efficacy*. New York: W.H. Freeman.

Bandura, A. (1998, August). *Swimming against the mainstream: Accentuating the positive aspects of humanity*. Paper presented at the meeting of the American Psychological Association, San Francisco.

Banks, E.C. (1993, March). *Moral education curriculum in a multicultural context: The Malaysian primary curriculum*. Paper presented at the biennial meeting of the Society for Research in Child Development, New Orleans.

Banks, J.A. (1995). *Multicultural education: Its effects on students' racial and gender role attitudes*. In J.A. Banks & C.A.M. Banks (Eds.), *Handbook of research on multicultural education*. New York: Macmillan.

Banks, J.A. (1997). Approaches to multicultural education reform. In J.A. Banks & C.A.M. Banks (Eds.), *Multicultural education*. Boston: Allyn & Bacon.

Banks, M.S., & Salapatek, P. (1983). Infant visual perception. In P.H. Mussen (Ed.), *Handbook of child psychology* (4th ed., Vol. 2). New York: Wiley.

Barker, R., & Wright, H.F. (1951). *One boy's day*. New York: Harper.

Baron, N.S. (1992). *Growing up with language*. Reading, MA: Addison-Wesley.

Barrett, D.E., Radke-Yarrow, M., & Klein, R.E. (1982). Chronic malnutrition and child behavior: Effects of calorie supplementation on social and emotional functioning at school age. *Developmental Psychology, 18,* 541–556.

Barton, L., Hodgman, J.E., & Pavlova, Z. (1999). Causes of death in the extremely low birth weight infant. *Pediatrics, 103,* 446–451.

Baskett, L.M., & Johnson, S.M. (1982). The young child's interaction with parents versus siblings. *Child Development, 53,* 643–650.

Bates, A.S., Fitzgerald, J.F., Dittus, R.S., & Wollinsky, F.D. (1994). Risk factors for underimmunization in poor urban infants. *Journal of the American Medical Association, 272,* 1105–1109.

Bates, E., & Thal, D. (1991). Associations and dissociations in language development. In J. Millder (Ed.), *Research on language disorders: A decade of progress*. Austin: Pro-Ed.

Bates, N.A., Rynn, M.A., Conway, D.H., Lischner, H.W., Hahnlen, N., & Bagarazzi, M.L. (1999, May). *Assesment of psychiatric comorbidity in children infected with human immunodeficiency virus, Type I*. Paper presented at the meeting of the Society for Pediatric Research, San Francisco.

Baumann, J.F., Hoffman, J.V., Moon, J., & Duffy-Hester, A.M. (1998). Where are teachers' voices in the phonics/whole language debate? Results from a survey of U.S. elementary classroom teachers. *The Reading Teacher, 51,* 636–650.

Baumrind, D. (1971). Current patterns of parental authority. *Developmental Psychology Monographs, 4* (1, Pt. 2).

Baumrind, D. (1989). *Sex-differentiated socialization effects in childhood and adolescence*. Paper presented at the biennial meeting of the Society for Research in Child Development, Kansas City.

Bayley, N. (1969). *Manual for the Bayley Scales of Infant Development*. New York: Psychological Corporation.

Bayley, N. (1970). Development of mental abilities. In P.H. Mussen (Ed.), *Manual of child psychology* (3rd ed., Vol. 1). New York: Wiley.

Beagles-Roos, J., & Gat, I. (1983). Specific impact of radio and television on children's story comprehension. *Journal of Educational Psychology, 75,* 128–137.

Beal, C.R. (1994). *Boys and girls: The development of gender roles*. Boston: McGraw-Hill.

Bechtold, A.G., Bushnell, E.W., & Salapatek, P. (1979, April). *Infants' visual localization of visual and auditory targets*. Paper presented at the meeting of the Society for Research in Child Development, San Francisco.

Bednar, R.L., Wells, M.G., & Peterson, S.R. (1995). *Self-esteem* (2nd ed.). Washington, DC: American Psychological Association.

Behrmann, M.M. (1994). Assistive technology for students with mild disabilities. *Intervention in School and Clinic, 30,* 70–83.

Bell, A.P., Weinberg, M.S., & Mammersmith, S.K. (1981). *Sexual preference: Its development in men and women*. New York: Simon & Schuster.

Bell, M.A., & Fox, N.A. (1992). The relations between frontal brain electrical activity and cognitive development during infancy. *Child Development, 63,* 1142–1163.

Bell, S.M., & Ainsworth, M.D.S. (1972). Infant crying and maternal responsiveness. *Child Development, 43,* 1171–1190.

Belle, D. (1999). *The after school lives of children*. Mahwah, NJ: Erlbaum.

Bellinger, D., Leviton, A., Waternaux, C., Needleman, H., & Rabinowitz, M. (1987). Longitudinal analysis of prenatal and postnatal lead exposure and early cognitive development. *New England Journal of Medicine, 316,* 1037–1043.

Belsky, J. (1981). Early human experience: A family perspective. *Developmental Psychology, 17,* 3–23.

Belsky, J. (1989). Infant-parent attachment and day care: In defense of the Strange Situation. In J.S. Lande, S. Scarr, & N. Gunzenhauser (Eds.), *Caring for children: Challenge to America*. Hillsdale, NJ: Erlbaum.

Belson, W. (1978). *Television violence and the adolescent boy*. London: Saxon House.

Bem, S.L. (1977). On the utility of alternative procedures for assessing psychological androgyny. *Journal of Consulting and Clinical Psychology, 45,* 196–205.

Benelli, C., & Yongue, B. (1995). Supporting young children's motor skill development. *Childhood Education, 72,* 217–220.

Bennett, W. (1993). *The book of virtues*. New York: Simon & Schuster.

Benson, P. (1993). *The troubled journey*. Minneapolis: The Search Institute.

Bergin, D. (1988). Stages of play development. In D. Bergin (Ed.), *Play as a medium for learning and development*. Portsmouth, NH: Heinemann.

Berk, S.F. (1985). *The gender factory: The apportionment of work in American households*. New York: Plenum.

Berko, J. (1958). The child's learning of English morphology. *Word, 14,* 150–177.

Berliner, D.C. (1997). Educational psychology meets the Christian right: Differing views of schooling, children, teaching, and learning. *Teachers College Record, 96,* 381–415.

Berlyne, D.E. (1960). *Conflict, arousal, and curiosity*. New York: McGraw-Hill.

Berndt, T.J. (1999). Friends' influence on children's adjustment. In W.A. Collins & B. Laursen (Eds.), *Relationships as developmental contexts*. Mahwah, NJ: Erlbaum.

Berndt, T.J., & Perry, T.B. (1990). Distinctive features and effects of early adolescent friendships. In R. Montemayor (Ed.), *Advances in adolescent research*. Greenwich, CT: JAI Press.

Bier, J.B., Oliver, T.L., Ferguson, A., & Vohr, B.R. (1999, May). *Human milk reduces outpatient infections in low birth weight infants*. Paper presented at the meeting of The Society for Pediatric Research, San Francisco.

Biller, H.B. (1993). *Fathers and families*. Westport, CT: Auburn House.

Billy, J.O.G., Rodgers, J.L., & Udry, J.R. (1984). Adolescent sexual behavior and friendship choice. *Social Forces, 62,* 653–678.

Bingham, C.R., & Crockett, L.J. (1996). Longitudinal adjustment patterns of boys and girls experiencing early, middle, and late sexual intercourse. *Developmental Psychology, 32,* 647–658.

Blachman, B.A., Ball, E., Black, R., & Tangel, D. (1994). Kindergarten teachers develop phoneme awareness in low-income inner-city classrooms: Does it make a difference? In B.A. Blachman (Ed.), *Reading and writing*. Mahwah, NJ: Erlbaum.

Blair, C., & Ramey, C. (1996). Early intervention with low birth weight infants: The path to second generation research. In M.J. Guralnick (Ed.), *The effectiveness of early intervention*. Baltimore, MD: Paul Brookes.

Block, J., & Block, J.H. (1988). Longitudinally foretelling drug usage in adolescence. Early childhood personality and environmental precursors. *Child Development, 59,* 336–355.

Bloom, L. (1998). Language acquisition in developmental context. In W. Damon (Ed.), *Handbook of child psychology* (5th ed., Vol. 5). New York: Wiley.

Blumenfeld, P.C., Pintrich, P.R., Wessles, K., & Meece, J. (1981, April). *Age and sex differences in the impact of classroom experiences on self-perceptions*. Paper presented at the biennial meeting of the Society of Research in Child Development, Boston.

Boekaerts, M., Pintrich, P.R., & Zeidner, M. (Eds.). (1999). *Handbook of self-regulation*. San Diego: Academic Press.

Bohlin, G., & Hagekull, B. (1993). Stranger wariness and sociability in the early years. *Infant Behavior and Development, 16,* 53–67.

Bolen, J.C., Bland, S.D., & Sacks, J.J. (1999, April). *Injury prevention behaviors: Children's use of occupant restraints and bicycle helmets*. Paper presented at the meeting of the Society for Research in Child Development, Albuquerque.

Bollerud, K.H., Chrisotopherson, S.B., & Frank, E.S. (1990). Girls' sexual choices: Looking for what is right. In C. Gilligan, N.P. Lyons, & T.J. Hanmer (Eds.), *Making connections*. Cambridge, MA: Harvard University Press.

Bonk, C.J., & Cunningham, D.J. (1999). Searching for learner-centered, constructivist, and sociocultural components of collaborative educational learning tools. In C.J. Bonk & K.S. King (Eds.), *Electronic collaborators*. Mahwah, NJ: Erlbaum.

Bonk, C.J., & King, K.S. (Eds.). (1999). *Electronic collaborators*. Mahwah, NJ: Erlbaum.

Bonvillian, J.D., Orlansky, M.D., & Novack, L.L. (1983). Developmental milestones: Sign language and motor development. *Child Development, 54,* 1435–1445.

Booth, A., & Dunn, J.F. (Eds.). (1996). *Family–school links*. Mahwah, NJ: Erlbaum.

Bornstein, M.H. (1999, April). *Culture, parents and children: Intranational and international study*. Paper presented at the meeting of the Society for Research in Child Development, Albuquerque.

Bornstein, M.H., & Arterberry, M.E. (1999). Perceptual development. In M.H. Bornstein & M.E. Lamb (Eds.), *Developmental psychology: An advanced textbook* (4th ed.). Mahwah, NJ: Erlbaum.

Bornstein, M.H., & Sigman, M.D. (1986). Continuity in mental development from infancy. *Child Development, 57,* 251–274.

Bouchard, T.J. (1995, August). *Heritability of intelligence*. Paper presented at the meeting of the American Psychological Association, New York, NY.

Bouchard, T.J., Lykken, D.T., McGue, M., Segal, N.L., & Tellegen, A. (1990). Source of human psychological differences: The Minnesota Study of Twins Reared Apart. *Science, 250,* 223–228.

Bowe, F. (2000). *Physical, sensory, and health disabilities*. Columbus, OH: Merrill.

Bower, B. (1985). The left hand of math and verbal talent. *Science News, 127,* 263.

Bower, T.G.R. (1989). *The rational infant: Learning in infancy*. New York: W.H. Freeman.

Bowlby, J. (1969). *Attachment and loss* (Vol. 1). London: Hogarth.

Bowlby, J. (1989). *Secure and insecure attachment.* New York: Basic Books.

Boyles, N.S., & Contadino, D. (1997). *The learning differences sourcebook.* Los Angeles: Lowell House.

Boys and Girls Clubs of America. (1989, May 12). *Boys and Girls Clubs in public housing projects: Interim report.* Minneapolis: Author.

Bracken, M.B., Eskenazi, B., Sachse, K., McSharry, J., Hellenbrand, K., & Leo-Summers, L. (1990). Association of cocaine use with sperm concentration, motility, and morphology. *Fertility and Sterility, 53,* 315–322.

Bray, J.H., & Berger, S.H. (1993). Developmental Issues in Stepfamilies Research Project: Family relationships and parent–child interactions. *Journal of Family Psychology, 7,* 76–90.

Bray, J.M., Berger, S.H., & Boethel, C.L. (1999). Marriage to remarriage and beyond. In E.M. Hetherington (Ed.), *Coping with divorce, single parenting, and remarriage.* Mahwah, NJ: Erlbaum.

Brazelton, T.B. (1956). Sucking in infancy. *Pediatrics, 17,* 400–404.

Brazelton, T.B. (1983). *Infants and mothers: Differences in development.* New York: Delta.

Brazelton, T.B. (1992). Optimistic infants. Preface to *Head Start: The emotional foundations of school readiness.* Arlington, VA: National Center for Clinical Infant Programs.

Brazelton, T.B. (1998, September 7). Commentary. *Dallas Morning News,* p. C2.

Brazelton, T.B., Nugent, J.K., & Lester, B.M. (1987). Neonatal behavioral assessment scale. In J.D. Osofsky (Ed.), *Handbook of infant development* (2nd ed.). New York: Wiley.

Bredekamp, S. (1987). *Developmentally appropriate practice in early childhood programs serving children from birth through age 8.* Washington, DC: National Association for the Education of Young Children.

Bredekamp, S. (1993). Reflections on Reggio Emilia. *Young Children, 49,* 13–16.

Bredekamp, S. (1997). NAEYC issues revised position statement on developmentally appropriate practice in early childhood programs. *Young Children, 52,* 34–40.

Bretherton, I., Stolberg, U., & Kreye, M. (1981). Engaging strangers in proximal interaction: Infants' social initiative. *Developmental Psychology, 17,* 746–755.

Brewer, W.F. (1996). Children's eyewitness memory research. In N.L. Stein, C. Brainerd, P.A. Ornstein, & B. Tversky (Eds.), *Memory for everyday and emotional events.* Hillsdale, NJ: Erlbaum.

Brislin, R. (1993). *Culture's influence on behavior.* Fort Worth, TX: Harcourt Brace Jovanovich.

Bronfenbrenner, U. (1979). Contexts of child rearing: Problems and prospects. *American Psychologist, 34,* 844–850.

Bronfenbrenner, U. (1986). Ecology of the family as a context for human development: Research perspectives. *Developmental Psychology, 22,* 723–742.

Bronfenbrenner, U. (1995, March). *The role research has played in Head Start.* Paper presented at the meeting of the Society for Research in Child Development, Indianapolis.

Bronfenbrenner, U., & Morris, P. (1998). The ecology of developmental processes. In W. Damon (Ed.), *Handbook of child psychology* (5th ed., Vol. 1). New York: Wiley.

Brook, J.S., Brook, D.W., Gordon, A.S., Whiteman, M., & Cohen, P. (1990). The psychological etiology of adolescent drug use: A family interactional approach. *Genetic, Social, and General Psychology Monographs, 116,* 110–267.

Brooks, J.B. (1999). *The process of parenting* (5th ed.). Mountain View, CA: Mayfield.

Brooks, J.G., & Brooks, M.G. (1993). *The case for constructivist classrooms.* Alexandria, VA: Association for Supervision and Curriculum.

Brooks-Gunn, J., & Chase-Lansdale, P.L. (1995). Adolescent parenthood. In M.H. Bornstein (Ed.), *Children and parenting* (Vol. 3). Hillsdale, NJ: Erlbaum.

Brooks-Gunn, J., & Paikoff, R. (1993). "Sex is a gamble, kissing is a game": Adolescent sexuality, contraception, and sexuality. In S.P. Millstein, A.C. Petersen, & E.O. Nightingale, (Eds.), *Promoting the health behavior of adolescents.* New York: Oxford University Press.

Brooks-Gunn, J., & Reiter, E.O. (1990). The role of pubertal processes. In S.S. Feldman & G.R. Elliott (Eds.), *At the threshold: The developing adolescent.* Cambridge, MA: Harvard University Press.

Brooks-Gunn, J., & Ruble, D.N. (1982). The development of menstrual-related beliefs and behaviors during early adolescence. *Child Development, 53,* 1567–1577.

Brooks-Gunn, J., & Warren, M.P. (1989). The psychological significance of secondary sexual characteristics in 9- to 11-year-old girls. *Child Development, 59,* 161–169.

Brooks-Gunn, J., Graber, J.A., & Paikoff, R.L. (1994). Studying links between hormones and negative affect: Models and measures. *Journal of Research on Adolescence, 4,* 469–486.

Brooks-Gunn, J., Klebanov, P.K., & Duncan, G.J. (1996). Ethnic differences in children's intelligence test scores: Role of economic deprivation, home environment, and maternal characteristics. *Child Development, 67,* 396–408.

Brophy, J. (1998). *Motivating students to learn.* Boston: McGraw-Hill.

Brown, A.L. (in press). Transforming schools into communities of thinking and learning about serious matters. *American Psychologist.*

Brown, A.L., & Campione, J.C. (in press). Psychological learning theory and the design of innovative environments. In L. Schuable & R. Glaser (Eds.), *Contributions of instructional innovation to understanding learning.* Mahwah, NJ: Erlbaum.

Brown, A.L., & Palincsar, A.M. (1989). Guided, cooperative learning and individual knowledge acquisition. In L.B. Resnick (Ed.), *Knowing and learning: Essays in honor of Robert Glaser.* Hillsdale, NJ: Erlbaum.

Brown, B.B. (in press). "You're going with whom?!": Peer group influences on adolescent romantic relationships. In W. Furman, B.B. Brown, & C. Feiring (Eds.), *Contemporary perspectives on adolescent romantic relationships.* Cambridge, UK: Cambridge University Press.

Brown, B.B., & Lohn, M.J. (1987). Peer-group affiliation and adolescent self-esteem: An integration of ego-identity and symbolic-interaction theories. *Journal of Personality and Social Psychology, 52,* 47–55.

Brown, B.B., & Mounts, N. (1989, April). *Peer group structures in single vs. multiethnic high schools.* Paper presented at the biennial meeting of the Society for Research in Child Development, Kansas City.

Brown, D. (1987). The status of Holland's theory of vocational choice. *Career Development Quarterly, 36,* 13–24.

Brown, J., & Allen, D. (1988). Hunger in America. *Annual Review of Public Health, 9,* 503–526.

Brown, R. (1973). *A first language: The early stages.* Cambridge, MA: Harvard University Press.

Brown, R. (1986). *Social Psychology* (2nd ed.). New York: Free Press.

Bruce, J.M., Olen, K., & Jensen, S.J. (1999, April). *The role of emotion and regulation in social competence.* Paper presented at the meeting of the Society for Research in Child Development, Albuquerque.

Bruner, J.S. (1996). *The culture of education.* Cambridge, MA: Harvard University Press.

Bryant, B.R., & Seay, P.C. (1998). The technology-related assistance to individuals with learning disabilities and their advocates. *Journal of Learning Disabilities, 31,* 4–15.

Bryon, Y.J., Pang, W., Wei, L.S., Dickover, R., Diange, A., and Chen, I. S.Y. (1991). Clearance of HIV infection in a perinatally infected infant. *New England Journal of Medicine, 332,* 833–838.

Buhrmester, D., & Carbery, J. (1992, March). *Daily patterns of self-disclosure and adolescent adjustment.* Paper presented at the biennial meeting of the Society for Research on Adolescence, Washington, DC.

Buhrmester, D., & Furman, W. (1987). The development of companionship and intimacy. *Child Development, 58,* 1101–1113.

Burchinal, M.R., Roberts, J.E., Nabors, L.A., & Bryant, D.M. (1996). Quality of center child care and infant cognitive and language development. *Child Development, 67,* 606–620.

Burton, L., & Allison, K.W. (1995). Social context and adolescence: Alternative perspectives on developmental pathways for African-American teens. In L.J. Crockett & A.C. Crouter (Eds.), *Pathways through adolescence.* Hillsdale, NJ: Erlbaum.

Burts, D.C., Hart, C.H., Charlesworth, R., Hernandez, S., Kirk, L., & Mosley, J. (1989, March). *A comparison of the frequences of stress behaviors observed in kindergarten children in classrooms with developmentally appropriate and developmentally inappropriate instructional practices.* Paper presented at the meeting of the American Educational Research Association, San Francisco.

Butterfield, L.J. (1999, May). *The Apgar legend lives.* Paper presented at meeting of the Society for Pediatric Research, San Francisco.

Bybee, J. (Ed.). (1999). *Guilt and children.* San Diego: Academic Press.

Byrnes, J.P. (1997). *The nature and development of decision making.* Mahwah, NJ: Erlbaum.

C

Cairns, R.B. (1983). The emergence of developmental psychology. In P.H. Mussen (Ed.), *Handbook of child psychology* (4th ed., Vol. 1). New York: Wiley.

Cairns, R.B. (1998). The making of developmental psychology. In R.M. Lerner (Ed.), *Handbook of child psychology* (5th ed., Vol. 1). New York: Wiley.

Calabrese, R.L., & Schumer, H. (1986). The effects of service activities on adolescent alienation. *Adolescence, 21,* 675–687.

Caldwell, M.B., & Rogers, M.F. (1991). Epidemiology of pediatric HIV infection. *Pediatrics Clinics of North America, 38,* 1–16.

Calvert, S. (1999). *Children's journeys through the information age.* Boston: McGraw-Hill.

Cameron, J.R., Hansen, R., & Rosen, D. (1989). Preventing behavioral problems in infancy through temperament assessment and parental support programs. In W.B. Carey & S.C. McDevitt (Eds.), *Clinical and educational applications of temperament research.* Amsterdam: Swets & Zeitlinger.

Campbell, F.A., & Ramey, C.T. (1994). Effects of early intervention on intellectual and academic achievement: A follow-up study of children from low-income families. *Child Development, 65,* 684–698.

Campos, J.J. (1994, Spring). The new functionalism in emotions. *SRCD Newsletter* (pp. 1, 7, 9–11, 14).

Campos, J.J., Langer, A., & Krowitz, A. (1970). Cardiac responses on the visual cliff in prelocomotor human infants. *Science, 170,* 196–197.

Canfield, R.L., & Haith, M.M. (1991). Young infants' visual expectations for symmetric and asymmetric stimulus sequences. *Developmental Psychology, 27,* 198–208.

Carey, S. (1999). Sources of conceptual change. In E.K. Skolnick, K. Nelson, S.A. Gelman, & P.H. Miller (Eds.), *Conceptual development.* Mahwah, NJ: Erlbaum.

Carle, E. (1977). *The grouchy ladybug.* New York: HarperCollins.

Carlson, K.S. (1995, March). *Attachment in sibling relationships during adolescence: Links to other familial and peer relationships.* Paper presented at the meeting of the Society for Research in Child Development, Indianapolis.

Carlson, V., Cicchetti, D., Barnett, D., & Braunwald, K. (1989). Disorganized/disoriented attachment relationships in maltreated infants. *Developmental Psychology, 25,* 525–531.

Carnegie Corporation. (1989). *Turning points: Preparing American youth for the 21st century.* New York: Author.

Carnegie Corporation. (1996). *Report on education for children 3–10 years of age.* New York: The Carnegie Foundation.

Carnegie Council on Adolescent Development (1995). *Great transitions.* New York: The Carnegie Corporation.

Carter, D.B., & Levy, G.D. (1988). Cognitive aspects of children's early sex-role development: The influence of gender schemas on preschoolers' memories and preference for sex-typed toys and activities. *Child Development, 59,* 782–793.

Carter-Saltzman, L. (1980). Biological and sociocultural effects on handedness: Comparison between biological and adoptive families. *Science, 209,* 1263–1265.

Case, R. (1987). Neo-Piagetian theory: Retrospect and prospect. *International Journal of Psychology, 22,* 773–791.

Case, R. (1999). Conceptual development in the child and the field: A personal view of the Piagetian legacy. In E.K. Skolnick, K. Nelson, S.A. Gelman, & P.H. Miller (Eds.), *Conceptual development.* Mahwah, NJ: Erlbaum.

Case, R., Kurland, D.M., & Goldberg, J. (1982). Operational efficiency and the growth of short-term memory span. *Journal of Experimental Child Psychology, 33,* 386–404.

Caspi, A., Henry, B., McGee, R.O., Moffitt, T.E., & Silva, P.A. (1995). Temperamental origins of child and adolescent behavior problems: From age three to age fifteen. *Child Development, 66,* 55–68.

Cassidy, J., & Berlin, L.J. (1994). The insecure/ambivalent pattern of attachment: Theory and research. *Child Development, 65,* 971–991.

Cassidy, J., & Shaver, P.R. (Eds.). (1999). *Handbook of attachment.* New York: Guilford.

Cauffman, B.E. (1994, February). *The effects of puberty, dating, and sexual involvement on dieting and disordered eating in young adolescent girls.* Paper presented at the meeting of the Society for Research on Adolescence, San Diego.

Cavett, D. (1974). *Cavett.* San Diego: Harcourt Brace Jovanovich.

CDC National AIDS Clearinghouse. (1998, October 7). *Teenagers and AIDS.* Atlanta: CDC National AIDS Clearinghouse.

Ceballo, R.E. (1999, April). *The psychological impact of children's perceptions of neighborhood danger and collective efficacy.* Paper presented at the meeting of the Society for Research in Child Development, Albuquerque.

Ceci, S.J. (1993, August). *Cognitive and social factors in children's testimony.* Paper presented at the meeting of the American Psychological Association, Toronto.

Ceci, S.J., Rosenblum, T., de Bruyn, E., & Lee, D.Y. (1997). A bio-ecological model of intellectual development. In R.J. Sternberg & E. Grigorenko (Eds.), *Intelligence, heredity, and environment.* New York: Cambridge.

Centers for Disease Control. (1988). HIV-related beliefs, knowledge, and behaviors among high school students. *Morbidity and Mortality Weekly Reports, 37,* 717–721.

Chan, W.S. (1963). *A source book in Chinese philosophy.* Princeton, NJ: Princeton University Press.

Chapman, W., & Katz, M.R. (1983). Career information systems in secondary schools: A survey and assessment. *Vocational Guidance Quarterly, 31,* 165–177.

Charlesworth, R. (1987). *Understanding child development* (2nd ed.). Albany, NY: Delmar.

Charlesworth, R. (1996). *Understanding child development* (4th ed.). Albany, NY: Delmar.

Chasnoff, I.J., Griffith, D.R., Freier, C., & Murray, J. (1992). Cocaine/polydrug use in pregnancy: Two-year follow-up. *Pediatrics, 89,* 284–289.

Chattin-McNichols, J. (1992). *The Montessori controversy.* Albany, NY: Delmar.

Chauhuri, J.H., & Williams, P.H. (1999, April). *The contribution of infant temperament and parent emotional availability to toddler attachment.* Paper presented at the meeting of the Society for Research in Child Development, Albuquerque.

Chen, C., & Stevenson, H.W. (1989). Homework: A cross-cultural examination. *Child Development, 60,* 551–561.

Cherlin, A.J., & Furstenberg, F.F. (1994). Stepfamilies in the United States: A reconsideration. In J. Blake & J. Hagen (Eds.), *Annual review of sociology.* Palo Alto, CA: Annual Reviews.

Cherlin, A.J., Furstenberg, F.F., Chase-Lansdale, P.L., Kiernan, K.E., Robins, P.K., Morrison, D.R., & Teitler, J.O. (1991). Longitudinal studies of effects of divorce in children in Great Britain and the United States. *Science, 252,* 1386–1389.

Chescheir, N.C., & Hansen, W.F. (1999). New in perinatology. *Pediatrics in Review, 20,* 57–63.

Chess, S., & Thomas, A. (1977). Temperamental individuality from childhood to adolescence. *Journal of Child Psychiatry, 16,* 218–226.

Chi, M.T. (1978). Knowledge structures and memory development. In R.S. Siegler (Ed.), *Children's thinking: What develops?* Hillsdale, NJ: Erlbaum.

Child Trends. (1996). *Facts at a glance.* Washington, DC: Child Trends.

Children's Defense Fund. (1990). *Children 1990.* Washington, DC: Children's Defense Fund.

Chomitz, V.R., Cheung, L.W.Y., & Lieberman, E. (1995, Spring). The role of lifestyle in preventing low birth weight. *The Future of Children, 5* (1), 121–138.

Chomsky, N. (1957). *Syntactic structures.* The Hague: Mouton.

Cicchetti, D., Ganiban, J., & Barnett, D. (1991). Contributions from the study of high risk populations to understanding the development of emotion regulation. In J. Garber & K. Dodge (Eds.), *The development of emotion regulation and dysregulation.* New York: Cambridge University Press.

Circirelli, V.G. (1994). Sibling relationships in cross-cultural perspective. *Journal of Marriage and the Family, 56,* 7–20.

Clark, S.D., Zabin, L.S., & Hardy, J.B. (1984). Sex, contraception, and parenthood: Experience and attitudes among urban black young men. *Family Planning Perspectives, 16,* 77–82.

Clarke-Stewart, K.A., & Fein, G.G. (1983). Early childhood programs. In P.H. Mussen (Ed.), *Handbook of child psychology* (4th ed., Vol. 2). New York: Wiley.

Clay, R.A. (1997, December). Are children being over-medicated? *APA Monitor,* pp. 1, 27.

Clements, D.H., & Nastasi, B.K. (1993). Electronic media and early childhood education. In B. Spodek (Ed.), *Handbook of research on the education of young children.* New York: Macmillan.

Clifford, B.R., Gunter, B., & McAleer, J.L. (1995). *Television and children.* Hillsdale, NJ: Erlbaum.

Clifton, R.K., Morrongiello, B.A., Kulig, J.W., & Dowd, J.M. (1981). Developmental changes in auditory localization in infancy. In R.N. Aslin, J.R. Alberts, & M.R. Petersen (Eds.), *Development of perception, Vol. 1.* Orlando, FL: Academic Press.

Clifton, R.K., Muir, D.W., Ashmead, D.H., & Clarkson, M.G. (1993). Is visually guided reaching in early infancy a myth? *Child Development, 64,* 1099–1110.

The Cognition & Technology Group at Vanderbilt. (1997). *The Jasper Project.* Mahwah, NJ: Erlbaum.

Cohen, H.J., Grosz, J., Ayooh, K., & Schoen, S. (1996). Early intervention for children with HIV infections. In M.J. Guralnick (Ed.), *The effectiveness of early intervention.* Baltimore, MD: Paul Brookes.

Cohen, S.E. (1994, February). *High school dropouts.* Paper presented at the meeting of the Society for Research on Adolescence, San Diego.

Colby, A., Kohlberg, L., Gibbs, J., & Lieberman, M. (1983). A longitudinal study of moral judgment. *Monographs of the Society for Research in Child Development* (Serial No. 201).

Cole, M. (1999). Culture in development. In M.H. Bornstein & M.E. Lamb (Eds.), *Developmental psychology: an advanced textbook* (4th ed.). Mahwah, NJ: Erlbaum.

Coleman, J.S. (1961). *The adolescent society.* New York: Free Press.

Coles, R. (1970). *Erik H. Erikson: The growth of his work.* Boston: Little, Brown.

Coll, C.T.G., Meyer, E.C., & Brillion, L. (1995). Ethnic and minority parenting. In M.H. Bornstein (Ed.), *Children and parenting* (Vol. 2). Hillsdale, NJ: Erlbaum.

College Board (1996, August 22). *News from The College Board.* New York: The College Entrance Examination Board.

College Board Commission on Precollege Guidance and Counseling. (1986). *Keeping the options open.* New York: College Entrance Examination Board.

Collins, F.S. (1999). Genetics: An explosion of knowledge is transforming clinical practice. *Geriatrics, 54,* 41–47.

Comer, J. (1993, March). *African-American parents and child development: An agenda for school success.* Paper presented at the biennial meeting of the Society for Research in Child Development, New Orleans.

Comer, J.P. (1988). Educating poor minority children. *Scientific American, 259,* 42–48.

Comer, J.P., Haynes, N.M., Joyner, E.T., & Ben-Avie, M. (1996). *Rallying the whole village: The Comer process for reforming urban education.* New York: Teachers College Press.

Compas, B.E., & Grant, K.E. (1993, March). *Stress and adolescent depressive symptoms: Underlying mechanisms and processes.* Paper presented at the biennial meeting of the Society for Research in Child Development, New Orleans.

Comstock, G., & Scharrar, E. (1999). *Television.* San Diego: Academic Press.

Conger, J.J. (1988). Hostages to the future: Youth, values, and the public interest. *American Psychologist, 43,* 291–300.

Conger, R.D., & Chao, W. (1996). Adolescent depressed mood. In R.L. Simons (Ed.), *Understanding differences between divorced and intact families: Stress, interaction, and child outcome.* Thousand Oaks, CA: Sage.

Conger, R.D., & Ge, X. (1999). Conflict and cohesion in parent-adolescent relations: Changes in emotional expression. In M.J. Cox & J. Brooks-Gunn (Eds.), *Conflict and cohesion in families.* Mahwah, NJ: Erlbaum.

Considine, R.V., Sinha, M.K., & Heiman, M.I. (1996). Serum immunoreactive–leptin concentrations in normal-weight and obese humans. *New England Journal of Medicine, 334,* 292–295.

Cooper, C., Lopez, E., Dunbar, N., & Figuera, J. (1996, March). *Identity, relationships, and opportunity structures: African-American and Latino youth in University Academic Outreach programs.* Paper presented at the meeting of the Society for Research on Adolescence, Boston.

Cooper, C.R., & Ayers-Lopez, S. (1985). Family and peer systems in early adolescence: New models of the roles of relationships in development. *Journal of Early Adolescence, 5,* 9–22.

Cooper, C.R., & Grotevant, H.D. (1989, April). *Individuality and connectedness in the family and adolescent's self and relational competence.* Paper presented at the meeting of the Society for Research in Child Development, Kansas City.

Cooper, C.R., Grotevant, H.D., Moore, M.S., & Condon, S.M. (1982, August). *Family support and conflict:*

Both foster adolescent identity and role taking. Paper presented at the meeting of the American Psychological Association, Washington, DC.

Cooper, M.L., Shaver, P.R., & Collins, N.L. (1998). Attachment styles, emotional regulation, and adjustment in adolescence. *Journal of Personality and Social Psychology, 74,* 1380–1397.

Coopersmith, S. (1967). *The antecedents of self-esteem.* San Francisco: W.H. Freeman.

Cornell, D. (1998, April 6). Commentary. *Newsweek,* p. 24.

Corrigan, R. (1981). The effects of task and practice on search for invisibly displaced objects. *Developmental Review, 11,* 1–17.

Courage, M.L., & Howe, M.L. (1999, April). *A new look at an old method: Long-term retention in three-month-olds.* Paper presented at the meeting of the Society for Research in Child Development, Albuquerque.

Cowan, C.P., Cowan, P.A., Heming, G., & Boxer, C. (1995). *Preventive interventions with parents of preschoolers on the children's adaptation to kindergarten.* Paper presented at the meeting of the Society for Research in Child Development, New Orleans.

Cowan, C.P., Cowan, P.A., Heming, G., & Miller, N. (1991). Becoming a family: marriage, parenting, and child development. In P.A. Cowan & E.M. Hetherington (Eds.), *Family transitions.* Mahwah, NJ: Erlbaum.

Cowan, C.P., Heming, G.A., & Shuck, E.L. (1993, March). *The impact of interventions with parents of preschoolers on the children's adaptation of kindergarten.* Paper presented at the biennial meeting of the Society for Research in Child Development, New Orleans.

Cowan, P.A., Powell, D., & Cowan, C.P. (1998). Parenting interventions: A family systems perspective. In W. Damon (Ed.), *Handbook of child psychology* (5th ed., Vol. 4). New York: Wiley.

Cowley, G. (1998, April 6). Why children turn violent. *Newsweek,* pp. 24–25.

Coy, K.C. (1999, April). *The development of positive affectivity in toddlerhood.* Paper presented at the meeting of the Society for Research in Child Development, Albuquerque.

Crawford, C. & Krebs, D.L. (Eds.). (1998). *Handbook of evolutionary psychology.* Mahwah, NJ: Erlbaum.

Crick, N.R., & Dodge, K.A. (1994). A review and reformulation of social information-processing mechanisms in children's social adjustment. *Psychological Bulletin, 115,* 74–101.

Crockenberg, S.B. (1986). Are temperamental differences in babies associated with predictable differences in caregiving? In J.V. Lerner & R.M. Lerner (Eds.), *Temperament and social interaction during infancy and childhood.* San Francisco: Jossey-Bass.

Crockett, J.B., & Kauffman, J.M. (1999). *The least restrictive environment.* Mahwah, NJ: Erlbaum.

Crockett, L.J., & Petersen, A.C. (1993). Adolescent development: Health risks and opportunities for health promotion. In S.G. Millstein, A.C. Petersen, & E.O. Nightingale (Eds.), *Promoting the health of adolescents.* New York: Oxford University Press.

Cronbach, L.J., & Snow, R.E. (1977). *Aptitudes and instructional methods.* New York: Irvington Books.

Cross, W.E., Clark, L., & Fhagen-Smith, P. (1999). African-American identity development. In R.H. Sheets & E.R. Hollins (Eds.), *Racial and ethnic identity in school practices.* Mahwah, NJ: Erlbaum.

Crowder, J. (1969). *Stephanie and the coyote.* Upper Strata, Box 278, Bernalillo, NM 87004.

Culatta, R., & Tompkins, J.R. (1999). *Introduction to special education.* Columbus, OH: Merrill.

Cummings, E.M. (1987). Coping with background anger in early childhood. *Child Development, 58,* 976–984.

Curtiss, S. (1977). *Genie.* New York: Academic Press.

Cushner, K. (1999). *Human diversity in action.* Boston: McGraw-Hill.

Cushner, K., McClelland, A., & Safford, P. (1996). *Human diversity and education* (2nd ed.). Burr Ridge, IL: McGraw-Hill.

D

D'Angelo, D.A., & Adler, C.R. (1991). A catalyst for improving parent involvement. *Phi Delta Kappan,* pp. 350–354.

Dale, P., & Dionne, G. (1999, April). *Lexical and grammatical development: A behavioral genetic perspective.* Paper presented at the meeting of the Society for Research in Child Development, Albuquerque.

Damon, W. (1988). *The moral child.* New York: Free Press.

Damon, W. (1995). *Greater expectations.* New York: The Free Press.

Damon, W., & Hart, D. (1992). Self-understanding and its role in social and moral development. In M.H. Bornstein & M.E. Lamb (Eds.), *Developmental psychology: An advanced textbook* (3rd ed.). Hillsdale, NJ: Erlbaum.

Dapretto, M. (1999, April). *The development of word retrieval abilities in the second year of life and its relation to early vocabulary growth.* Paper presented at the meeting of the Society for Research in Child Development, Albuquerque.

Darwin, C. (1859). *On the origin of species.* London: John Murray.

Davis, K. (1996). *Families.* Pacific Grove, CA: Brooks/Cole.

Davis, S.M., Lambert, L.C., Gomez, Y., & Skipper, B. (1995). Southwest Cardiovascular Curriculum Project: Study findings for American Indian elementary students. *Journal of Health Education, 26,* S72–S81.

de Villiers, J. (1996). Toward a rational empiricism: Why interactionism isn't behaviorism any more than biology is genetics. In M. Rick (Ed.), *Towards a genetics of language.* Mahwah, NJ: Erlbaum.

de Villiers, J.G., & de Villiers, P.A. (1999). Language development. In M.H. Bornstein & M.E. Lamb (Eds.), *Developmental psychology: An advanced textbook* (4th ed.). Mahwah, NJ: Erlbaum.

De Wolff, M.S., & van IJzendoorn, M.H. (1997). Sensitivity and attachment: A meta-analysis on parental antecedents of infant attachment. *Child Development, 68,* 571–591.

DeCasper, A.J., & Spence, M.J. (1986). Prenatal maternal speech influences newborn's perception of speech sounds. *Infant Behavior and Development, 9,* 133–150.

DeLoache, J.S., Cassidy, D.J., & Carpenter, C.J. (1987). The Three Bears are all boys: Mothers' gender labeling of neutral picture book characters. *Sex Roles, 17,* 163–178.

Deluca, P. (1999, April). *Does illness enhance children's understanding of the inside of the body, death, and illness contagion?* Paper presented at the meeting of the Society for Research in Child Development, Albuquerque.

Dempster, F.N. (1981). Memory span: Sources of individual and developmental differences. *Psychological Bulletin, 80,* 63–100.

Denham, S.A. (1998). *Emotional development in young children.* New York: Guilford.

Derman-Sparks, L., & the A.B.C. Task Force. (1989). *Anti-bias curriculum.* Washington, DC: National Association for the Education of Young Children.

Devoe, M., & Sherman, T. (1978). A microtechnology for teaching prosocial behavior to children. *Child Study Journal, 8,* 83–92.

Dewey, C.R. (1999, April). *Day care, family, and child characteristics: Their roles as predictors and moderators of language development.* Paper presented at the meeting of the Society for Research in Child Development, Albuquerque.

Dewey, J. (1933). *How we think.* Lexington, MA: D.C. Heath.

Dishion, T.J., & Li, F. (1996, March). *Childhood peer rejection in the development of adolescent problem behavior.* Paper presented at the meeting of the Society for Research on Adolescence, Boston.

Dixon, R.A., & Lerner, R.M. (1999). History and systems in developmental psychology. In M.H. Bornstein & M.E. Lamb (Eds.), *Developmental psychology: An advanced textbook* (4th ed.). Mahwah, NJ: Erlbaum.

Dodge, K.A. (1983). Behavioral antecedents of peer social status. *Child Development, 54,* 1386–1399.

Dorn, L.D., & Lucas, F.L. (1995, March). *Do hormone-behavior relations vary depending upon the endocrine and psychological status of the adolescent?* Paper presented at the meeting of the Society for Research in Child Development, Indianapolis.

Doubleday, C.N., & Droege, K.L. (1993). Cognitive developmental influences on children's understanding of television. In G.L. Berry & J.K. Asamen (Eds.), *Children and television.* Newbury Park, CA: Sage.

Downey, G., & Bonica, C.A. (1997, April). *Characteristics of early adolescent dating relationships.* Paper presented at the meeting of the Society for Research in Child Development, Washington, DC.

Doyle, J.A., & Paludi, M.A. (1998). *Sex and gender* (4th ed.). Boston: McGraw-Hill.

Drew, C., & Hardman, M.L. (2000). *Mental retardation* (7th ed.). Columbus, OH: Merrill.

Dryfoos, J.G. (1990). *Adolescents at risk: Prevalence and prevention.* New York: Oxford University Press.

Dryfoos, J.G. (1995). Full service schools: Revolution or fad? *Journal of Research on Adolescence, 5,* 147–172.

Dunn, J., & Kendrick, C. (1982). *Siblings.* Cambridge, MA: Harvard University Press.

Dunn, J., & Kendrick, C. (1982). *Siblings.* Cambridge, MA: Harvard University Press.

Dunn, L., & Kontos, S. (1997). What have we learned about developmentally appropriate education? *Young Children, 52 (2),* 4–13.

Dunphy, D.C. (1963). The social structure of urban adolescent peer groups. *Society, 26,* 230–246.

DuRant, R.H. (1999, April). *Exposure to violence, depression, and substance use and abuse and the use of violence by young adolescents.* Paper presented at the meeting of the Society for Research in Child Development, Albuquerque.

Durkin, K. (1985). Television and sex-role acquisition: 1. Content. *British Journal of Social Psychology, 24,* 101–113.

E

Eagly, A.H. (1995). The science and politics of comparing men and women. *American Psychologist, 50,* 145–158.

Eagly, A.H. (1996). Differences between women and men. *American Psychologist, 51,* 158–159.

Eagly, A.H., & Crowley, M. (1986). Gender and helping behavior: A meta-analytic review of the social psychological literature. *Psychological Bulletin, 100,* 283–308.

Earls, F. (1993). Health promotion for minority adolescents: Cultural considerations. In S.G. Millstein, A.C. Petersen, & E.O. Nightingale (Eds.), *Promoting the health of adolescents.* New York: Oxford University Press.

Early Childhood and Literacy Development Committee of the International Reading Association. (1986). Literacy development and pre-first grade. *Young Children, 41,* 10–13.

East, P., & Felice, M.E. (1996). *Adolescent pregnancy and parenting.* Hillsdale, NJ: Erlbaum.

Eccles, J.S., & Roeser, R.W. (1999). School and community influences on human development. In M.H. Bornstein & M.E. Lamb (Eds.), *Developmental psychology: An advanced textbook* (4th ed.). Mahwah, NJ: Erlbaum.

Eccles, J.S., Wigfield, A., & Schiefele, U. (1998). Motivation to succeed. In W. Damon (Ed.), *Handbook of child psychology* (5th ed., Vol. 3). New York: Wiley.

Edelman, M.W. (1992). *The measure of our success: A letter to my children and yours*. Boston: Beacon Press.

Edelman, M.W. (1995). The state of America's children. Washington, DC: The Children's Defense Fund.

Edelman, M.W. (1997, April). *Children, families and social policy*. Paper presented at the meeting of the Society for Research in Child Development, Washington, DC.

Edelman, M.W. (1997, April). *Families, children, and social policy*. Invited address, presented at the meeting of the Society for Research in Child Development, Washington, DC.

Educational Testing Service. (1992). *Cross-cultural comparison of children's learning and achievement*. Unpublished manuscript. Educational Testing Service, Princeton, NJ.

Egeren, L.V. (1999, April). *The development of the parenting alliance in first-time parents: Predictors of change patterns over the first six months*. Paper presented at the meeting of the Society for Research in Child Development, Albuquerque.

Eiferman, R.R. (1971). Social play in childhood. In R.E. Herron & B. Sutton-Smith (Eds.), *Child's play*. New York: Wiley.

Eiger, M.S. (1992). The feeding of infants and children. In R.A. Hoekelman, S.B. Friedman, N.M. Nelson, & H.M. Seidel (Eds.), *Primary pediatric care* (2nd ed.). St. Louis: Mosby Yearbook.

Eimas, P. (1995). The perception of representation of speech by infants. In J.L. Morgan & K. Demuth (Eds.), *Signal to syntax*. Hillsdale, NJ: Erlbaum.

Eisenberg, A., Murkoff, H., & Hathaway, S. (1989). *What to expect when you're expecting*. New York: Workman.

Eisenberg, A., Murkoff, H., & Hathaway, S. (1991). *What to expect when you're expecting* (2nd ed., rev.). New York: Workman.

Eisenberg, N. (Ed.). (1982). *The development of prosocial behavior*. New York: Wiley.

Eisenberg, N., Fabes, R.A., Karbon, M., Murphy, B.C., Wosinski, M., Polazzi, L., Carolo, G., & Juhnke, C. (in press). The relations of children's dispositional prosocial behavior to emotionality, regulation, and social functioning. *Child Development*.

Eisenberg, N., Martin, C.L., & Fabes, R.A. (1996). Gender development and gender effects. In D.C. Berliner & R.C. Calfee (Eds.), *Handbook of educational psychology*. New York: Macmillan.

Elias, M. (1998, June 23). For 50 years pediatrics has taken giant steps. *USA Today*, pp. 1, 2D.

Elicker, J. (1996). A knitting tale: Reflections on scaffolding. *Childhood Education*, 72, 29–32.

Elkind, D. (1970, April 5). Erik Erikson's eight ages of man. *New York Times Magazine*.

Elkind, D. (1976). *Child development and education: A Piagetian perspective*. New York: Oxford University Press.

Elkind, D. (1981). *Children and adolescents*. New York: Oxford University Press.

Elkind, D. (1981). *The hurried child*. Reading, MA: Addison-Wesley.

Elkind, D. (1985). Reply to D. Lapsley and M. Murphy's *Developmental Review* paper. *Developmental Review*, 5, 218–226.

Elkind, D. (1988, January). Educating the very young: A call for clear thinking. *NEA Today*, pp. 22–27.

Ellis, L., & Ames, M.A. (1987). Neurohormonal functioning and sexual orientation: A theory of homosexuality-heterosexuality. *Psychological Bulletin*, 101, 233–258.

Elman, J.L. (1999). The emergence of language: A conspiracy theory. In B. MacWhinney (Ed.), *The emergence of language*. Mahwah, NJ: Erlbaum.

Embretton, S.E., & Hershberger, S.L. (Eds.). (1999). *The new rules of assessment*. Mahwah, NJ: Erlbaum.

Emde, R.N., Gaensbauer, T.G., & Harmon, R.J. (1976). Emotional expression in infancy: A biobehavioral study. *Psychological Issues: Monograph Series*, 10, (37).

Emery, R.E. (1994). *Renegotiating family relationships*. New York: Guilford Press.

Emshoff, J., Avery, E., Raduka, G., Anderson, D.J., & Calvert, C. (1996). Findings from SUPER STARS: A health promotion program for families to enhance multiple protective factors. *Journal of Adolescent Research*, 11, 68–96.

Enger, E.D., Kormelink, R., Ross, F.C., & Otto, R. (1996). *Diversity of life*. Dubuque, IA: Wm. C. Brown.

Enright, R.D., Lapsley, D.K., Dricas, A.S., & Fehr, L.A. (1980). Parental influence on the development of adolescent autonomy and identity. *Journal of Youth and Adolescence*, 9, 529–546.

Epstein, J.L. (1992). School and family partnerships. *Encyclopedia of educational research* (6th ed.). New York: Macmillan.

Erickson, J.B. (1982). *A profile of community youth organization members, 1980*. Boys Town, NE: Boys Town Center for the Study of Youth Development.

Erickson, J.B. (1996). *Directory of American youth organizations* (2nd rev. ed.). Boys Town, NE: Boys Town.

Erikson, E.H. (1950). *Childhood and society*. New York: W.W. Norton.

Erikson, E.H. (1968). *Identity: Youth and crisis*. New York: W.W. Norton.

Erwin, E.J. (Ed.). (1996). *Putting children first*. Baltimore: Paul Brookes.

Etzel, R. (1988, October). *Children of smokers*. Paper presented at the American Academy of Pediatrics meeting, New Orleans.

Evans, I.M., Cicchelli, T., Cohen, M., & Shapiro, N. (1995). *Staying in school*. Baltimore: Paul Brookes.

Eyler, F.D., Behnke, M., Conlon, M., Woods, N.S., & Wobie, K. (1998). Birth outcome from a prospective, matched study of prenatal crack/cocaine use: I. Interactive and dose effects on health and growth. *Pediatrics*, 101, 229–237.

Eyler, F.D., Behnke, M.L., & Stewart, N.J. (1990). *Issues in identification and follow-up of cocaine-exposed neonates*. Unpublished manuscript, University of Florida, Gainesville.

F

Fagot, B.I., Leinbach, M.D., & O'Boyle, C. (1992). Gender labeling, gender stereotyping, and parenting behaviors. *Developmental Psychology*, 28, 225–230.

Falbo, T., & Poston, D.L. (1993). The academic, personality, and physical outcomes of only children in China. *Child Development*, 64, 18–35.

Famy, C., Streissguth, A.P., & Unis, A.S. (1998). Mental illness in adults with fetal alcohol syndrome or fetal alcohol effects. *The American Journal of Psychiatry*, 155, 552–554.

Fantz, R.L. (1963). Pattern vision in newborn infants. *Science*, 140, 296–297.

Fein, G.G. (1986). Pretend play. In D.G. Orlitz & J.F. Wohlwill (Eds.), *Curiosity, imagination, and play*. Hillsdale, NJ: Erlbaum.

Feiring, C. (1995, March). *The development of romance from 15 to 18 years*. Paper presented at the meeting of the Society for Research in Child Development, Indianapolis.

Feiring, C. (1996). Concepts of romance in 15-year-old adolescents. *Journal of Research on Adolescence*, 6, 181–200.

Feldman, D.H., & Piirto, J. (1995). Parenting talented children. In M.H. Bornstein (Ed.), *Handbook of parenting*. Hillsdale, NJ: Erlbaum.

Feldman, M.A. (1996). The effectiveness of early intervention for children of parents with mental retardation. In M.J. Guralnick (Ed.), *The effectiveness of early intervention*. Baltimore: Paul H. Brooks Pub.

Feldman, R., Greenbaum, C.W., & Yirmiya, N. (1999). Mother-infant affect synchrony as an antecedent of the emergence of self-control. *Developmental Psychology*, 35, 223–231.

Feldman, S.S., & Elliott, G.R. (1990). Progress and promise of research on normal adolescent development. In S.S. Feldman & G. Elliott (Eds.), *At the threshold: The developing adolescent*. Cambridge, MA: Harvard University Press.

Feldman, S.S., & Weinberger, D.A. (1994). Self-restraint as a mediator of family influences on boys' delinquent behavior. A longitudinal study. *Child Development*, 65, 195–211.

Ferguson, D.M., Harwood, L.J., & Shannon, F.T. (1987). Breastfeeding and subsequent social adjustment in 6- to 8-year-old children. *Journal of Child Psychology and Psychiatry*, 28, 378–386.

Field, T. (1990). *Infancy*. Cambridge, MA: Harvard University Press.

Field, T. (1992, September). Stroking babies helps growth, reduces stress. *Brown University Child and Adolescent Behavior Letter*, pp. 1, 6.

Field, T. (1998). Maternal depression effects on infants and early interventions. *Preventive Medicine*, 17, 200–203.

Field, T., Grizzle, N., Scafidi, F., & Schanberg, S. (1996). Massage and relaxation therapies' effects on depressed adolescent mothers. *Adolescence*, 31, 903–911.

Field, T., Sandberg, D., Quetel, T.A., Garcia, R., & Rosario, M. (1985). Effects of ultrasound feedback on pregnancy anxiety, fetal activity, and neonatal outcomes. *Obstetrics and Gynecology*, 66, 525–528.

Field, T., Scafidi, F., & Schanberg, S. (1987). Massage of preterm newborns to improve growth and development. *Pediatric Nursing*, 13, 385–387.

Field, T.M. (1992). Infants and depressed mothers. *Development and Psychopathology*, 4, 49–66.

Field, T.M. (Ed.). (1995). *Touch in early development*. Hillsdale, NJ: Erlbaum.

Fields, M.V., & Spangler, K. (2000). *Let's begin reading right: Developing appropriate beginning literacy*. Columbus, OH: Merrill.

Fields, R. (1998). *Drugs in perspective* (3rd ed.). Dubuque, IA: McGraw-Hill.

Finkel, D., Whitfield, K., & McCue, M. (1995). Genetic and environmental influences on functional age: A twin study. *Journal of Gerontology*, 50B, P104–P113.

Firlik, R. (1996). Can we adapt the philosophies and practices of Reggio Emilia, Italy, for use in American schools? *Young Children*, 51, 217–220.

Fishman, B. (1999, April). *Supporting student searches in inquiry-based learning*. Paper presented at the meeting of the American Educational Research Association, Montreal.

Flavell, J.H., Green, F.L., & Flavell, E.R. (1995, March). Young children's knowledge about thinking. *Monographs of the Society for Research in Child Development*, 60 (Serial No. 143, No. 1).

Flavell, J.H., Miller, P.H., & Miller, S.A. (1993). *Cognitive development* (3rd ed.). Englewood Cliffs, NJ: Prentice Hall.

Forrest, J.D., & Singh, S. (1990). The sexual and reproductive behavior of American women, 1982–1988. *Family Planning Perspectives*, 22, 206–214.

Fowler, J. (1998, August). Class in the classroom. *Plano Profile*, Plano, TX, pp. 50, 55–56.

Fowler, J.W. (1981). *Stages of faith: The psychology of human development and the quest for faith*. New York: HarperCollins.

Fox, N. (1997). *Attachment in infants and adults: A link between the two?* Paper presented at the meeting of the Society for Research in Child Development, Washington, DC.

Fraga, C.C., Motchnik, P.A., Shigenaga, M.K., Helbock, H.J., Jacob, R.A., & Ames, B.N. (1991). Ascorbic acid protects against endogenous oxidative DNA damage in human sperm. *Proceedings of the National Academy of Sciences of the United States*, 88, 11003–11006.

Fraiberg, S. (1959). *The magic years*. New York: Charles Scribner's Sons.

Frankenburg, W.K., Dodds, J., Archer, P., Shapiro, H., & Bresnick, B. (1992). The Denver II: A major revision and restandardization of the Denver Development Screening Test. *Pediatrics*, 89, 91–97.

Freedman, D.S., Dietz, W.H., Srinivasan, S.R., & Berensen, G.S. (1999). The relation of overweight to cardiovascular risks among children and adolescents: The Bogalusa Heart Study. *Pediatrics*.

Freedman, J.L. (1984). Effects of television violence on aggressiveness. Psychological Bulletin, 96, 227–246.

Freppon, P.A., & Dahl, K.L. (1998). Balanced instruction: Insights and considerations. *Reading Research Quarterly*, 33, 240–251.

Freud, A. (1958). *The ego and its mechanisms of defense*. New York: International Universities Press.

Freud, A., & Dann, S. (1951). Instinctual anxiety during puberty. In A. Freud (Ed.), *The ego and its mechanisms of defense*. New York: International Universities Press.

Freud, S. (1917). *A general introduction to psychoanalysis*. New York: Washington Square Press.

Fried, P.A., & Watkinson, B. (1990). 36- and 48-month neurobehavioral follow-up of children prenatally exposed to marijuana, cigarettes, and alcohol. *Developmental and Behavioral Pediatrics*, 11, 49–58.

Friedman, H.S., Tucker, J.S., Schwartz, J.E., Tomlinson-Keasey, C., Martin, L.R., Wingard, D.L., & Criqui, M.H. (1995). Psychosocial and behavioral predictors of longevity: The aging and death of the "Termites." *American Psychologist*, 50, 69–78.

Friedrich, L.K., & Stein, A.H. (1973). Aggressive and prosocial TV programs and the natural behavior of preschool children. *Monographs of the Society for Research in Child Development*, 38 (4, Serial No. 151).

Fugger, E.F., Black, S.H., Keyvanfar, K., & Schulman, J.D. (1998). Birth of normal daughters after Microsort separation and intrauterine insemination, in-vitro fertilization, or intracycloplasmic sperm injection. *Human Reproduction*, 13, 2367–2370.

Furman, W., & Buhrmester, D. (1992). Age and sex differences in perceptions of networks of personal relationships. *Child Development*, 63, 103–115.

Furman, W., & Wehner, E.A. (in press). Adolescent romantic relationships: A developmental perspective. In S. Shulman & W.A. Collins (Eds.), *New directions for child development: Adolescent romantic relationships*. San Francisco, CA: Jossey-Bass.

Furnival, R.A., Street, K.A., & Schunk, J.E. (1999). Too many pediatric trampoline injuries. *Pediatrics*, 103, e57.

Furstenberg, F.F., Jr., & Nord, C.W. (1987). Parenting apart: Patterns of childrearing after marital disruption. *Journal of Marriage and the Family*, 47, 893–904.

Furth, H.G., & Wachs, H. (1975). *Thinking goes to school*. New York: Oxford University Press.

G

Gadpaille, W.J. (1996). *Adolescent suicide*. Washington, DC: American Psychological Association.

Gage, N.L. (1965). Desirable behaviors of teachers. *Urban Education*, 1, 85–96.

Galambos, N.L., & Maggs, J.L. (1989, April). *The after-school ecology of young adolescents and self-reported behavior*. Paper presented at the biennial meeting of the Society for Research in Child Development, Kansas City.

Galambos, N.L., & Tilton-Weaver, L. (1996, March). *The adultoid adolescent: Too much, too soon*. Paper presented at the meeting of the Society for Research on Adolescence, Boston.

Galinsky, E., & David, J. (1988). *The preschool years: Family strategies that work—from experts and parents*. New York: Times Books.

Gallup, G.W., & Bezilla, R. (1992). *The religious life of young Americans*. Princeton, NJ: Gallup Institute.

Galotti, K.M., & Kozberg, S.F. (1996). Adolescents' experience of a life-framing decision. *Journal of Youth and Adolescence*, 25, 3–16.

Galotti, K.M., Kozberg, S.F., & Farmer, M.C. (1990, March). *Gender and developmental differences in adolescents' conceptions of moral reasoning*. Paper presented at the meeting of the Society for Research in Adolescence, Atlanta.

Gandini, L. (1993). Fundamentals of the Reggio Emilia approach to early childhood education. *Young Children*, 49, 4–8.

Ganger, J.B., Baker, A.K., Chawla, S., & Pinker, S. (1999, April). *The contribution of heredity to early vocabulary and grammatical development: A twin study*. Paper presented at the meeting of the Society for Research in Child Development, Albuquerque.

Gao, Y., Elliott, M.E., & Waters, E. (1999, April). *Maternal attachment representations and support for three-year-olds' secure base behavior*. Paper presented at the meeting of the Society for Research in Child Development, Albuquerque.

Garbarino, J. (1976). The ecological correlates of child abuse. The impact of socioeconomic stress on mothers. *Child Development*, 47, 178–185.

Garcia, E.E. (1992). "Hispanic" children: Theoretical, empirical, and related policy issues. *Educational Psychology Review*, 4, 69–93.

Gardner, H. (1983). *Frames of mind*. New York: Basic Books.

Gardner, H. (1993). *Multiple intelligences*. New York: Basic Books.

Gardner, H. (1999). *The disciplined mind*. New York: Simon & Schuster.

Gardner, L.I. (1972). Deprivation dwarfism. *Scientific American*, 227, 76–82.

Garmezy, N. (1985). Stress-resistant children: The search for protective factors. In J.E. Stevenson (Ed.), *Recent research in developmental psychopathology. Journal of Child Psychology and Psychiatry Book Supplement*, 4, 213–233.

Garmezy, N. (1993) Children in poverty: Resilience despite risk. *Psychiatry*, 56, 127–136.

Garrod, A., Smulyan, L., Powers, S.I., & Kilenny, R. (1992). *Adolescent portraits*. Boston: Allyn & Bacon.

Gaylor, E.E., Anders, T.F., & Goodlin-Jones, B.L. (1999, April). *Sleep problems in early childhood: Continuity from 12 months*. Paper presented at the meeting of the Society for Research in Child Development, Albuquerque.

Gelman, R. (1969). Conservation acquisition: A problem of learning to attend to relevant attributes. *Journal of Experimental Child Psychology*, 7, 67–87.

Gelman, R. (1972). Logical capacity of very young children: Number invariance rules. *Child Development*, 43, 75–90.

Gelman, R., & Brenneman, K. (1994). Domain specificity and cultural variation are not inconsistent. In L.A. Hirschfeld & S. Gelman (Eds.), *Mapping the Mind: Domain specificity in cognition and culture*. New York: Cambridge University Press.

Gelman, R., & Williams, E.M. (1998). Enabling constraints for cognitive development and learning. In W. Damon (Ed.), *Handbook of child psychology* (5th ed., Vol. 4). New York: Wiley.

George, C., Main, M., & Kaplan, N. (1984). *Attachment interview with adults*. Unpublished manuscript, U. of California, Berkeley.

Gergen, P.J., Fowler, J.A., Maurer, K.R., Davis, W.W., & Overpeck, M.D. (1998). The burden of environmental tobacco smoke exposure on the respiratory health of children 2 months through 5 years of age in the United States, Third National Health and Nutrition Examination Survey, 1988 to 1994. *Pediatrics*, 101, E8.

Gesell, A. (1934). *An atlas of infant behavior*. New Haven, CT: Yale University Press.

Gesell, A.L. (1928). *Infancy and human growth*. New York: Macmillan.

Gewirtz, J. (1977). Maternal responding and the conditioning of infant crying: Directions of influence within the attachment-acquisition process. In B.C. Etzel, J.M. LeBlanc, & D.M. Baer (Eds.), *New developments in behavioral research*. Hillsdale, NJ: Erlbaum.

Gibbs, J.C. (1993, March). *Inductive discipline's contribution to moral motivation*. Paper presented at the biennial meeting of the Society for Research in Child Development, New Orleans.

Gibbs, J.T. (1989). Black American adolescents. In J.T. Gibbs & L.N. Huang (Eds.), *Children of color*. San Francisco: Jossey-Bass.

Gibson, E.J. (1982). The concept of affordances in development: The renaissance of functionalism. In W. A. Collins (Ed.), *Minnesota Symposium on Child Psychology, Vol. 15*. Hillsdale, NJ: Erlbaum.

Gibson, E.J. (1989). Exploratory behavior in the development of perceiving, acting, and the acquiring of knowledge. *Annual Review of Psychology*, 39. Palo Alto, CA: Annual Reviews.

Gibson, E.J., & Walk, R.D. (1960). The "visual cliff." *Scientific American*, 202, 64–71.

Gibson, J.J. (1966). *The senses considered as perceptual systems*. Boston: Houghton Mifflin.

Gibson, J.J. (1979). *The ecological approach to visual perception*. Boston: Houghton Mifflin.

Gilligan, C. (1982). *In a different voice*. Cambridge, MA: Harvard University Press.

Gilligan, C. (1990). Teaching Shakespeare's sister. In C. Gilligan, N. Lyons, & T. Hammer (Eds.), *Making connections: The relational worlds of adolescent girls at Emma Willard School*. Cambridge, MA: Harvard University Press.

Gilligan, C. (1992, May). *Joining the resistance: Girls' development in adolescence*. Paper presented at the symposium on development and vulnerability in close relationships, Montreal.

Gilligan, C. (1996). The centrality of relationships in psychological development: A puzzle, some evidence, and a theory. In G.G. Noam & K.W. Fischer (Eds.), *Development and vulnerability in close relationships*. Hillsdale, NJ: Erlbaum.

Gilligan, C., & Attanucci, J. (1988). Two moral orientations. In C. Gilligan, J.V. Ward, J.M. Taylor, & B. Bardige (Eds.), *Mapping the moral domain*. Cambridge, MA: Harvard University Press.

Ginzberg, E. (1972). Toward a theory of occupational choice: A restatement. *Vocational Guidance Quarterly*, 20, 169–176.

Gipson, J. (1997, March/April). Girls and computer technology: Barrier or key? *Educational Technology*, 41–43.

Gladden, W.G. (1991). *Planning and building a stepfamily*. Huntington, NY: William Gladden Foundation.

Godwin, P. (1993). *I feel orange today*. New York: Firefly.

Gojdamaschko, N. (1999). Vygotsky. In M.A. Runco & S. Pritzker (Eds.), *Encyclopedia of creativity*. San Diego: Academic Press.

Goldfield, E.C., Kay, B.A., & Warren, W.H. (1993). Infant bouncing: The assembly and tuning of action systems. *Child Development*, 64, 1128–1142.

Goldin-Meadow, S. (1979). The development of language-like communication without a language model. *Science*, 197, 401–403.

Goldman, R. (1964). *Religious thinking from childhood to adolescence*. London: Routledge & Kegan Paul.

Goldsmith, H.H. (1988, August). Does early temperament predict late development? Paper presented at the meeting of the American Psychological Association, Atlanta.

Goldsmith, H.H. (1994, Winter). The behavior-genetic approach to development and experience: Contexts and constraints. *SRCD Newsletter, 1, 6,* 10–11.

Goldsmith, H.H., & Gottesman, I.I. (1981). Origins of variation in behavioral style: A longitudinal study of temperament in young twins. Child Development, 52, 91–103.

Goleman, D. (1995). *Emotional intelligence.* New York: Bantam.

Goleman, D. (1995). *Emotional intelligence.* New York: Basic Books.

Goleman, D., Kaufman, P., & Ray, M. (1993). *The creative spirit.* New York: Plume.

Golombok, S., Cook, R., Bish, A., & Murray, C. (1995). Families created by the new reproductive technologies: Quality of parenting and social and emotional development of children. *Child Development, 66,* 285–298.

Golova, N., Alario, J., Vivier, P.M., Rodriguez, M., & High, P.C. (1999). Literacy promotion for Hispanic families in a primary care setting. *Pediatrics, 103,* 999–997.

Gomel, J.N., Hanson, T.L., & Tinsley, B.J. (1999, April). *Cultural influences on parents' beliefs about the relations between health and eating: A domain alanysis.* Paper presented at the meeting of the Society for Research in Child Development, Albuquerque.

Goodman, R.A., Mercy, J.A., Loya, F., Rosenberg, M.L., Smith, J.C., Allen, N.H., Vargas, L., & Kolts, R. (1986). Alcohol use and interpersonal violence: Alcohol detected in homicide victims. *American Journal of Public Health, 76,* 144–149.

Goodnow, J.J. (1995, March). *Incorporating "culture" into accounts of development.* Paper presented at the meeting of the Society for Research in Child Development, Indianapolis.

Gordon, I. (1978, June). *What does research say about the effects of parent involvement on schooling?* Paper presented at the meeting of the Association for Supervision and Curriculum Development, Washington, DC.

Gorman, K.S., & Pollitt, E. (1996). Does schooling buffer the effects of early risk? *Child Development, 67,* 314–326.

Gottfried, A. E., Gottfried, A. W., & Bathurst, K. (1995). Maternal and dual-earner employment status and parenting. In M.H. Bornstein (Ed.), *Handbook of parenting* (Vol. 2). Hillsdale, NJ: Erlbaum.

Gottfried, A.E., & Gottfried, A.W. (1989, April). *Home environment and children's academic intrinsic motivation: A longitudinal study.* Paper presented at the biennial meeting of the Society for Child Development, Kansas City.

Gottfried, A.E., Gottfried, A.W., & Bathurst K. (1995). Maternal and dual-earner employment status and parenting. In M.H. Bornstein (Ed.), *Handbook of parenting* (Vol. 3). Hillsdale, NJ: Erlbaum.

Gottfried, E., Fleming, J.S., & Gottfried, A. (1999, April). *Parental motivation practices and academic intrinsic motivation: A longitudinal study from childhood through adolesence.* Paper presented at the meeting of the Society for Research in Child Development, Albuquerque.

Gottlieb, G. (1991). Experiential canalization of behavioral development theory. *Developmental Psychology, 27,* 4–13.

Gottlieb, G., Wahlsten, D., & Lickliter, R. (1998). The significance of biology for human development: A developmental psychobiological systems view. In W. Damon (Ed.), *Handbook of child psychology* (5th ed., Vol. 1). New York: Wiley.

Gottman, J.M., & Parker, J.G. (Eds.). (1987). *Conversations of friends.* New York: Cambridge University Press.

Gounin-Decarie, T. (1996). Revisiting Piaget, or the vulnerability of Piaget's infancy theory in the nineties. In G.G. Noam & K.W. Fischer (Eds.), *Development and vulnerability in close relationships.* Hillsdale, NJ: Erlbaum.

Graham, S. (1986, August). *Can attribution theory tell us something about motivation in Blacks?* Paper presented at the meeting of the American Psychological Association, Washington, DC.

Graham, S. (1990). Motivation in Afro-Americans. In G.L. Berry & J.K. Asamen (Eds.), *Black students: Psychosocial issues and academic achievement.* Newbury Park, CA: Sage.

Graham, S. (1992). Most of the subjects were white and middle class. *American Psychologist, 47,* 629–637.

Graham, S., & Harris, K.R. (1994). The effects of whole language on children's writing: A review of the literature. *Educational Psychologist, 29,* 187–192.

Grant, J. (1996). *The state of the world's children.* New York: UNICEF and Oxford University Press.

Grant, J. (1997). *State of the world's children.* New York: UNICEF and Oxford University Press.

Grant, J.P. (1993). *The state of the world's children.* New York: UNICEF and Oxford University Press.

Grant, J.P. (1996). *The state of the world's children.* New York: UNICEF and Oxford University Press.

Green, P. (1995, March). *Sesame Street: More than a television show.* Paper presented at the meeting of the Society for Research in Child Development, Indianapolis.

Greenberg, B.S., & Brand, J.E. (1994). Minorities and the mass media. In J. Bryant & D. Zillman (Eds.), *Media effects.* Hillsdale, NJ: Erlbaum.

Greenberger, E., & Steinberg, L. (1981). *Project for the study of adolescent work: Final report.* Report prepared for the National Institute of Education, U.S. Department of Education, Washington, DC.

Greenberger, E., & Steinberg, L. (1986). *When teenagers work: The psychological social costs of adolescent employment.* New York: Basic Books.

Greene, B. (1988, May). The children's hour. *Esquire Magazine,* pp. 47–49.

Greenfield, P.M., & Suzuki, L.K. (1998). Culture and human development: Implications for parenting, education, pediatrics, and mental health. In W. Damon (Ed.), *Handbook of child psychology* (5th ed., Vol. 4). New York: Wiley.

Greeno, J.G., Collins, A.M., & Resnick, L. (1996). Cognition and learning. In D.C. Berliner & R.C. Chafee (Eds.), *Handbook of educational psychology.* New York: Macmillan.

Greenough, W.T. (1997, April 21). Commentary in article, "Politics of biology." *U.S. News & World Report,* p. 79.

Greenough, W.T. (1999, April). *Experience, brain development, and links to mental retardation.* Paper presented at the meeting of the Society for Research in Child Development, Albuquerque.

Greenough, W.T., Wallace, C.S., Alcantara, A.A., Anderson, B.J., Hawrylak, R.B., Sirevaag, A.M., Weiler, I.J., & Withers, G.S. (1997, August). *The development of the brain.* Paper presented at the meeting of the American Psychological Association, Chicago.

Grodstein, F., Goldman, M.B., & Cramer, R.L. (1993). Relation of female infertility to consumption of caffeinated beverages. *American Journal of Epidemiology, 137,* 1353–1360.

Gross, R.T. (1984). Patterns of maturation: Their effects on behavior and development. In M.D. Levine & P. Satz (Eds.), *Middle childhood: Development and dysfunction.* Baltimore: University Park Press.

Grossmann, K., Grossmann, K.E., Spangler, G., Suess, G., & Unzner, L. (1985). Maternal sensitivity and newborns' orientation responses as related to quality of attachment in Northern Germany. In I. Bretherton & E. Waters (Eds.), Growing points of attachment theory and research. *Monographs of the Society for Research in Child Development, 50* (1–2, Serial No. 209).

Grotevant, H.D., & Durrett, M.E. (1980). Occupational knowledge and career development in adolescence. *Journal of Vocational Behavior, 17,* 171–182.

Grunwald, L., Goldberg, J., Berstein, S., & Hollister, A. (1993, July). The amazing mind of babies. *Life,* p. 52.

Gruskin, E. (1994, February). *A review of research on self-identified gay, lesbian, and bisexual youth from 1970–1993.* Paper presented at the meeting of the Society for Research on Adolescence, San Diego.

Guajardo, N.R., & Turley-Ames, K.J. (1999, April). *Social cognitive development: Theory of mind and counterfactual thinking.* Paper presented at the meeting of the Society for Research in Child Development, Albuquerque.

Guilford, J.P. (1967). *The structure of intellect.* New York: McGraw-Hill.

Gunnar, M.R., Malone, S., & Fisch, R.O. (1987). The psychobiology of stress and coping in the human neonate: Studies of the adrenocortical activity in response to stress in the first week of life. In T. Field, P. McCabe, & N. Scheiderman (Eds.), *Stress and coping.* Hillsdale, NJ: Erlbaum.

Gur, R.C., Mozley, L.H., Mozley, P.D., Resnick, S.M., Karp, J.S., Alavi, A., Arnold, S.E., & Gur, R.E. (1995). Sex differences in regional cerebral glucose metabolism during a resting state. *Science, 267,* 528–531.

Gustafson, G.E., Green, J.A., & Kalinowski, L.L. (1993, March). *The development of communicative skills: Infants' cries and vocalizations in social context.* Paper presented at the biennial meeting of the Society for Research in Child Development, New Orleans.

Gutherie, G.M., Masangkay, Z., & Gutherie, H.A. (1976). Behavior, malnutrition, and mental development. *Journal of Cross-Cultural Psychology, 7,* 169–180.

Guttentag, M., & Bray, H. (1976). *Undoing sex stereotypes: Research and resources for educators.* Burr Ridge, IL: McGraw-Hill.

H

Hack, M.H., Klein, N.K., & Taylor, H.G. (1995, Spring). Long-term developmental outcomes of low birth weight infants. *Future of Children, 5*(1), 176–196.

Haertsch, M., Campbell, E., & Sanson-Fisher, R. (1999). What is recommended for healthy women during pregnancy? *Birth, 26,* 24–30.

Hafner, A., Ingels, S., Schnieder, B., & Stevenson, D. (1990). *A profile of the American eighth grader: NELS: 88. Student descriptive summary.* Washington, DC: U.S. Government Printing Office.

Hahn, W.K. (1987). Cerebral lateralization of function: From infancy through childhood. *Psychological Bulletin, 101,* 376–392.

Haight, W.L., & Miller, P.J., (1993). *Pretending at Home.* Albany: State University of New York Press.

Haith, M.H. (1991, April). *Setting a path for the '90s: Some goals and challenges in infant-sensory and perceptual development.* Paper presented at the Society for Research in Child Development, Seattle.

Haith, M.M. (1993). Preparing for the 21st century: Some goals and challenges for studies of infant sensory and perceptual development. *Developmental Review, 13,* 354–371.

Haith, M.M., & Benson, J.B. (1998). Infant cognition. In W. Damon (Ed.), *Handbook of child psychology* (5th ed., Vol. 2). New York: Wiley.

Haith, M.M., Hazen, C., & Goodman, G.S. (1988). Expectation and anticipation of dynamic visual events by 3.5 month old babies. *Child Development, 59,* 467–479.

Hakim-Larson, J.A. (1995, March). *Affective defaults: Temperament, goals, rules, and values.* Paper presented at the meeting of the Society for Research in Child Development, Indianapolis.

Hakuta, K., & Garcia, E.E. (1989). Bilingualism and education. *American Psychologist, 44,* 374–379.

Hall, G.S. (1904). *Adolescence* (Vols. 1 & 2). Englewood Cliffs, NJ: Prentice Hall.

Hallahan, D.P., & Kaufmann, J.M. (1997). *Exceptional learners* (7th ed.). Boston: Allyn & Bacon.

Halonen, J., & Santrock, J.W. (1999). *Psychology: Contexts and applications.* Boston: McGraw-Hill.

Halonen, J., & Santrock, J.W. (1999). *Psychology: The contexts of behavior* (3rd ed.). Madison, WI: Brown & Benchmark.

Halpern, L.F., & Brand, K.L. (1999, April). *The role of temperament in children's emotion reactions and coping responses to stress.* Paper presented at the meeting of the Society for Research in Child Development, Albuquerque.

Hamburg, B.A. (1990). *Life skills training: Preventive interventions for young adolescents.* Washington, DC: Carnegie Council on Adolescent Development.

Hamburg, D.A. (1993). The opportunities of early adolescence. In R. Takanishi (Ed.), *Adolescence in the 1990s.* New York: Teachers College Press.

Hamburg, D.A. (1997). Meeting the essential requirements for healthy adolescent development in a transforming world. In R. Takanishi & D. Hamburg (Eds.), *Preparing adolescents for the 21st century.* New York: Cambridge University Press.

Hamburg, D.A., Millstein, S.G., Mortimer, A.M., Nightingale, E.O., & Petersen, A.C. (1993). Adolescent health promotion in the twenty-first century: Current frontiers and future directions. In S.G. Millstein, A.C. Petersen, & E.O. Nightingale (Eds.), *Promoting the health of adolescents.* New York: Oxford University Press.

Hammond, W.R. (1993, August). Participant in open forum with the APA Commission on Youth and Violence, meeting of the American Psychological Association, Washington, DC.

Hans, S. (1989, April). *Infant behavioral effects of prenatal exposure to methadone.* Paper presented at the biennial meeting of the Society for Research in Child Development, Kansas City.

Hansen, D. (1996, March). *Adolescent employment and psychosocial outcomes: A comparison of two employment contexts.* Paper presented at the meeting of the Society for Research on Adolescence, Boston.

Harkness, S., & Super, E.M. (1995). Culture and parenting, In M.H. Bornstein (Ed.), *Handbook of parenting* (Vol. 3). Hillsdale, NJ: Erlbaum.

Harlow, H.F., & Zimmerman, R.R. (1959). Affectional responses in the infant monkey. *Science, 130,* 421–432.

Harris, G., Thomas, A., & Booth, D.A. (1990). Development of salt taste in infancy. *Developmental Psychology, 26,* 534–538.

Harris, J.R. (1998). *The nurture assumption: Why children turn out the way they do: Parents matter less than you think and peers matter more.* New York: Free Press.

Harris, L. (1987, September 3). The latchkey child phenomena. *Dallas Morning News,* pp. 1A, 10A.

Hart, B., & Risley, T.R. (1995). *Meaningful differences.* Baltimore, MD: Paul Brookes.

Hart, C.H., Charlesworth, R., Burts, D.C., & DeWolf, M. (1993, March). *The relationship of attendance in developmentally appropriate or inappropriate kindergarten classrooms to first-grade behavior.* Paper presented at the biennial meeting of the Society for Research in Child Development, New Orleans.

Harter, S. (1982). The Perceived Competence Scale for Children. *Child Development, 53,* 87–97.

Harter, S. (1985). *Self-Perception Profile for Children.* Denver: University of Denver, Department of Psychology.

Harter, S. (1989). *Self-Perception Profile for Adolescents.* Denver: University of Denver.

Harter, S. (1990). Processes underlying adolescent self-concept formation. In R. Montemayor, G.R. Adams, & R.P. Gulotta (Eds.), *From childhood to adolescence: A transitional period?* Newbury Park, CA: Sage.

Harter, S., & Marold, D.B. (1992). Psychosocial risk factors contributing to adolescent suicide ideation. In G.

Noam & S. Borst (Eds.), *Child and adolescent suicide.* San Francisco: Jossey-Bass.

Harter, S., Alexander, P.C., & Neimeyer, R.A. (1988). Long-term effects of incestuous child abuse in college women. Social adjustment, social cognition, and family characteristics. *Journal of Consulting and Clinical Psychology, 56,* 5–8.

Harter, S., Waters, F., & Whitesell, N. (1996, March). *False self behavior and lack of voice among adolescent males and females.* Paper presented at the meeting of the Society for Research on Adolescence, Boston.

Hartmann, D.P., & George, T.P. (1999). Design, measurement, and analysis in developmental research. In M.H. Bornstein & M.E. Lamb (Eds.), *Developmental psychology: an advanced textbook* (4th ed.). Mahwah, NJ: Erlbaum.

Hartshorne, H., & May, M.S. (1928–1930). *Moral studies in the nature of character: Studies in the nature of character.* New York: Macmillan.

Hartup, W.W. (1983). Peer relations. In P.H. Mussen (Ed.), *Handbook of child psychology* (4th ed., Vol. 4). New York Wiley.

Hartup, W.W. (1996). The company they keep: Friendships and their development significance. *Child Development, 67,* 1–13.

Hartup, W.W., & Laursen, B. (1999). Relationships as developmental contexts: Retrospective themes and contemporary issues. In W. Andrew Collins & B. Laursen (Eds.), *Relationships as developmental contexts.* Mahwah, NJ: Erlbaum.

Hartup, W.W., & Stevens, N. (1997). Friendships and adaptation in the life course. *Psychological Bulletin, 121,* 355–370.

Harvey, E. (1999). Short-term and long-term effects of parental employment on children of the National Longitudinal Survey of Youth. *Developmental Psychology, 35,* 445–454.

Hawkins, J., Pea, R.D., Glick, J., & Scribner, S. (1984). "Merds that laugh don't like mushrooms." Evidence for deductive reasoning by preschoolers. *Developmental Psychology, 20,* 584–594.

Hawkins, J.A., & Berndt, T.J. (1985, April). *Adjustment following the transition to junior high school.* Paper presented at the biennial meeting of the Society for Research in Child Development, Toronto.

Hayes, C. (Ed.). (1987). *Risking the future: Adolescent sexuality, pregnancy, and childbearing* (Vol. 1). Washington, DC: National Academy Press.

Hayman, L.L., Mahon, M.M., & Turner, J.R. (1999). *Health behavior in childhood and adolescence.* Mahwah, NJ: Erlbaum.

Hazen, B.S. (1991). *Even if I did something awful.* New York: Atheneum.

Helping a teenager grow up gradually. (1983, July 8). *Boston Globe.*

Helson, R., Elliot, T., & Leigh, J. (1989). Adolescent antecedents of women's work patterns. In D. Stern & D. Eichorn (Eds.), *Adolescence and work.* Hillsdale, NJ: Erlbaum.

Henderson, J.M.T., & France, K.G. (1999, April). *Sleep patterns in the first year of life: Developmental pathways.* Paper presented at the meeting of the Society for Research in Child Development, Albuquerque.

Henderson, K.A., & Zivian, M.T. (1995, March). *The development of gender differences in adolescent body image.* Paper presented at the meeting of the Society for Research in Child Development, Indianapolis.

Henderson, V.L., & Dweck, C.S. (1990). Motivation and achievement. In S.S. Feldman & G.R. Elliott (Eds.), *At the threshold: The developing adolescent.* Cambridge, MA: Harvard University Press.

Henninger, M.L. (1999). *Teaching young children.* Columbus, OH: Merrill.

Hernstein, R.J., & Murray, C. (1994). *The bell curve: Intelligence and class structure in modern life.* New York: Free Press.

Hess, R.D., Holloway, S.D., Dicson, W.P., & Price, G.G. (1984). Maternal variables as predictors of children's school readiness and later achievement in vocabulary and mathematics in the sixth grade. *Child Development, 55,* 1902–1912.

Hetherington, E.M. (1989). Coping with family transitions: Winners, losers, and survivors. *Child Development, 60,* 1–14.

Hetherington, E.M. (1993). An overview of the Virginia Longitudinal Study of Divorce and Remarriage with a focus on early adolescence. *Journal of Family Psychology, 7,* 39–56.

Hetherington, E.M. (1995, March). *The changing American family and the well-being of children.* Paper presented at the meeting of the Society for Research in Child Development, Indianapolis.

Hetherington, E.M. (1999). *Coping with divorce, single parenting, and remarriage.* Mahwah, NJ: Erlbaum.

Hetherington, E.M. (1999). *Should we stay together for the sake of the children?* Unpublished manuscript, Dept. of Psychology, U. of Virginia, Charlottesville, VA.

Hetherington, E.M. (1999). Social capital and the development of youth from non-divorced, divorced, and remarried families. In W.A. Collins & B. Laursen (Eds.), *Relationships as developmental contexts.* Mahwah, NJ: Erlbaum.

Hetherington, E.M., & Clingempeel, W.G. (1992). Coping with marital transitions: A family systems perspective. *Monographs of the Society for Research in Child Development, 57*(2–3, Serial No. 227).

Hetherington, E.M., & Jodl, K.M. (1994). Stepfamilies as settings for child development. In A. Booth & J. Dunn. (Eds.), *Stepfamilies: Who benefits? Who does not?* Hillsdale, NJ: Erlbaum.

Hetherington, E.M., Bridges, M., & Insabella, G.M. (1998). What matters? What does not? Five perspectives on the association between marital transitions and children's adjustment. *American Psychologist, 53,* 167–184.

Hetherington, E.M., Cox, M., & Cox, R. (1982). Effects of divorce on children and parents. In M.E. Lamb (Ed.), *Nontraditional families.* Hillsdale, NJ: Erlbaum.

Heuwinkel, M.K. (1996). New ways of learning 5 New ways of teaching. *Childhood Education, 72,* 27–31.

Heward, W. (1996). *Exceptional children* (5th ed.). Upper Saddle River, NJ: Prentice-Hall.

Heward, W.L. (2000). *Exceptional children.* Columbus, OH: Merrill.

Higgins, A., Power, C., & Kohlberg, L. (1983, April). *Moral atmosphere and moral judgment.* Paper presented at the biennial meeting of the Society for Research in Child Development, Detroit.

Hightower, E. (1990). Adolescent interpersonal and familial precursors of positive mental health at midlife. *Journal of Youth and Adolescence, 19,* 257–275.

Hill, C.R., & Stafford, F.P. (1980). Parental care of children: Time diary estimate of quantity, predictability, and variety. *Journal of Human Resources, 15,* 219–239.

Hill, J.O., & Trowbridge, F.L. (1998). Childhood obesity: Future directions and research priorities. *Pediatrics, 101,* 570-574.

Hillebrand, V., Phenice, A., & Hines, R.P. (2000). *Knowing and serving diverse families.* Columbus, OH: Merrill.

Hinde, R.A. (1992). Developmental psychology in the context of other behavioral sciences. *Developmental Psychology, 28,* 1018–1029.

Hirsch, B.J., & Rapkin, B.D. (1987). The transition to junior high school: A longitudinal study of self-esteem, psychological symptomatology, school life, and social support. *Child Development, 58,* 1235–1243.

Hirsch-Pasek, K., Hyson, M., Rescorla, L., & Cone, J. (1989, April). *Hurrying children: How does it affect their academic, social, creative, and emotional development?* Paper presented at the Society for Research in Child Development meeting, Kansas City.

Hochschild, A.R. (1983). *The managed heart: Commercialization of feelings.* Berkeley, University of California Press.

Hoff-Ginsberg, E., & Lerner, S. (1999, April). *The nature of vocabulary differences related to socioeconomic status at two and four years.* Paper presented at the meeting of the Society for Research in Child Development, Albuquerque.

Hoff-Ginsburg, E., & Tardif, T. (1995). Socioeconomic status and parenting. In M.H. Bornstein (Ed.), *Handbook of parenting* (Vol. 1). Hillsdale, NJ: Erlbaum.

Hoffman, L.W. (1989). Effects of maternal employment in two-parent families. *American Psychologist, 44,* 283–293.

Hoffman, L.W., & Youngblade, L.M. (1999). *Mothers at work: Effects on children's well-being.* New York: Cambridge.

Hoffman, M.L. (1970). Moral development. In P.H. Mussen (Ed.), *Manual of child psychology* (3rd ed., Vol. 2). New York: Wiley.

Hogan, D.M., & Tudge, J. (1999). Implications of Vygotsky's theory for peer learning. In A. M. O'Donnell & A. King (Eds.), *Cognitive perspectives on peer learning.* Mahwah, NJ: Erbaum.

Hohnen, B., & Stevenson, J. (1999). The structure of genetic influences on general cognitive language, phonological, and reading abilities. *Developmental Psychology, 35,* 590–603.

Holland, J.L. (1987). Current status of Holland's theory of careers: Another perspective. *Career Development Quarterly, 36,* 24–30.

Hollins, E.R., & Oliver, E.I. (1999). *Pathways to success in school.* Mahwah, NJ: Erlbaum.

Holmbeck, G.N. (1996). A model of family relational transformations during the transition to adolescence: Parent-adolescent conflict and adaptation. In J.A. Graber, J. Brooks-Gunn, & A.C. Petersen (Eds.), *Transitions through adolescence.* Hillsdale, NJ: Erlbaum.

Holmbeck, G.N., Paikoff, R.L., & Brooks-Gunn, J. (1995). Parenting adolescents. In M.H. Bornstein (Ed.), *Children and parenting* (Vol. 1). Hillsdale, NJ: Erlbaum.

Holtzman, W.H. (Ed.). (1992). *School of the future.* Austin, TX: American Psychological Association and Hogg Foundation for Mental Health.

Hones, D.F., & Cha, S.C. (1999). *Educating new Americans.* Mahwah, NJ: Erlbaum.

Honig, A.S., & Wittmer, D.S. (1996). Helping children become more prosocial: Ideas for classrooms, families, schools, and communities. *Young Children, 51,* 62–70.

Hoot, J.L., & Robertson, G. (1994). Creating safer environments in the home, school, and community. *Childhood Education, 71,* 259.

Horowitz, F.D., & O'Brien, M. (1989). In the interest of the nation: A reflective essay on the state of knowledge and the challenges before us. *American Psychologist, 44,* 441–445.

Hotchner, T. (1997). *Pregnancy and childbirth.* New York: Avon.

Howes, C. (1988, April). *Can the age of entry and the quality of infant child care predict behaviors in kindergarten?* Paper presented at the International Conference on Infant Studies, Washington, DC.

Howes, C., & Clements, D. (1994). Adult socialization of children's play in child care. In H. Goelman (Ed.), *Play and child care.* Albany: State University of New York Press.

Howes, C., Hamilton, C.E., Matheson, C.C. (1994). Children's relationships with peers: Differential associations with aspects of the teacher-child relationship. *Child Development 65,* 253–63.

Howes, C., Rodning, C., Galluzzo, D.C., Myers, L. (1988). Attachment and child care: Relationships with mother and caregiver. *Early Childhood Research Quarterly 3* (4), 403–416.

Huebner, A.M., Garrod, A.C., & Snarey, J. (1990, March). *Moral development in Tibetan Buddhist monks: A cross-cultural study of adolescents and young adults in Nepal.* Paper presented at the meeting of the Society for Research in Adolescence, Atlanta.

Huesmann, L.R. (1986). Psychological processes promoting the relation between exposure to media violence and aggressive behavior by the viewer. *Journal of Social Issues, 42,* 125–139.

Huesmann, L.R., Eron, L.D., Klein, R., Brice, P., & Fischer, P. (1983). Mitigating the imitation of aggressive behaviors by changing children's attitudes about media violence. *Journal of Personality and Social Psychology, 44,* 899–910.

Hunt, C.E. (1999, May). *Sudden infant death syndrome (SIDS) in families: Risk factors for recurrence.* Paper presented at the meeting of the Society for Pediatric Research, San Francisco.

Hunt, M. (1974). *Sexual behavior in the 1970s.* Chicago: Playboy Press.

Hurt, H., Malmud, E., Brodsky, N.L., & Giannetta, J.M. (1999, May). *What happens when the child with in utero cocaine-exposure (COC) goes to school?* Paper presented at the meeting of the Society for Pediatric Research, San Francisco.

Huston, A. (1999, August). *Employment interventions for parents in poverty: How do children fare?* Paper presented at the meeting of the Society for Research in Child Development, Boston.

Huston, A.C. (1983). Sex-typing. In P.H. Mussen (Ed.), *Handbook of child psychology* (4th ed., Vol. 4). New York: Wiley.

Huston, A.C., McLoyd, V.C., & Coll, C.G. (1994). Children and poverty: issues in contemporary research. *Child Development, 65,* 275–282.

Huston, A.C., Seigle, J., & Bremer, M. (1983, April). *Family environment and television use by preschool children.* Paper presented at the Society for Research in Child Development meeting, Detroit.

Hyde, J.S. (1993). Meta-analysis and the psychology of women. In F.L. Denmark & M.A. Paludi (Eds.), *Handbook on the psychology of women.* Westport, CT: Greenwood.

Hyde, J.S., & Plant, E.A. (1995). Magnitude of psychological gender differences: Another side of the story. *American Psychologist, 50,* 159–161.

I

Idol, L. (1997). Key questions related to building collaborative and inclusive schools. *Journal of Learning Disabilities, 30,* 384–394.

Infante-Rivard, C., Fernandez, A., Gauthier, R., David, M., & Rivard, G.E. (1993). Fetal loss associated with caffeine intake before and during pregnancy. *Journal of the American Medical Association, 270,* 2940–2943.

Ingersoll, E.W., & Thoman, E.B. (1999). Sleep/wake states of preterm infants: Stability, developmental change, diurnal variation, and relation with caregiving activity. *Child Development, 70,* 1–10.

Inoff-Germain, G., Arnold, G.S., Nottelmann, E.D., Susman, E.J., Cutler, G.B., & Chrousos, G.P. (1988). Relations between hormone levels and observational measures of aggressive behavior of young adolescents in family interactions. *Developmental Psychology, 24,* 124–139.

Intons-Peterson, M. (1996). Memory aids. In D. Hermann, C. McEvoy, C. Hertzog, P. Hertel, & M. Johnson (Eds.), *Basic and applied memory research* (Vol. 2). Hillsdale, NJ: Erlbaum.

Irwin, C.E. (1993). The adolescent, health, and society: From the perspective of the physician. In S.G. Millstein, A.C. Petersen, & E.O. Nightingale (Eds.), *Promoting the health of adolescents.* New York: Oxford University Press.

Izard, C.E. (1982). *Measuring emotions in infants and young children.* New York: Cambridge University Press.

J

Jacobs, J.E., & Potenza, M. (1990, March). *The use of decision-making strategies in late adolescence.* Paper presented at the meeting of the Society for Research in Adolescence, Atlanta.

Jacobs, J.K., Garnier, H.E., & Weisner, T. (1996, March). *The impact of family life on the process of dropping out of high school.* Paper presented at the meeting of the Society for Research on Adolescence, Boston.

Jacobson, J.L., Jacobson, S.W., Fein, G.G., Schwartz, P.M., & Dowler, J. (1984). Prenatal exposure to an environmental toxin: A test of the multiple-effects model. *Developmental Psychology, 20,* 523–532.

Jacobson, J.L., Jacobson, S.W., Padgett, R.J., Brumitt, G.A., & Billings, R.L. (1992). Effects of prenatal PCB exposure on cognitive processing efficiency and sustained attention. *Developmental Psychology, 28,* 297–306.

Jalongo, M.R., & Isenberg, J.P. (2000). *Exploring your role: A practitioner introduction to early childhood education.* Columbus, OH: Merrill.

James, W. (1890/1950). *The principles of psychology.* New York: Dover.

Jaquay, C.M., Williams, A.M., & Bernieri, F.J. (1999, April). *The development of mother-child interactional synchrony.* Paper presented at the meeting of the Society for Research in Child Development, Albuquerque.

Jeans, P.C., Smith, M.B., & Stearns, G. (1955). Incidence of prematurity in relation to maternal nutrition. *Journal of the American Dietary Association, 31,* 576–581.

Jensen, R.A. (1969). How much can we boost IQ and scholastic achievement? *Harvard Educational Review, 39,* 1–123.

Ji, B.T., Shu, X.O., Linet, M.S., Zheng, W., Wacholde, S., Gao, Y.T., Ying, D.M., & Jin, F. (1997). Paternal cigarette smoking and the risk of childhood cancer among offspring of nonsmoking mothers. *Journal of the National Cancer Institute, 89,* 238–244.

Jiao, S., Ji, G., & Jing, Q. (1996). Cognitive development of Chinese urban only children and children with siblings. *Child Development, 67,* 387–395.

Johnson, D.D.L., Swank, P., Howie, V.M., Baldwin, C., & Owen, M. (1993, March). *Tobacco smoke in the home and child intelligence.* Paper presented at the biennial meeting of the Society for Research in Child Development, New Orleans.

Johnson, D.W. (1990). *Teaching out: Interpersonal effectiveness and self-actualization.* Upper Saddle River, NJ: Prentice-Hall.

Johnson, J.S., & Newport, E.L. (1989). Critical period effects in second language learning: The influence of maturational state on the acquisition of English as a second language. *Cognitive Psychology, 21,* 60–99.

Johnson, K., Strader, T., Berbaum, M., Bryant, D., Bucholtz, G., Collins, D., & Noe, T. (1996). Reducing alcohol and other drug use by strengthening community, family, and youth resiliency. *Journal of Adolescent Research, 11,* 36–37.

Johnson, M.H. (1998). The neural basis of cognitive development. In W. Damon (Ed.), *Handbook of child psychology* (5th ed., Vol. 2). New York: Wiley.

Johnson, M.H. (1999). Developmental neuroscience. In M.H. Bornstein & M.E. Lamb (Eds.), *Developmental psychology: An advanced textbook* (4th ed.). Mahwah, NJ: Erlbaum.

Johnson, M.K., Beebe, T., Mortimer, J.T., & Snyder, M. (1998). Volunteerism in adolescence: A process perspective. *Journal of Research on Adolescence, 8,* 309–332.

John-Steiner, V., & Mahn, H. (1996). Sociocultural approaches to learning and development: A Vygotskian framework. *Educational Psychologist, 31,* 191–206.

Johnston, L., Bachman, J., & O'Malley, P. (1990). *Monitoring the future.* Ann Arbor: University of Michigan, Institute for Social Research.

Johnston, L., O'Malley, P.M., & Bachman, J.G. (1997, December). *Report of Monitoring the Future Project.* Ann Arbor: Institute for Social Research, University of Michigan.

Johnston, L.D., O'Malley, P.M., & Bachman, J.G. (1992, January 25). *Most forms of drug use decline among American high school and college students.* News release, Institute for Social Research, University of Michigan, Ann Arbor.

Johnston, L.D., O'Malley, P.M., & Bachman, J.G. (1995). *National survey results on drug use from the Monitoring the Future Study, Vol. I: Secondary school students.* Ann Arbor, MI: Institute for Social Research, University of Michigan.

Jones, B.F., Rasmussen, C.M., & Moffit, M.C. (1997). *Real-life problem solving.* Washington, DC: American Psychological Association.

Jones, E.R., Forrest, J.D., Goldman, N., Henshaw, S.K., Lincoln, R., Rosoff, J.I., Westoff, C.G., & Wulf, D. (1985). Teenage pregnancy in developed countries: Determinants and policy implications. *Family Planning Perspectives, 17,* 53–63.

Jones, J.M. (1993, August). *Racism and civil rights: Right problem, wrong solution.* Paper presented at the meeting of the American Psychological Association, Toronto.

Jones, J.M. (1994). The African American: A duality dilemma? In W.J. Lonner & R. Malpass (Eds.), *Psychology and culture.* Needham Heights, MA: Allyn & Bacon.

Jones, L. (1984). White-black achievement differences: The narrowing gap. *American Psychologist, 39,* 1207–1213.

Jones, L. (1996). *HIV/AIDS: What to do about it.* Pacific Grove, CA: Brooks/Cole.

Jones, M.C. (1965). Psychological correlates of somatic development. *Child Development, 36,* 899–911.

Joseph, C.L.M. (1989). Identification of factors associated with delayed antenatal care. *Journal of the American Medical Association, 81,* 57–63.

Jozefowicz, D.M., Barber, B.L., & Mollasis, C. (1994, February). *Relations between maternal and adolescent values and beliefs: Sex differences and implications for occupational choice.* Paper presented at the meeting of the Society for Research on Adolescence, San Diego.

Juang, L.P., & Nyuyen, H.H. (1997, April). *Autonomy and connectedness: Predictors of adjustment in Vietnamese adolescents.* Paper presented at the meeting of the Society for Research in Child Development, Washington, DC.

K

Kagan, J. (1984). *The nature of the child.* New York: Basic Books.

Kagan, J. (1987). Perspectives on infancy. In J.D. Osofsky (Ed.), *Handbook on infant development* (2nd ed.). New York: Wiley.

Kagan, J. (1992). Yesterday's promises, tomorrow's promises. *Developmental Psychology, 28,* 990–997.

Kagan, J. (1998). The biology of the child. In W. Damon (Ed.), *Handbook of child psychology* (5th ed., Vol. 3). New York: Wiley.

Kagan, J., & Snidman, N. (1991). Temperamental factors in human development. *American Psychologist, 46,* 856–862.

Kagan, J., Kearsley, R.B., & Zelazo, P.R. (1978). *Infancy.* Cambridge, MA: Harvard University Press.

Kagitcibasi, C. (1996). *Human development across cultures.* Hillsdale, NJ: Erlbaum.

Kail, R., & Pellegrino, J.W. (1985). *Human intelligence.* New York: W.H. Freeman.

Kalichman, S.C. (1996). *Answering your questions about AIDS.* Washington, DC: American Psychological Association.

Kamerman, S.B. (1989). Child care, women, work, and the family: An international overview of child-care services and related policies. In J.S. Lande, S. Scarr, & N. Gunzenhauser (Eds.), *Caring for children: Challenge to America.* Hillsdale, NJ: Erlbaum.

Kamii, C. (1985). *Young children reinvent arithmetic: Implications of Piaget's theory.* New York: Teachers College Press.

Kamii, C. (1989). *Young children continue to reinvent arithmetic.* New York: Teachers College Press.

Kamler, J., Irwin, C.E., Stone, G.C., & Millstein, S.G. (1987). *Optimistic bias in adolescent hemophiliacs.* Paper presented at the meeting of the Society for Research in Pediatrics, Anaheim, CA.

Kandel, D.B. (1974). The role of parents and peers in marijuana use. *Journal of Social Issues, 30,* 107–135.

Kantrowitz, B. (1991, Summer). The good, the bad, and the difference. *Newsweek,* pp. 48–50.

Katz, L., & Chard, S. (1989). *Engaging the minds of young children: The project approach.* Norwood, NJ: Ablex.

Katz, P. (1987, August). *Children and social issues.* Paper presented at the meeting of the American Psychological Association, New York.

Keating, D.P. (1990) Adolescent thinking. In S.S. Feldman & G.R. Elliott (Eds.), *At the threshold: The developing adolescent.* Cambridge, MA: Harvard University Press.

Keener, D.C., & Boykin, K.A. (1996, March). *Parental control, autonomy, and ego development.* Paper presented at the meeting of the Society for Research on Adolescence, Boston.

Kelder, S.H., Perry, C.L., Peters, R.J., Lytle, L.L., & Klepp, K. (1995). Gender differences in the class of 1989 study: The school component of the Minnesota Heart Health Program. *Journal of Health Education, 26,* S36–S44.

Keller, A., Ford, L., & Meacham, J. (1978). Dimensions of self-concept in preschool children. *Developmental Psychology, 14,* 483–489.

Kellogg, R. (1970). *Understanding children's art: Readings in developmental psychology today.* Del Mar, CA: CRM.

Kennedy, A.M. (1987, June). Teen pregnancy: An issue for schools. *Phi Delta Kappan,* pp. 728–736.

Kennell, J.H., & McGrath, S.K. (1999). Commentary: Practical and humanistic lessons from the third world for perinatal caregivers everywhere. *Birth, 26,* 9–10.

Kessen, W., Haith, M.M., & Salapatek, P. (1970). Human infancy. In P.H. Mussen (Ed.), *Manual of child psychology* (3rd ed., Vol. 1). New York: Wiley.

Kiewra, K.A. (1989). A review of note-taking: The encoding-storage paradigm and beyond. *Educational Psychology Review, 1,* 147–172.

Kimmel, A. (1996). *Ethical issues in behavioral research.* Cambridge, MA: Blackwell.

King, N. (1982). School uses of materials traditionally associated with children's play. *Theory and Research in Social Education, 10,* 17–27.

Kinsey, A.C., Pomeroy, W.B., & Martin, E.E. (1948). *Sexual behavior in the human male.* Philadelphia: W.B. Saunders.

Kisilevsky, B.S. (1995). The influence stimulus and subject variables on human fetal responses to sound and vibration. In J.-P. Lecaunet, W.P. Fifer, M.A. Krasnegor, & W.P. Smotherman (Eds.), *Fetal development.* Hillsdale, NJ: Erlbaum.

Klaus, M., & Kennell, H.H. (1976). *Maternal-infant bonding.* St. Louis: Mosby.

Klaus, M.H., Kennell, J.H., & Klaus, P.H. (1993). *Mothering the mother.* Reading, MA: Addison-Wesley.

Kleinman, R.E., Murphy, J.M., Little, M., Pagano, M., Wehler, C.A., Regal, K., & Jellinek, M.S. (1998). Hunger in the United States: Potential behavioral and emotional correlates. *Pediatrics, 101,* E3.

Klerman, L.V. (1993). The influence of economic factors on health-related behaviors in adolescents. In S.G. Millstein, A.C. Petersen, & E.O. Nightingale (Eds.), *Promoting the health of adolescents.* New York: Oxford University Press.

Klish, W.J. (1998, September). Childhood obesity. *Pediatrics in Review, 19,* 312–315.

Klitzing, K.V., Simoni, H., & Burgin, D. (1999, April). *Mother, father, and infant: The triad from pre-natal representations to post-natal interactions.* Paper presented at the meeting of the Society for Research in Child Development, Albuquerque.

Klonoff-Cohen, H.S., Edelstein, S.L., Lefkowitz, E.S., Srinivasan, I.P., Kaegi, D., Chang, J.C., & Wiley, K.J. (1995). The effect of passive smoke and tobacco exposure through breast milk on sudden infant death syndrome. *The Journal of the American Medical Association, 293,* 795–798.

Knight, M. (1999). The Darwinian algorithm and scientific inquiry. *Contemporary Psychology, 44,* 150–152.

Kochanska, G. (1999, April). *Applying a temperament model to the study of social development.* Paper presented at the meeting of the Society for Research in Child Development.

Kochhar, C.A., West, L., & Taymans, J.M. (2000). *Handbook for successful inclusion.* Columbus, OH: Merrill.

Kohl, H.W., & Hobbs, K.E. (1998). Development of physical activity behaviors among children and adolescents. *Pediatrics, 101,* 549–554.

Kohlberg, L. (1958). *The development on modes of moral thinking and choice in the years 10 to 16.* Unpublished doctoral dissertation, University of Chicago.

Kohlberg, L. (1966). A cognitive-developmental analysis of children's sex-role concepts and attitudes. In E.E. Maccoby (Ed.), *The development of sex differences.* Palo Alto, CA: Stanford University Press.

Kohlberg, L. (1969). Stage and sequence: The cognitive-developmental approach to socialization. In D.A. Goslin (Ed.), *Handbook of socialization theory and research.* Chicago: Rand McNally.

Kohlberg, L. (1976). Moral stages and moralization: The cognitive-developmental approach. In T. Lickona (Ed.), *Moral development and behavior.* New York: Holt, Rinehart & Winston.

Kohlberg, L. (1986). A current statement of some theoretical issues. In S. Modgil & C. Modgil (Eds.), *Lawrence Kohlberg.* Philadelphia: Falmer.

Kolbe, L.J., Collins, J., & Cortese, P. (1997). Building the capacity of schools to improve the health of the nation. *American Psychologist, 52,* 256–265.

Kontos, S., & Wilcox-Herzog, A. (1997). Teachers' interactions with children: Why are they so important? *Young Children, 52,* 4–12.

Kopp, C.B. (1992, October). *Trends and directions in studies of developmental risk.* Paper presented at the 27th Minnesota Symposium on Child Psychology, University of Minnesota, Minneapolis.

Kotlowitz, A. (1991). *There are no children here.* New York: Anchor Books.

Kozol, J. (1991). *Savage inequalities.* New York: Crown.

Krementz, J. (1983). *How it feels when a parent dies.* New York: Knopf.

Krementz, J. (1989). *How it feels to fight for your life.* New York: Little, Brown.

Kuebli, J. (1994). Young children's understanding of everyday emotions. *Young Children, 49,* 36–47.

Kuebli, J. (1994, March). Young children's understanding of everyday emotions. *Young Children,* pp. 36–48.

Kuhl, P. (1997, April 28). Commentary. Talking to infants may boost their ability to think, studies find. *Dallas Morning News,* p. B8.

Kuhl, P.K. (1993). Infant speech perception: A window on psycholinguistic development. *International Journal of Psycholinguistics, 9,* 33–56.

Kuhn, D. (1998). Afterward to Volume 2: Cognition, perception, and language. In W. Damon (Ed.), *Handbook of child psychology* (5th ed., Vol. 2). New York: Wiley.

Kupersmidt, J.B., & Coie, J.D. (1990). Preadolescent peer status, aggression, and school adjustment as predictors of externalizing problems in adolescence. *Child Development, 61,* 1350–1363.

Kupersmidt, J.B., & Patterson, C. (1993, March). *Developmental patterns of peer relations and aggression in the prediction of externalizing behavior problems.* Paper presented at the biennial meeting of the Society for Research in Child Development, New Orleans.

Kurtz, D.A., Cantu, C.L., & Phinney, J.S. (1996, March). *Group identities as predictors of self-esteem among African American, Latino, and White adolescents.* Paper presented at the meeting of the Society for Research on Adolescence, Boston.

Kwak, H.K., Kim, M., Cho, B.H., & Ham, Y.M. (1999, April). *The relationship between children's temperament, maternal control strategies, and children's compliance.* Paper presented at the meeting of the Society for Research in Child Development, Albuquerque.

L

Ladd, G.W. (1999). Peer relationships and social competence during early and middle childhood. *Annual Review of Psychology.* Palo Alto, CA: Annual Review, Inc.

LaFromboise, T., & Trimble, J. (1996). Multicultural counseling theory and American-Indian populations. In D.W. Sue (Ed.), *Theory of multicultural counseling and therapy.* Pacific Grove, CA: Brooks/Cole.

LaFromboise, T.D. (1993). American Indian mental health policy. In D.R. Atkinson, G. Morten, & D.W. Sue (Eds.), *Counseling American minorities.* Madison, WI: Brown & Benchmark.

Lally, J.R., Mangione, P., & Honig, S. (1987). *The Syracuse University family development research program.* Unpublished manuscript, Syracuse University, Syracuse, NY.

Lamb, M.E. (1977). The development of mother-infant and father-infant attachments in the second year of life. *Developmental Psychology, 13,* 637–648.

Lamb, M.E. (1986). *The father's role: Applied perspectives.* New York: Wiley.

Lamb, M.E. (1994). Infant care practices and the application of knowledge. In C.B. Fisher & R.M. Lerner (Eds.). *Applied developmental psychology.* Boston: McGraw-Hill.

Lamb, M.E. (1998). Nonparental child care: Context, quality, correlates, and consequences. In W. Damon (Ed.), *Handbook of child psychology* (5th ed., Vol. 4). New York: Wiley.

Lamb, M.E., & Sternberg, K.J. (1992). Sociocultural perspectives in nonparental childcare. In M.E. Lamb, K.J. Sternberg, C. Hwang, & A.G. Broberg (Eds.), *Child care in context.* Hillsdale, NJ: Erlbaum.

Lamb, M.E., Frodi, A.M., Hwant, C.P., Frodi, M., & Steinberg, J. (1982). Mother- and father-infant interaction involving play and holding in traditional and nontraditional Swedish families. *Developmental Psychology, 18,* 215–221.

Lamb, M.E., Hwang, C.P., Ketterlinus, R.D., & Fracasso, M.P. (1999). Parent-child relationships: Development in the context of the family. In M.H. Bornstein & M.E. Lamb (Eds.), *Developmental psychology: An advanced textbook* (4th ed.). Mahwah, NJ: Erlbaum.

Landesman-Dwyer, S., & Sackett, G.P. (1983, April). *Prenatal nicotine exposure and sleep-wake patterns in infancy.* Paper presented at the biennial meeting of the Society for Research in Child Development, Detroit.

Lane, H. (1976). *The wild boy of Aveyron.* Cambridge, MA: Harvard University Press.

Lapsley, D.K. (1996). *Moral psychology.* Boulder, CO: Westview Press.

Lapsley, D.K. (1997). The adolescent egocentrism theory and the "new look" at the imaginary audience and personal fable. In R.M. Lerner, A.C. Petersen, & J. Brooks-Gunn (Eds.), *Encyclopedia of adolescence.* New York: Garland.

Lapsley, D.K., Enright, R.D., & Serlin, R.C. (1985). Toward a theoretical perspective on the legislation of adolescence. *Journal of Early Adolescence, 5,* 441–466.

Lareau, A. (1996). Assessing parent involvement in schooling: A critical analysis. In K.L. Alexander & D.R. Entwisle (Eds.), *Schools and children at risk.* Mahwah, NJ: Erlbaum.

Larson, R., & Richards, M. (1994). *Divergent realities: The emotional lives of mothers, fathers, and adolescents.* New York: Basic Books.

Larson, R.W., Clore, G.L., & Wood, G.A. (in press). The emotions of romantic relationships. In W. Furman, B.B. Brown, & C. Feiring (Eds.), *Contemporary perspectives on romantic relationships.* New York: Cambridge University Press.

Larson, R.W., Clore, G.L., & Wood, G.A. (in press). The emotions of romantic relationships: Do they wreak havoc on adolescents? In W. Furman, B.B. Brown, & C. Feiring (Eds.), *Contemporary perspectives in adolescent romantic relationships.* New York: Cambridge University Press.

Lazar, I., Darlington, R., & Collaborators. (1982). Lasting effects of early education: A report from the consortium for longitudinal studies. *Monographs of the Society for Research in Child Development, 47.*

Leach, P. (1990). *Your baby and child: From birth to age five.* New York: Knopf.

Leach, P. (1991). *Your baby and child: From birth to age five* (2nd ed.). New York: Alfred A. Knopf.

Leifer, A.D. (1973). *Television and the development of social behavior.* Paper presented at the meeting of the International Society for the Study of Behavioral Development, Ann Arbor, MI.

Lemery, K.S., Goldsmith, H.H., Klinnert, M.D., & Mrazek, D.A. (1999). Developmental models of infant and child temperament. *Developmental Psychology, 35,* 189–204.

Lenneberg, E. (1967). *The biological foundations of language.* New York: Wiley.

Lenneberg, E.H., Rebelsky, R.G., & Nichols, I.A. (1965). The vocalization of infants born to deaf and hearing parents. *Human Development, 8,* 23–37.

Lepper, M., Greene, D., & Nisbett, R.R. (1973). Undermining children's intrinsic interest with extrinsic rewards. *Journal of Personality and Social Psychology, 28,* 129–137.

Lepper, M.R., & Gurtner, J. (1989). Children and computers: Approaching the twenty-first century. *American Psychologist, 44,* 170–178.

Lester, B.M., & Tronick, E.Z. (1990). Introduction. In B.M. Lester & E.Z. Tronick (Eds.), *Stimulation and the preterm infant: The limits of plasticity.* Philadelphia: W. B. Saunders.

Lester, B.M., Freier, K., & LaGasse, K. (1995). Prenatal cocaine exposure and child outcome: How much do we really know? In M. Lewis & M. Bendersky (Eds.), *Mothers, babies, and cocaine.* Hillsdale, NJ: Erlbaum.

Leventhal, A. (1994, February). *Peer conformity during adolescence: An integration of developmental, situational, and individual characteristics.* Paper presented at the meeting of the Society for Research on Adolescence, San Diego.

Levesque, J., & Prosser, T. (1996). Service learning connections. *Journal of Teacher Education, 47,* 325–334.

Levin, J. (1980). *The mnemonics '80s: Keywords in the classroom.* Theoretical paper No. 86. Wisconsin Research and Development Center for Individualized Schooling, Madison.

Levine, J.A. (1996, June 17). Commentary. *Newsweek,* p. 61.

Levy, T.M. (Ed.). (1999). *Handbook of attachment interventions.* San Diego: Academic Press.

Lewis, C.G. (1981). How adolescents approach decisions: Changes over grades seven to twelve and policy implications. *Child Development, 52,* 538–554.

Lewis, M. (1997). *Altering fate: Why the past does not predict the future.* New York: Guilford Press.

Lewis, M., & Brooks-Gunn, J. (1979). *Social cognition and the acquisition of the self.* New York: Plenum.

Lewis, M., & Ramsay, D.S. (1999). Effect of maternal soothing and infant stress response. *Child Development, 70,* 11–20.

Lewis, R. (1997). With a marble and telescope: Searching for play. *Childhood Education, 36,* 346.

Lewis, R.B. (1998). Assistive technology and learning disabilities: Today's realities and tomorrow's promises. *Journal of Learning Disabilities, 31,* 4–15.

Lewis, V.G., Money, J., & Bobrow, N.A. (1977). Idiopathic pubertal delay beyond the age of 15: Psychological study of 12 boys. *Adolescence, 12,* 1–11.

Lieberman, E.E., Lang, J.M., Frigoletto, F., Richardson, D.K., Rengin, S.A., & Cohen, A. (1997). Epidural analgesic, intrapartum fever, and neonatal sepsis evaluation. *Pediatrics, 99,* 415–419.

Lifshitz, F., Pugliese, M.T., Moses, N., & Weyman-Daum, M. (1987). Parental health beliefs as a cause of nonorganic failure to thrive. *Pediatrics, 80,* 175–182.

Limber, S.P., & Wilcox, B.L. (1996). Application of the U.N. convention on the rights of the child to the United States. *American Psychologist, 51,* 1246–1250.

Lindbohm, M. (1991). Effects of paternal occupational exposure in spontaneous abortions. *American Journal of Public Health, 121,* 1029–1033.

Lindner-Gunnoe, M. (1993). Noncustodial mothers' and fathers' contributions to the adjustment of adolescent stepchildren. Unpublished doctoral dissertation. University of Virginia.

Linn, M.C., & Hsi, S. (1999). *Computers, teachers, peers—science learning partners.* Mahwah, NJ: Erlbaum.

Liprie, M.L. (1993). Adolescents' contributions to family decision making. In B.H. Settles, R.S. Hands, & M.B. Sussman (Eds.), *American families and the future: Analyses of possible destinies.* New York: Haworth Press.

Lipsitz, J. (1983, October). *Making it the hard way: Adolescents in the 1980s.* Testimony presented at the Crisis Intervention Task Force, House Select Committee on Children, Youth, and Families, Washington, DC.

Lipsitz, J. (1984). *Successful schools for young adolescents.* New Brunswick, NJ: Transaction.

Livesly, W., & Bromley, D. (1973). *Person perception in childhood and adolescence.* New York: Wiley.

Locke, J.L. (1993). *The child's path to spoken language.* Cambridge, MA: Harvard University Press.

Lockman, J.J., & Thelen, E. (1993). Developmental biodynamics: Brain, body, behavior connections. *Child Development, 64,* 953–959.

Long, T., & Long, L. (1983). *Latchkey children.* New York: Penguin.

Lonner, W.J. (1990). An overview of cross-cultural testing and assessment. In R.W. Brislin (Ed.), *Applied cross-cultural psychology.* Newbury Park, CA: Sage.

Lorch, E. (1995, March). *Young children's perception of importance in televised stories.* Paper presented at the meeting of the Society for Research in Child Development, Indianapolis.

Lorenz, K.Z. (1965). *Evolution and the modification of behavior.* Chicago: University of Chicago Press.

Lucey, J.F. (1999). Comments on a sudden infant death article in another journal. *Pediatrics, 103,* 812.

Luria, A., & Herzog, E. (1985, April). *Gender segregation across and within settings.* Paper presented at the biennial meeting of the Society for Research in Child Development, Toronto.

Luster, T.J., Perlstadt, J., McKinney, M.H., & Sims, K.E. (1995, March). *Factors related to the quality of the home environment adolescents provide for their infants.* Paper presented at the meeting of the Society for Research in Child Development, Indianapolis.

Lutz, D.A., & Sternberg, R.J. (1999). Cognitive development. In M.H. Bornstein & M.E. Lamb (Eds.), *Developmental psychology: An advanced textbook* (4th ed.). Mahwah, NJ: Erlbaum.

Lyon, G.R. (1996). Learning disabilities. *The Future of Children*, 6(1) 54–76.

Lyon, G.R., & Moats, L.C. (1997). Critical conceptual and methodological considerations in reading intervention research. *Journal of Learning Disabilities*, 30, 578–588.

Lyons, N.P. (1990). Listening to voices we have not heard. In C. Gilligan, N.P. Lyons, & T.J. Hanmer (Eds.), *Making connections*. Cambridge, MA: Harvard University Press.

M

Maas, J.B. (1998). *Power sleep*. New York: Villard.

Maccoby, E.E. (1984). Middle childhood in the context of the family. In *Development during middle childhood*. Washington, DC: National Academy Press.

Maccoby, E.E. (1987, November). Interview with Elizabeth Hall: All in the family. *Psychology Today*, pp. 54–60.

Maccoby, E.E. (1992). The role of parents in the socialization of children: An historical overview. *Developmental Psychology*, 28, 1006–1018.

Maccoby, E.E. (1993, March). *Trends and issues in the study of gender role development.* Paper presented at the biennial meeting of the Society for Research in Child Development, New Orleans.

Maccoby, E.E. (1996). Peer conflict and intrafamily conflict: Are there conceptual bridges? *Merrill-Palmer Quarterly*, 42, 165–176.

Maccoby, E.E. (1999). The uniqueness of the parent-child relationship. In W.A. Collins & B. Laursen (Eds.), *Relationships as developmental contexts*. Mahwah, NJ: Erlbaum.

Maccoby, E.E., & Jacklin, C.N. (1974). *The psychology of sex differences*. Palo Alto, CA: Stanford University Press.

Maccoby, E.E., & Martin, J.A. (1983). Socialization in the context of the family: Parent-child interaction. In P.H. Mussen (Ed.), *Handbook of Child Psychology* (4th ed., Vol. 4). New York: Wiley.

Maccoby, E.E., & Mnookin, R.H. (1992). *Dividing the child: Social and legal dilemmas of custody*. Cambridge, MA: Harvard University Press.

MacFarlane, J.A. (1975). Olfaction in the development of social preferences in the human neonate. In *Parent-infant interaction*. Ciba Foundation Symposium No. 33. Amsterdam: Elsevier.

MacWhinney, B. (Ed.). (1999). *The emergence of language*. Mahwah, NJ: Erlbaum.

Maddux, J.E., Roberts, M.C., Sledden, E.A., & Wright, L. (1986). Developmental issues in child health psychology. *American Psychologist*, 41, 24–34.

Mader, S. (1999). *Biology* (6th ed.). Burr Ridge, IL: McGraw-Hill.

Mahler, M. (1979). *Separation-individuation* (Vol. 2). London: Jason Aronson.

Main, M., & Solomon, J. (1990). Procedures for identifying infants as disorganized/disoriented during the Ainsworth Strange Situation. In M. Greenberg, D. Cicchetti, & E.M. Cummings (Eds.), *Attachment during the preschool years*. Chicago: University of Chicago Press.

Malinosky-Rummell, R., & Hansen, D.J. (1993). Long-term consequences of childhood physical abuse. *Psychological Bulletin*, 114, 68–79.

Malloy, M.H. (1999). Risk of previous very low birth weight and very preterm infants among women delivering a very low birth weight and very preterm infant. *Journal of Perinatology*, 19, 97–102.

Mandler, J.M. (1990). A new perspective on cognitive development. *American Scientist*, 78, 236-243.

Mandler, J.M. (1992). The foundations of conceptual thought in infancy. *Cognitive Development*, 7, 273–285.

Mandler, J.M. (1998). Representation. In W. Damon (Ed.), *Handbook of child psychology* (5th ed., Vol. 2). New York: Wiley.

Marcia, J. (1996). Unpublished review of *Adolescence* (7th ed.) by J.W. Santrock, Madison, WI: Brown & Benchmark.

Marcia, J.E. (1980). Ego identity development. In J. Adelson (Ed.), *Handbook of adolescent psychology*. New York: Wiley.

Marcia, J.E. (1994). The empirical study of ego identity. In H.A. Bosma, T.L.G. Graafsma, H.D. Grotevant, & D.J. De Levita (Eds.), *Identity and development*. Newbury Park, CA: Sage.

Margolin, L. (1994). Child sexual abuse by uncles. *Child Abuse and Neglect*, 18, 215–224.

Marr, D. (1982). *Vision*. New York: W.H. Freeman.

Martin, E.W., Martin, R., & Terman, D.L. (1996). The legislative and litigation history of special education. *The Future of Children*, 6(1), 25–53.

Martin, J. (1976). *The education of adolescents*. Washington, DC: U.S. Office of Education.

Matas, L., Arend, R.A., & Sroufe, L.A. (1978). Continuity in adaptation: Quality of attachment and later competence. *Child Development*, 49, 547–556.

Mathes, P.G., & Torgesen, J.K. (1999). All children can learn to read: Critical care for the prevention of reading failure. In J.W. Miller & M.C. McKenna (Eds.), *Literacy education in the 21st century*. Mahwah, NJ: Erlbaum.

Matsumoto, D. (1996). *Culture and psychology*. Pacific Grove, CA: Brooks/Cole.

McAdoo, H.P. (Ed.). (1999). *Family ethnicity* (2nd ed.). Newbury Park, CA: Sage.

McCall, R.B., & Carriger, M.S. (1993). A meta-analysis of infant habituation and recognition memory performance as predictors of later IQ. *Child Development*, 64, 57–79.

McClelland, D.C. (1955). Some social consequences of achievement motivation. In M.R. Jones (Ed.), *The Nebraska Symposium on Motivation*. Lincoln: University of Nebraska Press.

McDougall, P., Schonert-Reichel, K., & Hymel, S. (1996, March). *Adolescents at risk for high school dropout: The role of social factors.* Paper presented at the meeting of the Society for Research on Adolescence, Boston.

McFarlane, J., Parker, B., & Soeken, K. (1996). Abuse during pregnancy: Associations with maternal health and infant birth weight. *Nursing Research*, 45, 37–47.

McGrath, S., Kennell, J., Suresh, M., Moise, K., & Hinkley, C. (1999, May). *Doula support vs. epidural analgesia: Impact on cesarean rates.* Paper presented at the meeting of the Society for Pediatric Research, San Francisco.

McHale, J.L., Frosch, C.A., Greene, C.A., & Ferry, K.S. (1995, March). *Correlates of maternal and paternal behavior.* Paper presented at the meeting of the Society for Research in Child Development, Indianapolis.

McHale, J.P., Lauretti, A.F., & Kuersten-Hogan, R. (1999, April). *Linking family-level patterns to father-child, mother-child, and marital relationship qualities.* Paper presented at the meeting of the Society for Research in Child Development, Albuquerque.

McLanahan, S., & Sandefur, G. (1994). *Growing up with a single parent: What hurts, what helps?* Cambridge, MA: Harvard University Press.

McLoyd, V. (1998). Children in poverty: Development, public policy, and practice. In W. Damon (Ed.), *Handbook of child psychology* (5th ed., Vol. 4). New York: Wiley.

McLoyd, V.C. (1998). Children in poverty. In I.E. Siegel & K.A. Renninger (Eds.), *Handbook of child psychology* (5th ed., Vol. IV). New York: Wiley.

McLoyd, V.C. (1998). Children in poverty: Development, public policy, and practice. In W. Damon (Ed.), *Handbook of child psychology* (5th ed., Vol. 4). New York: Wiley.

McLoyd, V.C. (1999). Cultural influences in a multicultural society: Conceptual and methodological issues. In A.S. Masten (Ed.), *Cultural processes in child development*. Mahwah, NJ: Erlbaum.

McMillan, J.H. (1996). *Educational research* (2nd ed.). New York: HarperCollins.

Medrich, E.A., Rossen, J., Rubin, V., & Buckley, S. (1982). *The serious business of growing up*. Berkeley: University of California Press.

Mehler, J., Jusczyk, P.W., Lambertz, G., Halsted, N., Bertoncini, J., & Amiel-Tison, C. (1988). A precursor of language acquisition in young infants. *Cognition*, 29, 132–178.

Melby, J.N., & Vargas, D. (1996, March). *Predicting patterns of adolescent tobacco use.* Paper presented at the meeting of the Society for Research on Adolescence, Boston.

Meltzoff, A. (1999, April). *Infant memory development: Contribution of the deferred imitation paradigm.* Paper presented at the meeting of the Society for Research in Child Development, Albuquerque.

Meltzoff, A., & Gopnik, A. (1997). *Words, thoughts, and theories*. Cambridge, MA: MIT Press.

Meltzoff, A.N. (1988). Infant imitation and memory: Nine-month-old infants in immediate and deferred tests. *Child Development*, 59, 217–225.

Meltzoff, A.N. (1992, May). *Cognition in the service of learning.* Paper presented at the International Conference on Infant Studies, Miami Beach.

Meltzoff, A.N., & Moore, M.K. (1999). A new foundation for cognitive development in infancy: The birth of the representational infant. In E.K. Skolnick, K. Nelson, S.A. Gelman, & P.H. Miller (Eds.), *Conceptual development*. Mahwah, NJ: Erlbaum.

Meltzoff, A.N., & Moore, M.K. (1999). Resolving the debate about early imitation. In A. Slater & D. Muir (Eds.), *The Blackwell reader in developmental psychology*. Oxford, England: Blackwell.

Meredith, N.V. (1978). Research between 1960 and 1970 on the standing height of young children in different parts of the world. In H.W. Reece & L.P. Lipsitt (Eds.), *Advances in child development and behavior* (Vol. 12). New York: Academic Press.

Meyers, A.F., Sampson, A.E., Weitzman, M., Rogers, B.L., & Kayne, H. (1989). School breakfast program and school performance. *American Journal of Diseases of Children*, 143, 1234–1239.

Michel, G.L. (1981). Right-handedness: A consequence of infant supine head-orientation preference? *Science*, 212, 685–687.

Michelozzi, B.N. (1996). *Coming alive from nine to five: The career search handbook*. Mountain View, CA: Mayfield.

Miller, G. (1981). *Language and speech*. New York: W.H. Freeman.

Miller, J.G. (1995, March). *Culture, context, and personal agency: The cultural grounding of self and morality.* Paper presented at the meeting of the Society for Research in Child Development, Indianapolis.

Miller, J.W. (1999). Literacy in the 21st century: Emergent themes. In J.W. Miller & M.C. McKenna (Eds.), *Literacy education in the 21st century*. Mahwah, NJ: Erlbaum.

Miller, S.A., & Harley, J.P. (1996). *Zoology* (3rd ed.). Dubuque, IA: Wm. C. Brown.

Miller-Jones, D. (1989). Culture and testing. *American Psychologist*, 44, 360–366.

Mills, J.L., Holmes, L.B., Aarons, J.H., Simpson, J.L., Brown, Z.A., Jovanovic-Graubard, L.G., Conley,

M.R., Graubard, B.I., Knopp, R.H., & Metzger, B.E. (1993). Moderate caffeine use and the risk of spontaneous abortion and intrauterine growth retardation. *Journal of the American Medical Association, 269,* 593–597.

Millstein, G.B. (1988). *The potential of school-linked centers to promote adolescent health and development.* Washington, DC: Carnegie Council on Adolescent Development.

Millstein, S.G., Petersen, A.C., & Nightingale, E.O. (1993). (Eds.). *Promoting the health of adolescents.* New York: Oxford University Press.

Minnett, A.M., Vandell, D.L., & Santrock, J.W. (1983). The effects of sibling status on sibling interaction: Influence of birth order, age spacing, sex of the child, and sex of the sibling. *Child Development, 54,* 1064–1072.

Minuchin, P.O., & Shapiro, E.K. (1983). The school as a context for social development. In P.H. Mussen (Ed.), *Handbook of child psychology* (4th ed., Vol. 4). New York: Wiley.

Mischel, W. (1973). Toward a cognitive social learning reconceptualization of personality. *Psychological Review, 80,* 252–283.

Mischel, W., & Patterson, C.J. (1976). Substantive and structural elements of effective plans for self-control. *Journal of Personality and Social Psychology, 34,* 942–950.

Mitchell, A.S. (1999, April). *The nature of sibling relationships in adolescence: A sequential analysis of verbal and nonverbal behaviors in twins and nontwins.* Paper presented at the meeting of the Society for Research in Child Development, Albuquerque.

Moely, B.E., Santulli, K.A., & Obach, M.S. (1995). Strategy instruction, metacognition, and motivation in the elementary school classroom. In F.E. Weinert & W. Schneider (Eds.), *Memory performance and competencies.* Mahwah, NJ: Erlbaum.

Montemayor, R. (1982). The relationship between parent-adolescent conflict and the amount of time adolescents spend with parents, peers, and alone. *Child Development, 53,* 1512–1519.

Morgan, J.L., & Demuth, K. (Eds.). (1995). *Signal to syntax.* Hillsdale, NJ: Erlbaum.

Morrison, F. (1999, August). *School transition: An individual differences perspective.* Paper presented at the meeting of the American Psychological Association, Boston.

Morrison, G.S. (2000). *Fundamentals of early childhood education.* Columbus, OH: Merrill.

Morrongiello, B.A., Fenwick, K.D., & Chance, G. (1990). Sound localization acuity in very young infants: An observer-based testing procedure. *Developmental Psychology, 26,* 75–84.

Mortimer, J.T., Finch, M., Shanahan, M., & Ryu, S. (1992). Work experience, mental health, and behavioral adjustment in adolescence. *Journal of Research on Adolescence, 2,* 24–57.

Moshman, D. (1999). *Adolescent psychological development: Rationality, morality, and identity.* Mahwah, NJ: Erlbaum.

Mott, F.L., & Marsiglio, W. (1985, September/October). Early childbearing and completion of high school. *Family Planning Perspectives,* p. 234.

Mueller, N., & Silverman, N. (1989). Peer relations in maltreated children. In D. Cicchetti & V. Carlson (Eds.), *Child maltreatment.* New York: Cambridge University Press.

Mullis, I.V.S., Martin, M.O., Beaton, A.E., Gonzales, E.J., Kelly, D.L., & Smith, T.A. (1998). *Mathematics and science achievement in the final year of secondary school.* Chestnut Hill, MA: TIMSS International Study Center, Boston College.

Mumme, D.L., Fernald, A., & Herrera, C. (1996). Infant's responses to facial & emotional signals in a social referencing paradigm. *Child Development, 67,* 3219–3237.

Munsch, J., Woodward, J., & Darling, N. (1995). Children's perceptions of their relationships with coresiding and non-custodial fathers. *Journal of Divorce and Remarriage, 23,* 39–54.

Murray, V.M. (1996, March). *Sexual and motherhood statuses.* Paper presented at the meeting of the Society for Research on Adolescence. Boston.

Myers, N.A., Clifton, R.K., & Clarkson, M.G. (1987). When they were very young: Almost-threes remember two years ago. *Infant Behavior and Development, 10,* 123–132.

N

NAEYC. (1988). NAEYC position statement on developmentally appropriate practices in the primary grades, serving 5- through 8-year-olds. *Young Children, 43,* 64–83.

NAEYC. (1996). NAEYC position statement: Technology and young children—Ages three through eight. *Young Children, 51,* 11–23.

NAEYC. (1996b). NAEYC position statement: Responding to linguistic and cultural diversity—Recommendations for effective early childhood education. *Young Children, 51,* 4–12.

Nahas, G.G. (1984). *Marijuana in science and medicine.* New York: Raven Press.

Nash, J.M. (1997, February 3). Fertile minds. *Time,* pp. 50–54.

National and Community Service Coalition. (1995). *Youth volunteerism.* Washington, DC: Author.

National Assessment of Educational Progress. (1976). *Adult work skills and knowledge* (Report No. 35-COD-01). Denver: Author.

National Association for the Education of Young Children. (1986). Position statement on developmentally appropriate practice in programs for 4- and 5-year-olds. *Young Children 41,* 20–29.

National Association for the Education of Young Children. (1990). NAEYC position statement on school readiness. *Young Children, 46,* 21–28.

National Childhood Cancer Foundation. (1998). *Cancer in children.* Washington, DC: Author.

National Commission on Sleep Disorders. (1993, January). *Report of the National Commission on Sleep Disorders Research.* Washington, DC: U.S. Department of Health and Human Services.

National Health Interview Study. (1991). *Current estimates from the National Health Interview Survey.* Hyattsville, MD: National Center for Health Statistics.

Neisser, U., Boodoo, G., Bouchard, T.J., Boykin, A.W., Brody, N., Ceci, S.J., Halpern, D.F., Loehlin, J.C., Perloff, R., Sternberg, R.J., & Urbina, S. (1996). Intelligence: Knowns and unknowns. *American Psychologist, 51,* 77–101.

Nelson, K. (1999). Levels and modes of representation: Issues for the theory of conceptual change and development. In E.K. Skolnick, K. Nelson, S.A. Gelman, & P.H. Miller (Eds.), *Conceptual development.* Mahwah, NJ: Erlbaum.

Nelson, K.E., & Réger, Z. (Eds.). (1995). *Children's language* (Vol. 8). Hillsdale, NJ: Erlbaum.

Neuman, S.B., & Roskos, K. (1993). *Language and literacy learning in the early years.* Fort Worth, TX: Harcourt Brace.

Newacheck, P.W. (1989). Improving access to health services for adolescents from economically disadvantaged families. *Pediatrics, 84,* 1056–1063.

Newcomb, M.D., & Bentler, P.M. (1988). Substance use and abuse among children and teenagers. *American Psychologist, 44,* 242–248.

Newman, B.S., & Muzzonigro, P.G. (1993). The effects of traditional family values on the coming out process of gay male adolescents. *Adolescence, 28,* 213–226.

Newman, D.L., & Caspi, A. (1996, March). *Temperament styles observed at age 3 predict interpersonal functioning in the transition to adulthood.* Paper presented at the meeting of the Society for Research on Adolescence, Boston.

Newman, J. (1995). How breast milk protects newborns. *Scientific American, 273,* (6) 76–80.

Newson, J., Newson, E., & Mahalski, P.A. (1982). Persistent infant comfort habits and their sequelae at 11 and 16 years. *Journal of Child Psychology and Psychiatry, 23,* 421–436.

NICHD Early Child Care Research Care Network. (1997). Infant child care and attachment. *Child Development, 68,* 860–879.

Nicholls, J.G. (1984). Conceptions of ability and achievement motivation. In R.E. Ames & C. Ames (Eds.), *Motivation in education.* New York: Academic Press.

Nicklas, T.A., Webber, L.S., Jonson, C.S., Srinivasan, S.R., & Berenson, G.S. (1995). Foundations for health promotion with youth: A review of observations from the Bogalusa Heart Study. *Journal of Health Education, 26,* S18–S26.

Ninio, A., & Snow, C.E. (1996). *Pragmatic development.* Boulder, CO: Westview Press.

Noddings, N. (1992). *The challenge to care in schools.* New York: Teachers College Press.

Noll, S. (1991). *That bothered Kate.* New York: Puffin.

Nottelmann, E.D., Susman, E.J., Blue, J.H., Inoff-Germain, G., Dorn, L.D., Loriaux, D.L., Cutler, G.B., & Chrousos, G.P. (1987). Gonadal and adrenal hormone correlates of adjustment in early adolescence. In R.M. Lerner & T.T. Foch (Eds.), *Biological-psychological interactions in early adolescence.* Hillsdale, NJ: Erlbaum.

O

Obler, L.K. (1993). Language beyond childhood. In J.B. Gleason (Ed.), The development of language (3rd ed.). New York: Macmillan.

Offer, D., Ostrov, E., Howard, K.I., & Atkinson, R. (1988). *The teenage world: Adolescents' self-image in ten countries.* New York: Plenum.

Ogbu, J.U. (1989, April). *Academic socialization of Black children: An innoculation against future failure?* Paper presented at the meeting of the Society for Research in Child Development, Kansas City.

Olds, S.B., London, M.L., & Ladewig, P.A. (1988). *Maternal newborn nursing: A family-centered approach,* Menlo Park, CA: Addison-Wesley.

Oller, D.K. (1999, August). *Bilingual infants show neither advantages nor disadvantages over monolingual infants.* Paper presented at the meeting of the American Psychological Association, Boston.

Olley, J.G., & Gutentag, S.S. (1999). Autism: Historical overview, definition, and characteristics. In D.E.B. Zager (Ed.), *Autism.* Mahwah, NJ: Erlbaum.

Olson, H.C., & Burgess, D.M. (1996). Early intervention with children prenatally exposed to alcohol and other drugs. In M.J. Guralnick (Eds.), *The effectiveness of early intervention.* Baltimore: Paul H. Brookes.

Olson, M. (1999, May). *How will the sequencing of the human genome change biomedical research?* Paper presented at the meeting of the Society for Pediatric Research, San Francisco.

Olweus, D. (1980). Bullying among schoolboys. In R. Barnen (Ed.), *Children and violence.* Stockholm: Adaemic Litteratur.

Oser, F., & Gmunder, P. (1991). *Religious judgment: A developmental perspective.* Birmingham, AL: Religious Education Press.

Ostoja, E., McCrone, E., Lehn, L., Reed, T., & Sroufe, L.A. (1995, March). *Representations of close relationships in adolescence: Longitudinal antecedents from infancy through childhood.* Paper presented at the meeting of the Society for Research in Child Development.

Overton, W.F., & Byrnes, J.P. (1991). Cognitive development. In R.M. Lerner, A.C. Petersen, & J. Brooks-Gunn (Eds). *Encyclopedia of adolescence* (Vol. 1). New York: Garland.

P

Paikoff, R.L., Brooks-Gunn, J., & Warren, M.P. (1991). Effects of girls' hormonal status on depressive and aggressive symptoms over the course of one year. *Journal of Youth and Adolescence, 20*, 191–215.

Paikoff, R.L., Buchanan, C.M., & Brooks-Gunn, J. (1991). Hormone-behavior links at puberty, methodological links in the study of. In R.M. Lerner, A.C. Petersen, & J. Brooks-Gunn (Eds.), *Encyclopedia of adolescence*. New York: Garland.

Paloutzian, R.F. (1996). *Invitation to the psychology of religion* (2nd ed.). Needham Heights, MA: Allyn & Bacon.

Paloutzian, R.F., & Santrock, J.W. (1997). The psychology of religion. In J.W. Santrock, *Psychology* (5th ed.). Madison, WI: Brown & Benchmark.

Paludi, M.A. (1998). *The psychology of women.* Upper Saddle River, NJ: Prentice-Hall.

Paneth, N.S. (1995, Spring). The problem of low birth weight. *Future of Children, 5*(1), 19–34.

Panofsky, C. (1999, April). *What the zone of proximal development conceals.* Paper presented at the meeting of the Society for Research in Child Development, Montreal.

Papert, S. (1980). *Mindstorms: Children, computers, and powerful ideas.* New York: Basic Books.

Parcel, G.S., Simons-Morton, G.G., O'Hara, N.M., Baranowski, T., Kolbe, L.J., & Bee, D.E. (1987). School promotion of healthful diet and exercise behavior: An integration of organizational change and social learning theory interventions. *Journal of School Health, 57*, 150–156.

Parkay, F.W., & Stanford, B.H. (1999). *Becoming a teacher* (4th ed.). Boston: Allyn & Bacon.

Parke, R.D. (1995). Fathers and families. In M.H. Bornstein (Ed.), *Children and parenting* (Vol. 3). Hillsdale, NJ: Erlbaum.

Parke, R.D., & Buriel, R. (1998). Socialization in the family: Ethnic and ecological perspectives. In W. Damon (Ed.), *Handbook of child psychology* (5th ed., Vol. 3). New York: Wiley.

Parker, F.L., Abdul-Kabir, S., Stevenson, H.G., & Garrett, B. (1995, March). *Partnerships between researchers and the community in Head Start.* Paper presented at the meeting of the Society for Research in Child Development, Indianapolis.

Parker, S.J., & Barrett, D.E. (1992). Maternal Type A behavior during pregnancy, neonatal crying, and infant temperament: Do Type A women have Type A babies? *Pediatrics, 89*, 474–479.

Parmalee, A.H. (1986). Children's illnesses: Their beneficial effects on behavioral development. *Child Development, 57*, 1–10.

Parten, M. (1932). Social play among preschool children. *Journal of Abnormal and Social Psychology, 27*, 243–269.

Patterson, G.R., DeBaryshe, B.D., & Ramsey, E. (1989). A developmental perspective on antisocial behavior. *American Psychologist, 44*, 329–335.

Patterson, K., & Wright, A.E. (1990, Winter). The speech, language, or hearing-impaired child: At-risk academically. *Childhood Education*, pp. 91–95.

Paulson, S.E., Marchant, G.J., & Rothlisberg, B. (1995). *Relations among parent, teacher, and school factors: Implications for achievement outcome in middle grade students.* Paper presented at the meeting of the Society for Research in Child Development, Indianapolis.

Pearson, S. (1978). *Everybody knows that.* New York: Dial.

Pentz, M.A. (1994). Primary prevention of adolescent drug abuse. In C. Fisher & R. Lerner (Eds.), *Applied developmental psychology.* New York: McGraw-Hill.

Perkins, D., & Tishman, S. (1997, March). Commentary in "Teaching today's pupils to think more critically." *APA Monitor,* p. 51.

Perris, E.E., Myers, N.A., & Clifton, R.K. (1990). Long-term memory for a single experience. *Child Development, 61*, 1796–1807.

Perry, C., Hearn, M., Murray, D., & Klepp, K. (1988). *The etiology and prevention of adolescent alcohol and drug abuse.* Unpublished manuscript, University of Minnesota.

Perusse, D. (1999, April). *Normal and abnormal early motor-cognitive development: A function of exposure to shared environmental risks.* Paper presented at the meeting of the Society for Research in Child Development, Albuquerque.

Peskin, H. (1967). Pubertal onset and ego functioning. *Journal of Abnormal Psychology, 72*, 1–15.

Petersen, A.C. (1979, January). Can puberty come any faster? *Psychology Today*, pp. 45–56.

Petersen, A.C. (1993). Creating adolescents: The role of context and process in developmental trajectories. *Journal of Research on Adolescence, 3*, 1–18.

Peterson, C.C. (1974). *A child grows up.* New York: Alfred.

Peterson, K.S. (1997, September 3). In high school, dating is a world into itself. *USA Today*, pp. 1–2D.

Peterson, P.L. (1977). Interactive effects of student anxiety, achievement orientation, and teacher behavior on student achievement and attitude. *Journal of Educational Psychology, 69*, 779–792.

Peth-Pierce, R. (1998). *The NICHD Study of Early Child Care.* Washington, DC: National Institute of Child Health and Human Development.

Phillips, D., Friedman, S.L., Huston, A.C., & Weinraub, M. (1999, April). *The roles of work and poverty in the lives of families with young children.* Paper presented at the meeting of the Society for Research in Child Development, Albuquerque.

Phillips, D.A., Voran, K., Kisker, E., Howes, C., & Whitebook, M. (1994). Child care for children in poverty: Opportunity or inequity? *Child Development, 65*, 472–492.

Phinney, J.S. (1989). Stages of ethnic identity development in minority group adolescents. *Journal of Early Adolescence, 9*, 34–49.

Phinney, J.S., & Alipura, L.L. (1990). Ethnic identity in college students from four ethnic groups. *Journal of Adolescence, 13*, 171–183.

Piaget, J. (1932). *The moral judgment of the child.* New York: Harcourt Brace Jovanovich.

Piaget, J. (1952). *The origins of intelligence in children.* New York: International Universities Press.

Piaget, J. (1952a). Jean Piaget. In C.A. Murchison (Ed.), *A history of psychology in autobiography* (Vol. 4). Worcester, MA: Clark University Press.

Piaget, J. (1954). *The construction of reality in the child.* New York: Basic Books.

Piaget, J. (1962). *Play, dreams, and imitation in childhood.* New York: W.W. Norton.

Piaget, J. (1962). *Play, dreams, and imitation.* New York: W.W. Norton.

Piaget, J., & Inhelder, B. (1969). *The child's conception of space* (F.J. Langdon & J.L. Lunzer, Trans.). New York: W.W. Norton.

Pianta, R. (1999, August). *Promoting literacy before and after school entry: Classroom activities and transition practices.* Paper presented at the meeting of the American Psychological Association, Boston.

Pierce, K.M., Hamm, J.V., & Vandell, D.L. (1997, April). *Experiences in after-school programs and children's adjustment at school and at home.* Paper presented at the meeting of the Society for Research in Child Development, Washington, DC.

Pinger, R.R., Payne, W.A., Hahn, D.B., & Hahn, E.J. (1998). *Drugs.* Dubuque, IA: McGraw-Hill.

Pintrich, P.R. (1999, April). *Multiple goals, multiple pathways: The role of goal orientation in learning and achievement.* Paper presented at the meeting of the Society for Research in Child Development, Albuquerque.

Pleck, J.H. (1983). The theory of male sex identity. In M. Lewis (Ed.), *In the shadow of the past: Psychology portrays the sexes.* New York: Columbia University Press.

Pleck, J.H. (1995). The gender-role strain paradigm. In R.F. Levant & W.S. Pollack (Eds.), *A new psychology of men.* New York: Basic Books.

Plomin, R. (1993, March). *Human behavioral genetics and development: An overview and update.* Paper presented at the biennial meeting of the Society for Research in Child Development, New Orleans.

Plomin, R. (1996, August). *Nature and nurture together.* Paper presented at the meeting of the American Psychological Association, Toronto.

Plomin, R., & DeFries, J.C. (1998). The genetics of abilities and disabilities. *Scientific American, 278*, 40–48.

Plomin, R., DeFries, J.C., & McClearn, G.E. (1990). *Behavioral genetics: A primer.* New York: W.H. Freeman.

Plomin, R., Reiss, D., Hetherington, E.M., & Howe, G.W. (1994). Nature and nurture: Contributions to measures of the family environment. *Developmental Psychology, 30*, 32–43.

Poest, C.A., Williams, J.R., Witt, D.D., & Atwood, M.E. (1990). Challenge me to move: Large muscle development in young children. *Young Children, 45*, 4–10.

Pollitt, E.P., Gorman, K.S., Engle, P.L., Martorell, R., & Rivera, J. (1993). Early supplementary feeding and cognition. *Monographs of the Society for Research in Child Development, 58* (7, Serial No. 235).

Polloway, E.A., Patton, J.R., Smith, T.E.C., & Buck, G.H. (1997). Mental retardation and learning disabilities: Conceptual and applied issues. *Journal of Learning Disabilities, 30*, 297–308.

Posada, G., Lord, C., & Waters, E. (1995, March). *Secure base behavior and children's misbehavior in three different contexts: Home, neighbors, and school.* Paper presented at the meeting of the Society for Research in Child Development, Indianapolis.

Posner, J.K., & Vandell, D.L. (1994). Low-income children's after-school care: Are there benefits of after-school programs? *Child Development, 65*, 440–456.

Posner, M.I. (1999, April). *Relating mechanisms of cognitive and emotional regulation.* Paper presented at the meeting of the Society for Research in Child Development, Albuquerque.

Potvin, K., Champagne, F., & Laberge-Nadeau, C. (1988). Mandatory driver training and road safety: The Quebec experience. *American Journal of Public Health, 78*, 1206–1212.

Potvin, L., Champagne, F., & Laberge-Nadeau, C. (1988). Mandatory driver training and road safety: The Quebec experience. *American Journal of Public Health, 78*, 1206–1212.

Poulton, S., & Sexton, D. (1996). Feeding young children: Developmentally appropriate considerations for supplementing family care. *Childhood Education, 73*, 66–71.

Pressley, M. (1996). Personal reflections on the study of practical memory in the mid-1990s. In D. Hermann, C. McEvoy, C. Hertzog, P. Hertel, & M. Johnson (Eds.), *Basic and applied memory research* (Vol. 2). Hillsdale, NJ: Erlbaum.

Pressley, M. (1996, August). *Getting beyond whole language: Elementary reading instruction that makes sense in light of recent psychological research.* Paper presented at the meeting of the American Psychological Association, Toronto.

Pressley, M. (in press). *Effective reading instruction: The case for balanced teaching.* New York: Guilford Press.

Pressley, M., & Schneider, W. (1997). *Introduction to memory development during childhood and adolescence.* Mahwah, NJ: Erlbaum.

Price, R.H., Cioci, M., Penner, W., & Trautlein, B. (1990). *School and community support programs that enhance adolescent health and education.* Washington, DC: Carnegie Council on Adolescent Development.

Prinstein, M.M., Fetter, M.D., & La Greca, A.M. (1996, March). *Can you judge adolescents by the company they keep?: Peer group membership, substance abuse, and risk-taking behaviors.* Paper presented at the meeting of the Society for Research on Adolescence, Boston.

Provenzo, E.F., Brent, A., & McCloskey, G.N. (1999). *Computers, curriculum, and cognitive change.* Mahwah, NJ: Erlbaum.

Pueschel, S.M., Scola, P.S., Weidenman, L.E., & Bernier, J.C. (1995). *The special child.* Baltimore: Paul Brookes.

Q

Quadrel, M.J., Fischoff, B., & Davis, W. (1993). Adolescent (in)vulnerability. *American Psychologist, 48,* 102–116.

R

Rabin, B.E., & Dorr, A. (1995, March). *Children's understanding of emotional events on family television series.* Paper presented at the meeting of the Society for Research in Child Development, Indianapolis.

Raikes, H. (1996). A secure base for babies: Applying attachment concepts to the infant care setting. *Young Children, 51,* 59–67.

Raman, L. (1999, April). *Developmental differences in children's and adults' understanding of illness.* Paper presented at the meeting of the Society for Research in Child Development, Albuquerque.

Ramey, C.T., & Campbell, F.A. (1984). Preventive education for high-risk children: Cognitive consequences of the Carolina Abecedarian Project, *American Journal of Mental Deficiency, 88,* 515–523.

Ramey, C.T., & Ramey, S.L. (1998). Early intervention and early experience. *American Psychologist, 53,* 109–120.

Ramey, C.T., Bryant, D.M., Campbell, F.A., Sparling, J.J., & Wasik, B.H. (1988). Early intervention for high-risk children. The Carolina Early Intervention Program. In R.H. Price, E.L. Cowen, R.P. Lorion, & J. Ramos-McKay (Eds.), *14 ounces of prevention.* Washington, DC: American Psychological Association.

Ramsay, D.S. (1980). Onset of unimanual handedness in infants. *Infant Behavior and Development, 3,* 377–385.

Read, L. (1995). Amos Bear gets hurt. *Young Children, 50,* 19–23.

Reeves, T.C. (1999, April). *A model to guide the integration of the WWW as a cognitive tool in K–12 education.* Paper presented at the meeting of the American Educational Research Association, Montreal.

Reilly, R. (1988, August 15). Here no one is spared. *Sports Illustrated,* pp. 70–77.

Reinberg, H. Z., Giaconia, R.M., Silverman, A.B., & Friedman, A.C. (1994, February). *Early psychological risks for adolescent suicide ideation and attempts.* Paper presented at the meeting of the Society for Research on Adolescence. San Diego.

Remafedi, G., Resnick, M., Blum, R., & Harris, L. (in press). The demography of sexual orientation in adolescents. *Pediatrics.*

Reschly, D.J. (1996). Identification and assessment of students with disabilities. In *Special education for students with disabilities.* Los Altos, Ca: The David and Lucile Packard Foundation.

Rest, J. (1999). *Postconventional moral thinking.* Mahwah, NJ: Erlbaum.

Reynolds, A.J. (1999, April). *Pathways to long-term effects in the Chicago Child-Parent Center Program.* Paper pre-

sented at the meeting of the Society for Research in Child Development, Albuquerque.

Rice, M.L. (Ed.). (1996). Toward a genetics of language. Hillsdale, NJ: Erlbaum.

Richards, M.H., & Duckett, E. (1994). The relationship of maternal employment to early adolescent daily experiences with and without parents. *Child Development, 65,* 225–236.

Rickards, T. (1999). Brainstorming. In M.A. Runco & S. Pritzker (Eds.), *Encyclopedia of creativity.* San Diego: Academic Press.

Riddle, D.B., & Prinz, R. (1984, August). *Sugar consumption in young children.* Paper presented at the meeting of the American Psychological Association, Toronto.

Ridgeway, D., Waters, E., & Kuczaj, S.A. (1985). Acquisition of emotion-descriptive language: Receptive and productive vocabulary norms for ages 18 months to 6 years. *Developmental Psychology, 21,* 901–908.

Rimberg, H.M., & Lewis, R.J. (1994). Older adolescents and AIDS: Correlates of self-reported safer sex practices. *Journal of Research on Adolescence, 4,* 453–464.

Roberts, W., & Strayer, J. (1996). Empathy, emotional expressiveness, and prosocial behavior. *Child Development, 67,* 471–489.

Robinson, D.P., & Greene, J.W. (1988). The adolescent alcohol and drug problem: A practical approach. *Pediatric Nursing, 14,* 305–310.

Rock, E.A., Fessler, M.A., & Church, R.P. (1997). The concomitance of learning disabilities and emotional/behavioral disorders: A conceptual model. *Journal of Learning Disabilities, 30,* 245–263.

Rode, S.S., Chang, P., Fisch, R.O., & Sroufe, L.A. (1981). Attachment patterns of infants separated at birth. *Developmental Psychology, 17,* 188–191.

Rodewald, L., Maes, E., Stevenson, J., Lyons, B., Stokley, S., & Szilagyi, P. (1999). Immunization performance measurement in a changing immunization environment. *Pediatrics, 103,* 889–897.

Rodin, J. (1984, December). Interview: A sense of control: *Psychology Today,* pp. 38–45.

Roff, M., Sells, S.B., & Golden, M.W. (1972). *Social adjustment and personality development in children.* Minneapolis: University of Minnesota Press.

Rogers, A. (1987). *Questions of gender differences: Ego development and moral voice in adolescence.* Unpublished manuscript, Department of Education, Harvard University.

Rogers, C.S., & Morris, S.S. (1986, July). Reducing sugar in children's diets: Why? How? *Young Children,* pp. 11–16.

Rogoff, B. (1998). Cognition as a collaborative process. In W. Damon (Ed.), *Handbook of child psychology* (5th ed., Vol. 2). New York: Wiley.

Rogosch, F.A., Cicchetti, D., Shields, A., & Toth, S.L. (1995). Parenting dysfunction in child maltreatment. In M.H. Bornstein (Ed.), *Handbook of parenting* (Vol. 4). Hillsdale, NJ: Erlbaum.

Rohner, R.P., & Rohner, E.C. (1981). Parental acceptance-rejection and parental control: Cross-cultural codes. *Ethnology, 20,* 245–260.

Roopnarine, J.L., & Johnson, J.E. (2000). *Approaches to early childhood education.* Columbus, OH: Merrill.

Rose, A.A., Feldman, J.F., McCarton, C.M., & Wolfson, J. (1988). Information processing in seven-month-old infants as a function of risk status. *Child Development, 59,* 489–603.

Rose, A.J., & Asher, S.R. (1999, April). *Seeking and giving social support within a friendship.* Paper presented at the meeting of the Society for Research in Child Development, Albuquerque.

Rose, S., & Frieze, I.R. (1993). Young singles' contemporary dating scripts. *Sex Roles, 28,* 499–509.

Rose, S.A. (1995). From hand to eye: Findings and issues in infant cross-modal transfer. In D.J. Lewkowicz & R. Lickliter (Eds.), *The development of intersensory perception.* Hillsdale, NJ: Erlbaum.

Rosen, K.S., & Burke, P.B. (1999). Multiple attachment relationships within families: Mothers and fathers with two young children. *Developmental Psychology, 35,* 436–444.

Rosenblith, J.F. (1992). *In the beginning* (2nd ed.). Newbury Park, CA: Sage.

Rosenstein, D., & Oster, H. (1988). Differential facial responses to four basic tastes in newborns. *Child Development, 59,* 1555–1568.

Rosenthal, D.M., & Sawyers, J.Y. (1996). Building successful home/school partnerships: Strategies for parent support and involvement. *Childhood Education, 72,* 194–200.

Rosenwalks, Z. (1998, September 10). Commentary. *USA Today,* p. 1A.

Rosenzweig, M.R. (1969). Effects of heredity and environment on brain chemistry, brain anatomy, and learning ability in the rat. In M. Monosevitz, G. Lindzey, & D.D. Thiessen (Eds.), *Behavioral genetics.* New York: Appleton-Century-Crofts.

Rothbart, M.K. (1999, April). *Developing a model for the study of temperament.* Paper presented at the meeting of the Society for Research in Child Development, Albuquerque.

Rothbart, M.K., & Bates, J.E. (1998). Temperament. In W. Damon (Ed.), *Handbook of child psychology* (5th ed., Vol. 3). New York: Wiley.

Rothbart, M.L.K. (1971). Birth order and mother-child interaction, *Dissertation Abstracts, 27,* 45–57.

Rothstein, R. (1998, May). Bilingual education: The controversy. *Phi Delta Kappan,* pp. 672–678.

Rovee-Collier, C. (1987). Learning and memory in children. In J.D. Osofsky (Ed.), *Handbook of infant development* (2nd ed.). New York: Wiley.

Rowe, D.C., & Jacobson, K.C. (1999, April). *Genetic and environmental influences on vocabulary IQ: Parental education as moderator.* Paper presented at the meeting of the Society for Research in Child Development, Albuquerque.

Rubin, D.H., Krasilnikoff, P.A., Leventhal, J.M., Weile, B., & Berget, A. (1986, August 23). Effect of passive smoking on birthweight. *The Lancet,* 415–417.

Rubin, K.H., Coplan, R., Nelson, L., Cheah, C., & Leagacy-Sequin, D.G. (1999). Peer relationships in childhood. In M.H. Bornstein & M.E. Lamb (Eds.), *Developmental psychology: An advanced textbook* (4th ed.). Mahwah, NJ: Erlbaum.

Rubin, K.H., Maioni, T.L., & Hornung, M. (1976). Free play behaviors in middle and lower social class preschoolers: Parten and Piaget revisited. *Child Development, 47,* 414–419.

Rubin, K.H., Fein, G.G., & Vandenberg, B. (1983). Play. In P.H. Mussen (Ed.), *Handbook of child psychology* (4th ed., Vol. 4). New York: Wiley.

Rubin, Z., & Sloman, J. (1984). How parents influence their children's friendships. In M. Lewis (Ed.), *Beyond the dyad.* New York: Plenum.

Rumberger, R.W. (1983). Dropping out of high school: The influence of race, sex, and family background. *American Educational Research Journal, 20,* 199–220.

Rumberger, R.W. (1995). Dropping out of middle school: A multilevel analysis of students and schools. *American Educational Research Journal, 3,* 583–625.

Runco, M.A. (1999). Critical thinking. In M.A. Runco & S. Pritzker (Eds.), *Encyclopedia of creativity.* San Diego: Academic Press.

Rushton, J.P. (1988). Race differences in behavior: A review and evolutionary analysis. *Journal of Personality and Individual Differences, 9,* 1035–1040.

Rutter, M. (1979). Protective factors in children's response to stress and disadvantage. In M.W. Kent & J.E. Rolf (Eds.), *Primary prevention in psychopathology* (Vol. 3). Hanover, NH: University Press of New England.

Rutter, M., & Schopler, E. (1987). Autism and pervasive developmental disorders: Concepts and diagnostic issues. *Journal of Autism and Pervasive Developmental Disorders, 17,* 159–186.

Ryan, A.M., & Patrick, H. (1996, March). *Positive peer relationships and psychosocial adjustment during adolescence.* Paper presented at the meeting of the Society for Research on Adolescence, Boston.

Ryan-Finn, K.D., Cauce, A.M., & Grove, K. (1995, March). *Children and adolescents of color: Where are you? Selection, recruitment, and retention in developmental research.* Paper presented at the meeting of the Society for Research in Child Development, Indianapolis.

Rymer, R. (1992). *Genie.* New York: HarperCollins.

S

Saarni, C. (1999). *The development of emotional competence.* New York: Guilford.

Saarni, C., Mumme, D.L., & Campos, J.J. (1998). Emotional development: Action, communication, and understanding. In W. Damon (Ed.), *Handbook of child psychology* (5th ed., Vol. 3). New York: Wiley.

Sadker, M., & Sadker, D. (1994). *Failing at fairness.* New York: Touchstone.

Sagan, C. (1977). *Dragons of Eden.* New York: Random House.

Samaras, A.P. (1996). Children's computers. *Childhood Education, 72,* 133–136.

Samuels, M., & Samuels, N. (1996). *New well pregnancy book.* New York: Fireside.

Sanson, A., & Rothbart, M.K. (1995). Child temperament and parenting. In M.H. Bornstein (Ed.), *Handbook of parenting* (Vol. 4). Hillsdale, NJ: Erlbaum.

Santrock, J.W. (1999). *Life-span development* (7th ed.). Boston: McGraw-Hill.

Santrock, J.W., & Sitterle, K.A. (1987). Parent-child relationships in stepmother families. In K. Pasley & M. Thinger-Tallman (Eds.), *Remarriage and stepparenting.* New York: Guilford Press.

Santrock, J.W., Sitterle, K.A., & Warshak, R.A. (1988). Parent–child relationships in stepfather families. In P. Bronstein & C.P. Cowan (Eds.), *Fatherhood today: Men's changing roles in the family.* New York: Wiley.

Santrock, J.W., & Warshak, R.A. (1986). Development, relationships, and legal/clinical considerations in father custody families. In M.E. Lamb (Ed.), *The father's role: Applied perspectives.* New York: Wiley.

Savin-Williams, R.C., & Rodriguez, R.G. (1993). A developmental, clinical perspective on lesbian, gay male, and bisexual youths. In T.P. Gullotta, G.R. Adams, & R. Montemayor (Eds.), *Adolescent sexuality.* Newbury Park, CA: Sage.

Scales, P.C. (1992). *A portrait of young adolescents in the 1990s: Implications for promoting healthy growth and development.* Carrboro, NC: Center for Early Adolescence.

Scarr, S. (1984, May). Interview. *Psychology Today,* pp. 59–63.

Scarr, S. (1993). Biological and cultural diversity: The legacy of Darwin for development. *Child Development, 64,* 1333–1353.

Scarr, S. (1996). Best of human genetics. *Contemporary Psychology, 41,* 149–150.

Scarr, S., Lande, J., & McCartney, K. (1989). Child care and the family: Complements and interactions. In J. Lande, S. Scarr, & N. Guzenhauser (Eds.), *Caring for children: Challenge to America.* Hillsdale, NJ: Erlbaum.

Scarr, S., & Weinberg, R.A. (1980). Calling all camps! The war is over. *American Sociological Review, 45,* 859–865.

Scarr, S., & Weinberg, R.A. (1983). The Minnesota adoption studies: Genetic differences and malleability. *Child Development, 54,* 253–259.

Schaffer, H.R. (1996). *Social development.* Cambridge, MA: Blackwell.

Schiller, M. (1995). An emergent art curriculum that fosters understanding. *Young Children, 50,* 33–38.

Schnorr, T.M., & others. (1991). Videodisplay terminals and the risk of spontaneous abortion. *New England Journal of Medicine, 324,* 727–733.

Schoenbrodt, L., Kumin, L., & Sloan, J.M. (1997). Learning disabilities existing concomitantly with communication disorder. *Journal of Learning Disabilities, 30,* 282–296.

Schoendorf, K.C., & Kiely, J.L. (1992). Relationship of sudden infant death syndrome to maternal smoking during and after pregnancy. *Pediatrics, 90,* 905–908.

Schrag, S.G., & Dixon, R.L. (1985). Occupational exposure associated with male reproductive dysfunction. *Annual Review of Pharmacology and Toxicology, 25,* 467–592.

Schreiber, L.R. (1990). *The parent's guide to kids' sports.* Boston: Little, Brown.

Schunk, D.H. (1983). Developing children's self-efficacy and skills: The roles of social comparative information and goal-setting. *Contemporary Educational Psychology, 8,* 76–86.

Schunk, D.H. (2000). *Learning theories* (3rd ed.). Columbus, OH: Merrill

Schunk, D.H., & Zimmerman, B.J. (Eds.). (1994). *Self-regulation of learning and performance: Issues and educational applications.* Mahwah, NJ: Erlbaum.

Schwartz, D., & Mayaux, M.J. (1982). Female fecundity as a function of age: Results of artificial insemination in nulliparous women with azoospermic husbands. *New England Journal of Medicine, 306,* 304–406.

Schweinhart, L.J. (1999, April). *Generalizing from High/Scope longitudinal studies.* Paper presented at the meeting of the Society for Research in Child Development, Albuquerque.

Scott, P. (1997). Language. In P. Scott & C. Spencer (Eds.), *Psychology.* Cambridge, MA: Blackwell.

Scott-Jones, D. (1995, March). *Incorporating ethnicity and socioeconomic status in research with children.* Paper presented at the meeting of the Society for Research in Child Development, Indianapolis.

Scribner, S. (1977). Modes of thinking and ways of speaking: Culture and logic reconsidered. In P.N. Johnson-Laird & P.C. Wason (Eds.), *Thinking: Readings in cognitive science.* New York: Cambridge University Press.

Seefeldt, C. (1995). Art—A serious work. *Young Children, 50,* 39–45.

Selman, R.L. (1980). *The growth of interpersonal understanding.* New York: Academic Press.

Semaj, L.T. (1985). Afrikanity, cognition, and extended self-identity. In M.B. Spencer, G.K. Brookins, & W.R. Allen (Eds.), *Beginnings: The social and affective development of Black children.* Hillsdale, NJ: Erlbaum.

Serbin, L.A., & Sprafkin, C. (1986). The salience of gender in the process of sex-typing in three- to seven-year-old children. *Child Development, 57,* 1188–1209.

Serdula, M., Williamson, D.F., Kendrick, J.S., Anda, R.F., & Byers, T. (1991). Trends in alcohol consumption by pregnant women: 1985 through 1988. *Journal of the American Medical Association, 265,* 876–879.

Serow, R.C., Ciechalski, J., & Daye, C. (1990). Students as volunteers. *Urban Education, 25,* 157–168.

Shade, S.C., Kelly, C., & Oberg, M. (1997). *Creating culturally-responsive schools.* Washington, DC: American Psychological Association.

Sheets, R.H. (1995). Relating competence in an urban classroom to ethnic identity development. In R.H. Sheets & E.R. Hollins (Eds.), *Racial and ethnic identity in school practices.* Mahwah, NJ: Erlbaum.

Sheffield, V.C. (1999, May). *Application of genetic strategies and human genome project resources for the identification of human disease genes.* Paper presented at the meeting of the Society for Pediatric Research, San Francisco.

Shields, S.A. (1991). Gender in the psychology of emotion: A selective research review. In K.T. Strongman (Ed.), *International review of studies on emotion* (Vol. 1). New York: Wiley.

Shiono, P.H., & Behrman, R.E. (1995, Spring). Low birth weight: Analysis and recommendations. *The Future of Children, 5,* 4–18.

Shirley, M.M. (1933). *The first two years.* Minneapolis: University of Minnesota Press.

Shneidman, E. (1996). *The suicidal mind.* New York: Oxford University Press.

Siegel, B. (1997, April). *Developmental and social policy issues and the practice of educational mainstreaming and full inclusion.* Paper presented at the meeting of the Society for Research in Child Development, Washington, DC.

Siegel, L.S. (1989, April). *Perceptual-motor, cognitive, and language skills as predictors of cognitive abilities at school age.* Paper presented at the biennial meeting of the Society for Research in Children, Kansas City.

Siegler, R. (1996). Information processing. In J.W. Santrock, *Child development* (7th ed.). Madison, WI: Brown & Benchmark.

Sigel, I.E. (1998). Practice and research: A problem in developing communication and cooperation. In W. Damon (Ed.), *Handbook of child psychology* (5th ed., Vol. 4). New York: Wiley.

Silverberg, S.B., & Steinberg, L. (1990). Psychological well-being of parents with early adolescent children. *Developmental Psychology, 26,* 658–666.

Simkin, P., Whalley, J., Keppler, A. (1984). *Pregnancy, childbirth, and the newborn.* New York: Simon & Schuster.

Simmons, R.G., & Blyth, D.A. (1987). *Moving into adolescence.* Hawthorne, NY: Aldine.

Simons, J., Finlay, B., & Yang, A. (1991). *The adolescent and young adult fact book.* Washington, DC: Children's Defense Fund.

Simpson, R.L. (1962). Parental influence, anticipatory socialization, and social mobility. *American Sociological Review, 27,* 517–522.

Singer, D.G. (1993). Creativity of children in a changing world. In G.L. Berry & J.K. Asamen (Eds.), *Children and television: Images in a changing sociocultural world.* Newbury Park, CA: Sage.

Skinner, B.F. (1957). *Verbal behavior.* New York: Appleton-Century-Crofts.

Skinner, E.A., Wellborn, J.G., & Connell, J.P. (1990). What it takes to do well in school and whether I've got it: A process model of perceived control and children's engagement and achievement in school. *Journal of Educational Psychology, 82,* 22–32.

Slavin, R.E. (1989). Cooperative learning and student achievement. In R.E. Slavin (Ed.), *School and classroom organization.* Hillsdale, NJ: Erlbaum.

Slavin, R.E. (1997). *Educational psychology* (5th ed.). Boston: Allyn & Bacon.

Slavin, R.E. (1999). Reading by nine: What will it take? In J.W. Miller & M.C. McKenna (Eds.), *Literacy education in the 21st century.* Mahwah, NJ: Erlbaum.

Slobin, D. (1972, July) Children and language: They learn the same way all around the world. *Psychology Today,* pp. 71–76.

Slusser, W., & Powers, N.G. (1997). Breastfeeding update: Immunology, nutrition, and advocacy. *Pediatrics in Review, 18* (4), 111–114.

Small, S.A. (1990). *Preventive programs that support families with adolescents.* Washington, DC: Carnegie Council on Adolescent Development.

Snarey, J. (1987, June). A question of morality. *Psychology Today,* pp. 6–8.

Snarey, J. (1998). Fathers. In H.S. Friedman (Ed.), *Encyclopedia of mental health* (Vol. 1). San Diego: Academic Press.

Snider, B.A., & Miller, J.P. (1993). The land-grant university system and 4-H: A mutually beneficial relationship of scholars and practitioners in youth development. In R.M. Lerner (Ed.), *Early adolescence.* Hillsdale, NJ: Erlbaum.

Snow, C.E. (1996). Interactionist account of language acquisition. In M. Rice (Ed.), *Towards a genetics of language*. Mahwah, NJ: Erlbaum.

Snow, C.E. (1998). Social perspectives on the emergence of language. In B. MacWhinney (Ed.), *The emergence of language*. Mahwah, NJ: Erlbaum.

Snow, C.E. (1999). Social perspectives on the emergence of language. In B. MacWhinney (Ed.), *The emergence of language*. Mahwah, NJ: Erlbaum.

Solomon, B., Powell, K., & Gardner, H. (1999). Multiple intelligence. In M.A. Runco & S. Pritzker (Eds.), *Encyclopedia of creativity*. San Diego: Academic Press.

Sonenstein, F.L., Pleck, J.H., & Ku, L.C. (1989). Sexual activity, condom use, and AIDS awareness among adolescent males. *Family Planning Perspectives, 21,* 152–158.

Spearman, C.E. (1927). *The abilities of man*. New York: Macmillan.

Spear-Swerling, L., & Sternberg, R.J. (1994). The road not taken: An integrative theoretical model of reading disability. *Journal of Learning Disabilities, 27,* 91–103.

Spelke, E.S. (1979). Perceiving bimodally specified events in infancy. *Developmental Psychology, 5,* 626–636.

Spelke, E.S. (1988). The origins of physical knowledge. In L. Weiskrantz (Ed.), *Thought without language*. New York: Oxford University Press.

Spelke, E.S. (1991). Physical knowledge in infancy: Reflections on Piaget's theory. In S. Carey & R. Gelman (Eds.), *The epigenesis of mind: Essays on biology and cognition*. Hillsdale, NJ: Erlbaum.

Spelke, E.S., & Newport, E.L. (1998). Nativism, empiricism, and the development of knowledge. In W. Damon (Ed.), *Handbook of child psychology* (5th ed., Vol. 2). New York: Wiley.

Spelke, E.S., & Owsley, C.J. (1979). Intermodal exploration and knowledge in infancy. *Infant Behavior and Development, 2,* 13–28.

Spence, J.T., & Helmreich, R. (1978). *Masculinity and femininity: Their psychological dimensions*. Austin: University of Texas Press.

Spence, M.J., & DeCasper, A.J. (1987). Prenatal experience with low-frequency maternal voice sounds influences neonatal perception of maternal voice samples. *Infant Behavior and Development, 10,* 133–142.

Spencer, M.B. (1990). Commentary in Spencer, M.B., & Dornbusch, S. Challenges in studying ethnic minority youth. In S.S. Feldman & G.R. Elliott (Eds.), *At the threshold: The developing adolescent*. Cambridge, MA: Harvard University Press.

Spencer, M.B. (1999). Social and cultural influences on school adjustment: The application of an identity-focused cultural ecological perspective. In K. Wentzel & T. Berndt (Eds.), *Social influences on school adjustment*. Mahwah, NJ: Erlbaum.

Spencer, M.B., & Dornbusch, S.M. (1990). Challenges in studying minority youth. In S.S. Feldman & G.R. Elliott (Eds.), *At the threshold: The developing adolescent*. Cambridge, MA: Harvard University Press.

Spring, J. (1998). *The intersection of cultures*. Burr Ridge, IL McGraw-Hill.

Sroufe, L.A. (1985). Attachment classification from the perspective of infant-caregiver relationships and infant temperament. *Child Development, 49,* 547–556.

Sroufe, L.A. (1996). *Emotional development*. New York: Cambridge U. Press.

Sroufe, L.A., & Waters, E. (1976). The ontogenesis of smiling and laughter: A perspective on the organization of development in infancy. *Psychological Review, 83,* 173–198.

Sroufe, L.A., Egeland, B., & Carlson, E.A. (1999). One social world: The integrated development of parent-child and peer relationships. In W.A. Collins & B. Laursen (Eds.), *Minnesota symposium on child psychology*, vol. 31. Mahwah, NJ: Erlbaum.

Sroufe, L.A., Egeland, B., & Carlson, E.A. (1999). One social world: Integrated development of parent-child and peer relationships. In W.A. Collins & B. Laursen (Eds.), *Relationships as developmental contexts*. Mahwah, NJ: Erlbaum.

Sroufe, L.A., Waters, E., & Matas, L. (1974). Contextual determinants of infant affectional response. In M. Lewis & L. Rosenblum (Eds.), *Origins of fear*. New York: Wiley.

St. Pierre, R., Layzer, J., & Barnes, H. (1996). *Regenerating two-generation programs*. Cambridge, MA: Abt Associates.

Stallings, J. (1975). Implementation and child effects of teaching practices in Follow Through classrooms. *Monographs of the Society for Research in Child Development, 40* (Serial No. 163).

Stanhope, L., & Corter, C. (1993, March). *The mother's role in the transition to siblinghood*. Paper presented at the biennial meeting of the Society for Research in Child Development, New Orleans.

Stanley, K., Soule, B., & Copens, S.A. (1979). Dimensions of prenatal anxiety and their influence on pregnancy outcome. *American Journal of Obstetrics and Gynecology, 135,* 333–348.

Stattin, H., & Magnusson, D. (1990). *Pubertal maturation in female development: Paths through life* (Vol. 2). Hillsdale, NJ: Erlbaum.

Staub, E. (1996). Cultural-societal roots of violence. *American Psychologist, 51,* 117–132.

Stechler, G., & Halton, A. (1982). Prenatal influences on human development. In B.B. Wolman (Ed.), *Handbook of developmental psychology*. Englewood Cliffs, NJ: Prentice Hall.

Steinberg, L.D. (1986). Latchkey children and susceptibility to peer pressure: An ecological analysis. *Developmental Psychology, 22,* 433–439.

Steinberg, L.D., Fegley, S., & Dornbusch, S.M. (1993). Negative impact of part-time work on adolescent adjustment: Evidence from a longitudinal study. *Developmental Psychology, 29,* 171–180.

Steiner, J.E. (1979). Human facial expressions in response to taste and smell stimulation. In H. Reese & L. Lipsitt (Eds.), *Advances in child development and behavior* (Vol. 13). New York: Academic Press.

Stengel, R. (1996, April 22). Fly till I die. *Time,* pp. 34–40.

Stenhouse, G. (1996). *Practical parenting*. New York: Oxford University Press.

Stern, D.N., Beebe, B., Jaffe, J., & Bennett, S.L. (1977). The infant's stimulus world during social interaction: A study of caregiver behaviors with particular reference to repetition and timing. In H.R. Schaffer (Ed.), *Studies in mother-infant interaction*. London: Academic Press.

Sternberg, R.J. (1977). *Intelligence, information processing, and analogical reasoning: The componential analysis of human abilities*. Hillsdale, NJ: Erlbaum.

Sternberg, R.J. (1986). *Intelligence applied*. San Diego: Harcourt Brace Jovanovich.

Sternberg, R.J. (1995, May/June). The triarchic model applied to identifying, teaching, and assessing gifted children. *Roeper Review*, pp. 255–260.

Sternberg, R.J. (1999). Intelligence. In M.A. Runco & S. Pritzker (Eds.), *Encyclopedia of creativity*. San Diego: Academic Press.

Sternberg, R.J., & Nigro, C. (1980). Developmental patterns in the solution of verbal analogies. *Child Development, 51,* 27–38.

Sternberg, R.J., & Rifkin, B. (1979). The development of analogical reasoning processes. *Journal of Experimental Child Psychology, 27,* 195–232.

Sternglanz, S.H., & Serbin, L.A. (1974). Sex-role stereotyping in children's television programming. *Developmental Psychology, 10,* 710–715.

Steur, F.B., Applefield, J.M., & Smith, R. (1971). Televised aggression and interpersonal aggression of preschool children. *Journal of Experimental Child Psychology, 11,* 442–447.

Stevenson, H.C. (1998). Raising safe villages: Cultural–ecological factors that influence the emotional adjustment of adolescents. *Journal of Black Psychology, 24,* 44–59.

Stevenson, H.C. (in press). The confluence of the "both-and" in Black racial identity theory. In R. Jones (Ed.), *Advances in Black psychology*. Hampton, VA: Cobb & Henry.

Stevenson, H.G. (1995, March). *Missing data: On the forgotten substance of race, ethnicity, and socioeconomic classifications*. Paper presented at the meeting of the Society for Research in Child Development, Indianapolis.

Stevenson, H.W. (1995). Mathematics achievement of American children: First in the world by the year 2000? In C.A. Nelson (Ed.), *Basic and applied perspectives on learning, cognition, and development*. Minneapolis: University of Minnesota Press.

Stevenson, H.W., Lee, S., Chen, C., Stigler, J.W., Hsu, C., & Kitamura, S. (1990). Contexts of achievement. *Monograph of the Society for Research in Child Development, 55* (Serial No. 221).

Stillman, R. (1998, September 10). Commentary. *USA Today,* p. 1D.

Stipek, D., Rosenblatt, L., & DiRocco, L. (1994). Making parents your allies. *Young Children, 49,* 4–9.

Stocker, C., & Dunn, J. (1991). Sibling relationships in adolescence. In R.M. Lerner, A.C. Petersen, & J. Brooks-Gunn (Eds.), *Encyclopedia of adolescence* (Vol. 2). New York: Garland.

Stone, L. (1994). Teaching Sam to enjoy reading. *Young Children, 49,* 76–79.

Strasburger, V.C. (1995). *Adolescents and the media*. Newbury Park, CA: Sage.

Strauss, R.S., & Knight, J. (in Press). Influence of the home environment on the development of obesity in children. *Pediatrics*.

Streissguth, A.P., Martin, D.C., Sandman, B.M., Kirchner, G.L., & Darby, B.L. (1984). Intrauterine alcohol and nicotine exposure: Attention and reaction time in four-year-old children. *Developmental Psychology, 20,* 533–543.

Sue, S. (1990, August). *Ethnicity and culture in psychological research and practice*. Paper presented at the meeting of the American Psychological Association, Boston.

Sullivan, H.S. (1953). *The interpersonal theory of psychiatry*. New York: W.W. Norton.

Sullivan, K., & Sullivan, A. (1980). Adolescent-parent separation. *Developmental Psychology, 16,* 93–99.

Sullivan, L. (1991, May 25). U.S. secretary urges TV to restrict "irresponsible sex and reckless violence." *Boston Globe,* p.A1.

Suomi, S.J., Harlow, H.F., & Domek, C.J. (1970). Effect of repetitive infant-infant separations of young monkeys. *Journal of Abnormal Psychology, 76,* 161–172.

Super, D.E. (1976). *Career education and the meanings of work*. Washington, DC: U.S. Office of Education.

Susman, E. (1995). Unpublished review of *Adolescence* (6th ed.), by J.W. Santrock. Dubuque, IA: Brown & Benchmark.

Swanson, D.P. (1997, April). *Identity and coping styles among African-American females*. Paper presented at the meeting of the Society for Research in Child Development, Washington, DC.

Swanson, D.P., Spencer, M.B., & Petersen, A.C. (1998). Identity formation in adolescence. In K. Borman & B. Schneider (Eds.), *The adolescent years: Social influence and educational challenges*. Chicago: University of Chicago Press.

Swanson, J.M., McBrunett, K., Wigal, T., & Others. (1993). The effect of stimulant medication on ADD children. *Exceptional Children, 60,* 154–162.

Swarr, A.E., & Richards, M.H. (1996). Longitudinal effects of adolescent girls' pubertal development, perceptions of pubertal timing, and parental relations. *Developmental Psychology, 32,* 636–646.

T

Tager-Flusberg, H. (Ed.). (1994). *Constraints on language acquisition.* Hillsdale, NJ: Erlbaum.

Takahashi, K. (1990). Are the key assumptions of the "Strange Situation" procedure universal? A view from Japanese research. *Human Development, 33,* 23–30.

Takanishi, R. (1993). The opportunities of adolescence: Research, interventions, and policy. *American Psychologist, 48,* 85–87.

Tamarin, R. (1996). *Principles of genetics* (5th ed.). Dubuque, IA: Wm. C. Brown.

Tannen, D. (1990). *You just don't understand!* New York: Ballentine.

Tappan, M.B. (1998). Sociocultural psychology and caring psychology: Exploring Vygotsky's "hidden curriculum." *Educational Psychologist, 33,* 23–33.

Tapper, J. (1996, March). *Values, lifestyles, and crowd identification in adolescence.* Paper presented at the meeting of the Society for Research on Adolescence, Boston.

Taskinin, H. (1989). Spontaneous abortions and congenital malformations among the wives of men exposed to organic solvents. *Scandinavian Journal of Work, Environment, and Health, 15,* 345–352.

Taylor, S. (1999). *Health psychology* (4th ed.). Boston: McGraw-Hill.

Terman, D.L., Larner, M.B., Stevenson, C.S., & Behrman, R.E. (1996). Special education for students with disabilities: Analysis and recommendations. *The Future of Children, 6*(1) 4–24.

Terman, L. (1925). *Genetic studies of genius: Vol. 1. Mental and physical traits of a thousand gifted children.* Stanford, CA: Stanford University Press.

Terman, L.H., & Oden, M.H. (1959). *Genetic studies of genius: Vol. 5. The gifted group at mid-life.* Stanford, CA: Stanford University Press.

Teti, D.M., Sakin, J., Kucera, E., Caballeros, M., & Corns, K.M. (1993, March). *Transitions to siblinghood and security of firstborn attachment: Psychosocial and psychiatric correlates of changes over time.* Paper presented at the biennial meeting of the Society for Research in Child Development, New Orleans.

Tetreault, M.K.T. (1997). Classrooms for diversity: Rethinking curriculum and pedagogy. In J.A. Banks & C.A. Banks (Eds.), *Multicultural education* (3rd ed.). Boston: Allyn & Bacon.

Tharp, G.R., & Gallimore, R. (1988). *Rousing minds to life: Teaching, learning, and schooling in social context.* New York: Cambridge University Press.

Tharp, R.G. (1994). Intergroup differences among Native Americans in socialization and child cognition: An ethogenetic analysis. In P.M. Greenfield & R. Cocking (Eds.), *Cross-cultural roots of minority child development.* Mahwah, NJ: Erlbaum.

Thelen, E. (1995). Motor development: A new synthesis. *American Psychologist, 50,* 79–95.

Thelen, E. (1997, April 28). Commentary. Talking to infants may boost their ability to think, studies find. *Dallas Morning News,* p. B8.

Thelen, E., & Smith, L.B. (1998). Dynamic systems theory. In W. Damon (Ed.), *Handbook of child psychology* (5th ed., Vol. 1.). New York: Wiley.

Thoman, E.B., Denenberg, V.H., Sievel, J., Zeidner, L., & Becker, P.T. (1981). State organization in neonates: Developmental inconsistency indicates risk for developmental dysfunction. *Neuropaediatrica, 12,* 45–54.

Thomas, A., & Chess, S. (1991). Temperament in adolescence and its functional significance. In R.M. Lerner, A.C. Petersen, & J. Brooks-Gunn (Eds.), *Encyclopedia of adolescence* (Vol. 2). New York: Garland.

Thomas, K. (1998, November 4). Teen cyberdating is a new wrinkle for parents, too. *USA Today,* p. 9D.

Thompson, E.T., & Hughes, E.C. (1958). *Race: Individual and collective behavior.* Glencoe, IL: Free Press.

Thompson, R.A. (1999). The individual child: Temperament, emotion, self, and personality. In M.H. Bornstein & M.E. Lamb (Eds.), *Developmental psychology: An advanced textbook* (4th ed.). Mahwah, NJ: Erlbaum.

Thorton, A., & Camburn, D. (1989). Religious participation and sexual behavior and attitudes. *Journal of Marriage and the Family, 49,* 117–128.

Thurstone, L.L. (1938). *Primary mental abilities.* Chicago: U. of Chicago Press.

Tinsley, B.J., Findley, K.A., & Ortiz, R.V. (1999, April). *Parental eating socialization in middle childhood: A multi-ethnic perspective.* Paper presented at the meeting of the Society for Research in Child Development, Albuquerque.

Tobin, J.J., Wu, D.Y.H., & Davidson, D.H. (1989). *Preschool in three cultures.* New Haven, CT: Yale University Press.

Tomlinson-Keasey, C. (1990). The working lives of Terman's gifted women. In H.W. Grossman & N.L. Chester (Eds.), *The experience and meaning of work in women's lives.* Hillsdale, NJ: Erlbaum.

Tomlinson-Keasey, C. (1993, August). *Tracing the lives of gifted women.* Paper presented at the meeting of the American Psychological Association, Toronto.

Tomlinson-Keasey, C., Warren, L.W., & Elliott, J.E. (1986). Suicide among gifted women: A prospective study. *Journal of Abnormal Psychology, 95,* 123–130.

Tompkins, G. (1997). *Literacy for the 21st century: A balanced approach.* Upper Saddle River, NJ: Prentice-Hall.

Torgesen, J.K. (1995, December). *Prevention and remediation of reading disabilities.* Progress Report NICHD Grant HD 30983. Bethesda, MD: The National Institute of Child Health and Human Development.

Torgesen, J.K. (1999). Reading disabilities. In R. Gallimore, L.P. Bernheimer, D.L. MacMillan, D.L. Speece, & S. Vaughn (Eds.), *Developmental perspectives on children with learning disabilities.* Mahwah, NJ: Erlbaum.

Torney-Purta, J. (1993, August). *Cross-cultural examination of stages of faith development.* Paper presented at the meeting of the American Psychological Association, Toronto.

Toth, S.K., Conner, P.D., & Streissguth, A.P. (1999, April). *Psychiatric/behavioral and learning and memory problems in young adults with fetal alcohol syndrome and fetal alcohol effects.* Paper presented at the meeting of the Society for Research in Child Development, Albuquerque.

Toth, S.L., Manley, J.T., Cicchetti, D. (1992). Child maltreatment and vulnerability to depression. *Development and Psychopathology, 4,* 97–112.

Tousignant, M. (1995, April 11). Children's cure or adults' crutch? Rise of Ritalin prompts debate over the reason. *Washington Post,* p. B1.

Treffers, P.E., Eskes, M., Kleiverda, G., & van Alten, D. (1990). Home births and minimal medical interventions. *Journal of the American Medical Association, 246,* 2207–2208.

Trehub, S.E., Schneider, B.A., Thorpe, L.A., & Judge, P. (1991). Observational measures of auditory sensitivity in early infancy. *Developmental Psychology, 27,* 40–49.

Trimble, J.E. (1989, August). *The enculturation of contemporary psychology.* Paper presented at the meeting of the American Psychological Association, New Orleans.

Troiano, R.P., & Flegal, K.M. (1998). Overweight children and adolescents: Description, epidemiology, and demographics. *Pediatrics, 101,* 497–504.

Tsai, L.Y. (1999). Recent neurobiological research in autism: Myths, controversies, and perspectives. In D.E.B. Zager (Ed.), *Autism.* Mahwah, NJ: Erlbaum.

Tubman, J.G., & Windle, M. (1995). Continuity of difficult temperament in adolescence: Relations with depression, life events, family support, and substance abuse. *Journal of Youth and Adolescence, 24,* 133–152.

Tucker, L.A. (1987). Television, teenagers, and health. *Journal of Youth and Adolescence, 16,* 415–425.

Tuckman, B.W., & Hinkle, J.S. (1988). An experimental study of the physical and psychological effects of aerobic exercise on school children. In B.G. Melamed, K.A. Matthews, D.K. Routh, B. Stabler, & N. Schneiderman (Eds.), *Child health psychology.* Hillsdale, NJ: Erlbaum.

Turecki, S., & Tonner, L. (1989). *The difficult child.* New York: Bantam.

Turnbull, A., Turnbull, R., Shank, M., & Leal, D. (1999). *Exceptional lives: Special education in today's schools.* Columbus, OH: Merrill.

Tyack, D. (1976). Ways of seeing: An essay on the history of compulsory schooling. *Harvard Educational Review, 46,* 355–389.

U

U.S. Department of Education. (1993). *Violence in schools.* Washington, DC: Author.

U.S. Department of Education. (1996). *Number and disabilities of children and youth served under IDEA.* Washington, DC: Office of Special Education Programs, Data Analysis System.

U.S. Department of Health and Human Services. (1998). *Teen births decline.* Washington, DC: Author.

U.S. General Accounting Office. (1987, September). *Prenatal care: Medicaid recipients and uninsured women obtain insufficient care.* A report to the Congress of the United States, HRD-97-137. Washington, DC: Author.

Unger, R., & Crawford, M. (1992). *Women and gender* (2nd ed.). New York: McGraw-Hill.

Urberg, K.A., & Wolowicz, L.S. (1996, March). *Antecedents and consequents of changes in parental monitoring.* Paper presented at the meeting of the Society for Research on Adolescence, Boston.

V

Van den Berghe, P.L. (1978). *Race and racism: A comparative perspective.* New York: Wiley.

van den Boom, D.C. (1989). Neonatal irritability and the development of attachment. In G.A. Kohnstamm, J.E. Bates, & M.K. Rothbart (Eds.), *Temperament in childhood.* New York: Wiley.

Van Hoorn, J., Nourot, P.M., Scales, B., & Alward, K.R. (1999). *Play at the center of the curriculum.* Columbus, OH: Merrill.

van IJzendoorn, M.H., & Kroonenberg, P.M. (1988). Cross-cultural patterns of attachment: A meta-analysis of the Strange Situation. *Child Development, 59,* 147–156.

Vandell, D.L., & Corasaniti, M.A. (1988). Variations in early child care: Do they predict subsequent social, emotional, and cognitive differences? *Child Development, 59,* 176–186.

Vandell, D.L., & Pierce, K.M. (1999, April). *Can after-school programs benefit children who live in high-crime neighborhoods?* Paper presented at the meeting of the Society for Research in Child Development, Albuquerque.

Vandell, D.L., & Wilson, K.S. (1988). Infants' interactions with mother, sibling, and peer: Contrasts and relations between interaction systems. *Child Development, 48,* 176–186.

Ventura, S.J., Martin, J.A., Curtin, S.C., & Mathews, T.J. (1997, June 10). *Report of final natality statistics, 1995.* Washington, DC: National Center for Health Statistics.

Von Beveren, T.T. (1998). *Prenatal development and the newborn.* Unpublished manuscript, University of Texas at Dallas, Richardson, TX.

Voyer, D., Voyer, S., & Bryden, M.P. (1995). Magnitude of sex differences in spatial abilities: A meta-analysis and consideration of critical variables. *Psychological Bulletin, 117,* 250–270.

Vygotsky, L.S. (1962). *Thought and language.* Cambridge, MA: MIT Press.

Vygotsky, L.S. (1987). Thinking and speech. In R.W. Rieber & A.S. Carton (Eds.), *The collected works of L.S. Vygotsky.* New York: Plenum.

W

Waddington, C.H. (1957). *The strategy of the genes.* London: Allen & Son.

Wagner, B.M., Cole, R.E., & Schwartzman, P. (1993, March). *Prediction of suicide attempts among junior and senior high school youth.* Paper presented at the meeting of the Society for Research in Child Development, New Orleans.

Wakschlag, L.S., Chase-Lansdale, P.L., & Brooks-Gunn, J. (1996, March). *Not just "ghosts in the nursery": Contemporaneous intergenerational relationships and parenting in young African American families.* Paper presented at the meeting of the Society for Research on Adolescence, Boston.

Walder, T. (1991). Infant social referencing. In J. Garber & K. Dodge (Eds.), *The development of emotional regulation and dysregulation.* New York: Cambridge University Press.

Waldman, I.D., & Rhee, S.H. (1999, April). *Are genetic and environmental influences on ADHD the same magnitude throughout the range of symptoms as at the disordered extreme?* Paper presented at the meeting of the Society for Research in Child Development, Albuquerque.

Waldron, M.C., & Turkheimer, E. (1999, April). *Shared family events predict nonshared outcomes.* Paper presented at the meeting of the Society for Research in Child Development, Albuquerque.

Walker, L.J. (1991). Sex differences in moral development. In W.M. Kurtines & J. Gewirtz (Eds.), *Moral behavior and development* (Vol. 2). Hillsdale, NJ: Erlbaum.

Walker, L.J. (1996). *Review of Child Development, 8th ed.* Madison, WI: Brown & Benchmark.

Wallace-Broscious, A., Serafica, F.C., & Osipow, S.H. (1994). Adolescent career development: Relationships to self-concept and identity status. *Journal of Research on Adolescence, 4,* 127–150.

Waltzman, M.L., Shannon, M., Bowen, A.P., & Bailey, M.C. (in Press). Monkeybar injuries: Complications of play. *Pediatrics.*

Ward, C.D. (1996). Adult intervention: Appropriate strategies for enriching the quality of children's play. *Young Children, 51,* 20–25.

Warman, K.L., Silver, E.J., McCourt, M.P., & Stein, R.E.K. (1999). How does home management of asthma exacerbations by parents of inner-city children differ from NHLBI guideline recommendations? *Pediatrics, 103,* 422–427.

Warrick, P. (1992, March 1). The fantastic voyage of Tanner Roberts. *Los Angeles Times,* pp. E1,12,13.

Waterman, A.S. (1992). Identity as an aspect of optimal psychological functioning. In G.R. Adams, T.P. Gullotta, & R. Montemayor (Eds.), *Adolescent identity formation.* Newbury Park, CA: Sage.

Waterman, A.S. (1997). An overview of service-learning and the role of research and evaluation in service-learning programs. In A.S. Waterman (Ed.), *Service learning.* Mahwah, NJ: Erlbaum.

Waters, E., Merrick, S.K., Albersheim, L.J., & Treboux, D. (1995, March). *Attachment security from infancy to early adulthood: A 20-year longitudinal study.* Paper presented at the meeting of the Society for Research in Child Development, Indianapolis.

Watson, J.B. (1928). *Psychological care of infant and child.* New York: W.W. Norton.

Weaver, C. (in press). *Reconsidering a balanced approach to reading.* Urbana, IL: National Council of Teachers of English.

Weaver, R.F., & Hedrick, P.W. (1996). *Genetics* (2nd ed.). Dubuque, IA: Wm. C. Brown.

Webster, J., Lloyd, W.C., Pritchard, M.A., Burridge, C.A., Plucknett, L.E., & Byrne, A. (1999). Development of evidence-based guidelines in midwifery and gynaecology nursing, *Midwifery, 15,* 2–5.

Wegman, W.E. (1986). Annual summary of vital statistics—1985. *Pediatrics, 78,* 1672–1677.

Weikart, D.P. (1982). Preschool education for disadvantaged children. In J.R. Travers & R.J. Light (Eds.), *Learning from experience: Evaluating early childhood demonstration programs.* Washington, DC: National Academy Press.

Weikart, P.S. (1987). *Round the circle: Key experiences in movement for children ages 3 to 5.* Ypsilanti, MI: High/Scope Press.

Weikert, D.P. (1993). [Long-term positive effects in the Perry Preschool Head Start program]. Unpublished data, High Scope Foundation, Ypsilanti, MI.

Weinstein, N.D. (1984). Reducing unrealistic optimism about illness susceptibility. *Health Psychology, 3,* 431–457.

Weiss, B., Dodge, K.A., Bates, J.E., & Pettit, G.S. (1992). Some consequences of early harsh discipline: Child aggression and a maladaptive social information processing style. *Child Development, 63,* 1321–1335.

Weissburg, R.P., & Greenberg, M.T. (1998). School and community competence-enhancement and prevention programs. In W. Damon (Ed.), *Handbook of child psychology* (5th ed., Vol. 4). New York: Wiley.

Weizmann, F., Weiner, N.I., Wiesenthal, D.L., & Ziegler, M. (1990). Differential K theory and racial hierarchies. *Canadian Psychology, 31,* 1–13.

Wellman, H.M. (1990). *The child's theory of mind.* Cambridge, MA: MIT Press.

Wentworth, R.A.L. (1999). *Montessori for the millenium.* Mahwah, NJ: Erlbaum.

Wentzel, K.R., & Asher, S.R. (1995). The academic lives of neglected, rejected, popular, and controversial children. *Child Development, 66,* 754–763.

Wentzel, K.R., & Erdley, C.A. (1993). Strategies for making friends: Relations to social behavior and peer acceptance in early adolescence. *Developmental Psychology, 29,* 819–826.

Werker, J.F., & LaLonde, C.E. (1988). Cross-language speech perception: Initial capabilities and developmental change. *Developmental Psychology, 24,* 672–683.

Werner, E.E. (1979). *Cross-cultural child development: A view from planet earth.* Monterey, CA: Brooks/Cole.

Werner, E.E. (1989). High risk children in young adulthood: A longitudinal study from birth to 32 years. *American Journal of Orthopsychiatry, 59,* 72–81.

Wertheimer, M. (1945). *Productive thinking.* New York: Harper.

Wertheimer, R.F. (1999, April). *Children in working poor families.* Paper presented at the meeting of the Society for Research in Child Development, Albuquerque.

Whitaker, R.C., Wright, J.A., Pepe, M.S., Seidel, K.D., & Dietz, W.H. (1997). Predicting obesity in young adulthood from childhood and parental obesity. *New England Journal of Medicine, 337,* 869–873.

White, B., Castle, P., & Held, R. (1964). Observations on the development of visually directed reaching. *Child Development, 35,* 349–364.

White, C.W., & Coleman, M. (2000). *Early childhood education.* Columbus, OH: Merrill.

White, S.H. (1995, March). *The children's cause: Some early organizations.* Paper presented at the meeting of the Society for Research in Child Development, Indianapolis.

Whiting, B.B. (1989, April). *Culture and interpersonal behavior.* Paper presented at the biennial meeting of the Society for Research in Child Development, Kansas City.

Whiting, B.B., & Edwards, C.P. (1988). *Children of different worlds.* Cambridge, MA: Harvard University Press.

Wigfield, A., & Eccles, J.S. (1994). Middle grades schooling and early adolescent development: An introduction. *Journal of Early Adolescence, 14,* 102–106.

Wigfield, A., & Eccles, J.S. (1995). Middle grades schooling and early adolescent development. *Journal of Early Adolescence, 15,* 5–8.

Wilcox, B.L. (1999, April). *Youth policy.* Paper presented at the meeting of the Society for Research in Child Development, Albuquerque.

Wilfond, B.S. (1999, May). *Genetic testing in children: Ethics issues of research and clinical practice.* Paper presented at the meeting of the Society for Pediatric Research, San Francisco.

William T. Grant Foundation Commission. (1988, February). *The forgotten half: Non-college-bound youth in America.* Washington, DC: William T. Grant Foundation.

Williams, C.R. (1986). *The impact of television: A natural experiment in three communities.* New York: Academic Press.

Williams, J.E., & Best, D.L. (1982). *Measuring sex stereotypes: A thirty-nation study.* Newbury Park, CA: Sage.

Williams, J.E., & Best, D.L. (1989). *Sex and psyche: Self-concept viewed cross-culturally.* Newbury Park, CA: Sage.

Williams, M.F., & Condry, J.C. (1989, April). *Living color: Minority portrayals and cross-racial interactions on television.* Paper presented at the Society for Research in Child Development meeting, Kansas City.

Wilson, B.J., & Gottman, J.M. (1996). Attention—The shuttle between emotion and cognition: Risk, resiliency, and physiological bases. In E.M. Hetherington & E.A. Blechman (Eds.), *Stress, coping, and resilience in children and families.* Hillsdale, NJ: Erlbaum.

Wilson-Shockley, S. (1995). *Gender differences in adolescent depression: The contribution of negative affect.* M.S. Thesis, University of Illinois at Urbana-Champaign.

Windle, W.F. (1940). *Physiology of the human fetus.* Philadelphia: Saunders.

Windridge, K.C., Cert, P.G., & Berryman, J.C. (1999). Women's experiences of giving birth after 35. *Birth, 26,* 16–23.

Winne, P.H. (1995). Inherent details in self-regulated learning. *Educational Psychologist, 30,* 173–187.

Winne, P.H. (1997). Experimenting to bootstrap self-regulated learning. *Journal of Educational Psychology, 89,* 397–410.

Winner, E. (1986, August). Where pelicans kiss seals. *Psychology Today,* pp. 24–35.

Winner, E. (1996). *Gifted children: Myths and realities.* New York: Basic Books.

Winsler, A., Diaz, R.M., & Montero, I. (1997). The role of private speech in the transition from collaborative to independent task performance in young children. *Early Childhood Research Quarterly, 12,* 59–79.

Wintre, M.G., & Vallance, D.D. (1994). A developmental sequence in the comprehension of emotions: Intensity, multiple emotions, and valence. *Developmental Psychology, 30,* 509–514.

Witkin, H.A., Mednick, S.A., Schulsinger, R., Bakkestrom, E., Christiansen, K.O., Goodenbough, D.R., Hirchhorn, K., Lunsteen, C., Owen, D.R., Philip, J., Ruben, D.B., & Stocking, M. (1976). Criminality in XYY and XXY men. *Science, 193,* 547–555.

Wolfe, W.S., Campbell, C., Fongillo, E.A., Haas, J.D., & Melnick, T.A. (1994). Overweight school children in New York State: Prevalence and characteristics. *American Journal of Public Health, 84,* 807–813.

Wolff, P.H. (1969). The natural history of crying and other vocalizations in early infancy. In B.M. Foss (Ed.), *Determinants of infant development* (Vol. 4). London, England: Methuen.

Wong, D.L. (1997). *Essentials of pediatric nursing* (5th ed.). St. Louis: Mosby.

Woodrich, D.L. (1994). *Attention-deficit hyperactivity disorder: What every parent should know.* Baltimore: Paul Brookes.

Worobey, J., & Belsky, J. (1982). Employing the Brazelton scale to influence mothering: An experimental comparison of three strategies. *Developmental Psychology, 18,* 736–743.

Wright, J.C. (1995, March). *Effects of viewing Sesame Street: The longitudinal study of media and time use.* Paper presented at the meeting of the Society for Research in Child Development, Indianapolis.

Wright, J.L., & Shade, D.D. (Eds.). (1994). *Young children: Active learners in a technological age.* Washington, DC: NAEYC.

Wright, M.R. (1989). Body image satisfaction in adolescent girls and boys. *Journal of Youth and Adolescence, 18,* 71–84.

Wroblewski, R., & Huston, A.C. (1987). Televised occupational stereotypes and their effects on early adolescents: Are they changing? *Journal of Early Adolescence, 7,* 283–297.

Y

Yates, M. (1995, March). *Community service and political-moral discussions among Black urban adolescents.* Paper presented at the meeting of the Society for Research in Child Development, Indianapolis.

Yates, M. (1995, March). *Political socialization as a function of volunteerism.* Paper presented at the meeting of the Society for Research in Child Development, Indianapolis.

Yates, M. (1996, March). *Community service and political-moral discussions among Black urban adolescents.* Paper presented at the meeting of the Society for Research on Adolescence, Boston.

Yin, Y., Buhrmester, D., & Hibbard, D. (1996, March). *Are there developmental changes in the influence of relationships with parents and friends on adjustment during early adolescence?* Paper presented at the meeting of the Society for Research on Adolescence, Boston.

Yip, R. (1995, March). *Nutritional status of U.S. children: The extent and causes of malnutrition.* Paper presented at the meeting of the Society for Research in Child Development, Indianapolis.

Young, K.T. (1990). American conceptions of infant development from 1955 to 1984: What the experts are telling parents. *Child Development, 61,* 17–28.

Young, S.K., & Shahinfar, A. (1995, March). *The contributions of maternal sensitivity and child temperament to attachment status at 14 months.* Paper presented at the meeting of the Society for Research in Child Development, Indianapolis.

Z

Zelazo, P.R., Potter, S., & Valiante, A.G. (1995, March). *Effects of fetal cocaine exposure on neonatal information processing.* Paper presented at the meeting of the Society for Research in Child Development, Indianapolis.

Zeskind, P.S., Gingras, J.L., Campbell, K.D., & Donnelly, K. (1999, April). *Prenatal cocaine exposure disrupts fetal autonomic regulation.* Paper presented at the meeting of the Society for Research in Child Development, Albuquerque.

Zeskind, P.S., Klein, L., & Marshall, T.R. (1992). Adults' perceptions of experimental modifications of durations and expiratory sounds in infant crying. *Developmental Psychology, 28,* 1153–1162.

Zigler, E., & Styfco, S.J. (1994). Head Start: Criticisms in a constructive context. *American Psychologist, 49,* 127–132.

Zigler, E.F., & Finn-Stevenson, M. (1999). Applied developmental psychology. In M.H. Bornstein & M.E. Lamb (Eds.), *Developmental psychology: an advanced textbook* (4th ed.). Mahwah, NJ: Erlbaum.

Zill, N., Morrison, D.R., & Coiro, M.J. (1993). Long-term effects of parental divorce on parent–child relationships, adjustment, and achievement in young adulthood. *Journal of Family Psychology, 7,* 91–103.

Zimmerman, B.J., Bonner, S., & Kovach, R. (1996). *Developing self-regulated learners.* Washington, DC: American Psychological Association.

Zimmerman, B.J., Bonner, S., & Kovach, R. (1996). *Developing self-regulated learners.* Washington, DC: American Psychological Association.

Zimmerman, R.S., Khoury, E., Vega, W.A., Gil, A.G., & Warheit, G.J. (1995). Teacher and student perceptions of behavior problems among a sample of African American, Hispanic, and non-Hispanic White students. *American Journal of Community Psychology, 23,* 181–197.

Zolotow, C. (1972). *William's doll.* New York: Harper & Row.

Zubay, G.L. (1996). *Origins of life on the earth and in the cosmos.* Dubuque, IA: Wm. C. Brown.

Credits

PROLOGUE

1 "If I Had My Child to Raise Over Again," from the book *Full Esteem Ahead* © 1994 by Diane Loomans with Julia Loomans. Reprinted by permission of HJ Kramer, PO Box 1082, Tiburon, CA. All rights reserved.

CHAPTER 1

Figure 1.3 Reprinted with permission from "The State of America's Children Yearbook 1996." Washington, DC Children's Defense Fund, 1996.
Figure 1.14 THE GREATEST LOVE OF ALL, by Linda Creed and Michael Masser © 1977 EMI Gold Horizon Music Corp. and EMI Golden Torch Music Corp. All rights reserved. Used by permission WARNER BROS. PUBLICATIONS U.S. INC., Miami, FL. 33014
© The New Yorker Collection 1998 Lee Lorenz from cartoonbank.com. All rights reserved.

CHAPTER 2

THE FAR SIDE © 1982 FARWORKS, INC. Used by permission. All rights reserved.
© The New Yorker Collection 1978 Everett Opie from cartoonbank.com. All rights reserved.
THE FAR SIDE © 1984 FARWORKS, INC. Used by permission. All rights reserved.
Figure 2.8 CB Kopp/JB Krakow, THE CHILD, (page 648). © 1982 by Addison-Wesley Publishing Company, Inc. Reprinted by permission of Addison Wesley Longman.

CHAPTER 3

© The New Yorker Collection 1985 Jack Ziegler from cartoonbank.com. All rights reserved.
By permission of Johnny Hart and Creators Syndicate, Inc.

CHAPTER 4

DENNIS THE MENACE used by permission of Hank Ketcham and © by North America Syndicate.
Figure 4.2 From Charles Carroll and Dean Miller, *Health: The Science of Human Adaptation,* 5th ed. Copyright © 1991 Wm. C. Brown Communications, Inc. Dubuque, Iowa. All Rights Reserved. Reprinted by permission.
Figure 4.4 © 1979, 1984, 1991 by the Childbirth Education Association. Reprinted from *Pregnancy, Childbirth, and the Newborn: The Complete Guide* by Penny Simkin, Janet Whalley, and Ann Keppler with permission of its publisher, Meadowbrook Press, Deephaven, MN
Figure 4.5 From Moore, K.L., "The Developing Human: Clinically Oriented Embryology," 4th ed. Copyright © 1988 W.B. Saunders Company. Reprinted with permission.
Figure 4.8 From Queenan and Queenan, "A New Life: Pregnancy, Birth & Your Child's First Year." © 1986 Marshall Cavendish Ltd., London, England. Reprinted by permission.

Figure 4.10 John Karapelou © 1991 *Discover* Magazine.
Figure 4.13 Source: Data from Food and Nutrition Board, "Recommended Nutrient Increases for Adult Pregnancy," National Academy of Sciences, Washington, DC, 1980.

CHAPTER 5

Figure 5.1 From Kent M. Van De Graff and Stuart Ira Fox, "Concepts of Human Anatomy and Physiology," 3d ed. Copyright © 1992 Wm. C. Brown Communications, Inc. All Rights Reserved. Reprinted by permission.
Figure 5.2 From Virginia Apgar, "A Proposal for a New Method of Evaluation of a Newborn Infant" in "Anesthesia and Analgesia," 32:260–267. Copyright © 1975 International Anesthesia Research Society. Reprinted by permission of Williams & Wilkins.
Figure 5.3 From: "Cultural Perspectives on Child Development," by Wagner and Stevenson. Copyright ©1982 by W. H. Freeman and Company. Used with permission.

CHAPTER 6

Figure 6.2 From Jesse LeRoy Conel, "Postnatal Development of Human Cerebral Cortex" Copyright © Harvard University Press, Cambridge, MA Reprinted by permission.
Figure 6.8 From W.K. Frankenburg and J.B. Dodds, "The Denver Development Screening Test" in "Journal of Pediatrics" 71:181–191. Copyright ©1967 Mosby-Year Book, Inc. Reprinted by permission.
Figure 6.9 Sources: Data from R. Charlesworth, "Understanding Child Development" 2d ed. Delmar Press, Albany, NY, 1987; and G.J. Schirmir (ed.), "Performance Objectives for Preschool Children," Adapt Press, Sioux Falls, SD, 1974.
Figure 6.12 Adapted from "The Origin of Form Perception" by R.L. Frantz. Copyright © 1961 by Scientific American, Inc. All rights reserved.

CHAPTER 7

© 1981 Thaves. Reprinted with permission.
Figure 7.6 From R. Brown, et al., "The Child's Grammar from 1-3" in "Minnesota Symposium on Child Psychology" Vol. 2, J.P. Hill (ed.). Copyright © 1969 University of Minnesota Press. Reprinted by permission.

CHAPTER 8

Reprinted with special permission of North America Syndicate.
Figure 8.4 From: M.D. Ainsworth. "The development of infant mother attachment" in *"Review of Child Developmental Research,"* Vol. 3 B. Caldwell and H. Ricciut (eds.) Reprinted by permission of The University of Chicago Press.

CHAPTER 9

© The New Yorker Collection 1987 Lee Lorenz from cartoonbank.com. All rights reserved.
Figure 9.1 Source: National Center for Health Statistics, NHCS Growth Charts, "Monthly Vital Statistics Report."
Figure 9.2 Adapted from "Human Biology and Economy" by Alert Damon, Second Edition, by permission of W.W. Norton and Company, Inc.
Figure 9.3 Source: Data from G.J. Schiner (ed.) "Performance Objectives for Preschool Children," Adapt Press, Sioux Falls, SD, 1974
Figure 9.4 Source: Data from G.J. Schiner (ed.) "Performance Objectives for Preschool Children," Adapt Press, Sioux Falls, SD, 1974
Figure 9.6 From S. Goodman, "You and Your Child" Copyright © 1979 Mitchell Beazley Publishers, Ltd., London, England. Reprinted by permission.
Figure 9.7 Source: Food and Nutrition Board, 1980
Figure 9.8 From Virginia DeMoss, "Good, the Bad and the Edible" in *Runner's World,* June 1980 Copyright © Virginia DeMoss. Reprinted by permission
Figure 9.10 From: C.A. Aligne and J.J. Stoddard. Tobacco and Children: An economic evaluation of the medical effects of parental smoking. *Archives of Pediatric & Adolescent Medicine,* 151, 648-653. Copyright 1997. Reprinted by permission of the American Medical Association.

CHAPTER 10

© The New Yorker Collection 1988 Ed Frascino from cartoonbank.com. All rights reserved.
CALVIN AND HOBBES © 1986 Watterson. Dist. By UNIVERSAL PRESS SYNDICATE. All rights reserved.
© The New Yorker Collection 1989 Lee Lorenz from cartoonbank.com. All rights reserved.
Figure 10.2 Courtesy of D. Wolf and J. Nove
Figure 10.9 From J. Berko, "The Child's Learning of English Morphology" in "Word," 14:361. Copyright © 1958 International Linguistic Association, New York, NY. Reprinted by permission.
Figure 10.10 From "Position Statement on Developmentally Appropriate Practice in Programs for 4- and 5-year-olds" in *Young Children,* 41:23-27. Copyright © 1986 by the National Association for the Education of Young Children (NAEYC). Used by permission.

CHAPTER 11

Figure 11.1 From: Janet Kuebli, "Young children's understanding of everyday emotions," *Young Children,* March 1994. Copyright 1994. Reprinted by permission of the National Association for the Education of Young Children.
THE FAR SIDE © 1985 FARWORKS, INC. Used by permission. All rights reserved.

CALVIN AND HOBBES © 1993 Watterson. Dist. By UNIVERSAL PRESS SYNDICATE. All rights reserved.
© Martha F. Campbell
Figure 11.7 From: D.F. Robitaille and R.A. Garden. *The IDEA Study of Mathematics II: Contexts and outcomes of school mathematics.*

CHAPTER 12

Figure 12.2 Source: Data from R.E. Behrman and V.C. Vaughan (eds.), Nelson Textbook of Pediatrics. W.B. Saunders, Philadelphia, PA 1987
Figure 12.3 Sources: Data from B.J. Cratty, "Perceptual and Motor Development in Infants and Young Children," Prentice Hall, Inc. Englewood Cliffs, NJ, 1979; and L.F. Whaleyand D.L. Wong, "Essentials of Pediatric Nursing," 3d ed., C.V. Mosby Company, St Louis, MO 1988

CHAPTER 13

Figure 13.3 From Steven R. Yussen, et al., "The Robustness and Temporal Cause of Story Schemics Influence on Recall" Journal of Experimental Psychology Learning, Memory and Cognition, 14:173-179 Copyright 1988 by the American Psychological Association. Reprinted by permission.
Figure 13.7 Simulated items similar to those in the Wechsler Intelligence Scale for Children: Third Edition. Copyright © 1990 by The Psychological Corporation. Reproduced by permission. All rights reserved. "Wechsler Intelligence Scale for Children" and "WUSC-III" are registered trademarks of The Psychological Corporation. Reproduced by permission. All Rights Reserved.
Table 13.1 Adapted from E.H. Berger and M.J. Pollman, Multiple intelligences: Enabling diverse learning. *Early Childhood Education Journal,* 23, No. 4, 249-253. Copyright 1996. Reprinted by permission of Plenum Publishing Corporation.

CHAPTER 14

© 1986 Joel Pett, Phi Delta Kappan.
Figure 14.1 From R.L. Selman, "Social-Cognitive Understanding" in T. Lickona (ed.), Moral Development and Behavior, 1976. Reprinted by permission of Thomas Lickona.
Figure 14.4 From Janet S. Hyde, et al., "Gender Differences in Mathematics Performance: A Meta-Analysis" in "Psychological Bulletin," 107:139-155. Copyright 1990 by the American Psychological Association. Reprinted by permission.
Figure 14.5 From Janet S. Hyde, Half the Human Experience: The Psychology of Women, 5th ed. Copyright © 1995 by DC Heath and Company, Lexington MA Used by permission of Houghton Mifflin Company.

CHAPTER 15

15-23A From: "Teen Pregnancy Folo," *Parade,* May 25, 1997. Reprinted with permission from Parade, Copyright © 1997.
Figure 15.3 From J.M. Tanner, et al., "Standards from Birth to Maturity for Height, Weight, Height Velocity, and Weight Velocity: British Children 1965" in "Archives of Diseases in Childhood" 41. Copyright © 1966 British Medical Association, London, England. Reprinted by permission.

Figure 15.4 Adapted from "Growing Up" by J.M. Tanner. Copyright © 1973 by Scientific American, Inc. All rights reserved.
Figure 15.6 Source: Data from the Alan Guttmacher Institute, 1938

CHAPTER 16

Figure 16.2 From: Zimmerman, Bonner and Kovach. *Developing self-regulated Learners,* fig. 1, pg. 11. Copyright © 1996 by the American Psychological Association. Reprinted by permission.
Figure 16.3 From L. Dey, et al., "The American Freshman: Twenty-Five-Year Trends," 1991 A.W. Astin, et al., "The American Freshman: National Norms for Fall 1991," 1991; EL Dey et al., "The American Freshman: National Norms for Fall 1992," 1992 A.W. Astin, et al., "The American Freshman: National Norms for Fall 1993," 1993 and A.W. Astin, et al, "The American Freshman: National Norms for Fall 1994" 1994. All works © Higher Education Research Institute, UCLA.

CHAPTER 17

Figure 17.3 Source: Data from Dexter C. Dunphy, "The Social Stucture of Urban Adolescent Peer Groups" in "Sociometry," Vol. 26 American Sociological Association, Washington, DC 1963

PHOTO

PROLOGUE: ©BACHMANN / PHOTO NETWORK

SECTION OPENERS:
Section 1: © Ross Whitakker / Image Bank / Dallas
Section 2: © Petit Format / Nestle / Photo Researchers
Section 3: Courtesy of Northern Telecom
Section 4: © John P. Kelly / The Image Bank / Chicago
Section 5: © T. Rosenthal / Superstock
Section 6: © Ron Chapple / FPG International

CHAPTER 1

Opener: © Si Chi KO; p. 5 top: © SYGMA; p. 5 bottom: © AP/Wide World; 1.1: Photo: © Eric Lessing /Art Resource, NY/ Painting by A.I.G. Velasquez, Infanta Margarita Teresa in white garb, Kunsthistorisches Museum, Vienna, Austria; 1.2: Archives of the History of American Psychology / Louise Bates Ames Gift; 1.A: (top to bottom) © Telegraph Color Library/ FPG International; © Peter Turnley / Black Star; © Kevin Horan; © Alan S. Frank / Photo Researchers; © Joseph Rodriquez / Black Star; p. 12 top: National Association for the Education of Young Children/ © Robert Maust; p. 12 bottom Courtesy of Nancy Agostini; 1.3: both © Michael Melford / Image Bank / Chicago; p. 17: ©Westenberger/ Liaison / USA; 1.6: top to bottom © James Shaffer; © Michael Salas / Image Bank / Chicago; © Chromosohm Media / The Image Works; Courtesy of John Santrock; © Dr. Landrum B. Shettles; p. 22: © Duka / Photo Network

CHAPTER 2

Opener: © Ray Stott / The Image Works; p. 31: © Sharon Beals for Insight; p. 33: www. corbis.com / Bettmann; 2.3: (bottom left to top right) ©William Hopkins Jr.; © Suzanne Sasz/ Photo Researchers; © Suzanne Sasz / Photo Researchers; ©Melchoir DiGiacomo / Image Bank / Chicago; © Sam Zarember / Image Bank / Dallas; © Brett Froomer / Image Bank / Dallas; © Alan Carey / The Image Works; © Art Kane/The Image Works; p. 36: © Sarah Putnam/ Picture Cube; p. 38 left © Yves DeBraine / Black Star; p. 39 right: Courtesy of A.R. Luria /Dr. Michael Cole/ Laboratory of Comparative Human Cognition; p. 40: www.corbis.com / Bettmann; p. 41: Courtesy of Albert Bandura; 2.7: © Nina Leen /Time/ Life Magazine/ Time Inc.; 2.8: © David Austen / Stock Boston; p. 45: Courtesy of Urie Bronfenbrenner; p. 50: © Richard T. Nowitz / Photo Researchers

CHAPTER 3

Opener: © Brain Vikander; p. 63: © Enrico Ferorelli; 3.1: © John P. Kelly / Image Bank / Chicago; p. 66: main image and lower left inset Courtesy of the United Nations; upper right inset © Elaine Sulle / Image Bank / Chicago; 3.2: © Will and Deni McIntyre/ Science Source/ Photo Researchers; 3.3: top left © R. Heinzen / Superstock; 3.3: bottom left © Elyse Lewin / Image Bank / Dallas; 3.4: © Sundstrom / Liaison; 3.5: © Alexandria Tsiaras / Photo Researchers; p. 70: © 1998 Brooks Kraft / SYGMA; 3.7: © Andrew Eccles / Outline; p. 74 © Andrew Eccles / Outline; 3.9: © Will & Deni McIntyre / Photo Researchers; 3.10: © Jacques Pavlovsky / Sygma; p. 90 © Myrleen Ferguson / Photo Edit; p. 83 © Enrico Ferorelli; p. 84 © Joel Gordon

CHAPTER 4

Opener: © Lennart Nilsson; p. 89: PhotoDisc/Vol. 15; 4.1: © Russ Kinne / Comstock; p. 93 all © Lennart Nilsson; 4.4: © Petit Format / Nestle / Photo Researchers; inset-top © Lennart Nilsson; inset-middle and bottom © Petit Format / Nestle/ Photo Researchers; 4.7: Courtesy A.P. Streissguth, University of Washington School of Medicine; 4.8: © Will & Deni McIntyre / Photo Researchers; p. 102: © Chas Cancellare; p. 109: © Charles Gupton / Stock Boston; p. 110: (left) © David Young-Wolff / Photo Edit; p. 112: (right) © David Shaefer / Photo Edit

CHAPTER 5

Opener: © SIU/ Peter Arnold; p.120: © Charles Gupton / Tony Stone; p. 123: © Charles Gupton / Stock Boston; p. 125 © Stephen McBrady / Photo Edit; p. 127: © Charles Gupton / Stock Boston; p. 129: Courtesy of Dr. Tiffany Field 5.2: © Comstock; p. 132 © Michael Newman / Photo Edit; p. 134: © James G. White

CHAPTER 6

Opener: © Niki Mareschal / Image Bank / Dallas; p. 144 top left: © Hank Morgan / Photo Researchers; p. 144 bottom right: Courtesy of Steven and Cindi Binder; 6.5: © A. Glauberman / Photo Researchers; p. 149 © Bruce McAllister /

Name Index

A

Aarons, J.H., 102
Abbassi, V., 445
ABC Task Force, 279, 430
Abdul-Kabir, S., 275
Aboud, F., 400
Abramovitch, R., 305
Academic Software, 352
Acredolo, L.P., 164
Adams, A., 365
Adams, R.J., 161
Adamson, L.B., 193
Adato, A., 74
Adler, C.R., 46
Adler, T., 64
Ainsworth, M.D.S., 201, 207, 209, 210, 211, 223
Alan Guttmacher Institute, 452, 453, 454
Alario, J., 271
Alavi, A., 413
Albersheim, L.J., 21
Alberto, P., 350
Alcantara, A.A., 84
Alderman, M.K., 390
Alexander, A., 348
Alexander, G.R., 109
Alexander, P.C., 216
Alexandrova, E.O., 200
Aligne, C.A., 245
Alipura, L.L., 503
Allen, D., 244
Allen, J.P., 505
Allen, K.E., 242
Allen, M., 151
Allen, M.L., 10
Allen, N.H., 460
Allison, K.W., 518
Allison, L., 232
Alward, K.R., 314
Amabile, T.M., 382
Amato, P.R., 307, 308
America in Transition, 486
American Academy of Pediatrics (AAP) Committee on Environmental Health, 245
American Association for Protecting Children, 216
American College Health Association, 456
American Psychiatric Association, 347
Ames, B.N., 104
Ames, M.A., 454
Amiel-Tison, C., 163
Amsterdam, B.K., 205
Anda, R.F., 101
Anderman, E.M., 389
Anders, T.F., 239
Anderson, B.J., 84
Anderson, D.J., 461
Anderson, D.R., 265
Anderson, E., 420
Anderson, H., 348
Anselmi, D.L., 54
Appalachia Educational Laboratory, 350

Applefield, J.M., 320
Arboleda, T., 500
Archer, P., 237
Archer, S.L., 504
Arend, R.A., 209
Argyle, M., 479
Ariès, P., 6
Armsden, G., 506
Arnold, S.E., 413
Aronson, E., 429
Arterberry, M.E., 167
Asarnow.J.R., 423
Asher, J., 387
Asher, J.R., 424
Asher, S.R., 422
Ashmead, D.H., 155, 157
Astin, A.W., 476
Astrid, N., 102
Atkinson, R., 441
Attie, I., 461
Atwood, M.E., 235
Au, K., 385
Avery, E., 461
Ayers-Lopez, S., 313
Ayooh, K., 98

B

Bachman, G., 459, 460, 461
Bachman, J., 477
Bachman, J.G., 492, 494
Bagarazzi, M.L., 98
Bagwell, C.L., 512
Bailey, M.C., 247
Baillargion, R., 175
Bakeman, R., 134
Baker, A.K., 80
Bakkestrom, E., 72
Baldwin, C., 101
Baltes, P.B., 19, 21
Bandura, A., 41, 42, 48, 187, 403
Banks, E.C., 408
Banks, J.A., 429, 430
Banks, M.S., 161
Baranowski, T., 248, 336
Barber, B.L., 492
Barker, R., 422
Barnes, H., 428
Barnett, D., 217
Baron, N.S., 190
Barrett, D.E., 100, 149
Barton, L., 127
Baskett, L.M., 304
Bates, A.S., 109
Bates, E., 185
Bates, J.E., 203, 302
Bates, N.A., 98
Bathurst, K., 307
Baumann, J.F., 384, 385
Baumrind, D., 296, 301
Bayley, N., 149, 180, 181, 184
Beagles-Roos, J., 322
Beal, C.R., 13, 295
Beaton, A.E., 392
Bechtold, A.G., 166

Becker, P.T., 146
Bednar, R.L., 403
Bee, D.E., 248, 336
Beebe, B., 213
Beebe, T., 479
Beherman, R.E., 348
Behnke, M.L., 102
Behrman, R.E., 109, 128
Behrmann, M.M., 351
Beit-Hallahmi, B., 479
Bell, A.M., 454
Bell, M.A., 144
Bell, S.M., 201
Belle, D., 422
Bellinger, D., 104
Belsky, J., 131, 214, 220, 223
Belson, W., 320
Bem, S.L., 415
Ben-Avie, M., 430
Benelli, C., 237
Bennett, S.L., 213
Bennett, W., 478
Benson, J.B., 176, 361
Benson, P., 479
Bentler, P.M., 461
Berbaum, M., 461
Berenson, G.S., 341, 342
Berger, S.H., 308, 420
Berget, A., 104
Bergin, D., 315, 317
Berk, S.F., 214
Berko, J., 269
Berlin, L.J., 210
Berliner, D.C., 385
Berlyne, D.E., 315
Berndt, T.J., 313, 425, 484
Bernensen, G.S., 341
Bernier, J.C., 349, 350
Bernieri, F.J., 213
Berryman, J.C., 99
Berstein, S., 177
Bertoncini, J., 163
Best, D.L., 411
Bezilla, R., 480
Bier, J.B., 148
Biller, H.B., 215
Billings, R.L., 104
Billy, J.O.G., 512
Binet, A., 180, 371, 372, 383
Bingham, C.R., 453
Bish, A., 71
Blachman, B.A., 347
Black, R., 347
Black, S.H., 68
Blair, C., 128
Bland, S.D., 247, 342
Bloom, L., 192
Blue, J.H., 444
Blum, R., 453
Blumenfeld, P.C., 426
Blythe, D.A., 449
Bobrow, N.A., 450
Boekarts, M., 390
Boethel, C.L., 420
Bohlin, G., 201
Bolen, J.C., 247, 342
Bollerud, K.H., 454

Bonica, C.A., 514
Bonk, C.J., 392, 427
Bonner, S., 390, 475, 476
Bonvillian, J.D., 175
Boodoo, G., 377
Booth, A., 44, 308
Booth, D.A., 165
Borman-Spurrell, E., 505
Bornstein, M.H., 13, 167, 265
Bouchard, T.J., 64, 377
Bowe, F., 346
Bowen, A.P., 247
Bower, B., 239
Bower, T.G.R., 161
Bowlby, J., 21, 201, 207, 208, 209, 211, 223
Boxer, C., 213
Boykin, A.W., 377
Boykin, K.A., 505
Boyles, N.S., 345, 346
Boys and Girls Clubs of America, 513
Bracken, M.B., 70
Brand, J.E., 318
Brand, K.L., 202
Braunwald, K., 217
Bray, J.H., 308, 415, 420
Bray, J.M., 420
Brazelton, T.B., 84, 131, 154, 157, 222, 307
Bredekamp, S., 253, 274
Bremer, M., 318
Brenneman, K., 362
Brent, A., 392
Bresnick, B., 237
Bretherton, I., 201
Brewer, W.F., 366
Brice, P., 320
Bridges, M., 307, 308, 310, 420
Brillion, L., 518
Brislin, R., 67
Brodsky, N.L., 102
Brody, N., 377
Bromley, D., 400
Bronfenbrenner, U., 43, 44, 45, 46, 48, 275
Brook, D.W., 507
Brook, J.S., 507
Brooks, J.B., 301
Brooks-Gunn, J., 205, 311, 377, 444, 448, 449, 450, 459, 461, 506
Brophy, J., 388
Brown, A., 383
Brown, A.L., 366, 369
Brown, B.B., 510, 513
Brown, D., 490
Brown, J., 244
Brown, J.V., 134
Brown, P., 10, 151
Brown, R., 187, 189, 192, 269, 283
Brown, Z.A., 102
Bruce, J.M., 198, 289
Brummit, G.A., 104
Bruner, J.S., 370
Bryant, B.R., 351
Bryant, D., 461
Bryant, D.M., 82, 219
Bryden, M.P., 413

Subject